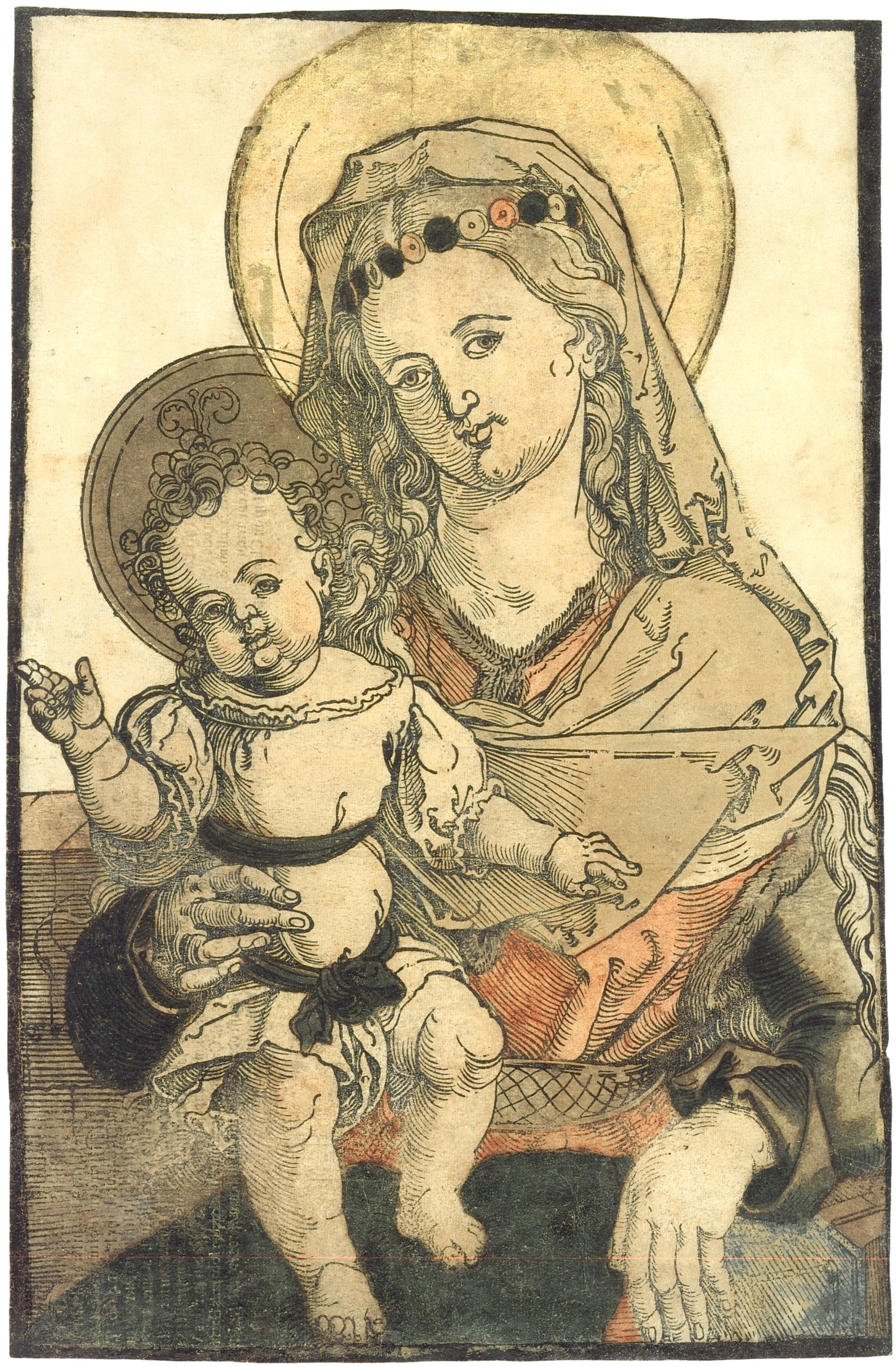

School of Dürer (Sebald Beham?), *Madonna and Child*, ca. 1520-25.

SIX CENTURIES OF MASTER PRINTS

Treasures from the
Herbert Greer French *Collection*

—

Edited by **Kristin L. Spangenberg**
with Essays by
David P. Becker, Suzanne Boorsch,
Jane Campbell Hutchison, George S. Keyes, Dennis Kiel,
Jane S. Peters, Timothy Riggs, Kristin L. Spangenberg,
and **Mark J. Zucker**

—

Cincinnati Art Museum, 1993

Cover detail: Antonio Pollaiuolo, *Battle of the Nudes*, ca. 1489?
Bequest of Herbert Greer French, 1943.118 (cat. 16).

Contents

Six Centuries of Master Prints: Treasures from the Herbert Greer French Collection

*Edited by Kristin L. Spangenberg
with essays by David P. Becker, Suzanne Boorsch, Jane Campbell Hutchison, George S. Keyes, Dennis Kiel, Jane S. Peters, Timothy Riggs, Kristin L. Spangenberg, and Mark J. Zucker*

This catalogue was supported in part by a grant from the National Endowment for the Arts, a federal agency.

Copyright 1993 by the Cincinnati Art Museum. All rights reserved. Printed in the United States of America.

ISBN 0-931537-15-0

Library of Congress Catalogue Card Number: 92-73973

*Editorial Services: CEP, Inc.
Typography and design: Noel Martin
Typesetting: Cobb Typesetting, Inc.
Printing: The Stinehour Press*

Color section made possible through funds donated by Mr. and Mrs. William D. Baskett and Mr. and Mrs. John J. Schiff.

Published on the occasion of the exhibition, "Six Centuries of Master Prints: Treasures from the Herbert Greer French Collection," held at the Cincinnati Art Museum, January 15, 1993, through April 11, 1993.

Foreword

The darkest days of that desperate struggle known as World War II came, for the United States, in 1942; however, that same year marked a high point for the Cincinnati Art Museum. The Herbert Greer French bequest of over eight hundred prints found a lasting home in the institution so revered and so long served by this titan collector. Today, the Herbert Greer French Collection still forms the treasured nucleus of this Museum's holdings of graphic art.

In the first months after my appointment in 1974 as the Museum's fifth director since its founding in 1881, I spent hours poring over the treasures in solander boxes that constitute the Herbert Greer French Collection. I audibly expressed awe and pleasure when first encountering this truly exquisite collection as Curator Kristin Spangenberg laid box after box before me. My reward for being one of the custodians of such riches held for the public good has been this: that I have never forgotten the pleasure that overwhelmed me upon opening the first box.

Over many years of assiduous sifting and refining, Mr. French developed his distinguished collection, the formation of which was inextricably woven into the collector's lengthy affiliation with the Museum. Over several decades, Herbert Greer French served as Curator of Prints (beginning in 1929), as Trustee (first elected in 1929), and as lender, exhibition organizer, and donor. His patronage to the Museum can be seen in the books he contributed to our library, in his purchase of the Allyn Poole collection of prints, and in the wing that opened in 1930 and bears his name. Finally, his generosity included not only his bequest of prints, but also the establishment of an endowment for the care and maintenance of the print department.

Although the Museum staged an exhibition in 1941 of Mr. French's prints, styled by then-director Walter H. Siple as "one of the most important in its history," no definitive catalogue was ever undertaken until now. To honor the fiftieth anniversary of the French bequest, the Museum sees realized what was first envisioned: a well-researched, extensive catalogue focusing on the choicest works in an extraordinary collection, the result of scholarship completed by a team of noted historians and curators, all specialists in their fields. Concurrent with the publication of this catalogue, the Museum is featuring an exhibition of these researched prints, to also celebrate its reopening after completion of the most extensive renovation and construction project in the Museum's history. Beyond this, the Museum plans to publish a checklist of the complete collection, extending the catalogue with this summary of the total French Collection.

Six Centuries of Master Prints: Treasures from the Herbert Greer French Collection adds to a growing, distinguished roster of publications devoted to the permanent collection that includes the following: Caroline R. Shine and Mary L. Meyer, *Art of the First Americans* (1976); Carol M. Macht and Deborah Long, *Cincinnati Landmarks* (1976); Millard F. Rogers, Jr., *Spanish Paintings in the Cincinnati Art Museum* (1978); Kristin L. Spangenberg, *French Drawings, Watercolors, and Pastels (1800-1950)* (1978); Denny T. Carter, *The Golden Age: Cincinnati Paintings of the Nineteenth Century Represented in the Cincinnati Art Museum* (1979); Ellen S. Smart and Daniel S. Walker, *Pride of the Princes: Indian Art of the Mughal Era in the Cincinnati Art Museum* (1985); Mary Ann Scott, *Dutch, Flemish, and German Paintings in the Cincinnati Art Museum* (1987); Otto Charles Thieme, *Simply Stunning: 200 Years of Fashion from the Cincinnati Art Museum* (1988); Kristin L. Spangenberg, *Photographic Treasures from the Cincinnati Art Museum* (1989); Otto Charles Thieme, *With Grace and Favour: Women's Fashionable Dress in the Edwardian and Victorian Eras, 1837-1911* (1993); and John Spike, *Italian Paintings from the Cincinnati Art Museum* (1993).

The Museum is indebted to many for their participation in and their contributions to this catalogue: special thanks to Kristin L. Spangenberg, curator of Prints and Photographs at the Cincinnati Art Museum, who, together with a team of scholars, shepherded the research project and the resulting catalogue; to the art historians and curators who shared their expertise on the fifteenth-through-twentieth-century prints presented in this catalogue and acknowledged in their catalogue entries; to Ann Cotter, coordinator of Publication and Photographic services; to Dennis Kiel, associate curator of Photographs, Design and Architecture; to Elizabeth Coombs, former associate conservator; to Joy Payton, associate coordinator of Photographic Services and Carol Schoellkopf, assistant coordinator of Publications; to Jorinne McKinnie, departmental assistant; and to Noel Martin, designer of this handsome publication.

The connoisseurship of Herbert Greer French was exalted. A casual view of the selected prints or a scholarly study of any of its masterpieces will confirm this estimate of one of the Cincinnati Art Museum's most distinguished and generous patrons, now honored by this catalogue and exhibition. Ultimately, it was Mr. French's exquisite taste and knowledge that formed his internationally renowned collection and earned him lasting praise from scholars, collectors, museum visitors, and all who love fine prints.

Millard Rogers, Jr.
Director

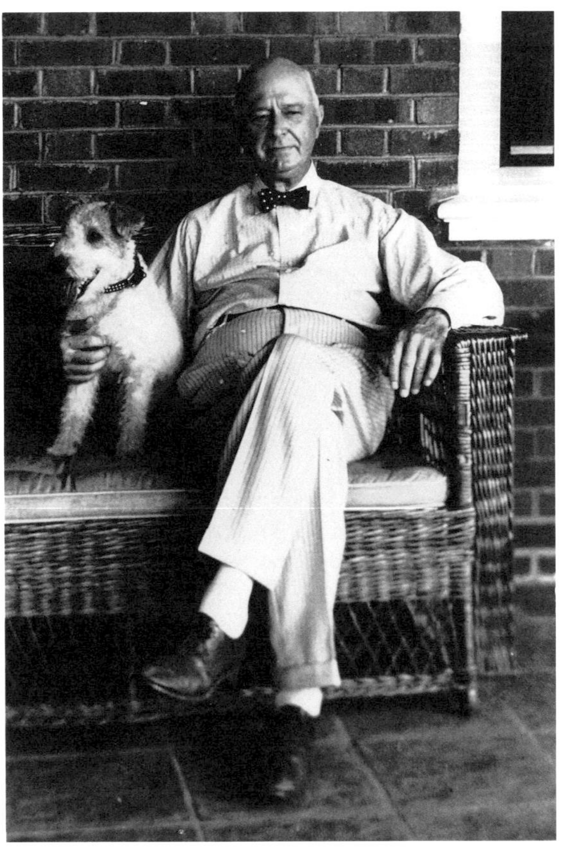

Herbert Greer French on the patio of his Reachmont Home, n.d., gelatin silver print, Courtesy of Procter & Gamble Corporate Archives, Cincinnati.

Acknowledgments

It is difficult, if not impossible, to properly thank all those who have generously given of their time, knowledge, and support to this project. I would like to express my gratitude to Millard F. Rogers, Jr. who recognized the international importance of this collection and supported this publication honoring the fiftieth anniversary of the bequest. Without his continuing and patient encouragement, the pursuit of this ambitious project and the allowance of time to research, write, and edit this catalogue and organize the accompanying exhibition would not have been realized.

Special thanks is due the contributing authors, David P. Becker, Suzanne Boorsch, Jane Campbell Hutchison, George S. Keyes, Dennis Kiel, Jane S. Peters, Timothy Riggs and Mark Zucker who enthusiastically undertook the challenge to bring their expertise and interpretation to the essays. Elizabeth Coombs, former associate conservator, paper, thoroughly examined all prints with the authors and expertly restored those requiring conservation.

On behalf of the authors, I would like to thank the staff of the following libraries and museum departments who answered their queries and facilitated the use of the materials in their custody: Mary R. Schiff Library and Archives, Cincinnati Art Museum; Stieglitz Archives, Collection of American Literature, Beinecke Rare Book and Manuscript Library, Yale University; British Museum, London; Cincinnati Historical Society; Avery Architectural and Fine Arts Library, Columbia University; Graphische Sammlung Albertina, Vienna; Department of Prints and Illustrated Books, The Metropolitan Museum of Art; Museum Boymans-van Beuningen, Rotterdam; the Department of Prints, Drawings, and Photographs, Museum of Fine Arts, Boston; National Gallery of Art, Washington; New York Public Library; Public Library of Cincinnati and Hamilton County; Rijksprentenkabinet, Amsterdam; Rijksbureau voor Kunsthistorische Documentatie, The Hague; Städelsches Kunstinstitut, Frankfurt-am-Main; Teylers Museum, Haarlem; University of Cincinnati; Print Study Room and Library, Yale Center for British Art.

I owe particular thanks to Melissa De Medeiros, librarian at M. Knoedler and Company, who facilitated my research on Herbert Greer French purchases and the provenance of his prints. Ruth-Maria Muthman of C. G. Boerner, Düsseldorf, graciously checked the auction records and provenance of prints sold by the company during the 1920s and 1930s in Leipzig.

Numerous curators and scholars unselfishly shared their knowledge and expertise without which this catalogue would have not been possible. The authors and I would like to thank in particular Mary Welsch Baskett, Peter Brunnell, Barbara Butts, Richard Campbell, Riva Castleman, Phillip Dennis Cate, Karen Chasp, Mitchell A. Codding, Marjorie B. Cohn, Ellen D'Oench, Douglas Druick, Ruth Fine, Robert H. Getscher, Pat Gilmour, Antony Griffiths, Maria Moris Hambourg, Sinclair Hitchings, Wolfgang Holler, Janet Isenhour, Colta Ives, Ellen Jacobowitz, Gregory Jecmen, Joseph R. Jones, David W. Kiehl, Martin Royalton Kisch, George Knox, Norman Kraeft, Armin Kunz, Jay A. Levenson, Patricia Lewis, Ger Luijten, Paul McCarron, Suzanne Folds McCullagh, Bram Meij, Matthias Mende, Hans Mielke, Edgar Munhall, Patrick Noon, Ilse O'Dell, Roy Perkinson, Konrad Renger, Andrew Robison, Dianne Russell, Brigitta Sandström, Eleanor Sayre, Peter Schatborn, Ulrike Schellhammer, Stephanie Stepanek, Margret Stuffmann, Christine Swenson, Kenneth Trapp, Carel van Tuyll van Serooskerken, and Roberta Waddell.

I would like to extend my special thanks to the exhibition's two research assistants, Karen Carter, who competently gathered exhibition and loan information for the authors' curatorial files and prepared a checklist of the entire collection, and Jay Pattison, who efficiently handled comparative photography orders and prepared the bibliography. The department secretary, Linda Pieper, expertly typed and revised portions of the manuscript.

I owe my sincere appreciation to many Cincinnati Art Museum staff members. My professional colleagues Glenn Markoe, Otto Charles Thieme, and John Wilson shared their expertise. Assistance and encouragement was given by other staff members who greatly influenced the contours of the exhibition: Elisabeth Batchelor, assistant director, Collections; Mary Ellen Goeke, head of Exhibitions and Registration; and Mark Rohling, chief preparator. Those who volunteered their time to the catalogue preparation were Joanne Schwartz in Prints, Drawings, and Photographs; and Janet Freeland and Nancy Howard in Publication and Photographic Services.

Kristin L. Spangenberg

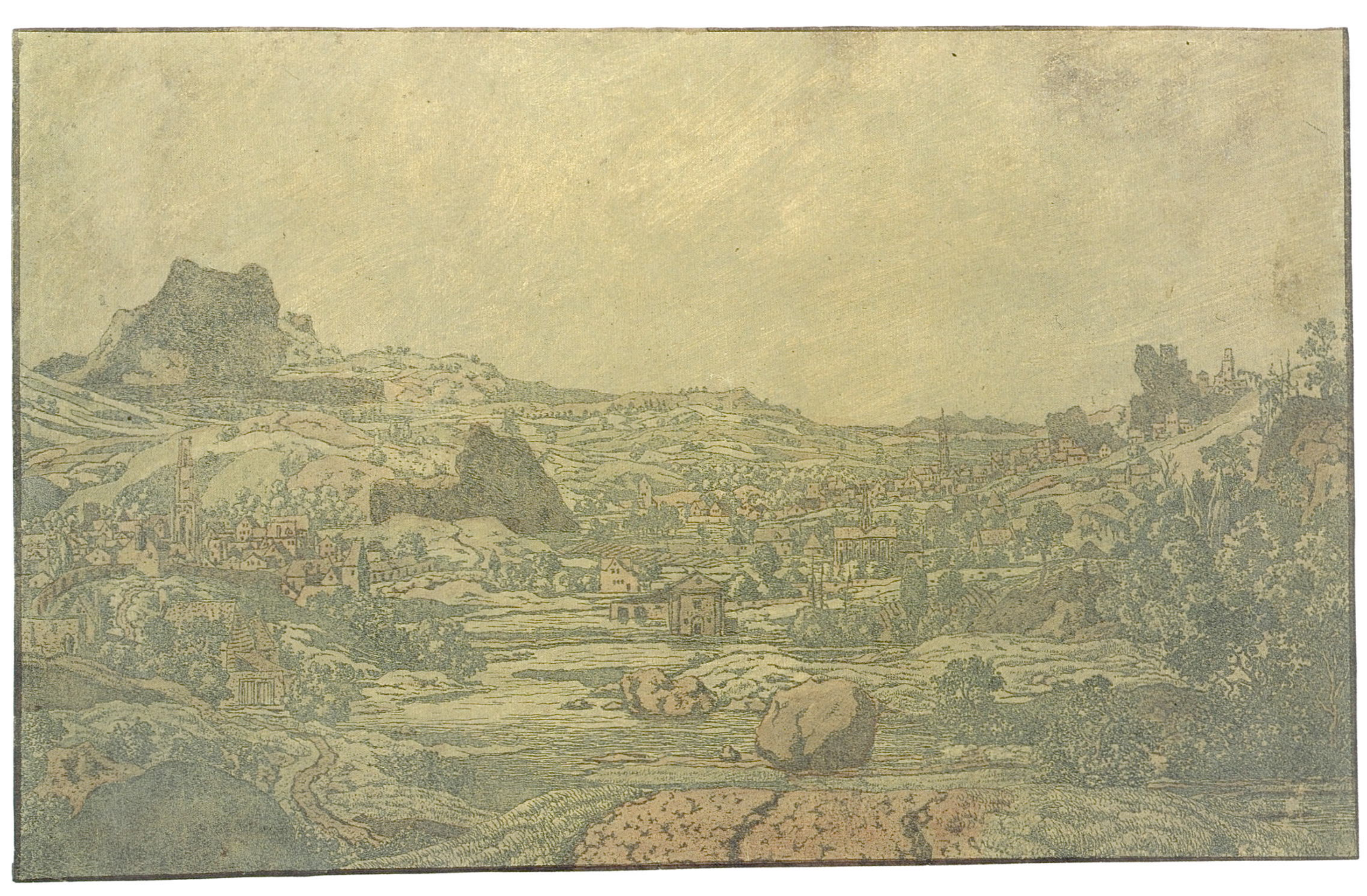

Hercules Segers, *Town with Four Towers*, ca. 1631 or later.

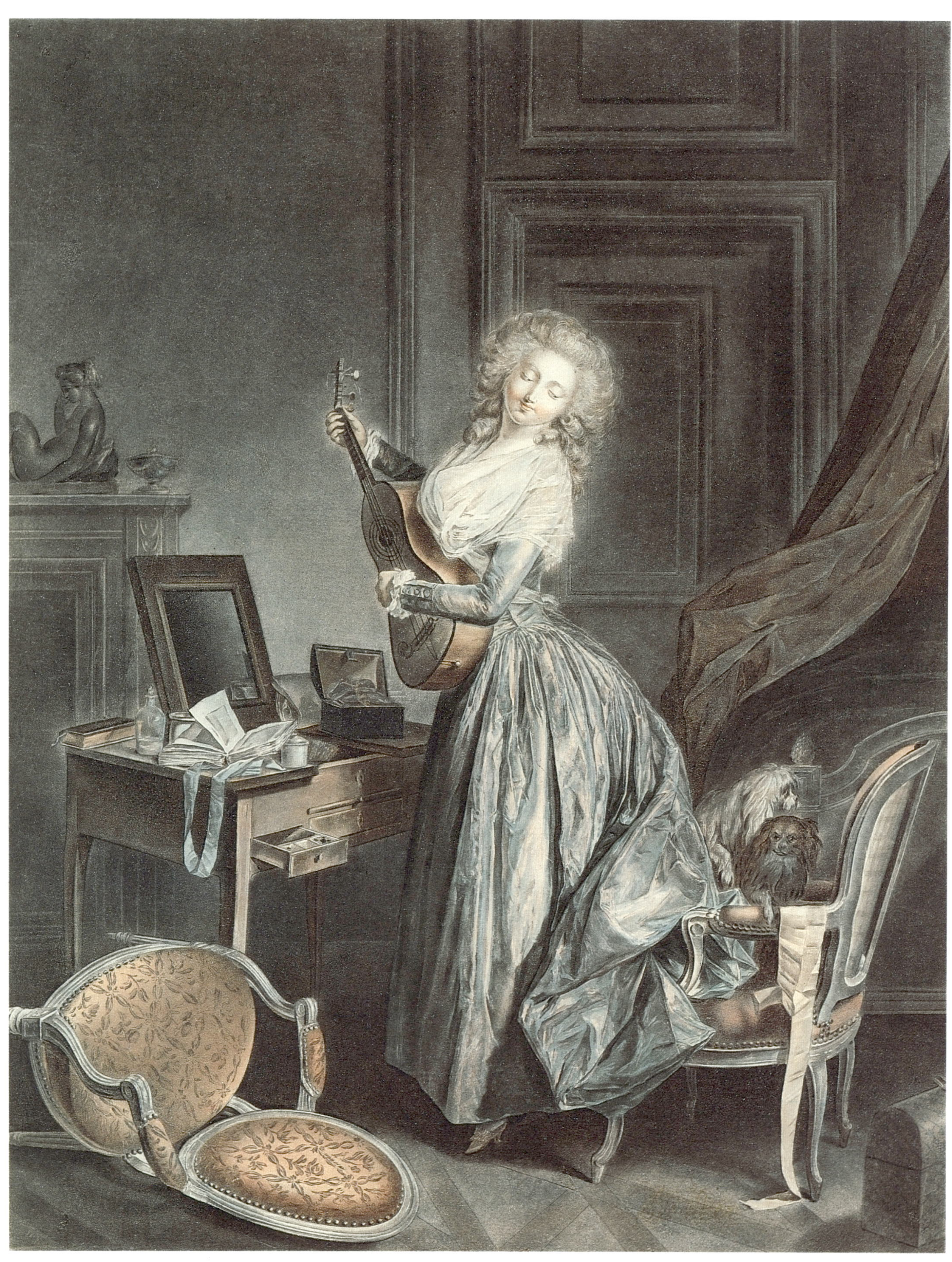

Jean-Francois Janinet, *The Guitar Player*, 1788-89.

Herbert Greer French

Herbert Greer French was one of Cincinnati's eminent citizens. As a vice-president of the Procter & Gamble Company, he was an outstanding figure in the business community, and was perhaps even more widely known for his distinguished leadership in artistic, cultural, and philanthropic activities. French possessed a rare combination of qualities. On the one hand, his judgment was sound and practical, and on the other, he possessed a deep feeling for beauty and quality in music, poetry, photography, and art. Few knew of his creative work – sensitive poems and songs – yet he was internationally known for the creation of an outstanding print collection.

French was born in Covington, Kentucky, on January 17, 1872, the son of Jeremiah Henry French and Katherine Smith French.[1] Two years later his family moved to Chicago, where his father became vice-president of the Chicago Board of Trade. In 1888, at the urging of William A. Procter, his father returned to Cincinnati to become treasurer of the Procter & Gamble Company. In 1893 French left his studies at the University of Cincinnati and joined the company as an under-clerk in the freight department at $40 per month. Two years later he transferred to the advertising department and from there went to the treasurer's office as an assistant cashier. In 1903, at the death of his father, he was made treasurer of the company. He was elected a vice-president in 1919 and was later made senior vice-president. His service to Procter & Gamble spanned nearly a half century and coincided with a period of corporate growth that saw this local industry become a giant of national and international importance. Needless to say, "his faith in Ivory soap was profound."[2]

Photo-Secession Photographer

In the spring of 1904 French was elected the only Cincinnati member of the Photo-Secession. Formed in 1902 by Alfred Stieglitz, the Photo-Secession, an informal organization of primarily American pictorial photographers, became the worldwide focal point for the finest in artistic photography in the first decade of the twentieth century. Although it is not known when French took up photography, as early as 1900 and 1901 he exhibited in the Third and Fourth Philadelphia Photographic Salons. Charles Fairman in his review of the 1901 Philadelphia Salon commented on French's entries:

Herbert Greer French. . . exhibited two pictures which were noticeable on account of their severe trimming. His "Chastened". . . was indeed a subject of curiosity, as no one seemed able to decide why such a narrow strip of a print should be so tentiously framed. His "Study of a Girl's Head". . . is a truly wonderful example of flesh tones and dainty lighting. . .[3]

At this early date, French was already an adherent of pictorialism. As with many pictorialist photographers, French was a serious amateur. His approach to focus and aesthetics falls within the formal pictorial ideas explored by many as the aesthetics of modernism. How he met Alfred Stieglitz remains a mystery. He may have been introduced by one of the founding members of the Photo-Secession, Clarence White of Newark, Ohio, who had a major exhibition at the Cincinnati Art Museum in 1900. In a January 4, 1904, letter to Stieglitz, White discussed French's work and in a subsequent letter on February 17, he mentioned that he had sent photographs by French to Stieglitz.[4] French's first correspondence with Stieglitz concerns details of a Cincinnati exhibition of Ohio Photo-Secessionists that he was organizing for May 1904.[5] On May 14 Stieglitz wrote of French that he had been elected to the Photo-Secession.[6]

An *Exhibition of Photographic Art* was arranged in cooperation with Stieglitz and shown at the Cincinnati Art Museum in February 1906. The appearance of such an estimable show in Cincinnati is tribute to French's commitment to the Photo-Secession and its aesthetic goals. In the preface to the seventy-five-piece exhibition checklist, French described the Photo-Secession as "a Society of protest against the use of photography as a purely mechanical means of reproduction; and its chief object is the establishment of photography as a recognized art medium."[7]

Between 1902 and 1909 French participated in over twenty major Photo-Secession shows in the United States and in Dresden, London, Paris, and Vienna. On January 26, 1906, French had the first one-man show at Stieglitz's "Little Galleries of the Photo-Secession" in New York.[8] He exhibited forty-five photographs illustrating Tennyson's version of the Arthurian legend, "Idylls of the King." In addition, he participated in four group exhibitions between 1905 and 1908. *Winged Victory* was exhibited in a 1907 group show and subsequently in Dresden in 1909.[9]

The last major exhibition outside of Cincinnati in which French participated was the *International Exhibition of Pictorial Photography* held at the National Arts Club, New York, in February 1909. J. Nilsen Laurvik, the reviewer for *Camera Work*, commented on his photographs:

Of like interest and importance were the delicate evocations of Herbert G. French, whose prints, almost breath-like in their subtlety of tone, furnished the most striking example of artistic reticence in the exhibition.[10]

Five of his photographs, including *Winged Victory*, were reproduced in the July 1909 issue of *Camera Work*, a quarterly of the organization, edited and published by Stieglitz.[11] Not only was French a subscriber to this important photographic periodical but he contributed financially to the Little Galleries' operation.

On September 13, 1910, French declined Stieglitz's request to show photographs in the *International Exhibition of Pictorial Photography* at the Albright Art Gallery in Buffalo which became the seminal show of the movement:

I have decided that, partly owing to lack of time, and partly to other reasons, which I can hardly outline in a letter but the value of which you may be able to surmise, I shall ask you to show no more of my work at any exhibitions whatsoever for the next few years. . . That you may always count on me to do anything in my power for the Photo-Secession goes without saying.[12]

French's activities as a photographer undoubtedly developed his discernment and visual acuity, which would play a major role in his future activities as a discriminating print collector. But there is no evidence to suggest that French continued to photograph. Indeed, in one of his last letters to Stieglitz, French wrote on February 13, 1938:

I have not kept up my photography but I have been very active in all phases of music and the arts in Cincinnati and have undertaken the task of seeing if I can not make collecting a fine art in itself. The early days in photography undoubtedly were a strong influence in my entering the field of etching and engravings. . .[13]

Herbert Greer French, *Winged Victory*, 1907, platinum print, Gift of Margaret L. Smith, 1979.345.

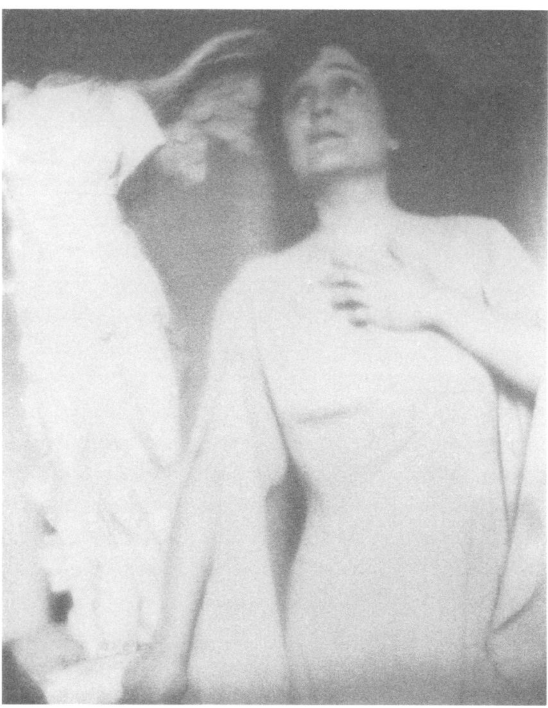

Philanthropic Leadership and Aesthetic Pursuits

A lifelong bachelor, French was committed to the welfare and education of the citizens of Greater Cincinnati. Owing to his untiring efforts and competent leadership as general chairman, the Community Chest had its most successful fund-raising campaign in its history in 1928. Again, in 1931, during the height of the Depression, he led a campaign that raised $2.42 million to help the unemployed. Although he never graduated from the University of Cincinnati, beginning in 1923, he served as a member of its Board of Trustees and as chairman of its finance committee and on various other committees.

He was not only active in humanitarian and civic affairs but he dedicated his time and energy as a leader of the city's cultural affairs. In 1929 French was president of the Cincinnati Institute of Fine Arts, formed in 1927, which raised money for the Cincinnati Symphony Orchestra and the Cincinnati Art Museum. He also served as the chairman of the institute's campaign to complete the $3.5 million endowment fund for the Taft Museum, the Pike Street home and art collection given by Mr. and Mrs. Charles P. Taft to the city.

As a man of many gifts and talents, French promoted the music, literature, and art of Cincinnati. As a youth, he studied voice at the College of Music, and for several years the richness of his baritone voice contributed to the performances of the Apollo Club and the May Festival Chorus. As a patron of music, he gave not only counsel but financial assistance to the Cincinnati Symphony Orchestra, upon whose Board of Trustees he sat for many years. He was sensitive, shy, gracious, and reticent, with a quiet humor. Despite his outward shyness, he was an enthusiastic member of the Cincinnati MacDowell Society, for whose dramatic and musical productions he served as creator, director, and actor. His interest in literature was equally broad. He was an active member of the Literary Club and privately published a collection of his poems under the title *Song of the Shores and Others* in 1925.

As a boy, French went bicycling west of Pleasant Ridge, a suburb of the city, and stopped at a farmhouse for a drink of water from an old-fashioned well. It was such a delightful place that he determined to buy it and decades later it became his home. Upon his death in 1942, this 275-acre Reachmont Farm was bequeathed to the City of Cincinnati and is enjoyed by all today as French Park.

Museum Trustee and Curator of Prints

Perhaps French's most lasting legacy was his many contributions to the Cincinnati Art Museum. In the early 1920s the Museum's second director, Joseph H. Gest, envisioned the establishment of a print department. With his encouragement, a group of prominent local collectors formed the Cincinnati Print and Drawing Circle on March 16, 1924. Their intent was to promote the understanding and enjoyment of prints among Cincinnatians and to foster the Museum's collection of prints and drawings. On March 22 the Circle opened an exhibition, *One Hundred Fine Prints from the 15th to the 20th Centuries*, at the Museum. The prints were lent by Cincinnati and New York financier Edward A. Seasongood. This exhibition and the purchase of a spurious Whistler from Emery H. Barton of Cincinnati piqued French's curiosity and prompted his serious study of the history of printmaking. He joined the Circle (now the Cincinnati Graphic Arts Forum) in 1925 and served as its president from 1930 to 1942. In 1926, at the age of fifty-four, he pursued his final aesthetic passion – to assemble a collection of engravings and etchings as a work of art.

> *He decided to begin his collection after much study of prints, their history and the place which they hold in the development of the fine arts. His desire was to bring together a representative expression of this phase of artistic achievement not according to the schools so much as provide the best work of the noblest exponent of the various definite periods.*[14]

He went on to explain that "his plan was to find the most brilliant and beautiful impression available..."[15]

In 1928 Gest established a print department and, with the endorsement of the Museum's trustees, invited French to become the first curator of prints. French not only accepted but, in 1929 during his first year as a trustee of the Museum, he donated $100,000 to build the French wing, which completed the quadrangle formed by the Mary Emery and Mary Hanna wings. When the wing opened in January 1930, its lower floors contained three print galleries and a print study room; the upper floor was used for general exhibition galleries. For the wing's inaugural exhibition, French lent ninety-three prints for the edification of Cincinnati print lovers. These prints were the first group in an ongoing series of prints lent to the Museum by French and by other Cincinnati collectors, including Allyn C. Poole and Mr. and Mrs. George Warrington. Simultaneously, the Museum's first study room formally opened, and Emily Poole was installed as assistant in charge of prints and drawings, a position French underwrote until his death.

As French was building his collection, he had the opportunity to study over 180 fine prints from the Seasongood Collection which were on extended loan for study and exhibition purposes from 1930 to 1939. Although this collection contained many rarities, French was able to secure impressions of seventy-five of the same prints in comparable or better impressions, including Giovanni Antonio da Brescia's *Hercules and the Nemean Lion* (cat. 36), Jacopo de' Barbari's *Three Captives* (cat. 34), and de rigueur for a gentleman's collection, Antonio Pollaiuolo's *Battle of the Nudes* (cat. 16). Ultimately, the Seasongood Collection was returned and sold at Parke-Bernet in New York in 1951.

In 1939 French purchased, as a gift to the Museum, 680 prints for $30,000 from the estate of the pioneer Cincinnati print collector and fellow trustee, Allyn C. Poole. This collection, begun early in the century, focused on prints from the sixteenth through twentieth centuries, with special emphasis on portraits, woodcuts, and lithographs, prints that complemented French's own collection, which he was assembling and planned to give to the Museum as a bequest. Among the comparative impressions selected for didactic purposes were Dürer's *The Four Horsemen* from the 1498 edition with Latin text, Rembrandt's *Faust in his Study* in the second state, and Toulouse-Lautrec's *The Jockey* from the first edition printed in black in 1899. Among the highlights of the purchase were twenty-four Dürer woodcuts, fourteen Rembrandts, eleven Hadens, twelve Whistlers, forty Toulouse-Lautrecs, nine Picassos, ninety-two chiaroscuro prints, and over one hundred portraits of artists and historical figures. French's purchase was the most important group of prints to enter the Museum's collection up to this time. Two years later French gave one hundred etchings by the Dutch landscape artist Allart van Everdingen to the Museum.

The Collection as a Work of Art

French's bequest of his personal collection, noted for its quality, connoisseurship, and scholarship, established the nucleus of a truly great print collection at the Museum. Arthur M. Hind, renowned keeper of prints and drawings at the British Museum, while lecturing in Cincinnati in 1949, paid tribute to French's legacy.

> *Mr. French was an outstanding collector, of fine discernment, who gathered works by Rembrandt, the early Italian masters, and all the great masters including the moderns.*[16]

French actively collected from 1926 to 1941, during the post-World War I years when great European auction houses, particularly C.G. Boerner in Leipzig, held frequent auctions, dispersing great rarities that would never again appear on the market. Among the important collections from which French acquired prints were the collections of Friedrich August II of Saxony (1927-37), Count Yorck von Wartenburg (1932), Prince Walburg-Wolfegg (1934), the Earl of Northwick (1933), and Oettingen-Wallerstein (1937). In addition, French had the perspicacity to acquire duplicates from the Albertina in Vienna, including *Melpomene* (cat. 5) by the Master of the E-Series Tarocchi, and *Landscape with a Road beside a Canal* (cat. 85) by Rembrandt from The Metropolitan Museum of Art.

French recognized that the provenance of connoisseurs like Jean-Pierre Mariette, William Esdaile, and Paul J. Sachs, and noted print scholars like Loys Delteil and Henri Beraldi, added to the luster of a particular impression and prestige to the overall collection. He stamped all of his prints in blue with his own collector's mark.

French acquired his prints from a number of sources: F.C. Bresler, Milwaukee; Albert Roullier, Chicago; Kennedy Galleries, New York; and over half from M. Knoedler and Company, New York. From the early 1920s Norman F. Wells, head of Knoedler's print department, regularly visited Cincinnati several times a year. It was in Wells that French found a man whose judgment and advice he valued. From 1927 onward until his death in 1939, French's personal vision for his collection was fired by the quality of Old Masters and moderns that Wells steered his way. Wells would often send batches of prints or comparative impressions for French to examine so that he could judiciously make up his own mind. Perhaps the biggest challenge that Wells directed to French was the opportunity to acquire the rarest of rarities, a color print, *The Town with Four Towers* (cat. 76), by Hercules Segers. French initially turned down the piece; however, Wells persisted, insisting that French study the artist. French ultimately bought *The Town* for $12,500, along with a stunning impression of *The Fall of Man* (cat. 1) by the Master E.S. for $6,250 on April 1, 1935.

Knoedler's supplied French with "waxed paper" to protect his prints, ordered solander boxes, coordinated conservation, searched rare references, and updated him on new print publications. From the 182 library books that accompanied French's bequest to the Museum, it is clear that books like P. G. Hamerton's *Etching and Etchers*, Arthur M. Hind's *A History of Engraving and Etching* and *Early Italian Engraving* (4 vols.), Frank Weitenkampf's *Famous Prints*, and *The Print Collector's Quarterly*, edited by Fritzroy Carrington and later Campbell Dodgson, guided his vision of his collection.

In order to enhance the quality of his collection, French traded over fifty pieces, upgrading impressions of Schongauer's *Annunciation*, Mantegna's *Mother and Child*, and Meryon's *Le Petit Pont* (cat. 123) twice before being satisfied with an impression on greenish paper (cat. 123). One of the emphases of his collecting was fifteenth-century European engraving. Although he acquired over one hundred prints from that period, he was only able to find a fragment done by the earliest engraver, the Master of the Playing Cards (fig. 7). Two of French's prints are unique: *Satire on Gossip during the Celebration of the Mass* by the Master of the Meshed Background (cat. 22) and *The Annunciation* (cat. 24) by Mair von Landshut. Twenty-three of his prints, including *The Fall of Man* (cat. 1) by the Master E.S., *Lovers on Horseback* (cat. 9) by the Master b g, and a first state impression of *Design for a Mantle-Clasp (Monile)* (cat. 10) by the Master W with the Key, are the only examples found in North America. Among the distinctive impressions are a striking one on blue paper of *St. Anne with the Virgin and Child and Four Angels* (cat. 25) by Mair von Landshut and an impression of *Christ Appearing to Mary Magdalene* (cat. 8) by Martin Schongauer, which was cited by Max Lehrs as one of the artist's most beautiful prints. In total he found thirty-seven fifteenth-century Italian engravings that Hind cites in his final three volumes of *Early Italian Engravings*, including Francesco Rosselli's *Moses on Mount Sinai* and the *Brazen Serpent* (cat. 15) and five of the seven engravings ascribed to Andrea Mantegna.

He collected twenty-eight engravings and fifteen woodcuts in superlative impressions by his favorite artist, Albrecht Dürer. When he lectured about Dürer, French told a tale of a magical green garment that enabled him to return to the sixteenth century in his imagination and befriend the artist.[17] He entitled this imaginary adventure, "With Verdure Clad," a phrase taken from one of Haydn's *Creation* arias. Together the two friends went to the Garden of Eden where Dürer engraved his magnificent *Adam and Eve* (cat. 33). French was thrilled to acquire a superlative impression of this print, an early state before the cleft in the tree was added, which once belonged to William Esdaile. Not only was he able to acquire fine impressions of Dürer's three *Meisterstuche* (cats. 47-49) but he

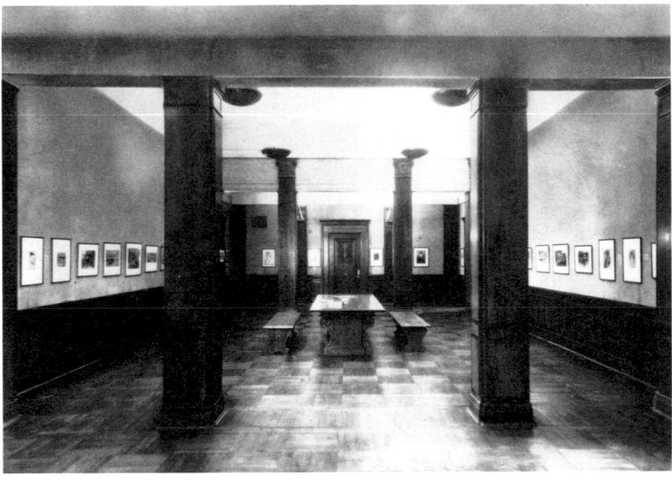

View of the print galleries in the new Herbert Greer French wing.

found an impression of one of his earliest etchings, *The Landscape with the Cannon* (cat. 52), before evidence of rust on the plate. The collection traces the development of pure landscape by the Little Masters like Augustin Hirschvogel and Hanns Lautensack and the first exponents of printmaking in France, Jean de Gourmont and Jean Duvet. French secured a fine impression of Lucas van Leyden's portrait *Emperor Maximilian I* (cat. 55), the earliest print combining engraving and etching. It is equally interesting to note that French did not buy examples of the school of Fontainebleau or mannerism, except Hendrick Goltzius' Düreresque *Pietà* (cat. 69).

For the seventeenth century he sought out five first state portraits (cats. 72-73) by Van Dyck, *Saint Catherine of Alexandria in the Clouds* (cat. 71) by Rubens, and a second state set of *The Miseries of and Misfortunes of War* (cat. 74) by Jacques Callot. In addition he sought Masters of the French school of portrait engravings, including Masson and Edelinck, and a host of Dutch seventeenth-century genre printmakers to complement his two-color Segers and forty-three etchings by another of his favorite artists, Rembrandt.

On February 11, 1929, the Cincinnati Enquirer carried the banner headline, "Etching Treasure is owned by Cincinnatian."

> *The eyes of international connoisseurs of art have been directed to Cincinnati as the inheritor of a rarely beautiful example of the most famous and the most stirring etching by the greatest master of all etching, "Christ Healing the Sick," by Rembrandt. . . . It was in order that Cincinnati might be the repository of this extremely fine impression of Rembrandt's so-called "hundred guilder print," and thus make it accessible to students and collectors from far and near for the purposes of study that French secured this print. . . . [It] is unique in its superb quality, a matchless impression of the greatest etching of all time in the nobility of its human message. . .* [18]

The impression, which he acquired from F.C. Bresler on October 1, 1928, came from a private European collection. This singular purchase, acquired for $15,000, was his most important purchase to that date, and marks his strong commitment to acquire master works for his collection. Trustee John W. Warrington recently recounted that French showed this print to him and other guests by candlelight as it would have been viewed during the artist's time. French went on to acquire a splendid group of Rembrandt portraits in the first state, including *Jan Asselyn* (cat. 83), *Jan Lutma, Goldsmith* (cat. 90), and an exquisite second state impression of *Jacob Haaringh* (cat. 89), along with numerous landscapes, the most important of which was *The Three Trees* (cat. 81).

The eighteenth-century Italian school is represented by first state impressions of etchings by the triumvirate of Canaletto (cat. 100),

Tiepolo (cat. 101), and Piranesi, represented by an early set of *Carceri* (cat. 102).

In 1935 French acquired a spectacular group of eighteenth-century French color prints. He acquired a total of eleven prints from the Cortlandt F. Bishop Collection auctioned at the American Art Association-Anderson Galleries in 1935, including one of four known impressions of Janinet's *The Guitar Player* (cat. 111) and an early impression before inscription of Debucourt's *The Public Promenade* (cat. 115), thus adding to his landmarks in the history of color. The collection includes highlights from the history of mezzotint, starting with Von Siegen's *Amelia Elisabeth, Landgravine of Hesse-Cassel* (cat. 80), Le Blon's portrait of *Ernst Wilhelm von Salisch* (cat. 97), the forerunner of four color printing, and Pelham's *Cotton Mather* (cat. 98), the first American example. Typical of collectors of his generation French bought a large group of eighteenth-century British mezzotints, all scratched-proof impressions, among them Green's *Mary Isabella, Duchess of Rutland* (cat. 108) and Smith's *Lieutenant Colonel Sir Banastre Tarleton* (cat. 109). His enthusiasm for Blake prompted him to acquire a beautiful hand-colored version of *Songs of Innocence* (cat. 112).

The expatriate Whistler was another of French's favorite artists. He acquired a total of twenty-six works by Whistler, including an evocative impression of *Nocturne* (cat. 135) and an early, previously undescribed state of *The Embroidered Curtain* (cat. 138). Hanging in French's office at the time of his death was *Riva Degli Schiavoni, Number Two* (cat 136), a proof before the edition by Whistler's contemporary and Cincinnati-area artist, Frank Duveneck.

As was popular at the time, French collected the major figures of the nineteenth-century French etching revival, including Bracquemond (cat. 124), Millet (cat. 126), Meryon (cats. 123, 125), and a unique first state drypoint of Rodin's *Victor Hugo* (cat. 137). The gift from Knoedler of Daumier's *Nadar Elevating Photography to Artistic Heights* (cat. 130) and the death of Allyn Poole, whose lithographs were donated to the Museum, led French to branch out in a new direction during his last years and add Daumier's masterpiece *Rue Transnonain, April 15, 1934* (cat. 122) and color lithographs by Redon (cat. 140) and Toulouse-Lautrec (cat. 139, 142) to his collection.

Like his contemporaries, French looked to Europe for prints of the established avant-garde: Cameron (cats. 143-144), McBey (cats. 145, 148), Griggs (cat. 147), and one of his last purchases, a classical-style Picasso (cat. 146). Although he did acquire contemporary American works by Martin Lewis (cat. 149) and by his personal friend John Taylor Arms (cat. 150), it is ironic that he never took an interest in American modernism as it evolved in the 1920s and 1930s, particularly as his old friend Alfred Stieglitz was one of its champions.

On September 27, 1941, the Museum celebrated his tremendous accomplishments with an *Exhibition of Prints of the Fifteenth, Sixteenth, Seventeenth, and Eighteenth Centuries from the Collection of Herbert Greer French*, showing 236 prints. Carl O. Schniewind, then recently appointed curator of prints and drawings at the Art Institute of Chicago, gave a testimonial lecture, "A Collection as a Work of Art," at the opening. Within less than a year, on June 25, 1942, at the age of seventy, French died. He bequeathed to the Museum his print collection, library, and a $250,000 endowment; the income of $100,000 was designated for the care and maintenance of the print department. French's passing and his generosity was a newsworthy event, and articles appeared in numerous art magazines and professional journals around the world.

French's high standards and tireless efforts to assemble a major print collection brought the best of European art and culture to the citizens of Cincinnati. He anticipated that future donors would expand and strengthen the collection, continually adding to it the

No.	ARTIST	TITLE	PRICE	Discount	NET
433	B. Montagna	"St. Jerome beneath an Arch of Rock."	2800."	600."	2200."
434	Raimondi	"Les Grimpeurs." (The Climbers.)	350."	100."	250."
435	G. Campagnola	"The Astrologer."	1.450."	400."	1.050."
436	Schongauer	"The Annunciation."	3.500."	1.320."	2.180."
437	Dürer	"Christ on the Cross." (large plate.)	2.000.	—	2.000."
438	Briscoe	"Typhoon: The Burst Topsail."	10.100." 225."	2.420." 25."	7.680." 200."
439	" "	"Heaving the Line."	225.	25."	200.
440	" "	"Making Sail."	225."	25."	200.
441	Hollar	"The Straight Canal."	36."	—	36.
442	Baroccio	"Virgin and Child in the Clouds."	45."	—	45."
443	Master E.S.	"The Fall of Man."	6750."	special price	6.250."
444	Seghers	"Landscape with a Town with Four Church Spires."	12.500."	"	12.500."
445	Whistler	"Weary."	2.750."		
446	" "	"Pierrot."	2400."	500"	9.400.
447	Rembrandt	"Landscape with a Ruined Tower and a Clear Foreground." H.244	4750." 29.800."	2.995."	36.511."
448	Schongauer	"Christ bearing His Cross."	7.500." 47.000."	1600." 4.595."	5.900." 42.411."

Page 13 from French's print purchase ledger.

Herbert Greer French collector's mark (Lugt S. 1307a).

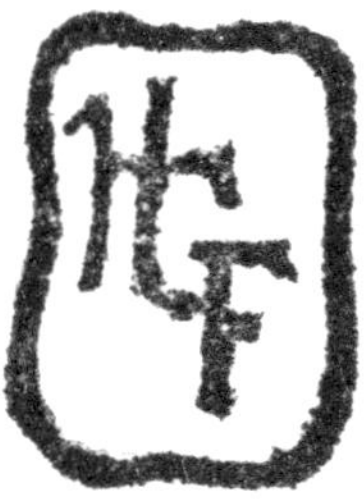

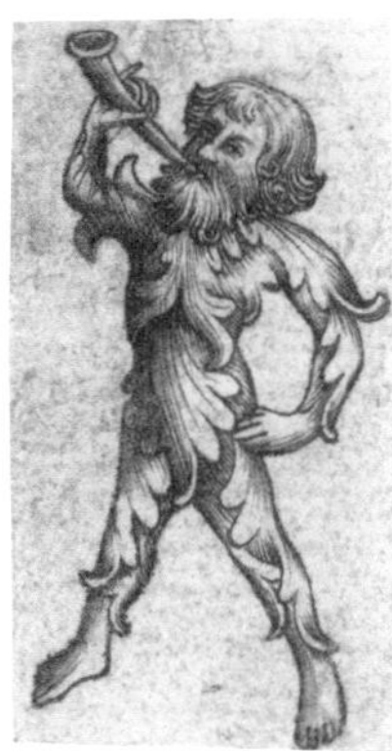

Master of the Playing Cards, *Man Clothed with Foliage and Blowing a Horn*, ca. 1446, engraving, 1943.145.

works of contemporary artists and exploring new areas of emphasis. Although the competition for print rarities was formidable, with curators like Henry P. Rossiter at the Museum of Fine Arts, Boston, and William M. Ivins, Jr. at The Metropolitan Museum of Art, New York, in the hunt, French is one of the legendary group of American collectors, including Lessing J. Rosenwald for the National Gallery, Washington, W. G. Russell Allen for the Museum of Fine Arts, Boston, and Herschel V. Jones for the Minneapolis Institute of Arts, who established world-class collections for joy and edification in the graphic arts.

Research and Revelations

At the time of French's death, his collection was internationally recognized for its connoisseurship, scholarship, and quality. The criterion for the 150 essays in this publication was to reexamine the aesthetic, scholarly, and physical aspects of the selected highlights from the collection.

Each author brought to the project critical judgment and historical expertise. Timothy Riggs discovered that the Flemish fifteenth-century illustration to the *Canticum Canticorum* (CAM 1943.45) was not a hand-colored woodcut but a die-stamped collotype reproduction from 1922, cut from a complete facsimile of the original work and published by the Marées-Gesellschaft in Berlin. The clues that led to his discovery were paper without laid lines, discreetly aged by coloring, the slight offset of the indentations from the ink lines, and the tear extending from the lower margin into the blue drapery of the bride. This tear extended further on the front than on the back of the sheet but had been disguised with watercolor.

Perhaps the most far-reaching revelation was related to French's pride and joy, Rembrandt's *Christ Healing the Sick,* popularly known as the "hundred guilder print." In comparing detail photographs with other impressions, George Keyes discovered in the lower left corner parallel hatching lines that did not appear on other impressions. This discovery touched off a microscopic examination of all areas of the print. Elizabeth Coombs, former Museum associate conservator for paper, suggested that there were dry brush strokes on the dog and the gourd slung on the woman's back. To clarify exactly what the Museum's impression was, the print was taken to the Museum of Fine Arts, Boston, and the Fogg Art Museum, Cambridge, and was compared with two other second state impressions and examined microscopically. The conclusion of the participating scholars, curators, and conservators was that the French impression had been discreetly and pervasively reworked by hand to the point where the mystical and atmospheric quality of the print had been greatly compromised. The second curiosity about the Museum's impression was its posthorn watermark, which had not appeared in the census of watermarks conducted by the National Gallery of Art. Rembrandt paper specialist Theo Laurentius eventually confirmed that the Museum's impression could indeed be seventeenth century.[19] After much deliberation, however, it was decided that Rembrandt's *Jan Asselyn* (cat. 83), another fine print, would replace *Christ Healing the Sick* in this catalogue.

Physical examination and X-rays of watermarks were equally revealing about several impressions. An X-ray of *The Nativity* (cat. 2) by the Master E.S. revealed that the entire upper edge had been added to a depth of 2 cm to 3 cm, with brushwork on the wall, roof, and angel. Likewise the *Betrayal of Christ* (cat. 13) by the Master IAM had been remargined and the signatures, upper and side border lines, horizontal hatching on both sides outside the pillars, and occasional lines in the outer pillars were added with pen and black ink. Two other pieces that were eliminated from the catalogue because of even more extensive areas of restoration worked with pen and ink were Jean Gourmont's *Nativity* (CAM 1943.258) and Benedetto Montagna's *St. Jerome Beneath an Arch of Rock* (CAM 1943.156). With new tools of physical examination now available, all major print collections housing sizable holdings of Old Master prints have retouched and restored impressions only now coming to light; the French Collection is no exception.

Perhaps equally challenging for the scholar and layman alike is the judicious reexamination of historic documents, or the lack thereof, in connection with the artists frequently grouped as the school of Mantegna and Andrea Mantegna himself. Certainly the evidence that the two artists, Giovanni Antonio da Brescia and Zoan Andrea are actually one in the same as discussed under *Hercules and the Nemean Lion* (cat. 36) is a revelation. Perhaps more stimulating is the scholarly position of Suzanne Boorsch that the seven engravings traditionally assigned to Mantegna were executed by a professional

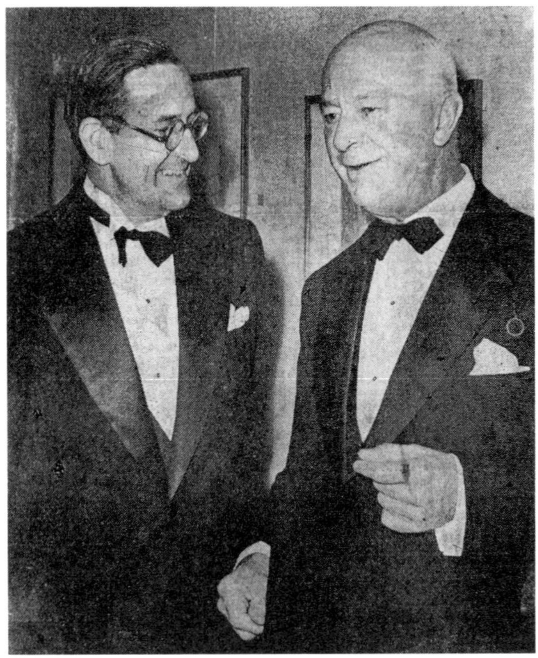

Carl O. Schniewind and Herbert Greer French at the opening of an *Exhibition of Prints of the Fifteenth, Sixteenth, Seventeenth, and Eighteenth Centuries from the Collection of Herbert Greer French* (*Cincinnati Times Star*, September 27, 1941).

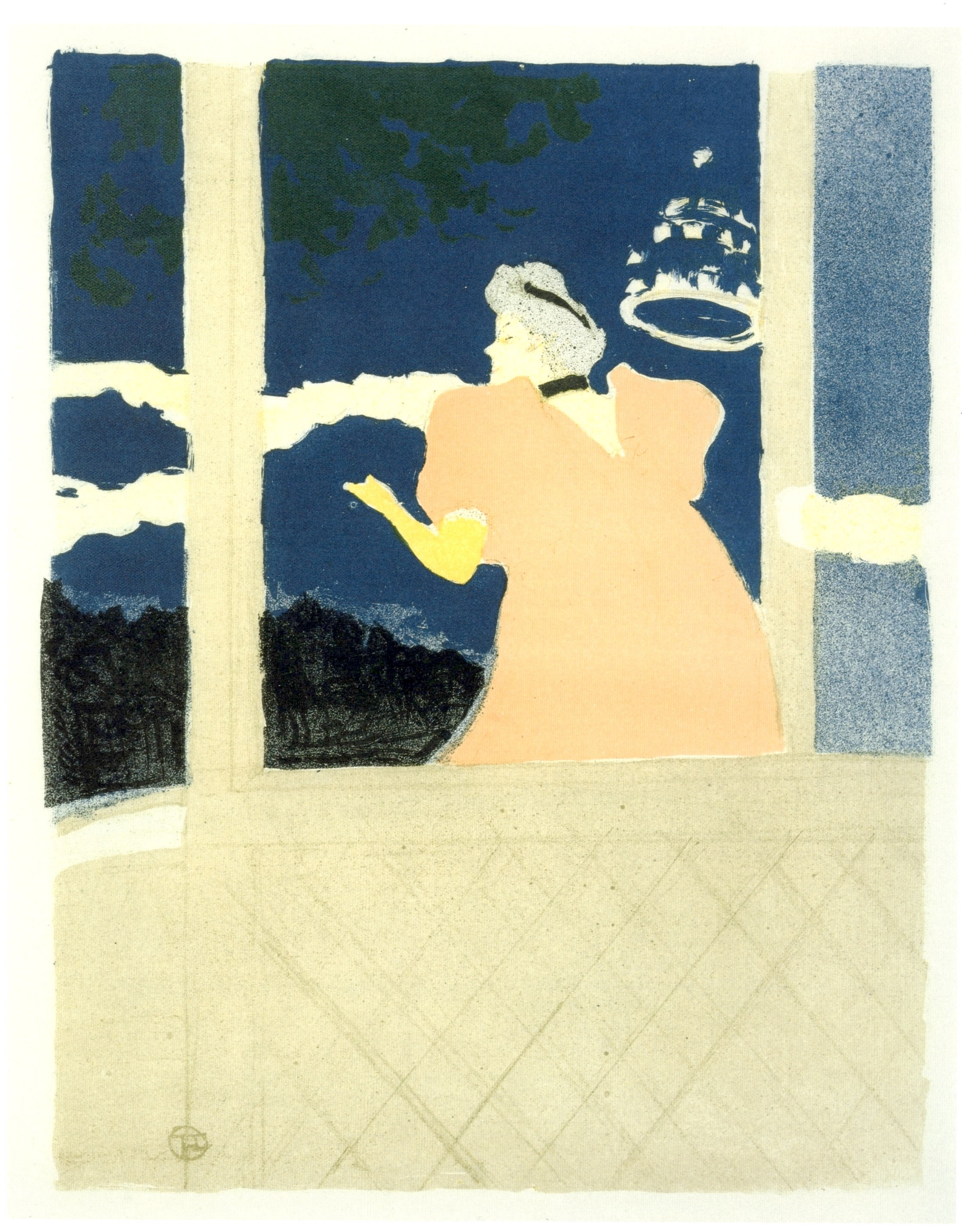

Henri de Toulouse-Lautrec, *At the Ambassadeurs – Café Concert Singer*, 1894.

engraver rather than the artist. Although this is not the first time that this challenge to the great artist theory has been put forth in this century, it represents the courage of a new generation of scholars to critically review aesthetic and historical premises that have been uncritically accepted and passed down over the years. All 150 entries published in this catalogue represent the authors' expertise and judgment, and it is hoped that they will stimulate further scholarly inquiry and debate, which was the underlying premise for undertaking this publication.

Kristin L. Spangenberg

1. Biographical material is derived from the Procter & Gamble Company Corporate Archives, Cincinnati.

2. This extract is taken from a memorial brochure produced at the time of French's death, presumably by the Procter & Gamble Company.

3. Charles E. Fairman, "The Fourth Philadelphia Photo-graphic Salon," *The Photographic Times,* no. 2 (March 1902): 107-108. "Study of a Girl's Head" is illustrated on p. 109.

4. Clarence White, Letter to Alfred Stieglitz, January 4, 1904, and February 17, 1904, Stieglitz Archives, *Collection of American Literature,* Beinecke Rare Book and Manuscript Library, Yale University, New Haven.

5. Herbert Greer French, Letter to Alfred Stieglitz, March 2, 1904, Stieglitz Archives.

6. Herbert Greer French, Letter to Alfred Stieglitz, May 16, 1904, Stieglitz Archives. This record mentions the date of Stieglitz's earlier letter.

7. Herbert Greer French, pref., *Exhibition of Photographic Art* (Cincinnati: Cincinnati Art Museum, 1906).

8. Weston J. Naef, *The Collection of Alfred Stieglitz: Fifty Pioneers of Modern Photography* (New York: Viking Press, 1978), 42.

9. Naef, *The Collection of Alfred Stieglitz,* 364, cat. 304.

10. J. Nilsen Laurvik, "International Photography at the National Arts Club, New York," *Camera Work* 26 (April 1909): 41.

11. Alfred Stieglitz, ed., *Camera Work* 27 (July 1909): pls. 1-5.

12. Herbert Greer French, Letter to Alfred Stieglitz, September 13, 1910, Stieglitz Archives.

13. Herbert Greer French, Letter to Alfred Stieglitz, February 13, 1938, Stieglitz Archives.

14. *Cincinnati Enquirer,* February 17, 1930.

15. *Cincinnati Enquirer,* February 17, 1930.

16. Charles Ludwig, "Collection in Art Museum Admired by British Visitor," *Cincinnati Times Star,* May 6, 1949.

17. Herbert Greer French. Lecture to the Literary Club, March 18, 1935, record of which is contained in The Cincinnati Historical Society.

18. *Cincinnati Enquirer,* February 11, 1929.

19. Theo Laurentius, Letter to Kristin L. Spangenberg, August 26, 1991.

Explanatory Notes

The one hundred fifty masterpieces and accompanying essays contained in this catalogue are organized chronologically by century so that the reader may assess the artistic achievement of each, independent of school or geographic origin. Images of these selected works are gathered into sections after the essay material and reproduced as close to actual size as possible. Related comparative images are found interspersed within each essay.

Each essay is followed by notes. Frequently cited books, exhibitions, and catalogues have been abbreviated, and complete citations may be referenced in these categories in the back of this catalogue.

Additionally, each essay begins with a description of the object and its exhibition and publication history presented in the following manner:

Titles: Translated into English.

Dates: Established from the prints or by external sources; appear after the title. *Ca.* (circa) precedes approximate dates.

Medium: Described with reference to the state of the print.

Measurements: Listed in centimeters, height preceding width. Measurements represent the plate mark or sheet for intaglio prints and composition for lithographs.

Catalogue Raisonnés: Appear under the author's name or in abbreviated form, followed by catalogue and state. Occasionally an exhibition catalogue, if now established under the author's name, will be located by author's name. For multi-volume catalogues the volume and page number are cited only when the artist appears under a different name.

Condition: Recorded when significant conditions affecting the image or sheet exist.

Signatures and Inscriptions: Transcribed from the work.

Accession Number: The year of acquisition to the Museum's collection is followed by a period and the number indicating the order in which it was received. For example, 1943.1 means that this object was the first work acquired in 1943.

Provenance: Listed chronologically by previous owner. All dealers' names appear in parentheses. Names of dealers have been abbreviated; for example, M. Knoedler & Company is simply referred to as M. Knoedler. Information pertaining to known auction sales follows each collector's name. Lot number, sale price, and buyer are cited where known. Collector and sale stamps recorded in Fritz Lugt's *Les Marques de la Collections le dessins et d'estampes* and the *Supplément* are referred to as *Lugt* and *Lugt S.*

Exhibitions: Those significant for dating, scholarship, or ownership of the Museum's impression have been listed under the place and date of first venue (i.e., Boston 1984), followed by item number. A full citation of the exhibition catalogue appears in the exhibition bibliography in the back of the catalogue.

References: All monographs or references cite specialized states, critical analyses, and commentaries about the Museum's impressions, with the exception of catalogue raisonnés (appear above) and exhibition catalogues (appear in back).

Illustrations: All works are reproduced actual size wherever possible.

xv

Master E. S.

Upper Rhenish active ca. 1450-1467

1. The Fall of Man

Engraving on antique laid paper, 19.0 x 14.2 cm (image) on 19.2 x 14.4 cm (sheet).
B. 1; Lehrs 1; Geisberg 1909 p. 8of; Geisberg 1924, p. 29; TIB 1.
Condition: Worm hole Adam's upper right arm filled.
Provenance: Ducal Museum, Gotha; (sale C.G. Boerner, Leipzig, May 2-3, 1932, no. 52, pl. 8, to Matthiesen for RM 9,200); (purchased from M. Knoedler, New York, March 1, 1935, for $6,250).
Bequest of Herbert Greer French, 1943.69.
Exhibitions: Cincinnati 1941, no. 20; Minneapolis 1956, no. 11; Philadelphia 1967, no. 19, illus.

Master E.S., the most influential of the first two generations of engravers, is the earliest printmaker to have been honored with a one-man show.[1] Ironically it now appears increasingly likely that "he" may have been a workshop or publishing house rather than a single artist.

It has traditionally been assumed that Master E.S., like the majority of the earliest-known engravers, trained initially as a goldsmith – an appropriate background, since the engraver's burin, a steel-shafted tool with two sharpened cutting edges on its diamond-shaped tip, was the same instrument employed by generations of goldsmiths (before the invention of the printing press) to add customized ornament to gold and silver objects made for royal or liturgical use. The engravings attributed to Master E.S. reveal not only an unusual virtuosity in handling the burin but also a frequent use of goldsmith's punches to create uniform patterns of tiny circles, stars, lozenges, and other shapes to decorate borders of clothing or arms and armor. Some of his plates, in fact, are designs for pure ornament of a type that were put to use by goldsmiths, woodcarvers, embroiderers, and other skilled artisans.

It was in Master E.S.'s workshop that engraving plates were "signed" for the first time – the Gothic letters *E*, *e*, *S*, or *ES* were placed on eighteen of the 318 known plates attributed to this artist. Sixteen of the plates were also dated: two in 1461, four in 1466, and ten in 1467. After the workshop closed – presumably at the time of death or incapacitation of the master – a number of the plates were acquired and reworked by Israhel van Meckenem; another plate even found its way to Italy to be reused.

Engravings made in Master E.S.'s atelier were the first to utilize the technique of cross-hatching and to display a rich variety of other burin effects, including stippling, to express subtleties of shading and texture. These innovations were a distinct improvement over the simple system of parallel lines employed by the earliest-known engraver, the Upper Rhenish Master of the Playing Cards,[2] and they laid the foundation for the distinctive modeling systems of Martin Schongauer (cats. 6-8) and Albrecht Dürer (cats. 33, 48).

Some of the prints from the workshop of Master E.S. were the first reproductions of identifiable paintings and sculptures: the epitaph fresco over the tomb of Otto III of Hachberg (in the Cathedral of Constance, dated 1445) is repeated in one of the monogrammed and dated engravings made for the Benedictine monastery of Einsiedeln (Switzerland).[3] Other engravings reflect the figure style of the Netherlandish sculptor Nicolaus Gerhaert of Leiden, who was active in Strasbourg in the 1460s.[4] Many of Master E.S.'s engravings were widely used in their turn as sources of inspiration for subsequent paintings, prints, and pieces of sculpture by such major artists as Hans Memling, Hugo van der Goes, Martin Schongauer, and Tilmann Riemenschneider.

In accordance with the nineteenth-century great man theory of art history, the earliest cataloguers of German fifteenth century engraving, including Adam Bartsch, Max Lehrs,[5] and Max Geisberg,[6] assumed that all of the signed engravings and those closely related to them in technique and style were the work of a single artist. Geisberg further speculated that Master E.S. had been responsible for up to five hundred individual engravings, including nearly two hundred "lost" compositions reflected in the work of other artists. Lehrs and Geisberg further hypothesized that the letters engraved on his plates were the artist's own initials – a strong possibility in light of the monograms of such later artists as Schongauer, Dürer, and Israhel van Meckenem, whose names were known. Consequently, archival searches were undertaken in several cities by various scholars in an effort to discover the artist's proper name. Several candidates were put forward, including Endres Silbernagel, Erhard Schön, Egidius Steclin, and Erwin von Stege (mintmaster to the Emperor Friedrich III), none of which has found universal acceptance.[7]

Several of the engravings have inscriptions written in the Alemannic dialect of southwestern Germany, while some of the watermarks on the papers used in Master E.S.'s workshop, including signed ones, can be traced to both south German and Swiss mills (the "walking bear" of the city of Bern is the most distinctive of these).

Holm Bevers quite plausibly suggests that the body of work known as the oeuvre of Master E.S. should probably be regarded as the output of a workshop[8] rather than of a single artist. If further research proves Master E.S. to have been a publisher or a medieval partnership rather than an individual engraver, the supposed chronology of the undated works will have to be reevaluated. Fritz Koreny cogently argues in favor of the traditional dating of the artist's prints. He points out that it coincides with the stylistic progress of engraving, from the parallel hatchings of Master E.S.'s predecessor, the Master of the Playing Cards, to the complex and systematic cross-hatching and double cross-hatching employed by Martin Schongauer, who by the early 1470s had supplanted Master E.S. as the most influential engraver of the period. According to Koreny, then, Master E.S.'s Fine Manner engravings with parallel modeling strokes would therefore remain his earliest, while those in his Broad Manner should continue to be regarded as closer in date to Schongauer's rise to fame.[9]

Since the dated plates are among those that, on the basis of their richer modeling style, scholars have traditionally identified as Master E.S.'s most fully developed work, it can still be assumed that the artist's death or retirement must have occurred by 1468.

The Museum's *Fall of Man* is one of the three best of eight known impressions and is the only example in an American collection. An early impression, its crisp contours and cast shadows are in perfect condition. The serpent's peacock-feather crest retains the fresh, drypointlike effect caused by waste copper left on the surface of the plate. The full effect of the highlights just inside the contours of Adam's back and down the side of the tree trunk is still striking in its contrast to the adjacent areas of modeled shadow. Two other prime impressions are in the Kupferstichkabinett, Berlin, and Kupferstich-Kabinett, Dresden. The Albertina in Vienna owns one of good quality, while impressions of lesser quality are in the British Museum, the London Guildhall Library, the Graphische Sammlung in Munich, and the Bibliothèque Nationale in Paris.

The Fall of Man could be more accurately titled *The Sixth Day of Creation.* Unlike the great Adam and Eve of Jan van Eyck from the Ghent altar painted some thirty years earlier, it locates the nude figures of the first parents in a fully landscaped Garden of Eden – a tradition harking back to illustrated manuscripts of the Bible rather than to contemporary monumental painting. Unlike contemporary depictions of Adam and Eve by Masaccio and others, Master E.S. does not emphasize the drama of the Expulsion, or Fall, although a half-consumed apple lies on the ground at the foot of the tree and Eve assumes the attitude of the classical Venus Pudica, attempting to cover breasts and pudenda with her hands. The presence of the many animals and birds in the print and the serene faces of Adam, Eve, and God lend an air of primal innocence to the scene.

God's physical resemblance to depictions of Christ recalls Paul's reference to the Son as "the last [or new] Adam" (I Cor. 15:22-45). It was also Paul's contention that Adam, unlike Eve, "was not seduced [by the serpent]" (I Tim. 2:11-14). In one hand God holds a closed codex, a reminder that Adam and Eve, who were virtually the only monogamous couple in the Old Testament, were not simply the perpetrators of original sin but also the bride and groom at the world's first wedding ceremony. Having created Adam "in His own image," God fashioned Eve from one of Adam's ribs and presented the couple to one another, telling them to "be fruitful and multiply, and replenish the earth, and subdue it" (Gen. 1:27-28). Adam's words on this occasion, "this is now bone of my bones, and flesh of my flesh. . . . Therefore shall a man leave his father and mother, and shall cleave unto his wife; and they shall be one flesh" (Gen. 2:23-34), were later reiterated by Paul (Eph. 6:31) in a New Testament passage that has become part of the Christian wedding service. Master E.S. underscored the theme of fertility by depicting both lion and lioness along with the first man and woman. The nude figures served as important models for other artists until supplanted by Albrecht Dürer's great *Adam and Eve*, engraved in 1504 (cat. 33).

Regarded by Lehrs as a relatively early work by Master E.S., *The Fall of Man* was partially copied by the Master of the Banderoles (*Fifth Day of Creation*) (P.II.13.2) and is thought to have influenced *The Fall of Man* from the Vienna diptych by Hugo van der Goes, an early work by the Flemish painter, undated but completed before 1470.[10] The distinctive side view of Adam was borrowed by Hieronymus Bosch for use in *The Fall of Man* panel of the Haywagon triptych (Prado, Madrid). – JH

1. Philadelphia 1967. A second exhibition of Master E.S.'s work was held in Munich and Berlin in 1986-87; see Munich 1986.

2. The Master of the Playing Cards, active circa 1435-1450, is represented in the French bequest by a fragment (CAM: 1943.745) – a tiny wild man that once formed one of the pips on a playing card. It is one of four engravings by the Master of the Playing Cards found in American collections.

3. It is also thought by many scholars that other compositions by Master E.S. reflect the influence of paintings by the mid-fifteenth-century Rhenish painter Hans Hirtz, some of whose work can be seen in Karlsruhe. Lilli Fischel, *Die Karlsruher Passion und ihr Meister* (Karlsruhe: G. Braun, 1952) 38-47; idem, "Le Maître E.S. et ses sources Strasbourgeoises," *Archives Alsaciennes* 14 (1935): 185-200.

4. For information about the Master E.S. as copyist see Lilli Fischel, *Nicolaus Gerhaert und die Bildhauer der deutschen Spätgotik* (Munich: F. Bruckmann, 1944), 155-76; Otto Wertheimer, *Nicolaus Gerhaert, seine Kunst und seine Wirkung* (Berlin, 1929), 89-92; Clemens Sommer, "Ein Werk aus der Passauer Zeit des Nicolaus Gerhaert von Leyden," *Oberrheinische Kunst* 2 (1926-27): 29-33.

5. Lehrs II:45-46; idem, *Die Spielkarten des Meisters E.S. 1466 in heliographischen Nachbildungen* (Berlin, 1891).

6. Max Geisberg, *Die Anfänge des deutschen Kupferstiches und der Meister E.S.*, vol. 2 of *Meister der Graphik* (Leipzig, 1909); idem, *Die Kupferstiche des Meisters E.S.*, vol. 10 of *Meister der Graphik* (Berlin, 1924).

7. The literature is listed and discussed in Alan Shestack, Philadelphia 1967, and in Holm Bevers, Munich 1986.

8. Bevers, Munich 1986, esp. 12-18.

9. Fritz Koreny, "Exhibition and Book Reviews – The Master E.S.," PQ. 4, no. 3 (1987): 304-08.

10. Bevers, Munich 1986, 23; Max J. Friedländer, *Early Netherlandish Painting* (Leiden, 1967), 4:4, no. 43; Erwin Panofsky, *Early Netherlandish Painting*, 2 vols. (Cambridge: Harvard University Press, 1953), vol. 2, fig. 456.

Master E. S.
Upper Rhenish active ca. 1450-1467

2. The Nativity.
Engraving on antique laid paper, 20.6 x 16.2 cm (image) on 21.0 x 16.7 cm (sheet).
B. 13; Lehrs 23; Geisberg 1909, p. 80; Geisberg 1924, pp. 28-29; TIB 13.
Watermark: Bunch of 42 grapes with central stem (Lehrs 48).
Condition: Entire upper edge added to depth of 2.0 cm (3.0 cm upper right) with brushwork on wall, roof, and angel.
Provenance: (T. O. Weigel, Leipzig, to Count Wartenburg); Count Yorck von Wartenburg (Lugt S. 2669); (his sale C.G. Boerner, Leipzig, May 2-3, 1932, no. 54, pl. 9, to Strölin for RM 12,500); (Alfred Strölin, Lausanne, consigned to Knoedler June 27, 1932); (purchased from M. Knoedler, New York, May 21, 1934, for $8,000).
Bequest of Herbert Greer French, 1943.67.
Exhibitions: Chicago 1941, no. 60; Cincinnati 1941, no. 21; Philadelphia 1967, no. 20.
References: *Die Kunst der Katalogbeschreibung.* C.G. Boerner, Düsseldorf, 1973, 16, illus.

As Shestack and Bevers have noted,[1] the iconography of this print follows the visionary account of the fourteenth-century mystic Birgitta of Sweden. It features a Madonna kneeling in awe to adore her newborn, the Infant Jesus, who lies directly on the ground, radiating beams of light. Secondary scenes in the background include (1) the annunciation to the shepherds by an angel bearing a banderole, or forked streamer, inscribed *Gl[o]ria in Ex[c]el[s]is Deo* (Glory be to God on High), and (2) the more unusual scene of the two midwives mentioned in the *Protoevangelium Jacobi* (the apocryphal gospel of the pseudo-St. James, also called the *Infancy Gospel of James*) and the Pseudo-Matthew.[2] According to these accounts, the first midwife, Rachel, who had been summoned by Joseph to assist with the birth, was astonished to discover Mary's virginity still intact. She rushed out to tell her friend Salome, the second midwife, who refused to believe the news that a virgin had given birth. Salome, who had been stricken with a withered hand, was cured only after she touched Christ's swaddling clothes. The theme of the two midwives is relatively rare in art; the best-known example is the Dijon altar of the Master of Flemalle. As Bevers has noted, the theme spread from the Netherlands into Upper Rhenish art, where it can be seen in an anonymous *Nativity* from around 1450 (Öffentliche Kunstsammlung, Basel), as well as in a wooden relief carving – the so-called *Molsheim Adoration* – from the circle of the great sculptor Nicolaus Gerhaert (Musée des Beaux Arts, Strasbourg).

Bevers has also called attention to strong stylistic affinities between the figures in this print and those by a follower of Konrad Witz, the leading painter in Basel in the late 1430s and 1440s. Bevers suggests that the reversal of the lettering on the angel's banderole may be an indication that the composition reflects a lost painting. This theory has much to recommend it: the sturdy carpentry, the wildly misunderstood perspective, and the stocky figures with too-voluminous drapery are entirely in keeping with the style of Konrad Witz and his disciples.

Eight impressions of this plate are known: the best impression, in the Kupferstich-Kabinett, Dresden, has the same watermark as the Museum's impression. Other impressions of fine quality are in the British Museum and in the Albertina, Vienna. The Museum's impression, when it belonged to Count Yorck, was described by Max Lehrs as one of the four best, despite the fact that it has a nearly invisible restoration at the top. It is the only impression in America. – JH

1. Alan Shestack, Philadelphia 1967, no. 20; Holm Bevers, Munich 1986, nos. 11, 28.
2. The *Protoevangelium Jacobi* is a work dating from the second century A.D. that exists in Greek, Syrian, Armenian, and Latin translations. The Pseudo-Matthew (not to be confused with the evangelist Saint Matthew) is a Latin composition dating from the fourth or fifth century A.D. entitled *The Gospel of St. Matthew*, a forgery pretending to have been written by the Apostle Matthew. It was translated into Latin by Jerome and is based on the *Protoevangelium*, however.

Master E. S.
Upper Rhenish active ca. 1450-1467

3. The Six of Birds ca. 1463.
From the set of Large Playing Cards.
Engraving on antique laid paper, 12.2 x 8.3 cm (sheet).
P.II.78.VI; Lehrs 265.
Condition: Trimmed within platemark.
Provenance: Ducal Museum, Gotha; (sale C.G. Boerner, Leipzig, May 2-3, 1932, no. 60, pl. 11 to Strölin for RM 1250); (Alfred Strölin, Lausanne, consigned to Knoedler June 7, 1932); (purchased from M. Knoedler, New York, October 6, 1934, for $2,150).
Bequest of Herbert Greer French, 1943.68.
Exhibitions: Chicago 1941, no. 69, illus.; Cincinnati 1941, no. 24; Philadelphia 1967, no. 59, illus.

Two decks of playing cards, one larger than the other, were designed and engraved in the workshop of Master E.S.[1] The Museum's *Six of Birds* is from the large deck, at least part of which can be shown to have been engraved during 1463.[2] This deck of forty-two cards from an original set of forty-eight cards in four suits – men, dogs, birds, and shields – still exists. Each suit originally had twelve cards (without aces). The cards are extremely rare today: seven have not survived at all, and thirty are known only in unique impressions. A number of cards, the court cards in particular, were copied in reverse by Israhel van Meckenem.

Very little is known about the games played with fifteenth-century cards. The number and types of suits varied quite widely: Master E.S.'s small deck, for example, had suits of animals, helmets, shields, and flowers, each consisting of thirteen cards, including aces.

Master E.S.'s dramatic and animated arrangements of birds on the individual cards are original. They suggest direct observation of bird behavior, although the types of birds depicted – falcons, herons, storks, and imaginary species – are the same as those engraved by the earlier Upper Rhenish Master of the Playing Cards (who flourished ca. 1435-55). Recent research has established strong links between the depictions of birds and beasts on playing cards and those of the

earlier model books employed by manuscript illuminators.[3]

It seems that Master E.S.'s cards were not colored and mounted on stiff paper for play but were preserved, sometimes untrimmed. Such cards were probably kept first as artists' models, both for other playing cards and for zoological and botanical motifs. The Nuremberg physician and humanist Dr. Hartmann Schedel (1440-1514), author of the *Weltchronik* (published in 1493), had mounted several playing cards by three different artists, including two by Master E.S., in the picture albums that he assembled at the close of the fifteenth century.[4] Four of the birds from this card were copied by Israhel van Meckenem for his *Six of Birds* (Lehrs 544). He copied the remaining two for his *Seven of Birds* (Lehrs 545).

Only four impressions of *The Six of Birds* survive: in addition to the Museum's fine impression, there are outstanding examples in the Pinacotheca Nazionale, Bologna, and in the Kupferstich-Kabinett, Dresden; the Louvre in Paris owns a heavily restored impression from the Rothschild Collection. – JH

1. On the history of playing cards, see Detlef Hoffmann, *Die Welt der Spielkarten. Eine Kulturgeschichte* (Munich, 1972), and W. L. Schreiber, *Die ältesten Spielkarten und die auf das Kartenspiel Bezug habenden Urkunden des 14. und 15. Jahrhunderts* (Strassburg, 1937).
2. The suit of shields can be dated exactly on the basis of the personal arms of the archbishop of Cologne, Ruprecht von der Pfalz (installed March 30, 1463), and the archbishop of Mainz, Dieter von Ysenburg (resigned October 5, 1463). See Ludwig Kämmerer, "Der Meister E.S. und die Heimat seiner Kunst," *JprK* 17 (1896): 152-53. For arguments against Kämmerer's dating, see Max Lehrs, "Eine wichtige Bereicherung des Dresdener Kupferstichkabinetts," in *Zeitschrift für bildende Kunst* 62 (1928-29): 3-6, 55-56. The argument is discussed in full by Alan Shestack, Philadelphia 1967, no. 59.
3. See Ann van Buren and Sheila Edmunds, "Playing Cards and Manuscripts: Some Widely Disseminated Model Sheets," AB 56 (1974): 12-30.
4. On Schedel's collection, see Béatrice Hernard, *Die Graphiksammlung des Humanisten Hartmann Schedel* (Munich: Prestel-Verlag, 1990).

Unidentified Artist
German ca. 1465

4. The Fourth and Fifth Angels Sound their Trumpets
(Rev 8: 12-13; 9: 1-3) ca. 1465.
Plate 12 for the *Apocalypse Johannis*.
Hand-colored woodcut on antique laid paper, 25.2 x 19.7 cm (image).
Schreiber IV. 180.12-IVh (Fourth edition).
Watermark: Gothic *P* with flower.
Condition: Losses and repairs left margin.
Provenance: (Purchased from M. Knoedler, New York, April 27, 1939, for $375).
Bequest of Herbert Greer French, 1943.48.
Exhibitions: Cincinnati 1941, no. 15.

The demand for books grew exponentially in Europe during the fourteenth and fifteenth centuries in response to the increase in the number of universities being founded. In addition, the number of grammar schools being established by the Brothers and Sisters of the Common Life began to multiply in the Netherlands and in Germany during this time. The demand for books finally became too great to be satisfied solely by scriptoria where manuscripts were painstakingly copied and illustrated by hand. The ultimate solution to the problem was printing books from cast type, using the press invented by Johannes Gutenberg in Mainz in the 1450s.

Blockbooks – booklets with both pictures and inscriptions printed entirely from woodcuts usually on only one side of a page – seem to have formed a transitional phase between handmade manuscripts and printed books. Scholars, however, have long disagreed as to which of these methods of book production came first, since no surviving blockbook can conclusively be proved to predate the invention of the printing press.[1] Since the majority of the earliest blockbooks were made in the northern Netherlands (some of the best of them in Haarlem) and were still being produced as late as the 1470s, blockbooks may actually have been inspired by the new printed books manufactured in Germany rather than the reverse.

In any case, the two forms of books served different purposes. The first books printed by Gutenberg, such as the famous forty-two line Bible, were unillustrated. Blockbooks, on the other hand, were primarily picture books, with text cut from the same block as the illustrations. The creators of blockbooks favored short subjects and kept the amount of text to a minimum. The *Decalogus* (*Ten Commandments*), *Canticum canticorum* (*Song of Songs*), *Exercitium super Pater Noster* (*Exercises on the Lord's Prayer*), *Sieben Todsünden* (*Seven Deadly Sins*), and *Ars moriendi* (*Art of Dying Well*) each spanned but a few pages and contained only a few lines of text per page. Two of the longer blockbooks produced were the forty-page *Biblia pauperum* (*Bible of the Poor [Cleric]*), a fourteenth-century book of exegesis that had previously existed in manuscript form, and the ever-popular *Apocalypsis Johannis* (*Book of Revelation*). The *Apocalypsis Johannis* went through six editions in the fifteenth century. The first three were Dutch; the last three are believed by most scholars to have been German. The example exhibited is from the fourth edition. In addition to the page from the fourth edition of the *Apocalypsis* discussed here, the Museum's collection includes a second page showing John prostrating himself before God and the raising of Drusiana from the dead (CAM 1943.50). An uncolored page from the second edition of a forty-eight page blockbook, *The Opening of the First and Second Seals* (CAM 1943.47), is also in the Museum's collection.

The Book of Revelation, or *Apocalypsis*, as it was called in the original Greek and in the Vulgate, relates a prophecy of the end of the world as envisioned on the island of Patmos by an author who called himself John. The author of the Book of Revelation has traditionally been identified as John the Evangelist, Christ's most youthful disciple. Addressing his remarks to seven early Christian churches in Smyrna, Ephesus, and elsewhere in the Near East – never dreaming that artists in later centuries would attempt to illustrate them – the author used the most cryptic and poetic imagery possible since Christianity was not yet a religion officially sanctioned by the Roman Empire.

> And the fourth angel sounded, and the third part of the sun was smitten, and the third part of the moon, and the third part of the stars; so as the third part of them was darkened, and the day shone not for a third part of it, and the night likewise.
>
> And I beheld, and heard an angel flying through the midst of heaven, saying with a loud voice, Woe, woe, woe to the inhabiters of the earth (Rev. 8:12-13).
>
> And the fifth angel sounded, and I saw a star fall from heaven unto the earth, and to him was given the key of the bottomless pit. And he opened the bottomless pit; and there rose a smoke out of the pit as the smoke of a great furnace; and the sun and the air were darkened. . . . And there came out of the smoke locusts upon the earth, and unto them was given power, as the scorpions of the earth have power (Rev. 9:1-3).

In his vision, John first speaks of the opening of the seven seals that produced, among other things, the four horsemen of the apocalypse (see Dürer, cat. 23). He further describes the souls of the martyrs; an earthquake; an eclipse of the sun; a torrent of falling stars; four angels holding the winds; and seven angels with trumpets. As these angels begin to sound their trumpets, further natural disasters occur: hail, fire mingled with blood, and the progressive destruction of the natural world. The fourth angel's trumpet call destroys the sun, the moon, and the stars. As the fifth angel sounds his trumpet, a bottomless pit (*puteus abyssi* in Latin, here a sarcophagus-like structure) opens, emitting locusts.

The angel who cries "woe to the inhabiters of the earth" (*ve ve hitantibus in terra*) is, in this anonymous blockbook, transformed into an eagle (upper right) – the apocalyptic symbol of John the Evangelist himself. Although the biblical quotation ends with the release of the locusts (Rev. 9:1-3), the designer of the woodcut has created the locusts as they are later described in verse 7:

> And the shapes of the locusts were like unto horses prepared unto battle; and on their heads were. . . crowns like gold, and their faces were as the faces of men. . . and the sound of their wings was as the sound of chariots of many horses running to battle (Rev. 9:7).

Roughly contemporary with the engraved work of Master E.S. (cat. 1), these woodcut figures appear old-fashioned and static with their stocky proportions, starchy drapery, and minimal landscape. Woodcut was considered the less important and cheaper of the two forms of printmaking in the fifteenth century. The production of most woodcuts involved a division of labor between the designer, who made the original drawing on the block of wood, and the *Formschneider*, who undertook the meticulous and monotonous task of cutting away the excess wood from both sides of each line, leaving the linework standing in relief. The printer in many cases could be a third person, and the person who added color yet a fourth.

The popularity of the blockbook *Apocalypsis* is confirmed by the fact that it quickly ran through six editions in the third quarter of the fifteenth century. The idea was revived and the imagery updated at century's end by the enterprising young Albrecht Dürer (cat. 23), godson of the greatest publisher in Germany. Dürer used Anton Koberger's cast type to print full pages of text on the reverse sides of his woodcut illustrations, thereby freeing up the picture space for more vivid imagery. – JH

1. For more information on blockbooks see A. J. J. Delen, *Histoire du livre et de l'imprimerie en Belgique des origines à nos jours* (Brussels, 1930), pt. 2, p. 42; Arthur M. Hind, *A History of Woodcut* (1935; reprint, New York, 1963); H. T. Musper, "Xylographic Books," in *The Book Through 5000 Years*, ed. H. D. L. Vervliet (London and New York, 1972); Gertrud Bing, "The Apocalypse Block-Books and Their Manuscript Models," *JWarb.* 5 (1942): 143-58; Adrian Wilson and Joyce Lancaster Wilson, *A Medieval Mirror: Speculum humanae salvationis 1324-1500* (Berkeley and Los Angeles, 1984) 89-111. The catalogue of an exhibition of blockbooks held at the Gutenberg-Museum in Mainz (1991) was not available at the time of writing.

Master of the E-Series Tarocchi

Ferrarese School ca. 1465

5. Melpomene ca. 1465 (no. 17 from the so-called *Tarocchi of Mantegna*).
Engraving on antique laid paper, 18.0 x 10.0 cm (platemark).
B.XIII.134.34; P.V.122.17; Hind E.I.17a.
Inscribed in margin lower left: ·D·; lower center: ·MELPOMEИE ·XVII·; lower right: ·17·
Provenance: Albertina duplicate; (purchased from M. Knoedler, New York, November 1, 1930, for $1,200).
Bequest of Herbert Greer French, 1943.38.
Exhibitions: Detroit 1958, no. 35; Houston 1960, no. 52.

For more than two hundred years a curious misnomer has obstinately clung to one of the most important series of early Italian engravings. Known as the *Tarocchi of Mantegna*, they are, in fact, completely unrelated to the great fifteenth-century painter of that name.[1] Nor do they have more than a few things in common with true *tarocchi*, popular Renaissance playing cards that have evolved into the modern set of tarot cards now principally used for fortune-telling.[2] The so-called *Tarocchi of Mantegna* comprise fifty images of uniform size, divided into five suits, or groups, of ten: (1) the Ranks and Conditions of Men (from beggar to pope); (2) the nine Muses and their leader, Apollo; (3) the Liberal Arts (including three extra disciplines – Poetry, Philosophy, and Theology – added to the classic trivium and quadrivium); (4) the Virtues (including three "genii," or personifications of cosmic powers, besides the seven traditional members of the group); and (5) the Planets and Spheres (including the three spheres that allegedly lie beyond the seven planets in the pre-Copernican cosmos). The exact purpose of this remarkable series has naturally been a matter for much speculation, but there is general agreement that it served more for instruction than for amusement.[3] No mere game of chance, we may think of the series as a sort of pictorial encyclopedia in miniature, giving visual form to a vast array of what once passed for knowledge of the universe and of humanity's position in it.

Study of the *Tarocchi* is complicated by the existence of two separate versions, identical to one another in format and imagery but stylistically rather diverse. Across the bottom of each print in both versions are inscriptions giving its title or subject, its number in the series (in Roman as well as Arabic numerals), and a capital letter denoting the group or suit to which it belongs. Numbers run consecutively in both versions from one to fifty, but the letters referring to the five groups show a significant variation between versions. In one set, the first five letters of the alphabet are inscribed in reverse order from *E* to *A*; in the other series, the letter *S* is mysteriously substituted for *E*. With this distinction in mind, the two versions have acquired the designations "E-Series" and "S-Series." Having debated the relationship between the series since the nineteenth century, scholars can now say with assurance that the E-Series preceded the S-Series, conjecturally by as many as twenty years, and that the latter is, in essence, a slightly modified and somewhat inferior copy of the former.[4]

Number 17 in the series, *Melpomene* belongs to group D, the Muses, goddesses led by Apollo and associated with creative inspiration in poetry, drama, song, and other arts. Specifically, she is the Muse of Tragedy and is here portrayed with a rather pained expression as she blows what one imagines to be a mournful sound on her horn. Like all of her sisters, she is garbed in a loose, billowing tunic whose style betrays its origins in Greco-Roman sculpture. Beside her, a blank disk apparently symbolizes one of the celestial spheres of the cosmos – the spherical orbits of the sun, moon, planets, and stars in classical astronomy. These celestial spheres were assigned to the Muses by a tradition at least as old as the fifth century.[5]

The Museum's impression of *Melpomene* is a fine example from the original E-Series. It is of special interest in view of the traces it retains of coloring by hand in gold, which adds a touch of luster to the image and provides valuable information on how such prints were occasionally treated.[6] The quality of the impression, moreover, beautifully reveals the refined craftsmanship of the anonymous master, who was, in all likelihood, active at Ferrara, an important artistic center in northeastern Italy. His designs are neatly and cleanly cut, with precise contours and delicate rectilinear cross-hatching incised with a high degree of regularity. Datable to circa 1465 – or, at any rate, prior to 1467, when several details from the series were copied in a Bolognese manuscript – the so-called *Tarocchi of Mantegna* are among the earliest and most elegant specimens of Italian engraving.[7]

They are also among the most important surviving relics of the splendidly civilized circle surrounding the court of the Este family in Early Renaissance Ferrara. In a recent essay, Marzia Faietti has shown just how intimately the so-called *Tarocchi* are connected with this ambience, an intellectual and cultural environment in which local scholars took a special interest in the Muses, and to which painters and a host of other artists and craftsmen contributed no small share.[8] Indeed, the engraved series shows close stylistic ties with mid-fifteenth-century Ferrarese painting, most notably with Francesco del Cossa's celebrated frescoes of 1469-70 in Ferrara's Palazzo Schifanoia. Among several other candidates, Cossa has even been cited as the possible designer of the *Tarocchi*,[9] but in all probability the anonymous engraver should himself be credited with having designed as well as executed this landmark in the history of printmaking. – MZ

1. For the question of whether Mantegna actually engraved any of the prints traditionally attributed to him, see Suzanne Boorsch's entry for *The Battle of the Sea Gods* (cat. 17). Whatever the case may be, he has no connection whatsoever with the so-called *Tarocchi*.

2. For early references to the misnomer, see Luigi Lanzi, *Storia pittorica della Italia* (Bassano: Remondini, 1795-96), 1:82; and Pietro Zani, *Materiali per servire alla storia dell'origine e de' progressi dell'incisione in rame e in legno* (Parma: Stamperia Carmignani, 1802), 70-71. Connections of the series with true *tarocchi* are analyzed by Hind 1:223-24. For *tarocchi* in general, see Michael Dummett, *The Game of Tarot* (London: Duckworth, 1980); and Ferrara 1987.

3. Arguments are reviewed by Hind 1:222-23. A classic study is that of Heinrich Brockhaus, "Ein edles Geduldspiel: 'Die Leitung der Welt oder die Himmelsleiter,' die sogennanten Taroks Mantegnas vom Jahr 1459-60," in *Miscellanea di storia dell'arte in onore di Igino Benvenuto Supino* (Florence: Olschki, 1933), 397-416.

4. On the dating of the S-Series, see Hind 1:225 ("about 1485"); and Jay A. Levenson, NGA, 81 and 89 (suggesting a date closer to that of the E-Series, "c. 1470[?]"). Recently, Suzanne Boorsch has made the provocative suggestion that the engraver of the S-Series may have been a certain Simone di Ardizone of Reggio Emilia, to whom no prints had hitherto been attributed (see London 1992, 66, n. 17). Simone is known from a famous letter, much discussed in the literature on Mantegna, that he wrote to Ludovico Gonzaga of Mantua on September 15, 1475. In this letter he describes himself as a "painter and engraver" and refers (among other things) to some stolen plates or prints that he had lately remade for a friend, the painter Zoan Andrea. Boorsch conjectures that Simone engraved the S-Series in 1475 as a replacement for the stolen E-Series; she promises to investigate the matter more thoroughly in the near future.

5. Jean Seznec, *The Survival of the Pagan Gods* (New York: Pantheon Books, 1953), 141. Among the Muses in the series only Thalia (Hind 16) lacks the disk, or sphere, for reasons explained by Seznec.

6. An impression of *Poetry* (Hind 27a) in the Metropolitan Museum of Art, New York, also has traces of gold coloring.

7. Evidence for the date of the E-Series is summarized by Hind 1:225.

8. See Faietti's long catalogue entry in Milan 1991, 431-37. Faietti summarizes most of the key issues regarding the so-called *Tarocchi*, and the catalogue as a whole provides copious information on the Muses in Ferrara. Another important recent study of the series is Claudia Cieri Via, "I Tarocchi cosidetti del 'Mantegna': Origine, significato e fortuna di un ciclo di immagini," in Ferrara 1987, 49-77.

9. Eberhard Ruhmer, *Francesco del Cossa* (Munich: Verlag F. Bruckmann, 1959), 81-82.

Martin Schongauer
Colmar 1445/50-1491 Breisach?

6. The Flight into Egypt 1470-75.
Engraving on antique laid paper, 25.6 x 17.0 cm (sheet).
B. 7; Lehrs 7.
Watermark: Profile head (fragment).
Signed on plate lower center: M☩S
Condition: Trimmed to or within platemark.
Provenance: Hermann Weber (Lugt 1383); Count Yorck von Wartenburg (Lugt s. 2669); (his sale C.G. Boerner, Leipzig, May 2-3, 1932, no. 80, pl. 16, to Alfred Strölin, Lausanne for RM 1,900); (Maurice Gobin, Paris, consigned to Knoedler, August 8, 1932);

(purchased from M. Knoedler, New York, September 29, 1933, for $3,400).
Bequest of Herbert Greer French, 1943.74.
Exhibitions: Cincinnati, 1934, no. 18; Cincinnati 1941, no. 38.

Martin Schongauer, whose workshop was in the Alsatian city of Colmar, was the most important European engraver before Albrecht Dürer and the first Northern printmaker to achieve wide distribution in Italy and Spain as well as in Germany and the Netherlands.[1] The most frequently imitated of late fifteenth-century engravers, his compositions were copied by painters, sculptors, goldsmiths, and other printmakers alike. He was the first graphic artist known to have trained primarily as a painter rather than as a goldsmith. It was to his studio that the young Albrecht Dürer traveled as a journeyman in 1492, unaware that Schongauer had died a few months earlier.

Schongauer, who signed his plates with his initials, *M* and *S*, separated by a goldsmithlike hallmark comprised of a cross and a crescent, is the earliest engraver whose life can partially be reconstructed from documentary evidence and the first to be commemorated in a painted portrait.[2] He was the son of the goldsmith Caspar Schongauer (who, like many fifteenth-century goldsmiths, was named for one of the three Magi). Caspar was a native of the wealthy Bavarian city of Augsburg, where his family belonged to the aristocracy. He settled in Colmar before 1445, the year in which he was granted the rank of master goldsmith and citizenship – a process that probably required a period of about five years' residency in the city. He and his wife, Gertrud, had four sons: Martin and Ludwig became painter-engravers and Jörg and Paul were goldsmiths.[3] Presumed to have been born in Colmar, Martin never applied for citizenship and probably acquired it by right of descent.

There has long been a scholarly controversy over Schongauer's birth date. He is thought by the majority of modern scholars to have been born about 1450-53, since it is known that he matriculated at the University of Leipzig in 1465. Most university students in the fifteenth century began their studies at the age of twelve or thirteen. Schongauer may originally have been destined for either the law or the priesthood, which were by far the most common occupations requiring university study in the fifteenth century. However, he seems to have remained in Leipzig for only one academic year. Schongauer is next documented in 1469 as co-tenant of a group of houses in Colmar where his workshop and living quarters were located; thus there is no archival evidence regarding his artistic training. It is possible that he may have been apprenticed to the local painter in Colmar, Caspar Isenmann, whose rare works betray Netherlandish influence. Schongauer may have gone as a journeyman to Flanders. A letter from the sixteenth-century Flemish painter-engraver Lambert Lombard to Giorgio Vasari alleges that Schongauer had been trained by the great Rogier van der Weyden, an allegation that is difficult to take at face value since Van der Weyden died in 1464. Schongauer's paintings and engravings do show the strong influence of Van der Weyden – an influence, however, that was widespread throughout western Germany. Van der Weyden's Beaune altarpiece inspired one of Schongauer's drawings, *Christ of the Last Judgment* (Louvre, Paris). Equally striking, however, is the influence of Van der Weyden's younger follower Dirk Bouts (1415/20-1475), who was active in the university city of Louvain. Bouts' *Entombment of Christ* (National Gallery, London) is reflected in the Museum's brilliant impression of Schongauer's engraving of the same subject (CAM 1943.73).

Schongauer's earliest dated painting, *The Rose Arbor Madonna*, painted for the Church of Saint Martin in Colmar, was done in 1473. His last, the enormous *Last Judgment* fresco on the west, north, and south walls of the Church of Saint Stephen in Breisach, was begun in 1488 and remained unfinished at the time of his death three years later. His activity as an engraver probably slackened after his 1488 move to Breisach, where the *Last Judgment*, the largest mural north of the Alps, would have had first claim on his attention.[4]

Schongauer's engraved oeuvre consists of 116 plates,[5] most of which are preserved in multiple impressions of good-to-superb quality, indicating that they were greatly admired and collected from the beginning. Unlike many fifteenth-century prints, they were never "improved" by their owners with hand coloring – a tribute to Schongauer's matchless skill with the burin as well as to his consistently fine printing. He controlled all of the refinements of cross-hatching and contour shading pioneered by Master E.S., whose monogram style may have inspired his own. But Schongauer raised engraving to the level of fine art with his superior sense of composition and graceful exaggeration of contours for decorative, almost calligraphic, effect.

Of the seventeen Schongauers in the French bequest, ten are notably fine impressions. Five came from the important collection of Count Yorck von Wartenburg (Lehrs 1, 2, 5, 7, 9) and two came from that of Prince Waldburg-Wolfegg (Lehrs 15, 38). Others include duplicates deaccessioned from the Albertina (Vienna) and one piece from the Fürstlich Hohenzollernsche Sammlungen (Sigmaringen, Germany).

One of Schongauer's most popular prints, *The Flight into Egypt* has survived in at least sixty impressions, only seven of which are of the first quality. The Museum's example, one of the best in an American collection, has one of the two earliest watermarks found on the prints. The earlier of the two monograms used by this artist, an *M* with straight sides, as well as the spatial uncertainties of the background and the disproportion between the Virgin Mary and the donkey she rides, mark this as one of Schongauer's earliest prints, probably datable to the years between 1470 and 1475. It was especially beloved by other artists for its exotic tropical foliage – a date palm, which angels are bending down so that Joseph may pick fruit, and a dragon tree (left). This cactuslike plant, native to the Canary Islands, has attracted much scholarly attention as evidence that Schongauer traveled in Spain and perhaps in Portugal during a portion of the missing years before 1469.[6] The tall plant in the lower left foreground, known by the folk name *Königskerze* (king's candle), was considered a medicinal herb in the Middle Ages.[7]

Among the artists influenced by this print were Albrecht Dürer, who included a very similar but correctly foreshortened composition in his great woodcut series of the *Life of the Virgin*, circa 1504 (B. 89) (CAM 1943.228); Hieronymus Bosch, who transplanted the dragon tree into the Eden panel of his so-called *Garden of Earthly Delights* triptych (Prado, Madrid); Gerard David, who copied the donkey in one of his paintings, *The Rest on the Flight to Egypt*; and Michael Wolgemut, who included it in his illustration of the Garden of Paradise for the Nuremberg Chronicle (1493). – JH

1. On Schongauer, see Lehrs 7; TIB 7; Julius Baum, *Martin Schongauer* (Vienna, 1948); Eduard Flechsig, *Martin Schongauer* (Strasbourg, 1951); Ulrich Middeldorf, "Martin Schongauers Klassischer Stil," in *Deutsche Beiträge zur geistigen Überlieferung* (Chicago, 1947), 94-114; Alan Shestack, Washington 1967; Charles I. Minott, *Martin Schongauer* (New York: Collectors Editions, 1971); Fedja Anzelewsky et al., Colmar 1991, 264, no. G.8; Sophie Renouard de Bussierre, Paris 1991, 116, no. 11.

2. Alte Pinakothek, Munich, no. 1027, attributed to Hans Burgkmair the Elder. Inscribed "HIPSCH [i.e., *hübsch*, or handsome] MARTIN SCHONGAUER MALER [painter]." Beneath the inscription are the Schongauer family arms and the only partially legible date, 14?3. According to Peter Streider, recent laboratory examination of the painting panel dates it from the sixteenth century, so it cannot have been done from life.

3. A fifth son, Caspar, is mentioned by only one early sixteenth-century author and is not otherwise documented.

4. Breisach, which today is on the right bank of the Rhine, near Freiburg im Breisgau, was on the left bank and, therefore, more easily accessible from Colmar in the fifteenth

century. (Since the fifteenth century, the course of the Rhine has been artificially altered.)

5. One of this number, *St. James the Great at the Battle of Clavijo*, has been doubted by some scholars, including Max Lehrs, who assigned it to Master AG. Alan Shestack and others, however, have made a compelling case for it as an early plate left unfinished by Schongauer and completed by someone else.

6. Several specimens of the dragon tree (*Dracaena draco*) are known to have been growing in the garden of the Monastery of Saint Augustine in Lisbon in the late fifteenth century. Schongauer is the first person to depict this type of tree, which was not described by botanists until 1576. (See Robert A. Koch, "Martin Schongauer's Dragon Tree," in *A Tribute to Wolfgang Stechow*, vol. 5 of *Print Review* [New York: Pratt Graphics Center, 1976], 114-19, and J. Schenk, "Martin Schongauers Drachenbaum," *Naturwissenschaftliche Wochenschrift* 19 [1920]: 775-80.) Schongauer's exclusive knowledge of the tree, his many depictions of Moors among the tormentors of Christ, and his unfinished engraving *St. James at the Battle of Clavijo* (B. 53; rejected by Lehrs but accepted as Schongauer by the majority of modern scholars) were cited most recently by Fedja Anzelewsky as evidence of Schongauer's trip to the Iberian peninsula (Paper presented at the International Colloquium Honoring the Five Hundredth Anniversary of Schongauer's Death, Colmar, October 1-3, 1991).

7. Hartmut Krohm and Jan Nicolaisen, Berlin 1991, 83-84, no. 3c.

Martin Schongauer
Comar 1445/50-1491 Breisach?

7. Christ Bearing His Cross (The large plate) ca. 1475.
Engraving on antique laid paper, 28.8 x 43.3 cm (platemark).
B. 21; Lehrs 9.
Signed in plate lower center: M ✝ S
Watermark: Small bull's head with St. Anthony's cross
(cf. Lehrs 38).
Condition: Trimmed just outside platemark.
Provenance: Johann Gottlob von Quandt (1860); Johann Peter Maria Cerroni (Lugt 1432); Count Yorck von Wartenburg (Lugt s. 2669); (his sale C.G. Boerner, Leipzig, May 2-3, 1932, no. 83, to Maison for RM 2500); (purchased from M. Knoedler, New York, October 28, 1935, for $5,900).
Bequest of Herbert Greer French, 1943.79.
Exhibitions: Chicago 1941, no. 83; Cincinnati 1941, no. 39.

Max Lehrs, former director of the Dresden Kupferstich-Kabinett, knew approximately seventy impressions of this plate, of which he considered only fifteen to be of the highest quality. The Museum's impression was cited in Lehrs' catalogue as one of the select fifteen when it was still at Klein-Oels in Count Yorck's collection (1925). The plate was the largest engraved at the time it was executed, when it cannot have been a simple matter to find an unflawed sheet of cast copper so large. The physical exertion required to ink and print an edition of it would have been considerable, even by today's standards. Owing to its unusual size, this print was difficult to store, and for this reason, it is almost never found without a vertical fold or with a full platemark. The Museum's impression shows traces of a vertical fold from the back, invisible from the front.

The plate seems to reflect a lost composition by Jan van Eyck — perhaps a mural painting, judging from its oblong shape. A Netherlandish drawing of the original composition in pen and bistre (Albertina, inv. 3.025, N.22) bears the erroneous attribution "Martin Schon" on its mount.[1] Because of its dramatic complexity and subject, a favorite among practitioners of the *Devotio moderna* popularized by Thomas à Kempis through his devotional book, *The Imitation of Christ* (1418), it was also one of Schongauer's most popular compositions. It was copied by a number of fifteenth-century engravers, including Israhel van Meckenem, Master W H, and Master I C, as well as by at least one nineteenth-century forger. It also influenced compositions by Albrecht Dürer and Raphael, among others. One of the earlier copies bears the date 1481, suggesting that the original was probably executed circa 1475. — JH

1. For a discussion of the extensive literature related to this drawing and its place in the Van Eyckian circle, see Fritz Koreny in Washington 1984, no. 22; Friedrich Winkler, "Über verschollene Bilder der Brüder van Eyck," *JprK.* 37 (1916): 287-301; Andreas Pigler, "Das Problem der Budapester Kreuztragung," *Phoebus* 11 (1951): 12-24. For further information on Schongauer's large *Christ Bearing the Cross*, see Colmar 1991, 366-69, no. G83; Paris 1991, 120-25, no. 13; Martin Schauder, Berlin 1991, 91-93, no. 9.

Martin Schongauer
Colmar 1445/50-1491 Breisach?

8. Christ Appearing to Mary Magdalene ca. 1480-90.
Engraving on antique laid paper, 15.9 x 15.8 cm (image) on 16.1 x 16.1 cm (sheet).
B. 26; Lehrs 15.
Signed on plate lower center: M ✝ S
Condition: Trimmed within platemark.
Provenance: Prince Waldburg-Wolfegg (Lugt 2542); (sale C.G. Boerner, Leipzig, May 14-15, 1934, no. 592, pl. 19, to Breiting for RM 1,500); (Alfred Strölin, Lausanne, consigned to Knoedler, August 17, 1934); (purchased from M. Knoedler, New York, October 6, 1934, for $2,900).
Bequest of Herbert Greer French, 1943.77.
Exhibitions: Cincinnati 1941, no. 42.

This scene, described in the gospels of Mark (16:9) and John (20:11-18), is also known as *Noli me tangere* (Don't touch me) — Christ's words to Mary Magdalene. She was the first to encounter him after his Resurrection when she came to his tomb bearing additional embalming spices in an alabaster jar. The wounds visible on Christ's hands and feet and in his side, his processional banner, and the symbolic use of dead and living trees in the landscape within and without the confines of the cemetery are all references to Christ's victory over death and the grave. Christ's appearance to the Magdalene, a repentant sinner, is of particular importance as a demonstration of divine forgiveness. French buyers would have been especially attracted to this print, since Mary Magdalene was believed to have died and been buried in Aix en Provence.[1]

This composition, one of a series of four identically sized square plates that illustrate scenes from the life of Christ, represents Schongauer's engraving style at its most refined.[2] Although certain earlier prints, such as the large *Christ Bearing the Cross* (cat. 7), are more immediately striking because of their richness of detail, *Christ Appearing to Mary Magdalene* and its companion pieces exhibit the tours de force of the engraver's art, a nearly superhuman control of the burin that permits the utmost economy of line. Lehrs, who had seen this impression at Wolfegg Castle, gave it three stars, signifying a print of the finest quality. — JH

1. See Hiltgart L. Keller, *Reclams Lexikon der Heiligen und der biblischen Gestalten* (Stuttgart: Philipp Reclam Jr., 1968), 361-64.

2. The other plates in the series are the square *Nativity* (Lehrs 4), *Baptism of Christ* (Lehrs 8), and *Christ Blessing the Virgin* (Lehrs 18). The National Gallery of Art in Washington owns the full set, collected by Lessing Rosenwald. See also Colmar 1991, 284-85, no. G17; Paris 1991, 160-61; and Berlin 1991, 88, no. 6.

Master b g
German active ca. 1470-1490

9. Lovers on Horseback
Engraving on antique laid paper, 14.1 x 16.3 cm (sheet).
B.VI.72.13, Lehrs 29.
Signed in plate lower center: b⍺ g
Condition: Trimmed to or within platemark.
Provenance: Ducal Museum, Gotha; (sale C.G. Boerner, Leipzig, May 14-15, 1934, no. 393, pl. 9, to Strölin for RM 620); (Alfred Strölin, Lausanne, consigned to Knoedler, July 14, 1934); (purchased from M. Knoedler, New York, September 21, 1936, for $1,300). Bequest of Herbert Greer French, 1943.179.
Exhibitions: Cincinnati 1941, no. 18.

The late fifteenth-century Middle Rhenish engraver who signed his plates with the lowercase letters *b* and *g*, separated by an *x*-and-crescent goldsmith's hallmark, is one of several printmakers who adopted Master E.S.'s practice of "copyrighting" his work by means of identifying marks or initials. The form of Master b g's monogram seems to have been influenced by that of his more famous contemporary, Martin Schongauer. Five of the master's forty-four known engravings are copies of compositions from Schongauer's *Passion of Christ* series. Unlike Schongauer, however, Master b g seems to have had little interest in religious subjects, preferring instead to depict secular scenes in the manner of the anonymous Housebook Master, also known as the Master of the Amsterdam Cabinet.[1] Seven of Master b g's engravings are copies after the Housebook Master's rare drypoints; another thirty have come to be regarded as reproductive engravings after lost compositions by this same master (Lehrs VIII:165-219).

As was the case with the earlier monogrammist Master E.S., scholars have made strenuous efforts to identify the Master b g – efforts complicated in the seventeenth, eighteenth, and nineteenth centuries by the misreading of the monogram as *b s*. Early on, scholars proposed that the hallmark between the initials was sufficiently similar to Martin Schongauer's to prove a family relationship, and the name of a supposed brother (Barthel Schongauer or Barthel Schoen), was created. Adam Bartsch points out that, although Martin Schongauer had four brothers, none was named Barthel nor anything else beginning with the letter *B*. Bartsch, therefore, lists the artist as an anonymous monogrammist in *Le Peintre graveur*, and there describes a dated engraving from his hand from 1479, a work that can no longer be located (B. VI:69).

In 1856 the original copperplate of one of Master b g's heraldic engravings – the merged coats of arms of two patrician families from Frankfurt, Rohrbach and Holzhausen – was discovered in the Holzhausen family archive, wrapped in a paper bearing the date 1467. The plate was acquired for the Berlin Kupferstichkabinett in 1973, and one of its four known fifteenth-century impressions (formerly owned by Count Maltzan) is in the National Gallery of Art, Washington.

The anonymous monogrammist was briefly identified in the 1860s as the Swabian painter Bartholomaus Zeitblom by Ernst Georg Harzen, the Hamburg print collector and dealer whose collection now forms the nucleus of the Kupferstichkabinett at the Hamburg Kunsthalle. Harzen also credited Zeitblom with the drypoints made by the Housebook Master.[2] It was his contention – an argument not entirely without merit – that the stylistic differences between the Housebook Master's delicate figures and Master b g's coarser ones could be explained by the technical differences between drypoint, in which a design is scratched into a soft, pewter or zinc plate with a needlelike tool, and a copperplate engraving made with a burin.

Bartholomaus Zeitblom ceased to be of interest when the Braunschweig scholar Eduard Flechsig correctly identified the monogram in 1911 as *b g* rather than *b s*. Flechsig noted that the *g* is based on the typefaces used in the late fifteenth century. As to the identity of the artist, Flechsig suggested the Frankfurt goldsmith Bartholomeus Gobel.

The subject of lovers riding double, one or both of whom may wear lovers' garlands on their heads, is familiar from the fourteenth-century German *Manesse* Codex which illustrates the love poetry of the *Minnesänger*, and from early fifteenth-century Franco-Flemish manuscript illumination. In the latter context, "riding out" in the forest constituted the month's "labor" for May, an allusion to the medieval cycle of monthly labors. The first day of May was the customary time for choosing lovers and/or for becoming engaged to marry. An elaborate scene with several pairs of lovers illustrating the month of May is depicted in the *Très riches heures*, illuminated for Jean, duke of Berry, by the Limbourg Brothers (ca. 1413-16). The subject was adapted to the graphic arts by the Housebook Master, who depicted a smaller entourage in *The Departure for the Hunt* (Lehrs 77), a rare drypoint known only in two impressions (Rijksprentenkabinet, Amsterdam, and Kupferstichkabinett, Berlin).

Master b g's lovers wear costumes and hairstyles identical to those worn by lovers in prints by the Housebook Master. The woman's collarless gown with laces at the neck, as well as the man's skintight hose and *Schnabelschuhe* (pointed shoes) – so castigated by preachers of the 1470s and 1480s – are examples. Max Lehrs consequently considers Master b g's work a reproductive copy of a lost drypoint by the Housebook Master. The depictions of the "laughing" horse, however, and the unchaperoned lovers, perhaps eloping, are features more typical of Master b g's own sense of humor, much bawdier than the Housebook Master's disposition. Either Master b g's print or its lost prototype was the inspiration for an early drawing by Albrecht Dürer (Winkler 54: Kupferstichkabinett, Berlin).[3]

The Museum's impression is the only one in America and one of five known to have survived. The best impression is in the Kupferstich-Kabinett, Dresden; others are in the Rothschild Collection (Louvre, Paris), in the Albertina in Vienna, and formerly in the Lichtenstein Collection.[4] Although trimmed slightly at the bottom, the linework of the Museum's impression is clear and the delicate shading on the riders' faces is still intact. Acquired by Mr. French in 1936, this impression was sold at C.G. Boerner (Leipzig) on May 14, 1934, when items from the collection of Friedrich August II, king of Saxony (d. 1854), and from "another old and princely collection" were auctioned off in a special sale.[5] This impression was never cited by Max Lehrs. The oversight is easily explained, in view of the fact that Lehrs was legally blind at the time of his writing the volume on the Master b g (1934) and, thus, relied upon his visual memory and old notes read to him by his daughter-in-law.[6] – JH

1. On this artist, see J. P. Filedt Kok, comp., *The Master of the Amsterdam Cabinet, or the Housebook Master* (Princeton: Princeton University Press, 1985). The artist is known as the Master of the Housebook, from a manuscript containing drawings by his hand, and as the Master of the Amsterdam Cabinet, from the largest collection of his rare drypoint work, which is housed in the Rijksprentenkabinet, Amsterdam.

2. Ernst Georg Harzen, "Über Bartholomaus Zeitblom, Maler von Ulm, als Kupferstecher," *N. Arch.* 6 (1860): 1-30, 97-124.

3. See Fedya Anzelewsky and Hans Mielke, *Albrecht Dürer: Kritisches Katalog der Zeichnungen im Berliner Kupferstichkabinett* (Berlin, 1984), no. 8.

4. Current location of the impression formerly in the Lichtenstein collection is unknown.

5. *Kupferstiche, Radierungen und Holzschnitte des XV-XVII. Jahrhunderts aus der Sammlung König Friedrich August II von Sachsen (gestorben 1854) und aus einer alten fürstlichen Sammlung, dazu einige andere Beiträge.* C.G. Boerner, Leipzig, May 14-15, 1934, no. 393.

6. I am indebted to one of Lehrs' successors, Dr. Werner Schmidt, former director of the Dresden Kupferstich-Kabinett, for this information.

Master W with the Key
Bruges active ca. 1465-1485

10. Design for a Mantle-Clasp (Monile)
Engraving on antique laid paper, 17.7 x 15.2 cm (sheet).
P. 41; Lehrs 50 i/ii; H. *Neth.* 50 i/ii.
Monogrammed in plate upper center: W ⚹
Condition: Trimmed within platemark.
Provenance: D.G. de Arozarena (1861); Count Yorck von
Wartenburg (Lugt S. 2669); (his sale C.G. Boerner, Leipzig, May
2-3, 1932, no. 66, illus. p. 14, to Matthiesen for RM 6,000);
(purchased from M. Knoedler, New York, October 28, 1935, for
$4,200).
Bequest of Herbert Greer French, 1943.61.
Exhibitions: Cincinnati 1941, no. 32.
References: *Die Kunst der Katalogbeschreibung*, C.G. Boerner,
Düsseldorf, 24, illus.

Nothing is known about the engraver known as Master W with the
Key, except what can be deduced from the prints that bear his
monogram or that can be attributed to him on stylistic grounds. It is
fairly certain that he worked in Bruges between about 1465 and
1485.[1] Bruges was at that time the principal city of Flanders (what is
now Belgium) and was under the control of the Dukes of Burgundy.
A large and elaborate engraving of the coat of arms of Charles the
Bold (Duke of Burgundy from 1467 to 1487) suggests that Master W
was in the service of the duke, and there is evidence that he
accompanied the duke on a military campaign.[2]

Almost certainly Master W, like many early engravers, was a
goldsmith. Almost half of the eighty-one engravings attributed to
him are designs for various forms of ornament, and even his figural
compositions frequently include ornate architectural settings. His
engraving technique derives from that of the Master E.S., likewise a
goldsmith (cats. 1-3), with its strongly marked outlines and shading
in patches of fine, uniform hatching. However, he was more ready
than Master E.S. to use curved hatching to follow the shape of a
surface, as, for example, in the curved wall surfaces of this print. At
times, as in the vaulted ceilings here, he uses a scratchy, informal
shading that suggests drypoint. It has been proposed that he may
have used a metal softer than copper, such as tin, to permit this
greater freedom in the use of line.[3]

This print is one of two engravings by Master W incorporating
elaborate architectural ornament in a circular composition. The
engravings have been identified as designs for a type of large
ornamental clasp called a morse, or *monile*. Part of the ecclesiastical
vestments of certain members of the Catholic clergy, the monile
fastens the cope, or *pluviale*, a cloaklike garment.[4] At first sight it
may seem incredible that this elaborate piece of architecture is the
design for what is essentially a large button, but a monile of similar
design, dated 1487 and signed by the goldsmith Reinecke vam
Dressche, is in the collection of the Kunstgewerbemuseum in Berlin
(fig. 10-1).[5] Made of silver, partially gilded and decorated in enamel,
the Berlin monile is 5½ inches in diameter (almost the same size as
the Museum's print) and more than an inch thick. The figures of
three saints and a kneeling donor are set in an elaborate architectural
frame that projects beyond the circular rim; the border is an
openwork tracery within a plain round moulding, very similar to
Master W's engraving.

Yet as complex as the Berlin monile is, Master W's engraving is
still more so. Reinecke vam Dressche placed his architecture in front
of the openwork border: it resembles an architectural facade, and
behind it we catch only glimpses of a dark hollow. Master W gives us
an architectural interior, which appears to be a small chapel, behind
the tracery border.

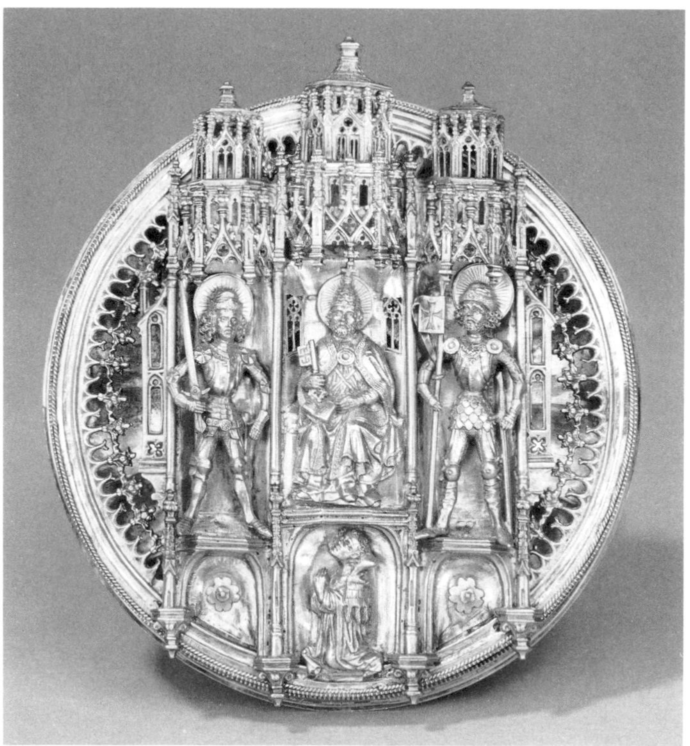

Figure 10-1. Reinecke vam Dressche, *Mantle-Clasp (Monile)*, 1487, silver
with gilding and enamel. Staatliche Museen Preußischer Kulturbesitz,
Kunstgewerbemuseum, Berlin.

To understand the full complexity of this architectural space, it
may help to break it down into separate elements. First, there is a
screen of tracery that links the border to two slender piers running
from the top to the bottom of the design; the piers and tracery are
fairly thin and flat and lie in roughly the same plane as the border.
Second, there is a scalloped floor that in part projects forward past
the tracery screen and in part lies behind it. This floor is supported
by brackets of sculptural foliage. The central bracket pushes
vigorously forward, while the foliage of the two side brackets seems
caged behind the openwork border. Finally, and most conspicuously,
an undulating back wall, penetrated by niches and pierced by
windows, lies entirely behind the tracery screen. The wall comes
forward to meet the screen at just those points where the scalloped
edge of the floor goes back.

The upper part of the design is dominated by the tracery screen, a
pattern of light, springy curves set off against a shadowy
background. The lower part is dominated by the scalloped edge of
the floor, a powerful contour dividing the white area of the floor
plane from the shaded region below. The middle part of the design is
dominated by a hierarchy of vertical divisions that articulate the
back wall. Two slender piers divide the entire space roughly into
thirds. The central "room" is subdivided by three again, with the
window bay flanked by niches; the window bay itself is divided into
three sections. In each side room, the division proceeds by twos: two
walls meet at an angle and each is divided into a window half and a
niche half. But because one of the walls is sharply foreshortened and
the other is seen broadside, there is also a threefold division: niche,
window, and foreshortened wall, with the foreshortened wall equal
to about half the wall seen broadside. As if this were not complex
enough, the large niches of the central room slip behind the piers to
form the niches in the foreshortened walls of the side rooms.
There is a similar three-against-two rhythm in the way each niche
is subdivided.

Yet all this analysis (which would become still more intricate if we
proceeded to the divisions of the vaulted ceiling) does not really

describe what we see when we look at the print any more than playing the separate melodic lines of a musical composition describes what we hear when they are played simultaneously. Looking at the print, we are aware of the result of all the interpenetrating patterns and rhythms: a simultaneous sense of awe-inspiring complexity and reassuring order.

Could Master W have carried out this design in gold and silver? He produced numerous engravings depicting goblets, monstrances, a bishop's crozier, and the like that are easy to envision as actual pieces of metalwork.[6] He also engraved views of Gothic halls and chapels that are clearly imaginary, not architecture to be built in stone but fantasies that could only be carried out, if at all, on a small scale in wood or metal or, better still, suited to form the background of a painted altarpiece or a miniature in a Book of Hours.[7]

This design seems to occupy a middle ground between a practical blueprint and a fantasy. Certain spatial contradictions, no doubt the result of Master W's limited understanding of perspective, begin to puzzle us as soon as we think of the design actually existing in three dimensions. Such contradictions could probably have been resolved with minor modification to the design. A more serious problem seems to be that the effect of the design depends so much on the apparent transparency of the windows: What would happen if they were opaque or blocked by the figures of saints? Master W's other design for a mantle-clasp, an ornate group of canopied niches, seems to await its figures, but in this print, the empty, spacious architecture is complete in itself. Perhaps, like many subsequent engravers of ornament, Master W allowed the pleasure of invention to take precedence over practical considerations. Ostensibly the design for a functional object, the print has become an end in itself, an exercise in abstract form.

Lehrs knew of five surviving impressions of this print, but the Museum's impression is the only one that he described as "excellent." It is one of two impressions from the first state, before Master W added some minor shading. – TR

1. The basic research on the Master W with the Key was done by Max Lehrs, *Der Meister W(key), ein Kupferstecher der Zeit Karls des Kühnen* (Dresden, 1895), and Wolfgang Boerner, *Der Meister W(key)* (Borna-Leipzig: R. Noske, 1927), and is summed up in Lehrs VII:1-101. Lehrs deduced that the master worked in Bruges on the basis of the watermarks on his prints (Lehrs VII:21-23).

2. Lehrs VII:4, 6-7.

3. Lehrs VII:16-17.

4. Joseph Braun, *The Catholic Encyclopedia*, s.v. "morse." Because the German term for this object (*Rauchmantelschliesse*) translates literally as something like "smoke-mantle-closure," it has sometimes been erroneously described in English as the fastening for a chimney-hood.

5. Wolfgang Scheffler et al., *Kunstgewerbemuseum Berlin, Ausgewählte Werke* (Berlin: Stiftung preussischer Kulturbesitz, Staatliche Museen, 1963), no. 48 (illustrated). Klaus Pechstein et al., *Deutsche Goldschmiedekunst vom 15. bis 20. Jahrhunderts aus dem germanischen Nationalmuseum* (Berlin: Verlag Willmuth Arenhövel, 1987), 12, fig. 3.

6. For example, Lehrs 49, 52-57, and 62 (reproduced in H. *Neth.* XII:49, 52-57, and 62).

7. For example, Lehrs 63-66 (reproduced in H. *Neth.* XII:63-66). 6. Lehrs saw this impression in the Count Yorck von Wartenburg Collection (Lehrs 79).

Master i.e.
German active ca. 1480-1500

11. The Martyrdom of St. Catherine
Engraving on antique laid paper, 28.4 x 20.5 cm (sheet).
P.II.151.44; Lehrs VI.46.41.
Watermark: Wheel of St. Catherine (cf. Lehrs 28).
Condition: Trimmed within platemark.
Provenance: (Alfred Strölin, Lausanne, consigned to Knoedler, May

25, 1932); (purchased from M. Knoedler, New York, May 26, 1932, for $1,050).
Bequest of Herbert Greer French, 1943.138.
Exhibitions: Cincinnati 1934, no. 26.

Master i.e., one of Martin Schongauer's many late fifteenth-century followers, was once thought to have been Schongauer's goldsmith brother Jörg[1] on the basis of his steady but unimaginative handling of the burin. The artist's name, Master i.e., is derived from the crudely inscribed monogram found on one of the fifty-five engravings attributed to his hand by Max Lehrs: a waist-length caricature of a peasant man holding a long sausage in both hands and a loaf of bread under one arm.

It is far from certain whether Lehrs' reverse reading of the monogram is correct, and equally unclear whether it represents the initials of the artist. This artist was formerly known as the Master of the Wheel of St. Catherine because of his frequent use of papers watermarked with a catherine wheel (Lehrs VI, watermark nos. 25-28). Other distinctive papers favored by this artist include the blessing hand, marked with the initials *B P* (Lehrs VI, watermark nos. 17-18).

Thirty-one of Master i.e.'s engravings are simply faithful copies of known prints by Schongauer, including the latter's series of the *Twelve Apostles* and the *Five Wise and Five Foolish Virgins* as well as a number of individual depictions of Madonnas and saints. The Schongauer prototypes chosen by Master i.e. include early works, such as *The Flight into Egypt* (cat. 6), engravings from Schongauer's middle period, such as *Death of the Virgin* (Lehrs 16), and late works such as the square *Baptism of Christ* (Lehrs 8). Master i.e.'s knowledge of Schongauer's entire oeuvre suggests that his workshop was probably located on the left bank of the Rhine near, or perhaps in, Colmar or nearby Isenheim. Furthermore, the fact that the Bibliothèque Nationale owns the best collection of the artist's work also suggests that the artist's studio may have been on the left bank of the Rhine in what today is French territory.

The Museum is fortunate to own two of the three most unique compositions by Master i.e., both from the Herbert Greer French Collection: *Madonna on a Grassy Bank with Three Angels* (Lehrs 10), a veritable sampler of engraving motifs adapted from various works by Schongauer and Master E.S., and *The Martyrdom of St. Catherine*. The third of his masterworks, *Christ in the Wilderness Served by Angels* (Lehrs 5), is represented in the National Gallery of Art, Washington, and the Georgia Museum of Art, The University of Georgia, Athens.

The Martyrdom of St. Catherine appears to be the earliest of several spectacular prints devoted to the protracted attempt to execute Catherine of Alexandria, a king's daughter and one of the two most popular female saints of the late Middle Ages. Catherine's overweening interest in Christian theology led her to engage in an ill-advised debate with the Emperor Maxentius (or Maximinus, according to *The Golden Legend*) and his fifty pagan orators on the subject of the stupidity of worshipping idols. The emperor, ever a poor loser, condemned the fifty orators to be executed and ordered Catherine to be tortured to death by a set of wheels fitted with saw blades. This diabolical apparatus was miraculously destroyed "with such violence that four thousand pagans were killed by its collapse."[2] Master i.e.'s engraving immortalizes this moment, without referring to Catherine's eventual death by beheading, a dramatic episode later chosen by Master M.Z., Albrecht Dürer, and Lucas Cranach.[3] Although *The Golden Legend* specifies that the wheel was actually destroyed by an angel of the Lord, all four artists chose to depict its destruction by hailstones, as specified in the German *Der Heiligen Leben und Leiden*, first published by Gunther Zainer in Augsburg

(1472) and quickly reprinted with woodcut illustrations in Nürnberg (1488) and Lübeck (1492.)

This very fine impression with plate tone is but one of five known.[4] In a letter from Dresden dated February 14, 1932, Lehrs describes the composition as "Master i.e.'s masterpiece. . . most likely done after a lost composition by Schongauer, from whose engravings certain details are taken." Lehrs also notes that only one impression had previously been placed at public sale: the heavily restored impression in the Durazzo Collection was sold to Baron Rothschild in 1872 and now belongs to the Louvre. A drawing copied from the print is found in the Reserve of the Cabinet des Estampes at the Louvre (B. 13 res).

According to Lehrs, a number of the secondary figures in this print were obviously adapted from Schongauer's works, most notably the head of the soldier under the lance at right, which comes from Schongauer's large *Christ Bearing the Cross* (cat. 7); others have their origins in *Christ before Pilate* (Lehrs 24) or *St. James at the Battle of Clavijo* (Lehrs V.376.1), considered by scholars to be an unfinished plate by Schongauer that was later completed by a follower.[5] – JH

1. Daniel Burckhardt, *Die Schule Martin Schongauers am Oberrhein* (Basel, 1888); see also Lehrs VI:9-54 and Max Lehrs, "Die deutsche und niederländische Kupferstich aus den Sachsischen Kunstsammlungen," *Rep. Kw.* 11 (1888): 64.

2. Catherine's story is told *in extenso* by the fourteenth-century Dominican author Jacobus de Voragine in *The Golden Legend*; see Granger Ryan and Helmut Ripperger, trans., *The Golden Legend* (1941; reprint, New York: Arno Press, 1969), 708-16.

3. See Master MZ's engraving (Lehrs 9); Albrecht Dürer's early woodcut (B. 120), and Lucas Cranach the Elder's triptych, the St. Catherine altar, of 1506 (Dresden).

4. Other impressions in public collections are to be found in the Fitzwilliam Museum, Cambridge, England, the British Museum, and the Bibliothèque Nationale, Paris.

5. For a discussion of the literature relating to the attribution of *St. James at the Battle of Clavijo*, see Alan Shestack, Washington 1967-68, no. 42; Colmar 1991, 256-59, no. G 5; and Paris 1991, 126-131, no. 14.

Master I A M of Zwolle

Dutch active ca. 1470-1490

12. The Madonna Seated, the Christ Child Holding a Cross

Engraving on antique laid paper, 21.8 x 17.7 cm (sheet).
B.VI.95.9; Lehrs 10.
Signed in plate lower center: · I · K · ↤↦
Condition: Trimmed within platemark.
Provenance: Friedrich August II (Lugt 971); (his sale C.G. Boerner, Leipzig, May 14-15, 1934, no. 408 [unsold]); (later sold to Alfred Strölin, Lausanne, July 1934, for rm 400); (consigned to Knoedler, July 16, 1934); (purchased from M. Knoedler, New York, November 1, 1934, for $950).
Bequest of Herbert Greer French, 1943.64.
Exhibitions: Chicago 1941, no. 108, illus.; Cincinnati 1941, no. 27, pl. 10.

One of the most gifted and intriguing of the late fifteenth-century engravers is the north Netherlandish artist whose plates are variously signed *I A* (the *A* is apparently an A-shaped hallmark rather than the first letter of the alphabet); *I M*; *I* [hallmark A] *M* ; *I A M*, with a small drawing of a medieval goldsmith's drill;[1] and simply *Zwoll*. Zwolle, a Hanseatic town in the Utrecht diocese, the northeast area of the modern Netherlands, is presumed to have been the location of the master's workshop.

A convincing case has now been made for the identification of Master IAM as Johan van den Minnesten, a municipal painter (*pictor nuncupatus*) active in Zwolle between 1462 and his death in 1504.[2] Unfortunately, none of Johan van den Minnesten's paintings

has survived, and none of the documents concerning him mentions his activity as an engraver. There is reason to believe that Van den Minnesten's son, who was also named Johan and who used the A-shaped hallmark, may have been the same "Master Johan the Printer" who was paid in 1545 for printing his (i.e., Johan the Younger's) engravings "to the welfare and honor of the City of Zwolle."[3] It is probable that *his* here refers to the younger Johan's ownership of his dead father's copperplates: such items were valuable and were normally willed by artists to their heirs.

Impressions of Master IAM's prints are relatively rare compared to those of such engravers as Martin Schongauer and Israhel van Meckenem. His oeuvre itself is much smaller, totaling only twenty-six engravings, a fact well in accordance with Johan van den Minnesten's major activity as municipal painter. Châtelet[4] has made the interesting suggestion, accepted and carried further by Filedt Kok,[5] that the work of the master may represent the first case of collaboration between a major painter and a professional, or purely reproductive, engraver. This division of labor, which had been the norm in the case of woodcut design from the very beginning, was destined to become quite common among engravers by the end of the sixteenth century. If Master IAM's prints were the result of a collaboration between painter and engraver, Filedt Kok suggests that the goldsmith's drill may have served as the engraver's signature or, alternatively, that the *I A* of the monogram may have stood for Johannes Aurifaber (literally, John the goldsmith) or possibly for Johannes Ludolphi, a goldsmith who settled in Zwolle in 1479. This collaborative theory would help to explain the dramatic stylistic changes between the deliberately simple composition, *The Madonna Seated, the Christ Child Holding a Cross*, with its uncomplicated linework, and the unusually virtuosic and elaborate *Betrayal of Christ*, with its dark background of multiple hatchwork, which sets off the main figures in white relief. It would also clarify the stylistic differences between a classical subject, such as *The Battle of Two Men with a Centaur* (Lehrs 23), so reminiscent of battle scenes by Pollaiuolo,[6] and the folk-inspired theme of *St. Christopher on Horseback* (Lehrs 16) or the airborne *St. George Battling the Dragon* (Lehrs 17).

Master IAM's rare prints have been cherished by collectors, beginning with late fifteenth-century artisans who used his designs to create paintings, sculpture, woodcuts, and dotted prints of their own. One of the most distinguished – and unexpected – of the master's collectors was the English diarist Samuel Pepys, who included the artist's *Pietà* (Lehrs 7) and *Last Supper* (Lehrs 2) in an album of New Testament subjects that he assembled in the closing years of the seventeenth century after his retirement from the admiralty.[7]

Generally considered one of the master's earliest, *The Madonna Seated, the Christ Child Holding a Cross* shows the strong influence of the style of Dirk Bouts, a Haarlem-born painter active in the Flemish university city of Louvain from about the mid-fifteenth century until his death in 1475. The print is known in only eight impressions, the Museum's being the only one in the United States. All eight are defective in one way or another, through trimming, overhandling, or plate wear, suggesting that the print must have been valued for its subject rather than collected as fine art.

The image of the Christ child, who holds a cross while still seated in his mother's lap, may strike the modern viewer as bizarre or anachronistic, but it is actually quite in keeping with the devotional tenets taught in the north Netherlandish schools of the Brothers and Sisters of the Common Life at the time: the purpose of Christ's incarnation was his Crucifixion; his death on the cross would expiate the sins of humanity. In his sermons and in his popular devotional book of the day, *The Imitation of Christ*, the subprior of the Windesheim monastery, Thomas à Kempis (1379/80-1471), urges his readers to prepare themselves to take up their own crosses by learning to bear their misfortunes without complaining. Zwolle, where Thomas à Kempis' remains were enshrined after his death, lies only a few miles from the site of the former Windesheim monastery, Mount Saint Agnes (Agnietenberg), where he had lived from 1399 until about 1408 and where his influence would have been particularly strong in Master IAM's day.[8] – JH

1. This drawing, formerly identified as either a weaver's shuttle or a burnisher, was identified as a drill by Wilhelm Buhler, "Signaturen des Meisters von Zwolle," *MGvK.* 50 (1927): 42-43. Cited in Alan Shestack, Washington 1967, no. 134.

2. This identification, first proposed by the archivist T. J. de Vries in his *Geschiedenis van Zwolle* (Zwolle, 1954), 1:137, was greeted with skepticism (see Shestack, Washington 1967, no. 134). However, a more complete and convincing argument has now been made by B. Dubbe, "Is Johan van den Mynnesten de 'Meester van Zwolle'?" *BvhR.* 18 (1970): 55-65. I am grateful to J. P. Filedt Kok for sending me a copy of this article and a copy of his own article, "Master IAM of Zwolle", in *Festschrift to Erik Fisher: European Drawings from Six Centuries* (Copenhagen: Royal Museum of Fine Arts, 1990).

3. *Gemeente Zwolle Jaarrekening, 1545, E. O. nitg. 6* (cited in Filedt Kok, "Master IAM of Zwolle," 341-356, n. 9.

4. Albert Châtelet, *Early Dutch Painting: Painting in the Northern Netherlands in the Fifteenth Century* (Amsterdam, 1980), 170.

5. Filedt Kok, "Master IAM of Zwolle," passim.

6. See Mark Evans, "Pollaiuolo, Dürer and the Master IAM of Zwolle," PQ. 3, no. 2 (1986): 109-16.

7. Cambridge University, Pepysian Library. On Pepys' print collection, see Jan van der Waals, "The Print Collection of Samuel Pepys," PQ. 1, no. 4 (1984): 236-57.

8. Elizabeth Finkenstaedt, "The Master IAM of Zwolle" (Ph.D. diss., Harvard University, 1963). This unpublished dissertation contains much interesting material regarding the relationship between the iconography of the master and the practices of the Brothers of the Common Life. See also, Elizabeth Finkenstaedt, "Two Netherlandish Engravings and the Windesheim Congregation in the Fifteenth Century," *Gesta* 8 (1969): 42-46. In this article, Finkenstaedt discusses *The Ecstasy of St. Bernard* (Lehrs 15) and *Young Man and a Pilgrim* (Lehrs 24).

Master I A M of Zwolle

Dutch active ca. 1470-1490

13. The Betrayal of Christ ca. 1485.

Engraving on antique laid paper, 35.6 x 27.2 cm (sheet).
B.VI.92.4; Lehrs 4; H. *Neth.* 4.
Watermark: Gothic *P* with flower.
Signed upper center: ZWOLL; lower center:

Condition: Trimmed and remargined. Both signatures, upper and side border lines, horizontal hatching both sides outside of pillars and occasional lines in outer pillars added with pen and black ink.
Provenance: Count Nostitz, Prague; (purchased from Harlow, McDonald, New York, July 10, 1933, for $2,400).
Bequest of Herbert Greer French, 1943.63.
Exhibitions: Cincinnati 1934, no. 30; Cincinnati 1941, no. 26.

This beautiful impression is one of about twenty that have survived. Unusually large and dramatically lighted for an engraving of the late fifteenth century, it was apparently created as part of an unfinished series of prints dealing with the Passion of Christ – always a popular theme for sets of prints since scenes of Christ's Passion were sequentially presented in illuminated Books of Hours of the time. Related prints from the series are *The Last Supper* (Lehrs 2)[1] and *The Agony in the Garden* (Lehrs 3),[2] similar in size, complex engraving style, dramatic lighting, and palpable architectural framework.

J. D. Passavant, writing in early nineteenth-century Germany, had already noted a resemblance between these three Passion scenes by Master IAM and contemporary wooden relief sculpture (P. II:179).

Passavant suggested that the compositions might not be the engraver's own but copies of some carved set of stations of the cross (the series of events leading up to Christ's Crucifixion). Max Lehrs also perceived a possible relationship with sculpture, but in reverse. Lehrs felt that the master's engravings were intended as designs for such sculpture. Furthermore, some documents relating to Johan van den Minnesten, the proposed master, have to do with his painting and gilding of three statues for a well-known sculptor of the day, Master Arndt of Calcar, in 1479.[3]

Richard Randall cites the stock of models used for a Flemish altarpiece carved in an Antwerp workshop for export to France as the influence for the screaming Malchus and the arresting soldier in this print. This altarpiece, from the Norman town of Blainville-Crevon, is now in the Walters Art Gallery in Baltimore.[4] A fresco by Gian Francesco da Tolmezzo in Provesano, datable to 1496 and largely inspired by the master's print (Lehrs 186), provides a terminal date for the plate, which was probably engraved about ten years earlier, in 1486. – JH

1. Of the eight surviving impressions of this plate, the only ones in America are in the Art Institute of Chicago and the Nelson-Atkins Museum in Kansas City.

2. Of the eight known impressions, the only one in America is in the Museum of Fine Arts, Boston.

3. B. Dubbe, "Is Johan van den Mynnesten de 'Meester van Zwolle'?" *BvhR.* 18 (1970): 57.

4. Richard H. Randall, Jr., "A Flemish Altar Made for France," *Journal of the Walters Art Gallery* 33-34 (1970-71): 9-33, esp. 25-28.

Francesco Rosselli

Florence 1448-after 1508 Florence

14. The Resurrection ca. 1485?

Plate 11 from *Life of the Virgin and Christ.*
Engraving on antique laid paper, 22.5 x 16.2 cm (platemark).
B.XIII.261.16;[1] P.V.52.11; Hind B.I.11 i/iii; TIB 2404.011 i/iii.
Watermark: Fleur-de-lis.[2]
Condition: Trimmed to platemark.
Provenance: (Purchased from M. Knoedler, New York, October 31, 1932, for $3,750).
Bequest of Herbert Greer French, 1943.39.
Exhibitions: Cincinnati 1934, no. 3; Cincinnati 1941, no. 4; Washington 1949; Minneapolis 1956, no. 80; Washington 1973, no. 82.

Younger brother of the well-known painter Cosimo Rosselli, Francesco was born in Florence in 1448 and died there at an unknown date in the first quarter of the sixteenth century. Widely traveled, he worked not only in Florence but also in Siena, in Venice, and even in Hungary. He was a versatile craftsman who seems to have begun his career as a manuscript painter before turning, eventually, to engraving.[3] Rosselli's contemporaries singled him out for special praise as a "cosmographer," which is to say a student of geography and a designer and printer of maps and city views. His surviving prints include eleven maps as well as a sizable fragment of a huge and remarkably accurate view of his native city; arguably his most significant work is nothing other than the earliest printed map to show the newly discovered American continents, a key monument in the history of cartography that Rosselli engraved for a Venetian publisher in 1506.[4]

In their own way, Rosselli's noncartographic prints are equally important. His artistic personality has emerged with a certain amount of clarity in recent years, and more than seventy-five engravings can now be assigned to him.[5] Among them are several well-known sets of prints, such as the six *Triumphs of Petrarch*, the fifteen scenes from *The Life of the Virgin and Christ*, and the thirty-six *Prophets and Sibyls*, in addition to a number of large, ambitious narrative subjects belonging to no particular series.[6] The original copperplates for most of these prints are tersely described in an extraordinary document – an inventory, dated 1527, that lists merchandise contained in the workshop of Francesco's son Alessandro, a mercer, or dealer in fabrics, who died in 1525.[7] The items named in the inventory cannot all be traced, and Alessandro's stock definitely included material by craftsmen other than his father. Still, many of the entries do correspond to surviving engravings attributable to a single hand, and it is reasonable to assume that Francesco was responsible for them.

Among his most notable projects was the aforementioned *Life of the Virgin and Christ*, a series to which *The Resurrection* belongs. Comprised of fifteen engravings (plus two additional engraved sheets of ornamental strips that were meant to be cut into segments and used to frame the principal scenes), the series portrays the major episodes in the lives of Mary and Jesus, from the Annunciation to the Virgin's Coronation in heaven. More than just simple illustrations of holy stories, however, the prints were specifically intended as aids for meditation when reciting the rosary. As such, their subjects were fixed by convention. Arranged chronologically in three groups of five, they depict the so-called Joyful Mysteries (events from Christ's infancy and youth), the Sorrowful Mysteries (scenes from Christ's Passion), and the Glorious Mysteries (miracles of glory and triumph over death, including the Resurrection, that occurred after the Crucifixion). Thus the set was produced with an eye to the Florentine market for devotional images, and it seems to have been something of a best-seller. After an initial edition that may have appeared in the mid- to late 1480s,[8] the prints were soon reissued in a slightly modified second state, then coarsely reworked in a third state, presumably after the turn of the century.

A fine specimen of the rare first state, the Museum's impression of *The Resurrection* typifies Rosselli's competent but rather impersonal manner of engraving. He presents his subject with admirable clarity, showing Christ rising from a tomb surrounded by the soldiers who had fallen asleep while guarding it. The figures recline in a variety of somewhat awkward poses, and the landscape, like that of other prints in the same series, consists of formulaic elements articulated with short, slightly curving dashlike strokes. As in all of Rosselli's prints, the modeling and shading of the figures are achieved exclusively by means of straight, widely spaced, oblique parallel lines, a highly disciplined system that seems to imitate a contemporary style of draftsmanship and that exemplifies the *Broad Manner* of late fifteenth-century Florentine engraving.[9] Pollaiuolo may (or may not) have been the inventor of this important new technique, as seen in his *Battle of the Nudes* (cat. 16). But Pollaiuolo produced no print other than the famous *Battle*, while Rosselli used the Broad Manner as the basis for an extensive body of work. In fact, he was not only the most persistent but virtually the sole practitioner of the Florentine Broad Manner – a circumstance, not generally recognized, that secures for him a major position in the development of early Italian engraving. – MZ

1. Mistakenly attributed to Nicoletto da Modena.

2. Fleurs-de-lis of various shapes and sizes are among the most common forms for watermarks. The present one, however, does not seem exactly to match any reproduced in standard references.

3. For Rosselli's manuscript paintings, see Mirella Levi d'Ancona, "Francesco Rosselli," *Commentari* 16 (1965): 56-76. Levi d'Ancona also publishes various documents concerning the artist and discusses his work as a miniaturist in Siena and Budapest.

4. Both the *View of Florence* and the world map of 1506 are catalogued by Hind B.III.18 and G.6. For Rosselli's maps in general, see S. Crinò, "I planisferi di Francesco Rosselli nell'epoca delle grandi scoperte geografiche: A proposito della scoperta di

nuove carte del cartografo fiorentino," *La Bibliofilia* 41 (1939): 384-405; and Roberto Almagià, "On the Cartographic Work of Francesco Rosselli," *Imago Mundi* 8 (1951): 27-34.

5. See especially Konrad Oberhuber, NGA, 47-59, and for a comprehensive discussion and complete catalogue of the noncartographic prints, the section on Rosselli in my forthcoming *Commentary* to TIB 24 (2404).

6. Hind obscured the unity of this group by placing its members in four different sections of his corpus on early Italian engraving (Hind B.I, B.II, B.III, and C.I-II); his caution also prevented him from attaching Rosselli's name to any of them.

7. Published most conveniently in Hind I:304-09. Plates for *The Life of the Virgin and Christ* may or may not be the ones listed on p. 307 as entry no. III.75 ("10 forme di rosai [rosaries] dopi, stanpe di ½ foglio chomune").

8. This date was determined in an important recent study by Madeline Cirillo Archer, "The Dating of a Florentine *Life of the Virgin and Christ*," PQ. 5 (1988): 395-402. Archer's findings strongly suggest that the dates traditionally assigned to the series, which ranged from circa 1465 to circa 1475, were much too early.

9. For a definition of the Broad Manner technique, see cat. 16.

Francesco Rosselli

Florence 1448-after 1508 Florence

15. Moses on Mount Sinai and the Brazen Serpent

ca. 1485-1500. Engraving on antique laid paper,
29.7 x 43.3 cm (platemark).
P.V.39.93; Hind B.III.5 i/iii.
Watermark: Eagle with trefoil crown (cf. Briquet 89).
Condition: Repaired vertical loss with retouching through center of sheet.
Provenance: Friedrich August II (Lugt 971); (his sale C.G. Boerner, Leipzig, November 8-9, 1932, no. 43, pl. 2, to Matthiesen for RM 4,800); (purchased from M. Knoedler, New York, July 26, 1937, for $5,250).
Bequest of Herbert Greer French, 1943.40.
Exhibitions: Chicago 1941, no. 126; Cincinnati 1941, no. 4; Washington 1949; Minneapolis 1956, no. 81; Washington 1973, no. 75, illus.

Moses on Mount Sinai and the Brazen Serpent belongs to a group of eight works within Rosselli's oeuvre that also includes scenes of *Solomon and the Queen of Sheba, David and Goliath, The Adoration of the Magi, The Last Judgment*, two slightly different versions of the biblical *Deluge*, and an elaborate religious allegory, *The Preaching of Fra Marco and the Seven Works of Mercy* (Hind B.III.1-8). These prints can be associated with one another by virtue of their approximately corresponding dimensions, the countless details they share in common, and the stylistic uniformity of their complex, multifigured compositions. Unlike the majority of Rosselli's other engravings, however, they were conceived independently and do not make up a unified series. That the artist of this impressive group of prints was none other than Francesco Rosselli now seems practically certain, not least because the plates from which they were pulled are listed in the inventory of 1527 (see cat. 14), which itemizes the contents of his son Alessandro's workshop.

Four of the plates in question[1] are inventoried sequentially rather than the expected eight because Rosselli followed the economical and not uncommon practice of utilizing both sides of his valuable copperplates. Thus *Moses on Mount Sinai* was evidently printed from the verso of a plate whose recto was engraved with a story of David killing Goliath, the relevant entry specifying "a death of Goliath, [and] on the other side the story of Moses, one royal folio in size."[2] Furthermore, the dimensions of a "royal folio" not only correspond well enough to those of *Moses on Mount Sinai*, they also correspond to surviving impressions of Rosselli's *David and Goliath* (fig. 15-1). As if to prove the case, both engravings exist in two states,

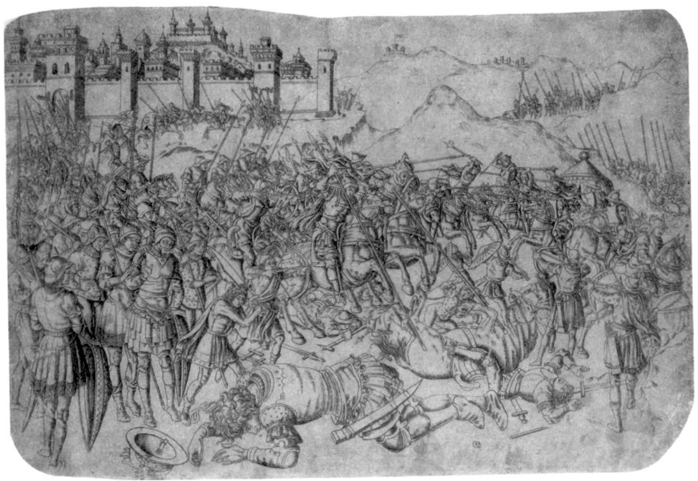

Figure 15-1. Francesco Rosselli, *David and Goliath*, engraving, Hind B.III.6. Louvre, Paris, Collection Edmond de Rothschild.

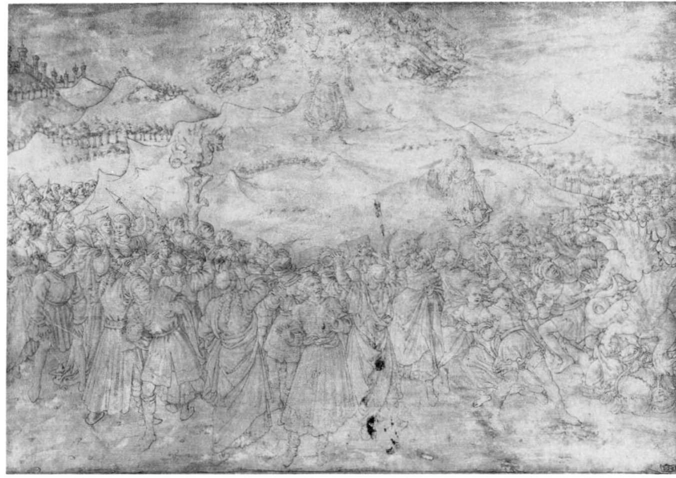

Figure 15-2. Maso Finiguerra, *Moses on Mt. Sinai and the Brazen Serpent*, ca. 1460-64, drawing. British Museum, London.

the second differing from the first only in the addition of inscriptions labeling the chief protagonists: David and Goliath in one case, Moses and Aaron in the other.

In spite of his skill as a craftsman, Rosselli was not always as original in his designs as we nowadays require an artist to be. Among the present group of engravings, for example, *The Last Judgment* derives, perhaps indirectly, from a painting by Fra Angelico, while both versions of *The Deluge* are based on a mid-fifteenth-century Florentine drawing now in Hamburg, sometimes ascribed to Maso Finiguerra (1426-1464).[3] From a drawing in the British Museum by the same hand (fig. 15-2),[4] Rosselli took a detail of a walled town on top of a distant mountain, transferring it (in reverse) to the mountainous background of his *Adoration of the Magi*. More significant for our purposes, the London drawing provided him with the complete composition for his engraving of *Moses on Mount Sinai and the Brazen Serpent*. Figure for figure, the two works correspond exactly: allowing for a few millimeters that were probably cut away along the left side of the drawing and across the bottom where the rocky ledge of the print is absent, even their dimensions are the same.

Notwithstanding Rosselli's dependence on the drawing, his engraving differs from its model in interesting ways. Surprisingly, he omitted the landscape with overlapping hills that appears in the distance on either side of Mount Sinai in the drawing. The omission is curious because Rosselli did include similar hills in the backgrounds of both his *Adoration of the Magi* (where they feature the aforementioned walled town) and *David and Goliath*. More curious still, *Moses on Mount Sinai* looks oddly incomplete in just those sections of its composition, the upper corners, where the mountainous landscape is missing. These empty areas do, however, show faint markings that seem to betray imperfect erasure from the plate with pumice, suggesting that Rosselli's initial inclination was to include the hills but that, for some unknown reason — perhaps to make the image appear more stark and emblematic — he eventually decided to remove them.

Other differences between print and drawing are less obvious but equally telling. A tendency toward decorative pattern is evident in the ornamental borders that Rosselli added above the hemlines of two figures at the left of the engraving, borders that recur with identical decoration elsewhere in his oeuvre.[5] A similar impulse no doubt prompted his addition of tiny patternistic circles on the bodies of the three dragons, just as we find them on the armor of soldiers in both *David and Goliath* and *The Resurrection* (cat. 14). The draftsman, moreover, shaded all his forms with a pale brown wash.

Rosselli, by contrast, modeled the figures with his signature Broad Manner shading and gave three-dimensional presence to the mountain and the foreground ledge with slightly curving strokes similar to the ones used for that purpose in *The Resurrection*.

Turning at last to the subject of our engraving, we see God proffering the tablets of the Law to Moses, recognizable by the two clusters of rays that emanate from his head. Farther down on Mount Sinai, at a respectable distance from Moses, kneels his elder brother Aaron, high priest of the Israelites, identified by inscription in the engraving's second state. All of this is conventional enough, but there is no precedent and no known explanation for combining this scene (from Exod. 31 or 34) with the story (from Num. 21:4-9) of the brazen serpent. Here the Lord sends "fiery serpents" to punish the Children of Israel for speaking against him, after which Moses "made a serpent of brass" at God's behest. Moses "put it upon a pole, and it came to pass that if a serpent had bitten any man, when he beheld the serpent of brass, he lived." Another seeming oddity, the substitution of dragons for serpents, is readily explained by the Latin word *draco*, although it does not occur in the Vulgate, which can carry either meaning. – MZ

1. Hind I.307.37-40.
2. Hind I.307.38: "1ª morte d'ugolia, da l'altra banda la storia di muisè, in un foglio reale."
3. Hamburg, Kunsthalle, no. 14867; pen and wash on parchment, 28.5 x 41.0 cm. See Bernhard Degenhart and Annegrit Schmitt, *Corpus der italienischen Zeichnungen, 1300-1450. Teil I: Süd- und Mittelitalien* (Berlin: Mann, 1968), 2:607-13, fig. 936; also NGA, fig. 4-9.
4. No. 1898-11-23-4; pen and wash on parchment, 28.2 x 41.6 cm. See A. E. Popham and Philip Pouncey, *Italian Drawings in the Department of Prints and Drawings in the British Museum: The Fourteenth and Fifteenth Centuries* (London: British Museum, 1950), 126-27, no. 210.
5. See, e.g., several of the *Prophets and Sibyls* as well as the *David and Goliath*.

Antonio Pollaiuolo

Florence 1431/32-1498 Rome

16. Battle of the Nudes ca. 1489?

Engraving on antique laid paper, 40.9/39.3 x 57.9 cm (sheet).
B. 2; P. 2; Hind 1; TIB 2501.001 ii/ii.
Inscribed on tablet hanging from left tree: ·OPVS·/·ANTONII·
POLLA/IOLI·FLORENT/TINI ("the work of Antonio Pollaiuolo
[the] Florentine").
Condition: Numerous repaired tears and losses throughout with
corresponding retouching with pen and ink.
Provenance: (Alfred Strölin, Lausanne, consigned to Knoedler, May
25, 1932); (purchased from M. Knoedler, New York, May 26, 1932,
for $4,200).
Bequest of Herbert Greer French, 1943.118.
Exhibitions: Cincinnati 1934, no. 14; Cincinnati 1941, no. 13, pl. 4.

Among the dozens of engravers active in Renaissance Italy, two
names, Mantegna and Pollaiuolo, stand out from all the rest. They
are the only major fifteenth-century artists to include printmaking
among their endeavors, albeit only as a sideline. Arguably the
greatest northern Italian painter of the Early Renaissance, Mantegna
may have cut seven or more plates with his own hand and he
certainly encouraged others to be executed under his guidance.[1]
Pollaiuolo, by contrast, made only one engraving during a forty-year
career in which his principal activities were in painting, metalwork,
and sculpture.[2] Born in Florence circa 1431-32, he seems to have
received his initial training as a goldsmith and, according to
tradition, to have worked as one of Lorenzo Ghiberti's assistants on
the Gates of Paradise. Emerging as an independent master in the late
1450s, he carried out major ecclesiastical and private commissions,
some of them for the Florentine Cathedral and Baptistery, others for
the palace of the Medici family. Moving to Rome in the early 1480s,
he produced two monumental bronze papal tombs, landmarks in the
history of sculpture, before his death in 1498.

Battle of the Nudes is not only Pollaiuolo's sole venture in the field
of printmaking, it is also unusual in other respects, being among the
largest of all fifteenth-century Italian engravings and one of the
earliest to be signed with the full name of the artist who designed and
executed it.[3] Given his background as a goldsmith, Pollaiuolo would
have possessed the necessary skills for engraving on copper; his
experience in painting and drawing would have prepared him for the
task of designing the complex, multifigured composition we see in
the *Battle*. A famous work in its day, it was widely influential,
generating several replicas in various media, stimulating numerous
partial copies, provoking countless artistic responses of a general
nature, and apparently selling so well in its initial issue that
Pollaiuolo had to recut the original plate to satisfy the demand for
additional prints. Some fifty-odd extant impressions – all but one of
them, including the Museum's impression, are of the reworked
second state[4] – bear witness to the popularity of what is surely the
most-celebrated engraving of the fifteenth century.

Such was the *Battle*'s reputation during the Renaissance itself that
it is one of the few prints to be mentioned by Vasari. In his *Life* of
Pollaiuolo, published in 1550 and again in 1568, Vasari explains:
"He had a more modern grasp of the nude than the masters who
preceded him, and he dissected many bodies to study their anatomy;
and he was the first to demonstrate the method of searching out the
muscles, in order that they might have their due form and place in his
figures; and of those [nude figures]. . . he engraved on copper a
battle."[5] As is so often the case, Vasari was fundamentally right in
his assessment of Pollaiuolo's accomplishments. He was a real
pioneer in the depiction of naked figures in action. Like no master
before him he understood what lies beneath the surface of the skin.
Pollaiuolo was certainly the first artist to give serious attention to
human anatomy and possibly the first to make anatomical
dissections.[6] In the *Battle*, he undertook to show how bodies move
and muscles bulge under conditions of stress and strain. In so doing,
he paved the way for Leonardo da Vinci, Michelangelo, and
Raphael, members of a younger generation who, in their own scenes
of combat, set out to rectify his anatomical errors, attaining greater
unity, fluency, and ease of movement while avoiding the jerky,
spasmodic motions of his figures and toning down their exaggerated
musculature. Artists, wrote Leonardo – perhaps with Pollaiuolo in
mind – should not "make their nudes wooden and without grace,
so that they seem to look like a sack of nuts rather than the surface
of a human being, or, indeed, a bundle of radishes rather than
muscular nudes."[7]

Despite these shortcomings, the magnitude of Pollaiuolo's
achievement remains impressive. With unprecedented intensity, he
explored the emotions of his figures no less than their strenuous
movements. As the combatants furiously seek to destroy each other,
we see their scowling faces and their frozen grins; we seem to hear
their shouts, their snarls, and their groans. Ferocious facial
expressions accompany violent physical activity, while the actions
themselves are ingeniously contrived to display what amounts to a
single naked body in ten different poses. At the far right, for
example, three figures are shown successively in standing, bending,
and reclining attitudes. Elsewhere the protagonists are self-
consciously arranged in pairs, most obviously in the center of the
composition where two swordsmen mirror each other as though they
were the same individual viewed from opposite directions.[8] A
minimum of overlapping helps us to examine, and hence to
comprehend, the form of an athletic nude in every conceivable
posture that it is capable of assuming.

Virtually all of Pollaiuolo's works show him to have been a keen
student of classical antiquity. He assimilated a vast array of visual
images found on antique coins and gems, in Roman sculpture, and in
all likelihood, on fragments of painted Greek pottery. So thoroughly
did he digest his sources, however, that one is hard pressed indeed to
identify them. Although scholars have never doubted that *Battle of
the Nudes* reflects Pollaiuolo's knowledge of ancient art, only
recently has one authority, Laurie Fusco, discovered a specific
classical model less uncertain than previous candidates: a group of
fragmentary marble statues, *Three Satyrs Strangled by a Serpent*.
Now in a private collection in Graz (Austria), the statues were
excavated at Rome in 1489, as we know from an on-the-spot letter
written to Lorenzo de' Medici by his agent.[9] If accepted, Fusco's
findings have implications beyond expanding our knowledge of the
material from which Pollaiuolo drew his inspiration. Her
observations suggest that Pollaiuolo executed the *Battle* in Rome
around 1489, contrary to the usual assumption that he engraved it in
Florence some fifteen to twenty-five years earlier.[10]

A tentative shift in date of up to two decades or more has, as Fusco
recognized, still further consequences, not only for the evolution of
Pollaiuolo's personal style but for the history of Italian engraving
itself. The relationship of Pollaiuolo's *Battle* to comparable prints
associated with Mantegna – above all to *The Battle of the Sea Gods*
(B. 17-18) (cat. 17) and the pair of *Bacchanals* (B. 19-20) – calls for
reevaluation. The role that Pollaiuolo played in the genesis of the so-
called Broad Manner of Florentine engraving also needs to be
considered anew. The Broad Manner is a technique first described a
century ago to distinguish a large group of Florentine prints, which
are now attributed to Francesco Rosselli (cats. 14-15), from a larger
and earlier Fine Manner group.[11] As the name implies, Fine Manner

prints are finely engraved; that is, their system of shading consists of short, very delicate lines placed extremely close to one another in clusters or patches or bands. Sometimes these lines are laid down in parallels and sometimes they crisscross each other rather haphazardly, but in either case, they produce dense areas of velvety shadow since few white spaces are visible between them. By comparison, the Broad Manner is a technique of greater regularity and discipline. Lines used for shading remain uniformly straight but are frequently longer than lines engraved in the Fine Manner. They normally run parallel to one another, are normally diagonal, and are normally spaced more widely or broadly. Moreover, given the wider spaces, an artist will often place so-called back strokes, or return strokes, obliquely between main diagonals, producing a zigzaglike effect that simulates a common method of shading found in contemporary pen and ink drawings.

In view of the uncertain dates of most fifteenth-century Italian engravings, we cannot say for sure whether Pollaiuolo was a follower or a leader in developing this distinctive manner. It seems unlikely to have been invented independently by Mantegna in Mantua, Rosselli in Florence, and Pollaiuolo in Florence or Rome. In the *Battle*, at any rate, Pollaiuolo varied his technique to a certain extent, employing long, oblique parallels to shade the ground, the vegetation, and the background; shorter parallels with return strokes to model the bodies; meshlike rectilinear cross-hatching to darken parts of the tree trunks; and sinuous, wiry, deeply incised contours to outline the nudes. The engraving's masterly craftsmanship is thus as remarkable as the complexity of its design. Those who first purchased impressions of the *Battle* must have studied and learned from its self-conscious display of technical virtuosity, endeavoring to comprehend the principles of the human body in motion from its artful disposition of figures as well.

Perhaps Pollaiuolo intended the *Battle* to serve a didactic function, to instruct as well as to delight its viewers, and to furnish a sort of demonstration piece or pattern sheet that might prove useful to fellow artists.[12] Granting this possibility, scholars occasionally wonder whether the print has any further significance. Most commentators have supposed that it does, making the traditional assumption that a work of fifteenth-century art must tell a recognizable story, illustrate a known classical text, or allude to an actual historical event.[13] To date, however, no proposal has been entirely convincing, and one may well question the value of further speculation in the absence of new evidence. Pollaiuolo probably had in mind a combat of Roman gladiators,[14] as suggested by, among other things, the chain that links the two central protagonists.[15] But rather than a specific gladiatorial contest with a specific, identifiable meaning, he seems to have conceived the notion of using a generalized scene of slaughter to portray nothing more – and nothing less – than the nature or essence of struggle. – MZ

1. For the theory that Mantegna actually executed none of the engravings associated with him, see Suzanne Boorsch's entry on *The Battle of the Sea Gods* (cat. 17), with reference to other opinions on this important question.

2. A print purporting to represent *Hercules and the Giants* (Hind 2) was evidently designed by Pollaiuolo although engraved by an unidentified north Italian follower of Mantegna; for extensive discussion, see Lilian Armstrong Anderson, "Copies of Pollaiuolo's 'Battling Nudes,'" AQ. 31 (1968): 154-67; and Mark Zucker, TIB 25 (*Commentary*): 18-20. Hind catalogued four other engravings under Pollaiuolo's name (Hind 3-6), but their relationship to the master is more remote and several different anonymous craftsmen were responsible for their execution. For Pollaiuolo's works in other media, see, most recently, Leopold D. Ettlinger, *Antonio and Piero Pollaiuolo: Complete Edition with a Critical Catalogue* (Oxford: Phaidon Press, 1978).

3. Somewhat larger than the *Battle* (about 70.0 x 50.0 cm) is the great *Interior of a Ruined Building with Figures*, signed with Bramante's name but executed by a Milanese goldsmith, Bernardo Prevedari, in 1481 (Hind 1). Given this circumstance, one may wonder whether even the *Battle of the Nudes* was made by a professional engraver rather than by Pollaiuolo himself. I am grateful to Suzanne Boorsch for raising this provocative issue with me in personal, unpublished communications. Her doubts demand further consideration, although Pollaiuolo's execution of the plate is assumed for the sake of convenience in this entry.

4. For the splendid first state from the Liechtenstein Collection, now in Cleveland, see Louise S. Richards, "Antonio Pollaiuolo: Battle of Naked Men," *The Bulletin of the Cleveland Museum of Art* 55 (1968): 63-70.

5. Giorgio Vasari, *Le Vite de' più eccellenti pittori, scultori ed architettori*, ed. Gaetano Milanesi (Florence: Sansoni, 1878-85), 3:295: "*Egli s'intese degl'ignudi più modernamente che fatto non avevano gli altri maestri innanzi a lui; e scorticò molti uomini per vedere la notomia lor sotto; e fu primo a mostrare il modo di cercare i muscoli che avessero forma ed ordine nelle figure; e di quelli [ignudi]. . . intagliò in rame una battaglia.*"

6. This supposition, partly based on Vasari's statement, was questioned by Laurie S. Fusco, NGA, 75-76, and in an unpublished lecture ("Did Pollaiuolo Dissect?") delivered at the meeting of the College Art Association (New Orleans, 1980). The issue has been reexamined with different conclusions by Bernard Schultz, *Art and Anatomy in Renaissance Italy* (Ann Arbor: UMI Research Press, 1985), 51ff, 63-65, and accompanying notes.

7. Martin Kemp, ed., *Leonardo on Painting* (New Haven and London: Yale University Press, 1989), 130.

8. For the use of reversed and pivoting figures by Pollaiuolo and other artists, see especially David Summers, "'Figure come Fratelli': A Transformation of Symmetry in Renaissance Painting," AQ., n.s., 1 (1977): 60-66; and Laurie Fusco, "The Use of Sculptural Models by Painters in Fifteenth-Century Italy," AB. 64 (1982): 175-94.

9. Laurie Fusco, "Pollaiuolo's Battle of Nudes: A Suggestion for an Ancient Source and a New Dating," in Mauro Natale, ed., *Scritti di storia dell'arte in onore di Federico Zeri* (Milan: Electa Editrice, 1984), 1:196-99. Fusco gives the date as 1488, but she has kindly informed me that it should be 1489; I am grateful to her for discussing this and related matters with me. On the general issue of Pollaiuolo's classical sources, see especially idem, "Antonio Pollaiuolo's Use of the Antique," *JWarb.* 42 (1979): 257-63 (with exhaustive summary of earlier opinions).

10. Opinions and arguments on the question of dating are summarized by Fusco (NGA, 72-74); prior to her discovery mentioned above, Fusco had argued for a date in the early 1470s.

11. E. Kolloff, s.v. "Baldini," in *Allgemeines Künstler-Lexikon (Zweite gänzlich neubearbeitete Auflage von Nagler's Künstler-Lexikon)*, ed. Julius Meyer (Leipzig, 1878), 2:574ff. See also Mark J. Zucker, "Fine Manner vs. Broad Manner in Two Fifteenth-Century Florentine Engravings," *The Metropolitan Museum Journal* 25 (1990): 21-26.

12. Ettlinger, *Pollaiuolo*, 33-34, is a recent proponent of this theory.

13. Fusco (NGA, 66-71) summarizes miscellaneous interpretations of the subject matter. Other provocative ideas are found in Patricia Emison, "The Word Made Naked in Pollaiuolo's *Battle of the Nudes*," AH. 13 (1990): 261-75; and J. R. Hale, *Artists and Warfare in the Renaissance* (New Haven and London: Yale University Press, 1990), 157-61.

14. In the early nineteenth century, Bartsch had already used the title *Les gladiateurs* (B. 2).

15. The enigmatic chain was wrongly described by Vasari (*Le Vite*, 3:293): "those [nude figures] all surrounded by a chain" ("*quelli [ignudi] tutti cinti d'una catena*"). For various conflicting interpretations of the chain, see Fusco (NGA, 66-68); Emison, "Word Made Naked," 265-66; Hale, *Artists and Warfare*, 159-61.

School of Mantegna
North Italian 15th century
after Andrea Mantegna (ca. 1430-1506)

17a. The Battle of the Sea Gods (left half) ca. 1490.
Engraving on antique laid paper, 29.7 x 42.2 cm (sheet).
B.XIII.239.18; Hind V.15.5; TIB 2506.004.
Watermark: Scales in circle (cf. Br. 2538 and 2554).
Inscribed on tablet: INVID / [indecipherable].
Condition: Trimmed within platemark.
Provenance: Bernhard Keller (Lugt 384); (purchased from M. Knoedler, New York, March 1, 1930, for $1,500).
Bequest of Herbert Greer French, 1943.120.
Exhibitions: Cincinnati 1934, no. 14.

17b. The Battle of the Sea Gods (right half) ca. 1490.
Engraving on antique laid paper, 29.9 x 38.7 cm (sheet).
B.XIII.239.17; Hind V.15.6; TIB 2506.005.

Condition: Trimmed within platemark; extensively retouched with pen and brown ink.
Provenance: (Purchased from M. Knoedler, New York, April 30, 1930, for $1,575).
Bequest of Herbert Greer French, 1943.121.
Exhibitions: Cincinnati 1934, no. 15.

Andrea Mantegna was born about 1430 near Padua. Before his twentieth birthday, he was recognized as a painter of rare genius; his youthful masterpiece, a cycle of frescoes in the Church of the Eremitani, Padua, showing the lives of saints Christopher and James, was unfortunately almost completely destroyed during the Second World War. In 1460 he accepted the invitation of Ludovico Gonzaga to become court painter in Mantua, the marquisate over which the Gonzaga ruled. Mantegna worked in this small north Italian city until his death in 1506 for Ludovico, his son Federico, his grandson Francesco, and especially, in the last decade and a half of Mantegna's life, for Francesco's well-educated and energetic wife, Isabella d'Este. Posterity knows Ludovico Gonzaga and his family as Mantegna painted them in the extraordinarily lifelike scenes on two walls of the so-called Camera Picta (formerly known as the Camera degli Sposi).

Mantegna took a great interest in the emerging medium of engraving, and about twenty-five of his compositions were reproduced in engravings during his lifetime. Many of these engravings, in turn, were copied relatively soon, so that the number of prints from the late fifteenth century or early sixteenth century made after his designs comes to more than fifty. It has long been thought that Mantegna made the best of these engravings himself. In preparing a recent exhibition on Mantegna, however, I came to the conclusion that it is unlikely that he did so; rather, in my opinion, the prints thought to have been engraved by him, including *The Battle of the Sea Gods*, were made by a professional engraver at his behest.[1]

Adam Bartsch, who published the first systematic catalogue of prints by engravers of the fifteenth through seventeenth centuries (in twenty-one volumes between 1803 and 1821), assigned twenty-three prints to Mantegna (B. XIII: 222-43). Since Bartsch, no one has doubted that these twenty-three compositions were Mantegna's, but subsequent writers have pared down the list of engravings believed to have actually been executed by him until, in 1901, Paul Kristeller maintained that Mantegna had made only seven prints.[2] During most of this century, scholars have followed Kristeller's view. A thorough study of the prints in question, however, has convinced me that Kristeller was much too exclusive and that, in fact, Bartsch's grouping of twenty-three had been by and large correct. Once it had become apparent to me that not just seven but over twenty prints had been made by the same engraver, it began to seem less and less likely that Mantegna would have actually produced these engravings with his own hand.

First, if he had done so, he would have been a complete anomaly among major artists of his day. Writing in his fundamental catalogue of early Italian engravings, Arthur Hind stated: "With a few exceptions, of which Antonio Pollaiuolo and Andrea Mantegna are the most notable, the early Italian engravers are artists of secondary importance, craftsmen who never had the same status which was held by the painters, sculptors and architects, in the society of the time" (Hind 1:15). Hind, however, apparently took it for granted that Mantegna had made the engravings himself; thus, he did not feel any obligation to suggest why Mantegna should have been such an exception.

Contemporaries praised Mantegna's art as early as the mid-1450s, when he was still in his twenties, steadily continuing their accolades until his death in 1506. A great number of encomia were written to him during his lifetime, but none of these has a word about engravings.[3] Yet it is not that laudatory poets of Mantegna's time simply ignored prints. Two other artists, both in Bologna, some fifty miles from Mantua, were praised for their prints: Francesco Francia in 1487[4] and Marcantonio Raimondi in 1504.[5]

One twentieth-century scholar did dispute Mantegna's authorship of these engravings. In a 1943 article, Erica Tietze-Conrat wrote, "not Mantegna himself but a professional engraver in his shop made these engravings under the master's supervision." She repeated this view in a book on Mantegna published in 1955.[6] Although Tietze-Conrat did not develop her argument at length, she mentioned the factor of time (even assuming that only seven prints were in question). She asserted that "the best engravings technically are those made by the best-trained engraver"[7] and pointed out that Mantegna is not known to have had any training in engraving.

What remains to be determined is the identity of the engraver. Although it may well prove possible in the future to establish this, there is not enough information in hand to do so at the present time.

The dates that have been suggested for the engravings of Mantegna's subjects have ranged widely. Of the seven prints that he assigned to Mantegna, Kristeller dated the earliest from the 1480s, when the artist was already in his fifties.[8] Hind had Mantegna making prints beginning in the 1450s and continuing sporadically until about 1500; he dated *The Battle of the Sea Gods* and the *Bacchanal*s about 1490 (Hind v:6). The authors of the 1973 National Gallery of Art catalogue gave the prints a twenty-five-year range, dating this print 1485-88,[9] while David Landau, in the London and New York exhibition catalogue of 1992, gave the prints roughly a fifteen-year span, seeing this one as a work of the 1470s.[10]

Vasari, in the second edition of his *Lives of the Artists*, published in 1568, wrote that printmaking came to Mantegna's attention when he was in Rome and that this was the reason he "gave a beginning to engraving many of his works" (*diede principio a intagliare molte sue opere*).[11] Between the publication of his first edition in 1550 and the second, Vasari had gained information on Mantegna previously unavailable to him, perhaps from a now lost letter from Girolamo Campagnola to Leonico Tomeo.[12] Thus, the statements that are new in Vasari's second edition have a strong claim to being trustworthy. Although Mantegna seems to have been looking to hire an engraver as early as 1475[13] and, consequently, Vasari was inaccurate to say that Mantegna first learned of engraving in Rome, the information that the engravings began to be made around the time of the Roman trip could have been something Vasari had newly learned.

Mantegna spent slightly over two years in Rome, from about July 1488 to September 1490, painting a chapel for Pope Innocent VIII (destroyed in 1780). Thus, if Vasari's statement can be relied upon, the earliest prints of Mantegna's designs would have been made at the time of or just after the Roman trip; it would seem more likely that the engravings would have been made after Mantegna's return to Mantua rather than while he was working for the pope. It is clear that at least some of the prints, including *The Battle of the Sea Gods*, were made by 1494. In this year, Albrecht Dürer (cat. 23) drew copies of the right half of this composition and also of *Bacchanal with Silenus* (both drawings now in the Albertina, Vienna).

While in Rome, Mantegna would have seen the monuments of ancient imperial glory – the triumphal arches, temples, baths, and theaters – that are still among the major attractions for tourists today. He would have seen smaller works as well, statuary and sarcophagi being gathered by collectors with humanistic, antiquarian interests. One such collection was that of the della Valle, a family of jurists, physicians, and scholars.[14] Two of Mantegna's famous mythological compositions, the present print and *Bacchanal with a Wine Vat* (Hind v.13.4), were inspired by two different sarcophagi in the della Valle Collection. *Bacchanal with Silenus*

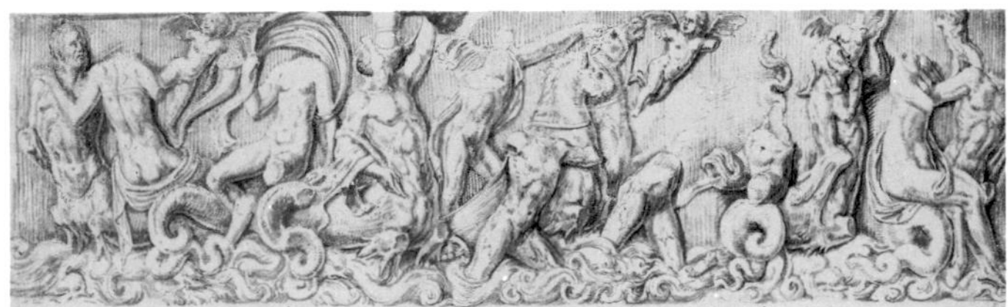

Figure 17-1. *Nereids and Tritons*, drawing after antique sarcophagus from *Codex Coburgensis*, f. 136, ca. 1550. Kunstsammlungen der Veste Coburg.

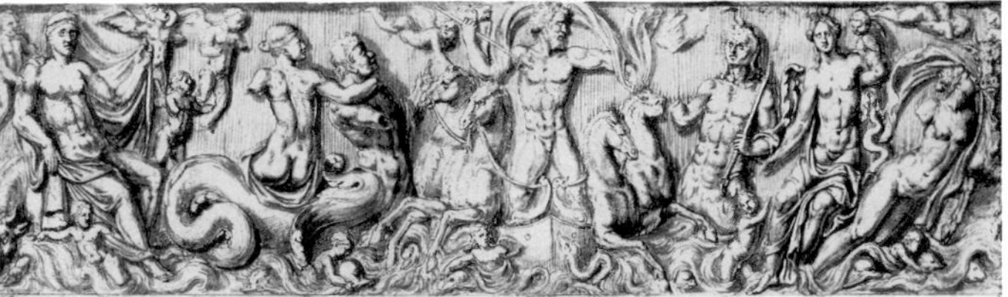

Figure 17-2. *Nereids and Tritons with the Triumph of Neptune*, drawing after antique sarcophagus from the *Codex Coburgensis*, f. 120, ca. 1550. Kunstsammlungen der Veste Coburg.

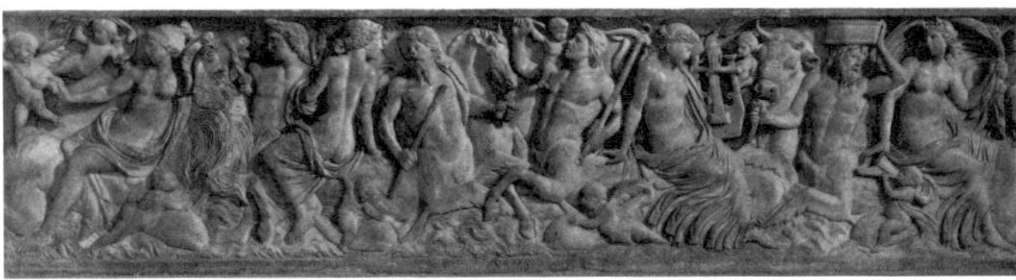

Figure 17-3. *Nereids and Sea-Centaurs with Sea-Creatures*, Roman sarcophagus front, mid 2nd century A.D., Louvre, Paris.

(Hind V.12.3) took its inspiration from another antique sarcophagus, at that time embedded in the wall of the Church of Santa Maria Maggiore (now in the British Museum).[15] Drawings of these sarcophagi by other artists could have been known to Mantegna before he went to Rome, but the extraordinary congruence of one of the main figures in *Bacchanal with a Wine Vat* with a figure from a Judgment of Paris sarcophagus would seem to rule out, in this case at least, any possibility of an intermediary; and it seems that that composition could not have existed before Mantegna's arrival in Rome.

The *sea-thiasos*, a gathering of sea creatures, was a common subject in classical reliefs, and Mantegna's inspiration for *The Battle of the Sea Gods* probably came from a number of these. The subject is printed on two sheets that join to form a continuous composition with more or less the proportions of a sarcophagus relief (the two sheets came into the Museum separately and thus are presented separately here). The sarcophagus in the della Valle Collection that has been accepted as its major visual source is in such poor condition today that it is best viewed in a drawing made about half a century after Mantegna would have seen it in Rome (fig. 17-1).[16] Any of the three figures near the center of the sarcophagus whose torsos lean toward its right edge might have inspired the figure of the man who is ready to swing two fish in the right half of Mantegna's *Battle of the Sea Gods*. They may also have inspired the pose of Envy, the emaciated hag in the left half who holds a plaque with her Latin name, *Invid[ia]*. The marine centaur positioned slightly to left of center could have inspired similar figures in the right half of Mantegna's composition, and Mantegna's seated women, especially the one with her back to the viewer in the right half, could also have been derived from those on the relief.

Two other reliefs that Mantegna surely would have seen in Rome, one showing Nereids and Tritons (Giardino della Pigna, Vatican) – also better seen in a Renaissance drawing (fig. 17-2) – and another showing Nereids and sea centaurs with sea creatures (fig. 17-3), could have been part of the inspiration for Mantegna's composition as well. Both of these reliefs include sea horses, for example, which the della Valle sarcophagus does not.[17]

Mantegna combined the figures inspired from these large reliefs with one from a classical source on an entirely different scale, a second-century B.C. sard intaglio known as the *Felix Gem* from the incised Greek signature, "Felix made it" (fig. 17-4). This gem was in the collection of Cardinal Francesco Gonzaga, as is known from an inventory taken after his death in 1483.[18] Mantegna's genius was to take from disparate sources, merging their elements into compositions that seemed entirely modern and entirely his own.[19]

In several compositions produced toward the end of his life, Mantegna created moralizing allegories, combining ideas from various classical texts just as he combined figures from a number of visual sources.[20] *The Battle of the Sea Gods* represents a similar intellectual fusion. Its subject has been analyzed by Michael Jacobsen as an allegory on the subject of envy: the sea creatures seem to refer to a specific race of artists, the Telchines, who lived on the Greek island of Rhodes.[21] In various antique texts that were known in Mantua in Mantegna's day, the Telchines were characterized as envious, spiteful, and given to fighting.

It is hard to know whether Mantegna meant this composition to be understood entirely seriously or more as an ironic joke: the use of fish as weapons and the rusticity of the other weapons led Lightbown, for example, to suggest that "the mood of the composition is one of angry and contemptuous burlesque," and that "the entire scene is a parody of a tourney."[22] The Telchines were primarily sculptors. Thus, if Jacobsen is correct that it is they who are depicted, this composition can be read as Mantegna's proclamation of victory in the ongoing competition between painters and sculptors. The fighting sea creatures would represent sculptors who are envious of Mantegna, an artist able to create "sculpture" using only two dimensions; furthermore, the "sculpture" that Mantegna created had the added virtue of recalling the antique works he had revered all his life.

In the catalogue of the London and New York exhibition of 1992, David Landau and I published a hitherto unknown copy of the left half of *The Battle of the Sea Gods*, which we attributed to the Master

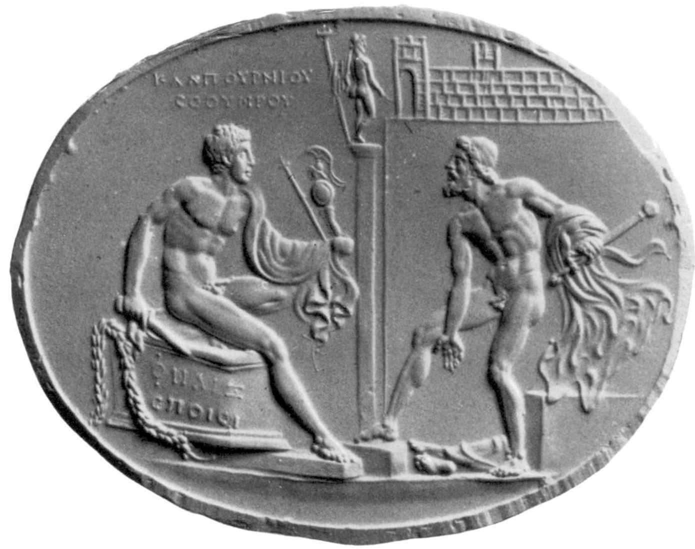

Figure 17-4. "Felix Gem," second half of 1st century B.C., sard intaglio. Ashmolean Museum, Oxford.

of 1515.[23] Both sides of the composition were copied by Daniel
Hopfer (H. *Ger.* 55-56). – SB

1. See London 1992, 56-66.

2. Paul Kristeller, *Andrea Mantegna* (London: Longmans, Green, and
Co., 1901), 386.

3. See Paul Kristeller, *Andrea Mantegna* (Berlin and Leipzig: Cosmos, 1902), 488-96;
and Chambers et al. in London 1992, 30.

4. Salimbeni, *Epitalamio nelle Pompe Nuziali di Annibale Bentivoglio* (Bologna,
1487), quoted in Hind I:304.

5. Giovanni Achillini, *Il Viridario*, written in 1504 and published in 1513, quoted in
Bernice F. Davidson, "Marcantonio Raimondi, The Engravings of His Roman Period,"
(Ph.D. thesis, Harvard University, 1954), 10, quoted in Lawrence 1981, xvi, n. 2.

6. Erica Tietze-Conrat, "Was Mantegna an Engraver?" GBA., 6th ser., 24 (1943):
378; idem, *Mantegna, Paintings, Drawings, Engravings* (London: Phaidon Press, 1955),
241-42.

7. Tietze-Conrat, *Mantegna*, 241.

8. Kristeller, *Andrea Mantegna* (London, 1901), 392ff.

9. NGA, 165-95.

10. London 1992, 285-87, no. 79.

11. Giorgio Vasari, *Le Vite de' più eccellenti pittori, scultori ed architettori*, ed.
Gaetano Milanesi (Florence: Sansoni, 1878-85), 5:396.

12. See Ronald Lightbown, *Andrea Mantegna* (Berkeley and Los Angeles: University
of California Press, 1986), 16, 393.

13. See London 1992, 48-52, 58.

14. For the della Valle Collection, see Bober and Rubinstein, 479-80.

15. For the sarcophagus that was one of the visual sources for the present print, see
Bober and Rubinstein, 131-33, no. 100. As recently first published by the present writer,
Bacchanal with a Wine Vat had as one of its visual sources a sarcophagus showing the
Judgment of Paris: see Boorsch in London 1992, 274-75; see also Bober and Rubinstein,
149-50, no. 119. For the sarcophagus that inspired some figures in *Bacchanal with
Silenus*, see Ruth Olitsky Rubinstein, "A Bacchic Sarcophagus in the Renaissance," *The
Classical Tradition: British Museum Yearbook* 1 (1976): 103-56; and Bober and
Rubinstein, 116-19, no. 83.

16. See Phyllis P. Bober, "An Antique Sea-Thiasos in the Renaissance," *Essays in
Memory of Karl Lehmann, Marsyas, Studies in the History of Art*, supp. 1, ed. Lucy
Freeman Sandler (New York, 1964), 43-48; Bober and Rubinstein, 131-33, no. 100.

17. Bober and Rubinstein, 131, 134, nos. 99, 103.

18. Clifford M. Brown, "Cardinal Francesco Gonzaga's Collection of Antique
Intaglios and Cameos: Questions of Provenance, Identification and Dispersal," GBA.,
6th ser., 101 (1983): 102-03.

19. Michael Vickers, "The 'Palazzo Santacroce Sketchbook': A New Source for
Andrea Mantegna's 'Triumph of Caesar,' 'Bacchanals' and 'Battle of the Sea Gods,'"
Burl. M. 118 (1976): 824-34, suggests the relief of a sea-thiasos, now in Munich, as a
visual source. He further suggests in "The Sources of Invidia in Mantegna's *Battle of the
Sea Gods*," *Apollo* 106 (1977): 270-73, that Mantegna's figure of Envy derives from a
woodcut by Erhard Reuwich in Breydenbach's *Peregrinations* (Mainz, 1886). These
derivations, while possible, are not compelling.

20. See, for example, London 1992, 427-30, no. 136; 453-56, no. 148.

21. Michael A. Jacobsen, "The Meaning of Mantegna's *Battle of Sea Monsters*,"
AB. 64 (1982): 623-29.

22. Lightbown, *Andrea Mantegna*, 241.

23. London 1992, 287-88, no. 80.

Unidentified Artist

Bolognese? School late 15th century

18. The Nativity

Niello on antique laid paper, 9.1 x 6.3 cm (platemark).
P.I.286.457; Dut.I.III.29.
Inscribed on tablet held by angel upper center (in reverse): GLORIA
IN / EXCELSIT [DEO] ("Glory be [to God] on high").[1]
Provenance: Friedrich August II (Lugt 971); (his sale C.G. Boerner,
Leipzig, November 8-9, 1932, no. 507, to Alfred Strölin for RM 100);
(Maurice Gobin, Paris, consigned to Knoedler, August 8, 1933);
(purchased from M. Knoedler, New York, September 29, 1933,
for $200).
Bequest of Herbert Greer French, 1943.170.
Exhibitions: Cincinnati 1941, no. 5.

This anonymous *Nativity* stands out from other Italian prints in the
Museum's collection, possessing a character uniquely its own. It is
obviously smaller than all the rest, and its diminutive size required a
finer, more miniaturistic technique. It is distinctive, moreover, in
exhibiting what appears to be a solid black sky, an effect obtained by
engraving the background of the plate with rectilinear cross-hatching
so dense that individual strokes are invisible to the naked eye.
Another idiosyncrasy may be noted in the inscription on a tablet
borne aloft by an angel near the top of the image. In spite of the care
with which each of the minuscule letters was incised, the message is
scarcely legible, insofar as it is written in reverse. One last factor
contributing to the exceptional nature of the print is its great rarity.
Apart from the Museum's impression, only a single additional
example has ever been recorded, and the latter was last seen when it
appeared at auction as long ago as 1866.[2]

Taken together, all of these factors suggest that *The Nativity* is
something other than a conventional engraving. In fact, it has always
been recognized as an engraving of a particular kind, a so-called
niello or, to be more precise, a *niello print*. The art of making nielli –
the plural of niello – has been practiced since antiquity. Nielli were
common in the Middle Ages and seem to have enjoyed a special
popularity in Italy during the Renaissance.[3] The heyday for making
nielli lasted from the middle of the fifteenth century to the beginning
of the sixteenth, a period corresponding to the time during which
most of the Italian engravings in the Museum's collection were
also produced.

Niello is a craft of the goldsmith or metalworker, its primary
purpose being the decoration of small-scale objects of silver or gold
by engraving designs directly on their surfaces or by affixing tiny
nielloed plaques to them with nails or rivets. Liturgical objects, such
as paxes, miniature altarpieces, chalices, crucifixes, and reliquaries,
were frequently so treated, as were objects of domestic usage and
personal adornment: caskets, knife handles, buckles, medallions,
and rings.

Having incised a design on a given surface, the metalsmith then
proceeded to cover the surface with a black powder known in
medieval Latin as *nigellum* – a word derived from the classical Latin
niger, or "black," whose diminutive *nigellus* means "blackish" or
"dark." Called *niello* in Italian, this black powdery substance was
normally composed of silver, copper, lead, sulfur, and borax. When
heated, it melted to the consistency of wax and was used to fill the
incisions. On cooling, it solidified, whereupon it was scraped off the
surface with a file and/or a pumice stone. In so doing, the
unengraved portions of the object were laid bare, while the engraved
lines retained the dark niello inlay. All that then remained to produce
the desired effect of a black enamellike design against a brightly
polished golden or silvery background was to reheat the object and
burnish it.[4]

Before going through this elaborate process, however, the artist
might decide to retain an exact record of his design so that he could
reproduce all or part of it in the future; or perhaps he might simply
wish to have a clearer view of the design he had just incised on the
gold or silver ground. Accordingly, he would sometimes ink the
surface and pull a very limited number of proofs, following the same
procedure that would be employed were he printing impressions
from an ordinary engraved plate of copper. Thus, he obtained one or
more prints – duplicates of the design in reverse – of the kind
preserved in the Museum's *Nativity*. Its dark, cross-hatched sky is
typical of nielli, and its reversed inscription suggests that the primary
function of the small, presumably silver plaque, now lost, was not a
plate for printing. Even the rarity of the print speaks in favor of its
being a niello, as do its modest dimensions. The intended purpose of

the original plaque can only be conjectured, but in view of its size, its arched top, its subject matter, and the absence of nail holes, the object presumably served as a pax. Paxes, tablets decorated with holy images, were kissed during the celebration of the Mass, immediately following recitation of the Agnus Dei and prior to the taking of communion. Suitably framed and held by means of a handle attached to the back, paxes played an important role in Catholic liturgy from the later Middle Ages onward, when their usage gradually supplanted the traditional kiss of peace exchanged by the priest and his congregation.

Italian Renaissance nielli and niello prints have been studied and repeatedly catalogued for nearly two hundred years, but knowledge of the field remains inadequate. Attributions to specific artists or even to regional schools are rarely reliable, and problems of identification are compounded by the existence of nineteenth-century forgeries. Evidence suggests that Florence and Bologna were the principal centers of production, and the style of *The Nativity* is compatible with an attribution to some unknown Bolognese craftsman active toward the end of the quattrocento. In the absence of definite evidence, however, it seems imprudent to be dogmatic about such matters. Moreover, the composition is conventional for the period, and the same is true for the treatment of the subject. Two angels herald the Nativity of Christ with the sound of trumpets; a third proclaims it with the opening words of the Gloria which are inscribed on his plaque. A fourth angel announces the event to a shepherd. Other shepherds arrive at the left to join Joseph and Mary in adoring the newborn child, in addition to three more angels and the traditional ox and ass. Above the ruined wall of the stable, leafy branches rise into the nighttime sky to symbolize new life growing out of decay – with the birth of the Redeemer, the New Dispensation (Christianity) supersedes the Old (Judaism). – MZ

1. Opening words of the great "Angelic Hymn" recited during the Roman Catholic Mass.

2. W. E. Drugulin sale, Sotheby's, June 18, 1866 (seventh day of sale), no. 1190. There seems to be no doubt that the Museum's impression is not the same as the one sold at Sotheby's in 1866. Dutuit unequivocally refers to two separate impressions known to him in 1888 (Dut. 1.111.29).

3. The best discussion of Renaissance nielli is found in A. M. Hind, *Nielli, Chiefly Italian of the XV Century: Plates, Sulphur Casts and Prints Preserved in the British Museum* (London: British Museum, 1936). For a more comprehensive treatment, see Marc Rosenberg, *Niello bis zum Jahre 1000 nach Chr. and Niello seit dem Jahre 1000 nach Chr.* (Frankfurt: Joseph Baer and Co., 1924-25).

4. Knowledge of the process derives principally from two sources: (1) the medieval treatise *De Diversis Artibus*, probably composed between 1110 and 1140 by a Benedictine monk, Roger of Helmarshausen, who styled himself Theophilus (John G. Hawthorne and Cyril Stanley Smith, eds., *On Diverse Arts: The Treatise of Theophilus* [Chicago and London: University of Chicago Press, 1983], 104-05, 108, 115-16; for the Latin text juxtaposed with an English translation, see C. R. Dodwell, ed., *Theophilus: The Various Arts* [London: Thomas Nelson and Sons, 1961], 80-82, 84, 92-93); and (2) Benvenuto Cellini's treatise *Dell'Oreficeria* (Carlo Milanesi, ed., *I Trattati dell'oreficeria e della scultura* [Florence: Le Monnier, 1857], 15-19; for an English translation, see C. R. Ashbee, trans., *The Treatises of Benvenuto Cellini on Goldsmithing and Sculpture* [London: Edward Arnold, 1898], 7-9). For a detailed technical discussion of the process, see A. A. Moss, "Niello," *Studies in Conservation* 1 (1953): 49-62.

Master FVB

Flemish active ca. 1480-1500

19. St. George and the Dragon ca 1480-90.

Engraving on antique laid paper, 18.0 x 13.0 cm (image) on 18.2 x 13.4 cm (sheet).
B. 33; Lehrs 42 i/ii; P. 33; H. *Neth.* 42 i/ii.
Watermark: Gothic *P* with flower.
Monogrammed in plate lower center: FVB.
Condition: Trimmed to or within platemark.

Provenance: Albertina duplicate; (purchased from F.C. Harlow, New York, December 17, 1936, for $4,050).
Bequest of Herbert Greer French, 1943.144.
Exhibitions: Cincinnati 1941, no. 25.

The goldsmith-engraver Matthäus Quadt von Kinckelbach wrote a pioneering history of German art in the form of a patriotic travel guide at the turn of the seventeenth century. In it he alleged that the inventor of engraving had been a certain "F. von Bocholt," a former shepherd "in Bergischen Land" (i.e., in southern Westphalia near Solingen and Bergisch-Gladbach – the former county of Berg).[1] Von Kinckelbach not only credited this F. von Bocholt with being the teacher of Israhel van Meckenem (cat. 20) and Wenzel von Olmütz but as the predecessor of Schongauer (cat. 6) and Dürer as well. Although J. D. Passavant disputed this claim, he retained the name of Franz von Bocholt at the suggestion of Johann Friedrich Christ.[2] Passavant was aware that the artist had copied Schongauer rather than inspired him and reported that a search of the Bocholt archives for documents relating to Franz von Bocholt proved fruitless owing to the disappearance of the city registers for the years 1459 through 1480.[3] (Master FVB's only apparent connection with Bocholt is that Israhel van Meckenem acquired and reprinted some of his plates after the master's death or retirement. However, this does not imply that Master FVB had ever visited Bocholt.)

Paul Kristeller[4] and Rosy Kahn[5] correctly identify many Netherlandish influences in the art of Master FVB, and in his catalogue raisonné of 1930, Max Lehrs suggests that Franz von Brugge (Frans of Bruges) would be a more appropriate name for this artist, noting the influences of Memling, Van der Weyden, and the Master of the St. Ursula Legend in his prints.[6] However, no Bruges documents have yet been discovered having to do with any goldsmith or engraver called Frans or any other name beginning with *F*. In light of this, modern scholars generally prefer to identify this artist only by the letters of the monogram that appear on his plates.

The Museum's splendid impression of *St. George and the Dragon*, considered by Lehrs to be one of Master FVB's best engravings, fully justifies his reputation as the most gifted of fifteenth-century Flemish engravers. The composition is similar to but more modern in feeling than that of the tiny panel in Washington attributed to the young Rogier van der Weyden (fig. 19-1). Master FVB's horse is better-proportioned than Van der Weyden's microcephalic creature, and his forward motion is convincingly depicted: his head turns daringly away from the picture plane. In addition, George's newer armor is more practical for riding, unlike Van der Weyden's long-skirted version, since it allows the wearer to assume a comfortable seat in the saddle. Master FVB's George, in contrast to Van der Weyden's recklessly bareheaded knight, prudently dons his helmet and closes his visor to do battle with a much larger and more repulsive dragon. With an impressive swing, the saint turns in the saddle to strike at the dragon with his sword, the dragon having already taken possession of his broken lance. Van der Weyden's impossibly tall and slender lance appears more appropriate for pole vaulting than for dragon-slaying, while Master FVB's lance is of proper length and heft.

Both compositions feature a somewhat improbable geology meant to suggest the peculiarities of the Near Eastern terrain where George's exploit allegedly took place. However, Master FVB's landscape, in contrast to Van der Weyden's, features a variety of young trees and shrubs, each revealing a different pattern of growth and executed with burin work that manages to suggest leaves animated by a breeze – an effect similar to the landscape backgrounds of such late fifteenth-century Netherlandish painters as Hugo van der Goes, Hans Memling, and Geertgen tot Sint Jans.

Master FVB was responsible for fifty-nine engravings. Since many

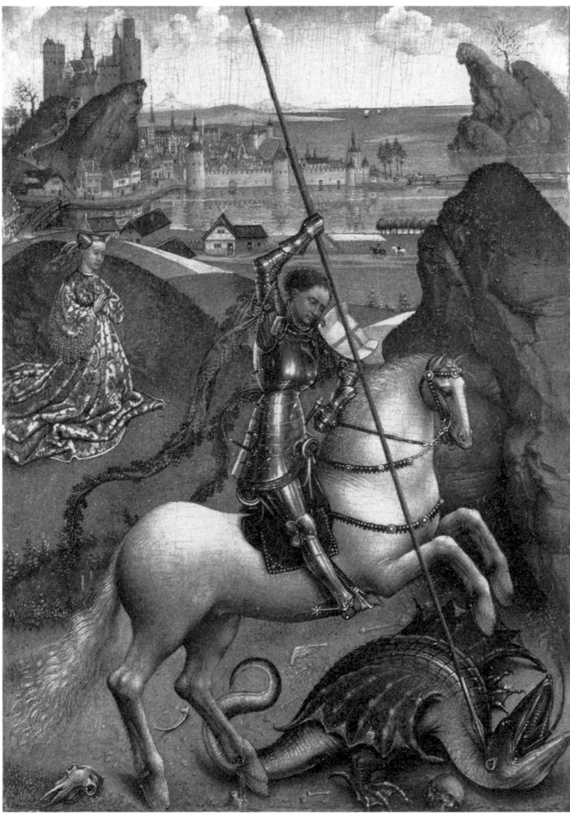

Figure 19-1. Rogier van der Weyden (attr.), *Saint George and the Dragon*, ca. 1432/35, oil on panel. National Gallery of Art, Washington, Ailsa Mellon Bruce Fund.

of them are based on Martin Schongauer's designs, he may have trained in Schongauer's Colmar studio before returning to or settling in Flanders. Some of his papers have the same watermarks as papers used by such Netherlandish engravers as the Bruges Master of the Boccaccio Illustrations, the east Netherlandish Master of the Banderoles, and the Master W with the Key (cat. 10), who is thought to have been a goldsmith employed at the Burgundian court of Charles the Bold.

The Museum's collection contains two engravings by Master FVB: this fine impression of *St. George and the Dragon* and a rarer but less fine print, the half-length *Madonna on a Crescent Moon* (Lehrs 11), formerly in the Ducal Museum in Gotha.[7]

It was Mr. French's and ultimately the Museum's good fortune to acquire one of the two equally beautiful impressions of *St. George and the Dragon* in the first state from the Albertina, Vienna. Other fine impressions of the first state are in Berlin, London, and Toledo (Ohio);[8] the remaining six are of lesser quality. Impressions of the second state, reworked in the shadows by Israhel van Meckenem, are in Washington, Boston, Cambridge (England), Paris, Vienna, and at Windsor Castle. – JH

1. Matthäus Quadt von Kinckelbach, *Teutscher Nation Herliqkeit* (Cologne, 1609); Christoph Gottlieb Von Murr, *Journal zur Kunstgeschichte und zur allgemeinen Literatur* (Nuremberg, 1775-84), 2:237; B. VI:80; Nagler I:549; P. II:186.

2. Johann Friedrich Christ, *Anzeige und Auslegung der Monogrammatum* (Leipzig, 1747), cited in Lehrs VII:102.

3. P. II:186. The search was undertaken by "Mr. C. Becker."

4. Paul Kristeller, *Kupferstich und Holzschnitt* (Berlin, 1905).

5. Rosy Kahn, *Lucas van Leyden* (Strassburg, 1918).

6. Lehrs VII:107ff.

7. The latter engraving, one of only four modern known, was printed by a Nuremberg dealer known for reprinting the plates of Master MZ and Wenzel von Olmütz on paper with the small Nuremberg arms watermark.

8. This fine first-state impression, formerly at Chatsworth, was acquired by the Toledo Museum of Art in 1987 (inv. 1987.169).

Israhel van Meckenem

Bocholt? 1440/50-1503 Bocholt
After Hans Holbein the Elder (1460/65-1524)

20. The Presentation in the Temple

Plate 8 from *The Life of the Virgin*.
Engraving on antique laid paper, 26.7 x 18.4 cm (sheet).
B. 37; Lehrs 57; H. *Ger.* 57.
Watermark: Gothic *P* with flower.
Signed in plate lower center: ·*Israhel·v·M·*
Condition: Trimmed within platemark.
Provenance: Albertina duplicate; (sale C.G. Boerner, November 15-16, 1928, no. 641, pl. 15, to Alfred Strölin for RM 3,400); (purchased from M. Knoedler, New York, November 1, 1930, for $2,600).
Bequest of Herbert Greer French, 1943.57.
Exhibitions: Cincinnati 1934, no. 34.

Israhel van Meckenem, the most prolific engraver of the fifteenth century, is documented as both an engraver and goldsmith who spent much of his working life in the small but wealthy city of Bocholt (Westphalia). The son of a goldsmith of the same name, he was one of the first printmakers to engage in reproductive engraving on a large scale: of over 620 engravings attributed to Van Meckenhem, more than three-quarters are copies or restrikes of works designed by other artists, including Master E.S., Master W with the Key, Master FVB, Martin Schongauer, Hans Holbein the Elder, and the young Albrecht Dürer.

Although it is known that Van Meckenem died in Bocholt on November 3, 1503, and was interred in the Church of Saint Georg,[1] the date of his birth is not recorded. His earliest known print, *Ornament with a Wild Man Battling a Woman* (Lehrs 605), is inscribed with a date (1465) and the statement that it was made in Cleves. Assuming that he must have been about twenty years old at the beginning of his career, art historians usually posit his birth date between 1440 and 1450; Paul Pieper, however, has suggested that the date may have been nearer to 1430.[2]

The family name, which uses the Dutch or Lower Rhenish "van," seems to have a geographic significance. According to Max Geisberg, the first to catalogue the artist's engravings, the name refers to the town of Meckenheim, near Bonn.[3] In view of the vagaries of medieval spelling, however, the possibility exists that the family may have had its origins in the village of Megchelen, between Bocholt and the modern Dutch border at Emmerich, or perhaps even in the cathedral city of Mechelen (Malines) in Brabant.[4]

Israhel the Elder is mentioned in the Bocholt archives in 1457 as the recipient of public charity. One gulden was given to the elder Van Meckenem as surety against persecution by the legal and ecclesiastical authorities: he apparently left his previous place of residence under a cloud of unpaid debts. His unusual first name, unknown outside the Van Meckenem family, suggests that there may have been a converted Jew among his ancestors. (Guild regulations ordinarily would not have permitted an observant Jew to work as a goldsmith, so it seems unlikely that he could have been Jewish himself.)

In any event, the elder Van Meckenem quickly obtained a position of respect and trust in Bocholt, and he began to receive annual payments from the city equal to the salary of an imperial goldsmith. He also fulfilled ecclesiastical commissions, one of which was a handsome monstrance for the parish church of Saint Georg, where his son was later buried.

After 1465 the family moved to the nearby ducal capital of Cleves, where "meister Isserhel" was paid two hundred marks (the equivalent of at least one thousand German marks in today's currency) to buy raw silver. It was at this time that Israhel the Younger made his first engraving. The younger Van Meckenem, however, seems to have left Cleves soon afterward, traveling south to work in the shop of Master E.S. (cat. 1). He seems to have remained with Master E.S., whose workshop cannot be precisely located, until the latter's death or retirement in 1468. He copied, retouched, and restruck a number of Master E.S.'s copperplates during his tenure in the master's studio. Although these activities have been regarded by generations of art historians as intellectually dishonest, it should be noted that the fifteenth century did not share our ideas about originality; furthermore, we have no reason to believe that Van Meckenem had not been specifically requested, either by his master or by his master's widow, to undertake this work in his capacity as journeyman.

By 1470 Van Meckenem had traveled to the episcopal city of Bamberg in Franconia, where he made and signed an Agnus Dei pyxis (Bayerisches Nationalmuseum, Munich) for Konrad Leen, vicar of the Marienkirche in Teuerstadt, before returning to Bocholt to establish a permanent workshop. A number of documents attest to his activity in Bocholt after 1480: some of these records concern commissions from the city council; others concern lawsuits instituted against his neighbors. Van Meckenem's wife, Ida, whom he married in the late 1480s, is the subject of still other documents, revealing that she had been fined for "unseemly speech" and for mocking and scolding public officials (fig. 20-1).[5]

On the day when the infant Christ was presented to the high priest in fulfillment of Old Testament Law, Mary also brought a purification offering to the temple – two turtledoves, according to the Franciscan *Meditations on the Life of Christ*. The doves are held by the young woman with long braids, at right. On the day of the presentation, an old man named Simeon recognized the child as the Messiah and asked to hold him, since God had promised Simeon that he would see the Messiah before he died. Calling the infant "the light to lighten the Gentiles, and the Glory of Thy people, Israel," Simeon then recited these words, which have since become a Christian benediction: "Now lettest Thou Thy servant depart in peace" (Luke 2:29). Van Meckenem engraved Simeon's blessing on the high priest's mantle border.

Although Israhel van Meckenem's composition is a reverse free copy of one panel of Hans Holbein the Elder's 1493 Weingarten

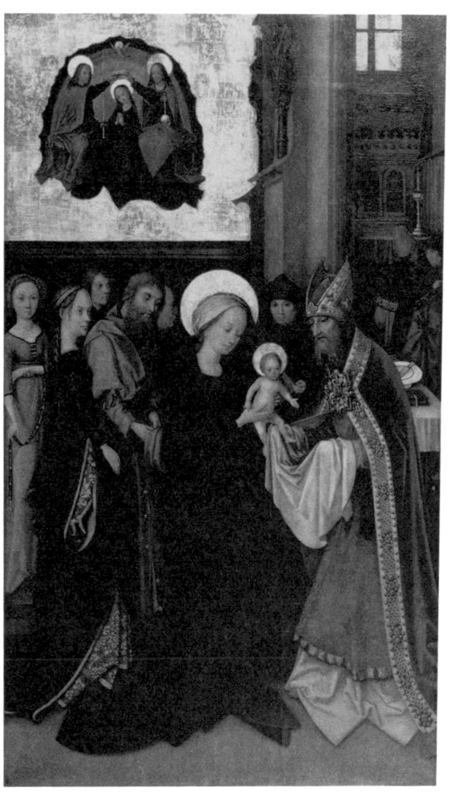

Figure 20-2. Hans Holbein the Elder, *Presentation in the Temple* from the Weingarten altar, 1493, oil on panel. Augsburg Cathedral.

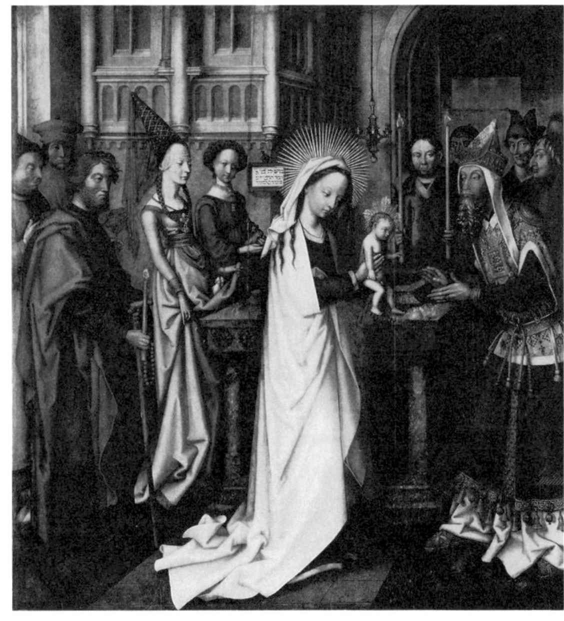

Figure 20-3. Hans Holbein the Elder, *Presentation in the Temple* from the Dominican church, Frankfurt, 1501, oil on panel. Kunsthalle, Hamburg.

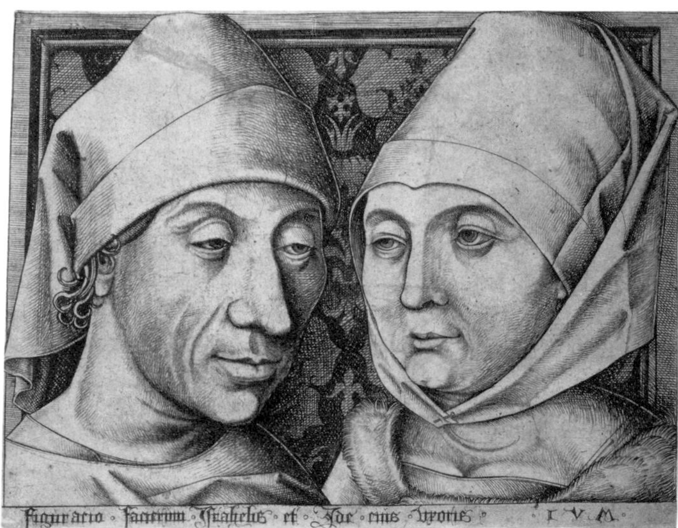

Figure 20-1. Israhel van Meckenem, *Double Portrait of Israhel van Meckenem and his Wife Ida*, ca. 1490, engraving, Lehrs 9. National Gallery of Art, Washington, Rosenwald Collection.

altar, now in the Augsburg Cathedral (fig. 20-2), Fritz Koreny shows that Van Meckenem's copies were often improvements over the elder Holbein's originals in the organization of space.[6] In fact, the elder Holbein (who was then a young artist) took Van Meckenem's reconfiguration into account in his later commission for the Dominican church in Frankfurt, circa 1500 or 1501 (now in the Kunsthalle in Hamburg), modifying his compositions in keeping with Van Meckenem's engraved interiors (fig. 20-3). As Koreny points out, Van Meckenem could easily have met the elder Holbein in Frankfurt in 1500, received drawings from him, and may have served as Holbein's reproductive engraver in a capacity that antici- pates Marcantonio Raimondi's (cat. 32) later work for Raphael.

Van Meckenem's composition, however, shows a theological as well as a spatial sophistication not evident in either of Holbein's commissions: namely, the juxtaposition of the primary subject – the presentation – with a smaller scene – the circumcision and naming of Jesus – in an adjoining chamber. In this upper space where the circumcision is in progress, we see a transition between the background vignettes introduced in the 1480s by the Flemish painter Hugo van der Goes and the sixteenth-century mannerist compositions of Pieter Aertsen and others. The smaller scene is used here to make the theological point that the ritual shedding of Christ's blood, witnessed first at the circumcision and later at the Crucifixion, symbolizes the transition from the Law of the Old Testament to the new Christianity. – JH

1. Although his tomb is no longer extant, a drawing of it (ca. 1600), which is now housed in the British Museum, is reproduced in Max Geisberg, "Israhel van Meckenem," PCQ. 17 (1930): 235.

2. On Van Meckenem's birth date, see Lehrs IX; Alan Shestack, Washington 1967, no. 152ff.; Paul Pieper, "Israhel van Meckenem als Goldschmied," *Unser Bocholt* (1953): 11ff; Hella Robels, "Israhel van Meckenem," in Cologne 1970, 144; and especially Marianne Bernhard, *Martin Schongauer: Handzeichnungen und Druckgraphik* (Munich: Südwest Verlag, 1980), 309-20.

3. Max Geisberg, *Verzeichnis der Kupferstiche Israhels van Meckenem*, vol. 58 of *Studien zur deutschen Kunstgeschichte* (Strassburg, 1905).

4. See Bernhard, *Martin Schongauer*, 309-20, for remarks on the close similarity between the coat of arms of the Netherlandish city of Mechelen and the arms carved on Van Meckenem's tomb.

5. See the document from the bishop of Münster to the Bocholt city council quoted in Bernhard, *Martin Schongauer*, 311.

6. Fritz Koreny, Bocholt 1972, 51-70, esp. 54-56.

Israhel van Meckenem

Bocholt? 1440/50-1503 Bocholt

21. Dance of the Daughters of Herodias 1495-1500.

Engraving on antique laid paper, 21.9 x 32.3 cm (sheet).
B. 9; Lehrs 367; H. Ger. 367.
Watermark: Gothic *P* with flower.
Signed in plate lower center: · *Israhel · v · M* ·.
Condition: Trimmed inside platemark.
Provenance: Joseph Grünling (Lugt 1863); Johann Gottlob von Quandt (1860); Count Yorck von Wartenburg, (Lugt S. 2669); (his sale C.G. Boerner, Leipzig, May 2-3, 1932, no. 17 to Mattheisen for RM 1,350); (purchased from M. Knoedler, New York, October 31, 1932, for $1,194).
Bequest of Herbert Greer French, 1943.53
Exhibitions: Cincinnati 1934, no. 32; Cincinnati 1941, no.47.

Max Lehrs knew forty examples of this print, which Max Geisberg considered one of Van Meckenem's masterpieces.[1] The depiction must have been extremely popular in its day, when the lower classes were occasionally permitted to pay admission to the grand balls of the nobility in order to watch the dancing. (Albrecht Dürer attended the imperial coronation ball in Cologne in 1520, although his class restricted him from the patrician dancing parties held in the Nuremberg city hall.)

The fateful occasion of the beheading of John the Baptist (background, upper left), Salome's presentation of the prophet's head on a platter to her mother (upper right), and Herodias' desecration of the head with her table knife are upstaged by a thoroughly contemporary grand ball featuring a three-piece band. The band's members are the city musicians from nearby Münster, recognizable, according to Geisberg, by their quatrefoil badges.[2] The band leader (center) plays both a one-handed flute called a *Schwegel*

and a snare drum known as a *Tämerlein*; his companions play the curved *Zink* (left) and the medieval trombone, or *Posaune*.[3]

Stately couples promenade in a variety of elegant fashions of the day. Many of the women, including Salome, the center of all three surrounding scenes, wear the tall peaked *hennin* and veil favored at the Burgundian court during the time of Margaret of York (1470s). Other women wear rounded headdresses, the more popular fashion in Germany. Some of the men are dressed in revealing doublets and hose, with scandalously vainglorious *Schnabelschuhe* (pointed shoes) also in evidence. Others wear long coats along with round-toed shoes, a style coming into vogue in the 1490s. A major domo is stationed at the door in the rear, behind the musicians, to control admission to the dance, while a palace guard, armed with a halberd, converses with a spectator behind the great bench that partially encloses the dance floor. Unconvincing as it seems, Geisberg and Heinrich Kohlhaussen have sought to identify the spectator as a self-portrait.[4] Hanspeter Landolt has identified the head of the guard with a drawing in a contemporary Westphalian sketchbook now in Paris (Louvre).[5]

The plate for this engraving was eventually cut in two, and the left half was printed separately, according to Henry Meier, who reported seeing two impressions taken from it.[6] In addition to the two engravings described in this catalogue, other noteworthy impressions by Israhel van Meckenem in the Museum's collection include Prince Waldburg-Wolfegg's *Annunciation* (Lehrs 54); the Albertina duplicate of *Organ Player and His Wife* (Lehrs 507 iii); *Couple Going to Church* (Lehrs 499); Count Yorck von Wartenburg's *Couple Seated on a Bed* (Lehrs 508) from Israhel's important *Daily Life* series; *The Children's Bath* (Lehrs 478); and the Albertina duplicate of *Ornament with the Stem of Jesse* (Lehrs 618). – JH

1. Max Geisberg, "Israhel von Meckenem," PCQ. 17 (1930): 235.

2. Max Geisberg, "Das alte Ratssilber," *Quellen und Forschungen zur Geschichte der Stadt Münster* 3 (1927):287.

3. Robert Nissen, "Silberne Boten und Spielmannsabzeichen und ihre Träger," *Westfalen* 47, no. 1 (1969): 20; cited by Robels in Cologne 1970, 145, no. 360.

4. Max Geisberg, *Verzeichnis der Kupferstiche Israhels van Meckenem*, vol. 58 of *Studien zur deutschen Kunstgeschichte* (Strassburg, 1905), no. 300; Heinrich Kohlhaussen, "Israhel van Meckenem als Schilderer niederrheinisch-westfälischen Lebens," in Bocholt 1953, 34.

5. Hanspeter Landolt, "Zu zwei Blättern mit Bildniszeichnungen," *Öffentliche Kunstsammlung Basel – Jahresbericht* (1968): 139, fig. 5.

6. Henry Meier, "Some Israhel van Meckenem Problems," PCQ. 27 (1940): 26-35, cited in Alan Shestack, Washington 1967, no. 232. According to Shestack, one such impression was formerly in the Firmin-Didot Collection, Paris.

Master of the Meshed Backgrounds

German active 1480-1500

22. Satire on Gossip During the Celebration of the Mass

Dotted print on antique laid paper, 36.9 x 25.9 cm (platemark).
Schreiber 2761; P.I.93-94.
Watermark: Small bull's head with ?
Inscribed across bottom: *Niemand kan[n] vol sagen noch schreiben + das schwatzen der bösen Me = /[ns]chen + Noch vi[e]l grosser Schann + Wann es tund die mann +* (Nobody can tell or write the frivolities of worthless women, but in men their shortcomings seem even worse.)
Condition: Trimmed to platemark.
Provenance: Ducal Museum, Gotha; (sale C.G. Boerner, Leipzig, May 2-3, 1932, no. 63, pl. 13, to Matthiesen for RM 4,000); (purchased from M. Knoedler, New York, September 29, 1933, for $2,200).

Bequest of Herbert Greer French, 1943.172.
Exhibitions: Cincinnati 1934, no. 5; Cincinnati 1941, no. 17.
References: Rathgeber, *Beschreibung. . . Gotha*, p. 87; Friedrich
Lippmann, *Kupferstiche und Holzschnitte in Nachbildung*, Berlin,
1892 (illustrated); W. L. Schreiber, *Die Meister der
Metallschneidekunst nebst einem nach Schulen geordneten Katalog
ihrer Arbeiten*, Strassburg, 1926, pp. 32-34.

The technique of making ornamental punchwork designs on copper
or bronze objects was highly developed in ancient times by both the
Greeks and the Chinese. With the invention of engraving and
printing shortly before the mid-fifteenth century, it was natural to
adapt the technique to the ornamentation of the engraver's cast
copperplates. Although a few such ornamented plates were viewed
as decorative objects in themselves, the majority were clearly
intended for printing. These relief prints on metal, also known as
dotted prints (*manière criblée*, in French; *Schrotblätter*, in German),
were created with scrapers and goldsmiths' punches. Unlike normal
engravings, they were printed in relief, white on black, with the ink
rolled on the surface of the plate rather than worked down into its
crevices as in normal copperplate engraving. Consequently, tonal
effects rather than contour lines carry the burden of description.

The technique, which yields more decorative than realistic results,
seems to have been used only during the last half of the fifteenth
century, mainly in the Rhine valley, from the eastern Netherlands
south to Lake Constance. As relief printing on metal was not a guild-
protected occupation, no names of the individual artists who
practiced this technique have been recorded. It is presumed that these
artists were active primarily as goldsmiths: the technique required
the use of goldsmiths' tools, and the art flourished particularly in
urban centers (Cologne, Basel, and Mainz) where substantial
numbers of goldsmiths were employed. Many makers of dotted
prints actually copied their compositional settings from such major
engravers of the time as Master IAM of Zwolle (cat. 12-13) and the
Master of the Berlin Passion.

The artist who made the Museum's dotted print is known in the
literature as the Master of the Meshed Backgrounds (*Maître au fonds
maillé*, in French; *Meister mit dem Maschenhintergrund*, in
German), a reference to a decorative effect in the backgrounds of
some of his earlier prints (not visible here) that resembles the curving
links of medieval chain mail.[1] According to Wilhelm Schreiber, this
master, who was active during the last quarter of the fifteenth
century, possibly living on into the early sixteenth, was one of the
last to create dotted prints. Two smaller and earlier examples of his
work are in the Rosenwald Collection, National Gallery of Art,
Washington.

This large and handsome dotted print, the only impression known,
has fascinated art historians for two centuries. J. D. Passavant was
the first to discover it during a visit to the castle at Gotha in Saxony.
Calling it an allegory of "the corruption of the human race," he
included a careful description of the print in the first volume of his
catalogue of master engravings. There he remarked that its execution
was excellent though without *une grande finesse* – a high
compliment, actually. Its naïveté would have appealed to Passavant,
a member of the early nineteenth-century group of young German
painters who called themselves Nazarenes. They admired sincerity
and religious fervor as practiced in medieval German art.

The theme of gossip during the Mass comes from a fourteenth-
century manuscript written by the Chevalier de la Tour Landry
(known in Germany as the Ritter von Thurn) for his daughter. A
printed edition of the German adaptation by Marquart von Stein
was published in Basel by Michael Furter in 1493 under the title
Exempel der Gottesfurcht und Ehrbarkeit (*Examples of the Fear of

God and of Respectability*). A satirical manual of good behavior,
Sebastian Brant's *Narrenschiff* (*The Ship of Fools*), was published in
Basel a few months later on Carnival Day in 1494. Our dotted print
seems likewise to have been influenced by this famous satire. The
chapter entitled "Noise in Church" describes a number of activities
depicted in this dotted print.

> One must not ask who they may be
> Whose dogs in church bark furiously .
> While people pray at mass or sing,
> Who bring a hawk that flaps its wings
> And rings its bell with tinkling gay,
> That one can neither sing nor pray.[2]

Brant goes on to deplore the fact that "affairs are aired and tongues
are loose." Most importantly, he writes about Christ's good example
in driving the money-changers from the Temple, a scene depicted
with vigor in the background of this print.

> Christ gave us all a good example,
> Coin-changers drove He from the temple,
> And men with pigeon-vending urge
> He chased in anger with a scourge.
> If now He'd oust the men of sin,
> But few would still remain within.[3]

It is remarkable that the artist was influenced by the moral content of
both Brant's and Von Stein's books rather than by their excellent but
small-scale woodcut illustrations, some of which have traditionally
been attributed to the young Albrecht Dürer. The dotted print, seen
in bird's-eye view, is an ambitious crowd scene laid in a huge vaulted
hall. Although the composition is incorrectly foreshortened, it
provides a good sense of the interior space in medieval churches,
where a number of more or less conflicting activities occur
simultaneously. At the left rear, a tonsured priest, assisted by his
acolyte, celebrates Mass at an altar elaborately adorned with
punchwork; behind them people in three pews pray, gossip, and
snooze. A guardian angel in full flight delivers a crown of life to the
obedient couple at left who listen attentively to the sermon of a
mendicant friar. Next to them, a demon tweaks the ears of the
disrespectful women who have brought a lapdog to church. An
enormous black Lucifer busily writes nonsense syllables on a
medieval blackboard – a huge piece of stretched cowhide held up
and tacked down by other monsters. In the foreground just above the
inscription stand those couples who come to church only to be seen:
a canon holding hands with a housewife, two men making a business
deal, a pair of young and fashionable lovers, and two wealthy young
men with a falcon and a leaping dog.

A *terminus ante* for this work can be set at 1494 (when *The Ship of
Fools* was published), a date in keeping with the round-toed shoe
that came into style about 1490 worn by the men in the foreground.
The clothing styles of the young people in the foreground were
identified by Schreiber as localized to the Strassburg area. – JH

1. The term was invented by Wilhelm L. Schreiber. See Schreiber and Schreiber,
Metallschneidekunst.
2. Edwin H. Zeydel, trans., *The Ship of Fools* (New York: Dover, 1962), 162-63.
3. Zeydel, *The Ship of Fools*, 163.

Albrecht Dürer

Nuremberg 1471-1528 Nuremberg

23. The Four Horsemen ca. 1497-98.

Plate for the *Apocalypse*.
Woodcut on antique laid paper, 39.2 x 28.3 cm (image).
Before the text.
B. 64; Meder 167-1b (before text); Panofsky 284; H. *Ger.* 167; TIB 1001.264 1a.
Watermark: Large imperial orb (Meder 53).
Monogrammed lower center: 𝔄
Provenance: (Purchased from M. Knoedler, New York, November 21, 1938, for $1,550).
Bequest of Herbert Greer French, 1943.212.
Exhibitions: Cincinnati 1941, no. 120.

The Four Horsemen is justifiably the most famous of Albrecht Dürer's fifteen woodcuts of the *Apocalypse*.[1] According to St. John's prophetic vision, each time the Lamb broke one of the first four seals of the scroll, a horseman was released to unleash cataclysmic forces upon the earth, and together, the riders "were given the authority over a quarter of the earth to kill by the sword, by famine, by plague" (Rev. 6:8). Whereas the biblical text treats each event separately, Dürer combines and compresses the four riders to dramatically increase their apocalyptic impact. The riders, aligned in a phalanx, cut a sharp diagonal across an ominous sky and plow into the powerful winds with such velocity that their mounts lift off the ground destroying everything in their paths. The first rider, representing war, takes the lead and aims a taut bow straight forward to attack and conquer. Just behind, the second aggressively wields a huge sword "to take away peace from the earth and set people killing each other" (Rev. 6:4). The third spreads famine; the scale he swings back like a discus to gather momentum is empty. The bearded, balding (but paradoxically vivacious) corpse of death, wrapped in a windblown shroud, brings up the rear. In place of his usual scythe, death vigorously harvests his victims with a pitchfork.[2] No one, according to the popular medieval *topos*, can escape him — neither emperor (with crown), nor hausfrau (with purse), nor monk (with tonsure). At his heels lies Hades in the form of a medieval hellmouth, ready to swallow up the growing heap.

The *Apocalypse*, the earliest of Dürer's "three large books," was published in separate German and Latin editions in 1498 and again in Latin in 1511.[3] It was the first time an artist had ever acted as his own publisher.[4] That his godfather, Anton Koberger (ca. 1445-1513), was the leading publisher in Germany undoubtedly facilitated this initiative. Dürer used Koberger's typeface and German translation. In addition his choice of the huge *Superregal* format (super book, as Koberger called it) and innovative layout of full-page woodcuts facing full pages of text was likely due to the example of Koberger's *Nuremberg Chronicle* (1493). Whether Dürer actually printed the volume in his godfather's workshop remains conjectural, but according to Ludwig Grote, the means existed to print both the text and image together at the same time on such a large full sheet.[5]

The relationship of the woodcuts to the text was also novel. Dürer made no attempt to relate his images to the text opposite them; it is printed continuously on the versos of the woodcuts. He regarded his woodcuts not as traditional illustrations to enhance a particular passage but as an independent sequence of visual images to be considered in relationship to one another rather than to the narrative. In a brief introduction to the 1498 edition, Dürer explains that he neither included every detail nor slavishly followed the organization of the book because it was his express hope that his

visual interpretation would encourage the faithful to probe its meaning even more deeply.[6]

Dürer undertook this edition of woodcuts at the outset of his career when he was still only in his mid-twenties. Even though he had trained as a painter in Michael Wolgemut's Nuremberg workshop, he must have learned a great deal there about woodcut production: Wolgemut (1434/7-1519) had a thriving sideline supplying publishers like Anton Koberger with some of the most progressive woodcut illustrations of his day.[7] Still, Dürer's early *Apocalypse* woodcuts have little in common with Wolgemut's, for during the period in which he was producing them, he literally revolutionized the art of the relief print.

Compared to any woodcut by the Wolgemut workshop (fig. 52-1), *The Four Horsemen* demonstrates how Dürer drastically increased the sheer number of lines of a woodblock. He synchronized hatchings yet varied their density and pliancy to create a richer range of light values and volumetric effects. In stark contrast to Wolgemut's uniformly flat and vacuous skies, for instance, Dürer's sky becomes spatial, energized, and boldly expressive through the manipulation of hatchings. He furthermore treated independent lines, such as contours, more calligraphically, seemingly defying the very grain of his block to endow them with elasticity to swell or taper. Comparison of his treatment of line to Schongauer's engravings (cats. 6-8) shows that Dürer brought to the woodcut some of the sophistication that had already been achieved with engraving. It is not surprising, then, that Dürer was the first printmaker to affix his monogram to his woodcuts. (Engravers had been monogramming their work for decades.) He transformed what had been a modest craft into an expressive art form.

Dürer's *Apocalypse* woodcuts differ from Wolgemut's as much in their underlying conception as in their technique. In 1495 Dürer returned from a prolonged stay in Italy. His exposure to Italian Renaissance art challenged him to explore more convincing spatial solutions, more clearly articulated and expressive figures, and more dynamic compositional structures. Without the example of Mantegna (cat. 17a), for instance, the commanding figure with the scales in *The Four Horsemen* would be inconceivable. His facial structure, his ardent expression, the vitality of his well-developed body, even the way he pivots to create a dynamic compositional axis all reflect knowledge of Renaissance art.

The question of who actually cut Dürer's early woodcut designs still lingers. Whether Dürer himself could have cut them is a matter of debate. In the traditional division of labor practiced in woodcut production, the responsibility for cutting the design into the block belonged to the *Formschneider* (block-cutter). While Wolgemut's *Formschneider* were the most experienced in Nuremberg, they would seemingly have been ill prepared to tackle the complexities and subtle refinements of Dürer's *Apocalypse* designs. A recent, compelling hypothesis proposes that Veit Stoss, the virtuoso sculptor newly returned to Nuremberg in 1496, may have played a facilitating role; Dürer's early extant blocks are as intricately carved as any low-relief sculpture.[8]

Dürer realized that printmaking could be lucrative and at the same time allow more creative freedom than commissioned paintings typically engendered. The intense piety of the population on the eve of the Reformation along with the eschatological fears at the close of the century heightened interest in St. John's terrifying predictions, making the *Apocalypse* an astute and opportune choice of subject on Dürer's part. In terms of its new woodcut technique, the effect of the series on fellow artists was inescapable: the sixteenth-century German woodcut designers represented in this catalogue — Burgkmair (cat. 37), Wechtlin (cat. 38), Cranach (cat. 46), Baldung (cat. 52), Sebald Beham (cat. 56) — all emulated the graphic language of Dürer's woodcuts, but none matched the subtlety or virtuosity of his technique.

There is no letterpress on the verso of the Museum's impression of *The Four Horsemen*, which never was bound in an edition of the *Apocalypse*. It is one of the impressions that Dürer intended as a single-leaf woodcut and, therefore, was pulled on thinner, smoother paper. For text editions, he selected a coarser, thicker paper in order to keep the letterpress from showing through to the image.[9] – JSP

1. *Apocalypse*, the Greek word for "revelation" or "unveiling," is another name for the Book of Revelation, the last book of the Bible. In his introduction to the 1498 edition, Dürer repeats the (then) commonly held assumption that the author of the Book of Revelation was St. John the Evangelist. *Martyrdom of Saint John*, which introduces the series, is the only woodcut not related to the biblical source. For illustrations see Washington 1971, nos. 92-106.

2. The German word for pitchfork, *Mistgabel*, literally translates as "fork" (*Gabel*) for "dung" (*Mist*), so death's pitchfork visually associates the heap of victims with barnyard fodder or worse. See Joseph Leo Koerner, "The Mortification of the Image: Death as a Hermeneutic in Hans Baldung Grien," *Representations* 10 (1985): 59.

3. In 1511 Dürer added a new title page to the *Apocalypse* and bound it with the other two of his "large books": *Large Passion* and *Life of the Virgin* (cat. 45). For facsimiles with text, see Horst Appuhn, *Albrecht Dürer. Die drei grossen Bücher.* (Dortmund: Harenberg Komunikation, 1979).

4. The colophon of the first edition of the *Apocalypse* reads (in translation): "Printed in Nuremberg by Albrecht Dürer, painter, in the year of our Lord 1498."

5. Ludwig Grote, *Albrecht Dürer. Die Apokalypse* (Munich, 1970), 3.

6. "*Des aber schickung der geschrifft oder ordnung des buchs wirt darumb von uns nit durch alle ding aufgeleget das dem unwissenden zeerfoerschen die begirde werde gesetzet. und dem suchenden die frucht der arbyt, vnd got die meysterschafft der lere werd behalten.*" (However, neither the transmission of the story nor the organization of the book will [therefore] be laid out detail for detail [*durch alle ding*], so that the desire of the uninstructed person may be inflamed to investigate [it further] and that he who seeks, will reap the fruit of his labor; so that the Lord may [in the end] remain the master of its teaching.) The passage is given in Grote, *Albrecht Dürer*, n.p. For the numerous interpretations of this series (with further literature), see Nuremberg 1971, 320-21, no. 596; Bialostocki, 265-89; and Alexander Perrig, *Albrecht Dürer oder die Heimlichkeit der deutschen Ketzerei* (Weinheim: VCH, Acta Humaniora, 1987), 1-23.

7. Wolgemut's 645 woodcuts for the *Nuremberg Chronicle* are his most famous and extensive undertaking. See the fascimile, *Die Schedelsche Weltchronik*, vol. 64 of *Die bibliophilen Taschenbücher* (Dortmund: Harenberg Kommunikation, 1978), and Elisabeth Rücker, *Die schedelsche Weltchronik. Das grösste Buchunternehmen der Dürer-Zeit* (Munich: Prestel Verlag, 1973).

8. Hutchison, 60.

9. For Dürer's selection of paper, see Boston 1971, 38.

Mair von Landshut

German ca. 1450-1510

24. The Annunciation ca. 1499.

Engraving on antique laid paper, 17.0 x 11.0 cm (platemark). Lehrs 4; P. 14; TIB 913.004.
Watermark: Landshut coat-of-arms (shield with three helmets, Lehrs 38).
Signed in plaque lower left: MAIR.
Condition: Trimmed to or with platemark.
Provenance: Ducal Museum, Gotha; (sale C.G. Boerner, Leipzig, May 2-3, 1932, no. 13, pl. 4, to Matthiesen for RM 1,250); (purchased from M. Knoedler, New York, October 31, 1932, for $1,877).
Bequest of Herbert Greer French, 1943.114.
Exhibitions: Cincinnati 1934, no. 12; Cincinnati 1941, no. 35.

Mair von Landshut, painter, engraver, and designer of woodcuts, is first mentioned in the Munich tax records of 1490 as "*Mair, maler von Freising*" (Mair, painter from Freising).[1] He is presumed to have collaborated with the official painter to the city of Munich, Jan Polack (literally, John the Polack, ca. 1450/60-1519), on the wings,

or outer panels, of the enormous altarpiece of Christ's Passion for the local church of Saint Peter. Mair is next mentioned in the Augsburg *Stadtgerichtsbuch* in 1497 as the brother-in-law of Michael Holbein, father of Hans Holbein the Elder. Gert von der Osten and Horst Vey note the influence of the elder Holbein's Weingarten altar (1493) on Mair's panel for the sacristy of Freising Cathedral (1495).[2]

Mair's early life and apprenticeship are undocumented, although he may have trained in the workshop of Michael Pacher in Brixen (modern Bressanone, Italian Tyrol) circa 1485; his *Crucifixion* may also have been painted there (Wallraf-Richartz Museum, Cologne, inv. no. 750).[3] Other paintings by his hand include *St. Oswald* (Bayerisches Nationalmuseum, Munich), *St. George and the Dragon* (Alte Pinakothek, Munich, inv. no. 9344), and *Ecce Homo*, dated 1502 (Museo Nazionale, Trento).

Mair's graphic oeuvre consists of twenty-two engravings and three woodcuts, most of them signed "Mair"; two of the woodcuts and eight of the engravings bear the date 1499, and one is also inscribed with the coat of arms of the Bavarian city of Landshut – a shield emblazoned with three helmets.[4] The Landshut arms appear as the watermark on the only known impression of *The Annunciation*. Other watermarks on papers used by Mair include the large bull's head with serpent and cross or rod, crown and flower, the high crown, and *K* in a circle.

Although nine of Mair's prints are unique and only four have survived in two impressions, five of his engraved plates survived and were restruck on late sixteenth-century papers (Lehrs VIII.427.44-47 – a shield bearing a salt-vat). The majority of the artist's prints seem to have been created in a short span of time, around 1499, in or near the brilliant court at Landshut, which at the time was an independent duchy ruled by Duke Georg "the Rich" of Bavaria-Landshut. The duke died in 1503 without leaving a male heir, touching off the War of the Landshut Succession. At this time, much of southern Germany was devastated by the armies of the Emperor Maximilian and the Swabian League. It is not known whether Mair survived the war.

The Museum's impression of *The Annunciation*, formerly in the Ducal Museum at Gotha (Germany), is the only one known.[5] It is printed on paper bearing the watermark of the coat of arms of the duchy of Landshut (Bavaria) – three helmets (two over one) on a shield. In his monograph on Mair, Franz Schubert dates this the earliest of Mair's prints because of its spatial clumsiness. He further suggests that it must have been influenced by a drypoint engraving of the same subject by the late fifteenth-century Housebook Master (Lehrs 8), a print having a vaguely similar interior setting, shaded with large quantities of coarse cross-hatching, and memorable chiefly for its strikingly ugly Madonna.[6] Both Mair's engraving and the Housebook Master's drypoint are interiors of the Virgin's bedchamber, but there the resemblance ends.

Mair von Landshut's *Annunciation* is remarkable for its ambitious but confused perspective, apparently the result of a desire to reference a number of rather complex theological issues. The Virgin Mary is shown here in her role as *Maria Ecclesia*, the personification of the Christian Church. Her *prié-dieu* (prayer desk) resembles a substantial stone pulpit; her canopied bed overlaps a stone altar set into a fragmented view of a full-blown Gothic chancel. A barred door, the closed portal of Ezekiel's vision as well as the *porta coeli* (gate of heaven), a well-known symbol of Mary's virginity, was Gabriel's means of entry into the room. Next to this door stands a prominent window, surely an allusion to Mary's intercessory role as *fenestra coeli* (window of heaven).[7] The foreground of the composition is further complicated by several ill-foreshortened sets of steps that distort the bed-altar area, giving it the elevation of a shrine. The Virgin's role as the Bride of Christ is underscored by the presence of a pot of carnations, here substituted for the more traditional Madonna lilies usually found in Annunciation scenes. – JH

1. Mair von Landshut, whose given name appears to have been Hans, was formerly confused with the painter Nicolaus Alexander Mair. On this issue and its extensive literature, see Alan Shestack, Washington 1967, no. 142. For examples of Mair's graphic work other than those mentioned above, see Jane C. Hutchison, TIB 9 (plate vol.), 346-57, and idem, TIB 9 (*Commentary*), pt. 2, 269-99.

2. Gert von der Osten and Horst Vey, *Painting and Sculpture in Germany and the Netherlands 1500-1600*, vol. 31 of *The Pelican History of Art* (Harmondsworth, Baltimore, and Ringwood, 1969), 118.

3. Franz Schubert, *Mair von Landshut* (Landshut, 1930). See also Max Lehrs, "Der deutsche und niederländische Kupferstich des fünfzehnten Jahrhunderts in den kleineren Sammlungen," *Rep. Kw.* 17 (1894): 191, no. 105.

4. Alfred Stange, *Deutsche Malerei der Gotik* (Munich, 1952-60), 10:124-130; Von der Osten and Vey, *Painting and Sculpture in Germany*, 118.

5. In addition to Lehrs, see also the Cincinnati Museum's acquisition announcement in *Burl. M.* 80 (March 1942): 76; *Cincinnati Museum Bulletin* 12 (October 1941): 69; and *Cincinnati Museum News*, n.s., 5 (May 1950): 111.

6. For the rare prints and drawings of this artist, see J. P. Filedt Kok, comp., *The Master of the Amsterdam Cabinet, or Housebook* (Princeton: Princeton University Press, 1985).

7. For more extensive discussion of Marian symbolism, see Carol J. Purtle, *The Marian Paintings of Jan van Eyck* (Princeton, 1982), passim. For the *fenestra coeli*, see especially the extensive discussion by Carla Gottlieb, "En ipse stat post parietum nostrum: The Symbolism of the Ghent Annunciation," *Bulletin des Musées Royaux des Beaux Arts de Belgique* 19 (1970): 79ff.

Mair von Landshut

German ca. 1450-1510

25. St. Anne with the Virgin and Child and Four Angels

1499.
Engraving on antique laid paper prepared with blue gouache, 23.8 x 16.6 cm.
B. 8; Lehrs 11; TIB 913.011.
Inscribed on tapestry lower center: · *1499* ·/HILF S ANN SELB TRIT ("Help, St Ann Seldbdritt")/ · MAIR ·.
Condition: Trimmed within platemark.
Provenance: Johann Gottlob von Quandt (1860); (Clément, Paris to Count Wartenburg); Count Yorck von Wartenburg (Lugt S. 2669); (his sale C.G. Boerner, Leipzig, May 2-3, 1932, no. 12, to Strölin for RM 1,550); (Alfred Strölin, Lausanne, consigned to Knoedler, June 14, 1932); (purchased from M. Knoedler, New York, June 14, 1933, for $2,000).
Bequest of Herbert Greer French, 1943.113.
Exhibitions: Cincinnati 1934, no. 11; Cincinnati 1941, no. 34; Minneapolis 1956, no. 71.

Mair's most striking contribution to the history of printmaking is neither his treatment of the human figure, which tends to be rather wooden, nor his unusually complicated, almost cubist stage settings; it is, rather, his bold experimentation with color. Many of his engravings are printed on paper first tinted with watercolor. After running the plates through the press on prepared paper, he often applied delicate strokes of white, yellow, or red pigment with a small brush to form highlights, adding depth and interest to his compositions. Mair's images, consequently, are strongly suggestive of the effects of chiaroscuro drawing, which, in the late fifteenth century, was becoming increasingly popular in southern Germany, particularly among artists of the Holbein family, Mair's in-laws in Augsburg. Mair's subtly hand-colored prints form a transition between the sometimes clumsily hand-tinted woodcuts produced in the early fifteenth century and the development of the true chiaroscuro woodcut in the early years of the sixteenth century by

Lucas Cranach the Elder (cat. 46), Hans Baldung Grien (cat. 53), and Hans Burgkmair (cat. 37).

Nine early and several modern impressions of *St. Anne with the Virgin and Child and Four Angels* are known, two of them now in Boston and Detroit; however, the Museum's impression is the finest and the only one utilizing color. On a dark blue prepared paper, the print's pristine and unfaded condition suggests that it was kept for many years between the pages of an album or manuscript. Brownish coloration on the verso of the sheet is glue residue. The faint imprint of lettering over the glue indicates contact with a printed page.

Although an impression of this print was listed by Paul Behaim, an early seventeenth-century Nuremberg collector, in his handwritten catalogue of 1618 (now in the Kupferstichkabinett, Berlin), the history of this blue impression can only be traced with certainty as far back as the nineteenth century. At this time, it belonged to two important collections: Quandt (1860) and Count Yorck von Wartenburg (1861-69).[2] In 1894 Max Lehrs reported a drawing related to it in the Durazzo Collection.[3]

The subject of Anne with her daughter, the Virgin Mary, and the Christ child formed a sort of maternal trinity, a religious theme conveniently titled *Anna Selbdritt* in German (a term for which there is no exact English equivalent). Images of this sort were called *Andachtsbilder* (literally, images for thinking about) and were used much in the manner of older Byzantine icons: they required the viewer's mental participation in order to complete their religious meanings. Anne's role as the (possibly virginal) mother of Mary was an issue of immense theological interest in the late fifteenth century after the publication of the 1494 treatise on the Immaculate Conception by Johannes Trithemius, honoring the elevation of St. Anne's Day to a full-fledged day of obligation in the Catholic Church calendar. – JH

1. Lehrs's reading of *HILF* as *HILE* and his interpretation of *HILE* as an abbreviation for *heilige* (saint) makes no sense in view of the S (for *sankt*) that follows. Mair's *e* is differently formed (see *Selb* in the inscription).

2. Lugts. 2669. The print was sold from the Quandt Collection in 1860 to Clément, who in turn sold it in 1861 to Count Yorck von Wartenburg.

3. Max Lehrs, "Der deutsche und niederländische Kupferstich des funfzehnten Jahrhunderts in den kleineren Sammlungen," *Rep. Kw.* 17 (1894): 191, no. 105.

Master LCz

German active ca. 1480-ca. 1505

26. The Temptation of Christ ca. 1500.

Engraving on antique laid paper, 22.6 x 16.9 cm (sheet).
B. 1; Lehrs 2; TIB 912.002.
Watermark: Large bull's head with caduceus and cross.
Monogrammed in plate lower center: · L· Gⅉ ·
Condition: Trimmed to platemark.
Provenance: Earl of Northwick (Lugt S. 2709a); (his sale C.G. Boerner, Leipzig, May 22-24, 1933, no. 501); (purchased from M. Knoedler, New York, September 21, 1936, for $1,550).
Bequest of Herbert Greer French, 1943.178.
Exhibitions: Cincinnati 1941, no. 29.

The late fifteenth-century artist who signed ten of his twelve known engravings with the monogram LCz was the most talented German engraver active between the death of Martin Schongauer and the emergence of the young Albrecht Dürer. That he completed so few engravings seems to indicate that his primary source of income came from another profession. Since one of the master's plates, dated 1492, depicts a design for a piece of jewelry – a pendant or brooch of a maiden taming a unicorn (Lehrs 12) – it was formerly thought that he must have been a goldsmith. Modern scholars, however, are inclined to think that Master LCz was probably a painter.

Nineteenth-century art historians, assuming that the master was Dutch, thought that perhaps his name was Corneliszoon: *z*. is the standard abbreviation for *zoon*, or "son (of)."[1] This theory was soon abandoned when it became apparent that the sources of the master's style and iconography were entirely German. Lucas Cranach the Elder's father was then believed to have been this artist, but it was later discovered that Cranach's father's name was Hans Maler.[2] Subsequently, the intriguing suggestion was made that LCz was the earliest monogram utilized by Lucas Cranach the Elder himself.[3]

The most widely accepted belief concerning the master's identity, however, involves the identification of the engraver with an anonymous Bamberg painter formerly known as the Master of the Strache Altar.[4] This composite artist may have been a Bamberg painter named Lorenz Katzheimer who is documented in 1505 as having been sentenced to eight days in jail for brawling. Some of Lorenz Katzheimer's paintings, datable to the late 1480s, are in Berlin, Budapest, Darmstadt, and Nuremberg. Lorenz was almost surely a close relative of the better-known Bamberg painter Wolfgang Katzheimer (active ca. 1465-1508),[5] who, among other things, painted a group of Bamberg architectural views in watercolor and gouache (Kupferstichkabinett, Berlin). Wolfgang's work established an important precedent for Dürer's landscape watercolors.

The central event of Master LCz's *Temptation of Christ* is taken from Matthew (4:1-11). After Christ had fasted forty days in the wilderness, Satan taunted him, suggesting that he use his powers to turn stones into bread. When Christ refused, saying "man does not live by bread alone," Satan then unsuccessfully attempted to persuade Christ to jump from the roof of the Temple in Jerusalem (depicted here in the distant center). In a final effort to deflect Christ from undertaking his ministry, Satan took Jesus to the top of a high mountain and offered "all the kingdoms of the world, and all the glory of them." This final temptation is represented in the upper left landscape.

In Christian churches, Christ's forty days of fasting in the wilderness are commemorated yearly during the Lenten season. Thus prints of this subject would have had an annual market during the late fifteenth century, just as prints of Christ's Nativity and Resurrection exhibited their own seasonal demand at Christmas and Easter.

Ten of Master LCz's twelve known engravings are signed with his monogram, but only two are dated – the brooch design of 1492 mentioned above and a sudarium (Veronica's veil) of 1499. *The Temptation of Christ*, with its unusually sensitive feeling for landscape and atmosphere, is surely one of the master's most mature works. Most scholars date it to circa 1500 or later.[6] Master LCz's position as a transitional figure between Schongauer and Dürer is seen clearly in this work. The face and drapery of Christ reflect the strong influence of Martin Schongauer's late *Virgin Mary* (Lehrs 3). The city view, with its great domed temple, seems to have been inspired by Erhard Reuwich's view of Jerusalem in Bernhard von Breydenbach's best-selling *Peregrinationes in Terram Sanctam* (*Travels in the Holy Land*), which was published in Mainz in 1486. The figure of Satan, inspired by one of the nightmarish creatures in Schongauer's *Temptation of St. Anthony* (Lehrs 54), prefigures Dürer's own furry monster with bat's wings depicted in his 1514 master engraving, *The Knight, Death and the Devil* (cat. 47).

Alan Shestack correctly identifies the immediate inspiration for the layout of the landscape, framed between a cliff and a grove of trees, as Master E.S.'s engraving *St. John on Patmos* (Lehrs 150). Master LCz's dramatic use of light and shade and his enormous virtuosity with the burin in creating varied effects of texture, however, transformed Master E.S.'s airless world into one of luxurious foliage, exotic architecture, and specific natural detail. A mass of oak leaves and a lively squirrel crown tree trunks that Master E.S. would surely have topped with all-purpose medieval foliage. A grinning wolf, a sinister serpent, and a lizard are allusions to the wily Satan. This rich landscape setting is less a derivation from Master E.S. than a harbinger of the early sixteenth-century Danube school.

A mountain goat, symbolic of obstinacy and unbelief, peers down from a ledge near the top of the cliff overlooking Jerusalem. A very similar goat on a similar outcropping in the distant background of Dürer's *Adam and Eve* of 1504 (cat. 33) caused Max Lehrs to date Master LCz's print 1505, no doubt theorizing that Dürer, the greater artist, must also have been the most original.[7] Erica Tietze-Conrat later moved the date back to 1500, declaring that the influence must have run the other way.[8] Shestack ended the argument over the primogeniture of the goat by discovering a third and clearly senior goat in a woodcut from the *Swabian Chronicle* (1486) that could have been known to either artist.[9]

Reciprocal influences between the young Dürer and Master LCz would be easily explained if the older engraver can, indeed, be identified as Lorenz Katzheimer: Nuremberg is located in the episcopal see of Bamberg. Many scholars theorize that the composite Master LCz/Lorenz Katzheimer/Strache Altar Master trained as a painter in the Nuremberg studio of Hans Pleydenwurff and Michael Wolgemut, where Dürer became an apprentice in 1486.

About twenty impressions of this print are known. The earliest and the best have the large bull's head with caduceus and cross watermark found on the Museum's example. Nearly all impressions are in European museums. Amsterdam, Berlin, Munich, and Paris have particularly fine impressions, as does the National Gallery of Art in Washington. – JH

1. P. II:288-90; Carl von Lützow, *Geschichte des deutschen Kupferstiches und Holzschnittes* (Berlin, 1891). For additional discussion, see Lehrs VI:320-24 and Jane C. Hutchison in TIB 9 (*Commentary*) pt. 2:253-67.

2. Nagler, *Mon.* IV.328.1008; Eberhard Schenk-Gotha, "Der Meister LCZ," *Zeitschrift für Kunst* 1 (1947): 26-30.

3. Eberhard Freiherr Schenk zu Schweinsberg, in Dieter Koepplin and Tilman Falk, *Lukas Cranach – Gemälde, Zeichnungen, Druckgraphik*, 2 vols. (Basel and Stuttgart, 1974), 2:760-61, n. 31.

4. Bernard Saran, *Der Meister LCz. Ein Wegbereiter Albrecht Dürers in Bamberg* (Stettin, 1938). Saran's theory is accepted by Alan Shestack, in *Master LCz and Master W B* (New York, 1971).

5. Fedja Anzelewsky, in *Zeitschrift des deutschen Vereins für Kunstwissenschaft* 19 (1965): 146-50. Also discussed in Koepplin and Falk, *Lukas Cranach*, 760-61, n. 31.

6. The date of circa 1500 is accepted by Martin Weinberger ("Über die Herkunft des Meisters LCZ," in *Festschrift Heinrich Wölfflin* [Munich, 1924], 169-82), Lehrs, and Shestack.

7. Max Lehrs, "Master LCz," PCQ. 9 (1922): 8-9.

8. See Erica Tietze-Conrat, "Die Flucht nach Egypten, eine Dürerstudie," *MGvK.*, 49 (1926): 65-67.

9. Thomas Lirer, *Chronik von allen Königen und Kaisern* (Ulm: Konrad Dinckmut, 1486). Hain 10117.

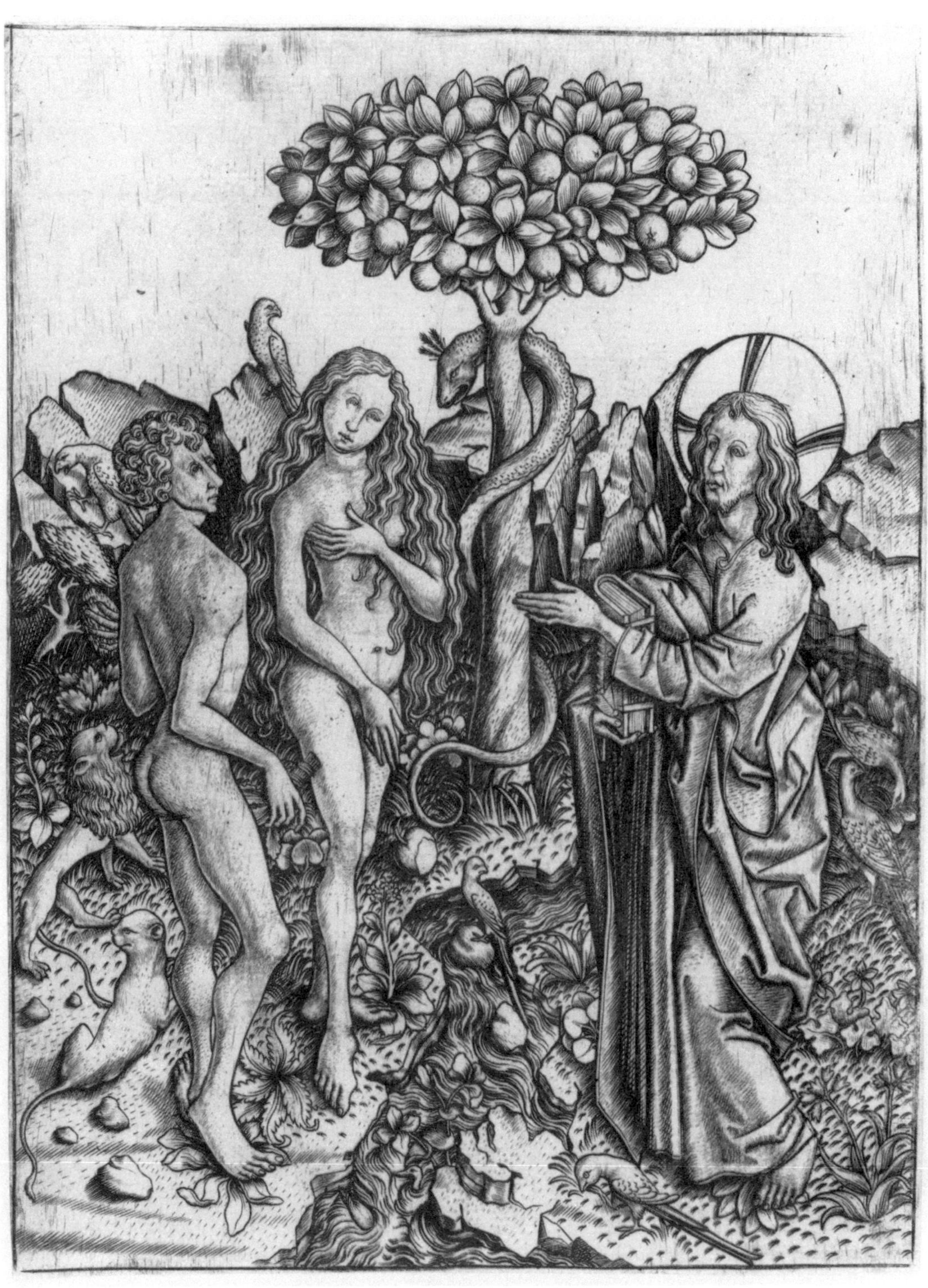

Plate 1. Master E.S., *The Fall of Man*.

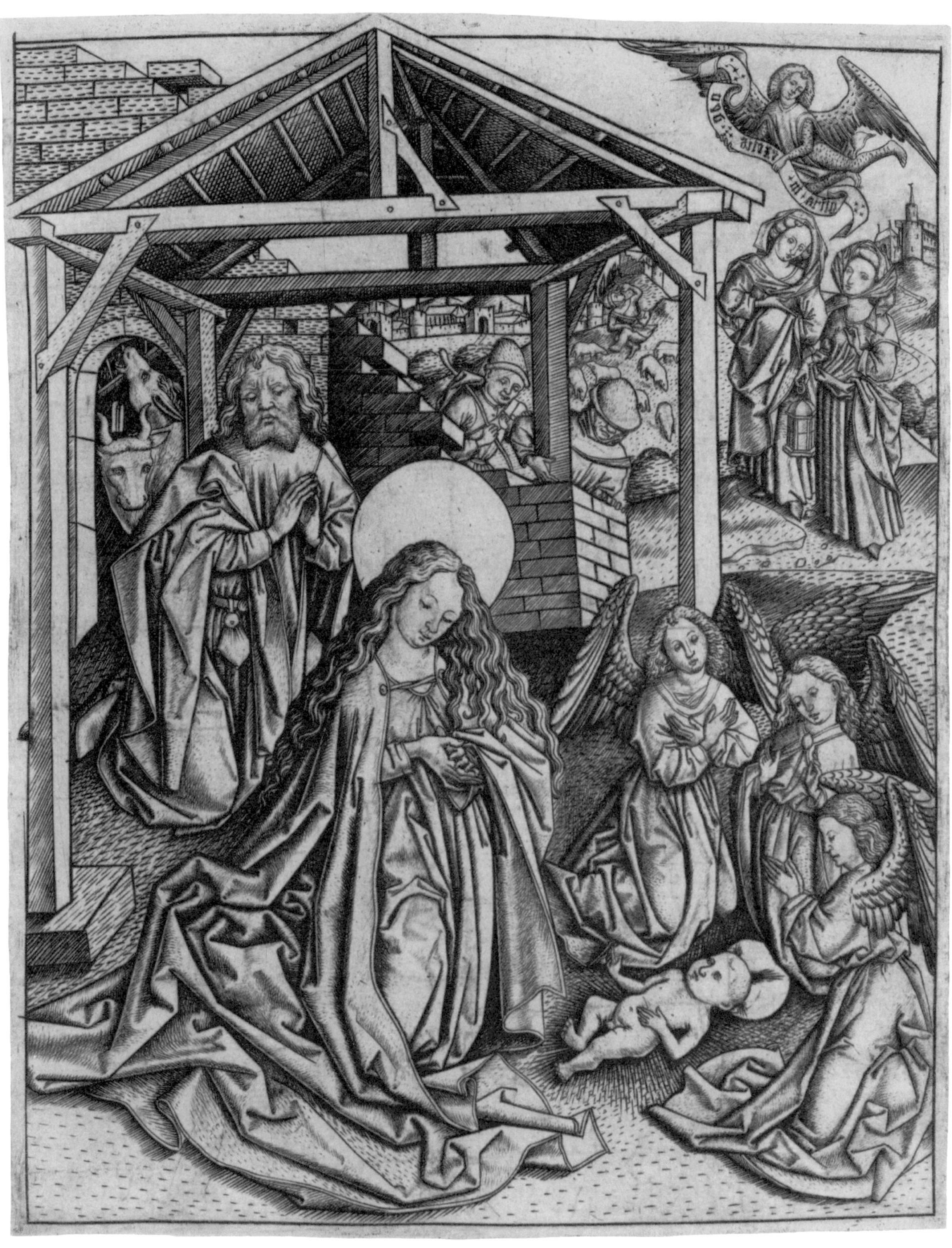

Plate 2. Master E.S., *The Nativity*.

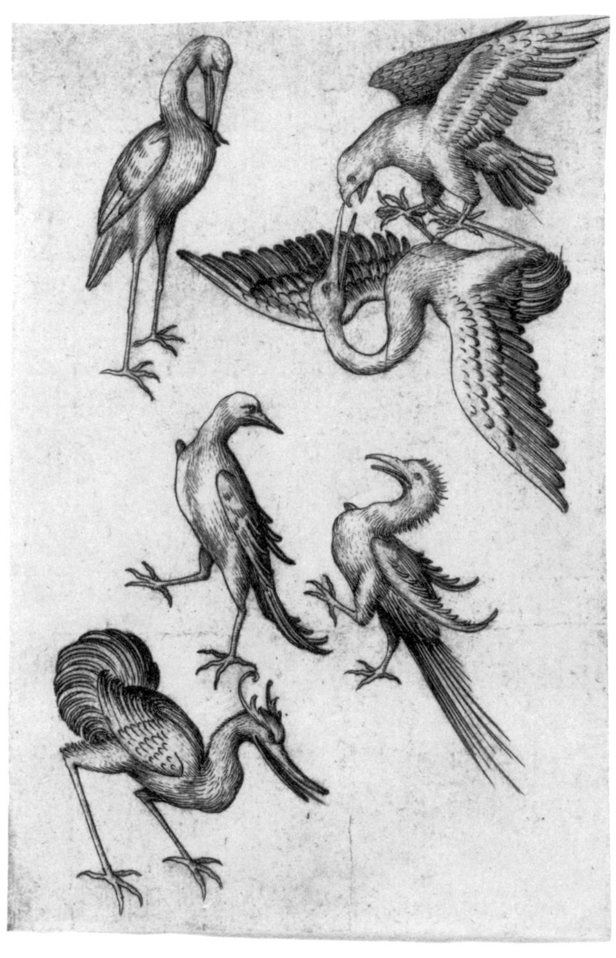

Plate 3. Master E.S., *The Six of Birds*, ca. 1463.

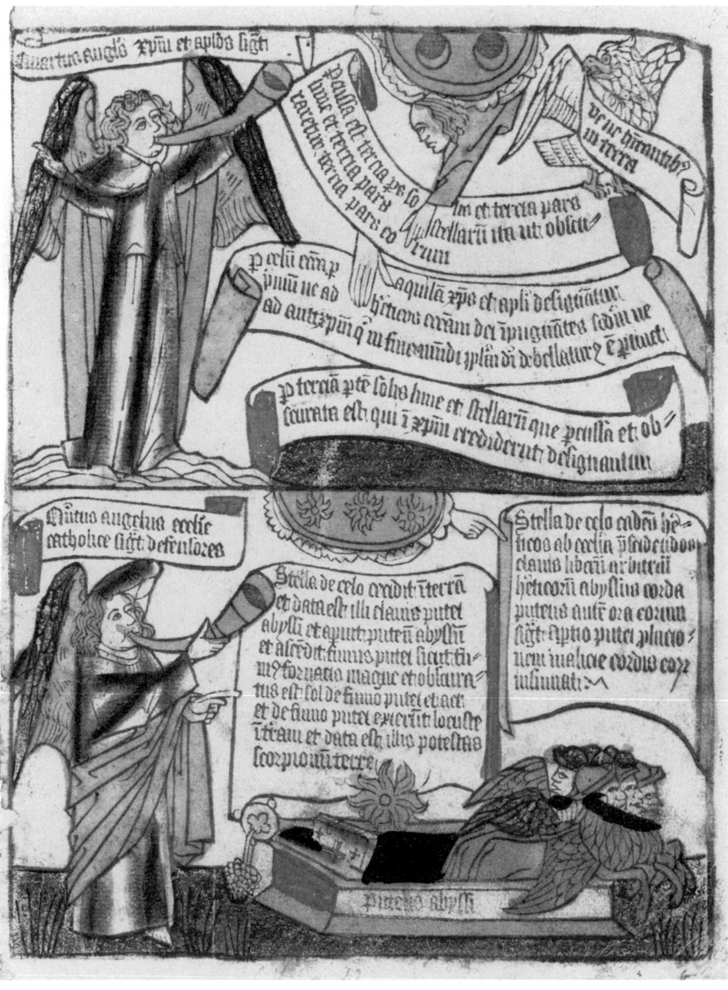

Plate 4. Unidentified Artist, *The Fourth and Fifth Angels Sound their Trumpets*.

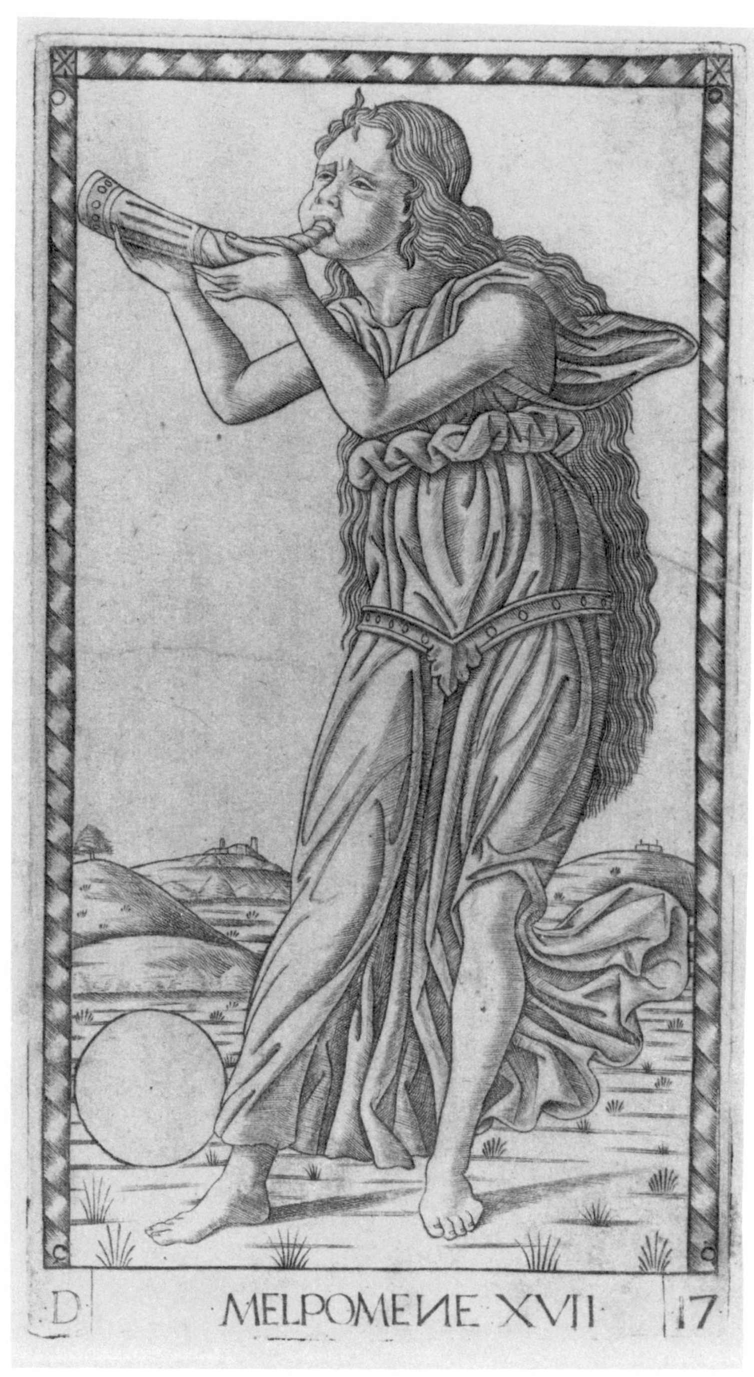

Plate 5. Master of the E-Series Tarocchi, *Melpomene*, ca. 1465.

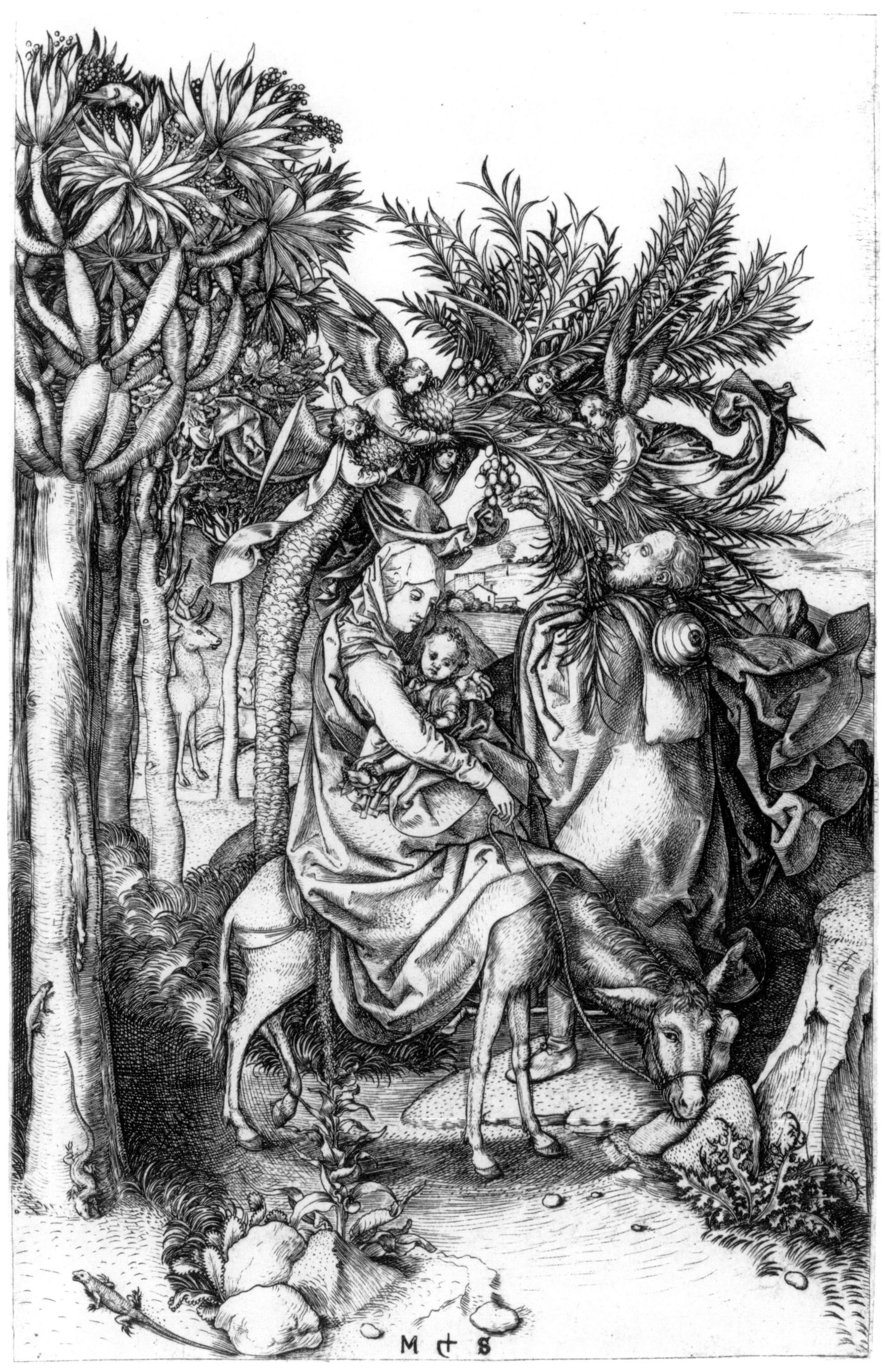

Plate 6. Martin Schongauer, *The Flight into Egypt*, 1470-75.

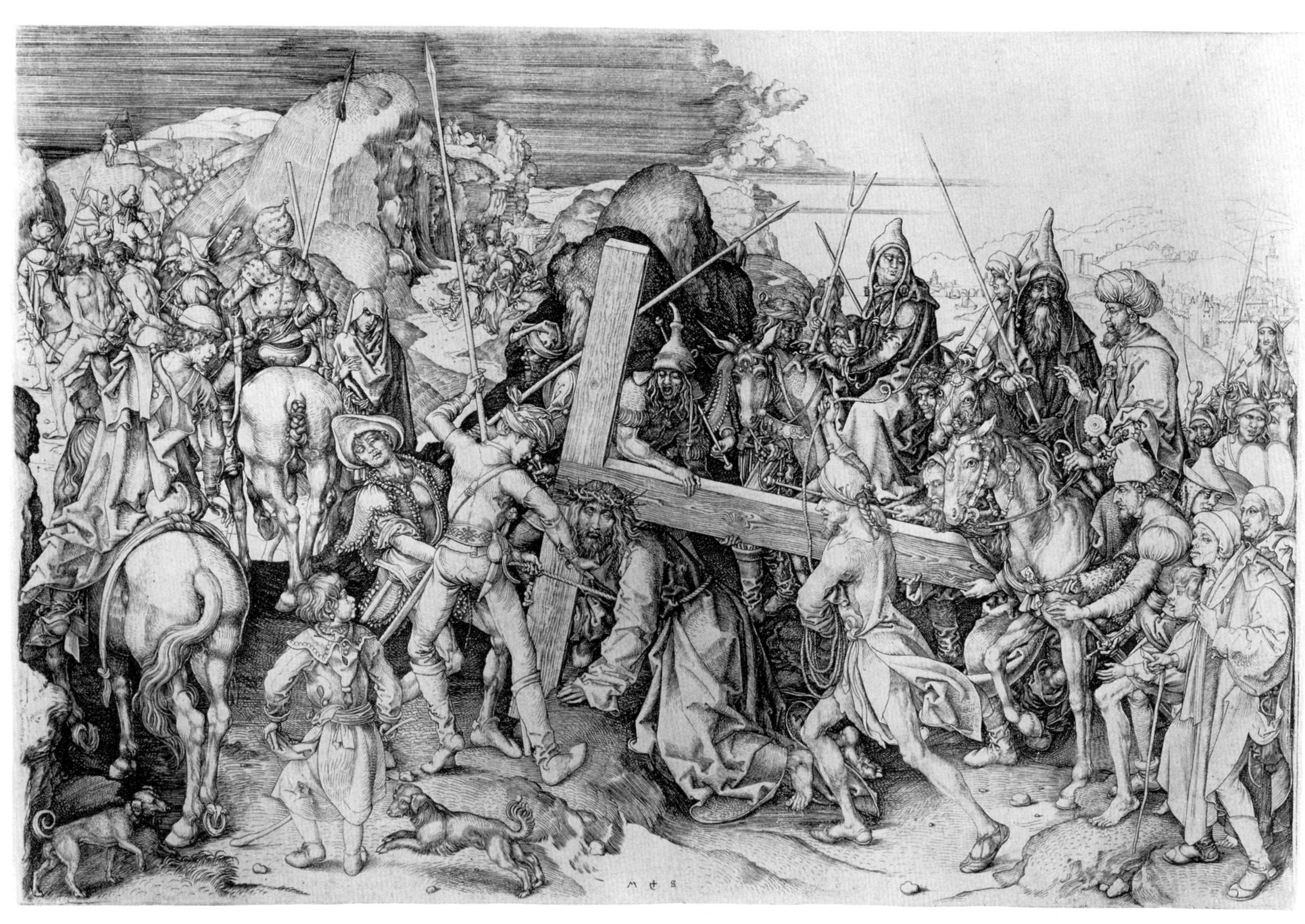

Plate 7. Martin Schongauer, *Christ Bearing His Cross* (The large plate), ca. 1475.

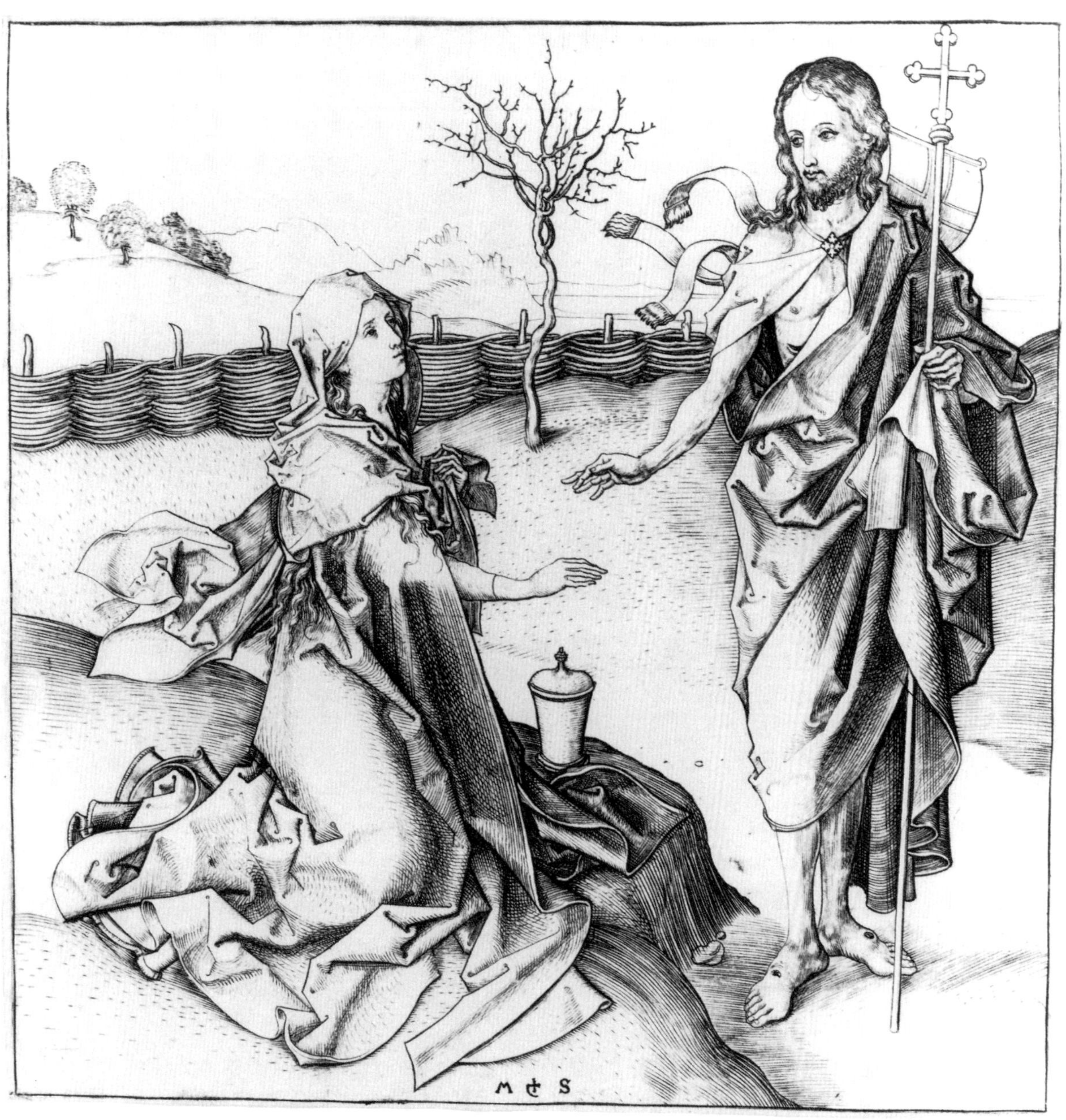

Plate 8. Martin Schongauer, *Christ Appearing to Mary Magdalene*, ca. 1480-90.

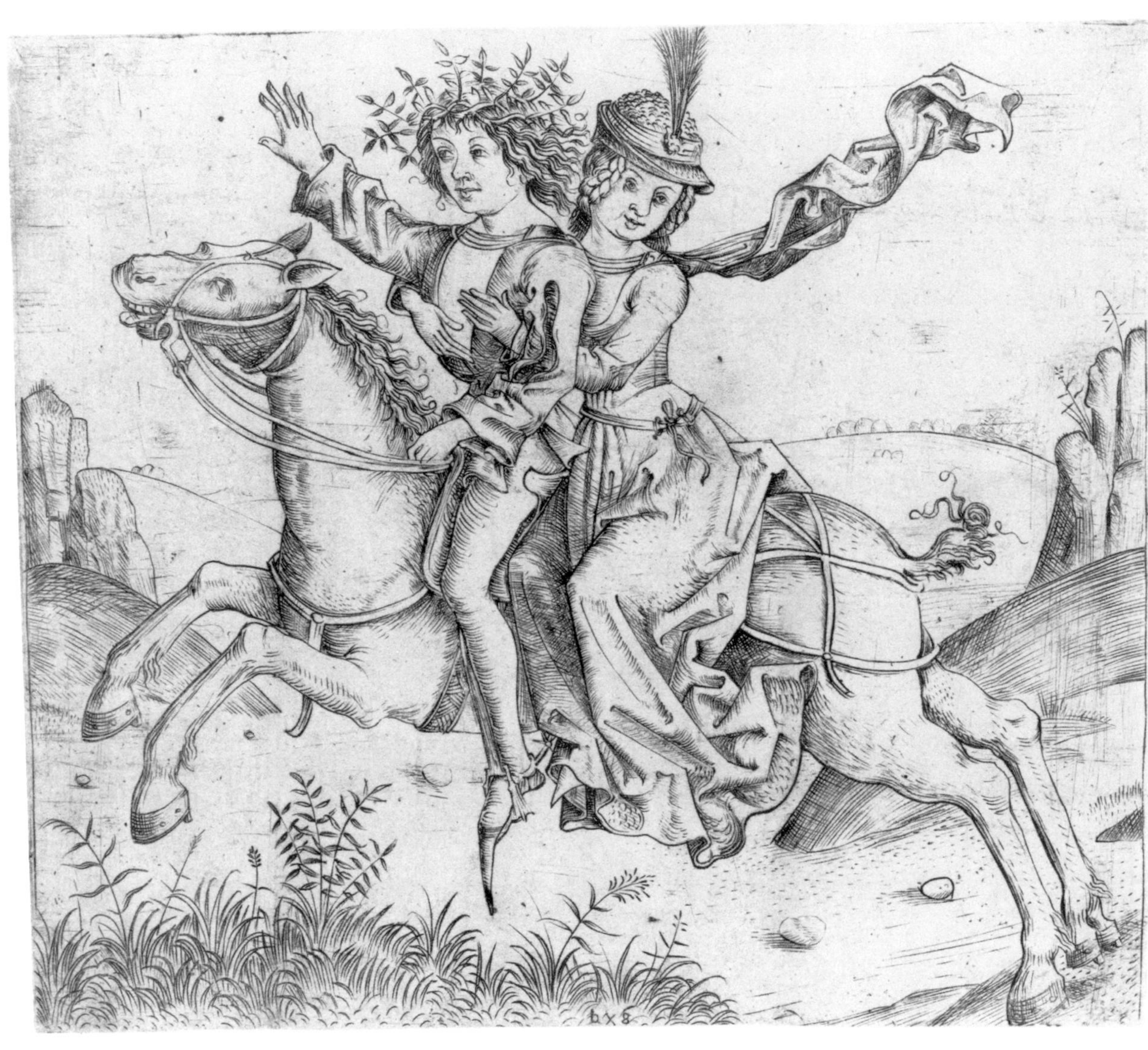

Plate 9. Master b g, *Lovers on Horseback*.

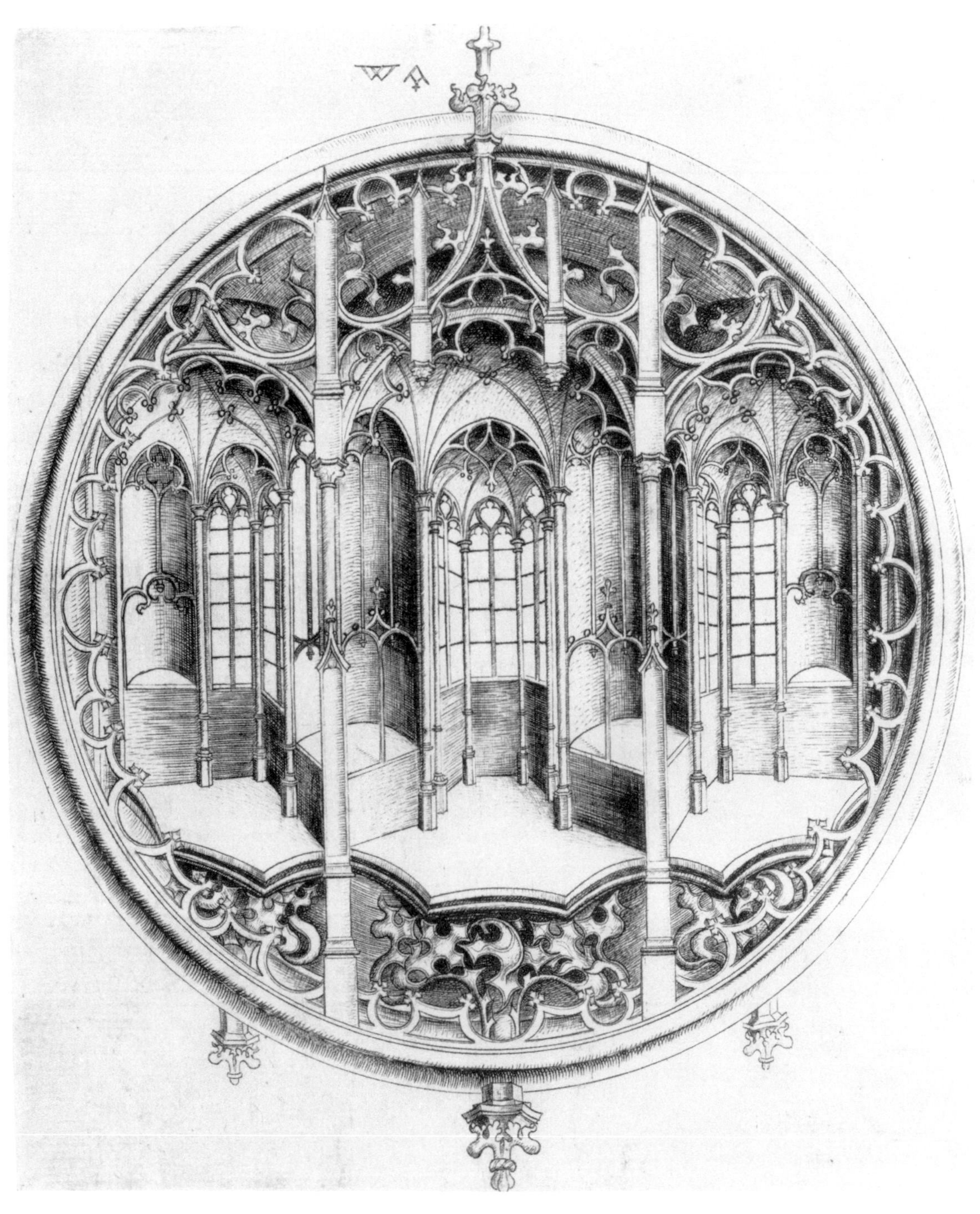

Plate 10. Master W with the Key, *Design for a Mantle-Clasp (Monile)*.

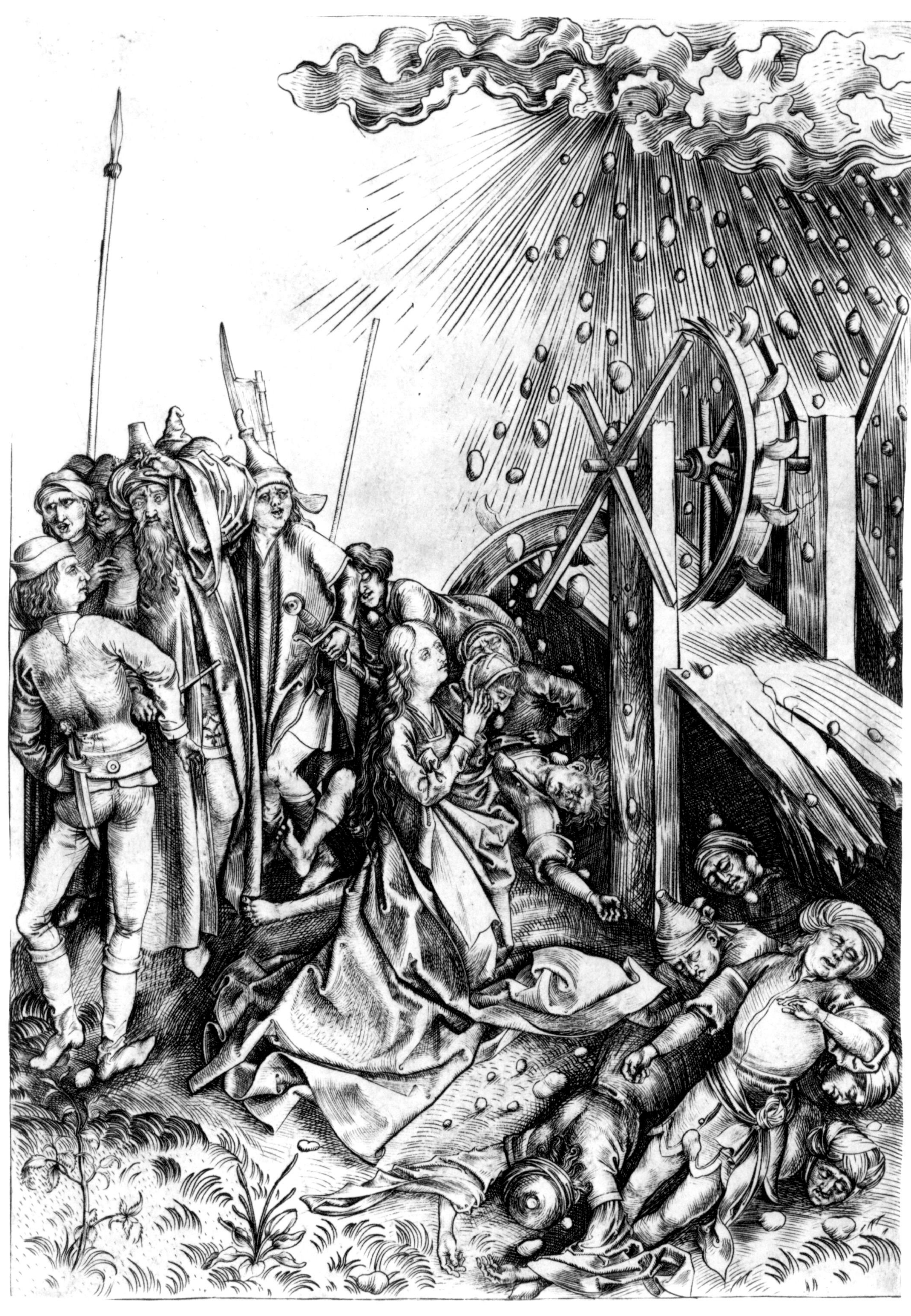

Plate 11. Master i.e., *The Martyrdom of St. Catherine*.

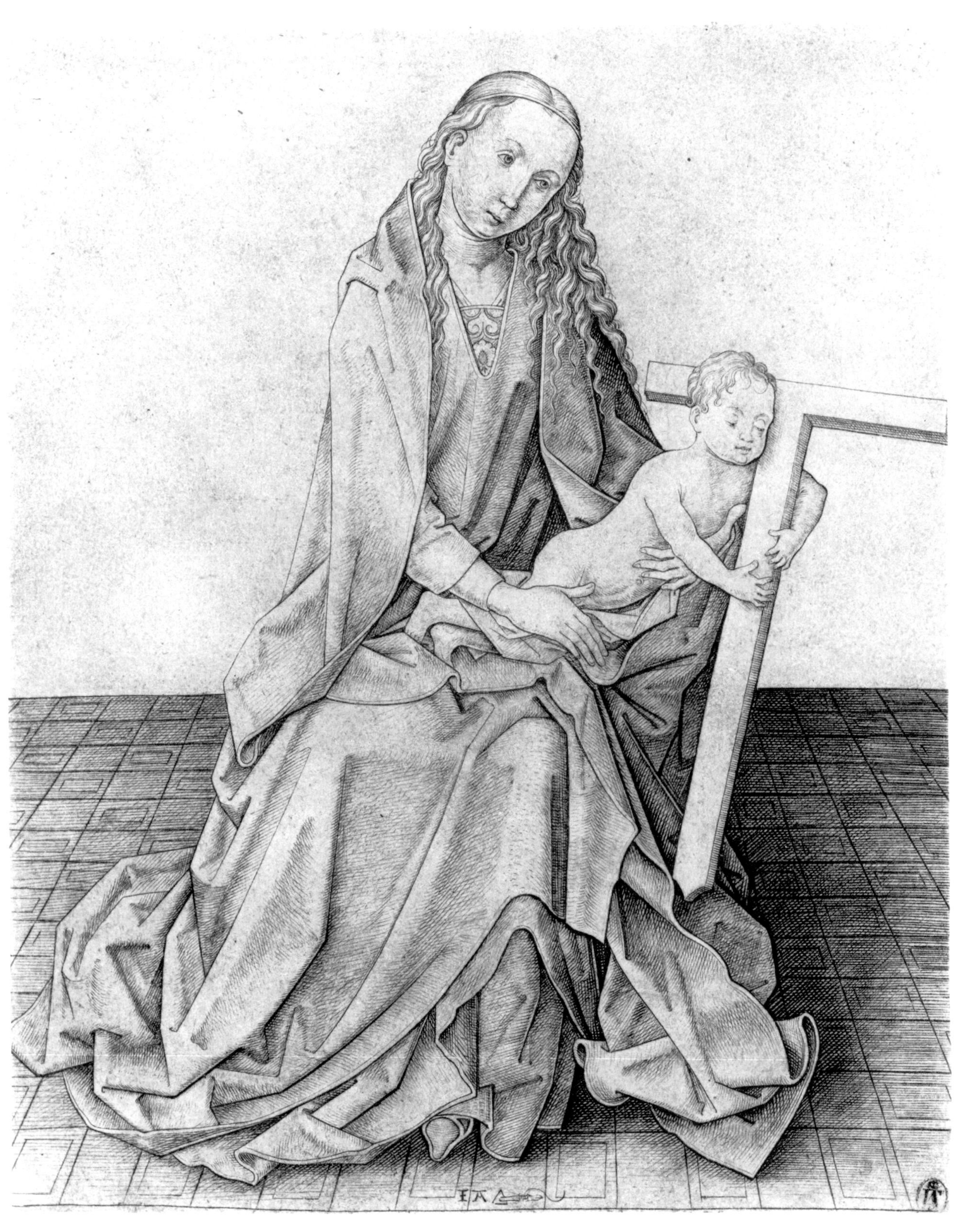

Plate 12. Master I A M of Zwolle, *The Madonna Seated, The Christ Child Holding a Cross*.

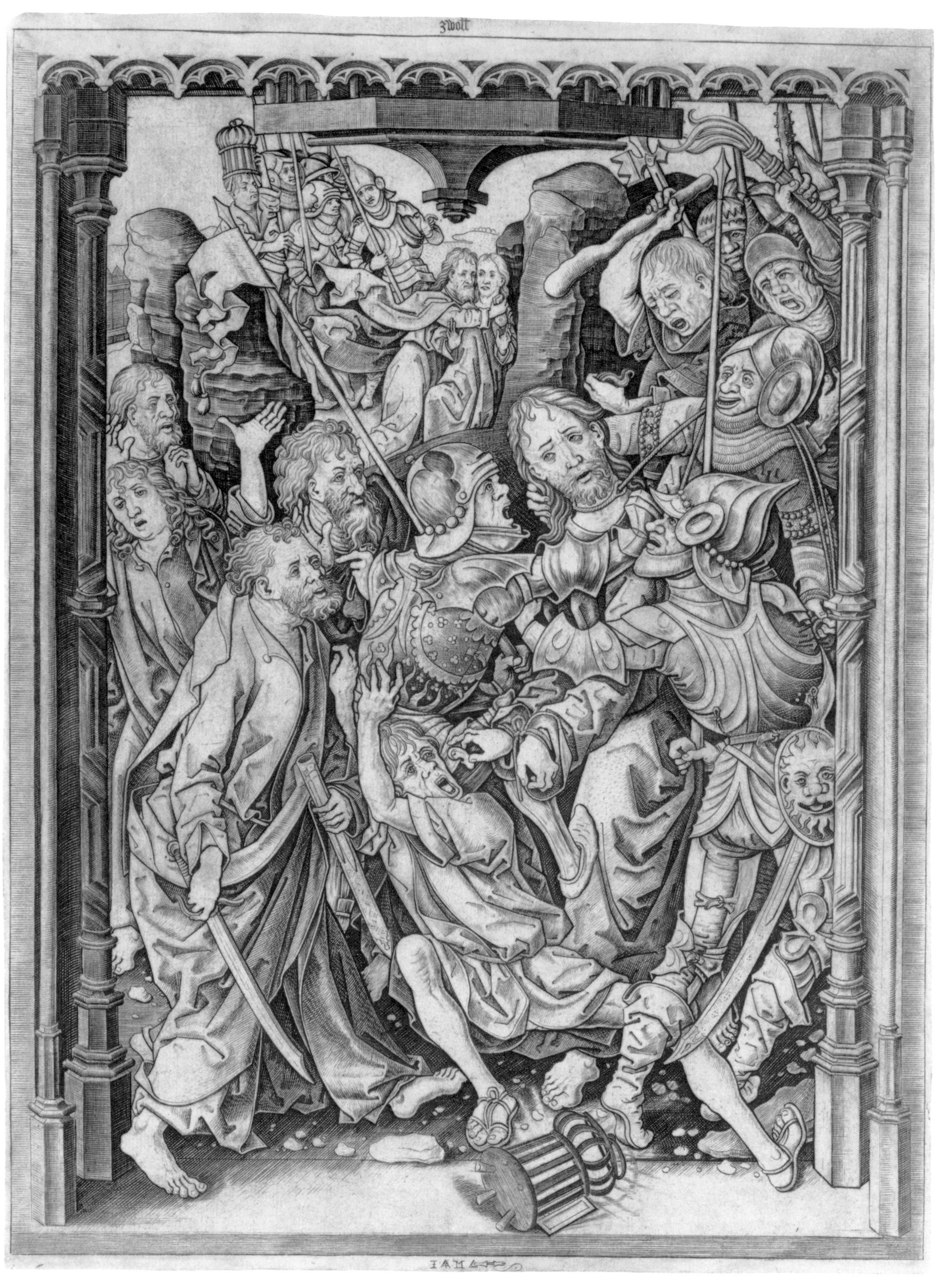

Plate 13. Master I A M of Zwolle, *The Betrayal of Christ*, ca. 1485.

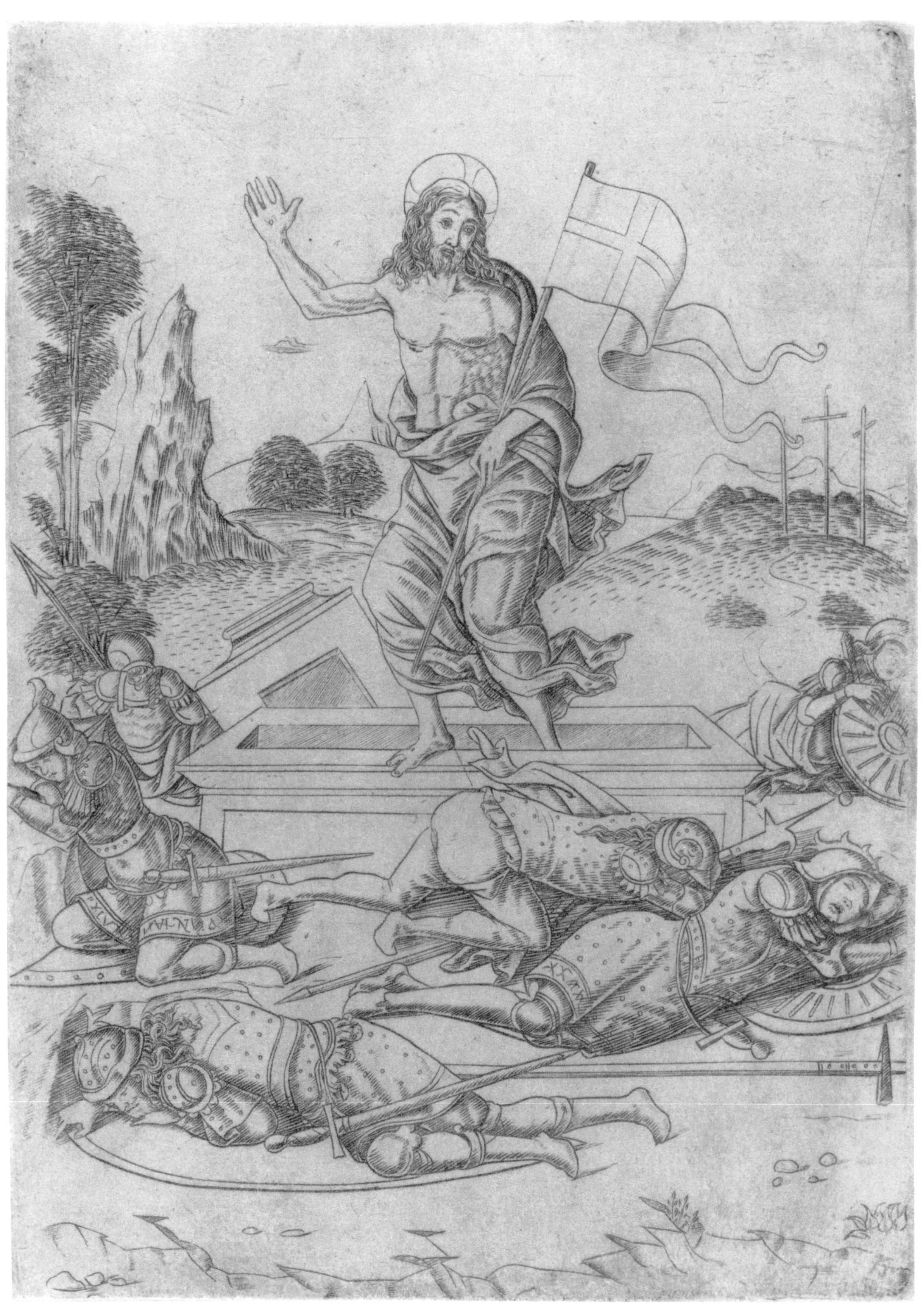

Plate 14. Francesco Rosselli, *The Resurrection*, ca. 1485?

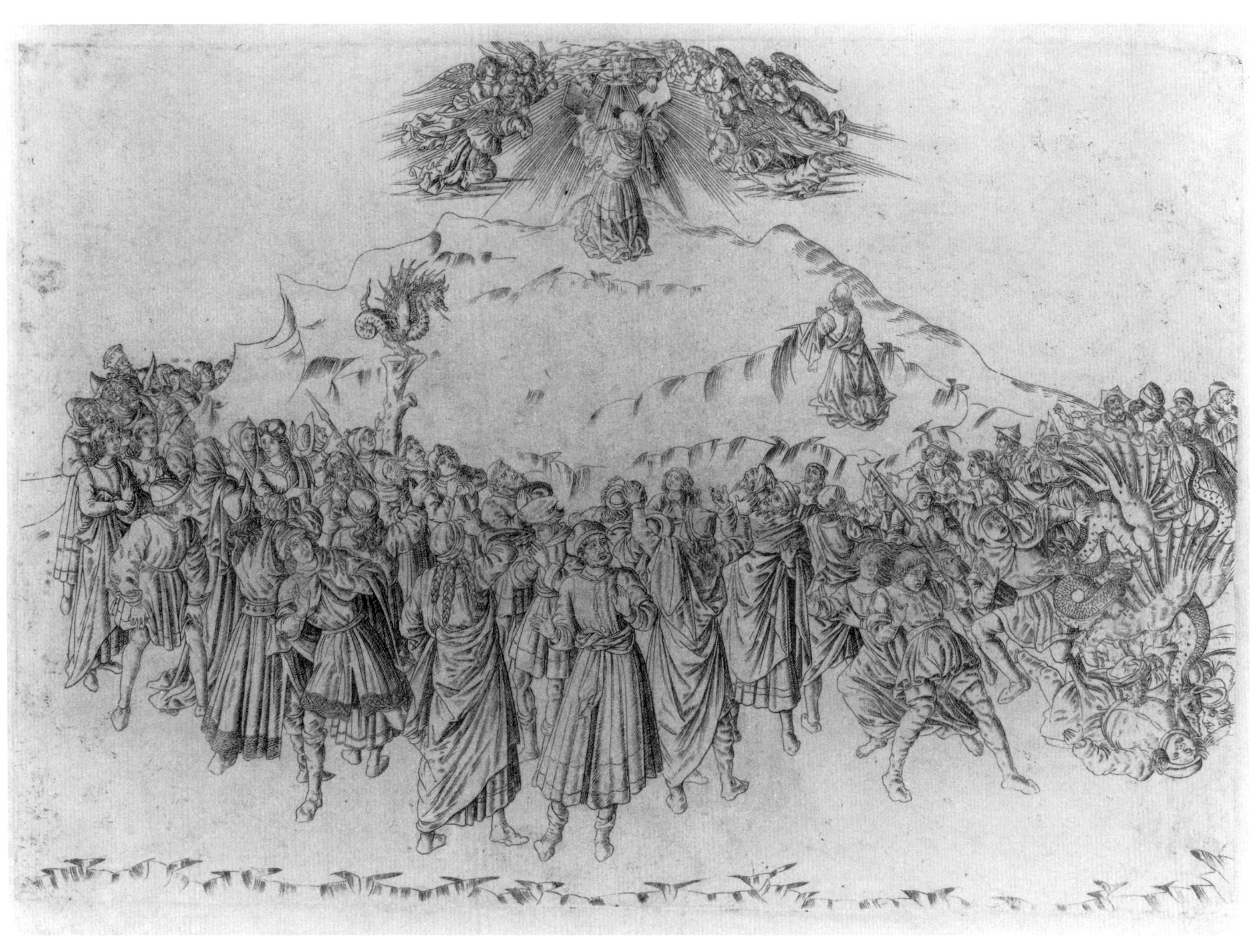

Plate 15. Francesco Rosselli, *Moses on Mount Sinai and the Brazen Serpent*, ca. 1485-1500.

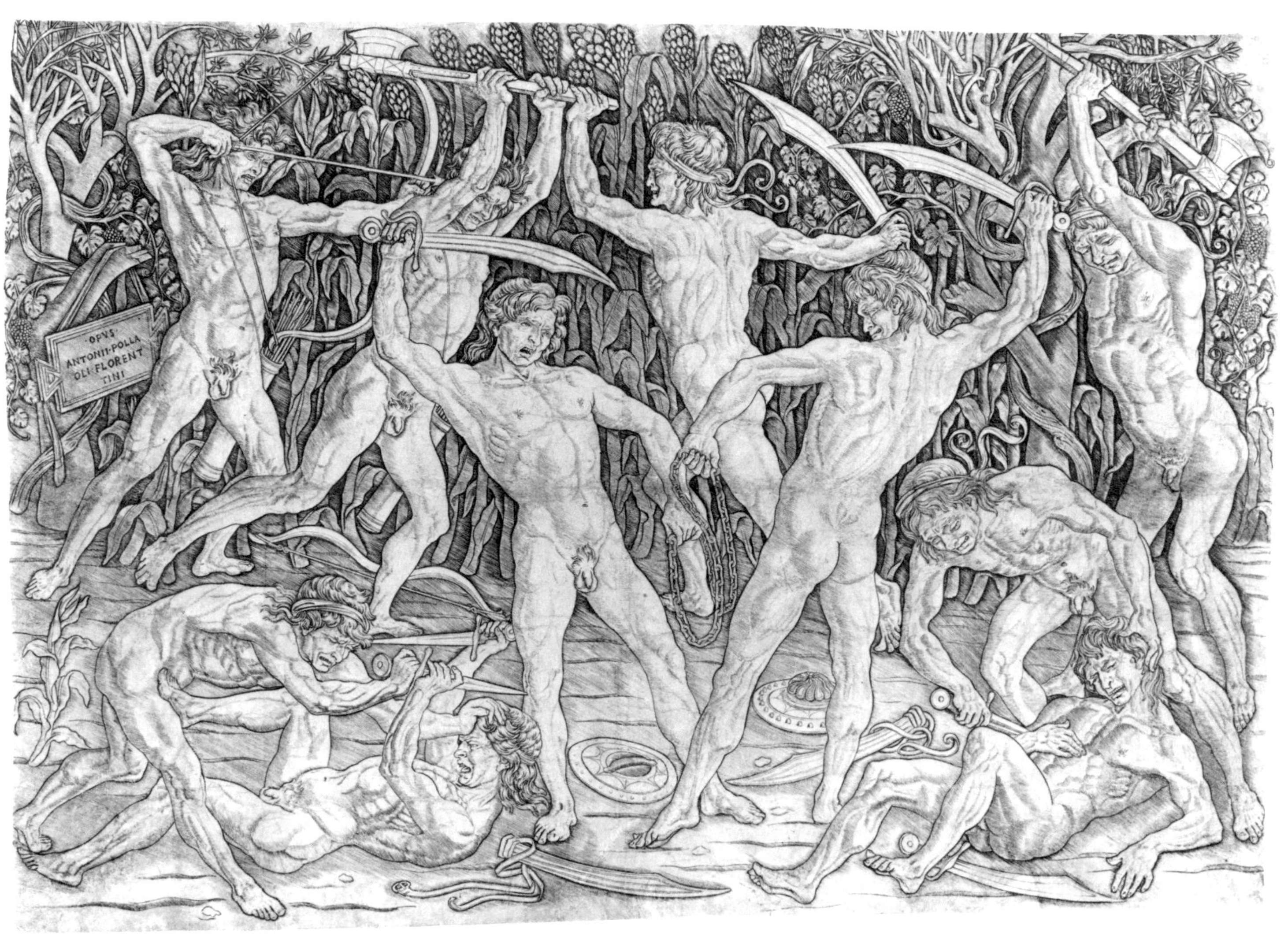

Plate 16. Antonio Pollaiuolo, *Battle of the Nudes,* ca. 1489?

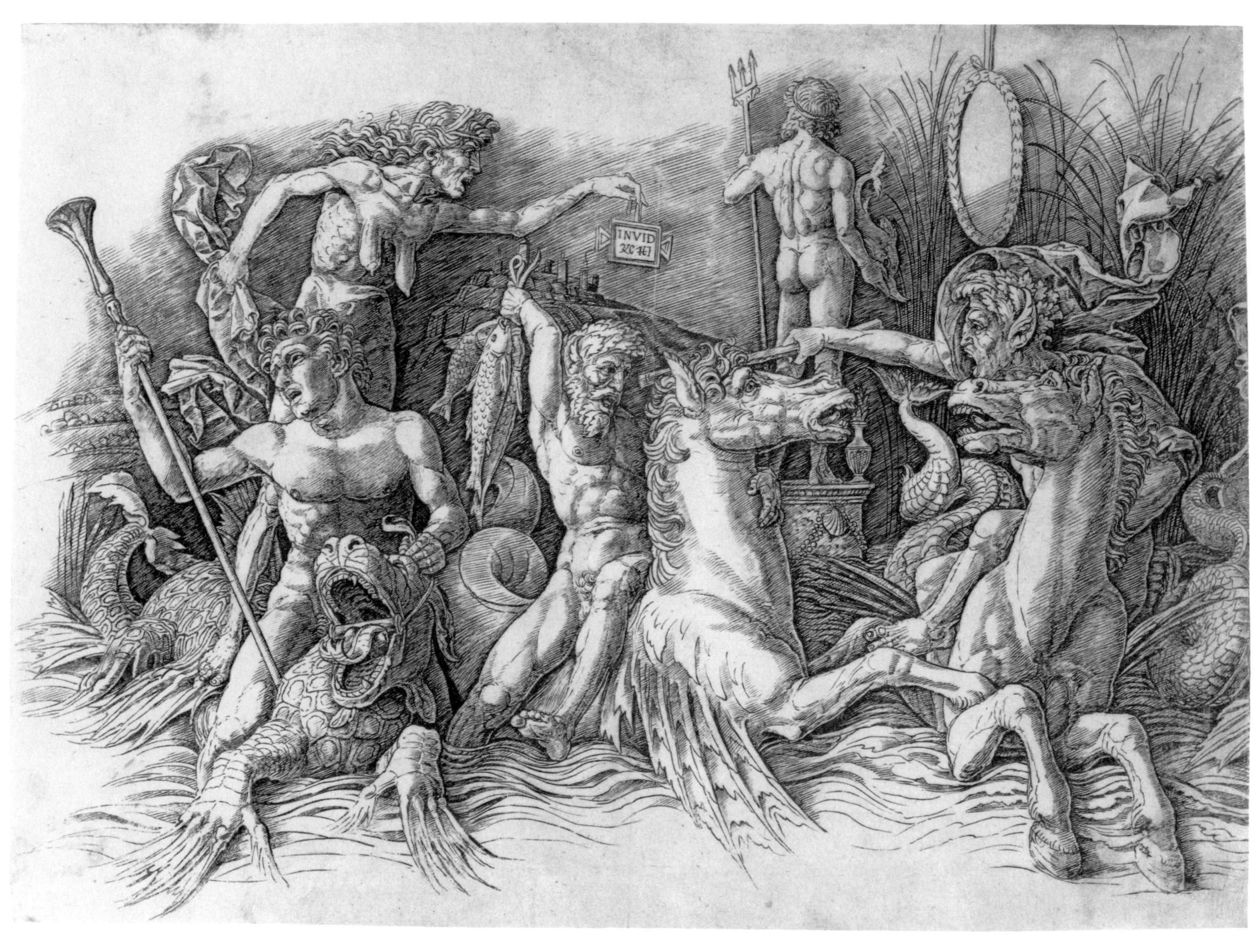

Plate 17a. School of Mantegna, *The Battle of the Sea Gods* (left half), ca. 1490.

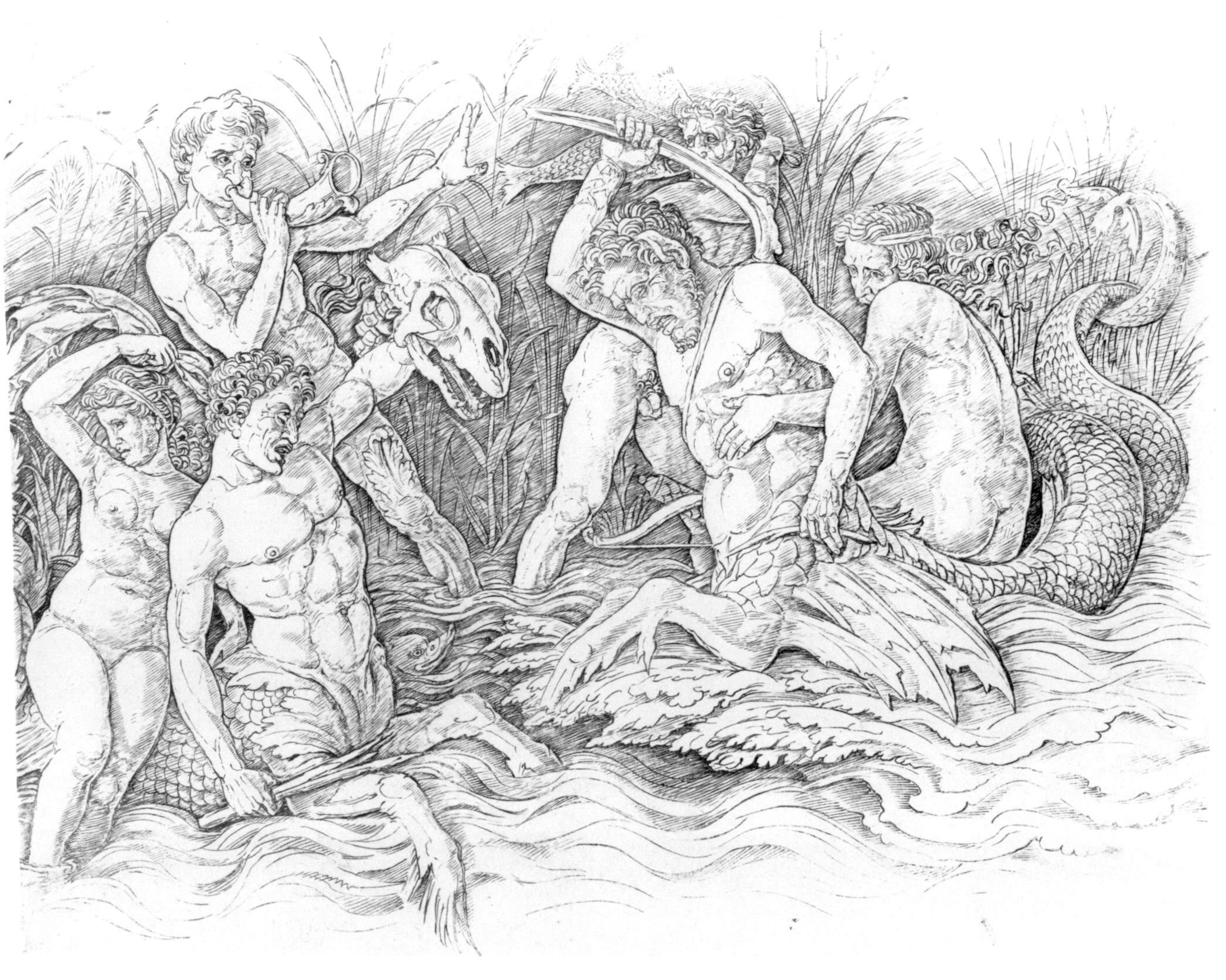

Plate 17b. School of Mantegna, *The Battle of the Sea Gods* (right half), ca. 1490.

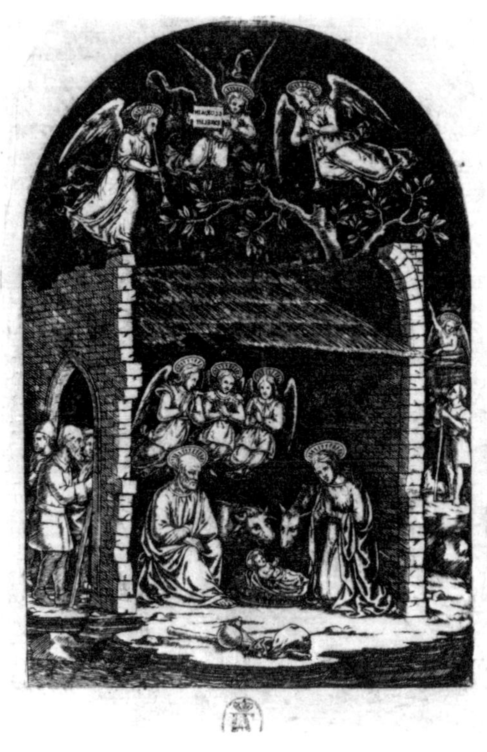

Plate 18. Unidentified Artist, *The Nativity*.

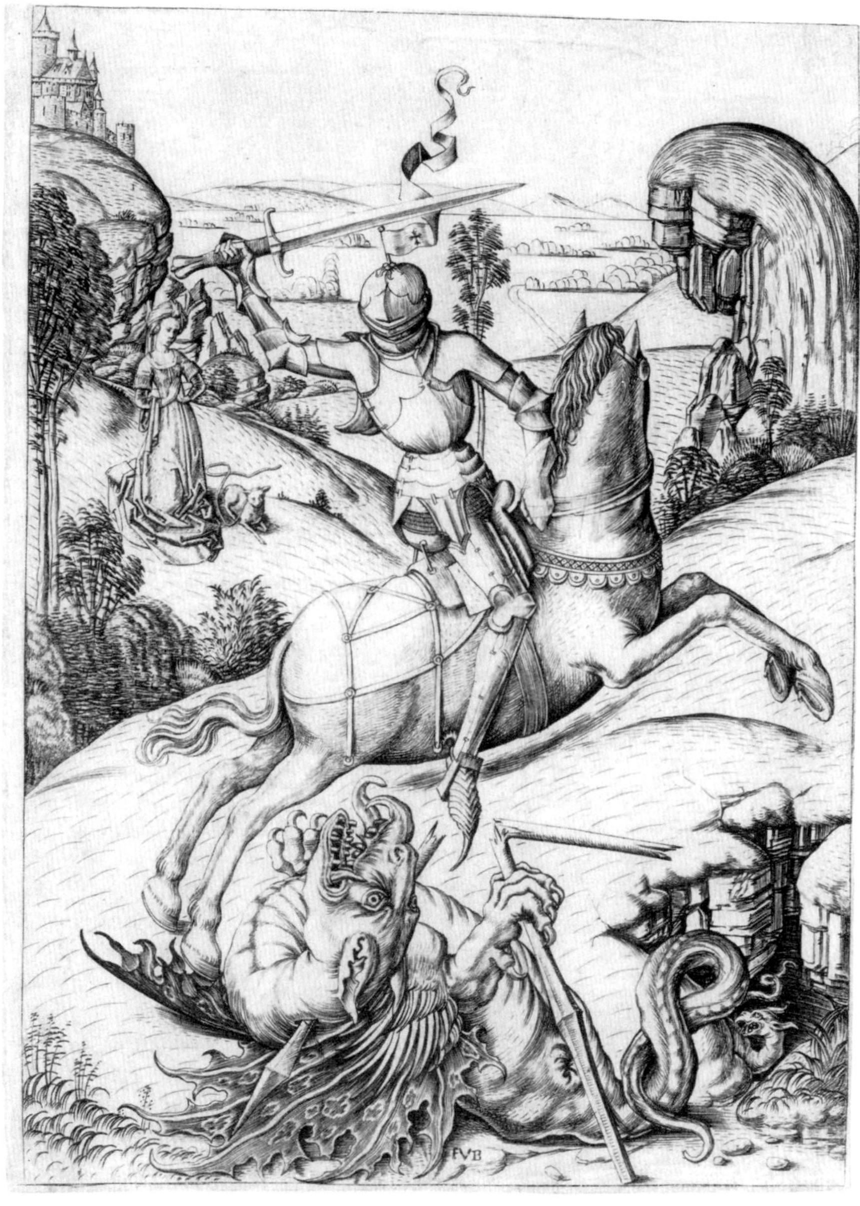

Plate 19. Master FVB, *St. George and the Dragon*, ca. 1480-90.

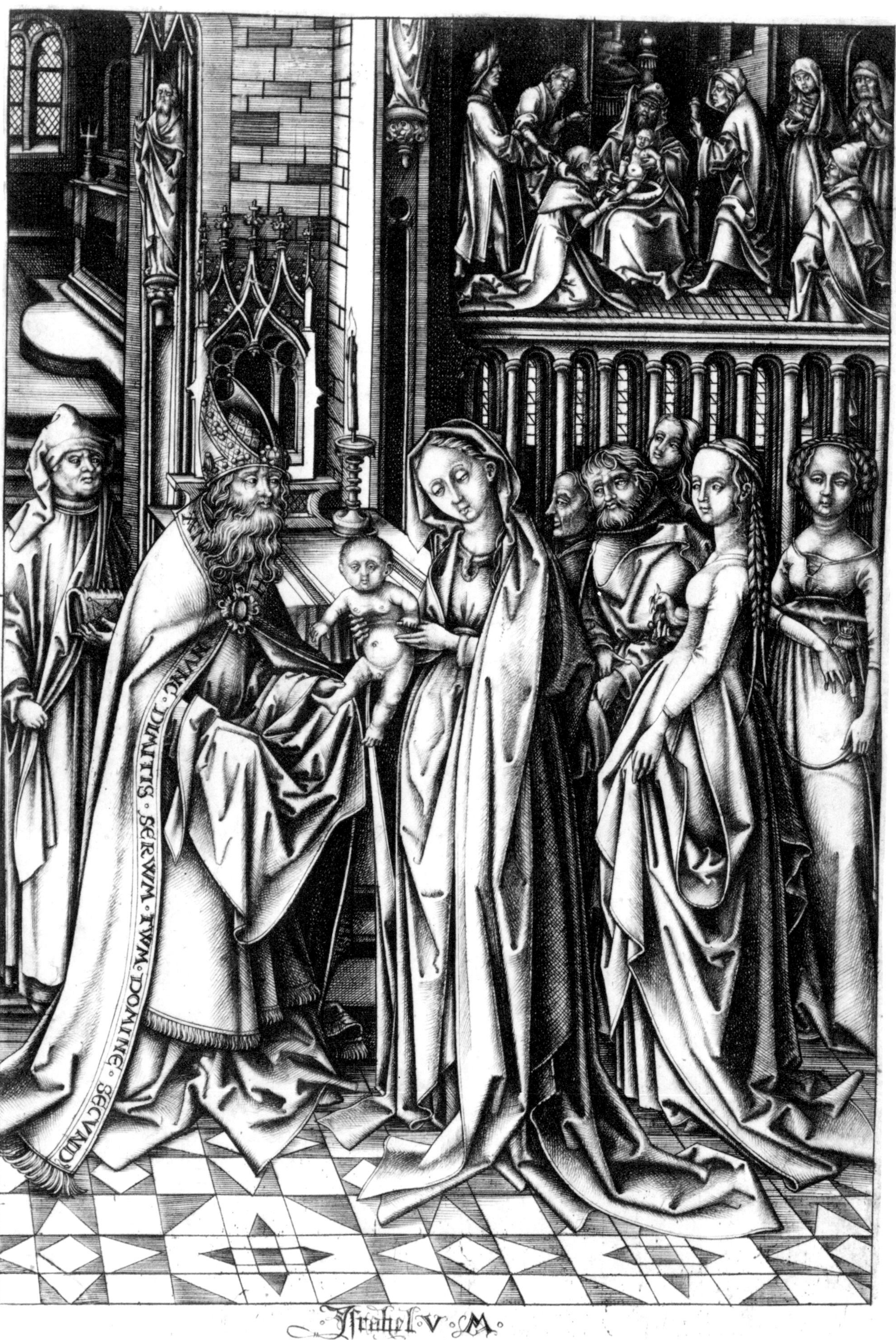

Plate 20. Israhel van Meckenem, *The Presentation in the Temple*.

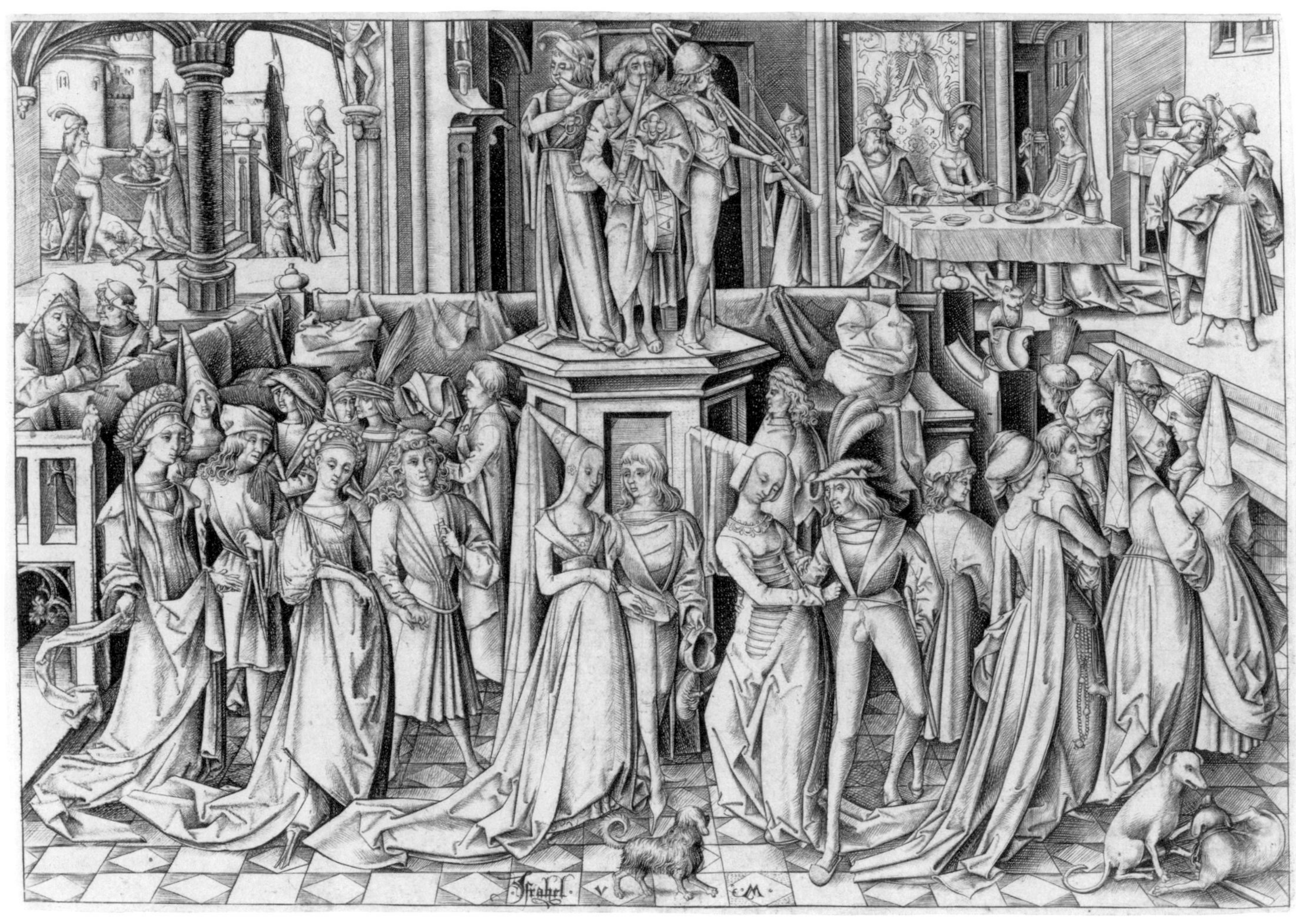

Plate 21. Israhel van Meckenem, *Dance of the Daughters of Herodias*, 1495-1500.

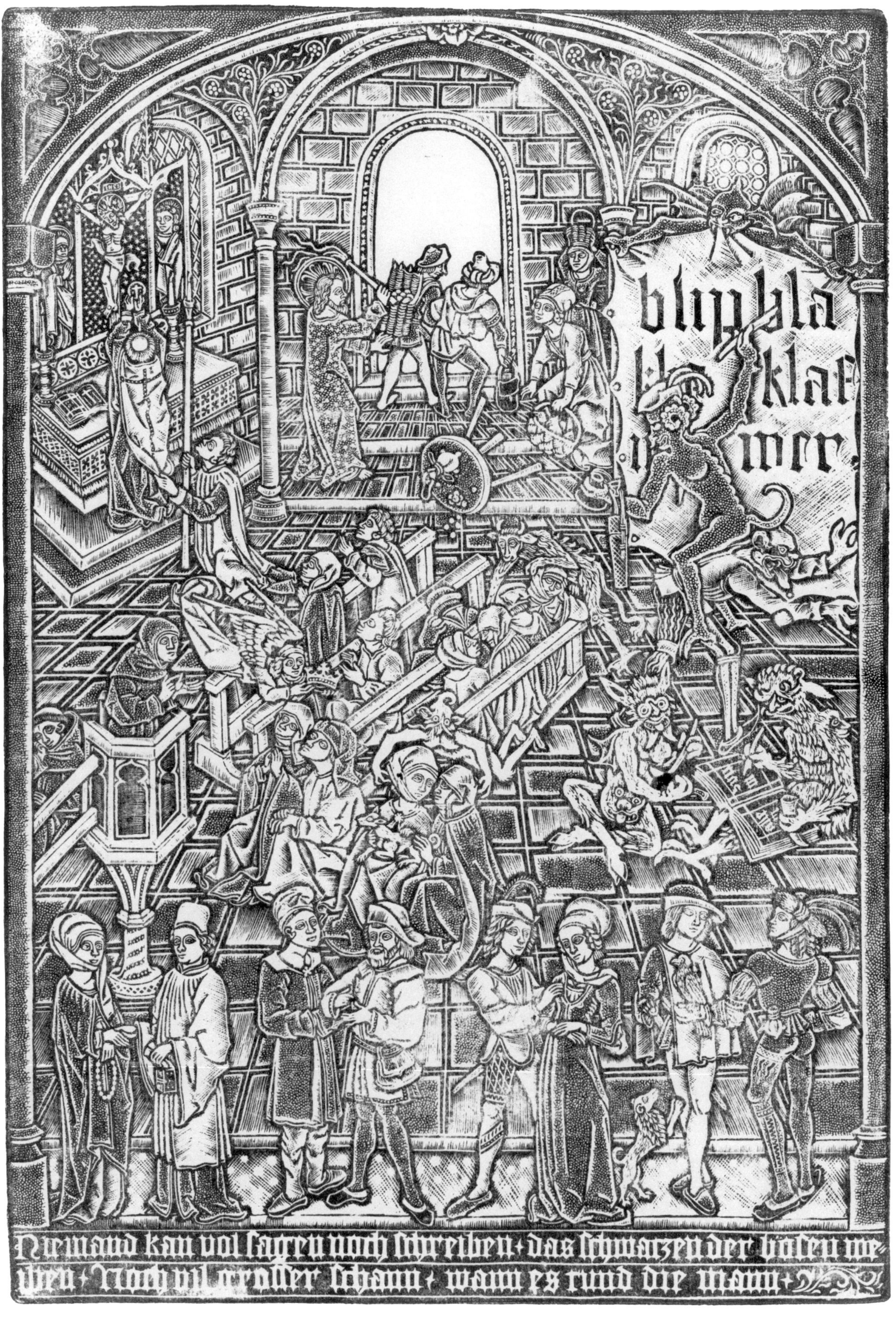

Plate 22. Master of the Meshed Backgrounds, *Satire on Gossip During the Celebration of the Mass*.

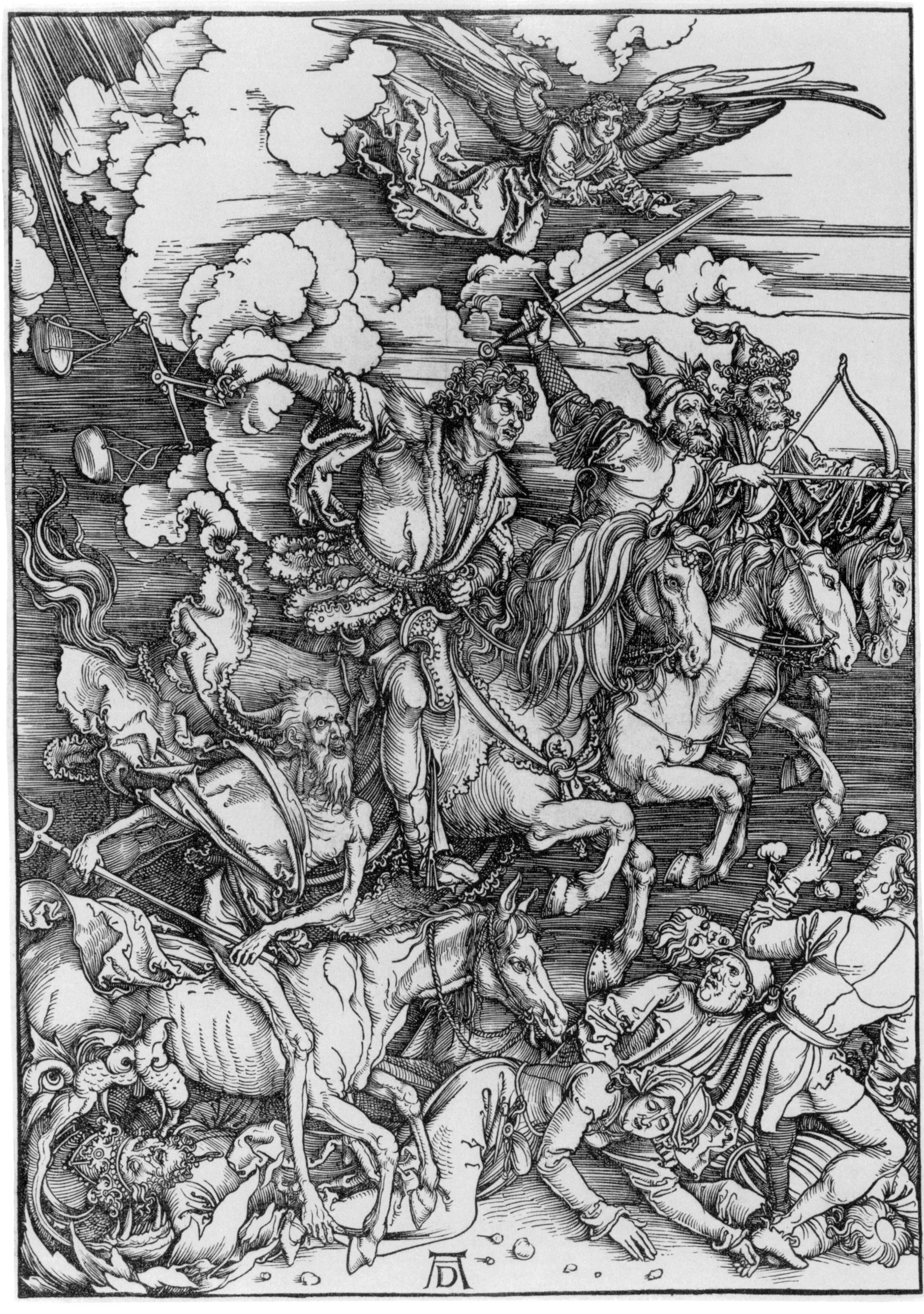

Plate 23. Albrecht Dürer, *The Four Horsemen*, ca. 1497-98.

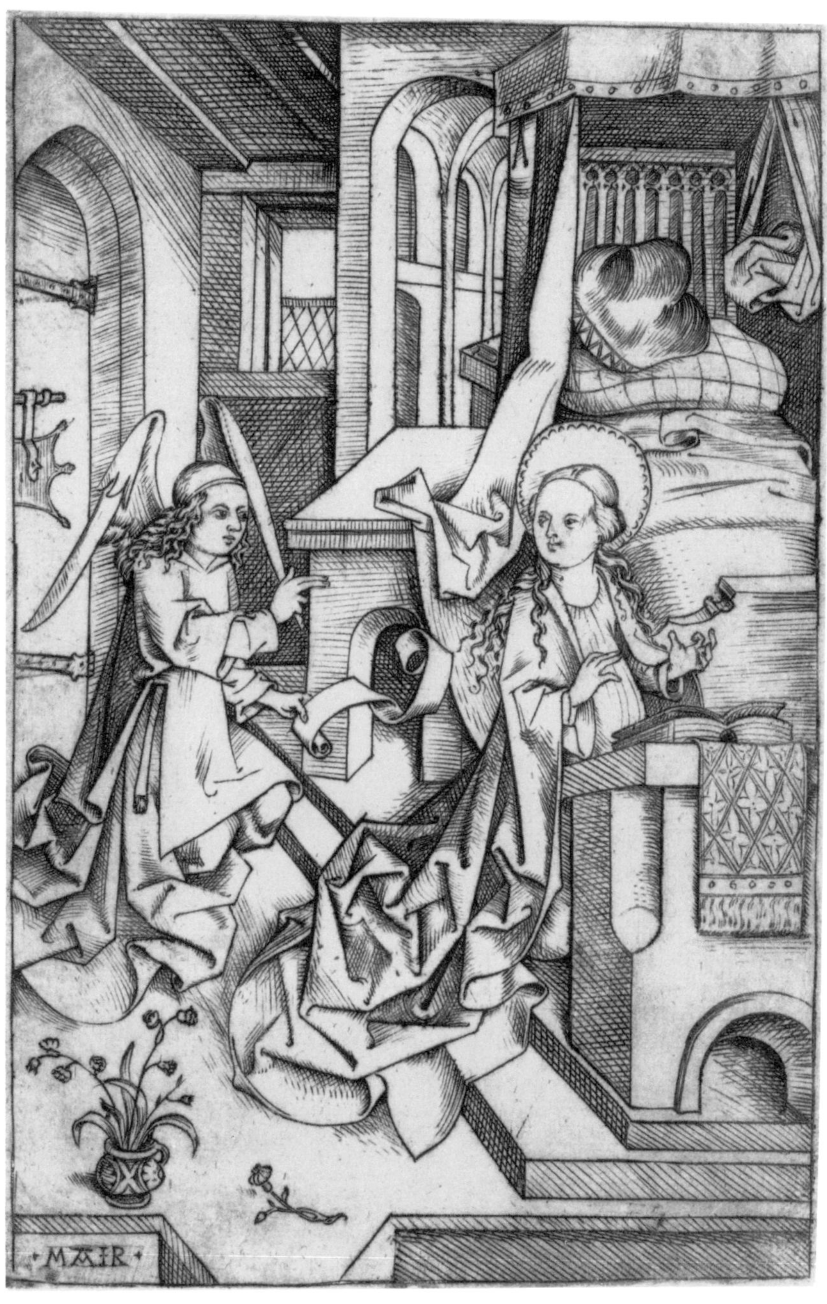

Plate 24. Mair von Landshut, *The Annunciation*, ca. 1499.

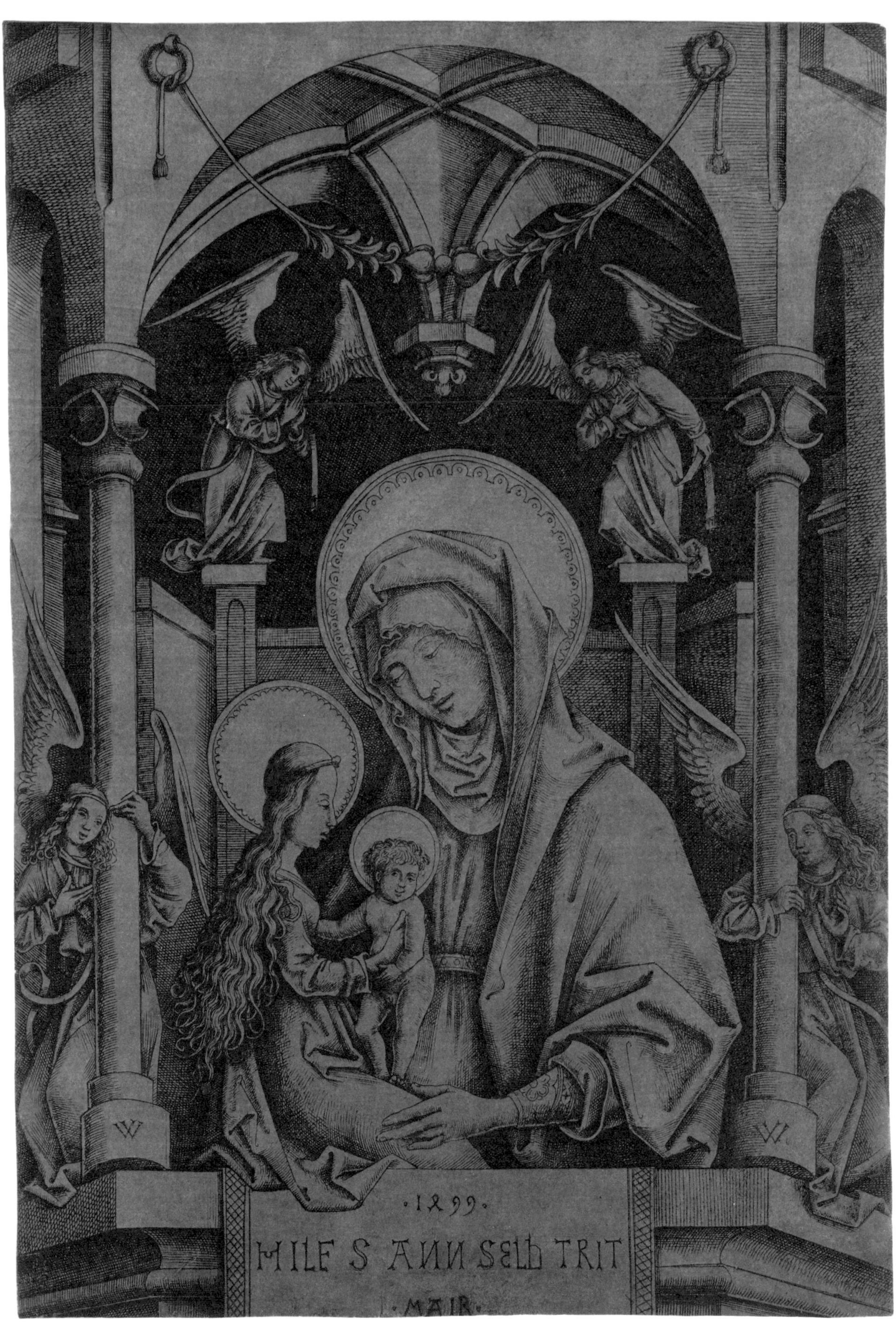

Plate 25. Mair von Landshut, *St. Anne with the Virgin and Child and Four Angels*, 1499.

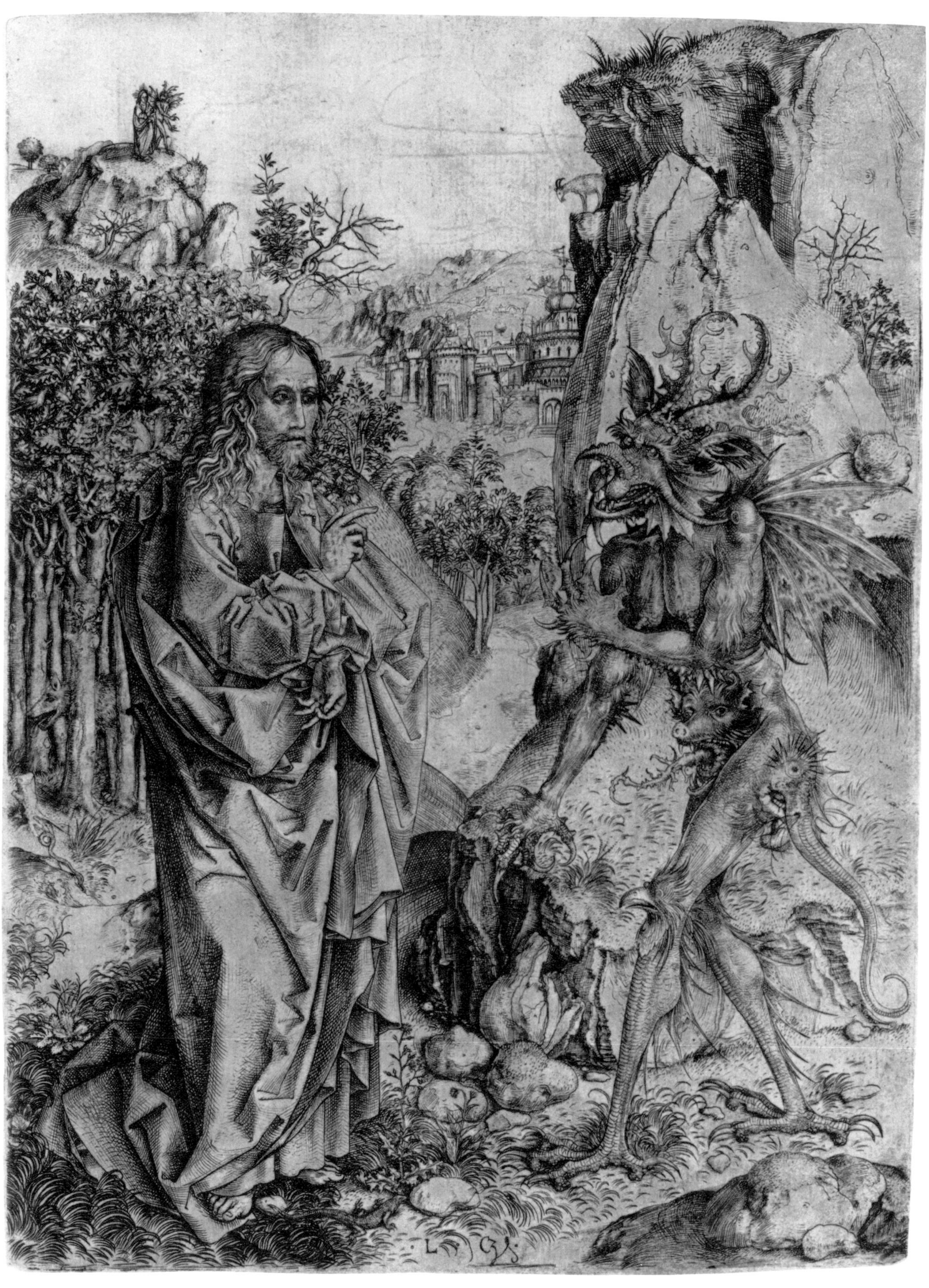

Plate 26. Master L Cz, *The Temptation of Christ*, ca. 1500.

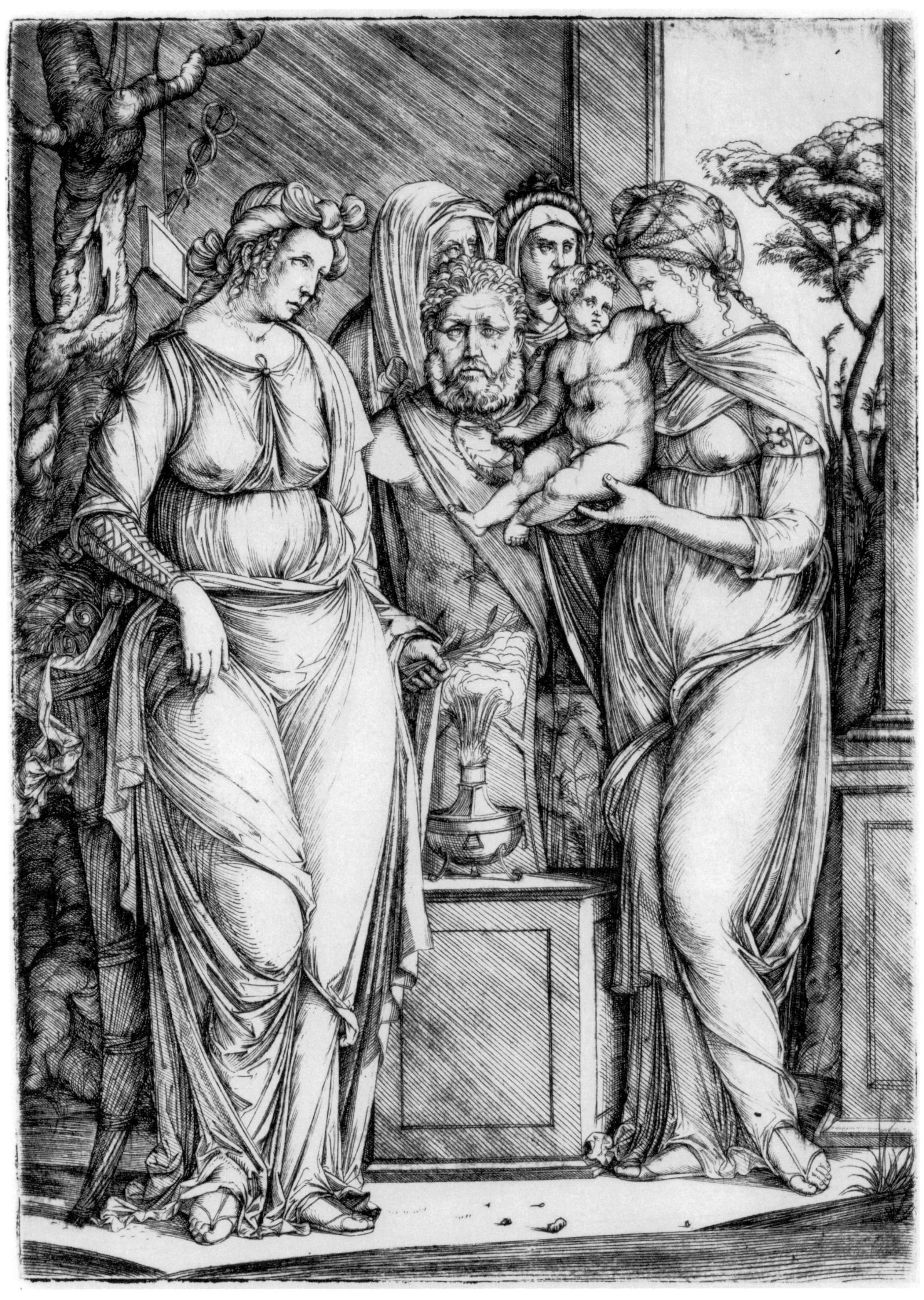

Plate 27. Jacopo de' Barbari, *Sacrifice to Priapus*, ca. 1499-1501.

Jacopo de' Barbari

Venice? ca. 1460/70-by 1516 Malines or Brussels

27. Sacrifice to Priapus (large plate) ca. 1499-1501.

Engraving on antique laid paper, 23.1 x 16.7 cm (platemark).
B.VII.525.19; Hind 23.
Watermark: Bull's head with cross and serpent (cf. Briquet 15375).
Provenance: (Purchased from M. Knoedler, New York, October 6, 1934, for $2,750).
Bequest of Herbert Greer French, 1943.104.
Exhibitions: Cincinnati 1941, no. 53.

Although a relatively large number of documents exist concerning Jacopo de' Barbari, the date and place of his birth and death are uncertain.[1] Our first knowledge of Jacopo places him in Venice during the last years of the fifteenth century, where he was apparently hired by Anton Kolb, a merchant from Nuremberg, to design an immense woodcut map of Venice. The map, on six blocks with overall dimensions of 132.7 x 281.1 cm, gives a bird's-eye view of the city with accuracy astonishing for its day. The actual gathering of data and the drawing of views were probably compiled by a number of surveyors, but the ensemble – plus vignettes of his own design depicting Mercury, Neptune, and the Winds – was put together by Jacopo.[2] In 1500 he received a one-year appointment as a painter to the Emperor Maximilian I, and subsequently he worked for Friedrich the Wise, Elector of Saxony, and Joachim I, Elector of Brandenburg. Toward the end of the decade, he was in the Netherlands, working for Count Philip of Burgundy. He may have returned to Italy in the entourage of the count in 1508 and 1509.[3] The last years of his life were spent in Brussels and Malines in the service of Margaret of Austria, daughter of Emperor Maximilian I and Regent of the Netherlands. In 1516 Jacopo was referred to as having died.

Jacopo's oeuvre includes twenty-nine engravings, of which twenty-seven are signed with a caduceus; until 1820, in fact, he was known as the Master with the Caduceus, although why he used this device is still to be discovered.[4] Such signatures are often simply a name in pictorial form, as is the sign of Giovanni Battista Palumba, long known as the Master I.B. with a Bird (see cat. 43). Pierre-Jean Mariette suggested the name "Luca Catutie" or "Catuche" on the basis of inscriptions on two engravings, but there is now no way of knowing just what these inscriptions were or on what information they were based.[5] Levenson suggested that the caduceus might have been chosen because it is the sign of Mercury, the patron of artists.[6]

At Jacopo's death, twenty-three copper engraving plates were left in Margaret's possession, which could indicate that Jacopo had engraved as many as forty-six subjects; it seems to have been common practice to engrave both sides of a plate, and some of Jacopo's images were almost certainly on reverse sides of a single plate (see cat. 34).[7] The second side of the plate need not have been engraved immediately after the first, however; the engraving whose dimensions most nearly coincide with those of *Sacrifice to Priapus* is *Presentation in the Temple* (so titled by Levenson, following Kristeller, but called *Adoration of the Magi* by Bartsch and Hind; B.VII.517.2, Hind 1),[8] an image generally agreed to have been made

considerably later in Jacopo's life. Thus, the second side of a number of plates may never have been engraved; on the other hand, that one of his prints, *A Centaur Pursued by Dragons* (Hind 28), is known in a single impression suggests that other prints might have been made of which no impression is now known. A thirtieth print that has been proposed as Jacopo's, however, *Head of a Woman* (Hind 30), is difficult to reconcile with the rest of his oeuvre.[9]

Jacopo's paintings, of which less than a dozen are known,[10] and his prints have a distinctive, virtually unmistakable style: his figures have small heads and somewhat shapeless bodies, with sloping shoulders and thick torsos supported by slender legs. It has been widely accepted that Jacopo was interested in the study of human proportions. In 1523 Albrecht Dürer wrote, "I find no one who has written anything about how to make a canon of human proportions except for a man named Jacobus, born in Venice and a charming painter."[11] Dürer wrote that he was young when he met this "man named Jacobus," and it is traditionally believed that this Jacobus was Jacopo de' Barbari, although to look at Jacopo's figures it is hard to believe that he was attempting to create an idealized norm.[12]

None of Jacopo's engravings is dated, but stylistic evolution and evidence of influence from sources with known dates – the prints of Dürer, for example – have made it possible to sort them into a rough chronology. *Sacrifice to Priapus*, the larger of two images Jacopo made that treat this subject, is thought to have been executed just around the turn of the sixteenth century. The paper on which the Museum's excellent early impression is printed, as well as that of the Washington impression and of some others, was most probably made in Italy, but as these Italian papers were used in the German-speaking areas to the north, this fact alone cannot prove where the

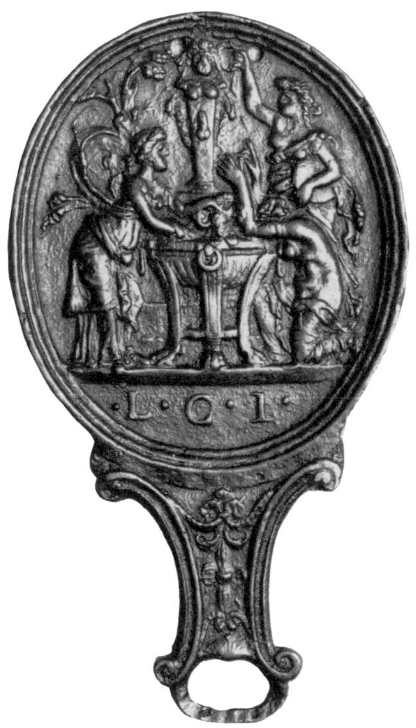

Figure 27-1. Romano-Mantuan, *Sacrifice to Priapus*, before 1480, lamp cover incorporating bronze plaquette. Victoria and Albert Museum, London.

print was made.[13] In any case, on stylistic grounds, the print is judged to be one of Jacopo's earliest engravings.

Priapus was an ancient god of fertility, usually represented during the Renaissance as a herm with a large, erect phallus, which is concealed here by the smoke from an incense burner. If indeed a plaquette (fig. 27-1) known in numerous versions, perhaps by Cristoforo di Geremaia, to be dated before 1480, it is the earliest representation of the subject of a sacrifice to Priapus in Renaissance art known to me.[14] The subject was widely diffused through a woodcut (fig. 27-2) in the *Hypnerotomachia Poliphili* (*The Strife of Love in a Dream of Poliphilo*), a long, idiosyncratic, allegorical proto-novel in Italian illustrated with 170 woodcuts, published by the famous Aldus Manutius in Venice in 1499; the book was written by Francesco Colonna, a Dominican monk.[15]

Jacopo's print is one of several Italian works made around the turn of the century that shows a sacrifice to Priapus, and a parallel interest in the story of Priapus and Lotis seems to have emerged around the same time. This story was told by Ovid in the *Fasti*, but it was popularized in the first Ovid published in Italian, which also was the first with illustrations, the edition by Lucantonio Giunta in Venice in 1497.[16] The story is depicted soon again in an engraving by Giovanni Battista Palumba (B.XIII.247.6, Hind V.257.7); the most famous rendition of the subject is Giovanni Bellini's *Feast of the Gods*, painted for Alfonso d'Este, duke of Ferrara, in 1514 (now in the National Gallery, Washington).[17]

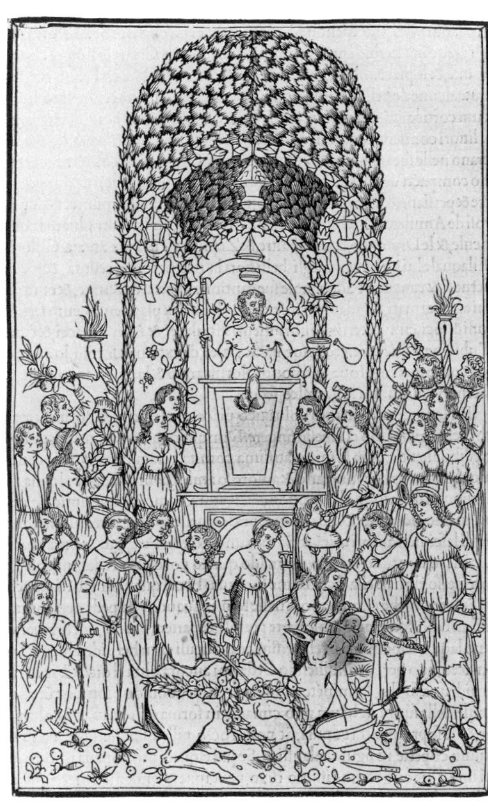

Figure 27-2. *Sacrifice to Priapus*, woodcut from Francesco Colonna, *Hypnerotomachia Poliphili* (Venice: Aldus Manutius, 1499), leaf M6 recto. The Metropolitan Museum of Art, New York, Gift of J. P. Morgan, 1923.

Jacopo's composition seems to conflate the Christian celebration of the Presentation in the Temple – a subject based in Hebrew tradition – with the pagan worship of the god of fertility. The figure of the woman at the left seems to provide further evidence that the *Hypnerotomachia* was known to Jacopo, as it is close in pose to a woodcut (fig. 27-3) on a page immediately preceding the *Sacrifice*. The gnarled trees at the left, while owing something to Dürer, as Levenson points out, also bear a close resemblance to trees in the

Figure 27-3. *Flavae Messi. S.*, woodcut from Francesco Colonna, *Hypnerotomachia Poliphili* (Venice: Aldus Manutius, 1499), leaf M5 recto. The Metropolitan Museum of Art, New York, Gift of J. P. Morgan, 1923.

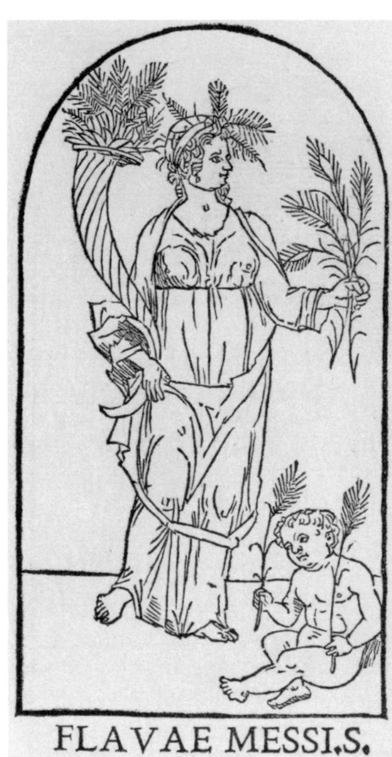

Hypnerotomachia. Jacopo's print also reflects certain works by Mantegna, for example, *The Circumcision and Presentation in the Temple*, now in the Uffizi.[18] Although this painting itself was almost certainly not accessible to Jacopo, it was copied in drawings; a drawing of the *Virgin with the Child* from this painting, in fact, is still extant.[19] Jacopo's composition as a whole seems to reflect Mantegna's *Presentation in the Temple* (Gemäldegalerie, Staatliche Museen, Berlin)[20] or a version of the same subject by Bellini (Galleria Querini-Stampalia, Venice).[21] Finally, the cornucopia standing on its small end and also perhaps the motif of the crown of leaves, here held by the child, seem to echo Mantegna's famous *Bacchanal with a Wine Vat* (B.XIII.240.19, Hind V.13.4).

Agostino Veneziano engraved a copy of *Sacrifice to Priapus* (B.XIV .252.336) in reverse, with considerable changes. – SB

1. The information here about Jacopo de' Barbari and the chronology of the prints is based on Jay A. Levenson, NGA, 341-81; idem, "Jacopo de' Barbari and Northern Art of the Early Sixteenth Century" (Ph.D diss., New York University, 1978). I am very grateful to Jay Levenson for generously lending me his copy of the dissertation. I am also grateful to Mark Zucker for letting me consult his unpublished manuscript about Jacopo.

2. See Levenson, NGA, 553-54; Juergen Schulz, "Jacopo de' Barbari's View of Venice: Map Making, City Views, and Moralized Geography Before the Year 1500," AB. 60 (1978): 425-74; David Chambers in London 1983, 392-93; Martin Kemp in Washington 1991, 253-55, no. 151.

3. This is suggested by Levenson, "Jacopo de' Barbari," 34-35; David Landau also, apparently independently, proposed that Barbari made a return trip to Venice (London 1983a, 306).

4. According to Levenson, "Jacopo de' Barbari," 46, François Brulliot was the first to identify the Master with the Caduceus as Jacopo de' Barbari (*Table Générale des Monogrammes, Chiffres, Lettres Initiales et Marques Figurées* [Munich, 1820], cols. 75-80, no. 80).

5. According to Levenson, "Jacopo de' Barbari," 45, n. 14, the information was reported by Jules Renouvier in a letter to Rudolph Weigel of February 20, 1854.

6. Levenson, NGA, 341, n. 1.

7. An inventory that lists eleven "fairly large," five medium-sized, and seven small plates was published by Jules Finot, *Inventaire sommaire des archives départmentales antérieures à 1790, Nord, Archives civiles*, ser. B (Lille, 1895), 8:212; reprinted in Levenson, "Jacopo de' Barbari," 366.

8. Levenson pointed out: "The bearded man wearing a hood has an appearance that is more priestly than royal, and the old woman at the right, who would represent Hannah in the *Presentation*, would be entirely out of place in an *Adoration*, which

requires Joseph to accompany the Virgin Mary. The schematic architecture, moreover, is more suggestive of the altar of the Temple than of the manger" (Levenson, "Jacopo de' Barbari," 255). The uncertainty concerning the subject, however, is evidence of the idiosyncratic iconography that is a hallmark of Jacopo's work.

9. David Landau (London 1983a, 307, no. P3) affirmed the attribution to Jacopo, but Hind expressed reservations and both Levenson (NGA, 341, n. 1) and Zucker, in his unpublished notes on Jacopo, rejected it. The fact that at 33.7 x 26 cm it is nearly twice the size of *Mars and Venus* (28.8 x 17.9 cm), the largest of the prints universally given to Jacopo, would also make it an anomaly in his oeuvre.

10. Levenson, "Jacopo de' Barbari," 174-208.

11. Hans Rupprich, ed., *Dürer, Schriftlicher Nachlass* (Berlin: Deutscher Verein für Kunstwissenschaft, 1956-69), 1:103; translation as in Levenson, NGA, 345.

12. Levenson (NGA, 345, n. 19) also wrote: "Actually, Jacopo's preserved oeuvre does not seem to contain a single figure constructed according to a scheme of proportions."

13. See Briquet, 770-71, for discussion of similar watermarks. See NGA, 356, 570; see Hind for other watermarks.

14. Anthony Radcliffe, "Two Early Romano-Mantuan Plaquettes," in *Italian Plaquettes*, ed. Allison Luchs, vol. 22 of *Studies in the History of Art* (Washington: National Gallery of Art, 1989), 93-103.

15. Francesco Colonna, *Hypnerotomachia Poliphili* (Venice 1499). Modern critical ed. (2 vols.) by Giovanni Pozzi and Lucia A. Ciapponi (Padua: Antenore, 1980). The *Sacrifice to Priapus* is on fol. m6 recto of the original and vol. 1, p. 189, of the 1980 edition.

16. Le Prince d'Essling, *Les livres à figures vénitiens* (Florence: Librairie Leo S. Olschki; Paris: Librairie Henri Leclerc, 1907), 1:220-27, no. 223; Max Sander, *Le livre à figures italien* (New York: G. E. Stechert and Co., 1941), 2:911, no. 5330.

17. For this painting see, most recently, David Bull and Joyce Plesters, *The Feast of the Gods, Conservation, Examination, and Interpretation*, vol. 40 of *Studies in the History of Art*, Monograph Series 2 (Washington: National Gallery of Art, 1990), with previous bibliography on p. 105; for Priapus in the Renaissance, see also Fritz Saxl, "Pagan Sacrifice in the Italian Renaissance," *JWarb.* 2 (1938-39): 346-67; Godelieve Denhaene, "Lambert Lombard relit le mythe de Priape," in Mauro Natale, ed., *Scritti di storia dell'arte in honore di Federico Zeri*, 2 vols. (Milan: Electa, 1984), 362-70; and Philippe Morel, "Priape à la Renaissance: Les guirlandes de Giovanni da Udine à la Farnésine," *Revue de l'Art* 69 (1985): 13-28.

18. Ronald Lightbown, *Andrea Mantegna* (Berkeley and Los Angeles: University of California Press, 1986), 413, no. 15.

19. See Ekserdjian in London 1992, 163, no. 18; Lightbown, *Andrea Mantegna*, 482-83, no. 181.

20. Lightbown, *Andrea Mantegna*, 404-05, no. 7.

21. See Giles Robertson, *Giovanni Bellini* (Oxford: Clarendon Press, 1968), 75-76.

Girolamo Mocetto

Murano ca. 1470-1531 Venice
after Andrea Mantegna (ca. 1430-1506)

28a. Judith Putting the Head of Holofernes into a Sack

ca. 1500.
Engraving on antique laid paper, 33.7 x 21.4 (sheet).
B. 1 i/ii; Hind 10 i/ii; Romano 22 i/ii; TIB 2505.001 i/ii.
Watermark: Cardinal's hat (cf. Briquet 3404).
Condition: Figures tinted with pale brown wash. Entire background added with brushwork reinforcing the outlines and occasionally extending into the figures, except for the areas between the maid's ankles and between her right foot and Judith's drapery, which are part of the original sheet.
Provenance: Albertina duplicate; Herschel V. Jones, Minneapolis? (1928); Tessie Jones, Newburgh, NJ (consigned to Knoedler, February 28, 1940); (purchased from M. Knoedler, New York, April 17, 1940, for $2,400).
Bequest of Herbert Greer French, 1943.164.
Exhibitions: Cincinnati 1941, no. 62, pl. 18; Detroit 1958, no. 45; Washington 1973, no. 251.

28b. Judith Putting the Head of Holofernes into a Sack

ca. 1500.
Engraving on antique laid paper, 33.5 x 21.6 cm (platemark).
B. 1 ii/ii; Hind 10 ii/ii; Romano no. 22 ii/ii; TIB 2505.001 ii/ii.

Watermark: Wheel with teeth (cf. Briquet 13244-13568).
Inscribed verso with pen and ink: *P. Mariette, 1698*; with pencil: *Mantegna inv. & sc.*
Condition: Trimmed to platemark. Brushwork strengthening grass and tree foliage, shading in background, figures' contours, drapery, and the sack and extending line of hills right.
Provenance: Pierre Mariette (Lugt 1788); Albertina duplicate; Herschel V. Jones, Minneapolis (1928); Tessie Jones, Newburgh, NJ (consigned to Knoedler, February 28, 1940); (purchased from M. Knoedler, New York, April 17, 1940, for $1,600).
Bequest of Herbert Greer French, 1943.165.
Exhibitions: Cincinnati 1941, no. 63.

Girolamo Mocetto, a painter and engraver, is more important as the latter than the former. His known paintings, few in number, are derivative in form and middling, at best, in quality.[1] Because of a misread document, for years scholars thought that Mocetto was as much as a full generation older than he really was. A recent reexamination of the document in question by Luigi Zecchin,[2] however, has established that Mocetto was not born in the 1450s, as supposed by Arthur Hind, Konrad Oberhuber, and others,[3] but probably about 1470. The misreading resulted from the fact that a document of 1458 is mentioned in a document of 1493 in which Girolamo is named; thus, it was erroneously assumed that he was alive by the earlier date. Girolamo's grandfather is known to have been married in 1445. If we can assume that his father was born within five years of that marriage, and that Girolamo was born when his father was twenty or a little older, Girolamo's birth would fall around 1470.[4] This revised chronology fits better with other information we have about Girolamo: that he married a Venetian woman in 1494, that none of his works seems to predate the 1490s, and that he made a will — leaving what he had to his son, Domenico — and seems to have died in 1531.[5]

Mocetto made seventeen engravings; the only datable ones, four plans and views of the town of Nola, were published in Ambrosius Leo, *De Nola Opusculum*, Venice, 1514. Of the others, one, *The Battle between the Israelites and the Amalekites*, is printed from three plates to fit side by side on three sheets for a total dimension of about 28 x 115 cm; two others are on two plates, and most of the rest are also sizable, so Mocetto's engraved work is more substantial than this restricted number suggests.[6]

Mocetto's style is looser and freer than that of any other Italian engraver of the time; Oberhuber pointed out that "he is one of the very few engravers active around 1500 for whom Dürer's prints seem to have meant little."[7] His style has an undisciplined and even, to a certain extent, naive quality that imparts to the prints an idiosyncratic charm. Mocetto's style varies little from one print to another, and although his engravings have been divided into groups according to the author of the design — Mantegna, Bellini, and Mocetto himself — this division is more a convenience than an indication of any really evident stylistic development.

Four of Mocetto's prints are after designs by Mantegna (for a biographical note on Mantegna, see cat. 17). As Zucker pointed out, *Judith Putting the Head of Holofernes into a Sack* and *St. John the Baptist* (Hind 9) were almost certainly engraved on opposite sides of the same plate; *Calumny of Apelles* (Hind 12) and *Metamorphosis of Amymone (Allegory of Mantua)* (Hind 13), on another.[8] All of these designs can be dated on stylistic grounds to the last decade or so of Mantegna's life (he died in 1506). Because of these four prints, it has been speculated that Mocetto spent some time in Mantua, and it is certainly possible that he did; the watermark on the Museum's impression of the first state of this print, usually dating in the first years of the sixteenth century, in fact, argues in favor of this thesis: it also occurs on early impressions of several other prints after Mantegna's designs presumed to have been made in Mantua.[9]

Judith was a Jewish heroine who risked her life to save her town – and, by extension, her people – from destruction. When Bethulia was under siege by the Assyrian general Holofernes, Judith, a beautiful young widow, left the city and went with her maid to the enemy camp, declaring that she had deserted her people and would help the Assyrians. Holofernes, dazzled by her beauty, allowed Judith to stay in his camp; after three days, he invited her to dine alone with him in his tent. He became very drunk, and when he had fallen asleep, Judith cut off his head with his own sword.

The theme of Judith was treated many times by Mantegna toward the latter part of his life. Two of his paintings and two designed by him for his funeral chapel, a beautiful drawing by his hand, showing Judith partially from the back, two additional compositions represented in prints, and the composition shown here bring to eight the known treatments of this subject by Mantegna.[10] All of these, except one of the two from the funerary chapel, depict the moment when Judith puts the severed head of Holofernes into a sack. This was the dramatic center of the story: the crucial deed had been accomplished, but its revelation was still to come. In the medieval tradition, Judith was an antetype of the Virgin; her triumph over Holofernes was seen to prefigure that of Mary over Satan. Judith personified Chastity and Humility and sometimes Justice; thus, this moment depicted by Mantegna symbolized at once the triumph of these virtues over their opposites, Lust, Pride, and Tyranny. For Mantegna the story resonated with many of the themes that preoccupied him toward the end of his life, all having to do with the struggle between virtue and evil.

The composition of the print by Mocetto is known in three nearly identical drawings (now in Chatsworth, Washington, and Rotterdam), none of them autograph but all presumed to derive from an original by Mantegna probably dating from the 1490s.[11] The print reverses the orientation of the drawings.

A very few impressions are known of the first state of this print, before a background was added. The sheet of paper as seen here is not all one but the result of an extraordinarily skillful combining of the original print, trimmed to or into the outlines of the figure group, with another piece of paper. A close examination of the outer lines shows that many had been cut off and thus had to be inked in by hand on the new piece of paper. Nonetheless, the print is definitely an example of the first state, as is proved by the lack of background showing in the area between Judith's right shoulder and the arc of drapery above and the right foot of the maid and Judith's dress. In the second state, Mocetto added a landscape background, presumably of his own invention, to Mantegna's original design, probably to give the composition a more finished look.

The same composition is represented in another print of the sixteenth century. Although Bartsch (under the Mocetto print and also XV.13.9) and Hind called this later print a copy of the Mocetto, it seems more likely to be a version derived from Mantegna's design independently, because some details differ and it is significantly smaller. The composition was also reproduced in a plaquette by Andrea Riccio.[12] – SB

1. Serena Romano, in *Ritratto di fanciullo di Girolamo Mocetto* (Modena: Edizioni Panini, 1985), 105-06, lists ten paintings to be definitively attributed to Mocetto.

2. Luigi Zecchin, "I Mozetta, vetrai muranesi del Quattrocento," *Rivista della Stazione Sperimentale del vetro* (1978): 111-15.

3. Hind V:159, NGA, 382; David Landau in London 1983a, 310; TIB 25 (*Commentary*): 39.

4. See Romano, *Ritratto*, 25, for a full discussion of the misunderstanding.

5. Konrad Oberhuber, in fact, found the early date troubling, writing that it seems to be "astonishingly early for an artist who lived until 1531, and whose known works do

not seem to be datable before the 1490s" (NGA, 382, n. 1).

6. Hind lists twenty-two subjects, giving each plate of the multiplate prints a separate number (Hind V:159-71). Mark J. Zucker, in TIB 2505.004, doubted his no. 2, *The Coronation of the Virgin*, and I think it is by Giovanni Antonio da Brescia: its style is less self-assertive than Mocetto's, more regular and unexciting as Giovanni Antonio's tends to be; further, its small dimensions, 11.0 x 13.7 cm, are completely out of place among Mocetto's large plates.

7. NGA, 383.

8. Zucker, TIB 2505.001, 008, 015, 016.

9. See London 1992, appendix II, 471-84, watermark no. 3.

10. See London 1992, 403-05, no. 129; 411-13, no. 133; 435-44, nos. 140-144.

11. See Ekserdjian in London 1992, 441-42, no. 143.

12. Leo Planiscig, *Andrea Riccio* (Vienna: Anton Schroll and Co., 1927), 436, 490, fig. 521.

Giovanni Antonio da Brescia

North Italian active ca. 1495-ca. 1520
after Andrea Mantegna (ca. 1430-1506)

29. Triumphs of Caesar: The Elephants ca. 1500

Engraving on antique laid paper, 27.6 x 26.1 cm (sheet).
B. 8 (and 12, copy); Hind V.23.14a.
Watermark: Orb and cross (cf. Briquet 3057-68).
Condition: Abrasion through elephant's belly covered with gray pigment.
Provenance: (Purchased from M. Knoedler, New York, March 1, 1930, for $850).
Bequest of Herbert Greer French, 1943.98.

Giovanni Antonio da Brescia was a prolific engraver working at the end of the fifteenth and during the first two decades of the sixteenth century. Recent research by David Landau and myself has shown that this engraver used two different monograms.[1] Early in his career he used "ZA" on twenty prints; but at a certain point, in or around 1507, he began using a Latinized and more complete monogram, "IO. AN. BX," for "Ioannes Antonius Brixianus." This monogram is seen on twenty-six of Giovanni Antonio's later images.

Our research into the wealth of anonymous prints reproducing designs by Andrea Mantegna increasingly revealed an extraordinary similarity in style between what had been thought to be the work of two separate engravers: the one who signed "ZA," whose name was thought to be Zoan Andrea, and the one who signed many prints in the abbreviated Latinized form given above. Since a few works were signed in a fuller form, the name of this engraver, Giovanni Antonio da Brescia, was never in doubt. A study of watermarks on the papers on which all these engravings were printed also revealed that many engravings attributed to these two artists were printed on the same papers (many fine impressions, in fact, were printed on paper with the orb and cross watermark seen on the Museum's print[2]). Finally, we realized that an engraving plate monogrammed "ZA" had been reused for an image with the Latinized monogram.

The practice of burnishing out an image on an engraved plate in order to reuse it was probably more common in the late fifteenth and early sixteenth century than is now realized, since copper was expensive. Giovanni Antonio, however, seems to have burnished out his images less carefully than most engravers, and in several instances lines from one image, imperfectly erased, are visible in subsequent ones. That the feet of Judith in Giovanni Antonio's *Judith with the Head of Holofernes*, monogrammed "ZA" (Hind V.63.5, as Zoan Andrea), are still visible in *Venus, after the Antique*, monogrammed "IO. AN. BRIXIAS." (Hind V.41.14, as Giovanni Antonio da Brescia) (figs. 29-1 and 2), when added to the affinity of style and similarities of watermarks discussed above, is decisive evidence that the letters

Figure 29-1. Giovanni Antonio da Brescia, *Judith with the Head of Holofernes* (detail), ca. 1506-07, engraving. British Museum, London.

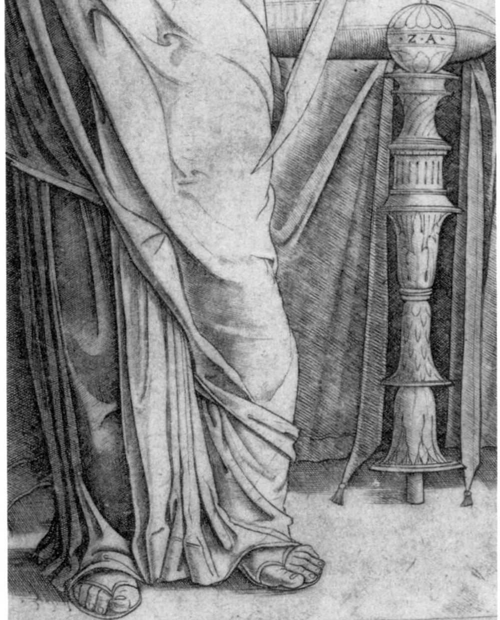

Figure 29-2. Giovanni Antonio da Brescia, *Venus* (detail), ca. 1510, engraving. British Museum, London.

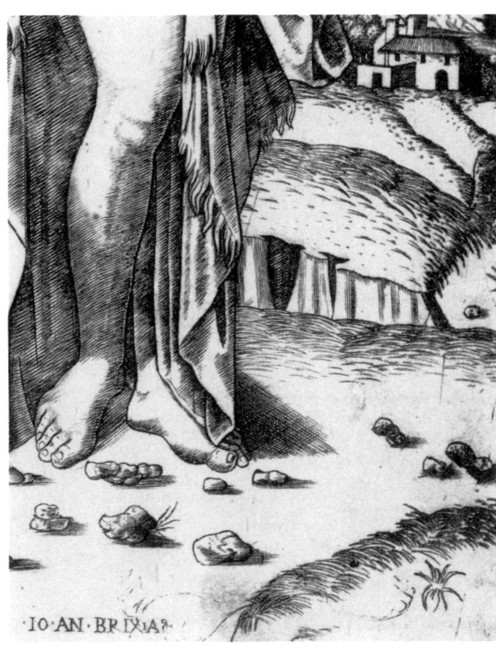

ZA stood for Zovanni (or Zoan) Antonio, not Zoan Andrea (the soft G being pronounced as a Z in north Italian dialect). Thus, the prints bearing these two monograms and also the unmonogrammed ones that for centuries have been associated on stylistic grounds with one or the other of these two engravers are all by Giovanni Antonio. Zoan Andrea, a painter working in Mantua during the 1470s, was not an engraver at all. At least 150 prints are to be attributed to Giovanni Antonio; a list as complete as possible will be published in the near future by this author.

This major realignment of the engravings, however, has still provided no solid biographical information about the engraver; the prints themselves provide all the facts that are known. As set forth in the 1992 *Andrea Mantegna* catalogue, much of his oeuvre consists of copies of other prints;[3] among the earliest are engravings after designs by Mantegna, but Giovanni Antonio also copied prints by Dürer and by Marcantonio Raimondi. His earliest dated engravings are his copy of Dürer's *Virgin and Child on a Grassy Bank* (H. *Ger.* 31) and an *Ornament Panel*, both monogrammed "ZA" and dated 1505 (Hind v.69.24, 26); the latest datable one is the attributed *Portrait of the Emperor Charles V*, which cannot have been made earlier than 1519 (the year Charles was elected Holy Roman Emperor). Giovanni Antonio is assumed to have gone to Rome: he engraved an image of the Laocoon, unearthed there in 1506, and a newly excavated statue of Venus (the print on which the feet from the earlier *Judith* are still visible); he also copied at least seven prints by Marcantonio, one of which is dated 1516.

The Elephants reproduces a drawing by Andrea Mantegna (cat. 17), court artist for the ruling Gonzaga family in Mantua. Mantegna's drawing was made in preparation for the major commission of his later life: nine large canvases roughly nine by nine feet illustrating the *Triumphs of Caesar*, now in the British royal collection. All his life Mantegna was fascinated by classical antiquity, and this series of paintings gave him the opportunity to exercise his prodigious inventive powers to recreate a quintessential Roman manifestation, the triumphal procession. When these paintings were begun and finished is not certain, although some were in existence by 1486, and Mantegna may have worked on them into the sixteenth century.[4]

The print is close to the final design for the fifth of Mantegna's nine canvases, *Trumpeters, Youths Leading Oxen, Elephants with Attendants*, although differences from the final design make it clear that this and the six other engravings related to the *Triumphs* (which, however, show only three different subjects in all) were derived from preliminary drawings, not the finished paintings. A passage from Suetonius, quoted in a fifteenth-century work by Flavio Biondo, *Roma Triumphans*, seems to have been Mantegna's chief textual source. It states that Caesar "ascended the Capitol by the light of forty elephants on the right and the left bearing lamps,"[5] although the lamps themselves are more products of Mantegna's fancy than convincing archeological recreations.

The seven engravings related to *Triumphs* are by three different hands. Two, in my opinion, are by the same hand as cats. 17a, b; three, of which two are copies of the preceding prints, are by Giovanni Antonio; and David Landau and I have tentatively attributed the other two to the young Giulio Campagnola.[6] Giovanni Antonio's engraving of *The Elephants* does not follow a known earlier version, but because his other two prints of *Triumphs* subjects are such close copies of earlier ones, it seems likely that for this image, too, an earlier version existed, of which no impression is known to survive. Similarly, the other print by Giovanni Antonio in this exhibition (cat. 36) may also be a copy of an earlier print no longer known to us. – SB

1. See Boorsch in London 1992, 56-66.

2. See London 1992, appendix II, 471-84, watermark 22.

3. See Boorsch in London 1992, 60.

4. See Hope in London 1992, 350-72; and Andrew Martindale, *The Triumphs of Caesar* (London: Harvey Miller, 1979), passim.

5. Quoted by Hope in London 1992, 365.

6. See Boorsch in London 1992, nos. 117, 118, 120, 121, 123, 126, 127; for Giulio Campagnola, see Hind v:189-205; Oberhuber in NGA, 390-413; Mark Zucker, TIB 25 (*Commentary*):463-95.

Alart du Hameel

's-Hertogenbosch? 1450/78-1506 Antwerp

30. Gothic Baldacchin

Engraving on antique laid paper, 38.9 x 12.7 cm (platemark);
40.6 x 25.6 cm (sheet).
B. 6; Lehrs 10.
Watermark: Hand with flower (cf. Lehrs 16).
Signed in plate upper center:
Condition: Ink and watercolor.
Provenance: (Alfred Strölin, Lausanne, consigned to Knoedler, May
25, 1932); (purchased from M. Knoedler, New York, May 26, 1932,
for $1,750).
Bequest of Herbert Greer French, 1943.136.
Exhibitions: Cincinnati 1934, no. 25; Cincinnati 1941, no. 33.

Alart du Hameel is the only fifteenth-century Netherlandish engraver
whose name and activity are documented. The date and place of his
birth are unknown, but it seems probable that he was born a native
of 's-Hertogenbosch about 1450. Hameel was a practicing architect
there from 1478 to 1494 without having applied for naturalized
citizenship – a legal requirement for those born elsewhere. He often
inscribed the word *bosche* on his engraving plates, a fact that led his
earliest catalogers and at least one sixteenth-century copyist to the
erroneous conclusion that his engravings were copies after lost
works by his more famous contemporary, Hieronymus Bosch. Adam
Bartsch first realized that *bosche* was a geographic reference rather
than a signature, noting correctly that it appears even on plates
having nothing in common with Bosch's style and iconography
(B. VI:345).[1]

Alart du Hameel is first mentioned in 1478 as the architect of the
Church of Saint Jan in 's-Hertogenbosch.[2] Another document from
1478 mentions the reception of Alart, his sister Nicolaä, and his
apprentice Jan Heyns as honorary members of the socially exclusive
Brotherhood of Our Lady – the pious and charitable organization
into which Hieronymus Bosch was later initiated (1486). Alart's
membership *honoris causa* (because of services performed for Our
Lady) may mean that he designed the Lady Chapel on the northeast
side of Saint Jan's, the most imposing Gothic-style stone structure in
the northern Netherlands.

The small tombstone of Alart's first wife, Margriet van
Auweninghen (d. 1484), can still be seen in the south aisle of Saint
Jan's. After her death, Alart married Gosina, an illegitimate daughter
of Jan Heim, the high sheriff of 's-Hertogenbosch. Alart's sister
Nicolaä married his apprentice Jan Heyns, who later succeeded him
as architect.

From 1485 to 1493, Alart was also consultant to the builders of
the Church (now Cathedral) of Our Lady in Antwerp. He designed a
sacrament tower (1485-87), completed by the sculptor Thomas Best,
and was consultant for an altar (1493) and the bell tower
finial (1500).

Despite numerous trips to Antwerp to fulfill his architectural
duties, Alart continued to maintain his residence in 's-Hertogenbosch and to be active in projects for Saint Jan's until the end of 1494
or beginning of 1495. At this time he submitted his formal
resignation to accept positions as chief mason to the city of Louvain
and chief architect of its collegiate Church of Saint Peter (1497), for
which he designed the portico of the south transept. He was also
charged with the installation of the sculptures on the facade of an
elegant new city hall and with furnishing the castle known as the Hof
van Camerijk for the state visit of Maximilian and his son, Philip the
Handsome (1499). He also remodeled Louvain's Norbertine Abbey

(1502) and was commissioned to make an engraved portrait of Philip
the Handsome (1504), which has not survived.

In 1502 Alart resigned his municipal office in Louvain to become a
naturalized citizen of Antwerp, a center of international commerce
and finance whose rising fortunes were a great attraction for artists
in the early sixteenth century.

On December 12, 1505, Alart made his will. He requested burial in
the Lady Chapel of Saint Walpurga's Church in Antwerp (destroyed
1843) and left 1½ silver marks to his wife and seventy-five Rhenish
gulden (gold) to a son, Sebastian. Alart probably died in 1506: a
document dated January 27, 1507, provides for a memorial Mass to
be said at Saint Jan's for "the late" Master Alart, a Mass endowed by
Jan Heyns, executor of Alart's will.

Alart's twelve engravings, some signed simply "bosche" and
others "HAMEEL" or "Alart du Hameel" and many also inscribed
with his mason's hallmark, show a wide stylistic range as well as an
unusual variety of subject matter. His most popular print, a large
Last Judgment (Lehrs 2), and *The War Elephant* (Lehrs 7) are
reminiscent of the panoramic settings and schematic figures of
Hieronymus Bosch and may perhaps have been inspired by two
Bosch paintings of these subjects, now lost, which were in the
collection of Philip the Handsome. Others, such as the two unique
engravings *The Brazen Serpent* in Vienna (Lehrs 1) and *The Apostle
Peter* in Munich (Lehrs 3), may have been inspired by, or intended as
designs for, works of sculpture. Such compact narrative compositions
as *The Brazen Serpent* and *The Vision of Constantine* (Lehrs 5) recall
the style of the greatest Dutch wood sculptor of the late fifteenth
century, Adriaen van Wesel. Van Wesel had done work for the Lady
Chapel in Saint Jan's, 's-Hertogenbosch. One of Alart's engravings
depicts a monstrance, perhaps related to the one he designed for
Saint Jan's in 1484-85. Its influence can be seen in a monstrance from
the Church of Our Lady of the Immaculate Conception in Oss. The
standing St. Peter, depicted on a console, is reminiscent of stone
carving and is probably associated with the commission for the
unfinished portico of Saint Peter's Church in Louvain.

The Museum's impression of *Gothic Baldacchin* is the finest of the
four now known. In an autograph letter from 1932, Max Lehrs, then
director of the Dresden Kupferstich-Kabinett and author of the
definitive catalogue of fifteenth-century Northern European
engravings, states:

> This important engraving belongs to the exceedingly scarce work
> of the famous Dutch architect. It is of unusually fine conservation
> and has – as the only impression – a paper margin of more than a
> hand's width. The watermark of the large hand with a flower is
> also found in the more or less cut down impressions in London
> and Vienna. Also the third known impression at Dresden is very
> much cut down.

It is not known whether the baldachin was designed for Saint Jan's
Church in 's-Hertogenbosch or whether it formed a stage in the
development of the sacrament tower that Alart had designed for the
Church of Our Lady in Antwerp. The inclusion of a partial ground
plan (upper right) suggests that it refers to a freestanding structure,
such as a sacrament tower, rather than to a baldachin for the portico
of Saint Peter's, Louvain. – JH

1. For other examples of Alart's work, see Jane C. Hutchison in TIB 9 (Plates), 338-43
and (*Commentary*), pt. 2, 231-51.

2. C. J. A. C. Peeters, *De Sint Janskathedraal te 's-Hertogenbosch* (The Hague:
Staatsuitgeverij, 1985), passim. Peeters' work supercedes all previous information
concerning Alart's life. The author has shown that Alart must have been the chief
architect, not a subordinate of Gerard Symons, as previously supposed. (Symons was
merely a witness to the contract, not one of the parties involved.) See also A. M.
Koldewij, ed., 's-Hertogenbosch 1990.

Master MZ (Mattaus Zaisinger?)

German active ca. 1500

31. The Embrace 1503.

Engraving on antique laid paper, 15.5 x 11.7 cm (platemark).
B.VI.378.15; Lehrs 16.
Monogrammed on tablet lower right: *mz* (in reverse).
Provenance: Endris (Lugt 812); Friedrich Kalle (Lugt 1021); Julian
Marshall (Lugt 1494); Marseille Holloway (Lugt 1875); Franz von
Hagens; (his sale C.G. Boerner, Leipzig, May 2-3, 1927, no. 557, to
M.A. McDonald, New York, for RM 2,200); (purchased from M.
Knoedler, New York, April 1, 1930, for $1,375).
Bequest of Herbert Greer French, 1943.101.

Master MZ is the name given to the enigmatic Bavarian engraver
who signed his plates with the initials MZ. Master MZ's earliest
engraving, *St. Sebastian* (Lehrs 6), was influenced by one of Martin
Schongauer's prints. However, soon after its completion, probably in
the mid-1490s, he seems to have discovered Dürer's early work.
Master MZ's handling of both indoor and outdoor lighting is the
most sophisticated prior to Dürer's own. He was one of the first of
many artists influenced by Dürer, who opened a workshop in
Nuremberg, in nearby Franconia, late in 1495.

Sixteen of the twenty-two known engravings by Master MZ were
identified and assembled by the early seventeenth-century
Nuremberg collector of Dürer's work, Paul Behaim. Behaim's
handwritten inventory, dated 1618, is now in the Kupferstichkabinett, Berlin.[1] Without elaborating his reasons or identifying the
location of the artist's workshop, Behaim called the artist Matheus
Zingel or Zaszinger. The art historian Joachim von Sandrart
(1606-88), founder of the Nuremberg Academy, included the
engraver in his collection of biographies of famous German artists
(*Der Teutsche Academie der edlen Bau-, Bild-, und Mahlerey-
Künste*, Nuremberg, 1675). Sandrart interpreted the monogram as
standing for Martin Zink, Zatzinger, or Zasinger and identified this
engraver as a favorite with Nuremberg collectors.[2]

Documents relating to a Matthaus Zaisinger, or Zaysinger, have
recently been discovered in Munich, where Zaisinger was recorded
as having been a printer (1505), a goldsmith (1498, 1508), and an
official of the ducal mint (1520 to ca. 1555). Johann Michael Fritz
demonstrates that the documents, some of which are dated from the
1570s, may refer to two different individuals, father and son, thus
explaining the master's unusual longevity.[3]

Many scholars believe that specific scenes from the court of the
Bavarian Duke Albrecht IV and his wife, Kunigunde of Austria, can
be identified in two of Master MZ's most popular engravings. The
interior setting for *The Grand Ball* (Lehrs 17), which survives in at
least seventy impressions – twenty of them on early papers – was
thought by Friedrich Hofmann to represent the *Neuveste* (the New
Fortress, no longer extant) in Munich.[4] Its pendant, *The Tournament*
(Lehrs 18), of which fifty impressions are known – fifteen of them
early impressions – bears a minuscule Bavarian coat of arms. Dated
1500, it is the earliest-known print representing a tournament.

Master MZ's unusually light and sketchy manner of working the
burin; his truly extraordinary handling of light, shade, and aerial
perspective; his unerring sense of court fashion; and his powerful
black chalk drawings led Friedrich Winkler[5] and Max Lehrs[6] to
conclude that this artist initially trained as a painter rather than as a
goldsmith, a line of thought most recently explored, with mixed
results, by Miklós Moyzer.[7] For this and other reasons, it seems
prudent to retain the monogram MZ as the artist's designation.

The Embrace is one of Master MZ's most original and
provocative compositions. The handling of indoor lighting here is
the most subtle prior to Dürer's master engraving of 1514, *St. Jerome
in His Study* (cat. 48). MZ's theme, however, is one of worldly – and
quite possibly adulterous – love. The rich furnishings of the
chamber, with its elegantly carved table, window canopy, convex
mirror, and *Lüsterweibchen* (chandelier with female torso and stag
antlers), together with the outdoor clothing worn by the lovers and
the open landscape seen through the window, give the impression
that the setting may be a nobleman's hunting lodge or *Lusthauschen*
(summer house). Indeed, the juxtaposition of the embracing lovers
and the stag's antlers, a well-known symbol of cuckoldry, would
seem to indicate that an illicit tryst is being depicted. The scene has
recently been interpreted as an allegory of transitoriness,[8] a theme
that fits well with the known use of the convex mirror as a *vanitas*
motif in the early sixteenth century. In perceiving something furtive
about the assignation, Charles Talbot calls attention to the curious
lack of warmth in the woman's facial expression and in an embrace
that oddly fails to disturb the rippling folds of the man's cape.[9]

As Dürer also realized, the graphic arts offered artists a far greater
opportunity to experiment with subject matter than was the case
with paintings. Most paintings were still commissioned and favored
depictions of religious themes. The sale of prints at fairs and other
public occasions provided an outlet for worldly subjects as well as
for scenes from mythology and modern literature. A subject depicted
in contemporary dress that could be appreciated on several levels, as
is true of *The Embrace*, would be guaranteed a wide audience.

Craig Harbison calls attention to the underlying theme of
sexuality in Jan van Eyck's famous double portrait of Giovanni
Arnolfini and his bride (1434).[10] Master MZ's engraving of an
embracing couple, no longer identifiable as individuals, could have
had a similar appeal among the wider audience to which printmakers
addressed their work. This audience had been exposed to engravings
and woodcuts portraying themes of erotic love and the power of
women well before the end of the fifteenth century.

Of the more than thirty known impressions of *The Embrace*, only
a few are as fine as the Museum's. Both an early and a complete
impression, this engraving still has the three-dimensional stone
threshold that has sometimes in other impressions been trimmed
away from the foreground. (Other prime impressions are in
museums in Braunschweig, Coburg, Dresden, Copenhagen, London,
Paris, and Pavia.)

None of the best early impressions has a watermark. It seems
clear, from the plate wear evident in many of the others and from the
late papers on which they were printed, that a substantial demand
for the print survived the death of this artist and that the plate was
printed posthumously. The rear view of the man in Master MZ's
engraving was used as a model by an unknown early sixteenth-
century Bavarian artist for a figure in a painting of the Crucifixion
now in the Hungarian National Museum in Bucharest.[11] – JH

1. Berlin Kupferstichkabinett, ms. 79C.32.
2. A. R. Peltzer, ed., *Joachim von Sandrart's Academie der Bau-, Bild-, und Mahlerey-
Künste von 1675. Leben der beruhmten Maler. Bildhauer und Baumeister* (Munich: G.
Hirth's Verlag, 1925; reprint, Westmead, Farnborough, Hants. U.K.: Gregg
International Publishers, 1971), 60, 317.
3. See Johann Michael Fritz, *Gestochene Bilder, Gravierungen auf deutschen
Goldschmiedearbeiten der Spätgotik* (Cologne and Graz, 1966); Max Frankenberger,
Die altmünchner Goldschmiede und ihre Kunst (Munich, 1912).
4. Friedrich Hofmann, "Der gotische Tanzsaal in der Neuveste," in *Beiträge zur
Geschichte der deutschen Kunst. I: Oberdeutsche Kunst der Spätgotik und
Reformationszeit*, ed., E. Buchner and E. Feuchtmayr (Augsburg, 1924), 1:120ff.
5. Friedrich Winkler, *JprK.* 40 (1939): 30.
6. Max Lehrs, "Der Meister MZ," PCQ. 16 (1929): 237; Lehrs VIII, 330-78.
7. Miklós Moyzer, "Um Meister MZ," *Acta Historiae Artium* 21, no. 3/4 (1975):
371-428. For further discussion, see Jane C. Hutchison in TIB 9 (*Commentary*), pt. 2,
301-27.

8. F. Bächtiger, *Vanitas Schicksalsdeutung in der deutschen Renaissancegraphik* (Munich and Zurich, 1970), 72. See also Anthony F. Janson, "The Convex Mirror as Vanitas Symbol," *Source* 4, no. 2/3, (1985): 51ff.

9. Christiane Andersson and Charles Talbot, eds., Detroit 1983, 316, no. 178.

10. Craig Harbison, "Sexuality and Social Standing in Jan van Eyck's Arnolfini Double Portrait," *Renaissance Quarterly* 43, no. 2 (Summer 1990) 249-91.

11. See Maria Matache, *Catalogue of the Universal Art Gallery* (Bucharest, 1974), 77.

Marcantonio Raimondi

Bologna ca. 1480/82-by 1534 Bologna

32. The Nativity ca. 1503-04.

Engraving on antique laid paper, 37.4 x 27.2 cm (platemark).
B.16; Delaborde 7 ii/ii.
Watermark: LLAR.
Monogrammed on cushion under Christ Child's head: MAF.
Condition: Trimmed to platemark. Added brushwork in figures.
Provenance: (Purchased from M. Knoedler, New York, November 21, 1938, for $325).
Bequest of Herbert Greer French, 1943.153.
Exhibitions: Cincinnati 1941, no. 70.

Although Marcantonio Raimondi is best known for his prints after drawings by Raphael (1483-1520), his early work and a number of late prints represent inventions of other artists. Marcantonio was born between 1480 and 1482, probably in the small town of Argine near Bologna, into a family documented in the region as far back as the fourteenth century. He trained with the painter, goldsmith, and niellist Francesco Francia, and ties between the two were so close that he was sometimes called Marcantonio Francia. Marcantonio, however, never seems to have made paintings; one document calls him *aurifex* (goldsmith), but no work by him other than drawings or prints is known.[1]

Late in 1506 both Dürer and Michelangelo were in Bologna, and it is possible that Marcantonio met them both. Around this time he began copying some of Dürer's woodcuts from the series *Life of the Virgin*, begun in 1502. Marcantonio made seventeen engraved copies of the series of twenty; since two of the three that he did not copy are dated 1510, he probably had stopped making these copies before that date. Marzia Faietti has recently suggested that Marcantonio was in Venice between 1507 and 1508 rather than in 1506, as had been thought, and that some or possibly all of these copies were made there.[2]

Marcantonio then set out for Rome, stopping in Florence, probably in 1509.[3] Once in Rome, he began reproducing compositions by Raphael, making several dozen before the latter artist died. He set up a workshop and seems to have been associated with two engravers, Marco Dente and Agostino Veneziano, who may have begun as his apprentices. For nearly four centuries, until the technology of photography made reproductive engraving obsolete, the engravings by Marcantonio and his workshop were the medium by which most people knew Raphael's works.

Luck was not with Marcantonio after Raphael's death, however. Late in 1524, he began engraving twenty erotic subjects drawn by Raphael's artistic heir, Giulio Romano.[4] Giulio had gone to Mantua earlier that same year, so it was Marcantonio who was jailed by order of Pope Clement VII for the propagation of pornography. He was soon released for this offense but was ruined during the Sack of Rome in 1527. He returned to Bologna; since he is referred to in the past tense in a work of Pietro Aretino of 1534, it is assumed he had died by that date.

The Nativity, although not dated, can be seen on stylistic grounds to be one of Marcantonio's earliest engravings.[5] He had not yet achieved the technical means of creating a convincing image by black lines alone. Although in certain areas, such as the shading on the thighs of the kneeling shepherd, he has developed a systematic method for conveying form, in the body of the child and in many of the landscape elements, the strokes seem haphazard and ineffective. At this early stage, Marcantonio's compositions tend to have an additive, pastichelike quality, apparent in the figures in *The Nativity*; a certain naïveté is also evident in the manner in which a tree on the hill in the background is bent to fit under the arch.

Considering Marcantonio's early relationship with Francia, it is no surprise that several elements in *The Nativity* derive from the older artist's work; Marcantonio, however, recombined his sources into new configurations rather than taking over a composition wholesale. The Virgin, the pose of the child, and architectural elements in the background are similar to those in two paintings by Francia, *The Adoration of the Child* and *Nativity, Infancy, and Passion of Christ*, both in the Pinacoteca Nazionale, Bologna;[6] the young standing shepherd is also similar to a figure in the latter painting. The kneeling shepherd at the left may derive from an antique source, a freestanding statue or a sarcophagus relief, known to Marcantonio in actuality or through a drawing. Although no prototype has been identified for them, Joseph in his turban and the shepherd in the background also appear to have been borrowed rather than invented for this composition.

This plate is probably the largest Marcantonio had made up to this time. As it was common practice to engrave two sides of the same plate, it is conceivable that *Allegory of Human Life* of about the same date (B.XIV.274.360)[7] was engraved on the other side. The Museum's impression is the second state of the engraving; the only difference is the addition of a halo around the head of the Virgin (but not the heads of the child and Joseph, as Delaborde mistakenly wrote). – SB

1. The most recent concise biography of Marcantonio is that of Corinna Giudici in Bologna 1988, 355-57.

2. Marzia Faietti in Bologna 1988, 150-54, no. 31.

3. Giudici, Bologna 1988, 356.

4. Lynne Lawner, *I Modi, The Sixteen Pleasures: An Erotic Album of the Italian Renaissance. Guilio Romano, Marcantonio Raimondi, Pietro Aretino and Count Jean-Frederic-Maximilien de Waldeck* (Evanston: Northwestern University Press, 1988).

5. For this print, see Bologna 1988, 110-12, no. 11; Lawrence 1981, 52-53, no. 1.

6. See Bologna 1988, 110, 112; Andrea Emiliani et al., eds., *La Pinacoteca Nazionale di Bologna* (Bologna: Cappelli editore, 1967), figs. 102-103.

7. Delaborde 160; Bologna 1988, 104-105, no. 8.

Albrecht Dürer

Nuremberg 1471-1528 Nuremberg

33. Adam and Eve 1504.

Engraving on antique laid paper, 24.5 x 19.1 cm (platemark).
B. 1; Meder 1-2c; Dodgson 39 iv/v; Panofsky 108; H. *Ger.* 1 iv/v; TIB 1001.001 S2.
Watermark: Bull's head (Meder 62).
Inscribed: ALBERT/DVRER/NORICVS/FACIEBAT/AD·1504 (Albrecht Dürer of Nuremberg made [this]. (A.D. stands for both Anno Domini [In the year of our Lord] and Albrecht Dürer).
Condition: Trimmed to platemark.
Provenance: William Esdaille (Lugt 2617); G. Jones, London (1840); Thomas Miller Whitehead (Lugt 2449); Sotheby, London (1848); (purchased from F.H. Bresler, Milwaukee, September 28, 1929, for $11,000).
Bequest of Herbert Greer French, 1943.193.

Exhibitions: Cincinnati 1930, (no. 20); Cincinnati 1934, no. 38; Cincinnati 1941, no. 103.

When Albrecht Dürer "engraved" his full name in Latin on the *cartello* hanging from a tree in his *Adam and Eve*, he was paying tribute to Pollaiuolo and at the same time vying with him. Some fifteen years earlier, the Italian Renaissance artist had similarly signed a cartello in his masterpiece, the *Battle of the Nudes* (cat. 16). Like Pollaiuolo, Dürer highlighted his nudes by setting them against a dark foil – here a densely forested paradise. Dürer likewise consulted classical prototypes: Adam is based upon a classical Apollo; Eve, upon a classical Venus. In his construction of the first couple's proportions, in his subtle refinements of their rippling muscles and supple flesh, in his presentation of their balanced contrapposto poses, and in his unmatched skill with the burin, Dürer indeed outdid his Florentine predecessor.[1] *Adam and Eve* was Dürer's most complex and accomplished engraving to date, the culmination of several years' study of the human figure.[2]

Ever since his exposure to Italian Renaissance art during a trip to Italy (1494-95), Dürer had experimented with the nude, seeking a canon of ideal human proportions. His figures from this early period already reflect the influence of Renaissance artists such as Pollaiuolo and Mantegna. After Jacopo de' Barbari, the Renaissance artist from Venice who resided in Nuremberg in 1500, failed to provide Dürer with such a canon, he turned to Vitruvius, the classical authority on the matter.

By 1500 Dürer's theoretical studies of proportion and his attempts at mathematically constructing the human body were on the increase. His development of the male nude, leading up to the Adam in this 1504 engraving, can be traced through his drawings, particularly those known as "the Apollo group." Eve likewise is the product of Dürer's analysis of female proportions, which can be seen in his drawings and in the engraved *Nemesis* from circa 1502, (fig. 52-2).[3] In many instances, Dürer first geometrically constructed the proportions of a figure on one side of a sheet of paper, then traced the resulting contours onto the verso. The inspiration guiding his proportions was the classical figure – the *Apollo Belvedere* for his Adam, the Medici *Venus* for his Eve.

While Dürer's emulation of classical figures and his search for a theoretical-mathematical foundation for their proportions might have been typical for an Italian Renaissance artist, they were exceptional for a German artist of his day. Nuremberg was, however, fast becoming a major intellectual center, and Dürer's intellectual pursuits were nurtured by his humanist friends, most particularly Hartmann Schedel, Sebald Schreyer, Willibald Pirckheimer, and the arch-humanist Conrad Celtis.[4] These men sought to revive classical learning in Germany. They knew classical languages and between them amassed outstanding libraries and classical coin collections. Dürer collaborated with these friends on iconographic projects and illustrated their publications. It was through them that Dürer increased his knowledge of the classical world, medieval philosophy, and contemporary Florentine Neoplatonic thought, knowledge that informs his work from this period of the Munich *Self-Portrait* (1500) and the *Nemesis*.[5] Celtis wrote four epigrams in 1500 justly honoring Dürer not as a craftsman but an artist-savant. Besides comparing him to the ancients, Phidias and Apelles, and finding him superior to Italian artists, Celtis wittingly proclaimed Dürer the new *Albertus Magnus* (Albert the Great). What the thirteenth-century German Albertus Magnus had done for philosophy, Albrecht Dürer, artist, would do for painting and "symmetry" (art based on harmony and mathematical proportion).[6]

Adam and Eve was one of the first prints in which Dürer combined his studies of classically inspired male and female nudes into a single composition. In his most complete extant preparatory drawing for this engraving, the artist literally pasted together two sheets of single figures with backing strips so that Adam and Eve might interrelate, though they do not actually touch (fig. 33-1).[7] In the drawing Dürer had not yet arrived at his final interpretation of the subject. Adam and Eve each hold a forbidden fruit – here a fig[8] – Adam extending his to Eve as if the Fall were already a *fait accompli*.

Dürer's engraved solution, by contrast, depicts Adam and Eve *before* the actual Fall. In this context, Dürer's classical figures match and even amplify the meaning of the Christian theme: their masculine and feminine beauty visually embodies the state of perfection that Adam and Eve shared before their corruption. To a late medieval audience fixated on Adam and Eve's culpability for bringing death into the world, this image of the first couple imbued with the elixir of life must have seemed novel. Here, still unaware of their nakedness, the two turn their sensuous torsos unashamedly toward the viewer, enabling Dürer to chart the undulations of their muscles and the texture of their flesh with hairline hatchings that dissolve under exposure to light. Adam and Eve's balanced and complementary contrapposto poses – the product of the two studies Dürer initially juxtaposed in his preparatory drawing – heighten the suggestion of the state of perfect equilibrium they enjoyed in paradise. Dürer underscores this equilibrium through the inclusion of four animals in his composition. Each represents one of the four humors, or bodily fluids, whose excess, according to a long-held belief, controlled human disposition. The four humors were in perfect balance before the Fall in Adam and Eve; afterward that equilibrium gave way to predominance of one: to melancholy, represented in the engraving by the gloomy elk; to phlegm, symbolized here by the sluggish ox; to sanguinity, epitomized by the sensuous rabbit; or to choler, as evidenced by the cruel cat.[9]

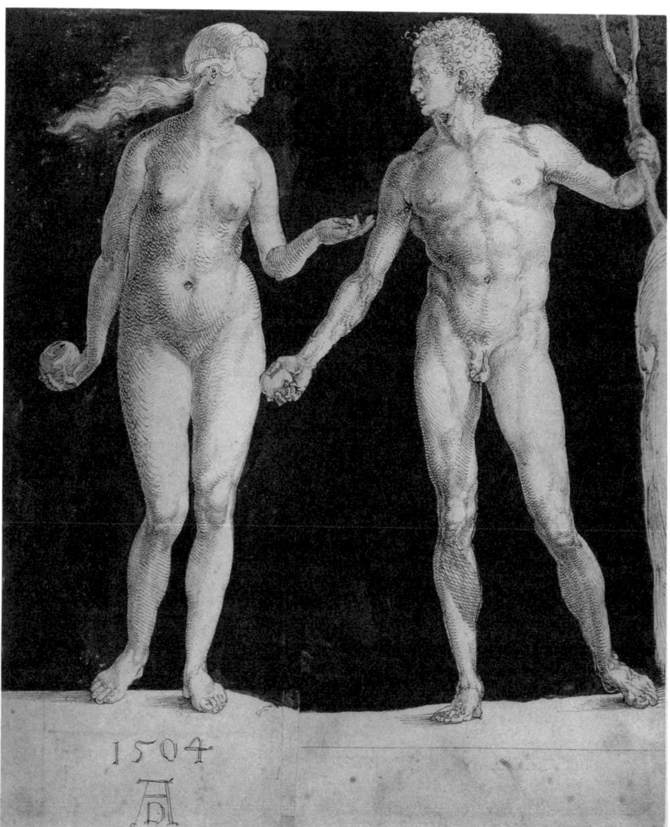

Figure 33-1. Albrecht Dürer, *Adam and Eve*, 1504, pen and brown ink and wash on two sheets pasted together. The Pierpont Morgan Library, New York, I,257d.

In the drawing Eve does not yet hold a second fig to share with the serpent. In the engraving she does and, through the addition of three mirrored oppositions, becomes more tightly implicated as instigator of the impending Fall: it is Eve who takes the fruit from the fig tree, the Tree of Knowledge. Adam, by contrast, firmly holds a branch of the Tree of Life, appropriately a mountain ash (according to Physiologus, it repelled snakes).[10] Dürer contrasts the serpent, which receives the fateful fruit from Eve, with the parrot perched above Adam. The parrot was associated with the Virgin, who, as the second Eve, redresses Eve's sin.[11] Paralleling Eve, a cat, coyly poised on its haunches, is ready to entrap the mouse at Adam's feet. The lone goat on the distant rocky precipice presages the sin with which the couple will burden humankind once they have tasted the forbidden fruit.[12]

In the engraving Dürer removes the tainted fig that Adam held in the drawing. Instead, he invests his Adam-Apollo with an inherent dignity, central to the Renaissance humanists' notion of man as the divine likeness, the mirrored image of God (Gen. 1:26).[13] Adam is centered here precisely between the forces of good (mountain ash, parrot) and the forces of evil (fig tree, serpent). Just as Pico della Mirandola places Adam at the center of the universe in his *Dignity on the Oration of Man* (1486), Dürer acknowledges that the choice between mortality and immortality is still Adam's to make. – JSP

1. For Pollaiuolo and Dürer, see Panofsky, 87.

2. The Museum's impression is of the fourth, or earliest, complete and corrected state of the engraving. The first two states record early stages of the yet unfinished plate, from which Dürer took proof impressions to check his progress. In the third state, the engraving is complete, but he had not yet corrected the number 5 of the date, which appears upside down and in reverse.

3. For an analysis of Dürer's approach to constructing human proportions in these drawings, see Robert Keil, "Zu Dürers frühen Proportionszeichnungen des menschlichen Körpers," *Pantheon* 43 (1985): 54-61; see also Jay A. Levenson in Washington 1991, 290-91, no. 195.

4. For humanism in Nuremberg, see Jeffrey Chipps Smith, "Art and the Rise of Humanism," in Austin 1983, 39-44; and Fedja Anzelewsky, "Dürers Stellung im Geistesleben seiner Zeit," in *Dürer-Studien* (Berlin, 1983), 179-216.

5. The humanistic influence on the Munich *Self-Portrait* from 1500 (with further literature) is explored by Fedja Anzelewsky, "Das Selbsbildnis von 1500," in *Dürer-Studien*, 90-100, and by Dieter Wuttke, "Dürer und Celtis: Von der Bedeutung des Jahres 1500 für den deutschen Humanismus: 'Jahrhundertfeier als symbolische Form'," *Journal of Medieval and Renaissance Studies* 10, no. 1 (1980): 73-129. Panofsky, 81, explores the influence of Neoplatonic writers on the *Nemesis*.

6. Dieter Wuttke, "Humanismus als integrative Kraft. Die Philosophia des deutschen 'Erzhumanisten' Conrad Celtis. Eine ikonologische Studie zu programmatischer Graphik Dürers und Burgkmairs," *Artibus et historiae* 11 (1985): 69.

7. For a convincing argument that the Pierpont Morgan Library drawing was not, as some believe, the final preparatory drawing for the engraving, see Charles Talbot, Washington 1971, 50-52, no. XII; see also Rainer Schoch, New York 1986, 293-94, no. 120.

8. Dürer may have selected the fig rather than the more customary apple tree because the Bible states that after the Fall, Adam and Eve sewed fig leaves to cover themselves (Gen. 3:7).

9. Panofsky, 85.

10. For the mountain ash, see Rainer Schoch, New York 1986, 294-95, no. 121.

11. The parrot serves as an attribute of the Virgin in some works, particularly in Annunciation scenes. According to Panofsky and Purtle, the correlation may be due to the parrot's ability to address Mary, as Gabriel in the Annunciation, with the greeting *ave*. See E. Panofsky, *Problems in Titian, Mostly Iconographic* (New York, 1969), 28-29, and Carol Purtle, *The Marian Paintings of Jan van Eyck* (Princeton, 1982), 92. If the connection of the parrot with *ave* is correct, then it is closely tied to the notion of Mary as the antidote to Eve's curse, as expressed in the prayer *Ave maris stella* (written for the feast of the Annunciation): "Taking that sweet Ave/Which from Gabriel came/Peace confirm within us/Changing Eva's name." See Marina Warner, *Alone of All Her Sex* (New York, 1983), 60.

12. In the Old Testament (Num. 7:28), a goat was used for the sin offering ("And a buck goat for sin"); in the Last Judgment, the goat is cursed and consigned to hell (Matt. 25:41). The reference in the engraving may be to the scapegoat, known in German as the *Sündenbock* (sin goat), that annually carried all the sins of the people of Israel into the wilderness (Lev. 16:22).

The scapegoat was a familiar concept in the popular culture of sixteenth-century Germany. For scapegoating rituals, see Robert W. Scribner, "Ritual and Reformation" in *The German People and the Reformation*, ed. R. Po-Chia Hsia (Ithaca, 1988), 138. In his description of *Europe* (1458), for example, Aeneas Silvius (1405-1464; Enea Silvio Piccolomini) described the tradition of the "Halberstadter Adam," where the community of Halberstadt annually selected a man, whom they named Adam, to be their scapegoat and carry all their sins during the forty days of Lent. See Gerald Strauss, *Sixteenth Century Germany: Its Topography and Topographers* (Madison, 1959), 14. Dürer need not have known this particular Thuringian tradition, although the works of Silvius, "the apostle of humanism in Germany," were well known to humanists in Nuremberg. See Augustus Buck, "Enea Silvio Piccolomini und Nürnberg" in *Albrecht Dürers Umwelt. Festschrift zum 500. Geburtstag Albrecht Dürers am 21. Mai 1971* (Nuremberg: Nürnberger Forschungen, 1971), 20-28. Perhaps the goat that inhabits the distant precipice of other Northern scenes of temptation (of Adam and Eve, Christ, or hermetic saints) likewise refers to the sin goat (the *Sündenbock*), or scapegoat.

13. For Dürer's interpretation of Adam, see Joseph Leo Koerner, "The Mortification of the Images Death as a Hermeneutic in Hans Baldung Grien," in *Representations* 10 (1985): 72-75.

Jacopo de' Barbari

Venice? ca. 1460/70-by 1516 Malines or Brussels

34. Three Captives ca. 1505.

Engraving on antique laid paper, 15.9 x 9.8 cm (platemark).
B.VII.524.17; Hind 15.
Inscribed: [CADUCEUS]
Condition: Trimmed to platemark.
Provenance: Earl of Northwick (Lugt S. 2709a); (his sale C.G. Boerner, Leipzig, May 22-24, 1933, no. 47, to Colnaghi, London for RM 1,000); (purchased from M. Knoedler, New York, February 2, 1934, for $1,400).
Bequest of Herbert Greer French, 1943.103.
Exhibitions: Cincinnati 1941, no. 52, pl. 16; Minneapolis 1956 (not in catalogue); Washington 1973, no. 267.

Many of Jacopo's images have odd, often puzzling aspects and iconographic idiosyncrasies that have yet to be explained, and this engraving is among these. Affinities with two drawings by Bernardino da Parenzo, called Parentino, a Paduan artist, have been pointed out, but these drawings, which depict captives similarly bound to trees or columns, are clearly allegories of victory, within a classical context established by the inclusion of a personification of Victory or Fame and the inscription "S.P.Q.R." on shields.[1] Jacopo's composition has no hint of classical reference: his captives are isolated in a Germanic forest, leafless and forbidding. The setting, with its disturbing, disorienting quality, adds to the feeling of helplessness and doom. This emotive effect recalls the expressionistic rendition of natural settings in the works of Jacopo's contemporaries, such as Albrecht Altdorfer (see cat. 57) and others of the Danube School, working in Regensburg and Vienna in the first years of the sixteenth century.

Jay Levenson suggested that the combination of figures in Jacopo's print is too close to the Bernardino da Parenzo drawings to be coincidence and thus that Barbari knew either these drawings or compositions close to them. Since the Bernardino drawings relate to frescoes in the Church of Santa Giustina, Padua,[2] not far from Venice, it is entirely possible that Jacopo had seen the frescoes or similar works.

Levenson dated this print about 1505[3] because of its affinities with Dürer's *Satyr Family* (H. *Ger.* 65), which bears that date; it is not possible to say whether Barbari's or Dürer's print was made earlier. By 1505 Barbari was living in Wittenberg, but as prints traveled easily it can be assumed that Dürer and Jacopo each continued to be aware of the other's work.

The Museum's impression is a rich one, obviously among early pulls from the plate before it became worn.[4] Arthur Hind was the first to suggest that this image might have been engraved on the back of the same plate as *Apollo and Diana* (B.VII.523.16, Hind 14), a suggestion that seems probable given that the plate dimensions are the same (16 x 10 cm), and Levenson assigned the two images approximately the same date (although, as stated in cat. 27, an engraver would not necessarily use the two sides of a plate in quick succession). The print was copied, in reverse and slightly reduced, in an etching by Hieronymus Hopfer (H. *Ger.* 43). – SB

1. Jay Levenson, "Jacopo de' Barbari and Northern Art of the Early Sixteenth Century" (Ph.D. diss., New York University, 1978), 244-45. The Parentino drawings are published in Alberta de Nicolò Salmazo, *Bernardino da Parenzo, un Pittore "Antiquario" di Fine Quattrocento* (Padua: Editrice Antenore, 1989), figs. 23-24; Popham and Pouncey, 114, no. 185; and James Byam Shaw, *Drawings by Old Masters at Christ Church, Oxford* (Oxford: Clarendon Press, 1976), 186-87, no. 696.

2. See de Nicolò Salmazo, *Bernardino da Parenzo*, fig. 33.

3. NGA, 350.

4. Levenson, "Jacopo de' Barbari," 243, includes the Museum's impression among four "best impressions" of those he had seen (twenty-five impressions are listed by Hind).

Nicoletto da Modena

Modena? active ca. 1480-ca. 1522

35. The Fate of an Evil Tongue ca. 1507.

Engraving on antique laid paper, 29.1 x 20.4 cm (platemark).
B. 37; Hind 33; TIB 2508.037.
Watermark: Fleur-de-lis in circle (cf. Briquet 7099 or 7100?).
Inscribed in pier left center: C (tower) / F? / NIC·MUT; on vertical face of second stone pedestal: LINGUA PRAVORUM PERIBIT.
Condition: Trimmed to platemark.
Provenance: Albertina duplicate; Herschel V. Jones, Minneapolis (1928); Tessie Jones, Newburgh, NJ (consigned to Knoedler February 28, 1940); (purchased from M. Knoedler, New York, April 17, 1940, for $1,600).
Bequest of Herbert Greer French, 1943.159.
Exhibitions: Cincinnati 1941, no. 73.

Nicoletto da Modena, one of the most prolific of the early Italian engravers, is an enigmatic figure. His known oeuvre of 114 works has been roughly sorted chronologically, most recently and thoroughly by Mark Zucker.[1] Because many of these works are known in very few impressions (sometimes in only one), it is reasonable to infer that some of Nicoletto's prints have not survived and thus that his oeuvre was considerably larger than the number now given to him. Zucker has also recently rediscovered and republished a large *St. Roch* by Nicoletto, important in itself and made more so by its being dated 1522, extending the known time of the engraver's activity to that year and bringing the total number of dated prints by Nicoletto to three.[2] The other two are Nicoletto's copy of Dürer's *Four Witches*, dated 1500 (B. 62, Hind 98),[3] and *St. Anthony Abbot*, dated 1512 (B. 24, Hind 55).

An artist named Nicoletto was a decorative designer at the Ferrarese court during the 1480s, and there is a strong possibility that this artist is identical with the engraver.[4] No particular activity is documented for Nicoletto in the 1490s, but he is known to have been working in Padua in 1506.[5] In the following year he was apparently in Rome, since a graffito on the then recently excavated Golden House of Nero reads "Nicholeto da Modena/Ferara 1507" (Modena was at the time under the rule of the Este family of Ferrara).[6] No other documentation concerning Nicoletto is now known.

Zucker has aptly called Nicoletto "one of the most engaging printmakers of his period,"[7] and Sheehan has discerningly written:

"Nicoletto's engravings show consistent delicacy and fineness of technique. The fact that he often engraved his lines quite lightly has surely contributed to the rarity of good, early examples, and the harsh, late impressions which one frequently encounters have unfortunately done little to enhance his reputation."[8]

Nicoletto's development, as Zucker pointed out, "mirrors – indeed helps to define – the general course of Italian engraving in the period of transition from the Early to the High Renaissance."[9] His early works, several of which were based on compositions by Mantegna, reflect the drawing style of that artist (cat. 17), with shading in more or less parallel lines and little or no cross-hatching; he then began to show the influence of prints coming to Italy from the German-speaking areas to the north, particularly those by Schongauer and Dürer. In his niellolike works he was probably influenced by Francia,[10] and during his last decade or so, the influence of Marcantonio is discernible. Other than Mantegna, in only a few instances have the designers of Nicoletto's figures or compositions been suggested. Filippino Lippi, for example, has been proposed as the source for the figure of *Apelles* (Hind 29); others could doubtless be identified. A large number of Nicoletto's engravings consist of a figure from mythology or Christian hagiography isolated in front of classicizing ruins; many of these figures seem to have been inspired by, or taken from, larger compositions by other artists and given architectural settings by Nicoletto.

Throughout all these changes and varying influences, however, Nicoletto's handling of the burin remained relatively constant; it was always fluid and versatile, and all of his prints are characterized by a feeling of spontaneity. Technically, the prints provide evidence of an experimental outlook: the plates Nicoletto used seem often to have been relatively soft so that the edges of the engraved lines not only are not sharp but seem almost to crumble. In some prints, unwiped ink was apparently left on the surface of the plate, creating completely tonal areas, and many early impressions show the use of burr for a rich surface effect. At least one print, an impression of *The Fate of an Evil Tongue* (Metropolitan Museum of Art), is printed in blue ink.

Unlike a good many of Nicoletto's images, as mentioned above, *The Fate of an Evil Tongue* exists in a fairly large number of impressions – at least sixteen are known. The print illustrates the second half of Proverbs 10:31: "The mouth of the just shall bring forth wisdom: the tongue of the perverse shall perish" (*lingua pravorum peribit* is the exact text of the Vulgate). Thus the subject is an allegory against slander or calumny akin to the moralizing allegories of Mantegna (cat. 17), Botticelli, and other Italian artists around the turn of the sixteenth century. There may well have been some specific impetus for the creation of this composition, but if so, it is as yet unknown. No other depiction of this particular subject seems ever to have been made (with the exception of a copy of this print on a majolica plate, now in the Victoria and Albert Museum).[11] Why the designer of the composition – whether Nicoletto or some anonymous artist – chose to show the perverse tongue not only pulled from the mouth of the offender but subjected to forging on a hot anvil has yet to be discovered, but the idea is extraordinary. The charm of its rendition, however – with seven putti dressed in soft leather or fur shoes, minimally draped, earnestly at work while two others, flanking a sort of dragon, sleep soundly in the foreground – causes the composition in the end to be more curious than horrifying.

Its general visual source was surely a depiction of the forge of Vulcan, known from antiquity on sarcophagi and gems and painted by numerous Renaissance artists; Zucker mentioned a painting by

Figure 35-1. *Youths Beating an Anvil*, woodcut from Gafurius Franchinus, *Theorica Musicae* (Naples: Franciscus di Dino Florentinus, 1480). The Newberry Library, Chicago, The John M. Wing Foundation.

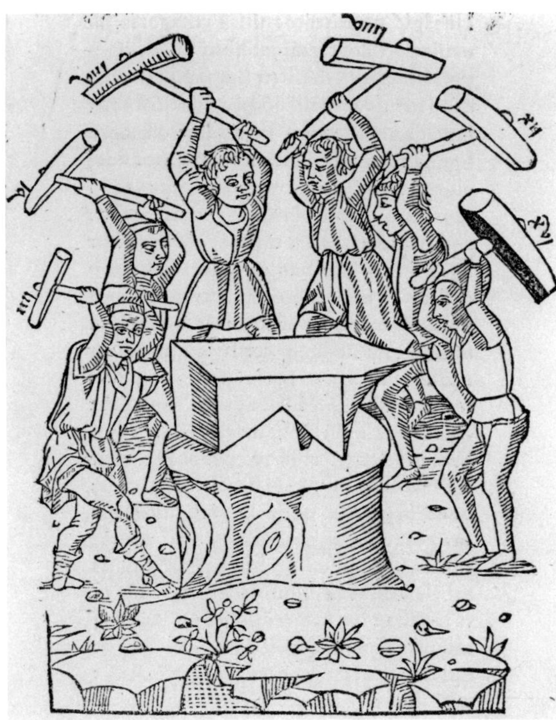

Tura in the Palazzo Schifanoia in Ferrara.[12] Another possible source, which was most probably known in Ferrara, is a woodcut from Gafurius Franchinus, *Theorica Musicae* (Naples: Franciscus di Dino Florentinus, 1480) (fig. 35-1); Eleanor of Aragon, Duchess of Ferrara from 1471 until her death in 1493, was Neapolitan, and thus relations between Ferrara and Naples were close. Although the woodcut is much simpler, certain similarities – the youth of the figures and the direction and placement of the anvil – suggest that the book illustration was the germ for the more developed composition of the engraving (see cat. 27 for another engraving possibly inspired by a woodcut book illustration).

In this engraving Nicoletto has achieved rich surface animation without losing compositional interest. The main subject holds the center of the composition, but in the background, a large barren tree with spiky, intertwined branches,[13] semiruined classical buildings with a great variety of vegetation growing from or behind them, and, in the far distance, a delicately engraved view of fortified buildings by the sea also demand attention. All of these details are typical of Nicoletto's work and make this one of his most characteristic as well as one of his most successful prints.

The shield above the signature shows a tower with a *C* and an *F* at the left and what seems to be a reverse *C* and something that looks like a question mark at the right; the significance of these markings has yet to be explained. – SB

1. Mark J. Zucker, TIB 25 (*Commentary*): 157-253.
2. Mark J. Zucker, "Nicoletto da Modena's Late Works Reconsidered," PQ 8 (1991): 28-36.
3. Dürer's print is H. *Ger.* 69.
4. See M. M. Licht, "A Book of Drawings by Nicoletto da Modena," *Master Drawings* 8 (1970): 379-87.
5. Paolo Sambin, "Nuovi documenti per la storia della pittura in Padova dal XIV al XVI secolo," *Bolletino del Museo Civico di Padova* 51 (1962): 112, 124-26.
6. Nicole Dacos, *La Découverte de la Domus Aurea et la formation des grotesques à la Renaissance* (London: Warburg Institute; Leiden: E. J. Brill, 1969), 148.
7. Zucker, TIB 25 (*Commentary*): 157.
8. NGA, 469.

9. Zucker, "Late Works Reconsidered," 28.
10. See Zucker, TIB (*Commentary*) 2508.074-89.
11. Bernhard Rackham, *Catalogue of Italian Maiolica at the Victoria and Albert Museum*, with emendations and additional bibliography by J. V. G. Mallet (London: Her Majesty's Stationery Office, 1977), 195, no. 582.
12. Zucker, TIB 25 (*Commentary*): 198; for the Tura, see Ranieri Varese, *Atlante di Schifanoia* (Ferrara: Edizione Panini, 1989), 355.
13. Sheehan in NGA, 474, and Zucker, TIB 25 (*Commentary*): 196-98, state that the group of trees is copied from Giovanni Battista Palumba's *Satyr Family* (B.XIII.248.7, Hind V.256.6), but it is not clear to me that this borrowing could not have been the other way around.

Giovanni Antonio da Brescia

North Italian, active ca. 1495-ca. 1520
after Andrea Mantegna (ca. 1430-1506)

36. Hercules and the Nemean Lion 1507 or later.

Engraving on antique laid paper, 26.1 x 23.4 (sheet).
B. 11; Hind 2.
Inscribed: ·D[(IVE)]/ HERC[ULI]/ IN/VICTO·
Condition: Trimmed within platemark. Monogram IO·AN·BX· trimmed off lower center. Repaired breaks Hercules' left foot and to right of head above inscription.
Provenance: (Purchased from F.C. Harlow, New York, November 29, 1940, for $1,750).
Bequest of Herbert Greer French, 1943.100.
Exhibitions: Cincinnati 1941, no. 56; Washington 1973, no. 202.

Hercules and the Nemean Lion reproduces a design by Andrea Mantegna that is also known in two drawings. Neither drawing, however, is by Mantegna's hand,[1] but all three of these works presumably derive from the same original. In style and proportion the design would seem to date at the earliest from the 1490s; that is, when Mantegna was in his sixties.

This episode shows Hercules in battle with the fearful lion of Nemea, a beast impervious to weapons. Hercules finally strangled the lion with his bare hands, the first of his classical twelve labors; in subsequent deeds, Hercules is almost always shown wearing the lion's skin. Another image of Hercules designed by Mantegna to the same scale, *Hercules and Antaeus*, is known in several prints.[2] The two designs almost certainly were made around the same time and for the same ultimate purpose. They may have been part of a larger series of the labors of Hercules for some decoration now lost. In the vault of the Camera Picta, for instance, the first major commission Ludovico Gonzaga gave to Mantegna and on which he worked between 1465 and 1474, five episodes from the story of Hercules, along with scenes of Orpheus and Orion, are depicted in monochrome in spandrels. A document mentions that Mantegna also designed some Hercules subjects for a now lost Gonzaga villa at Cavriana, in the countryside surrounding Mantua, during the 1460s. Later in Mantegna's life, however, no commission for Hercules subjects is known.

The inscription DIVO HERCULI INVICTO, sometimes abbreviated, as here, appears in various forms on several prints after Mantegna's designs. In the catalogue for the recent Mantegna exhibition, I showed that this inscription must have been a dedication to Ercole d'Este, duke of Ferrara from 1471 to 1505 and father of Isabella d'Este.[3] Isabella became Mantegna's principal patron after she married Francesco Gonzaga in 1490. The form of Giovanni Antonio's monogram on this print (trimmed off the Museum's impression), however, almost certainly indicates that it was made in 1507 or later, after Ercole's death. The most likely explanation for this anomaly is that Giovanni Antonio's engraving is a copy of an earlier print, made only in a few impressions, of which none has survived. (The same may also be true with respect to the other print by Giovanni Antonio represented in this exhibition, cat. 29). Giovanni Antonio made two other prints of Hercules subjects after Mantegna's designs, and both of these are known to copy an earlier print, most likely by the engraver of cats. 17a, b.[4] The fact that one of these copied compositions exists in only four impressions is evidence that some of these prints were not produced in large quantities. Most of Giovanni Antonio's prints that reproduce Mantegna's designs were copies of existing prints, and it seems likely that *Hercules and the Nemean Lion* also was a copy of a print, rather than deriving directly from a drawing.

The comparable plate size of *The Laocoon* (Hind 20), 28.2 cm x 25.0 cm, suggests that it could have been engraved on the verso of the same plate. – SB

1. Christ Church, Oxford, inv. no. 0266; see Ekserdjian in London 1992, no. 96. Louvre, Paris, inv. no. RF 39030.

2. Hind v.25.17, as Mantegna school; copy by Giovanni Antonio da Brescia, Hind v.36.1; see London 1992, nos. 93, 94. Another version is by Nicoletto da Modena, Hind v.113.1.

3. Boorsch in London 1992, 301.

4. Hind v.36.1, which copies Hind v.25.17 and Hind v.36.3, which copies 36.3a. See also London 1992, nos. 86, 87, 93, 94.

Hans Burgkmair

Augsburg 1473-1531 Augsburg

37. St. George 1508.

Woodcut on antique laid paper, 32.2 x 23.0 cm (image).
B. 23; Dodgson *B.M.* 14 v/vii; H. *Ger.* 253 vi/vi; TIB 23.
Inscribed: DIVVS · GEORGIVS / CHRISTIANORUM · / MILITVM · PRO · / PVGNATOR · [St. George, Champion of Christian Soldiers].
Condition: Trimmed to image.
Provenance: Friedrich August II (Lugt 971); Josef Wünsch; (his sale, C.G. Boerner, Leipzig, May 4-6, 1927, no. 218, illus. p. 39, to Colnaghi for RM 400); (purchased from M. Knoedler, New York, April 27, 1939, for $975).
Bequest of Herbert Greer French, 1943.III.
Exhibitions: Cincinnati 1941, no. 78.

St. George, dressed in armor, mounted, and facing right, dominates Burgkmair's woodcut. St. George's cross, a Greek (+ -shaped) cross within a circle, decorates the crest of his helmet, his breastplate, and the caparison of his steed. The soldier looks down at the lamb and the king's daughter kneeling before him, whom, according to *The Golden Legend*, he saved from sacrifice to the dragon. The monster itself lies dead beneath his feet, coiled around a portion of the lance still lodged in its throat. By placing the group beneath a triumphal arch[1] rather than in a narrative context, Burgkmair makes clear that St. George, not the legend of his defeat of the dragon, is the true subject of the print. The inscription in the upper left celebrates him more specifically as the model *miles christianus* (Christian soldier).[2] St. George's noble lineage and military daring earned him the role of patron saint of chivalry; knights taking their chivalric vows were dubbed in his name. His cult thereby became closely associated with the crusades.

Burgkmair designed *St. George* as a pendant for a woodcut that depicts a matching equestrian knight facing left, likewise beneath a triumphal arch (fig. 37-1). The double-headed imperial eagle on the banner behind the rider and the inscription "Maximilian, Holy Roman Emperor" (IMP.CAES.MAXIMIL.AVG) identify George's counterpart as the Habsburg ruler Maximilian I (1459-1519).[3]

Maximilian, himself commonly called the last of the chivalric knights, held St. George in highest esteem and identified this crusading saint with his own long-standing campaign to rid Europe of the heathen Turks. In 1493, in his efforts to organize a new crusade, Maximilian established a Brotherhood of St. George; and in 1503 he reactivated the knightly Order of St. George, which his father, Emperor Friedrich III, had founded in 1468.[4] The members of both these groups displayed the cross of St. George on their official costume. By pairing *St. George* with the emperor's portrait, Burgkmair associated Maximilian closely with his personal hero and the Order of St. George.

The immediate motivation for Burgkmair's *St. George* and *Maximilian I* was to commemorate the Habsburg monarch's newly acquired status: in 1508, the year these prints were made, Maximilian, the Roman king, was proclaimed "Roman Emperor elect" in Trent. The title *electus imperator* in actuality fell short of the ultimate status of Holy Roman Emperor, which could be conferred only in the papal city itself; and at the time, the Venetians effectively blocked Maximilian's passage through their territories to Rome. At the ceremony in Trent, Maximilian specifically called upon the Order of St. George to accompany him to Rome. The pendant woodcuts were calculated to advertise the two primary objectives that Maximilian envisioned for the Order of St. George: first and foremost, to assure his imperial coronation in Rome as Holy Roman Emperor; and second, to help him defend Western Christendom in a crusade against the Turks. In the equestrian portrait, Maximilian is presented not as emperor elect but, *fait accompli*, with full imperial status as Holy Roman Emperor (*Caesar Augustus*).[5]

The person responsible for commissioning the two woodcut designs and devising their iconographic program was likely Conrad Peutinger (1465-1547), a humanist, secretary for the city of Augsburg, and advisor in legal and artistic affairs to Emperor

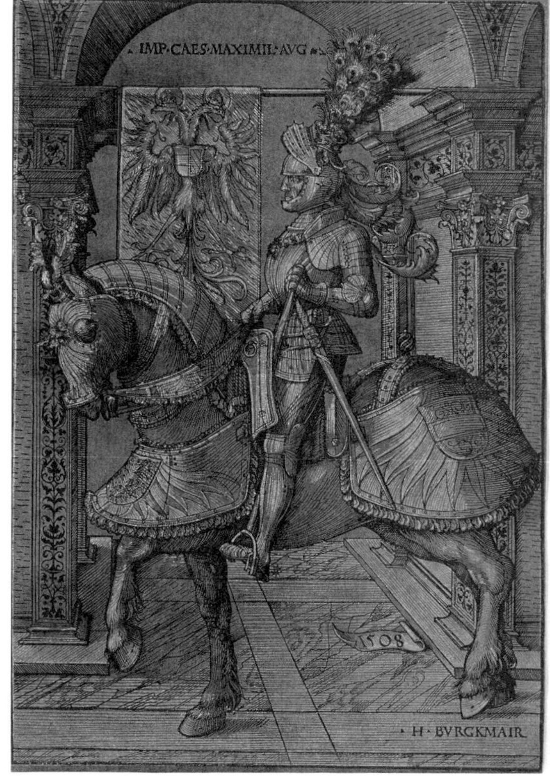

Figure 37-1. Hans Burgkmair, *Equestrian Portrait of Emperor Maximilian I*, 1508, woodcut, H. *Ger.* 323. The Cleveland Museum of Art, John L. Severance Fund, 50.72.

Maximilian.[6] Hans Burgkmair was the logical choice for the designs since he was at the time Augburg's leading artist. He received his training as a painter first from his father, Thoman Burgkmair, and thereafter from Martin Schongauer in Colmar (cats. 6-8). It is curious that even though Schongauer was the most outstanding German engraver of the fifteenth century, Burgkmair never attempted a single engraving. Woodcuts, by contrast, were his print medium; he designed eight hundred during his career. Maximilian was the first ruler to exploit the propagandistic potential of prints, mostly to eulogize himself and his rule. *St. George* was one of the earliest of nearly three hundred designs Burgkmair would make in this capacity, including those for imperial publications like the *Genealogy* (1509-12), *Theuerdank* (1517), and *Weisskunig* (not published until 1775) and those for Maximilian's monumental print assemblages like the *Triumphal Arch* (1517) and *Triumphal Procession* (not published until 1526).

The Museum's woodcut involves a single block, the customary line block. When the block was originally cut in 1508, its makers experimented by combining it with other blocks and printing surfaces to create sumptuous effects worthy of its imperial message. It was initially combined with a second line block that was covered with a sticky substance rather than ink so that a metallic color (gold and/or silver dust) would adhere to the printed lines. The two blocks – the black and metallic line – were printed together on vellum, normally reserved for costly manuscript illumination, and were also printed on hand-tinted blue paper. The highlights created by the metallic block must have originally appeared even richer on the colored ground than on vellum.[7] When Peutinger sent impressions of both woodcuts to Maximilian's governor-general, Friedrich the Wise, elector of Saxony (see cat 46), it was not just for political purposes; he sought Friedrich's opinion about the artistic success of the new printing venture.[8]

Further experimentation with *St. George* and *Maximilian I* led to the first true *chiaroscuro* (*chiaro-scuro*, light-dark) woodcuts. The technique involved two blocks, but instead of using the metallic line block, a new *tone* block was cut and inked with a color (impressions printed with slate gray, red, and green exist). The tone block of the chiaroscuro versions was printed first, covering much of the paper's surface to serve as a middle tone (as hand-tinted surfaces had done previously). The areas of the paper left untouched now read as white highlights. The original black line block was then printed on the toned surface. The effect is similar in appearance to the Museum's slightly later chiaroscuro woodcut by Hans Wechtlin (cat. 38). Jost de Negker (active in Augsburg from 1508?-44), whose name appears in letterpress on some chiaroscuro impressions of Burgkmair's two prints, is thought to have developed the technique in collaboration with Burgkmair and to have cut the tone block.[9] Their chiaroscuro technique immediately caught on. Within a few years, Lucas Cranach (Friedrich the Wise's court artist), Hans Baldung, Hans Wechtlin, and Albrecht Altdorfer had all tried it.[10]

The Museum's impression is later than those just discussed. There is no tone block, and the date, MCVIII, formerly on the right wall beneath the tooled panel, has been removed from the block. Tilman Falk suggests that this later impression was issued for the diet held in Augsburg in 1518 at which Maximilian was present. Like the earlier states of *St. George*, this sixth, and final, state is very rare.[11] – JSP

1. According to Tilman Falk, *Hans Burgkmair. Studien zu Leben und Werk des Augsburger Malers* (Munich: Bruckmann KG, 1968), 71, the architectural motifs, free variations on motifs from the interior of San Marco in Venice, were taken from sketches that Burgkmair must have made during an undocumented trip to Italy in 1507.

2. IHS, the Greek abbreviation for Jesus, centered in the tooled panel of the wall, reinforces the association of St. George as a soldier for Christ. So does the inclusion of the pelican feeding its young (with its own blood), a symbol of Christian sacrifice that is woven into the horse's caparison.

3. For a thorough discussion of the companion print, *Maximilian I*, with reproductions of three different impressions (figs. 1, 7-8) and further literature, see Larry Silver, "Shining Armor: Maximilian I as Holy Roman Emperor," *Museum Studies* 12, no. 1 (1985): 8-29.

4. For Maximilian's close identification with St. George (a "St. George in the flesh") and initiatives involving the Brotherhood and the Order of St. George, see Walter Winkelbauer, "Kaiser Maximilian I. und St. Georg," *Mitteilungen des Österreichischen Staatsarchivs* 7 (1954): 523-50.

5. The print of the Habsburg ruler was a political fiction. Maximilian was never officially crowned in Rome, and the Trent proclamation had not changed his status. He therefore remained in reality Roman king (king of the Germans), technically Roman Emperor elect, but not a bona fide Holy Roman Emperor. See Hermann Wiesflecker, "Maximilians I. Kaiserproklamation zu Trient (4. Februar 1508). Das Ereignis und seine Bedeutung," in *Österreich und Europa. Festgabe für Hugo Hantsch zum 70. Geburtstag* (Graz, 1965), 15-38; idem, *Kaiser Maximilian I* (Munich: R. Oldenbourg Verlag, 1981), 4:6-15.
The two prints were effective propaganda to suggest otherwise. They signaled the onset of a great deal of imperial imagery and implied that the elect status was considered sufficient to identify Maximilian as Holy Roman Emperor by projecting Maximilian into that office. The strategy worked; none of the subsequent emperors was crowned in Rome. Maximilan's successor, Charles V, was in fact the last emperor even to be crowned by a pope at all.

Maximilian, however, honored the tradition that the imperial title was legitimized only by coronation in Rome. In 1508 he still believed he would be officially crowned in Rome with the help of the Order of St. George. His identification with the Order of St. George was such that he formally joined the knightly order in 1510 after the death of his second wife, Bianca Maria Sforza, and presided as its leader.

6. Peutinger's role as instigator of this project was proposed by Anton Reichel, *Die Clair-Obscur-Schnitte des XIV. XVII. und XVIII. Jahrhunderts* (Vienna, 1926), 12-17, and supported by Falk, *Hans Burgkmair*, 70-71. For Peutinger's relationship with Maximilian, see Josef Bellot, "Konrad Peutinger und die literarisch-künstlerischen Unternehmungen Kaiser Maximilians," *Philobiblon* 11 (1967): 171-90.

7. A convenient summary of states and repositories owning them is in Hollstein (H. Ger. 253). Details on the motivation for Burgkmair's *St. George* and its variations are summarized in Stuttgart 1973, nos. 21-22c. See also N. G. Stogdon, *Catalogue VIII: German and Netherlandish Woodcuts* (London, 1991), no. 21.

8. The motivation for Peutinger's commission and Burgkmair's experiment was Lucas Cranach's *St. George in a Landscape* (H. Ger. 81), a woodcut similarly employing a second metallic line block on a colored ground that had been produced for Friedrich the Wise one year earlier. For the role of Cranach's print, see Basel 1974, 1:63-64, no. 14. Peutinger's correspondence to Friedrich the Wise about Burgkmair's two woodcuts is cited in both Harold Joachim, "Maximilian I by Burgmair," *The Art Institute of Chicago Quarterly* 55, no. 1 (1961): 8; and Silver, "Shining Armor," 10.

9. Stuttgart 1973, nos. 21-22.

10. For facsimile reproductions of these chiaroscuro woodcuts, see Reichel, *Die Clair-Obscur-Schnitte*, pls. 1-25. These are also reproduced in Walter L. Strauss, *Chiaroscuro: The Clair-Obscur Woodcuts by the German and Netherlandish Masters of the XVITH and XVIITH Centuries* (Greenwich, Conn.: New York Graphic Society Ltd., 1973), esp. nos. 1-57.

11. Besides the Museum's impression (formerly in the Dresden collection of Friedrich August II), the hand-colored impression from Gotha that is now in Vienna is the only other one known. See Stogdon, *Catalogue VIII*, no. 21.

Hans Wechtlin

Strasbourg ca. 1480/85-ca. 1526 Strasbourg

38. Knight and Halberdier ca. 1512.

Chiaroscuro woodcut (black line block and greyish-blue tone block) on antique laid paper, 26.8 x 18.0 cm (image).
B. 10; Ge. 1497; Strauss *Chiaroscuro*, 27.
Watermark: Small bull's head (cf. Briquet 15158).
Monogrammed on tablet lower left: *Io V*.
Condition: Trimmed to image.
Provenance: (Purchased from M. Knoedler, New York, December 31, 1936, for $1,375).
Bequest of Herbert Greer French, 1943.269.

A mounted knight and a halberdier emerge from a thick, wooded area and head left. Like Burgkmair's *St. George* (cat. 37), the knight wears Maximilian armor, so named for the "last of the knights" himself, Maximilian I, the Holy Roman Emperor (1439-1519). This style of armor, which was in vogue between 1500 and 1530, is recognizable by the knight's longish, wide-fluted skirt of steel (with its front section removed to make way for the saddle) and by his broad, flat *sabaton* (armored footgear). The bushy panache of his helmet fans out, echoing the shape of the treetops behind, and serves as a dramatic foil to make him the central focus. The foot soldier, who runs alongside, carries a halberd – a versatile, vicious, long-handled ax equipped with a spike for stabbing and a hook for pulling down riders.[1]

Wechtlin probably borrowed the idea for the monogrammed tablet that lies on the ground from Dürer, who likewise placed his signature on a cartellino (cat. 33). On Wechtlin's, two pilgrim staffs cross and intersect the stem of a stylized flower (a thistle or eryngium?). The letters *Io* and *V* on either side of this mark prompted art historians to identify the artist at first as Johann Ulrich or even Johann Ulrich Pilgrim. Later it was discovered that the initials stand for Joannes Veuchtelin (Hans Wächtlin, Wechtle, Wechtlin), an artist who designed several series of woodcut illustrations between 1506 and 1526 for Strasbourg publications. Little is known about Wechtlin. In 1505-06 he served as painter at the court of Duke René II in Nancy, and in 1506 he was in Wittenberg. In 1514 he became a citizen of Strasbourg and twice, in 1516 and 1519, he was mentioned in connection with painters' associations there, but no paintings by him are known, and most drawing attributions remain tentative.[2]

Wechtlin's reputation lies with nineteen undated single-leaf woodcuts that are roughly contemporary with his book illustrations (ca. 1505-15).[3] These reveal that he was one of the earliest German printmakers besides Dürer and Burgkmair to experiment with Italian Renaissance content and form, which is demonstrated by the fact that four of his single-leaf prints depict classical subjects, several of his nudes derive from Italian Renaissance prints, and many of his architectural elements incorporate Italian Renaissance motifs.[4] His approach to woodcut design is otherwise quite predictably modeled upon Dürer's early woodcuts. Comparison of his *Knight and Halberdier* with Dürer's *Knight on Horseback and Lansquenet* (B. 131) demonstrates just how much Wechtlin depended on the Nuremberg master for his graphic forms.[5]

Wechtlin was also one of the first printmakers to experiment with the chiaroscuro woodcut (*chiaro-scuro*, light-dark) to achieve chromatic effects. This technique originated in Germany circa 1508 (see discussion under cat. 37), and of the approximately sixty chiaroscuro woodcuts produced there during the first decades of the sixteenth century, Wechtlin made twelve, more than any of his German contemporaries. The technique requires a line block and at least one *tone* block. Using his tone block, Wechtlin first printed the grayish blue color on the Museum's impression of *Knight and a Halberdier*, establishing the white highlights (the unprinted areas of the paper) in the process. Afterwards, he printed his line block with black on top of the toned sheet and must have devised a way to register the block on the paper to make the black lines align with the white exactly as desired. The contrasts created by the white highlights enliven surfaces, bringing sheen to armor and stronger definition to textures like foliage and plumes. In other chiaroscuros, Wechtlin capitalized on the tone block's potential to create deep, atmospheric landscapes and to evoke a mood. He only signed eleven of his prints with his monogram; significantly all are chiaroscuros.

For *Knight and Halberdier* Wechtlin selected imagery that was popular in early sixteenth-century Germany. Maximilian's frequent calls for a crusade and his preoccupation with the Order of St. George popularized the image of the knight, who was often depicted in the guise of St. George, the model Christian soldier. In fact, the

earliest experiments in the history of the chiaroscuro woodcut may have inspired Wechtlin's subject since they each feature an equestrian knight: Lucas Cranach's *St. George in a Landscape* from 1507[6] and Burgkmair's pair from 1508, *St. George* (cat. 37) and *Maximilian I* (fig. 37-1). The foot soldier also figured prominently from about 1500 to 1530 particularly in the art from the circle of Maximilian.[7] The emperor was the one, after all, who first established the infantries of German *Landsknechte* (i.e., hired mercenaries) to satisfy his need for a standing army.

The equestrian knight, who represented the traditional mode of warfare, and the German foot soldier, who represented a more modern one, appeared side by side in art during the last decade of Maximilan's life. The two are featured together, for instance, on the reverse of several commemorative medals issued between 1508 and 1514 to celebrate Maximilian's promotion to Holy Roman Emperor (1508); Maximilian himself is the equestrian knight, his faithful companion is a mercenary who runs at his side.[8] Even though the companion soldiers on the medals act more aggressively than Wechtlin's, trampling their foe underfoot to symbolize imperial might and triumph, his steadfast *Knight and Halberdier* derives from this genre of imagery. The historical coexistence of aristocratic knight and mercenary *Landsknecht*, as chronicled by Wechtlin's chiaroscuro, was short-lived, not outlasting Maximilian by very long. In Wechtlin's print, the mercenary soldier is visually subordinated to the knight, but in the tactics of Renaissance warfare, he would replace his armored predecessor; the one-on-one equestrian combats of knights would soon give way to the hand-to-hand onslaughts of massive regimented phalanxes of mercenary infantrymen.[9] – JSP

1. For costume terminology, see Helmut Nickel, *Warriors and Worthies: Arms and Armor through the Ages* (New York: Atheneum, 1969), 56-60, 117-19; and Christiane Andersson, Detroit 1983, 73-75.

2. For information on Wechtlin, see Heinrich Röttinger in *ThB.*, s.v. "Wechtlin."

3. For reproductions of eighteen of Wechtlin's woodcuts, see Ge. 1481-98. Campbell Dodgson added one woodcut to Geisberg's list in "Rare Woodcuts in the Ashmolean Museum – V," *Burl. M.* 69 (1936): 81.

4. For the influence of Italian Renaissance art on several of Wechtlin's prints, see Otto Pannewitz in Karlsruhe 1986, 1:392-95, F 27-F 29. The more recent consensus that Marcantonio Raimondi's work (B.XIV.242.322) influenced Wechtlin's (B. 7) reverses the relationship originally proposed by Röttinger in *Th.B.*, s.v. "Wechtlin"; and idem, "Hans Wechtlin und der Helldunkelschnitt," *Gutenberg Jahrbuch* (1942-43): 107-15. See Karlsruhe 1959, 134; and Strauss, *Chiaroscuro*, 48, no. 24.

5. It is questionable, on the other hand, whether Dürer's *Knight on Horseback and Lansquenet* (B. 131) served as the immediate source for Wechtlin's subject, as suggested by Röttinger, *Th.B.*, 233; and Strauss, *Chiaroscuro*, 54. In strong contrast to Wechtlin, Dürer does not present the chivalric ideal of an undaunted knight; indeed there is no reason to identify his rider as a knight at all.

6. Lucas Cranach's *St. George* (H. *Ger.* 81) is not strictly a chiaroscuro woodcut since it does not employ a tone block, but his experiment of printing two blocks (one with black, the other with white) on hand-colored paper was pivotal in motivating Burgkmair and Jost de Negker to create similar effects with a tone block soon thereafter (see discussion under cat. 37). Since Wechtlin was in Wittenberg in 1506, he may have been privy to these developments from the start. Anton Reichel reproduces Cranach's print in color in *Die Clair-Obscur-Schnitte des* XVI., XVII. *und* XVIII. Jahrhunderts (Wien, 1926), pl. 1; for more information, see Koepplin, Basel 1974, 1:63-66.

7. For the depiction of the German *Landsknecht*, see John R. Hale, "The Soldier in Germanic Graphic Art of the Renaissance," in *Art and History*, ed. R. T. Rotberg and T. K. Rabb (Cambridge: Cambridge University Press, 1988), 85-114; idem, *Artists and Warfare in the Renaissance* (New Haven: Yale University Press, 1990), 1-72; and Keith Moxey, "Mercenary Warriors and the 'Rod of God,' " in *Peasants, Warriors and Wives: Popular Imagery in the Reformation* (Chicago: University of Chicago Press, 1989), 67-100.

8. The medals are reproduced in Erich Egg, *Die Münzen Kaiser Maximilians I* (Innsbruck, 1968), 152-55, nos. 6-11.

9. Moxey, "Mercenary Warriors," 71; and Peter Krenn, "Heerwesen, Waffe und Turnier unter Kaiser Maximilian I," Innsbruck 1969, 86-91.

Giulio Campagnola

Padua ca. 1482-ca. 1515/18 Venice

39. The Astrologer 1509.

Engraving on antique laid paper, 9.6 x 15.4 cm (platemark).
B. 8 copy c; P. 8; Hind 9 ii/iii; TIB 2518.011 ii/iii.
Watermark: Mermaid in a circle (cf. Briquet 13887).
Inscribed on disc lower left with numbers *3, 21, 40, 0, 43, 50* and initial C? with date *1509*; identified with pen and brown ink upper center: IVLIVS CĀPAGNOLA.
Condition: Brush and brown wash throughout landscape.
Provenance: Edme Durand (Lugt 741); Friedrich August II (Lugt 971); (his sale C.G. Boerner, Leipzig, November 8-9, 1932, no. 247, pl. 18 to Maison for RM 1,050); (purchased from M. Knoedler, New York, November 1, 1934, for $1,050).
Bequest of Herbert Greer French, 1943.90.
Exhibitions: Cincinnati 1941, no. 61; Washington 1949; Minneapolis 1956, no. 91; Washington 1973, no. 281; Washington 1988, 51, 259, no. 29, fig. 19.
References: NGA 1973, 393-94, fig. 19-4.

An aura of enchantment surrounds Giulio Campagnola's engraving known as *The Astrologer*. Reclining before a hummock surmounted by a stand of trees, a maguslike philosopher ponders the measurement he makes on a disk or sphere. The disk, inscribed with solar and lunar emblems and a series of enigmatic numbers in addition to the date, 1509, appears below a diagrammatic image of a scale that possibly represents the astrological sign of Libra. Nearby a dragon, diabolical in significance though unintentionally comical in expression, is flanked by symbols or reminders of mortality: on one side, a skull and crossbones; on the other, a blasted stump. The scene is set on a strip of landscape behind which looms an imaginary city on a lagoon whose watery locale along with the forms of its principal building vividly call Venice to mind. According to one distinguished scholar, the print "might well be named *Sage, Death, and Devil*,"[1] but its meaning remains elusive. Doubtless intended to stimulate agreeably melancholic thoughts on the part of reflective viewers, the engraving is suggestive rather than explicit. Part idyl, part elegy, it weaves its subtle spell by poetic rather than prosaic means.

The author of this extraordinary work, Giulio Campagnola, was a prodigy of sorts. Born in Padua circa 1482, he must have been tutored by his father, Girolamo, a humanist and, it seems, an amateur artist.[2] At age fifteen, Giulio is described as being talented in poetry, singing, and playing the lute; adept in Greek, Latin, and Hebrew letters; and expert in the arts of painting, manuscript illumination, engraving, and the cutting of gems. We learn all this from an admittedly biased letter written by a relative to one of Francesco Gonzaga's counselors in Mantua, recommending that the boy be taken on at the court where he might have the opportunity to study under Mantegna.[3] Whether the petition was successful or not, by January 1499 Giulio – now about seventeen years old – was in residence at another of the princely north Italian courts, that of Ercole d'Este in Ferrara. At an unknown date, he moved from Ferrara to Venice, where he probably remained for the rest of his brief career. We find him there in 1507 and again in 1515, when he is mentioned in the will of Aldo Manuzio, renowned printer and publisher. Giulio seems to have died soon thereafter: there are no further references to him in contemporary records and one of his unfinished plates, *Shepherds in a Landscape* (Hind 6), was completed by Domenico Campagnola, Giulio's pupil and adopted son, in 1517 or 1518.

Although various extant drawings testify to his exceptional skill as a draftsman, and although a number of paintings, rather heterogeneous in style, have also been ascribed to his hand, Giulio's modern reputation rests mainly on his engravings.[4] He produced fewer than twenty engravings, but they comprise some of the finest, most fascinating, most important, and most influential of all surviving Italian Renaissance prints. The earliest among them perhaps may be two or three traditionally associated with the school of Mantegna; one or two later ones also show Giulio working on the basis of Mantegna's inventions.[5] Still near the outset of his career, Giulio turned for inspiration to Albrecht Dürer's early engravings (of ca. 1495-98), prints that seem to have flooded the Venetian market, judging from the magnitude of their impact on local engravers.[6] In the most characteristic works of his maturity, including *The Young Shepherd* (cat. 40) as well as *The Astrologer*, Giulio was almost wholly under the sway of Giorgione (ca. 1478-1510), the greatest Venetian painter of the first decade of the sixteenth century.

Scholars have long debated the nature of Giulio's relationship to Giorgione, but whatever it may have been, the Giorgionesque character of *The Astrologer* is undeniable. The engraving's mysterious, poetic mood is typical of Giorgione, as is its asymmetrical design and the relationship of the figure to the landscape. The facial type of the bearded sage and even the obscure, possibly astrological, subject matter recall numerous Giorgionesque pictures, most notably the master's own *Three Philosophers*, now in Vienna (fig. 39-1). More remarkable still, Giulio was able to devise a sort of graphic equivalent of Giorgione's painting style, with its vaguely defined, impressionistic forms achieved by a novel method of applying oil paint to canvas. Giulio's early engravings remain traditional in their linearity, notwithstanding the variety of strokes and flicklike marks that he learned to employ by imitating Dürer. In fact, a somewhat Düreresque technique of engraving may still be seen in *The Astrologer*, especially in its first state (fig. 39-2). Here Dürer's method of depicting a rolling terrain with bands of undulating parallel lines is more apparent than in the Museum's second-state impression, in which Giorgionesque softness results from the addition of countless dots throughout the foreground landscape.

Obtained by pricking the plate with the point of the burin or graver, these dots are found to one or another degree in all of Giulio's mature works (cf. also cat. 40). His only dated print, *The Astrologer* (1509), falls about midway through the artist's career. In

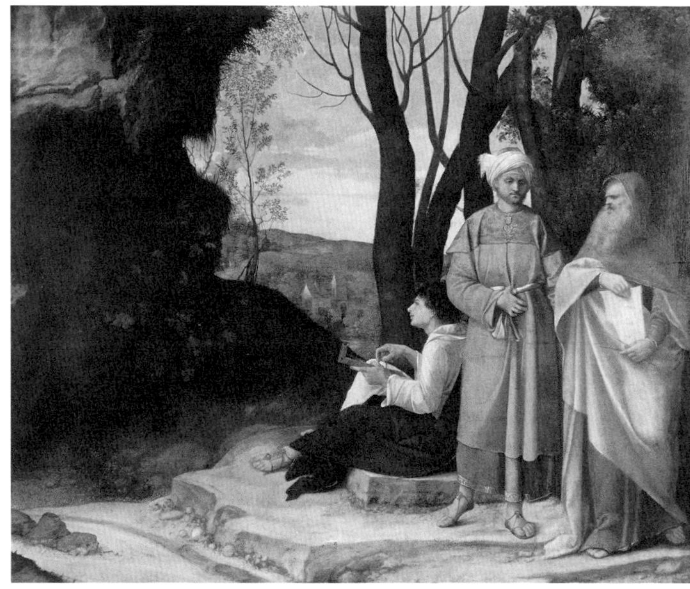

Figure 39-1. Giorgione, *The Three Philosophers*, 1507-08, oil on canvas. Kunsthistorisches Museum, Vienna.

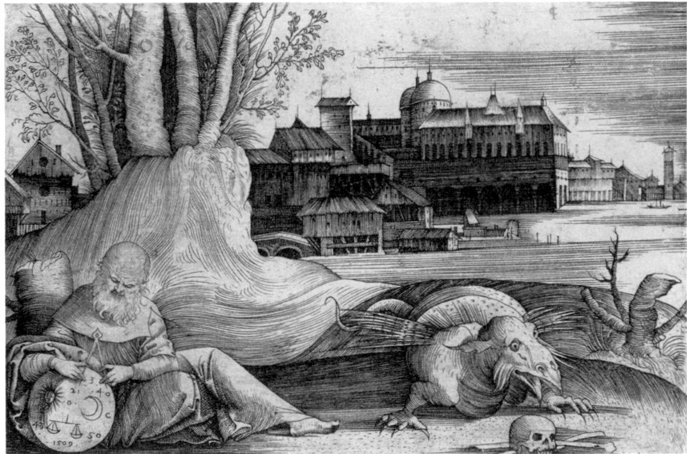

Figure 39-2. Giulio Campagnola, *The Astrologer*, 1509, engraving, Hind 9 i. Kupferstichkabinett, Staatliche Museen Preuβischer Kulturbesitz, Berlin.

it he combines his stippling technique with pure line in more or less equal proportion. A few years later, in such exquisitely delicate engravings as *Venus Reclining in a Landscape* (Hind 13) and *Stag at Rest, Chained to a Tree* (Hind 14) (fig. 44-1), Giulio would go further still, abandoning conventional linework altogether and rendering even contours in his revolutionary dotted manner.

As tributes to the desirability and enduring popularity of *The Astrologer*, at least five different printmakers copied it during the first half of the sixteenth century (Hind 9a-e), and the date on the original plate was eventually altered to 1569 for a third state, issued more than fifty years after Giulio's death. Only one example of the first state (fig. 39-2) has survived, but the Museum's second-state impression is as fine as any. Aside from its outstanding quality, it has certain special characteristics, being lightly tinted with a brown wash that imparts an attractive golden brown tone to the image. Another distinguishing feature is the signature in the sky. Carefully inscribed by hand in pen and ink, it resembles authentic printed signatures by Giulio, who may have drawn it in himself.[7] An impression of *The Astrologer* in Paris (Bibliothèque Nationale) has the same handwritten signature, which also occurs on at least four other impressions of three different Campagnola engravings.[8] – MZ

1. Edgar Wind, *Giorgione's Tempesta* (Oxford: Clarendon Press, 1969), 27.

2. Documentation pertaining to Giulio's life is conveniently collected by Hind v:189-90. For a summary of all material on the artist, see E. Safarik, DBI 17 (1974): 318-21, with exhaustive bibliography; for Girolamo Campagnola, see idem, DBI 17 (1974): 317-18.

3. Excerpt from the letter of September 10, 1497, from Michael de Placiola, Giulio's "cugnado," to Ermolao Bardelino, in Hind v:190, n. 1(ii); complete text published by Alessandro Luzio, "Giulio Campagnola, fanciullo prodigio," *Archivio storico dell'arte* 1 (1888): 184-85.

4. For Giulio's drawings, see the references cited in TIB 25 (*Commentary*): 465, n. 1; for paintings attributed to him, see Giuseppe Fiocco, "La giovinezza di Giulio Campagnola," *L'Arte* 18 (1915): 138-56, and Hind v:192. Literature on the engravings is extensive, but the basic studies are Émile Galichon, "Giulio Campagnola, peintre-graveur du xvie siècle," GBA. 13 (1862): 332-46; Paul Kristeller, *Giulio Campagnola: Kupferstiche und Zeichnungen* (Berlin: Graphische Gesellschaft, 1907); Hind B.M., 489-500; Hans Tietze and Erica Tietze-Conrat, "Giulio Campagnola's Engravings," PCQ. 29 (1942): 179-207; Hind v:189-205; NGA, 390-413; TIB 25 (*Commentary*): 463-90.

5. Cf. Giulio's *St. John the Baptist* (Hind 12), based on a Mantegna design; the figures of the boy and the eagle in Giulio's *Ganymede* (Hind 4), but not the Düreresque landscape beneath them, may also derive from Mantegna. For engravings usually placed with the Mantegna school but possibly by the young Giulio, see London 1992, nos. 83, 118, 123.

6. Cf. Giulio's *Penance of St. John Chrysostom* (Hind 3), after Dürer's engraving of the subject (B. 63). Giulio's *Tobias and the Angel, Saturn, Ganymede*, and his fragmentary *Landscape* (Hind 1-2, 4-5) all have landscapes copied from Dürer, whose technical conventions are likewise imitated.

7. Compare the engraved signatures on Giulio's *Tobias and the Angel, Saturn, Penance of St. John Chrysostom, Ganymede, St. John the Baptist*, and *Stag at Rest* (Hind 1-4, 12, 14). By contrast, the first state of *The Astrologer* (fig. 39-2) has a printed monogram consisting of the superimposed letters *I* and *C*, also found on second-state impressions of Giulio's *Old Shepherd* (Hind 8); important, though tentative, conclusions are drawn from the presence of these monograms by David Landau, London 1983a, 312, nos. P8-P9.

8. I.e., a first-state impression of *The Old Shepherd* (Hind 8) in the Bibliothèque Nationale, Paris; second-state impressions of *The Young Shepherd* (Hind 10) in Bologna and London (the latter illustrated in Hind VII: pl. 778); and an impression of the *Venus Reclining* (Hind 13, known only in a single state) in the Cleveland Museum of Art (illustrated in NGA, fig. 19-10).

Giulio Campagnola
Padua ca. 1482-ca. 1515/18 Venice

40. The Young Shepherd ca. 1510.

Engraving on antique laid paper, 13.2 x 7.8 cm (sheet).
B. 6; H. 10 ii/ii; TIB 2518.009 ii/ii.
Condition: Trimmed within platemark.
Provenance: Sir Joshua Reynolds (Lugt 2364); (purchased from M. Knoedler, New York, September 15, 1930, for $3,600). Bequest of Herbert Greer French, 1943.88.
Exhibitions: Cincinnati 1934, no. 7, pl. 5; Cincinnati 1941, no. 60, pl. 17; Minneapolis 1956, no. 96; Washington 1973, no. 282; Washington 1988, 50, 259, no. 27, fig. 15.
References: NGA, 400, fig. 19-11.

Similar in many respects to *The Astrologer* (cat. 39) and, in all likelihood, contemporary with it if not slightly later in date, *The Young Shepherd* also typifies Giulio Campagnola's mature style of engraving. Like *The Astrologer*, it is markedly Giorgionesque in spirit, so much so that commentators have often held that it is based on or adapted from Giorgione, perhaps even reproducing one of his lost designs.[1] While its invention should probably be credited to Giulio himself, the print's dreamy atmosphere, its velvet-soft forms, and its bucolic subject place it firmly within Giorgione's circle.

Although the title of the work should be retained for the sake of tradition – it has been in use since the beginning of the nineteenth century – no sheep are present to testify unequivocally to the seated boy's occupation.[2] On the other hand, the simple pair of flutes that he holds are common attributes of shepherds, who tend to be associated with such rude instruments in Italian Renaissance art. Indeed, the print may be regarded as a pendant of sorts to another by Giulio, *The Old Shepherd* (Hind 8) (fig. 40-1). In it an elderly man

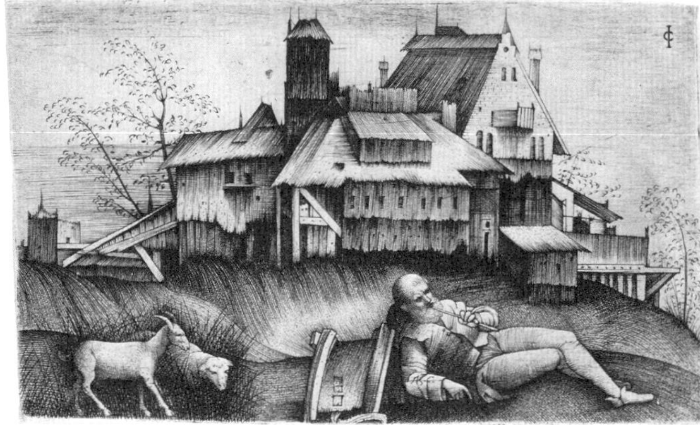

Figure 40-1. Giulio Campagnola, *The Old Shepherd*, ca. 1510-16, engraving, Hind 8. The Metropolitan Museum of Art, New York, Harris Brisbane Dick Fund, 1937.

plays a pipe while reclining in a landscape before a group of rustic buildings as a sheep and a goat browse nearby. The two works have similar dimensions, but in view of *The Old Shepherd*'s horizontal format, they cannot literally be taken as companion pieces. They do, however, embody a meaningful contrast of youth and age, a contrast explored in *The Young Shepherd* itself, where a bearded old man appears to lie sleeping at the feet of the boy. Implicit in the opposition of alert youth and somnolent age is that of life and death, a theme restated in the contrast between the leafy branches sprouting from the adjacent tree and the leafless dead ones below them. No doubt significant in this context are the flutes, for music above all other arts is associated with the passage of time. *The Young Shepherd*, then, is a kind of pastoral elegy, expressing in visual terms sentiments inherent to poetry and song – sentiments not unlike those already encountered in Giulio's *Astrologer*, with its somber, reflective mood.

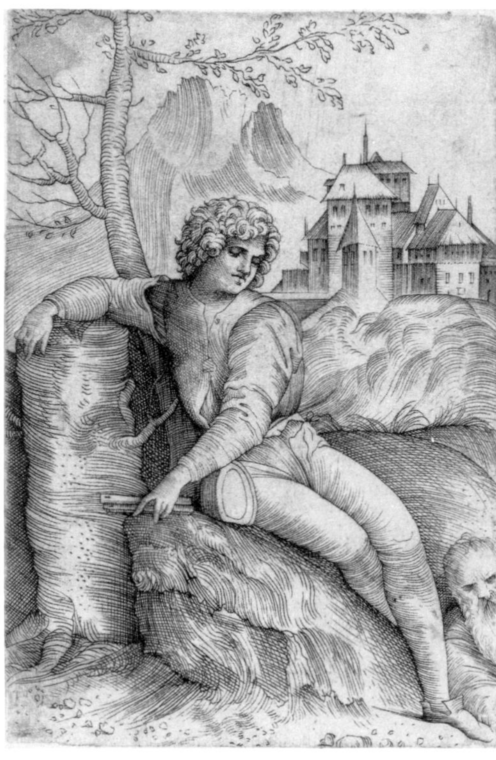

Figure 40-2. Giulio Campagnola, *The Young Shepherd*, ca 1510, engraving, Hind 10 i. British Museum, London.

Like *The Astrologer*, *The Young Shepherd* shows Giulio's virtuosity in obtaining tonal gradations of unprecedented richness and subtlety. His achievement is based on the combination of traditional line engraving with stippling, although the balance has now shifted decisively to the dotted manner. Again, the print exists in two different states, the first of which, still faintly reminiscent of Dürer in its curvilinear cross-hatching and its clusters of wavy parallels, consists of nothing but line and a few Düreresque flick-marks sprinkled over the surface of the tree stump (fig. 40-2). In the Museum's impression of the second state, however, Giulio's linework is virtually obscured by dots, although those lines that do remain visible – on the youth's clothing, for example, as well as on the rock upon which he is seated and the mountain in the background – are especially effective in suggesting both surface pattern and three-dimensional form.

Two early sixteenth-century engraved copies of *The Young Shepherd* (Hind 10a-b) attest to its contemporary appeal. Strangely enough, one of them, signed by Agostino Veneziano, derives from the undotted first state of Giulio's engraving.[3] Although the latter

survives only in a single impression (the London impression here illustrated), Agostino's copy suggests that Giulio put first-state impressions of his print into circulation, regarding them as finished, self-sufficient works rather than as trial proofs. The same may well be true of Giulio's *Astrologer*, which presents an even more satisfactory image in its undotted state (fig. 39-2) than does *The Young Shepherd*. – MZ

1. See, for example, Ludwig Justi, *Giorgione* (Berlin: Dietrich Reimer, 1926), 2:296; George Martin Richter, *Giorgio da Castelfranco, Called Giorgione* (Chicago: University of Chicago Press, 1937), 258; Konrad Oberhuber, NGA, 400.

2. Alfredo Petrucci prefers to call the engraving *Il flautista giovinetto* or *Il pagetto* (*The Young Flautist* or *The Page-boy*) (*Panorama della incisione italiana: il cinquecento* [Rome: Carlo Bestetti, 1964], 87).

3. Illus. TIB 25 (plate vol.): 249. Before leaving Venice in 1515 or 1516, the young Agostino also made copies of Giulio's *Old Shepherd* and *Astrologer* (Hind 8b, 9d; illus. TIB 25 [plate vol.]: 251, 254).

Marcantonio Raimondi

Bologna ca. 1480/82-by 1534 Bologna

41. The Climbers 1510.

Engraving on antique laid paper, 28.8 x 22.8 cm (sheet).
B. XIV.361.487; Delaborde 196.
Watermark: Cardinal's hat?
Dated on paper lower center: 1510.
Condition: Trimmed to or within platemark. Mounted on thin Japanese paper. Skinned patches verso.
Provenance: (Purchased from M. Knoedler, New York, November 1, 1934, for $250).
Bequest of Herbert Greer French, 1943.152.
Exhibitions: Cincinnati 1941, no. 71.

The Climbers, the last dated print by Marcantonio, was made relatively early in his career (cat. 32).[1] It is one of three prints in which he reproduced figures from a famous and enormously influential composition by Michelangelo of 1504-05, the cartoon for a section of *The Battle of Cascina*. This cartoon (a full-sized drawing constituting the last stage in the preparation for a fresco) was on view in the Palazzo della Signoria in Florence when Marcantonio passed through the city on his way from Venice to Rome about 1509. *The Battle of Cascina* was conceived as a pendant to Leonardo's *Battle of Anghiari*, the cartoon for which was completed just prior to Michelangelo's. Each *Battle* was to be painted on one half of a long wall of the Sala del Gran Consiglio in the palazzo.[2] Michelangelo's patriotic commemoration of a 1364 Florentine victory over Pisa was a timely subject at the beginning of the sixteenth century because Florence and Pisa were again at war.

Michelangelo finished only the cartoon for *The Bathers*, not the rest of the composition of *The Battle of Cascina*, presumably because he was called to Rome by Pope Julius II to begin work on the pope's tomb (another ill-fated project). What is now known of Michelangelo's composition may represent less than half of what was projected, the rest to have shown arriving cavalry and battle scenes. The composition was never painted in fresco. Because the cartoon was greatly admired, it was moved around, cut into pieces, and eventually destroyed within a decade of its creation. The entire composition of *The Bathers*, however, has come down to us through a painted copy by Aristotile da San Gallo (fig. 41-1) made in 1542 from an earlier drawing.

The Bathers shows a group of nineteen Florentine soldiers hastily climbing out of the river Arno to dress for battle – a moment that allowed Michelangelo to show off his mastery in depicting the male

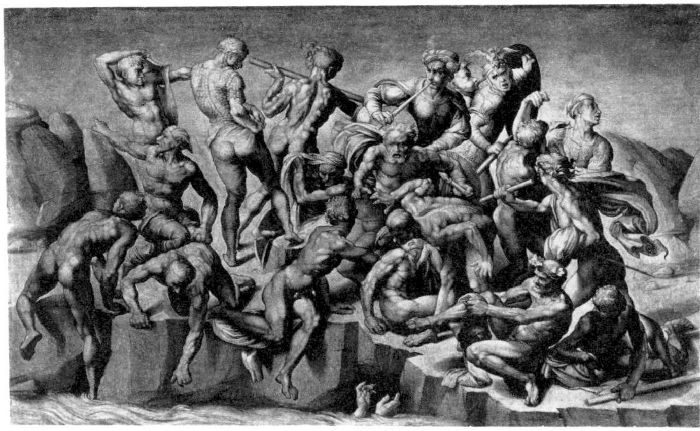

Figure 41-1. Aristotile da Sangallo, copy after Michaelangelo's *Battle of Cascina, The Bathers*, 1542, grisaille. Viscount Coke and the Trustees of Holkham Estate, Holkham Hall.

nude figure; it was recently that he had completed the great marble *David*. The engraving reuses a figure Marcantonio had earlier isolated in one of the two other prints mentioned above. Both of these prints (B.472 and B.488), which only show one figure, can, on stylistic grounds, be dated earlier than this engraving. For *The Climbers* Marcantonio took a group of three interrelated figures from the left side of Michelangelo's composition and placed them in an incongruous setting – the landscape of Lucas van Leyden's precocious engraving of 1508, *Mohammed and the Monk Sergius* (H. *Neth.* 126) (fig. 41-2). Marcantonio eliminated the tree on the right to make room for the pointing man, changed the consternated group in the background of Lucas' print to Pisan soldiers hidden in the woods, and made the foreground into a shallow river bank. On the riverbank, Marcantonio engraved a piece of paper with his date.

In copying a print by Lucas van Leyden (see cats. 54-55), Marcantonio indicated his interest in and admiration for the work of the young Netherlandish artist. His own style at this time reflected the influence of both Dürer and Lucas: Dürer's in the clarity of the modeling and in the employment of a greater variety of burin strokes

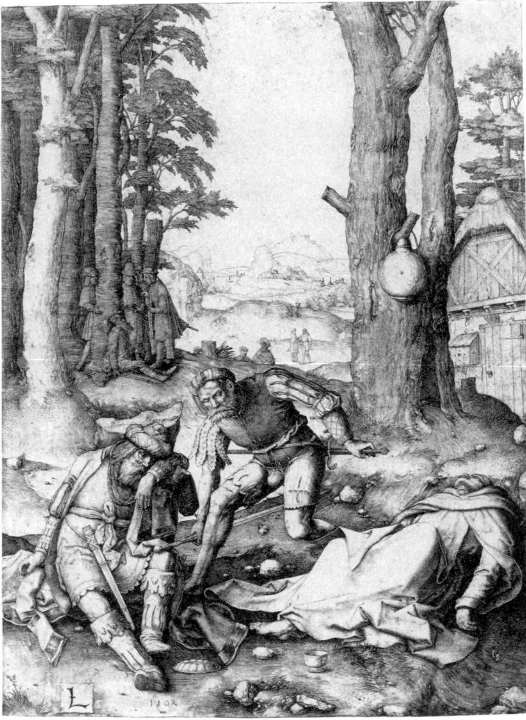

Figure 41-2. Lucas van Leyden, *Mohamet and the Monk Sergius*, 1508, B. 126 i. The Metropolitan Museum of Art, New York, Rogers Fund, 1921.

and Lucas' in a striving for delicate tonal effects. Marcantonio's technique had developed, and greater systematization and control of the burin are exhibited here than in *The Nativity* of some seven years earlier (cat. 32). Although *The Climbers* is still a pastiche, the blending of sources is much more skillful than in the earlier print, and excepting the Northern flavor of the trees and building, the figures on the whole are comfortably placed in their appropriated setting. – SB

1. For this print, see also Lawrence 1981, 90-93, no. 19.
2. For Michelangelo's drawings for the *Battle*, see Cecil Gould, *Michelangelo, Battle of Cascina* (Newcastle upon Tyne: University of Newcastle upon Tyne, 1966), unpaginated; Howard Hibbard, *Michelangelo* (New York: Harper and Row, 1974), 74-84; Michael Hirst, *Michelangelo and His Drawings* (New Haven and London: Yale University Press, 1988), 125; see also Charles de Tolnay, *The Youth of Michelangelo* (Princeton: Princeton University Press, 1943), 209-19.

Cristofano Robetta

Florence 1462?-after 1522

42. The Virgin and Child with St. John and Three Angels ca. 1500-20.

Engraving on antique laid paper, 24.8 x 17.8 cm (platemark).
B. 13; Hind 19 i/ii; TIB 2521.021 i/ii.
Condition: Trimmed to platemark.
Provenance: Count Franz von Sternberg-Manderscheid; Friedrich August II (Lugt 971); (his sale C.G. Boerner, Leipzig, November 8-9, 1932, no. 639, pl. 23, to Matthiesen for RM 3,500); Dr. Meller, Vienna; (purchased from Harlow, McDonald, New York, May 5, 1933, for $2,000).
Bequest of Herbert Greer French, 1943.142.
Exhibitions: Cincinnati 1934, no. 27; Cincinnati 1941, no. 69, pl. 19.

One of the more appealing Italian engravers of the early sixteenth century, Robetta is in all probability the artist identified as Cristofano di Michele, born in Florence in 1462 to a shoemaker or hosier (*calzaiuolo*) named Michele di Cristofano Martini. In 1480, at eighteen years of age, Cristofano was working in his father's shop, which suggests that he began his artistic studies at an unusually advanced age and did not undergo a normal apprenticeship. If true, these circumstances may explain why none of his surviving works can be dated prior to the very end of the fifteenth century and why even the most accomplished of them retain a touch of awkwardness. Be that as it may, by 1498 he was operating as a goldsmith, like Pollaiuolo (cat. 16) and other Florentine engravers before him. Robetta's name is thereafter linked with this occupation in documents from 1516 to 1522, and he was possibly still alive as late as 1535.[1] Apart from these meager records, the only references to him in a Renaissance source are two passing remarks from Vasari's *Life* of the sculptor Giovanni Francesco Rustici.[2] Here we learn that the "goldsmith Robetta" belonged to a dining club, the Company of the Cauldron, along with such noted Florentine painters as Andrea del Sarto and Domenico Puligo, in addition to Rustici and several lesser-known artists.

Understandably, Robetta's engravings show no kinship with works by fellow members of the company, for most of his compatriots were much younger than he. Sarto, for example, was born in 1486 and Puligo, in 1492, and their paintings present a fully evolved High Renaissance style. By contrast, Robetta's manner is fundamentally rooted in late fifteenth-century Florentine painting, which is to say, in the Early Renaissance art of his own generation. He took frequent inspiration from older artists, among them Pollaiuolo (b. 1431-32) and Botticelli (b. 1445), and especially from his near contemporary, Botticelli's pupil, Filippino Lippi (b. 1457-58).[3] Filippino's influence, coupled with that of his master, is paramount in Robetta's *Virgin and Child with St. John and Three Angels*, where the figures' attenuated proportions, their lissome grace, and the linear complexity of the angels' windblown drapery – fragmented by myriad thin, convoluted folds – testify to their origins in paintings by Botticelli and Filippino of the 1480s and 1490s.

None of Robetta's engravings can be dated with precision, but he surely produced this fully mature work sometime during the first two decades of the sixteenth century, thereby extending the life of a style already fading from fashion. Just as distinctive as the figure and drapery style is the ornamental character of the design as a whole, which betrays the mind and hand of a goldsmith accustomed to making decorative objects and to working in small scale with precious and semiprecious materials. Robetta situated his figures on rising terrain that clings to the surface as much as it recedes into space. Covered with wavy striations and anchored in the foreground by virtually abstract formations sprinkled with flicklike marks, this strange landscape quivers with vitality. Normal expectations are confounded as earth and rock lose their sense of solid substance, alternately taking on the semblance of rolling sea or turbulent sky or pure two-dimensional pattern.

Thus Robetta adhered to principles of late quattrocento Florentine design, perpetuating them idiosyncratically into the opening decades of the sixteenth century. He may even be said to have preserved an indigenous technique by working in a late variant of the so-called Fine Manner. Characterized by short, straight, closely laid lines, delicately incised, the technique often produces bands or patches of shading of the kind we see on flesh and drapery in Robetta's print. Ever since Florentine goldsmiths began to engrave copperplates for printing in the 1460s, the Fine Manner predominated in local workshops, notwithstanding the development of the rival Broad Manner, popularized by Francesco Rosselli in the 1480s and 1490s. Around the turn of the century, however, native traditions changed decisively under the impact of German imports. The arrival of what must have been large quantities of engravings executed between 1495 and 1501 by the young Albrecht Dürer caused a sensation among practitioners of the craft all over Italy. While various Florentines, including Robetta, were already familiar with prints by his Northern predecessors, they had never seen anything quite like Dürer's astonishingly rich, detailed, and naturalistic engravings. These works had a catalytic effect on Italian engravers, few of whom remained immune to their influence.

To one degree or another, all of Robetta's mature prints show the influence of Dürer, sometimes to the point of being larded with motifs adopted wholesale from readily identifiable models. *The Virgin and Child* is less derivative than other of Robetta's works, but the handling of the landscape is thoroughly in Dürer's manner. Rocks and hummocks are marked with characteristic dots, flicks, and short, rounded dashes; the sloping hill is defined by imitative masses of sweeping, undulating strokes; and Düreresque clouds are set off by a large, blank (unfinished?) area and by Düreresque bands of long horizontal lines. Yet where Dürer used these devices to suggest nature's own forms and textures, Robetta produced something more akin to ornamental pattern and abstract design.

Robetta thus emerges as an original artist, despite his obvious eclecticism. Basing his figures and their arrangement on Florentine sources, he borrowed elements of landscape from Dürer and combined aspects of traditional Florentine technique with the technical conventions of a foreigner. In *The Virgin and Child*, one of the most beautiful of the thirty-five to forty engravings by or attributed to him, Robetta takes the best features from both worlds and synthesizes them in a manner uniquely his own. – MZ

1. For all known documents pertaining to Robetta, see Paolo Minucci del Rosso, "Di alcuni personaggi ricordati dal Vasari nella Vita di Gio. Francesco Rustici," *Archivio storico italiano*, 4th ser., 3 (1879): 475-82. Since various documents refer to Robetta as Cristofano di Michele di Cristofano, he is probably identical with the son of the *calzaiuolo*, Michele di Cristofano. If, however, the identification should prove to be mistaken, one might date his birth more plausibly fifteen to twenty years later than 1462. In the present entry I retain the traditional view of Robetta's parentage and birthdate, but further study may oblige me to revise my opinion and some of the conclusions that follow from it.

2. Giorgio Vasari, *Le Vite de' più eccellenti pittori, scultori ed architettori*, ed. Gaetano Milanesi (Florence: Sansoni, 1878-85), 6:609, 611.

3. E.g., Robetta's *Hercules and the Hydra* and *Hercules and Antaeus* (Hind 34-35) are based on Pollaiuolo; his *Adoration of the Magi*, *Vision of St. Bernard*, and *Two Muses* (Hind 10, 21, 27), on Filippino.

Master I. B. with the Bird

(Giovanni Battista Palumba?)
Roman? School active ca. 1500-1510

43. Leda and Her Children ca. 1510.
Engraving on antique laid paper, 15.4 x 12.4 cm (platemark).
B. 3; Hind 10; TIB 2507.005.
Signed on tablet lower left: IB (followed by a bird).
Condition: Trimmed to platemark.
Provenance: Friedrich August II (Lugt 971); (his sale C.G. Boerner, Leipzig, November 8-9, 1932, no. 439, pl. 8); (purchased from Harlow, McDonald, New York, July 10, 1933).
Bequest of Herbert Greer French, 1943.169.
Exhibitions: Cincinnati 1934, no. 29.

Master I.B. with the Bird received his odd sobriquet, among the more colorful nicknames to have been bestowed upon a printmaker, for an obvious reason. All but one of his fourteen engravings[1] and all but one of his twelve known woodcuts[2] are signed with the letters *IB* (with or without punctuation) followed by a small bird shown in profile. Needless to say, scholars have long puzzled over the master's identity, attempting to solve the problem through learned argument and bold conjecture.[3] Most of these scholarly endeavors begin with the plausible assumption that the bird is a rebus for the surname of an artist whose given names begin with the initials *I* and *B* in Latin or Italian. Although small doubts continue to linger, Augusto Campana seems to have found the solution in a manuscript by the minor Roman humanist Evangelista Maddaleni dei Capodiferro. Now in the Vatican Library, this codex is a collection of some five hundred Latin and Italian poems, one of which, an epigram datable to circa 1503, almost certainly alludes to a surviving engraving by Master I.B.[4] The epigram's title refers to the master by the literary name of Dares; but in a marginal note Maddaleni gives his real name: "Io[h]anne[s] Baptista [i.e., Giovanni Battista in the vernacular] Palumba." Thus the engraver's first two names accord with the initials *I* and *B*, while his family name neatly corresponds with the Italian *palombo*, a variety of pigeon.

To have rescued Master I.B. with the Bird from the limbo of anonymity is cause for real satisfaction. Nevertheless, the achievement should not be overrated, inasmuch as no further information concerning Giovanni Battista Palumba has turned up in the fifty-odd years since Campana's discovery. We are therefore at liberty to reconstruct the artist's development in whatever way seems most compatible with the evidence available, that being mainly the prints themselves. They do not, unfortunately, tell us anything definite about Palumba's origins. He may have come from Bologna or perhaps from Lombardy, but at any rate, the locus of his activity during the first decade or so of the sixteenth century was probably

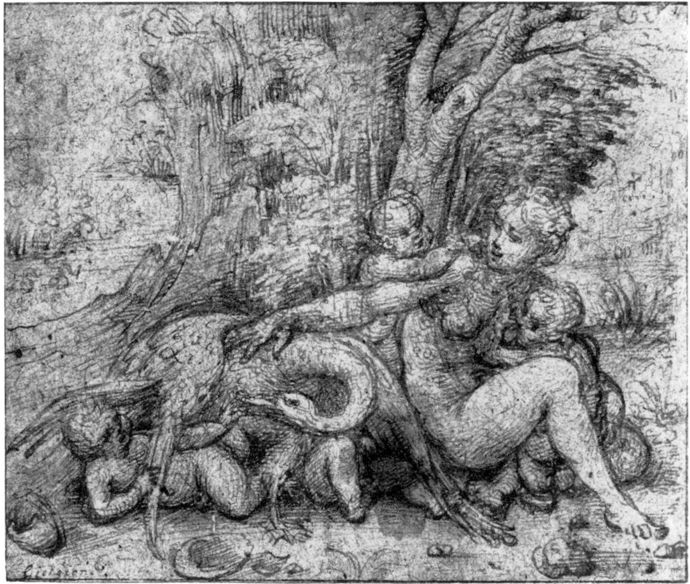

Figure 43-1. Master I.B. with the Bird (attr.), *Leda and Her Children*, ca. 1510, drawing. British Museum, London.

Rome, a hypothesis confirmed by Maddaleni's epigram.

At the height of his career, conjecturally around 1510, Master I.B. produced the engraving *Leda and Her Children*. One of his most admired works, it illustrates the myth in which Zeus (or Jupiter) comes to Leda in the guise of a swan. Leda, in due course, lays a pair of oversized eggs, from which spring Castor and Pollux, the "heavenly twins" of the constellation Gemini, as well as Clytemnestra, doomed to murder her husband Agamemnon, and Helen, fated to provoke the Trojan War. Oblivious to the dire consequences of this tryst, Master I.B. treated the subject in a playful vein. Bits of eggshell lie here and there as the precocious newly hatched children exhibit a range of infantile behavior. One of them suckles at Leda's breast, another presents her with a butterfly, and the remaining two cavort with the swan who, entangled with his offspring, turns to nip a child on the fingers while receiving a wifely caress from the smiling Leda. This delightful, pseudoclassical family outing takes place before a spectacular ruin that contemporary Romans would have instantly recognized as the famous late antique nymphaeum on the Esquiline hill, then known as the Temple of Minerva Medica. Although its ruinous state is absurdly anachronistic, the picturesque structure serves to set the scene in pagan antiquity and, assuming that the master had firsthand knowledge of the building, bears witness to his presence in Rome.

Like so many of his contemporaries throughout Italy, Master I.B. takes Albrecht Dürer as a point of departure for his style of engraving. He often borrowed details of landscape or other elements of staffage from Dürer's engravings and almost always utilized his graphic conventions. *Leda* includes no direct quotations, but most of its landscape is unabashedly Düreresque, from the flicklike markings of the foreground, to the undulating striations of the middleground, to the feathery trees and lightly engraved mountains in the distance. It was equally characteristic of the master's generation of engravers to stay closer to home for the figural portions of their compositions. Here the classically inspired female nude and accompanying putti arrange themselves into the sort of tightly knit pyramidal configuration universally associated with principles of Italian High Renaissance design.

Indeed the central group of interconnected figures can be traced (by an unknown route) to a series of themes and variations on the subject of Leda and her children that Leonardo da Vinci had

developed a few years earlier.[5] Especially close to a putative model in Leonardo is a drawing in the British Museum (fig. 43-1), tentatively attributable to Master I.B.'s own hand.[6] It shows the composition in reverse of the engraving, includes a wholly different landscape as well as a mound of rocks and trees in place of the classical ruin, and varies from I.B.'s ultimate solution in a number of other ways. Doubts concerning its authorship notwithstanding, the drawing documents an early stage in the evolution of a design that, in its final form, represents a harmonious fusion of Leonardo and Dürer. – MZ

1. I follow Konrad Oberhuber in rejecting I.B.'s authorship of an engraving of *Venus and Cupid* (Hind 15) but do not agree with his other attributions (NGA, 508-09) to the author of this print, whom Oberhuber dubs Master IRs.

2. For the woodcuts, see especially Friedrich Lippmann, *The Woodcuts of Master I.B. with the Bird* (Berlin: International Chalcographical Society, 1894); J. Byam Shaw, "The Master I.B. with the Bird," PCQ. 19 (1932): 285ff; 20 (1933): 174-78; Oberhuber, NGA, 443-45, n. 13.

3. Opinions summarized and evaluated by Hind V:248-53.

4. The print in question (Hind 9) shows Leda copulating with the swan, and the epigram, an elegiac couplet, reads "*De Laeda a Darete impressa. / Laeda videbatur vix concubuisse Tonanti / Ni foret arte nova iuncta sine arte Iovi*" (loosely translated: "On Leda printed by Dares. / It seems that Leda would hardly have coupled with the Thunderer / Had she not by the new art [of engraving?] been joined to this artless Jove"). See Augusto Campana, "Intorno all'incisore Gian Battista Palumba e al pittore Jacopo Rimpacta (Ripanda)," *Maso Finiguerra* 1 (1936): 164-72.

5. The issue is discussed by Oberhuber, NGA, 450-52.

6. No. 1862-10-11-199; pen and ink, 12.5 x 15.1 cm. Discussion of the drawing in Oberhuber, NGA, 452.

Master of the Beheading of St. John the Baptist

Milanese? School active ca. 1500-1525

44. Doe Resting ca. 1510-20?

Engraving on antique blue gray laid paper, 18.3 x 13.5 cm (sheet).
P.V.166.17 and P.VI.259.74; Hind 3.
Condition: Trimmed to platemark; added lower right corner; repaired vertical tear bisecting sheet; retouched with pen and black ink.
Provenance: (Alfred Strölin, Lausanne, consigned to Knoedler, June 14, 1932); (purchased from M. Knoedler, New York, May 8, 1933 for $1,350).
Bequest of Herbert Greer French, 1943.168.
Exhibitions: Cincinnati 1934, no. 28; Paris 1935; Cincinnati 1941, no. 12, pl. 3; Washington 1949; Washington 1973, no. 236; Austin 1980, no. 127.

This delicate and beautiful work was engraved by one of the many early Italian printmakers who has left us no definite clues to his identity. Author of four engravings (and a possible fifth one, less reliably attributed), he takes his nickname from *The Beheading of St. John the Baptist* (Hind 1), a key member of his small but distinctive oeuvre.[1] After a certain amount of confusion among nineteenth-century print specialists, scholars have tentatively agreed to localize the master in or near Milan, the great Lombard metropolis in northwestern Italy, where he would have been active during the first quarter of the sixteenth century.[2] His works show affinities with paintings and drawings by Leonardo da Vinci, whose style forms the basis of the entire early sixteenth-century Lombard school of painting; and insofar as paintings can legitimately be compared to prints, his engravings have also been related to the painted work of such Milanese followers of Leonardo as Cesare da Sesto and Marco d'Oggiono.

It must be admitted, however, that Milanese engraving of the Renaissance is something of a *terra incognita*.[3] Late fifteenth-century craftsmen are mostly anonymous and appear to have been a rather conservative lot; nor did a common style emerge among engravers of the master's generation. In some respects, moreover, the master's works find their closest counterparts in those of Giulio Campagnola and his following – that is to say in northeastern, rather than northwestern, Italian engraving. Indeed the *Doe Resting* was actually attributed to Giulio when, 150 years ago, it made its first appearance in the scholarly literature.[4] The master's style is certainly analogous to and was possibly influenced by Giulio's idiosyncratic approach to the medium. Both men's works are characterized by an amazing lightness of touch, by great refinement, and by a sensitivity to soft, velvety form, effects obtained by suppressing continuous lines and downplaying emphatic contours in favor of short, delicate strokes of the burin.

On the other hand, the master's engravings remain quite distinct from those of Giulio Campagnola. Comparing the *Doe Resting* with Giulio's *Young Shepherd* (cat. 40), for example, we note that Giulio's system of uniform stippling results in an overall tonal unity, yet scarcely differentiates among the textures of rock, earth, bark, or, for that matter, flesh or cloth. Eschewing this somewhat inflexible dotted manner, the Master of the Beheading of St. John the Baptist approached nature far more closely. In modeling the doe with minute flicks, he produced a graphic equivalent of the actual substance of its hide; and he varied the length and character of his strokes throughout the print to suggest diversity, rather than uniformity, in the tree trunks, twigs, leaves, grasses, and stones. Infinitely more attuned to the wonder of nature's variety and abundance than Giulio, the master created a little corner of the world that teems with life. Leafless branches twist and turn, plants appear to wave in the breeze, ducks skim across an unruffled sea, frogs enliven the foreground space, and a pair of birds flutters at the end of a branch as a snake slithers up in their direction.

The *Doe Resting* is commonly held to be based on an engraving by Giulio Campagnola, *Stag at Rest, Chained to a Tree* (Hind 14), and there is no denying that the two images are of the same general type

(fig. 44-1). Even so, their stylistic differences are as marked as those between the *Doe Resting* and *The Young Shepherd*, and the master's print has neither the abstract, timeless setting nor the obviously contrived composition of Giulio's emblematic *Stag*. On the contrary, in view of its extraordinary naturalism, one is tempted to think of the *Doe Resting* as being nothing beyond what it seems to be: a straightforward, unpretentious image derived from the artist's loving attention to nature, produced for a clientele that shared a common outlook. But Renaissance prints customarily offer more than a slice of life, and it may well be that the *Doe Resting*, after all, was originally understood to have additional significance. This idea finds some support in another engraving by the master, *Stag Browsing* (Hind 4) – an unfinished work of similar dimensions, identical in style and format but presenting a contrasting subject (fig. 44-2). Although each engraving is self-sufficient, together they may function as pendants, or companion pieces, complementing one another and inviting the viewer to contemplate the meaningful relationship between an active male and a passive female of the same species. If such were the master's intention, he expressed it with remarkable subtlety and restraint. Additional layers of meaning, assuming they are really present, in no way detract from the primary appeal of these engravings as intimate, unassertive glimpses of nature. – MZ

1. Colin Eisler, *The Master of the Unicorn: The Life and Work of Jean Duvet* (New York: Abaris Books, 1979), 323, doubts that the *Doe Resting* and the associated *Stag Browsing* (fig. 44-2) are by the same hand as the eponymous *Beheading*, but his reservations seem to me to be unwarranted.

2. I cannot accept Jacquelyn Sheehan's theory (NGA, 437) that the master may have also worked in Mantua among the followers of Mantegna nor that he might have been responsible for two "Mantegna school" prints, *The Man of Sorrows* and *Hercules and the Hydra* (Hind 26-27).

3. No comprehensive study has been undertaken since Paul Kristeller's classic *Die lombardische Graphik der Renaissance* (Berlin: Bruno Cassirer, 1913).

4. P.V.166.17 (subsequently listing it a second time under the name of Jean Duvet, P.VI.259.74).

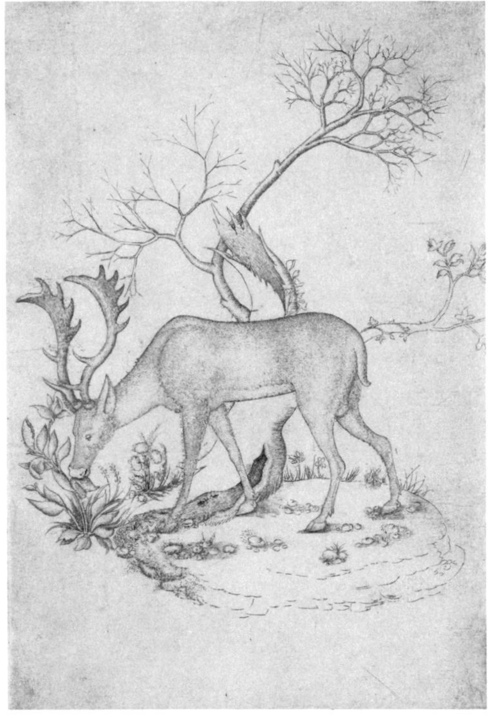

Figure 44-1. Master of the Beheading of St. John the Baptist, *Stag Browsing*, engraving, Hind 4. Museum of Fine Arts, Boston, S. Ballard, H.G. Curtis and G.P. Gardner Funds.

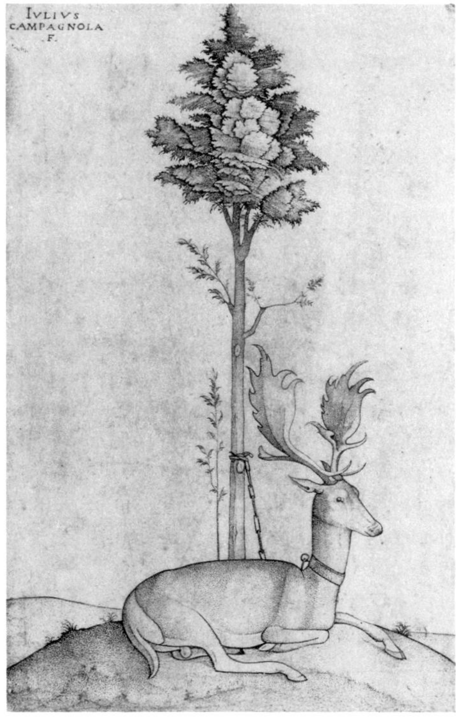

Figure 44-2. Giulio Campagnola, *Stag at Rest, Chained to a Tree*, engraving, Hind 14. British Museum, London.

Albrecht Dürer

Nuremberg 1471-1528 Nuremberg

45. Madonna on the Crescent ca. 1510-11.

Title page for *Life of the Virgin*.
Woodcut on antique laid paper, 22.0 x 19.1 cm (sheet)
B. 76; Meder 188 proof; Panofsky 296; H. *Ger.* 188; TIB 1001.276
Watermark: Bull's head (Meder 70).
Condition: Trimmed to edge of image at right.
Provenance: (Purchased from F.H. Bresler, Milwaukee, November 13, 1930, for $1,350).
Bequest of Herbert Greer French, 1943.215.
Exhibitions: Cincinnati 1941, no. 122.

> In the year 1511 [Albrecht Dürer] represented the whole life of Our Lady in twenty sheets of the same size, executing it so well, that it would not be possible. . . to do better.
>
> – Giorgio Vasari (*Lives of the Artists*)[1]

The years around 1500 brought growing emphasis to the veneration of the Virgin Mary, Pope Sixtus IV (1414-84) having recently conferred new importance on the doctrine of the Immaculate Conception.[2] Although this doctrine had been forcefully opposed in the Middle Ages by St. Bernard and did not become Catholic dogma until 1854, Sixtus' constitution of 1483 threatened anyone who did not believe in it with excommunication.[3] By 1497 the great universities, first Paris and Bologna, later Mainz, Cologne, and Vienna, decreed that henceforth no one should be admitted to their faculties who refused to take an oath to defend the doctrine of Mary's Immaculate Conception. A new phrase had also been added to the Hail Mary, asking that the Virgin "pray for us now and at the hour of our death," emphasizing Mary's role as intercessor with Christ on behalf of sinners.[4]

At about the time of his father's death in 1502, Dürer seems to have made the first in a series of twenty full-page woodcuts that he would later publish in 1511 as the third of his large picture books, *Life of the Virgin*. At least seventeen of the woodcuts had been finished and marketed as single sheets before Dürer left for his second trip to Italy in 1505.[5] We know this from Marcantonio Raimondi's engraved copies with forged Dürer monograms, two of which bear the date 1506 (B. 621-37).[6]

After his return, Dürer completed the series and designed its visionary title page, *Madonna on the Crescent*, and had all twenty woodcuts printed in book form by Hieronymus Höltzel. As he had done earlier with *The Apocalypse* (cat. 23), Dürer retained his own name as the book's publisher. For the frontispiece, he chose an image based on a vision of John the Evangelist on the island of Patmos (Rev. 12:1-5):

> And there appeared a great wonder in Heaven; a woman clothed with the sun, and the moon under her feet, and upon her head a crown of twelve stars. . . . And she brought forth a man child, who was to rule all nations. . . and her child was caught up unto God, and to His throne.

The apocalyptic woman "clothed with the sun" was identified in Christian theology as the Virgin Mary, and the reference to her son, who later vanquishes a dragon representing Satan, was thought to signify Christ. Dürer's depiction of the apocalyptic woman as a seated, nursing Madonna combines the visionary language of John with the image of the Madonna of Humility – "humble and exalted," as Dante says – who is traditionally shown nursing while sitting on the ground.

Since the New Testament contains relatively little material concerning the life of Christ's mother, Dürer commissioned the poet Benedictus Chelidonius (Benedict Schwalbe), a monk in Nuremberg's Benedictine monastery of Saint Egidius, to write the brief text for this volume. Chelidonius wrote the twenty-six-line Latin poem that appears recto and verso on the title page of the book as well as the eight-line poem at the end of the volume that dedicates the book to Caritas Pirckheimer, abbess of Nuremberg's Franciscan convent of Saint Clara. Caritas was the older sister of Dürer's best friend, Willibald Pirckheimer.

Before the Reformation, Saint Clara's convent, where Sister Caritas had been mistress of novices before her elevation to abbess, was the institution where young girls of Nuremberg's "better" families were sent to be educated. Dürer was undoubtedly aware of the potential value of his folio-sized and beautifully crafted scenes from the life of the Virgin for classroom use. Mary's maidenly purity and motherly love made her the ideal role model for young women. Dürer directs attention to these qualities by choosing to illustrate the nursing but apocalyptic Madonna enthroned in a setting of cumulus clouds. The artist's interest in the Virgin Mary would have been amplified and enhanced by his knowledge of the fifteen mysteries of the rosary – scenes that he glorified in a major altarpiece painted in 1506 for the German church in Venice (*Altarpiece of the Rose Garlands*, now in the National Gallery, Prague). The final mysteries of the rosary, the "glorious" ones, culminate in the coronation of the Virgin after her bodily assumption into Heaven.

Dürer's series was not only the most beautiful but also the most extensively detailed life of the Virgin Mary available in the graphic arts at the time; yet despite its unusual number of prints, it is remarkable for its theological accuracy. The events treated do not include any of the more bizarre miracles that had been credited to the Virgin before the Reformation but are geared instead to the feast days of the liturgical year and to the mysteries of the rosary. The soundness of its "scholarship," from the clerical point of view, was to become one of the chief reasons why Dürer, a generation after his death, won high praise for his series from the Council of Trent, despite his many friendships with leaders of the Reformation, including Spengler, Melanchthon, Karlstadt, and Martin Luther's protector, Friedrich the Wise, and despite his membership in a study group led by Luther's own confessor, Johann von Staupitz. Dürer's *Life of the Virgin* was completed and published six years before the beginning of the Reformation, a decade before Luther addressed the question of the Virgin's theological role in his commentaries on the Magnificat (1521) and the Hail Mary (1522).

Cincinnati owns a complete set of proof impressions for *Life of the Virgin* (CAM 1943.214, 216-34), purchased *en bloc* by Mr. French, as well as this brilliant rare proof state of the title page (before the addition of text printed from movable type) on warm-toned paper resulting in a radiant light. Other proof sheets of this page are in the British Museum, the Art Institute of Chicago, and the Staatsgalerie in Stuttgart. – JH

1. Giorgio Vasari, *Le Vite de' più eccellenti pittori, scultori ed architettori*, ed. Gaetano Milanesi (Florence: Sansoni, 1878-85), 5:398-409.
2. The doctrine of the Immaculate Conception does not refer to Christ but to his mother, the Virgin Mary, who was also thought to have been born of a virginal mother.
3. *Grave nimis* (September 4, 1483). See also Mirella Levi d'Ancona, *The Iconography of the Immaculate Conception in the Middle Ages and Early Renaissance*, vol. 7 of *Monographs on Archaeology and Fine Arts* (New York, 1957).
4. On this and other aspects of the cult of the Virgin in Germany, see Stephan Beissel, S.J., *Geschichte der Verehrung Marias in Deutschland* (Freiburg im Breisgau, 1909), passim.
5. The existence of Dürer's first trip to Italy, made in 1494-95 shortly after his wedding, was most recently questioned by Alastair Smith ("Germania and Italia: Albrecht Dürer and Venetian Art," *Journal of the Royal Society of Arts* 127 [April

1979]: 273-90). Smith's argument rests upon faulty logic and an incomplete knowledge of Dürer's oeuvre.

6. On the dating of the individual woodcuts from Dürer's series, see Ernst Heidrich, "Zur Chronologie des Dürerschen Marienlebens," *Rep. Kw.* 29 (1906): 227-41; Bernward Deneke, Nuremberg 1971, 195-97, 329-30, nos. 376 and 601; Charles Talbot, Washington 1971, 178-83; Barbara S. Shapiro, Boston 1971, 86-113, nos. 63-82; Walter L. Strauss, TIB 10 (Commentary):346-75.

Lucas Cranach the Elder
Kronach 1472-1553 Weimar

46. Friedrich the Wise in Prayer before the Madonna and Child ca. 1512-15.
Hand colored woodcut on antique laid paper, 36.8 x 22.9 cm (image).
B. 77; Ge. 566; H. *Ger.* 72; Geisberg/Strauss 566; Koepplin and Falk 341.
Signed in lower center margin: *Hans Guldenmundt.*
Provenance: Ducal Museum, Gotha; (sale C.G. Boerner, Leipzig, November 14-15, 1933, no. 176, to Richard Zinser for RM 1,300); (purchased from M. Knoedler, New York, 1941, for $2,850). Bequest of Herbert Greer French, 1943.97.

Friedrich III (1463-1525), a prince of Saxony from the Ernestine branch of the Wettin dynasty, succeeded his father in 1486, and as a leader of Saxony and a German elector, he became one of the most influential rulers in early sixteenth-century Germany. Emperor Maximilian I appointed him head of the *Reichsregiment* (Imperial Council of Regency) and *Reichs-Erzmarschall* (Imperial Governor-General) in 1500 and 1507, respectively. Friedrich was himself considered a candidate for Roman king, but he declined the opportunity and was, instead, a pivotal player in the election of Charles V in 1519. His political caution and tact earned him the epithet Friedrich the Wise. An avid patron of the arts, he turned Wittenberg into an important art center, commissioning paintings from Dürer (cats. 48-49) and Burgkmair (cat. 37) and employing such artists as the Venetian Jacopo de' Barbari (1503-05) at court (cats. 27, 34).[1] In 1505 Friedrich engaged Lucas Cranach as court artist. Cranach had already worked in 1501 at the Veste Coburg, one of Friedrich's familial residences, but it was his growing reputation as a book illustrator and painter for humanists in the imperial circle in Vienna that made him an attractive choice.[2]

Cranach was the only major German Renaissance artist to ever serve as a full-time in-house court artist, a position that he retained for life, working and prospering after Friedrich's death under his successors Johann the Steadfast (1463-1532) and Johann Friedrich I the Magnanimous (1503-1554). Besides his annual salary of one hundred guilders (and a yearly set of summer and winter court attire), Cranach was paid for individual paintings and for the costs of some materials.[3] By 1507 he had two apprentices in what would become an extremely busy workshop. Five years later he had built a house on Wittenberg's marketplace – with eighty-four heatable rooms! – suitable enough to host the exiled king of Denmark (1523). In 1520 he obtained, with electoral privilege, an apothecary's license and held a monopoly on the sale of medicine, herbs, sugar, and wine in Wittenberg. Cranach served the town as councilman and as mayor (three times), and by 1528 he was its second richest citizen.[4]

The reputations of Friedrich the Wise and Lucas Cranach were closely linked with the Reformation. Friedrich founded the University of Wittenberg (1502), where Luther taught theology. It was at the University's Castle Church of All Saints that Luther triggered the Reformation by posting, in 1517, his *Disputation on the Power and Efficacy of Indulgences*, better known as the ninety-five theses. Friedrich would later protect the reformer by securing a safe public hearing for him in Worms in 1521, by concealing him in Wartburg Castle after he was declared an outlaw, and above all by allowing Wittenberg to become the center of the reform movement.

Cranach was Luther's friend and portraitist. He served as witness for Luther's marriage (1525), and Luther was his daughter's godfather (1520). He illustrated Luther's publications, such as the *Passional Christi and Antichrist* (1521) and the *September Testament* (1522). The artist also provided the public with much sought-after prints of the reformer, portraying him as monk, as scholar, and in his disguise as *Junker Jörg* (Squire George) with beard and a full crop of hair.[5]

The Museum's woodcut of *Friedrich the Wise in Prayer before the Madonna and Child* predates the Reformation. It reveals Friedrich as a devout Catholic, steeped in the very habits of late medieval piety that Luther would later criticize. As an avid collector of relics, he brought many back from a pilgrimage to the Holy Land in 1493. Cranach illustrated them in the *Wittenberg Heiligtumsbuch* (1509-10), a guidebook to Friedrich's reliquaries in which 5005 relics are inventoried. The many indulgences attached to these relics financially benefitted the University of Wittenberg and its Castle Church, where the relics were deposited. The best-known indulgence was connected with the annual public display of Friedrich's entire collection in the church on All Saints' Day – it remitted 1443 years in purgatory.[6]

Friedrich actively promoted the cult of the Virgin in Wittenberg. He donated a chapel next to the choir in Castle Church in her honor, and at his request, Pope Julius II issued a special relic-related indulgence for the church in 1510 to honor the Virgin, Saint Anne, and the Eucharist. The papal bull refers to special Masses honoring the Virgin, specifically requiring a procession to the high altar with a *Bild*, or reliquary, containing her relics. The reliquary in question is probably the one illustrated in the *Heiligtumsbuch* – a silver statuette of Mary and the Christ child sharing a cluster of grapes – that contains fifty-six of her relics (among them a drop of her milk, four strands of her hair, three fragments of her cloak, and seven particles of her blood-stained veil).[7] The woodcut, along with the numerous paintings by Cranach's workshop of the Madonna with her grape-consuming child, is a further manifestation of the strong pre-Reformation emphasis on the Madonna at Wittenberg.[8] The woodcut may have served as a devotional souvenir for the faithful who sought Wittenberg's indulgences and perhaps as a subtle reminder of the stipulation that they pray for the Saxon prince's salvation.

The depiction of Friedrich piously kneeling in prayer before the Virgin was not meant to suggest that the saint and donor actually share the same space. Like the many Netherlandish versions of this devotional image, the Virgin and child instead visualize and make concrete the substance of the elector's meditations.[9] An illumination depicting Friedrich kneeling before the apocalyptic Madonna from one of his Netherlandish manuscripts may have prompted Cranach to appropriate this devotional type for his woodcut. Unlike the illuminated version, the elector in the Museum's woodcut is unaccompanied by a protective saint. He is also in closer physical proximity to the object of his prayers – the Madonna and the sacrament of the Eucharist (evoked by the grapes that the child holds and by the Virgin's wistful gaze implying her foreknowledge of his fate).[10]

Although Cranach designed *Friedrich the Wise,* the Museum's impression was not actually printed in his workshop. His authorship is designated by the emblematical figure situated on the front ledge of the print: the crowned, winged serpent that holds a ring in its mouth. Cranach frequently used this image, which derives from the

78

coat of arms that Friedrich bestowed on him in 1508, to sign his own work and his workshop's.[11] He curiously omitted the double coat of arms of electoral Saxony, however, which as court artist he normally included on his prints as a kind of copyright protection.[12]

Hans Guldenmund (active ca. 1490-1560), a print dealer and printer in Nuremberg, signed his name in the lower margin. He must have obtained Cranach's unprotected woodblock and later, in the 1540s, printed an edition adding his own name.[13] Guldenmund's early career as a *Briefmaler*, whose primary function was to color prints by hand, has been documented, and large numbers of prints from his shop, like the Museum's impression, were colored by hand. In this case, the coloring camouflages the fact that, by the time this impression was pulled, the block was already somewhat worn. There are only two known impressions from this late Guldenmund edition; the Museum's is the only one that is colored.[14] – JSP

1. For Friedrich the Wise, see Ingetraut Ludolphy, *Friedrich der Weise* (Göttingen: Vandenhoeck and Ruprecht, 1980); for his role as art patron, see Robert Bruck, *Friedrich der Weise als Förderer der Kunst*, vol. 45 of *Studien zur deutschen Kunstgeschichte* (Strassburg, 1903).

2. Koepplin suggests that Conrad Celtis (1459-1508), who knew the Saxon elector and was teaching at the University of Vienna in 1504, may have recommended Cranach. See Dieter Koepplin, Basel 1974, 1:185.

3. Werner Schade, *Cranach: A Family of Master Painters* (New York: Putnam, 1980), 23.

4. Biographical documentation on Cranach is given in Basel 1974, 2:19-29; for different interpretations of some documents, see Schade, *Cranach*, 41-45.

5. For reproductions see Johannes Jahn, *Lucas Cranach d. Ä. Das gesamte graphische Werk* (Munich: Rogner and Bernhard, 1972): the *Passional*, 555-83, the *Heiligtumsbuch*, 460-544, the Luther portraits, 207-10, 405.

6. For the indulgences, see Koepplin, Basel 1974, 1:186-90, 218-20; see also Roland H. Bainton, *Here I Stand: A Life of Martin Luther* (New York: Abingdon Press, 1950), 53-55.

7. For the indulgences related to the Virgin, see Basel 1974, 1:186-90, 218-20; and Paul Kalkoff, *Ablass und Reliquienverehrung in der Schlosskirche zu Wittenberg* (Gotha: Friedrich Andrea Perthes, 1907), esp. 11-12, 95-96 (Latin text of the papal bull). The woodcut of the reliquary is reproduced in Jahn, *Lucas Cranach*, 526.

8. For reproductions of the Madonna and child paintings with the eucharistic grapes, see Max J. Friedländer and Jakob Rosenberg, *The Paintings of Lucas Cranach* (Secaucus, N.J.: Weltfleet Press, 1978), nos. 29-30, 34, 37-39, 86, 130-31, 162-63, 386-90, 392.

9. For the meaning of devotional images of a donor in prayer before the Madonna and child, see Carol Purtle, *The Marian Paintings of Jan van Eyck* (Princeton: Princeton University Press, 1982), esp. 59-74.

10. Cranach's nearly contemporary painting of *Friedrich Adoring the Apocalyptic Madonna* (ca. 1515) is likewise based on the devotional type depicted in the elector's slightly earlier Netherlandish illumination. For reproductions of both, see Basel 1974, vol. 2, nos. 339-40, figs. 268-70. Cranach may have seen other examples of this devotional image while on his trip to the Netherlands in 1508. Cranach based the Madonna (and landscape background), however, on his own painting of *Adoration of the Magi* (Gotha, ca. 1512-14), which is reproduced in Schade, *Cranach*, pl. 92.

11. For the possible meaning of Cranach's winged serpent, see Schade, *Cranach*, 27.

12. For the copyright privilege, see Talbot, Detroit 1983, no. 119.

13. For Guldenmund, see *Neue deutsche Biographie*, s.v. "Guldenmund, Hans"; ThB., s.v. "Guldenmund, Hans." W. Fries lists works published by Guldenmund in "Der nürnberger Briefmaler Hans Guldenmund," *Zeitschrift für Buchkunde* 1 (1924): 39-48. Guldenmund published a number of portraits of the family of Friedrich's successor, Johann Friedrich I, around 1546; his reissue of the Friedrich the Wise woodcut probably occurred about that time.

14. The Museum's impression is the one from a collection in Gotha that Campbell Dodgson mentions in Dodgson *B.M.* 2:314, no. 117. Impressions from the earlier edition, without Guldenmund's name, are also very rare. For Coburg's early impression, see Coburg 1972, no. 59, fig. 18.

Albrecht Dürer

Nuremberg 1471-1528 Nuremberg

47. Knight, Death and the Devil 1513.
Engraving on antique laid paper, 24.6 x 18.9 cm (sheet).

B. 98; Meder 74c?, Dodgson 70; Panofsky 205; H. *Ger.* 74; TIB 1001.098c.
Dated and monogrammed on tablet lower left: s[alus]·1513·/
Condition: Trimmed to within platemark.
Provenance: Purchased from Kennedy, New York, 1929.
Bequest of Herbert Greer French, 1943.199.
Exhibitions: Cincinnati 1930, (no. 18); Cincinnati 1934, no. 39; Cincinnati 1941, no. 109.

In 1513 and 1514, still under the spell of Venetian light and atmosphere that had suffused his work since his return from a second stay in Italy (1505-07), Dürer created his three so-called *Meisterstiche* (master prints): *The Knight, Death and the Devil*[1] (called by Heinrich Wölfflin "perhaps the best known picture in German art"); *St. Jerome in his Study* (cat. 48); and *Melencolia I* (cat. 49). Nearly identical in size and complexity of technique, the three prints have often been regarded as a suite representing three basic approaches to life: secular morality and theological and secular scholarship, respectively. It is clear, however, from Dürer's travel diary of his journey to the Netherlands (1520-21) that he made no connection between them himself; in fact, he often sold, bartered, or gave away the three prints separately.

In the engraving known as *The Knight, Death and the Devil*, an armored rider, accompanied by his faithful dog, is set off against a tangled Gothic landscape that culminates in a fortified castle. Ignoring Death, who holds an hourglass to call attention to the brevity of life, and having bypassed the grotesque, pig-snouted devil, the knight in his determination is reminiscent of Italian Renaissance images of *condottiere*, such as Verocchio's monument to Colleoni (Venice) and Donatello's *Gattamelatta* (Padua), both of which Dürer had recently seen during his Italian travels. Nearer home, of course, Dürer would also have been familiar with the chiaroscuro woodcuts of Lucas Cranach the Elder from circa 1507 (B. 56) (Kupferstich-Kabinett, Dresden) and Hans Burgkmair from 1508 (B. 32) (Universitätsbibliothek, Innsbruck) that depict St. George on horseback in full parade armor.

Dürer's war horse, a highly disciplined "pacer," is deliberately contrasted to Death's dispirited nag and represents the latest stage of his study of the proportions of horses – a topic that had also interested Leonardo da Vinci. Leonardo's failed project for the Sforza monument in Milan may have been known to Dürer through drawings or early engraved copies.[2] Dürer's geometric construction of the knight's horse is preserved in a double-sided drawing in Milan (Bibliotheca Ambrosiana).[3]

When he wrote of this print in a travel diary of his journey to the Netherlands (1520-21), Dürer titled it simply *Reuter*, not *Ritter* (the *Rider*, not the *Knight*), and never commented on its inner meaning. The first to attempt an analysis of its content, a generation after the artist's death, was Giorgio Vasari, who thought it an allegory of *Fortitudo*, or human strength of character, by no means an impossible suggestion.[4] During the seventeenth century it was mentioned both as a "ghostly Rider," allegedly seen by one Philipp Rink in the forest near Nuremberg,[5] and by Dürer's biographer, Joachim von Sandrart (1675), as "the Christian knight."[6] By the eighteenth century, it had begun to be viewed as a robber-knight, the companion of Death and the devil rather than their opponent, "whose business in life [was] the perpetration of evil deeds."[7]

The engraving was given its present title, *The Knight, Death and the Devil*, in 1778 by Goethe's friend Heinrich Hüsgen, who saw Death and the devil as "symbols and outcomes of [the knight's] godless way of life."[8] By the early nineteenth century, the knight was identified by Schlegel (1803) and Adam Bartsch (1808) as a representation of the German knight Franz von Sickingen

(1481-1523), an early supporter of Martin Luther whose forces were defeated by the troops of the archbishop of Trier in 1522, marking the last use of German knights as an effective force in modern warfare. Bartsch also reports that in his day the print was sometimes known as *Le Manège* (*Horsemanship*, or the art of riding).[9]

In 1814, at the end of the Napoleonic era, the print was given a heroic interpretation in Friedrich de la Motte Fouqué's romantic novel, *Sintram and His Companions*, in which a young Scandinavian knight chooses death in order to avoid the temptations of the devil. In 1835 Carl Gustav Carus compared Dürer's knight to Goethe's *Faust*.[10]

The most widely accepted modern interpretation of the print as a work inspired by the 1504 publication of Erasmus' *Enchiridion militis Christiani* (*Handbook of the Christian Soldier*) was first suggested by Hermann Grimm in 1875.[11] Dürer would have certainly been made aware of this book by his humanist friend Pirckheimer, who corresponded with Erasmus. The determination with which Dürer's rider pointedly ignores the presence of Death and the way in which the devil has been characterized as a ridiculous creature are in keeping with Erasmian thought. Dürer's later reference in his Netherlandish diary to Erasmus as "thou knight of Christ" seems to support this identification. In any event, both Erasmus and Dürer would have been aware of Paul's letter to the Ephesians (Eph. 6:10-18), urging them to "put on the whole armour of God [and the] helmet of salvation, [take up the] sword of the Spirit [in order to] stand against the wiles of the devil [and do combat against] the rulers of darkness of this world [and] against spiritual wickedness in high places." The idea of a heroic and Christian rider would, of course, have also been familiar to Dürer from the famous medieval equestrian statue in the Bamberg Cathedral – the seat of the diocese in which Nuremberg was located and the place where his friend Canon Lorenz Behaim was employed.

During the nineteenth century, Dürer's images were put to use by Friedrich Nietzsche, Richard Wagner, and others as a symbol of the German struggle for unification, finally attained with the establishment of the Second Reich in 1871. In 1870 Nietzsche gave an impression of *The Knight, Death and the Devil* to Wagner for Christmas, commenting in *The Origins of Tragedy* that Dürer's knight "who goes on his dread journey alone. . . undaunted by his horrible companions and yet totally without hope," could be compared to the philosopher Schopenhauer. He remarked elsewhere in 1871 that "Dürer's image of Knight, Death and Devil [is] a symbol of our [Teutonic] being."[12] In 1918, during World War I, Thomas Mann spoke of "that Nordic-Germanic atmosphere of solid simplicity surrounding the engraving of *Knight, Death and Devil*," while Ernst Bertram characterized Nietzsche himself as "a Dürerian knight. . . who, like Schopenhauer and Luther's 'free Christian men' is beholden to nobody."[13]

A still more bellicose knight appeared in German art historical writings of the 1930s, when the most popular Dürer book of the era characterized the knight in this print as "the descendant of the giant heroes of the Nordic myths, and a forefather of the Prussian officer."[14] In an address given at the University of Erfurt in 1936, its author said, "Heroic souls love this engraving as Nietzsche did and as Adolf Hitler does today. They love it because it personifies victory."[15]

During World War II, Erwin Panofsky, writing in exile in the United States, reintroduced Grimm's Erasmian interpretation of Dürer's knight. This interpretation has remained the most widely accepted one, despite more recent reexaminations of the case for the robber-knight by Sten Karling and others.[16] – JH

1. The literature is extensive; see especially the monograph by Heinrich Theissing, *Dürers Ritter, Tod und Teufel. Sinnbild und Bildsinn* (Berlin, 1978); Ursula Meyer,

"Politische Bezüge in Dürers 'Ritter, Tod und Teufel,'" *Kritische Berichte* 6 (1978): 27-41 (English translation in PCN. 9 [May-June 1978]: 36); Hans Schwerte, *Faust und das Faustische. Ein Kapittel deutscher Ideologie* (Stuttgart, 1962); Sten Karling, "Riddaren döden och djävulen," *Konsthisthorisk Tidsskrift* 39 (1970): 1-13; R. J. Clements, "Dürer's 'Knight, Death and Devil': Five Literary Readings," *Canadian Review of Comparative Literature* 4 (1979): 1-8; Mario Scalini, "Il 'Reuther' di Albrecht Dürer: Tipologia e Simbologia di un Armamento," *Antichita* 23 (1984): 15-18; Bialostocki, esp. 211-42. See also the following exhibition catalogues: Wulf Schadendorf, in Nuremberg 1971, no. 503; Charles Talbot et al., Washington 1971, no. 58; Charles Talbot, Detroit 1983, no. 153; Sue W. Reed, Boston 1971, nos. 179-82; Jean Michel Massing, Washington 1991, no. 196.

2. Massing, Washington 1991, 292.

3. The body of the horse is geometrically constructed on one side of the drawing; its outline was then traced through to the other side of the page.

4. Vasari's interpretation was later taken over by the nineteenth-century English critic John Ruskin (Bialostocki, *Dürer and His Critics*, 211-12, n. 46.)

5. *Stammbuchregister* of the Scheurl family (1664), cited in Hans Schwerte, *Faust und das Faustische*, 248.

6. Joachim von Sandrart, *L'Academia Todesca della Architectura, Scultura et Pictura, oder Teutsche Akademie der edlen Bau-, Bild-, und Mahlerey-Künste* (Nuremberg, 1675), 105.

7. Heinrich Conrad Arend, *Das Gedächtnis der Ehren eines der vollkommensten Kunstlers seiner und aller nachfolgenden Zeiten, Albrecht Dürer* (Goslar, 1728), para. 11; quoted in full in Bialostocki, 212; and David Gottfried Schober (1769), cited by Schwerte, *Faust*, and Bialostocki, 212.

8. Heinrich Hüsgen, *Raisonnierendes Verzeichnis aller Kupfer- und Eisenstiche von Albrecht Dürer* (Leipzig, 1778); cited in Schwerte, 251. Hüsgen was the proud owner of the lock of Dürer's hair that had been clipped at the time of the artist's death to send to a former pupil, Hans Baldung Grien.

9. Bialostocki, 213.

10. Bialostocki, 213-17.

11. Hermann Grimm, "Dürers Ritter, Tod und Teufel," *Preussische Jahrbücher* 36 (1875): 543-49; Bialostocki, 217.

12. Bialostocki, 225-36.

13. Bialostocki, 236-37.

14. Bialostocki, 239.

15. Waetzoldt, quoted in Bialostocki, 240.

16. Sten Karling, "Riddaren, döden och djävulen," *Konsthistorisk Tidskrift* 39 (1970): 1-13 (with English summary). Cited in Talbot et al., Washington 1971, 144, no. 58. See also Ursula Meyer, "Political Implications of Dürer's 'Knight, Death and Devil,'" PCN. 9, no. 2 (May-June 1978): 35-39.

Albrecht Dürer
Nuremberg 1471-1528 Nuremberg

48. St. Jerome in His Study 1514.
Engraving on antique laid paper, 24.9 x 19.1 cm (platemark)
B. 60; Meder 59a?; Dodgson 74; Panofsky 167; H. *Ger.* 59; TIB 1001.060.
Dated and monogrammed on tablet lower right: *1514*/⒜
Condition: Trimmed to platemark.
Provenance: Alexander Beugo, Lugt 81; purchased from Knoedler, New York, 1929.
Bequest of Herbert Greer French, 1943.205.
Exhibitions: Cincinnati 1930, (no. 22); Cincinnati 1934, no. 42; Cincinnati 1941, no. 113, illus no. 27

The second of Dürer's so-called master prints depicts Jerome at work in his sun-dappled study – a chamber closely resembling a room in Dürer's spacious house located near Nuremberg's Tiergartnertor. Jerome (A.D. 340-420), one of the four Latin fathers of the Roman Catholic Church, is best known for translating the Bible from its original Hebrew and Greek sources into the Latin edition known as the Vulgate. He enjoyed tremendous prestige in Northern Europe as a patron saint of biblical humanistic studies and is perhaps shown here as an example of the *vita contemplativa*.

Engrossed in writing what appears to be a letter, Dürer's Jerome, interestingly, has no reference materials on his work table. (Many of

Jerome's letters were available in printed editions in Dürer's day.[1]) The three bound volumes shelved on the ample window seat nearby seem to suggest that his work as translator had been completed. The enormous gourd hanging from the ceiling (upper right) further suggests that his *Commentaries on the Book of Jonah* (ca A.D. 396) were also finished and that he may now be engaged in lengthy debate with St. Augustine. Augustine was the recipient of much of Jerome's correspondence in the years A.D. 403 and 404.[2] As Peter Parshall has shown, their disagreement had to do with the translation of the Hebrew word *kikayon* (castor oil plant) – a vine that is said to have grown up to shelter Jonah from the sun (Jon. 4:6). Jerome translated this Hebrew word as *hedera* (ivy). The earlier Latin substitution for *kikayon*, which is native to Palestine, was *concurbita* (gourd).[3] Jerome's ivy rather than Augustine's gourd was adopted by Erasmus in his new edition of the Vulgate, published in 1522.

St. Jerome's choice of ivy, as Parshall notes, was an indication of his knowledge of natural history as well as of his determination to establish the plausibility of biblical events. It might also be added that it was evidence of Jerome's having translated "by the sense," rather than word for word – a concept to which Dürer's best friend, Willibald Pirckheimer, Germany's leading translator of Greek texts into Latin and German, was himself devoted.[4]

While Dürer's *Knight, Death and the Devil* was destined to enjoy greater fame in years to come, *St. Jerome in His Study* is truly an "engraver's engraving," a work of unprecedented subtlety. Unlike the knight, who dominates the plane of the picture, Jerome retreats as far as possible from the viewer in order not to be interrupted at his work. A human skull, a *memento mori*, lies on the sunny windowsill; and an hourglass hangs next to a cardinal's hat on the wall behind. Jerome was not actually entitled to this high ecclesiastical office, as Erasmus was later to prove in his authoritative biography of the saint, published in 1517. (In 1521, after a meeting with Erasmus in Antwerp, Dürer dressed Jerome in a simple scholar's beret in a half-length painting now in Lisbon.)

The viewer's access to the room via a staircase is hinted at in the foreground. Access to the study, however, is blocked by the majestic presence of the lion from whose wounded foot, according to legend, Jerome had removed a thorn. The lion and a little dog, symbolic of fidelity, doze together in the warm sunshine; Herbert Friedmann has suggested that this peaceable kingdom motif, unique in the iconography of Jerome, may express the artist's deep-seated desire for a reconciliation between modern humanistic scholarship and the papacy.[5]

The print was widely imitated: Jerome's study served as the setting for a 1526 portrait of Cardinal Albrecht von Brandenburg by Lucas Cranach the Elder (The John and Mabel Ringling Museum of Art, Sarasota, Florida) as well as for Wolfgang Stuber's engraved portrait of Martin Luther (Albertina, Vienna, ca. 1584). And Crispin van de Passe appropriated the gourd, inappropriately, for his engraving of St. Mark (Museum of Fine Arts, Boston).

Dürer's composition was developed over a period of several years, from the woodcut version of *St. Jerome in His Cell* (B. 114) (Rosenwald Collection, National Gallery of Art, Washington), which is set in a curtained alcove, to the drypoint of 1512, *St. Jerome by a Pollard Willow* (also in the Rosenwald Collection). This drypoint transports the saint, with only his lion, crucifix, and lapdesk, outdoors into brilliant and corrosive sunshine. In *St. Jerome*, however, the effects of light are incredibly subtle. The sunlight filters through mullioned windows to produce the afterglow on the window embrasure so admired by Vasari: "The phenomenon is as pictorial and subtle as the treatment is graphic and simple: the 'bull's-eyes' themselves are rendered by outlines with hatchings, and

their shadows by short horizontal hatchings without outlines. That is all."[6] – JH

1. One of Dürer's earliest commissions as a journeyman, in fact, had been a design for a woodcut frontispiece for Nicolaus Kessler's edition of the *Epistolare beati Hieronymi* (Basel, August 8, 1491). In 1514 a new edition of Jerome's letters was being prepared by Erasmus of Rotterdam, part of the complete works of Jerome that he was editing for Johannes Froben's press in Basel. Peter Parshall, "Albrecht Dürer's *St. Jerome in his Study*: A Philological Reference," AB. 53 (1971): 303-05.

2. See Y. M. Duval, "Saint Augustin et le commentaire sur Jonas de Saint Jerome," *Revue des etudes Augustiniennes* 12 (1968): 9-40.

3. Parshall, "Albrecht Dürer's *St. Jerome*," 303.

4. Dürer makes frequent reference in his own letters to Pirckheimer to the concept of translating or reading "by the sense." These letters were written in 1506 and 1507. On Pirckheimer as translator, see Hutchison, 48ff.

5. Herbert Friedmann, *A Bestiary for St. Jerome* (Washington, 1980), 101-14.

6. Giorgio Vasari, *Le Vite de' più eccellenti pittori, scultori ed architettori*, ed. Gaetano Milanesi (Florence: Sansoni, 1878-85), 5:409, cited in Talbot et al., Washington 1971, 147, no. 60.

Albrecht Dürer

Nuremberg 1471-1528 Nuremberg

49. Melencolia I 1514.

Engraving on antique laid paper, 24.2 x 18.0 cm (sheet).
B. 74; Meder 75-2a; Dodgson 73 ii; H. *Ger.* 75 iia;
TIB 1001.074 S2a.
Dated and monogrammed in plate lower right: *1514*/ 🄰🄳
Condition: Trimmed within platemark.
Provenance: P. Mariette 1668; "G – Veggio, 1854"; purchased from Bresler, Milwaukee, 1929.
Bequest of Herbert Greer French, 1943.204.
Exhibitions: Cincinnati 1930, (no. 21); Cincinnati 1934, no. 41; Cincinnati 1941, no. 112.

After Dürer's death, *The Knight, Death and Devil* (cat. 47) became his most famous work in Germany. His *Melencolia I* was to achieve a similar status among English and French writers of the romantic period. In England its celebrity came as a natural consequence of the late sixteenth- and seventeenth-century fascination with the melancholic. Both Alexander Pope's description of "Malancholy" and Milton's "Il Penseroso" may have been based on Dürer's engraving. William Blake is said to have owned an impression of *Melencolia I* that he kept always with him; and James Thomson used a description of it to conclude his lengthy poem, *The City of Dreadful Night* (1870-74). In France *Melencolia I* was the subject of another long poem, *Melancholia* (1834), by Theophile Gautier. Gautier described the engraving as a "spiritual self-portait" of the artist, a concept later expanded by Erwin Panofsky in his 1943 monograph. For Sainte-Beuve, Gerard de Nerval, Charles Blanc, and others, the engraving seemed to reflect the influence of the medieval Faust legend.[1] The Museum's impression of *Melencolia I*, once owned by the important French art historian, collector, and dealer, Pierre Jean Mariette (1694-1774), remained in France until 1853.

Gautier and Panofsky both believed *Melencolia I* to be autobiographical – an idea seemingly supported by the many mathematical references in the print that surely reflect Dürer's well-known interest in euclidean geometry.[2] However, Dürer's surviving travel diary and personal letters as well as the testimony of those who knew him give the definite impression that the artist was an unusually industrious and articulate man, a man with a keen sense of humor who was unanimously considered good company. And as Giehlow noted many years ago, it was the Emperor Maximilian, not Dürer, who was known to suffer from melancholia.[3] Dürer did have one self-described low point in his life: in 1514 he attended his mother in her last illness and witnessed her death.[4]

The idea that mental depression and its corollary, apathy, could have a heroic aspect was relatively new in Europe in 1514. These conditions had heretofore been identified with a deadly sin, sloth, and were listed in contemporary medical books as symptoms of disease.[5] Melancholy as an attribute of intelligence must have come to Dürer's attention through his friend Pirckheimer. At his father's request, Willibald Pirckheimer had purchased the definitive treatise on the treatment of melancholy and its relationship to [literary] genius – Marsilio Ficino's *De vita triplici* (1489).[6] Pirckheimer had known Marsilio Ficino's nephew since his student days in Italy. Ficino, who based his work on Aristotle's observation that creative people are frequently pensive, attributed this particular mindset to the influence of the planet Saturn. Saturn was thought to possess the power to bestow either bad luck or good fortune and wealth. Dürer seems to have digested this: a preparatory drawing for the putto in the print bears a notation in Dürer's handwriting: "keys mean power, purse means wealth."[7]

Melencolia I, which represents the life of the scientist and craftsman, is the antithesis of the serene and sun-filled *St. Jerome in His Study*. The contrast seems to have been a conscious one, an opposition of divine and worldly knowledge: on several occasions, Dürer sold or gave away impressions of these prints in pairs. Jerome, engrossed in his work, occupies a neat and orderly office; Melancholy, an enormous winged figure, sits idly brooding in the midst of a clutter of attributes symbolizing geometry, architecture, mathematics, and astronomy. As Panofsky notes, the setting of *Melencolia I* is in many ways identical to that depicted in a woodcut entitled *Typus Geometriae* that had appeared in the 1504 and 1508 editions of Gregor Reisch's *Margarita Philosophica*. In this woodcut illustration, a lady seated at a table presides over a still life of drafting equipment, carpenters' tools, and astronomical instruments.[8]

Melancholy's skin is swarthy, and she wears a wreath of lovage[9] on her head to relieve a dryness in the brain brought on, no doubt, by an excess of black bile; a clyster (enema syringe) is glimpsed beneath the hem of her gown (lower right), denoting an additional source of relief from dryness elsewhere in the body. The contemporary belief in the four humors – the sanguine, the phlegmatic, the choleric, and the melancholic – were thought to be caused by an imbalance in any one of the body's four fluids – blood, phlegm, yellow bile, and black bile. Medieval physiology held that too much black bile caused melancholy.

Melancholy and her companion, a writing putto seated on a millstone, are ensconced in an unusual building site, the foot of a tower still under construction. A Jupiter square – a table of numbers (here including the date 1514) that, when added in any direction, yields the same sum – is inscribed on the base of the tower. A bell for sounding the hours, a pair of balances for measuring weights, an hourglass (an item common to all three of Dürer's master prints), a caliper (in Melancholy's hand), a carpenter's plane and saw, and a goldsmith's brazier represent the ability of scientist, artist, and craftsman to deal with the physical properties of geometric solids, Dürer's allusion to the natural world.

Konrad Hoffmann has argued that the title of the print refers to the bat, a traditional medieval symbol of pride and despair. In Dürer's engraving, it is seen carrying a banderole, appropriately inscribed "Melencolia I," fleeing before the brilliant light of the comet in the background.[10] He interprets the juxtaposition of bat, comet, and rainbow – the Old Testament demonstration of divine providence – congregating above the body of water in the background, as Dürer's response to Johannes Stoffler's prediction

that a deluge would be set off by a planetary conjunction in the watery sign of Pisces in February 1524.[11] Stoffler recorded this prediction in his widely influential *Almanach* (Ulm, 1499). Rejecting Panofsky's contention that Dürer's literary source was the as yet unpublished treatise of Agrippa von Nettesheim (*De occulta philosophia*, 1531), which divided melancholy genius into "Inspiratio" and "Ratio," Hoffmann offers the more probable thesis that Dürer's bat represents Melencolia I, the "black" melancholy of traditional belief, while the winged figure personifies the beneficent "melancholia generosa," or noble melancholy.

Melencolia I is known in two states: the first, extremely rare, contains an error in the Jupiter square; the Museum's fine second-state impression has the correction of the numeral 9 in the square below the bell. – JH

1. See Raymond Klibansky, Erwin Panofsky, and Fritz Saxl, *Saturn and Melancholy: Studies in the History of Natural Philosophy, Religion and Art* (New York, 1964); Bialostocki, esp. 189-218, where generous quotations from the cited works can be found.

2. Dürer's personal copy of Bartolommeo Zamberti's new edition of Euclid (Venice, 1505), now in the library at Wolfenbüttel, is inscribed on the flyleaf: "I bought this book at Venice for one ducat in the year 1507 – Albrecht Dürer." On Dürer as mathematician, see G. Staigmüller, *Dürer als Mathematiker* (Stuttgart, 1891).

3. Karl Giehlow, "Dürers Stich, 'Melencolia I' und der maximilianische Humanistenkreis," *MGvK.* 26 (1903): 29-41; *MGvK.* 27 (1904): 6-18, 57-78.

4. Dürer's account of his mother's death (April 26, 1514) is recorded in a notebook that he called his *Gedenkbuch*; his reference to the "great distress" from which Luther's teachings subsequently rescued him is contained in a letter written to Georg Spalatin early in 1520. See Hutchison, 121-25.

5. Panofsky, 160.

6. Panofsky, 156-71.

7. British Museum, London (Winkler 3). Other drawings related to this print are *Seated Woman* (Berlin) (Winkler 621); *Two Views of a Child's Head* (London) (Winkler 619); *Balance in Two Views* (Berlin) (Winkler 620); *Truncated Rhomboid* (Dresden) (Tietze 585); *Compasses and Molder's Form* (Tietze 586). Winkler also reproduces a copy of a lost study of the dog (Winkler 3, pl. 15). Washington 1971, 146, n. 7.

8. Panofsky, 161, fig. 219.

9. Lottlisa Behling, "Betrachtungen zu einigen Dürer-Pflanzen," *Pantheon* 23 (1965): 277-84.

10. Konrad Hoffmann, "Dürer's 'Melencolia,'" *PCN.* 9, no. 2 (May-June 1978): 33-35.

11. Hoffmann, "Dürer's 'Melencholia,'" 35.

Benedetto Montagna

Vicenza ca. 1480-1555/58 Vicenza

50. Vulcan, Apollo, and Cupid ca. 1515-20.

Engraving on antique laid paper, 18.4 x 13.0 cm (sheet).
B. 24; P. 47; Hind 39; TIB 2512.037.
Watermark: Cardinal's hat (cf. Briquet 3404).
Signed in the sky: BENEDETO / MONTAGNA.
Condition: Trimmed within platemark.
Provenance: Albertina duplicate; (purchased from M. Knoedler, New York, February 2, 1934, for $2,800).
Bequest of Herbert Greer French, 1943.154.
Exhibitions: Cincinnati 1941, no. 67.

Born in Vicenza around 1480, Benedetto was the son of Bartolomeo Montagna, the most important Vicentine painter of the Renaissance. When Bartolomeo died in 1523, Benedetto inherited the family workshop and spent the rest of his life painting pictures of no great merit. During the first half of his career, however, a twenty-year period that seems to have begun circa 1500, Benedetto was one of the foremost printmakers active in the Veneto, responsible for more than fifty surviving engravings, most of them signed or monogrammed. They show the influence of Bartolomeo Montagna's paintings and drawings and, not unexpectedly for a master of Benedetto's generation, are much indebted to Albrecht Dürer. Benedetto adopted aspects of Dürer's technique, appropriated some of his settings with modifications, lifted details from his engravings, and turned out faithful copies of five or six of them.[1]

In *Vulcan, Apollo, and Cupid* we find Benedetto at an advanced stage in his career as an engraver. The setting of the work, with its rustic buildings, its prominent well, and above all, its deep perspectival plunge, recalls Dürer's engraving of *The Nativity* (B. 2), dated 1504, a print that Benedetto had previously copied in an engraving of his own (Hind 51). But Dürer's graphic conventions are so thoroughly digested that *Vulcan, Apollo, and Cupid* does not appear to be especially derivative. Rather, Benedetto may be said to have taken advantage of virtually every technical device available to an engraver of his generation. Straight lines and curved, cross-hatching and parallel shading, dots, flicks, and wavy striations are all used to evoke a wide variety of naturalistic surfaces. The sky is left blank – except for the artist's signature – to create the effect of light, space, and air. The tonal character of the engraving is further enhanced by the unusual blue-gray paper on which the Museum's impression is printed, lending color and warmth to an image already notable for its textural richness. In all of this one senses the inspiration of Giulio Campagnola along with that of Dürer, as though Benedetto were striving to compete with the suggestive, atmospheric works of the great Venetian engraver who was his exact contemporary.

Vulcan, Apollo, and Cupid belongs to a group of eight engravings, conjecturally datable to circa 1515-20, that portray selected scenes from Ovid's *Metamorphoses*.[2] Probably the most famous collection of myths surviving from the ancient world, the *Metamorphoses* was translated into Italian and accompanied by fifty-nine woodcut illustrations in a Venetian edition published in 1497.[3] All but one of Benedetto's Ovidian engravings depend upon these woodcuts, each of which invariably includes several episodes that make up the particular myth selected for depiction. From these "continuous narratives" Benedetto excerpted single incidents and modified them almost, but not quite, beyond recognition. Thus, the figures of Vulcan and Apollo in the present engraving as well as the anvil between them and the hammer on the ground nearby are loosely based on their counterparts in the left-hand portion of the woodcut illustrating two scenes from Ovid (*Metamorphoses*, bk. 4, ll. 167-89) (fig. 50-1).[4] Benedetto's alterations and additions are, however, so extensive that the engraving amounts to a substantially original composition; significantly, too, it is entirely independent of its model in style.

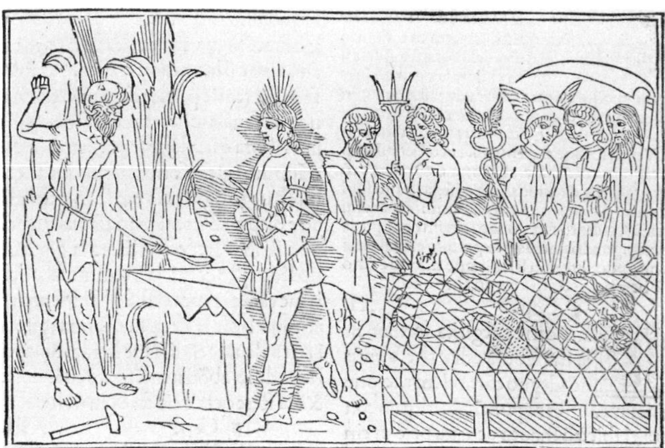

Figure 50-1. *Apollo at the Forge of Vulcan and Mars and Venus Caught in Vulcan's Net*. Woodcut from Ovid, *Metamorphoseos vulgare* (Venice: Christofolo de Pensa, 1501), leaf d4 recto. The Metropolitan Museum of Art, New York, Rogers Fund, 1922.

In Benedetto's excerpt (corresponding to ll. 173-76), we see Apollo in the guise of a handsome youth crowned with laurel and accompanied by Cupid, who plays no role in the woodcut nor indeed in the myth as recounted by Ovid. Approaching Vulcan, blacksmith of the gods, Apollo informs him that his wife, Venus, has unfaithfully taken up with Mars; whereupon "Vulcan's mind reeled and the work upon which he was engaged fell from his hands"[5] – a reaction nicely conveyed by Vulcan's upraised arm, poised as if in midstroke, and his hammer fallen useless beside him.

Unlike the Venetian woodcuts, Benedetto's illustrations were never published in book form. Instead, they must have been issued individually to attract connoisseurs with a recently acquired taste for fine prints with classical subjects. Quite likely these were the same enthusiasts who collected Giulio and Domenico Campagnola's engravings, such as the ones catalogued here (cats. 39, 40, 51), men with enough sophistication to appreciate things that have no intrinsic worth and serve no practical purpose. Thus *Vulcan, Apollo, and Cupid* as well as other prints of a similar type by Benedetto and his contemporaries are not only valuable in their own right, they are also of interest for what they seem to tell us about the rise of a new class of patron and the new social climate in which such patronage might thrive. – MZ

1. Benedetto's copies of Dürer are Hind 48-49, 51-53; a copy of Dürer's *Virgin and Child on a Grassy Bank* (Hind 50) is a doubtful attribution.

2. Remaining members of the group are Hind 38, 40-44, 46; other closely related engravings are Hind 34-37, 45, 47. Among other things, all of these works include the same signature isolated in an otherwise blank sky, a formula borrowed from Giulio Campagnola's engravings.

3. *Ouidio metamorphoseos vulgare. . . . Stampato in Venetia per Zoane rosso uercellese ad instantia del nobile homo miser Lucantonio Zonta fiorentino del* MCCCC.LXXXXVII (Hain 12166); reprinted Parma: F. Mazalis, 1505. See Friedrich Lippmann, *The Art of Wood-Engraving in Italy in the Fifteenth Century* (London: B. Quaritch, 1888), 106-08; Hind V:173-74; and especially Fitzroy Carrington, "Benedetto Montagna and the 'Metamorphoses' of Ovid," PCQ. 28 (1941): 212-32, illustrating the cuts relevant to Montagna's compositions and quoting the relevant passages from Ovid.

4. Fol. 28 of the 1497 Venice edition; fol. 44v of the 1505 Parma edition. For the passage in question, see Ovid, *Metamorphoses*, trans. Frank Justus Miller, 3rd ed., rev. by G. P. Goold (Cambridge: Harvard University Press, and London: William Heinemann Ltd., 1977), 1:190-91.

5. Ovid, *Metamorphoses*, 191.

Domenico Campagnola
Venice 1500-1564 Padua

51. Battle of Naked Men 1517.
Engraving on antique laid paper, 22.1 x 23.0 cm (platemark).
B. 10; P. 11; Hind 4; TIB 2519.013.
Signed and dated lower left: DOMINICVS / CĀPAGNOLA / .1517.
Provenance: Karl Ferdinand Friedrich von Nagler (Lugt 2529); Kupferstichkabinett, Staatliche Museen, Berlin, duplicate (Lugt 1606); (purchased from M. Knoedler, New York, April 27, 1938 for $525).
Bequest of Herbert Greer French, 1943.260.
Exhibitions: Washington 1973, no. 292.

In this complex scene of battling nudes, Domenico Campagnola operates within a tradition begun by Pollaiuolo in Florence a generation earlier (cf. cat. 16), modifying it according to the standards of his own time and place. More than half a century younger than Pollaiuolo, Campagnola, a Venetian rather than a Florentine, was more adept at integrating his frantically struggling protagonists with their forestlike setting. His naked men – and their horses – move with greater freedom and flexibility. Uninterested in the contrived pairings and groupings of combatants that Pollaiuolo had devised to impose artificial order on the chaos of battle, Campagnola designed a seething mass of humans, animals, and landscape, all merging together in a unified whole that throbs with a passionate energy.

Born in Venice to German parents in 1500, Domenico was trained and apparently adopted by Giulio Campagnola, from whom he learned the art of engraving and from whom he took his name. He developed into a versatile printmaker, creating innovative woodcuts in addition to engravings; an influential draftsman, responsible for numerous fine drawings; and a prolific, if rather uninspired painter, active principally in Padua (near Venice) from circa 1520 to his death in 1564. Domenico's activity as an engraver is limited to the beginning of his career when, at age seventeen or eighteen, he designed and executed a small but extraordinary group of engravings, thirteen of which (including the present one) are signed and dated 1517, a fourteenth being dated to the following year.[1]

For the most part, Domenico's style is surprisingly little indebted to Giulio Campagnola. Unlike the meditative passivity of Giulio's figures and their ideal, generalized forms, Domenico's are impulsive in their movements and often distorted for expressionistic purposes. Where Giulio's compositions radiate idyllic calm, Domenico's pulsate with emotional intensity. These differences reflect a broader change, usually associated with painting, in the tenor of Venetian art during the second decade of the sixteenth century – a shift from the dreamy lyricism of Giorgione, who died in 1510 after the briefest of careers, to the powerful drama of Titian, then arriving at his early maturity. In all fundamental ways, Giulio's engravings are imbued with the spirit of Giorgione; Domenico's, by contrast, take Titian as their point of departure.

This is certainly the case with the *Battle of Naked Men*, which is based on pictorial ideas developed by Titian during the years immediately preceding Domenico's engraving. In 1513 Titian was commissioned to paint a large canvas, now known to have represented the Battle of Spoleto, for the Doge's Palace in Venice. Although he did not produce the picture until 1537-38 – it was later destroyed by fire – he was working on preparatory drawings in 1514 and perhaps as late as 1516. Domenico, whose style of draftsmanship is closely dependent on Titian's, may well have had access to the latter's studies for the project, such as the remarkable chalk drawing now in the Louvre, the only sketch for *The Battle of Spoleto* that has chanced to survive.[2] In 1514-15, moreover, Titian turned out a related design in a huge woodcut, *The Submersion of Pharaoh's Army in the Red Sea*,[3] parts of which have much the same character as Domenico's engraving of 1517. Lurking further behind the *Battle of Naked Men* as models of a more general kind are such classic battle scenes as the pair designed in 1503-06 by Michelangelo and Leonardo da Vinci for the Palazzo Vecchio in Florence (see cat. 41). But Titian, rather than Leonardo or Michelangelo, surely stands behind Domenico as his direct source of inspiration.[4]

Unlike his immediate predecessors, Domenico seems not to have portrayed a specific historical skirmish but a visceral image of the essence of conflict.[5] A century ago Émile Galichon identified the engraving's subject as the mythological battle of centaurs and Lapiths.[6] What he saw as centaurs are, of course, men on horseback, but Galichon's insight has a fundamental validity: the nudity of the soldiers removes them from real space and time, suggesting, rather, a generic combat *all'antica*. Whatever such subjects may have meant to those who first purchased Renaissance battle prints "in the antique manner," their appeal within their time – a time of incessant warfare on the Italian peninsula – was widespread. Analogous contemporary versions were also made by Nicoletto da Modena (in Emilia) and the Master of 1515 (in Lombardy?); and some forty impressions of Domenico's *Battle of Naked Men* – more than any of

his other engravings and far more than usual for early Italian engravings in general – still survive to document its popularity.[7]

Much of the print's effectiveness is attributable to Domenico's expressive technique. Dense thickets of cross-hatching create vibrating patches of darkness that contrast sharply with brilliant patches of light. Clusters of lines seem to twist and streak across the ground. Small flicklike markings lend texture and pattern to earth, rock, fur, and hide. And the tangled skeins of hair, manes, and tails conjure up an improbable image of Domenico scribbling on the copperplate instead of cutting deliberately into it. Such apparent spontaneity of execution is almost without parallel in early Italian printmaking, although some of the technical conventions can be traced to Albrecht Dürer's engravings, to Jacopo de' Barbari's, and even to Titian's famous woodcut mentioned above. In the final analysis, however, recognition of Domenico's sources scarcely diminishes one's appreciation of his original approach to them. – MZ

1. For documentation on Domenico's life, see Rosita Colpi, "Domenico Campagnola (nuove notizie biografiche e artistiche)," *Bollettino del Museo Civico di Padova* 31-43 (1942-54): 81-111; also, Lionello Puppi, DBI 17 (1974): 312-17, with exhaustive bibliography. For citation of specialized literature on the paintings and drawings as well as the woodcuts and engravings, see Mark Zucker, TIB 25 (*Commentary*): 497-98, 515.

2. For this drawing, see London 1983a, 292-93, no. D72, with citation of previous literature.

3. "Arguably the greatest woodcut ever made," according to David Landau, London 1983a, 321, it is known only in impressions printed in 1549; see David Rosand and Michelangelo Muraro, Washington 1976, 70-87, no. 4.

4. The complicated issue of the engraving's putative sources is reviewed, with citation of specific opinions, in my commentary to TIB 2519.013.

5. Paraphrased from J. R. Hale, *Artists and Warfare in the Renaissance* (New Haven and London: Yale University Press, 1990), 162.

6. Émile Galichon, "Domenico Campagnola: Peintre-graveur du XVIᵉ siècle," GBA. 17 (1864): 540-42, no. 11.

7. For the versions by Nicoletto and the Master of 1515, see Hind V.124.43 and Hind V.285.17. For impressions of Domenico's print (as of 1948), see Hind V:211, listing 39 of them. Certain other early Italian engravings also exist in forty or more impressions, most notably Pollaiuolo's *Battle of the Nudes* (cat. 16) and several related to Mantegna; evidently Domenico's *Battle* was quite as popular an image as these famous prints.

Albrecht Dürer
Nuremberg 1471-1521 Nuremberg

52. The Landscape with the Cannon 1518.
Etching on iron on antique laid paper, 22.0 x 32.1 cm (sheet).
B. 99; Meder 96a (before rust); Dodgson 86; Panofsky 206; H. *Ger.* 96 i/ii; TIB 1001.099 S1.
Watermark: High crown (Meder 31).
Dated and monogrammed in plate upper left: *1518* / 𝔄𝔇
Condition: Trimmed within platemark.
Provenance: (Purchased from M. Knoedler, New York, May 25, 1927, for $400).
Bequest of Herbert Greer French, 1943.207.
Exhibitions: Cincinnati 1941, no. 115.

In 1515 Albrecht Dürer began to experiment with etching, a new intaglio printmaking technique that had come into existence a few years earlier.[1] Dürer made six etchings in all, *The Landscape with the Cannon* of 1518 being his largest and last. Etched lines are inherently more blunt, raw, and wiry than their engraved counterparts; consequently, Dürer could not make them swell or taper with the machinelike precision used to create the rich range of tonal transitions capable of being produced with a burin (cf. cats. 47-49). Instead he used his etching needle to make thicker, looser, more assertive lines that contrast sharply with the white of the paper. He exploited this potential to heighten the emotional tension in etchings like the 1515 *Agony in the Garden* (B. 19) and the 1516 *Abduction on a Unicorn* (B. 72). In the case of *The Landscape with the Cannon*, his alternation of strong lights and darks helps convey the depth and lay of the terrain. Like other etchers before midcentury, Dürer used hammered iron for his plates, a metal that is far more susceptible to rust than the copperplate used for engraving. According to Campbell Dodgson, impressions of *The Cannon* that are free from rust, like the Museum's, are rare.[2]

The iconography of *The Landscape with the Cannon* is still a mystery. Jan Bialostocki considers it an *allégorie réelle*, a complex or unusual allegory under the guise of realism that Dürer may have intended for a small, learned audience.[3] The artist presents us with a cannon positioned somewhat precariously on a high precipice in the left foreground. The arms of Nuremberg inscribed on the tool box at the end of the gun's barrel identify it as artillery produced in Nuremberg's renowned metal foundries; it is a vintage model from around 1450-80.[4] Three German halberdiers guard the immediate vicinity, ostensibly because of the presence of a group of foreign dignitaries (right), among them a Hungarian soldier with bow and quiver and, more prominently, a Turk, to whom Dürer has given his own facial features.[5] The siege weapon itself is not, however, aimed at any visible target in the calm landscape that stretches into the distance below. The figure raising his whip on the left may even be supervising the removal of the machine from its station, its back wheels already angled and pulled away from the stone brace by the force of an unseen agent.[6]

In 1518 when Dürer made this print, the eastern borders of the empire, including Hungary, were threatened by the Turks. That year the artist was part of the Nuremberg delegation to the imperial diet in Augsburg, where efforts were made to mobilize the German estates for war against the Turks. Whether these contemporary events had any bearing on Dürer's subject remains speculative.[7] Whatever the purpose of the cannon and its attendant figures, nothing threatens the tranquility of the landscape setting. It is nearly

a pure landscape, filling three-fourths of the page, and even though it is Dürer's only etched landscape, it set a precedent for the German landscape tradition known as the Danube style. Almost immediately afterward etching became *the* print medium for landscape portrayal (see, for example, Hirschvogel, cat. 63, and Lautensack, cat. 65).[8]

As with so many things, Dürer was at the forefront of German landscape depiction. His endeavors must have been partly stimulated by the "geographical renaissance" in which Nuremberg played a pivotal role at the turn of the century.[9] Rediscovery of Ptolemy's *Geographia* and Tacitus' classical account of Germany (*Germania*), as well as more recent geography books like Aeneas Sylvius' *Germania* (1457), sparked the patriotic desire of German humanists to study their land and history more closely themselves.[10] Conrad Celtis, the German arch-humanist who was planning an updated, more accurate *Germania Illustrata*, proposed that travel and study of German geography be incorporated into the educational curriculum. In a 1492 oration, he chided his German audience: "Consider it. . . the height of shame to know nothing about the topography, the climate, the rivers, the mountains. . . of our regions and country."[11]

Dürer was intimate with a circle of Nuremberg humanists – Conrad Celtis, Willibald Pirckheimer, Sebald Schreyer, and Hartmann Schedel – who actively promoted the study of cosmography. As a young artist, he participated in the production of two early geography books that had been instigated by these scholars: Schedel's record-breaking *Nuremberg Chronicle* (1493), where geography, cartography, and art were rolled into one huge volume, and the *Quatuor Libri Amorum* (1502), in which Celtis dedicated a poem to each of four geographical regions in Germany.[12] The woodcuts of topographical views illustrating these publications provided Dürer with a rich visual source, albeit more descriptive than artistic, for a variety of pure landscapes depicted from different vantage points. In them, three basic types of landscape can be distinguished. Large-scale city views are shown with pictorial details from ground level or a slightly raised viewpoint to distinguish street patterns. Planimetric small-scale maps of vast areas are presented, by contrast, from multiple and directly vertical viewpoints. Finally, medium-scale regional views, composite landscapes fashioned from the first two, combine the pictorial realism of the local city view with a panoramic expanse viewed from a highly elevated vantage point (see, for example, fig. 52-1, View of Sarmatia from the *Nuremberg Chronicle*).[13]

The availability of these visual models helps to explain Dürer's ability to manipulate his landscape views with such facility early on in his career. Owing to his travels, his careful nature studies, his scientific interests (such as mathematical perspective), his mastery of graphic techniques, and his pure artistic talent, however, Dürer's landscape studies and settings quickly surpassed these fledgling woodcuts, transforming landscape into a fully dimensional and representational art form. The scope of the world beneath the feet of his engraved *Nemesis* from 1502 (fig. 52-2), for instance, is equivalent to a regional view surveyed from a vantage point almost as steep as a small-scale map in the geography books mentioned above. Dürer must have observed the Tyrolean region of Klausen depicted in this print from a high mountain peak during his trip to Italy (1494-95). Instead of the conventionalized waterways and molehill-like mountains of the landscapes illustrated in the earlier geography books, he created an individualized portrait of the region's complex and variegated terrain, unifying it through a careful attention to light and spatial projection.

Even though Dürer probably considered the landscape settings of his finished works subordinate elements, he had become an accomplished landscapist by the time he etched *The Landscape with*

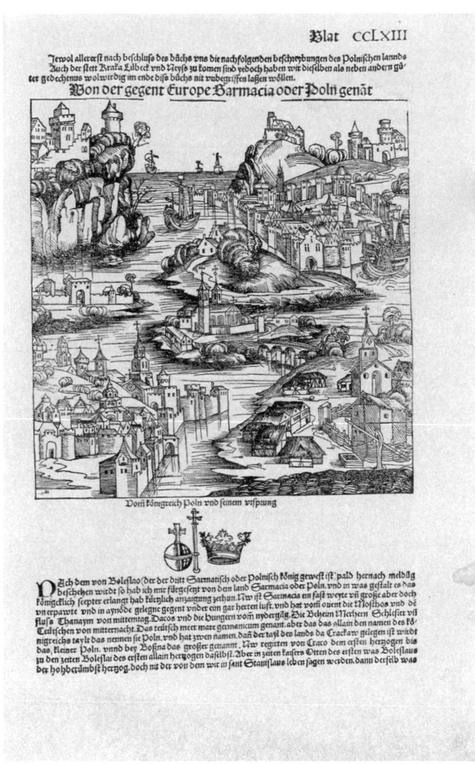

Figure 52-1. Michael Wolgemut, *View of Sarmartia*, woodcut illustration for *Nuremberg Chronicle*, 1493. Library of Congress. Rosenwald Collection.

Figure 52-2. Albrecht Dürer, *Nemesis*, ca. 1501-02, engraving, B.77.
Cincinnati Art Museum, Bequest of Herbert Greer French (1943.188).

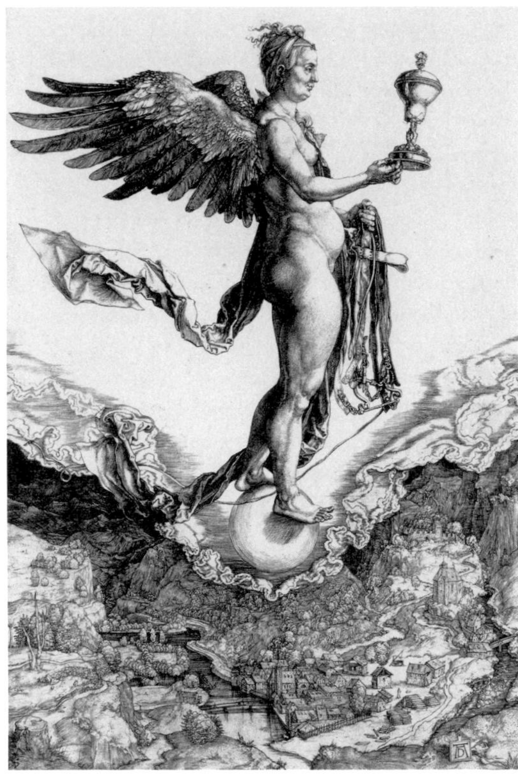

the Cannon. Extant drawings prove that he had, by 1518, developed
a portfolio of pure landscape studies, many of identifiable localities.
Among these is a silverpoint of a Franconian hamlet near Bamberg,
Kirchehrenbach (fig. 52-3), that he probably sketched on a visit to
the bishop of Bamberg in 1517.[14] In approach it is not unlike the local
city views of earlier geography books, but it is more dimensional and
atmospheric. He subsequently used it as the basis for the town that
occupies the midground of this etching. His overall approach to the
landscape of *The Cannon* might be categorized, like the *Nemesis*, as
a composite regional view. Here, from the high foreground ledge
that contains the cannon, the quasi-cartographic panorama of the
Franconian valley and the distant Ehrenburg mountain ridge is
surveyed in all its varied detail from a steeply elevated vantage point.

Dürer's regional view would become, to one degree or another,
almost formulaic for Danube-style landscapists. Both Hirschvogel
and Lautensack, for instance, likewise employ a high bank in the
foregrounds of their river landscapes from which to overlook the
expanse traversed by the river below. The preference of German

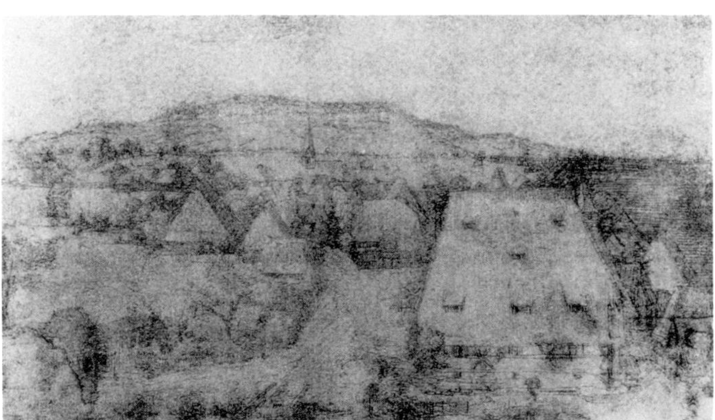

Figure 52-3. Albrecht Dürer, *Kircherenbach near Forchheim* (*A View of the
Hamlet Reuth near Bamberg*), ca. 1517, silverpoint on paper or parchment.
Location unknown. Formerly Koenigs Collection, no. D-I-121.

artists for these regional vistas may have been conditioned by their
understanding of the German word for landscape, *Landschaft*.
According to Rainer Gruenter, *lantschaft*, in its everyday usage in the
sixteenth century, did not mean a view of nature, as we think of it
today, nor an isolated city view, as might be found among Dürer's
drawing studies, but a geographical or political region, a territorial
entity.[15] For Dürer, then, the *Landschaft* of *The Cannon* may have
conceptually encompassed not just Kirchehrenbach but necessarily
the whole region of which it formed a part. – JSP

1. Etching was originally a process practiced by armorers. The earliest-dated etching
is by Urs Graf (1513). For a brief history, see Arthur M. Hind, *A History of Engraving
and Etching from the 15th Century to the year 1914*, 3rd rev. ed. (New York, 1923),
esp. 105-10.

2. Dodgson, 86.

3. Jan Bialostocki, "Myth and Allegory in Dürer's Etchings and Engravings," in *The
Message of Images: Studies in the History of Art* (Vienna: IRSA, 1988), esp. 136-38.

4. For the date on the cannon, see Charles Talbot, Washington 1971, 152, nn. 2-3.

5. For his Turk, Dürer used the central figure from a pen and watercolor study of
three Turks, now in the British Museum. He had copied the group of three from a study
for Gentile Bellini's 1496 painting of *Procession of the Relic of the True Cross*. Hans
Schwarz's portrait medal of Dürer could not have provided the artist's features, as some
sources have suggested, because it was not cast until 1520. For literature on the medal,
see Hermann Maué, New York 1986, 419, no. 216.

6. For this reading of the supervisor's action, see Pieter Strieder, Nuremberg 1978,
170, no. 210. For a different one, see Talbot, Washington 1971, 152, no. 69.

7. For those who connect the print with the Turkish threat, see Bialostocki, "Myth
and Allegory," 137, and Talbot, Washington 1971, 152.

8. For Dürer's influence on the Danube style, see Charles Talbot, New Haven 1969,
esp. 13, 20-26.

9. Gerald Strauss coined the term "geographical renaissance" and discusses the
developments in *Sixteenth-Century Germany: Its Topography and Topographers*
(Madison: University of Wisconsin Press, 1959), esp. 3-59; see also Karin Alexis, "The
Landscape Genre in Northern Europe: The Emergence of a New Secular Symbol,"
Athanor 2 (1982): 11-17.

10. The *Geographia* by Ptolemy (second century A.D.) was published in a Latin
edition for the first time in the mid-fifteenth century. Dürer's close friend Pirckheimer
also edited and printed an edition in 1525. The *Germania* by Cornelius Tacitus (ca. A.D.
55-117) was discovered in the mid-fifteenth century and published in Nuremberg in
1473. The *Germania* by the Italian Aeneas Silvius (in Italian, Enea Silvio Piccolomini,
1405-1464), served as a model of cultural history for the German humanists. A
condensed version of his *Europa* was incorporated in the *Nuremberg Chronicle* (1493).

11. Strauss, *Sixteenth-Century Germany*, 20. The complete text of Celtis' oration at
the University of Ingolstadt (1492) is translated in Lewis W. Spitz, *The Northern
Renaissance* (Englewood Cliffs: Prentice-Hall, 1972), 15-27; see also idem, *Conrad
Celtis: The German Arch-Humanist* (Cambridge: Harvard University Press, 1957).

12. It is thought that Dürer may have designed several of the woodcuts for the
Nuremberg Chronicle. He was apprenticed to Michael Wolgemut when the workshop
produced the 645 woodcuts for Anton Koberger, the publisher. (Koberger was Dürer's
godfather.) See Adrian Wilson, *The Making of the Nuremberg Chronicle* (Amsterdam:
Nico Israel, 1976), esp. 199; Elisabeth Rücker, *Die schedelsche Weltchronik. Das grösste
Buchunternehmen der Dürer-Zeit* (Munich: Prestel Verlag, 1973); and a facsimile, *Die
Schedelsche Weltchronik*, with an epilogue by Rudolf Pörtner, *Die bibliophilen
Tasrchenbücher*, no. 64 (Dortmund, 1978). For Dürer's contribution to Celtis' *Quatuor
Libri Amorum*, see Jeffrey Chipps Smith, Austin 1983, 103, no. 10; and Fedja
Anzelewsky, "Die Philosophie," in *Dürer-Studien: Untersuchungen zu den
ikonographischen Grundlagen seiner Werke zwischen den beiden Italienreisen* (Berlin:
Deutscher Verlag für Kunstwissenschaft, 1983), 118-33.

13. The three landscape categories are distinguished and illustrated in Karen S.
Pearson, "The Multimedia Approach to Landscape in German Renaissance Geography
Books," in Sandra Hindman, ed., *The Early Illustrated Book: Essays in Honor of
Lessing J. Rosenwald*, (Washington, 1982), 117-35.

14. The identification of the view as Kirchehrenbach in the drawing (Winkler 479)
has been accepted ever since it was proposed by O. Mitius, "Die Landschaft auf Dürers
Eisenradierung 'Die grosse Kanone' vom Jahre 1518," *Mitteilungen aus dem
Germanischen Nationalmuseum* (1911), 141-49. Recently, however, it has been
identified as Reuth, near Bamberg, by Albert J. Elen, *Missing Old Master Drawings
from the Franz Koenig Collection* (The Hague: SDU Publishers, 1989), 109, no. 155.

15. Rainer Gruenter, "Landschaft. Bemerkungen zur Wort- und
Bedeutungsgeschichte," in Alexander Ritter, ed., *Landschaft und Raum in der
Erzählkunst* (Darmstadt: Wissenschaftliche Buchgesellschaft, 1975), 192-207, esp.
192-93. See also Charles Talbot, "Topography as Landscape in Early Printed Books," in
Sandra Hindman, ed., *The Early Illustrated Book: Essays in Honor of Lessing J.
Rosenwald* (Washington, 1982), 105-16.

Hans Baldung

Schwäbisch-Gmünd 1484/85-1545 Strasbourg

53. Adam and Eve 1519.

Woodcut on antique laid paper, 25.6 x 9.9 cm (image).
B. 2.; GE. 58; H. *Ger* 2; Mende 73.
Monogrammed on tablet lower right: ᴴᴮ ; dated lower left: *1519*.
Provenance: P. von Baldinger-Seidenberg (Lugt 212); Paul J. Sachs
(Lugt 2091); (purchased from Goodman-Walker, October 3, 1934,
for $250).
Bequest of Herbert Greer French, 1943.262.

Hans Baldung's *Adam and Eve* from 1519 is the last and most
gripping of his three single-leaf woodcut versions of the subject.[1] He
eliminated his earlier references to a densely wooded paradise, with a
serpent conspicuously coiled around the Tree of Knowledge, in order
to concentrate on the protagonists. Adam, like a predator, desirously
stalks Eve from behind in this constrictive, narrow format. Eve
grimaces uncomfortably and recoils in an attempt to evade his
advances. Pinned visually between Adam, his foot blocking her way,
and the tree of her downfall, Eve is thrust forward, forced to expose
her newly realized nakedness and sexuality to the viewer.

Throughout much of his career, Baldung explored themes similar
to this one that ally female carnality with demonic forces and the
macabre. In his choice and presentation of such themes, he is one of
the most individualistic, innovative German Renaissance artists to
follow the footsteps of Albrecht Dürer.[2] He spent five years in
Dürer's Nuremberg workshop (1503-07). Baldung came there as a
trained journeyman artist from Strasbourg, and under Dürer's
tutelage developed a graphic language for his prints and drawings as
well as a fascination with the classically derived female nude.[3] The
two artists were on sufficiently collegial terms that Dürer entrusted
the younger Alsatian with his workshop during a second sojourn to
Italy (1505-07). The two remained in contact until Dürer's death.

By the time Baldung had designed this *Adam and Eve*, he had been
a citizen of Strasbourg for a decade, producing paintings and designs
for woodcuts and stained glass from his own workshop. His highly
educated and influential family undoubtedly proved an asset to his
business and provided him automatic entry into the humanist circles
of this cosmopolitan city, for whom he would design some of his
four hundred or more woodcut illustrations. With his monumental
winged altarpiece for the Freiburg Cathedral (1512-17), Baldung
established his reputation as a painter.[4] Later, after the Reformation
was introduced into Strasbourg in 1529 and commissions for
altarpieces ceased, Baldung continued to prosper. The emotional
intensity and expressiveness of works executed prior to 1529, such as
Adam and Eve, however, would largely give way to a style marked
by an ambiguous aesthetic detachment more in keeping with
mannerist tastes.

The Fall was a pivotal theme for Baldung. He illustrated it many
times in his career and explored its meaning through other subjects
as well. While in Nuremberg, Baldung must have followed Dürer's
progress on his engraving of *Adam and Eve* (1504) and been privy to
the deliberations underlying its presentation (cat. 33). No doubt
Dürer's print had a profound effect on the young printmaker.
Baldung's earliest woodcut of Adam and Eve from 1511 (fig. 53-1) in
fact, assumes an audience sufficiently sophisticated to discern that
his version alludes to Dürer's while simultaneously transforming it.
With this 1519 version, Baldung distanced himself from Dürer's
model to accentuate more forcefully the contrast between their
interpretations.

Dürer's engraving presents Adam and Eve before the Fall, when

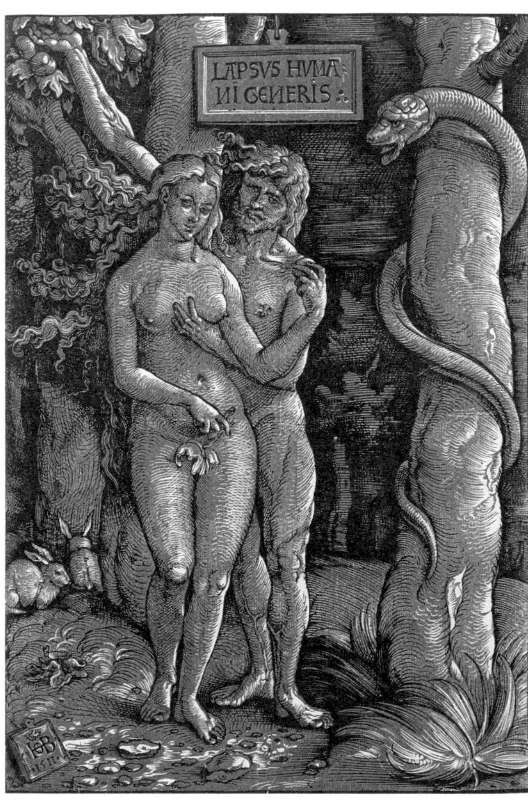

Figure 53-1. Hans Baldung, *Adam and Eve*, 1511, chiaroscuro woodcut with
olive gray tone block, B. 3. Kupferstichkabinett, Staatliche Museen
Preußischer Kulturbesitz, Berlin.

each epitomized a perfected ideal in a state of innocence. Sexuality
does not enter into the couple's consciousness. In Baldung's
woodcut, by contrast, it does; and the implications behind the Fall
become crucial factors in its interpretation. In his version, Adam and
Eve, who have already partaken of the forbidden fruit, are no longer
separated as in Dürer's composition. Newly aware of their
nakedness (Gen. 3:7), the two are aroused; their sexuality forces
them to interact. Adam approaches Eve from behind, possessively
takes hold of her shoulder, and poises a figleaf strategically over her
genitals, its stems shooting up phallically suggestive buds. Eve's
maidenly long tresses are now bound up upon her head in a matronly
manner, her virginal innocence lost.[5]

At the same time that the bite of the apple stimulated their sexual
appetites, it brought death into being. God had warned Adam and
Eve of the mortifying consequences of eating the forbidden fruit,
"Thou shalt die the death" (Gen. 2:17), and human mortality can be
traced directly to their corruption: "Scripture teaches us that death
comes, first of all, from Paradise, from the bite of the forbidden fruit".[6]

The theme of the inevitability of death, as Joseph Koerner has
shown, pervades Baldung's work. The female in Baldung's paintings
of *Death and the Woman*, for instance, unwittingly entices death and
thereby becomes the victim of her own attraction.[7] Like Eve who
unwillfully seduces Adam, her sexuality becomes the cause of her
own undoing. Through the original sin, Adam is similarly both the
cause of death and its victim. In Baldung's later painting, *Eve, the
Serpent, and Death*, Adam literally takes the form of death's
putrefying corpse.[8] In this woodcut of Adam and Eve, the mortal
threat of the couple's sexual encounter is implied by Eve's aversion
to her abductor. She pulls away from Adam and drops her left arm,
as if wishing, too late, to be rid of the venomous apple that is already
having its effect.

Ultimately, Baldung's print is not just about Adam and Eve but
also about us. It is a *memento mori*. Their transgression is ours.

Baldung makes our fallen state explicit in his earlier woodcut version of the Fall by inscribing a tablet with "The Fall of Mankind" (*Lapsus Humani Generis*) (fig. 53-1). Together Adam and Eve stand beneath the inscription and fixate on us, as if transmitting to us their carnality and morbid affliction.

In the Museum's later woodcut, Baldung discards this didactic approach altogether. Instead he subtly involves us, making us active and culpable participants. We, like Adam, experience Eve's fatal seduction. Our encounter is with Eve alone, not with them both. Eve's body is turned toward us, not toward Adam. She exposes herself intimately to us and reacts erotically to our presence. We become partners to her carnal desires, and, as if ravished by our gaze, she turns her head painfully away from us. Through our confrontation with Eve, we, like Adam, sealers of our own fates, are implicated in the Fall.

Baldung would also succumb to Eve's wiles and thus included his personal epitaph here. At the base of the Tree of Knowledge, he placed his monogram, HBG (*Hans Baldung* [*Grien*]) – not on his usual *cartellino*, or hangable tablet, but on a stone slab.[9] Immediately after the Fall, God warned the serpent that "she [Eve] shall crush thy head" (Gen. 3:15).[10] Eve, as she pivots, presses her left foot down on that slab – Baldung's own headstone – and Baldung, like all humankind, is linked to Eve through death. – JSP

1. For Baldung's two earlier single-leaf versions, see fig. 53-1 and Mende, no. 33.

2. For introductions to Baldung's life and context, see Alan Shestack, "An Introduction to Hans Baldung Grien," and Linda C. Hults, "Baldung and the Reformation," in New Haven 1981, 3-18, 38-55.

3. See Charles W. Talbot, "Baldung and the Female Nude," in New Haven 1981, 19-37.

4. Baldung resided in Freiburg im Breisgau during the five years he was occupied on this lucrative commission. For illustrations and further literature, see Gert von der Osten, *Hans Baldung Grien. Gemälde und Dokumente* (Berlin: Deutscher Verlag für Kunstwissenschaft, 1983), 99-118, pls. 64-87.

5. For further examples of Baldung's refiguration of prints by Dürer, see Thomas DaCosta Kaufmann, "Hermeneutics in the History of Art: Remarks on the Reception of Dürer in the Sixteenth and Early Seventeenth Centuries" in *New Perspectives on the Art of Renaissance Nuremberg,* ed. Jeffrey Chipps Smith (Austin, 1985), esp. 28-33.

6. This English translation (from Martin Luther, *Werke* [Weimar, 1883-1901], 32:284) is taken from Joseph Leo Koerner, "The Mortification of the Image: Death as a Hermeneutic in Hans Baldung Grien," *Representations* 10 (1985): 77. Koerner's analysis of the theme of death in Baldung's work forms the basis for the interpretation of Baldung's *Adam and Eve* presented here. For other analyses of this woodcut with further literature, see Otto Pannewitz, Karlsruhe 1986, 1:382 (F4); New Haven 1981, 243-44, no. 75; and Washington 19906, no. 72.

7. For illustrations of Baldung's versions of *Death and the Woman*, see Von der Osten, *Hans Baldung Grien*, nos. 10, 24, 44, 48. Of these, the version in Basel from circa 1517-20 (Von der Osten, *Hans Baldung Grien*, no. 48) most closely resembles the *Adam and Eve* woodcut in structure and meaning. For further discussion of the Basel version, see Koerner, "Mortification of the Image," 78-80, 85-87; and Dieter Koepplin, Basel 1978, 23-30, no. 6.

8. *Eve, the Serpent and Death (as Adam)* is discussed by Koerner, "Mortification of the Image," 90-92; and by Robert A. Koch, *Hans Baldung Grien: Eve, the Serpent, and Death* (Ottawa, 1974), esp. 22-29.

9. The *G* in Baldung's monogram, HBG, stands for Grien (Green). It is speculated that Baldung was given the nickname while still in Dürer's workshop, that he unofficially adopted it, and by 1510, that he had integrated it into his monogram. See Shestack, New Haven 1981, 6.

10. For different readings of how the biblical passage (Gen. 3:15) relates to Eve and Baldung's monogram, see New Haven 1981, 244.

Lucas van Leyden

Leiden 1489/94-1533 Leiden

54. The Dance of St. Mary Magdalene 1519.

Engraving on antique laid paper, 28.9 x 39.5 cm (sheet).
B. 122; Dut. 122 i/ii; H. *Neth.* 122 i/iii.

Watermark: Gothic *P*.
Signed and dated on cartello lower center: *1519* L.
Condition: Trimmed within platemark.
Provenance: Louis Galichon (Lugt 1060); (purchased from M. Knoedler, New York, April 17, 1940, for $1,800).
Bequest of Herbert Greer French, 1943.134.
Exhibitions: Cincinnati 1941, no. 86, illus. 22.

Lucas van Leyden was the most important and influential printmaker in the Netherlands during the pivotal period when artists trained in Northern medieval canons apprehended and amalgamated southern Renaissance ideas. Like his German counterpart, Albrecht Dürer, to whom he is often unfavorably compared, Lucas' engravings, etchings, and woodcuts found a market with his contemporaries and inspired his principal successors, Pieter Bruegel the Elder, Hendrik Goltzius (cat. 69), and Rembrandt (cat. 77), to create masterpieces of their own. The majority of Lucas' prints depict religious subjects, innovatively reinterpreted in secularized narratives reinforced by pictorial elements – subtleties of light and shadow and atmospheric and linear perspective. Lucas' mature prints successfully integrate secular figures in narrative sequences with convincing perspectival landscapes, thus establishing him as a pioneer of the Dutch genre tradition.

Karel van Mander, the first biographer of Dutch painters, in his *Schilderboeck* (1604), gives Lucas' birth date as 1494. This date would make his first engraving, *Mahomet and the Monk Sergius* (1508) (fig. 41-2), evidence of an extremely precocious talent.[1] E. Pelinck suggests that Van Mander misinterpreted information he received from Lucas' grandson regarding Lucas' birth. Pelinck relates that Lucas began to engrave at the age of fourteen rather than nine, making his birth date 1489.[2] Regardless which date is accepted, the young Lucas was a gifted child prodigy with which to be reckoned.

According to Van Mander, Lucas received his first formal training in the studio of his father, Hugo Jacobsz., and subsequently studied with another Leiden painter, Cornelis Engebrechtsz.[3] The means by which Lucas learned engraving is undocumented. One can only speculate that he trained with a goldsmith or armorer, since the engravers' trade in Leiden was undeveloped. The large number of his prints dated between 1508 and 1530, however, permits the study of the development of his engraving style and helps establish a chronology for his painting. His youthful engravings seem to borrow more from the paintings of Gerard David and Hugo van der Goes than from the engraving tradition of his predecessors. *Mahomet and the Monk Sergius* (B. 126), his first dated print of 1508, reveals a reasonably sophisticated presentation of the popular medieval theme of Mahomet's drunkenness and supposed misdeed. Lucas' preoccupation with foreshortening and a planar recession restrict the dramatic action to the frontal plane. The spectator's viewpoint is inconsistent, and the feet and hands are disproportionately small. One year later *The Conversion of St. Paul* (B. 107) introduced the large horizontal format with a sequential pictorial subject. This composition gives primary emphasis to the blinded Saul led toward Damascus over the conversion of Paul depicted in the left middle ground. *The Conversion* was followed by *Ecce Homo* (B. 71) in 1510 and *Calvary* (B. 74) in 1517, each a tour de force of linear and aerial perspective, respectively, that direct attention back to the primary votive focus.

The visual provocation of Lucas' *Dance of St. Mary Magdalene* corresponds with the controversies of Catholic orthodoxy of his day. Could one and the same person begin life as a courtesan and miraculously become a repentant hermit? Was Mary Magdalene three Marys rolled into one, as accepted by Catholic legend, or three separate Marys, as proposed by the French humanist Jacques Lefèvre d'Étaples in 1517?[4] Lucas treated the subject of the Magdalene on at least three earlier occasions: *The Repentant Magdalene*, circa 1505-06 (B. 123); *Mary Magdalene in the Clouds* of 1518 (B. 124), and *Christ Appearing to the Magdalene* of 1519 (B. 77). In *The Dance of St. Mary Magdalene*, Lucas juxtaposes the extremes of earthly excess and heavenly ecstasy. With artistic ingenuity he appeals to a varied audience by combining courtly dance, stag hunt, and religious legend in an unprecedented and controversial composition counter to votive tradition for the Magdalene.[5] In the foreground, a scene of earthly decadence is depicted, with an elegantly dressed Magdalene, her halo symbolizing her future sainthood, promenading with a young courtier to the music of drum and flute – an episode commonly portrayed in German, French, and English passion plays of the late fifteenth and early sixteenth centuries.[6] The secular life of the Magdalene does not appear in the Bible; it was, however, a vehicle for moral instruction through popular songs and didactic examples concerning sin and repentance. The well-organized composition recalls Israhel van Meckenem's sequential portrayal in his *Dance of the Daughters of Herodias* (cat. 21). The vastness of the naturalistic landscape, with its high middle ground, light, and shade, draws attention around the central figures to the stag hunt and, finally, to the ascent of four angels with the penitent Magdalene in the upper center. The mountainous background is an accurate portrayal of La Sainte-Baume, site of a cave where she retired to a hermitlike existence in southern France.[7]

In the best impressions of *The Dance of St. Mary Magdalene*, there are no strong contrasts of light and shadows; instead there is a harmonious, atmospheric quality. Connoisseurs have not always fully appreciated this subtler aspect of Lucas' prints executed between 1512 and 1520. French found an early impression in which the slipped stroke on the dog to the right of the rightmost tree and the slipped stroke across the hilltop to the right of the freestanding tree at left still prints.[8] He preferred a print quality based on Dürer's mature engraving style rather than the silvery chiaroscuro as found in the impression at the Philadelphia Museum of Art. – KLS

1. Ellen Jacobowitz and Stepanie Loeb Stepanek, Washington 1983, 11.

2. Jacobowitz and Stepanek, Washington 1983, 11.

3. Jacobowitz and Stepanek, Washington 1983, 12.

4. Craig Harbison, "Lucas van Leyden, The Magdalen and the Problem of Secularization in early Sixteenth Century Northern Art," *Oud Holland* 98, no. 3 (1984): 120.

5. Peter Parshall, "Lucas van Leyden's narrative style," *Nederlands Kunsthistorisch Jaarboek* 29 (1978): 224.

6. Parshall, "Lucas van Leyden's Narrative Style," 225.

7. Robert A. Koch, "La Sainte-Baume in Flemish Landscape Painting of the Sixteenth Century," GBA, 6th ser., 66 (November 1965): 273.

8. Jacobowitz and Stepanek, Washington 1983, 192.

Lucas van Leyden

Leiden 1489/94-1533 Leiden

55. Emperor Maximilian I 1520.

Engraving and etching on antique laid paper, 26.1 x 19.5 cm (sheet).
B. 172; Dut. 172; H. *Neth.* 172.
Watermark: Crowned shield with blazing sun, letter *b*, and flower (Briquet 13979).
Signed on cartello upper left: L *1520*.
Condition: Trimmed within platemark.
Provenance: (Purchased from M. Knoedler, New York, February 16, 1931, for $3,500).
Bequest of Herbert Greer French, 1943.128.
Exhibitions: Cincinnati 1934, no. 24; Cincinnati 1941, no. 87.

In his diary, Albrecht Dürer recounts his historic meeting with his contemporary and competitor during June of 1521:

I was invited to be the guest of Master Lucas, who engraves in copper; he is a small man and native of Leiden in Holland, he was at Antwerp. . . . I made a portrait of Master Lucas van Leyden in silverpoint.[1]

The reason for Lucas' trip to Antwerp is not recorded. It could have been to sell his prints at the Antwerp market, where, in fact, they sold better than Dürer's, or the opportunity to meet Dürer himself, whose work he greatly admired. Lucas exchanged his complete graphic oeuvre for eight guldens' worth of Dürer's prints.[2] This trade would have included Lucas' posthumous portrait of *Emperor Maximilian I* (after Dürer's own woodcut [B. 154] of 1519 [fig. 55-1] or one of its contemporary replicas).[3] Dürer had attended the imperial diet in Ausburg in June 1518, where he made a charcoal drawing from life of the emperor for whom he had worked since 1512 on various propagandistic woodcut cycles to glorify his person for posterity.[4]

Lucas copied the unimpeachable portrait drawing, but he altered the setting. Borrowing a detail or fragment from another artist's work was an acceptable practice at the time. Lucas undoubtedly planned to capitalize on the popularity of memorial portraits of the Holy Roman Emperor. The most powerful man in Europe, Maximilian had consolidated his own power in the imperial office and passed it on to his Habsburg descendants at his death on January 12, 1519.

Emperor Maximilian I is the only print by Lucas for which a drawing (fig. 55-2), now in the Fondation Custodia, Paris, exists.[5] Lucas drops Dürer's iconic image by eliminating the honorific titles and by placing the bust-length portrait in an architectural setting. He does not lose sight of the imperial nature of the portrait: he places an emphasis on the accoutrements of the office, among them an enlarged chain of the Order of the Golden Fleece, and in the foreground, an embroidered panel thrown over a bannister depicts the double-headed imperial eagle and two stylized pomegranates, the

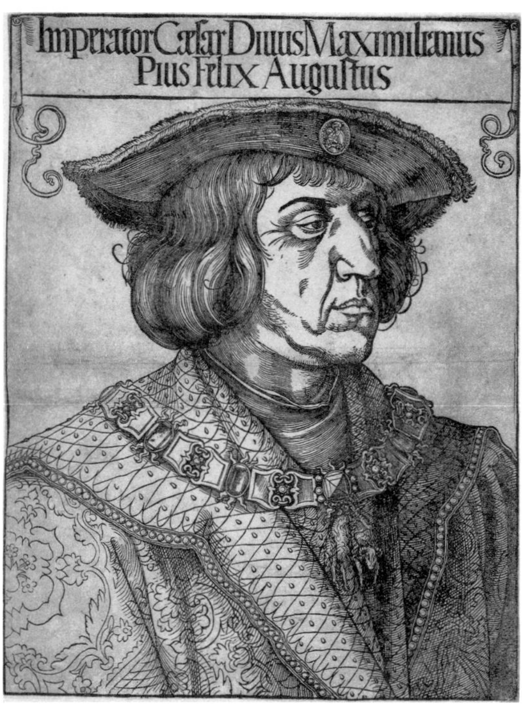

Figure 55-1. Albrecht Dürer, *Portrait of Emperor Maximilian I*, 1519, woodcut. Museum of Fine Arts, Boston. Harvey D. Parker Collection.

Figure 55-2. Lucas van Leyden, *Maximilian I*, pen and gray ink, brushpoint and graphite. Fondation Custodia, (coll. F. Lugt), Institut Néerlandais, Paris.

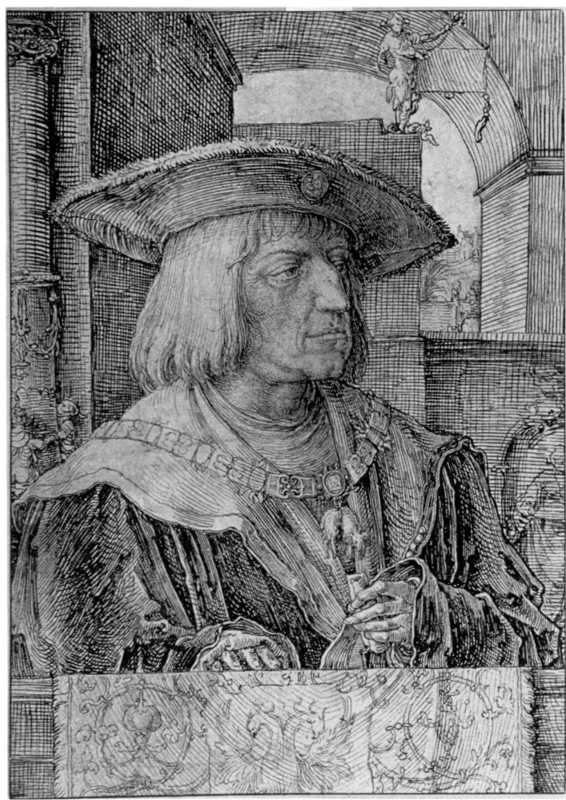

personal emblem of Maximilian. Since this is a memorial portrait, Lucas adds three fools with horned headdresses, allusions to the transitoriness of life. The introduction and posing of the hands, one against the top of the bannister, is a pictorial motif derived from early Netherlandish portraiture. Dürer's straightforward woodcut presents an austere, mature, and august image of the emperor. Lucas' interpretation is far more youthful, contemplative, and humane.

This portrait would not have been possible without Lucas' pioneering experiments in etching. His *Maximilian* is considered a landmark in the history of etching: it is the first etching on copper rather than iron and the first to combine etching and engraving in a single print. In 1520 he executed six etchings.[6] While the medium offered spontaneity and rapid execution, allowing Lucas to draw directly through the protective coating on the plate, he appears to have been uncomfortable with his newly invented technique to achieve the accuracy or subtlety that he attained with engraving. He engraved the face to convey three-dimensionality through the subtle gradation of light and shadow. He did, however, etch the hands; then he reworked them with engraving. Other areas with added engraving include the robe, the chain, the tapestry, the pillar, the arch, and the castle on the hill in the background. A comparison with Lucas' original drawing shows that he enhanced the formal presence of Maximilian by eliminating the distracting niche figures and by widening the composition. The shadows are carefully orchestrated to direct the focus to the dignified and self-assured countenance of the emperor, who was an enlightened patron of the arts and sciences and the last of the Christian knights.

Lucas' final years reflect several influences. His meeting with Dürer shifted his attention to greater detail, dramatic presentation, and appropriation of motifs. He likewise took a greater interest in the Italianate style through his contact with Jan Gossaert, one of the first Netherlandish artists to bring the Italian Renaissance manner north. Gossaert's style was characterized by a greater emphasis on sculpturesque and animated nude figures, and increased ornamentation. Lastly, Lucas adapted from Marcantonio Raimondi a new system, using broad, fluid cross-hatching to describe shape and volume. Thus Lucas' career ended with a style that ushered in the monumental sculpturesque forms of the Italian High Renaissance into the Netherlands. – KLS

1. Ellen S. Jacobowitz and Stephanie Loeb Stepanek, Washington 1983, 210.
2. Jacobowitz and Stepanek, Washington 1983, 210.
3. Jacobowitz and Stepanek, Washington 1983, 199.
4. Larry Silver, "Prints for a Prince: Maximilian Nuremberg and the Woodcut," in *New Perspectives on the Art of Renaissance Nuremberg: Five Essays*, ed. Jeffrey Chipps Smith (Austin: The Archer M. Huntington Art Gallery, 1985), 8.
5. Karel Boon et al., *L'Epoque de Lucas de Leyde et Pierre Bruegel* (Paris: Fondation Custodia, 1980-81), 148-50.
6. Ad Stijnman, "Lucas van Leyden and Etching," PQ. 5, no. 3 (1988): 256-57.

School of Dürer (Sebald Beham?)

Nuremberg 1500-1550 Frankfurt am Main

56. Madonna and Child ca. 1520-25.

Hand colored woodcut on antique laid paper, 43.5 x 29.5 cm (sheet).
P. 240 copy [Dürer].
Watermark: Indecipherable.
Condition: Hand-applied colors have changed; the Virgin's headdress was once blue, greens have darkened, and reds have faded. There is abrasion and cracking in the green cushion, Virgin's halo. Christ's halo may have darkened (?). Discoloration and printed text verso both show through to recto.
Provenance: Fürstlich Hohenzollernsches Museum, Sigmaringen (Lugt 2759, no mark); Ralph King, Cleveland (Mrs. Ralph King consigned to Knoedler, January 12, 1939); (purchased from M. Knoedler, New York, March 6, 1939, for $3,000).
Bequest of Herbert Greer French, 1943.254.
Exhibitions: Cincinnati 1941, no. 76.

This large devotional image likely served as a cheap substitute for a painting. The Madonna's fur-lined garment, now orange, was originally red. Her headdress and book were darker blue. The green of Christ's sash and cushion, on the other hand, has darkened, so today they contrast with the other translucent, faded colors. Minute traces of gold paint still spot Christ's halo, and gold leaf originally adorned the Madonna's halo, covering Christ's at the point of their intersection.

The original opaque colors once concealed that this impression was pulled from a block already well worn. Where lines no longer printed darkly and evenly or had broken down altogether (such as along the Virgin's belt), color disguised the true condition of the block. Perhaps the color also helped mask the fact that the verso of this sheet had been previously employed for another purpose. Today – even in reproductions – letters of a text, which run lengthwise along the left edge, can be readily discerned where they emboss the image surface. The text, a German translation of Fernando Alvares Seco's description of Portugal cannot have been printed before 1561.[1] Thus, the woodblock for the *Madonna and Child* was already at least forty years old by the time it was used to pull the Museum's unique impression.[2]

The Museum's woodcut is deceptively similar to *Madonna and Child in a Landscape*, exemplified here by the impression in Bremen (fig. 56-1). The two are so similar that they have been mistaken for one another.[3] Still Bremen's differs from Cincinnati's in three respects: (1) the depiction has been slightly extended on all sides, (2) a background landscape has been added, and (3) it was cut from two blocks instead of one. J. D. Passavant is the only cataloguer to distinguish between the two woodcuts. He thought that Cincinnati's version was a copy of Bremen's, but actually, just the reverse is true. A copyist normally attempts to improve upon his model by regularizing lines and hatchings. The *Formschneider* (block-cutter) of the Bremen woodcut rounded out the circles of the Madonna's halo, which are awkward and flattened in the Cincinnati version, and systematized the hatchings of her fur collar, thereby divulging that Cincinnati's is the earlier of the two, not vice versa.[4]

The identity of the designer of the Cincinnati-Bremen woodcuts is not certain. The earliest print cataloguers attributed the design to Albrecht Dürer; a plug with his monogram was inserted into the woodblock (on the wall near the Virgin's right elbow) in the second state of the *Madonna and Child in a Landscape* (Bremen version).[5] Even without his monogram, the connection with Dürer is clear because the Cincinnati-Bremen Madonna derives from his 1518 *Virgin as Queen of Angels* (fig. 56-2).[6] The chapelet of roses or beads that encircles the Madonna's head in these images alludes to the rosary, a string of beads representing garlands of roses (*rosarius*) used to keep count of prayers. Devotion to the rosary, which the Dominicans and their confraternities aggressively promoted in Germany in the early sixteenth century, was closely tied to the veneration of the Virgin – the rosary prayer cycle includes 150 repetitions of Ave Marias.[7] Instead of adopting Dürer's eucharistic theme (grapes) or quasi-heavenly context (coronation as Queen of Heaven), the Cincinnati-Bremen designer places the Madonna before a stone wall to indicate a *hortus conclusus* (the enclosed garden from *Song of Songs* 4:12), a common symbol for her purity.

Most scholars have rejected the attribution of the Cincinnati-Bremen woodcuts to Dürer in favor of an artist working in his circle. Hans Süss von Kulmbach (ca. 1480-1522), who studied with Dürer, and Sebald Beham (1500-1550), a younger Nuremberg printmaker who was profoundly influenced by him, have each been proposed. The Kulmbach attribution is more controversial. Friedrich Winkler, who established Kulmbach's print oeuvre, singled out *Madonna and Child in a Landscape* (Bremen version) as one of his most successful woodcuts.[8] More recently, however, Barbara Butts has contested Kulmbach's entire output of nearly a hundred woodcuts – including the Cincinnati-Bremen Madonna – as being too disparate and tenuous.[9]

Sebald Beham's name has been linked intermittently since the nineteenth century with the Cincinnati-Bremen Madonna.[10] Beham's habit of freely appropriating or varying Dürer's compositions would tend to support his authorship; many of his engravings (*Virgin with a Pear*, B. 18; *Melencolia*, B. 144) and woodcuts (*The Fall of Mankind*, Ge. 163; *St. Christopher*, Ge. 213) depend wholly or in part on Dürer's work.[11] Approximately a dozen prints of the Madonna and child theme are ascribed to him and, like the Cincinnati-Bremen Madonna, they are all stylistically characteristic of the Dürer school. Of these, Beham's *Nursing Madonna* (Ge. 194), which scholars date close to circa 1520-21, resembles the Cincinnati-Bremen Madonna most closely.[12] It is probable that Beham designed the Cincinnati-Bremen Madonna about the same time, while he was actively exploring this theme but before his temporary ouster from Nuremberg in 1525 for flirting with radical religious beliefs.[13]

As one of the Nuremberg Little Masters (*Kleinmeister*), Beham's miniature engravings often receive more attention than his woodcuts.[14] His woodcuts of secular subjects (peasants, genre scenes, satires, etc.) are better known than his devotional ones, particularly those he supplied for Hans Sach's popular broadsheets between 1520-30. In stark contrast to the minute scale of his engravings, Beham's woodcuts can be unusually large in format. Two of his

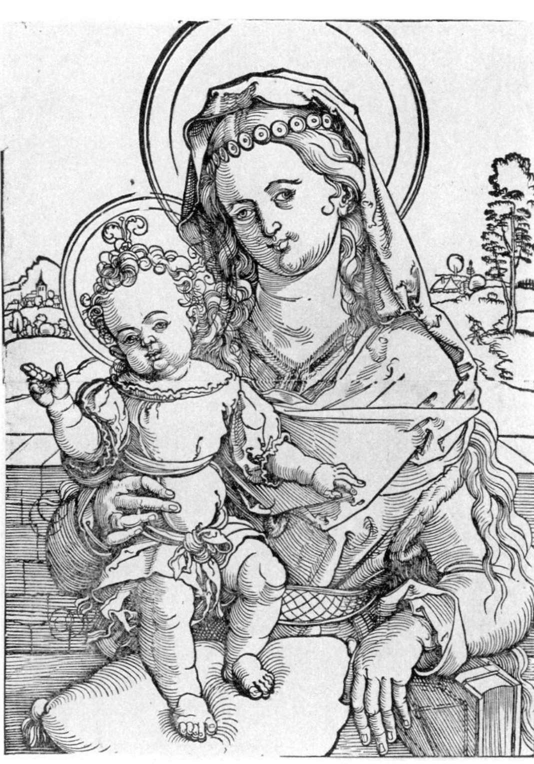

Figure 56-1. Sebald Beham, *Madonna and Child in a Landscape*, ca. 1520-25, woodcut (two blocks), Pauli 866 i. Kunsthalle, Bremen.

Marian woodcuts (Ge. 966, Ge. 798) approach or exceed the size of the Museum's *Madonna and Child*, and like the Bremen version, a number of his large woodcuts are composed of more than one block that have been printed together on a single sheet of paper.

The Cincinnati-Bremen design served as the model for a later woodcut, a *Madonna and Child* that is attributed to Erhard Schön and signed by its publisher, "Hanns Guldenmundt zu Nurnberg" (fig. 56-3). Schön eliminated the stone wall, clarified the

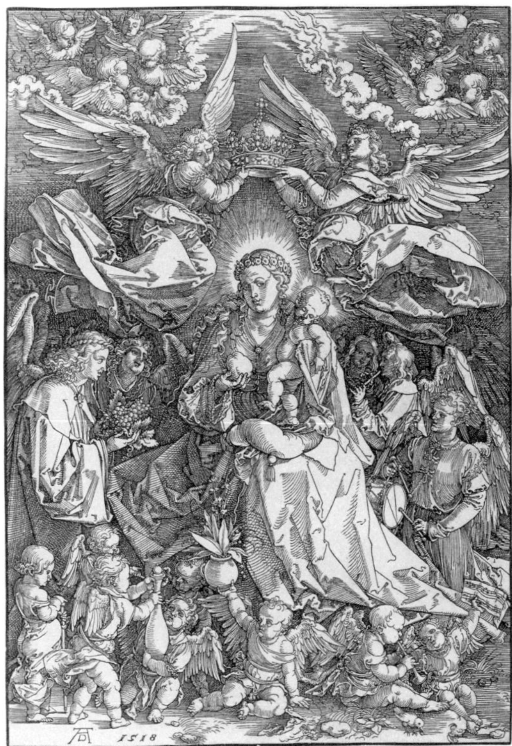

Figure 56-2 Albrecht Dürer, *Virgin as Queen of Angels*, 1518, woodcut, B. 101. Museum of Fine Arts, Boston, Stephen Bullard Fund.

Figure 56-3. Erhard Schön, *Madonna and Child with God the Father and the Holy Spirit*, ca. 1530, hand-colored woodcut. Albertina, Vienna.

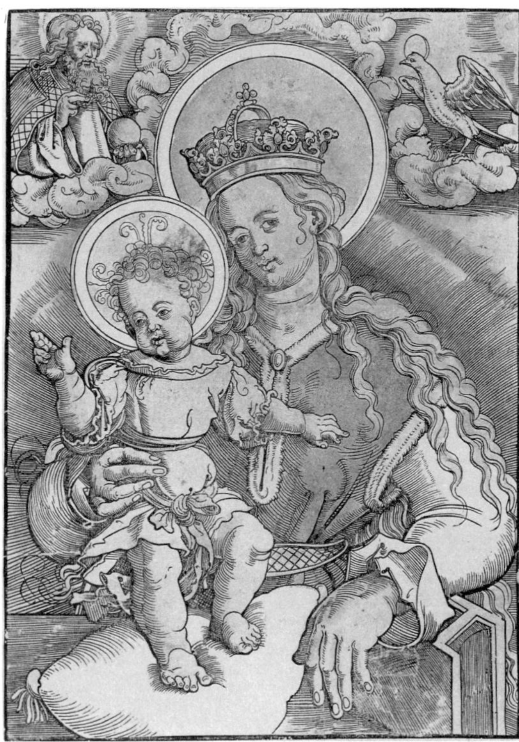

construction of the Virgin's bodice, and exchanged her beaded chapelet for a crown, but he otherwise followed the Cincinnati-Bremen figures.[15] The Museum's impression of Beham's little-known *Madonna and Child* thus provides an important link in this cluster of related images. – JSP

1. The earliest edition of Seco's map of Portugal was published in Latin in Rome in 1561, establishing a *terminus a quo* for the Museum's impression. According to Mitchell A. Codding of the Hispanic Society of America, the German text on its verso "corresponds exactly with the first and third paragraphs, the second paragraph having been omitted, of the Latin text on the verso of a map of Portugal by Fernando Alvares Seco from a Latin edition of *Theatrum orbis terrarum* by Abraham Ortelius." Many publishers besides Ortelius (e.g., Jode, Hondius, Mercator, Bleau) copied Seco's map either as a single-leaf or in atlas form. The precise German edition for which the Museum's textual fragment was destined has not yet been identified. The text that runs across the width of the Hispanic Society's Latin folio of Ortelius, like the German text that runs along the side of the Cincinnati impression, measures 43.5 cm. The Museum's text was printed askew so that the lines are cut off on the right, probably rendering the sheet unsatisfactory for publication.

My special thanks to Mitchell Codding of the Hispanic Society of America and to Joseph R. Jones of the University of Kentucky for their help in identifying this text.

2. The Museum acquired the impression from the Hohenzollern collection that is listed in Gustav Pauli, *Hans Sebald Beham, ein kritisches Verzeichnis seiner Kupferstiche, Radierungen, und Holzschnitte. Mit Nachträgen, sowie Ergänzungen und Berichtungen von Heinrich Röttinger*, vols. 33, 134, 246 of *Studien zur deutschen Kunstgeschichte* (Baden-Baden, 1974), no. 886ii. This edition is a reprint that combines Pauli's original catalogue raisonné [1901], his supplement to it [1911], plus Röttinger's supplement [1933]. Pauli's list of six more impressions of this *Madonna and Child* is incorrect. Five of them can still be traced and they are not from the same woodblock as Cincinnati's, making it likely that the Museum's impression is unique (see n. 3). Information about the sixth (in Gotha?) is unavailable.

3. Pauli, not noticing the differences between the two woodcuts, catalogued both the Cincinnati and Bremen impressions in *Hans Sebald Beham* under no. 886i (see n. 2). Whereas Cincinnati's appears to be unique, the repositories in Berlin, London, Nuremberg, and Vienna own impressions of the same woodcut as Bremen's.

4. Hans Mielke of the Kupferstichkabinett in Berlin, in correspondence (HM, letter to KLS, February 7, 1991) with the Museum, was the first to establish the priority of Cincinnati's woodcut.

5. Early cataloguers who attribute the Cincinnati-Bremen design to Dürer include Bartsch (B.VII.178.app.14) and Passavant (P. 240). Catalogues of Dürer's graphic oeuvre that reject his authorship include Joseph Heller, *Das Leben und die Werke Albrecht Dürer's*, 2 pts. in 3 vols. (Bamberg, 1827), nos. 1996-7; and TIB 10:444 [B. app.14 (178)].

The three collections with impressions of the second state with Dürer's monogram (H. Ger. 886ii) are London, Paris (Bibliothèque Nationale), and Vienna.

6. The Cincinnati-Bremen Madonna makes clear that its designer was also very familiar with Dürer's drawings. The Christ child, for instance, is close in type to Dürer's in *Half-Length Madonna and Child* in Leningrad (Winkler 551) or *Madonna and Child on the Grassy Bench* in Windsor Castle (Winkler 534).

7. The English word for bead even derives from the German word for prayer (*Gebet*). For the relationship between the prayer beads, roses, and the Virgin Mary, see Eithne Wilkins, *The Rose-Garden Game* (New York: Herder and Herder, 1969), esp. 105-25. The chapelet of beads or roses became a popular attribute of the Virgin after Dürer painted the *Feast of the Rose arlands* (1505). The Madonna is so adorned in at least three more of Beham's prints.

8. Friedrich Winkler, *Hans von Kulmbach. Leben und Werk eines fränkischen Künstlers der Dürerzeit*, vol. 14 of *Die Plassenburg Schriften für Heimatforschung und Kulturpflege in Ostfranken* (Bayreuth: Julius Steeger and Co., 1959), 88-91. Although Geisberg ascribed the design to a Meister der Celtis-illustrationen (Master of the Celtis Illustrations) in the original German edition of his catalogue (Ge. 781), Walter Strauss, in the revised English edition, followed Winkler's proposal and reattributed it to Kulmbach. See Max Geisberg, *The German Single-Leaf Woodcut: 1500-1550*, 5. vols., rev. ed. Walter L. Strauss (New York: Hacker Art Books, 1974), no. 891-3.

9. My thanks to Barbara Butts for sharing the results of her Kulmbach research in "'Dürerschüler' Hans Süss von Kulmbach" (Ph.D. diss., Harvard University, 1985), 131-44. Further discussion of this attribution will be published in a catalogue raisonné of Kulmbach's graphic oeuvre by Barbara Butts and Matthias Mende.

10. Among those who support the attribution to Beham are Pauli, *Hans Sebald Beham*, 886; Campbell Dodgson, *Catalogue of Early German and Flemish Woodcuts Preserved in the Department of Prints and Drawings of the British Museum*, 2 vols. (London, 1903-11), 1:461.105 (Sebald Beham, ca. 1525); H. Ger. 886; and Pieter Strieder in Nuremberg 1961, no. 132 (Sebald Beham, ca. 1521). Until Beham's graphic work is systematically and critically reviewed, this attribution to him can only be tentative.

11. For Dürer's influence on Beham, see Pauli, *Hans Sebald Beham*, esp. 2-8; Nuremberg 1978, nos. 101, 169; and Lawrence 1988, nos. 11, 27, and 49B.

12. Like the Cincinnati-Bremen Madonna, Beham's *Nursing Madonna* was influenced by various prints and drawings by Dürer, among them the 1518 *Virgin and Queen of the Angels*. Five of Beham's other Madonna and Child prints, which are stylistically similar, contain dates of 1520 or 1521.

13. In 1525, while still in Nuremberg, Beham, his brother, Barthel, and Georg Pencz, were all brought to trial for their professed heretical views. Because they denied the validity of the sacrament, the historical existence of Christ, and the divine authority of Scripture, they were temporarily expelled from the city and later became labeled the "three godless painters." Because of this sensational event, their art has been interpreted as radical by many art historians. For fully developed arguments of this view, see Herbert Zschelletzschky, *Die 'drei gottlosen Maler' von Nürnberg, Sebald Beham, Barthel Beham, and Georg Pencz.* (Leipzig: VEB E.A. Seemann Verlag, 1975). For the revisionist view that the Little Masters' "personal religious convictions were irrelevant to their artistic production," see Keith Moxey, "The Beham Brothers and the Death of the Artist," *The Register of the Spencer Museum of Art* 6, no. 6 (1989): 25-29.

14. For the German Little Masters' intaglio production, consult Lawrence 1988; and for comments about their woodcuts, see the review of the Lawrence 1988 exhibition by Larry Silver, "Less Is More: The 'Kleinmeister' in Kansas," PCN. 19, no. 6 (1989): 213-16.

15. The figures of God the Father and the Holy Spirit, which occupy the upper corners of the Schön-Guldenmundt version, may have been inspired by another woodcut of the *Madonna and Child* that is ascribed to Sebald Beham in Pauli, *Hans Sebald Beham*, no. app. 888a; and H. Ger. 888a. (This woodcut is reproduced in Geisberg, *German Single-Leaf*, no. 966 [and attributed there to Michael Ostendorfer].)

Albrecht Altdorfer
Regensburg(?) ca. 1480-1538 Regensburg

57. Madonna and Child with St. Anne at the Cradle ca. 1515-25.

Engraving on antique laid paper, 6.2 x 5.5 cm (sheet).
B. 14; H. Ger. 15; Winzinger *Graphik* 128; TIB 14.
Monogrammed in plate on cradle: 𝕬
Condition: Trimmed within platemark.
Provenance: Lawson Thompson; (purchased from M. Knoedler, New York, October 23, 1939, for $156).
Bequest of Herbert Greer French, 1943.141.
Exhibitions: Cincinnati 1941, no. 75.

In this engraving, not even 2¹/₂ inches high, Albrecht Altdorfer permits hardly more than a peek into an interior. A bed curtain forms a backdrop that hides all but the bed's footrest, restricting our view to the foreground, itself not much deeper than the length of the cradle it contains. An older woman, bundled in a fur cap and layers of clothing that add to her aging bulk, bends almost reverently to prepare the linens in the cradle. A younger woman waits nearby, ready to deposit the child there. The halos radiating from the three provide the sole clue that this is not just a commonplace scene of burgher life but Anne, the Virgin Mary, and the Infant Christ.

Albrecht Altdorfer placed his monogram within its own dimmer halo on the edge of the cradle. At the time that he engraved this scene, circa 1520, he was an active, respected civic leader and the leading artist in Regensburg. Nothing is documented about his origins or early training before he became a citizen of this Bavarian city in 1505, but by 1517 he had become a member of its large outer council and, in 1526, of its small inner council. A strong indication of Altdorfer's professional commitment as an artist is the fact that he actually refused the city's highest post as mayor in 1528 in order to complete a commission for Duke Wilhelm of Bavaria, probably *Battle of Alexander*, one of his most important paintings.[1] Among Altdorfer's other important patrons was Emperor Maximilian I, who involved him with other German artists, such as Dürer, Cranach, and Burgkmair, in a number of collaborative projects ranging from colored ink drawings (*Prayerbook of Maximilian*, ca. 1515) and designs for woodcuts (*Triumphal Arch*, ca. 1515) to miniatures on parchment (*Triumphal Procession*, ca. 1513-16).[2]

Altdorfer has long been categorized as a leader of the Danube school, although scholarly efforts have reached no clear consensus about the formative influences, participating members, or geographical boundaries of such a movement. Doubts have in fact recently been raised whether this so-called Danube school ever existed at all.[3] The features ascribed to the movement were largely appropriated from Altdorfer's art and are exemplified by the nine small pure landscapes – the first of their kind in German graphic art – that he etched between 1515 and 1522 (see fig. 57-1). With them he helped launch the tradition of expansive, organic, mood-filled Danube style landscape that can be traced from the work of his brother, Erhard Altdorfer, to etchings by the next generation, Augustin Hirschvogel (cat. 63) and Hanns Lautensack (cat. 65).

The autonomy and freedom that characterize the wiry, calligraphic lines of Altdorfer's etched landscapes contrast with his engravings. *Madonna and Child with St. Anne at the Cradle* attests

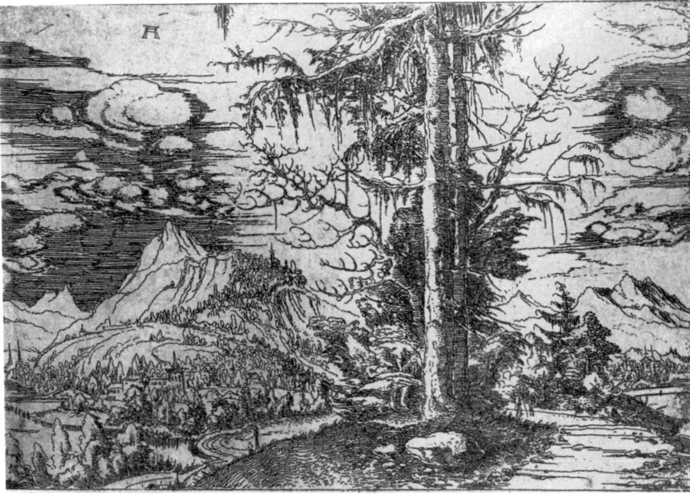

Figure 57-1. Albrecht Altdorfer, *Landscape with Double Pine*, ca. 1520, etching, Winzinger *Graphik* 179. Louvre, Paris. Collection Edmond de Rothschild.

Figure 57-2. Barthel Beham, *Virgin and Child at the Window*, ca. 1528-30, engraving, B. 8. Cincinnati Art Museum, Bequest of Herbert Greer French (1943.267).

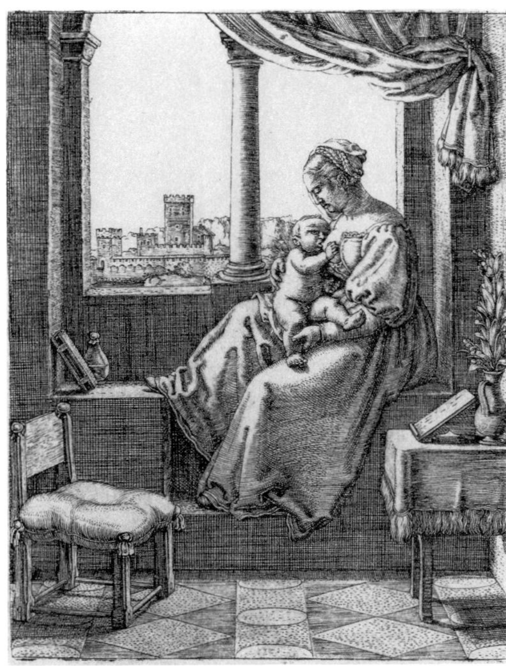

to Altdorfer's close study of Dürer's engraving technique and a decade of practice in controlling the burin to create precise systems of razor-thin hatchings (cf. Dürer, *St. Jerome in His Study*, cat. 48). The *Madonna and Child* also attests to his preference for things small; indeed, many of his engravings are even half its size. Whether this predilection stems from his (hypothetical) training as a miniaturist or whether it may have been a response to a growing market for visual images that were small enough to paste into increasingly popular portable books or to organize into volumes of newly developing print collections remains speculative.[4] The minute scale of Altdorfer's prints, however, did catch on with the next generation of engravers who, precisely because of the size of their engravings, became known as the German Little Masters.

The tiny size of Altdorfer's prints accommodates his Danube style inclination to cast his subjects in a down-home, folksy idiom. Although the art of the Italian Renaissance and the work of Dürer influenced Altdorfer, he typically eschewed any suggestion of classical monumentality. It is instructive to compare Altdorfer's little print with Barthel Beham's slightly larger and later *Nursing Madonna at the Window* (fig. 57-2). Both stage their holy scenes in a genre setting, but the Nuremberg master's work betrays the classicizing influence of Dürer and Italian art while Altdorfer's maintains a familiar, colloquial tone. Beham's Madonna, even while nursing, sits straight in dignified fashion, her form clearly articulated, her gestures firm and confident. Altdorfer's Madonna, by contrast, shrinks modestly beneath her heavy garments, her stance hesitant. The architectural elements of Beham's interior enframe his Madonna, making her the central focus, and posit her above the background townscape. Altdorfer's interior provides us with no such clues. The diminutive figures themselves humbly defer to the simple cradle on the floor.

What has not yet been fully explained is why Altdorfer, cognizant of Italian Renaissance precepts, bucked the tide of Renaissance influence propagated by Dürer to concentrate on landscape rather than figures, to avoid classical models for his figures, to seek out the humble and mundane rather than the proud and heroic, and to subordinate the world of objective appearances to the exploration of

93

mood and subjective feeling.[5] He was an individualist, and his originality, as demonstrated by his *Madonna and Child*, extends to iconographical as well as to stylistic concerns.

Even though Anne may submit to Mary in this engraving, she is its true subject. At this time she represented an important cultural symbol in Northern Europe, and her cult was at an all-time high. Her veneration was encouraged by the Church, the urban middle class, Christian humanists, and even Reformers. Her relics were sought (and even stolen); shrines were constructed in her honor; brotherhoods were devoted to her; processions were held on her feast day; treatises and poems were written about her. Her popularity was partially due to her versatility as a saint. She responded to so many needs, particularly those dealing with familial matters at a time when the concept of family was growing in importance. She was the patron saint of marriage and the family, and because of her legend, she gave hope to pregnant women and infertile couples alike.[6] As has recently been shown, she was revered as "the ideal model of a spouse, mother and widow fitting into the pattern of norms and values of the urban middle class.[7]

During this period, Anne was frequently featured in two different contexts. One was the Holy Kinship, which visually embodies the doctrine of the *trinubium* by presenting her as the matriarch of her extended family (from three marriages). In the other, known by its German term *Anna Selbdritt*, a subject used to represent the doctrine of the Immaculate Conception, Anne usually holds both the grown Virgin Mary and the Infant Christ – together on her lap or separately on each arm. Altdorfer's achievement here was to present Anne less as she was doctrinally understood than as she was popularly perceived. He devised a more natural setting for the three generations of *Anna Selbdritt* in which Anne could carry out the matronly role that endeared her to the popular imagination. – JSP

1. Documents on Altdorfer are published in Franz Winzinger, *Altdorfer. Die Gemälde* (Munich: R. Piper and Co., 1975), 145-51; see also AKL, s.v. "Altdorfer, Albrecht."

2. More information on these works can be found in Franz Winzinger's publications: *Albrecht Altdorfer. Zeichnungen. Gesamtausgabe* (Munich: R. Piper and Co., 1952), *Albrecht Altdorfer. Graphik. Holzschnitte, Kupferstiche, Radierungen. Gesamtausgabe* (Munich: R. Piper and Co., 1963), and *Die Miniaturen zum Triumphzug Kaiser Maximilians I*, 2 vols. (Munich: R. Piper and Co., 1972-73). For more recent discussions, see Jacqueline and Maurice Guillaud, Paris 1984; and Hans Mielke, Berlin 1988.

3. For Pierre Vaisse's survey of the research on the Danube school that leads him to conclude that such a movement never did actually exist, see Paris 1984, 149-64.

4. Winzinger discusses his possible training as a miniaturist in *Die Gemälde*, 8. For external causes that may have encouraged the production of small-sized prints, see Stephen H. Goddard, Lawrence 1988, 13-29.

5. For the theory that Altdorfer, reflecting contemporary German political and humanist concerns, may have deliberately sought to distinguish his work from Italianate art, see Pierre Vaisse, Paris 1984, 161-62.

6. For Anne (with further literature), see Kathleen Ashley and Pamela Sheingorn, "Introduction" in *Interpreting Cultural Symbols: Saint Anne in Late Medieval Society* (Athens: University of Georgia Press, 1990), 1-68; for the Reformers' appropriation and transformation of the theme of Anne and the Holy Kinship, see Christiane D. Andersson, "Religiöse Bilder Cranachs im Dienste der Reformation," in Lewis W. Spitz, ed., *Humanismus und Reformation als kulturelle Kräfte in der deutschen Geschichte*, vol. 51 of *Veröffentlichungen der historischen Kommission zu Berlin* (Berlin: Walter de Gruyter, 1981), 43-79, esp. 45-49; and Peter-Klaus Schuster, Hamburg 1983, no. 119.

7. Ton Brandenbarg, "St. Anne and Her Family: The Veneration of St. Anne in Connection with Concepts of Marriage and the Family in the Early Modern Period," in Lène Dresen-Coenders, ed., *Saints and She-Devils: Images of Women in the Fifteenth and Sixteenth Centuries* (London: Rubicon Press, 1987), 121.

Jean de Gourmont

Carquebut ca. 1483-after 1551 Lyon

58. Laocoön ca. 1525-30?
Engraving on antique laid paper, 10.6 x 15.4 cm (sheet).
B. 16; RD. 20.
Monogrammed on stone lower right: ℑᵷ
Condition: Trimmed just inside platemark.
Provenance: Alexandre-Pierre-François Robert-Dumesnil (Lugt 2200); (purchased from M. Knoedler, New York, May 21, 1934, for $275).
Bequest of Herbert Greer French, 1943.259.

Jean de Gourmont was born into a family of painters, printers, publishers, and engravers. The younger brother of two printers, Robert and Gilles, he worked with them in Paris from 1508 to 1520 and was elected a master artisan there in 1508. It is assumed that Gourmont received training as a goldsmith because his engraving technique reveals the discipline, and two of his prints depict Eligius, the patron saint of metalsmiths. Another shows the interior of a shop with two goldsmiths quarreling. Although it is not known when Gourmont moved to Lyon, it is known that he worked there during the 1520s: two of his prints are dated 1522 and 1526 in the plate. A painting of workers in a wine cellar, dated 1537, is in the Städelsches Kunstinstitut, Frankfurt, and another attributed to him of the Nativity is in the Louvre.[1] In 1546 a series of ornamental prints with Gourmont's characteristic monogram was issued under this elaborate title: *Livre des Moresques, très utile et nécessaire à tous orfèvres, tailleurs, grav., etc.* (*Book of Moresques* [arabesque ornaments], *Very Useful and Necessary for All Goldsmiths, Tailors, Engravers, etc.*).[2] Two of his pen drawings, one of the Flagellation and another of the Holy Family, are in the Pierpont Morgan Library, New York.[3]

Gourmont's total engraved oeuvre, excluding the series of arabesque ornaments mentioned above, consists of less than thirty subjects.[4] All highly finished, most are quite small, often circular. His work has been described as a French translation of the spirit of the German Little Masters, treated in an original guise (cf. Albrecht Altdorfer, cat. 60).[5]

Placing almost miniature figures within quite decorative architectural settings, Gourmont's work often indulges in inventive feats of perspective. He looks toward Italy for classical architectural models, and some of his figural groups also demonstrate Italian influences as here in the *Laocoön*. Religious scenes, saints, and classical figures number among his subjects. Several of Gourmont's compositions show children casually seated in classical galleries; one, a monkey chained to a column. Gourmont's prints are usually initialed in the plate with his monogram: an interlaced *J* and *G*; at times the words A LION (at Lyon) are added.

The principal subject of this print derives from the famed classical statue, discovered in Rome in 1506, now in the Vatican collections. Although much scholarly debate surrounds the sculpture, it is increasingly felt to date from the second half of the first century A.D. and to be a reconstruction of an earlier two-figure group composed of only the father and the younger son.[6] Laocoön was a Trojan priest who warned the inhabitants of the city against accepting the gift of a wooden horse from the Greeks, which he correctly suspected was a trick. In retaliation, Athena (Minerva) sent two serpents out of the water to kill Laocoön and his two sons. The story is vividly described by Virgil in the *Aeneid*.[7]

The discovery of the sculpture at the height of the Renaissance was a celebrated event, for observers knew instantly that it was the work described by Pliny as the work of three sculptors and "of all paintings and sculptures the most worthy of admiration."[8] Artists flocked to see it installed at the Belvedere Palace in the Vatican, and prints and drawings reproducing it were circulating through Europe soon afterward.[9]

Since its discovery the sculpture has been the subject of much scholarly debate concerning its interpretation, expressing as it does the horrid retribution for defying the will of the gods in spite of the priest's patriotic defense of his city. During the Counter-Reformation, the statue was recommended as a model for renderings of suffering martyrs, and it became a specific political symbol during the reign of Pope Julius II.[10] It has always been admired for its amazingly lifelike quality and for its depiction of ultimate agony.

While obviously dependent on the antique sculpture for his model, Gourmont did not literally reproduce it. He chose instead to recreate the event on the seashore before the city of Troy. He transformed Laocoön's two sons from young men into near-infants and also considerably loosened up the tightly bound figural group. His representation, in fact, probably depends upon an engraving by Marco Dente da Ravenna (active 1515, d. 1527), a member of Marcantonio Raimondi's workshop. That engraving (B. 243) also shows the group on the shore before Troy near an altar with a sacrificial fire in front of a grand temple specifically dedicated to Minerva. Fragments of sculpture with inscriptions lie about, ships are anchored offshore, and more structures are seen in the far left distance. Laocoön is posed on top of the altar with both arms flung out and with one leg kneeling in an attitude signifying prayer.[11] In most respects, Dente's engraving follows Virgil's text (referring to it in an inscription on the print), but his depiction reflects a much earlier prototype in a manuscript illumination in the Vatican Library.[12]

Gourmont's representation actually follows that of Marco Dente remarkably closely. Both prints, unlike the statue, represent Laocoön's sons as quite young. Both prints would have been engraved fairly close in time: Dente's dating from before his death in 1527; Gourmont's only dated prints being executed in the 1520s. It is significant that Dente also engraved a quite straightforward representation of the statue alone, datable to circa 1520-25 (B. 353). Another even more likely source for Gourmont is an anonymous engraving, signed with the initials "BF," that precisely duplicates in reverse the exact setting Gourmont uses for the Laocoön group. The only print known by this engraver, it is listed in Bartsch with the anonymous engravers around Marcantonio Raimondi; he declares that it was copied from Gourmont's print.[13] However, it is difficult to understand why a copyist would not include the figures; it seems more likely that Gourmont himself is the copyist, combining his various Italian sources into his own creation. Such a source would explain the anomaly within Gourmont's works of such a totally open space, unenclosed by a customary architectural setting.

Typically, for Gourmont, the scene is otherwise deserted and ruined. The drama itself takes place before the altar of Neptune, upon which the priest has just placed his offering. The letters and symbols seen on the side of the altar are not clear and may have been meant merely to evoke ancient inscriptions.[14] Gourmont inserts a statue in a grand colonnade, which is the major architectural focus of the engraving. The figure resembles one of several antique works of Venus, in particular a form known as Venus Pudica (Modest Venus), in which the goddess holds her hand across her genital area.[15] The print is lit by harsh sunlight, and the unsettled atmosphere is reinforced by the disturbed waves, windswept trees, and contorted smoke from the altar fire (the latter extends its tendrils toward the garment of the Venus statue). Although Gourmont's prints are not well known today and are comparatively rarely encountered, Mr.

French acquired four different subjects, including the large *Nativity* (B. 1, RD. 2).[16] This impression of the *Laocoön* was once in the collection of the famed connoisseur and cataloguer of French prints, A. P. F. Robert-Dumesnil. – DPB

1. The Frankfurt painting is reproduced in Carlo Ragghianti, "Pertinenze francesi nel Cinquecento," *Critica d'arte*, n.s., 27, no. 122 (1972): 21, fig. 11 (reproduced in color on the cover). Ragghianti also tentatively attributes a *Flagellation* in the National Museum at Warsaw to Gourmont. The Louvre *Nativity*, first attributed by Pierre-Jean Mariette in the eighteenth century, is reproduced in Charles Sterling and Hélène Adhémar, *Musée National du Louvre – Peintures école française xive, xve et xvie siècles* (Paris: Editions des Musées Nationaux, 1965), no. 97, pls. 210-15.

2. Two plates are reproduced in Rudolf Berliner and Gerhart Egger, *Ornamentale Vorlageblätter des 15. bis 19. Jahrhunderts*, 3 vols. (Munich: Klinkhardt and Biermann, 1981), vol. 2, nos. 421-22. Another ornament print is also reproduced in Berliner and Egger (no. 420). Each carries Gourmont's characteristic monogram.

3. The former is reproduced in New York 1959, no. 8, pl. 6; the latter in *Major Acquisitions of the Pierpont Morgan Library 1924-1974 – Drawings* (New York: Pierpont Morgan Library, 1974), no. 22. A related drawing is cited there as being in the Bibliothèque Nationale, Paris.

4. The traditional listings of Gourmont's prints are Bartsch (listing sixteen prints) and Robert-Dumesnil (twenty-three prints, with a supplement of eight more). Some of these prints are now attributed to Gourmont's nephew, Jean de Gourmont II. The most accurate listing is contained in the I.F.F. *1500* vol. I, in which twenty-nine prints are listed by Gourmont.

5. Arthur M. Hind, *A History of Engraving and Etching* (New York: Dover Publications, 1963), 101-02.

6. For a concise history of the discovery, influence, and scholarly study of the Laocoön group, with further bibliography, see Francis Haskell and Nicholas Penny, *Taste and the Antique – The Lure of Classical Sculpture 1500-1900* (New Haven and London: Yale University Press, 1981), 243-47.

7. Virgil *Aeneid* 2:40-56, 199-231. Robert Fitzgerald, trans. *The Aeneid* (New York: Vintage Books, 1984), 34-35, 40-41.

8. Haskell and Penny, *Taste and the Antique,* 243.

9. For a partial list of graphic works after the Laocoön group, see Phyllis Pray Bober, *Drawings after the Antique by Amico Aspertini* (London: Warburg Institute, University of London, 1957), 62. Printed reproductions of the sculpture are the subject of an extended discussion of the means of graphic representation by William M. Ivins, Jr.; see his *Prints and Visual Communication* (Cambridge and London: M.I.T. Press, 1968), pls. 73-77. The statue was literally aped in a woodcut attributed to Niccolò Boldrini (1510-aft. 1566) representing the figures as apes themselves (reproduced in David Rosand and Michelangelo Muraro, Washington 1976, 188-90, no. 40). This print is still not satisfactorily understood (see Patricia A. Emison, New Haven 1986, 20-22).

10. See Hans Henrik Brummer, *The Statue Court in the Vatican Belvedere* (Stockholm: Almqvist and Wiksell, 1970), 117-19.

11. Brummer, *The Statue Court,* 116-17.

12. Vatican Library, ms. Vat. lat. 3225, fol. 18v; reproduced in Brummer, *The Statue Court,* 116, fig. 104.

13. B.XV.545.1; it is also reproduced and discussed in Stefania Massari, *Guilio Bonasone* (Rome: Edizioni Quasar, 1983), 1:109, no. 170c.

14. If one stretches, it may possibly be read as "TRO/RIA/N," which, by another stretch, could refer to Troy. I am grateful to John Herrmann and Annewies van den Hoek for looking at this inscription. There is no inscription in the print by the Master BF.

15. Such as the so-called Celestial Venus in the Uffizi, Florence, reproduced in Haskell and Penny, *Taste and the Antique,* 320.

16. However, Gourmont was often featured among French sixteenth-century printmakers available in U.S. print dealers' catalogues during the 1920s and 1930s (taken from a random sampling of M. Knoedler & Co. catalogues of the period). At the time of his purchase of this print, Knoedler sent Mr. French some seventeen Gourmonts for purchase consideration!

Dirk Jacobsz Vellert

Antwerp active ca. 1511-1547

59. St. Luke Painting a Portrait of the Virgin 1526.

Engraving on antique laid paper, 16.9 x 12.1 cm (sheet).
B. 9; Popham 9; H. *Neth* 9.
Inscribed on footstool lower left: D V (flanking a star); dated and signed lower center: *1526 + in + ivli + 28.*
Condition: Trimmed inside platemark.

Provenance: Fürstlich Hohenzollernsches Museum Braunschweig, Sigmaringen (note by French); (purchased from M. Knoedler, New York, September 21, 1936, for $575).
Bequest of Herbert Greer French, 1943.265.
Exhibitions: Hartford 1949, no. 108; Washington 1983, no. 139, illus.

The sixteenth century was a period of crisis in the art of Flanders; during most of this century, artists were struggling to reconcile native traditions with the new styles of the Renaissance emanating from Italy. But to an artist like Dirk Vellert, working in Antwerp in the early years of the century, it must have seemed less a crisis than an exhilarating broadening of horizon. Antwerp was entering a period of rapid commercial expansion that would make it a world economic capital by 1550 and the primary center for art in Flanders.[1]

It has been suggested that Vellert was born in Amsterdam, in the northern Netherlands; but by 1511 he had settled in Antwerp. His work reflects the characteristics of Antwerp art, amalgamating influences from a wide variety of sources with a strong emphasis on a rich, decorative style. Although active as a painter, he was primarily a designer and a maker of stained-glass windows, presiding over a flourishing workshop that produced designs for churches in England and Germany as well as in the Netherlands.[2]

When Albrecht Dürer traveled to the Netherlands in 1520-21, he met Vellert on at least two occasions and gave him prints. While Dürer was in Antwerp, Lucas van Leyden also visited the city.[3] The visits of these two artists, the most famous engravers of their time, may have inspired Vellert to begin experimenting with both etching and engraving in 1522. Over the next five years he produced eighteen prints, a modest number considering that only six measured more than a couple of inches across. This suggests that he may have been more interested in trying out the medium than in making it a commercial venture; after 1526 he abandoned engraving until 1544, when he issued one final print. Despite his limited and sporadic involvement with engraving, Vellert acquired a mastery of the technique surpassed only by Lucas van Leyden among the Netherlandish artists of his generation.[4]

Perhaps Vellert selected this subject because in 1526 he was dean of the Antwerp Guild of Saint Luke, the painters' trade organization.[5] The legend that Luke, the author of the Third Gospel, had made a portrait of the Virgin naturally led to his becoming the patron saint of artists.[6] Earlier Flemish painters, like Rogier van der Weyden and Jan Gossaert, had shown Luke simply making a drawing of the Virgin. Vellert places far more emphasis on the tools of the painter's trade: Luke works at an arch-topped panel propped on an easel, resting his brush hand on a staff (called a maulstick) to steady it. The flask on the windowsill behind him probably alludes to the tradition that Luke was also a physician: it is the kind of vessel that sixteenth-century doctors used to examine their patients' urine.[7] The ox kneeling beside Luke (his emblem as an evangelist) is not usually found in earlier depictions of him as an artist, but it calls to mind Jerome's lion, making a parallel between the painter-physician-saint and the scholar-saint.

The result of five years of intermittent activity as a printmaker and the last engraving Vellert was to make for almost two decades, *St. Luke Painting a Portrait of the Virgin* was perhaps deliberately intended as a demonstration of his mastery of the burin. It is his most elaborately constructed engraving and his largest up to that time. Like Dürer's *St. Jerome in His Study* (cat. 48), though less subtle, it is a study in light effects: the even lighting of the foreground is juxtaposed against the bright scene outside the window and the half-light of the background chamber. Technically, however, the print is much more reminiscent of Lucas van Leyden than of Dürer, with its silvery-gray tonality and its comparatively limited range of textures.[8]

Humans, animals, still life, elaborate ornament in the new Renaissance style, a view through a window into a courtyard bordered with a variety of architecture and offering the glimpse of a tree, a view through a door into a carefully constructed chamber recalling the study in Dürer's *St. Jerome* – it is as if Vellert were deliberately showing off the variety of things he could depict, filling the composition with remarkable density. In Lucas van Leyden's prints, such as *The Dance of St. Mary Magdalene* (cat. 54), objects are clearly separated or they clearly overlap; here, by contrast, contours brush against one another or collide. The ox seems to nuzzle the easel and to touch the basket with its knee. The sprightly, nervous folds of the Virgin's skirt form such a strongly decorative pattern that while they seem to rest on the stone floor at one moment, at another they seem to rise straight up in the air, brushing the edge of the elaborate footstool that bears the artist's initials. Objects that are spatially quite distant from one another are hooked together as their contours touch. The halo of the Virgin almost seems to loop around the leg of the servant standing in the background and just grazes the lower corner of the open door; the arched top of the panel on Luke's easel seems to become a doorway in the building beyond the window. Vellert repeats circular and spherical forms almost obsessively – overtly in the ornament and architecture of the background, less obviously in the rounded surface of a shoulder, a tucked-up bed curtain, or the servant's fur cap.[9]

The taste for a rich, tapestrylike surface design appears in other Flemish artists of the time, but in Vellert it may have been reinforced by his experience as a designer of windows. Stained-glass windows were no longer the flat, intensely colored designs of the Middle Ages: artists imitated the complex spaces and rounded, sculptural figures of contemporary painting. But although some shading could be indicated in a window by painting on the glass, it was not possible to suggest the subtle blurring of distant objects through atmospheric perspective – on glass, all parts of the design are equally sharp and clear. The grid of iron bars and lead strips that supports the glass emphasizes the flat surface of the glass-picture, compelling the artist to reconcile any composition in depth with a strong two-dimensional pattern. And since different elements of the picture were usually separate pieces of glass, there was a tendency to fit them together like a jigsaw puzzle; besides, it was good economy to make a single strip of leading serve as the contour of two objects.

Max Friedländer describes Vellert as possessing "that dangerous type of skill that causes its owner to become complacent and careless."[10] Certainly there are suggestions of egotism and ostentation in Vellert's work. His habit of dating works not merely to the year but to the day (July 28 for this print) suggests a self-conscious preoccupation with his own activity as an artist. Certainly, too, he was more adept at filling a space with ornament than at conveying religious feeling or emotion. But there is nothing complacent or careless about the way that this print is composed. The profusion of objects and the interlocking of background and foreground could easily have been oppressive or unsettling, but the overall impression is actually orderly and restful. The figures of Luke and the Virgin dominate the composition, partly because of the clarity with which the profiles of their faces are set off against darker areas, partly because their comparatively lightly shaded and simply drawn figures contrast with the packed-in detail and dense shading of the background. The print may say little about Luke as a saint, but it is a worthy homage to him as an artist. – TR

1. On the economic rise of Antwerp see Fernand Braudel, *The Perspective of the World*, vol. 3 of *Civilization and Capitalism* (New York: Harper and Row, 1984), 143-57.

2. There is no definitive study of Vellert as an artist. A summary of earlier literature is given in Ellen S. Jacobowitz and Stephanie Loeb Stepanek, Washington 1983, 318-19. On Vellert's stained-glass painting and his origins in Amsterdam, see H. Wayment, *The Windows of Kings College Chapel, Cambridge: Corpus Vitrearum Medii Aevi, Great Britain* (London: Oxford University Press, 1972), 1:18-19. Stimulating characterizations of his style can be found in Julius Held, *Dürers Wirkung auf die niederländische Kunst seiner Zeit* (The Hague: Martinus Nijhoff, 1931), 88-96; and Max J. Friedländer, *Jan van Scorel and Pieter Coeck van Aelst*, vol. 12 of Early Netherlandish Painting, comments and notes by H. Pauwels and G. Lemmens, trans. Heinz Norder (Leyden: A. W. Sijyhoff; Brussels: La Connaissance, 1975) (first published 1935), 27-31.

3. *Albrecht Dürer: Diary of his Journey to the Netherlands 1520-1521*, with an introduction by J. A. Goris and G. Marlier (Greenwich, Conn.: New York Graphic Society Ltd., 1971), 81, 89, 96.

4. A. E. Popham, "The Engravings and Woodcuts of Dirick Vellert," PCQ. 12 (1925) 343-68; Jacobowitz and Stepanek, Washington 1983, 318-25; H. *Neth.* XXXIII:187-209.

5. Ph. Rombouts and Th. van Lerius, eds., *De Liggeren en andere historische archieven der Antwerpsche Sint Lucasgilde* (1864-1876; reprint, Amsterdam: N. Israel, 1961), 1:107.

6. Louis Réau, *Iconographie de l'art chrétien* (Paris: Presses universitaires de France, 1958), vol. 3, pt. 2, pp. 828-32.

7. A similar flask appears in a later painting of the subject by Maerten van Heemskerck, discussed in J. P. Filedt Kok, W. Halsema-Kubes, and W. Th. Kloek, eds., The Hague 1986, 265-66.

8. Jacobowitz and Stepanek, Washington 1983, 322.

9. Friedländer, *Jan van Scorel*, 28, connects Vellert's fondness for circular motifs with the design of round compositions in stained glass.

10. Friedländer, *Jan van Scorel*, 28.

Heinrich Aldegrever

Paderborn 1502-ca. 1555/61 Soest

60. Jan of Leyden 1536.

Engraving on antique laid paper, 31.4 x 22.7 cm (platemark).
B. 182; H. *Ger.* 182 ii/ii; TIB 182.
Watermark: Little jug with crown (cf. Briquet 12629).
Inscribed in plate upper margin: JOHAN · VA [N] · LEIDEN · EY [N] · KONINCK · DER · WEDERDOPER · /THO · MONSTER · WAERHAFTICH · CO [N] TER [FEIT] · [Jan of Leyden, King of the Anabaptists in Münster, truthfully portrayed]; on ledge below: HAEC · FACIES · HIC · CVLTVS · ERAT · CV [M] · SEPTRA · TENERE [M] · REX · αναβαπτιςων sed · breve · te [m] pvs · ego · [This was my appearance, this my official attire, while I bore the scepter as King of the Anabaptists – but only for a short time.] [HENRICVS · ALDEGREVER · SVZATIE [NSIS] · FACIEBAT · ANNO · M · D · XXXVI · [Heinrich Aldegrever of Soest made this in 1536] GOTTES · MACHT · IST · MYN · CRACHT [God's power is my strength]; monogrammed in plate center left: 𝔄
Condition: Trimmed to or just outside platemark.
Provenance: Lessing Rosenwald (Lugt S. 1760b); (purchased from M. Knoedler, New York, December 31, 1936, for $1,150).
Bequest of Herbert Greer French, 1943.268.

Jan Bockelson of Leyden (1509-1536), better known as Jan of Leyden, a Dutch tailor by trade and would-be playwright, is presented half-length against a neutral background, facing left and turned in a three-quarter view. He cuts a commanding figure: his torso dominates the space; his beret actually invades the field of the inscription above; his elbow protrudes over the ledge. As the inscriptions imply, Heinrich Aldegrever depicted Jan of Leyden as the Anabaptist convert who reigned as king of the Anabaptists in Münster from 1534 to 1535. Jan of Leyden bears his scepter; his motto, "God's power is my strength," is incised into the ledge below. Nothing about his demeanor might suggest that his rule resulted in some of the most gruesome events of the Reformation.

Aldegrever was the leading artist in Westfalia when he engraved this portrait. Soon after settling in Soest (ca. 1535), Westfalia's most important commercial city, he joined the painters' guild there and became a respected, life-long citizen. His activities as painter, goldsmith, and stained-glass painter are less well substantiated than his printmaking. During two periods, 1527-41 and 1549-55, he produced nearly three hundred engravings, many of which found practical application as designs for decorative arts.[1] In 1531 Soest instituted the Reformation. Aldegrever himself was of Protestant persuasion and participated in the city's reform. Of his seven identifiable engraved portraits, two feature prominent reformers, Martin Luther and Philipp Melanchthon (B.184, B. 185), and as Gisela Luther has shown, his selection of religious and profane themes was informed by a Protestant outlook.[2]

Aldegrever placed his monogram on the left side of Leyden's portrait. With its small *G* embedded within a larger *A*, his monogram is a conscious imitation of Dürer's. Dürer's engraving technique and print compositions exerted a profound and continual influence on Aldegrever's art. Dürer's younger Nuremberg followers, Barthel and Sebald Beham, who were Aldegrever's contemporaries, also influenced his work: he shared the Behams' propensity for making miniature engravings and, thus, has been grouped with these younger Nuremberg printmakers as one of the German Little Masters.[3] In terms of its size, the Jan of Leyden portrait is exceptionally large. In terms of its presentation, however, it testifies to Aldegrever's debt to the Nuremberg school. He probably did not make his preparatory drawing directly from life (fig. 60-1)[4] but by insisting on documenting Leyden's true likeness (*waerhaftich conterfeit*), Aldegrever was following Dürer's lead and the Renaissance concern that the image, if not the sitter himself, should endure in perpetuity. His portrait format (three-quarter view, neutral background, Latin inscription) likewise finds its precedent in Dürer's engravings.[5] For some of Leyden's costume details, on the other hand, Aldegrever turned to Barthel Beham's 1531 engraved portrait of Emperor Charles V (fig. 60-2).[6]

That Jan of Leyden wears the same fur-lined beret (with laces) and the same damask design as Beham's Charles V was probably not fortuitous. The inscription on Aldegrever's portrait states this is Leyden's official state attire (*hic cultus erat*), attire befitting the king of the Anabaptists and made all the more regal by analogy to the emperor. Other references to Leyden's status that blend fact with fiction are recorded in the print: his crown surmounts the coat of

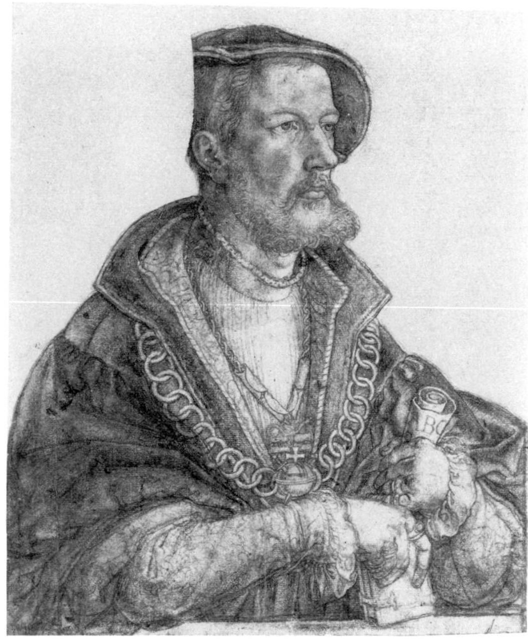

Figure 60-1. Heinrich Aldegrever, *Jan of Leyden*, probably 1635, black chalk with red chalk on parts of the face. British Museum, London.

Figure 60-2. Barthel Beham, *Charles V*, 1531, engraving, B. 8. Kupferstichkabinett, Hamburger Kunsthalle.

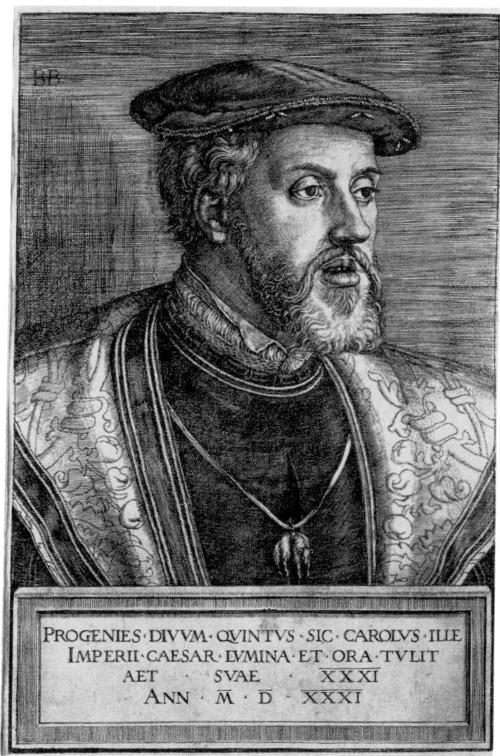

arms in the upper left, and his coat of arms displays an imperial orb. The orb, pierced by two swords (one of the spirit, the other of vengeance), symbolizes universal Anabaptist rule and appears two more times in the print: on the tip of Leyden's scepter and on the larger of two chains around his neck. The letters of the alphabet on the band that loops around the royal insignia on the wall, like the scroll in Leyden's right hand, refer to his self-proclaimed prerogative to assign names to all newborns in Münster in alphabetical order.[7]

By the time Aldegrever had made this engraving (1536), Leyden had already met a cruel death.[8] He joined the growing Anabaptist community of Münster in 1534, the year in which the sect, under the leadership of their "prophet" Jan Matthys (d. 1534), took over the city, driving out unconverted Protestants and Catholics alike and setting up their godly kingdom of "New Jerusalem." Anabaptists (literally, "re-baptizers") repudiated infant baptism in favor of the baptism of believers. A radical wing of the Reformation, Anabaptism found its most extreme expression in Münster. Leyden succeeded Matthys as prophet and shortly thereafter proclaimed himself "King of New Zion" and ruled in all due pomp in an increasingly arbitrary, tyrannical manner. He enforced a communistic sharing of property and goods, instituted polygamy, terrorized the populace, and executed dissenters. All the while Münster was under siege by the combined forces of its former bishop, Franz von Waldeck (ca. 1491-1553), and Landgrave Philip von Hessen (1504-1567).

Leyden's fanatical rule ended in grisly revenge. When the opposition retook Münster in June 1535, the Anabaptist king was imprisoned along with two fellow sectarian leaders, Berndt Knipperdolling (whom Aldegrever portrayed in a matching engraving [B. 183]) and Bernd Krechting. The prisoners were paraded separately throughout the region and, in January 1536, were brutally tortured and executed in Münster's town square. Their decaying corpses then hung in iron cages from Saint Lambert's Church for public view. Because of the Münster fiasco, Anabaptists throughout Europe suffered further persecution and disrepute. Aldegrever's engraving must have satisfied an intense demand for the image of this infamous personality. Although the artist presented the

Anabaptist king in a dignified, stately pose, the inscription clarifies that the purpose of the portrait was to make an example of Leyden by underscoring the consequences of his fanaticism. He was king, after all, only for a short time (*sed breve tempvs*).

Aldegrever's engraving of John van Leyden was easily his most influential. It provided the source for nearly all subsequent representations. Geisberg records over thirty intaglio prints that directly or indirectly depend on it, dating well into the eighteenth century.[9] – JSP

1. For biographical information on Aldegrever, see Herbert Zschellestzschky, *Das graphische Werk Heinrich Aldegrevers*, vol. 292 of *Studien zur deutschen Kunstgeschichte* (Strassburg, 1933), 5-11; and, more recently, the *AKL*, s.v. "Aldegrever, Heinrich." Although documents refer to Aldegrever as a painter, only two paintings can be attributed to him with certainty. See Rolf Fritz, *Heinrich Aldegrever als Maler* (Dortmund, 1959); and Münster 1985, no. 3. For the difficulties in establishing him as a goldsmith, see Carde H'loch, Unna 1986, 45-55. For his graphic oeuvre, see Zschelletzschky, *Das graphische Werk*. The exhibition catalogue Unna 1986 provides a rich study of the application of Aldegrever's designs in the decorative arts of the period.

2. Gisela Luther, *Heinrich Aldegrever, ein westfälischer Kupferstecher des 16. Jahrhunderts*, Bildhefte des Westfälischen Landesmuseums für Kunst und Kulturgeschichte no. 15 (Unna, 1982), esp. 10-18.

3. Stephen H. Goddard, Lawrence 1988, 13.

4. For the preparatory drawing, see John Rowlands, *The Age of Dürer and Holbein: German Drawings 1400-1500* (Cambridge, 1988), 168-69, no. 138.

5. Dürer's portraits of Friedrich the Wise (1524) (B. 104), Willibald Pirckheimer (1524) (B. 106), and Philip Melanchthon (1526) (B. 105) provide the best comparison.

6. Jochen Luckhardt, Münster 1985, 20-21.

7. Max Geisberg established that while some of the accoutrements of the portrait are historically verifiable, others are a product of Aldegrever's style of ornament (*Die münsterischen Wiedertäufer und Aldegrever*, vol. 76 of *Studien zur deutschen Kunstgeschichte* [Strassburg, 1907], 13-28). Actual artifacts, such as jewelry, coins, and documents, from the short period of Leyden's rule are featured in the exhibition catalogue Münster 1983.

Aldegrever's blend of fact and fantasy is exemplified by Leyden's small inner chain in the engraving. Leyden wore, in fact, many gold chains. Four recognizable Anabaptist coins are curled around the base of the inner chain. The pendant hanging from it, however, is a practical, multipurpose utensil akin to a sixteenth-century Swiss army knife that folded out at the top to form a dog whistle (the serpent form) and at the bottom to provide an earspoon and nailknife for hygienic purposes. Aldegrever featured such a utensil in several prints (for example, see Lawrence 1988, no. 60).

8. For the sequence of events of the short Anabaptist rule in Münster, see Gerd Dethlefs, "Das Wiedertäuferreich in Münster 1534/1535," in Münster 1982, 19-36; and R. Po-chia Hsia, "Münster and the Anabaptists," in *The German People and the Reformation*, ed. R. Po-chia Hsia (Ithaca: Cornell University Press, 1988), 51-69.

9. Geisberg, *Die münsterischen Wiedertäufer*, 53-55.

Jean Duvet
Dijon ca. 1485-after 1562 Langres

61. The Marriage of Adam and Eve ca. 1540-55.
Engraving on antique laid paper, 29.8 x 21.3 cm (sheet).
B. 1; RD. 1; Eisler 35 ii/ii; TIB 1.
Signed lower left: IONA·/NNES·/DUVET·/FAC·
Condition: Trimmed within platemark.
Provenance: Friedrich August II (Lugt 971); (his sale C.G. Boerner, Leipzig, May 22-24, 1933, no. 384, to Colnaghi, London for RM 520); (Alfred Strölin, Lausanne, consigned to Knoedler, July 13, 1933); (purchased from M. Knoedler, New York, September 29, 1933, for $1,750).
Bequest of Herbert Greer French, 1943.173.
Exhibitions: Cincinnati 1934, no. 10; Cincinnati 1941, no. 88.

The densely fevered compositions of the French engraver Jean Duvet exert a powerful attraction for modern viewers conditioned to expressionist views of the world. Although earlier commentators disparaged his unrefined technique and muddled compositions, later writers recognize an isolated genius who weaves powerful, rough-hewn imagery into a visionary art reminiscent of other mystical "misfits" such as Segers (cats. 75-76), Blake (cat. 112), Goya (cats. 116, 119), and Redon (cat. 140). Duvet can now be appreciated as an honest reporter of his emotions and of the texts he illustrated without intervention of academic constraint.[1] Hidden under layers of accumulated detail, his mature work reveals a familiarity with the prints of Dürer and with the figural prototypes of Raphael (1483-1520) and Mantegna, as transmitted through prints.[2] Although he is credited as one of the earliest French printmakers to incorporate Italian Renaissance models into his work, Duvet's provincial status and eccentric style militated against his making a strong personal mark on the mainstream.

According to his own witness, Duvet was born around 1485.[3] The son of a Dijon goldsmith, he apprenticed in this trade, acquiring further skills as engraver, gilder, enamelist, and the designer of ceremonial pageants. In 1509 he was accepted as a master craftsman of Dijon and possibly executed his first engravings at that time. His first dated print is *The Annunciation* of 1520 (Eisler 12). Duvet assisted in the designs for the ceremonial visit of Francis I to the nearby city of Langres in 1521 and was fully in charge of Francis' even more elaborate entry into the same city in 1533.

The facts of Duvet's life during the 1530s and 1540s are quite sketchy, and scholars have speculated about a possible residence in Geneva during this time. Dijon and Langres were centers of conservative Catholic power. The harassment of Protestant believers in those cities caused many artists to move to nearby Geneva to escape persecution. Although there are records of a Jean Duvet in Geneva at this time, the evidence that this person can be identified with our artist is inconclusive.[4]

Duvet probably began both his *Apocalypse* and *Unicorn* (cat. 62) series during the late 1540s, securing a royal privilege, or copyright, from Francis I for the former set in 1556. The *Apocalypse* was eventually issued with a letterpress text in Lyon in 1561.[5] The latest documentary reference to Duvet is his presence at a town meeting in Langres in 1562.

The inscription on the tablet hanging on the tree in this print identifies its subject as God blessing the union of Adam and Eve (Gen. 1:28).[6] Duvet chose to depict hosts of heavenly soldiers surrounding the composition's three central figures (God and the first couple). These triumphant soldiers, who are seen trampling Satan and the defeated rebel angels, hold branches and banners of the cross, symbolic of the victory of Christ. Adam and Eve, whose future progeny are glimpsed behind the figure of God, also each hold a branch. The Tree of Knowledge is at the very top of the composition.[7] Wearing a miter topped by a cross, the richly attired figure of God as priest joins the couple. Diane Russell points out the rarity of this subject in the visual arts, identifying its iconography as a prefiguration of the marriage of Christ and the Roman Catholic Church.[8] Colin Eisler associates this scene with Duvet's designs for pageants devised for triumphal entries, specifically *mystères* (mystery plays) such as *Les Rameaux* (The Branches).[9]

The exact purpose of this plate within the full context of Duvet's work is unclear. *The Marriage of Adam and Eve* precisely matches the tabletlike format of his *Apocalypse* series but is not itself part of it. Along with another plate, *Moses Surrounded by the Patriarchs* (Eisler 36), it may have served as an introduction to a projected series for an illustrated book of Genesis. Eisler dates *The Marriage* to the 1540s or early 1550s, a period when Duvet was working on his *Apocalypse*. All characteristic marks of his style are present in this engraving. The almost oppressive mass of detail that falls just short of an incoherent jumble is accomplished by a combination of strong figural outlines and short, rough jabs of the engraver's burin to define surface forms. The figure of God blends into the background and Adam and Eve become the principal anchors of the composition, their unadorned bodies carefully sculpted with very delicate and clearly defined strokes. Their forms project into space as if standing on pedestals. The Museum's very fine impression of *The Marriage* reveals these subtly suggested details. Later printings lose this effect, rendering the figures mere voids among the background crowds.

Eisler identifies several graphic prototypes that served Duvet in assembling the basis of his composition. Perhaps his primary source, at least for the three central figures, is Dürer's woodcut *Marriage of the Virgin* (B. 82); specific models include Dürer's 1504 *Adam and Eve* (cat. 33) for Adam and a figure from Marcantonio Raimondi's *Three Graces* (B. 340) for Eve.[10] These examples clearly demonstrate the wide circulation and considerable influence of graphic images throughout artists' workshops in Europe during this time, prints then being the primary bearers of visual ideas.

Mr. French acquired four other Duvet prints: one from the *Apocalypse* series (*A Star Falls and Makes Hell to Open* [Eisler 43]) and three plates from the *Unicorn* series (cat. 62), now in the Museum's collection. – DPB

1. See William M. Ivins, Jr., "Jean Duvet," *The Arts* 9, no. 5 (May 1926): 261-69, for an articulate statement of this transition in critical favor.

2. Eisler (pp. 3-5) speculates on a trip to Italy, but there is no documentary or visual proof of such a visit.

3. In his *Self-Portrait as St. John* (Eisler 65), dated 1555 in the plate, he inscribed his age as "presently 70."

4. Among modern scholars, Eisler (pp. 11-17) and A. Blunt (review of Eisler in *Burl. M.* 122, no. 927 [June 1980]: 443) argue in favor of Duvet's residency in Geneva; H. Zerner (review of Eisler in *AB.* 63, no. 2 [June 1981]: 333-34) and R. May (Langres 1985, 8-13), argue against it.

5. Only six original copies with text of the *Apocalypse* are known today. One quite rich is at the Cleveland Museum of Art (see Eisler, 102-03, n. 36).

6. Eisler's translation of the inscription reads: "The marriage of Adam and Eve and their blessing from God and other mysteries here contained are taken from the first chapter of Genesis."

7. In addition to pointing out the imagery of branches relating to the cross, Eisler (p. 238) also mentions the larger metaphorical image of the tree and its branches as symbols of the relationship of God to worshippers, described in John (15:1-5).

8. Washington 1990b, 114, no. 62.

9. Eisler, p. 238.

10. Eisler, p. 238. He speculates that Dürer's model may have come to Duvet through a print of the marriage of the Virgin by Caraglio after Parmigianino (B. 1), which was itself copied by at least two French printmakers. Both Dürer and Parmigianino employed arched architectural motifs, and the latter included an arched top to the composition itself.

Jean Duvet
Dijon ca. 1485-after 1562 Langres

62. The Unicorn Purifies the Water with His Horn
ca. 1540-60.
Engraving on antique laid paper, 22.4 x 39.7 cm (platemark).
B. 42; RD. 59; Eisler 68 ii/ii; TIB 42.
Watermark: Bunch of grapes (cf. Briquet 13084-85).
Condition: Trimmed to platemark.
Provenance: (Purchased from M. Knoedler, New York, October 28, 1935, for $1,150).
Bequest of Herbert Greer French, 1943.175.
Exhibitions: Cincinnati 1941, no. 91.

Almost half of Duvet's known oeuvre of over seventy plates derives from only two series of prints. One group of twenty-four images constitutes illustrations for the Book of Revelation, also known as the Apocalypse; six other images relate to the mythical unicorn and its magical powers. The *Unicorn* series exerted such power that Duvet was christened "Master of the Unicorn" as early as the seventeenth century.[1] Although Duvet's seemingly hallucinatory images from his *Apocalypse* series are actually quite literal interpretations of the biblical text (as visionary as that text is), his apparently straightforward approach to a completely mythical subject in the *Unicorn* series poses numerous questions of style and iconography.

Both series date from Duvet's mature period – the 1540s and 1550s – and were probably developed concurrently.[2] Unlike the *Apocalypse*, the *Unicorn* series was never officially published as a numbered series or with a text, although Eisler cites a unique impression of *The Capture of the Unicorn* (Eisler 33) in Vienna that includes a letterpress caption, a possible indication that publication may have been considered.[3]

The rich symbolism surrounding the unicorn was a natural subject for Duvet's interests. Traditionally a symbol of salvation and purity, the unicorn encompasses the classical and the Christian, the mystical and the erotic. A unicorn's horn was thought from classical times to possess healing powers. Often depicted in medieval and Renaissance tapestries, illuminated manuscripts, decorative sculptures, and prints, the unicorn was first fully described in the *Physiologus*, a fifth-century classical text by Eustathius. This text elaborated upon the lore of this untamed animal, whose horn could purify whatever it touched and who could only be subdued by a virgin. In time, the symbolism of the unicorn became associated instead with the virginity of Mary and with Christian salvation.[4] The ironic juxtaposition of its religious significance with often erotic and profane images of betrothals and marriages cannot be denied.[5]

The six plates in Duvet's series (Eisler 32-34, 66-68) consist of *The Unicorn Purifying the Water with His Horn, The King and Diana Receiving Huntsmen, A King Pursued by a Unicorn, The Capture of the Unicorn, The Unicorn Borne on a Triumphal Car, and The Triumph of the Unicorn*. Although the series is loosely constructed around the pursuit, capture, and eventual triumph of the ferocious unicorn, the immediate inspiration for Duvet's conception of the series is not known. Several commentators have attempted to connect the prints with the ascension of Henry II to the throne of France and his relationship with Diane de Poitiers, relating her to the goddess Diana, who is featured in the prints. Eisler tentatively accepts this interpretation, whereas Blunt finds no conclusive reason to do so.[6]

Stylistically, Eisler relates the *Unicorn* series to festival designs by Duvet.[7] He further stresses the particular importance of tapestry designs for the plates in addition to the more general influence of tapestry aesthetic on Duvet's style.[8] The series also reflects a widespread interest in depicting the hunt and the numerous wild animals to be met with in Northern forests. In fact, Duvet had copied a hunting subject from a Fontainebleau print by Master L.D., *Death of a Stag* (Eisler 29).

The Unicorn Purifies the Water with His Horn illustrates the purported power of the unicorn's horn as an antidote to any poison. Horns believed to be those of unicorns (usually from the narwhal) were used during the medieval period to guarantee uncontaminated food for princely tables.[9] The many animals in attendance await the unicorn's purification of the water (traditionally poisoned by a serpent) so that they may drink. Somewhat set apart, the peacock with its spread tail, seen at the right, is a conventional symbol of immortality.[10] All the animals are rendered with a striking naturalism, most skillfully exemplified in the dramatically foreshortened body of the unicorn itself. An intriguing graphic prototype can be seen in a north Italian print (formerly attributed to Duvet) by the so-called Master of the Beheading of St. John the Baptist, an allegory of a combat between animals (Hind 2). It includes a unicorn, quite naturalistic depictions, and a shorthand

stippling technique, not unlike Duvet's, to delineate surface texture.[11]

Colin Eisler also points out prototypes for Duvet's menagerie in two Fontainebleau prints by Jean Mignon after Luca Penni, *The Creation of Eve* and *The Temptation*, datable to the mid-1540s.[12] Eisler sees precedents for the dense forests in the *Unicorn* series in prints by Northern artists such as Hans Baldung.[13] Another more direct borrowing from a German print is the tiny goat on the mountaintop at the upper right, which has been lifted from Dürer's *Adam and Eve* (B. 1) (cat. 33) of 1504. The printmaker has cleverly "signed" his plate with a swan (lower right) that plucks some down (duvet) from its breast.

The density of this plate and the formality of the composition are characteristic of Duvet. The unicorn occupies center stage front in a triangular area of water separating the ranks of animals. Thick woods lie behind them. A coastal vista appears in the distance beyond a formal arched bridge, complete with a column and statue. The rectangle outlined in the tree's leaves at the top edge of the plate remains blank in at least two known impressions. It was later filled with branches and leaves but was perhaps meant for an inscription at one time. Mr. French acquired two other prints from the *Unicorn* series, *The King and Diana Receiving Huntsmen* (Eisler 32) and *The Triumph of the Unicorn* (Eisler 67). – DPB

1. Eisler, 111.
2. While Anthony Blunt (*Art and Architecture in France 1500-1700*, 4th rev. ed. [Middlesex: Penguin Books Ltd., 1982], 120) places the *Unicorn* series in the 1540s, before the *Apocalypse*, Eisler (113) separates the group into two "campaigns," with nos. 32-34 coming earlier and nos. 66-68 coming toward the end of his career, about 1560.
3. Eisler, 112.
4. For a lengthier discussion of the evolution of the myths surrounding the unicorn, see Eisler, 117-19.
5. See James Hall, *Dictionary of Subjects and Symbols in Art* (New York: Harper and Row, 1974), 327-28.
6. Eisler, 115; Blunt, 415, n. 77.
7. Eisler, 119, figs. 53-57.
8. Eisler, 151-53.
9. Munich 1965, no. 93. Indeed, Pope Clement VII gave a unicorn horn to his niece Catherine de Médicis upon her marriage to the future Henry II of France. (François Courboin, *Histoire illustré de la gravure en France*, [Paris, 1923-29], 1:132).
10. Ruth H. Schlesinger, Ithaca 1973, no. 71.
11. Reproduced in Eisler, 114, fig. 47.
12. Eisler, 308; illus. 114-15, figs. 48-49.
13. Eisler, 116, figs. 50-51.

Augustin Hirschvogel

Nuremberg 1503-1553 Vienna

63. River Landscape with Large Tree at Left 1546.

Etching on antique laid paper, 14.3 x 21.3 cm (sheet).
B. 73; Schwarz 73; H. Ger. 46 ii/ii; TIB 73.
Watermark: Crowned Imperial eagle with initials MM.
Condition: Trimmed to or within platemark.
Dated and monogrammed in block lower right: 15HAF46.
Provenance: (Purchased from M. Knoedler, New York, November 8, 1929, for $700).
Bequest of Herbert Greer French, 1943.237.
Exhibitions: Cincinnati 1930 (no. 30); Cincinnati 1934, no. 48; Cincinnati 1941, no. 81.

Although Augustin Hirschvogel made over three hundred etchings, he is best remembered for thirty-five pure landscapes that he etched between 1545 and 1549.[1] *River Landscape with Large Tree at Left* is a fine representative to exemplify Hirschvogel's penchant for horizontal formats in which he typically charts the course of a quiet river like this one, as it meanders past shorelines dotted with hills, towns, castles, and high promontories. The tranquil mood of this river scene prevails in nearly all Hirschvogel's landscapes. Nothing stirs in his clear, open skies. Any signs of human activity, if present at all, are negligible. In this etching, one lone boat quietly floats on the still water.

Augustin Hirschvogel was nearly forty before he began to etch. It is significant that he, unlike most other etchers at the time, trained as a stained-glass painter not as a painter. His father, Veit Hirschvogel the Elder (1461-1525), ran the leading stained-glass workshop in Nuremberg and served as the city's official glazier, a position retained in the family until nearly the end of the century. Augustin's training and early production took place during the years that his father's workshop was shifting from a medieval to a Renaissance style of stained glass, a style strongly influenced by the art of Albrecht Dürer. Augustin proved to be the most progressive stained-glass painter in the workshop. His early drawing style, modeled upon the Dürer school, closely resembles that of his contemporaries, Sebald Beham and Georg Pencz; whereas his stained glass is distinguished by its illusionistic and painterly effects, created in part by the tonal qualities achieved with silver stain.[2]

While etching had up to this point played only a minor role in the oeuvre of most printmakers, it is the only printing technique Hirschvogel ever tried. He probably turned to it because of its similarities with stained glass, and conversely, his experience with stained glass undoubtedly conditioned his approach to etching both in terms of style and technique.[3] Stylistically, the abstract calligraphic freedom of many of his wiry, etched lines finds its source in lines from his stained glass, scratched through dark matted tones of paint with a finely pointed needle to release thin lines of light. Spontaneous flourishes in Hirschvogel's *River Landscape*, such as the lines that dangle from trees or that fancifully sprout in bowlike coils from grasses, stem from the tendency in stained glass to treat line as playful ornament.

Stained glass and etching are created through chemical processes: just as the final color of silver stain depends on the concentration of silver nitrate and the intensity and length of firing of the glass, etched lines depend on mordant action and the length of time that they are exposed to an acid bath. The actual processes are different, but Hirschvogel, having already dealt with problems of timing and chemical effects on stained glass, would have been inclined to experiment with multiple bites in etching. In *River Landscape*, he must have exposed the thick, dark contour lines of the foreground trees to the biting process much longer than the faint lines of the distant mountain range.[4] The contrast between them, although abrupt, nevertheless heightens the suggestion of airy depth. His efforts at tonal gradations with multiple bites represent a very early stage in the development of a technique that would be exploited in much more subtle and complex ways in the following century by master etchers like Rembrandt (cat. 81).

The Reformation, accepted by Nuremberg in 1525, dealt a severe blow to the Hirschvogel workshop by putting an end to its commissions for monumental church windows. Since Augustin's less innovative elder brother, Veit the Younger, took over the Hirschvogel workshop in 1526 and the market for small stained-glass panels (*Kabinettscheiben*) was apparently insufficient to support both brothers, Augustin was left to his own devices. In 1537 he left Nuremberg, returning only briefly before a permanent move to Vienna in 1544.[5] In the interim, he traveled widely through Habsburg territories and practiced mathematics, cartography, and etching. In his three late etched self-portraits (B. 39, B. 40, Schwarz 140), Hirschvogel presents himself not as a craftsman from Nuremberg but as a learned mathematician surrounded by Latin inscriptions, compass, and globe.

Hirschvogel innovatively combined his skills as mathematician-cartographer-etcher in depictions of Vienna etched for the city between 1547 and 1552 (B. 80, B. 81, Schwarz 143). His were the first views of Vienna ever to be produced according to a given scale, and his circular ground plan is significant in the history of cartography because it was the first ever made by triangulation, a system of surveying that Hirschvogel himself had developed. For art historians, it is significant that the plates for the ground plan were made of copper. Although copperplates were regularly used for engravings, iron had up to this time been used for etchings. Dürer's *Landscape with the Cannon* (cat. 52) and Erhard Altdorfer's *Mountain Landscape* (CAM 1943.146), for example, were both etched on iron, whereas Hirschvogel's *River Landscape* was etched on copper. Copperplates are less prone to rust than iron and produce a cleaner, sharper line. Hirschvogel appears to be one of the first etchers to make regular use of copperplates.[6]

Hirschvogel's objective, topographical views documenting Vienna were an isolated experiment. When it came to his other landscapes, the technically innovative etcher-cartographer instead turned for inspiration to the tradition established by his predecessors, Albrecht Dürer (cat. 52) and the Danube-style landscapists. Like them, he constructed a composite view in his *River Landscape* by juxtaposing the tree and pathway of the high bank in the immediate foreground with the river valley that stretches out below. The tree, placed so close to the front plane that its leafy crown has been cropped, serves as a convenient spatial device to summarize the immediate foreground, establish a high vantage point, and provide an anchor from which to gauge the vast distance to the horizon. Hirschvogel's expansive regional views not only align his landscape work with the Danube style but also visually correspond with the German notion of *lantschaft* (landscape) in the sixteenth century.[7]

Hirschvogel was influenced by the work of both early Danube-style artists, Albrecht Altdorfer and Wolf Huber. Albrecht Altdorfer's nine landscapes (see fig. 57-1) etched around 1520 supplied Hirschvogel with a virtual primer of natural motifs, graphic conventions, and spatial formulae from which to draw. Altdorfer's landscapes are more animated, more expressive of nature's flux and tensions, more densely described; Hirschvogel's, by comparison, are more restrained, almost devitalized, more sparse and abstract.

Hirschvogel also freely borrowed motifs and entire compositions from Huber's pure landscape designs. An unfinished pen-and-ink copy of a Huber drawing in Brunswick (fig. 63-1) contains the same

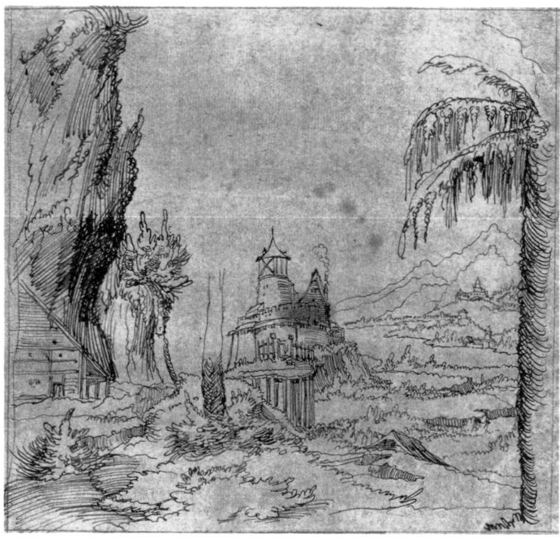

Figure 63-1. Circle of Wolf Huber, *Mountain Landscape*, pen with ink on reddish tinted paper. Herzog Anton Ulrich-Museum, Braunschweig.

landscape scene as this *River Landscape*. Whether the Brunswick drawing was Hirschvogel's immediate source is unclear because Hirschvogel's etching is not a literal copy. As a stained-glass painter, he was adept at revising and varying compositions.[8] It is instructive to see how he gave this landscape his personal stamp. He opened Huber's compact, enclosed vertical scene, giving it a horizontal orientation. Spatially he tempered Huber's dynamic diagonal inroads into the midground with his formulaic foreground tree and overlapping grassy hillocks parallel to the picture plane. He reordered the focus and scale by widening the river, pulling it forward, and making it a major thematic element. Meanwhile the rock cliff, so bold in the drawing, is reduced to little more than a backdrop for the half-timber structures on the right. Indeed by the time Hirschvogel had affixed his foreshortened monogram, HAF ([A]ugustin [H]irsch [F]ogel), to the plate, he had virtually transformed Huber's prototype to make it consistent with his own style and vision.[9] – JSP

1. For reproductions of Hirschvogel's work, see Schwarz, 2:71-93.

2. Gottfried Frenzel distinguishes the different hands and styles of the Hirschvogel stained-glass workshop in "Veit Hirschvogel: Eine Nürnberger Glasmalereiwerkstatt der Dürerzeit," *Zeitschrift für Kunstgeschichte* 23 (1960): 193-210. For Hirschvogel's early drawings and stained glass, see J. S. Peters, "Early Drawings by Augustin Hirschvogel," *Master Drawings* 17 (1979): 359-92; idem, "Frühe Glasgemälde von Augustin Hirschvogel," *Anzeiger des Germanischen Nationalmuseums* (1980): 79-89.

3. Annegrit Schmitt explains how the differences in training of Hirschvogel as stained-glass painter and of Lautensack as goldsmith-engraver contributed to the differences in their respective etching styles in *Hanns Lautensack* (Nuremberg, 1957), 35-36.

4. The Museum's staff examined each of its etchings by Hirschvogel under magnification and found that, like *River Landscape*, multiple bites were used to create these etchings as well (B. 55, 66, 75).

5. Biographical information and documents about Hirschvogel are found in Schwarz, 1:3-22, 131-43.

6. While Lucas van Leyden's portrait of Maximilan I from 1520 (cat. 55) was the first instance of etching on a copperplate, it was made in combination with engraving and represents an isolated experiment. As Schmitt pointed out in *Hanns Lautensack*, 19-20, n. 38, Hirschvogel was the earliest etcher to make consistent use of copperplates. On the change from iron to copper, see also W. Wegner, *Reallexikon zur deutschen Kunstgeschichte*, s.v. "Eisenradierung." Hirschvogel's copperplates for the ground plan of Vienna are still housed in the Historisches Museum in Vienna. See Vienna 1953, 19-21, 36, nos. 15, 37. The differences between the lines produced from the iron plates of Dürer's and Altdorfer's etchings and those from Hirschvogel's copper become more obvious under magnification.

7. For the sixteenth-century German concept of landscape and the formative influences on the German regional landscape view, see the discussion under Dürer (cat. 52). The term Danube style is used here to indicate stylistic affinities between such artists as Altdorfer, Huber, and Hirschvogel. For recent opinions that dismiss the notion that these artists participated in a movement referred to as the Danube school, see Pierre Vaisse, "Remarks on the Danube School" in Jacqueline and Maurice Guillaud, eds., Paris 1984, 149-64.

8. For the design abilities of stained-glass painters, see Gottfried Frenzel, "Entwurf und Ausführung in der Nürnberger Glasmalerei der Dürerzeit," *Zeitschrift für Kunstwissenschaft* 15 (1961): 31-59.

9. Franz Winzinger considers this a preparatory drawing by Hirschvogel (in *Wolf Huber. Das Gesamtwerk*, 2 vols. [Munich: Hirmer Verlag, 1979], no. 234). Halm's attribution of the drawing to the circle of Wolf Huber is more commonly accepted and appropriate. See Peter Halm, Passau 1953, no. 71 (copy of Huber from ca. 1510-1515); and Hans Werner Schmidt, *Die deutschen Handzeichnungen bis zur Mitte des 16. Jahrhunderts*, no. 9 of *Kunsthefte des Herzog Anton Ulrich-Museums* (Brunswick, 1965), 16, no. 43 (copy of Huber).

Hieronymus Cock
Antwerp 1510?-1570 Antwerp

64. The Marvelous Windings of the Labyrinth 1558.
From the series *Varia Variarum Regionum Typographicae Adumbrationes* (*Various Printed Sketches of Different Places*, also called *Landscape with Biblical and Mythological Scenes*).

Etching on antique laid paper, 19.9 x 29.1 cm (platemark).
H. *Neth.* 21; Riggs 50.
Watermark: Crowned eagle? (cf. Briquet 115).
Inscribed in plate lower left: *Labyrinthi mirabiles ambages* (the marvelous windings of the labyrinth).
Provenance: (Purchased from M. Knoedler, New York, September 20, 1939, for $45).
Bequest of Herbert Greer French, 1943.275.

Matthys Cock. . . was an excellent painter of landscape. He was also the first who began to make landscapes in a better style, with more variations, in the manner of the modern Italians and the ancients, and was remarkably decorative and inventive in arranging or uniting [the different parts of the landscape]. He painted excellent things in tempera and oil color. About Hieronymus Cock, his brother, I have little to say: for he gave up making art, and began to trade in it instead: he had pictures painted, purchased paintings in oil and tempera, and employed engravers and etchers. Nevertheless he himself was a very inventive landscapist, and etched several things, but also many of his brother Matthys' compositions, in particular twelve little landscapes that everyone still enjoys looking at.

The Marvelous Windings of the Labyrinth belongs to the series of twelve little landscapes described in this passage from Carel van Mander's *Lives of Eminent Netherlandish and German Painters*, first published in 1604.[1] A number of landscape drawings have been attributed to Matthys Cock, some closely related to prints in the series, but none of them signed. If it were not for Van Mander we might be unaware of Matthys' contribution to the print series, for his name appears neither on the individual prints nor on the title page.[2]

Judging by the compositions of these prints and the drawings attributed to Matthys, his landscapes – panoramic views often including fantastic rock formations – derive from the early sixteenth-century Flemish tradition of artists like Joachim Patenier and Herri met de Bles. But as Carel van Mander suggests, the transitions between foreground and background are more subtly managed in Matthys' compositions than in earlier landscapes. Hills and valleys flow smoothly together, and even the bizarre rocks, like those in the background of this print, seem to grow more naturally out of the earth than in earlier Flemish landscape.

Matthys' brother Hieronymus Cock is best known as a publisher, issuing more than eleven hundred prints between 1548 and 1570. As a printmaker, he produced sixty-two etchings; the series of twelve landscapes, issued in 1558, was his last and most notable achievement in the medium.[3] Etching had been used as a printmaking technique since the beginning of the sixteenth century, but Hieronymus uses it more freely than Lucas van Leyden (cat. 55) or even Augustin Hirschvogel (cat. 63). His jagged, broken contours are ostentatiously unlike the controlled lines of the engraver. They strikingly resemble the hasty pen strokes of his own and his brother's drawings, well suited to delineating the irregular forms of rocks, trees, and foliage. He also skillfully varies the weight of his lines, biting some of them in the etching acid longer than others in order to get effects of atmospheric perspective. Lightly bitten lines add distance to the mountains at the right in this print, whereas the combination of light and deeply bitten lines in the foreground offers a rich variety of light and shade.

Within the series of twelve landscapes, *The Labyrinth* is something of an anomaly. Each of the other landscapes, picturesque views of hills, valleys, and seacoast, includes a few small figures enacting a biblical or mythological story. This print, by contrast, seems to dispense with such narratives (the figures are anonymous and wear contemporary dress), and picturesque landscape elements are pushed aside to enframe the vast formal pattern of the labyrinth, set on a circular island.

Labyrinth patterns date from prehistoric times and had significance in both pagan and Christian religion (patterns very similar to this one were incorporated into the pavement of many Gothic cathedrals).[4] In classical mythology, the labyrinth is associated with the story of the Minotaur, a monster living at the center of a labyrinth on the island of Crete; and Cock's print has often been called *The Cretan Labyrinth*, suggesting a mythological subject on the pattern of the other prints in the series. This labyrinth, however, is no prison for a monster but a pleasure garden and has nothing in common with the labyrinth of Crete except that it, too, is set on an island. Garden labyrinths first appeared in the mid-sixteenth century, both in art and in actual garden design.

In contrast to an ordinary maze, which requires the visitor to choose between branching paths, a labyrinth is formed by a single path doubling back on itself again and again in a complicated design. If you were to enter the gate at the left, you would need only patience to get to the center; but before getting there, you would have covered every square foot of ground on the island. The pleasure of walking in such a place is not in solving a puzzle but in allowing the path itself to surprise you: after turning only seven corners, you seem to be at the point of reaching center; but after circling around it, the path swings away, and after another twenty-three turns, you are practically back at the gate where you started. Having completely frustrated you, the path then suddenly gives in and leads you to the center in just three more turns. This alternation of advance and retreat, frustration and success, may be one reason why the labyrinth was associated with the vicissitudes of love and courtship in the sixteenth and seventeenth centuries.[5] It is significant that most of the figures within the labyrinth are couples, and the scenes of hunting, feasting, and music making in the foreground are also appropriate to a garden of love. In substituting a contemporary theme for the biblical and mythological stories of the other landscapes, *The Labyrinth* is perhaps the most innovative print in the series. – TR

1. Carel van Mander, *Het Leven der Doorluchtighe Nederlandtsche en Hoogduytsche Schilders/Das Leben der niederländischen und deutschen Maler*, ed. and trans. Hanns Floerke from the 1617 edition (Munich and Leipzig: Georg Muller, 1906), 1:248-49. English translation by T.R.

2. *Variae Variarum Regionum Typographicae Adumbrationes in Publicum Pictorum Usum a Hieronymo Cock Delineatae, in Aes Incisae et Aeditae. Veelderleye ordinantien van lantschappen, met fyne historien daer in gheordineert, wt den ouden ende niewen testamente, ende sommighe lustighe Poeteryen, seer bequaem voer Schilders, ende andere liefhebbers der consten: Nu eerst niew in de printe ghebracht, ende ghemaect by Ieronymus Cock Schilder. Men salse vinden Thantwerpen inde vier winden. Met Gratie ende privilegie. Imprimé en Anvers auprès la bourse neuve au quatre vens, en la mayson de Hieronymus Cocq Paintre, 1558.* The Flemish version of the title reads in full: "Numerous sketches of landscape, with fine stories set into them, from the Old and New Testaments, and certain pleasant fictions [myths], very convenient for painters and other lovers of the arts: Now brought for the first time into print, and made by Hieronymus Cock, painter. You can find them in Antwerp at the Sign of the Four Winds. Copyright."

3. Timothy Riggs, *Hieronymus Cock, Printmaker and Publisher* (New York: Garland Publishing, Inc., 1977). On Cock as etcher, see 127-33.

4. Hermann Kern, *Labyrinthe: Erscheinungsform und Deutungen; 5000 Jahre Gegenwart eines Urbilds* (Munich: Prestel-Verlag, 1982).

5. The sixteenth-century labyrinth as garden of love is discussed in detail in Kern, *Labyrinthe*, 328-41.

Hanns Lautensack

Bamburg ca. 1520-1564/66 Vienna

65. River Landscape with Three Figures ca. 1558-59.

Etching on antique laid paper, 20.0 x 29.3 cm (platemark).
P. 67; Schmitt 77, H. *Ger.* 12.
Watermark: Anchor in circle (cf. Briquet 553).

Condition: Trimmed to or just outside platemark.
Provenance: (Purchased from M. Knoedler, New York, November 1, 1934, for $350).
Bequest of Herbert Greer French, 1943.241.

Hanns Lautensack's known work falls into two periods: his earlier Nuremberg period (ca. 1544-54) and his later Viennese period (1554-64). While Lautensack was still a child, his father, Paul Lautensack (ca. 1478-1558), a painter, musician, and religious mystic, moved his family from Bamberg to Nuremberg. It was there that Hanns likely trained as a goldsmith. All that remains of his artistic production is a handful of drawings and a modest number of prints – one engraving, seventy-eight etchings, and three woodcuts.[1]

Lautensack's only engraving, a mounted battle dated 1546, is sufficiently accomplished to suggest that he had had prior experience with a burin and the engraving technique. After 1546, however, he would use engraving only to add finishing touches to his etched portraits. His first two dated etchings from 1544 contain blotches, extreme contrasts in line, and conspicuous rust spots, indicating that the etching process was then still new to him (H. *Ger.* 6, 8). By 1551, he had mastered the etching technique and had switched from iron to copper, thereby reducing the tendency of his plates to rust. For the next decade Lautensack continued to produce etchings – primarily portraits and landscapes – and after 1561, he ceased making prints altogether. *River Landscape with Three Figures* is one of his latest, most accomplished landscapes, made while he was residing in Vienna.

Judging from his etched portraits, Lautensack's patrons from his earlier Nuremberg period were primarily prominent citizens of the city and distinguished Bavarian families. Although he retained the established convention of presenting the sitter in an interior, posed half-length behind a ledge (cf. Aldegrever, cat. 60), Lautensack's portraits give the genre a new twist. On the back wall next to the customary coat of arms, he introduced a window that opens into a deep landscape vista, an addition that provides a dynamic compositional balance, a source of airy light, and above all, room for the sitter to breathe.[2]

These small background views, rendered with as much care and detail as the sitters themselves, betray Lautensack's penchant for landscape: half of his entire graphic oeuvre is devoted to it. In the 1550s Nuremberg artists had not yet developed a tradition of pure landscape. For them, landscapes generally served a supportive role for narrative scenes. It was the Danube-style artists, Albrecht Altdorfer of Regensburg and Wolf Huber of Passau, who a generation earlier had developed the theme of autonomous landscape in German art, primarily in their prints and drawings (cf. Albrecht Altdorfer, fig. 57-1), and it is to their work that Lautensack turned for inspiration. His *River Landscape with Three Figures* exemplifies how he, like these earlier Danube-style masters, attempted to evoke panoramic, airy depths and to create scenes combining romantic features of German topography – river valleys, Neuschwanstein-like castles perched high on boulders, half-timber houses nestled in woods, distant Alpine peaks. In Lautensack's expansiveness, even the boldest of these motifs appears diminutive and takes on a fairy tale character. What distinguishes Lautensack's Danube-style landscapes, including this *River Landscape*, from the earlier generation of landscapists is his insistence on surface description. Whereas Altdorfer's and Huber's best works record nature's moods and the artist's response to them, Lautensack concentrates on the material stuff of the scene.

One of Lautensack's major early achievements is his pair of etched city views of Nuremberg from 1552. As topographical portraits they contrast with his Danube-style landscapes both in their scale and objectivity. They were modeled on two topographical views of Vienna that Augustin Hirschvogel, a Nuremberg predecessor, had etched and sent to Nuremberg's city council in 1547.[3] Lautensack followed Hirschvogel's format, making each print from three plates, but he enlarged them so that each composite view (one from the east, the other from the west) measures nearly five feet in length. Like Hirschvogel he faithfully recorded the city's skyline and identified each of its major structures by name, but he went further: he enlivened his views with descriptions of the tilled contours of the terrain surrounding the city walls and the daily activities of its farmers and travelers, including himself (smack in the middle!) making studies for the project. Hirschvogel's views were made to aid Vienna in its plans for new fortifications; Lautensack's, to eulogize Nuremberg. To this end, Lautensack added modern strapwork cartouches inscribed with Latin verses praising the city. His views of Nuremberg were the first of their kind and among the best German city portraits of the sixteenth century.[4]

Lautensack's move to Vienna in 1554 was a turning point in his career that resulted in new patronage and, correspondingly, in new kinds of artistic projects. As illustrator, he supplied the humanist Wolfgang Lazius with an etched allegorical-topographical view of the Turkish siege of Vienna (1529) to accompany an historical account of the city. As portraitist, he was called upon to etch official portraits of the imperial family (Maximilian, archduke of Austria, in 1555; Ferdinand I in 1556), which he enclosed in highly ornate, allegorical frames.[5]

Prior to Lautensack's arrival in Vienna, Augustin Hirschvogel (d. 1552), whose city portraits had influenced Lautensack, was the most prominent printmaker in Vienna, and the two artists are invariably compared. Both began their careers in Nuremberg and finished their careers in Vienna. Both made etching their primary printmaking technique (rather than engraving), thereby anticipating the growth in its popularity later in the century, and both switched from iron to copperplate.[6] Together they represent the final phase of the so-called Danube style, but comparison of the Museum's impressions of their two ostensibly similar river landscapes (cf. Hirschvogel, cat. 63) demonstrates how different their approaches really were. Whereas Hirschvogel minimized detail, allowing the white of the page to assert itself, Lautensack relished nature's textures. Hirschvogel summarized foliage almost indifferently with undifferentiated strokes; Lautensack distinguished a myriad of leafy forms. As Annegrit Schmitt points out, their respective approaches may have been conditioned by their training. Hirschvogel, the stained-glass painter, picked up the etching needle to release lines seemingly spontaneously, practically allowing them to take their own free course; Lautensack, the goldsmith-engraver, treated the needle like a burin to impose a variety of fine weblike linear systems.[7]

Lautensack's *River Landscape*, like his other large landscape etchings from circa 1558-59, reflects two late developments in his treatment of landscape. Looking beyond the German tradition to contemporary Netherlandish landscape portrayal, especially to the circle of Matthys and Hieronymus Cock,[8] Lautensack first eliminated the sharp juxtaposition of foreground and background seen in his earlier landscapes and developed a continuously unrolling midground. In *River Landscape*, the waterway provides a spatial conduit that runs diagonally from the foreground to the horizon (as if out to sea as in Netherlandish scenes). Second, although he reintroduced figures into his Danube-style landscapes, he scaled them down so that they integrate *into* the landscape and help to articulate the foreground space, as do the two travelers here who approach the man resting at the foot of the foreground tree.

In the past, *River Landscape* was thought to illustrate the parable of the Good Samaritan, but even if Lautensack intended to portray this parable, the subject remains incidental. His inclusion of the three figures serves primarily to heighten the feeling of the grandeur of nature. – JSP

1. In her monograph on Lautensack, Annegrit Schmitt argues that documents refer to the artist not as Hans Sebald Lautensack, as frequently cited, but as Hanns Lautensack. His monogram, HLS, should thus be interpreted as [H]anns [L]auten [S]ack. For her arguments on Lautensack's early training as goldsmith, see Schmitt, 7-8. For a woodcut not included in Schmitt's catalogue raisonné that has been rediscovered, see H. Schwarz, "A Unique Woodcut by Hanns Lautensack," *Pantheon* 22 (1964): 143-50.

2. For reproductions of the Nuremberg portraits, see Schmitt, figs. 4-7. Lautensack could have adopted this spatial solution of a window opening from painted portraits, where it had been in use much earlier.

3. For the city views of Nuremberg, see Schmitt, 50-51, figs. 65-66; see also Jeffrey Chipps Smith, Austin 1983, 75, 254-57, nos. 163-64. For Hirschvogel's views of Vienna, see Schwarz, 1:20, n. 82, 185; 2:90, figs. 80-81.

4. Smith, Austin 1983, 75.

5. One plate of the Turkish siege is reproduced in Schmitt, fig. 9; for the Viennese aristocratic portraits, see H. Ger. 55, 57, 61.

6. For the change from iron to copperplate in etching between 1540 and 1550, see W. Wegner, *Reallexikon zur deutschen Kunstgeschichte*, s.v. "Eisenradierung"; Schmitt, *Hanns Lautensack*, 19, n. 38; and Ilse O'Dell-Franke, *Kupferstiche und Radierungen aus der Werkstatt des Virgil Solis* (Wiesbaden: Franz Steiner Verlag, 1977), 34-35. For the changeover from engraving to etching as technique of preference, see O'Dell-Franke, *Kupferstiche*, 39.

7. Schmitt, 34-36.

8. Schmitt groups *River Landscape* with seven others similar in dimension that are Lautensack's largest and most mature landscapes (several are dated 1558 or 1559). See Schmitt, figs. 74-81. For arguments for the Netherlandish influence, see Schmitt, see also Konrad Oberhuber, Vienna 1967, 139, no. 183.

Jost Amman
Zurich 1539-1591 Nuremberg

66. Gaspard de Coligny 1573.
Etching with engraving on antique laid paper, 36.8 x 27.0 cm (platemark).
B. 17 ii, Becker 112, A. 2 ii/ii, H. *Ger.* 2 ii/ii, TIB 17 ii/ii.
Watermark: Jug with crown and flower.
Inscribed in cartouche upper center: *Effigies Gasparis de Colig/ni, D. de Castilione·Amir/alii Franciae* [Portrait of Gaspard de Coligny of Châtillon, Commander of the French Admiralty]; in border lower center: *Fecit Norimbergae Jost Amman Tigurinus, 1573* [Made in Nuremberg by Jost Amman of Zurich]
Provenance: Count von Oettingen-Wallerstein (Lugt S. 2715a); (his sale C.G. Boerner, Leipzig, June 16-17, 1937, no. 6, to Colnaghi, London, for rm 21); (purchased from M. Knoedler, New York, October 11, 1937, for $125).
Bequest of Herbert Greer French, 1943.270.

Amman presents Gaspard II de Coligny of Châtillon (1519-1572) in terms of the power he wielded before his untimely death in 1572. Coligny was from a noble Burgundian family and pursued a military career as had his father, the Maréchal de Châtillon (Gaspard I de Coligny, d. 1522). With the help of his influential maternal uncle, Constable Anne de Montmorency (1493-1567), a wealthy chief minister, Coligny was appointed colonel-general of the French Infantry in 1547. After military successes in northern France, he was awarded the high post of commander of the French Admiralty (1552). Later in the decade, after having converted to Calvinism, Coligny worked for the Huguenot (e.g., French Calvinist) cause in the French civil wars, supporting measures that fostered religious coexistence and tolerance in France. In 1569 he became leader of the Huguenot armies,[1] and it is in this capacity that Amman depicts him.

Coligny stands, his left hand on hip, dressed in richly etched armor with a modish Spanish high collar. He turns to face the viewer with a noble and confident demeanor. Signs of his rank and prowess are nearby: he grasps his commander's mace in his right hand; the hilt of his sword is poised close to his left; his helmet, with its bushy panache, and his left gauntlet rest on the table before him. A carving of Michael slaying the dragon on the pendant that hangs from his neck attests to his knighthood in the Order of St. Michael. Coligny's profile dominates the horizon of the landscape vista opening behind him, where above in the sky a wingless figure of Victory extends a wreath to crown him with the fame of martyrdom. Amman has enclosed the portrait within an oval frame, cordoning it off from its highly ornate strapwork margins in such a way that Coligny commands the entire space.

This is the largest, most elaborate of Jost Amman's etched portraits and the only one in which the artist specifies his nationality and full name. Even though he etched the portrait "in Nuremberg," he was "from Zurich" (Tigurinus). In Zurich Amman had received a humanist education in the Collegium Carolinum, where his father was professor of classical languages and logic. Even though he later trained as a stained-glass painter, family connections brought him into contact with other important humanists and contemporaries, including the botanist-artist Conrad Gessner.[2] Before Amman actually took up permanent residence in Nuremberg – marrying there in 1574 – he seems to have traveled widely and gained diverse experience as a designer (1557-74). Knowledge of his itinerary is spotty, but his training, travels, and/or journeyman's work took him to Basel (1557); to Schaffhausen (1559), where he likely was in touch with Tobias Stimmer; and possibly to Paris, where he may have become acquainted with the French printmaker Étienne Delaune.[3] His purpose for going to Nuremberg in 1561 was probably to meet Virgil Solis, whose influence can already be detected in his first drawing (1556).[4] Solis at the time ran the most productive and successful print workshop in the city.

When Solis died in 1562, Amman must have recognized his opportunity to fill the vacuum for designer and printmaker in Nuremberg. By the 1570s he had established the leading printmaking workshop in this free imperial city, an accomplishment that earned him citizenship there in 1577.[5] Like Solis, he supplied ornamental designs for goldsmiths and jewelry makers. In contrast to Solis, whose intaglio work comprises mostly engravings, Amman followed a later sixteenth-century trend by turning to etching, often adding finishing touches to his plates with a burin as in the Coligny portrait. Amman's main occupation, however, was designing single-leaf woodcuts and countless book illustrations.[6] Beginning in 1563 he provided the Frankfurt publisher Sigmund Feyerabend with illustrations for over fifty books. His education must have enabled him to bring to the many texts that he illustrated an understanding exceeding that of most craftsmen. The sheer spectrum of subjects that Amman undertook to illustrate, from religious to classical, to such contemporary topics as costume, trades, war, geometry, emblems, and sport, makes his oeuvre a significant cultural document of his time.

The Coligny portrait is itself a document of a crucial juncture in Reformation history. Like Aldegrever's portrait of Jan of Leyden, made nearly forty years earlier (cat. 60), Amman's portrait chronicles a bloody massacre of Protestants. But whereas Aldegrever subtly exposed an infamous perpetrator, Amman's purpose was to commemorate Coligny as a hero. Coligny's murder in Paris triggered the St. Bartholomew's Day Massacre, the bloodiest and most horrific massacre of the second phase of the Reformation. On the day of his murder, August 24, 1572, St. Bartholomew's Day (appropriately the patron saint of butchers), some two thousand Huguenots were killed in Paris. The bloodbath would spread to Orléans, Rouen, Lyons, Bourges, and elsewhere in France.[7] The massacre followed the marriage of the Huguenot leader, Henry of Navarre (the future Henry IV), to the Catholic Marguerite de Valois, sister of Charles IX. This political marriage was ironically intended to symbolically cement the coexistence of French Protestants and Catholics after a decade of intermittent civil war. Coligny, who was in Paris for the marriage festivities, had become a political liability to the French royal family.

Amman recorded the events leading up to the massacre of the Huguenots in the cartouche below. On the left, the assassin, Maurevert, who had been hired by the queen mother, Catherine de Medici, fires his arquebus from an upper window and wounds Coligny, who reads a petition (August 22, 1572). On the right, a German mercenary fatally stabs Coligny in an apartment where he was recuperating (August 24, 1572, 4 A.M.). Below in the courtyard stands Henry, duke of Guise, a personal enemy of Coligny and leader of the Catholic opposition. At the behest of the royal family, the duke was to oversee the assassination. He commands that Coligny's body be thrown from the window for identification. The body shown being dragged into the main street in Amman's print may be Coligny's as well: according to reports, his body was mutilated, dragged through the streets for three days, and then hanged by the feet for public viewing. (The duke allegedly severed Coligny's head and, after showing it to the king and queen mother, sent it to Rome to his uncle, the cardinal of Lorraine, and the pope.) In the center, Amman shows the extermination of the Huguenots, who were killed and thrown into the Seine following Coligny's assassination.

News of the massacre, a heated topic, quickly reached Germany and Switzerland through diplomats, Huguenot refugees, and published accounts. Amman must have had access to an image of Coligny, perhaps a print or medallion, and to firsthand or published versions of the events. The details of Coligny's death and the massacre that followed were collected in *De Furoribus Gallicis (French Fury)*, a propagandist account by Huguenot activist François Hotman, published in Latin, Italian, French, English, and German in 1573, the year that Amman made his print.[8] Regardless of today's historical debate about the facts and fiction of the St. Bartholomew's Day Massacre, Amman's portrait contributed to the image of Coligny as hero and martyr for the sixteenth-century Protestant community. – JSP

1. For Coligny, see J. Shimizu, *Conflict of Loyalties: Politics and Religion in the Career of Gaspard de Coligny, Admiral of France, 1519-1572* (Geneva: Librarie Droz, 1970).

2. Amman's connection with Gessner is treated in Ilse O'Dell-Franke, "Die Nachwirkung von Dürers Tierdarstellungen auf Arbeiten Jost Ammans," *Jahrbuch der kunsthistorischen Sammlungen in Wien* 82-83 (1986-87): 91. For a brief biographical synopsis of Amman, see O'Dell, Stuttgart 1979, 1:194; Jeffrey Chipps Smith, Austin 1983, 275; and AKL, s.v. "n, Jost."

3. O'Dell establishes a direct connection between Delaune's and Amman's work and, even though documentary proof is lacking, provides strong arguments that Amman may have gone to Paris and been in contact with Delaune in "Étienne Delaune and Jost Amman: Drawings after Prints and Prints after Drawings," PQ. 7, no. 4 (1990): 419. Amman's own style of ornament, used for title pages and frames, as found in the Coligny portrait, was influenced by the Fontainebleau style of French mannerist ornamentation.

4. For Amman's early drawings after prints by Virgil Solis and Tobias Stimmer, see Ilse O'Dell-Franke, "Federkunststücke von und nach Jost Amman," *Kunst und Antiquitäten* 6 (1986): 20-25.

5. O'Dell-Franke convincingly argues against the traditional assumption that Amman took over Solis' workshop in *Kupferstiche und Radierungen aus der Werkstatt des Virgil Solis* (Wiesbaden: Franz Steiner, 1977), 22-23.

6. The most complete catalogue of Amman's prints is still Andresen (A.1:109-448). According to him, Amman made a matching portrait intaglio of Coligny's second wife, Jacobine de Coligny (A. 3, Jacqueline de Montbel). For reproductions of Amman's work, see TIB 20, pts. 1-2; and for the most recent extensive treatment of Amman's graphic work, see Ilse O'Dell, *Jost Ammans Buchschmuck-Holzschnitte für Sigmund Feyerabend. Die dekorative figürliche Bilderschmuck, die Technik seiner verwenden in den Drucken von 1563-1599 und seine Nachwirkung* (Wiesbaden: Otto Harrassowitz, in press). O'Dell provides proof that Amman not only designed woodcuts, but in some

instances also cut his own blocks in "Jost Ammans 'Mummereyen' für Ottavio Strada," *Zeitschrift für schweizerische Archäologie und Kunstgeschichte* 47 (1990): 244-50.

7. The literature on the St. Bartholomew's Day Massacre is voluminous. For analyses with further literature see R. Kingdon, *Myths about the St. Bartholomew's Day Massacre 1572-1576* (Cambridge: Harvard University Press, 1988); N. M. Sutherland, *The Massacre of St. Bartholomew and the European Conflict 1559-1572* (London: Macmillan, 1973); and A. Soman, ed., *The Massacre of St. Bartholomew: Reappraisals and Documents* (The Hague: Martinus Nijhoff, 1974).

8. L. Spitz analyses the impact of the massacre on Germany in "Imperialism, Particularism and Toleration in the Holy Roman Empire," in Soman, ed. *The Massacre*, 71-95. For Hotman's account, see Donald R. Kelley, "François Hotman: A Revolutionary's Ordeal* (Princeton: Princeton University Press, 1973), esp. 205-38. A German translation of Hotman's book was published by Christoph Egenolf's heirs in 1573 in Frankfurt, where Amman had many contacts. See Günther Richter, "Christian Egenolfs Erben 1555-1667," *Archiv für Geschichte des Buchwesens* 7 (1967): 449-1130, no. 356.

Hieronymus Wierix

Antwerp 1553-1619 Antwerp

67. Henry III, King of France by 1589.

Engraving on antique laid paper, 35.6 x 25.1 cm (sheet).
Nagler 9; Alvin 1918, MH. *Wierix* 1827a.
Watermark: Basel coat of arms with countermark.
Signed in plate right center above shoulder: *Ieronimus W. fe.*, 4-line French text below sitter: *Peintre afin . . . dans ses yeux.*
Condition: Trimmed to or just inside platemark.
Provenance: Karl Ferdinand Friedrich von Nagler (Lugt 2529); Kupferstichkabinett, Staatliche Museen, Berlin (Lugt 1606, gift of Von Nagler in 1935, and Lugt 2398); (probably sale, Lepke, Berlin, November 6-11, 1873, lot 1048); Baron Adalbert Von Lanna, (Lugt 2773); (his sale, Gutekunst, Stuttgart, May 11-22, 1909, lot 3010, to Boerner for RM 410); (C.G. Boerner, Leipzig, June 16-17, 1937, lot 400); (purchased from M. Knoedler, New York, October 11, 1937, for $275).
Bequest of Herbert Greer French, 1943.271.

Hieronymus and Jan Wierix were among the most prolific Netherlandish printmakers active in Antwerp during the later years of the sixteenth and the early years of the seventeenth centuries. The indefatigable cataloguer M. Mauquoy-Hendrickx lists a total of 2333 prints by members of the Wierix family.[1]

Although four years younger than his brother Jan, Hieronymus was the more precocious talent. The two brothers appear to have apprenticed at the same time with a still-unidentified master. They also began their professional careers together by working for the celebrated Antwerp publisher Christophe Plantijn, and they entered the Antwerp Guild of Saint Luke jointly, between 1572 and 1573. Hieronymus received his first payment from Plantijn on March 14, 1570.

Hieronymus Wierix was a temperamental personality prone to acts of violence, including drunken assault and manslaughter. Court records in Antwerp amply document his renegade activities. From these records, we know that Plantijn was forced to pay a fine of eighteen florins on September 23, 1574, on behalf of Hieronymus, who was found by the city's night patrol drunk and without a lantern. It appears that Plantijn eventually ceased to patronize the Wierix brothers, because of their unpredictable behavior, subsequently replacing them with more compliant employees.

Hieronymus' first dated print is from 1577. At about this time, he worked principally for the Antwerp publisher Willem van Haecht, a rhetorician who devised complex satirical and allegorical subjects that Wierix engraved after the drawings of such distinguished artists

as Martin van Cleef, Ambrosius Francken, Frans Pourbus, and Martin de Vos. Van Haecht was loyal to his troublesome but gifted engraver. On one occasion, he provided bail for Wierix when he was thrown into prison in 1579 for fatally striking a female tavernkeeper in a fit of drunken anger; on March 24, 1580, Wierix was released from prison. Throughout the 1580s, the Wierix brothers found ample work, although in a letter of January 2, 1587, Plantijn decried their poor working habits and debauched lives. The brothers, it seems, would work for a few days only to earn sufficient cash that then might be dissipated in taverns. Their would-be patron was forced again and again to seek them out, straighten out their affairs, and return them to sobriety. But seek them out he did, for the Wierix brothers, particularly Hieronymus, were recognized as prodigious talents. Their superb engravings lent cachet to the fine-quality illustrated books for which Antwerp's publishers, like Plantijn, were famous throughout Europe.

On June 12, 1587, Hieronymus married Dympne de Backer, who bore him several children. Although their marriage may not have been placid, Hieronymus does seem to have settled down. He developed a large and active workshop and maintained a number of apprentices.

Henry III, King of France is a superb example of Hieronymus Wierix's virtuoso engraving style. The linear precision, the controlled luminosity, and the subtle rendering of texture mark this print as a masterpiece of mannerist portraiture. The Museum's impression is flawlessly preserved, and it retains the requisite depth of tone associated with fine early pulls from the engraved plate.

Hieronymus' portrait of Henry actually copied an engraving by his brother Jan.[2] This version betrays his intention to produce a magnificent likeness that would outclass his brother's engraving. He produced the image in the same direction and proudly signed it above the sitter's left shoulder. Jean Adhémar discovered the original copperplate for Hieronymus' *Henry III* in the Musée de Montauban, France. Its reverse side was used as the support for a late mannerist painting, *Allegory of Taste*.[3]

Henry III's assassination in 1589 brought an end to the Valois dynasty in France. On his deathbed Henry III recognized Henry of Navarre, the future Henry IV, as his successor to the throne, thereby inaugurating the Bourbon dynasty. By formally declaring himself a Roman Catholic in 1593, Henry IV brought the troubled epoch of Catherine de Médicis to a close. – GK

1. MH. *Wierix*, 3 vols. in 4 sections (Brussels: Bibliothèque Albert Ier, 1978-83). The majority of these are by the three Wierix brothers, Anton, Hieronymus, and Jan, sons of the elder Anton Wierix.

2. MH. *Wierix*, vol. 3, no. 1827. Jan's engraving, in turn, may have been based on the engraved *Portrait of Henry III* by Thomas de Leu after a drawing in the Bibliothèque Nationale in Paris. This drawing is attributed to J. Decourt by Jean Adhémar and C. Monlin, "Les Portraits dessinés du XVIᵉ Siècle au Cabinet des Estampes," GBA. 82 (September 1973): 170, no. 376. Jan Wierix paired this portrait with an identically framed *Portrait of King Philip II of Spain* (MH. *Wierix*, no. 1892).

3. Jean Adhémar, "Sur un Cuivre gravé et peint du Musée de Montauban", GBA. 55 (January 1960): 57-59.

Federico Barocci

Urbino ca. 1535-1612 Urbino

68. Madonna and Child in the Clouds ca. 1581.

Etching and engraving on antique laid paper, 15.3 x 10.7 cm (platemark).
B.2.
Signed in plate lower left: · F · B · V · F ·
Condition: Trimmed to platemark.

Provenance: Carl Theodor Thiemann (Lugt S. 642c); (purchased from Frederick Keppel, New York, February 6, 1935, for $45). Bequest of Herbert Greer French, 1943.263.

A painter whose sweet rational style was a near-perfect instrument for Counter-Reformation needs and values, Federico Barocci spent most of his highly successful and productive life in his native Urbino, a small city not far from the Adriatic coast, more or less due east of Florence. Barocci was a student of his father, Ambrogio, a sculptor, and then of Battista Franco, who worked in Urbino off and on between 1545 and 1551. It has been suggested that Franco, who is better known today for his prints than for his paintings, taught etching to Barocci, but if he did, Barocci may have had to relearn the technique at a later date: it was not until nearly three decades after Franco left Urbino definitively for Venice that the younger artist made prints himself.

Barocci spent most of the decade of his twenties – from the mid-1550s to the mid-1560s – in Rome, working with the brothers Taddeo and Federico Zuccaro, decorating, among other things, the so-called Casino of Pius IV, an elegant small retreat within the gardens of the Vatican. According to his biographer, Giovanni Bellori,[1] Barocci may have been poisoned by artists envious of his talent, although this is an overfamiliar *topos* in artists' biographies. Whatever the truth, after his stay in Rome Barocci returned to Urbino and worked there and in neighboring cities diligently for nearly fifty more years. He received commissions from popes, the Holy Roman Emperor, the King of Spain, and the Duke of Tuscany. Barocci's method was to work out a composition thoroughly, making numerous studies from models, and today an oeuvre of some two thousand drawings remains. His large production of paintings, virtually all of religious subjects, has for the most part remained in the places for which it was made – the churches and palaces of the small cities of northeastern Italy, and thus it is less well known, especially in the Western Hemisphere, than is the oeuvre of many of his contemporaries.

Barocci made only four prints, two small and two large. His paintings had been made known through reproductive engravings, the best of which were by Cornelis Cort, a Netherlander who worked in Venice with Titian and then in Rome from the mid-1560s until his death in 1578. It is certainly plausible that after Cort's death Barocci wanted to continue to have his paintings reproduced, and his two large prints, the *Perdono of St. Francis of Assisi* (B. 4) and the *Annunciation* (B. 1), serve this function: they replicate paintings completed in 1576 and 1584. The smaller etchings also reuse motifs from earlier paintings: the figure of the saint in the *Stigmatization of St. Francis* (B. 3) is the same as that in the *Perdono*, and the *Madonna and Child in the Clouds* reproduces figures from an altarpiece, now lost, made in the 1560s for the Church of the Capuchins in Fossombrone; even the angels' heads in the corners are the same as those in the *Perdono*. Nonetheless, these two prints are sketchier in feeling and approach much more closely the ideal of a spontaneous drawing that comes to life on a metal plate.

Based on an analysis of the technique of the four etchings, Louise Richards concluded that the *Stigmatization* was probably first.[2] Next, close in time to each other, were the *Madonna* and the *Perdono*; the latter is dated 1581. The *Madonna* was copied in engraving by Agostino Carracci, whose print is dated 1582. Last would have been the *Annunciation*, Barocci's greatest print, most probably made after 1584 when the painting was finished. It is not known why Barocci stopped making prints, but perhaps the demand for his paintings made it difficult for him also to do this time-consuming work.

Smallest of the plates, the *Madonna* is less than one-half the size of the *Stigmatization*. Close examination of the print is thus needed to perceive the artist's free use of a combination of line and stipple and his achievement of darker lines through the use of stopping out and reetching – a technique that Barocci seems to have innovated, but examination is rewarded by an understanding of the bold means by which Barocci created this, the most captivating of his prints. – SB

1. Giovanni Pietro Bellori, *Le vite de pittori, scultori ed architetti moderni* (Rome, 1692); see English translation in Cleveland 1978, 11-24. For a concise biography, see Reed in Boston 1989, 89-90.
2. Richards in Cleveland 1978, 93-94.

Hendrick Goltzius
Mühlbracht (now Bracht) 1558-1616/17 Haarlem

69. Pietà 1596.
Engraving on antique laid paper, 18.8 x 12.9 cm (platemark).
B. 41; Dut. 41 ii/ii; Hirschmann 50 ii/ii; H. *Neth.* 50 ii/ii; Strauss 331 ii/ii; TIB 301.041 ii/ii.
Watermark: Crowned shield with fleur-de-lis.
Monogrammed in plate lower center: HG
dated on rock cropping: *A°96*.
Provenance: Heinrich Friedrich De La Motte-Fouquet (Lugt 778); Carl Schlosser (Lugt 636); Charles Deering (Lugt 516); (purchased from Albert Roullier, Chicago, November 4, 1935, for $350). Bequest of Herbert Greer French, 1943.264.

Herbert Greer French acquired many prints by Dürer – only one by Hendrick Goltzius. It is not difficult to understand why this was the one. Ever since its creation, the *Pietà* of Goltzius has been renowned as one of the most remarkable imitations of one artist by another in the history of Western art.

In the early 1570s when Goltzius' career began, printmaking had been transformed from a simple craft into something like an industry. Division of labor meant that a print was frequently the product of several hands. An artist made a drawing; an engraver copied it on a copperplate; a printer printed the plate; and a publisher coordinated their efforts, paid them for their work, and reaped his profits by marketing the print internationally. The Flemish city of Antwerp, where Hieronymus Cock (cat. 64) had set up the first great print publishing business in Northern Europe, was the world capital of print production by Goltzius' time. Although he himself lived not in Flanders but in the northern Netherlands (settling in Haarlem in 1577), much of his early work was done for Antwerp publishers.[1] Whether inventing the subjects of his prints or reproducing the designs of other artists, Goltzius began by working in a rather anonymous style; there was little to distinguish his earliest work from that of many other industrious technicians in late sixteenth-century Antwerp. By the time he was twenty-one, however, his virtuosity revealed itself in a series of remarkable miniature portraits, primarily designed by himself, and his reproductive engravings were distinguished by a silky brilliance.[2] Soon after, he enjoyed an international reputation with a series of prints influenced by and, in some cases, reproducing the work of Bartholomeus Spranger and Cornelis van Haarlem. These artists worked in the hyperelegant style of late mannerism, depicting male figures of bombastic musculature and female nudes of more-than-serpentine grace. Goltzius rendered them with a line that swells and tapers to produce dazzling patterns of light and shade (fig. 69-1).

By 1590, when he interrupted his production of engravings for a year's trip to Italy, Goltzius was already moving away from the extreme mannerist style. After 1600 he would move away from

Figure 69-1. Hendrick Goltzius, *The Dragon Devouring the Companions of Cadmus* (detail), 1588, engraving, H. *Neth* 130. Ackland Art Museum, The University of North Carolina at Chapel Hill, Burton Emmett Collection, 58.1.691.

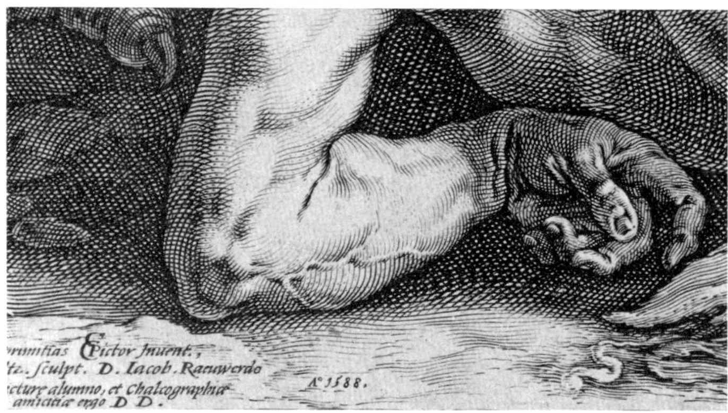

engraving to concentrate on painting, delegating to several brilliant pupils the labor of making prints from his drawings. Among his last engravings, however, are several that pay homage to the whole engraving tradition and, in particular, to its acknowledged "old masters" in Germany and the Netherlands, Dürer and Lucas van Leyden.[3]

In 1593 and 1594 Goltzius issued a series of engravings depicting the life of the Virgin, known as the *Meesterstukjes*, or Master Prints.[4] Each of the six prints in this series was designed in the style of a different artist. Four of them imitate Italian painters, but the two most famous prints in the series are *The Circumcision*, in the manner of Albrecht Dürer, and *The Adoration of the Magi*, in the manner of Lucas van Leyden. Here Goltzius imitated not only the composition and figure types of the artists but their distinctive engraving techniques. According to Goltzius' friend and biographer Carel van Mander, before the series as a whole was issued, the artist circulated impressions of these two prints with his own monogram removed and the paper artificially aged. He delighted in the wonder of collectors and artists that previously unknown prints by Dürer and Lucas had suddenly appeared almost a century after their deaths.[5] In 1596, when he engraved the *Pietà*, Goltzius was beginning another masquerade, a series of twelve prints in the style of Lucas van Leyden, depicting the Passion of Christ.[6]

The *Pietà* depends on two late engravings by Dürer of the Madonna and child: *The Virgin Nursing the Infant* of 1519 (B. 36) for Mary's tilted, veiled head and the general configuration of the upper part of her body and *The Virgin with the Swaddled Infant* of 1520 (B. 35) for the setting, the nocturnal lighting, and the geometric simplicity of Mary's skirt.[7] The figure of Christ is borrowed from the dead Christ in Dürer's large woodcut of 1511, *The Trinity* (B. 122). The configuration of the entire group, and perhaps the arrangement of drapery over the Virgin's head, is based on the famous sculpture by Michelangelo in Saint Peter's, which Goltzius must have seen on his trip to Rome in 1590-91.[8] Yet Goltzius has blended the elements from these four sources into a seamless whole, and he has scrupulously avoided copying any detail exactly.

In both the *Meesterstukjes* and the *Passion* series, Goltzius offers clues to the informed viewer that these are prints from the end of the sixteenth century, not the beginning. The *Meesterstukjes* are large prints, the figures on a scale far larger than Dürer or Lucas had ever engraved. The *Passion* is on a Lucasian scale, but the dedication tablet in the first plate has an inscription in the unmistakably ornate and flashy calligraphy of Goltzius' time (Goltzius must have known that, unlike Dürer, Lucas never inserted an inscription into a print other than the date and his initial *L*). The *Pietà* is another matter.

Not that it is an attempt to deceive – Goltzius' monogram and the date '96 are clearly visible in the foreground – but it is almost as if Goltzius were saying "If I had not signed this so plainly, would you have realized that it was not by Dürer?" It would doubtless have amused Goltzius that a copy of his print by another engraver was altered by an unscrupulous publisher who replaced Goltzius' monogram with Dürer's.[9]

Even in the choice of subject Goltzius is ingeniously devious. The Pietà – the Virgin Mary with the dead Christ on her lap – was a subject first depicted by German artists around the year 1300. Dürer, however, the quintessential German artist of the Renaissance, never made a print of the subject. The most famous Pietà created in Dürer's time was by an Italian, Michelangelo. Dürer, who never visited Rome, may not have known Michelangelo's sculpture, but he was certainly aware of Michelangelo's work in general: his own late work was influenced by it. Erwin Panofsky cites the Michelangelesque qualities of both the Dürer engravings of the Madonna that Goltzius was using for models here and describes *The Virgin Nursing the Infant* as "evoking the idea of a *Pietà* rather than of a Madonna."[10] In short, we have Goltzius engraving for Dürer, sixty-seven years after his death, the subject that Dürer as a German artist should have engraved (but never did), using as a model the Italian work of art that should have influenced Dürer (if he ever saw it) and the style that Dürer would have used when he was most under the influence of that work's creator. Goltzius himself may not have been aware of all these connections, but it seems likely that he would have relished them. – TR

1. The principal sources for Goltzius are Carel van Mander, *Het Leven der Doorluchtighe Nederlandtsche en Hoogduytsche Schilders/Das Leben der niederländischen und deutschen Maler*, ed. and trans. Hanns Floerke from the 1617 edition (Munich and Leipzig: Georg Muller, 1906), 2:222-61; Otto Hirschmann, *Hendrick Goltzius als Maler, 1600-1617* (Quellenschriften zur Holländischen Kunstgeschichte) (The Hague: Martinus Nijhoff, 1916); Hirschmann; E. K. J. Reznicek, *Die Zeichnungen von Hendrick Goltzius, mit einem beschreibenden Katalog* (Utrecht: H. Dekker and Gumbert, 1961); Strauss 1977.

2. Reznicek, *Die Zeichnungen*, 1:51-54.

3. Reznicek, *Die Zeichnungen*, 1:94-105. On Goltzius' imitation of other artists, see Walter Melion, "Hendrick Goltzius' Project of Reproductive Engraving," AH. 13 (1990): 458-87.

4. B. 15-20; Hirschmann 9-14; Strauss 1977, nos. 574-87 passim.

5. Van Mander, *Het Leven*, 2:246.

6. B. 27-38, Hirschmann 21-32, Strauss 1977, nos. 610-63 passim.

7. See Clifford S. Ackley, Boston 1980, 12-15, for a fine analysis of the Goltzius print in relation to Dürer and Michelangelo.

8. Goltzius could also have used several engravings of the *Pietà* as sources, in particular one by Agostino Carracci. Diane DeGrazia Bohlin, Washington 1979, 82-83.

9. Hirschmann 50, copy.

10. Erwin Panofsky, *The Life and Art of Albrecht Dürer* (Princeton: Princeton University Press, 1955) (first published 1943), 200.

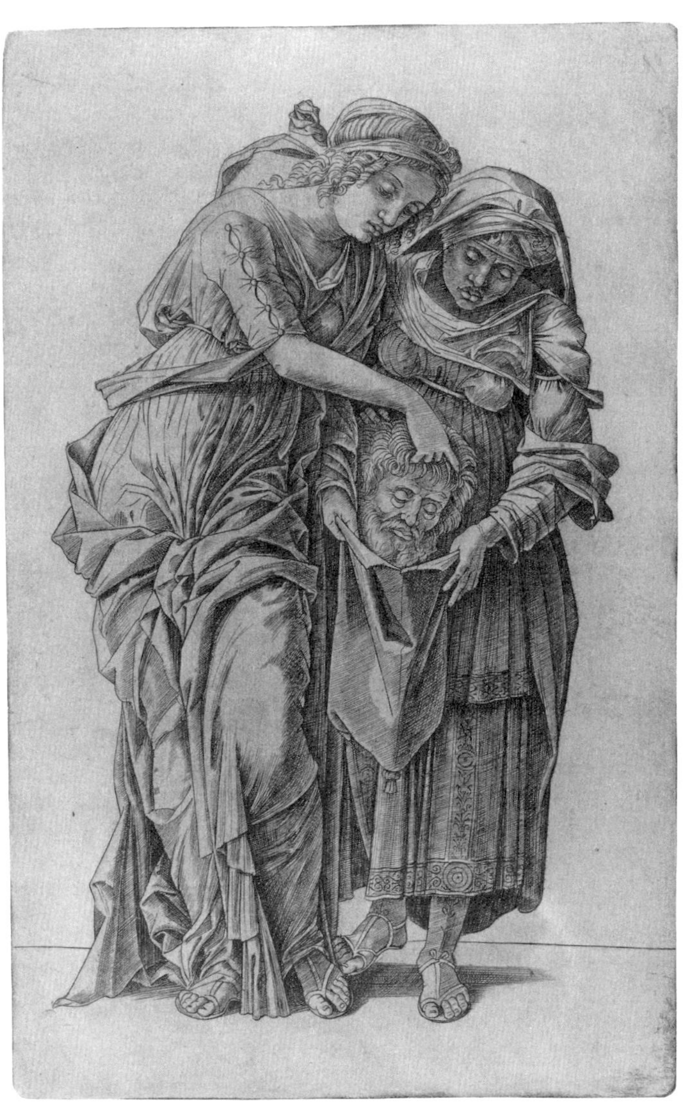

Plate 28a. Girolamo Mocetto, *Judith Putting the Head of Holofernes into a Sack*, ca. 1500.

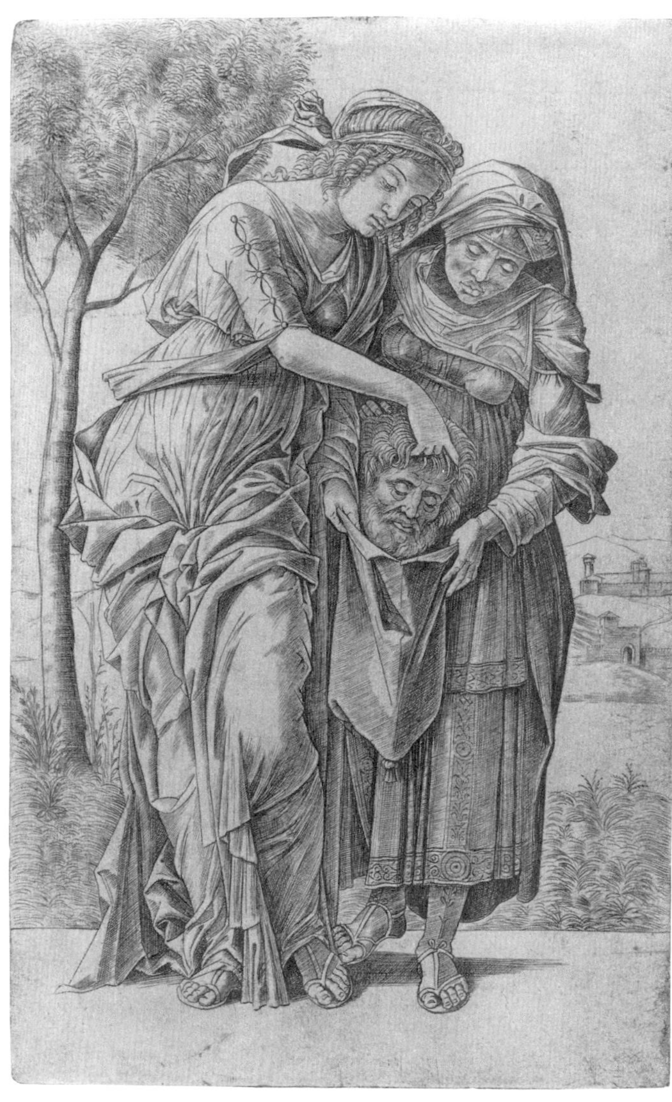

Plate 28b. Girolamo Mocetto, *Judith Putting the Head of Holofernes into a Sack*, ca. 1500.

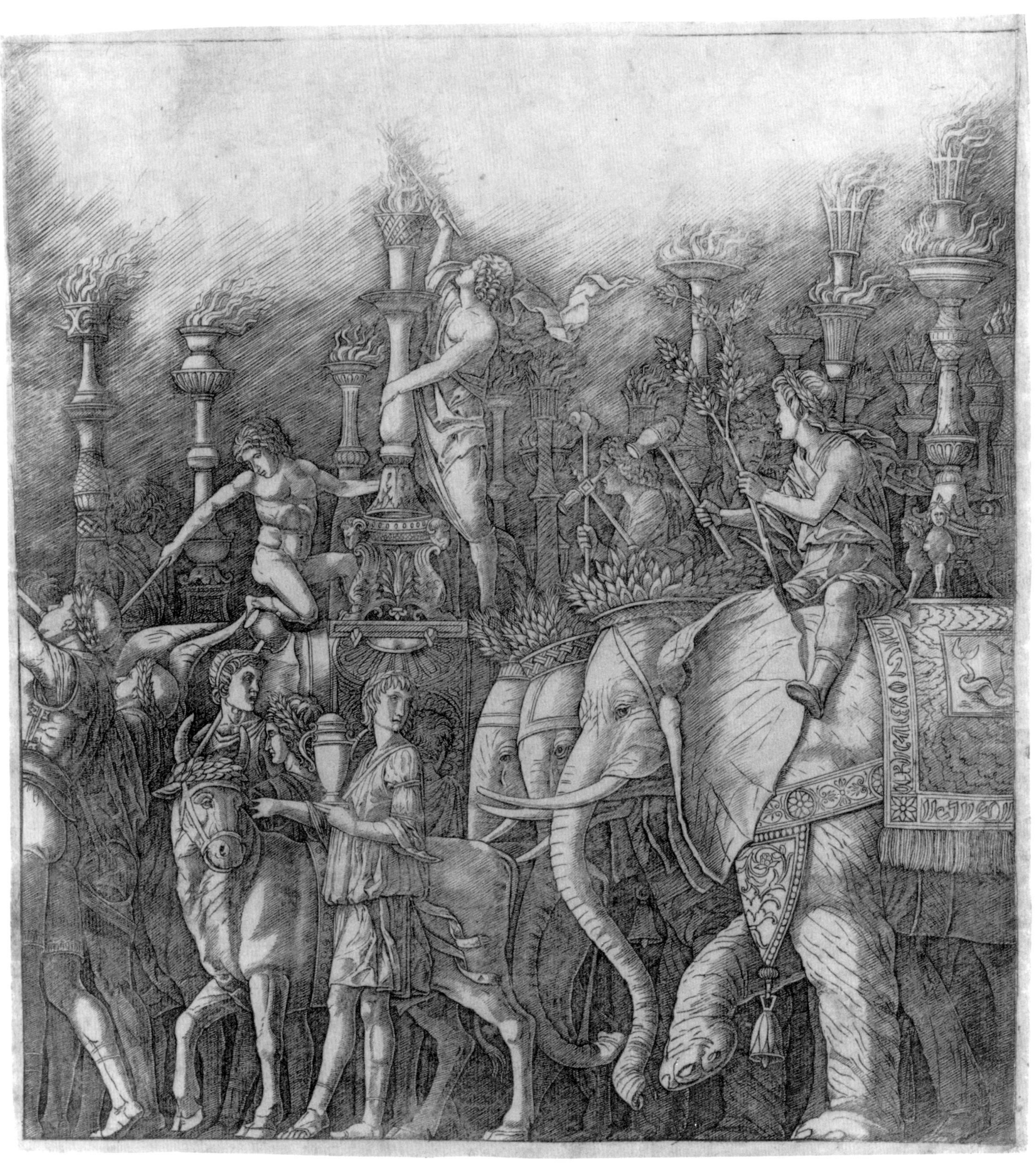

Plate 29. Giovanni Antonio da Brescia, *Triumphs of Caesar: The Elephants*, ca. 1500.

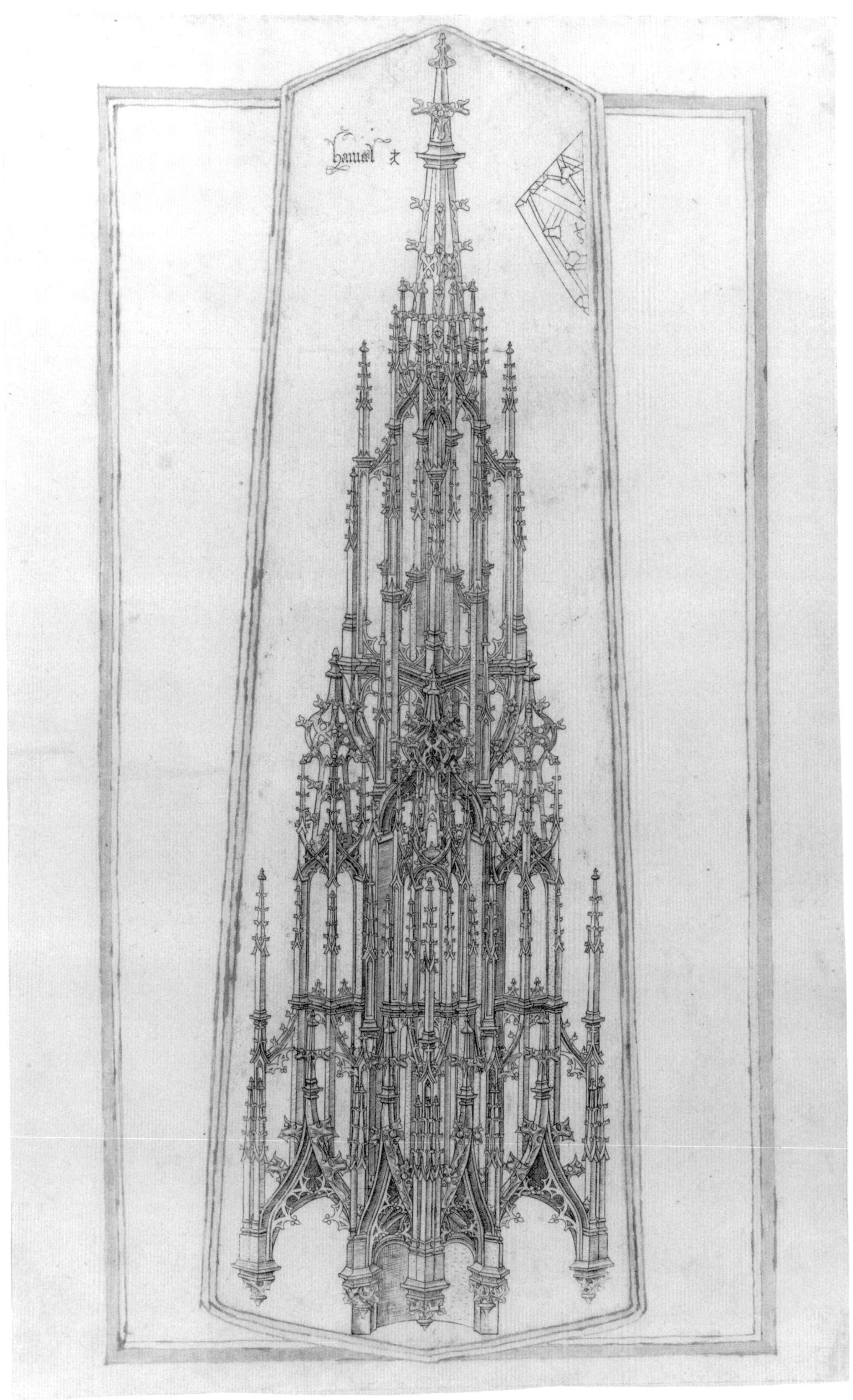

Plate 30. Alart du Hameel, *Gothic Baldacchin*.

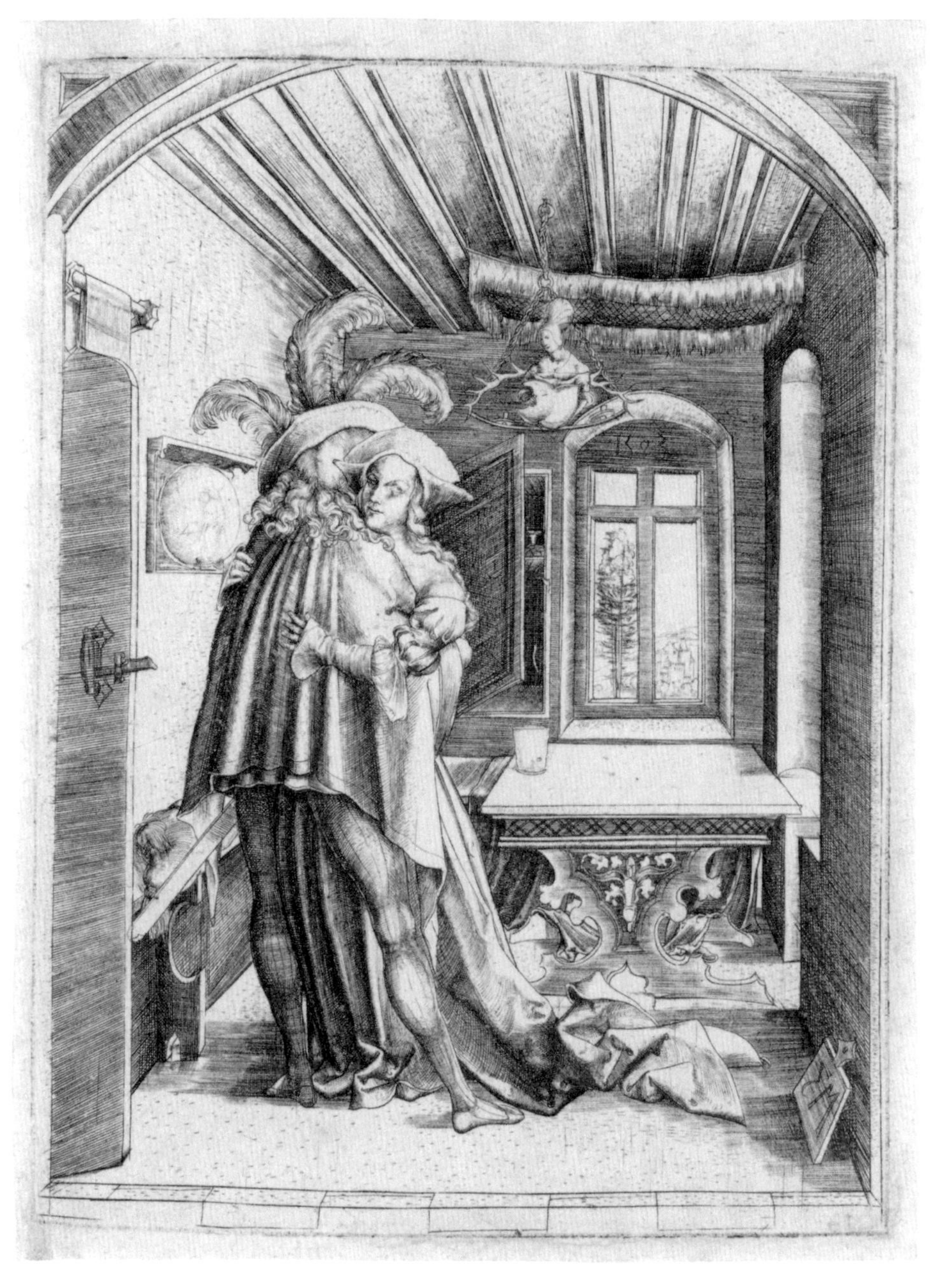

Plate 31. Master M Z (Mattaus Zaisinger?), *The Embrace*, 1503.

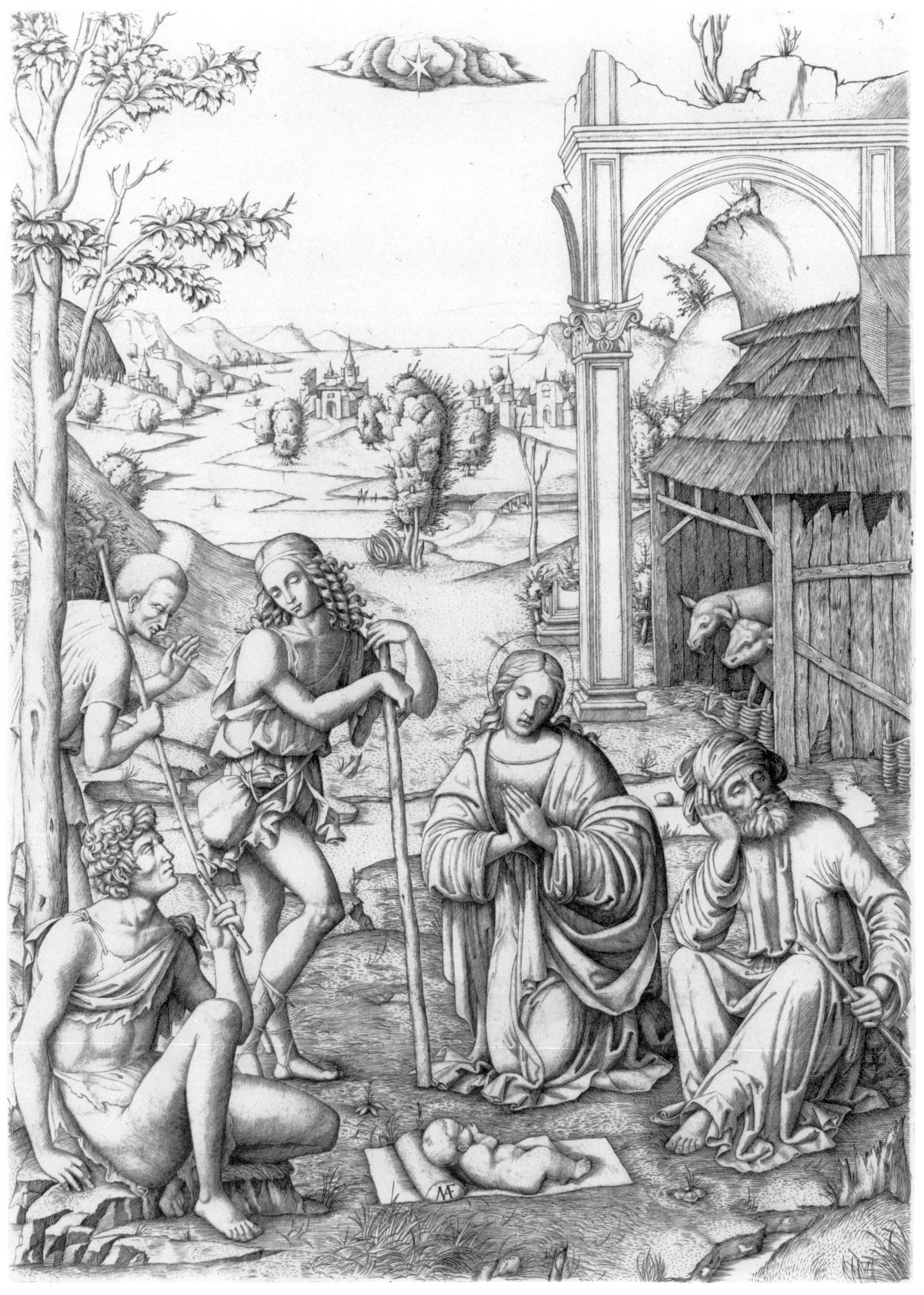

Plate 32. Marcantonio Raimondi, *The Nativity*, ca. 1503-04.

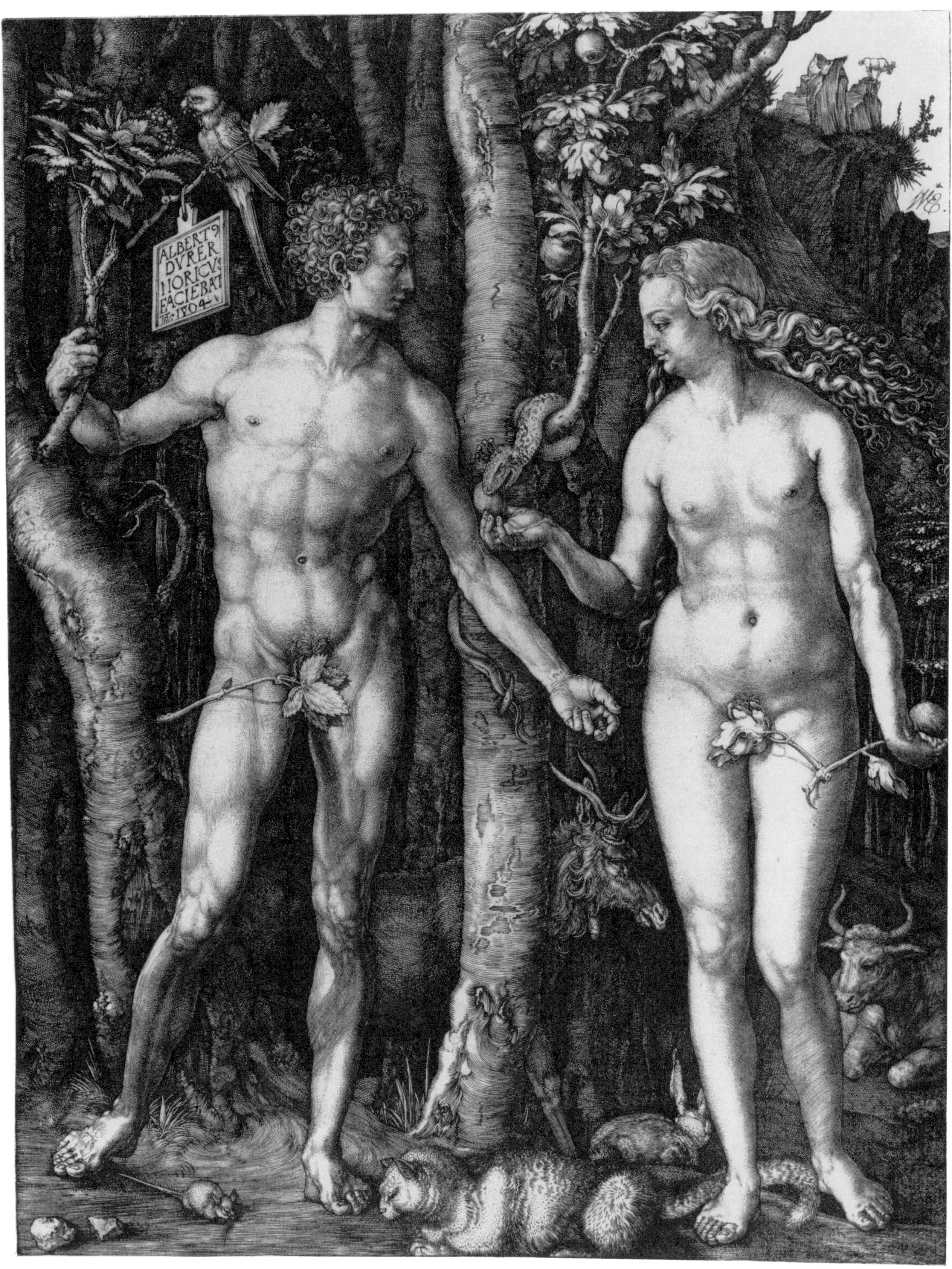

Plate 33. Albrecht Dürer, *Adam and Eve*, 1504.

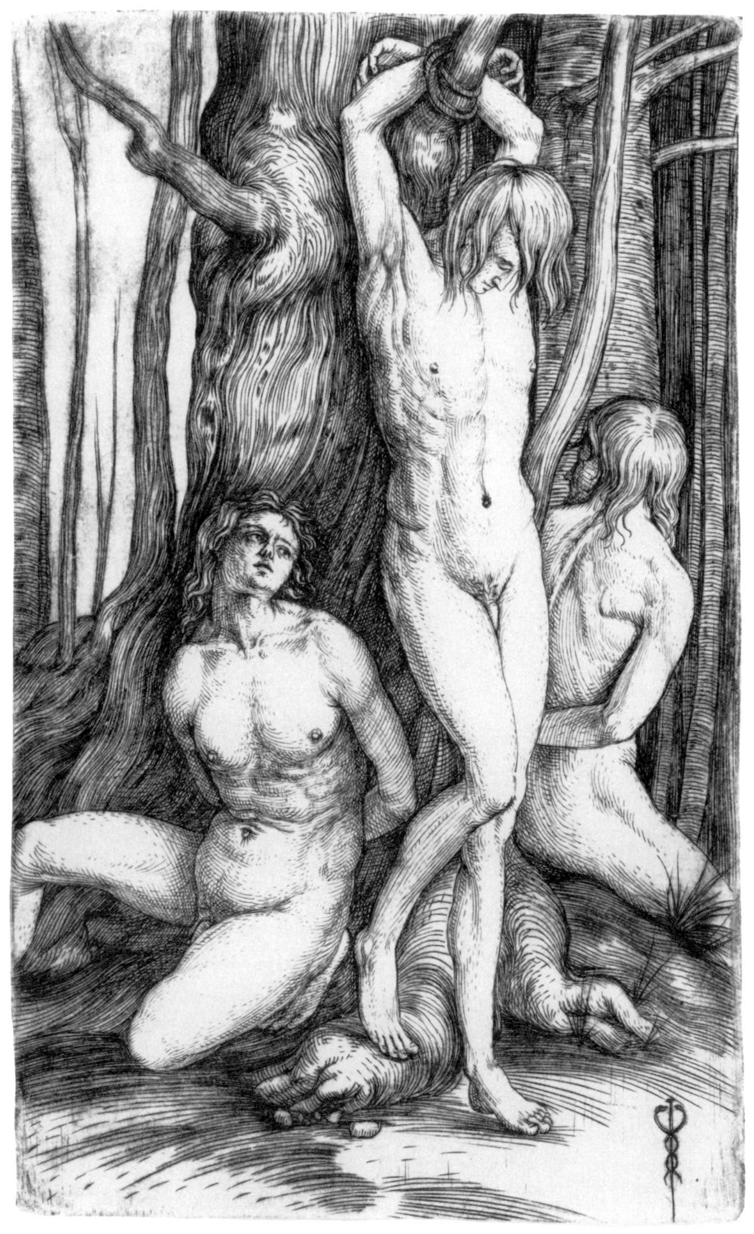

Plate 34. Jacopo de' Barbari, *Three Captives*, ca. 1505.

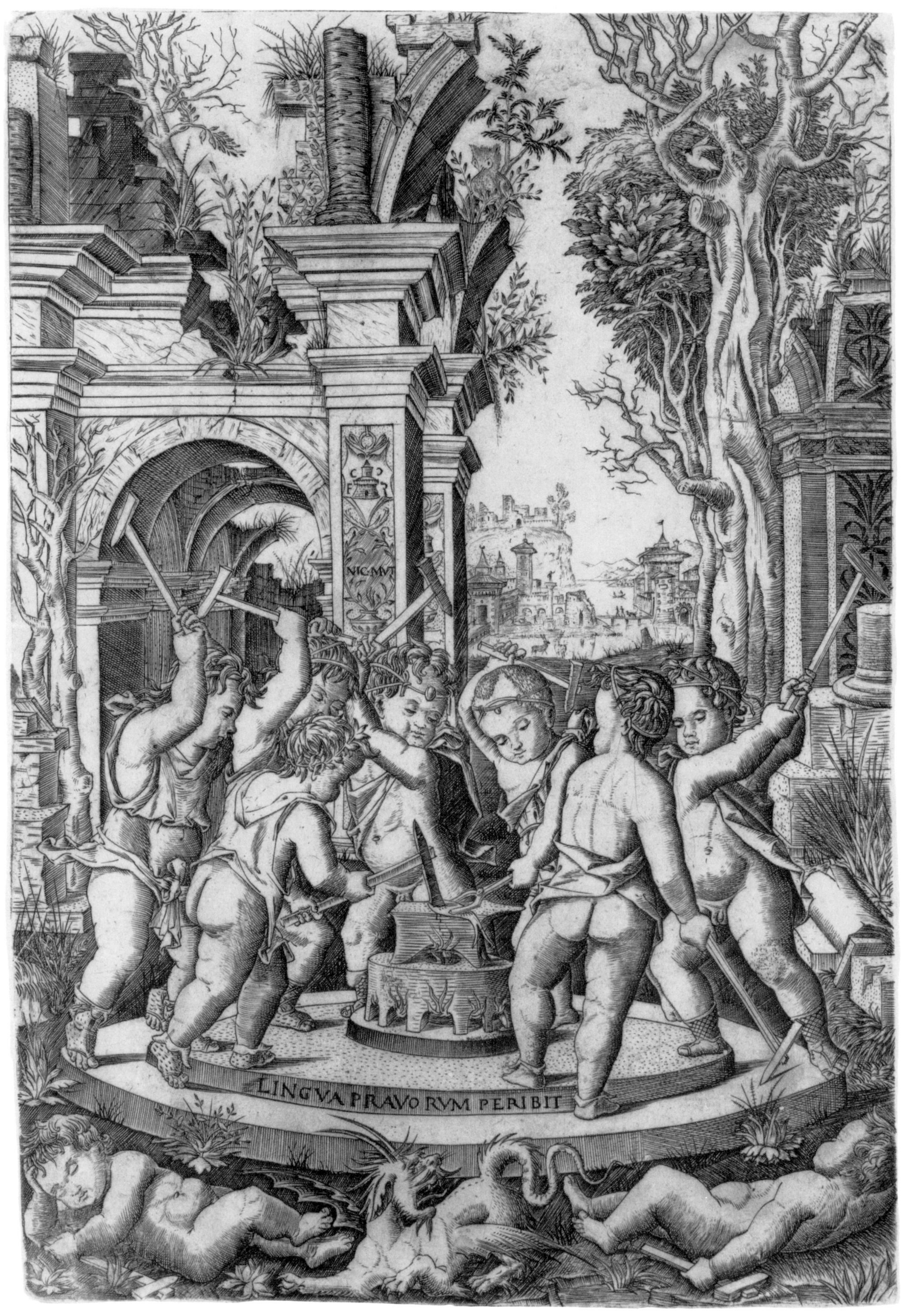

Plate 35. Nicoletto da Modena, *The Fate of an Evil Tongue*, ca. 1507.

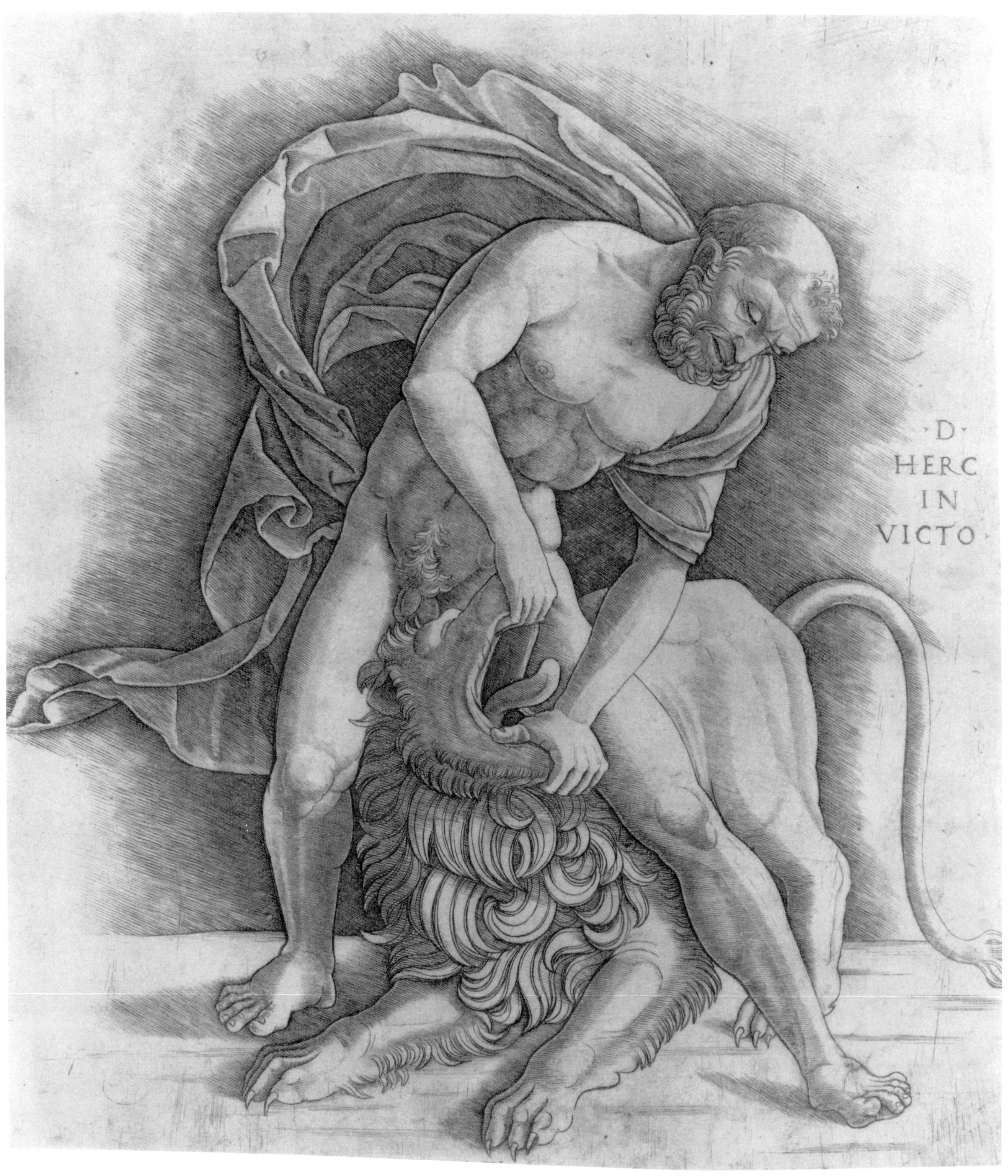

Plate 36. Giovanni Antonio da Brescia, *Hercules and the Nemean Lion*, 1507 or later.

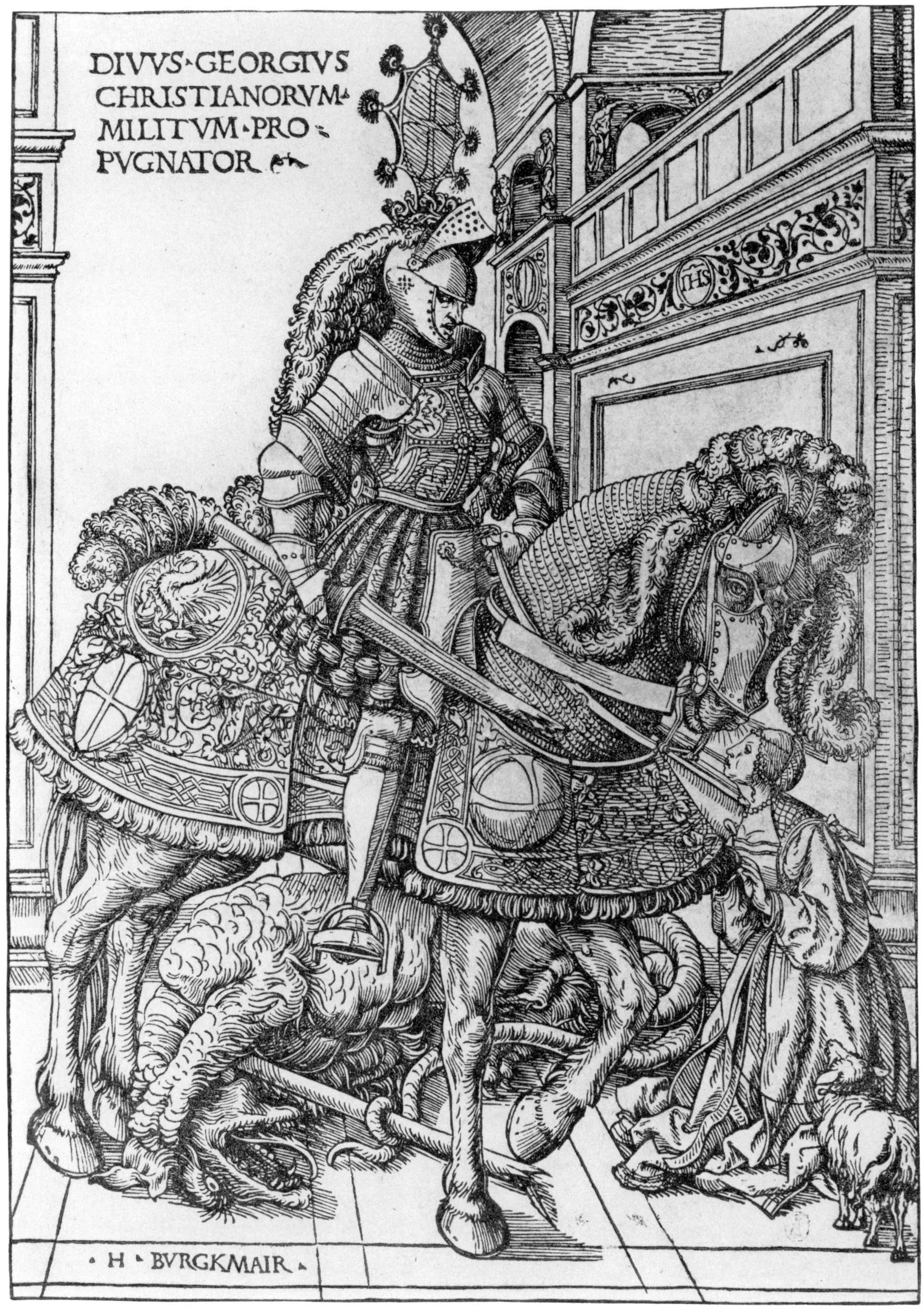

Plate 37. Hans Burgkmair, *St. George*, 1508.

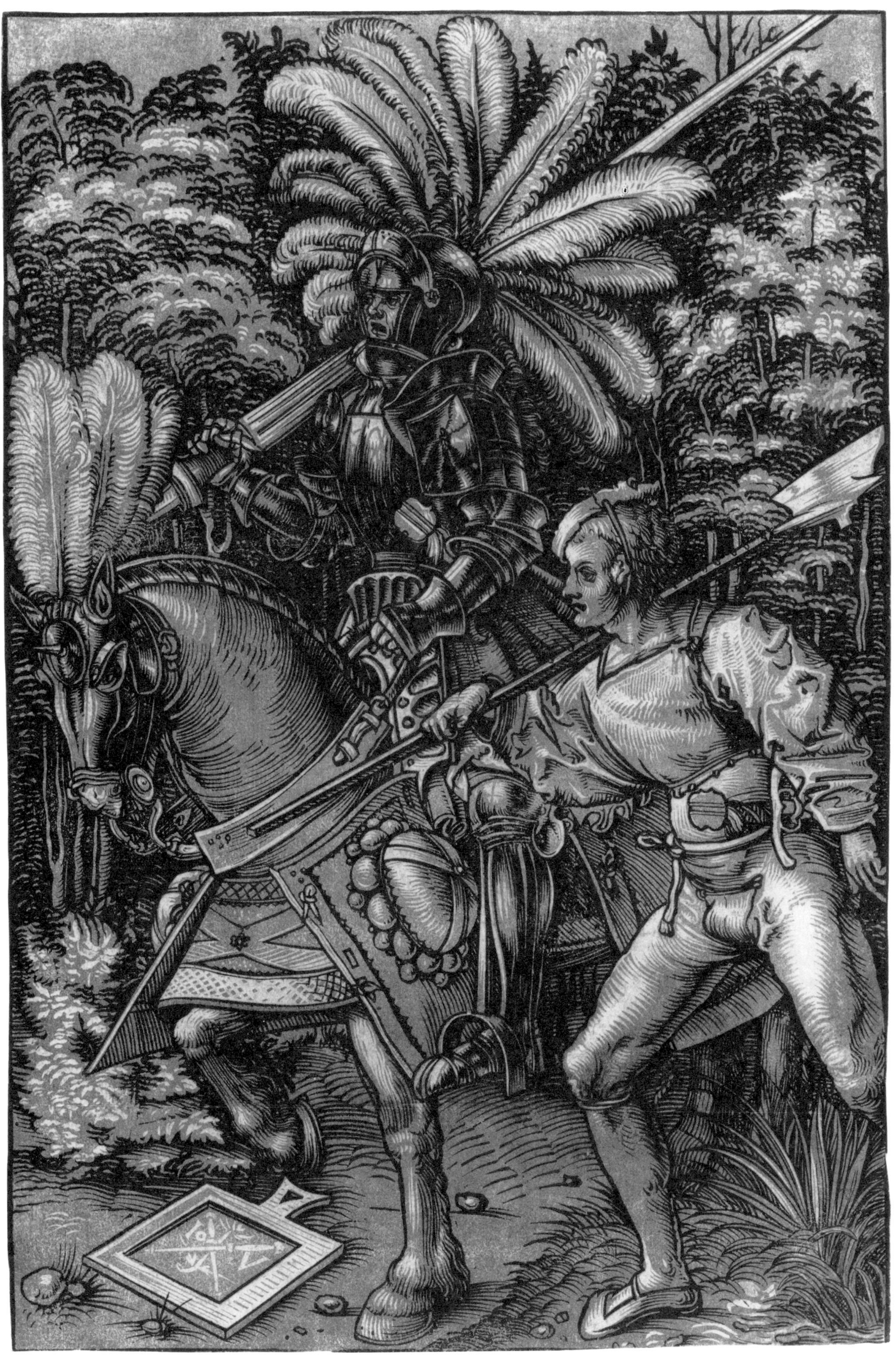

Plate 38. Hans Wechtlin, *Knight and Halberdier, ca. 1512.*

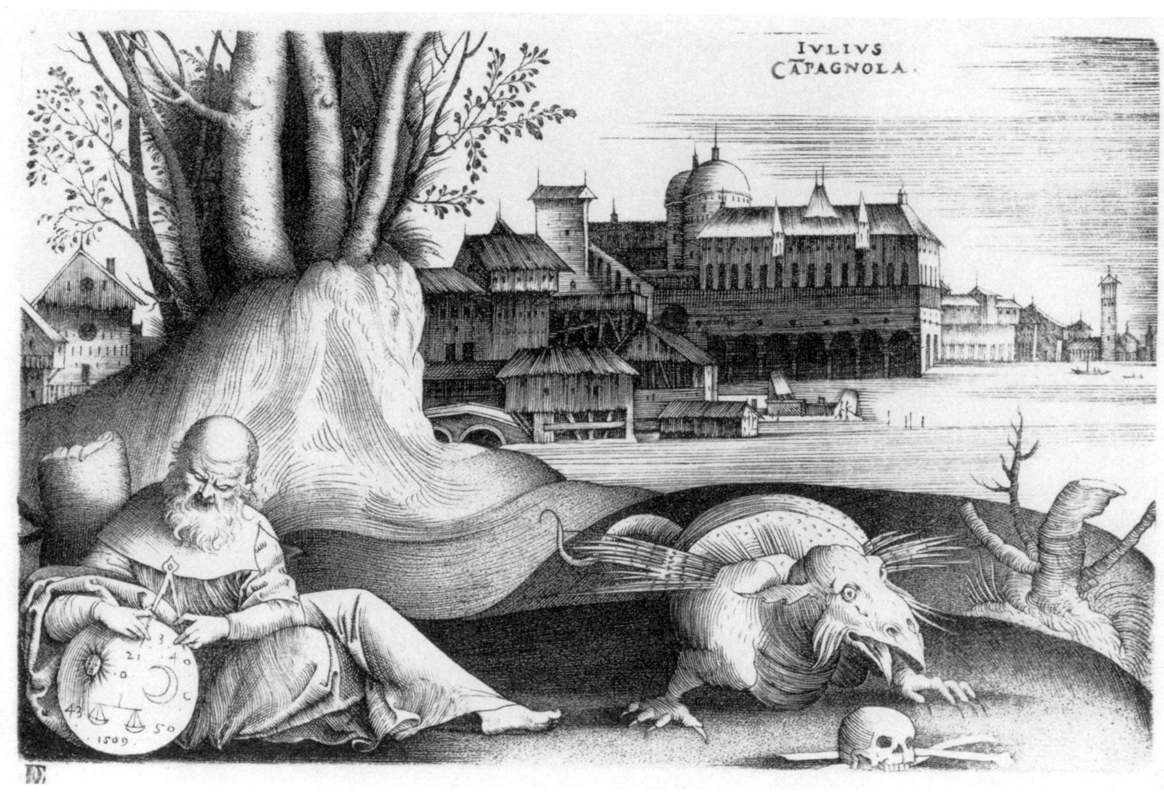

Plate 39. Giulio Campagnola, *The Astrologer*, 1509.

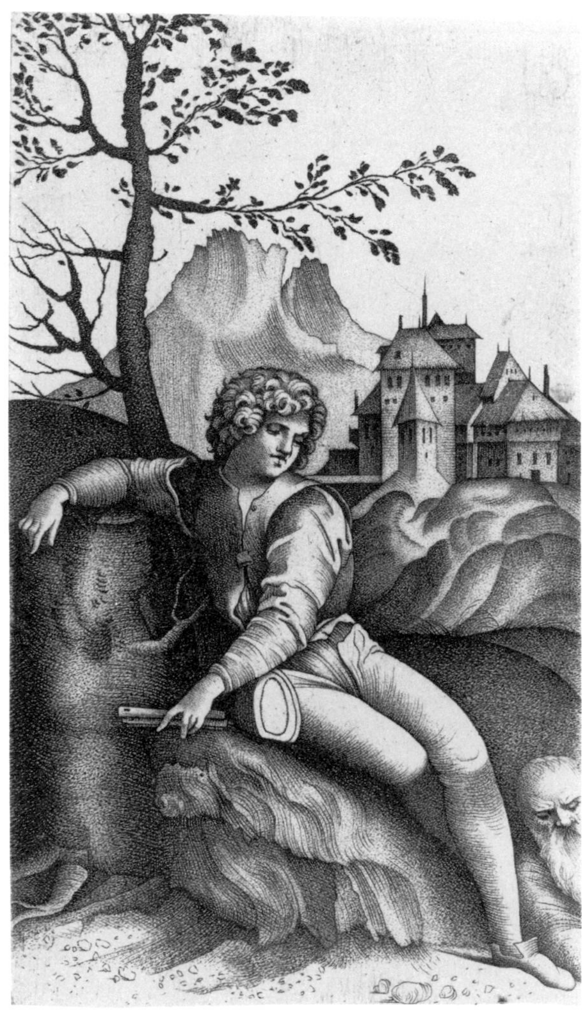

Plate 40. Giulio Campagnola, *The Young Shepherd*, ca. 1510.

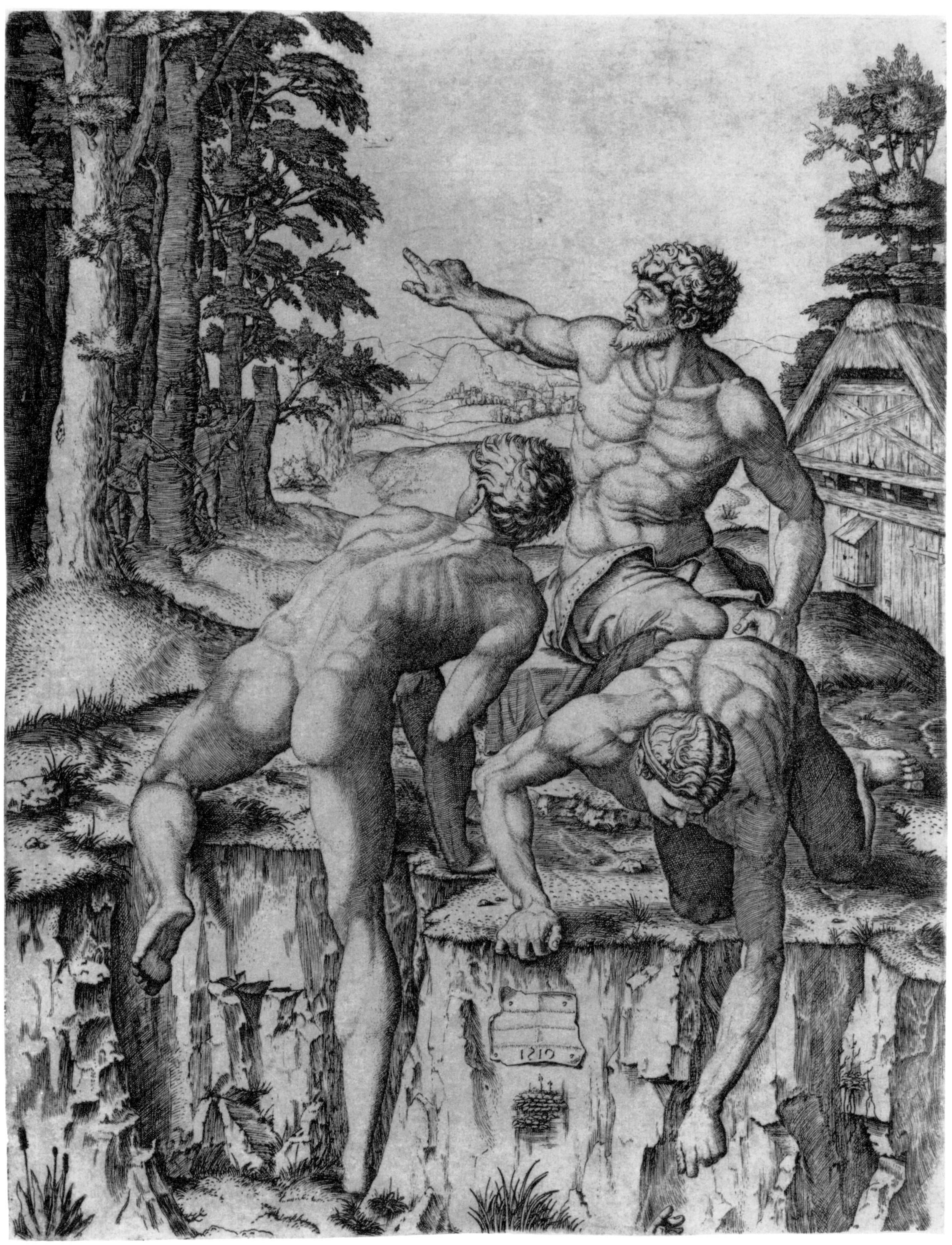

Plate 41. Marcantonio Raimondi, *The Climbers*, 1510.

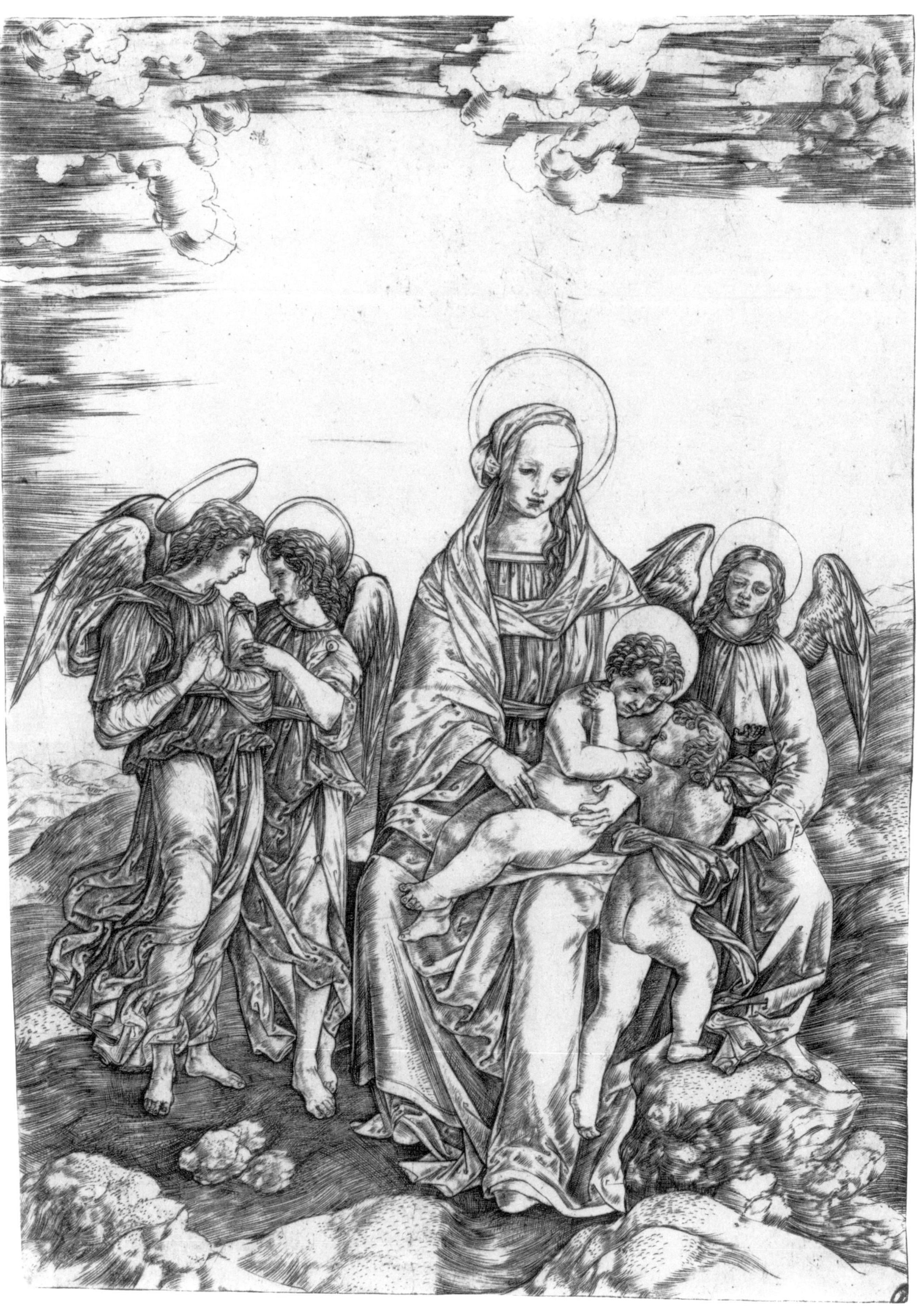

Plate 42. Cristofano Robetta, *The Virgin and Child with St. John and Three Angels*, ca. 1500-20.

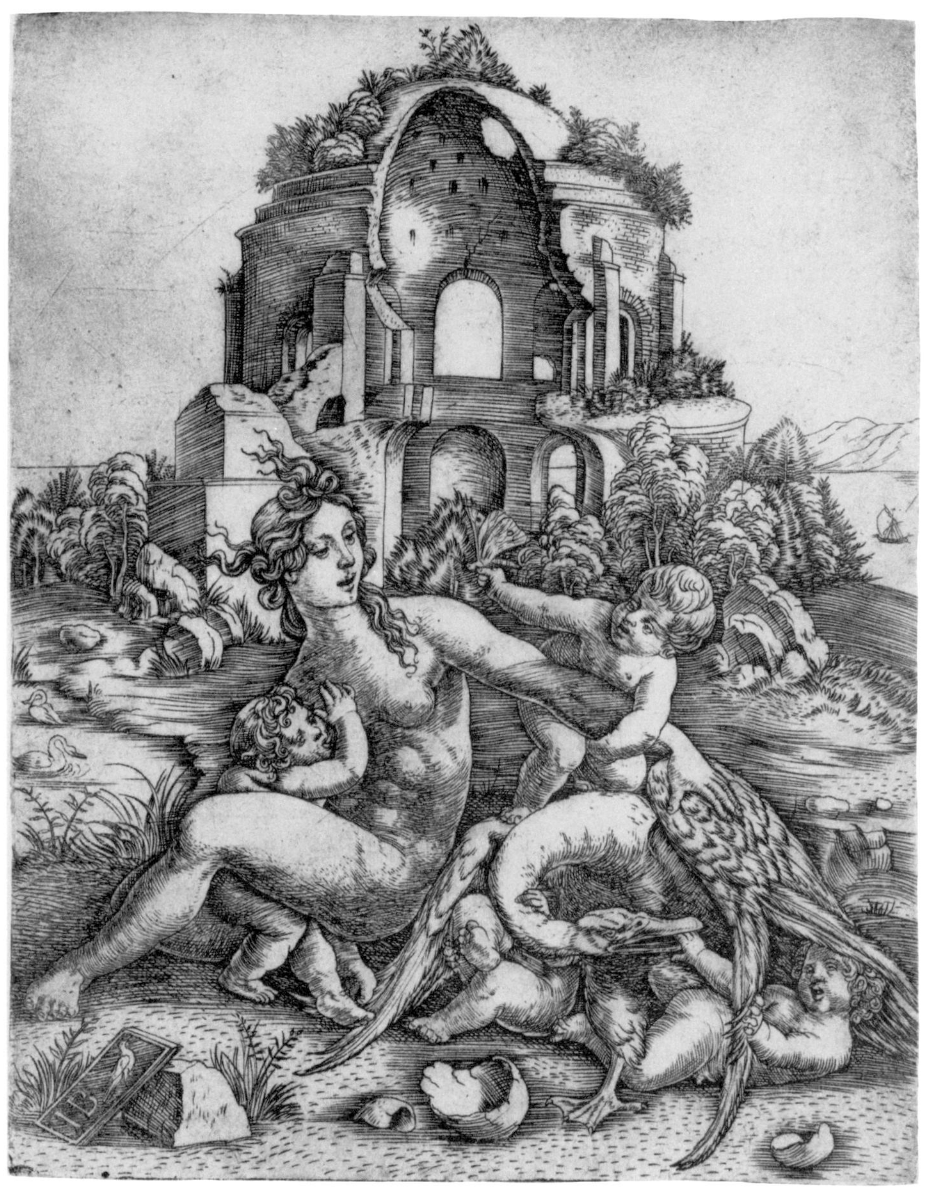

Plate 43. Master I. B. with the Bird (Giovanni Battista Palumba?), *Leda and Her Children*, ca. 1510.

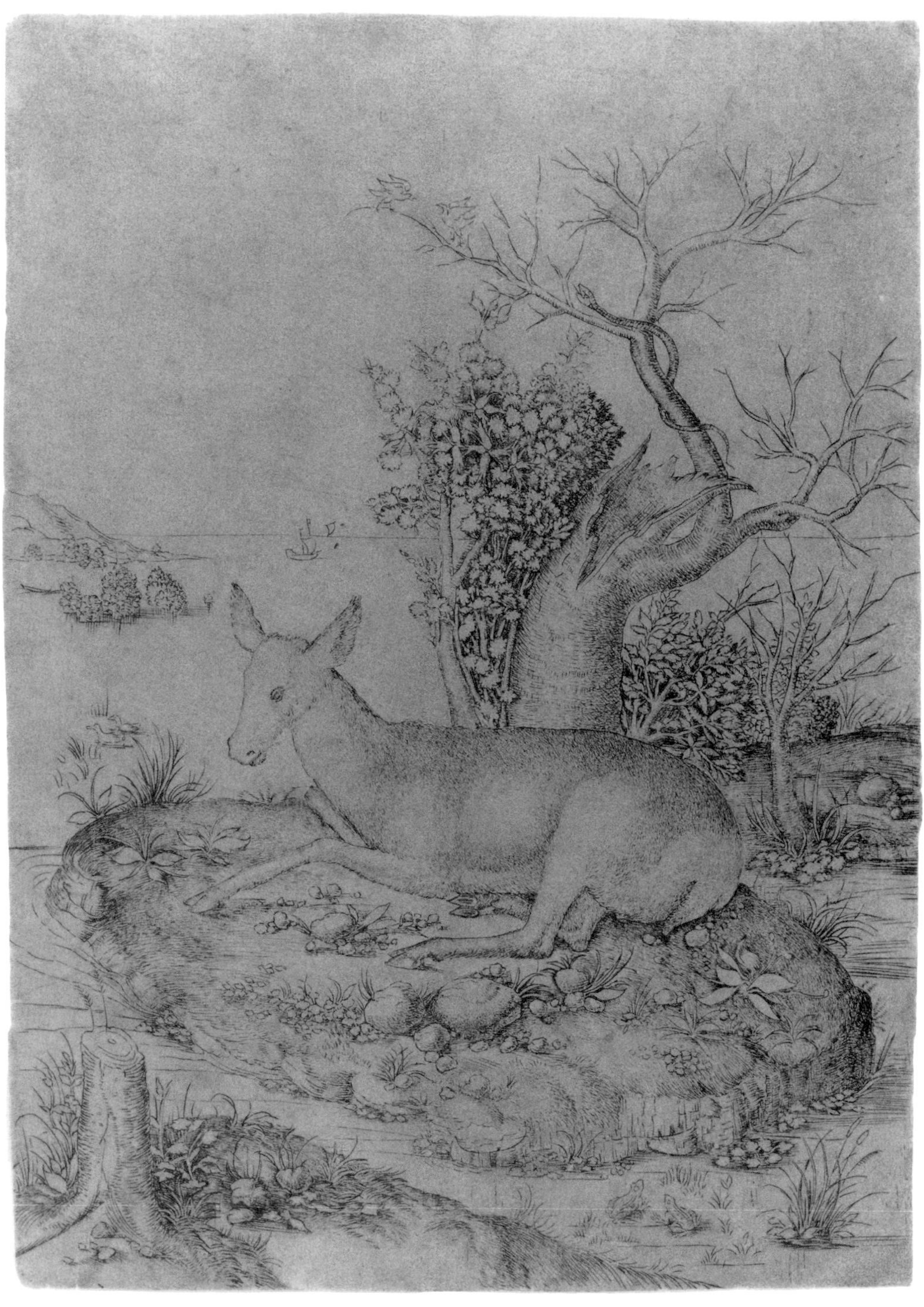

Plate 44. Master of the Beheading of St. John the Baptist, *Doe Resting*, ca. 1510-20?

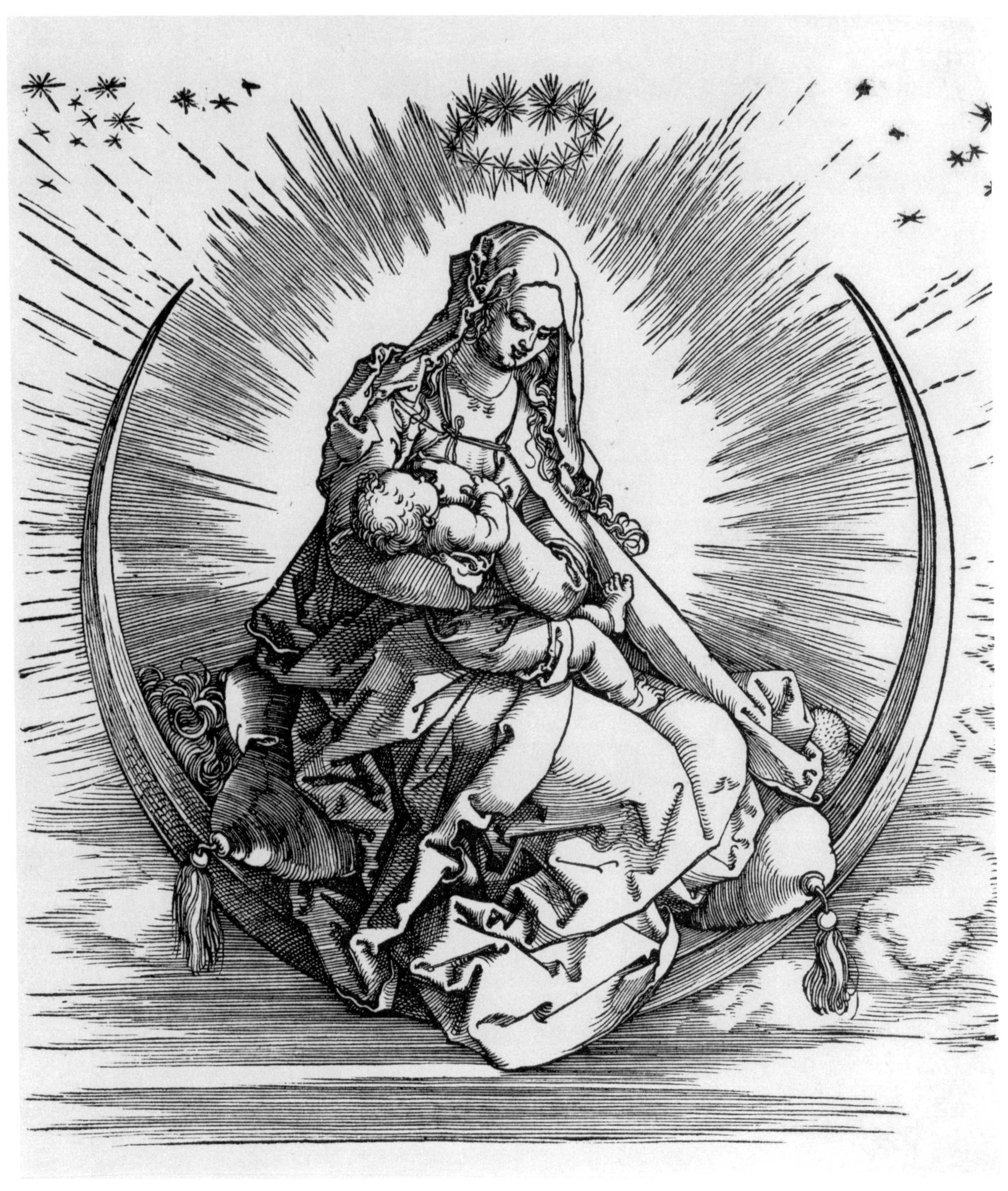

Plate 45. Albrecht Dürer, *Madonna on the Crescent*, ca. 1510-11.

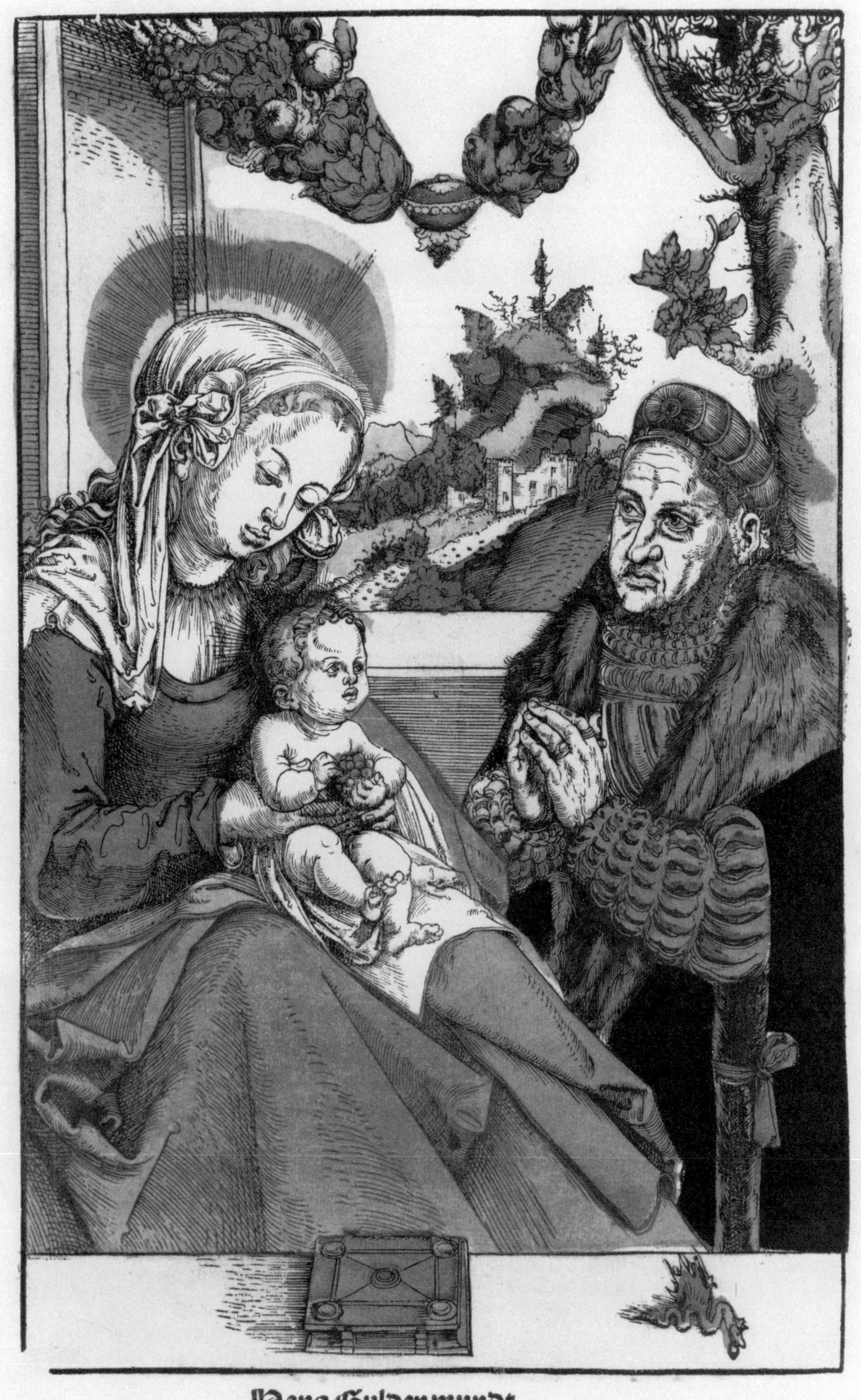

Plate 46. Lucas Cranach the Elder, *Friedrich the Wise in Prayer before Madonna and Child*, ca. 1512-15.

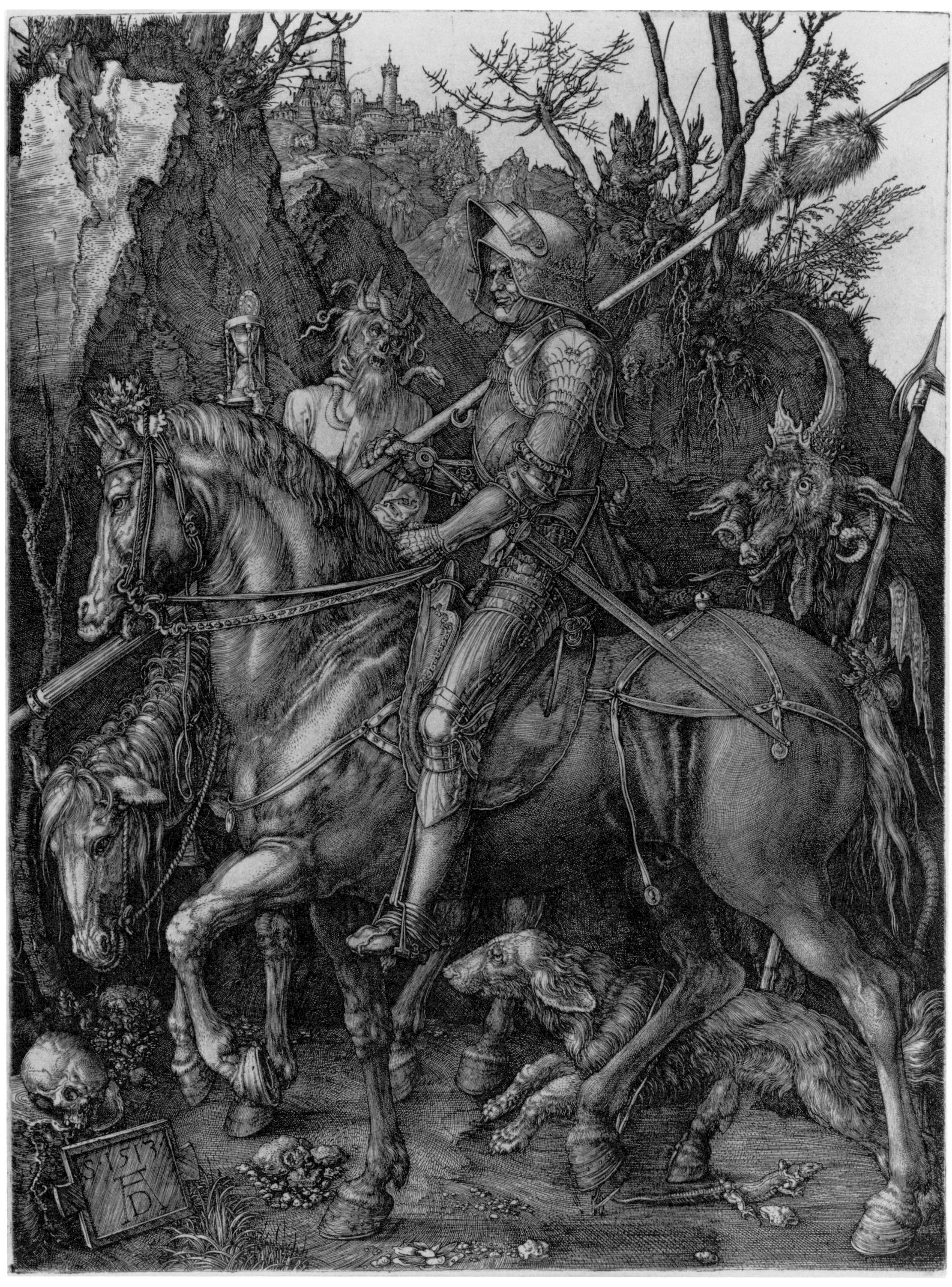

Plate 47. Albrecht Dürer, *Knight, Death and the Devil*, 1513.

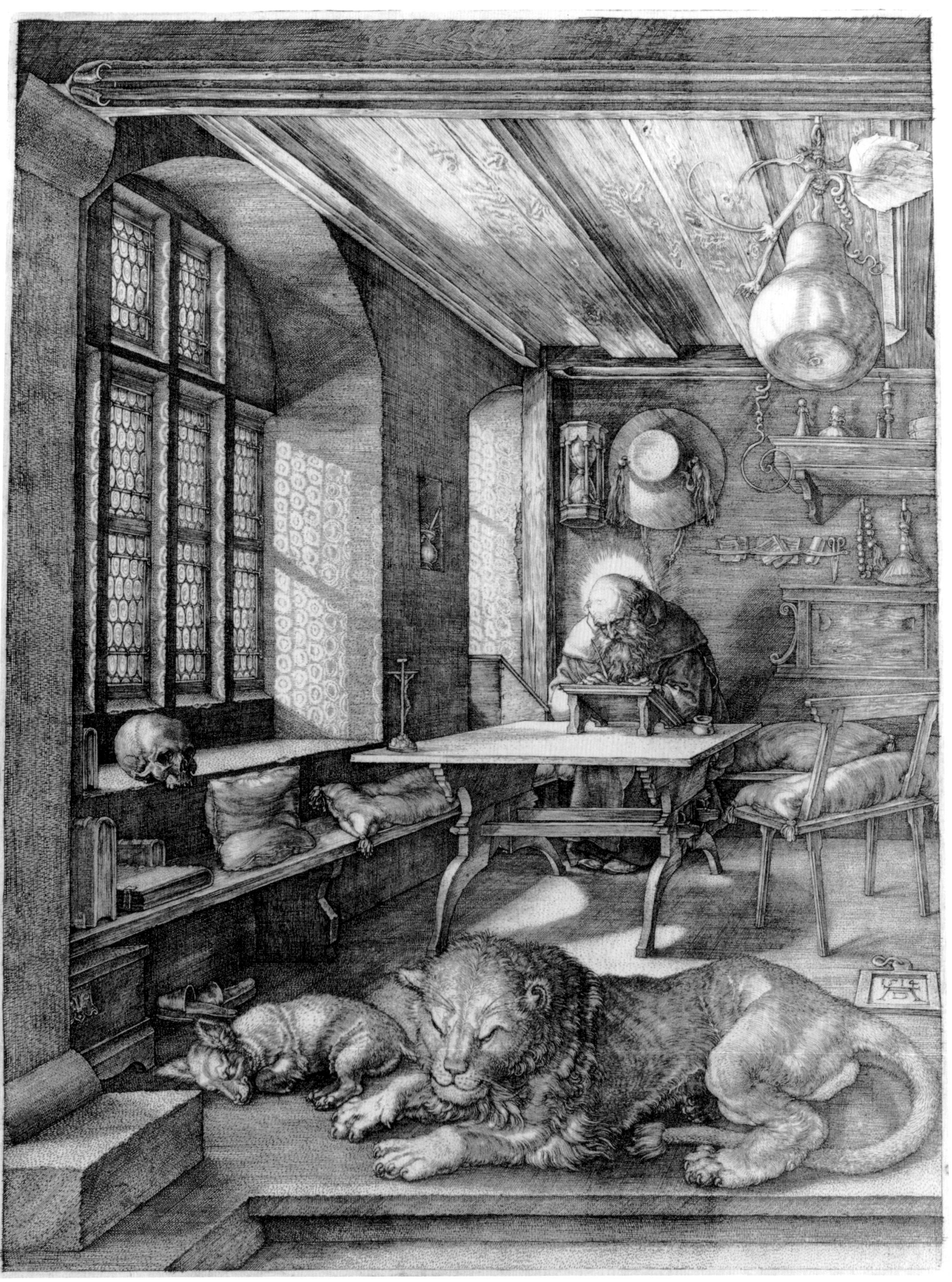

Plate 48. Albrecht Dürer, *St. Jerome in His Study*, 1514.

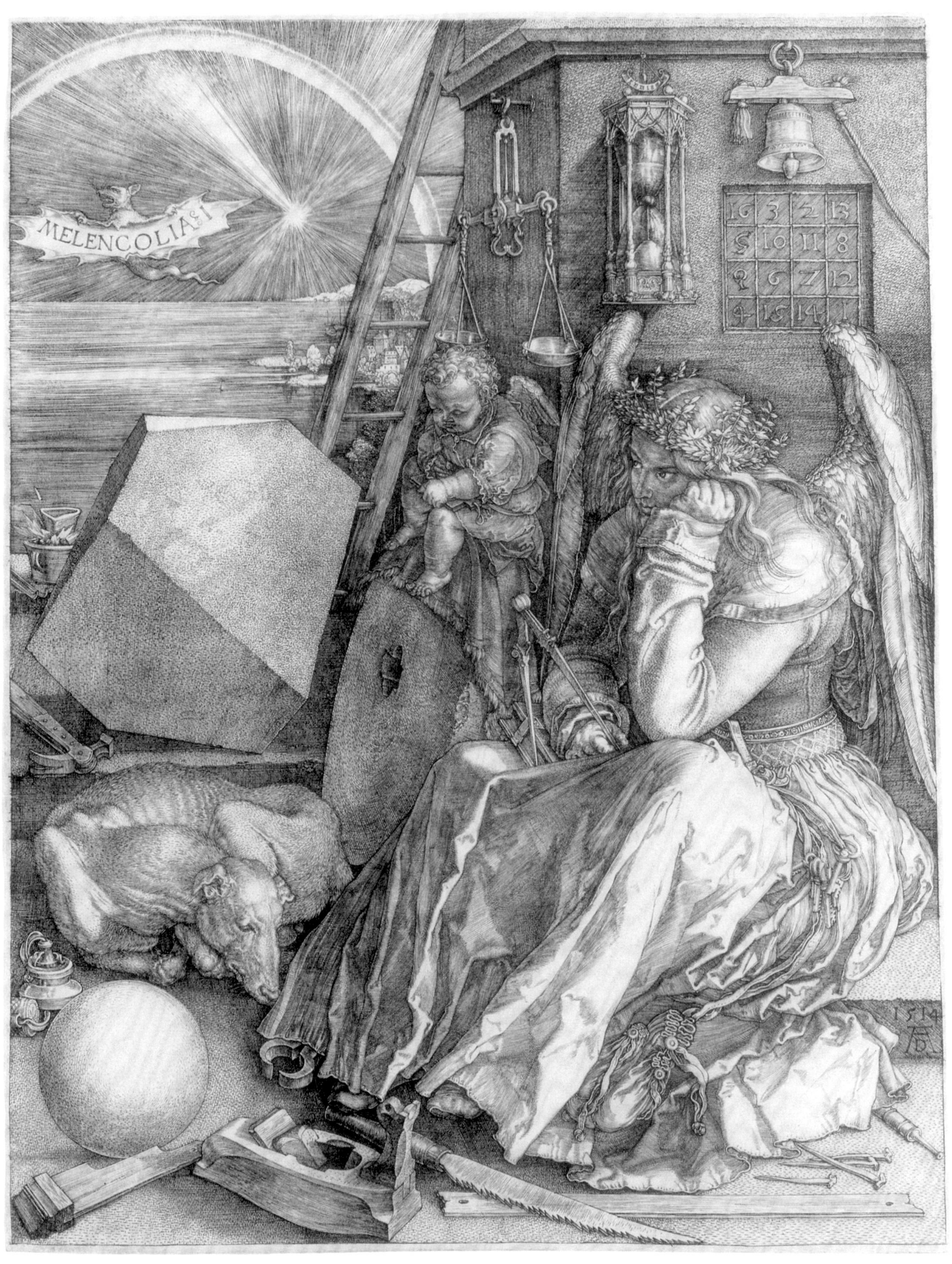

Plate 49. Albrecht Dürer, *Melencolia I*, 1514.

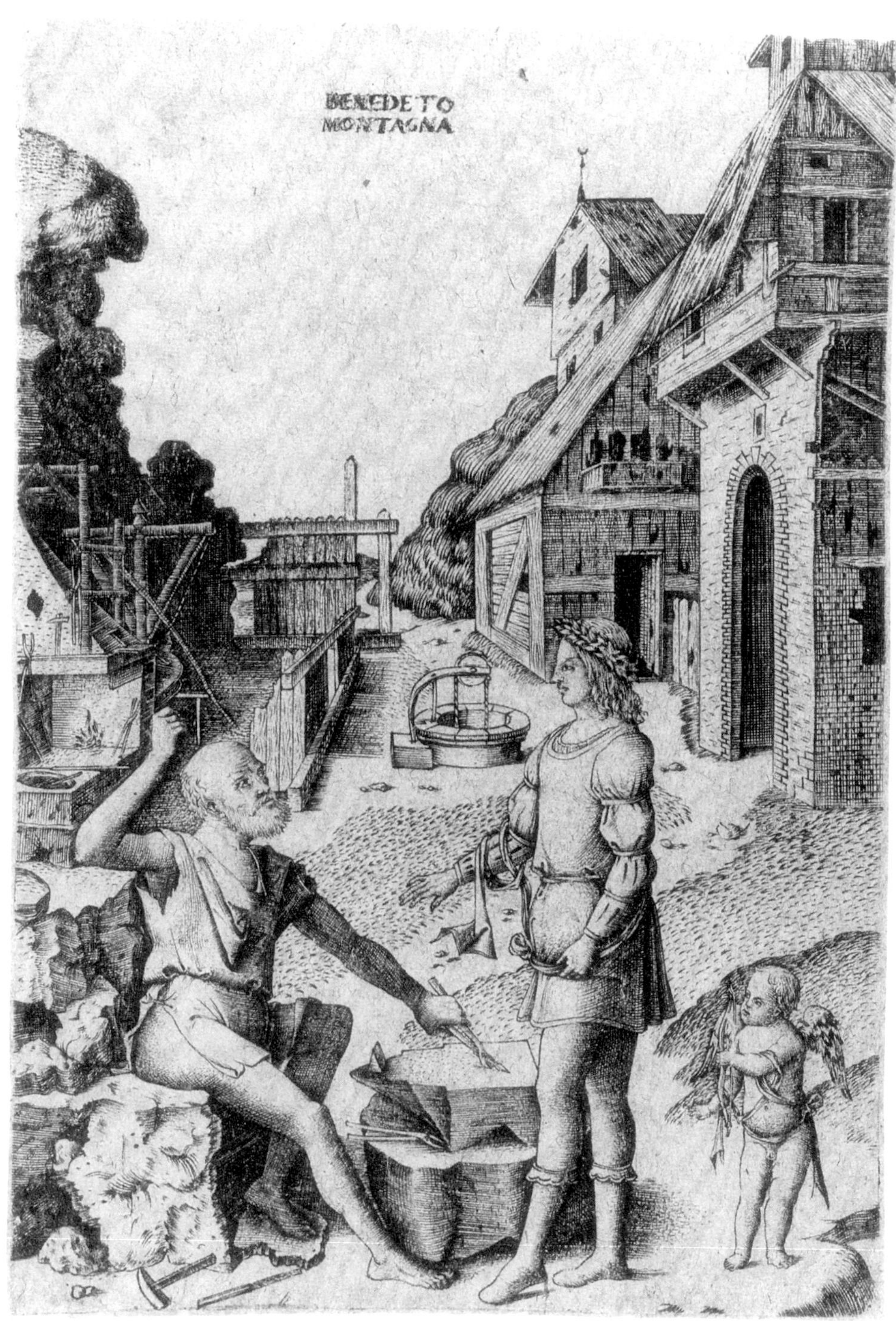

Plate 50. Benedetto Montagna, *Vulcan, Apollo, and Cupid*, ca. 1515-20.

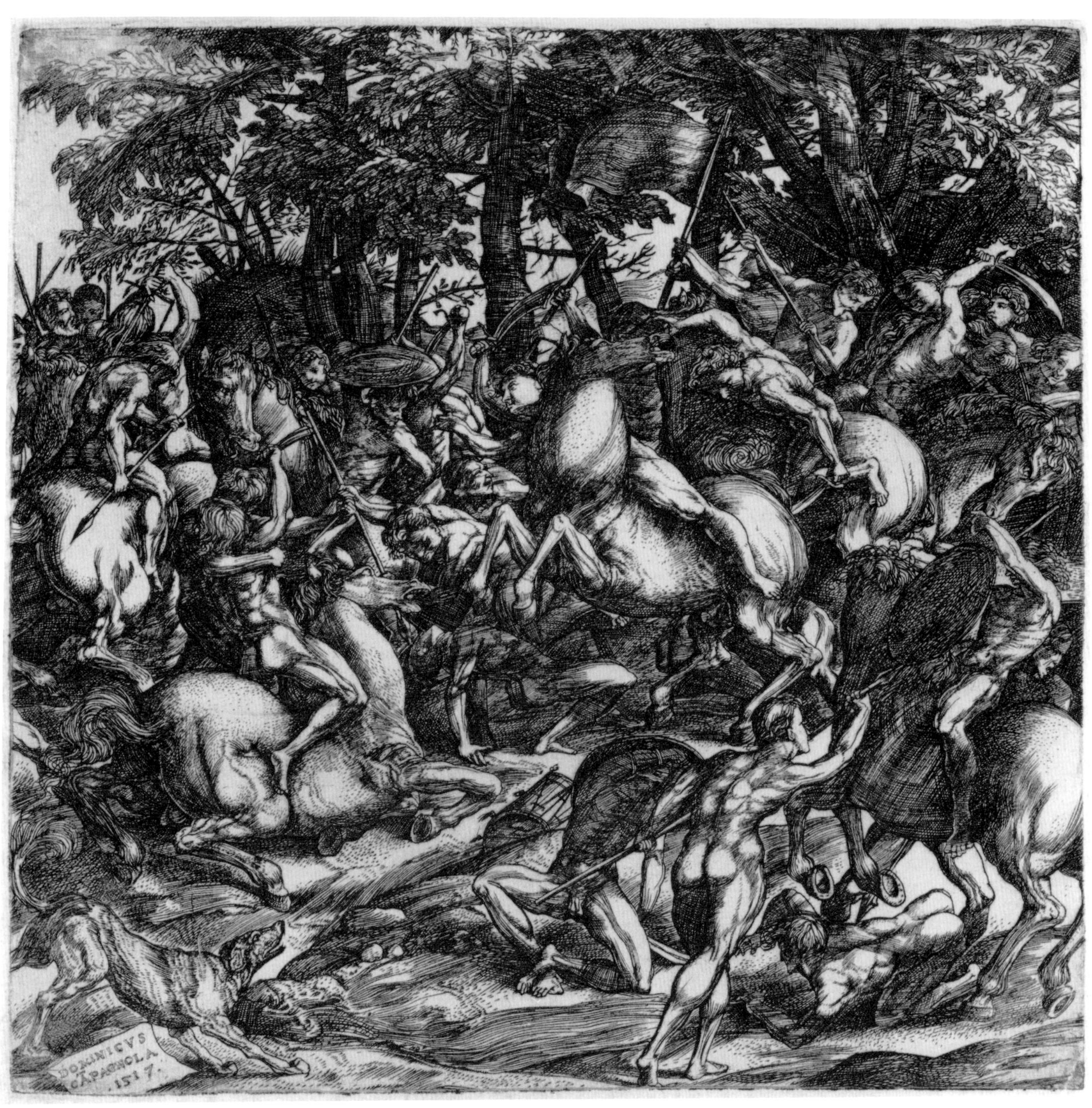

Plate 51. Domenico Campagnola, *Battle of Naked Men*, 1517.

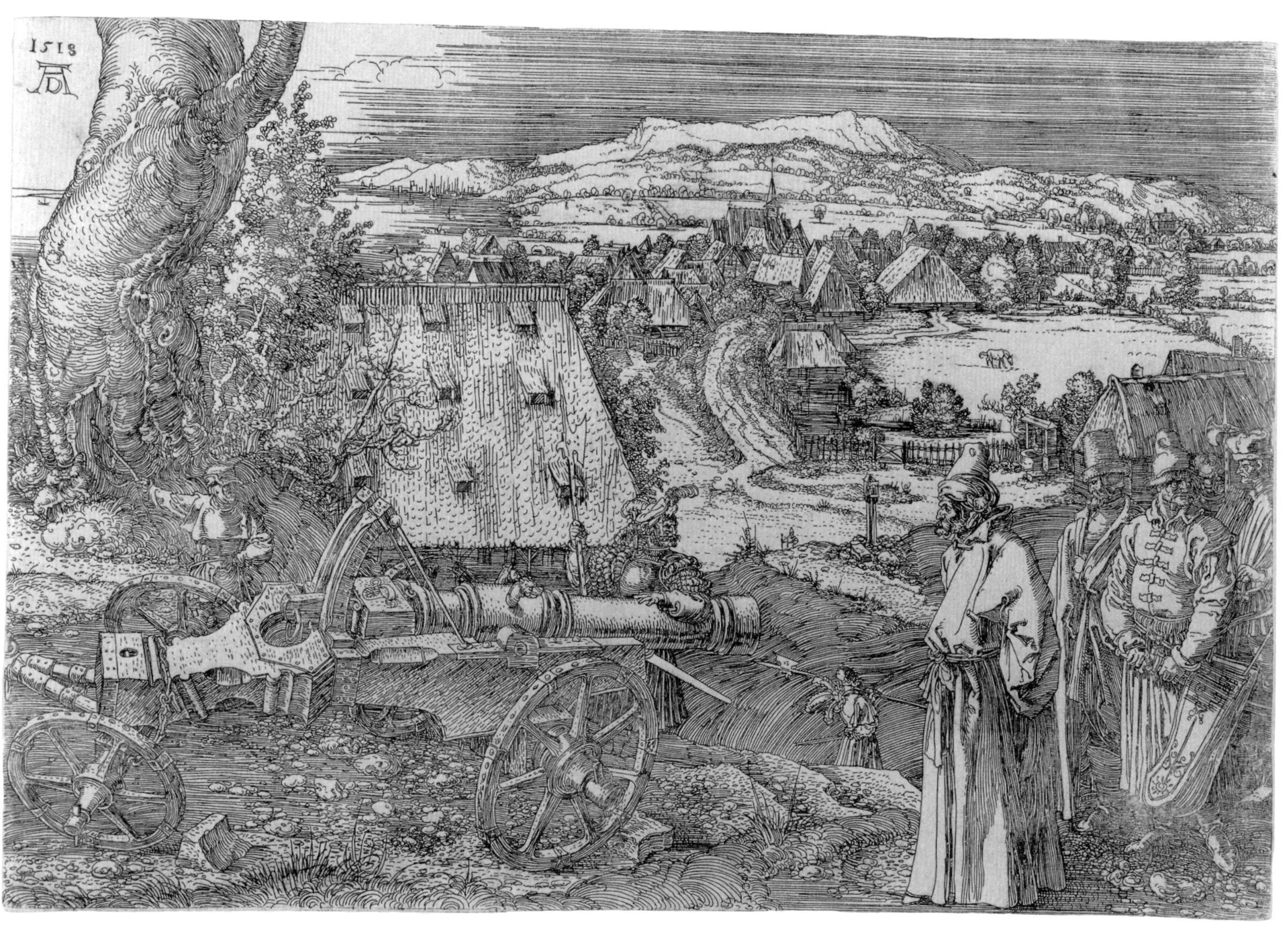

Plate 52. Albrecht Dürer, *The Landscape with the Cannon*, 1518.

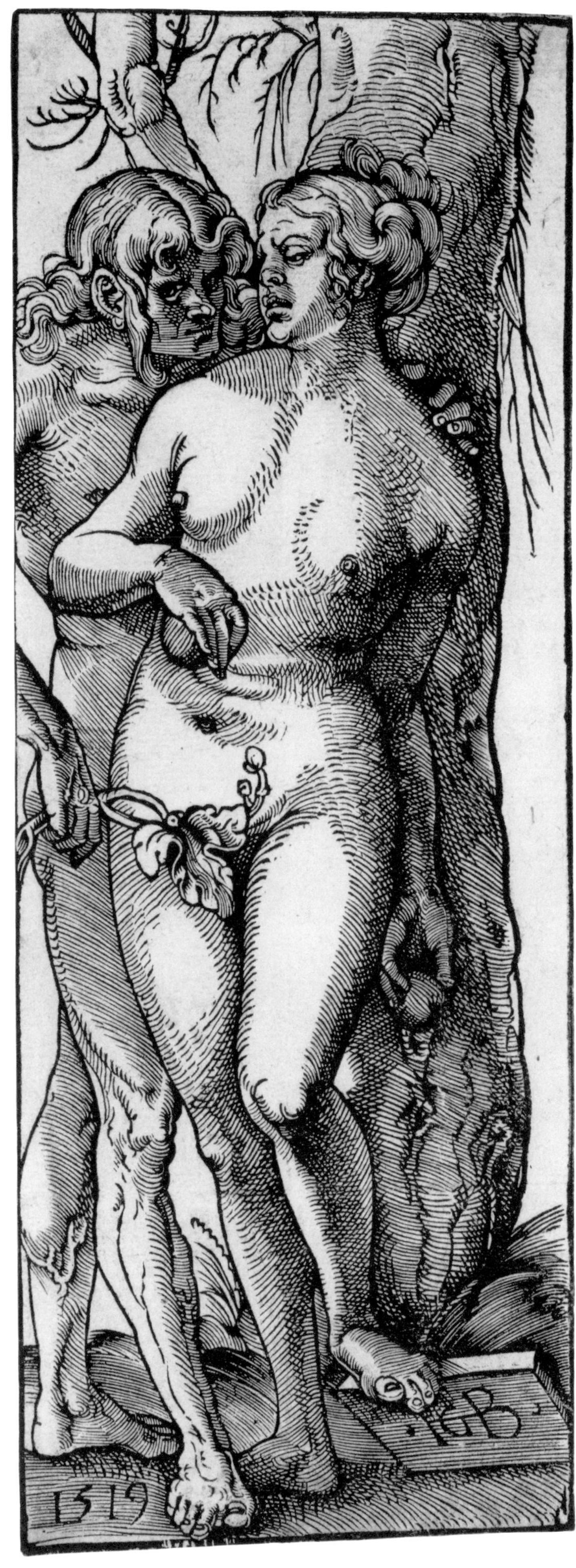

Plate 53. Hans Baldung, *Adam and Eve*, 1519.

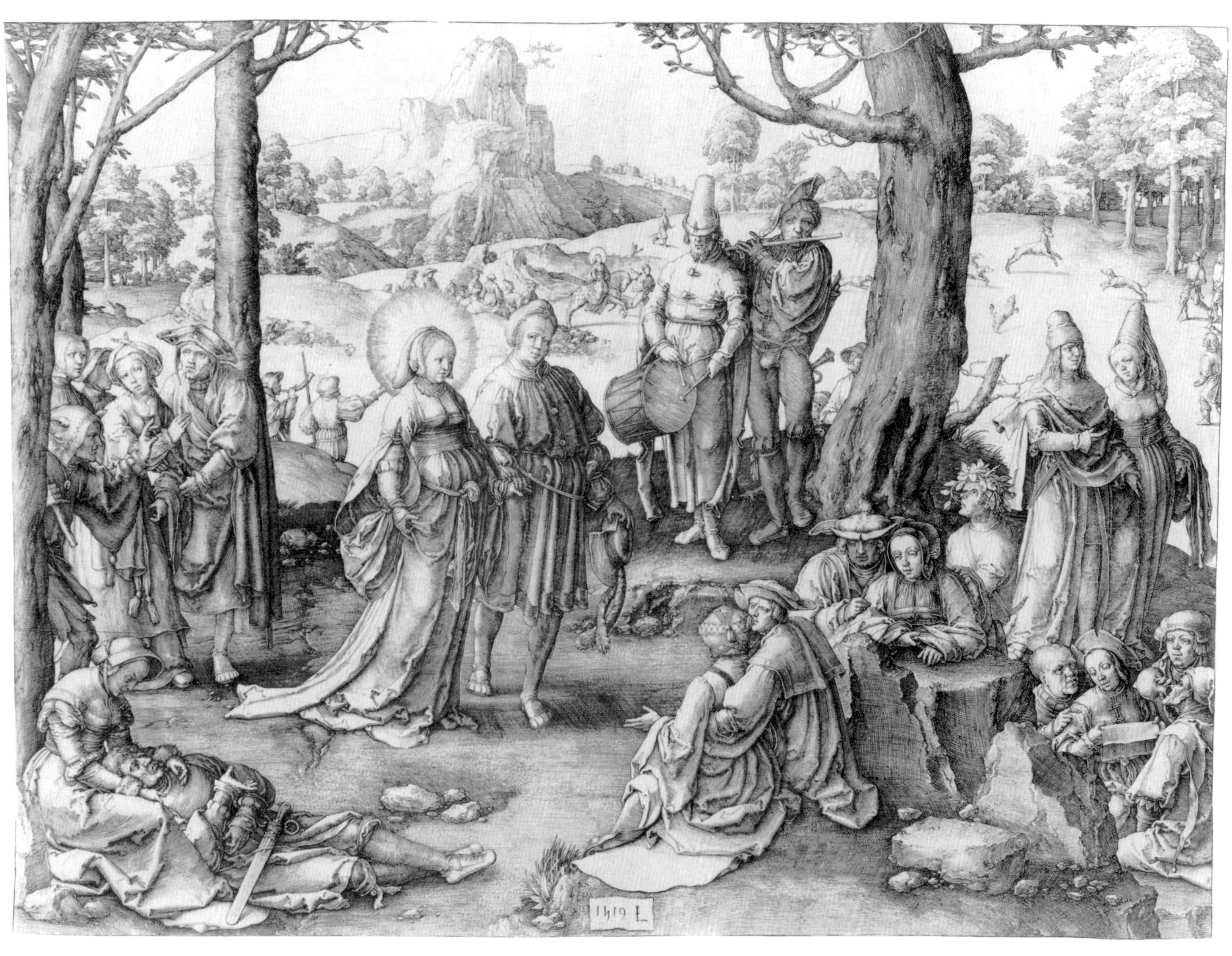

Plate 54. Lucas van Leyden, *The Dance of St. Mary Magdalene*, 1519.

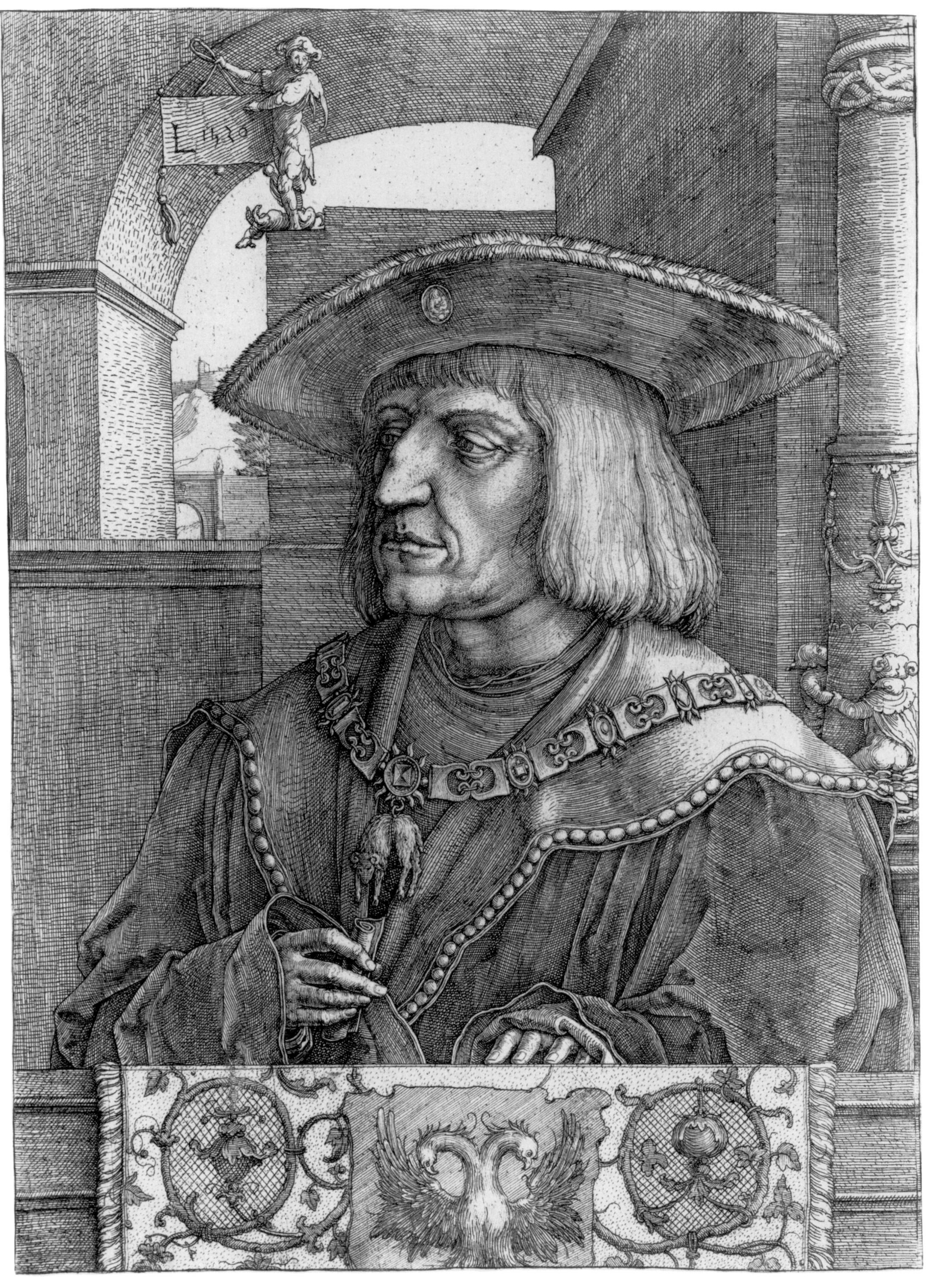

Plate 55. Lucas van Leyden, *Emperor Maximilian I*, 1520.

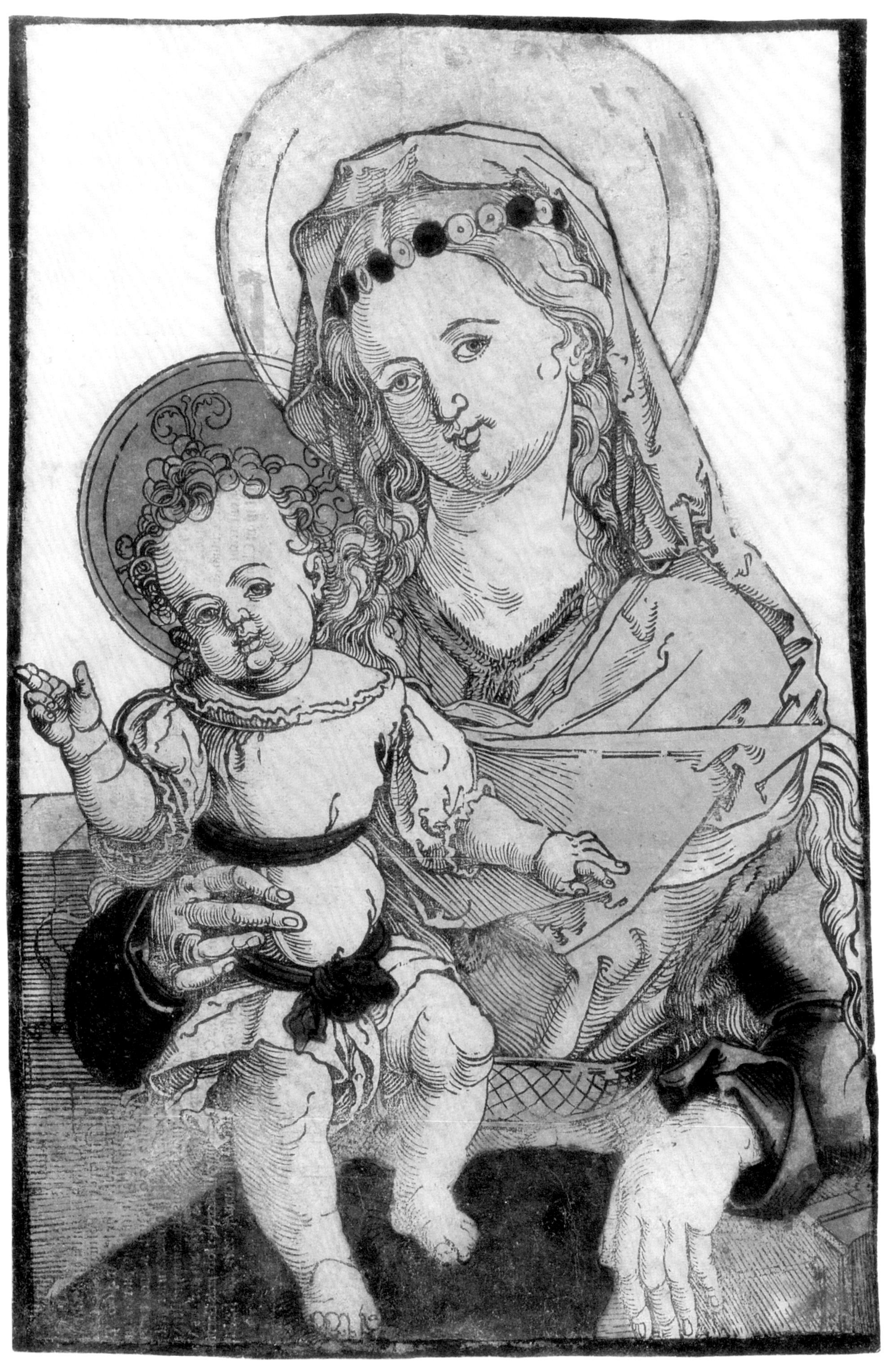

Plate 56. School of Dürer (Sebald Beham?), *Madonna and Child*, ca. 1520-25.

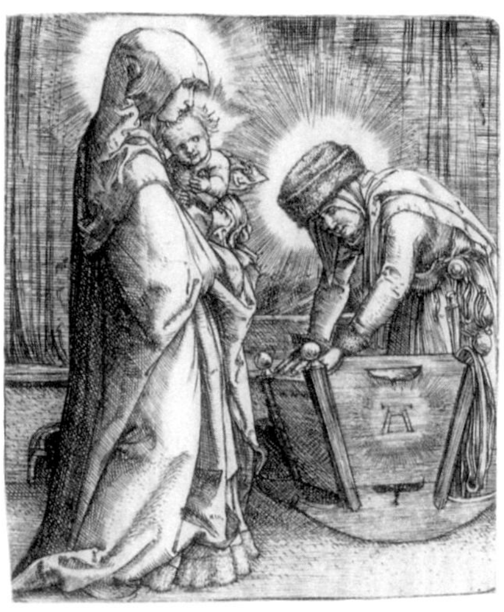

Plate 57. Albrecht Altdorfer, *Madonna and Child with St Anne at the Cradle*, ca. 1515-25.

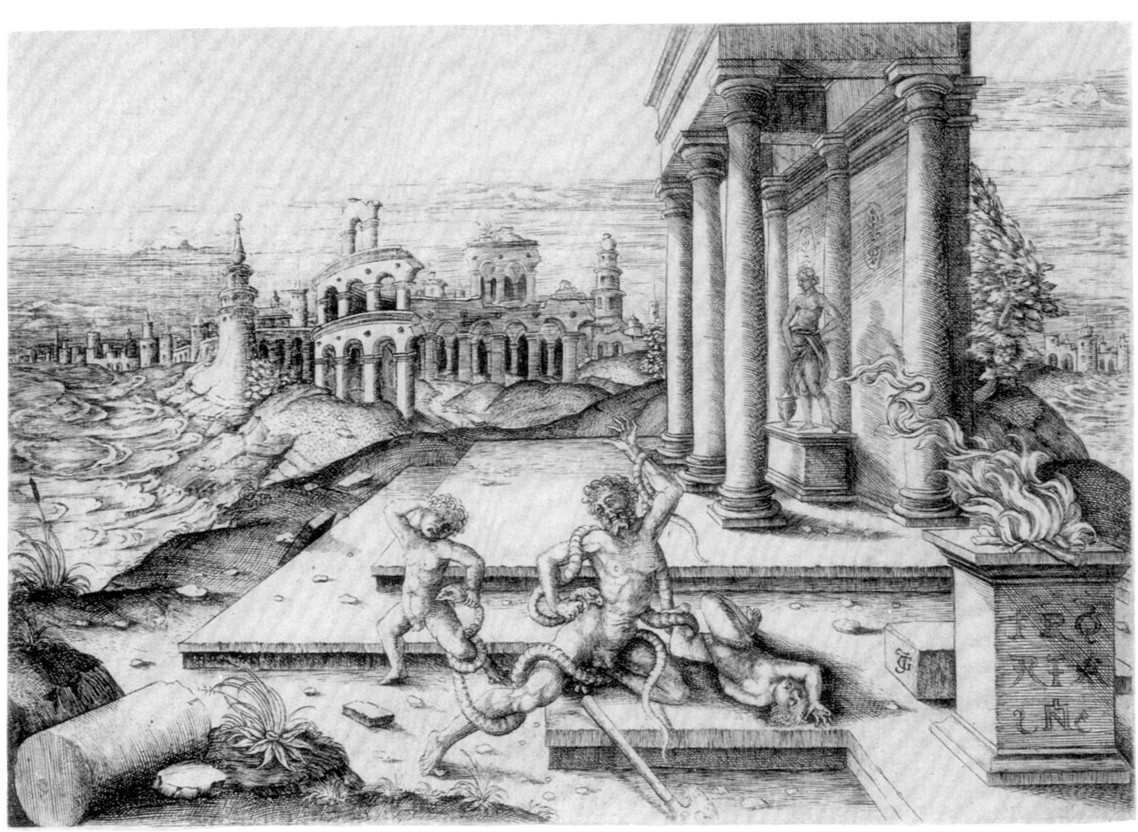

Plate 58. Jean de Gourmont, *Laocoön*, ca. 1525-30?

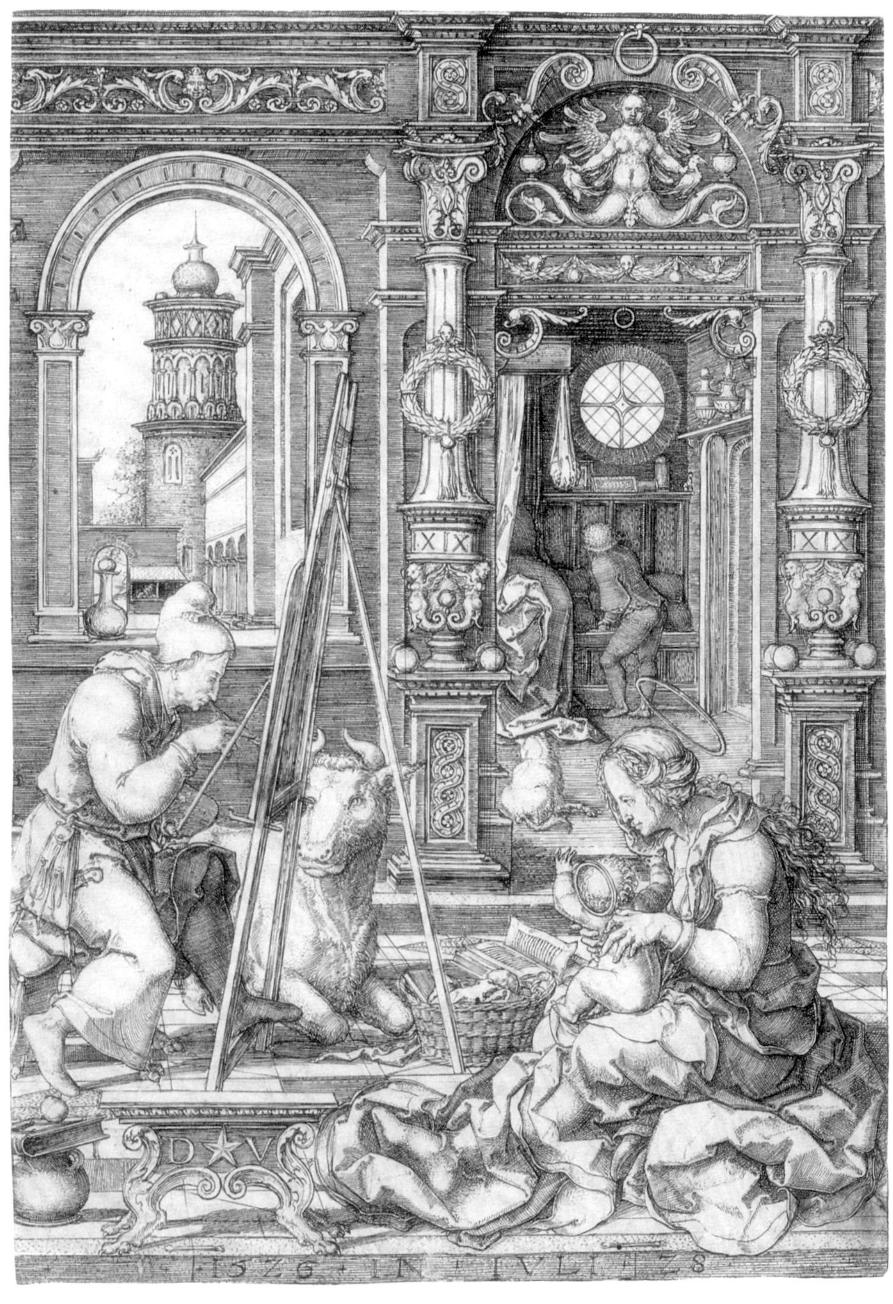

Plate 59. Dirk Jacobsz Vellert, *St. Luke Painting a Portrait of the Virgin*, 1526.

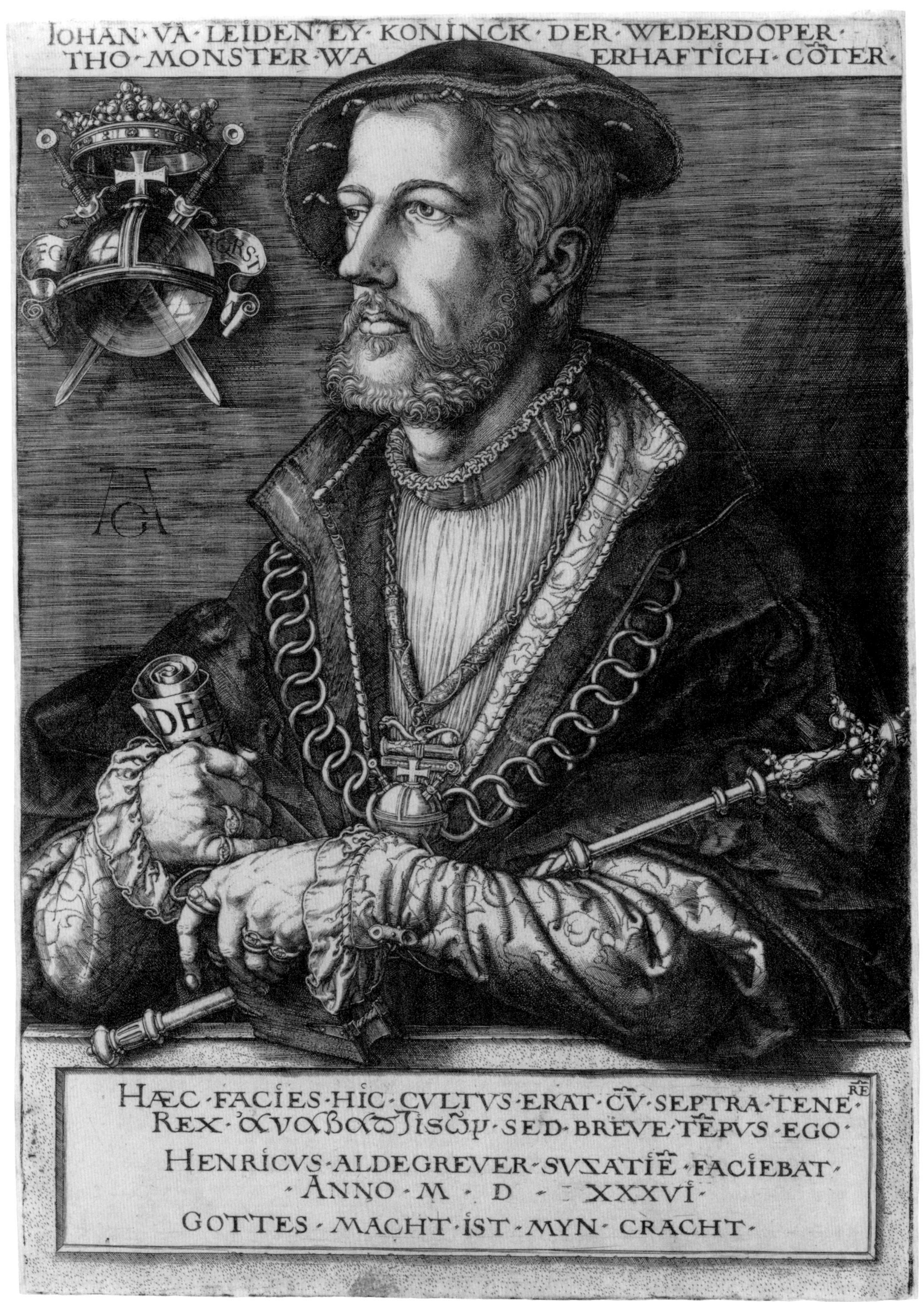

Plate 60. Heinrich Aldegrever, *Jan of Leyden*, 1536.

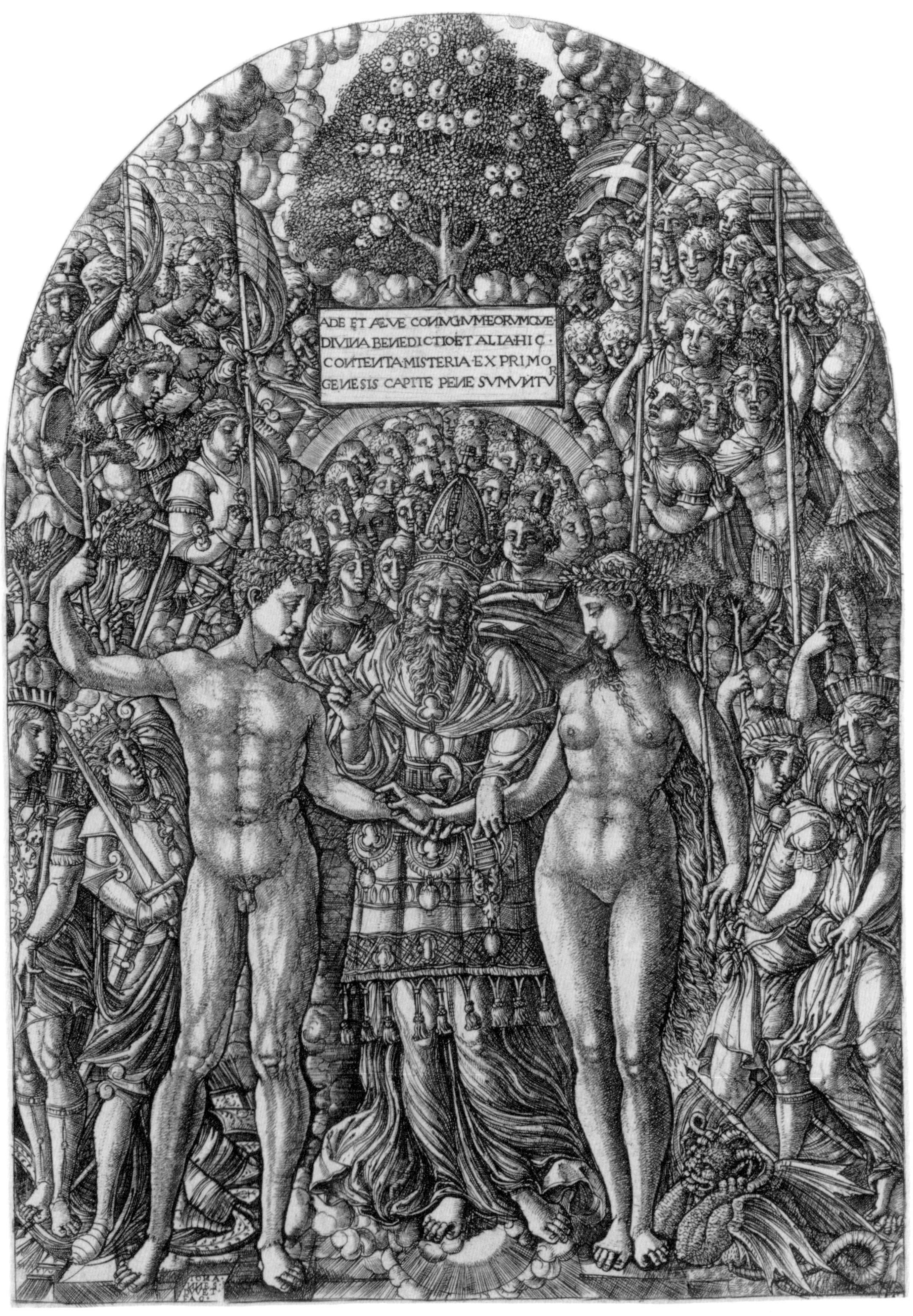

Plate 61. Jean Duvet, *The Marriage of Adam and Eve*, ca. 1540-55.

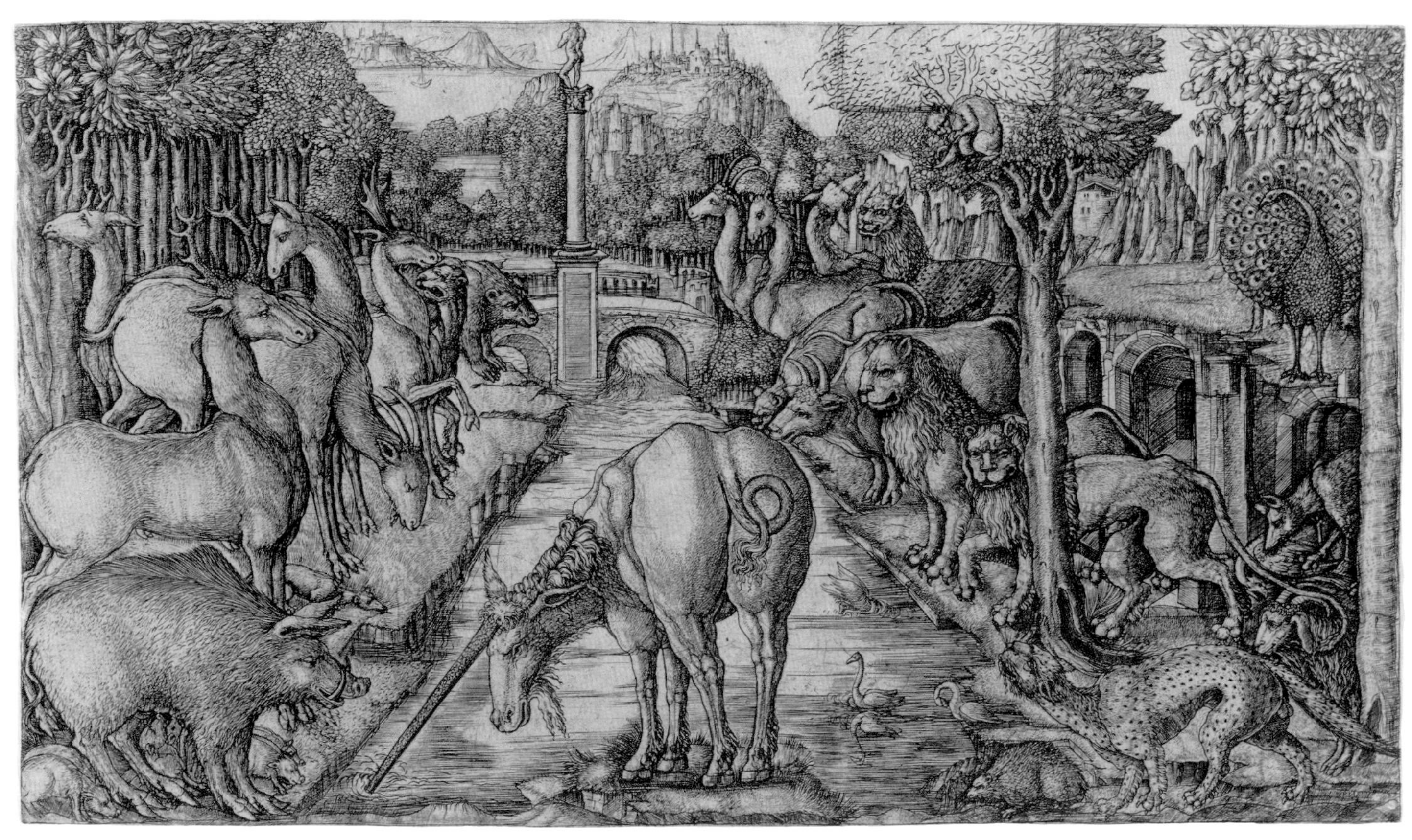

Plate 62. Jean Duvet, *The Unicorn Purifies the Water with his Horn*, ca. 1540-60.

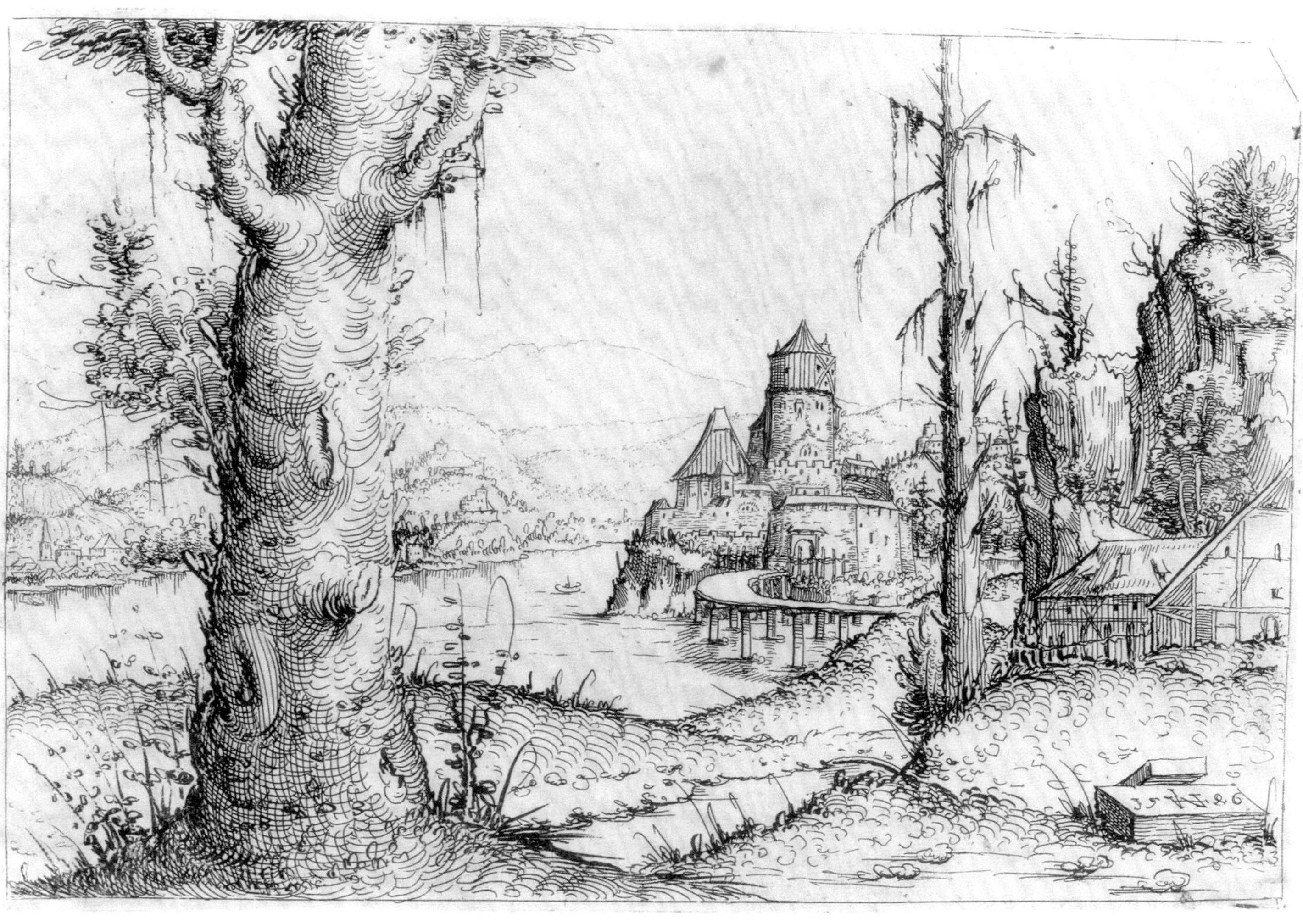

Plate 63. Augustin Hirschvogel, *River Landscape with large Tree at Left*, 1546.

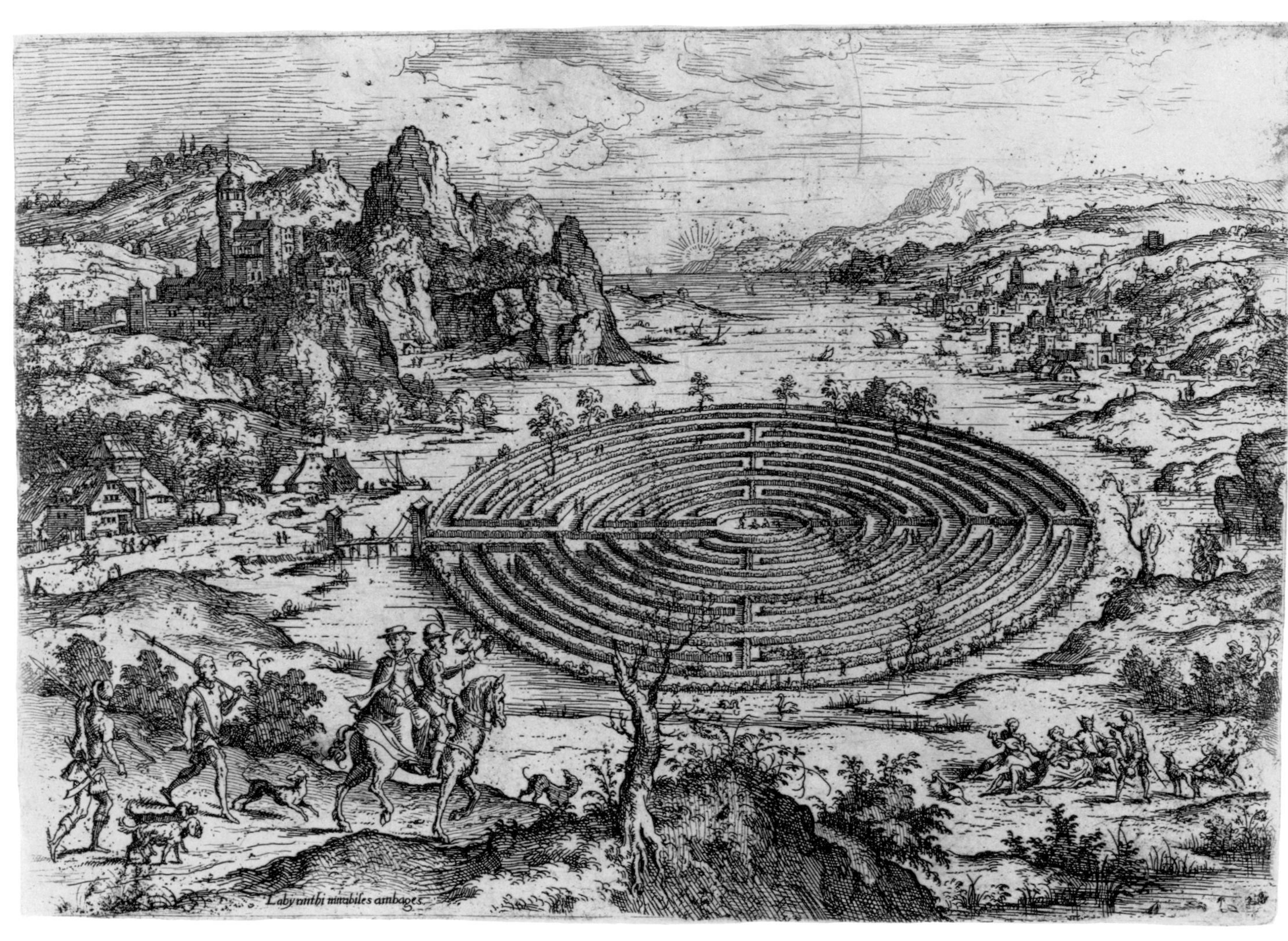

Plate 64. Hieronymus Cock, *The Marvelous Windings of the Labyrinth*, 1558.

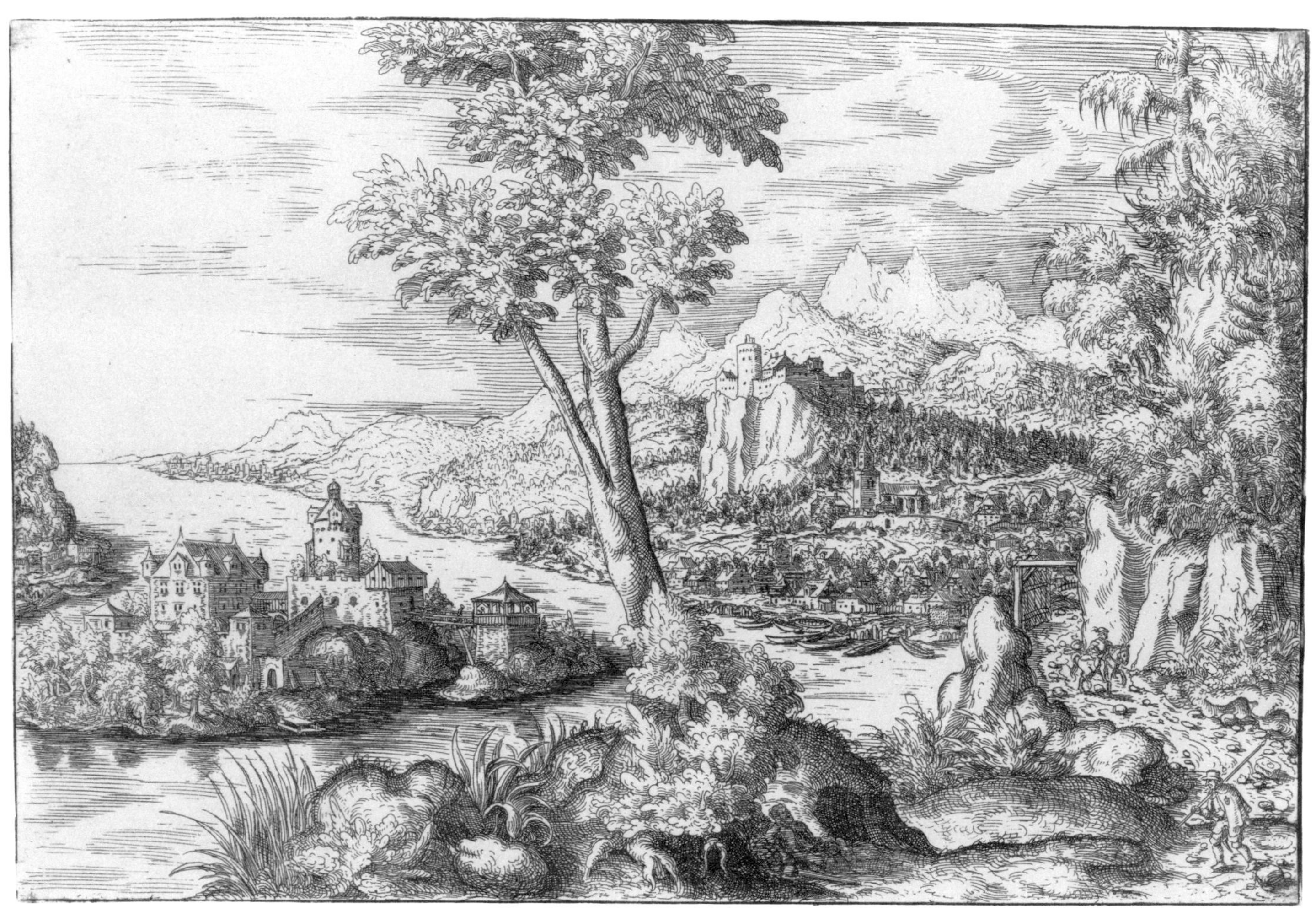

Plate 65. Hanns Lautensack, *River Landscape with Three Figures*, ca. 1558-59.

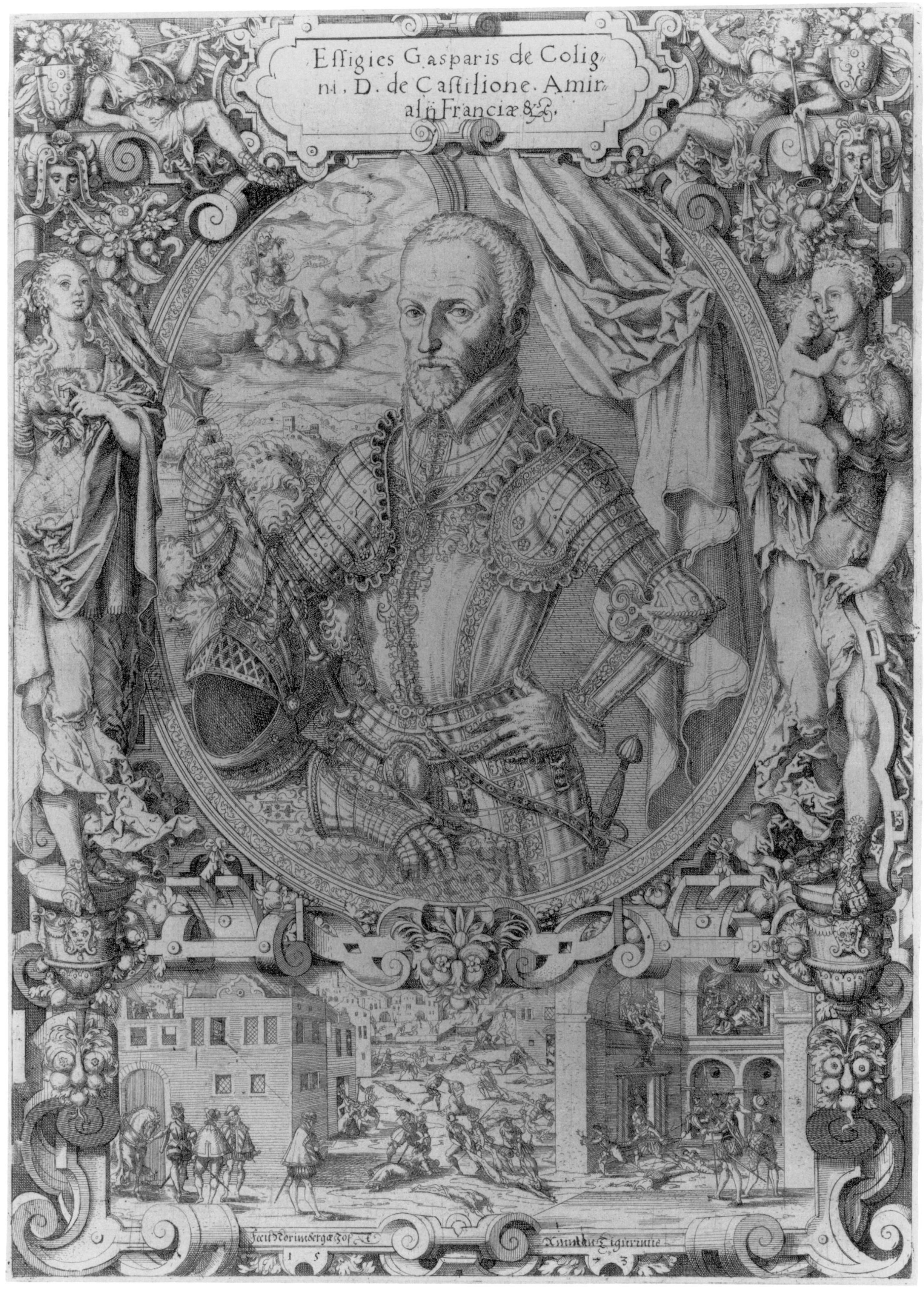

Plate 66. Jost Amman, *Gaspard de Coligny*, 1573.

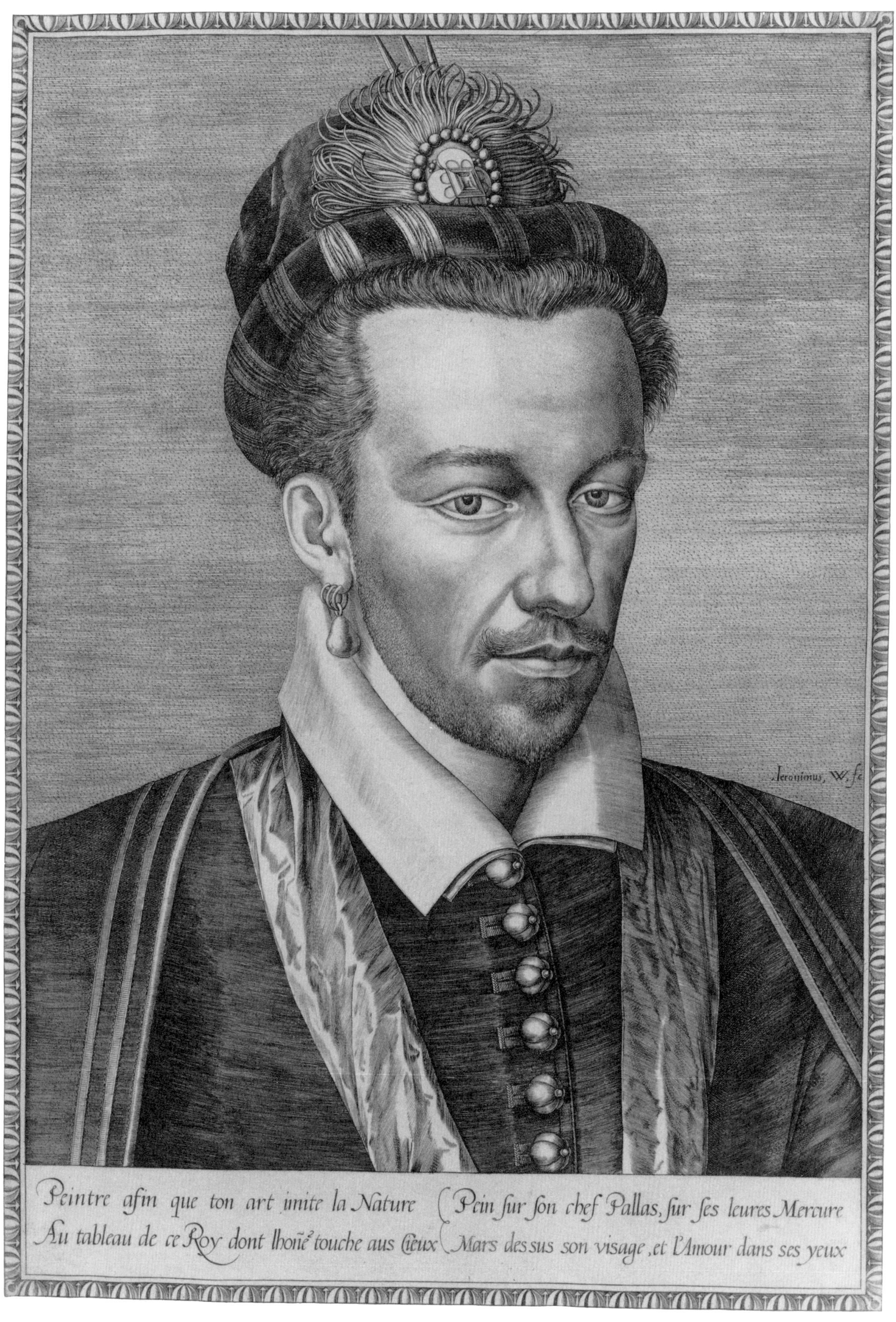

Plate 67. Hieronymus Wierix, *Henry III, King of France*, by 1589.

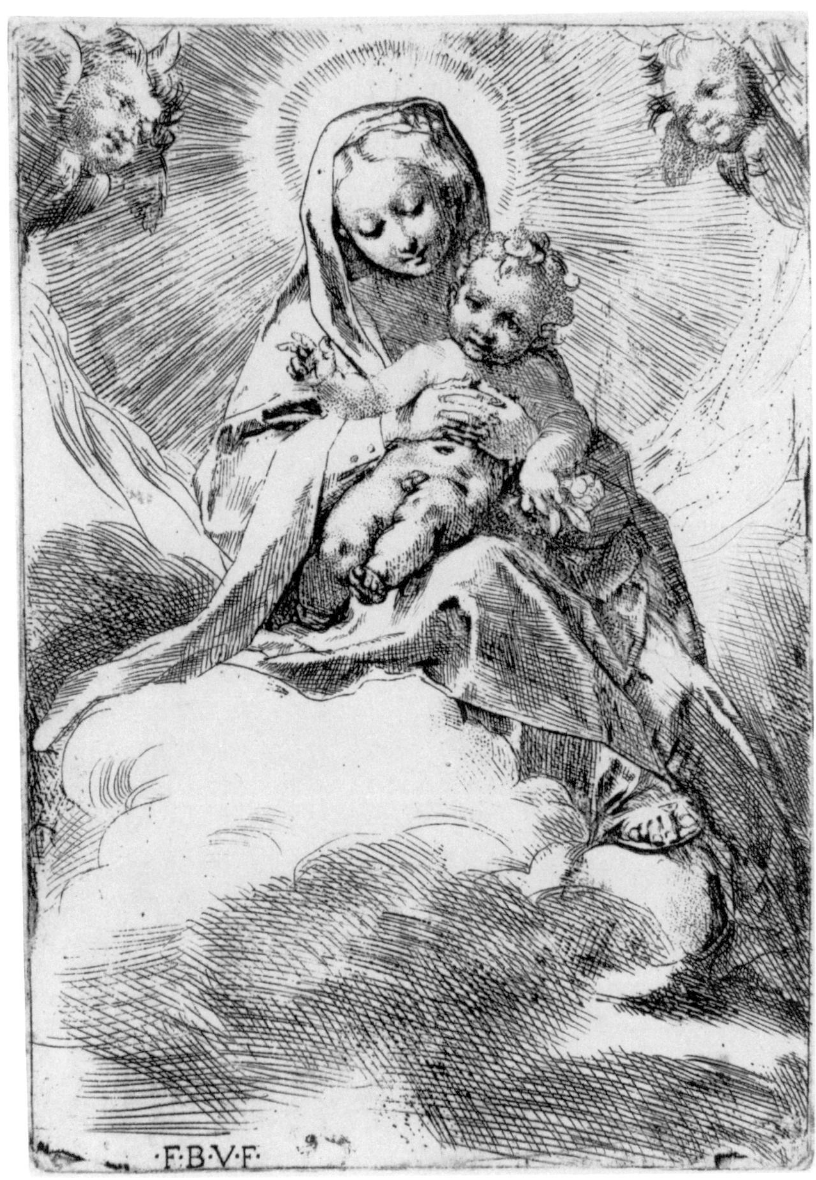

Plate 68. Federico Barocci, *Madonna and Child in the Clouds*, ca. 1581.

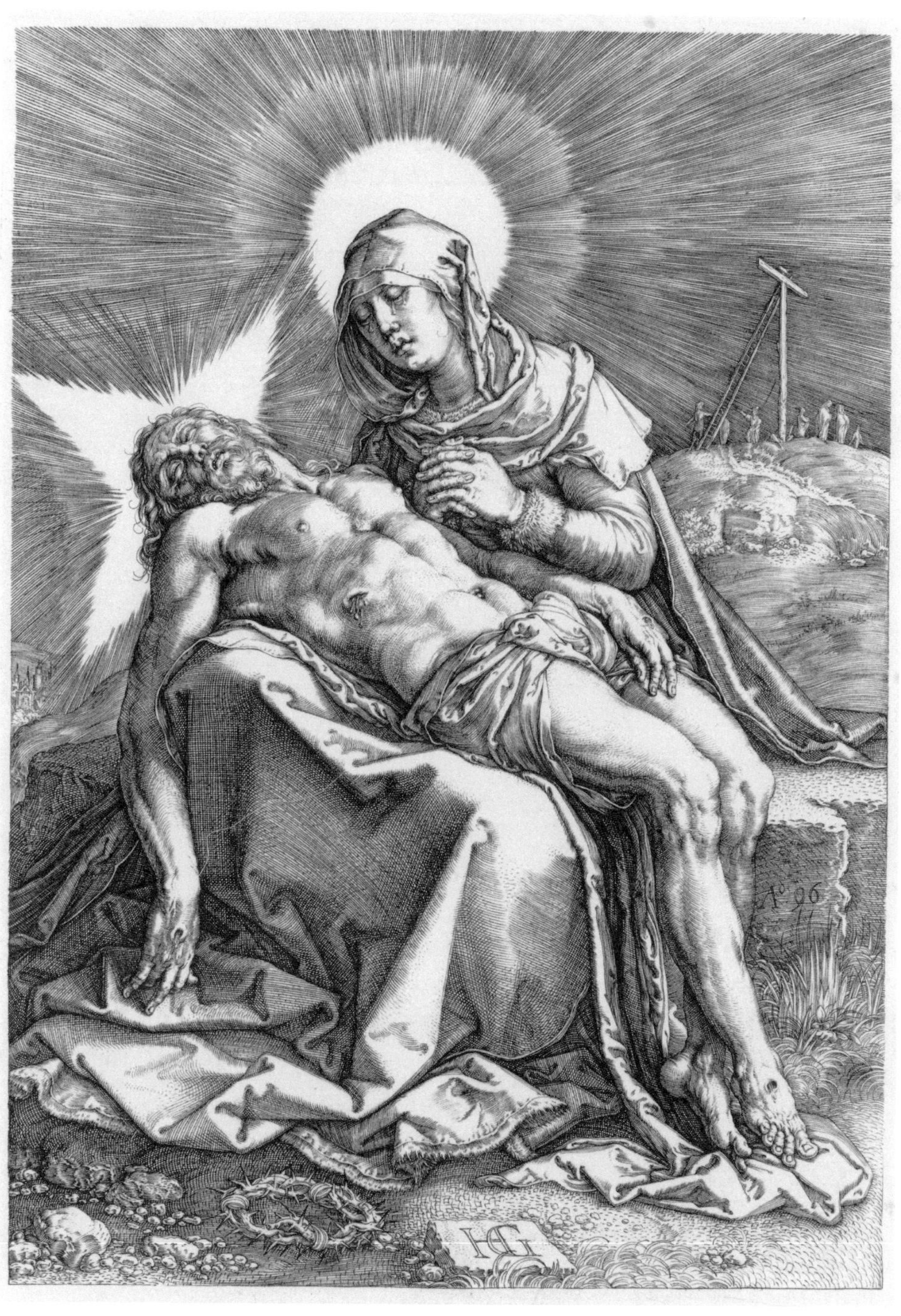

Plate 69. Hendrick Goltzius, *Pietà*, 1596.

Jan van de Velde II

Rotterdam 1593-1641 Enkhuizen
after Willem Buytewech (ca. 1591/92-1624)

The Four Elements

70a. Earth

Etching on antique laid paper, 19.2 x 29.0 cm (platemark).
H. *Neth.* 18 i/iv; Fr.-v.d. K. 134.
Watermark: Crowned crest.
Signed in plate lower center: *J. V. Velde. fec. et excud.*; titled in lower center: TERRA flanked by 4-line Latin text: *Terra suas . . . Ceres.*; lower right: WB (in ligature).
Bequest of Herbert Greer French, 1943.381.

70b. Air

Etching and engraving on antique laid paper, 18.5 x 28.3 cm (platemark).
H. *Neth.* 19 i/iii; Fr.-v.d. K. 135.
Watermark: Crowned crest.
Signed in plate lower right: *J. V. Velde fecit et excud.*; titled lower center: AER flanked by 4-line Latin text: *Aer . . . greges*; in lower right: WB (in ligature).
Bequest of Herbert Greer French, 1943.378.

70c. Fire

Etching and engraving on antique laid paper, 185 x 291 cm (platemark).
H. *Neth.* 20 i/v; Fr-v.d. K. 136.
Watermark: Crowned crest.
Titled in plate lower center: IGNIS flanked by 4-line Latin text: *Ignis alit . . . fovet.*; signed in lower right: *J. V. Velde fec. et. excud.* WB (in ligature).
Bequest of Herbert Greer French, 1943.379

70d. Water

Etching and engraving on antique laid paper, 18.4 x 28.6 cm (platemark).
H. *Neth.* 21 i/iv; Fr.-v.d. K. 137.
Signed in plate lower center: *J. V. Velde. fec. et excud.*; titled lower center: AQVA flanked by 4-line Latin text: *Frugum . . . aqua.*; lower right: WB (in ligature).
Bequest of Herbert Greer French, 1943.380.
Provenance: (Set purchased from M. Knoedler, New York, September 27, 1929, for $107).

Jan van de Velde II, son of the famous Dutch calligrapher and writing master, Jan van de Velde I, was born in Rotterdam in 1593. He moved to Haarlem in 1613 where he apprenticed with Jacob Matham, the stepson of Hendrick Goltzius. Jan joined the Haarlem Guild of Saint Luke in 1614, two years after Willem Buytewech, Hercules Segers, and Jan's cousin, Esaias van de Velde, became members. During the following three years, Jan produced a huge number of etchings, mostly landscapes, after his own designs. The majority of these were published in Amsterdam. In 1618 he married Christina Non in Enkhuizen but returned to Haarlem. After his marriage, Jan shifted the nature of his print production, principally reproducing the designs of other artists, including Willem Buytewech, Frans Hals, Pieter Molyn, Pieter Saenredam, and Cornelis Claesz. van Wieringen. In pursuing this course of action, Jan followed the example of his teacher, Jacob Matham, who was almost exclusively a reproductive engraver. But in place of Matham's *svelte* international mannerist style, Jan van de Velde II worked in a strongly realist vein. He was a prolific printmaker, with more than 470 prints to his credit. Jan moved to Enkhuizen in 1636 and died there in 1641. Van Gelder postulates that the printmakers Willem Akersloot and Cornelis van Kittensteyn were Van de Velde's pupils.[1]

Jan van de Velde's prints after Willem Buytewech (ca. 1591/92-1624) are among his finest and most notable works. Moreover, these prints after Buytewech's preparatory designs are an invaluable source of knowledge about Buytewech's productivity because most of his preparatory drawings for prints are now lost. Jan's prints after Buytewech date several years after Buytewech had moved from Haarlem to Rotterdam (1617). Thus, these two artists, who surely knew each other in Haarlem, maintained a close working relationship after Buytewech's departure. The Museum's set *The Four Elements* is undated, but it is so similar to a second suite, dated 1622,[2] that Jan must have produced both series of prints at virtually the same time.

Traditional representations of the four elements – earth, water, fire, and air – produced by mannerist printmakers in the Low Countries such as Jacques de Gheyn II or Maerten de Vos, employed large-scale single figures, either pagan deities or simply mortal humans, whose activities identified them as personifying one of the four elements.[3] The setting reinforced the connection between the figure and its corresponding element. A maidservant placing a skewer in a kitchen fireplace denoted fire; a hunter whose dogs pursue rabbits denoted earth; a fisherman with his catch symbolized water; a falconer symbolized air.

As Egbert Haverkamp-Begemann notes, Buytewech transformed conventional representations of earth, water, fire, and air in two fundamental ways. He abandoned the single figure personification of these abstractions and replaced it with the types of genre scenes that appeared in the backgrounds of certain mannerist suites of the four elements. By eliminating the prominent single foreground figure and replacing it with a many-figured genre scene, Buytewech achieved an unprecedented degree of realism that is reflected in the two sets of *The Four Elements*[4] reproduced by Jan van de Velde.

In the Museum's set, he depicts a cattle market at the edge of a Dutch town to personify earth. Peasants and members of the aristocracy mingle around several cows and pigs before a vista of cultivated countryside. Fisherfolk displaying their catch along the shoreline personify water. To the right a beached fishing vessel lies before a large, dilapidated fire tower, and a vast vista of beach and dunes extends beyond the bustling foreground activities. Fire is represented by three cannons set into earthworks to the left of a dirt track. Buytewech's preparatory drawing for *Fire*, formerly on loan to the Hermitage in St. Petersburg, represents the subject in broad daylight, with the ramparts of a distant rivertown visible along the horizon.[5] Van de Velde transformed Buytewech's design into a starry nocturne. A firing cannon provides an eerie, flickering light source that fleetingly illuminates the figures and cart at right. In creating this nocturne, Jan van de Velde drew inspiration from Adam Elsheimer's *Flight into Egypt*, now in Munich. Jan may have known the painting firsthand because it may have been in Hendrick Goudt's possession in Utrecht.[6] Otherwise, he would have relied on Goudt's engraving after Elsheimer's design. In creating such an extraordinary range of velvety blacks, Jan does seem to have studied Goudt's engraving technique closely. If anything, his own achievement in *Fire* is an even greater virtuoso performance than Goudt's.[7] *Air*, the last print in the series, illustrates a carriage surrounded by a party of falconers on foot and on horseback. The carriage passes between two posts supporting armorial lion sculptures. This allusion to the approach to an aristocratic country house is a fitting reminder that falconry was a sport reserved for the rich and titled. The actual quarry is seen at the upper left center, where two falcons attack a heron. The Latin captions in the bottom margin of each print allude to the elements as the source of material abundance and as life-sustaining forces.[8] – GK

1. J. G. van Gelder, *Jan van de Velde 1593-1641 teekenaar-schilder* (The Hague, 1933), 71-72.

2. Egbert Haverkamp-Begemann, *Willem Buytewech* (Amsterdam, 1959), nos. CP 37-40; H. *Neth.* 22-25.

3. Several suites of *The Four Elements*, including that by De Gheyn and others by Claes Jansz. Clock, Frederick Bloemaert after the designs of his father, Abraham Bloemaert, and Nicolas de Bruyn after Maerten de Vos, are illustrated in "Die Sprache der Bilder" Braunschweig 1978, nos. 5a-d (Clock); 5e-h (Bloemaert); 12e-h (De Bruyn after M. de Vos); and 12i-l (De Gheyn). Haverkamp-Begemann, *Willem Buytewech*, 16, also refers to a set of *The Four Elements* by Crijpijn de Passe in which each scene is dominated by an amorous couple; H. *Neth.* 524-27.

4. Haverkamp-Begemann, *Willem Buytewech*, 16.

5. Illustrated in Rotterdam 1974, pl. 128.

6. Haverkamp-Begemann, *Willem Buytewech*, 198.

7. This is not the sole nocturne in Jan van de Velde's graphic oeuvre. His suite of *The Four Times of Day* (H. *Neth.* 71-74) includes three landscapes depicted at night or in quasinocturnal lighting conditions. *The Star of the Kings* (H. *Neth.* 149) and *Shrove-Tuesday* (H. *Neth.* 150) after Pieter Molyn are also notable, but Jan's masterpiece in this vein is *The Sorceress* (H. *Neth.* 152) of 1626.

8. Haverkamp-Begemann translates each Latin quatrain into Dutch in *Willem Buytewech*, 197-98. This information is also cited in Rotterdam 1974, 142-45.

Peter Paul Rubens

Siegen, Westphalia 1577-1640 Antwerp

71. Saint Catherine of Alexandria in the Clouds 1630s?

Etching and engraving on antique laid paper, 29.8 x 19.9 cm (platemark).
Basan 15; Dut. 15 ii/iii; H. *Neth.* 1 iii/iii.
Watermark: Fool's bauble.
Signed in plate lower left: *P. Paul. Rubens fecit.* Notation in pencil on reverse: S.C. *11296*.
Provenance: Spencer Churchill? (note on verso, S.C. *11296*; see Lugt 2709a); (purchased from M. Knoedler, New York, October 11, 1937, for $225).
Bequest of Herbert Greer French, 1943.346.
Exhibitions: Cincinnati 1941, no. 17, pl. 35.

Ever since printmaking began, important painters and sculptors, such as Rembrandt and Delacroix, have taken up the medium and become fascinated with it; others, Rubens and Ingres among them, experimented with it once or twice and then gave it up. Rubens is an especially interesting example because he was closely associated with printmakers throughout his life. Having an engraving made from a painting or drawing was the usual way for him to encounter printmaking. Early in his career, he made drawings for engraved book illustrations and title pages; later he was clearly interested in prints as a way of publicizing his paintings.[1] Beginning in 1619, if not before, Rubens commissioned at least fifty-seven engravings after his paintings; and by closely supervising the work of several engravers, correcting trial proofs of the engravings with pen or brush, he

fostered the development of a "Rubens-style" of engraving.[2] In the 1630s he collaborated with Christoffel Jegher to produce twenty-four woodcuts.[3] Most scholars today, however, believe that Rubens made at most three etchings himself, and only *St. Catherine of Alexandria in the Clouds* has been accepted almost universally as his work.[4]

According to legend, Catherine of Alexandria was condemned by the Emperor Maximin to be tortured on a spiked wheel. When an angel descended and shattered the instrument of torture, Maximin had her beheaded with a sword. Accordingly, she is commonly shown with a palm branch, emblematic of martyrdom, the sword, and the broken wheel. Rubens designed this figure originally for a ceiling painting, one of thirty-nine monumental canvases that he had made for the Jesuit church in Antwerp in 1620-21.[5] He retained the *modelli*, or painted preliminary designs, for these paintings in his studio; and in the 1630s, when he began working with Jegher, he used two of them as the basis for woodcuts. Most probably the Museum's etching dates from the same period.[6] It may seem curious that Rubens should have made prints from compositions of this type, with their perspective arranged for a view from below, but the ceilings had been one of his largest and most highly regarded public commissions, and he may have felt that the fame of the paintings would enhance the market for his prints. It is also possible that the choice of subject for the woodcuts derives from Rubens' deep response to Titian, who had also created both great ceiling paintings and woodcut designs.[7]

In the ceiling painting, which was almost square, Catherine stands over the fallen Emperor Maximin. For the etching, Rubens simplified the design and concentrated on the vertical figure of the saint, who treads on the broken wheel instead of the emperor. The three states of the etching help to reconstruct the stages of its creation. The first, known only from a counterproof in the Metropolitan Museum of Art, shows the entire composition completed in etching, but the effect was probably rather flat and gray.[8] It is difficult to assess exactly how the etching looked by itself, because the counterproof has been extensively worked over by Rubens in black chalk (or charcoal) and pen and ink.[9] He used the chalk to spread shadow over broad areas of the figure's drapery, rubbed in to create a tone. Individual strokes of chalk are visible in only a few places. Pen and ink were used to apply sharper accents of shadow and were occasionally used to add something to the composition: additional foliage to the palm branch and a couple of square pegs on the side of the broken wheel.

In the second state, which seems to be almost as rare as the first, the changes indicated with pen and chalk have been carried out in engraving.[10] Here, also, there are two kinds of work. Bold, slightly awkward strokes of the burin fill in and deepen patches of shadow. Finer strokes add subtlety to the flesh tones with the "lozenge-and-dot" technique that had been perfected by professional engravers of the late sixteenth century: two sets of cross-hatchings come together at an angle to form diamond-shaped patches, and as a final refinement, dots are placed in the centers of some of the patches to darken the area just a little more.

Most scholars have concluded that Rubens treated the etching just like an engraving made under his direction: he corrected a proof and left the alteration of the plate to the professional. It is a truism of the history of printmaking that, after etching became popular in the middle of the sixteenth century, only professional printmakers made use of the engraver's burin to any significant extent. Perhaps it is more truism than true. The elaborate patterns of shading that characterize professional engravings may indeed have required years of practice to achieve, but it is possible to conceive that a novice engraver – at least a novice with the hand and eye of Rubens – could have managed the irregular but vigorous burin work that shades in the drapery and clouds.

In favor of Rubens' own participation is the fact that in a few minor but significant details the burin work departs from the model laid out in pen and ink and chalk on the counterproof. Rubens extended the saint's palm branch in pen; the burinist left the palm branch alone but extended the rays of her halo. In reworking the broken wheel, Rubens drew in a fourth square peg along its side; the burinist ignored this but added a shadow to the first peg. One suspects that a conscientious professional would have followed Rubens' indications and would not have introduced variations of his own; Rubens himself, however, would have felt free to change his mind and deviate from the model he had just laid out.

Against this view it could be argued that the fine "lozenge-and-dot" engraving that delicately shades the face and arms of the figure is precisely the kind of meticulous, practiced work that a professional engraver would have produced but for which Rubens would have lacked the skill or the patience. All the same, it is tempting to imagine a scenario in which Rubens begins work on the print with one or another of his printmaking colleagues at hand to offer instruction or assistance. The first trial proof shows that the print is much too gray and flat; Rubens works up a counterproof in pen and chalk and then takes the burin in hand himself. Perhaps he finishes the job; perhaps, after trying his hand at a few patches of shading, he hands the plate over to an assistant.[11]

Whether Rubens himself added the engraving of the second state or only supervised it, it appears that he did not issue the print. The third state bears the inscription "*P. Paul. Rubens fecit*" but lacks the declaration of copyright ("*Cum privilegio*") that Rubens was authorized to use to protect his prints from plagiarism. It may be that the plate came into the hands of a publisher only after Rubens' death.[12] It is interesting that Rubens should have abandoned a print that had evidently been created with considerable care. Perhaps, after all, he was disappointed in the medium. The idea of etching as a way of making freely sketched prints (such as Rembrandt was making by the early 1630s) clearly did not appeal to him. Instead, he seems to have been aiming at something between the informality of a drawing and the careful finish of an engraving. Once the burin work had been added, the print became still more engravinglike but without the high finish of a true engraving. Having satisfied his curiosity about the medium of etching, Rubens may have concluded that the print would add nothing to his towering reputation and thus set the plate aside. But Rubens' second-best is worth the best of many other artists, and we can be grateful to the publisher (whoever it was) who added Rubens' name to the plate and printed it in quantity for the first time.

Although the Museum's impression bears Rubens' name, it differs from ordinary impressions of the third state. In the lower right corner of the print and in a few other places are marks of foul biting, black dots accidentally etched into the plate where the etching ground broke down. These were later burnished away and are not normally found in the third state; the Museum's impression could thus be described as an extremely early impression from the third state or an intermediate state between those usually described as second and third. – TR

1. The most serious recent studies of Rubens' interaction with printmakers are Konrad Renger, "Rubens dedit deicavitque: Rubens' Beschäftigung mit der Reproduktionsgrafik, I. Teil: Der Kupferstich; II. Teil: Radierung und Holzschnitt – Die Widmungen," *Jahrbuch der Berliner Museen* 16 (1974): 122-75 and 17 (1975): 166-213; Ingeborg Pohlen, *Untersuchungen zur Reproduktionsgraphik der Rubenswerkstatt*, vol. 6 of *Beiträge zur Kunstwissenshaft* (Munich: Richard A. Klein, 1985).

2. Renger, "Rubens," 1:124-75. Pohlen, *Untersuchungen*, 182-301, catalogues the engravings commissioned by Rubens.

3. Mary L. Meyers, "Rubens and the Woodcuts of Christoffel Jegher," *The Metropolitan Museum of Art Bulletin* (Summer 1976): 7-25. Renger,

"Rubens," 2:172-99. H. *Neth.* IX:181-92.

4. A. M. Hind, "Rubens as Etcher," PCQ. 10 (1923): 61-80. Hind accepts only *St. Catherine* as by Rubens. See also C. G. Voorhelm Schneevoogt, *Catalogue des estampes gravées d'après P. P. Rubens* (Haarlem: Les Heritiers Loosjes, 1873), 114, "Saintes no. 35"; Frank van den Wijngaert, *Inventaris der Rubeniaansche prentkunst* (Antwerp: De Sikkel, 1940), 88, no. 595 (Van den Wijngaert doubts R.'s authorship); Hans Vlieghe, *Saints 1*, vol. 8 of *Corpus Rubenianum Ludwig Burchard* (London and New York: Phaidon Press, 1972), 116-17, no. 75.

5. J. R. Martin, *The Ceiling Paintings for the Jesuit Church in Antwerp*, vol. 1 of *Corpus Rubenianum Ludwig Burchard* (London and New York: Phaidon Press, 1968), 144-47.

6. Martin, *The Ceiling Paintings*, 146-47, points out that the etching and woodcuts are based on the *modelli* rather than the ceiling paintings themselves. Renger ("Rubens," 2:168) points out that the pen work on the counterproof of the etching in the Metropolitan Museum of Art in New York is characteristic of Rubens' style in the 1630s.

7. On Rubens' complex response to Titian, see Mary Crawford Volk, "On Rubens and Titian," *The Ringling Museum of Art Journal* (1983): 140-49.

8. Hollstein erroneously cites a second impression of the first state in the British Museum. In a letter to Riggs (November 1, 1991), Anthony Griffiths has confirmed that there is no such impression in the British Museum.

9. In examining the proof in the Metropolitan Museum of Art, I could not be sure whether the medium was black chalk or charcoal; I have referred to it as chalk for the sake of simplicity, but its exact nature is irrelevant here. What matters is that it is a broadly applied means of adding shadow. (Hind and Renger mention only the work in ink.)

10. I know of only the impression in the British Museum, reproduced in John Rowlands, London 1977, 107, no. 144.

11. It is interesting that there is no consensus on which of the engravers associated with Rubens might have added the burin work. Lucas Vorsterman has been mentioned (Henri Hymans, *Histoire de la gravure dans l'école de Rubens* [Brussels: F. J. Olivier, 1879], 141), but if the etching dates from the 1630s, it was done when Rubens and Vorsterman were no longer on good terms. Pierre-Jean Mariette suggests "Bolswert" without specifying to which of the Bolswert brothers he is referring (P. J. Mariette, *Abecedario* [Paris: J. B. Dumoulin, 1858-59], 5:108). Stylistically Boetius A. Bolswert seems plausible to me.

12. Renger, "Rubens," 2:168.

Sir Anthony van Dyck
Antwerp 1599-1641 London

72. Self Portrait, mid 1620s-36.
Etching on antique laid paper, 24.3 x 15.6 cm (platemark).
Dut. 3 i/iv; Mauquoy-Hendrickx 4 i/vii.
Watermark: Two interlaced c's over cross of Lorraine, crowned (Mauquoy-Hendrickx 1).
Condition: Trimmed just outside platemark.
Provenance: (Purchased from M. Knoedler, New York, April 1, 1931, for $4,500).
Bequest of Herbert Greer French, 1943.373.
Exhibitions: Cincinnati 1934, no. 55; Cincinnati, 1941, no. 164, pl. 43.

Born in Antwerp to a wealthy merchant family, Van Dyck was apprenticed at the age of eleven to the painter Hendrik van Balen (1575-1632) for two years. He was admitted to the painters' guild in 1618. At that time he began an active collaboration in the studio of Rubens, quickly achieving favored status and completing independent commissions. During the year from 1620 to 1621 he worked in England. After an extensive sojourn in Italy and Sicily, he had returned to Antwerp by 1627 through France. In 1632 Van Dyck left his native city to reside permanently in England, where he was appointed "Principal Painter in Ordinary" to the court of Charles I, being knighted for his services in the same year. Except for brief trips to Antwerp, Brussels, and Paris, he spent the rest of his life in England.

Engraved portrait prints became vastly popular during the sixteenth century and were avidly collected, often compiled into large albums.[1] In response to this trend, publishers began issuing volumes of portraits – from Roman emperors to "illustrious" Frenchmen (and, very occasionally, Frenchwomen). There had been earlier precedents for compilations of portrait prints by a single printmaker, but Van Dyck's series of printed portraits commonly known as the *Iconography* was the first to be executed primarily after the designs of a single artist, and his characterful and elegant renderings eclipsed earlier stock types.[2]

Van Dyck's enduring fame as an original printmaker rests on a small number of portrait etchings that he executed in conjunction with his larger series. As conceived by Van Dyck, an ideal "iconographic" collection of European notables would consist of portraits in identical format in three classes: princes and generals, statesmen and philosophers, and artists and collectors. Most of his subjects were living in the southern Netherlands, many in Antwerp. He worked on his models over a period of years, from perhaps as early as the mid-1620s until at least 1636. These models included both preliminary drawings and, in many cases, *grisaille* oil sketches.[3] All the subjects in the *Iconography* were, however, eventually engraved by professional printmakers, most of whom belonged to the large circle of engravers employed by Rubens. In certain cases, the oil sketches seem the more detailed sources for the engravers; in others, highly finished drawings, clearly incised for transfer, would seem to be the final preparatory studies.[4] The precise role of Van Dyck's oil sketches and his drawings remains somewhat obscure.

Curiously, Van Dyck's own etchings did not appear in early issues of the set, being incorporated into the published *Iconography* only after his death. He kept the plates of his etchings in his studio, and early impressions from them are extremely rare. His purpose in etching these few portraits is not known. It is not known whether he prepared them as ideal models for engravers of other subjects in the *Iconography* or as purely personal exercises to be sold individually.[5] Most of them are masterfully understated yet focused depictions of the faces of fellow artists. Mr. French acquired no less than five rare first-state impressions of these etchings before details of dress or setting were added. They include this self-portrait, the portrait of the diplomat Philippe Le Roy (cat. 73), and those of three fellow artists – Frans Snyders, Justus Sustermans, and Lucas Vorsterman.

The first "editions" of the *Iconography*, issued by the Antwerp publisher Martin Van den Enden, apparently consisted of eighty portraits (of which fifty-two were of fellow artists). These undated collections were published without a frontispiece; they probably appeared between the end of 1635 and the artist's death in 1641. At that time, these eighty plates and those of Van Dyck's own etchings were acquired from his estate by the publisher Gilles Hendricx, who issued sets of the *Iconography* that included one hundred portraits and a frontispiece beginning about 1645-46.[6]

After it was thoroughly elaborated by the engraver Jacob Neeffs (ca. 1610-1660), the self-portrait shown here was utilized by Hendricx as the frontispiece to his edition of the series. Neeffs placed the artist's head on a round pedestal flanked by busts of Minerva and Mercury.[7] The pedestal was inscribed with the title for the series, advertising Van Dyck's portrayal "from life" of the subjects included. Hendricx's name as publisher was also added.[8] Portraits of a wide range of personalities continued to be added to the *Iconography* by later publishers into the eighteenth century, bringing the number of portraits to over two hundred. The plates for the *Iconography* were acquired by the Calcographie du Louvre in 1851.

The deceptive simplicity of the pose in this unadorned state of his *Self-Portrait* and the technique reveal Van Dyck's skills at portraiture. The placement of the head within the blank rectangular format of the plate is especially apposite (allowing the viewer to supply the missing figure), as is its direct, informal over-the-shoulder gaze toward the viewer. Evidenced particularly in his artist portraits,

this quality of casual grace, revealed through the figure, is seen as Van Dyck's conscious effort to reflect the inner source of artistic genius.[9] No preparatory drawing or oil sketch is known for this etching (it may have been drawn directly on the plate from his mirrored reflection). Van Dyck most effectively incorporated etched dots (stippling) to supplement his fluid linear technique, achieving subtle variations in the surface texture of his faces, a technique pioneered in Italy by Federico Barocci (ca. 1535-1612).[10] Van Dyck's assured depictions set universal standards for later portrait etching, especially in the nineteenth-century etching revival works of Seymour Haden and James McNeill Whistler and their followers. – DPB

1. Such a collection is described in Jan van der Waals, "The Print Collection of Samuel Pepys," *PQ.* 1 (December 1984): 236-57, esp. p. 251 (an album page of portraits from the collection is reproduced on p. 250, fig. 139).

2. Some earlier series included those by Theodor de Bry, Domenicus Custos, and Hendrik Hondius. See, for instance, Erik Larsen, *The Paintings of Anthony van Dyck* (Freren: Luca Verlag, 1988), 479.

3. For drawn studies, see Horst Vey, *Die Zeichnungen Anton van Dycks* (Brussels: Arcade, 1962), vol. 1, nos. 242-81; Joaneath Spicer, "Unpublished Studies for Van Dyck's Iconography," *Master Drawings* 23-24 (Winter 1986): 537-44; and Christopher Brown, *The Drawings of Anthony van Dyck* (New York: Pierpont Morgan Library, 1991), 190-213, nos. 54-63. The Duke of Buccleugh owns some forty oil studies for the *Iconography* (three are reproduced in Arthur M. Hind, *Van Dyck – His Original Etchings and His Iconography* [Boston and New York: Houghton Mifflin, 1915], 51, 53, 73); ten more are in the Alte Pinakothek, Munich (see Hind, *Van Dyck*, 42-47). The attribution to Van Dyck of several of the oil sketches is the subject of much debate, but most scholars feel that the finest of them are certainly autograph. Most recently, Christopher Brown (*The Drawings of Anthony van Dyck*, 192-93), who is undertaking a study of the oil portrait sketches, argues for Van Dyck's close collaboration with the engravers and supervision at all stages of the process. It should be noted that a small number of portraits in the *Iconography* are taken from depictions by other artists, among them *Erasmus* (after Hans Holbein) and *Jacques Callot*.

4. See Spicer, "Unpublished Studies," 537-44, and Julius S. Held, in Washington 1990c, no. 92, for two recent discussions of the preparatory process for the engravings. See also n. 3 above. Dr. Spicer is working on a full study of the *Iconography*.

5. See Christopher Brown, *The Drawings of Anthony van Dyck*, 190.

6. The publishing history and original makeup of copies of the *Iconography* still remains quite obscure, with conflicting evidence deduced from existing copies of the collection, many of which have undoubtedly been assembled from different sources (see Spicer, "Unpublished Studies," 537, 542, n. 2, 4, and 6).

7. This motif is derived from Rubens' design for the printer's mark of Jan van Meurs (Marie Mauquoy-Hendrickx, *L'Iconographie d'Antoine van Dyck* [Brussels: Palais des Académies, 1956], 1:55; it is reproduced in J. Richard Judson and Carl van de Velde, *Book Illustrations and Title-Pages*, vol. 21 of *Corpus Rubenianum Ludwig Burchard* [London and Philadelphia: Harvey Miller/Heyden, 1978], 1:255, no. 60; 2: fig. 204). Mauquoy-Hendrickx has also noted (*L'Iconographie*, 53) a source in a cartouche by Agostino Mitelli.

8. The full title reads ICONES / PRINCIPVM / VIRORVM DOCTORVM / PICTORVM CHALCOGRAPHORVM / STATVARIORVM NEC NON AMATORVM / PICTORIAE ARTIS NVMERO CENTVM / AB / ANTONIO VAN DYCK / PICTORE AD VIVVM EXPRESSAE / EIVSQ:SVMPTIBVS AERI INCISAE (One Hundred Portraits of Princes, Men of Letters, Painters, Printmakers, Sculptors as well as Amateurs of the Pictorial Arts done from Life by Anthony van Dyck, Painter, and Engraved at his Expense in Copper). Hind (*Van Dyck*, 95) refers to a proof of the *Self-Portrait* in the British Museum with drawn additions for the pedestal; Mauquoy-Hendrickx (54-55) feels the additions are not by Van Dyck himself.

9. See Spicer, "Unpublished Studies," 537, and Jeffrey M. Muller, "The Quality of Grace in the Art of Anthony van Dyck," in Washington 1990c, 27-36, esp. p. 29.

10. See Boston 1989b, 89-98.

Sir Anthony van Dyck

Antwerp 1599-1641 London

73. Philippe Le Roy, Baron de Broechem ca. 1630-36.

Etching on antique laid paper, 24.1 x 15.5 cm (platemark).
Dut. 6 i/viii; Mauquoy-Hendrickx C i/ix.
Watermark: Two interlaced C's over cross of Lorraine, fleur-de-lis above (cf. Mauquoy-Hendrickx 1 bis).

Provenance: Heinrich Wolff (Lugt 1392); Belle da Costa Greene, New York (consigned to Knoedler 1933); (purchased from M. Knoedler, New York, November 1, 1933, for $2,750).
Bequest of Herbert Greer French, 1943.375.
Exhibitions: Cincinnati 1934, no. 56; Cincinnati 1941, no. 165.

Born in Lièges, Philippe Le Roy (ca. 1596-1679) became one of the highest representatives of the Spanish government in the Netherlands during the seventeenth century. He was variously commissioner of armaments (*poudres et salpêtres*), commissioner-general of supplies, and superintendent of taxes, later becoming a financial advisor and eventually the commissioner of finances for Archduke Ferdinand, governor of the Netherlands. He was appointed a knight of the Holy Roman Empire by Ferdinand in 1647. Le Roy acquired several properties near Antwerp and, in 1671, became the Baron of Broechem.

Van Dyck's etching of his friend Le Roy was ultimately based on a full-length oil, dated 1630, now in the Wallace Collection, London.[1] Consistent with his other original etchings, this portrait was not included in any editions of the *Iconography* that were published during Van Dyck's lifetime (cf. cat. 72), although it clearly was executed in conjunction with it. Further, this particular plate was *never* published in any subsequent edition of the *Iconography*; another version of Le Roy's portrait, which was engraved by Lucas Vorsterman and Paulus Pontius, was substituted instead (Mauquoy-Hendrickx 185).[2]

Again, as in his *Self-Portrait* (cat. 72), Van Dyck achieves an extraordinarily direct portrayal with deceptive simplicity. He places the subject's head and shoulders on the plate with the rest of the figure clearly in mind, either to be later added or to remain unseen. The figure's presence is felt, however, in this rare first-state impression. It is conceivable that the plate's prominent spot of so-called *false biting*, where the acid bit through the ground in an unintended place, caused the other version of Le Roy's portrait, the Vorsterman-Pontius version, to be engraved for the *Iconography*. The Museum's impression is cited by Mauquoy-Hendrickx among sixteen first states that she knew of at the time of her catalogue; it once was part of a celebrated collection of Van Dyck's *Iconography* formed by Heinrich Wolff, a German physician and print collector.[3]

Van Dyck's portrait etching style presents an intriguing contrast to that of Rembrandt (cat. 89-90), whose portrayals are more psychologically penetrating but not perhaps as suave in their quickly grasped fluency. Neither subscribed to the icy clarity of traditional portrait engraving that became the standard in the late seventeenth century, particularly in France (see cats. 93-94).

In addition to *Self-Portrait* and *Philippe Le Roy*, Mr. French acquired three other first-state impressions of Van Dyck's portrait etchings – portraits of Frans Snyders, Justus Sustermans, and Lucas Vorsterman. – DPB

1. Reproduced in Erik Larsen, *The Paintings of Anthony Van Dyck* (Freren: Luca Verlag, 1988), 1:283, fig. 272; and *Summary Illustrated Catalogue of Pictures* (London: Wallace Collection, 1979), 83. The Wallace Collection also owns the pendant painting of Le Roy's wife, Marie de Raet. The preparatory design for the Le Roy portrait (and, hence, indirectly, for the etching) is known only through a copy in Antwerp (Horst Vey, *Die Zeichnungen Anton van Dycks* [Brussels: Arcade, 1962], no. 179, pl. 216).

2. Another anonymous engraving was also included in later editions of the *Iconography* (Mauquoy-Hendrickx 167); this plate is actually a copy of the Vorsterman-Pontius engraving.

3. See the biographical entry in Lugt (1392); the Museum's impression is perhaps the one cited in Wolff's 1877 sale for RM 2100.

Jacques Callot
Nancy 1592-1635 Nancy

74. The Miseries and Misfortunes of War 1633.

74.1 Title Page
74.2 Recruitment of Troops
74.3 The Battle
74.4 Scene of Pillage
74.5 Plundering a Large Farmhouse
74.6 Destruction of a Convent
74.7 Plundering and Burning a Village
74.8 Attack on a Coach
74.9 Discovery of the Criminal Soldiers
74.10 The Strappado
74.11 The Hanging
74.12 The Firing Squad
74.13 The Stake
74.14 The Wheel
74.15 The Hospital
74.16 The Dying Soldiers
74.17 The Peasants Avenge Themselves
74.18 The Distribution of Rewards

Eighteen etchings on antique laid paper, ea. ca. 8.3 x 18.4 cm (platemark).
Lieure 1339 iii/iii; 1340-55 ii/iii; 1356 iii/iv.
Watermark: Posthorn in shield, initials below on 7, 9, 10-12, 16-18 (cf. Washington 1975, 334).
Condition: Variously trimmed to or within platemark.
Provenance: (Purchased from Barton or F. H. Bresler, Milwaukee, September 16, 1927, for $200).
Bequest of Herbert Greer French, 1943.382-399.

The graphic images of brutality and violence seen in this series have exerted an influence out of all proportion to their near-miniature format. Celebrated since their creation, *The Miseries and Misfortunes of War* was itself often reprinted, and printmakers throughout Europe directly copied it.[1] Callot's imagery specifically inspired later artists, including Romeyn de Hooghe (1645-1708) and, perhaps most notably, Francisco Goya (cats. 116,119), whose *Disasters of War* is in many ways a response to Callot's earlier set. Callot's view of war is essentially a close-up, similar in some ways to modern-day television reportage of atrocity. Hyatt Mayor has written that "the wars that he packed tight to bursting in his little etchings did not resemble those vast impersonal conflicts that mobilized whole populations. . . . Callot's war was as intimate as our commando raids or underground sabotage."[2] No viewer can mistake the directness of these scenes, despite the calligraphic elegance of their lines.

In his relatively brief career, Callot etched an astonishing number of prints, over fourteen hundred. He was born to a prominent family in the independent duchy of Lorraine. At the age of fifteen, he was apprenticed to a local goldsmith, but he traveled to Italy soon thereafter and learned engraving in Rome from the French expatriate Philippe Thomassin (1561/62-1622) and etching probably from the Florentine Antonio Tempesta (1555-1630). Callot moved to Florence in 1612, where he developed his etching style and subject matter, which included festival and theatrical designs, military subjects, landscape, and scenes from daily life. Collaborating at first with Tempesta, Giulio Parigi, and Remigio Cantagallina, he soon was fully independent, often employed by the Medici court.

After the death of Cosimo 'de Medici II in 1621, Callot returned to Nancy, serving the dukes of Lorraine and other patrons, including the courts of Spain and France and independent print publishers. He visited the Netherlands and Paris during the late 1620s. His varied output encompassed many religious compositions (such as *The Temptation of St. Anthony* from 1635 [Lieure 1416]), portraits, including hundreds of saints, military battles (bird's-eye views rendered in large multiple plates), and more pictures of daily life depicting beggars, bohemians, and gypsies.

Callot was a professional printmaker and a major technical innovator. He pioneered the use of a hard varnish as an etching ground that allowed the precise application of line during the drawing and biting processes. He also refined an oval-pointed etching tool, the *échoppe*, into a means of varying the widths and appearances of his lines. Callot combined the freedom (and speed) of etching with the desired precision of the engraved line. These innovations formed a central part of Abraham Bosse's influential treatise on etching, published in Paris in 1645.[3] Callot further refined the use of multiple bitings to achieve varying widths of line for shading and depth.

The complete title of this set is *The Miseries and Misfortunes of War Represented by Jacques Callot Lorraine Noble and Published* [brought to light] *by Israel, his Friend, in Paris in 1633 with the Privilege of the King*. It is commonly referred to as the large *Miseries*: Callot had earlier etched a similar set in a smaller format but left it incomplete and without a title page.[4] Each plate in this larger set was supplied with a six-line verse explanation, probably written by the Abbé Michel de Marolles (1600-1681), the famed print collector and, though prolific, the less celebrated verse writer.[5] The sequentially numbered plates were often bound in small albums or else were mounted together in larger blank volumes, as was the custom for collecting prints during the seventeenth and eighteenth centuries. Some seven compositional drawings by Callot for the *Miseries* series have survived, and a large group of tiny figural studies used in the plates is in the Hermitage, Saint Petersburg.[6]

It is difficult, if not impossible, to attach any specific historical reference or interpretation to this series. Although the French invasion of Callot's native Lorraine took place in 1633 and parts of Europe were often taken over by warring armies during this time, the lack of *any* exact identification of site or insignia argues against attaching an anti-French or antiwar interpretation to the series. In the inventory of Callot's studio after his death and in other contemporary accounts, the series was commonly called *Soldier's Life*. Diane Wolfthal has most recently pointed out contemporary texts that explicate the contrasting glories and miseries of warfare and that specify the just and unjust behaviors of soldiers.[7] The actual sequence of images in the set focuses such a reading without explaining, perhaps, Callot's almost dispassionate view of the phenomenon of war itself.

Callot begins the series with a title page, replete with the ornamental finery of soldiers, flags, banners, and military trappings, and two panoramic plates: the recruitment of new soldiers into orderly ranks and a smoke-filled battle scene. The next five plates turn from the glories of things military to the excesses of soldiers who indulge in extracurricular pillage, robbery, murder, and rape. The fifth plate, an especially gruesome scene of the plundering of a farmhouse composed as a stage set, leaves nothing to the imagination. The sixth plate shows the destruction of a convent, the robbery of its goods, and the abduction of its inhabitants. These and other scenes of entire villages being terrorized evidently reflect regular occurrences in Callot's time.

The captions make clear who the culprits are, and the next five plates show the pursuit of the rogue soldiers culminating in their own torture and death. The fourteenth plate shows a soldier who had ambushed travelers becoming the "plaything of a wheel." The fifteenth and seventeenth plates reveal wounded and destitute soldiers receiving no sympathy from the people whom they have terrorized, becoming, in fact, victims of their former victims. Callot's final etching in the series, presumably the moral of the story, shows a ruler dispensing rewards to virtuous soldiers. Its caption specifies that those who committed excesses shall receive "shame, scorn and the extreme penalty."

From the beginning of his career, Callot had depicted numerous military subjects, including naval battles, sets of formal military exercises, and, on a wholly different scale, three multiplate aerial views of military and naval sieges. While some of these commissions came from the Spanish and French courts, Callot issued *The Miseries and Misfortunes of War* at his own initiative through his favored Parisian agent and publisher, Israel Henriet. Some graphic prototypes for Callot's series occur both in his own and in others' work. He incorporated specific vignettes from the margins of his siege prints, and some prints, such as the contemporary *Punishments* (Lieure 1402) and *Martyrdom of St. Sebastian* (*The Ordeal by Arrows*, Lieure 670), are particularly comparable. Graphic scenes of violence by such Netherlandish artists as Esaias and Jan van de Velde, David Vinckboons, and Claes Jansz. Visscher, along with other depictions of military subjects by German artists Jost Amman and Hans Burgkmair, are in some cases direct prototypes.[8]

Callot's mature technique is amply evident in these plates. He employed a broad universe of figural poses and gestures and effectively utilized subtle variations in biting to achieve a gradual recession of spatial depth. Plates such as the pillaging of the inn (cat. 74.4) and the capture of the soldiers (cat. 74.9) progress from heavily bitten dark framing lines in the foreground, through highlighted figures in the middle ground, to the subtlest, most lightly bitten landscape features in the far distance. By utilizing discrete figural groupings, Callot skillfully inserted large numbers of people in his small plates without their appearing jumbled or crowded.

The Museum's set of *The Miseries* is from the first published state, after the insertion of the verses and numbering of the plates. The impressions fully reveal the nuances of Callot's etching style, retaining the richness of his strongly etched figures, the finest lines from the smoking fires of battle, and the wispiest features of the distant landscape. Mr. French acquired only three other Callot etchings: *St. Amond Preaching* (Lieure 406), *The Fair at Gondreville* (Lieure 561), and *The Passage of the Red Sea* (Lieure 665), now all part of the Museum's collection. – DPB

1. See H. Diane Russell et al., Washington 1975, 246. The copperplates are in the Musée Historique Lorrain, Nancy.

2. A. Hyatt Mayor, "The Etchings of Jacques Callot," *The Massachusetts Review* 3, no. 1 (Autumn 1961): unpaginated.

3. For a brief technical overview with illustrations from Bosse's treatise, see Russell et al., Washington 1975, xviii-xxiv.

4. Lieure 1333-38; all the scenes represented in the smaller set were included in the larger, except the peaceful view of life in the soldiers' camp (Lieure 1333). The title plate was later supplied by Abraham Bosse.

5. The verses are translated in Russell et al., Washington 1975, 250, 253-254, 257, 259-60.

6. Daniel Ternois, *Jacques Callot – Catalogue complet de son oeuvre dessiné* (Paris: DeNobele, 1962), nos. 914-52.

7. Diane Wolfthal, "Jacques Callot's *Miseries of War*," *AB*. 59, no. 2 (1977): 222-33. She offers an excellent overview of previous interpretations of the series. The most recent review of the subject is Hilliard Goldfarb, "Callot and the Miseries of War: The Artist, His Intentions and His Context," in Hanover 1990, 13-26.

8. See Goldfarb, Hanover 1990, 20-21.

Hercules Segers

Haarlem ca. 1589/90-ca. 1638 The Hague?

75. Ruins of the Abbey of Rijnsburg (small version).

Etching in black ink on plain weave cloth prepared opaque gray with added double brown wash borderline, 9.6 x 17.3 cm (sheet).
Springer 53; HB. 47 Ic; H. *Neth* 47 Ic.
Condition: Trimmed within platemark bottom only.
Provenance: (Purchased from M. Knoedler, New York, May 19, 1937, for $3,650).
Bequest of Herbert Greer French, 1943.345.
Exhibitions: Cincinnati 1941, no. 160; New Brunswick 1983, no. 113, illus. 126.

Hercules Segers is one of the most eccentric and experimental printmakers of the European tradition. His total surviving oeuvre consists of 183 impressions from fifty-four plates, many printed on cloth. In fact, his first biographer, Samuel van Hoogstraeten, described Segers as "printing paintings."[1] Moreover, Segers hand colored his prints and cropped impressions to create a range of images that stress the uniqueness of each; consequently, his prints, although often multiples taken from the same plate, assume the character of monotypes.

Hercules Segers, son of a cloth merchant, Pieter Segers, was born in Haarlem in 1589 or 1590. The elder Segers had earlier emigrated from Flanders to Haarlem but moved again with his family to Amsterdam in 1596. There Hercules apprenticed with Gillis van Coninxloo, the celebrated landscape artist. When Coninxloo died in December 1606, Hercules Segers and his father bought several art works at Coninxloo's estate auction. After his father's death in 1612, Segers returned to Haarlem and joined its artists' guild, whose members at the time included Willem Buytewech and Esaias van de Velde. By late 1614 Segers was back in Amsterdam to secure custody of an illegitimate daughter. In 1615 he married Anneken van der Bruggen, sixteen years his senior, and in 1619 he bought a house on the Lindengracht in Amsterdam for the considerable sum of about four thousand guilders. By the late 1620s Segers had fallen into debt and, in 1631, was forced to sell his house. He moved to Utrecht the same year and supported his artistic pursuits by becoming an art dealer. In 1633 he moved to The Hague where he continued to deal, albeit on a larger scale. He must have died by 1638: in a document from that time, a certain Cornelia de Witte is mentioned as the widow of one Hercules Pietersz., presumably Segers. Although Segers is best known as a printmaker, he was also a landscape and still life painter of repute: the stadholder Frederick Henry acquired landscape paintings by Segers in 1632,[2] and a Segers landscape was once offered to the Danish king. Moreover, Rembrandt owned several pictures by Segers, including *Mountain Landscape*, now in the Uffizi in Florence, which he later reworked. Rembrandt not only collected Segers prints, he acquired the original copperplate of *Tobias and the Angel* (HB. 1), later transforming it into *The Flight into Egypt* (B. 56) (CAM 1943.300).

The cloistered Abbey of Rijnsburg was built by the count of Holland as the final burial place for members of his distinguished family. The Spanish destroyed the abbey during their protracted siege of Leiden (1573-74), and the last remnants of its ruins finally disappeared at the beginning of the nineteenth century.

Medieval ruins figure prominently in the graphic works of several leading Dutch landscape artists active at the beginning of the seventeenth century, including Claes Jansz. Visscher, Willem Buytewech, Esaias and Jan van de Velde, and Segers. Such ruins may allude to the transitory nature of human life and human endeavor.

On the other hand, Dutch artists may have used medieval ecclesiastical and feudal buildings, often left in ruins by the mercenary armies of Spain, to evoke a sense of Holland's past and as glorious remnants from an earlier age. Such subjects offered appealing pictorial opportunities to landscape artists and appear in sketchbooks and in suites of landscape prints extolling the beauties of the Dutch countryside.[3]

Segers produced two etchings of the Abbey of Rijnsburg. In both he depicts its large hall with the remains of its arcades leading to a stepped-gabled end wall. Vegetation and grass carpet what was once flooring and sheep graze among the building's former precincts. Segers printed the small version of *Ruins of the Abbey at Rijnsburg* in two states. The Museum's impression is one of four surviving impressions in the first state. Like the other three, it was printed in black ink on cloth prepared with gray watercolor.[4] Segers used cotton fabric instead of paper in prints lacking tone. Egbert Haverkamp-Begemann notes that in using cloth Segers enriched the graphic arts by introducing a prime feature of painting – a cloth support. Conversely, he transcribed qualities of printmaking to painting by seeming to print paintings.[5]

The Museum's impression of *Ruins* lacks any added tone: Segers indicated shadow solely by the relative density of the lines defining the shrubbery and the inner wall of the left arcade. By contrast, in one impression in Amsterdam, Segers used gray, bluish gray, and yellow washes to create a lively sense of modulated light throughout the scene (HB. 47 Ia). The front of the projecting wall and a strip across the foreground were tinted yellow; deeper gray washes were added across most of the ruins, generating a pronounced yet transparent shadow. The impression in the National Gallery of Art in Washington has gray and blue washes (HB. 47 Id). Specifically, Segers applied gray wash to the upper section of the stepped end wall and in a strip across the foreground up to and including the lower half of the standing man. He added a blue wash below the strip of gray in the foreground and throughout most of the buildings. He modulated blue and gray washes on the projecting arcades, imbuing the architecture with a plasticity less evident in the Museum's impression. Although it is perhaps the least evocative of those that survive in the first state, its limpid, pervading light is remarkable. This impression provides a standard of objectivity against which those with added washes must be gauged. The impressions in the second state printed on pink or green prepared paper are much more tonal and coloristic in effect (HB. 47 IIe, Dresden; HB. 47 IIf, Paris).

Segers produced a larger version of *Ruins of the Abbey of Rijnsburg* (HB. 46) in which the artist printed the subject in light yellowish ink on darkly tinted prepared papers.[6] The resulting images, several of which seem to have been conceived as nocturnes, are hallucinatory in effect. Haverkamp-Begemann believes that both versions of this subject were based on the same design, probably a drawing.[7] In the small version, a few curious blank zones to the right of the projecting arcade at center may suggest that it followed the larger version. The most conspicuous difference between the two versions is the representation of the chimney above the fireplace on the second level of the ruins in the right middle distance. In the small version its upper section directly above the fireplace mantel lacks supporting masonry and seems, therefore, to float in a void. The window above the arched doorway immediately to the right of the central projecting arcade is left blank; in the large version, it frames foliage.

A precise chronology of Segers' prints remains an elusive and probably unresolvable problem. Segers' changing domicile may have had some bearing on the present dating of *Ruins*. By 1633 Segers had moved to The Hague and would have found Leiden and its neighboring villages and ruins easily accessible. Nonetheless, the dating of either version of *Ruins* remains a vexing puzzle, as indicated by the broad parameters of Haverkamp-Begemann's suggested date, 1622/23-31 or perhaps later.[8] – GK

1. S. van Hoogstraeten, *Inleyding tot de Hooge Schoole der Schilderkonst* (1678), 312. For an English translation of Hoogstraeten's text, see HB., 23-24. In preparing this biographical sketch I also refer to Clifford S. Ackley, Boston 1980, 55, and A. Chong, Amsterdam 1987, 484-85.

2. During the seventeenth century, the stadholder of Holland was the supreme military commander of the land forces of the Dutch republic. Although nominally an office appointed by the States General, the position was *de facto* an hereditary one reserved for the leading members of the Orange Nassau family.

3. A key example of this phenomenon is the suite of twelve etchings by Claes Jansz. Visscher entitled *Plaisante Plaetsen* (*Pleasant Places*), published about 1611-12, in which Visscher includes a view of the Huis ter Kleef, a fortified castle in the environs of Haarlem. The Huis ter Kleef was destroyed by the Spanish army during the siege of Haarlem. For a discussion of the importance of Visscher's prints, see Ackley, Boston 1980, 61-62, nos. 35, 36, illus.

4. The impressions in the second state are printed on prepared paper rather than cloth. For a complete listing and description of each impression, see HB., 91.

5. HB., 47. The author also stresses that Segers would deliberately crop each impression, another idiosyncratic feature of his printmaking. Measurements can vary considerably from one impression to another, thus endowing each with unique compositional and visual effects.

6. Six impressions in a single state survive.

7. HB., 90.

8. HB., 53.

Hercules Segers
Haarlem ca. 1589/90-ca. 1638 The Hague?

76. Town with Four Towers ca. 1631 or later.
Etching and drypoint, printed in green on antique laid paper prepared with an olive green tint, with added pink washes, 20.1 x 32.6 cm (sheet).
Springer 26; HB. 29g; H. *Neth.* 29g.
Watermark: Indecipherable.
Annotations in sanguine on verso [reproduce].
Condition: Trimmed within platemark top only; single brown ink borderline across top and left side which has been reinforced along the bottom and right side.
Provenance: (D.A. Hoogendijk, Amsterdam); (Colnaghi, London, 1935); (purchased from M. Knoedler, New York, March 1, 1935, for $12,500).
Bequest of Herbert Greer French, 1943.344.
Exhibitions: Cincinnati 1941, no. 161; Minneapolis 1956, no. 156.

Town with Four Towers is one of Segers' seminal prints. In it the artist tries to reconcile his interest in vast mountain scenery with a landscape more strongly defined by human habitation. This departure from his usual austere mountain panoramas nevertheless is predicated on them, suggesting that *Town with Four Towers* dates later than the majority of his landscape prints, including all of his arid mountain scenes.

In this etching, Segers combines native Dutch architecture with references to Italy and Rome. Specifically, he includes a pedimented building in the middle ground that recalls the Church of Santa Maria del Priorato in Rome. By contrast, the tall spire dominating the town at the left alludes to the Church of Our Lady in Amersfoort, a town that Segers represented in another print (HB. 30). The vast, rolling landscape is neither Dutch nor Italian but purely imaginary. The artist's means of delineating this landscape deserves close analysis because it may provide a clue in dating this important print. In it Segers employed a system of shading in which he combined patches of oblique parallel hatching in drypoint with hand-colored details to

accent the landscape. Moreover, Segers often alternated zones of oblique shading with areas free from wash. The result is a patchwork quilt of alternating dark and lighter zones. Reinforced by hand-colored washes, this landscape attains complex visual effects unlike virtually any of Seger's other prints. The coloristic system devised for this print is unique and explains why he produced so many impressions of *Town with Four Towers* with such closely related coloristic effects.

Segers's combination of Dutch and Mediterranean motifs in this print finds analogies in two landscape paintings now in Rotterdam.[1] These paintings are generally dated late and provide circumstantial support for dating *Town with Four Towers* to about 1631 or later. *Town with Four Towers* is also closely related to Segers' two panoramic views of Amersfoort and Wageningen (HB. 30 and 31). In both prints, but more evident in *Panoramic View of Amersfoort*, Segers employed dense oblique drypoint shading to create the type of alternating patchwork of light and dark across an open landscape that also appears in *Town with Four Towers*.[2] His interest in delineating space in such a manner finds perfect resolution in the vast rising vista in *Town with Four Towers*. The artist leads the eye from the broadly defined masses in the foreground to the land beyond where isolated crags emerge from largely cultivated, rolling countryside. In his more austere mountain panoramas, the viewer perceives the subject from a high vantage point. By lowering the viewpoint, Segers sets the observer before an open foreground stage, the vista rising up beyond it. The resulting continuous flow of space enables Segers to focus more on individual detail than was possible in his earlier panoramas or in his sweeping views of Amersfoort and Wageningen. The unfolding landscape in *Town with Four Towers* is kindred to Segers's late landscape paintings and suggests that it should be dated late and recognized as a synthesis of his landscape idiom.

The Museum's print is one of nine impressions of this subject that exist in a single state. It is exceptionally well preserved and bears no trace of abrasion.[3] Unlike *The Enclosed Valley* (HB. 13) for which Segers produced impressions ranging enormously in mood through experimental coloring and cropping, most impressions of the *Town with Four Towers* are similar in mood and coloration. All but one are printed in green, either on unprepared paper or on paper prepared with a white or pale green body color. In certain impressions, the artist first hand colored specific zones in red then applied an olive green body color over the entire surface. This green body color can vary considerably in opacity and transparency. Nonetheless, five impressions, including three in Amsterdam and those in London and Cincinnati, are similar in coloring. Examined together they suggest that Segers was striving to attain closely related visual effects.

Of the six impressions of *Town with Four Towers* in Amsterdam, three are comparable to the Museum's impression, two diverge significantly from it, and one is a radical departure from all remaining examples. The impression most similar to that in Cincinnati is printed in green on unprepared white paper and is hand colored throughout with navy green body color and patches of red watercolor (HB. 29a). Many of the isolated red zones have been partially masked by the green body color, but Segers left certain prominent objects – the central field in the foreground, the two boulders beyond it, and the two churches in the middle ground – untouched by the green overlay. In one respect this Amsterdam impression differs considerably from the others. In it Segers added a thin blue wash across the entire horizon to produce pronounced atmospheric effects. The second impression in Amsterdam (HB. 29c) is printed in dark bluish green on a navy green prepared paper with added hand-colored washes in olive green and brown. The sky evokes a sense of atmospheric pall yet is surprisingly transparent, the result being that the horizon glows with light. This luminosity suggests a vast sense of depth. This impression, like Cincinnati's, is notable for its spatial clarity. The third Amsterdam impression (HB. 29b), printed solely in green on grayish white prepared paper, emphasizes the stark contrast between light and shadow throughout the landscape. By applying a thin, transparent grayish white wash across the sky and suggesting the formation of cumulus clouds, Segers again achieved pronounced atmospheric effects. Segers attained an absolutely monochrome effect in the fourth Amsterdam impression (HB. 29d). It is printed in dark green on white paper and is hand colored in a deep olive green body color. The subject is extremely muted in effect, the green body color so thickly applied that the sky lacks all transparency and suggests an oppressive atmospheric pall. The fifth Amsterdam impression (HB. 29f) is printed in dark bluish green ink on green prepared paper. Segers represented the sky in a metallic blue gouache with patches of modulated white and cream that have since turned a sickly yellow.[4] The last impression in Amsterdam (HB. 29e) is printed in dark green ink on paper now a brownish green. Segers hand tinted details in red, but these are now largely obscured by the darkened paper. He also added a deep bluish green across the upper zone of the sky with a grayish blue to light blue gouache across the horizon and accentuated the silhouette of the distant mountains with white chalk. This image is totally atmospheric, its detail largely obliterated. It is particularly evocative and seems to depict the subject at dusk.

The single impression in the British Museum (HB. 29h) is most similar to that in Cincinnati's collection. It is printed in green ink on unprepared paper. Segers colored certain details a delicate red and coated the entire print with a deep olive green body color. Although detail appears more pronounced in the Museum's impression, which results in a greater sense of spatial clarity, in coloration the impressions in Cincinnati and London are similar and both manifest analogous, albeit not identical, visual effects. The slight differences display the artist's subtle modulation of related atmospheric conditions. Segers strove to create similar visual effects in three impressions in Amsterdam (particularly HB. 29a, 29c, and 29d). Thus, five impressions differ from one another only slightly and convey closely related atmospheric qualities. Together they indicate the specific direction that Segers was pursuing in his concept of landscape at the height of his career. – GK

1. *Old Paintings 1400–1900* (Rotterdam: Museum Boymans-van Beuningen, 1972), 46–47, illus. Both pictures, which Alan Chong dates to the 1620s, are also included in Amsterdam 1987, nos. 100, 101, pls. 29, 40.

2. Segers also employs this type of drypoint shading in a number of his mountain panoramas, including *Rocky Landscape: A Church Tower in the Distance* (HB. 7, state II), *Rocky Mountains, Tree Stumps in the Foreground* (HB. 8), *The Enclosed Valley* (HB. 13, state II), *Rocky Mountains, a Forked Tree at One Side* (HB. 15, state II), *Mountain Gorge Bordered by a Road* (HB. 17, state II), *Mountain and Ravines* (HB. 19), *River Valley with a Waterfall: Version I* (HB. 21, state II), and *Distant View with a Branch of a Pine Tree* (HB. 27, states II and III). Six of these subjects lack this oblique shading in the first state. Hypothetically, this shading could have postdated the early states of these prints by many years. As Segers evolved this method of shading in prints like his *Panoramic View of Amersfoort* and *Town with Four Towers*, he might have wished to apply it to some of his earlier mountain panoramas.

3. For a complete listing, see HB., 29a–29i.

4. Unfortunately this impression has suffered egregiously, with disfiguring staining transforming most of the sky and all but destroying the artist's intended effects. The metallic blue sky would have provided a remarkable foil to the murky landscape below.

Rembrandt Harmensz. van Rijn

Leiden 1606-1669 Amsterdam

77. The Death of the Virgin 1639.

Etching and drypoint on antique laid paper, 39.1 x 31.4 cm (sheet).
B. 99; Hind *Rem.* 161 ii/iv; Münz 208 ii/iii; H. *Neth.* 99 ii/iii.
Signed and dated in plate lower left: *Rembrandt f. 1639.*
Condition: Trimmed to or within platemark.
Provenance: (Purchased from M. Knoedler, New York, September 15, 1930, for $950).
Bequest of Herbert Greer French, 1943.276.

The Death of the Virgin is one of Rembrandt's pivotal prints. In it he displays a new approach to printmaking that differs from his earlier large prints and employs etching with remarkable freedom and variety. By combining summarily sketched areas with others of considerable detail, the artist evokes the visionary and the supernatural. This stylistic shift partially reflects Rembrandt's changed social and professional circumstances during the late 1630s.

Rembrandt was born in Leiden in 1606. Son of a miller, he attended the Leiden Latin school and, at age fourteen, matriculated at Leiden University. He abandoned his studies to become an artist and studied first with Jacob van Swanenburgh in Leiden from about 1621 until 1623. In 1624 Rembrandt went to Amsterdam, where he worked with Pieter Lastman for about six months. Lastman, one of the leading painters in the city, left an indelible mark on Rembrandt and introduced him to the realm of history painting. Rembrandt returned to Leiden and set up a studio with a colleague, Jan Lievens. Both artists came to the attention of Constantijn Huygens, who would later prove instrumental in securing commissions for Rembrandt from the stadholder Frederick Henry. In Leiden Rembrandt first attracted students, including Gerrit Dou, but by 1632 he had moved back to Amsterdam permanently. Not a citizen of the city when he arrived, Rembrandt lived and maintained a studio in the home of Hendrik van Uylenburgh, an art dealer. There Rembrandt met Uylenburgh's niece, Saskia, whom he married in 1634. Of their four children, only Titus van Rijn, born in 1641, lived to maturity. Saskia died in 1642 after what may have been an extended illness. Rembrandt and Saskia bought a grand house on the Jodenbreestraat (now the Rembrandthuis). During this period, Rembrandt was a voracious collector. His financial obligations became ever more pressing, and by the mid-1650s Rembrandt faced financial ruin. He was forced to declare bankruptcy and liquidate his holdings. In 1657-58 the contents of his house, including his vast art collection, were sold at auction. Inventories drawn up at the time offer a unique glimpse into Rembrandt's encyclopedic collection. Hendrickje Stoffels, his companion during the later years, bore Rembrandt a daughter, Cornelia. Because Rembrandt and Hendrickje never married, she was called before a tribunal of the Dutch Reformed Church and ostracized, although she later conceded that Cornelia should be baptized. In 1659 Hendrickje and Titus formed a partnership to protect Rembrandt's diminished finances. The family eventually moved to the Rozengracht in the unfashionable Jordaan district of Amsterdam. There Rembrandt spent the last decade of his life. Henrickje died in 1663, and Titus predeceased his father by several months. Only a granddaughter, Titia, outlived him. Rembrandt died in 1669 and was buried in the Westerkerk in Amsterdam.

Rembrandt's decision to move permanently to Amsterdam reflects his ambition to establish his reputation in the largest and wealthiest city in the Dutch republic. His work prior to about 1630 tended to be modest in scale yet remarkable for its precise detail. No doubt

Rembrandt's initial contact with Lastman inspired him to compose history subjects, focusing on narrative clarity and the virtuoso display of expression. Thus fostered, Rembrandt's interest in representing sentiment applied not only to his history paintings but to portraiture as well. His first triumph in exploring a full range of expression is *The Anatomy Lesson of Dr. Nicolas Tulp* (1632), a life-sized group portrait conceived as a dialogue between the famous surgeon and his students, who respond powerfully to his learned discourse.

In a number of large-scale religious prints from the early to mid-1630s and in certain religious paintings, Rembrandt explores narrative conventions. The paintings, including *The Blinding of Samson* (1636) and a series of scenes from the Passion of Christ that were acquired by Frederick Henry on the recommendation of his secretary, Constantijn Huygens, were conceived in an exuberant baroque idiom. These paintings may have been produced partly in response to the celebrated religious paintings of Peter Paul Rubens, known in the Dutch republic through large, highly finished reproductive engravings produced under Rubens' supervision. The marketing and dissemination of Rubens' ideas through such reproductions also seems to have affected Rembrandt's printmaking activities during the mid-1630s. Rembrandt produced three large-scale religious prints during this time: *The Raising of Lazarus* from about 1632 (B. 73), *The Descent from the Cross* dated 1633 (B. 81-II),[1] and *Christ before Pilate* from 1636 (B. 77). *The Descent from the Cross* is an adaptation of Rembrandt's painting from the Passion series. The arched format of *The Raising of Lazarus* links it to the same series, whereas Rembrandt conceived of *Christ before Pilate* as an independent invention for which he produced a preparatory grisaille (Br. 546), now in the National Gallery in London.

These three prints are remarkable for their precisely rendered detail. The almost compulsive descriptive capacity of these works manifests a direction that Rembrandt subsequently abandoned. Ultimately, this enormously time-consuming goal proved antithetical to Rembrandt's aspirations as printmaker. Instead of offering him greater freedom of expression, precise rendering shackled his expressive capacity.

Dated 1639, *The Death of the Virgin*, Rembrandt's first large-scale print following *Christ before Pilate*, manifests a radically different approach to the medium.[2] Christopher White discusses the unique importance of *The Death of the Virgin* and stresses the wonderful freedom of its execution. Tone and detail are perfectly blended in this image, an image both pictorial and linear at the same time.[3] White also ascertains that Rembrandt drew inspiration from several sources, including Dürer's woodcuts from *The Life of the Virgin* and Dirck Crabeth's stained-glass window, *The Death of the Virgin*, in the Oude Kerk in Amsterdam.[4] Moreover, as White also indicates, Saskia had been bedridden during this very period. Rembrandt produced a number of sketches of his wife convalescing. His familiarity with her sickroom would certainly have influenced his interpretation of *The Death of the Virgin*, particularly in terms of the tender ministrations to the sick and the wide range of emotional response countenanced by this subject. Rembrandt's etching includes certain features that differ from the historical antecedents cited by White. The Virgin reclines on an ornate canopied bed within a large chamber that assumes the scale of a throne room. Despite its size and costly furnishings, the artist avoided defining the interior space in rigorous architectural perspective. The faintly defined ceiling beams are largely obliterated by a supernatural vision of a host of angels appearing in a burst of light. This miraculous light source illuminates the bed and the figures surrounding the Virgin, although none is cognizant of this divine revelation. The attendant figures include a high priest, an acolyte, a seated scribe reading at a table in the left foreground, several women, and a physician who takes the Virgin's pulse. Rembrandt expanded the range of participants ministering to the Virgin, no longer restricting the number to twelve apostles, which better places the subject in the realm of normative experience. This accessibility is underscored by the poignant expression of pathos conveyed in the faces and hand gestures of the figures gathered at the foot of the bed: the clasped hands of the standing woman, the praying hands of the woman behind her, and the outreached left hand of John the Evangelist sharply framed by the dark curtain behind it.

Certain features imply that Rembrandt may have been familiar with other representations of the death of the Virgin, including Martin Schongauer's engraving (Lehrs 363), Hugo van der Goes' painting, now in Bruges, or a variant thereof,[5] and Pieter Bruegel the Elder's composition,[6] engraved by Philip Galle. The onlookers in Schongauer's engraving communicate an emotional intensity with their febrile hands and expressive gazes. Their frenetic activity contrasts with the emotional restraint of the figures in Dürer's 1510 woodcut, *Death of the Virgin* (B. 93). Moreover, Schongauer conspicuously includes two kneeling apostles at the foot of the bed reading from the Scriptures. Although Dürer includes a similar pair of figures, their activity calls less attention to itself. By contrast, Rembrandt magnifies and modifies this motif.

Hugo van der Goes' painting contains one feature not found in the prints of Schongauer and Dürer: a supernatural vision of Christ, accompanied by angels, appearing in a burst of light in the Virgin's bedchamber. While not obliterating the setting to the degree found in Rembrandt's etching, it is an analogous vision to which the participants below remain oblivious.

Bruegel's composition includes several features that may have stimulated Rembrandt. Bruegel elaborates on the setting and its furnishings. The figures in attendance include patriarchs, martyrs, confessors, and holy virgins, as well as the twelve apostles.[7] The main source of supernatural light seems to emanate from the Virgin and fills the canopied bed. Rembrandt employs this lighting in a different way, with the divine light source from above playing on the limp figure of the Virgin.

The Museum's impression of *The Death of the Virgin* is in the second state. The armchair at the right has been darkened with drypoint.[8] In the third state, fine vertical, parallel hatching was added to the nearest footpost of the bed.[9]

Of Rembrandt's roughly three hundred etchings only twenty-eight have bottom margins. Most contain the artist's monogram or signature, often followed by the date.[10] He signed and dated *The Death of the Virgin* at the bottom left yet retained the blank margin in all three states. Whether Rembrandt ever envisaged adding text to the margin remains impossible to ascertain. From the artist's point of view, perhaps, the blank space served as an important pictorial foil to the subject above. *The Death of the Virgin*, Rembrandt's most ambitious print to date, was a watershed in his career as printmaker. In it he liberated his instincts as an etcher and concentrated on tonal values and the interplay of light and shadow. Rembrandt expressed a full range of grief, from anguish to resignation, but he also infused this outpouring of emotion with the supernatural, creating a religious subject of great pathos. – GK

1. The first version of this print, B. 81-I, failed to bite properly, and Rembrandt abandoned the plate. See Christopher White, *Rembrandt as an Etcher* (London 1969), 33-34.

2. As noted by White, *Rembrandt as an Etcher*, 43.

3. White, *Rembrandt as an Etcher*, 43.

4. White, *Rembrandt as an Etcher*, 45, fig. 39.

5. Max J. Friedländer, *Early Netherlandish Painting* (New York, 1969), vol. 4, no. 14, pl. 22.

6. For Bruegel's grisaille of *Death of the Virgin*, Upton House in Warwickshire, see

W. Stechow, *Pieter Bruegel the Elder* (New York: Harry N. Abrams, n.d.), 25.

7. Stechow, *Pieter Bruegel*, 24.

8. Hind *Rem.*, 161, believed in the existence of an earlier intermediate state in which the bottom margin contained noticeable scratches that he thought were subsequently removed. The degree to which these show up or are absent seems to be determined by the inking and wiping of this section of the plate. Christopher White and Karel Boon (H. *Neth.* 99) query the existence of this supposed intermediate state and eliminate it in their listed sequence of states.

9. This hatching wore away so completely that it is often difficult to distinguish between characteristic impressions of the second and third states. One guideline is the degree of wear evident elsewhere in the plate. However, the copperplate of *The Death of the Virgin* proved to be remarkably resistant to wear. The resulting number of still passable posthumous pulls from this plate is remarkably high.

10. In certain instances, B. 28, 81, 88, and 90, the artist filled this space prominently with his signature.

Claude Lorrain

Chamagne 1600-1682 Rome

78. The Shipwreck ca. 1638-41.

Etching on antique laid paper, 12.6 x 17.9 cm (sheet).
RD. 7 ii/ii; Mannocci 35 ii/v.
Inscribed with number lower left: 3; signed lower center: CL inv.
Condition: Trimmed within platemark.
Provenance: (Purchased from M. Knoedler, New York, September 12, 1927, for $54).
Bequest of Herbert Greer French, 1943.351.
Exhibitions: Washington 1982, no. 44B, illus.

Perhaps the most consistently celebrated European landscape painter of all time, Claude Lorrain has also been accorded the highest rank within the realm of printmaking. Etching slightly over thirty landscapes and seascapes, Claude pushed the medium in unconventional ways to evoke in pure black and white an unerring sense for the light of day within the ideal landscape.[1] At times seeming almost sketchy in execution (especially in later dull impressions), his etchings masterfully use this lack of definition and "finish" to unify their overall effect. Working at exactly the same time as Rembrandt (cats. 81, 84-85), Claude showed a similar willingness to experiment and feel his way through the medium with few, if any, precedents.

Born Claude Gellée in the independent duchy of Lorraine (seven years after his countryman Jacques Callot, cat. 74), Claude had made his way to Rome by the age of thirteen, either as an apprentice craftsman or pastry cook.[2] He seems to have studied painting with Agostino Tassi, spending two years in Naples, from 1618, and afterward working in Rome for Tassi for several years. After spending two years in Lorraine, from 1625, he returned to Rome in October 1627 and remained there for the rest of his life, venturing only into the nearby countryside for sketching trips. At this time, Rome was a major center of artistic activity, and many Northern artists traveled there to further their classical and aesthetic education. In the midst of this large colony of expatriate artists, Claude quickly achieved a reputation for landscape painting. From the mid-1630s forward, he served a steady stream of popes, cardinals, nobles, and foreigners, all eager to commission works from him. He worked steadily until a few weeks before his death. About three hundred paintings by him are known; the Cincinnati Art Museum owns *Artist Studying from Nature* (CAM 1946.102).[3]

Claude's first etchings date from about 1630, but it is not known how or from whom he learned the technique. Both the rough draftsmanship and the technique of staged bitings (stopping-out the etching action in various phases) point to the early influence of Adam Elsheimer (a German painter who had lived in Rome) and

Callot.[4] After etching the majority of his plates during the 1630s, Claude seems to have put aside the medium except for two large plates, which were executed around 1650, and three more, which were produced in the early 1660s. Although there were many printers and print publishers in Rome at this time, Claude seems never to have officially published any of his landscape etchings and probably printed the majority of them himself. A printing press was listed among the contents of his studio at his death.[5]

Claude's fame as a painter has assured that a considerable amount of praiseworthy attention has been given to his etchings over the centuries, although he has been occasionally criticized for a lack of technical finesse. Writing in the eighteenth century, William Gilpin lamented that Claude's "execution is bad; there is a dirtiness in it, which is disgusting," and he called his etchings "below his character."[6] Only slightly later, however, Goethe described Claude's etchings as "the true ideal, which can so use real means of expression that the truth which emerges gives the illusion of actuality."[7] In the next century, Turner perceived Claude as a rival whose achievements he had to surpass, both in his paintings and in his series of ideal landscape prints, the *Liber Studiorum* (cat. 117), in imitation of Claude's own *Liber Veritatis*.[8] The British print critic E. S. Lumsden, writing in 1929, cited *Dance by the Waterside* (Mannocci 13, also in the French Collection, CAM 1943.347) as being "as true to nature as any of the contemporary Dutch landscapes except those of Rembrandt." Lumsden also remarked on Claude's "bigness of design," so unlike the Northern love of particularity.[9] Finally, William Ivins (in a twist on Goethe's statement) declared that Claude's etchings "have a dreamlike quality that would have been difficult for a more realistic draughtsman to attain."[10]

The Shipwreck is not a typical work within Claude's etched oeuvre. The majority of his etchings reflect his influential pastoral landscape style and are not full of such drama. He etched only one other sea storm, in 1630 (Mannocci 6), and one of his later etchings, circa 1650-51, depicts a herd in a landscape dominated by an approaching storm (Mannocci 40). Such subjects, although not unknown, are comparatively rare in his paintings. There were certainly precedents and an active tradition of marine painting at this time, especially in Northern art but also in Italy, as in the work of Claude's master Tassi and in works by Filippo Napoletano (ca. 1585-1629).[11] Mannocci points out that Claude had experienced a storm at sea during his return to Italy in 1627.[12] His sea storms provided the prototypes for a series of twenty-eight etchings of similar subjects by his contemporary and friend Dominique Barrière (ca. 1610-1678), dated 1646.[13]

For its composition *The Shipwreck* seems to depend on a lost painting, executed circa 1638-39 for the Duke of Bracciano, Paolo Giordano Orsini, perhaps illustrating the duke's motto, *contra ventos et undas* (against wind and waves).[14] The painting is recorded in a drawing from the *Liber Veritatis* that varies from the etching in that the principal ship is smaller in scale and differently placed.[15] The other elements in the etching are essentially identical to the drawing, although another small ship has been added in the far distance. In addition to the general precedents cited above, Diane Russell relates the motif of an imperiled ship set below a high rock and castle to a fresco by Paul Bril (1554-1626) in the Church of the Scala Santa, Rome. She also interprets the theme of the sea storm as an allegorical representation of the "sea of life."[16]

Claude's vivid etching strokes and the prominent slanting rain in the sky add tempestuous energy to the scene.[17] Only the earliest impressions such as this one reveal diagonal strokes of burnishing in the upper left corner, the result of an attempt to lighten that area of the plate. The Museum's print shows the great range of Claude's etched lines, from the finest strokes of rain and sea foam to the heavily etched foreground. Subtler qualities, such as the sculptural presence of the waves and the figures silhouetted on the rock, are lost in later printings. In late impressions, the figures become mere cutouts and the area of sky and water at left practically disappears. Claude's etchings were reprinted often after his death until well into the early nineteenth century.

The Museum's impression of *The Shipwreck* is an ideally fresh and early printing of the presumed second state of the plate. Mannocci assumes there must have been impressions before the addition of the numeral 3 that appears in the left margin and before the burnishing of the initials "*CL inv.*" at the bottom center of the image; however, no such are known to him. Only four impressions of this state are recorded, the others being in Amsterdam (Rijksprentenkabinet), Paris (Bibliothèque Nationale), and San Francisco (Achenbach Foundation).

Mr. French acquired fine impressions of four other Claude etchings: *Harbor Scene with Rising Sun* (Mannocci 15), *The Cowherd* (Mannocci 18), *The Shipwreck* (Mannocci 35), and *Harbor Scene with a Lighthouse* (Mannocci 37), now all a part of the Museum's collection. – DPB

1. In 1637 he also etched one series of thirteen festival designs to commemorate the coronation of Ferdinand III of Hungary as king of the Romans. See Lino Mannocci, *The Etchings of Claude Lorrain* (New Haven and London: Yale University Press, 1988), nos. 21-33, and also Peter Krüger, "The *Feux d'artifice* by Claude Lorrain," PQ. 7, no. 4 (December 1990), 424-33.

2. Two recent, clear biographies are in H. Diane Russell, Washington 1982, 47-59; and Mannocci, *Etchings*, 3-6.

3. Marcel Röthlisberger, *Claude Lorrain – The Paintings*, 2 vols. (New Haven: Yale University Press, 1961), no. 44, repr. fig. 107. The Cincinnati painting is closely related to Claude's etching of the same subject (Mannocci 36, CAM 1947.480).

4. For Elsheimer's influence, see Mannocci, *Etchings*, 94; also see Sue Welsh Reed, Richard Wallace et al., Boston 1989b, 151-52.

5. See Mannocci, *Etchings*, 20-22, for a discussion about a possible publishing project for twelve of his plates at the end of the 1630s.

6. Mannocci, *Etchings*, 12.

7. Mannocci, *Etchings*, 12.

8. Claude's *Liber* was an album of drawings that he intended as a record of his major painted compositions. By the eighteenth century it was in England and was reproduced in a series of mezzotints by Richard Earlom in 1777.

9. Mannocci, *Etchings*, 15.

10. Mannocci, *Etchings*, 15.

11. Mannocci, *Etchings*, 57.

12. Mannocci, *Etchings*, 57.

13. *Differentes vues de mer* (*Various Seaviews* – I.F.F. 1600 I.272-73.2-29).

14. Mannocci, *Etchings*, 216. Mannocci does not agree with a suggestion by Röthlisberger that the etching was first commissioned to illustrate the motto, with the drawing and painting following.

15. Reproduced in Mannocci, *Etchings*, 216, fig. 194, and Michael Kitson, *Claude Lorrain: Liber Veritatis* (London: British Museum, 1978), no. 33. Only two other drawings in the *Liber* depict sea storms (Kitson nos. 72 and 74); they are datable circa 1643-44.

16. H. Diane Russell, Washington 1982, 392.

17. One is reminded of the stormy sky in Rembrandt's etching *The Three Trees* (cat. 81), dated 1643.

Wenceslaus Hollar

Prague 1607-1677 London

79. **Design for a Chalice** 1640.

Etching on antique laid paper, 46.9 x 24.0 cm (sheet).
Parthey 2643; Pennington 2643.
Watermark: Crowned armorial shield.
Inscribed across bottom: *Tabulam hanc, olim ab* ANDREA MANTENIO *cum penna delineatam, et nunc/Londini in Ædibus Arundelianis conseruatam, Wenceslaus Hollar, Bohem, aqua forti æri insculpsit 1640* (This picture, formerly drawn by Andrea

Mantegna with the pen, and now preserved in London at Arundel House, Wenceslaus Hollar of Bohemia has engraved in brass with acid, 1640).
Provenance: Herschel V. Jones, Minneapolis (1928); Tessie Jones, Newburgh, New Jersey (consigned to Knoedler, May 13, 1940); (purchased from M. Knoedler, New York, June 19, 1940, for $175). Bequest of Herbert Greer French, 1943.329.
Exhibitions: Cincinnati 1941, no. 180, pl. 27.

The diversity of names by which Hollar is known reflects his cosmopolitan career. In his native city of Prague, he is Vaclav Hollar; in Germany, where he came to maturity as an artist, he is Wenzel Hollar; and the English, who adopted him as they adopted Hans Holbein, call him Wenceslaus. Born in what is now Czechoslovakia but was then called Bohemia, Hollar left Prague at the age of twenty and, for the next ten years, traveled around Germany, growing increasingly skillful in the topographic landscape that would become one of his specialties. A major turning point in his career occurred in 1636 when he met the English nobleman Thomas Howard, Earl of Arundel, in Cologne. Arundel, who was traveling to Vienna and Prague on a diplomatic mission from Charles I of England to the court of the Holy Roman Emperor, engaged Hollar as a draftsman to record the journey; and when Arundel returned to England, Hollar accompanied him.[1] In London Hollar formed part of Arundel's enormous household, and on a portrait of Arundel that he etched in 1639, Hollar describes himself as Arundel's engraver. Hollar's position in Arundel's household should not be construed as his being a servant in the "Upstairs, Downstairs" sense of the word. Arundel was one of the great political powers in England: for Hollar being attached to his household was probably analogous to being a consultant for the Democratic National Committee or the lobbying group of a major industry. Hollar's contemporary John Aubrey described him as one of Arundel's "gentlemen"; in fact, his family had claim to a minor title of nobility in Bohemia that Arundel had had confirmed by the emperor at the time of his mission to Prague.[2]

Arundel's lifelong aim was to increase the power and dignity of his family, which had fallen under a cloud because of their adherence to the Catholic religion and the involvement of some members of the previous generation in plots against the crown. The vast collections of art that he assembled not only served his own delight but increased his prestige as a patron of the arts. And just as a twentieth-century corporation will underwrite a university research project or the production of a televised opera, Arundel supported scholars, architects, and artists.[3]

Much of what Hollar produced during this time, including the many English landscapes and city views for which he is particularly famous, seems unconnected with Arundel's patronage, but this print is clearly associated with the earl. According to George Vertue, an early biographer of Hollar, Arundel "had several gravers constantly at work with a design to make a large volume of prints of all his pictures, drawings and other rarities."[4] *Design for a Chalice* is one of four prints representing objects from Arundel's collection that Hollar produced during the period from 1637-41, but he was probably making drawings of many others. He later issued at least fifty-nine prints whose inscriptions indicate that they reproduce works in the earl's collection. By the time these later prints were issued, however, Arundel and his wife were in exile, casualties of the English civil war; their collection was being sold off; and Hollar was no longer associated with them.[5]

It may seem surprising that so much effort should have been lavished on the reproduction of a drawing when Arundel possessed magnificent paintings and works of sculpture, but paintings and sculpture in the house of a great nobleman were on semi-public display already.[6] The drawing, hidden in a portfolio, would have been seen by few, and only its reproduction in a print would call the attention of a large audience to its undeniable splendor.

Now in the British Museum, the drawing is no longer attributed to Mantegna but to an anonymous Venetian artist working in the third quarter of the fifteenth century (1450-75).[7] It is thus roughly contemporary with another design for goldsmith's work in this exhibition, the *Design for a Mantle-Clasp*, by the Master W (cat. 10), and it is interesting to note the different approaches of the two artists. The Italian has meticulously shaded the chalice so as to indicate its solid roundness; one could easily imagine that the drawing is a record of an actual object rather than a design for one. Even the different techniques of metalwork that would be employed are clearly distinguishable: relief (perhaps *repoussé* work) in the upper portion, cast figures and ornament around the stem, and engraving (probably niello work) around the base.

The semicircle at the top of the design probably represents the Communion wafer, since the chalice is a cup designed for the celebration of the Mass. It is decorated with motifs appropriate to the coming of Christ and the foundation of Christianity. On the stem of the cup are eight figures in niches, of which four can be seen in the drawing: one is Paul, another probably John the Evangelist; presumably the other six would have been apostles. The base is divided into twelve sections (six visible in the drawing), with elaborate engraved decoration, including a half-length figure in each section and two smaller figures below. The twelve apostles would be an appropriate base for such a cup, but the turbans and exotic costumes of the figures suggest that they belong to the Old Testament (prophets or ancestors of Christ), particularly if the niche-figures above are conceded to be apostles. Around the bowl of the cup is a band of panels showing the Passion of Christ: running from left to right (because of Hollar's reversal of the composition) they are the resurrection of Lazarus, the entry into Jerusalem, the garden of Gethsemane, the betrayal of Christ, Christ on trial, and the flagellation of Christ. (On the other side of the cup, six more scenes would doubtless have included the bearing of the cross, the Crucifixion, and the Resurrection.) It is probably deliberate that the Last Supper, a crucial episode in the drama, is omitted: the cup itself and the Mass in which it would be used would represent the Last Supper.

Given such a drawing, what were the qualities that Hollar brought to the task of reproducing it? An English acquaintance, Francis Place, described him as "a very passionate man easily moved. He has often told me, he was always uneasie if not at work."[8] Like his somewhat older contemporary Jacques Callot (see cat. 74), Hollar was one of those etchers who produced an enormous body of work (more than twenty-six hundred prints in all). Also, like Callot, Hollar tightly controlled his line, making prints with the highly finished appearance of engravings. But where Callot's line races, leaps, and dances, Hollar's walks. It is easy to see this print as the creation of a workaholic, but the passion is less obvious. Still, Hollar seems to have had the ability to focus his gaze on a thing, whether a building, a woman's dress, or a drawing, with a quiet intensity that would carry him through the meticulous labor of drawing on the plate and manipulating the etcher's acid. Step by step, one line after another is laid down. Individually none is any more lively than a paving stone, but each fits with the others, and when Hollar is done, the road is there, smooth and well built, to the goal he set.

Two centuries after Hollar's death the etcher Seymour Haden paid tribute to his unassuming technical proficiency:

If anyone want[s] truth without pretension let him go to Hollar. If he want[s] perfection of "biting" and the precise degree of gradation required, let him also go to Hollar. If he want[s] to live in the time illustrated, let him again go to Hollar. . . . People sometimes say to me, "What is it you see in Hollar?" and I always answer – "Not quite but nearly everything."[9]

Haden was probably thinking in particular of Hollar's sober landscapes and city views, so different from his own romantic Rembrandtism (cat. 129). But "truth without pretension" and "the precise degree of gradation required" are equally applicable to his rendition of intricate ornament and subtle passages of light and shade in this print. – TR

1. The best recent studies of Hollar are the catalogue raisonné by Pennington and two exhibition catalogues: Antony Griffiths and Gabriela Kesnerová, London 1983b; and Hans Mielke, Berlin 1984. Pennington builds upon the foundation of the nineteenth-century catalogue by Parthey.
2. John Aubrey, *"Brief Lives," Chiefly of Contemporaries, Set Down by John Aubrey between the Years 1669 and 1696*, ed. Andrew Clark (Oxford: Clarendon Press, 1898), 1:301, 407-08. Pennington, xxiii.
3. The basic biography of Arundel is Mary F. S. Hervey, *The Life, Correspondence and Collections of Thomas Howard, Earl of Arundel* (Cambridge: Cambridge University Press, 1921), which has not been superseded by the recent book by David Howarth, *Lord Arundel and his Circle* (New Haven and London: Yale University Press, 1985).
4. *The Walpole Society* 18 (1930) (Vertue's note books, 1) 47.
5. Pennington, xxvii-xxviii.
6. Hervey, *Life, Correspondence and Collections*, 255-57, describes the display of the collections at Arundel House. See also Pennington, xxv.
7. Popham and Pouncey, 1:197, no. 327; 2: pl. 280.
8. *The Walpole Society* 18 (1930) (Vertue's note books, 1) 34-35.
9. Francis Seymour Haden, *About Etching* (London: Fine Art Society, 1879), 44-45.

Ludwig von Siegen
Utrecht 1609-1680? Wolfenbüttel

80. Amelia Elisabeth, Landgravine of Hesse-Cassel 1642.
Mezzotint on antique laid paper, 45.6 x 33.4 cm (sheet).
Nagler 1 i/ii; Sm. I i/ii.
Watermark: Crowned shield with fleur-de-lis and initials WR and IHS with cross and initials LR.
Inscribed below: AMELIA ELISABETHA, D. G. HASSIAE LANDGRAVIA *etc.*/ COMITESSA HANOVIAE MVNTZENB:/ Illustrissimo ac Cel:[ssimo] Pr:ac Dño Dño WILHELMO VI. D. G. HASSIAE LANDGR: *etc. hanc Serenissimae Matris/ et Incomparabilis Heroinae effigiem, ad vivum á se primum depictam novoá; jam sculpturae modo expressam dedicat conse=/cratá; L.á.S. Aõ Dñj* M.D. C. XLII[I] (Amelia Elisabeth, by the grace of God Landgravine of Hesse etc, Comtesse of Hanover-Müntzenberg. To the illustrious and celebrated Prince and Master William VI, by the grace of God Landgrave of Hesse etc. this portrait of the earnest mother and incomparable heroine which has been first depicted [i.e. drawn or painted] from life, and then engraved in a new manner, is dedicated and consecrated by L[udwig] von S[iegen] Anno Domini 1642)[1].
Provenance: Friedrich August II (Lugt 971); (purchased from M. Knoedler, New York, September 21, 1936, for $1,100).
Bequest of Herbert Greer French, 1943.377.

Seventeenth-century Dutch painters and printmakers sought to depict chiaroscuro and convey atmospheric depth. Prints became the purveyors of an artist's reputation throughout Europe at a time when print collecting and printmaking were fashionable pastimes. Although a variety of relief and intaglio techniques existed, a nonlinear graphic process that could systematically translate a painting's tonal values and surface textures eluded artists, engravers, and publishers. By 1642 the search to convey dark pictorial tonalities hit a climax in the dramatic tenebrous effects achieved by the dense, irregular mesh of etching and drypoint lines in Rembrandt's *Saint Jerome in a Dark Chamber* (H. *Neth.* 105). This high point coincided with the invention of the mezzotint, the most painterly of the intaglio techniques, with its mechanically executed tones of dense, velvety black. Mezzotint became the process of choice for reproductive portrait prints in eighteenth-century England and was popularly known as *la manière anglaise*. Ludwig von Siegen is credited with mezzotint's primitive beginning. This new discovery in printmaking occurred amidst the religious and political turmoil of the Thirty Years' War (1618-48).

Ludwig von Siegen was probably born at the family's castle at Sechten near Cologne in 1609, not in Utrecht as is often stated, the son of Johann von Siegen and Anna Perez de Breil. He was baptized in Cologne on May 2, 1609.[2] Although being part of the archbishopric of Cologne, Sechten was under the jurisdiction of the landgrave of Hesse-Cassel. Johann had to withdraw from Catholic Cologne because of his Protestant beliefs and was living in Holland. As former vassal of Hesse-Cassel he nevertheless petitioned Landgrave Moritz in 1617 to allow his stepson Marcus to attend the *Collegium Mauritianum*, where aristocratic youths received their education and military training. When the contact with the Hessian court had been newly established, Johann von Siegen became chancellor of the *Collegium Mauritianum* and an advisor to the landgrave in 1620. The following year his son Ludwig, whose mother had died in 1619, was enrolled in the school, where he received an education reserved for the privileged upper classes. When Moritz von Hesse-Cassel retired in 1627, his son Wilhelm V became the new landgrave of Hesse-Cassel.[3] He dissolved the school and Johann von Siegen returned to Holland that year. Ludwig had already left school to begin studying law at the *Hohe Schule* (high school) in Herborn in 1626.[4]

Little is known about Ludwig von Siegen's whereabouts or activities between 1629 and 1639. In August 1639 Siegen delivered a letter from his father to the dowager landgravine Amelia[5] Elisabeth, requesting a position at court and service in the army for the duration of the war and subsequent peace. Amelia Elisabeth (d. 1651) married Wilhelm V, landgrave of Hesse-Cassel in 1619. After her husband's death in 1637, she ruled during her son's minority with courage and intelligence until 1650. The landgravine accepted his application and made the lieutenant-colonel *kammerjunker* (chamberlain) to her son Wilhelm VI. His responsibilities as aide, secretary, guard, and companion to his royal charge allowed him to pursue his artistic interests while tutoring the young nobleman. By 1641 his anti-Reformation views came into open friction with the strict Calvinist court at Hesse-Cassel and he moved to Amsterdam, which was noted for its religious tolerance. There he announced his conversion to Roman Catholicism. Amsterdam at the time was the leading commercial and artistic center in Europe. From Amsterdam he continued to supply the dowager landgravine with portraits, designs for medals and coins, and a painted copy after Honthorst of her husband, Wilhelm V.

Von Siegen's communications to Amelia Elisabeth are filled with complaints about the goldsmith's quality of workmanship and the need for additional support, since in the time needed to design one coin he could execute four or five paintings. In 1640 Von Siegen witnessed the move of Wilhelm V's body to the state crypt. In a letter of December 9, 1641, Amelia Elisabeth commissioned a print after his wash drawing of the funeral procession. In his follow-up letter of March 6, 1641, he detailed costs of a comparable commission. In the same letter he revealed that he was working on a portrait of the landgravine.

Underdessen ich sunst ein werck, dass nit gering ist, und zu J. F. Gn. renommée und ewigen gedächtniss strecket, under handen angefangen habe, wozu mich dan underschiedliche vornehme J. F. Gn. wohl affectionirte leuth auch zu vollenführen ahngetrieben, welches, und nach deme noch anders folgende zu J. F. Gn. Ehre, so ich nur nit sonderlich darob gehindert werde, ich gerne verfertigen wolle, da daz eine allein eines vierteljahres werck sein wirdt.[6] (Meanwhile, among other things, I have started a work which is not minor and which will be to the fame and eternal memory of your highness. Various Noblemen who hold high affection for your highness also urge me to finish this work which I would very much like to do and after which others may follow to the honor of your highness, if I am not hindered – because only one such work would take a quarter of a year to complete.[7])

He goes on to point out "wie bey langwierigen und vielen arbeitten auch daz essen, wen man etwaz hatt, nit ubel zu passe kombt"[8] (for all these lengthy and many works, it is not bad to have some food, if one has some). The response to this letter was not encouraging as the landgravive had only just found out about his conversion to Catholicism. On August 19, 1642, Von Siegen sent the young landgrave Wilhelm VI this mezzotint along with an accompanying letter.

Weile aber ich gantze newe jnvention oder sonderbahre, noch nie gesehene arth hierinnen erfunden von solchem kupffer (nit wie von gemeinen mit thausenden) alhier nur etlich wenige wegen subtilheit der arbeit abdrucken habe lassen können, und deswegen nur etlichen zu verehren habe. . . . hab ich J. F. Gn. als einen extraordinari liebhabern der kunst, auch solch ein rar noch nie gesehenes kunststück vor andern zu underthenigen Ehren zu dediciren nit vorbei gekont. Dieses Werck, wie es gemacht werde, kan noch kein kupferstecher oder künstler aussdrücken noch errathen.[9] (Since I have found this completely new invention and peculiar, previously unseen mode, I could only have printed very few impressions from this copperplate [not thousands as could have been done from the ordinary ones] very few because of the subtleness of the work, and, therefore, I have only a few to dedicate. . . . Nevertheless I could not pass up dedicating such a rare and previously unseen artwork in humble honor before anyone else to your highness who is an extraordinary connoisseur of art. This work, the way it is made, no engraver or artist could explain nor guess.)

He describes the three existing methods of printmaking with copperplates. One is engraving, the second is etching, and the third is with metal punches. He proceeds to point out that

diese arth ist deren keine, wie wohl auch lauter kleine puncktlin und kein einziger strich oder Zugh daran ist, wan es schon an etlichen orthen strichweise scheinet, so ist's doch all punctirt.[10] (This manner is none of those, because it is all made up of many small dots and there is not one line or stroke in it, and if it seems like a line in some places it is not – it is made up of small dots.)

Her formidable portrait is a formal presentation using the conventional bust-length formula of the day. Von Siegen built up his image using a variety of roulettes, a tool with a toothed wheel that revolves around an axle attached to a handle that leaves rows of dotted wells and burrs when drawn across the plate. He used a scraper and burnisher to eradicate errors and polish highlights. He did not, however, work in a subtractive method from dark to light. He conveyed the stiffness of her collar and the softness of her curls with a range of intermediate tones executed with a variety of

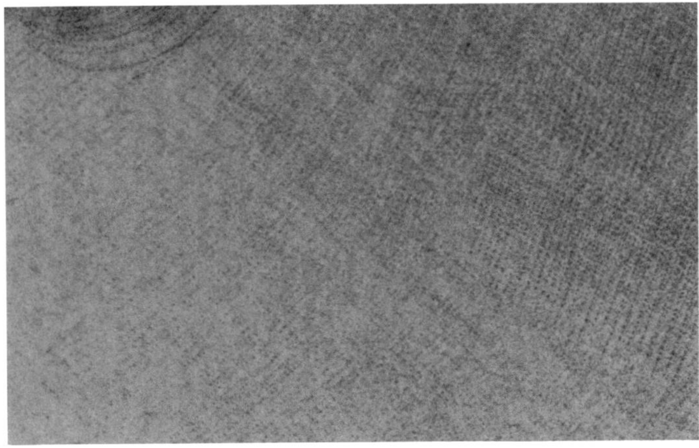

Figure 80-1. Ludwig von Siegen, *Amelia Elizabeth, Landgravine of Hesse-Cassel* (detail).

roulettes. There are telltale zigzag dot patterns typical of the tool, which eventually became known as a "mezzotint rocker," on her left shoulder immediately below her hair (see detail, fig. 80-1). In the first state, the date of 1642 is changed to 1643 with the addition of a pen stroke. In the following state the number is added to the plate.

In 1643 Von Siegen executed a portrait of Elizabeth of Bohemia and, in 1644, portraits of William II of Orange and his wife, Henrietta Maria, all after paintings by Honthorst. These early prints were likewise executed in an additive manner.

During the following decade, he resumed his military career in the armies of the bishop of Hildesheim and the archbishop of Cologne, without disclosing his new process. In January of 1654 he was installed as a retired colonel with duties to the elector of Mainz, which enabled him to return to his artistic activity. His presence at the diet of the Holy Roman Emperor in Regensburg in 1654 may have been in the service of his patron or as an independent observer. He executed a large mezzotint of Emperor Ferdinand III from memory, which he distributed to the other heads of state along with a description of his new art. He hoped commissions for mezzotint portraits would come from the other heads of state; however, none of the attendees offered any encouragement. That same year he produced *Saint Bruno*, which he dedicated to the Carthusian order in Cologne. In it he displayed full mastery of the mezzotint technique, further demonstrated in his last print, *The Holy Family*, after Annibale Carracci, in 1657.

There remains the question as to how the technique was disseminated. John Evelyn, in his *Sculptura* (1662), claimed that Prince Rupert was its inventor. His specially commissioned illustration, *Head of the Executioner*, accompanied the first mention of the process.[11] Although there is no documented meeting between Rupert and Von Siegen, they could have met during their earlier military days at the Palatine court. Rupert could have known about the portrait *Amelia Elisabeth* through his cousin Wilhelm VI or about Von Siegen's second mezzotint of his mother, *Elizabeth of Bohemia*. Prince Rupert's first mezzotint, *Portrait of Titian* (1657), was preceded by Theodor Casper von Fürstenberg's *Leopold Wilhelm, Archduke of Austria*. An amateur, Fürstenberg, canon of Mainz, would have learned the technique directly from Von Siegen, proving Evelyn incorrect. It appears that the dissemination of the mezzotint technique began in Mainz. No further artistic endeavors are known after Von Siegen's *The Holy Family*. Von Siegen's final years appear to have been encumbered with lawsuits. In 1666 he was involved in a lawsuit concerning an estate in the village of Bodenstedt near Peine. In 1671 in the rank of major he petitioned the duke of Wolfenbüttel for permission to go to the Netherlands to settle an inheritance, which dragged on until 1676. We do not know for certain the date of his death, which presumably occurred in Wolfenbüttel.[12] – KLS

1. I would like to thank Armin Kunz for the translations and for his assistance in preparing this entry.

2. ThB. 30:596.

3. Paul Seidel, "Ludwig von Siegen Der Erfinder des Schabkunstverfahrens," *JprK.* 10 (1889): 36.

4. ThB. 30:596.

5. The spelling of the name in German is Amalie.

6. Seidel, "Ludwig von Siegen," 42.

7. The intention of the translation is to follow the original text by Ludwig von Siegen as closely as possible and to give the reader not only the exact information but also the flavor of the courteous and flowery language of baroque German.

8. Seidel, "Ludwig von Siegen," 42.

9. Seidel, "Ludwig von Siegen," 42.

10. Seidel, "Ludwig von Siegen," 42.

11. John Evelyn, *Sculptura* (London: G. Beedle, 1662), 147.

12. Seidel, "Ludwig von Siegen," 45; ThB. 30:596.

Rembrandt Harmensz. van Rijn

Leiden 1606-1669 Amsterdam

81. The Three Trees 1643.

Etching, drypoint, and burin with sulphur tint on antique laid paper, 21.4 x 28.1 cm (platemark).
B. 212; Hind *Rem.* 205; Münz 152; H. *Neth.* 212.
Watermark: Strasbourg lily on crowned shield with initials PR and countermark WK.[1]
Signed and dated in plate lower left: *Rembrandt f 1643*.
Provenance: (Purchased from M. Knoedler, New York, September 15, 1930, for $12,000).
Bequest of Herbert Greer French, 1943.285.
Exhibitions: Cincinnati 1934, no. 59; Cincinnati 1941, no. 146.

The Three Trees, dated 1643, is Rembrandt's largest and most complex landscape print. In creating this remarkable image, Rembrandt employed etching, burinwork, and drypoint.[2] As Christopher White noted in 1969, we only know this print in its finished state.[3] Nonetheless, certain adjustments, such as the remains of further diagonal lines at the top left center, indicate that Rembrandt made changes in the plate before he considered it finished.

This landscape print, more than any other, parallels the direction Rembrandt was exploring in his landscape paintings of the 1630s, including *The Bridge* (Amsterdam),[4] *Landscape with the Good Samaritan* (Kraków),[5] and *Landscape with a Castle* (Paris).[6] Their cosmic character, charged by the dramatic interplay of light and shadow, violent stormy activity and the onset of clearing weather, the vast panoply of nature and the most intimate detail of quotidian human activity, is embraced in *The Three Trees*.

This most spiritual of Rembrandt's landscape prints is not only encyclopedic in its range of detail but is also patient of many levels of interpretation. Ostensibly it represents a view of the environs of Amsterdam. As early as 1915, Frits Lugt identified the subject as the Diemerdijk or Sint Anthonisdijk east of Amsterdam,[7] yet any reference to actuality is transformed by the knoll in the right foreground. This knoll provides the viewer with a purely imaginary but ideal topographical vantage point from which to survey the flat panorama surrounding it.

Jan Bialostocki alludes to the symbolic character of *The Three Trees* in his recent assessment of Rembrandt's iconography:

Even a landscape so pure as the one called *Three Trees*, which shows a storm as opposed to the peaceful countryside, contains some moral meaning, most likely obvious to anyone educated in the metaphors of preachers' rhetoric, emblem books and Cats' poetry.[8]

This train of thought has led several art historians to offer an extremely close emblematic reading of the subject. In an interpretation of *The Three Trees* as a manifestation of God's divine will, Christopher Brown goes so far as to posit that the three trees symbolize the three crosses on Golgotha.[9] A. Ziemba offers a less extreme, but more thoughtful, reading of the subject. He sees the three trees as personifying the three virtues of fortitude, constancy, and humility in their struggle against destiny.[10] He supports his thesis by citing literature from the period in which trees are emblematic of virtue: the deep roots of virtue, victorious over tribulation, metaphorically embody the capacity of prayer to nourish the soul. For Ziemba, the three trees in Rembrandt's print embody life's struggle against adversity and death, a struggle that in itself manifests God's will. As seen from this vantage point, the entire landscape becomes a pantheistic vision of the evolution of nature linked to a cycle of change. The outward appearance of nature is often determined by the interplay of oppositions, including violent weather pitted against the stasis of calm.[11] Ziemba further observes that the wind direction from the right implies that the squall, moving off to the left, will be superseded by clearing weather. Intense sunlight plays on the tree crowns in spectacular *contre jour* lighting. This opposition between the primordial forces of light and dark, clearing weather and stormy gloom, infuse certain of Rembrandt's landscape paintings with symbolic meaning. By inference, lightness and darkness in these pictures symbolize the polarity between good and evil.[12]

Although this moralizing tenor is evident in *The Three Trees*, its infinite detail invites further exploration and awaits discovery, and to a significant extent, its experiential quality defines its character.[13] Each detail is perfectly integrated. Each zone offers startling discoveries. Lovers, hidden amid the tangle of shrubs in the right foreground, are unobserved by the fisherman and his wife to the left. Beyond the right-hand tree, a horse-drawn cart filled with people moves across the crest of the knoll to the left of a seated artist, sketching. Beyond the knoll, a herdsman tends his cattle on the flats. Others walk through the landscape. Two figures stand, silhouetted against the distant water, just to the left of center.

Man's role in the world, although dwarfed by the immensity of nature, remains an integral feature of Rembrandt's larger universe. Through farming, animal husbandry, harnessing the wind, and a network of international trade, we witness attempts to rein in the fruitfulness of the earth and still find time for recreation, trysting, and contemplation. *The Three Trees* measures the immensity of nature yet includes a place for humanity. – GK

1. This watermark is virtually identical to that found in several Rembrandt prints cited in Washington 1990a, 279-80, nos. 18 and 21. It is also extremely close to the watermark found on a Rembrandt drawing in the Rijksprentenkabinet in Amsterdam. See Amsterdam 1985, no. 27, illus. on p. 237; cf. Heawood 1663.

2. Rembrandt also used sulphur tint, restricted to the bottom left-hand area, to add a mottled gray tone across the zone beyond the water, extending into the distant flat panorama.

3. Christopher White, *Rembrandt as an Etcher* (London, 1969), 200.

4. Cynthia P. Schneider, *Rembrandt's Landscapes* 1990, 169-71, no. 1, pl. 6.

5. Schneider, *Rembrandt's Landscapes* 1990, 178-81, no. 4, pl. 2.

6. Schneider, *Rembrandt's Landscapes* 1990, 181-83, no. 5, pl. 4.

7. Frits Lugt, *Wandelingen met Rembrandt in en om Amsterdam* (Amsterdam, 1915), 147.

8. Jan Bialostocki, "A New Look at Rembrandt Iconography," *Artibus et Historiae* 10 (1984): 14.

9. Christopher Brown, London 1986, 226, no. 112.

10. A. Ziemba, "Rembrandts Landschaft als Sinnbild Versuch einer ikonologischen Deutung," *Artibus et Historiae* 15 (1989): 123-24.

11. Ziemba, "Rembrandts Landschaft," 124-25. White also discusses the elemental, even cataclysmic, forces in nature that characterize this print (*Rembrandt as an Etcher*, 199).

12. Ziemba, "Rembrandts Landschaft," 117.

13. Clifford S. Ackley stresses the infinite variety found in *The Three Trees* (Boston 1980, 199, no. 133).

Ferdinand Bol

Dordrecht 1616-1680 Amsterdam

82. Portrait of an Officer 1645.

Etching on antique laid paper, 13.7 x 11.2 cm (platemark).
B. *Rem.* 11; Dut. 12; Rov. 11; H. *Neth.* 12 i/ii.
Signed and dated in plate upper left: *f BoL/1645* (6 reversed).
Condition: Trimmed just outside platemark.
Provenance: Kupferstichkabinett, Staatliche Museen, Berlin (Lugt 1606); (probably sale, Amsler and Ruthardt, Berlin, May 15, 1906, lot 1001 for RM 60); Paul Davidsohn (Lugt 654); (his sale, C.G. Boerner, Leipzig, May 3-8, 1920, lot 692 to Gutekunst for RM 1,600); (purchased from F.H. Bresler, Milwaukee, September 26, 1927, for $145).
Bequest of Herbert Greer French, 1943.319.
Exhibitions: Cincinnati 1930 (no. 2); Cincinnati 1941, no. 135.

Ferdinand Bol's activities as an etcher stemmed from his apprenticeship with Rembrandt. Of all Rembrandt's pupils, Bol emulated his style of printmaking with the greatest facility and success but produced only a handful of etchings.[1] Bol's activity as a printmaker spanned a very few years: all but two of his dated prints are from 1642-45.

Born in Dordrecht in 1616, Bol may have first studied with the Dordrecht painter Jacob Gerritsz. Cuyp. At some point during the later 1630s, Bol moved to Amsterdam and entered Rembrandt's studio. According to Blankert, he stayed with Rembrandt until about 1641.[2] His first signed and dated works are from 1642. These include three of his etchings (H. *Neth.* 6, 9, and 14). Bol's earliest paintings are strongly influenced by Rembrandt, who continued to be a source of inspiration up to about 1650.[3] In 1652 Bol applied for citizenship in Amsterdam, probably motivated by his hope to secure decorative commissions for the new Amsterdam town hall. In this he was successful because, in 1656, Bol received the substantial sum of fifteen hundred guilders for this project for his painting *Pyrrhus and Fabricius*. During the years from 1659-64, Bol received many prestigious commissions, including several notable group portraits, and he had pupils, including the distinguished painters Cornelius Bisschop and Godfried Kneller. Bol's second wife, Anna van Erckel, whom he married in 1669, was extremely wealthy, and it appears that he gave up painting for less arduous patrician pursuits immediately after this marriage. Bol died in 1680 and was buried in the Zuiderkerk in Amsterdam.

The majority of Bol's etchings are strongly characterized figure studies. They reflect Rembrandt's interest in expression and his fascination with exotic costumes. Bol's religious subjects were often executed on an ambitious scale and emulate Rembrandt's most important works of the later 1630s.[4] Although they do not attain the same degree of profundity exhibited in Rembrandt's work, Bol's religious subjects display a proficiency in presenting biblical narratives in an arresting manner. His religious prints are also an

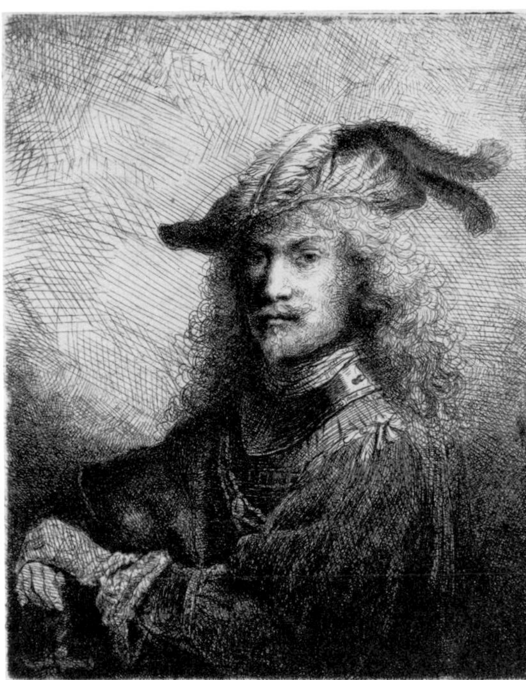

ambitious assimilation of Rembrandt's ideas. In his later years, Bol
became a reputed portraitist whose large-scale, somewhat
stereotyped manner of portraying persons diverged from
Rembrandt's, conforming closely instead to the classicizing spirit
that became progressively fashionable in Holland after 1650.

Portrait of an Officer is one of Bol's most distinguished etchings,
comparable in importance to the 1651 *Woman with a Pear* (H. *Neth.*
15). It displays his skillful use of the etcher's needle to create a
network of energetic, wiry lines. Bol experimented with the
stopping-out process to enrich his prints with subtle tonal values.
The Museum's impression of *Portrait of an Officer* was recognized
by one of its former owners, Paul Davidsohn, the celebrated Berlin
collector, as a unique proof in a hitherto undescribed first state prior
to considerable reworking. In the second state (fig. 82-1), shading
was added to both sides of the head. A more significant alteration,
not previously cited in the literature, was the radical transformation
of the sitter's left wrist and cuff. In the second state Bol covered the
left wrist with a loose, falling cuff that calls greater attention to the
officer's hands. This alteration clarifies their pose, and the hands,
resting on a sword hilt, underscore the man's military demeanor.
Moreover, the added hatching to the left of the officer's face mutes
the original luminous white backdrop, thereby integrating this broad
zone with the general play of light and shadow on the figure. Not
coincidentally, this shading also directs more attention to the
sitter's hands.

The sitter, with his gorget and double-plumed hat, relates to
contemporary portrait likenesses by Bol, including several
traditionally considered to be self-portraits.[5] These may be fantasy
portraits in which the artist creates an imaginary figure garbed in
exotic finery and exuding youthful good looks and panache. The
somewhat dandified character of the sitter in *Portrait of an Officer*
finds antecedents in a number of Rembrandt's portraits in which he
presents himself or other sitters wearing gorgets, plumed hats, and
chains of nobility. In the case of Rembrandt's self-portraits, the artist
assumes a purely imaginary station in life.[6] Rembrandt's etched *Self-
Portrait* (B. 20) of 1638 is a compelling prototype for Bol because of
its similarity in technique, scale, and presentation. In his *Portrait of*

an Officer, Bol captures the sitter's quizzical, searching expression,
in a manner analogous to that in Rembrandt's *Self-Portrait*.[7] – GK

1. Hollstein (H. *Neth.* III) lists a total of twenty-four items, including at least five
problematic attributions. D. M. Tsurutani, "The Etchings of Ferdinand Bol," *Allen
Memorial Art Museum Bulletin* (1975-76), 38:46-47, only accepts sixteen authentic Bol
etchings. A. Blankert, *Ferdinand Bol (1616-1680) Rembrandt's Pupil* (Doornspijk:
Davaco, 1982), 14, also rejects Bartsch/Hollstein 1, *The Sacrifice of Abraham*.
2. Blankert, *Ferdinand Bol*, 19. Bol's father died in 1641. The son likely came into a
substantial inheritance that would have enabled him to set himself up independently in
Amsterdam.
3. Blankert, *Ferdinand Bol*, 18.
4. Such as *The Blinding of Samson* (Br. 501) of 1636, now in Frankfurt, and *The Feast
of Balshazzar* (Br. 497), in London.
5. Blankert, *Ferdinand Bol*, 131-33, nos. 60-65, pls. 60-63, 65, 70. He questions the
traditional assumption that these related likenesses are, in fact, self-portraits.
6. These include his *Self-Portrait* (Br. 8) of 1629 in the Isabella Stewart Gardner
Museum, Boston; a fantasy likeness (Br. 24) in the Mauritshuis, The Hague; his
celebrated self-portrait in his double portrait with Saskia (Br. 30) in Gemäldegalerie Alte
Meister, Staatliche Kunstsammlungen, Dresden, in which a sword hangs prominently in
its sheath from Rembrandt's waist. Other similar pictures include the so-called
Rembrandt's Father (Br. 79) in the J. Paul Getty Museum and his *Standard Bearer* (Br.
433) of 1636 in the Rothschild Collection, Louvre, Paris. For further discussion of
Rembrandt's self-portraits see H. Perry Chapman, *Rembrandt's Self Portraits*
(Princeton: Princeton University Press, 1990).
7. A drawing by Bol, *A Young Man with a Hat and Sword*, offers parallels to this
etching. The drawing is reproduced in W. Sumowski, *Drawings of the Rembrandt
School* (New York: Abaris, 1979), vol. 1, no. 224x. Unlike the etching, the sitter is seen
en face and stands with his sword hilt placed before his waist.

Rembrandt Harmensz. van Rijn

Leiden 1606-1669 Amsterdam

83. Jan Asselyn (*Krabbetje*) 1647.

Etching, drypoint, and burin on Japanese paper, 21.5 x 17.0 cm
(platemark).
B. 277; Hind *Rem.* 227 iii/iii; Münz 71 iii/iii; H. *Neth.* 277 iii/iii.
Signed and dated lower right: *Rembrandt f 16 (..)*.
Condition: Trimmed to or just outside platemark.
Provenance: Possibly Arthur Pond, London; Sir Edward Astley
(Lugt 2775); (purchased from M. Knoedler, New York, April 1,
1931, for $3,900).
Bequest of Herbert Greer French, 1943.311.
Exhibitions: Cincinnati 1941, no. 147.

The subject of this portrait, Jan Asselyn (ca. 1615-1652), was an
Amsterdam artist noted for his Italianate landscape paintings. After
spending an undetermined amount of time in Rome, Asselyn had
certainly returned to Amsterdam by 1647 where he developed a
distinctive strain of landscape distinguished by its conspicuous
architectural motifs and lively staffage. He and another artist, Jan
Both, were the leading second generation Dutch Italianate landscape
painters.[1] While in Rome Asselyn was a member of the *Bentvogels*,
a confraternity of expatriate artists – mostly Dutch and Flemish –
residing in the Eternal City. Each had a nickname. Asselyn was
dubbed *Krabbetje*, the "little crab," a reference to his deformed
left hand.

Rembrandt's portraits of the artists *Jan Asselyn* and *Jan Lutma*
(cat. 90) evolved in opposite directions. In *Jan Asselyn*, instead of
further elaborating the setting, he reduced its role as the print
evolved from its first to its third and final state. In the first state,
Rembrandt etched the painter's easel behind the sitter, putting on it a
large landscape. He found this representation visually distracting
and in the second state largely removed the easel and the painting. In
the third state, Rembrandt removed all remaining references to the
easel. We can only surmise why he chose to transform *Jan Asselyn* in

this manner. However, one point is evident; namely, if we lacked knowledge of its earlier states, there would be no reason to believe that the sitter in this etching was an artist. In the third state, Rembrandt depicts a burgher, dressed in modish black attire, who stands next to a table covered with books. The sitter, we surmise, is both affluent and learned.[2] He is also supremely self-confident. Notice Asselyn's firm gaze and jaunty pose: one hand akimbo and the other emphatically pressed onto the table. The portrait is highly finished and monumental in effect. With the exception of a blank bottom margin, the image is almost square in format, conveying a spaciousness and amplitude appropriate to the sitter's forceful gestures.[3]

Rembrandt devoted considerable attention to *Jan Asselyn*. For example, he printed many impressions on Japanese paper, the Museum's impression being a particularly beautiful example.[4] Unlike *Jacob Haaringh* (cat. 89), another of Rembrandt's portraits, whose thick sheet of Japanese paper was particularly absorbent, the artist here selected a thin sheet that responded differently to the ink. The drypoint, although pronounced, is not blurred. Moreover, the finely hatched lines defining the robe, face, and tablecloth have printed sharply. Rembrandt left a transparent ink film across the entire plate to give the portrait a delicate, silvery tone that softens the light and lends a wonderful luminosity to the print.

The Museum's impression bears the stamp of the distinguished eighteenth-century British collector Sir Edward Astley. Astley acquired many of Rembrandt's prints from the English artist Arthur Pond, whose collection can be traced back, in part, to that of Jacob Houbraken. Houbraken, in turn, acquired Rembrandt's work from Willem Six in 1734. Six's collection may have partly stemmed from that of his uncle, Jan Six, Rembrandt's friend and patron. Many of Astley's most prized Rembrandt prints are now in the British Museum, and although Astley owned impressions of *Jan Asselyn* in all three states, ironically, not one of these found its way into the British Museum.[5] – GK

1. For discussion of this aspect of Dutch landscape painting see W. Stechow, *Dutch Landscape Painting of the Seventeenth Century* (London: Phaidon, 1966), 91-92, 153, 158. For Asselyn, see C. Steland Stief, *Jan Asselyn* (Amsterdam: Van Gendt, 1971).

2. H. Perry Chapman (*Rembrandt's Self Portraits* [Princeton: Princeton University Press, 1990], 83) comes to the same conclusion.

3. The existence of the bottom margin retained in all three states may suggest that Rembrandt or the sitter envisaged the inclusion of an identifying caption in this blank space. If such an inscription was ever intended, Rembrandt never added it. One possible reason for its inclusion may have been Asselyn's untimely death, which could also explain why Rembrandt never strengthened his signature nor completed the date at the bottom right. In fact, the area just to the right of the sitter remains unresolved. Rembrandt barely indicates a chair rail that he never developed nor eliminated in either the second or third state. Although of marginal visual consequence, this detail may indicate that Rembrandt stopped reworking the portrait even though he pulled several magnificent impressions in the third state.

4. Christopher White and Karel Boon (H. *Neth.* XVIII:130) include a listing of impressions on Japanese paper known to them.

5. The Rijksprentenkabinet in Amsterdam possesses, among its rich holdings of *Jan Asselyn*, impressions bearing Astley's stamp in states I and II.

Rembrandt Harmensz. van Rijn

Leiden 1606-1669 Amsterdam

84. Landscape with Trees, Farm Buildings, and a Tower

ca. 1651.
Etching and drypoint on antique laid paper, 12.2 x 32.0 cm (platemark).
B. 223; Hind 244 *Rem.* iv/iv; Münz 168 iv/iv; H. *Neth.* 223 iv/iv.
Watermark: Strasbourg lily on crowned shield with initials EC (bottom fragment).

Condition: Trimmed to platemark.
Provenance: Städelsches Kunstinstitut, Frankfurt-am-Main (Lugt 2357 and 2396); (sale, Baer. . . Goldschmidt, Frankfurt-am-Main, September 16, 1839, lot 1891); (purchased from M. Knoedler, New York, April 1, 1935, for $4,510).
Bequest of Herbert Greer French, 1943.292.
Exhibitions: Cincinnati 1941, no. 151.

Landscape with Trees, Farm Buildings, and a Tower, one of Rembrandt's most monumental and imposing landscape subjects, is notable for its size and its unusual format. Datable to about 1651, it integrates into a single image the enormous range of the artist's investigations into landscape at a point of feverish interest in the subject.[1] Not only does Rembrandt focus on the play of light on the trees but he combines this light with a turbulent, cloudy sky that envelops the distant trees in deep shadow. This powerful contrast animates the flat landscape of Holland, which becomes a stage for the unfolding drama of changing weather. This image is particularly remarkable because of the conspicuous visual impact of the largely empty, undifferentiated foreground. Like *Landscape with a Road beside a Canal* (cat. 85) and so many other landscape prints and drawings from the early 1650s, Rembrandt screens much of the architecture with trees and shrubs, the perfect means for representing the effects of changing light.

The building with the tower has been identified as the *Huys met het Toorentje*, property of the family of Jan Uytenbogaert. It stood on the Amstelveensche Weg, due south of Amsterdam. Jan Uytenbogaert was receiver general of Amsterdam and an acquaintance of Rembrandt. In fact, Rembrandt made a large portrait of Uytenbogaert weighing precious goods (B. 281). In a drawing now in Malibu, Rembrandt represents the same building set farther into the distance.[2]

Landscape with Trees exists in four states. Impressions of the second state are exceedingly rare. Those in the third state are only slightly more common. The vast majority of surviving impressions, including the Museum's impression, are in the fourth and final state. Although Rembrandt introduced only modest changes in each state, each brought the print to a greater degree of concentration in two ways: (1) by eliminating the cupola in the third state, the architecture becomes less conspicuous and the roof lines of the buildings conform more closely to the height of the trees; and (2) the amalgamated profile of buildings and vegetation, rising above and from the land, becomes an emphatic, albeit densely packed, horizontal mass. Moreover, the added shading to the drawbridge and gate at the left further enriches the deep pockets of shadow in the landscape below the cloud front at the left.

Rembrandt printed more impressions of the fourth state than any other, but he varied the inking of many of these fourth-state impressions to attain remarkable atmospheric effects. In certain instances, he wiped the plate clean; in others, he left much surface tone. No two impressions with tone are identical. In order to transform the mood and the outward visual effect of each impression, Rembrandt often adjusted the wiping of the plate to place certain zones in bright light and casting other areas, by contrast, in an atmospheric pall. Notable impressions in Amsterdam (fourth state), London (third state), New York (Pierpont Morgan Library, first and third states), and Washington (fourth state) convey a sultry atmosphere. The National Gallery of Art in Washington has a second impression of the fourth state in which the artist indicates clouds above the buildings at center and right.[3] Other impressions, including the Museum's, are far more cleanly wiped.[4] Nonetheless, even these contain experimental wiping and are more varied than one might initially realize. In the case of the Museum's impression,

Rembrandt wiped the tree crowns clean but left a thin film of ink across the foreground and the sky, particularly in the area of the clouds at the left. The resulting image focuses on the intense light that seems to glow from the trees and the blank foreground. Barely affected by the gathering clouds at the left, the sunlight radiates across the landscape. This effect is intentional and contrasts with far denser atmospheric effects found in several impressions with much more modulated surface tone. The Museum's impression, while not exhibiting pronounced evidence of Rembrandt's experimental approach to inking, is, in fact, a superb representation of this very phenomenon. It is only in juxtaposition with other more richly inked examples that one can appreciate the distinctive character of Cincinnati's impression. Rembrandt strove for different visual effects that, although visually inconspicuous, are no less valid in their ultimate impact. – GK

1. For further discussion of this shift in interest see cat. 85.
2. J. Paul Getty Museum. For further discussion of this drawing and the identification of the subject, see Cynthia P. Schneider, Washington 1990a, 253-54, no. 81, illus.
3. National Gallery of Art, Washington, inv. 1955.6.12.
4. Other cleanly wiped impressions of the fourth state are in Amsterdam (Rijksprentenkabinet, Collection De Bruijn), Budapest, London, New York (the Metropolitan Museum of Art), and Washington.

Rembrandt Harmensz. van Rijn

Leiden 1606-1669 Amsterdam

85. Landscape with a Road beside a Canal ca. 1652.

Drypoint on antique laid paper, 7.5/7.9 x 21.1 cm (platemark).
B. 221; Hind *Rem.* 264; Münz 170; H. *Neth.* 221.
Condition: Trimmed just outside platemark.
Provenance: George Hibbert (Lugt 2849); (his sale, Th. Philipe, London, April 17-May 3, 1809, lot 190 to Earl of Aylesford for £6); Heneage Finch, 5th Earl of Aylesford (Lugt 58); Samuel Woodburn, London; Kupferstichkabinett, Staatliche Museen, Berlin (Lugt 1606 and 2482); (sale, Amsler and Ruthardt, Berlin, May 4, 1903, lot 1855, for RM 2,130); George Coe Graves, New York (1920); The Metropolitan Museum of Art, New York (Lugt 1943 [inv. no. 20.46.10, gift of George Coe Graves, 1920, exchanged, March 15, 1935]); (purchased from M. Knoedler, New York, September 21, 1936, for $1,750).
Bequest of Herbert Greer French, 1943.297.
Exhibitions: Ann Arbor 1960, no. 54.

Rembrandt first experimented with drypoint in landscape in his etching *The Three Trees* of 1643 (cat. 81). Circa 1652 he produced two landscapes purely in drypoint, *Landscape with a Road beside a Canal* and *Clump of Trees with a Vista* (B. 222). Both convey a directness of observation and feeling to suggest that they may have been executed *en plein air*.[1] E. F. Gersaint mentions that Rembrandt took copperplates with him on his walks in the countryside outside Amsterdam.[2] These vividly realized drypoint landscapes may represent the type of prints that the artist executed directly from nature.

Drypoint produces rich tone through the burr, as the result of ink held by the irregular deposits of scraped up metal next to the lines scratched into the copperplate. Drypoint enables an artist to pull only a few rich tonal impressions before the burr wears away. The fugitive nature of this technique assures that only a handful of fine impressions can be made before the copperplate shows the inevitable consequences of wear. Each drypoint impression has the capacity to assume the distinctive qualities of a monotype, which is particularly relevant in the case of Rembrandt's drypoints because there is every

reason to believe that he alone would have pulled fine impressions from the plate.

The impressions of *Landscape with a Road beside a Canal* that I have studied suggest that Rembrandt strove for three general effects. The exceptional impression in Amsterdam[3] is uniquely rich in burr but lacks surface tone; the impressions in London and New York[4] are notable for their subtle balance between burr and delicate silvery tone, the result of a network of fine vertical scratches most evident across the center of the sky. By contrast, the Museum's impression, which uniquely represents the third general effect, is truly idiosyncratic in character. First, Rembrandt generated a pronounced tone across the sky by leaving a swath of residual ink that reinforces the sky's mesh of vertical hatchings. Second and more remarkable still, the artist smudged the rich burr of the clump of trees partly in shadow to the right of the farmhouse. The blurring of these tree crowns into the sultry sky above resulted in a unique visual effect that caught the artist's imagination.

During the 1640s Rembrandt produced several landscape etchings that immortalize farm dwellings sketched on walks in the vicinity of Amsterdam.[5] He represented these dwellings in limpid light, without evoking suggestive, blurring atmospheric effects. By about 1650, however, Rembrandt shifted his focus to the evocative play of pervading light modified by subtle atmospheric effects. As a result, he became progressively more interested in landscape subjects that allowed him to register light in its infinite variety. Instead of focusing on clearly delineated buildings, he selected complex groupings of farm dwellings largely screened by trees. Thus his landscape prints of the early 1650s tend to focus principally on trees oscillating in strong, raking light. His subjects frequently seem charged by breezes or strong winds that provide great potential for capturing changing light effects. *Landscape with a Road beside a Canal* is unusual in representing a sultry but essentially still day. It finds innumerable parallels in Rembrandt's contemporaneous landscape drawings, including magnificent examples from the collection of Nicolai Flinck, once together at Chatsworth and now partially dispersed.[6] As in his drypoint landscapes, in these drawings the artist largely obscures the farm buildings with shrubs and trees. Despite its modest size, *Landscape with a Road beside a Canal* is a complex composition, with vistas partially screened by three clusters of vegetation of unequal mass. To the left, vegetation partially obscures a sailboat. The shrubs beyond the field in strong light lead toward taller trees before and to the right of the farm at center. By contrast, the trees in the right foreground form a bold coulisse that sets off a view to a distant village church. This intricate delineation of space is enhanced by the pronounced atmospheric effect that subtly modifies the play of light across the landscape.

The Museum's impression has a remarkable provenance that one must surmise was partially triggered by its idiosyncratic character. Its first documented owner was the English collector George Hibbert, at whose sale in 1809 it was acquired by the fifth Earl of Aylesford for the substantial price of six guineas. It subsequently entered the collection of the Kupferstichkabinett in Berlin but was sold as a "duplicate" in 1903. The New York collector George Coe Graves acquired the landscape and presented it, along with other notable Rembrandt prints, to the Metropolitan Museum of Art in 1920. However, in 1929 Mrs. H. O. Havermeyer bequeathed another impression of this subject to the Metropolitan – the one recently exhibited in Washington.[7] At some point after 1929, the Metropolitan Museum of Art sold the former Hibbert-Aylesford-Berlin impression. Herbert Greer French had the perspicacity to acquire it for his own collection from M. Knoedler in 1936. This remarkable history of "upgrading" from museum collections raises interesting questions about the changing taste in determining quality in Rembrandt's prints. The more we learn about Rembrandt's highly personal approach to printing, inking, and paper selection, the more we have to conclude that Hibbert and the Earl of Aylesford, two distinguished English collectors of Rembrandt's prints, displayed a remarkable sympathy for the artist's experimental techniques and did not err in adding this truly unique landscape drypoint to their respective collections. By an extraordinary series of coincidences, Herbert Greer French was able to continue this tradition of adventurous buying, the ultimate measure of a creative collector with a flair for the unusual. – GK

1. Christopher White, *Rembrandt as an Etcher* (London, 1969), 191; Washington 1990a, 127.

2. As noted by Cynthia P. Schneider, Washington 1990a, 127.

3. Rijksprentenkabinet, Amsterdam, illustrated in H. *Neth.* XIX:181.

4. Metropolitan Museum of Art (illustrated in Washington 1990a, no. 25) and the Pierpont Morgan Library, New York.

5. For an illuminating discussion of the various types of farm dwellings that Rembrandt studied, see B. Bakker, Washington 1990a, 33-59.

6. For examples, see Washington 1990a, nos. 13, 14, 17, 67-69, all illus.

7. See n. 3.

Adriaen van Ostade
Haarlem 1610-1685 Haarlem

86. The Anglers
Etching on antique laid paper, 11.4 x 16.6 cm (platemark).
B. 26; Dut. 26; Davidsohn 26 iv/v; Godefroy 26 iv/vii; H. *Neth.* 26 iv/vi; TIB 26.
Watermark: Fleur-de-lis (fragment).
Signed in water lower right: *AvO* (in ligature).
Provenance: (Purchased from F.H. Bresler, Milwaukee, February 15, 1929, for $155).
Bequest of Herbert Greer French, 1943.339.
Exhibitions: Cincinnati 1930 (no. 84).

Adriaen van Ostade was born in Haarlem in 1610, son of the weaver Jan Hendricx van Eyndhoven. Arnold Houbraken claimed that Ostade studied with Frans Hals around 1627, at the time when Adriaen Brouwer was also in Hals' studio. Ostade's work betrays no influence from Hals, but he was deeply impressed by the peasant genre subjects of Brouwer. Virtually Ostade's entire repertoire of several hundred paintings and drawings and fifty etchings is devoted to such genre themes. Ostade only rarely produced portraits, biblical subjects, and landscapes. He must have entered the Haarlem painters' guild by 1634 and was subsequently elected *hoofdman* of the guild in 1647 and 1661, becoming deacon in 1662. He had several pupils, including his brother Isack, Cornelis Bega, and Cornelis Dusart. Ostade married Machteltje Pietersdr. on July 26, 1638. She died childless in 1642. Fifteen years later the widower Ostade remarried. His second wife, Anna Ingels, was from a wealthy Roman Catholic family. After her death in 1666, Ostade came into a substantial inheritance. After his death in 1685 Ostade's daughter put up the contents of his studio at auction. This included fifty of his etching plates and all the impressions of his prints still on the premises.[1]

The Anglers, one of Ostade's most felicitous landscape compositions, has always been considered one of his most desirable prints. As noted above, Ostade's landscapes are rare, and this is his only print that can be classified as a pure landscape. Like *Slaughtering the Hog* (cat. 87), *The Anglers* is notable for its sense of intimacy and its marvelous interplay between landscape and man's presence in the natural world. The almost whimsical wooden bridge becomes the perfect measure of man's ability to adapt to Holland's watery landscape. The two peasants fishing are as integral to the landscape as the pair of ducks under the bridge or the farmhouse nestled among trees beyond it to the right. This image is quintessentially Dutch with its proverbial fishermen, as true to Holland today as they were to the seventeenth century, embodying patience and relaxation. The stillness of the scene, as gauged by the unruffled water, is further underscored by the glowing light across the middle distance.

Ostade was not the only Dutch artist to portray such rustic bridges. Painters Jan van Goyen and Pieter Molyn depicted analogous rustic monuments.[2] Nonetheless, Ostade's print, which Godefroy dates to about 1653,[3] has attained a unique reputation within the larger tradition of Dutch art because his rare landscapes are so distinctive. In developing the composition for *The Anglers*, Ostade may have drawn inspiration from a drawing, now in Berlin, by his younger brother Isack (1621-1649).[4] The drawing depicts a similar bridge but sets it before a totally different background.[5]

The Anglers exists in several states, some of which have nothing to do with Ostade. The Museum's impression is Paul Davidsohn's fourth state in which the artist added fine, \\\ oblique hatching in the space under the sloping ramp between the riverbank at the left and the wooden piling that supports this ramp. This is the only alteration that distinguishes the fourth state from the Davidsohn/Godefroy third state.[6] Dutuit describes a first state prior to the borderline, but Davidsohn doubts whether this state ever existed.[7] In the second state, the artist added a fine borderline and his monogram.[8] He reworked the plate more substantially in the third state, adding horizontal lines in the sky at the upper right, completing the outline of the peasant, and darkening the light space on the bucket. Although Hollstein cites Amsterdam, Frankfurt, Haarlem, London, and Vienna as possessing this third state, in fact, they, like Cincinnati, have impressions in Davidsohn's described fourth state.[9]

Ostade's reworking of the composition is less substantial here than in *Slaughtering the Hog* but the copperplate for *The Anglers* suffered wear more quickly, particularly in terms of the fine horizontal hatching in the sky directly under the bridge and at the upper right. The Museum's impression is richly printed with subtle contrasts between deep shadow and pervading light, still coherently defined. The suggestion of tone, the deep platemark, and the sheen of the paper are a measure of the quality of this impression. – GK

1. The biographical data on Adriaen van Ostade is drawn from B. Schnackenburg, *Adriaen van Ostade Isack van Ostade Zeichnungen und Aquarelle*, 2 vols. (Hamburg: Ernst Hauswedell and Co., 1981), 13-16; Clifford S. Ackley, Boston 1980, 157; and C. von Bogendorf-Rapprath, Philadelphia 1984, 281-82.

2. Van Goyen produced a fine drawing, *Anglers on a High Bridge*, dated 1651, now in Groningen. See J. Bolten, *Dutch Drawings from the Collection of Dr. C. Hofstede de Groot* (Utrecht: Oosthoek, 1967), 66, no. 29, illus. A similar drawing by Pieter Molyn, now in the Lugt Collection, Fondation Custodia, Institut Néerlandais, Paris, is dated 1655. For this and other related material by Molyn, see C. van Hasselt, Brussels 1968, 104-05, no. 103, illus. Esaias van de Velde anticipated this subject early in the seventeenth century. See G. S. Keyes, *Esaias van de Velde* (Doornspijk: Davaco, 1984), nos. 133, D79, D90, D117 bis, E16, E32. More frequently Esaias places wooden and stone bridges spanning streams in rocky, hilly country.

3. Louis Godefroy, *The Complete Etchings of Adriaen van Ostade* (San Francisco: Alan Wofsy Fine Arts, 1990).

4. Schnackenburg, *Adriaen van Ostade*, 186, no. 559, illus.

5. Schnackenburg (*Adriaen van Ostade*, 186) states that Adriaen van Ostade's preparatory study for *The Anglers*, although listed in three eighteenth-century inventories, is now lost.

6. An enormous amount of confusion exists in distinguishing between states III and IV because Davidsohn and Godefroy, followed by Hollstein, focus on the addition of the fine oblique lines on the riverbank under the left-hand sloping ramp of the bridge. This oblique shading is already found in state II, although certain impressions are inked in such a way that these lines are not always clearly visible. At the time of writing I was unable to consult the impressions in Oxford and Paris to ascertain whether they conform

to Davidsohn's described state III. In fact, the firm C.G. Boerner, Düsseldorf, *Neue Lagerliste Nr. 82* ("Adriaen van Ostade Die schönsten Radierungen"), 1985, 34, no. 23, queries the very existence of Godefroy's described third state. To the best of my knowledge, the fourth, fifth, and seventh states, as described by Godefroy, do not exist. See Godefroy, *The Complete Etchings*, 98.

7. Sale Paul Davidsohn, C.G. Boerner, Leipzig, November 22-26, 1920, 172.

8. Impressions in the Rijksprentenkabinet, Amsterdam, and the British Museum, London.

9. Two impressions in this state in the National Gallery of Art, Washington, include one formerly in the Davidsohn Collection.

Adriaen van Ostade

Haarlem 1610-1685 Haarlem

87. Slaughtering the Hog

Etching on antique laid paper, 11.2 cm (image) on 11.8 x 11.6 cm (platemark).
B. 41 i/ii; Dut. 41 iii/v; Davidsohn 41 iv/viii; Godefroy 41 iv/viii; H. *Neth.* 41 iv/viii; TIB 41.
Inscription: Signed in plate lower left: *AvOstade* (in ligature).
Condition: Trimmed just outside platemark.
Provenance: Walter Francis, 5th Duke of Buccleuch (Lugt 402); (his sale, Christie's, London, April 19-22, 1887, lot 1677 or 1678 to Wunderlich); Baron Adalbert Von Lanna (Lugt 2773); (his sale, Gutekunst, Stuttgart, May 11-22, 1909, lot 2357 to Keppel for RM 160); General Brayton Ives; (his sale, New York, American Art Association, April 6-14, 1915, lot 936); Paul J. Sachs (Lugt 2091); (purchased from M. Knoedler, New York, May 17, 1927, for $190). Bequest of Herbert Greer French, 1943.338.
Exhibitions: Cincinnati 1930, (no. 83); Cincinnati 1941, no. 140; Boston 1980, no. 104, illus.

Slaughtering the Hog is one of Adriaen van Ostade's most distinguished prints, notable for its tondo format and unusual lighting. Like so many of his etchings, it exists in many states that remain to be clearly described. According to Paul Davidsohn, the Museum's impression is in the fourth state.[1] The first state is unfinished and survives in a single known impression (Haarlem). Impressions of the second state consulted by the author in Amsterdam, Frankfurt, London, New York (Metropolitan Museum of Art), Rotterdam (ex Davidsohn), Vienna, and Washington (National Gallery of Art) indicate that the artist brought the original conception to completion.[2]

In the Davidsohn/Godefroy third state the artist further strengthened the borderline. This reworking is most evident at the top left where it frames the sky.[3] In the fourth state, subtle changes were made throughout. The differences between the third and fourth states not cited in the literature deserve mention in order to precisely define the changes that occurred in the elusive third state.[4] The changes found in the Museum's impression and in one in the British Museum conform to the description of the Davidsohn/Godefroy fourth state.[5]

The plate was subjected to substantial reworking in the fifth state, as described by Davidsohn/Godefroy, which involved many changes not cited in the literature.[6] To my mind, the Davidsohn/Godefroy sixth through eighth states involve changes having nothing to do with Adriaen van Ostade. I also suspect that the vicissitudes to which the plate was subjected at this stage may involve more than the three states described by Davidsohn and Godefroy.[7] I cite these changes in such detail because this print was progressively transformed into a quasinocturne. The lighting on the figures is mysterious, as if emanating from an open fire, yet no evidence for such a source exists.[8] Nonetheless, the pictorial device is most effective because the light and the deep shadows enveloping it create a scene of startling intimacy. It also concentrates our attention on the moment when the peasant slits the throat of the hog. The woman at left waits, her long-handled pan ready to catch the blood of the slaughtered animal. Ostade's subtle use of light to such mysterious effect enhances the composition's dramatic concentration: figures of all ages witness the slaughter of an animal that represents a source of nourishment during the long winter months when the land remains dormant. Not surprisingly this subject was traditionally associated with the month of November in series of prints or drawings representing the twelve months. But as Clifford S. Ackley notes, Ostade's print is not part of a series.[9] Instead, the artist isolates this single labor and monumentalizes the activity by presenting it in such unusual light and by choosing a circular compositional format. – GK

1. Sale Paul Davidsohn, C.G. Boerner, Leipzig, November 20-26, 1920, in which the catalogue cites eight states. Godefroy 41 also lists eight states.

2. An impression in this state is reproduced in C.G. Boerner, Düsseldorf, *Neue Lagerliste Nr. 82* ("Adriaen van Ostade die schönsten Radierungen"), 1985, no. 43.

3. The impression in the Museum Boymans-van Beuningen, Rotterdam, conforming to H. *Neth.* 41 state III involves a single change, the completed borderline. In all other respects it is the same as state II and is prior to the completion of the sky and added vertical lines on the gable. Curiously, the Rotterdam impression has been trimmed to the borderline and set into a second surrounding sheet of paper that has a platemark with rounded corners. I was unable to consult the collections in Paris to confirm whether they possess impressions involving the same degree of reworking as that in Rotterdam. Hollstein cites British Museum, London and Albertina, Vienna as repositories of this print in the third state, but this is an error. Both are fourth state impressions identical to that in Cincinnati.

4. These include the following: (1) further horizontal hatching in the interior of the wooden pail under the pump creating cross-hatching; (2) horizontal hatching added to the shaft of the pump below the spigot and fine vertical hatching added to the lip of the spigot and below it on the illuminated section of the shaft; (3) the window of the house below the vine and above the peasant kneeling on the pig is covered in dense vertical-horizontal cross-hatching plus /// oblique hatching to its left-hand section that largely obliterates it; (4) vertical hatching is added on the wall just above the back of the peasant kneeling on the pig; (5) the sky to the right of the farm is fully shaded in (already noted as a change that occurred in the third state); (6) the barrel at the left is darkened by swelling parallel curved hatching that follows its contours; (7) the roof, gable, and shaded part of the house below the vine are largely reworked by pronounced vertical and oblique parallel shading; 8) foliage of the tree to the left of the chimney has been darkened by \\\ oblique hatching. Impressions in this state are in Cincinnati, London, and Vienna.

5. Davidsohn's description, although summary, is accurate; whereas Godefroy fails to note any reworking to the image, and his fifth state conflates features that had already occurred in state IV.

6. As noted, the plate corners are rounded. The reworking in the fifth state includes the following: (1) the gable is darkened and the upper window is all but obliterated; (2) the chimney to the right of the gable is darkened on the front side with dense vertical hatching and on the right side with oblique cross-hatching; (3) the shadow between the child immediately beyond the man slaughtering the pig and the wall is darkened by added vertical and oblique hatching; (4) the back of the peasant kneeling on the pig has further horizontal hatching; (5) the planks or posts leaning against the house beyond the pump are darkened by further oblique hatching; (6) the entire shadow under the pig is reinforced by horizontal hatching; (7) the shaded area of the house behind the standing peasant at the left and including his back are darkened principally by dense vertical hatching reinforced by horizontal and oblique shading; (8) the upper section or plank behind the basket on the barrel at the left is redefined by dense vertical/horizontal cross-hatching and the wall above it is darkened by dense \\\ oblique hatching. Impressions in this state are in Amsterdam, Frankfurt, London, and Vienna (cited as Dutuit state III and Davidsohn/Godefroy state V). Another is reproduced in C.G. Boerner, Düsseldorf, *Neue Lagerliste Nr. 82*, 1985, 68 – 69, no. 44.

7. Impressions in Amsterdam, Rotterdam, and Vienna conforming to Davidsohn/Godefroy state VI involve considerably more reworking than the catalogue description implies. It includes the following: (1) hatching parallel to the roof line darkens the roof of the farmhouse; (2) further parallel hatching on the back and left arm of the peasant slaughtering the pig; (3) added cross-hatching on the child immediately beyond this man and on the peasant peering over this child, and their hats have been darkened; (4) new oblique cross-hatching added on the house wall under the arbor; (5) oblique cross-hatching on wooden slat fence reducing the areas catching light; (6) fine parallel horizontal lines on the support to the wooden shaft of the pump handle; (7) barrel at left is darkened further; (8) the foreground is darkened by dense \\\ oblique shading.

8. Ostade's preparatory study for this print is in the Royal Museum of Fine Arts in Brussels (inv. 1581). See B. Schnackenburg, *Adriaen van Ostade Isack van Ostade Zeichnungen und Aquarelle*, 2 vols. (Hamburg: E. Ernst Hauswedell and Co., ca. 1981), 91, no. 52, illus. The lighting in the drawing does not convey the sense of mystery and intimacy so evident in the etching. In a small picture, signed and dated 1637, now in the Städelsches Kunstinstitut in Frankfurt am Main (inv. 1231), Ostade represents the subject in torchlight, although the actual light source is screened by the figures standing around the peasant kneeling on the pig.

9. Clifford S. Ackley, Boston 1980, 162, no. 104.

Reinier Nooms ("Zeeman")
Amsterdam ca. 1623-1664 Amsterdam

88. A States Yacht and a Guard-ship or Wadden Convoy Ship ca. 1660.
From *Various Ships and Views of Amsterdam*.
Etching on antique laid paper, 13.5 x 25.1 cm (platemark).
B. 78; Dut. 78 i/iii; TIB 606.078 S2.
Watermark: Cadeucus.
Titled in plate lower center: *Een Staten Iacht, Een uijtlegger of Watte Convoijer. 4.*
Provenance: (Purchased from Harlow, McDonald, New York, March 17, 1933, for $20).
Bequest of Herbert Greer French, 1943.366.
Exhibitions: Cincinnati 1941, no. 163.

Reinier Nooms, nicknamed the Seaman (*Zeeman*), is one of the most gifted of the seventeenth-century Dutch peintre-graveurs. He produced more than 170 etchings, many of which describe Dutch sailing vessels and other boats with an extraordinary degree of accuracy. Nooms' ability to infuse his compositions with a certain pictorial élan makes them a unique contribution to the Dutch "golden age." Nooms was also a prolific draftsman whose characteristic marines were executed with a brush and east india ink. Many of his surviving drawings are finished preparatory studies for prints, carefully indented for transfer.

Virtually nothing is known about the life of this significant master. He is documented in Amsterdam in 1653 and in 1663, and on March 8, 1658, he declared that he was about thirty-five years old. Nooms died in 1664. On December 9, 1667, three years after his death, his widow drew up an inventory of her possessions as part of a marriage contract to Dirck van der Helm. This inventory cites several paintings by Nooms in addition to his library, which included several nautical treatises.

The vast majority of Nooms' prints were conceived in series that fall into three broad categories: representations of various types of ships, accurate topographical views of Amsterdam and Paris, and imaginary Italianate coastal views. A number of these series were published in Amsterdam; others were issued in Paris. The series *Various Ships and Views of Amsterdam*, to which *A States Yacht and a Guard-ship or Wadden Convoy Ship* belongs, probably ranks as his most significant achievement as an etcher.[1]

The marine prints in the *Various Ships* series contain pairs of related ships. Each is usually depicted under full sail under optimum weather conditions, thus enabling Nooms to demonstrate the maneuverability of each vessel while displaying the skillful seamanship of its crew. His accuracy of representation is remarkable and is enhanced by the vivacity of his presentation. Employing light and shadow to great effect, Nooms subtly explored tonal values while stressing the weight and three-dimensionality of the ships as they plough through choppy water. In *A States Yacht and a Guard-ship or Wadden Convoy Ship* Nooms places his subjects before a distant seaport, probably along one of the vast estuaries that comprise so much of the Dutch republic.

States yachts, fast-sailing ships reserved for important dignitaries, were used in their official capacity by members of either the Dutch States General or the provincial states. A transom stern with a stateroom aft, another room amidships, and a pantry and galley in the forecastle were typical amenities. The states yacht in the Museum's print has a rather outmoded spritsail; the convoy ship, by contrast, has a gaff rig. An armed convoy designed for shallow waters,[2] *Watte Convoyer* refers to the Waddenzee, one of the inland seas of the Dutch republic, part of a network of estuaries in the province of Zeeland. – GK

1. *Verscheyde Schepen en Gesichten van Amstelredam*, issued in three parts (B., Dut. 63-98). Excepting the title pages for the three sections, these prints exist in two states. In the first state, each is numbered but is prior to the letter placed before the number. These letters denote the section of the series to which each print belongs.

2. The technical information on these two types of ships is drawn from I. de Groot and R. Vorstman, *Maritime Prints by the Dutch Masters* (London, 1984), 84.

Rembrandt Harmensz. van Rijn
Leiden 1606-1669 Amsterdam

89. Jacob Haaringh ("Young Haaringh") 1655.
Etching, drypoint, and burin on Japanese paper, 19.9 x 14.4 cm (platemark).
B. 275; Hind *Rem.* 288 ii/v; Münz 75 ii/v; H. *Neth.* 275 ii/v.
Signed and dated in window lower center: *Rembrandt f 1655* (6 reversed).
Provenance: Henry Graves, Jr.; (purchased from M. Knoedler, New York, June 29, 1936, for $3,500).
Bequest of Herbert Greer French, 1943.316.
Exhibitions: Ann Arbor 1960, no. 70.

Rembrandt's *Jacob Haaringh* is one of his most extraordinary prints. The dense mesh of lines defining the background wall establishes a murky, dimly lit interior from which the salient features of the sitter barely emerge. Rembrandt concentrates on the sitter's face, his left hand, and the patch of daylight glimpsed through the window. Haaringh's right hand is almost indistinguishable. The background and Haaringh's attire are etched with a dense hatching that approximates the black, velvety sheen of mezzotint engraving, a medium that never interested Rembrandt despite his fascination with dark tonal effects.

In the first state of *Jacob Haaringh*, Rembrandt produced an image in which the pervading darkness of the interior predominates. His satisfaction with this portrait is evident in the experimental range of inking and selection of papers used. He also signed and dated the print in its first state, albeit summarily indicated and barely legible.

In the second state, Rembrandt made several adjustments to the subject, of which only the most major have been cited in the literature. First, he added a bar across the lower section of the window and reinforced the signature and date. Through burnishing he also transformed Haaringh's left hand, redefining the cuff and lightening the hand. Not previously noted, Rembrandt also darkened the right stile of the chair. More important, he reworked the sitter's face and hair. Supplementary vertical shading in the forehead and right cheek, the substantial redefinition of Haaringh's left earlobe, and further slight adjustments to certain locks of wavy hair, all in drypoint, add a visual intensity to Haaringh's visage and enhance this haunting image. The Museum's impression of this portrait is exceptional because of the velvety sheen that results from the way the thick sheet of Japanese paper absorbed the ink.[1]

The mysterious ambiance, the focus on the sitter's face, and the restricted glimpse into the wider world of daylight through the narrow window raise fundamental questions about the meaning of this portrait. Haaringh seems introverted, even vulnerable. The deliberate focus on his face reveals a slight man of spare countenance whose steady gaze makes us accept his inherent dignity. His hands are static – Haaringh makes no emphatic gesture with either – in fact, his right hand is only barely distinguishable from the general darkness. Both hands rest on chair arms and display a lack of nervousness belied by the sitter's rather febrile gaze.

David Smith brilliantly analyzes the visual and psychological components of many of Rembrandt's portraits, including his famous representations of Jan Six.[2] Smith stresses the dichotomy between the private and public personas of Rembrandt's sitters. Rembrandt's portraits of Jan Six are singularly germane to our discussion of *Jacob Haaringh* because of the way Rembrandt interprets the activities and gestures of his subject. In contrast to Jan Six, whom, in his celebrated painting now in the Six Collection in Amsterdam, Rembrandt portrayed as a private man about to step into the public realm or as enlightened collector, author, and bibliophile in his celebrated etching (B. 285) of 1647, Jacob Haaringh is immutably drawn into a private world. Nonetheless, our glimpse into Haaringh's private universe also reveals an intimation of the wider world beyond the confines of his room. Of equal significance, the artist's presentation of the sitter in three-quarter length *en face* creates an intense bond between the observer and the observed. The dark, hushed ambiance is the perfect foil, concentrating attention onto the sitter. Who was Jacob Haaringh? A lawyer from Utrecht, he was the son of Thomas Haaringh, bailiff to the court of insolvents who oversaw Rembrandt's bankruptcy proceedings in 1657 and 1658. Rembrandt produced a monumental printed likeness of *Old Haaringh* (B. 274), very different in mood from the portrait of his son, Jacob.

Rembrandt's representation of Jacob Haaringh is among the first in his oeuvre in which the contrast between darkened interior and intense spotlighting on the face and hands of the sitter is so pronounced. Rembrandt evolved this style of presentation in several of his greatest painted portraits from the same period. His celebrated *Self Portrait* in the Frick Collection, New York, is arguably the most ambitious of these, but even later pictures, such as his haunting 1661 *Portrait of Jacob Trip*, now in London, come even closer to the mood of Rembrandt's likeness of Haaringh. Jacob Trip's static pose is less a pose of relaxation than the inertia of old age. In fact, Rembrandt depicted Trip only months before the sitter's death, his sallow pallor and fragility a premonition of imminent mortality. The seated three-quarter length format offered Rembrandt innumerable pictorial possibilities in presenting his subjects and, in many respects, he first developed it for his portrait *Jacob Haaringh*. Despite its diminutive size, it should be recognized as one of the artist's outstanding portraits. – GK

1. This is in direct contrast to the equally splendid visual effects found in *Jan Asselyn* (cat. 83), in which the thin sheet of Japanese paper results in a distinctive, glossy sheen.
2. David R. Smith, "*I Janus*: Privacy and the Gentlemanly Ideal in Rembrandt's Portraits of Jan Six," AH. 11, no. 1 (March, 1988): 42-63; idem, "Carel Fabritius and Portraiture in Delft," AH. 13, no. 3 (June 1990): 151-74, esp. 158, 160.

Rembrandt Harmensz. van Rijn

Leiden 1606-1669 Amsterdam

90. Jan Lutma, Goldsmith 1656.
Etching and drypoint on antique laid paper, 19.8 x 14.9 cm (platemark).

B. 276; Hind *Rem.* 290 i/iii; Münz 77 i/iii; H. *Neth.* 276 i/iii.
Watermark: Crowned double headed eagle.
Condition: Trimmed just outside platemark.
Provenance: Alfred Morrison (Lugt 151); (purchased from F.H. Bresler, Milwaukee, April 7, 1931, for $12,750).
Bequest of Herbert Greer French, 1943.317.
Exhibitions: Cincinnati 1934, no. 66; Cincinnati 1941, no. 158.

Rembrandt's depictions of fellow artists comprise a significant subgroup of portrait likenesses that offers an important comparison to his better-known self-portraits. Only a few of Rembrandt's self-portraits allude to his profession as an artist.[1] His representations of other artists shed light on Rembrandt's interpretation of creative genius.

In *Jan Lutma*, Rembrandt represents an Amsterdam silversmith (1584 – 1669) celebrated for his distinctive style. Lutma developed ornamental patterns of biomorphic shapes characterized as lobate or auricular. These flowing organic patterns were integral to many types of decorative art. For example, Dutch picture frames of the period with carved and gilded lobate motifs are generically known as "Lutma" frames.[2] In this print, Rembrandt places a silver dish in Lutma's characteristic lobate style on a table next to a hammer and graver's tools in a jar. These tools of Lutma's trade forge a link between inspiration and practice, suggesting that an artist's creative drive can only be realized by employing skills acquired through discipline and training.

Rembrandt depicts Jan Lutma, three-quarter length, in a fine armchair with stiles capped by lion's heads. Unlike Jacob Haaringh (cat. 89) who appears in a darkened chamber, Lutma sits in a light-filled room. In the first state of this print, the light source is undefined, but in the second state, Rembrandt transformed the background by setting a window into an arched casement. He also signed and dated the print: *Rembrandt/f 1656*. Rembrandt made other minor adjustments to the area immediately to the left of the back of the armchair. By adding shading along much of its right stile, Rembrandt merged the chair with the shaded wall at the left.

Rembrandt printed several impressions of the first state of *Jan Lutma* on Japanese papers that print with a lustrous sheen. By contrast, the Museum's impression is on a European paper. Although wiped clean, traces of residual surface tone add an almost transparent film that envelops the subject in glowing light. The tone sets off the vibrant display of drypoint most evident in the sitter's robe and on the silver dish. The boldly defined bulk of the sitter's robe and the sparkling light on the dish are enhanced by the strong light that seems to have two sources: the background window and the right side. In particular, this lighting system enhances the role of the chair as a visual foil to Lutma's head, which is caught in a strong, raking light.

One recent Rembrandt scholar perceives *Jan Lutma* as introspective in mood:[3] one is especially struck by the intimacy established between subject and viewer. Lutma gazes out at the observer. His grave countenance conveys a probity and a sense of conviction underscored by his immobile yet relaxed pose. His hands reinforce the mood of repose.[4] The silversmith ponders his handiwork as he handles a statuette in his right hand. Despite the stillness and monumentality so apparent in this print, its two points of activity – the sitter's alert gaze and his hand holding the sculpture – are powerful psychological gestures. Both invite the viewer to fathom the sitter's thoughts about art and artistic creativity that, by inference, also reflect Rembrandt's concerns as an artist. It is not known whether *Jan Lutma* was commissioned, but Rembrandt's sympathetic likeness suggests that he admired the silversmith not only as an artist, but as a dignified and distinguished compatriot. – GK

1. For example, *Self Portrait at a Window*, dated 1648 (B. 22), depicts Rembrandt as a draftsman or more probably as an etcher; the *Self Portrait* at Kenwood House in London (Br. 52), as a painter holding his palette; and the etching of about 1639, *The Artist Drawing from a Model* (B. 192), as a draftsman. For Rembrandt's self-portraits, see H. Perry Chapman, *Rembrandt's Self Portraits* (Princeton: Princeton University Press, 1990). Chapman (p. 82) argues that Rembrandt depicts himself as an etcher rather than a draftsman in his *Self Portrait at a Window*.

2. A fine example is illustrated in Amsterdam 1984, cat. 34, on a pair of portraits by Cornelis Jonson van Ceulen representing Jaspar Schade and his wife, Cornelia Strick van Linschoten, now in the Rijksmuseum Twenthe, Enschede.

3. Clifford S. Ackley, Boston 1980, 203, no. 137.

4. In certain respects Rembrandt's magisterial *Self Portrait* of 1658 in the Frick Collection in New York (Br. 50) is similar in presentation to the slightly earlier *Jan Lutma*. The massive hands, the steady gaze, and the monumental three-quarter length format are analogous in both works. The mysterious setting and dramatic spotlighting in the painting differ and transform the relationship between the subject and viewer. Nonetheless, certain features of *Jan Lutma* continued to preoccupy Rembrandt in his later painted portraits, including the 1658 *Self Portrait*.

Cornelis Pietersz. Bega

Haarlem ca. 1631/32-1664 Haarlem

91. Tavern Interior (Le Cabaret) 1660-61.

Etching on antique laid paper, 22.5 x 17.4 cm (platemark).
B. 35; Dut. 35; H. *Neth.* 35; TIB 35.
Watermark: Indecipherable.
Condition: Trimmed just outside platemark.
Provenance: Edward Peart (Lugt 891); (his sale, Christie's, London, April 12, 1822); Joseph Maberly (Lugt 1845); (his sale, Sotheby's, London, May 26-30, 1851, lot 26 [7 Bega items] to Colnaghi); (purchased from F.H. Bresler, Milwaukee, February 15, 1929, for $121).
Bequest of Herbert Greer French, 1943.322.
Exhibitions: Cincinnati 1930, (no. 1); Minneapolis 1956 (not in catalogue)

Cornelis Bega, born in Haarlem about 1631 or 1632, was the son of the gold and silversmith Pieter Jansz. Begeijn (or Begga) and Maria Cornelisdr., the illegitimate daughter of the reputed mannerist artist Cornelis Cornelisz. van Haarlem. In an inventory from 1639, Cornelis Cornelisz. left Maria a substantial part of his estate, including all of his red chalk drawings as well as half of his household effects.[1] Arnold Houbraken states that Bega was Adriaen van Ostade's best pupil.[2] In 1653 Bega traveled with his compatriots Vincent Laurensz. van der Vinne and Joost Boelen in Germany, Switzerland, and France. By June of that year Bega was back in Haarlem, where he joined the Guild of Saint Luke in 1654. He died of the plague in Haarlem on August 27, 1664, and was buried in the Church of Saint Bavo.

Bega's choice of low-life peasant subjects, including tavern interiors, shows the impact of his teacher, Adriaen van Ostade; but as a draftsman, Bega's choice of medium and style differs fundamentally from Ostade's. Instead of producing diminutive pen-and-wash studies, Bega preferred red and black chalk. Quite likely his choice was influenced by the many red chalk drawings by Cornelis Cornelisz. that were readily available to him. Bega's drawings tend to be finished chalk studies of individual figures, often drawn on blue paper.

Bega also produced about thirty-five etchings,[3] which fall into two distinct groups. The vast majority are small studies of individual peasants; the remainder are considerably larger multifigured genre scenes depicting peasants relaxing in taverns. *Tavern Interior*, one of the artist's most imposing multifigured etchings, contains five peasants. Two men and a young woman in the foreground are cast in

strong light in contrast to two seated men deep in conversation in half-shadow beyond. The dark neutral background projects the entire subject in sharp relief. Bega calls attention to two major activities associated with public houses – drinking and smoking. These two temptations of the flesh were vehemently criticized by the Calvinist clergy of the Dutch Reformed Church. The two men in the foreground have earthenware tankards. The man at right also holds a clay pipe. Neither speaks; instead, they both gaze intently at the young woman, who may or may not be finishing a yarn. Although not clearly visible to the viewer, this woman's open décolletage offers her companions an enticing view of her ample bosom.

Mary Ann Scott believed that Bega must have used live models or sketches for the individual figures and composition of *Tavern Interior*.[4] In fact, Bega's red chalk study, *Seated Woman in Right Profile*, now in a Dutch private collection, is quite close in pose and attire to the seated barmaid in this etching.[5] Even though the model is seated in an armchair and lacks the frizzy hair of the woman in the print, her relaxed right arm and her similar blouse and vest find close parallels with the female figure in *Tavern Interior*.

Like so many female tavernkeepers represented in seventeenth-century Dutch genre paintings, Bega's women were often the dispensers of sexual favors or the objects of sexual abuse. By succumbing to the blandishments of money and alcohol, many young barmaids fell into disrepute. This is the subject of Jan Steen's *Tavern Scene with a Pregnant Hostess*, now in Philadelphia.[6] Scott discusses Bega's unusual focus on peasant women as objects of potential and actual abuse.[7] Bega treats the theme of abused women principally in his paintings but recapitulates his ideas in certain etchings, including *Tavern Interior*. In its starkness, the dark ambiance in this print focuses our attention onto the human protagonists with uncompromising clarity. In the case of *Tavern Interior*, Scott believes that the barmaid, whose drooping eyelids betray her intoxication, struggles to maintain an upright posture. Moreover, Scott argues that the two men encourage her to consume more alcohol. Bega does not elucidate any further course of action to the degree that Scott claims;[8] nonetheless, certain details in the print allude to the woman's dereliction of duty. The broom cast on the floor at the left next to the wide-brimmed hat and the cast-off shoes are signs that she rejects industriousness for sloth. Scott also cites the dish whose glowing embers were used to light clay pipes as a well-known metaphor for the flames of lust kindled by the intoxicating influences of alcohol and tobacco.[9] – GK

1. The biographical data on Bega is drawn from Mary Ann Scott, "Cornelis Bega (1631/32-1664) As Painter and Draughtsman" (Ph.D. diss., University of Maryland, 1984); Philadelphia 1984, 132.

2. A. Houbraken, *De Groote Schouburgh der Nederlantsche Konstschilders en Schilderessen*, vol. 1 (Amsterdam, 1718), 349-50.

3. H. *Neth.* I lists forty items, but Clifford S. Ackley, Boston 1980, 256, rejects H. *Neth.* 36-40. Scott, "Cornelis Bega," 252, reattributes *Group at a Fireplace* (B. 23) to R. van Oosterzaen.

4. Scott, "Cornelis Bega," 74.

5. P. Schatborn, Amsterdam 1981, 106, no. 10, illus. Also cited in Scott, "Cornelis Bega," 379, no. D28. Scott links this drawing to nine others representing the same model. Certain of these relate to Bega's paintings in Bordeaux (*Bordello Scene*, Scott, no. 101, which she dates to about 1660) and Brussels (*Merry Company in a Tavern*, Scott, no. 123, signed and dated 166[1]). This helps confirm a date of about 1660-61 for *Tavern Interior*. Neither author cites the similarity of *Seated Woman in Right Profile* with *Tavern Interior*.

6. P. C. Sutton, "Jan Steen Comedy and Admonition," *Bulletin of the Philadelphia Museum of Art* 78 (Winter-Spring 1981-82): 32, 34, pl. 8.

7. Scott, "Cornelis Bega," 185-90.

8. Scott, "Cornelis Bega," 74.

9. Scott, "Cornelis Bega," 178.

Johannes (Jan) Thomas

Ypres 1617-1678 Vienna
after Anthony van Dyck (1599-1641)

92. Achilles Disguised as a Woman 1659.

Etching and mezzotint on antique laid paper, 21.0 x 22.4 cm
(platemark).
Nagler 10; W. 9; H. *Neth.* 14.
Watermark: Basilisk (cockatrice) with Basel crozier over three circles
(cf. Heawood 843, 846).
Inscribed below composition: ACHILLES INTER VIRGINES HABITU
MULIEBRI DELITESCENS, EX GALEA SIBI PRAE DONIS CETERIS
ELECTA ULYSSIS ASTU DETEGITUR/ *Spectatissimo Eximióq. Viro,
Dno. Ludovico Malo, observationis ergô dedicat humillimè Joann:
Thomas 1. Jan: 1659* (Achilles, hiding away among the maidens in
the costume of a woman, was detected by choosing a helmet for
himself in preference to other gifts, through the cleverness of Ulysses.
Johannes Thomas most humbly dedicates this [print] to that most
worthy and distinguished man, his lordship Ludovicus Malus
[Ludwig Mahl?], because of his attention. 1 Jan. 1659).
Condition: Lower left margin replaced, upper left corner repaired.
Provenance: Fritz Reiss (Lugt 2178); (purchased from M. Knoedler,
New York, June 12, 1939, for $150).
Bequest of Herbert Greer French, 1943.403.

Johannes Thomas was one of the first practitioners of the mezzotint
technique, invented in the early 1640s by Ludwig von Siegen (cat. 80)
and improved by Prince Rupert of the Palatinate (Ruprecht von der
Pfalz) and Wallerant Vaillant.

Thomas, a pupil of Rubens, practiced both painting and etching in
his native Antwerp but spent the later part of his life in Vienna in the
service of the Emperor Leopold I.[1] In 1658 he was in Frankfurt to
attend the emperor's coronation; there Prince Rupert and Vaillant
were experimenting with mezzotint, and Thomas almost certainly
learned the technique directly from them, making his first mezzotint
the same year.[2]

In its fully developed form, mezzotint is a process of working from
dark to light. The entire surface of a metal plate is roughened with a
special tool (the *rocker*) so that it prints a deep, velvety black. The
artist then creates an image by selectively smoothing and burnishing
areas to produce highlights and middle tones out of the dark ground.
To achieve an evenly roughened surface, the rocker must be passed
over the entire plate repeatedly in several different directions, a
laborious, mechanical process.

Early mezzotinters were less systematic in the way they worked. In
this print, Thomas first etched the main lines of the image; then he
used the rocker to add shadows as the composition required. Broad
areas of shading, like the rock on which the helmet rests, could be
put in using the rocker alone, but for more intricate details of
shading, highlights were scraped or burnished. The folds of drapery
show this most clearly. The print is crude by comparison with the
later mezzotints of Valentine Green (cat. 110) or John Raphael Smith
(cat. 111): the tracks of the rocker show up as diagonal lines running
in various directions through the image and some of the transitions
of light and shade are rather abrupt. Although less suave than other
mezzotints, it is also more personal, clearly revealing the processes
by which it was created and the individuality of the artist's hand. A
viewer accustomed to twentieth-century expressionist art may
actually find it more approachable than the smooth and flawless
mezzotints of the eighteenth century.

The inscription on the print identifies the subject as an early
episode from the story of the Trojan War. The goddess Thetis,
mother of the hero Achilles, knew that if he joined the Greek army to
make war on Troy he would achieve great fame but die in combat;
therefore, she persuaded him to go to the palace of Lycomedes, king
of Scyros, and to live among the king's daughters disguised as a
woman. The clever Ulysses came to Scyros in search of Achilles. To
detect him in his disguise, Ulysses brought a quantity of jewels,
dresses, and similar things, ostensibly as gifts for the ladies of the
court. Concealed among the feminine articles, however, were
weapons of war. Achilles revealed his sex and identity by seizing the
weapons and thereupon agreed to join the Greeks.[3]

Although no inscription acknowledges it, Thomas' print closely
reproduces a painting by Van Dyck, now in the collection of the
Duke of Marlborough. Van Dyck's painting, however, has been
connected with a completely different story, an episode from
Jerusalem Delivered by Torquato Tasso.[4] In Tasso's poem, set at the
time of the First Crusade, the Lady Erminia is prompted by Cupid to
seek her wounded lover, Tancred, among the Crusaders. She dresses
herself in armor so that she can leave Jerusalem unrecognized.[5] The
figure does, in fact, fit Erminia's story better than that of Achilles,
who is usually described as grasping a sword and shield rather than a
helmet. Furthermore, Van Dyck's painting is actually the portrait of
a noblewoman, probably English. While there would be nothing
unusual in such a woman having herself portrayed in the guise of the
virtuous Erminia, it would have been remarkable, indeed, for her to
be depicted as Achilles.

There is no way to know whether Thomas had seen Van Dyck's
painting or a drawing made from it and whether he misunderstood
the subject or deliberately chose to reinterpret it as Achilles. Whether
accidentally or deliberately, the resulting image emphasizes a side of
the Achilles story mentioned by several ancient authors. While in
hiding at the court of Lycomedes, Achilles is said to have become the
lover of one of the king's daughters, who bore him a son; in revealing
himself to Ulysses, therefore, he was not only accepting death in
battle but abandoning his love.[6] This print portrays a pensive
Achilles at the moment of decision, pulled backward by Cupid but
indicating his choice with the gesture of his right hand.

The Ludovicus Malus to whom Thomas dedicated the print has
not yet been identified, and one can only guess why Thomas chose to
compliment him on his *observatio*, a word that can mean attention
or watchfulness, in the sense of surveillance. Perhaps he was a
statesman who would have been pleased to think that his
watchfulness compared to the cunning of Ulysses, but it is equally
likely that he was an amateur of the arts, attentive to the
development of the new printmaking technique. – TR

1. W. II:709-10; ThB. XXXIII:64-65; H. *Neth.* XXX:87-99.
2. Jane Bayard, New Haven 1976, 3; Wax, 18.
3. Robert Graves, *The Greek Myths* (Harmondsworth: Penguin Books, 1960), 2:280.
4. Van Dyck's painting, now in the collection of the Duke of Marlborough, is
reproduced in Oliver Millar, London 1982, 85-86, no. 42. The print is in reverse to the
painting; the only other major difference is that the painting shows a peaceful landscape
behind the figure of Cupid rather than the uniform dark background of the print.
5. Torquato Tasso, *Jerusalem Delivered*, trans. Edward Fairfax (New York: The
Colonial Press, 1901), 125.
6. This theme is most fully developed in the *Achilleid* of the Roman poet Statius.
Statius, with an English Translation by J. H. Mozley, M.A. (Cambridge: Harvard
University Press; London: William Heinemann, 1928).

Antoine Masson

Loury 1636-1700 Paris
after Nicolas Mignard (1606-1668)

93. Guillaume de Brisacier 1664.

Engraving on antique laid paper, 34.8 x 26.4 cm (sheet).
RD. 15 i/iv.

Watermark: Large coat of arms with scrollwork, containing two five-pointed stars, three circles, etc. (cf. Heawood 686).
Inscribed, signed, and dated in plate lower center: *N. Mignard Avenionensis Pinxit-Ant Masson Sculpebat 1664.*
Condition: Trimmed just within platemark.
Provenance: Alfred Morrison (Lugt 151); (his sale, C.G. Boerner, November 10-12, 1927, no. 804, to Colnaghi, London for RM 150); (purchased from M. Knoedler, New York, April 16, 1928, for $740). Bequest of Herbert Greer French, 1943.330.
Exhibitions: Cincinnati 1930 (no. 38); Cincinnati 1934, no. 67; Cincinnati 1941, no. 175, pl. 26.
References: M. Holloway, *The Collection of Engravings, formed between the years 1860-68, by Alfred Morrison* (London: 1868), no. 1575.

The seventeenth-century French school of portrait engraving has been consistently ranked at the height of the development of the specialized portrait print. Masters of this school, such as Jean Morin, Robert Nanteuil, Gerard Edelinck (cat. 94), Claude Mellan, and Masson himself, established the standard toward which all subsequent portrait engravers strived. The very rich tradition of French portraiture thrived under the strong arts sponsorship of Louis XIV, who particularly favored the translation of painted portraits of notables into widely circulated printed tokens of their power and status. Inheriting a tradition of scientific and historical interest in the visages of emperors, kings, and religious figures, the seventeenth century refined and expanded the informational medium of the portrait print into a political and social tool of high technical sophistication.

The French school combined a classical sensibility of presentation with a penetrating gaze at the outer visage to achieve a striking model of cool, "photographic" realism. In contrast, the British were beginning their love affair with the warm-toned mezzotint (see Pelham, cat. 98, and Green, cat. 108), and the Italians, such as Ottavio Leoni, were exploring the medium of etching for their portraits. At this time in the Netherlands, two of the greatest masters of portrait etching – Van Dyck (cats. 71-72) and Rembrandt (cats. 89-90) – were working in a tradition of technical freedom and psychological penetration that also differed from their French counterparts.[1] During the eighteenth century, French portrait paintings (and the engravings after them) became ever more obsessed with accessory details; such works were characterized by Mayor as "full-length effigies in robes of office, treading on a baroque litter of professional paraphernalia."[2]

Robert Nanteuil (1623-1678) has usually been accorded top honors by critics and collectors for the sobriety of his presentation and the understated finesse of his execution. He engraved over two hundred portraits, including eleven of Louis XIV and fourteen of Cardinal Mazarin. Mr. French acquired only three Nanteuil portraits, but among them he secured *Pompone de Bellièvre*,[3] which at the time he was collecting was considered one of the "top three" prints that any self-respecting collection *must* have; the other two were Edelinck's *Philippe de Champaigne* (cat. 94) and this portrait by Masson.

Antoine Masson was born near Orléans, the son of an armorer. He first learned that trade, which undoubtedly included its engraved decoration, but virtually nothing is known of any further artistic training. Masson eventually settled in Paris, where he became a member of the Royal Academy in 1679, well after his career as an engraver was established.[4] While some sixty-four of his approximately seventy prints were portraits, he was also well known for several religious compositions after other artists, in particular *Supper at Emmaus* after Titian (RD. 5), known as "The Tablecloth"

for the skill of his depiction of that article.

Masson has been consistently featured in the literature for his bravura technical skills at reproducing objects that at times compete with the depictions of the subjects themselves. But it seems that critics of the time highly prized such verisimilitude in depicting accoutrements in addition to accurately conveying the likeness of the sitter.[5] Writing a century later, Diderot recommended Masson's engravings in order to "learn how one represents feathers, skin, hair, leather, silk, embroidery, linen, drapery, metal and wood."[6] This portrait of Guillaume de Brisacier is popularly known as "The Gray-Haired Man"; writers have continually marveled at Masson's compulsive depiction of every hair on his subject's head. A nineteenth-century commentator wrote that "one feels the lightness of his beautiful grey hair; his collar is truly lace."[7] On the other hand, one critic earlier in this century severely criticized Masson for making his likenesses so convincing that they "verge on caricature," and he found grave fault with the De Brisacier portrait for its too-brilliant contrasts and the "sensational qualities" of the hair.[8]

Guillaume de Brisacier (1607-1675) served in various clerical and financial positions in the diplomatic service, eventually being appointed private secretary to Queen Marie Thérèse, a privileged position that he subsequently lost for accepting bribes.[9] Masson's engraving is after a painting by Nicolas Mignard (1606-1668). After working in Lyons and Rome, Mignard settled in Avignon for twenty years until moving to Paris to work for Louis XIV. He became a Royal Academician in 1663 and taught at the academy until his death (which actually occurred in De Brisacier's home). Mignard painted religious subjects and portraits and executed some nine etchings.[10]

This impression of *Guillaume de Brisacier* is a brilliant one of the first state, before the sitter's name and title ("*Secretaire des Commandements de la Reine*") were engraved within the oval border. The format of Masson's print follows the classic French model, with its severely simple stone frame placed on a plinth; the laurel leaves seem an almost busy addition. De Brisacier's coat of arms falls beneath the oval frame. Typically, the areas behind the sitter and around the frame are totally unadorned, leaving Masson's obsessively detailed head of hair to stand clearly featured as is particularly evident in this impression. Resembling nothing so much as fine spaghetti, many of De Brisacier's hairs are delineated by two thin black lines enclosing a white "line," thus creating the hair's grayish effect. Masson's technique also includes the finest, most precise flicks of the engraver's burin to define the nose and much of the face. The standard cross-hatching technique of engraving is to be found on the face only in the shaded portions of the cheek and chin. – DPB

1. Two of the best short introductions to the function and variations of portrait prints during their heyday are by A. Hyatt Mayor, *Prints and People* (New York: The Metropolitan Museum of Art, 1971), nos. 282-92, and Michel Melot, "The Portrait: An Ideological Product," in Michel Melot, Antony Griffiths, Richard S. Field, and André Béguin, *Prints – History of an Art* (New York: Skira/Rizzoli, 1981), 76-79.

2. Mayor, *Prints and People*, no. 291.

3. Ch. Petitjean and Ch. Wickert, *Catalogue de l'oeuvre gravé de Robert Nanteuil* (Paris: Loys Delteil et Maurice Le Garrec, 1925), no. 16.

4. W. McAllister Johnson, *French Royal Academy of Painting and Sculpture Engraved Reception Pieces: 1672-1789* (Kingston: Agnes Etherington Art Centre, 1982), 70, no. 17.

5. See Johnson, *French Royal Academy*, 8-11, for a discussion of the role and characteristics of the most-developed academic portrait engraving of the period.

6. Quoted in Richard Campbell, "The Portrait Print: Traditions and Transformations," Baltimore 1984, 29.

7. [Henri Herluison] *Notice sur Antoine Masson graveur orléanais suivi du catalogue de l'oeuvre de Masson* (Orléans: Herluison, 1866), 13. According to his own testimony, the nineteenth-century Italian portrait engraver Giuseppe Longhi copied De Brisacier's hair for his portrait of George Washington (see Charles Sumner, *The Best Portraits in Engraving*, 4th ed. [New York: Frederick Keppel, 1875], 14).

8. T. H. Thomas, *French Portrait Engraving of the XVIIth and XVIIIth Centuries* (London: G. Bell and Sons, 1910), 65-66. Thomas declares that Masson "goes to immense pains to show single hairs. . . a piece of technical buffoonery quite unworthy of an engraver of Masson's calibre."

9. The most reliable source for De Brisacier's life is found in the *Dictionnaire de biographie française* (Paris: Letouzey et Ané, 1933ff.), 7:350. The often heard story that he was imprisoned in the Bastille for forging a document over the queen's signature in order to obtain a duke's title actually belongs to his son, Mathieu de Brisacier (d. 1686), who succeeded him as secretary to the queen (*Dictionnaire*, 351).

10. The fullest account of Mignard's works is Antoine Schnapper, Avignon 1979; the De Brisacier portrait is no. 81. The current whereabouts of the painting are unknown; it is postulated from Masson's print, which cites its model as "painted (*pinxit*) [by] N. Mignard of Avignon." Nicolas and the well-known Pierre Mignard were brothers.

Gérard Edelinck

Antwerp 1640-1707 Paris
after Philippe de Champaigne (1602-1674)

94. Portrait of Philippe de Champaigne 1676.

Engraving on antique laid paper, 39.7 x 33.5 cm (platemark).
RD. 164 ii/ii.
Dated in plate lower right: *1668*; inscribed and signed below image:
Philippus de Champaigne Bruxellensis Pictor Regius, et Regiae Pictorum Academiae Rector:/Eximiae hujus artis excellentiâ, et christianâ pietate aeque insignis/Se ipse pinxit G. Edelinck sculpsit. 1676./Cum pri. R. (Philippe de Champaigne of Brussels, Painter to the King, and Director of the Royal Academy of Painters: equally notable by excellence in this distinguished art, and by Christian piety. He himself painted it. G. Edelinck engraved it. 1676. Copyright).
Provenance: Gift to Herbert Greer French, (as first state, ca. 1932).
Bequest of Herbert Greer French, 1943.343.
Exhibitions: Cincinnati 1941, no. 169.

The work of Gérard Edelinck represents the synthesis of two major engraving traditions, the Rubens school (deriving from the group of engravers who were trained by Rubens to reproduce his paintings) and the French portrait engraving tradition, most purely exemplified by the work of Robert Nanteuil. By Edelinck's time, reproductive engravers had spent almost two centuries finding increasingly sophisticated ways of harmonizing two goals: on the one hand, to space and weight their lines in such a way that each patch of shading accurately matched the tone of a corresponding patch of color in the paintings or drawings they were reproducing; on the other, to make each group of shading lines an orderly and beautiful pattern in itself. Yet, paradoxically, the more successful the engraver, the more his own personality was subordinated to that of the artist whose work he was reproducing. Looking at this print from a distance, we hardly notice the individual lines. It is not just that the lines are fine in relation to the size of the print – Dürer and Lucas van Leyden had engraved with equal delicacy – but because the lines are laid down with such mechanical regularity, the eye misses the small variations that enliven the surfaces of earlier prints and reads each patch of shading as a mass. If we expect a work of art to be the vivid expression of an artist's individuality, Edelinck's print must disappoint us, for it is the product of two artistic personalities and both express themselves only within a very narrowly defined set of formal rules.

Engraved two years after the death of Philippe de Champaigne, Edelinck's print reproduces a lost self-portrait.[1] It can be seen as a memorial to the older artist, a friend of Edelinck's (he had been a witness at Edelinck's marriage in 1672) whose paintings he

frequently reproduced.[2] The inscription – laying equal weight on the subject's official honors, his artistic skill, and his Christian piety – epitomizes a view of the successful artist as good citizen, with a clearly established rank in a hierarchical society. Edelinck and Philippe de Champaigne – both transplanted Flemings who found government patronage, financial success, and official recognition at the French court – would surely have approved of this view.

Philippe de Champaigne was born and received his early training in Brussels but came to Paris before he was twenty. By 1628 he was the favored painter of Marie de Medici, the mother of Louis XIII, and had attracted the patronage of the king's powerful minister, Cardinal Richelieu. This court patronage was followed by many commissions from private citizens and from the Roman Catholic Church.[3] The self-portrait was painted near the end of his life (1668), when Champaigne had come under the influence of the Jansenists, an austere reform movement within the Church. Ironically, the very idea of a self-portrait runs counter to the tenets of Jansenism, which advocated the distrust and suppression of the self (several Jansenist leaders would not permit their portraits to be made). Yet if by Jansenist standards Champaigne's portrait is a surrender to worldly vanity, it is nevertheless a humbler image than its model, the famous self-portrait by Nicolas Poussin in the Louvre. Whereas Poussin depicts his own paintings stacked behind him and grasps a portfolio of drawings as if it were the scepter of a king, Champaigne appears in a landscape with the city of Brussels in the distance, affirming his Flemish roots rather than his artistic prowess.[4]

Edelinck received his early training as an engraver in Antwerp, where he is recorded to have been the pupil of a minor engraver, Gaspard Huybrechts. He is also said to have studied with Cornelis Galle the Younger, whose father had been one of Rubens' preferred engravers and who continued the tradition of the Rubens school. Arriving in Paris at the age of twenty-six, Edelinck worked in the studios of several French engravers, including Robert Nanteuil, whose niece he later married. One of his prints attracted the attention of Charles Le Brun, first painter to Louis XIV. Le Brun in turn recommended him to the king's minister, Jean-Baptiste Colbert, who was responsible for royal patronage of the arts. Colbert commissioned Edelinck to reproduce paintings in the royal collections, and from then on, his career was a succession of official commissions and honors. He reproduced paintings of a variety of types, but more than two-thirds of his prints were portraits.[5]

Although when compared to the etchings of Van Dyck or Rembrandt Edelinck's style may seem cold and impersonal, he was praised by eighteenth- and nineteenth-century connoisseurs of engraving for warmth and vivacity.[6] To understand what they meant, it may help to scrutinize small details in the print, even to use a magnifying glass. Although each patch of shading is tightly controlled and uniform, different surfaces are rendered with a wide variety of different types of line. The hair is depicted with long parallel lines that mimic individual strands of hair and, at the same time, broaden and narrow to suggest highlights and shadows, color and volume. At the jaw, systems of bold, smoothly curving lines that map the volume of the cheek are intersected by a flock of tiny irregular strokes that suggest a short, stubbly beard. The distant church (fig. 94-1) is defined in an almost impressionistic manner by slightly quavering vertical and horizontal cross-hatching, and minute interruptions in the shading create halos of light around the back-lit trees in front of the church.

Moving back to contemplate the print as a whole, we can see how these varied types of shading blend like the instruments in a large symphony orchestra to create overall tones that we read as dark cloth, shadows on a tree trunk, or luminous evening sky. In a time and place when the ideal of personal conduct was not self-expression

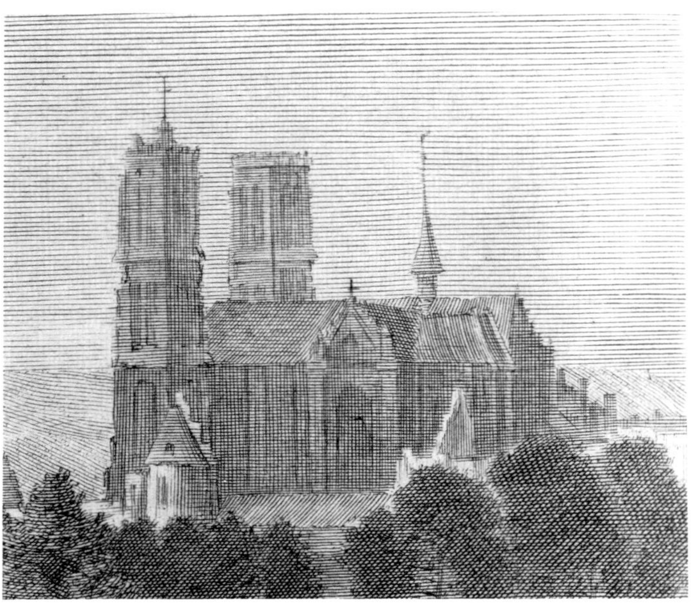

Figure 94-1. Gérard Edelinck, *Portrait of Philippe de Champagine* (detail).

but graceful conformity to rigorous and elaborate codes of etiquette, Edelinck practiced a supremely well-mannered engraving style. – TR

1. Bernard Dorival, *Philippe de Champaigne, 1602-1674, la vie, l'oeuvre et le catalogue raisonné de l'oeuvre* (Paris: Léonce Laget, 1976), 2:164-65, pl. 328-29.

2. L. Dussieux et al., eds., *Mémoires inédits sur la vie et les ouvrages des membres de l'Académie royale de peinture et sculpture publiées d'après les manuscrits conservés à l'École impériale des Beaux-Arts* (Paris: F. de Nobele, 1968), 2:51; Henri Delaborde, *Les Artistes célèbres: Gérard Edelinck* (Paris: J. Rouam, 1886), 22-28, 58; Dorival, *Philippe de Champaigne*, 1:57-59.

3. Dorival, *Philippe de Champaigne*, 1:39-55.

4. Dorival, *Philippe de Champaigne*, 1:98, 129-30, 165.

5. L. Dussieux et al., *Mémoires inédits*, 2:46-60; RD. VII:169-336; Henri Delaborde, *Les Artistes célèbres*, 11-74; Roger-Armand Weigert, I.F.F. 1600 4:7.

6. L. Dussieux et al., *Mémoires inédits*, 2:51; RD. VII:169-70 (quoting a certain M. Levesque); Delaborde, *Les Artistes célèbres*, 56-58, 90-93.

Nicolaes Berchem

Haarlem 1620-1683 Amsterdam

95. The Cows at the Watering Place 1680.

Etching on antique laid paper, 27.7 x 37.8 cm.
B. 1; Dut. 1 iii/v; H. *Neth.* 1 iii/v; TIB 1.
Watermark: Crowned shield with fleur-de-lis and countermark IHS/
ET (cf. Churchill 428).
Signature and address in plate lower left: *Delineavit et Sculpt: per
NBerchem/et in lucem edit: per NVisscher cum Privil:*
Provenance: (Purchased from Harlow, McDonald, New York,
March 17, 1933, for $50).
Bequest of Herbert Greer French, 1943.369.

Nicolaes Pietersz. Berchem was born in Haarlem in 1620, the son of the Haarlem still-life painter, Pieter Claesz, who was also his first teacher. Berchem subsequently studied with several artists, including Jan van Goyen, Claes Moeyaert, Pieter de Grebber, Jan Wils, and putatively with Jan Baptist Weenix. He entered the Haarlem painters' guild in 1642 as a master and, by August of that year, had three registered pupils. He married Catrijne Claesdr. de Groot in 1646. About three years later, Berchem journeyed with Jacob van Ruisdael to the German border region of Westphalia, where both artists sketched the castle of Bentheim and traveled as far as Burgsteinfurt, the birthplace of Pieter Claesz.

Berchem's many magnificent Italianate landscapes and coastal views suggest that he must have traveled to Italy. No surviving documentary evidence confirms a sojourn to the Mediterranean, although the fact that Berchem is not documented in the Netherlands between 1649 and 1656 might indicate a period when he could have resided in Italy. From 1657 until the mid-1670s, Berchem resided principally in Haarlem, but he moved to Amsterdam in 1677 and died there in 1683.

Berchem had many pupils, including Abraham Begeyn, Karel Dujardin, Dirk Maas, Jan van der Meer the Younger, Hendrik Mommers, Willem Romeyn, and two notable Dutch genre painters, Pieter de Hooch and Jacob Ochtervelt.[1] He painted the staffage in certain landscapes by Jacob van Ruisdael, Meindert Hobbema, and Jan Hackaert. Berchem was a prolific artist who produced hundreds of paintings[2] and drawings as well as about sixty etchings. Early in his career, he was influenced by Jan Both and Jan Asselyn, the two leading Dutch Italianate artists of the second generation. Later he came under the spell of Adam Pynacker, whose elegant baroque style and large-scale figures appealed to Berchem.

The Cows at the Watering Place, dated 1680 in the second state, is Berchem's most celebrated print. It represents one of his favorite subjects, Italian peasants accompanying their flocks to a watering place by antique ruins. Despite the obvious reference to decay and the passing of time, Berchem celebrates the sheer joy of living with figures relaxing in a festive mood. One woman soaks and washes her feet while her companions converse.

Most of Berchem's prints are representations of domesticated animals – cows, sheep, and goats. He, along with Karel Dujardin, Paulus Potter, and Adriaen van de Velde, is one of the three or four greatest animal painters of the Dutch school. All four produced magnificent etched suites of animals. In the case of *The Cows at the Watering Place*, Berchem incorporates animals into a larger composition of great elegance. The ample, open foreground is hemmed in by massive ruins and steep hills jutting up immediately behind. Berchem virtually omits the far distance, only offering a glimpse of remote hills, largely screened by the peasants at right. Clifford S. Ackley felicitously describes the "balletic grace" of the subject while stressing Berchem's reliance on strong contrasts and rhythmic, calligraphic contours.[3]

The large, elegantly posed figures and the bucolic mood of this and related subjects appealed enormously to French artists of the rococo, above all, to François Boucher. Eighteenth-century collectors prized Berchem virtually above all other Dutch landscape painters. For this reason, most of his finest paintings are found in European public collections that trace their origins to the eighteenth century. Berchem's prints, no less desirable, were issued long after his death in many posthumous editions printed from worn plates. Fine impressions, such as that in the Museum's collection, convey a depth of inking and clarity of light that demonstrate the artist's brilliant technique before his copperplates began to show the telltale signs of wear. – GK

1. Certain of these masters also produced prints. The most distinguished of these is Karel Dujardin, but Abraham Begeyn, Dirk Maas, and Jan van der Meer the Younger also experimented with etching.

2. C. Hofstede de Groot, *Beschreibendes und kritisches Verzeichnis der Werke der hervorragendsten holländischen Maler des XVII. Jahrhunderts*, vol. 9 (Esslingen/Paris, 1926), lists more than 850 pictures by the artist.

3. Clifford S. Ackley, Boston 1980, 293, no. 205.

Seventeenth century continued on page 211.

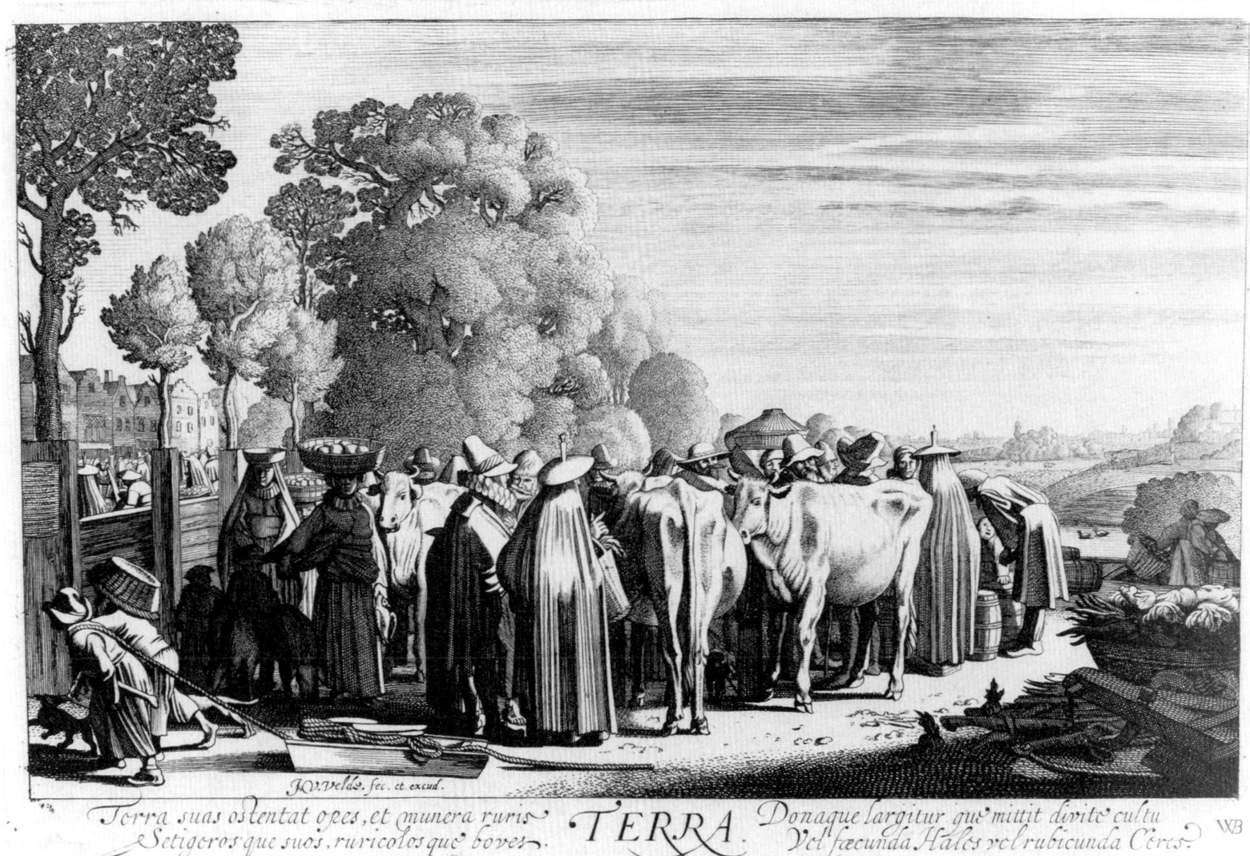

Plate 70a. Jan van de Velde II, *Earth*, from *The Four Elements*.

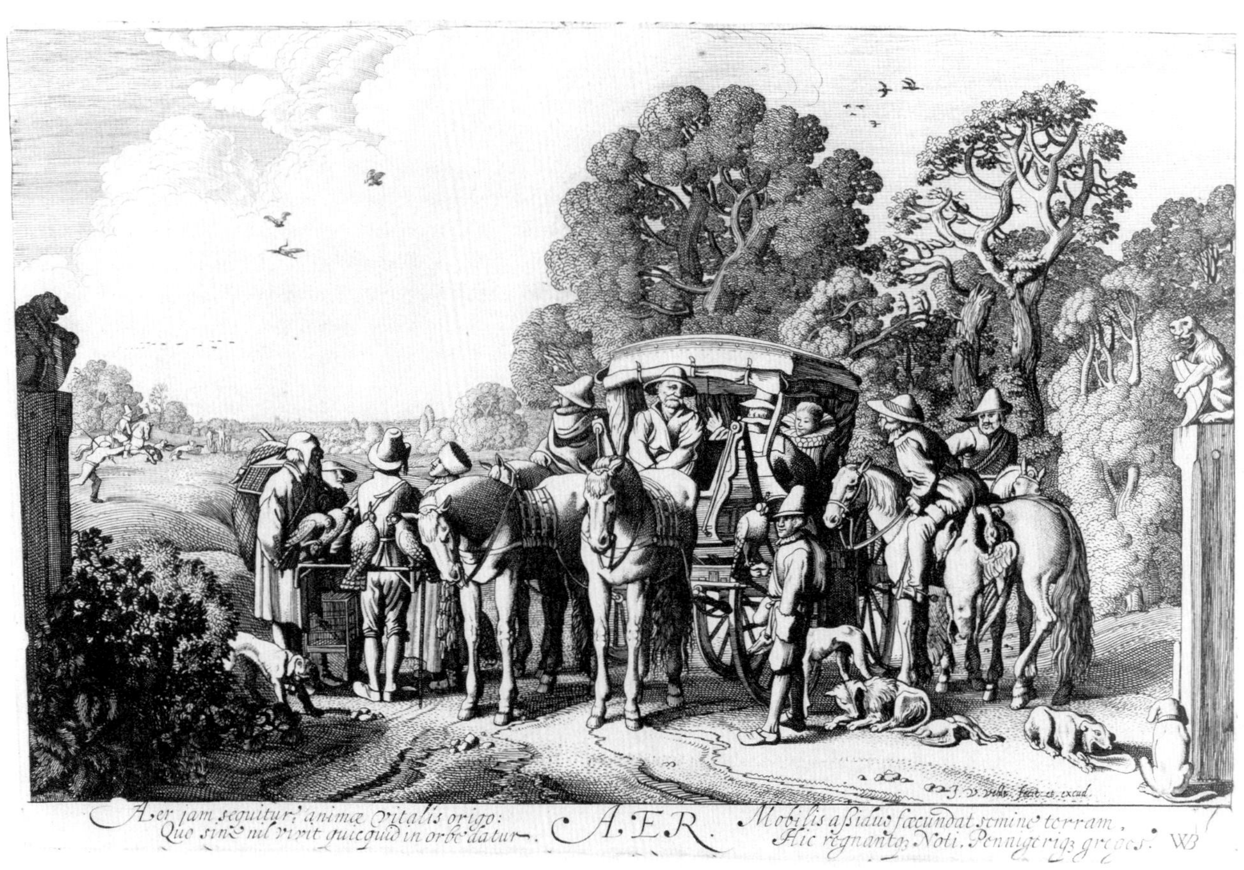

Plate 70b. Jan van de Velde II, *Air*, from *The Four Elements*.

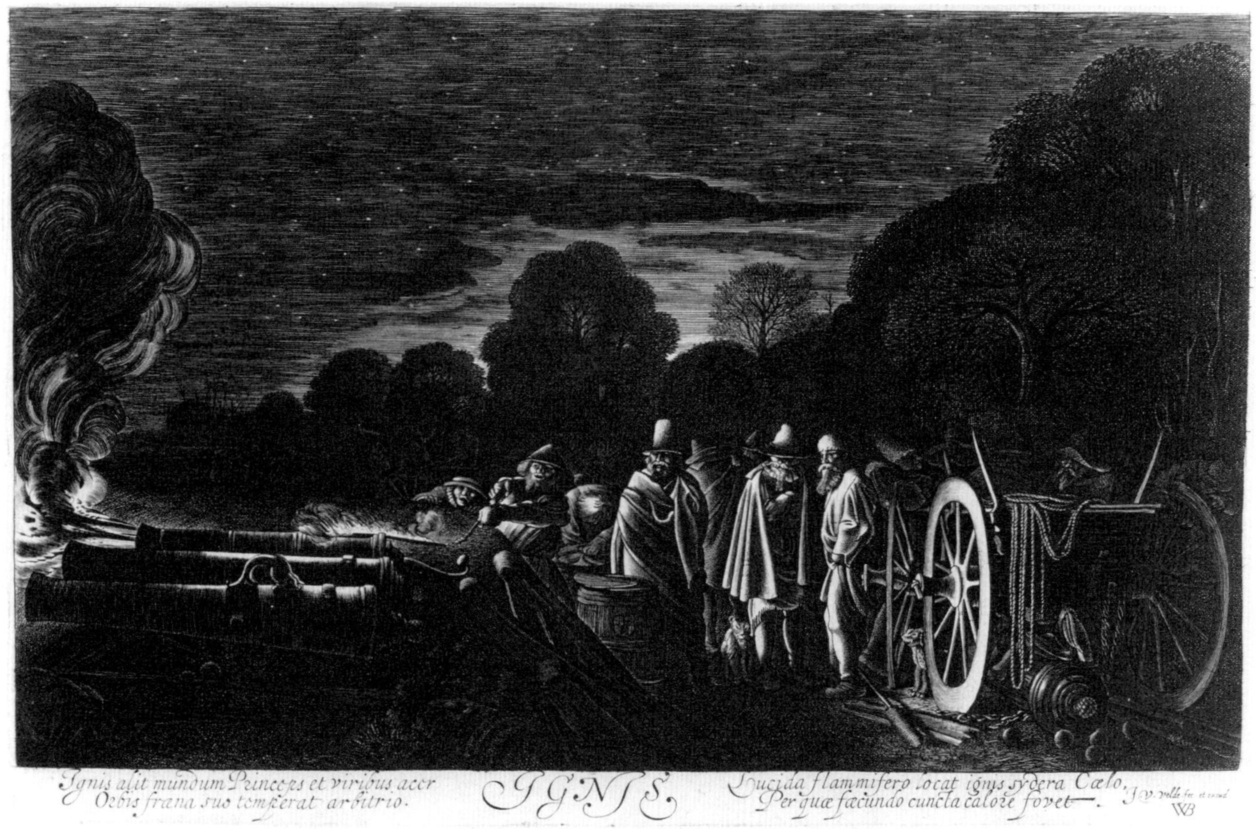

Plate 70c. Jan van de Velde II, *Fire*, from *The Four Elements*.

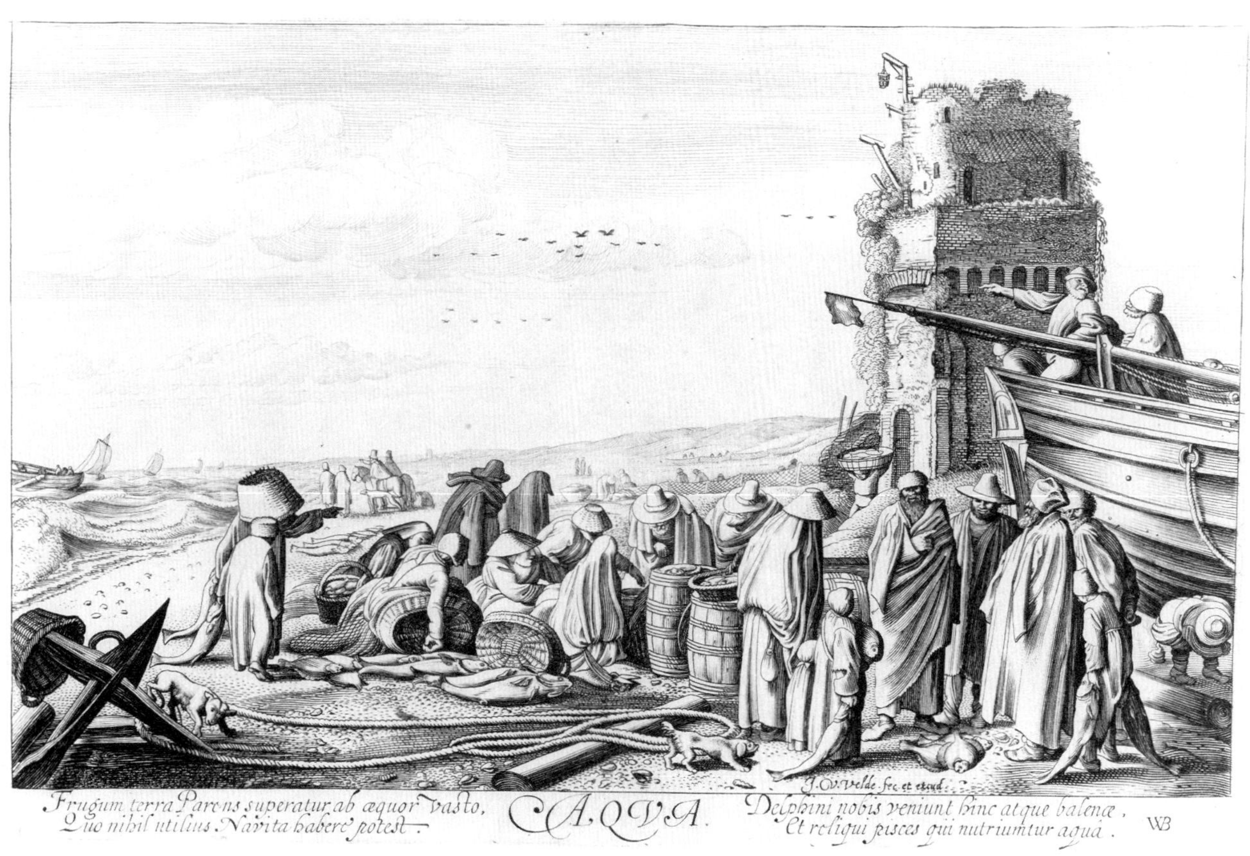

Plate 70d. Jan van de Velde II, *Water*, from *The Four Elements*.

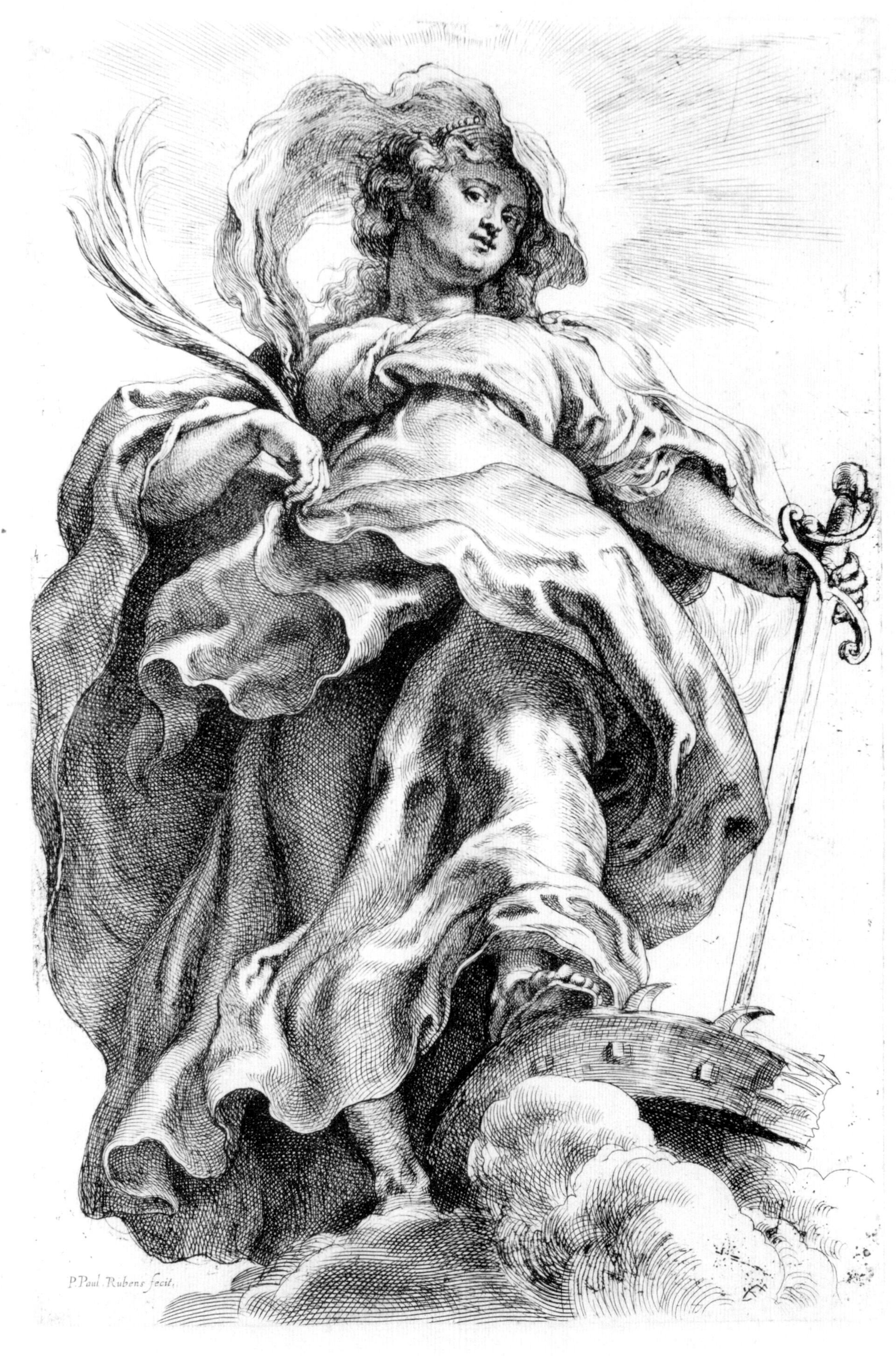

Plate 71. Peter Paul Rubens, *Saint Catherine of Alexandria in the Clouds*, 1630s?

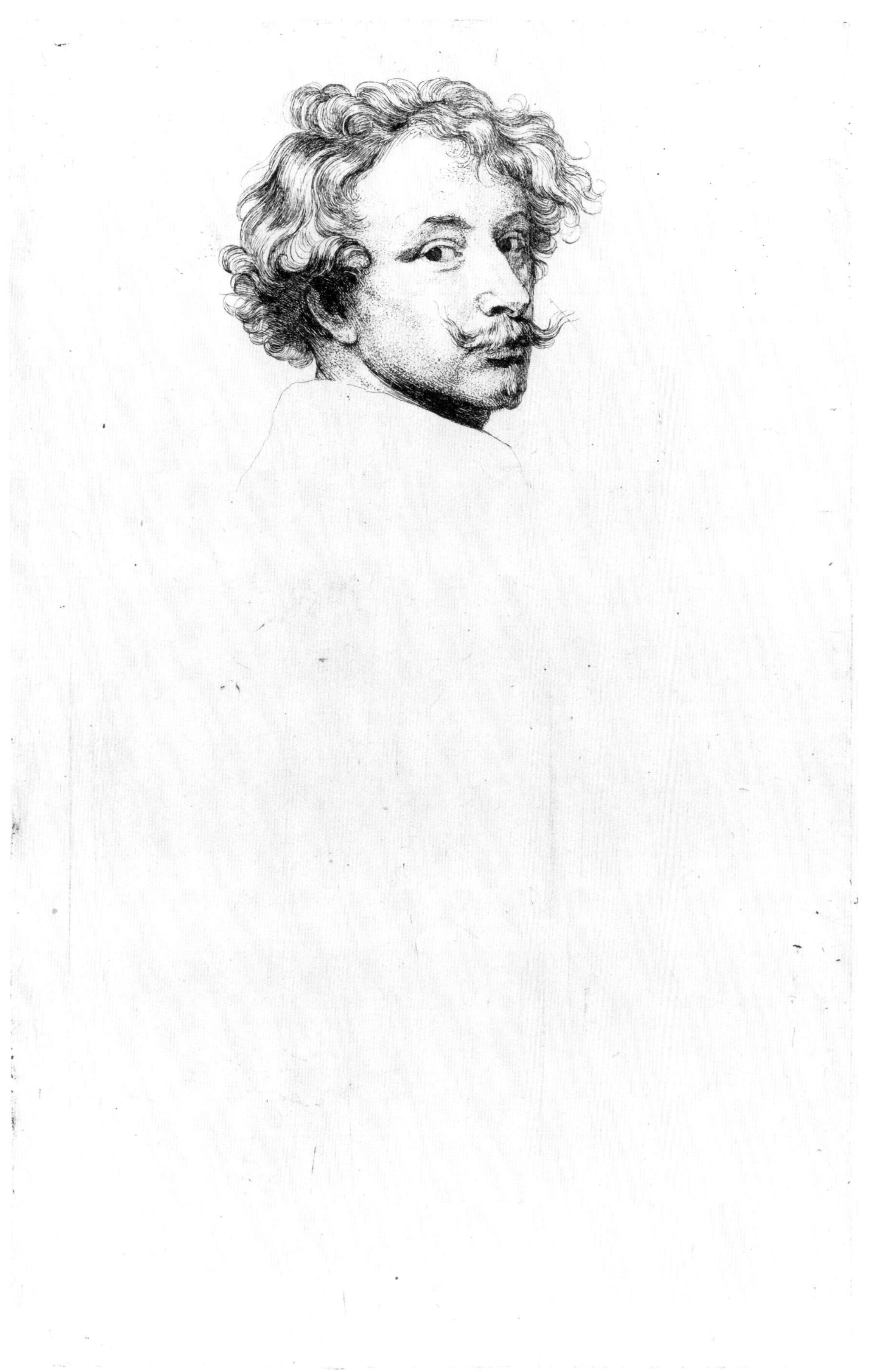

Plate 72. Sir Anthony van Dyck, *Self Portrait*, mid 1620s-36.

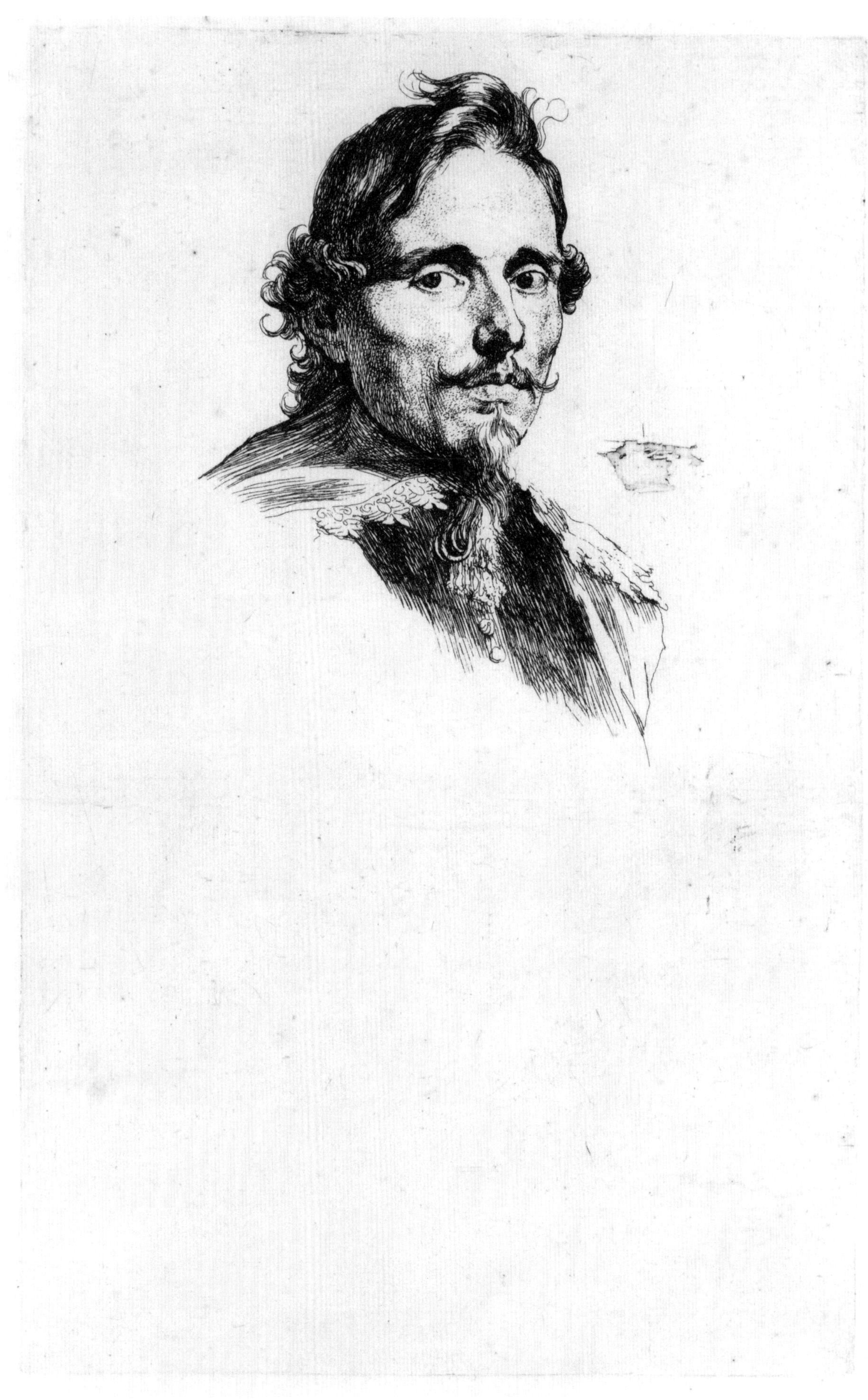

Plate 73. Sir Anthony van Dyck, *Philippe Le Roy, Baron de Broechem*, ca. 1630-36.

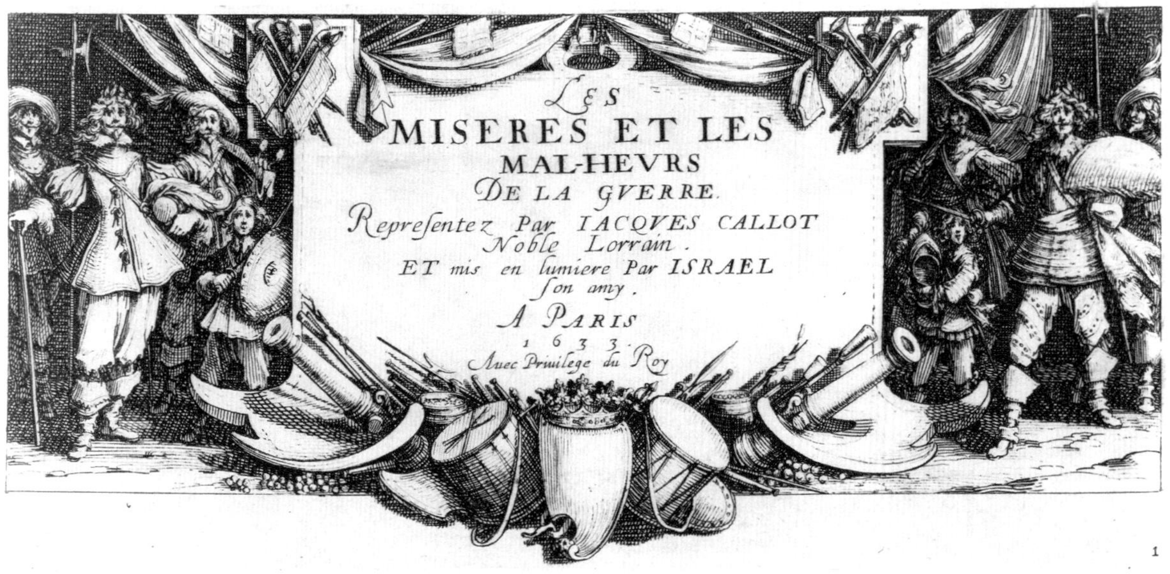

Plate 74.1. Jacques Callot, Title Page, from *The Miseries and Misfortunes of War*, 1633.

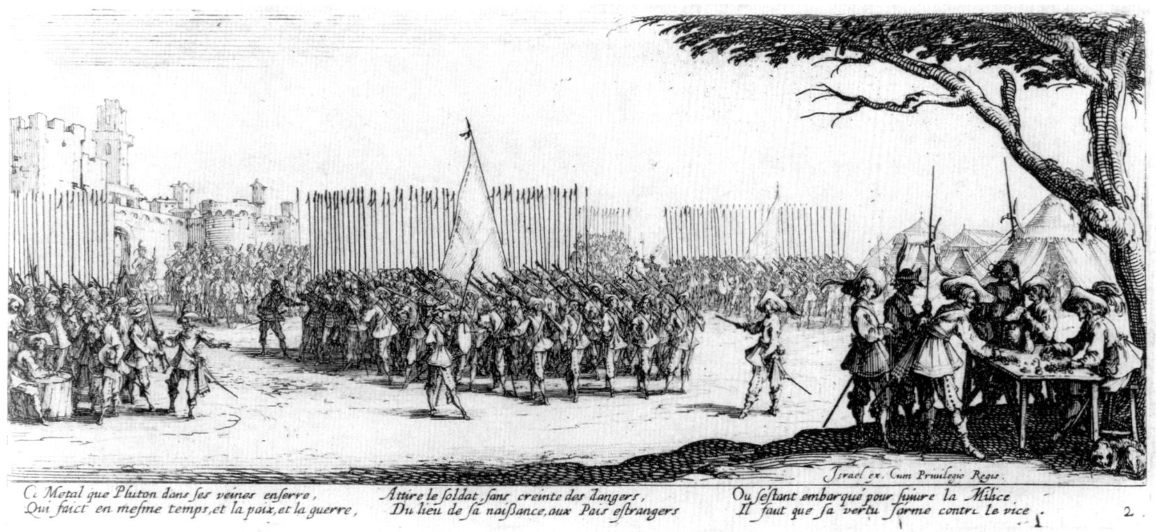

Plate 74.2. Jacques Callot, *Recruitment of Troops*, from *The Miseries and Misfortunes of War*, 1633.

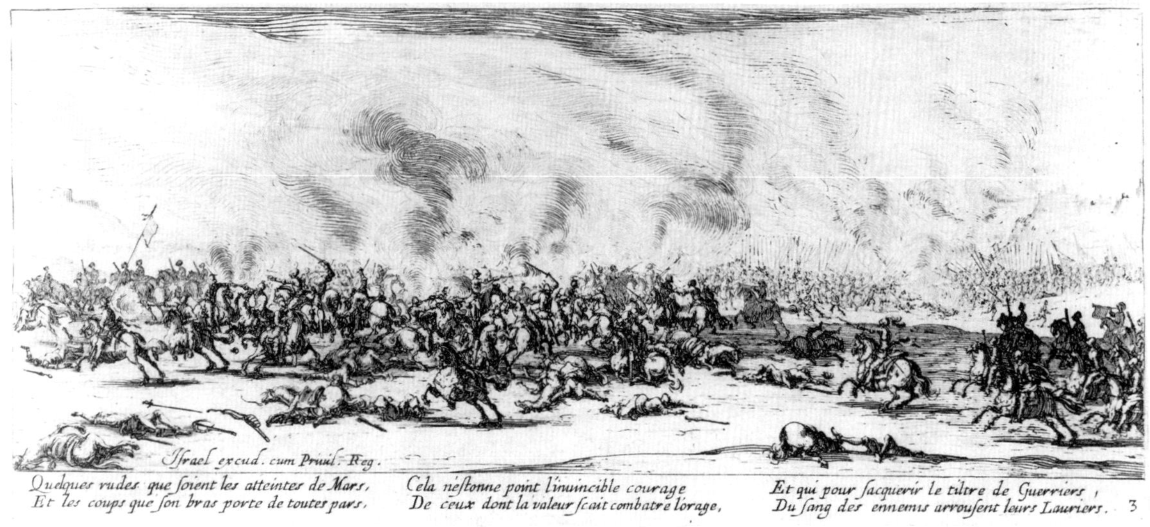

Plate 74.3. Jacques Callot, *The Battle*, from *The Miseries and Misfortunes of War*, 1633.

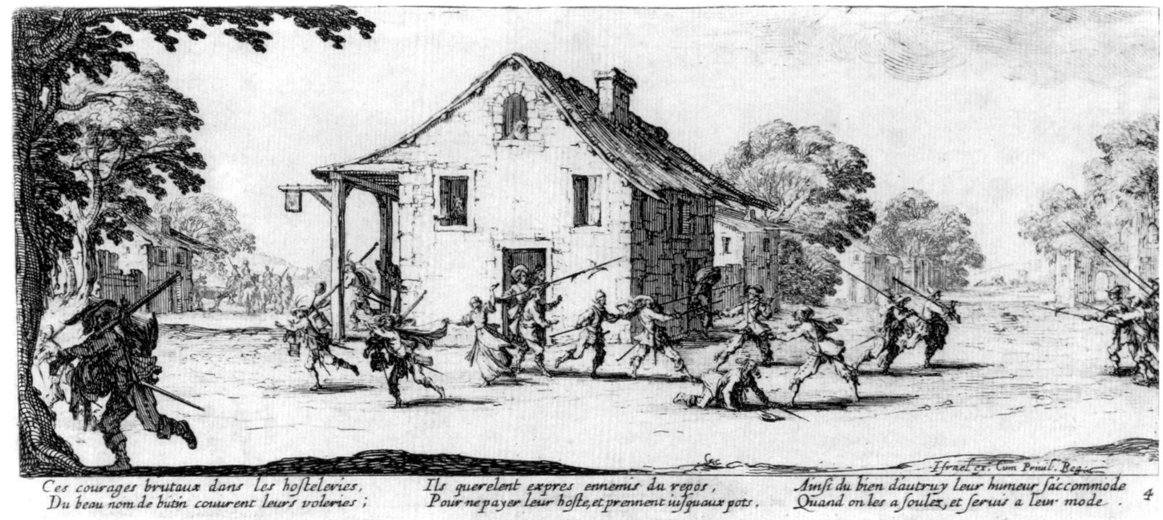

Plate 74.4. Jacques Callot, *Scene of Pillage*, from *The Miseries and Misfortunes of War*, 1633.

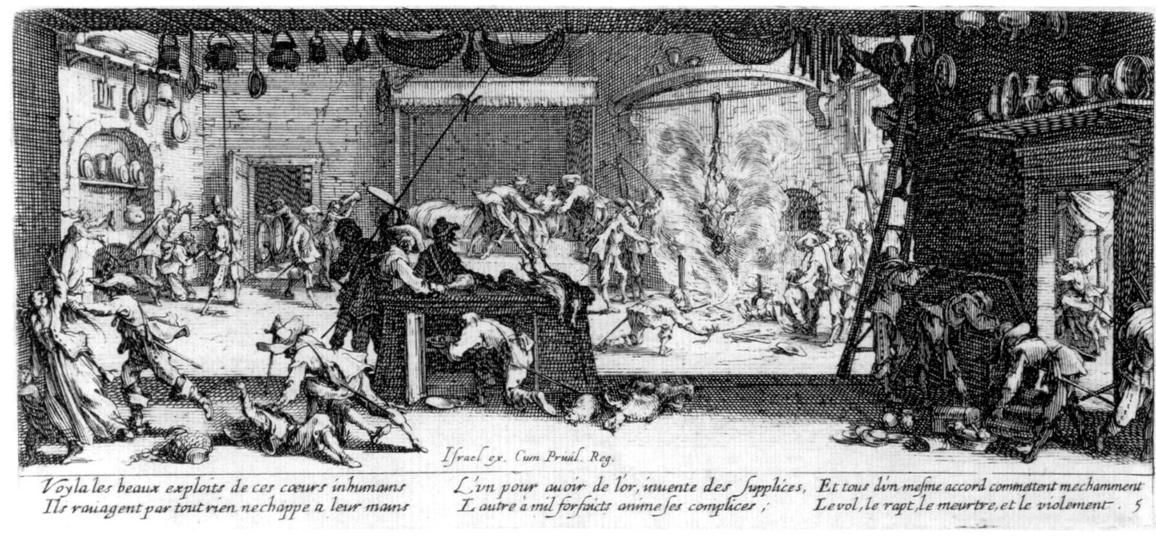

Plate 74.5. Jacques Callot, *Plundering a Large Farmhouse*, from *The Miseries and Misfortunes of War*, 1633.

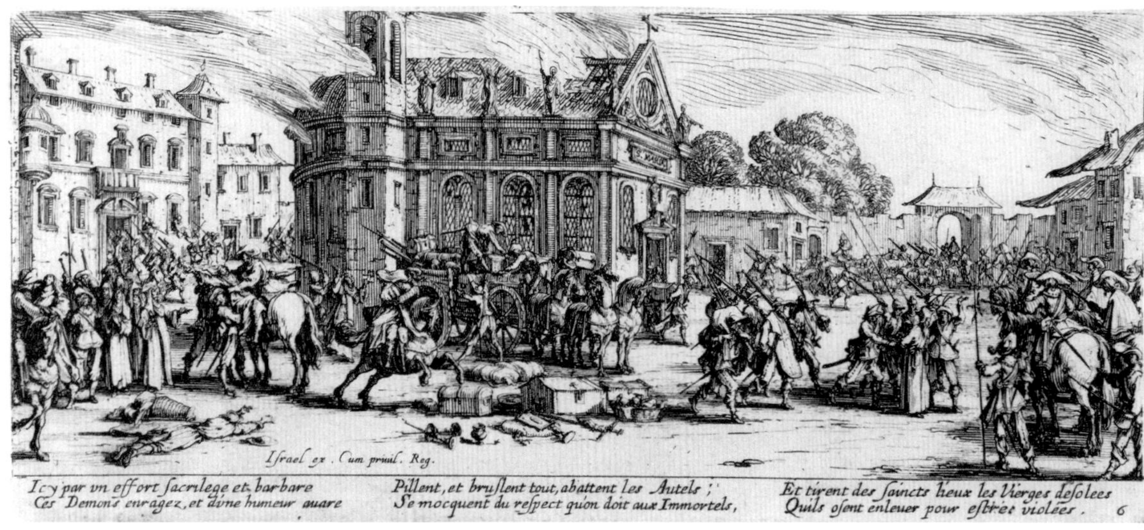

Plate 74.6. Jacques Callot, *Destruction of a Convent*, from *The Miseries and Misfortunes of War*, 1633.

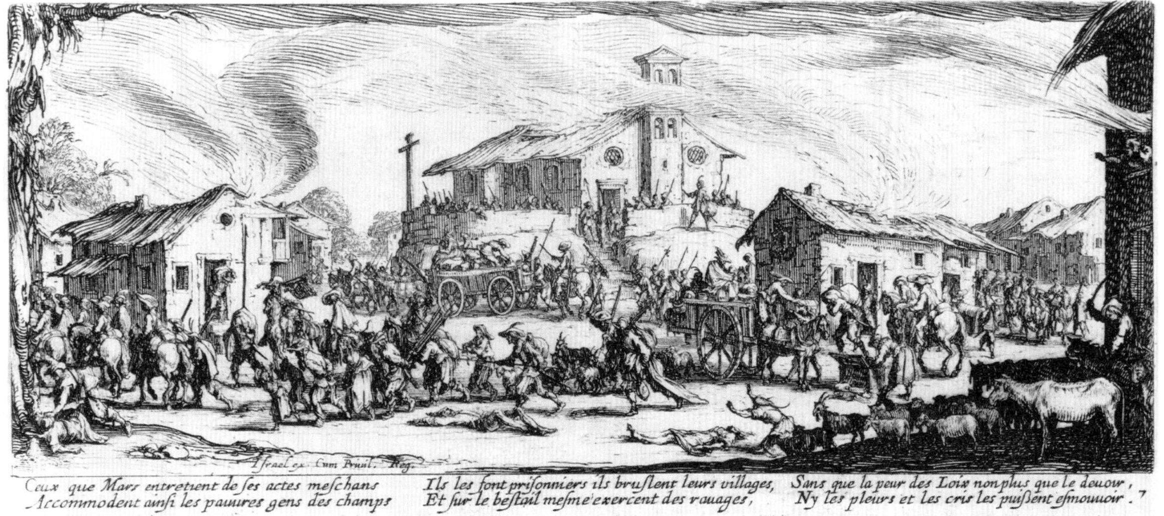

Plate 74.7. Jacques Callot, *Plundering and Burning a Village*, from *The Miseries and Misfortunes of War*, 1633.

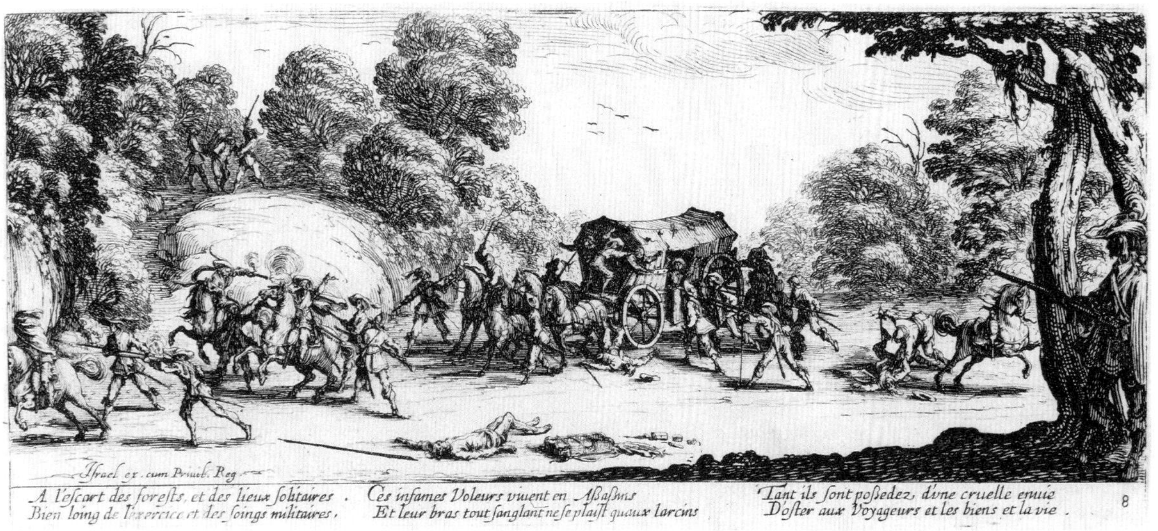

Plate 74.8. Jacques Callot, *Attack on a Coach*, from *The Miseries and Misfortunes of War*, 1633.

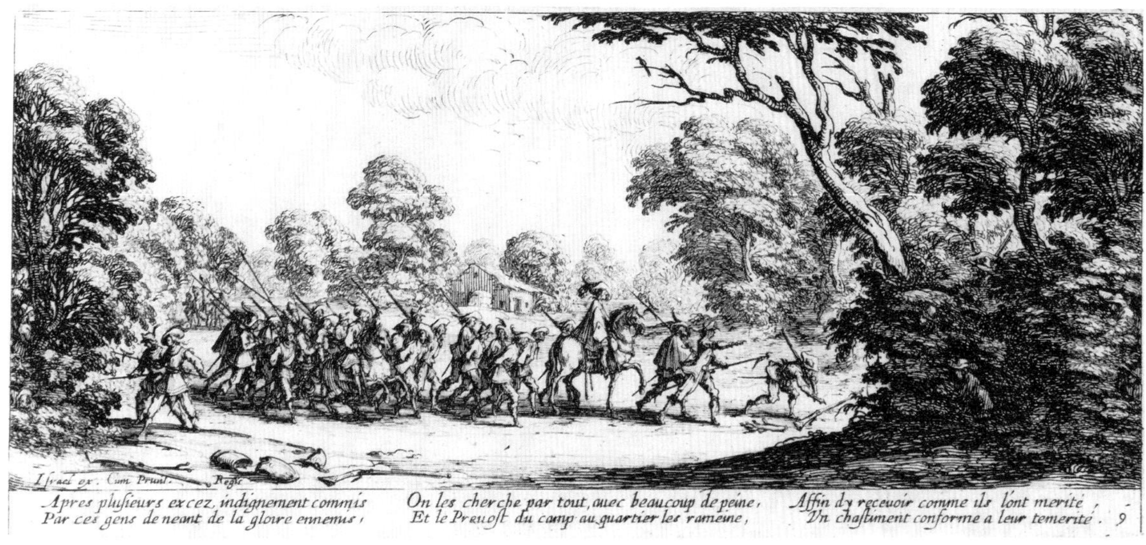

Plate 74.9. Jacques Callot, *Discovery of the Criminal Soldiers*, from *The Miseries and Misfortunes of War*, 1633.

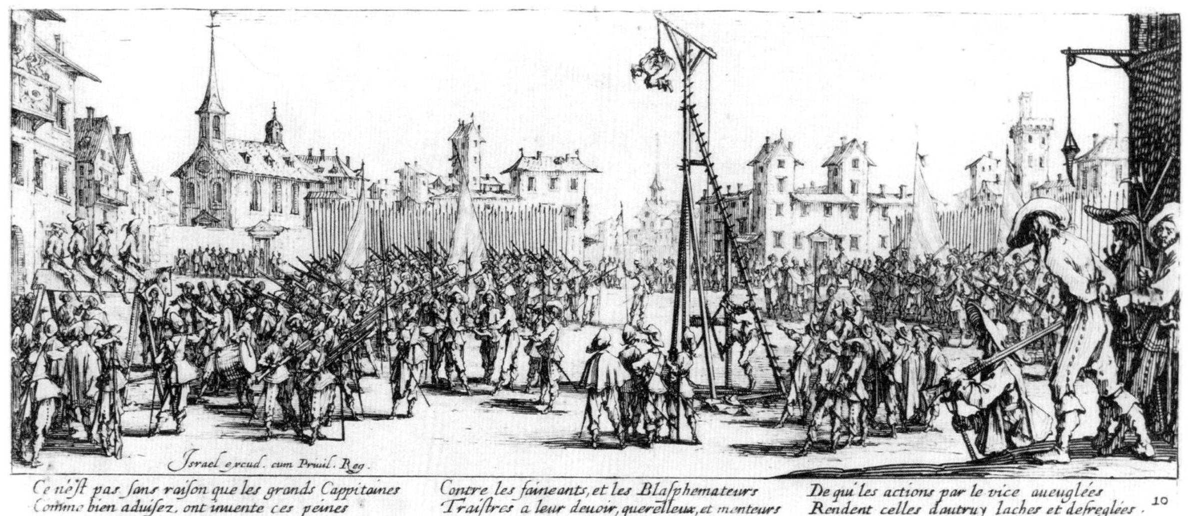

Plate 74.10. Jacques Callot, *The Strappado,* from *The Miseries and Misfortunes of War*, 1633.

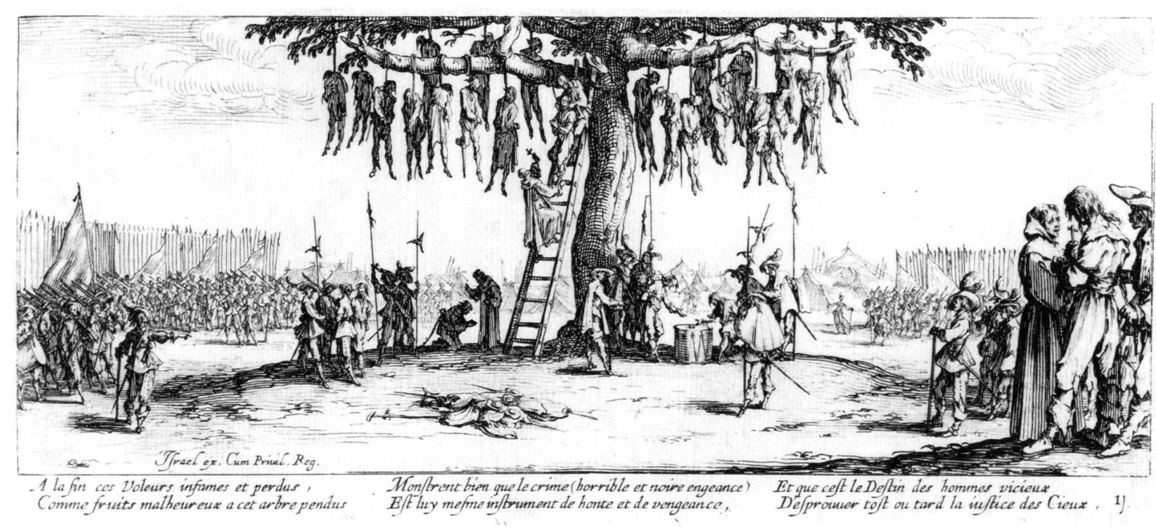

Plate 74.11. Jacques Callot, *The Hanging,* from *The Miseries and Misfortunes of War*, 1633.

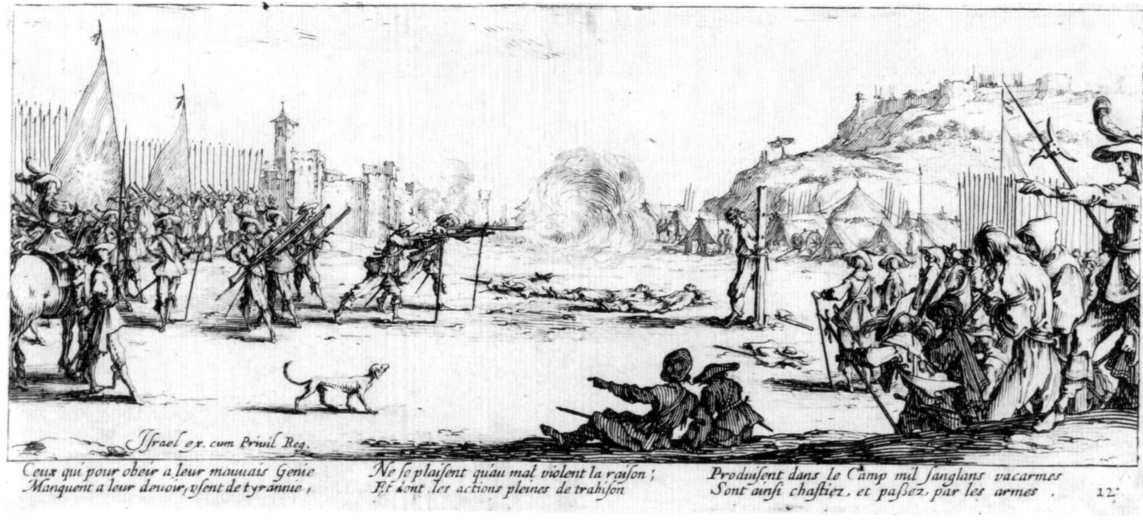

Plate 74.12. Jacques Callot, *The Firing Squad,* from *The Miseries and Misfortunes of War*, 1633.

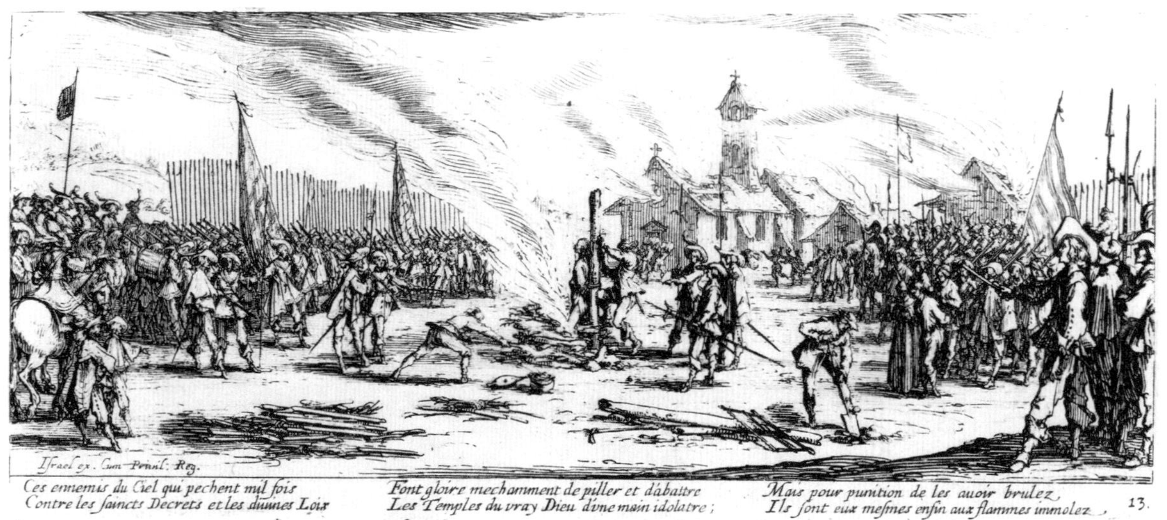

Plate 74.13. Jacques Callot, *The Stake*, from *The Miseries and Misfortunes of War*, 1633.

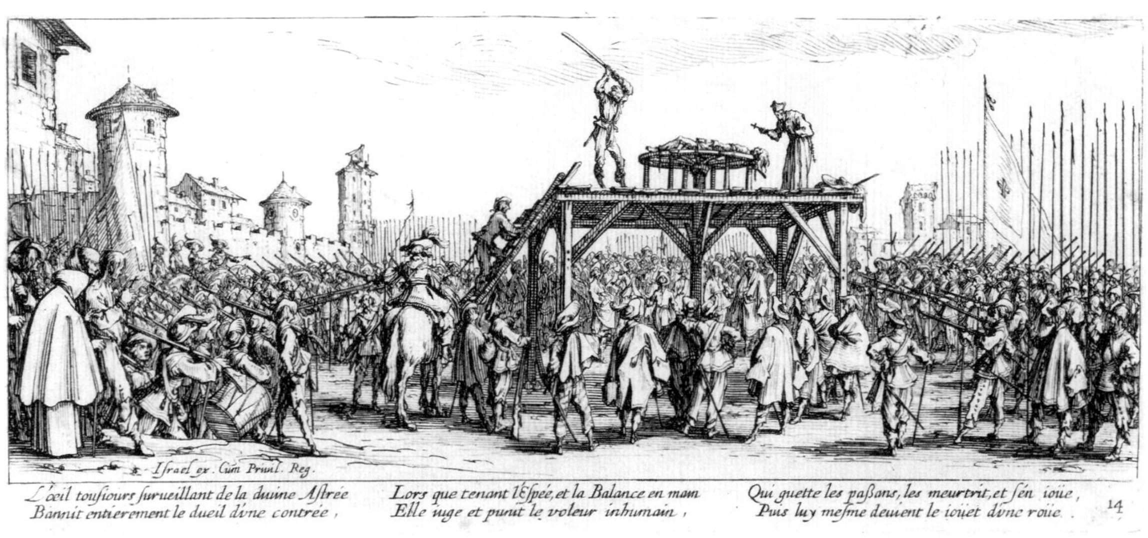

Plate 74.14. Jacques Callot, *The Wheel*, from *The Miseries and Misfortunes of War*, 1633.

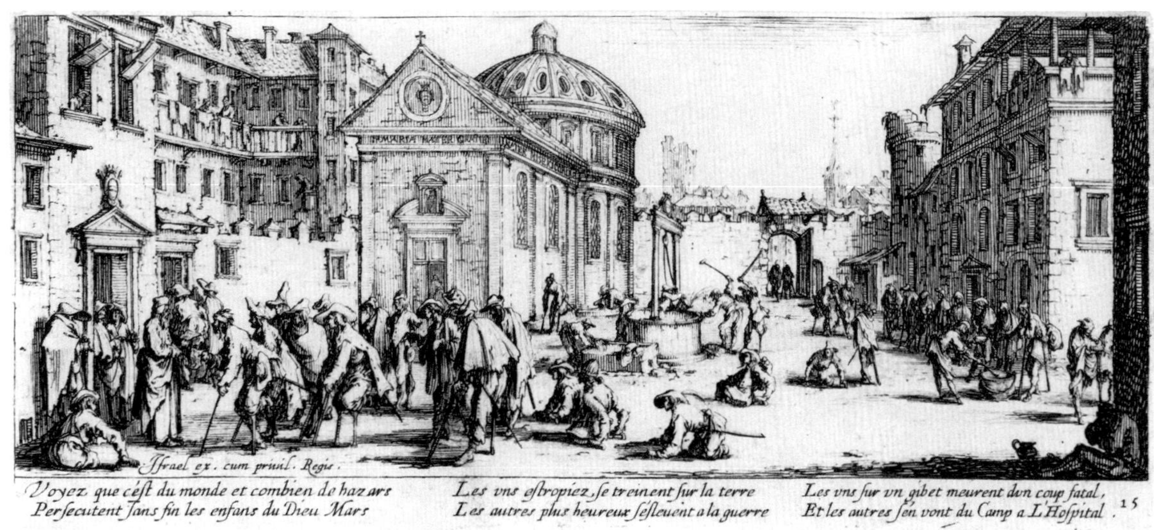

Plate 74.15. Jacques Callot, *The Hospital*, from *The Miseries and Misfortunes of War*, 1633.

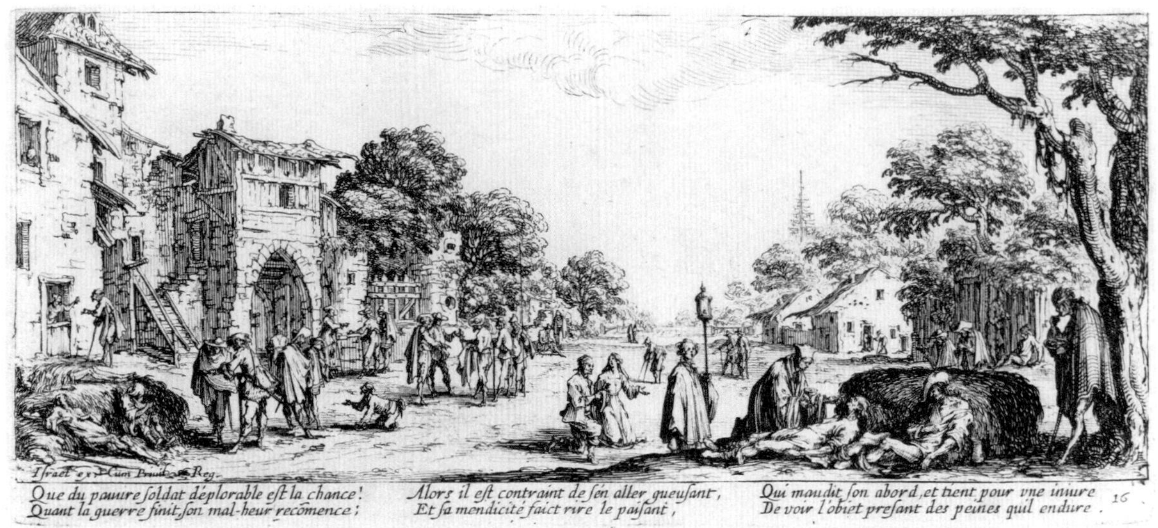

Plate 74.16. Jacques Callot, *The Dying Soldiers*, from *The Miseries and Misfortunes of War*, 1633.

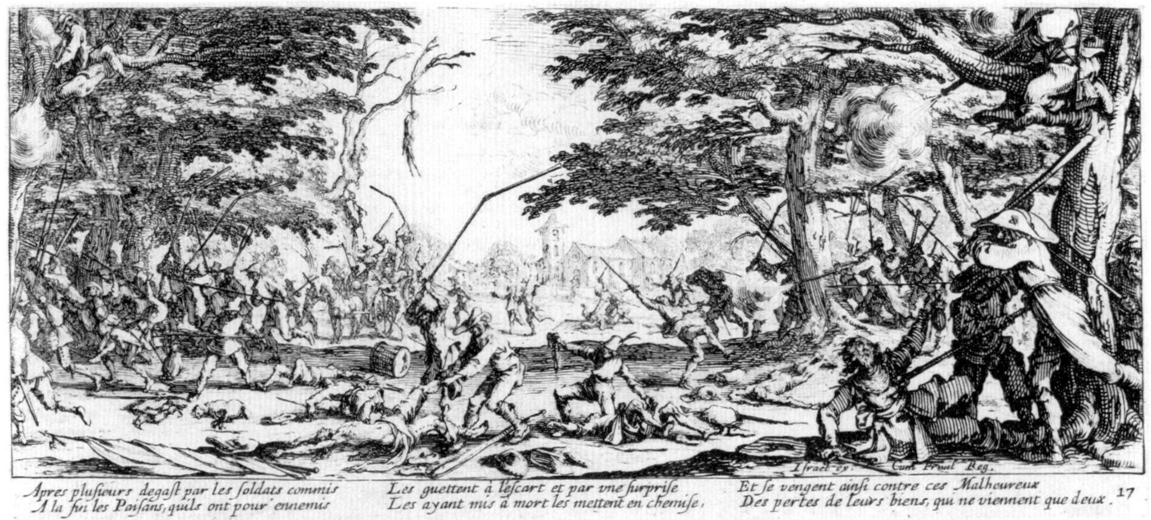

Plate 74.17. Jacques Callot, *The Peasants Avenge Themselves*, from *The Miseries and Misfortunes of War*, 1633.

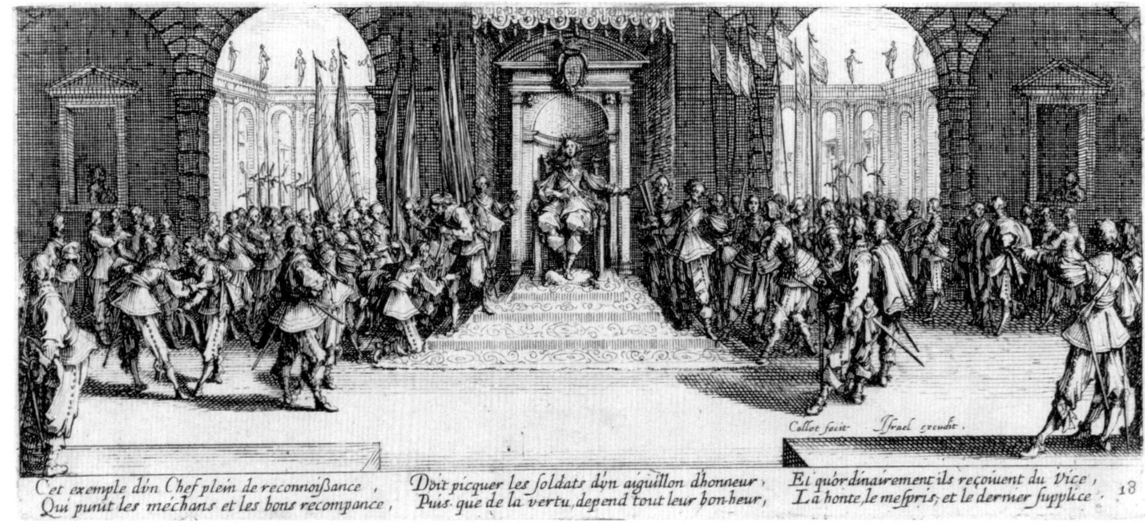

Plate 74.18. Jacques Callot, *The Distribution of Rewards*, from *The Miseries and Misfortunes of War*, 1633.

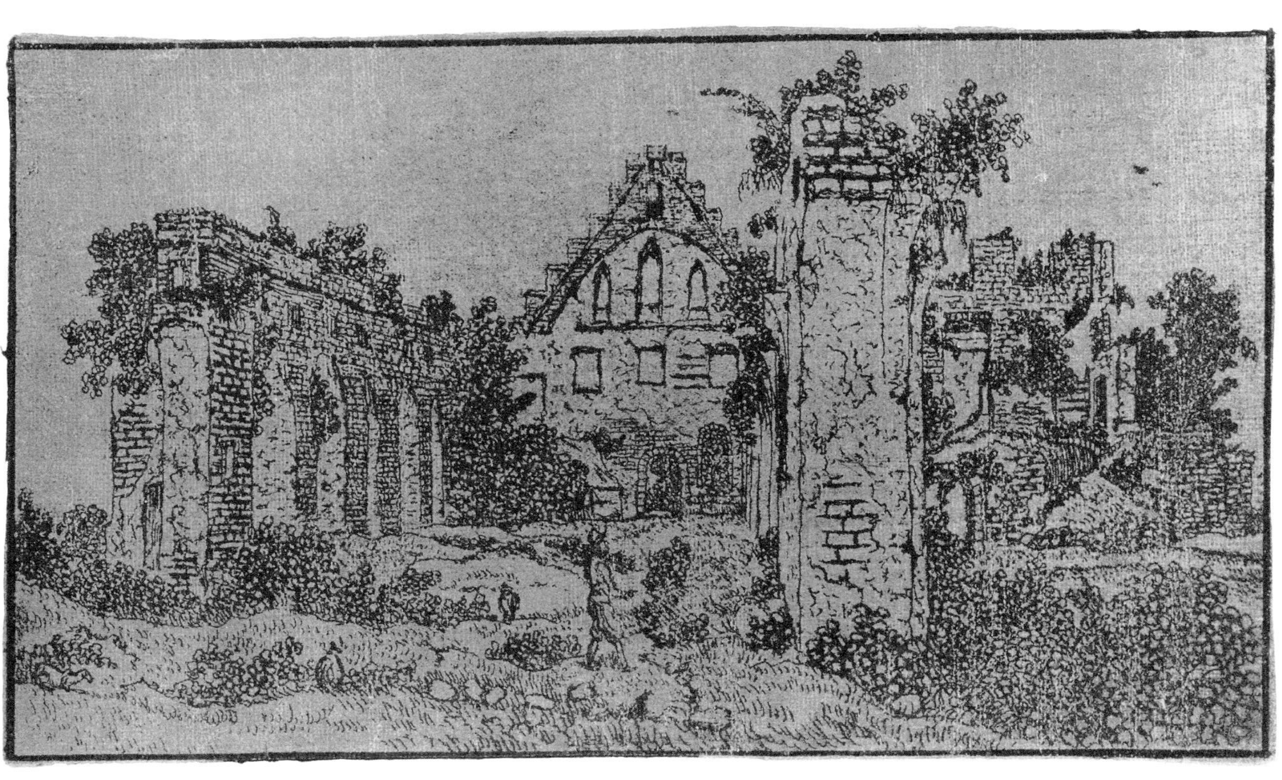

Plate 75. Hercules Segers, *Ruins of the Abbey of Rijnsburg* (small version).

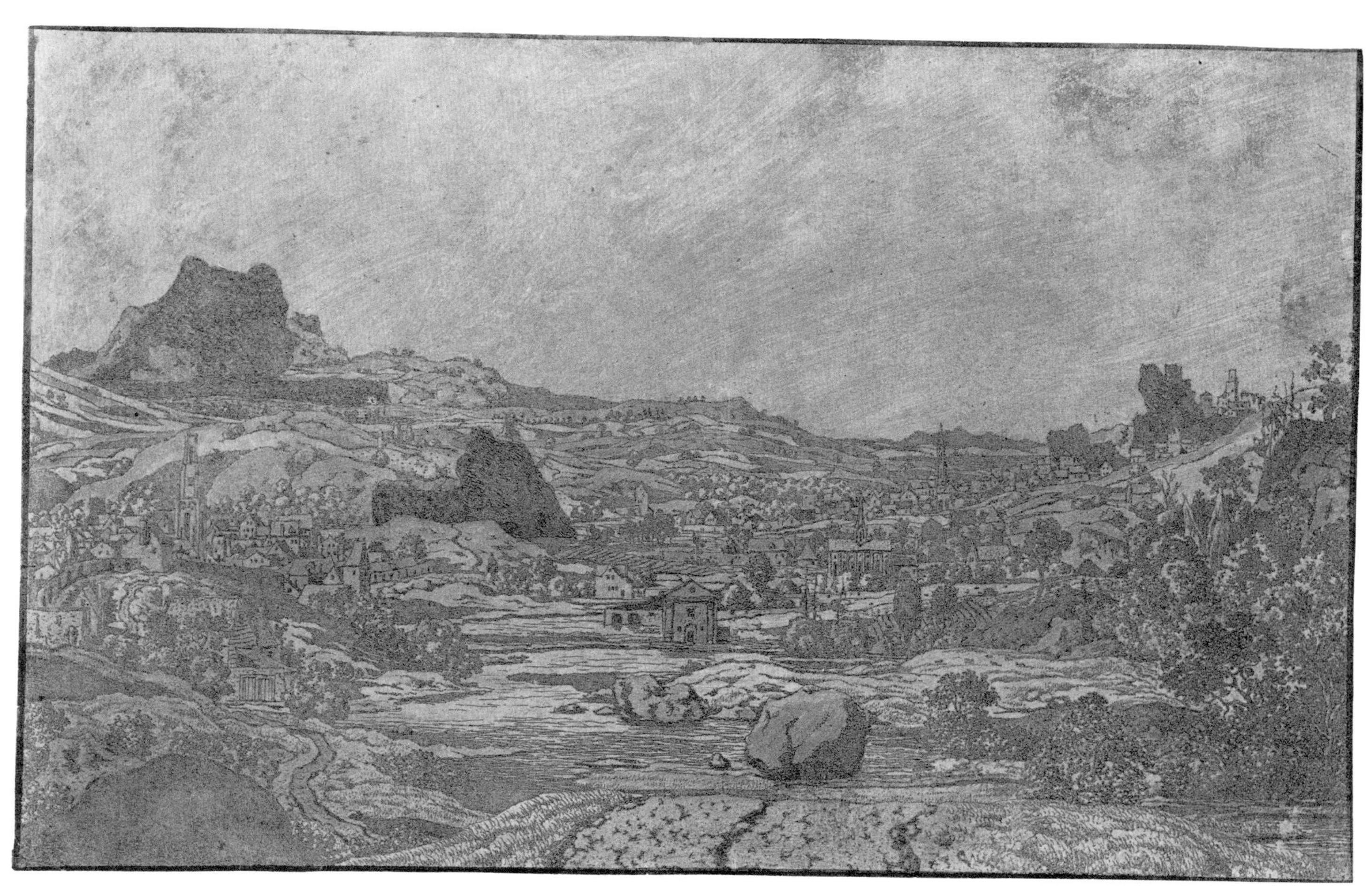

Plate 76. Hercules Segers, *Town with Four Towers*, ca. 1631 or later.

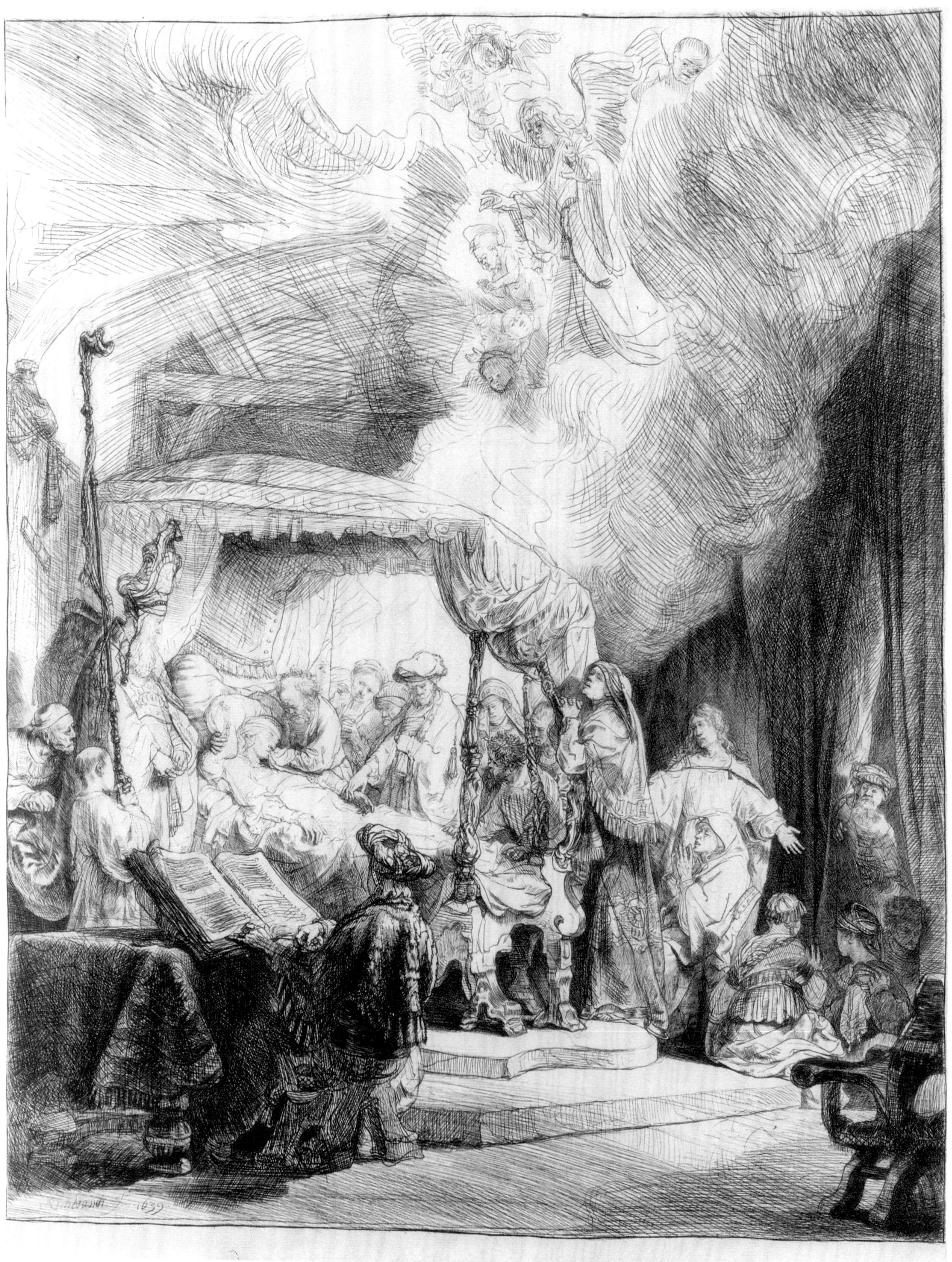

Plate 77. Rembrandt Harmensz. van Rijn, *The Death of the Virgin*, 1639.

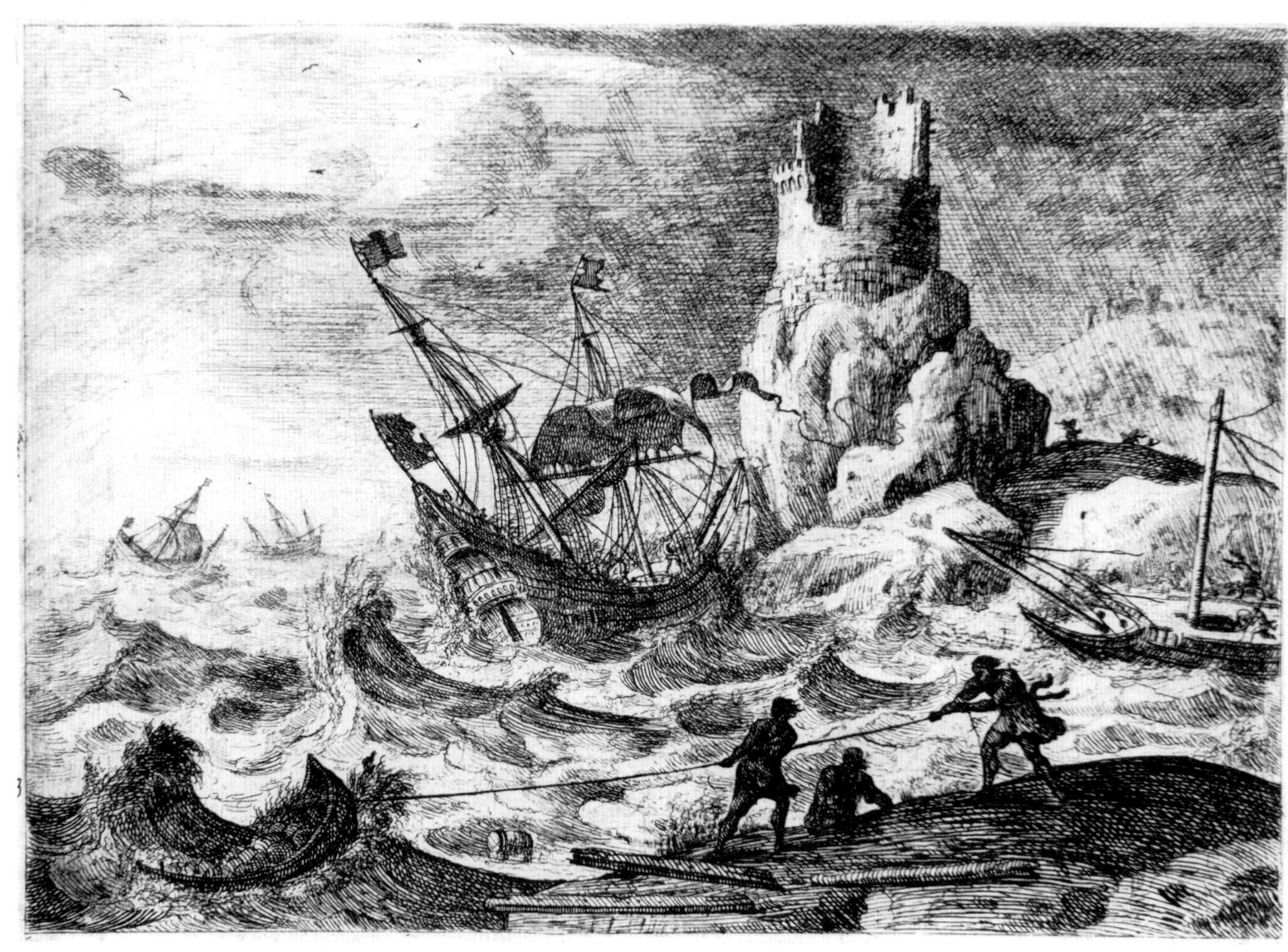

Plate 78. Claude Lorrain, *Shipwreck*, ca. 1638-41.

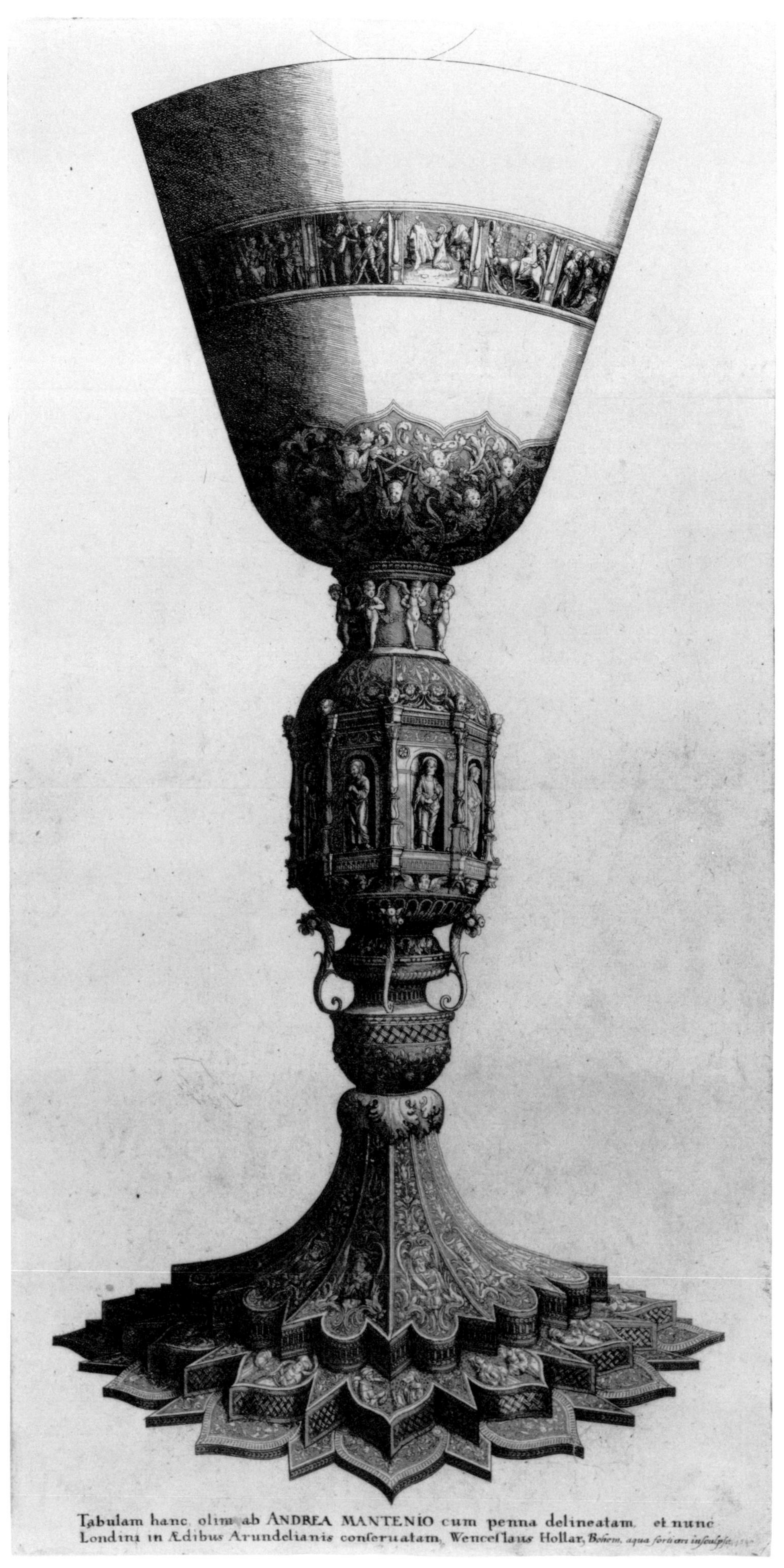

Plate 79. Wenceslaus Hollar, *Design for a Chalice*, 1640.

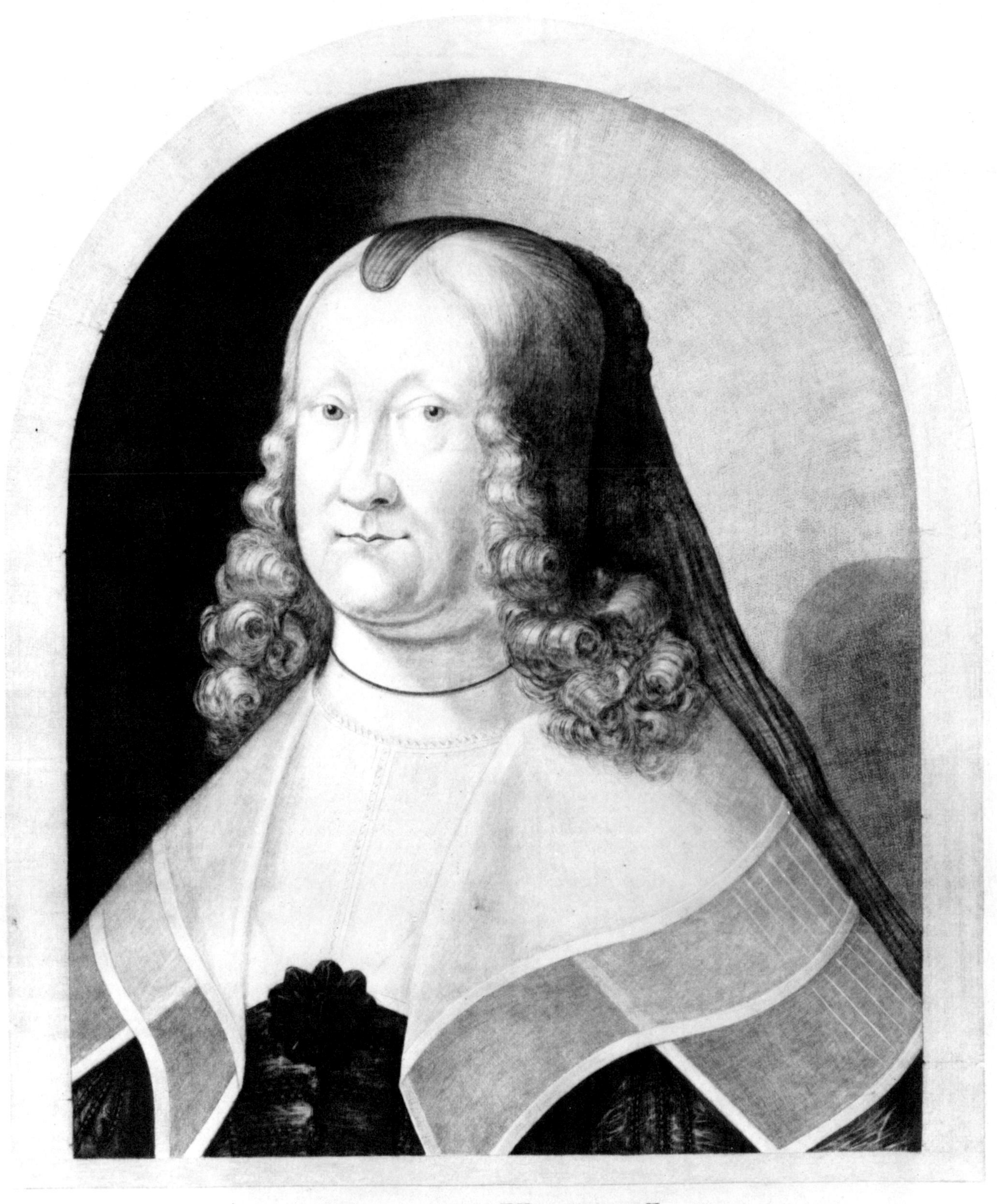

Plate 80. Ludwig von Siegen, *Amelia Elisabeth, Landgravine of Hesse-Cassel*, 1642.

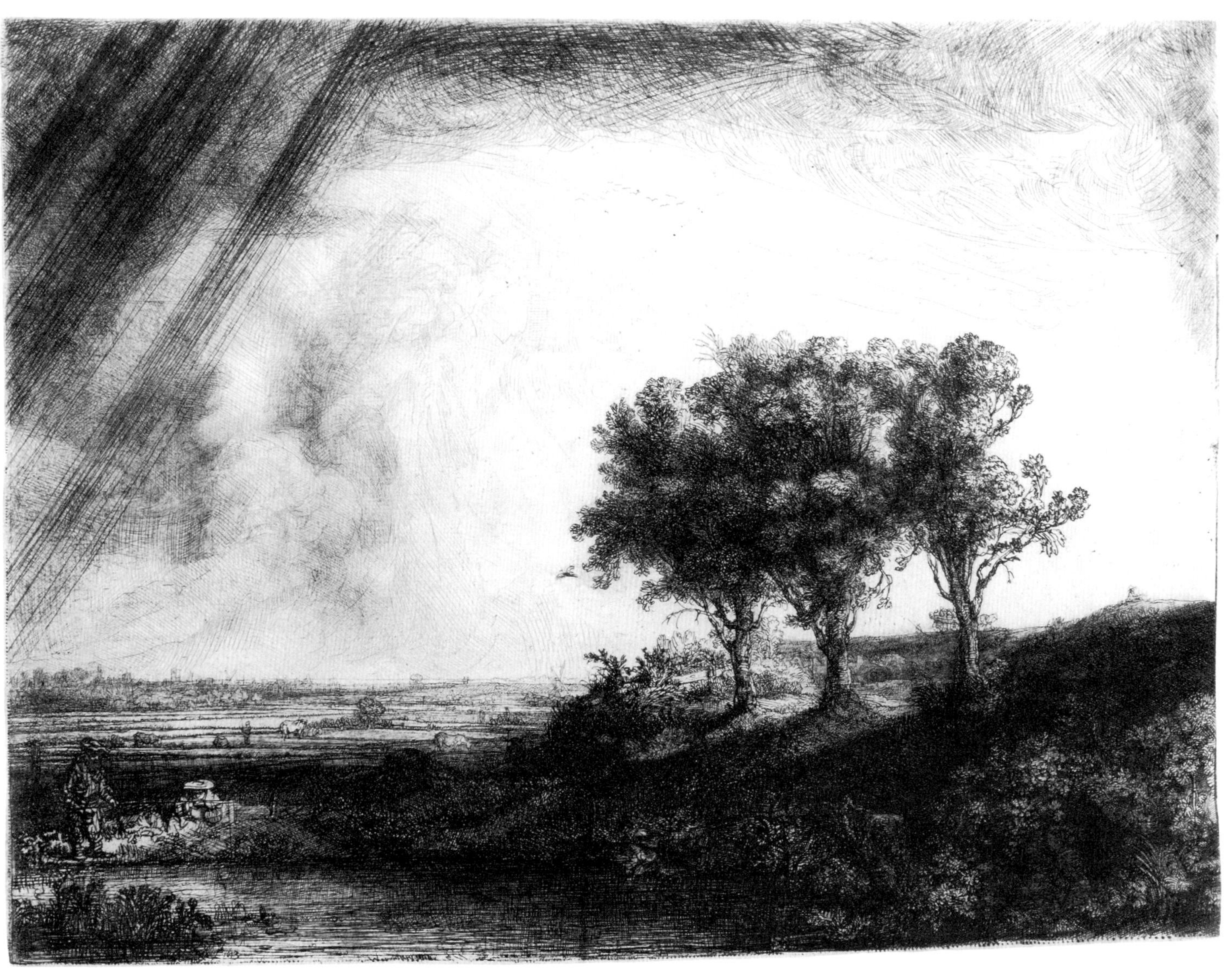

Plate 81. Rembrandt Harmensz. van Rijn, *The Three Trees*, 1643.

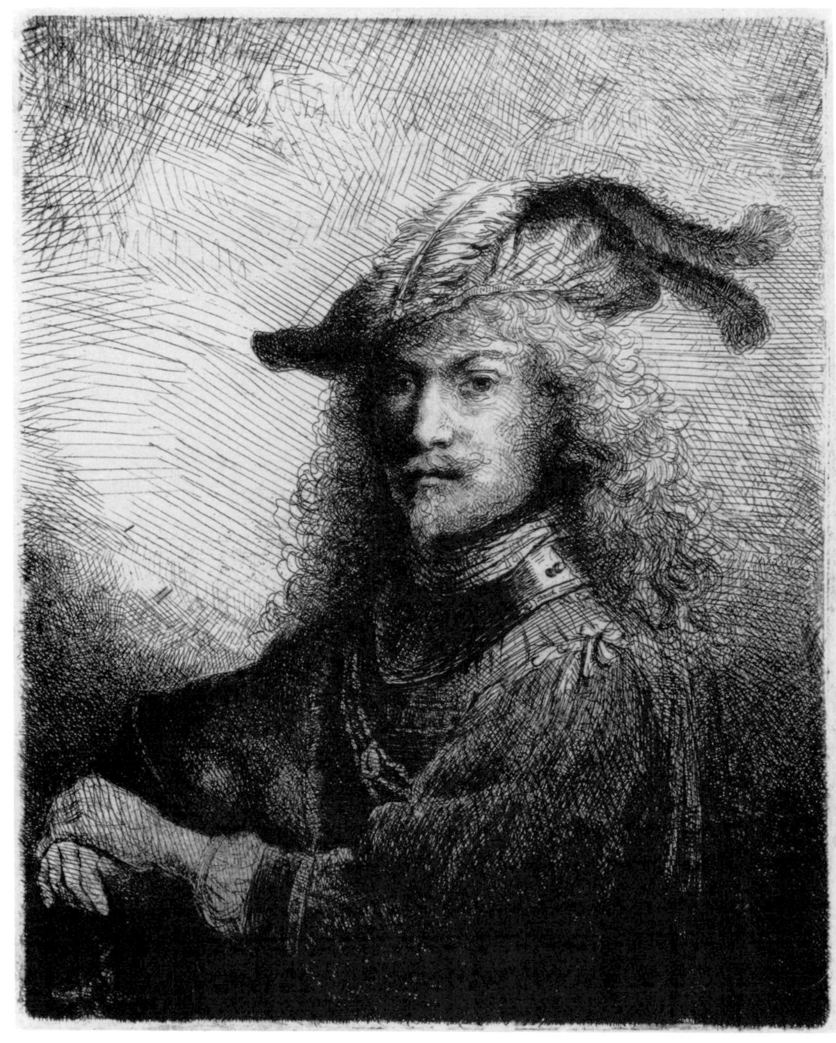

Plate 82. Ferdinand Bol, *Portrait of an Officer*, 1645.

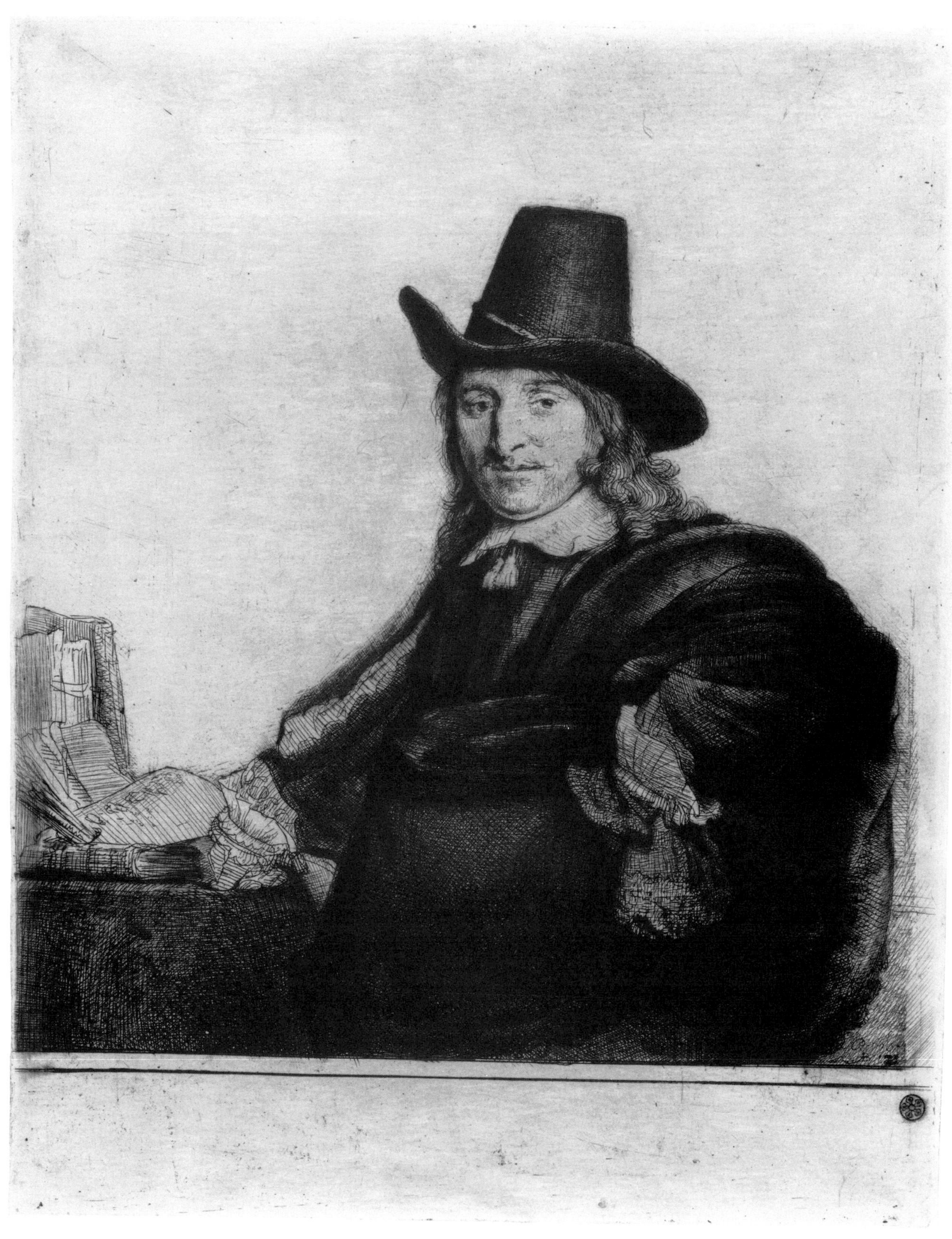

Plate 83. Rembrandt Harmensz. van Rijn, *Jan Asselyn (Krabbetje)*, 1647.

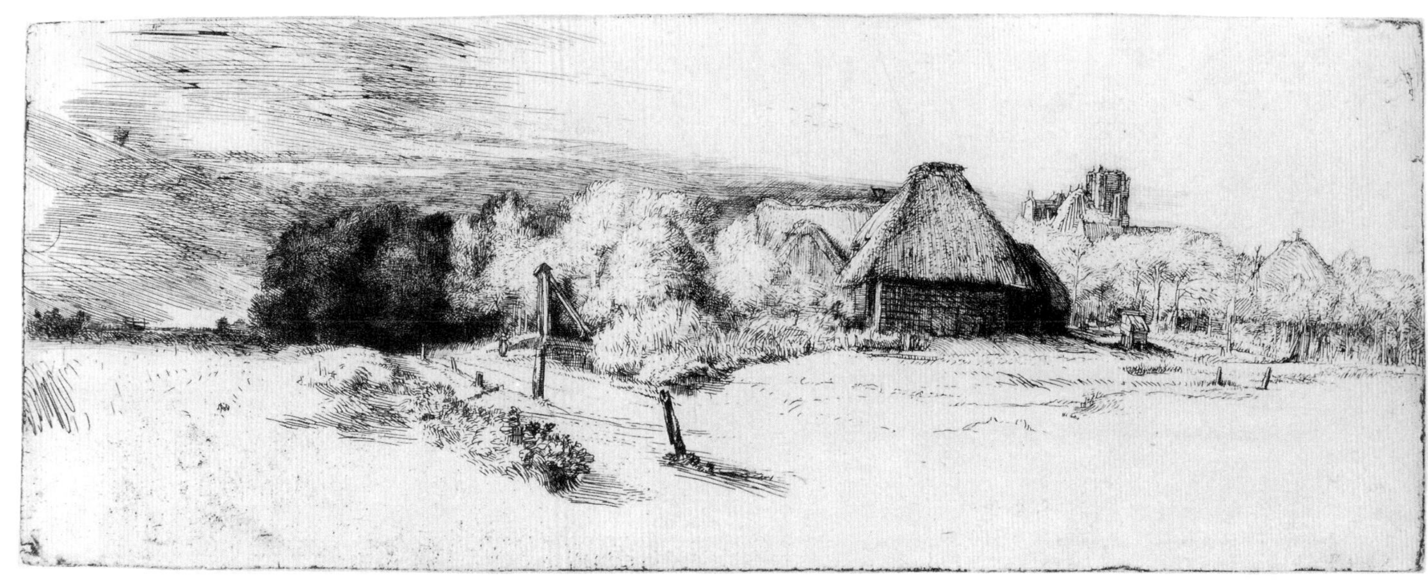

Plate 84. Rembrandt Harmensz. van Rijn, *Landscape with Trees, Farm Buildings, and a Tower*, ca. 1651.

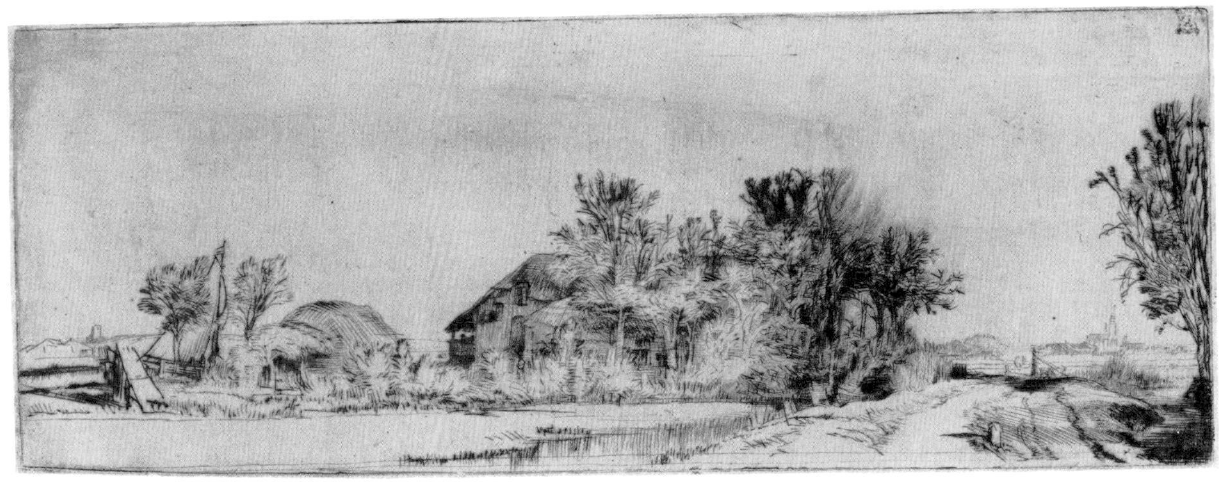

Plate 85. Rembrandt Harmensz. van Rijn, *Landscape with a Road beside a Canal*, ca. 1652.

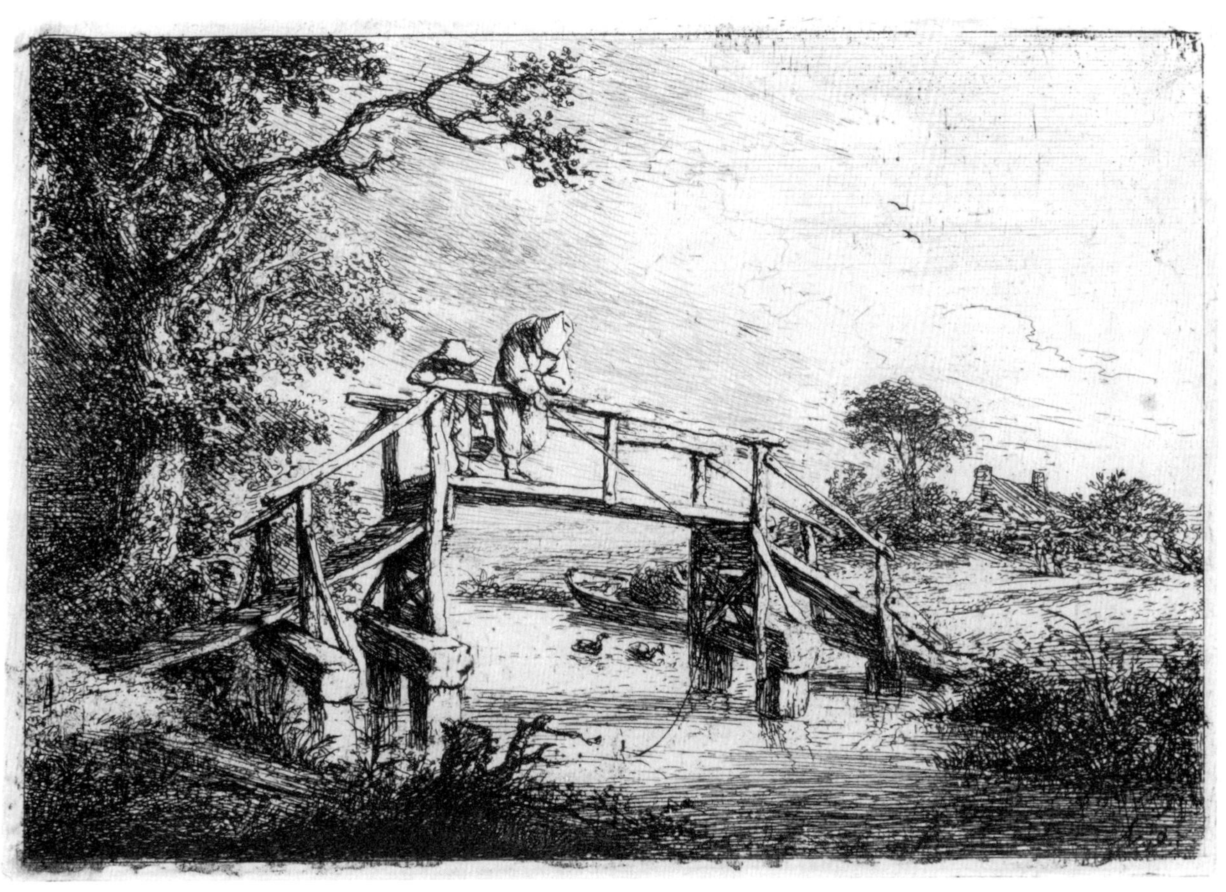

Plate 86. Adriaen van Ostade, *The Anglers*.

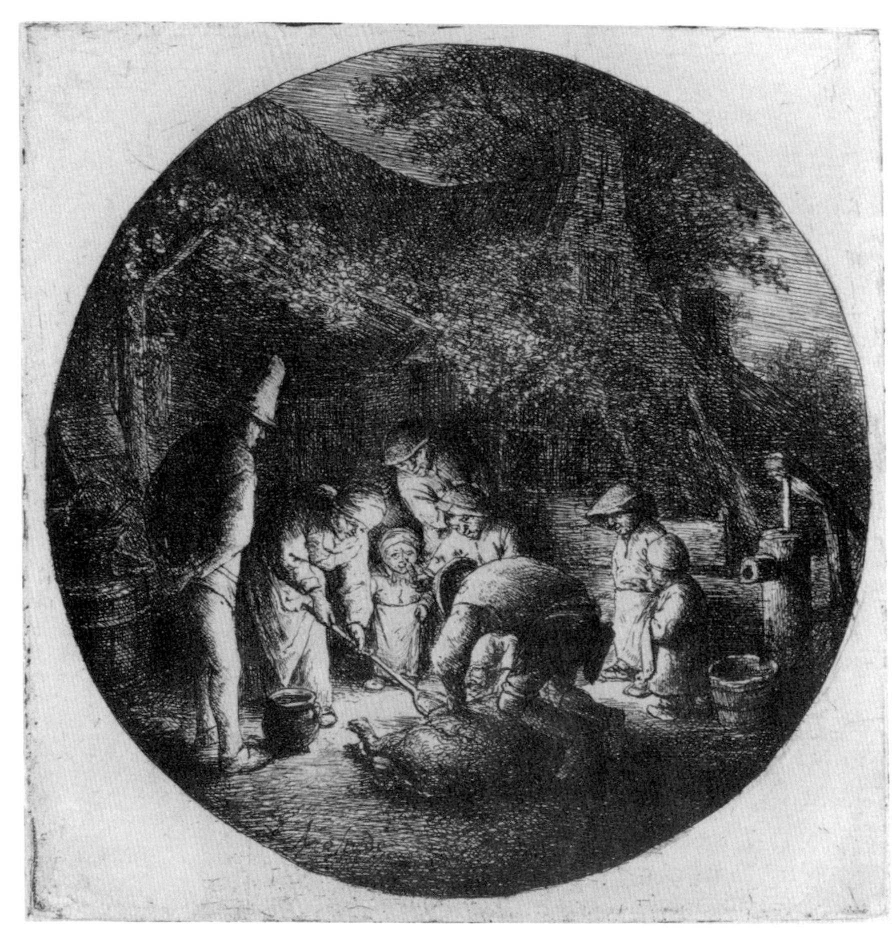

Plate 87. Adriaen van Ostade, *Slaughtering the Hog*.

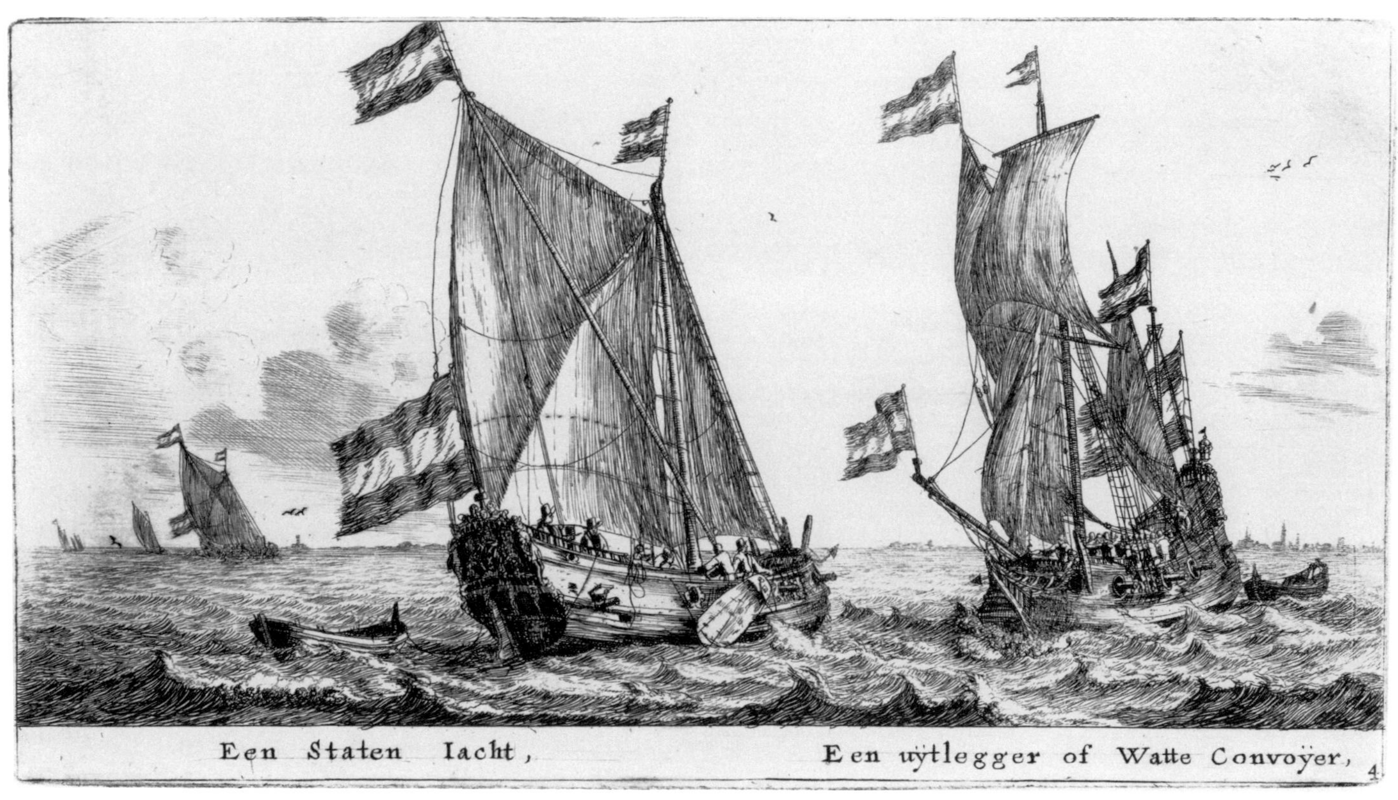

Plate 88. Reinier Nooms ("Zeeman"), *A States Yacht and a Guard-ship* or *Wadden Convoy Ship*, ca.1660.

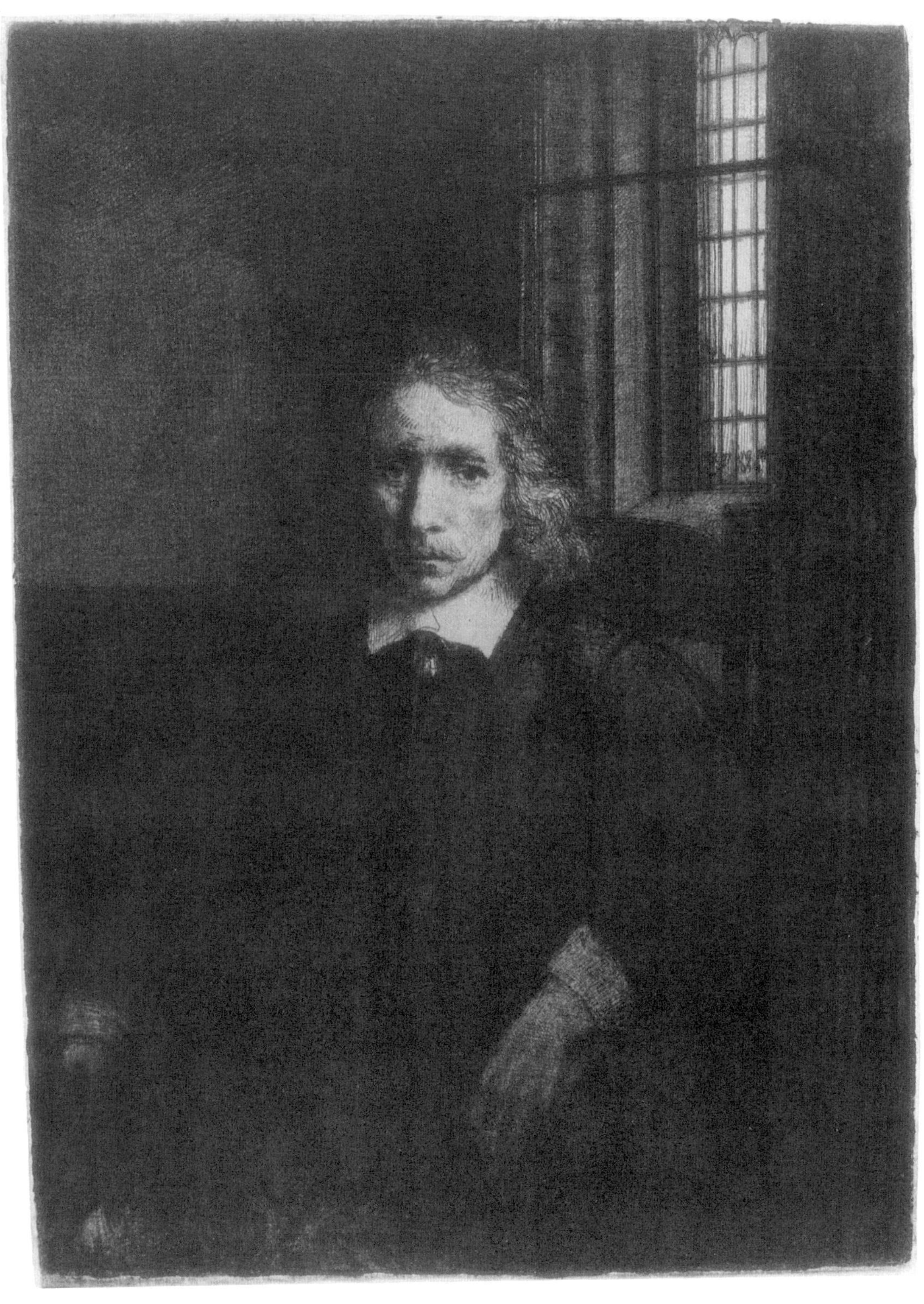

Plate 89. Rembrandt Harmensz. van Rijn, *Jacob Haaringh (Young Haaringh)*, 1655.

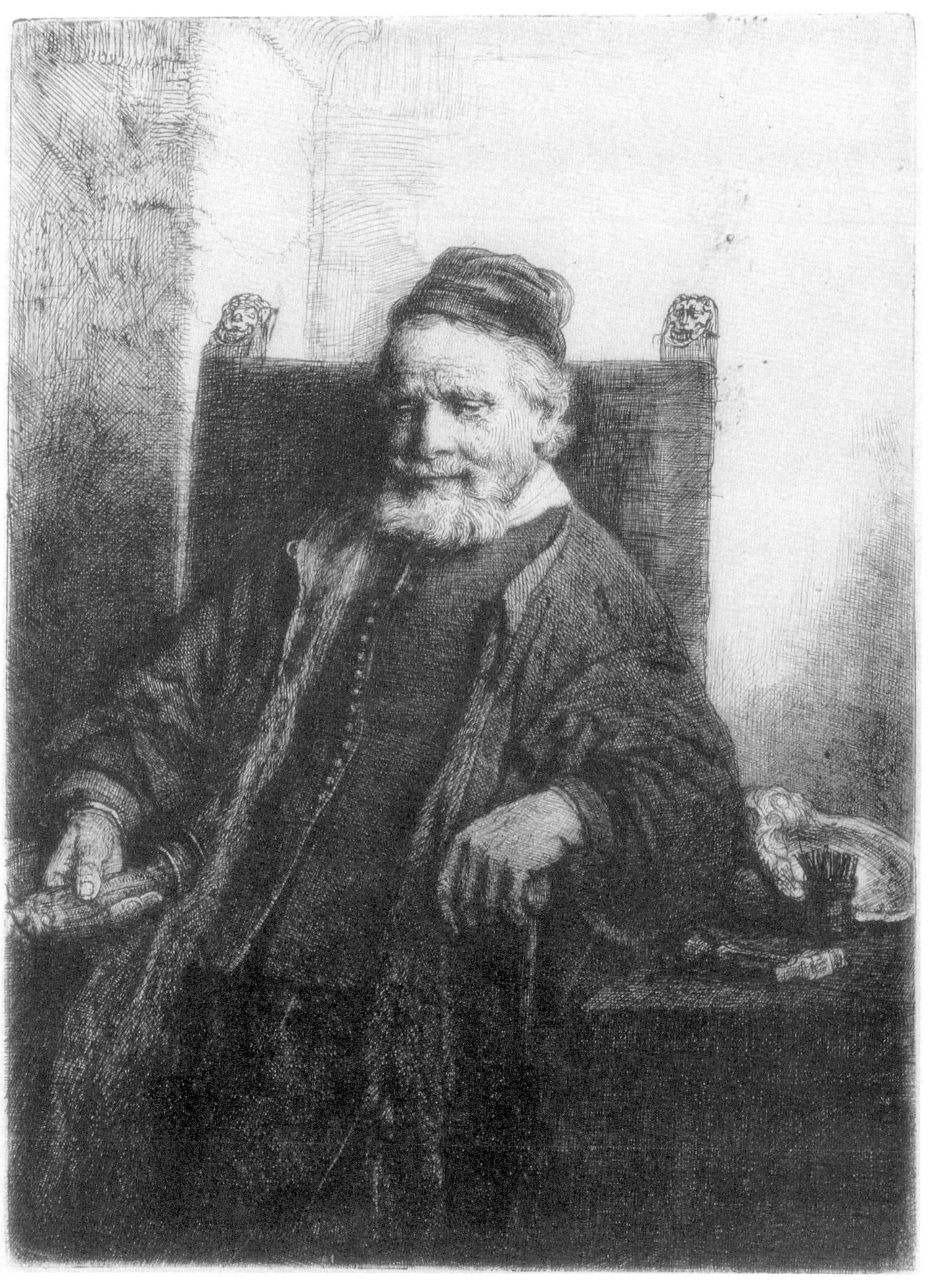

Plate 90. Rembrandt Harmensz. van Rijn, *Jan Lutma, Goldsmith*, 1656.

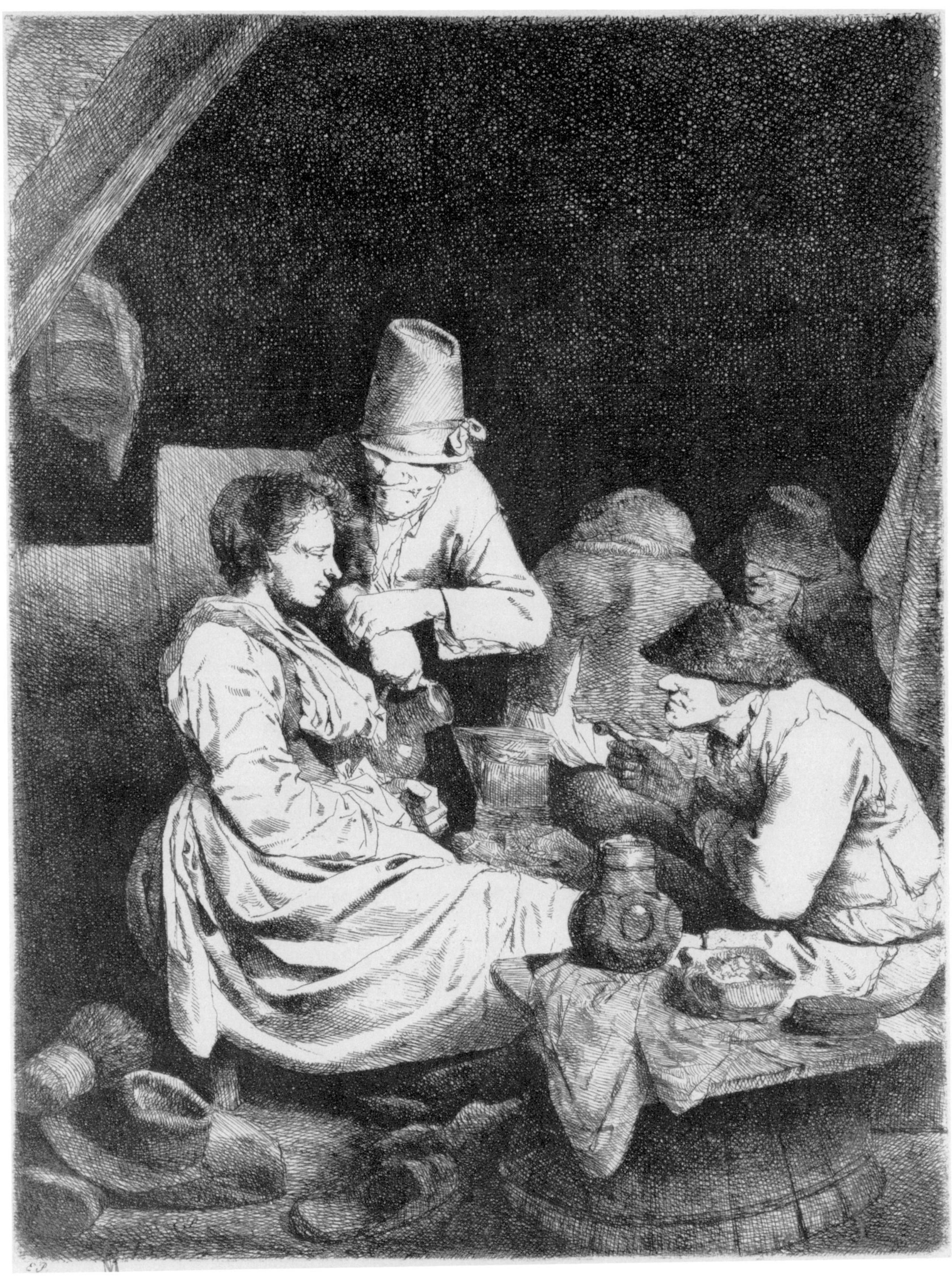

Plate 91. Cornelis Pietersz. Bega, *Tavern Interior (Le Cabaret)*, 1660-61.

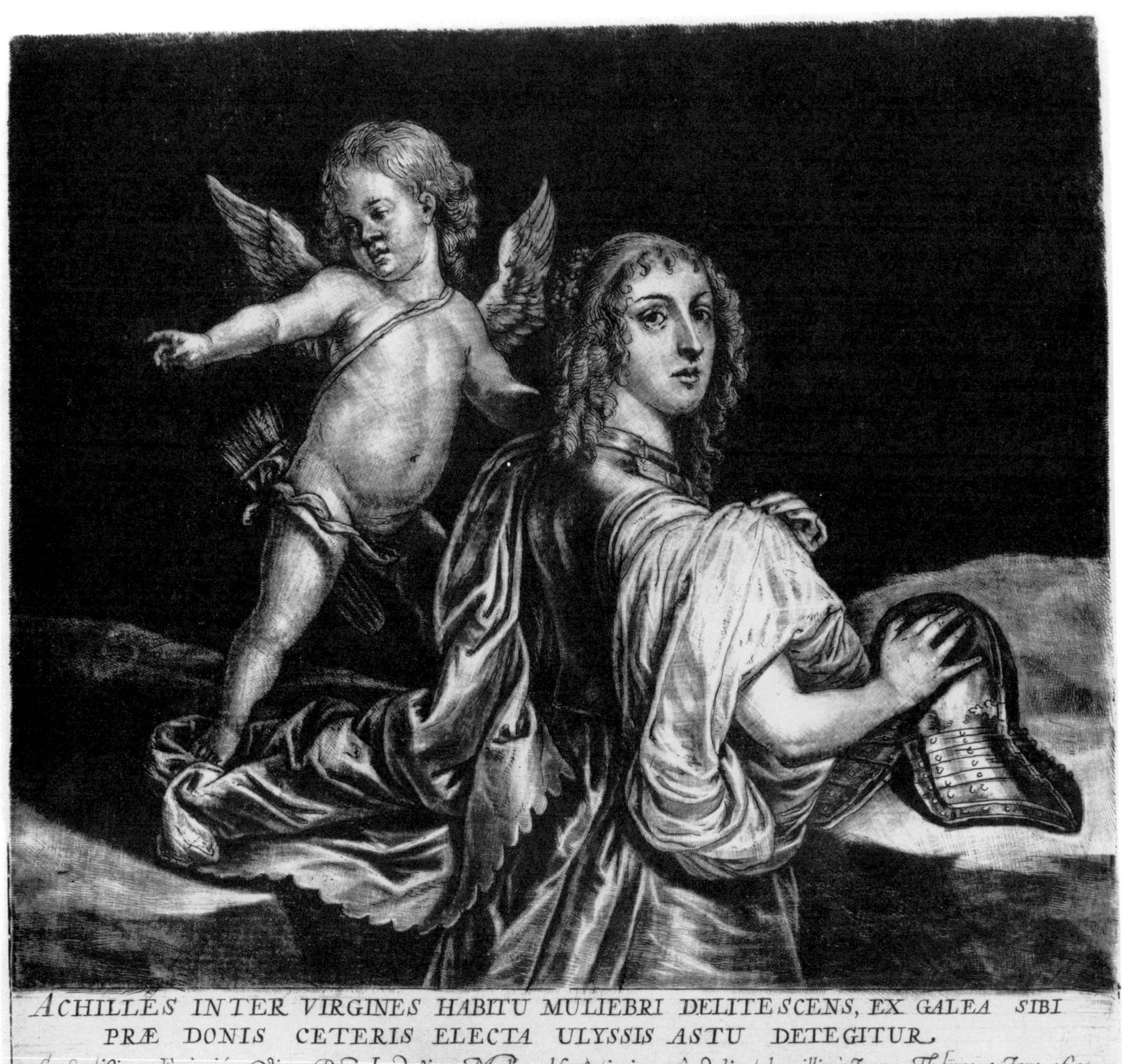

Plate 92. Johannes (Jan) Thomas, *Achilles Disguised as a Woman*, 1659.

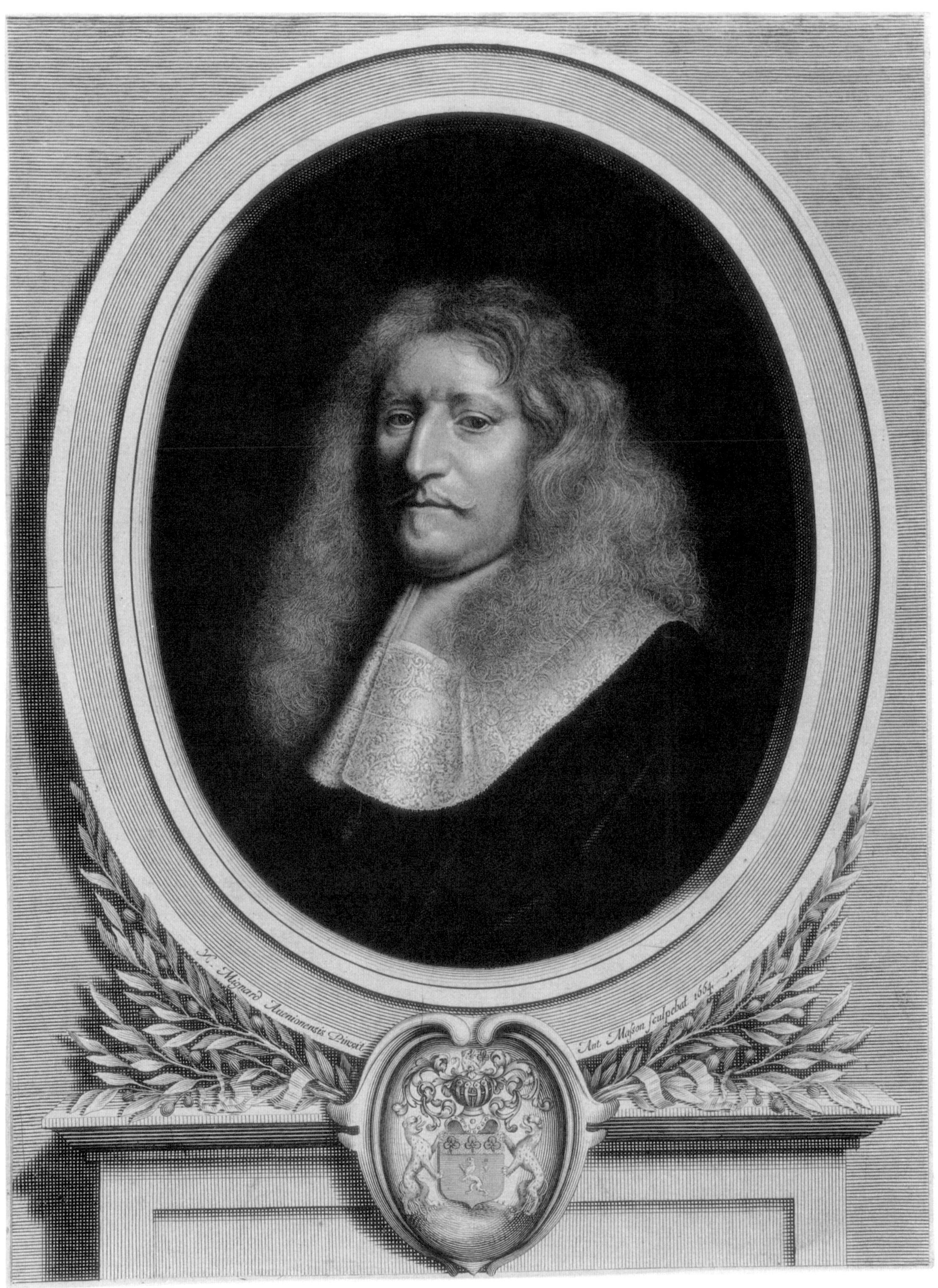

Plate 93. Antoine Masson, *Guillaume de Brisacier*, 1664.

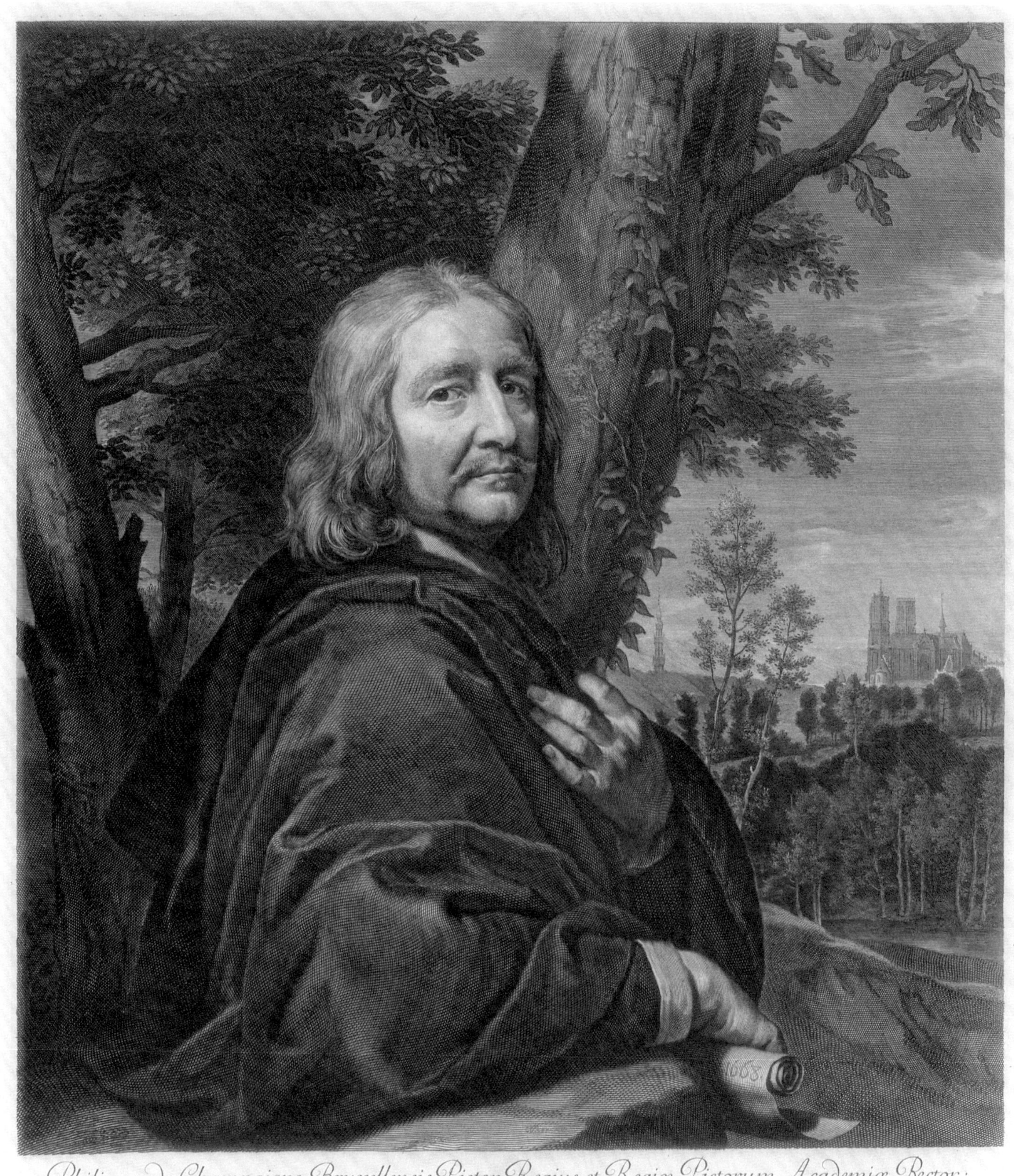

Plate 94. Gérard Edelinck, *Portrait of Philippe de Champaigne*, 1676.

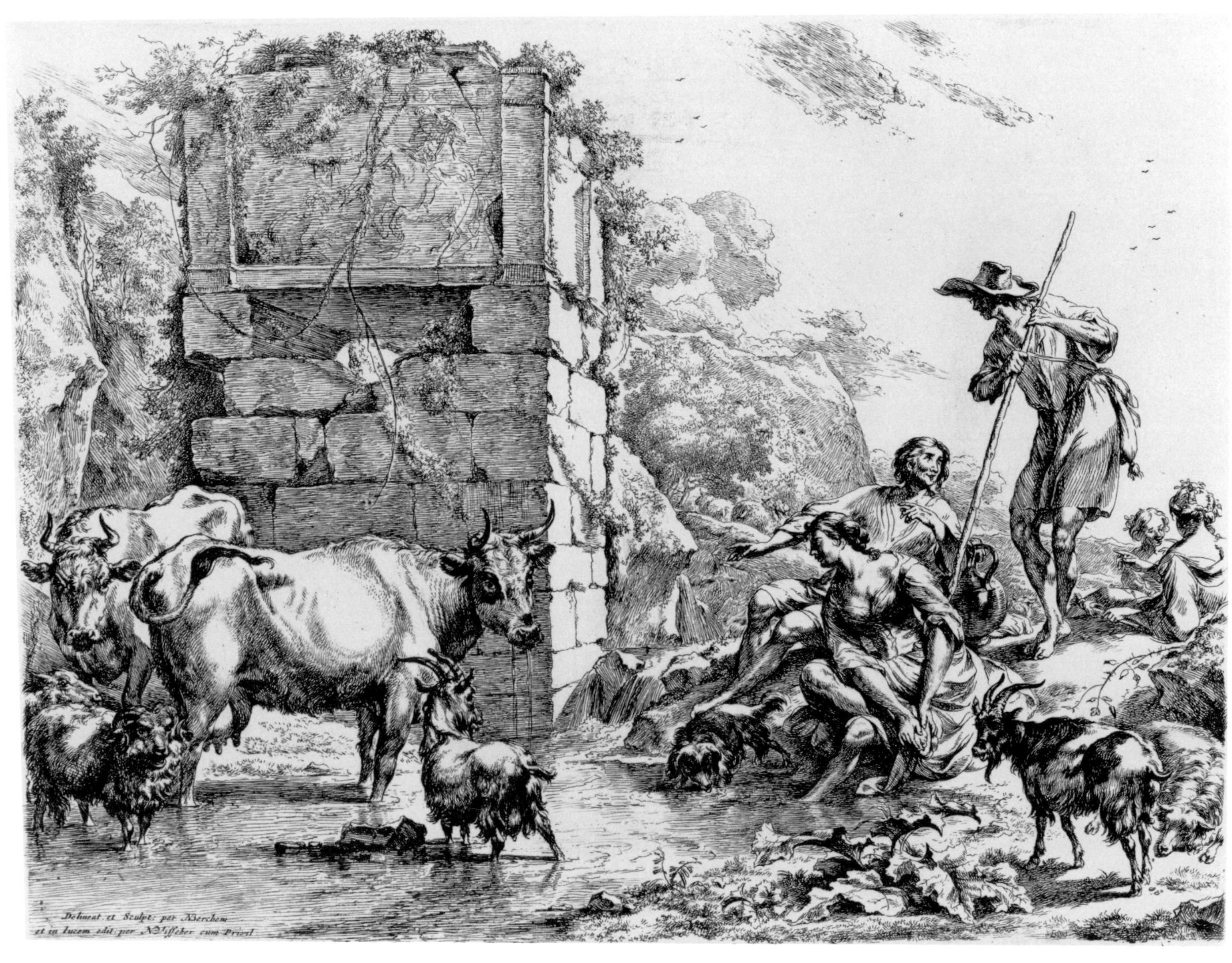

Plate 95. Nicolaes Berchem, *The Cows at the Watering Place*, 1680.

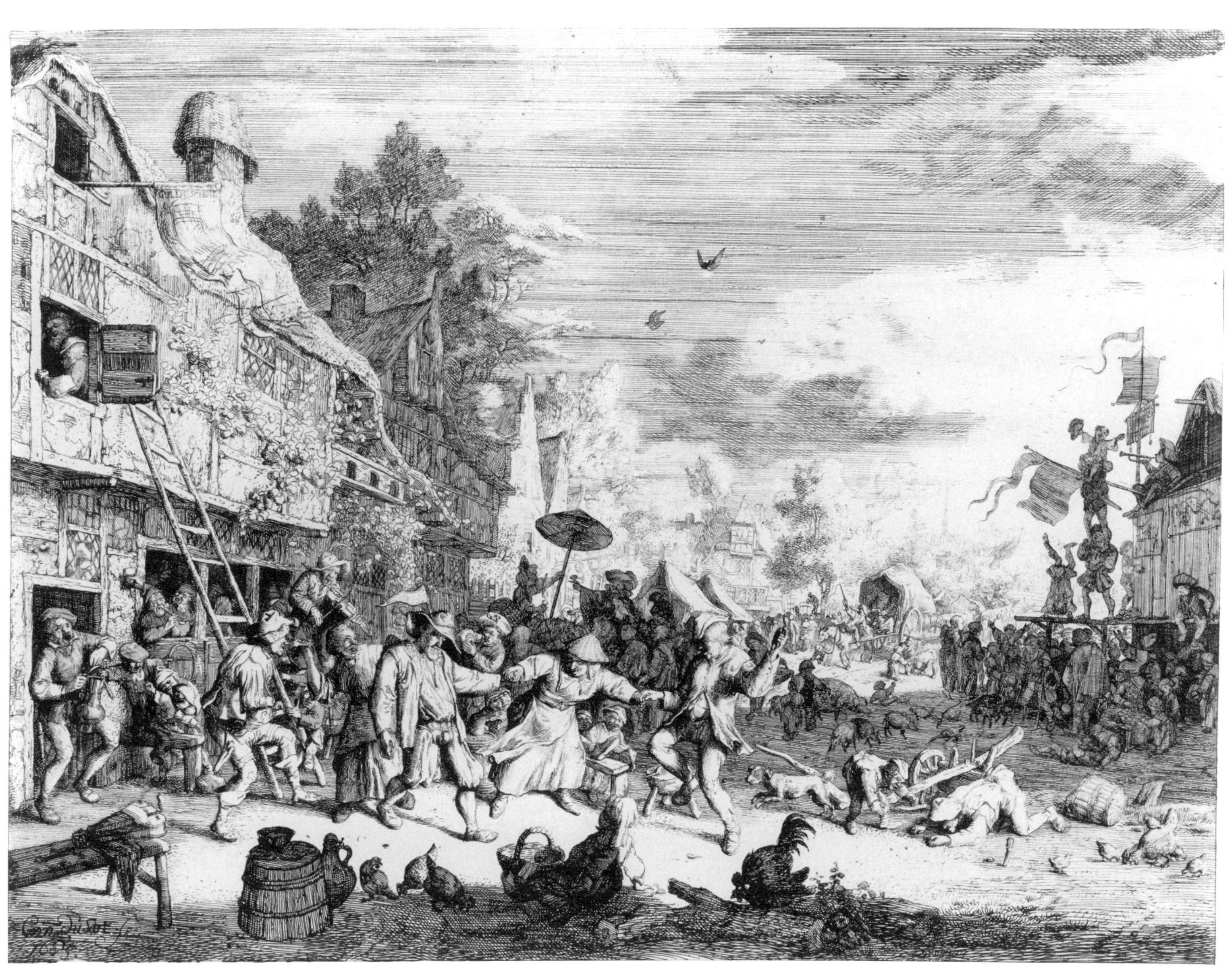

Plate 96. Cornelis Dusart, *The Village Festival*, 1685.

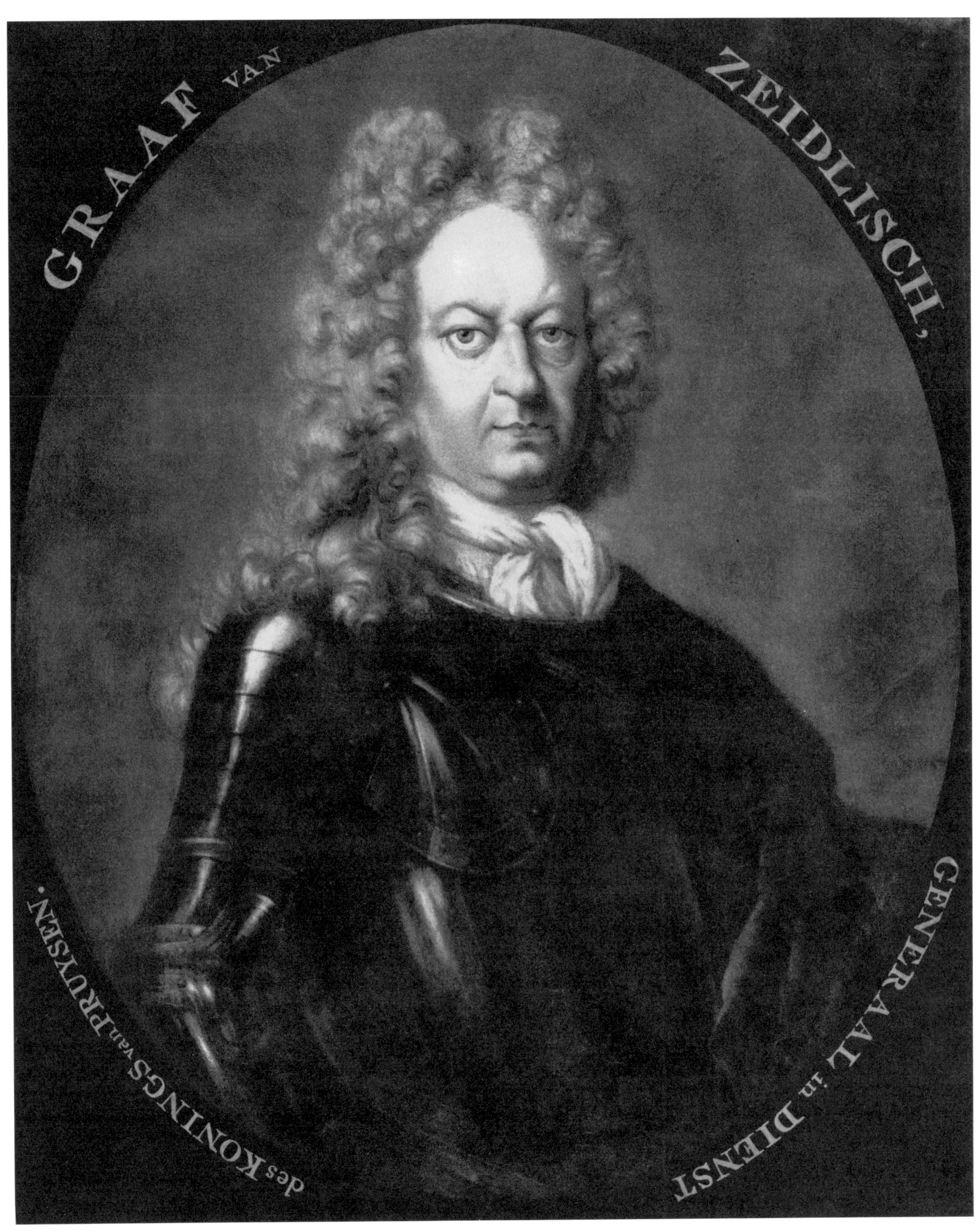

Plate 97. Jacob Christoph le Blon, *Ernst Wilhelm von Salisch*, ca. 1710.

Cornelis Dusart

Haarlem 1660-1704 Haarlem

96. The Village Festival 1685.

Etching on antique laid paper, 25.2 x 33.5 cm (sheet).
B. 16; Dut. 16 ii/ii; H. *Neth.* 16 ii/iii; TIB 16.
Watermark: Bunch of grapes.
Signed and dated lower left: *Corn duSart fe / 1685.*
Condition: Trimmed within platemark.
Provenance: J. M. (Lugt 1493, unidentified collector); (purchased
from The Fine Arts Society, London, October 22, 1928, for $125).
Bequest of Herbert Greer French, 1943.323.
Exhibitions: Cincinnati 1941, no 138; Boston 1980, no. 202.

Cornelis Dusart was born in Haarlem in 1660 and died there on
October 1, 1704. He entered the studio of Adriaen van Ostade and
remained deeply influenced by him for the rest of his life. On January
10, 1679, Dusart joined the Guild of Saint Luke, serving as the
guild's *hoofdman* in 1692. He never married and lived with two
aunts from 1693 until his death. Apparently Dusart inherited many
of the contents of Ostade's studio. A number of drawings by Adriaen
and Isack van Ostade were listed in Dusart's estate inventory. Other
references suggest that Dusart completed or retouched works by the
Ostade brothers.

Dusart produced about fourteen or fifteen etchings. His real forte
as a printmaker was mezzotint engraving. His satirical subjects and
suites in mezzotint display a superb mastery of the medium. It is easy
to see how Dusart translated his magnificent, highly finished chalk
and watercolor drawings into mezzotints.[1]

The Village Festival, signed and dated 1685, represents a street
scene before a tavern whose name, the Golden Tankard (*Gulde
Schenk Kan*), appears on a banner fluttering from the open window
in the gable at left. Peasants throng onto the unpaved street to dance
and imbibe. A group, gathered around an open stage erected at the
right, watches a troupe of acrobats perform. Across from them,
before a half-timbered house at the center, a quack doctor peddles
wares under an umbrella. In the distance, a horse-drawn wagon rolls
into town. The street, a teeming stage, reflects a favorite subject of
Netherlandish artists from Bruegel onwards; that is, peasant
kermisses, or "festivals." Dutch painters, such as David Vinckboons,
Adriaen van de Venne, Adriaen van Ostade, and Jan Steen,
contributed to this popular tradition. Dusart drew inspiration from
Ostade but also captured the zesty, uninhibited spirit of Steen in this
large etching. The sheer energy of the dancing peasants and the
intensity of their expressions are kindred to Steen's. The charming
detail of an unattended hurdy-gurdy isolated on a bench in the left
foreground indicates that an itinerant street performer has taken
time off from work to join the general merriment.[2] – GK

1. Ackley indicates that Dusart's activity as a mezzotint engraver is inextricably linked
to that of Jacob Gole, another of the greatest mezzotint artists of the Dutch school. Gole
was a print publisher in Amsterdam who produced many mezzotints after Dusart's
designs. See Clifford S. Ackley, Boston 1980, 287.

2. Dusart's preparatory study, indented for transfer, is in the Albertina, Vienna, as
noted by Ackley, Boston 1980, 288, no. 202.

Eighteenth Century

———

Jacob Christoph le Blon

Frankfurt 1667-1741 Paris

97. Ernst Wilhelm von Salisch ca. 1710.

Color mezzotint with additional hand-coloring and glazing on
parchment, 36.7 x 30.3 cm (image) on 38.2 x 31.6 cm (sheet).
Singer 42.
Inscribed with brush and opaque pink wash around oval: GRAAF
VAN ZEIDLISCH, GENERAAL *in* DIENST *des* KONINGS *van* PRUYSEN.
Condition: Additional hand-coloring and glazing.
Provenance: Prince of Oettingen-Wallerstein (Lugt 2715a, no mark);
(his sale C.G. Boerner, Leipzig, June 16-17, 1937, lot 774, pl. 11, to
Colnaghi, London, for RM 780); (purchased from M. Knoedler, New
York, October 11, 1937, for $1,200).
Bequest of Herbert Greer French, 1943.501.

Jacob Christoph Le Blon is considered the pioneer who invented,
described, and practiced the principles of three- and four-color
printing that form the basis of today's commercial printing. The life
and work of the artist and his inventions have been clouded over the
centuries by falsehoods previously published as reliable information.
Otto Lilien in his recent book on Le Blon has separated fact from
fiction and unearthed additional original documents to delineate the
artist's career. Le Blon's baptism on May 23, 1667, is recorded in the
town archives of Frankfurt am Main.[1] He came from a long line of
booksellers and engravers. His time in Rome as a pupil of Carlo
Maratti has yet to be verified. In 1702 Le Blon settled in Amsterdam,
where he married Gerarda Vloet in 1705.[2] Correspondence from
1706 through 1712 between the Dutch philologist and art collector
Lambert Ten Kate and the painter and etcher Hendrick van
Limborch records Le Blon's publication of a booklet on human
proportions in 1707 and his experiments with color mixing in
1708-09. Ten Kate also mentions his problems of printing a
copperplate on February 10, 1710.[3] His printmaking activity is
further corroborated by the diary of Zacharias Conrad von
Uffenbach who mentions Le Blon's color printing during a visit to
Amsterdam with his brother, Johann Friedrich, on February 11, 1711.

We called on. . .a German born painter Le Blon. His special
invention, to print engravings like miniature paintings was praised
enthusiastically. But he had only one single example, the penitent
Magdalena which however was unrivaled. It was printed on
parchment and one could not believe it to be an engraving but a
painting. It was also quite incomprehensible how the distribution
of the colours succeeded without confusion. Mr. Le Blon made a
great secret about it; he said it would be for great gentlemen who
would have to pay him handsomely before he made his invention

public. . . .Mr. Le Blon assured us that last December he produced
a portrait of Prince Eugenio which succeeded so well, that the
Prince liked it very much.[4]

No portrait of the Austrian general, Prince Eugenio of Savoy, has
ever been found. Perhaps Uffenbach confused the portrait with that
of Ernst Wilhelm van Salisch. Johan van Gool wrote in his *De
Nieuwe Schouburgh der Nederlantsche Kunstschilders en
Schilderessen* of 1750:

> He [Le Blon]. . .invented the art of printing paintings. The first
> proof of this new discovery was a portrait of the well known
> General Sales who was Governor of Breda for a long time. The
> print was made after a painted portrait which the General liked
> very much.[5]

Ernst Wilhelm van Salisch (1649-1711) was a general in the service of
Frederick I and Governor of Breda from 1696 until his death.[6]

Following the death of his wife in 1716, Le Blon moved to London
in 1717-18, where mezzotint had been established since the 1680s. He
received a royal privilege from George I on February 5, 1719, for "A
New Method of Multiplying Pictures and Draughts by a Natural
Coloris with Impression."[7] With royal privilege in hand, Le Blon
formed the "Picture Office" in 1721. He was readily able to attract
capital investors to exploit his invention for copying oil paintings.
Mismanagement and unrealistic expectations led to the liquidation
of the company by 1725. In May of that same year, the London
bookseller John Wilford announced that Le Blon's bilingual (English
and French) *Coloritto; or, the Harmony of Colouring in Painting*
was available.[8] Here Le Blon concisely described his invention for the
first time.

> Painting can represent all *visible* Objects, with three Colours,
> *Yellow*, *Red*, and *Blue*; for all other Colours can be compos'd of
> these *Three*, which I call *Primitive*; for Example. *Yellow* and *Red*
> make an *Orange Colour*. *Red* and *Blue* make a *Purple* and *Violet
> Colour*. *Blue* and *Yellow* make a *Green Colour*. And a *Mixture* of
> those *Three* Original Colours makes a *Black*, and all *other*
> Colours whatsoever; as I have demonstrated by my Invention of
> *Printing* Pictures *and* Figures *with their* natural *Colours*.
> I am only speaking of *Material* Colours, or those used by *Painters*;
> for a *Mixture* of *all* the primitive *impalpable* Colours, that cannot
> be felt, will not produce *Black*, but the very Contrary, *White*; as
> the Great Sir ISAAC NEWTON has demonstrated in his *Opticks*.[9]

In 1704 Newton published his *Opticks: or a treatise of the
Reflexions, Refractions, Inflexions and Colours of Light*, in which
he discussed the additive color of light. This publication may have
been the catalyst for Le Blon's investigation into the substractive
nature of pigments. While he did discuss the need for suitable
pigments in *Coloritto*, Le Blon did not discuss the need to use
mezzotint, the only process available to provide continuous tone, or
the need to previsualize the color separations.

Le Blon undertook another ill-fated venture in 1727. He secured a
patent to weave tapestries using his discovery and began with the
ambitious intention of producing woven copies of Raphael's
cartoons at Hampton Court Palace. In the face of bankruptcy he fled
to Paris circa 1736, where he petitioned Louis XV for a twenty-year
privilege on November 12, 1737.[10] He then sold half the privilege to
the merchant François Claude Descatillon for start-up costs. In less
than two years he trained assistants in the art of mezzotint and
executed a portrait of Louis XV that was publicized in the *Mercure
de France* in September 1739.[11] In less than four months after Le
Blon's death on May 15, 1741, Jacques Gautier Dagoty, one of his
former assistants, secured a privilege for three-color printings on

September 5, 1741. Under protest from Descatillon and the guardian
of Le Blon's minor daughter, the privilege was revoked two months
later. Gautier purchased the rights and spent the following years
attempting to discredit Le Blon's innovation, claiming that he was
the inventor of four-color printing.

In 1901 Hans W. Singer published the only monograph on Le
Blon's rare prints. His list of forty-nine or fifty prints, including those
for which there is only documentary evidence, needs to be
reexamined in light of new evidence. If we are to believe that Van
Gool's 1750 account is correct, the portrait *Ernst Wilhelm von
Salisch* is Le Blon's earliest-known color print. Two other
impressions are known, both printed on parchment, one in the
British Museum and the other in the Kupferstich-Kabinett, Staatliche
Kunstsammlungen, Dresden. The London and Dresden impressions
are inscribed in gold in the lower left, "*V. K. ad viv pinxit*" and in the
lower right "*J. C. Le Blon fecit*." The Museum's impression is
inscribed around the oval with "GRAFF VAN ZEIDLISCH,
GENERAAL *in* DIENST *des* KONINGS *van* PRUYSEN" lettered in brush
and opaque pink wash on the opaque black ground, hiding the
overrun of the mezzotint. Only after Singer saw the impression in the
collection of Count Oettingen-Wallerstein in Maihingen (French/
Museum impression) was he able to solve the puzzle of the sitter's
identity. According to him, Die Kirche in Zessel (Kreis Oels,
Schlesien) has a portrait of the general and his wife.[12] Technical
examination reveals that the print, lacking a platemark, is printed
with three mezzotint plates in black, red, and yellow, with areas of
light etching in the hair and on the scarf. This beautiful impression
has been enhanced by thin transparent washes in red, yellow, and
gray on the figure and a blue wash on the armor. Darker shadow
areas have been enriched by a water-soluble glazing to simulate the
oil painting from which it was copied.

At this early juncture, Le Blon had not fully resolved his technical
problems. Only a full technical examination of his oeuvre and a
chronology of his prints will answer whether he was able to fully
realize his theory for multicolor printing as published in *Coloritto*.
This, however, does not diminish his importance in introducing the
concept of three- and four-color printing. – KLS

1. Otto M. Lilien, *Jacob Christoph Le Blon 1667-1741: Inventor of Three- and Four-Colour Printing* (Stuttgart: Anton Hiersemann, 1985), 12.

2. Lilien, *Jacob Christoph Le Blon*, 19.

3. Lilien, *Jacob Christoph Le Blon*, 20.

4. Lilien, *Jacob Christoph Le Blon*, 22.

5. Lilien, *Jacob Christoph Le Blon*, 23.

6. For limited biographical information see *Gothaisches Genealogisches Taschenbuch der Uradeligen Häuser* (Gotha: Justus Berthes, 1912), 713.

7. Lilien, *Jacob Christoph Le Blon*, 138.

8. Lilien, *Jacob Christoph Le Blon*, 96.

9. Reproduced in Lilien, *Jacob Christoph Le Blon*, 188.

10. Lilien, *Jacob Christoph Le Blon*, 68.

11. Lilien, *Jacob Christoph Le Blon*, 72.

12. Hans W. Singer, "Jakob Christoffel Le Blon," *MGvK.* (1901):18.

Peter Pelham

London ca. 1697-1751 Boston

98. Cotton Mather 1727.

Mezzotint on antique laid paper, 34.8 x 25.0 cm (platemark).
Sm. 26 i/ii
Inscribed in plate lower center: *Cottonus Matherus / S. Theologiæ
Doctor, Regiæ Societatis Londinensis Socius, / et Ecclesiæ apud
Bostonum Nov-Anglorum nuper Præpositus. / Ætatis Suæ* LXV,
MDCCXXVII. *P. Pelham ad vivum pinxit ab Origin, Fecit et excud.*

Provenance: (Purchased from M. Knoedler, New York, September
29, 1933, for $750).
Bequest of Herbert Greer French, 1943.376.

Peter Pelham was a member of the second generation of English
mezzotint artists who were active during the early part of the
eighteenth century.[1] Mezzotint had become a popular printmaking
process, especially in England, because of its ability to reproduce the
tonal range and dramatic chiaroscuro effects of oil painting. The
earliest form of mezzotint was developed in 1642 by an amateur
Dutch printmaker, Ludwig von Siegen, who used a series of roulette
wheels to pit the plate with tiny holes to hold the ink for his portrait
Amelia Elisabeth, Landgravine of Hesse-Cassel (cat. 80). After the
Restoration in 1660, Prince Rupert, who created a tool similar to the
modern-day rocker, introduced the process to Great Britain.[2] As
engravers migrated to London for more information on the
technique and as printsellers began turning over a substantial profit,
England established itself as the center for mezzotint, which was
being called "la manière Anglaise" by the turn of the century.
Competition became so stiff, however, that an established mezzotint
engraver, such as Peter Pelham, who produced at least twenty-five
portraits between 1720 and 1726, had difficulty making ends meet.
Although many took on other activities or jobs, Pelham decided to
try his luck in America, a change that was also prompted by the
death of his youngest child.

Peter Pelham was born in London around 1697. As a teenager, he
was apprenticed to the Huguenot John Simon, one of the city's
leading mezzotint engravers who had fled France to avoid religious
persecution. Because Simon had a working relationship with the
immensely popular German artist Sir Godfrey Kneller, successor to
Peter Lely as court painter to Charles II, Pelham could turn to the
finest portrait paintings of the day to use as his models. When he
settled in Boston in 1627, Pelham was the first mezzotint engraver to
arrive in America. He had hoped that the market for his work would
be strong, but unlike his home country, there were no portrait
painters in the Massachusetts colony as talented as Kneller to copy.
Furthermore, printmaking materials were often inferior and/or
unavailable. Pelham initially succeeded, however, by enlisting as his
first subject the Puritan reverend Cotton Mather, possibly the most
famous citizen in all of New England. Mather (1663-1728) was the
son of Increase Mather, D.D., and the grandson of Richard Mather,
both nonconformist divines. After graduating from Harvard (where
his father was president), Mather became minister of Boston in 1684,
was made a doctor of divinity by the University of Glasgow in 1710,
and was elected a fellow of the Royal Society four years later. He was
especially well known for his treatises and published work on
witchcraft, having served as an investigator and advisor on the
subject during the Salem trials in 1692.

Pelham's 1727 portrait of Cotton Mather was the first mezzotint
known to have been made in America.[3] The plate was copied from
Pelham's own painting of Mather, completed just months before the
preacher's death in February of the following year. Two weeks after
Mather's passing, Pelham made the mezzotint available to the
public.[4] The Museum's first-state impression of *Cotton Mather*
portrays the divine in a frontal pose, facing slightly to the viewer's
left, complete with wig and black overcoat. Pelham's use of a bust-
length portrait in an elongated oval was a favorite compositional
prototype of Sir Godfrey Kneller and may have been his inspiration
for this pose. Pelham also occasionally focused his lighting toward
the top portion of the face, creating, very much like the Kneller
portrait, "a kind of penumbra around the head."[5] Because of the
nature of the engraving process, mezzotint portraits often appear
somewhat sober and static when compared with their more fluid
counterparts on canvas. Pelham attempted to offset this tendency by
adding, with the upward corners of the mouth, a possible hint of a
smile. Furthermore, the rich, velvety blacks of the overcoat, set off
against the soft tonality of the background and the subtle highlights
around the shoulders, create an illusion of depth and impart a
measure of intensity to the image.

Pelham was very successful with this mezzotint. However, with
few personalities like Mather in the New England area, he was
forced to supplement his income by other means. At various times
throughout his career, Pelham served as a dancing master and taught
reading, writing, arithmetic, penmanship, needlework, glass
painting, drawing, and music. In 1731 he held the first documented
public musical concert in America where an admission was charged.[6]
Pelham married his third wife, Mary Copley, in 1748 and became
stepfather to John Singleton Copley.[7] With the assistance of his new
stepson, Pelham's output of mezzotint portraits during the last three
years of his life was at its most productive.[8] – DK

1. Other noted mezzotint engravers who were part of this group included John Smith,
George White, and the two John Fabers (father and son).

2. There is still some debate among historians whether or not Prince Rupert actually
met Von Siegen. For information on this controversy see Wax, 16-17. When he arrived in
England, Prince Rupert shared his secret with John Evelyn, who decided to call the
process "metzotint." Later he decided that the term was not very proper and wanted it
changed. See Antony Griffiths, "Early Mezzotint Publishing in England – 11: Peter Lely,
Thompson and Browne," PQ. 7 (1990): 131, n. 1.

3. It is interesting to note that while Cotton Mather's portrait is the first known
mezzotint in the New World, a woodcut of his grandfather made by John Foster, circa
1670, is considered to be the earliest print made in English-speaking America. See
Richard B. Holman, "Seventeenth-Century American Prints" in *Prints in and of America
to 1850* (Charlottesville: University Press of Virginia, 1970), 24.

4. For details on how the subscription "Proposals" were advertised in the newspaper,
see Andrew Oliver, "Peter Pelham (c. 1697-1751): Sometime Printmaker of Boston," in
Boston Prints and Printmakers 1670-1775 (Boston: Colonial Society of Massachusetts,
1973), 135-38.

5. J. Douglas Stewart, *Sir Godfrey Kneller and the English Baroque Portrait* (Oxford:
Clarendon Press, 1983), 9-10.

6. Wax, 92.

7. Pelham's first wife, Martha, died around 1734, leaving him three sons: Peter was
born in London in 1721; Charles, in London in 1722; and William, in Boston in 1729.
His second wife, whom he married in October 1734, was Margaret Lowrey, possibly the
widow of Isaac Lowrey. According to Andrew Oliver, no records can be found of
Margaret Lowrey's death. See Oliver, "Peter Pelham," 142, 158.

8. "Pelham engraved fourteen mezzotint portraits in America: six after his own
design, six after paintings by his friend John Smibert, one after a portrait by John
Greenwood, and one based on a painting by Joseph Highmore." See Wax, 94.

Georg Friedrich Schmidt
Berlin 1712-1775 Berlin
and Nicolas de Larmessin
Paris 1684-1755 Paris
after Nicolas Lancret (1690-1743)

99. The Avaricious Wife and the Gallant Swindler 1738.
Etching and engraving on antique laid paper, 32.7 x 36.7 cm
(platemark).
Portalis & Beraldi 7; Bocher 2 i/iv; I.F.F. 1700 XII.411.66.
Watermark: Initials ITD and stone well [manufacturer's mark for
Dupuy Auvergne].
Condition: Trimmed to platemark; repaired tears near center of
woman's dress and left edge.
Provenance: Polignac; Alfred Morrison (Lugt 151); (purchased from
M. Knoedler, New York, November 21, 1938, for $125).
Bequest of Herbert Greer French, 1943.492.
Exhibitions: Cincinnati 1941, no. 226.

The Avaricious Wife and the Gallant Swindler is from a set of prints illustrating stories by the seventeenth-century French poet Jean de la Fontaine (1621-1695). Known collectively as the "Suite de Larmessin," the majority of the prints were engraved after paintings by Jean Baptiste Pater (1695-1736) and Nicolas Lancret (1690-1743). The painters Nicolas Vleughels (1668-1737), Sébastien le Clerc (1676-1763), and François Boucher (1703-1770) also contributed to the series. Larmessin apparently commissioned the first subjects from Pater in 1733; eight of these were engraved by Pierre Filloeul (active 1730-1750) before Pater's death in 1736.[1] Larmessin's series can be viewed as a response to Jean de Jullienne's series of over three hundred prints after the works of Antoine Watteau, begun in the 1720s and finished by 1739.[2]

Beginning in 1737, Lancret took over a major part of the La Fontaine series. He painted at least twelve subjects, all of which were later engraved by Larmessin, including this plate. Lancret, along with Watteau, had studied under Claude Gillot, and as a consequence of their interaction in Gillot's studio, became strongly influenced by Watteau's style and subject matter. Larmessin made rather a specialty of engravings after Lancret, executing some seventeen others during his career, including sets after Lancret's *Four Stages of Life*, *Four Times of Day*, and *Four Seasons*. He was a member of a dynasty of Parisian engravers and printsellers that included his father and uncle, both also named Nicolas. He engraved several royal commissions, including the *Sacre de Louis XV à Reims* in 1723; a large series of plates after Raphael; and many portraits. He was admitted into the Royal Academy in 1730 and received a pension as royal engraver in 1754.[3] Larmessin was a very active print publisher as well, operating a large studio.[4]

Jean de la Fontaine's works were enormously popular in eighteenth-century France, chiefly through his *Fables* and his *Contes et nouvelles*, from which this subject and the entire "Suite de Larmessin" is drawn. Their often licentious nature was certainly a prime attraction, but their inherent grace and La Fontaine's central place in the French school of the previous century, a school that also included Racine and Molière, certainly added to the popularity. The *Contes et nouvelles* were first published in 1665, but they were not illustrated until an Amsterdam edition was issued with etchings by the Dutch printmaker Romeyn de Hooghe (1645/46-1708) in 1685.[5] The influence of these quite small-format pictures was strongly felt in the next century as most subsequent illustrators looked to their baroque inventiveness for inspiration and quite often for direct prototypes. Indeed, Lancret's painting of an avaricious wife and a suave swindler illustrates the same episode and setting from La Fontaine as De Hooghe's etching; Lancret merely switched the disposition of the three characters slightly.

The tale illustrated here (credited by La Fontaine to Boccaccio) concerns the young scoundrel Gulphar's pursuit of the attractive wife of a moneylender. The one obstacle to their rendezvous was her avaricious nature, "not a rare thing in those days," according to the author. Finding his offer of two hundred crowns accepted, Gulphar borrowed the sum from the husband, explaining his need for an emergency business loan. When the husband was away, Gulphar offered the money to the wife, saying, for appearance's sake, that she could bestow it on her husband upon his return. Conditions satisfied, she then entertained all of Gulphar's desires; he begged her in the following days for his money's worth – with interest. Larmessin shows Gulphar later smoothly explaining to the husband that, as he had not needed the money after all, he had returned it to his wife in full satisfaction of the loan. The tricked wife is seen clenching her fists in frustration. La Fontaine then reports that Gulphar went about broadcasting his success from the rooftops.[6] Interestingly, for the celebrated 1762 Fermiers-Généraux edition of

the *Contes* (of which the Museum owns a copy in its John J. Emery Collection, CAM 1971.684.1 [between 81-82]), Charles Eisen chose a slightly earlier moment in the story to illustrate. Just prior to the swindler's revelation, the unaware wife coyly signals discretion to the suave paramour, while the oblivious husband tends to his ledgers (fig. 99-1).[7] The quite small format of Eisen's plate is a perfect example of the increasingly popular miniaturized prints and vignettes that were used to illustrate books in the second half of the century.

The present whereabouts of Lancret's original painting for this plate is not known, but it can be assumed to have been similar in format to others in the series,[8] which seem to have been painted on copper and were consistently equal in size to the engravings after them.[9] It is assumed that all the paintings were specifically commissioned by Larmessin for his projected print series; indeed, it is recorded that Pater's paintings for the series were offered for sale by their engraver at the former's death.[10] Lancret's painting for this subject was exhibited along with three others for the La Fontaine series in the official Salon of 1738. In addition to being responsible for engraving all the La Fontaine subjects after Lancret's paintings, Larmessin engraved four others after Boucher, four after Vleughels, and two after Le Clerc. In addition to his prints and to Filloeul's after Pater, other engravers who took part in the set were Nicolas Tardieu, L[ouis?] Le Grand, Dominique Sornique, and Pierre Aveline. The final title page of the suite was *Collection des Contes de la Fontaine, Graves par de Larmessin, et filloeul d'après les Tableaux de Lancret et Paterre. Se vend à Paris*; it is undated. Though sets vary in makeup, complete series would seem to include thirty-four subjects published by Larmessin, with four more added later.[11]

As was often the practice in large engraving studios, occasionally other engravers would do most (if not virtually all) of the work on a plate, with the credit going to the head of the studio. Such was

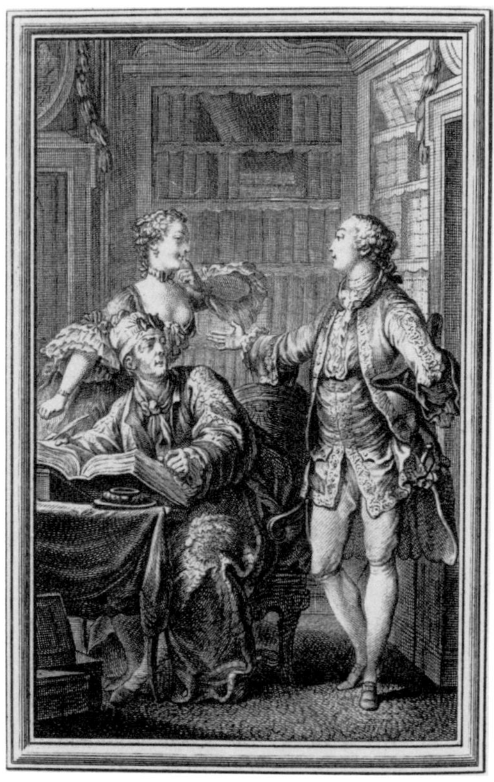

Figure 99-1. after Charles Eisen, *Avaricious Wife and Gallant Swindler*, 1762, etching and engraving from Jean de la Fontaine, *Contes et nouvelles en vers* (Amsterdam [i.e. Paris], 1762), vol. I. Cincinnati Art Museum, Gift of Mr. and Mrs. John J. Emery (1971.684.1).

apparently the case with *The Avaricious Wife:* the second state
carries the name of Georg Friedrich Schmidt as its engraver. Schmidt
(1712-1775) worked primarily in Germany for the Prussian court,
but he resided in Paris from 1737 to 1743 and apparently worked for
Larmessin. An early catalogue raisonné of Schmidt's prints identifies
three of the La Fontaine plates as having been engraved by him, with
twelve proofs only of each print actually bearing his name; after
these few proofs, Larmessin substituted his name as engraver on the
plate in all subsequent states.[12] Schmidt has been cited as modeling
for Lancret's painting as the young gallant, with the painter's brother
modeling for the husband.[13] Two later engraved copies of this
illustration exist, one appearing greatly reduced in a 1743 edition of
the *Contes et nouvelles* primarily illustrated by Charles Nicolas
Cochin.[14]

The somewhat intimate, "cabinet-size" format of this print is
intermediate between the grander reproductive prints after religious
or history paintings and the evolving vignette style of literary
illustration. Though this is one of a set of prints that would have
been bound either together or kept loose in a portfolio, one can also
imagine a collector framing several for decorating a small room. This
series is valuable today for providing a particularly accurate picture
of the interiors and fashions of the reign of Louis XV, some forty
years before the famous *Monument du costume* (cat. 107). The
Cincinnati impression of *The Avaricious Wife* is of the first state
before any inscription. In addition to naming the designer,
engraver(s), and publisher, later states carried a four-line verse,
written by a M. Roy, summarizing the subject. It is a crisp, bright
impression revealing Larmessin's somewhat rigorous, academic style
(as transmitted through Schmidt), resembling that of the classic
portrait engravings of the previous century (Larmessin himself was
well known as a portrait engraver). The freer line of Delaunay's
version of Fragonard's *Swing* (cat. 110) is not seen here and even
more distant is Saint-Aubin's rough draftsmanship (cat. 103). – DPB

1. Florence Ingersoll-Smouse, *Pater* (Paris: Les Beaux-Arts, 1928), 74-75, nos.
470-80, figs. 185-92. See also I.F.F. 1700, IX:182.

2. The series is fully catalogued in Émile Dacier, Jacques Herold, and Albert Vuaflart,
Jean de Jullienne et les graveurs de Watteau au XVIIIe siècle, 4 vols. (Paris: Société pour
l'Étude de la Gravure Française, 1921-29).

3. See I.F.F. 1700, XII:386-88.

4. See Maxime Préaud, Pierre Casselle, Marianne Grivel, and Corinne Le Bitouzé,
Dictionnaire des éditeurs d'estampes à Paris sous l'Ancien Régime (Paris: Promodis,
1987), 199-200.

5. Jean de la Fontaine, *Contes et nouvelles en vers* (Amsterdam: Desbordes, 1685);
see John Landwehr, *Romeyn de Hooghe as Book Illustrator* (Amsterdam: Van Gendt;
New York: A. Schram, 1970), 149, no. 62.

6. Jean de la Fontaine, *Fables, Contes et nouvelles,* vol. 1 of *Oeuvres complètes* (Paris:
Gallimard, 1954), 436-38.

7. Eisen had rejected an earlier version of the scene virtually identical to De Hooghe's
and Lancret's prototypes. Both of Eisen's solutions are reproduced in Gordon N. Ray,
The Art of the French Illustrated Book 1700 to 1914 (New York: The Pierpont Morgan
Library; Ithaca: Cornell University Press, 1982), 1:57.

8. Georges Wildenstein, *Lancret* (Paris: Les Beaux-Arts, 1924), no. 644. This print is
reproduced as fig. 166. Wildenstein 645 (a 1785 sale reference to a lost version of this
subject) could be the original; it is the same size as the engraving.

9. Wildenstein 637-79, figs. 155-68; included in his listings are other versions and
copies. At least one original painting is in the Louvre (Wildenstein 648, fig. 161), and
another is in the Wallace Collection, London (Wildenstein 666, fig. 159); see also John
Ingamells, *The Wallace Collection – Catalogue of Pictures III [French before 1815]*
(London: Wallace Collection, 1989), no. P 409, who cites ten of Lancret's painted
models as surviving).

10. Ingersoll-Smouse, *Pater,* 74.

11. Henry Cohen (with additions by Seymour de Ricci), *Guide de l'amateur de livres à
gravures du xviiie siècle,* 6th ed. (Paris: A. Rouquette, 1912), cols. 556-57, has the
clearest description of the suite and its participants. The earliest plates appeared in 1733;
Larmessin worked on the Lancret plates until at least 1743. Cohen-de Ricci indicates
that the four additional prints (after paintings by Charles Eisen) were added by
Larmessin's successor publisher, Buldet. The title cited is taken from the copy in the
Widener Collection at the National Gallery, Washington, cited as unique in [Edward
Clayton], *French Engravings of the Eighteenth Century in the Collection of Joseph
Widener, Lynnewood Hall* (London: Chiswick Press, 1923), 4:592-603, no. 335. I am
indebted to Gregory D. Jecman at the National Gallery for the transcription of this title.

12. [Aug. Guilaume Crayen], *Catalogue raisonné de l'oeuvre de feu George Frédéric
Schmidt* (London: 1789), no. 102. Under his no. 103, Crayen quotes extensively from a
letter of J. G. Wille, dated March 22, 1783, attesting to being present in Larmessin's
studio when this "arrangement" took place. For another instance of such a case in the
French Collection, see the Bartolozzi/Knight portrait of *Miss Farren* (cat. 114).

13. See [Crayen], *Catalogue raisonné,* no. 102, and Portalis and Beraldi, 2:533.

14. Cohen-de Ricci (*Guide,* col. 557); see also Emmanuel Bocher, *Les graveurs
françaises du xviiie siècle,* fasc. 4 [Nicolas Lancret] (Paris: Librairie des Bibliophiles et
Rapilly, 1877), 7, no. 2(C), which cites a 1745 edition.

Giovanni Antonio Canal
called Canaletto
Venice 1697-1768 Venice

100. The Portico with the Lantern early 1740s.
Etching on antique laid paper, 30.0 x 43.3 cm (platemark).
Bromberg 10 ii/iii; Vesme 10 i/iii.
Watermark: Half moon with crown shield with three stars
(Bromberg 1).
Signed lower center: *A. Canal f.*v.
Provenance: (Purchased from Albert Roullier, Chicago,
February 27, 1928, for $149).
Bequest of Herbert Greer French, 1943.470.
Exhibitions: Cincinnati 1930 (no. 8).

Giovanni Antonio Canal, called Canaletto, was considered one of
the most-celebrated Venetian artists of his time by discerning foreign
connoisseurs. His *vedute,* or views, of Venice were avidly
commissioned and collected by well-to-do young Englishmen who
had made the Grand Tour. In 1762 the British consul in Venice,
Joseph Smith (1645-1770), who had been an astute connoisseur,
ardent collector, and art agent, sold his library and collection of
paintings, drawings, prints, coins, and gems to George III for the
English royal collection. Included in this sale were a remarkable
group of approximately fifty paintings, 142 drawings, and fifteen
rare or unique etchings by Canaletto.[1] Because Canaletto did not
paint portraits, still lifes, or religious, mythological, or genre subjects
but rather canals, churches, and plazas, he was not highly revered by
his own townspeople and was only elected to the Venetian Academy
in 1763, five years before his death.

Canaletto was born in Venice on October 28, 1697, the son of
Benardo Canal, a *pittore da teatro* (stage scenery designer and
painter), in whose studio he received a thorough foundation in
draftsmanship, architecture, and perspective. According to
Canaletto's early biographers, his name appears for the first time
along with his father's on opera libretti performed in Venice between
1716 and 1718. Two years later, in 1720, their names appear on the
libretti for two Scarlatti operas in Rome. That same year his name
first appears on the list of members of the Venetian painting guild. It
was not until 1725 that we encounter Canaletto's first documented
commission, a commission for Stefano Conti of Lucca through
Alessandro Marchesini.[2]

The earliest dated transaction between Smith and Canaletto dates
to the 1730 purchase of two paintings by Samuel Hill, Shenstone
Park, Staffs.[3] In a letter from Smith to Hill on July 17, 1730, he
mentions prints after paintings by Canaletto.[4] These prints,
undoubtedly fourteen engravings after Canaletto by Antonio
Visentini, were made after paintings owned by Smith that had been
published in 1735 under the title *Prospectus Magni Canalis*

Venetiarum by the firm of Giambattista Pasquali in which Smith had an interest.[5] During the 1730s through the mid-1740s, Smith was Canaletto's patron and principal agent. He had the organization to pack and ship goods to England. A passionate collector, he shrewdly utilized his library and collection and the *Prospectus* to secure commissions from the constant stream of English tourists to Venice. On June 6, 1744, Smith was appointed English consul to Venice. In honor of this appointment, Canaletto included a dedication to Smith on the title plate for a group of etchings:

> Views / some representing actual sites, others imaginary / by / Antonio Canal / and by him etched and set in perspective / humbly dedicated / to the most illustrious / Joseph Smith / Consul of His Britannic Majesty to the Most Serene / Republic of Venice / as a sign of esteem and homage.[6]

One can only speculate about the date at which the etchings were started; however, it seems most likely they were begun after 1735 and published after June 6, 1744, but before Canaletto traveled to England in 1746.[7] Thirty-one unnumbered prints were eventually published without the name of a publisher, although the publisher was probably Smith. It may have been Smith who encouraged Canaletto to explore printmaking after the 1740 outbreak of the War of Austrian Succession, which had had the effect of reducing foreign commissions. Only *Imaginary View of Venice* carries the date of 1741. Ruth Bromberg's recent study of Canaletto's prints proposes a chronology based on stylistic grounds. She places *The Portico with the Lantern*, considered his masterpiece for the quality of its line and luminosity, circa 1741.[8] Most of the prints were executed in multiple states, suggesting that the artist became intimately involved with the evolution of each image in order to capture the graphic equivalent of Venetian light.

In *The Portico with the Lantern* Canaletto varied the thickness, length, direction, and spacing of his lines, leaving untouched areas of the house with the *altana* (open terrace) and the left foreground to convey the dazzling intensity of light. The quavering parallel lines define breezy clouds and exude the sensation of a moisture-laden atmosphere. Although the design was fully realized in the first state (fig. 100-1), in the second state Canaletto intensifies the aerial perspective and emphasizes the expansive vista. Canaletto heightened the roof of the temple at the right and strengthened the lines on the reinforced timber wall in the middle foreground. He further dramatized the shadowy areas in the right foreground by rebiting the lines and selectively adding areas of cross-hatching.

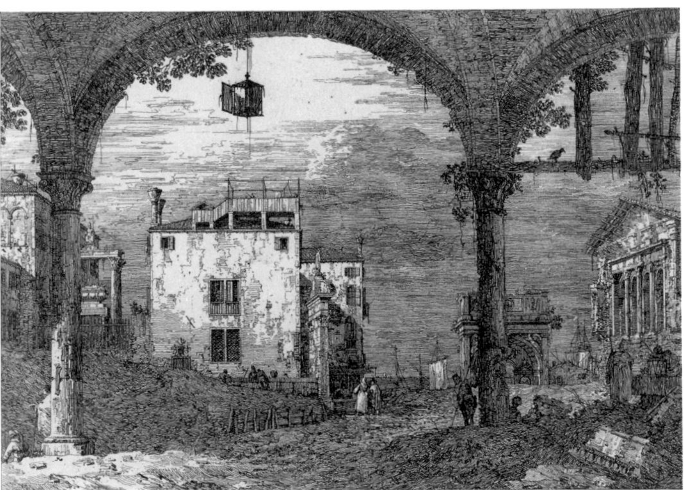

Figure 100-1. Antonio Canal, called Canaletto, *Portico with the Lantern*, ca. 1741, etching, Bromberg 10 i. Courtauld Institute Galleries, London.

Canaletto's family was in a class immediately below patrician; he used the shield with chevron over the door of the house to the left of the window.

Eleven of the etchings depict sites on the mainland, including views along the Brenta River and canal and scenes of Padua and its environs. *The Portico with a Lantern* is a *veduta ideata*, combining visual reality with artistic imagination. The classical temple at right and the triumphal arch at the edge of the lagoon seen through a Roman portico are part of the stock-in-trade antique ruins that Canaletto freely incorporated into the image. In addition, he inserted Gothic and Palladian elements such as the bishop's tomb at left.

The *veduta ideata* opened up new pictorial possibilities for Canaletto to which he would return in 1755 after his stay in England of nearly a decade. Canaletto did not resume etching; he did, however, execute twelve drawings of ducal ceremonies and festivals between 1763 and 1766 that were engraved by Giovanni Battista Brustonloni and published by Lodovico Furlanetto.[9] The artistic issue of neo-Palladianism and *invenzione-fantasia* were to be transformed in the third quarter of the eighteenth century into artistic doctrine by the Academy. Canaletto, in the painterly etchings and imaginary subjects of his *veduta ideata*, anticipated the growing eighteenth-century literary and philosophical interest of Francesco Milizia and Ludovico Antonia Muratori in the role of *invenzione-fantasia*, as an intrinsic part of the creative artistic process.[10] – KLS

1. Bromberg, 2.

2. J. G. Links, *Canaletto and His Patrons* (New York: New York University Press, 1977), 12-19.

3. W. G. Constable, *Canaletto*, 2 vols. 2nd ed., rev. by J. G. Links (Oxford: Claredon Press, 1989), 17.

4. Constable, *Canaletto*, 688.

5. Constable, *Canaletto*, 662-64.

6. Bromberg, 1.

7. Bromberg, 27.

8. Bromberg, 27.

9. Constable, *Canaletto*, 673-74.

10. Burr Wallen, Santa Barbara 1979, 30.

Giovanni Battista Tiepolo

Venice 1696-1770 Madrid

101. Adoration of the Magi 1740s.

Etching on antique laid paper, 40.3 x 29.2 cm (platemark).
Vesme 1 i/iv; Rizzi 27 i/iv.
Watermark: F?
Signed on slab lower left: *Tiepolo*.
Provenance: (Purchased from M. Knoedler, New York, September 28, 1929, for $300).
Bequest of Herbert Greer French, 1943.404.
Exhibitions: Cincinnati 1930 (no. 77).

The last and greatest in a line of Venetian decorative artists, Giovanni Battista Tiepolo, whose career spanned over half a century, blended high baroque illusionism with the pageantry of religious, historical, and mythological subjects. An heir to Titian, Tintoretto, and Veronese, Tiepolo traveled to Germany and Spain and throughout northern Italy to execute great fresco cycles in churches, palaces, and villas; his paintings and altarpieces journeyed to collections in Sweden and Russia. His patrons, church, state, and wealthy patricians, commissioned paintings of gods, saints, and heros that dizzily ascend or descend through airy space. Tiepolo's embodiments of secular and sacred myths are realized by luminous effects and opulent color.

The sixth child of Domenico and Orsetta Tiepolo, Giovanni Battista was born in Venice on March 5, 1696. Circa 1710 he entered the school of Gregorio Lazzarini (1655-1730), a competent portrait and history painter. In 1717 his name appears in the *Fraglia*, or guild of Venetian painters, and his first recorded painting, *Crossing the Red Sea*, was shown at San Rocco. During this period, he executed drawings for reproductive engravings of sixteenth-century paintings in churches and in the Doge's palace, which were published in *Il Gran Teatro di Venezia* (1717).[1] In 1719 he married Cecilia Guardi, the sister of Francesco and Antonio Guardi, who often served as his model. His first major commission outside of Venice was to decorate the chapel of the Confraternity of the Most Holy Sacrament in Udine. He subsequently executed a major series of frescoes for the Dolfin palace of the Patriarch of Aquileia. The 1730s brought further fresco commissions, beginning with an entire secular heaven for the Palazzo Archinto in Milan and culminating with his masterful design for the ceiling fresco *St. Dominic Distributing the Rosary* for the church of Santa Maria del Rosario (the Gesuati) in Venice (1737-39).

Already by 1724 Tiepolo had executed drawings after Roman sculpture, which were later engraved by Andrea Zucchi for Scipione Maffei's *Verona Illustrata* (1732).[2] Tiepolo's own etched oeuvre consists of thirty-five securely identified prints. His etchings fall into two series, the *Vari Capricci* (ten) and the *Scherzi di Fantasia* (twenty-three), and two single prints, *Adoration of the Magi* and *St. Joseph Holding the Infant Christ*. Although there seems to be a general consensus that the *Adoration* stylistically relates to the *Scherzi*, there has been an ongoing scholarly debate on the dating and interpretation of both series. In 1971 Lina Frerichs published four important documents, associated with the French print connoisseur Pierre-Jean Mariette, that established that the *Scherzi* series was executed by the end of 1757, although it was never published during Tiepolo's lifetime.[3] The following year Maria Santifaller located the missing copy of *Diversarum Iconum* in Dresden with the manuscript date of 1743 on the title page.[4] This copy had belonged to the printmaker and connoisseur Anton-Maria Zanetti, who bound into the second undated volume a set of the *Capricci*, which he presumably had commissioned. It has been previously known that sets of the *Capricci* had been bound in copies of his *Raccolta di varie stampe a chiaroscuro*, issued in 1749.[5] Therefore for both sets there now exists a terminal date. Russell, in her *Rare Etchings by G. B. and G. D. Tiepolo*, suggests that the *Scherzi* should be dated to the late 1740s and into the Würzburg years of the early 1750s.[6] She considers the *Capricci* earlier for its conceptual and compositional beauty; whereas the *Scherzi*, she notes, shows a greater variety and subtlety in linear vocabulary. Frerichs, Terisio Pignatti, and Santifaller all likewise maintain that the *Scherzi* series comes after the *Capricci*.[7] George Knox, in his revision of the *Catalogue of the Tiepolo Drawings in the Victoria and Albert Museum* and in *Etchings by the Tiepolos*, reiterates his 1972 position that the prints must be seen in context with related drawings and suggests that all were done circa 1743.[8] Aldo Rizzi, in *The Etchings of the Tiepolos*, assigns a date of 1735-40 and, like Knox, gives the *Scherzi* precedence.[9] All of these judgments are based on subjective theses of stylistic development. What is needed now is a systematic study of all of Zanetti's *Raccolta*, the watermarks on the *Capricci* and *Scherzi*, and their related drawings.

The largest plate by Tiepolo, *Adoration of the Magi* is unique in the artist's oeuvre because it is believed to illustrate a lost work. De Vesme's proposal in 1906 that it reproduces a lost painting of 1766 for the Palacio Real, Aranjuez, Spain, persists in the literature.[10] The subject has subsequently been linked with the altarpiece for the Church of the Benedictines at Schwarzach (1753).[11] In 1972 Santifaller pointed out the analogous compositional relationship to

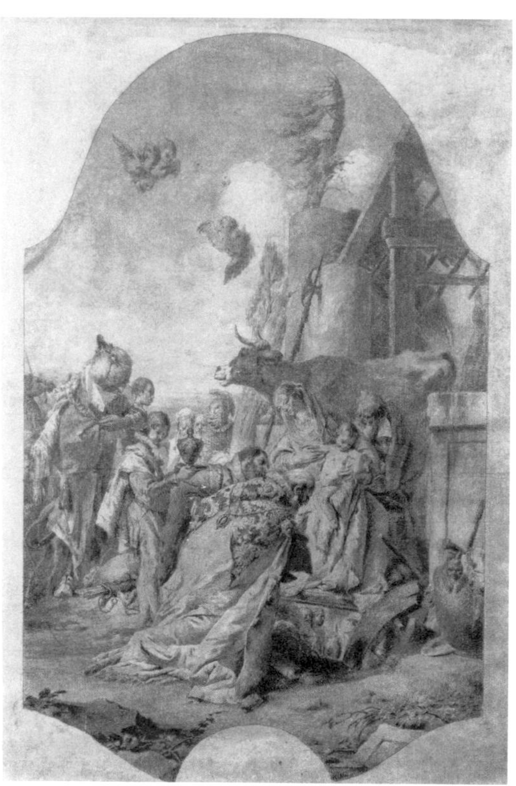

Figure 101-1. Giovanni Raggi (attr.), copy after Giovanni Battista Tiepolo, *The Adoration of the Magi*, ca. 1735-40, pen and wash heightened with white over black chalk on white paper toned brown. Private Collection.

Tiepolo's altarpiece, *Rest on the Flight into Egypt* (1742-45) for the Church of S. Massimo, Padua.[12] Four lively finished compositional variations in ink and wash on the theme of the Adoration exist in Berlin, Cleveland, New York, and San Francisco that probably predate the etching and last painting.[13] Circa 1970 an uninspired copy (fig. 101-1) bearing remarkable fidelity to the etching, except for its Baroque profile that Knox attributed to Giovanni Raggi, Tiepolo's studio assistant from 1732/33 to 1741, came on the market.[14] The evidence seems to suggest a date in the 1740s, earlier rather than later.

Tiepolo's grandiose and sumptuous treatment of the subject betrays a knowledge of Paolo Veronese's *Adoration of the Magi*, which hung in the Church of San Silvestro, Venice, in the eighteenth century. Russell suggests that the iconography of the *Adoration* symbolizes both the era of the Old Testament that is inferred by the presence of the satyr vase and classical relief and the New Testament revelation of Christ's divinity explicit in the attitudes of the Magi and Joseph and the star's three radiating beams, which may represent the Trinity.[15] She further points out that the turbaned figure betrays the Eastern origin of the priestly figures and that the columns and halberd allude to Christ's future flagellation.[16] More importantly, Tiepolo has transposed the style and apparatus of rococo fresco decoration to etching. His leitmotif of the balanced, triangular figure grouping derives from decorative ceiling schemes. Its central focus is on the Madonna and child on the raised dais. Areas of visual density are counterbalanced by expanses of white paper. There is a variety of line: hooking and parallel hatching subtly describe texture and form, light and dark. These traits, along with the signature, link the print to the *Scherzi*. However, the vigorous debate on the dating of the *Scherzi* remains.

In 1762 Tiepolo and his two sons, Domenico and Lorenzo, traveled to Madrid, where they painted *The Apotheosis of Spain*, ceiling frescos for the throne room of the royal palace, and undertook a series of altarpieces for the royal chapel at Aranjuez. On March 27, 1770, Tiepolo died suddenly in Madrid. – KLS

1. Michael Levey, *Giambattista Tiepolo: His Life and Art* (New Haven and New York: Yale University Press, 1986), 9.

2. Filippo Redrocco "Giambattista Tiepolo illustratore di libri" in *Giambattista Tiepolo: il e segno l'enigma* (Gorizia: Castello di Gorizia, 1985), 66.

3. Lina Christina Frerichs, "Nouvelles sources pour la connaissance de l'activité de graveur des trois Tiepolo," *Nouvelles de l'estampe* 4 (1971): 213-28; idem, "Mariette et les eaux-fortes des Tiepolos," GBA. 6, no. 78 (October 1971): 233-52.

4. Maria Santifaller, "Carl Heinrich von Heinecken e le acqueforti di Giambattista Tiepolo a Dresda," *Arte Veneta* 26 (1972): 145-53.

5. Santifaller, "Carl Heinrich von Heinecken," 146.

6. H. Diane Russell, Washington 1972, 22.

7. Frerichs, "Mariette"; Terisio Pignatti, *Le acqueforti dei Tiepolo* (Florence, 1965); Maria Santifaller, "Giambattista Tiepolos Radierung 'Die Anbetung der Konige'," *Pantheon* 30, no. 6 (November/December 1972): 492.7.228.

8. George Knox, *Catalogue of the Tiepolo Drawings in the Victoria and Albert Museum*, 2nd ed., rev. (London: Victoria and Albert Museum, 1975), 22; idem, Ottawa 1976, 16-17.

9. Aldo Rizzi, *The Etchings of the Tiepolos* (New York: Phaidon, 1971), 80.

10. Alexandre De Vesme, *Le peintre-graveur italien* (Milan: Ulrico Hoepli, 1906), 382.

11. Russell, Washington 1972, 28.

12. Santifaller, "Carl Heinrich von Heinecken," 487.

13. Russell, Washington 1972, 28-29.

14. George Knox, *Tiepolo a Bicentenary Exhibition 1770-1970* (New York and London: Garland Publishing Inc., 1970), no. 22.

15. Russell, Washington 1972, 27.

16. Russell, Washington 1972, 29.

Giovanni Battista Piranesi
Mogliano near Venice 1720-1778 Rome

102a. The Drawbridge 1749-50.
Plate 7 from *Invenzioni Capric di Carceri all Acqua Forte*.
Etching, engraving, and scratching on antique laid paper,
55.3 x 41.2 cm (platemark).
Hind PIR. 1922 7 i/iii; Focillon 30; Robison 33 i/vi (2nd issue 1750-ca. 1758).
Watermark: Fleur-de-lis in circle with the letter *F* (Robison 5).
Signed in lower left: *Piranesi f.*
Provenance: (Set of 14 purchased from M. Knoedler, New York, January 20, 1939, for $875).
Bequest of Herbert Greer French, 1943.450.

102b. The Drawbridge 1761.
Plate 7 from *Invenzioni Capric di Carceri all Acqua Forte*.
Etching, engraving, and scratching on antique laid paper,
55.7 x 41.2 cm (platemark).
Hind PIR. 1922 7 ii/iii; Focillon 30; Robison 33 iv/v.
Watermark: House with 3 birds (not in Robison).
Signed in lower left: *Piranesi f.*
Provenance: (Purchased from M. Knoedler, New York, September 12, 1927, for $53).
Bequest of Herbert Greer French, 1943.460.
Exhibitions: Cincinnati 1930 (no. 54).

Rome was the most important tourist center in eighteenth-century Italy for young noblemen, affluent dilettantes, writers, artists, and architects who often stayed in the city years at a time to study the architectural and archaeological significance of its ancient monuments. Giovanni Battista Piranesi introduced his European contemporaries through his prints to the splendors of the Eternal City's ancient and modern public monuments, and new excavations in Rome and its environs.

Piranesi was born on October 4, 1720, the son of a stonemason and builder, Angelo Piranesi. Reports on his early training and stays in Rome have been carefully scrutinized by Andrew Robison in his recent book in light of Piranesi's first major publication, *Prima Parte di Architteture, e Prospettive*.[1] It is most probable that his maternal uncle, Matteo Lucchesi, a Venetian waterworks engineer and later Palladian architect, taught Piranesi drawing.[2] While it is tempting to accept unconfirmed reports that he studied stage design with Ferdinando Bibiena in Bologna, it is more likely that he knew Bibiena's *L'Architettura Civile* (1711) or its pocket-sized student reprint, *Direzioni a' Giovani Studenti nel Disegno dell'Architettura Civile* (1731-32), and the latest ideas in Giuseppe Bibiena's *Architteture, e Prospettive* (1740).[3] Piranesi had his first opportunity to study Roman antiquity during his first trip to Rome in September 1740 as a draftsman in the retinue of Marco Foscarini, Venetian ambassador to the papal state. Early biographers agree that he studied stage design and perspective under Domenico and Giuseppe Valeriani and learned the basics of etching under Giuseppe Vasi. At the age of twenty-three he published *Prima Parte de Architteture, e Prospettive*, containing thirteen etchings of imaginary temples, palaces, ruins, and a prison. The first edition went through numerous revisions in content and the plates through various states during its six issues between 1743 and 1749.[4] Piranesi returned to Venice in 1744 and again in 1745-47, where he could have known the etchings of Canaletto (cat. 100) and Giovanni Baptista Tiepolo (cat. 101). Stylistically their vibrant light and scribbly hatching influenced his publication of the *Grotteschi*, a series of four prints that were executed shortly after his permanent return to Rome in 1747. As the local distributor for the Venetian printseller Joseph Wagner, Piranesi set up shop on the Corso, opposite the Academie de France, where he came in contact with progressive art and architecture students. The four *Grotteschi* are allegories on the transitoriness of life in which he explores the chaotic juxtaposition of decaying ancient bones, human artifacts, and the architectural ruins of a lapsed Arcadia, symbolizing the lost splendor of ancient Rome.

Within two years, 1749-50, Piranesi issued his final provocative series of early architectural fantasies entitled *Invenzioni Capric di Carceri all Acqua Forte*. Its appearance and reissue in 1761 as a dramatically different set mark two critical periods in Piranesi's creative and intellectual growth and signal the major role architectural fantasies would play in his oeuvre. These brilliant theatrical innovations spring from his foundation in baroque stage design and from his Venetian *capriccio*, explored in 1743 in the plate *Carcere oscura* and published in *Prima Parte*. In the fourteen plates of the *Carceri*, Piranesi interpreted monumental enclosed spaces and endless vistas with ponderous arches, grandiose staircases, and wooden bridges with a breadth of imagination and a fluent etching technique. Cyclopean stone walls dissolve under shafts of illumination and opaque clouds of smoke. Piranesi executed his subjects swiftly, blocking in large geometrical forms and describing surfaces with fluent parallel hatching, leaving traces of pedimenti. On a technical level, he utilized a wide repertoire of tonal techniques, including scratching, sulphur tint, open bite, and burnishing. With its massive columns, cylindrical towers, monumental arches, winding stairs, open drawbridge, and instrument of torture, *The Drawbridge* is one of his most complex architectural compositions. A related drawing is in the Kunsthalle, Hamburg.[5] Piranesi brought all these forms into delicate equilibrium with mass, space, and scale. Tiny figures are overwhelmed by their surroundings. All the impressions from the Museum's complete set of fourteen plates carry the watermark of a fleur-de-lis in a circle with the letter *F*.[6] This set, the second issue of the first edition with the publisher's name spelled Bouchard on the title plate (Robison 29ii), was published between 1750 and circa 1758.[7]

The second edition, reissued with two additional plates under the title *Carceri d'Invenzione* was a radical departure from the first edition. Piranesi's intensive reworking of the composition was in keeping with his polemical obsessions with Roman achievement in the Greco-Roman controversy. Piranesi described textures in intensified shadows and with dense meshes of cross-hatching, clarified shapes with heavy outlines, reduced illumination, and eliminated the smoke screen. In *The Drawbridge* (102b) he added an additional drawbridge at center, rings and chains in the lower left, a new platform at the lower right, and additional figures to humanize the cavernous space. No longer is there any pretense to spatial ambiguity; instead he has supplanted it with spatial impossibility. Robison points out that the revised *Carceri* are "fantasies on the severe magnificence of ancient Roman architecture and justice, rediscovered by his contemporaries and given their due admiration."[8] Today the plates reside at the Calcongrafia Nazionale, Rome.

The 1761 reissue must be seen in context with the prodigious amount of work that Piranesi published in the 1750s. Using the dowry from his wife, Angelica, whom he married in 1752, he published *Le Antichità romane* with papal imprint in 1756, for which he was elected to the Society of Antiquaries in London. Within five years, on the threshold of architectural commissions at the Lateran and on the Aventine, he published *Della Magnificenza ed Architettura de' Romani*, in which he defended Roman art and architecture against the attack of "Greek" excellence. His final project at the time of his death in 1778, *Différentes vues de quelques restes de trois édifices de l'ancienne ville de Pesto*, took him to Paestum, where he responded to the magnificence of Greek architecture. During his brilliant career, which spanned four decades, he executed nearly one thousand prints, making him throughout Europe and America a highly influential international figure for architecture and the applied arts, archaeological and topographical illustration, theoretical writing, and the restoration of antiquities over the next century. With the rise of the industrial age around 1850, glass and iron replaced marble and, consequently, the need to interpret antiquity. – KLS

1. Robison, 10.
2. Robison, 9.
3. Robison, 12-13.
4. Robison, 23.
5. Robison, 41, illus.
6. Robison, 216, WM no. 5.
7. Robison, 139.
8. Robison, 53.

Gabriel-Jacques de Saint-Aubin

Paris 1724-1780 Paris

103. View of the 1753 Salon at the Louvre 1753.

Etching on antique laid paper, 14.7 x 17.8 cm (platemark).
Dacier (1914) 10 i/iii; Dacier (1931) 794 ii/iv.
Signed in plate lower left: *gabriel de S ͭ aubin*; titled in plate lower center: VUE DU SALON DU LOUVRE EN LANNÉER 1753.
Condition: Trimmed just outside platemark.
Provenance: Henri Beraldi (Lugt S. 230); (his sale Paris, December 12-13, 1927, lot 37, for FR 16,200); Marcel Mirault (Lugt 1892a); (his sale Paris, May 18, 1938, lot 95, for FR 16,100); (purchased from M. Knoedler, New York, November 21, 1938, for $750).
Bequest of Herbert Greer French, 1943.497.
Exhibitions: Cincinnati 1941, no. 235; Minneapolis 1956, no. 178; Middletown 1975, no. 13, pl. 13; Baltimore 1984, no. 33, illus. p. 121.

Gabriel-Jacques de Saint-Aubin was an anomaly among eighteenth-century French printmakers. He came from an artistic family: his brothers Augustin (1736-1807) and Charles-Germain (1721-1786) were well-known designers and engravers, but Gabriel steadfastly refused to conform to accepted canons of art practice and instead pursued his own interests, which were apparently dominated by an obsession to sketch everywhere he went. (The contemporary painter Jean-Baptiste Greuze [1725-1805] once remarked that Saint-Aubin had a "priapism of drawing.") Having tried and failed to win the grand prize for painting at the Royal Academy several times while a student there in the early 1750s, Saint-Aubin rarely exhibited publicly again and secured no prestigious commissions or appointments during his life. From 1747 he did teach at Jacques-François Blondel's art school; his subjects included human proportion, "historical" attributes, and allegory. He apparently sold very little of his work, leaving a studio cluttered with eighty paintings, thousands of drawings and sketches, some one hundred art sales catalogues annotated with marginal sketches, and a small number of etchings, which were never numerous and today are extremely rare.[1]

Only some fifty etchings are known by Saint-Aubin, but their unique qualities of observation and execution serve both as remarkable documents of the age and as eloquent works in their own right. The famous nineteenth-century art critics and connoisseurs Edmond and Jules de Goncourt wrote in their influential book on eighteenth-century art that Saint-Aubin deserved a place in art history for his etchings alone, citing his mastery of that notoriously unpredictable medium.[2] The subject matter of his etchings reflected his restless observation of city life, including garden parties, street fairs, parades, theatrical productions, and café scenes. He also etched a dark portrait of the celebrated criminal who was tortured and executed for stabbing Louis XV in 1757[3] and a number of allegorical compositions.

Citing *View of the 1753 Salon at the Louvre* as a "little marvel and the plate 'par excellence' of the eighteenth century," the De Goncourt brothers enumerate almost every figure in the crowded scene, singling out natural attitudes and preoccupied airs as each converses with one another or has eyes only for the pictures on the walls. In describing Saint-Aubin's skillful use of light and shadow, the brothers also compare *View of the 1753 Salon* to a Rembrandt.[4] At the time, Salon exhibitions, sponsored by the Royal Academy of Painting and Sculpture and installed in the Salon Carré of the Louvre, constituted, in effect, the official state view of "accepted" art and exerted a most powerful influence on careers, sales, and reputations. Lasting through the nineteenth century, Salons often served inadvertently as catalysts for progressive art movements that formed in reaction to the monolithic character of the Salon. Saint-Aubin's evocative view of the 1753 Salon recreates one of the last years during which he had tried to win its grand prize for students.

Saint-Aubin's depiction was not intended to represent an official panorama of the particular paintings that were then on view; in fact, not one painting is readily identifiable.[5] Instead, Saint-Aubin's viewpoint puts the observer in the middle of the scene, standing on a dimly lit staircase leading up to the exhibit area. His skillful treatment of light, both penetrating the staircase from a lower floor and brightly illuminating the upper room through the high windows at the right, is achieved with a simplicity of draftsmanship that reveals a sure knowledge of the relative strength of line necessary to achieve particular values when etched in an acid bath. He has further burnished the wall of paintings at the left a bit to brighten that area. The figures standing on the stairs at the left are solidly sculptured by the light. One might wonder if Saint-Aubin was sardonically allegorizing the light of official recognition bathing favored paintings being viewed by those who emerge from the shadows of ignorance.

An amusing eyewitness account of the 1777 Salon written by the art critic Pidansat de Mairobert could equally well serve to describe Saint-Aubin's view (or, indeed, the many views of nineteenth-century Salons by Honoré Daumier):

> You emerge through a stairwell like a trapdoor, which is always choked despite its considerable width. Having escaped that painful gauntlet, you cannot catch your breath before being plunged into an abyss of heat and a whirlpool of dust. Air so pestilential and impregnated with the exhalations of so many unhealthy persons should in the end produce either lightning or plague. Finally you are deafened by a continuous noise like that of the crashing waves in an angry sea. But here nevertheless is a thing to delight the eye of an Englishman: the mixing, men and women together, of all the orders and all the ranks of the state.[6]

The dramatic space so grandly illuminated in this relatively small-format print has reminded some scholars of Piranesi (cat. 102), who first developed his own architectural fantasies in Rome during the 1740s.[7] Piranesi influenced many French artists then resident at the French Academy there, who may well have brought his prints, in particular his series of imaginary prison interiors, *Carceri*, first issued 1749-50, back to Paris.[8] Saint-Aubin has anchored his carefully constructed space within a grid, or scrim, of vertical and horizontal etched lines. There is, in a way, more believability – certainly more life – in his rougher surface technique than, for instance, in the rigidly precise lines of *The Little Godparents* (cat. 107).

A careful ink wash and crayon preparatory drawing by Saint-Aubin is recorded for this etching, in a private collection.[9] In the unique first state (now in the National Gallery of Art, Washington), the chiaroscuro so evident in the Museum's impression is not developed: the triangular shadow in the foreground is not present, the wall of paintings on the left has not yet been burnished, and the stairwell is merely murky, without the evocative treatment of filtered and reflected light evident here. The figures in the Museum's impression are also much more sculpturally realized.[10] Fourteen years later, when Saint-Aubin wished to issue a view of the 1767 Salon, he took this plate, burnished out the paintings, and re-etched images that corresponded to the ones on exhibit in that year.[11] – DPB

1. The basic biographical and art historical study on Saint-Aubin is Dacier 1931; the most recent study is Victor Carlson, Ellen D'Oench, and Richard S. Field, Middletown 1975.

2. Edmond and Jules de Goncourt, *L'Art du xviiie siècle*, 3 vols. (Paris: G. Charpentier, 1881-82), 125.

3. The latter portrait of Damiens (Dacier 1931, no. 197) is reproduced in Baltimore 1984, no. 34.

4. Baltimore 1984, 127-28.

5. Occasionally Saint-Aubin could produce such an accurate reporting of the works in a particular Salon, such as his watercolor view of the 1765 Salon (reproduced in Thomas E. Crowe, *Painters and Public Life in Eighteenth-Century Paris* [New Haven and London: Yale University Press, 1985], 161, fig. 8). A more customary engraved view of a Salon is reproduced in Crowe, *Painters*, 2, fig. 1.

6. Quoted in Crowe, *Painters*, 4.

7. Middletown 1975, 12-13.

8. See Robison 1986, esp. 37-44.

9. Dacier 1931, no. 793; see Suzanne Folds McCullagh, *The Development of Gabriel de Saint-Aubin as a Draughtsman* (Cambridge: Harvard University Press, 1981), 137.

10. The National Gallery impression is reproduced in Middletown 1975, no. 12, next to the Museum's impression, affording an illuminating lesson in Saint-Aubin's treatment.

11. See Baltimore 1984, no. 33; an impression of this state is in the Paul Prouté archives, Paris.

Jean-Honoré Fragonard
Grasse 1732-1806 Paris

104. Dance of the Satyrs 1763.
Plate 4 from *Bacchanals*.
Etching on antique laid paper, 14.3 x 20.9 cm (platemark).
Wildenstein 6 i/ii; I.F.F. 1700 5 i/ii.
Watermark: Indecipherable fragment.
Signed in plate on stone lower left: *Frago*.
Provenance: (Purchased from M. Knoedler, New York, February 1, 1929, for $200).
Bequest of Herbert Greer French, 1943.517.

After moving to Paris as a young boy, Fragonard apprenticed briefly with François Boucher (1703-1770) and Jean-Baptiste-Siméon Chardin (1699-1779) before returning to Boucher's studio to study intensively with him from 1748 until 1753. At that time, he entered the École Royale des Elèves Protégés, having won the prestigious Prix de Rome the previous year. The prize led to a period of study at the French Academy in Rome; after further study at the École Royale, Fragonard left for Italy in 1755. He spent almost six years there, studying Old Master paintings and classical antiquities and developing his drawing and painting skills. He indulged a great interest in landscape draftsmanship, often working with his fellow student Hubert Robert (1733-1808); their graphic styles at this time in their careers were occasionally very similar. The two young artists also traveled and worked with the Abbé de Saint-Non, Jean-Claude Richard (1727-1791), a wealthy amateur artist and patron who came to Italy in 1759.[1]

Following an extended summer journey through Italy with Saint-Non, Fragonard returned to Paris in 1761. After being initially received into the Royal Academy in 1765 with a large history painting and showings at the Salons of that year and 1767, he made no attempt to exhibit there again or to secure full membership in the academy, preferring instead to work independently and to depend on private commissions. He journeyed to Holland in the late 1760s and made a lengthy trip through Central Europe to Italy from 1773 to 1774. Aside from a two-year stay in Grasse for his health in the early 1790s, Fragonard remained in Paris for the rest of his life; after the Revolution, he was instrumental in organizing the Louvre.

Fragonard's own prints consist of some twenty-five etchings, sixteen of which are based on sketches that he had made in Italy from Old Master paintings.[2] These latter sixteen were executed in the early 1760s at the same period as the set of four *Bacchanals*, after his return from Italy. One of his first independent etchings was an almost miniature view of an overgrown Italianate park, *The Little Park* (Wildenstein 1), composed of a delicate tracery of lightly etched lines, seemingly made of spun sugar.[3] Although comparable in technique to the *Bacchanals* and probably etched after his return to Paris, it is conceivable that *The Little Park* is a first brilliant assay in the etching medium done while still in Italy.

Although it is not known where or with whom Fragonard learned to etch, it is evident that he was strongly influenced by the light-filled, freely drawn style of such Italian painter-printmakers as Giovanni Benedetto Castiglione (1609-ca. 1665) and especially the Tiepolos, Giovanni Battista (cat. 101) and his son Giovanni Domenico (1727-1804). Prints such as Castiglione's vegetation-filled *Animals Entering the Ark* (B. 1), *Tobit Burying the Dead* (B. 5), or Giovanni Domenico Tiepolo's *Flight into Egypt* series (Vesme 1-27), first published in 1753, reveal a freedom of etched line quite comparable to that in the *Bacchanals*. Fragonard would undoubtedly have seen etchings by all these masters during his

Italian stay. His friend Robert certainly learned etching while still in Italy; in the very same year, Robert executed a series of prints in Rome, *Evenings in Rome* (Les soirées de Rome) (Baltimore 1984, no. 54) remarkably similar to *Bacchanals* in spirit and technique.[4]

Fragonard's *Bacchanals*, a set of four playfully erotic scenes populated with nymphs and satyrs, is an unusual combination of fantasy, ornament, classical allusion, and landscape vignette. At least one of the illusionistic stone reliefs is distantly related to an actual antique marble sculpture from the Villa Mattei, Rome.[5] All the scenes reflect Fragonard's study of classical art, but they also certainly exist on a level beyond mere antiquarianism and enjoy lives of their own. A notebook, now in the Fogg Art Museum, Harvard University, contains sketches attributed to Fragonard that closely relate to the set.[6] Eunice Williams states that these sketches were probably commissioned by the Abbé de Saint-Non, circa 1760-61; Saint-Non made etched copies of them for his own volume of prints entitled *Recueil de griffonis* (*Selection of Sketches*), circa 1765-75.[7]

Dance of the Satyrs is a perfect example of what was referred to in the eighteenth century as "free" etching (*eau-forte libre*), which was not subject to the very controlled etching and engraving style preferred for reproductive prints or for the detailed vignettes used in book illustrations. Though certainly successful in its own right as an evocation of the lushly described painting, the Delaunay etching after Fragonard's *Swing* (cat. 110) is a very different kind of print than those etched by Fragonard himself. Especially in an area such as the upper left corner of *Dance of the Satyrs*, the fourth plate in the set, the etched lines more resemble a twentieth-century abstract expressionist drawing than an eighteenth-century print. The lushness of Fragonard's vegetation surrounding his domestic/erotic scenes serves to particularize them and bring them to life, as though the viewer stumbled upon them in a corner of an actual garden. Fragonard's technique of very lightly delineating his figures, often with delicate flicks of his etching needle, combined with his sprightly draftsmanship, further enlivens them. He brilliantly exploits the viewer's confusion of apparently looking at a stone relief while, at the same time, seeing cavorting satyrs and nymphs ready to spring out of their marble confines. His figures inspired later eighteenth-century sculptors, including a direct copy of the first plate by Johan Tobias Sergel (1740-1814).[8]

The lightness of Fragonard's touch is amply displayed in this impression from the very rare first state of the set before numbers were added at the lower right and before their publication by François-Etienne Joubert in Paris during the Revolution.[9] Mr. French also acquired impressions of the three other plates in the set. After *Bacchanals*, Fragonard waited fifteen years before returning to the etching medium. He reproduced one of his large ink wash drawings and experimented with even freer approaches to etching.[10] He also collaborated at this time with his student and sister-in-law, Marguerite Gérard (1761-1837), on at least five etchings.[11] – DPB

1. For Fragonard's relationship with Saint-Non, see Pierre Rosenberg, New York 1988a, 118-20.

2. Wildenstein 7-22; see also Rosenberg, New York 1988a, 120.

3. Reproduced and discussed in Victor Carlson, John Ittmann et al., Baltimore 1984, no. 46.

4. Reproduced and discussed in Baltimore 1984, no. 54.

5. Rosenberg, New York 1988a, 155.

6. Baltimore 1984; the Fogg inventory nos. are 1979.70.8, .13, and .17. Not all the drawings in the album can be given to Fragonard; see Eunice Williams, *Drawings by Fragonard in North American Collections* (Washington: National Gallery of Art: Cambridge: Fogg Art Museum, 1979), 44, no. 9. Rosenberg (New York 1988a, 154, repr. figs. 1-4) does not feel any of the above drawings are by Fragonard, tentatively attributing them instead to Saint-Non. For another group of related drawings, see Paul Culot, "Dessins et eaux-fortes de la suite des bacchanales de Jean-Honoré Fragonard," *De Gulden Passer* 52 (1974): 67-78; an attribution of this group to Fragonard does not seem very convincing.

7. Baltimore 1984, 152; three are reproduced in Rosenberg, New York 1988, 157, figs. 5, 7, and 8.

8. Reproduced in Rosenberg, New York 1988a, 157, fig. 10.

9. The second state of pl. 1 is titled *Suite d'Eaufortes gravées en Italie par Fragonard. à Paris chez Joubert, rue des Mathurins, aux deux piliers d'or*. Early impressions of the first state also reveal the remnants of a curious inscription in reverse ("*Bergeret invenit et fecit. . .* "), implying a connection in the early 1760s with the patron of his later Italian trip, Jacques-Onésyme Bergeret (Rosenberg, New York 1988, 156). For Joubert (active 1787-95), see Maxime Préaud, Pierre Casselle, Marianne Grivel, and Corinne Le Bitouzé, *Dictionnaire des éditeurs d'estampes à Paris sous l'Ancien Régime* (Paris: Promodis, 1987), 180.

10. See Baltimore 1984, nos. 76-77.

11. Baltimore 1984, no. 78.

Louis-Marin Bonnet

Paris 1736-1793 Saint-Maudé
after François Boucher (1703-1770)

105. Head of a Young Woman 1767.

Chalk manner color etching and engraving on antique laid paper, (five plates), 29.0 x 21.8 cm (sheet).
Herold 10 i or ii/iv; Jean-Richard 340; I.F.F. 1700 III.143.9.[1]
Watermark: Indecipherable.
Condition: Trimmed with platemark.
Provenance: Cortlandt F. Bishop (Lugt s.2270b); (his sale Anderson Galleries, New York, November 21, 1935, lot 21); (purchased from M. Knoedler, New York, December 16, 1935, for $440).
Bequest of Herbert Greer French, 1943.416.
Exhibitions: Cincinnati 1941, no. 206, pl. 44; Ann Arbor 1975.

The second half of the eighteenth century in France saw a particularly intense period of technical experimentation in the facsimile reproduction of other works of art, particularly drawings, via printmaking. As the vogue for collecting drawings and pastels grew, a concerted effort was made to duplicate these works, thus accommodating the broadening market for such products. The two main strands of this experimentation involved the reproduction of the textures of the drawing media in printmaking and the introduction of increasingly sophisticated color-printing techniques. Although Jakob Christoffel Le Blon (cat. 97) had taken his highly developed color mezzotint process to Paris by 1735, the technique never really caught on in France. His theories of color printing, however, undoubtedly served as a foundation for the future printing innovations of Bonnet and others.

In the 1740s Jean-Charles François (1717-1769) began issuing prints that attempted to reproduce specific drawing techniques as illustrations for a series of didactic drawing manuals. His earliest experiments, which were undertaken in the 1740s, utilized only standard engraving tools, but he then combined these experiments with etching and with new ways of making irregular marks in imitation of the scumbled surfaces of chalk drawings. In the mid-1750s he adapted tools that he had used as an apprentice to an ornamental metalworker – punches (*poinçons*), toothed wheels (*roulettes*), and blunt devices with clusters of teeth (*mattoirs*) – to expand the character of marks that could be made on a printing plate. Later, François devised his own tools whose irregular patterns of teeth allowed him to make remarkably effective facsimiles of chalk drawings.[2] His drawing manual, *L'Amour du dessein*, was published to considerable acclaim in 1757.[3] During that year, Bonnet apprenticed with François, absorbing many new techniques as a basis for his own innovations during the next decade.

Bonnet had learned engraving from Louis-Claude Legrand (1723-1807) before he entered François' studio. After leaving the latter's employ, he worked briefly with another innovator in color printing, Gilles Demarteau (1722-1776). Bonnet worked steadily to develop a technique for printing multiple-color facsimiles of drawings, striving particularly to imitate pastel drawings. He went to Saint Petersburg, where he attempted to set up a course in chalk manner engraving at the Russian Academy of Fine Arts, but by 1767 he had returned to Paris. In Paris he published his first multiple-color prints. He soon achieved considerable success and made rather a specialty of engraving facsimiles after drawings by the very popular François Boucher. Of almost twelve hundred prints listed in the Herold catalogue raisonné (of which a good number were undoubtedly executed by studio assistants), some ten percent were after Boucher.[4] There was an extensive market for prints after Boucher's compositions, particularly after his drawings, and the artist actively encouraged such reproductions. Many collectors also eagerly lent works they owned to printmakers for copying.[5]

Among other innovations, Bonnet invented a stable non-oxidizing white ink that enabled him to reproduce the white chalk highlights so integral to the drawings and pastels of the period.[6] But his greatest technical advance was the creation of a reliable method of printing registration that permitted the overlaying of multiple colors of ink to achieve accurate color facsimiles of chalk and pastel drawings. Bonnet achieved this effect only after he first succeeded in printing two-color black-and-white prints (often printing them on colored papers), then three-color prints. The Museum's *Head of a Young Woman* is only the second pastel-manner print that Bonnet produced. It appeared just one month after his first experiment with the technique – another head of a young woman after a Boucher pastel.[7]

On May 18, 1767, Bonnet announced the successful reproduction of this Boucher pastel as his first print *"aux trois crayons"* (i.e., in the traditional red, black, and white chalks), in the journal *Avant-Courier*. Five months later he announced that the same print could be obtained in "pastel"; with the addition of two color plates, he had rendered the portrait in a fuller range of colors. The Museum's portrait was announced in the journal *Mercure* in November of the same year; it is sometimes referred to as Bonnet's "Second Head." The first two states of this plate were printed from five plates – black, blue, red, yellow, and white – in a remarkable, even deceptive evocation of a pastel drawing. Bonnet also issued this print in three colors – black, red, and white – at less than half the price of the full-color "pastel".[8]

The later states of the Museum's portrait indicate that Bonnet reproduced a pastel by Boucher then in the collection of the "painter Baudouin," probably Pierre-Antoine Baudouin (1723-1769), his son-in-law and a favorite student of Boucher. The identity of the sitter is unknown, and the present location of the pastel is also not recorded. Two years later, Bonnet was to execute his most-noted tour de force of color printing after Boucher, *Head of Flora* (Herold 192), which depicts Baudouin's wife. That print is often regarded as the pinnacle of French color printing in the chalk manner; it was printed from eight plates.[9] – DPB

1. According to the Museum's files and the Bishop sale catalogue, this impression is described as a "proof before all letters," which would indeed be Herold's first state of four. However, it is trimmed to just outside the seventh border, eliminating the area in the margin where all later inscriptions of draftsman, printmaker, and publisher appear; no inscriptions ever appear in the area visible on the Museum's impression (the later inscriptions are reproduced in Pierrette Jean-Richard, *L'Oeuvre gravé de François Boucher*, vol. 1 of *Musée du Louvre. . . Inventaire général des gravures école française* (Paris: Editions des Musées Nationaux, 1978), cat. 340. As the coloring of the printing is reduced by the third state, this can only be placed as either the first or second state.

2. Several of these tools are reproduced in J. Herold, *Louis-Marin Bonnet – Catalogue de l'oeuvre gravé* (Paris: Société pour l'Etude de la Gravure Française, 1935), illus.; and Antony Griffiths, *Prints and Printmaking* (London: British Museum Publications, 1980), 83, fig. 69.

3. This account owes a great deal to the discussion by John Ittmann in Victor Carlson, John Ittmann et al., Baltimore 1984, esp. 22-24, nos. 39, 40, and 62-64

4. Jean-Richard, *L'Oeuvre*, 106; the Rothschild Collection at the Louvre contains sixty-seven of them (all in Jean-Richard, *L'Oeuvre*, nos. 315-81).

5. The sheer number of such prints can be gauged by referring to Jean-Richard, *L'Oeuvre*, passim, in which almost fifteen hundred prints in the Rothschild Collection in the Louvre are meticulously catalogued – and he was not able to acquire every print made after Boucher!

6. Baltimore 1984, 192.

7. Jean-Richard, *L'Oeuvre*, 339.

8. Herold, 61, under no. 10.

9. It is reproduced in color in Baltimore 1984, no. 63.

Jean-Michel Moreau *le jeune*
Paris 1741-1814 Paris
after Jean-Baptiste Greuze (1725-1805)

106. Philosophy Asleep 1778.
Etching with touches of engraving on antique laid paper, 48.0 x 34.4 cm (platemark); 40.9 x 31.1 cm (image).
Bocher 251, undescribed proof before i/iii; L.D. 1 (under Aliamet), proof a.
Watermark: Indecipherable.
Condition: Repaired breaks left margin.
Provenance: Henri Beraldi; (his sale Rousseau, Paris, December 12-13, 1927, lot 136, illus.); Cortlandt F. Bishop (Lugt s. 2770b); (his sale Anderson Galleries, New York, November 21, 1935, lot 152); (purchased from M. Knoedler, New York, December 16, 1935, for $880).
Bequest of Herbert Greer French, 1943.506.
Exhibitions: Baltimore 1984, no. 72, illus 219.

Moreau was a very successful designer of book illustrations and single prints; the list of his own prints and those after his designs extends to almost two thousand subjects. He first studied painting with Louis-Joseph Le Lorrain (1715-1759), whom he accompanied to Saint Petersburg in 1758 to teach at the Fine Arts Academy there. Returning to Paris after Le Lorrain's death the next year, Moreau then entered the studio of the engraver Jacques-Philippe Le Bas (1707-1783). In 1770 he was appointed designer of the royal "Menus-Plaisirs," later becoming engraver to the king's "cabinet." He traveled to Italy in 1785. Moreau was elected a full member of the Royal Academy in 1789, and was actively involved in the arts during the Revolution. The stylistic evolution of Moreau's work is a fascinating transition from the highest rococo to a much more severe neoclassical style, reflective of his trip to Italy and the ever-increasing strictures of the time.[1] He designed well-known series of illustrations to accompany the works of Rousseau, Molière, and Voltaire, in addition to his famous series of prints illustrating high fashion, *Monument du costume*, from 1776 and 1783 (cat. 107).

During the early part of his career, Moreau's engraved projects primarily included prints after subjects by Rembrandt, Gravelot, and the Comte de Caylus, in addition to Jean-Baptiste Greuze (1725-1805). Greuze was a highly successful painter whose often moralistic subjects appealed greatly to the public and to the influential critic and thinker Denis Diderot. Diderot singled out Greuze for particular praise. His compositions were engraved in great numbers and were often hung in parlors as admonitory examples of family morality and piety.

Moreau etched several other subjects after Greuze, including *The Education of a Young Savoyard* (Bocher 250); a pair entitled *Proper Education* and *Household Peace* (Bocher 174-75), dating from 1765-66; and the very famous subject pair of 1777 and 1778, *The*

Ungrateful Son and *The Punished Son* (Bocher 191-92).[2] *Philosophy Asleep* is ultimately based on a pastel by Greuze that was exhibited in the Salon of 1765, but the print was not executed until over ten years later; its appearance was advertised in the *Mercure de France* in January of 1777. A finished drawing in reverse to the print, executed in pen and black ink with wash and white heightening, has traditionally been attributed to Greuze.[3] However, Edgar Munhall considers its dry, slavish detail uncharacteristic of Grueze's customary preparatory studies, and he speculates that it could be a preparatory drawing made by Moreau after the original pastel.[4] Several preliminary studies by Greuze for his pastel are known, among them a sketch in the Hermitage, Saint Petersburg; three head studies in museums at Tournus, Caen, and Karlsruhe; and a study for the sleeping dog in Dijon.[5]

Though not specifically stated on the print, its subject is Greuze's wife, Anne-Gabrielle Babuti, whom he married in 1759 (and whom he divorced in a celebrated case of "husband-abuse" in 1793).[6] The final state of the print is dedicated to Babuti by the engraver Jacques Aliamet (1726-1788), its publisher. The conceit for *Philosophy Asleep* has never been fully elucidated. Victor Carlson sees it as an ironic statement: the real-life Madame Greuze, as he notes, was "far from the embodiment of philosophical virtues."[7] Her obviously displayed beauty and very rich attire, however, also lend this portrayal an indulgent air. In later states of the print, her dress is further unbuttoned, imparting a slightly more risqué quality to the subject. Traditional apparatus that define philosophy – globe and volumes of Newton, Epicurus, Plato, Descartes, and Copernicus – lie on the table beside her.[8] The representation of sleep and absorption was not uncommon in eighteenth-century art, actually figuring prominently in Greuze's work.[9] In his commentary on the 1765 Salon, Diderot did not remark on the pastel's subject but spent much time on Greuze's preoccupation with his wife's throat.[10]

Although signed in later states with only the names of Greuze as designer and Aliamet as "directing" the work (*direxit*), the attribution to Moreau for the preliminary etching of the print has been generally accepted.[11] As Moreau was already well established as an engraver and designer of prints and other illustrations, it is not clear why he did not sign (or was not allowed to sign) this print (or another "directed" by Aliamet after Greuze, *Education of a Young Savoyard*, mentioned above). Although Moreau's etching can well stand on its own, Aliamet nonetheless added various engraved touches, and subtly changed the sleeping woman's expression.[12] In Moreau's print, her eyelids are distinctly upturned; Aliamet reverses this feature, in addition to rather hardening the expression of her lips, turning them downward also. These details in the finished compositional drawing are reflected exactly in Moreau's etching, but in the portrait head study in Karlsruhe they are as in Aliamet's version.

The Museum's impression of a proof of the etched state is a rich example of Moreau's skill with the etching needle, particularly in the bravura treatment of the rich fabric of dress, pillow, and cloth and the subtle shading on the woman's face. (Although this state of the print is most often referred to as a pure etching, it has additional engraved touches, there being actually very few absolutely pure etchings in eighteenth-century French printmaking.) Mr. French acquired another print by Moreau, *The Honest Model* of 1770 (Bocher 239), after Pierre-Antoine Baudouin (1723-1769). – DPB

1. Several groups of Moreau drawings for his later book illustrations dating from 1805-08 are in the John J. Emery Collection in the Cincinnati Art Museum; see Cincinnati 1978, nos. 74-103.

2. The three are reproduced in Paris 1985, nos. 59-61.

3. This sheet, formerly belonging to the Baron Hatvany, has passed through several auctions, the most recent known to this writer being Christie's, London, July 6, 1965, lot

111 (repr.). It is also reproduced in Denis Diderot, *Salons*, 2nd ed., ed. Jean Seznec (Oxford: Clarendon Press, 1975-79), vol. 2, pl. 53.

4. Edgar Munhall, personal communication to Becker, July 1991. One problem with the drawing being by Moreau is that the figure's dress is as it appears in *later* states of the print, more unbuttoned than in Moreau's etched version.

5. See Paris 1985, 60, under no. 64. The Karlsruhe head study is reproduced in Edgar Munhall, Hartford 1976, 21, fig. 11, as is the Dijon dog pastel study (no. 45). The Saint Petersburg study is reproduced in Leningrad 1977, no. 66.

6. See Victor Carlson, Baltimore 1984, 218, no. 72.

7. Carlson, Baltimore 1984, 218, no. 72.

8. See Cesare Ripa, *Baroque and Rococo Pictorial Imagery* (New York: Dover, 1971), emblem 198 (based on an edition of Ripa's *Iconologia* printed in Augsburg by Johann Georg Hertel ca. 1758-60).

9. See especially Michael Fried, *Absorption and Theatricality – Painting and Beholder in the Age of Diderot* (Chicago: University of Chicago Press, 1988), 32-35, 55-61, for similar sleeping subjects by Greuze of the period of *Philosophy Asleep*.

10. See Diderot, *Salons*, 2:153.

11. A proof of the first state in the Bibliothèque Nationale, Paris, carries the manuscript inscription "Madame Greuze, gravè à l'eau-forte par J. M. Moreau d'après le portrait de Mr. Greuze." (I.F.F. 1700 I.43.55, s.v. "Aliamet").

12. The final state of the print is reproduced in Emile Dacier, *La gravure de genre et de moeurs* (Paris and Brussels: G. Van Oest, 1925), no. 79, pl. 51. Dacier remarks in his entry on the print (p. 79) that Aliamet only finished the plate and that it can't be said that he made it any better.

Jean-Charles Baquoy

Paris 1721-1777 Paris
after Jean-Michel Moreau *le jeune* (1741-1814)

107a. The Little Godparents 1777.
Plate for *Monument du Costume.*
Etching on antique laid paper, 41.2 x 32.3 cm (platemark).
Bocher 1353 i/vii; L.D. 224 proof a; I.F.F. 1700 I.492.372.
Watermark: Indecipherable.
Provenance: Cortlandt F. Bishop (Lugt S. 2770b); (his sale Anderson Galleries, New York, November 21, 1935, lot 157); (purchased from M. Knoedler, New York, December 16, 1935, for $715).
Bequest of Herbert Greer French, 1943.505.

Jean-Charles Baquoy *and* Charles-Emmanuel Patas

Paris 1744-1802 Paris
after Jean-Michel Moreau *le jeune*

107b. The Little Godparents 1777.
Plate from *Monument du Costume.*
Etching and engraving on antique laid paper, 41.0 x 31.0 cm (sheet).
Bocher 1353 iv/vii; L.D. 224 ii/iv.
Watermark: I T DUPUY[well-tower]AUVERGNE 1742[1].
Signed in plate lower left: *J.M. Moreau le Jeune del. 1776*; lower right: *C. Baquoy ine. [sic] aqua f. Patas terminavit 1777.*
Condition: Trimmed within platemark.
Provenance: (Purchased from M. Knoedler, New York, April 1, 1930, for $525).
Bequest of Herbert Greer French, 1943.504.
Exhibitions: Cincinnati 1941, no. 233.

The suite of prints commonly known as *Monument du costume* was a consciously conceived record of the fashions and mores of a particular society (and class) at a particular period – in this case the decade of the 1770s in Paris. It appeared in three installments from 1774 to 1783. The first set of twelve prints was engraved after designs by Sigmund Freudeberg (1745-1801) and issued with the title *Suite d'estampes pour servir à l'histoire des moeurs et du costume des François dans le dix-huitième siècle* (*Suite of Prints to Serve as the History of Customs and Costume of the French in the Eighteenth Century*). Since the first set did not have great commercial success, the sought-after printmaker and book illustrator Jean-Michel Moreau (see cat. 106) was commissioned to design the next two sets of prints.

The second and third series appeared in 1776 and 1783, respectively, each containing twelve prints after Moreau. Every plate was accompanied by a brief letterpress text describing the scene depicted, with occasional comments on particular decorative or fashion details. A thin "plot line" transpires through the series: the first two sets describe the activities of a young woman named Céphise, her marriage, the birth of her child, and incidents from her married life. The third series depicts scenes of society's upper crust, in particular the activities of a young man-about-town. All three series were reprinted together in 1789 under the more familiar title of the *Monument du costume physique et moral de la fin du dix-huitième siècle, ou tableaux de la vie* (*Material and Moral Monument of the End of the Eighteenth Century, or Pictures of Life*), accompanied by a very flowery new text attributed to Nicolas-Edme Restif de la Bretonne (1734-1806).[2]

The Little Godparents was the sixth print in the second set of *Monument du costume* and was executed in two stages, as was often the custom at the time. Jean-Charles Baquoy did the preliminary etching of the entire design, and Charles-Emmanuel Patas added the finely detailed touches of engraving and other accents for the final print. The Museum is fortunate to possess two different states of *The Little Godparents*: one, a very early proof of the plate in pure etching; the other, an early impression of the fully finished subject that exhibits the participation of both printmakers. All authorities remark on the extraordinary rarity of impressions of the early etched states from this series.[3]

The printmaker Baquoy was a member of a family of printmakers. He worked for various Parisian book publishers and participated in such famed projects as Ovid's *Metamorphoses* and La Fontaine's *Fables*, the latter illustrated by Jean-Baptiste Oudry (1686-1755). Some 405 prints engraved by Baquoy are listed in the collection of the Bibliothèque Nationale.[4] Patas, who studied with Baquoy, worked primarily as an engraver of book illustrations. It is conceivable that Patas' participation in this print occurred literally because of Baquoy's sudden death in February 1777. Baquoy executed one other subject for the *Monument* series: the birth announcement of the heroine's child, *It's a Son, Monsieur!* (Bocher 1352).

In *The Little Godparents*, Baquoy illustrates the departure of the party for the christening of Céphise's son. The godparents, Céphise's sister Aurore and their cousin, a young chevalier, descend the staircase of a grand Parisian mansion.[5] A nurse with the newborn baby and various other figures follow. The two godparents are dressed in their best finery, and the accompanying text expresses the families' hope that "a more enduring sentiment" will grow out of the young couple's companionship at this event.[6] Moreau's composition effectively contrasts the decorative details of the figures' dress and attitudes with the simplified strength of the two undecorated columns framing the group. The large scale of the coach wheel serves to emphasize the small stature of the young godparents; its form and the pattern of the spokes are reflected in the swirling ornamentation of the stair railing. The finished plate is a tour de force of engraving skills, delighting in the bravura treatment of illuminating this nocturnal scene: a single torch held by the footman at the far left.

The Museum's two impressions of differing states help illustrate the process of building up the dense and complex line structure necessary to produce the final engraved result, including the

extremely subtle lighting effects. The very preliminary etched state is even earlier than the first state cited in the Rothschild Collection in the Louvre.[7] Additional work in the Louvre impression is especially visible in the background wall, the stair railing above the figures (and the wall below it), the bodice of the nurse holding the baby, and the spokes of the coach wheel. The Museum's etching reveals the very earliest stage of filling in details and shading the composition, immediately after the first outline of the elements would have been transferred from Moreau's drawing. Moreau's very detailed, "finished" drawings for each print were customarily executed in very thin-lined pen and ink with precisely controlled nuances of shading done in ink wash, all in the exact format and size of the intended print. Such highly finished drawings were necessary for the engravers to follow Moreau's intentions exactly; several drawings for this series have survived (the present location of the drawing for this subject is not known, however). Interestingly, some of the drawings are in the same direction as the prints; some are reversed.[8] In addition, Moreau often composed his figures through larger-scale studies executed in colored chalks from life.[9] The designer would often, although not always, have personally supervised the engraving process and approved each stage of the evolving print.[10]

The final print after Moreau's drawing, as seen in the brilliant early impression in the Museum's collection, represents the height of finesse in the printmaking skills in the latter part of the eighteenth century in France. These prints also reveal the perfect collaboration between draftsman and printmaker characteristic at this time. The understated ease with which the figures in this print are delineated by the light of one torch is intentionally deceptive, as the eye is instead occupied with the costumes and attitudes of the characters. – DPB

1. See Pierrette Jean-Richard, *L'Oeuvre gravé de François Boucher dans la collection Edmond de Rothschild* (Paris: Editions des Musées Nationaux, 1978), s.v. "Filigranes – Dupuy."

2. The entire series is described bibliographically in Henry Cohen (additions by Seymour de Ricci), *Guide de l'amateur de livres à gravures du xviii siècle*, 6th ed. (Paris: A. Rouquette, 1912), cols. 352-56, 881; all the prints are reproduced in L.D., frontispiece and pls. 47-81; and [Edward Clayton] *French Engravings of the Eighteenth Century in the Collection of Joseph Widener, Lynnewood Hall* (London: Chiswick Press, 1923), 4:492-562, pls. 1-36. The latter volume has a particularly lengthy introduction (508-17 and 540 – 42) to the two Moreau series. Some early states of the Moreau prints are reproduced in Paris 1985, nos. 65-99.

3. For instance, see Clayton, *Widener*, 488. Mr. French acquired two other subjects from the *Monument* series: *The Awakening* by Antoine-Louis Romanet after Freudeberger (CAM 1943.491) and two different states of *The Precautions* by Pierre-Antoine Martini after Moreau (CAM 1943.502-03).

4. I.F.F. 1700:I. 441-95.

5. Said to be modeled after the town house of the Marquis d'Entraques, now 12 Rue de Tournon (Clayton, *Widener*, 526).

6. The text is translated in Clayton, *Widener*, 526.

7. Paris 1985, no. 71 (repr.)

8. Several of them are recorded in Paris 1985, under nos. 65, 67, 76, 80. Two are reproduced in London 1968, nos. 477-78, figs. 308, 310; another in a sale catalogue for Christie's, London, June 27, 1967, no. 108. A drawing cited in the Museum's files as being a study for *The Little Godparents* is not, in this writer's opinion, by Moreau (see Charles E. Slatkin Gallery, *Exhibition of Drawings by Old and Modern Masters* [New York: ca. 1956], repr. pl. 18); while depicting a similar subject of figures entering a carriage, they are clearly not children. Subject-wise, it resembles another plate in the series, *Les précautions* (Bocher 1349), but the draftsmanship resembles that of an artist such as Fragonard more than Moreau.

9. Paris 1985, under nos. 67, 74, 92, 95. One is reproduced in London 1968, no. 475, fig. 27; and two others (for two separate figures in the same print), in a sale catalogue for Drouot, Paris, June 14-15, 1956, nos. 58-59.

10. Different examples and types of drawings for printmaking are illustrated in David P. Becker, *Drawings for Book Illustration – The Hofer Collection* (Cambridge: The Houghton Library, Harvard University, 1980); and Braunschweig 1987.

Valentine Green

Worcestershire 1739-1813 London
after Sir Joshua Reynolds (1723-1792)

108. Mary Isabella, Duchess of Rutland 1780.

Plate from *Beauties of the Present Age.*
Mezzotint on antique laid paper, 63.5 x 38.7 cm (platemark).
Sm. 115 i/iii.
Scratched in plate in lower left margin: *Painted by Sir Joshua Reynolds*; lower right: *Engrav'd by V. Green Mezzotinto Engraver to his Majesty & to the Elector Palatine*; lower center: *Publish'd July 1st 1780 by V. Green No 29 Newman Street, Oxford Street.*
Provenance: (Purchased from M. Knoedler, New York, September 21, 1936, for $1,750).
Bequest of Herbert Greer French, 1943.463.
Exhibitions: Cincinnati 1941, no. 189.

The importance of the mezzotint school in England during the first quarter of the eighteenth century owed much to Sir Godfrey Kneller, the most copied portrait painter prior to the arrival of Sir Joshua Reynolds. After Kneller's death in 1723, very few mezzotints were produced, and the craft suffered a serious decline that lasted almost thirty years. This lack of competition eventually encouraged James McArdell, Richard Houston, and other Irish mezzotint engravers to begin emigrating from Dublin to London in 1747.[1] At the same time, the emergence of a number of new British painters, such as Francis Cotes and Joshua Reynolds, increased the demand for engravers to reproduce their work. McArdell's first mezzotints after Reynolds in 1754 opened the door to what has commonly been referred to as the great age of the portrait mezzotint.

By 1770 the monopoly held by the Irish was finally being challenged by many young and extremely skillful British mezzotint engravers. The most ambitious among them was Valentine Green. The son of a dancing master, Green was born in Salford near Evesham in 1739. He began his career as an apprentice to William Phillips, the Evesham town clerk, but left Phillips after two years and without his father's approval to train with the potter and line engraver Robert Hancock. Learning the rudiments of mezzotint from Hancock and devoting himself to perfecting the craft, Green arrived in London in 1765 as an accomplished mezzotint engraver. His early work, devoted primarily to historical plates after Joseph Wright of Derby and the American painter Benjamin West, obviously served him well. In 1767 Green was elected a fellow of the Incorporated Society of Artists. Six years later, he received an appointment as mezzotint engraver to George III and became one of six associate engravers of the Royal Academy the following year. Green was also made mezzotint engraver to Charles Theodore, elector palatine of the Rhine, in 1775.[2]

Valentine Green's best-known work, however, came from his association with Sir Joshua Reynolds after 1778. Based on the success of John Faber's *Beauties at Hampton Court of 1690-91* after Sir Godfrey Kneller, Green developed a plan to produce a similar portfolio with reproductive prints of Reynolds' full-length portraits of women. After getting the painter's approval, he proposed a series of six plates titled *Beauties of the Present Age* and even offered to extend the number in accordance with public demand. As a result, the completed series included nine portrait mezzotints that Green offered to subscribers for twelve shillings per print; fifteen to the general public.

The Museum's striking impression of *Mary Isabella, Duchess of Rutland*,[3] a first-state scratched letter proof, was published in 1780 and is one of the first six images in Green's original proposal.[4] The

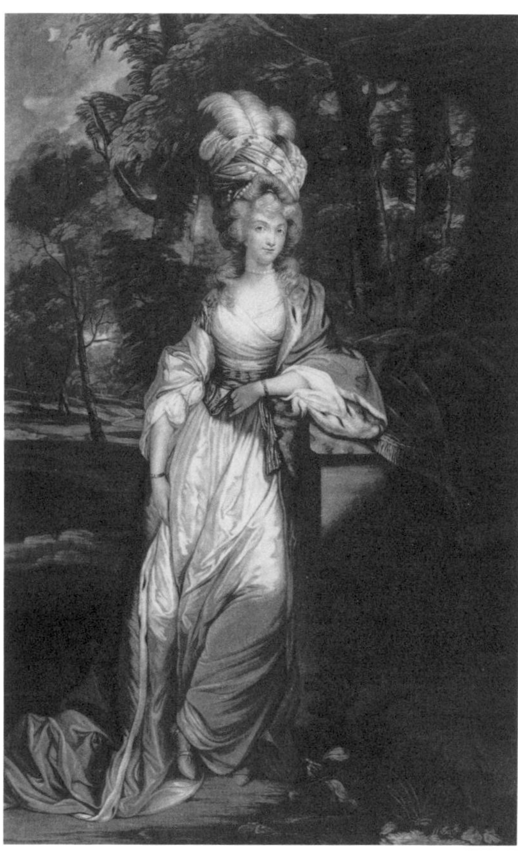

Figure 108-1. Valentine Green (?), *Frederica Charlotta, Duchess of York 1793* (reworked portrait of Mary Isabella, Duchess of Rutland), 1793, mezzotint. Print Collection, The New York Public Library.

print portrays the youngest daughter of Charles, fourth duke of Beaufort, who was also the wife of Charles, fourth duke of Rutland, leaning gently against a rectangular pedestal, her tall, slender frame poised before a wooded landscape. "The beautiful duchess," as she was often called, is adorned in an elegant long flowing gown, a decorative muslin kerchief, and an exquisite high headdress with feathers. Green created the soft and delicate effect of his ground by characteristically rocking the plate in many different directions with a finely toothed tool. Together with the precision and refinement of his scraping technique, the *Duchess of Rutland* is an excellent example of the high quality Green consistently maintained throughout the production of his prints.

Maintaining these standards was not often easy. Because the burr of the mezzotint plate tends to wear down with each subsequent printing, the artist had the somewhat difficult job of reconditioning the plate as it began to lose contrast. However, because this process was much easier to accomplish in mezzotint than in engraving, the practice of altering portions of the mezzotint plate became a common one.[5] Thirteen years after the *Duchess of Rutland* was published, the plate went through a third state in which the engraver, presumably Green, changed the image of the figure from Mary Isabella to Frederica Charlotte, duchess of York (fig. 108-1). In addition to the obvious alterations made to the face and hair, Green used a delicate and expert hand to rescrape the bodice and dress up the figure with bracelets and pearls. As Carol Wax notes:

> The skill with which the transformation was made is even more impressive when one considers that the *Duchess of Rutland* was an extremely popular image and that the number of impressions printed from the plate would have worn the ground, thus exacerbating the difficulty of regrounding areas so that the fresher burrs would not be conspicuous.[6]

By the end of the 1780s, Green had become extremely successful and was able to hire many assistants and travel to such places as Flanders, Germany, and Holland. However, he became involved in an elaborate enterprise that unfortunately proved to be his financial downfall. In 1789 the duke of Bavaria gave Green and his son, Rupert, permission "to Engage and Publish Prints from all, or any of the Pictures in the Gallery at Dusseldorf to their own use and benefit at their own risk and expence."[7] Taking on the financial responsibilities themselves, the Greens commissioned a group of artists to copy the paintings. In 1793 fourteen of the completed mezzotints were exhibited in Spring Gardens, London. Public response was disappointing and the future of the project looked precarious at best. Green perservered, nonetheless, until French forces destroyed the Düsseldorf gallery in 1798 during Napoleon's campaign against Austria. Although three-fourths of the paintings had already been reproduced, the final demise of the project was due in part to Green's own miscalculations of the financial risks involved.

Green never fully recovered from the Düsseldorf incident, and his son's death in 1804 devastated him even further. Despite the fame and notoriety he received throughout his career as one of the masters of mezzotint engraving, Valentine Green was nearly bankrupt when he died in 1813. – DK

1. This group included Charles Spooner, Richard Purcell, Edward Fisher, and later James Watson and John Dixon. See Wax, 42.

2. In addition to being an artist and draftsman, Green was also a dedicated historian. He authored a book in 1764 called *Survey of the City of Worcester* that included sixteen illustrations (ten of which were original designs by Green) engraved by his former master, Robert Hancock. By 1775 Green was an elected member of the Society of Antiquaries. See Wax, 47.

3. Sir Joshua Reynolds' painting of the duchess of Rutland was exhibited at the Royal Academy in 1781. Twenty-five years later it was destroyed in a fire at Belvoir Castle. See Ellis K. Waterhouse, *Reynolds* (Boston: Boston Book and Art Shop, 1955), 72.

4. Based on the pricing in Alfred Whitman, *British Mezzotinters: Valentine Green* (London: A.H. Bullen, 1902), 74-94, the first six prints in Green's proposal included *Lady Elizabeth Delme with Two Children* (1779); *Lady Jane Halliday* (1779); *Lady Louisa Manners* (1779); *Jane (Fleming), Countess of Harrington* (1780); *Georgiana (Spencer), Duchess of Devonshire* (1780); and *Mary Isabella (Somerset), Duchess of Rutland* (1780). *Ann (Montgomery), Viscountess Townshend* (1780); *Lady Elizabeth Compton* (1781); and *Mary Amelia (Hill), Countess of Salisbury* (1781) were the three plates added later.

5. For a detailed description of the altered mezzotint and how it was produced, see Wax, 70-1, 233-39.

6. Wax, 234. According to Wax, some of the tone was also restored with drypoint stippling. The bracelets were added with small rockers or roulettes and with drypoint.

7. Whitman, *British Mezzotinters*, 17.

John Raphael Smith

Derby 1752-1812 London
after Sir Joshua Reynolds (1723-1792)

109. Lieutenant Colonel Sir Banastre Tarleton 1782.

Mezzotint on antique laid paper, 64.2 x 39.5 cm (platemark).
Sm. 161 i/iii.
Watermark: T[well-house]DUPUY FIN/AUVERGNE 1742.
Scratched in plate lower left margin: *Painted by S. Joshua Reynolds/ Published Octr 11 1782 by J R Smith N. 23*; lower center: *Col. Tarleton*; lower right: *Engraved by J R Smith / opposite the Pantheon Oxford Street London.*
Provenance: Fritz Reiss (Lugt 2178); (purchased from M. Knoedler, New York, September 21, 1936, for $1,100).
Bequest of Herbert Greer French, 1943.481.
Exhibitions: Cincinnati 1941, no. 194.

John Raphael Smith was an expert painter, an important print dealer, and quite possibly the finest mezzotint engraver of his time. Because he rejected any artistic guidance from his father, the landscape painter Thomas Smith of Derby, John Raphael was apprenticed to a linen draper when he was ten. After his father died in 1767, Smith traveled to London where he attempted to earn a living by "scraping" mezzotints. Although initial response from print dealers was enthusiastic, he inevitably was forced to support himself by working in a linen shop. The neoclassical painter Angelica Kauffmann visited the shop and showed enthusiastic support for Smith's art. With Kauffmann's help, he was introduced to members of the London print community. Shortly thereafter, Smith handed the linen business over to his wife, purchased a print shop just down the street, and decided to pursue a full-time career in painting and printmaking. By 1775 exhibitions of his mezzotints after Thomas Gainsborough, Benjamin West, and especially Sir Joshua Reynolds at the Society of Artists had established Smith's name in the art world. Although probably best known for his translations of Reynolds' paintings, Smith understood the economic advantages of working from other models and, therefore, produced plates after James Barry, Sir Thomas Lawrence, George Romney, Francis Wheatley, Joseph Wright of Derby, and Johann Zoffany as well as his good friend George Morland.

John Raphael Smith was a very smart and congenial businessman, a prodigious worker, and a jack-of-all-trades. Not only did he receive substantial fame as a mezzotint engraver, Smith was also quite adept at painting and pastel portraiture. His popularity as a print dealer and publisher enabled him to bring in William and James Ward, John Young, Charles Howard Hodges, and other pupils to assist him in the studio and further increase his output. Smith's success had much to do with his willingness as well as his ability to adapt to the latest trends. When the market called for color, Smith had no problems selling tinted versions of his own prints. Both J. M. W. Turner and Thomas Girtin, in fact, were part of Smith's color production line early in their careers. Production of plates with idealized, sentimental subject matter began as quickly as the so-called "fancy" prints became fashionable in the late eighteenth century. Unlike Valentine Green, who proved to be somewhat of a purist when it came to printmaking, Smith altered his grounding techniques for greater flexibility and incorporated the stipple technique whenever it proved more advantageous.[1]

During the 1780s, Smith reached his creative peak, having perfected both the technical as well as aesthetic aspects of the mezzotint process. One of his masterpieces during this period was *Lieutenant Colonel Sir Banastre Tarleton*, after Sir Joshua Reynolds.[2] Born in 1754, Tarleton was the third son of John Tarleton, Esq., mayor of Liverpool. He traveled to America with Lord Cornwallis in 1776 and was with him at the surrender at Yorktown. Although considered one of the heroes of the American Revolution, Tarleton's apparent inclination toward cruelty severely damaged his reputation. In May 1780 Colonel Buford's regiment, which had begun its retreat to Virginia, was pursued and slaughtered by Tarleton. Throughout the Revolution, the term "Tarleton's quarter" became synonymous with wholesale butchery. Nonetheless, the lieutenant colonel was extremely popular when he returned to England, and his portrait was painted by a number of artists, including Reynolds and Gainsborough.

With expert handling of the mezzotint rocker and scraping tools, Smith exhibited in the Museum's outstanding first state, scratched letter proof impression, a broad spectrum of tones that range from the tenebrious underside of the cannon to the radiant glow of the billowing smoke. In her biography of Smith, Julia Frankau wrote about his painterly manipulation of the plate:

I am struck by his precision and accuracy, by the "quality" – there is no other word to be found for it – that he gets into his plate. . . . It is painting, not engraving, that one finds in "Colonel Tarleton."[3]

Smith portrayed the controversial Tarleton with spirit and vigor. Positioned to display his battle scarred right hand with its several missing fingers, the uniformed figure is surrounded by the accoutrements of combat: a sword, cannons, and two horses being restrained by a groom. For dramatic effect, the flag of the loyalist American Legion can be seen waving violently in the background. William Carey wrote in 1827 that Sir Joshua Reynolds praised the print, maintaining that "It has everything but the colour of my picture."[4] The success of *Lieutenant Colonel Tarleton* was a primary reason for Smith's appointment as mezzotint engraver to the Prince of Wales in 1784.

Smith ran into severe financial difficulties late in his career. Much of this problem has often been blamed on his tendency to overindulge in drink and gambling. The actual reason, however, appears to have been politically motivated. A good portion of Smith's profit came from the exportation of shiploads of prints to France. When the French Revolution began, his income from this overseas print trade was lost. As a result, Smith changed his artistic focus during the early nineteenth century from printmaking to producing pastels.[5] – DK

1. Wax, 50.

2. Reynolds' painting of Tarleton, the model for Smith's mezzotint, is in the National Gallery, London.

3. Julia Frankau, *John Raphael Smith: His Life and Works* (London: MacMillan and Co., Limited, 1902), 39.

4. Rudolph Ackermann, *Repository of Arts, Literature, Commerce, Manufactures, Fashions and Politics* (1813) 9:52.

5. Wax, 50.

Nicolas de Launay

Paris ca. 1739-1792 Paris
after Jean-Honoré Fragonard (1732-1806)

110. The Swing's Lucky Chances 1782.

Etching on antique laid paper, 54.9 x 43.2 cm (sheet)
L.D. 85 unfinished proof a or b; I.F.F. 1700 223.
Watermark: Indecipherable.
Condition: Trimmed to or just within platemark.
Provenance: G. Mühlbacher, Paris; (his sale Paris, March 1, 1881, lot 332 for FF 1,100); Henri Beraldi, Paris; (his sale Rousseau, Paris, December 12-13, 1927, lot 144, for FF 10,000); Cortlandt F. Bishop (Lugt 2770b); (his sale Anderson Galleries, New York, November 21, 1935, lot 86); (purchased from M. Knoedler, New York, December 16, 1935, for $550).
Bequest of Herbert Greer French, 1943.521.
Exhibitions: Baltimore 1984, no. 88, illus. 255.
References: Henri Beraldi, *Mes estampes* (Lille: Danel, 1884), 41; Henri Beraldi, *Estampes et livres 1872-1892* (Paris: L. Conquet, 1892), 38.

The Swing's Lucky Chances reproduces one of the best-known paintings of the eighteenth century and was itself equally celebrated among print collectors of the period. Writing about the painting, Donald Posner called it "surely the most famous picture of a swinger in the history of art."[1] Now in the Wallace Collection, London, the painting was commissioned from Jean-Honoré Fragonard (cat. 104) in 1767 and was probably finished fairly quickly.[2] The identity of the patron is still not definitively known, but the circumstances of the commission are recorded in some detail; it seems that a certain gentleman wished a painting depicting his mistress being pushed on a swing by a bishop [!], high enough to reveal her skirts to her lover hiding in the bushes underneath her.[3] Fragonard substituted an older man for the bishop; it is not known if the two central figures are actual portraits of the persons involved.

Fragonard's unconventional painting was a decisive step in declaring his independence so quickly after his triumph with a traditional large history painting only two years previously in the Salon of 1765; albeit *The Swing* achieved its own great success at the time for both its technique and its risqué subject matter. Posner has thoroughly described the painting's surface titillations and the underlying symbolism of the rhythmic motions of the swing, the woman's tossing off of her shoe, the statuary, and the lover's outstretched arm holding his flower-filled hat.[4] The print is very faithful to the painting (though in reverse to it), with only the addition of a plume to the woman's hat, probably indicating that De Launay worked from another version of the Wallace Collection painting.[5]

De Launay published this print himself, advertising it in the *Gazette de France* on April 2, 1782. He dedicated it personally to Fragonard, calling himself Fragonard's "very humble and very obedient servant" in an inscription in a later state of the print. De Launay seems to have spent his entire career in Paris, first studying with Louis-Simon Lempereur (1728-1807), another extremely successful reproductive engraver. De Launay was accepted into the Royal Academy in 1777, exhibiting there until the year before his death. He was elected an official member in 1789, and the next year was elected to the Academy of Fine Arts in Denmark. De Launay was employed by many painters of so-called "gallant" subjects, such as Baudouin and Lavreince (see cat. 111) as well as Fragonard, and he engraved many of the most famous book illustrations of the period. H. W. Lawrence described De Launay as "the most eminent engraver of his time," singling out his "almost incredible perfection of technique,. . . no trace of aught that is not light and careless is discernible in the charming frivolity of his expression."[6]

The Museum's impression of *The Swing* is of the very first state, before any inscriptions and before all the complex engraved details that fill the shadows, particularly in the woman's dress, were added. Such early "pure etching" proofs of eighteenth-century line engravings were madly collected by people eager to acquire the rarest items. (These were not so much collected to reveal the artistic working processes, although that aspect is what most intrigues and informs the modern viewer.) Because of the incredible detail in these engravings, printmakers customarily would lay down the entire composition first in the much less time-consuming etching technique, before methodically filling in details with the sharpened engraver's burin. At times, two separate specialists would execute different phases (see cat. 107a, b). Although still quite controlled, the etched lines here betray an easy grace that enlivens the already dense composition. The amazing lushness of the vegetation in Fragonard's painting is well translated by De Launay, who also preserved the subtle, changing values of light that effectively highlight the woman's form emerging from the shadows underneath the trees. While clearly "unfinished," the Museum's proof dazzles the eye with its greater contrasts and the clarity of its printing from such an early state of the plate. In addition to the later inscriptions below the image, which specify the title, the painter, the engraver, and the address of De Launay as the publisher, Pierre Philippe Choffard (1730-1809) designed a sprightly vignette bearing Fragonard's initials below the image.[7] – DPB

1. Donald Posner, "The Swinging Women of Watteau and Fragonard," AB. 64 (1982): 82.

2. John Ingamells, *The Wallace Collection – Catalogue of Pictures III (French before 1815)* (London: Trustees of Wallace Collection, 1989), 161-65, no. P430; Posner, "The Swinging Women," 82, n. 25.

3. Ingamells, *The Wallace Collection*, 163; Posner, "The Swinging Women," 82-83.

4. Posner, "The Swinging Women," 84-88. For a more sarcastic use of the swinging motif in the early nineteenth century, see Goya's late capricho of an old man swinging, datable circa 1824-28 (Boston 1989a, 392-93, no. 179).

5. Ingamells (*The Wallace Collection*, 165) indicates that De Launay's print is engraved after an intermediary drawing by Pierre-Philippe Choffard, who is credited with the design of a vignette later added in the bottom margin of the print. Earlier writers have suggested that De Launay worked after another painted replica of the subject formerly in the Rothschild Collection, which does contain a plume on the woman's hat (I.F.F. 1700 XII:529; Victor Carlson, Baltimore 1984, 254).

6. L.D., xviii.

7. Reproduced in L.D., pl. 13.

Jean-François Janinet

Paris 1752-1814 Paris
after Nicolas Lavreince (1737-1807)

III. The Guitar Player 1788-89.

Color etching and engraving (4 colors) on antique laid paper
35.1 x 27.7 cm (image).
I.F.F 1700 XII.17.25.
Condition: Remargined, including border line and platemark. Small repaired and inpainted losses all corners of plate. Three small repaired tears in plate area.
Provenance: Artist's portfolio until 1878; Greffulhe; Rousseau; Cortlandt F. Bishop (Lugt 2770b); (his sale Anderson Galleries, New York, November 21, 1935, lot 112, illus.); (purchased from M. Knoedler, December 16, 1935, for $4,180).
Bequest of Herbert Greer French, 1943.426.
Exhibitions: Cincinnati 1941, no. 222; Baltimore 1984, no. 94, illus. 267.

Janinet received his first artistic training from his father, a gem engraver, but more relevant to his eventual career as a printmaker was a period of apprenticeship with Louis-Marin Bonnet (cat. 105), which began about 1771. During this apprenticeship, Janinet learned the basics of "crayon-manner" color printmaking techniques. Striking out on his own in 1772, Janinet produced several series of standard chalk-manner prints for artists' drawing manuals, but he soon began to search for ways to reproduce the transparent effects of watercolor washes. He invented his own engraving tools and refined a way to control the registration necessary to print multiple plates for a composite color image. During 1774 he collaborated with Bonnet once again in developing ways to print gold ink, although it was necessary to conceal their use of strictly regulated gold leaf from the authorities.[1] Gold ink was used for the borders of prints and as highlights over other colors.

Janinet's highly successful imitation of the effects of watercolor and gouache washes (his so-called "lavis" manner) has been referred to in the literature as color aquatint. John Ittmann emphasizes that the effects which resemble aquatint in Janinet's most famous multiple-plate color prints were achieved by the hand application of engraving tools. Tools with dense clusters of fine points (called *mattoirs*) were used to create "delicately textured surfaces capable of catching just enough ink to print in filmy layers of color."[2] He used etching only to lay down the outlines of his compositions quickly, before filling in tonal areas of color.

Janinet used his consummate color printing skills to engrave prints after compositions by some fifty artists, including genre subjects, landscapes, topographical views, and portraits. As in many other cases, his work reflects the abrupt changes that the revolutionary period brought to artistic taste and employment. After establishing his reputation during the late 1770s and 1780s by engraving fashion plates and "gallant" subjects (including a very gaudy portrait of Marie Antoinette in 1777),[3] Janinet altered his style, producing severe neoclassical compositions and a patriotic series of fifty-two plates illustrating the *Principal Events since the Opening of the Estates-General* (1789-91). He also executed many prints of topographical views of Paris, including many valuable records of public and private architecture of the time.[4]

Together with his productive printmaking career, Janinet's biography is noted for one spectacular misadventure involving the attempted launching of an air-balloon from the Luxembourg Gardens on July 11, 1784. When the craft burst into flames before getting off the ground, the infuriated crowd, who had paid admission to witness the event, forced Janinet and his collaborator hastily to flee the scene. This mishap provided much satirical material for weeks afterward (I.F.F. 1700 XII:3). During the ensuing period, Janinet produced his most sophisticated color prints, including *The Guitar Player*.

One of the great treasures of Mr. French's eighteenth-century French print collection, both in terms of rarity and technical finesse, *The Guitar Player* is one of but four known impressions. Never published by Janinet and unknown to early cataloguers, all four impressions were discovered together in 1878 in a portfolio of works from his studio that had remained intact (I.F.F. 1700 XII:18). The Bibliothèque Nationale, Paris, owns one impression printed in color and one proof printed only in black; one other color impression is in the Widener Collection, National Gallery of Art, Washington.[5] None of the known impressions carries a printed inscription. Ittmann surmises that publication of the print was prevented by the outbreak of the Revolution: he dates its preparation to late 1788 or early 1789.[6]

The Guitar Player reproduces a painting by Niclas Lafrensen, a Swedish-born painter (known in France as Nicolas Lavreince) of society genre (i.e., bedroom) subjects and a resident of Paris until 1791, when he returned to Sweden.[7] It most probably belongs with a group of three other similar subjects engraved by Janinet after Lavreince: *The Comparison*, 1786 (I.F.F. 1700 20); *The Embarrassing Confession*, 1787 (I.F.F. 1700 24); and *The Indiscretion*, 1788 (I.F.F. 1700 28).[8] All are of comparable format and very similar subject matter, involving titillating scenes of women exchanging confessions, reading love notes, and comparing breasts(!).

The subject of the Museum's image is perhaps a bit more discreet on the surface but certainly amenable to indelicate interpretation. With her boudoir and dress in some disarray, a young woman is seen playing a guitar. She looks down at her two spaniels, who sit glowering (somewhat suggestively) in an armchair. The atmosphere suggests the glow from a just-concluded sexual rendezvous. The statue on the mantelpiece has been identified as a Venus by Jean-Marie Marin (1759-1834).[9]

The technical accomplishments in Janinet's print actually threaten to overwhelm all iconographic and aesthetic readings of the image. One can only imagine what enthusiastic commentaries would surround this print if it had appeared at the time it was executed. The shimmering surface of the woman's dress dominates the print. Janinet managed to reproduce the *moiré* effect of its silk fabric (the green palette is shot through with a reddish brown reflective layer underneath). In a continual effort to reproduce the qualities of drawings before the advent of photography, Janinet's achievement is truly remarkable and eminently adapted to the genre after which he was working.

Mr. French's enthusiasm for Janinet's place within eighteenth-century color printmaking led him to acquire five other Janinet prints, including another pair after Lavreince, the undated *Ha! The Pretty Little Dog* and *The Little Word of Advice* (I.F.F. 1700 212, 223) (CAM 1943.430-431).[10] He also acquired two of Janinet's earliest works in his "lavis" manner, a pair of Roman views after Hubert Robert (1733-1808) dated circa 1776, and a portrait of Benjamin Franklin of 1789 (I.F.F. 1700 170, 172, and 58 [CAM 1943.429, .428, .429], respectively).[11] Mr. French had an abiding interest in the evolving techniques of color printing, a category of prints that has suffered extremes in taste and market value; however, even while collecting at the top of the market, Mr. French was able to assemble a remarkable group of prints illustrating the history of the medium. This impression of *The Guitar Player* came from the Cortlandt F. Bishop Collection, famous for its eighteenth-century French prints and books.[12] – DPB

1. See John Ittmann, Baltimore 1984, nos. 65-66, for a discussion of printing with gold leaf and its attendant legal problems.

2. Baltimore 1984, 258, no. 90. Ittmann notes that in rare instances Janinet may have used aquatint in a few monochrome prints. His multiple-plate color prints are so effective that they require extremely close inspection, often under magnification, to determine their exact media. The practical use of aquatint had been developed in France only very recently, during the 1760s (Ittmann, Baltimore 1984, 188-90, nos. 60-61); see also Antony Griffiths, "Note on Early Aquatint in England and France," PQ. 4, no. 3 (September 1987): 257, n. 11, where he quotes the studio inventory of the contemporary printmaker Laurent Guyot (1756-1808) as containing twenty-three roulettes and 157 "*champignons pour le lavis et le pointillé.*" Literally a mushroom, a *champignon* was a tool resembling one used to make the delicate color "for wash and stippled tone." Griffiths repeats the assertion that the vast majority of the color prints by Bonnet, Janinet, and Debucourt that have been described as aquatints are, in fact, not. For classic instances of aquatint in the present exhibition, see Goya (cats. 116, 119) and Delacroix (cat. 120).

3. Illustrated in Baltimore 1984, 205, no. 66.

4. Janinet has never had a monographic catalogue of his prints. The fullest listing, with a biography, is contained in I.F.F. 1700 XII:1-94, which includes prints *not* in the Bibliothèque Nationale.

5. Ittmann, Baltimore 1984, 266, n. 1.

6. Ittmann, Baltimore 1984, 266, n. 4.

7. For a list of over sixty prints by various artists after Lavreince, see Emmanuel Bocher, *Nicolas Lavreince*, vol. 1 of *Les gravures françaises du xviiiᵉ siècle* (Paris: Librairie des Bibliophiles, 1875).

8. *The Embarrassing Confession* is illustrated in Baltimore 1984, 264-65, no. 93.

9. [Edward Clayton] *French Engravings of the Eighteenth Century in the Collection of Joseph Widener, Lynnewood Hall* (London: Chiswick Press, 1923), 307.

10. The latter is illustrated in Loys Delteil, "Jean-François Janinet," *P. Conn.* 2, no. 2 (December 1921): 157.

11. The Cincinnati impression of one of the Roman views (I.F.F. 1700 172) (CAM 1943.428) is illustrated in Baltimore 1984, 258-59, no. 90.

12. An indication of its perceived value and rarity at the time of Mr. French's purchase is given by the fact that it was reproduced in color as the frontispiece for the Bishop sale catalogue, Anderson Art Galleries, New York, November 21, 1935. For Bishop, see cat. 115, n. 10.

William Blake

London, 1757-1827 London

Songs of Innocence ca. 1789.

Twenty-eight hand-colored relief etchings (Bentley copy S, ca. 1808).

112a. Title Page (plate 2).

Hand-colored relief etching on wove paper 12.1 x 7.4 cm. (platemark).
Binyon 182 (1943.559.2).
Numbered with pen and ink upper right margin: 2; inscribed, dated,

and signed in plate: SONGS / *of / Innocence / 1789 / The Author & Printer W. Blake.*

112b. Laughing Song (plate 14).

Hand-colored relief etching 11.1 x 6.6 cm (platemark).
Binyon 194 (1943.559.14).
Numbered with pen and ink upper right margin: *14*; printed center: *Laughing Song.*
Provenance: Probably T.F. Dibdin?; (purchased by Bernard Quartich, London, June 1920, his sale catalogue December 1920 for £350 [without plate 2] and again March 1922, lot 108, for £400); Mrs. Phoebe A.D. Boyle, 1923; (her sale, Anderson Galleries, New York, November 19, 1923, lot 46, for $1,100, to G.D. Smith); G.C. Smith, Jr., 1927; (his sale Parke-Bernet, New York, November 2, 1928, lot 16, for $2,300, to Gannon); (Scribner's Rare Book Department to Roullier, ca. 1941); (purchased from Albert Roullier, Chicago, January 21, 1941, for $3,960).
Bequest of Herbert Greer French, 1943.559.1-28.
Exhibitions: Cambridge, Mass., 1930, no. 2.
References: John E. Grant and Mary Lynn Johnson, "Illuminated Books in the Cincinnati Art Museum," *Blake Newsletter* 26, (Fall 1973) 41.

In *Songs of Innocence*,[1] Blake gave the pastoral mode, one of the great traditions of English verse, a new direction and vision. His achievement, according to David Bindman, "was to endow the pastoral genre with some of the Neo-Platonic elevation it had enjoyed in the Renaissance, but of which little survived by the end of the eighteenth century."[2] The elements of nature became "symbols of Innocence," a state of being that Blake could especially identify with childhood.[3]

In February 1787, Blake became emotionally distressed over the tragic loss of his younger brother Robert. At the time of Robert's death, Blake had been searching for a way to combine his illustrations and poetry together on a single copperplate. Shortly thereafter, the problem was resolved with guidance apparently coming from Robert's spirit. J. T. Smith, who knew both brothers personally, recorded what he knew of the discovery:

> Blake, after deeply perplexing himself as to the mode of accomplishing the publication of his illustrated songs, without their being subject to the expense of letterpress, his brother Robert stood before him in one of his visionary imaginations, and so decidedly directed him in the way in which he ought to proceed that he immediately followed his advice.[4]

In truth, Blake's moment of inspiration may have actually resulted from the print he was working on. Known as *The Approach of Doom*, the composition, significantly enough, was based on a design created by his brother. He began by engraving the plate in the traditional manner, but later relief-etched the central section, allowing the engraved area to print in white line. In a prospectus given in 1793, Blake made "large claims" about inventing the process, and although relief printing itself dates back to the early eighteenth century,[5] the idea of printing an etched plate containing both design and text from a relief surface rather than intaglio was clearly his own.

One of five children, William Blake was born in the Carnaby Market area of London in 1757. At age ten, he was enrolled by his father, James, a hosier by profession, into Henry Pars' drawing school for industrial designers. Four months before his fifteenth birthday, Blake began a seven-year apprenticeship with James Basire, engraver to the Society of Antiquaries and the Royal Society of the Arts, who worked in an old-fashioned linear manner.[6] During his apprenticeship with Basire, Blake was sent to make drawings at Westminster Abbey, where he quickly developed a love for Gothic art. Throughout the 1780s, Blake earned a living as a reproductive engraver, producing numerous plates after the neoclassical book illustrations of Thomas Stothard, as well as developing a small but loyal following for his poetry. With the publication of his art in mind, he ventured into the publishing business with James Walker, a friend from the Basire workshop. When the company failed shortly thereafter, Blake began his search for an economic way to bypass letterpress and print both text and design together.

After his discovery and three rather unsatisfactory experiments with the new relief process, Blake was far more successful with the printing of *Songs of Innocence*,[7] a collection of verses pertaining to childhood innocence that is filled with symbolic references to a higher, more spiritual plane. According to Blake, "Christ is ever present in childhood, so He is present in the text and design of the *Songs*."[8] As his perception of the songs continued to change over the years, so did the order, number, and hand-coloring of the plates.[9] For this reason, Blake/'s original plan for mass-producing the books was unsuccessful. Moreover, his meticulous handling of each plate has often been likened to that of a medieval illuminator. Blake was no doubt inspired by the illuminated manuscripts he had an opportunity to view at Westminster Abbey.

The Museum's *Songs of Innocence*, which has been identified as copy S,[10] contains twenty-eight pages that were printed on wove paper primarily in shades of brown, gray, and black. The watermark "J WHATMAN/1808" is visible on the verso of *Infant Joy* (plate 25).[11] Although a frontispiece was originally included when the Museum's copy was published, the current plate, because of its smaller size, dissimilar stitch-holes, and muddied color, appears to have come from another source.[12] The layering of paint throughout the remaining plates is rather heavy, which is not uncommon for those copies that Blake printed in the early nineteenth century. In the *Title Page* (plate 2), for example, the entire image area has been hand colored with various shades of blue, yellow, green, orange, pink, and brown. Blake reinforced the border along with most of the objects and type with outline, while painting over the white-line striations of the figures and chair, the landscape, and the flamelike forms coming from "Songs" to make them barely visible. As a subtle decorative touch, the stump of the tree and its branches, the words "of" and "Innocence," and the area with Blake's "Author & Printer" identification have been gilded with a metallic pigment.

The *Title Page* consists of a seated adult (possibly a mother or nurse) with an open book on her lap that she is showing to two children. Many of the compositional motifs included in the *Songs* were based on a number of children's books with which Blake was familiar from his years as a copy engraver. This particular arrangement, in fact, is very similar to the illustration found on the frontispiece of John Newbery's *A Little Pretty-Pocket Book, Intended for the Instruction and Amusement of Little Master Tommy, and Pretty Miss Polly*, published in 1767.[13] Likewise, the configuration of adult, book, and two children can also be found in several illustrated books from the same period by the brothers Bewick.

To the right of the three figures, a spiraling vine climbs up the trunk of an apple tree, a motif that also appears in John Huddlestone Wynne's 1772 publication *Choice Emblems. . . for the Improvement and Pastime of Youth*. In the Museum's copy, Blake, in what may have been a moment of whimsy, has reversed the direction of the spiral by painting over the printed line to make the vine go counterclockwise.[14] The tree branches extend upward, taking on the appearance of flames that flow out of and surround the word "SONGS."[15] In keeping with the childhood theme, tiny human figures

have been placed in playful if not allegorical poses on several of the letters, to watch and/or possibly guide the innocent children as they begin their fall into Experience.

The pastoral scene Blake created for *Laughing Song*, plate 14 in the Museum's copy S version of *Songs of Innocence*,[16] consists of seven youths (six girls and one boy) seated around a table in an arbor.[17] The boy, standing in the center with his back to the viewer, holds a goblet in his right hand and a plumed hat in his left. In the Museum's plate, a layering of wash covers the entire scene with colors that are appropriately festive for the occasion. The shades of bright orange worn by the boy and the blue, pink, and green dresses of the young girls are set against a background of yellow-green trees and bushes that themselves are surrounded by hints of a blue-gray and pink sky. Blake was apparently fond of this symmetrically arranged composition. It was based on an engraving that he had made after Thomas Stothard for "Drinking Songs, Song I" from Joseph Ritson's *A Select Collection of English Songs* of 1783. Although the central figure in the print is seated facing front, the most obvious similarities between the two engravings include the plumed hat and elevated glass. Furthermore, the poses of the remaining members of the group are almost exact and, in some cases, indicate a direct borrowing for *Songs of Innocence*.[18] In 1796 he duplicated the general design again, this time in watercolor, as the 479th (out of 537) illustration produced for Edward Young's *Night Thoughts*. This version includes a number of angels that were added to the joyous gathering.[19]

In the margins surrounding the type, Blake added several spiraling vines and a variety of birds, while delicately coloring the space in pink, orange, and yellow. The use of marginal decoration was a pattern often found in illuminated books and may have been the inspiration for their inclusion in *Songs of Innocence*. While the color of the birds in the Museum's *Laughing Song* is generally the same (orange bodies with blue wings), their basic shapes have been identified by David Erdman, although somewhat conjecturally, as swallows (to the left and right of the title and above the vine in the lower left corner), a crane or swan (above "Song"), birds of paradise (flying, diving, and perching at the bottom center), an eagle, lapwing, and a dove (all three in the bottom right corner). Interestingly enough, one of the small winged objects found after the verse "painted birds laugh in the shade" is a common housefly, a motif used by Blake to symbolize his sympathy for the helpless.[20] – DK

1. Mr. French collected a number of books by William Blake. Along with *Songs of Innocence*, the list includes *Illustrations of the Book of Job* (cat. 121), proof impressions for *Thornton's Pastoral of Virgil* (CAM 1943.580), *Thornton's Pastoral of Virgil*, Volume I (CAM 1943.561), *Thornton's Pastoral of Virgil*, Volume II (CAM 1943.579), and *Young's Night Thoughts* (CAM 1943.560).

2. David Bindman, *Blake as an Artist* (Oxford): Phaidon Press Limited, 1977), 58.

3. S. Foster Damon, *William Blake: His Philosophy and Symbols* (Boston: Houghton Mifflin Company, 1924), 39-42.

4. As quoted in Bindman, 14.

5. Bindman, 14. Blake was not alone in his experimentation with printing processes. For a discussion on some of the other experiments see Bindman, *Blake as an Artist*, 41-43.

6. According to Albert Boime, it is most likely that, by sending his son to Pars' school and having him work with Basire, Blake's father "had hoped to reap some benefit from this course of action beyond gratifying his son's ambition to become an artist; an industrial designer and engraver could have served a useful function in the hosiery business." See Albert Boime, "William Blake's Graphic Imagery and the Industrial Revolution," *Arts Magazine* 59 (June 1985): 110.

7. *Songs of Innocence*, first published as a separate work in 1789, was combined with *Songs of Experience* in 1794.

8. Bindman, *Blake as an Artist*, 60.

9. Bindman, *Blake as an Artist*, 474. Some of the plates alternate between *Innocence* and *Experience*. Blake eventually fixed the order of *Innocence* in the 1820s.

10. John E. Grant and Mary Lynn Johnson, "Illuminated Books in the Cincinnati Art Museum," *Blake Newsletter* 26 (Fall 1973): 41, 43.

11. Fragments of the "J WHATMAN" watermark appear on *The Little Black Boy* (plate 8) and *A Cradle Song* (plate 15).

12. Grant and Johnson, "Illuminated Books," 41.

13. Essick, 138.

14. The vine on the tree of *The Little Black Boy* (plate 8) was also reversed, this time making it go clockwise.

15. In some copies, these forms were painted green and resemble plant leaves.

16. Grant and Johnson, "Illuminated Books," 41.

17. Blake sometimes eliminated or obscured the third figure from the left, as is the case in *Laughing Song* in the second copy S version of *Songs of Innocence and of Experience* in the Museum's collection (CAM 1969.509).

18. Essick, 139.

19. Damon, *Philosophy and Symbols*, 214, 272.

20. David V. Erdman, *The Illuminated Blake* (London: Oxford University Press, 1975), 56.

Louis le Coeur

Paris active ca. 1784-1823 Paris
after Jacques-François-Joseph Swebach called Swebach-Desfontaines (1769-1823)

113. The Bastille Ball 1790.

Color etching and engraving on antique laid paper, 40.3 x 32.0 cm (platemark).

I.F.F. 1700 XIII.471.16.

Inscribed in plate below image lower left: *Swebach Desfontaines del.*; lower right: *Le Coeur sculp.*; lower center: BAL DE LA BASTILLE / *Ce fut précisément sur les ruines de cet affreux monument du despotisme que le Français célébra le premier anniversaire de la liberté. La / célérité des préparatifs de cette fête dut etonner sans doute, mais comment exprimer le sentiment qu'on éprouvait en lisant cette inscription: / Ici l'on danse. / A Paris, chez l'Auteur, rue St. Jacques, No. 55.*
Provenance: (Purchased from M. Knoedler, New York, October 11, 1937, for $300).
Bequest of Herbert Greer French, 1943.433.
Exhibitions: Cincinnati 1941, no. 228.

Little biographical information is known of Le Coeur. He is assumed to have been born in the second half of the eighteenth century, and the period of his greatest activity in Paris was from 1784 to 1815. He is traditionally thought to have studied printmaking with Debucourt (cat. 115), although Ittmann points out that Le Coeur had already produced several color prints before Debucourt began making prints in 1785.[1] In addition to his direct printmaking activities, Le Coeur also published his own prints. He engraved primarily compositions after other artists, including portraits, topographical views, "gallant" subjects, and, as *The Bastille Ball* illustrates, a small number of topical scenes from the period of the French Revolution.[2]

This unusual nighttime view is one of a pair of prints Le Coeur produced in connection with the Festival of the Federation held in Paris on July 14, 1790. The festival commemorated both the first anniversary of the fall of the Bastille and the establishment of the National Federation. Both prints reproduce compositions by Jacques-François-Joseph Swebach, often called Swebach-Desfontaines, a painter of landscapes, battles, and genre scenes. Originally from Metz, Swebach worked primarily in Paris and was an active chronicler of revolutionary and Napoleonic history. He later became painter to the imperial porcelain manufacturer at Sèvres.

One of the pair commemorates the grandest and most massive event that occurred during the festival on the Champ de Mars on July 14, 1790, when over three hundred thousand spectators witnessed the marquis de Lafayette (1757-1834) pronounce the oath of the National Federation in front of the king and representatives of the eighty-three counties of France. Le Coeur's print of the ceremony records the crowds and the triumphal arch and altar, which were built on very short notice for this occasion.[3]

The Bastille Ball, Le Coeur's other print from the pair, is a view of the grand ball held as part of the three-day-long festivities on the ruins of the infamous prison. The inscription on the print translates: "Bastille Ball. It was precisely on the ruins of that frightful monument of despotism that the French celebrated the first anniversary of liberty. The swiftness of the preparations for this festival no doubt were astonishing, but how to express the feeling experienced upon reading this inscription: Here one dances."

The ball took place on the leveled ruins of the Bastille, a vast terrace surrounded by a ring of trees – eighty-three in all – each carrying a plaque with the name of a French county. Le Coeur's print seems to very accurately reflect the decorations for the ball, given several contemporary accounts. Strings of lanterns, the aspect of the decor most evident in Le Coeur's print, are suspended between the trees. The foundations of eight projecting towers are each fashioned into leafy bowers sheltering small cafés; in the center stands a platform for musicians. On the top of this platform, a huge pole that had actually been used as a battering ram in the assault the year before supports a tent, from which a banner with the word "Liberty" is hung. Suspended above the entrance to the ball appeared an inscription – "Here one dances (*Ici l'on danse*)" – whose irony and poignancy struck every visitor and commentator.[4]

The joyous yet peaceful spirit of the vast crowds was also remarked upon, considering the massive crush of visitors from all over the country who no doubt strained the city's hospitality. These manifestations of good feeling admirably fit the often-expressed purpose of the celebrations for the new "federation": they were an attempt to forge a new unity and a spirit of partnership between the national capital and government with the people in outlying departments.[5]

Le Coeur's print of the ball is an intriguing object both technically and compositionally. The print is striking for the sobriety of its treatment and color. The viewer stands at some distance from the dancers, not in the midst of the revelers nor far enough back to take in a panoramic view of the entire scene. One needs to look very closely to distinguish the celebrants, themselves dressed in restrained fashions when compared to the styles witnessed at such balls a few years previously. Almost half of Le Coeur's print is covered with tonalities of very dark green and black, colors which are difficult to achieve without becoming very muddy. The upper half of the print is distinctively energized by decorative garlands of illuminated lanterns. The contemporary engraver Johann-Georg Wille (1715-1808) declared in his memoirs that "a great number of prints represented this ball, and [Le Coeur's was] certainly the most original and picturesque."[6] A contemporary anonymous print shows the ball decorations from a further distance, silhouetting the entire edifice of trees and bowers and forming an echo, or shadow, of the solid stone fortress that had once stood there.[7] Mr. French acquired one other Le Coeur color print, *Le Colin-Maillard*, or *Blindman's Buff* (I.F.F. 1700 31) (CAM 1943.432), a much more typical "gallant" subject. – DPB

1. John Ittmann in Baltimore 1984, 282.

2. The most complete list of Le Coeur's prints is contained in I.F.F. 1700 XIII:465-83 and I.F.F. 1800 II:222-24.

3. I.F.F. 1700 XIII:471.17; the inscription reads [in translation] "Federal oath of 14 July 1790. View of the Altar of the Fatherland and part of the Champ de Mars at the instant when M. de la Fayette in the name of all the National Guards of France pronounces the oath to be ever faithful to the Nation, the Law and the King, etc." Le Coeur dedicated his print to Lafayette, "Major-General of the Federation." It is reproduced in Pierrette Jean-Richard and Gilbert Mondin, Paris 1989a, no. 30. For other

views of the Champ de Mars ceremony, see, among others, Werner Hofmann, ed., *Europa 1789* (Cologne: DuMont, 1989), 229-30. A good brief description of the event is in Samuel F. Scott and Barry Rothaus, eds., *Historical Dictionary of the French Revolution* (Westport, Conn.: Greenwood Press, 1985), 1:381-83. See also Richard A. Etlin, "L'Architecture et la fête de la Fédération Paris 1790," in Jean Ehrard and Paul Viallaneix, eds., *Les fêtes de la Révolution – Colloque de Clermont-Ferrand (Juin 1974)* (Paris: Société des Etudes Robespierristes, 1977), 131-54.

4. The origin of the motto is given to the dramatist Jean-Louis Brousse Desfaucherets (1742-1808) in Paris 1989b, 2:412, under no. 532.

5. The above account of the ball is taken from two sources: Georges Duplessis, ed., *Mémoires et Journal de J.-G. Wille*, (Paris: Veuve Jules Renouard, 1857), 2:259, and the profusely illustrated, near-contemporary history of the Revolution, *Collection complète des tableaux historiques de la révolution française* (Paris: Pierre Didot l'Aîné, 1802), 1:161-64.

6. Duplessis, *Mémoires*, 259.

7. Illustrated in color in Hofmann, *Europa 1789*, no. 277, color pl. 20. It is also illustrated in Paris 1989b, vol. 2, no. 533, along with a drawing (no. 532) by Pierre-François Palloy that illustrates all the plaques that adorned the trees at the ball with their inscriptions.

Charles Knight

London 1743-after 1826 London
after **Sir Thomas Lawrence** (1769-1830)

114a. Miss Farren 1791.

Stipple etching on antique laid paper, 55.6 x 35.5 cm (platemark).
Tuer 1662; Vesme & Calabi 1075 i/vi.
Watermark: Dovecote fragment and indecipherable maker's name
Inscribed in plate below image: *T Lawrence Pinxt: C Knight Sculpt: 1791. / Miss Farren /* LONDON Publish'd Feby: 25 1791 by IJEFFRYES Ludgate Hill.
Provenance: (Purchased from M. Knoedler, New York, October 11, 1937, for $325).
Bequest of Herbert Greer French, 1943.475.

Charles Knight

London 1743-after 1826 London

and Francesco Bartolozzi

Florence 1727-1815 Lisbon
after **Sir Thomas Lawrence** (1769-1830)

114b. Miss Farren 1791-92.

Stipple etching and engraving on antique laid paper, 55.6 x 35.5 cm (platemark).
Tuer 1662; Vesme & Calabi 1075 iv/vi.
Watermark: Dovecote and indecipherable maker's mark.
Inscribed in plate below image: *T. Lawrence Pinxt. Publish'd Jany 1. 1792 by Bull & Jeffryes Ludgate Hill London. F. Bartolozzi Sculpt.* R·A·*Engraver to his Majesty.*
Provenance: Arnold Collection; Frederic R. Halsey (Lugt 1308); (his sale Anderson Galleries, New York, Part IV, January 8, 1917, lot 102); (purchased from M. Knoedler, New York, April 18, 1936, for $175).
Bequest of Herbert Greer French, 1943.476.
Exhibitions: Cincinnati 1941, no. 183, pl. 38.

The only serious competition for mezzotint that emerged in England during the second half of the eighteenth century was the stipple print, derived from the "crayon manner" developed in France in the 1750s and 1760s (cat. 105). Stipple prints similarly utilize a technique of building up nonlinear tones by means of a mass of dots and flicks of varying sizes made with customized tools, produced in a combination of etching and engraving. Stippling wasn't used in England to copy slavishly the appearance of chalk drawings as it was

in France, however. More often it was utilized to reproduce watercolors or oils, being very suitable for color printing, usually by daubing different ink colors directly together onto the plate in one application, a method known as *à la poupée*. Stipple prints were very often used as decorative home furnishings, being referred to somewhat disparagingly as "furniture art."[1] The earliest English practitioner of the stipple print was William Wynne Ryland (1733-1783), who trained in Paris in the crayon manner and developed stipple in England after 1774.

The chief exponent of the medium was, in fact, Francesco Bartolozzi. Bartolozzi trained a sizable studio of engravers in the technique. Among his students was Charles Knight. Bartolozzi, the son of a goldsmith, trained at the Florence Academy. He learned engraving there and then apprenticed with the Venetian engraver Joseph Wagner from 1745, executing prints after contemporary masters. He was commissioned to come to England in 1764 to engrave copies of the large collection of Guercino drawings in the royal collection.

Settling in London, Bartolozzi joined the Society of Artists in 1765 and became a founding Royal Academician in 1769 (nominally on his qualifications as a painter, because engravers as yet did not qualify for full membership). He was also appointed official engraver to the king in that year. He established a large business engraving copies after Old Master and contemporary works (especially the works of artists G. B. Cipriani [1727-1785] and Angelica Kauffmann [1740-1807]) and was employed by private collectors and publishers alike. Bartolozzi developed a particular skill in stippling: over twenty-two hundred prints are listed under his name, although quite a few were probably executed by his assistants as is the case here. In 1802 Bartolozzi was summoned by the prince regent of Portugal to be the director of the art academy at Lisbon. He died there in 1815.

Little is known of the life of Charles Knight, who was born in London and spent his entire career there, establishing himself in Hammersmith. After working in Bartolozzi's studio, he practiced on his own for many years, his last dated print being made in his eighty-third year. There is no catalogue of Knight's engraved work, although quite a few prints are cited in Thieme, Becker et al. (ThB. 20:588-89).

The French Collection contains two impressions of this portrait print. The first state was completed and signed by Charles Knight, while presumably in the employ of Bartolozzi; the second Cincinnati impression, dated January 1, 1792, is of the fourth? state, after Knight's name had been effaced and after considerable engraved additions, presumably by Bartolozzi himself, had been made. (Bartolozzi's name appears on this and subsequent states.[2]) Later editions were published in 1797 (on the occasion of Miss Farren's marriage) and in 1806, by which time the plate had considerably weakened.

Elizabeth (or Eliza) Farren was born in Cork, Ireland, about 1759 and became a celebrated actress, appearing first in Bath in 1773. After appearances in other provincial cities, she debuted in London in 1777. She married Edward Smith, twelfth earl of Derby, on May 1, 1797, retiring from the stage at that time. She died in 1829. This print is based on an oil painting by Sir Thomas Lawrence (1769-1830), now in the Metropolitan Museum of Art, New York.[3] It was finished in 1790 and exhibited in the Royal Academy that year, along with another full-length portrait of Queen Charlotte.[4] These two major works helped to establish Lawrence's reputation as the successor to Sir Joshua Reynolds (1723-1792). The Farren portrait was very popular, prompting one reviewer to remark:

> We have seen a great variety of pictures of Miss Farren, but we never before saw her mind and character upon canvas. It is completely Elizabeth Farren; arch, spirited, elegant and engaging.[5]

The sitter had complained to Lawrence that she appeared very thin and that he "must make it a little *fatter*, at all events, diminish the *bend* you are so attached to."[6] Lawrence's composition was eventually the source for at least six engravings, including the Knight-Bartolozzi version.[7] Miss Farren was the subject of a number of other portraits, including paintings by Johann Zoffany (1734/35-1810) and, perhaps, Richard Cosway (1742-1821); drawings by John Downman (ca. 1750-1824), Edward F. Burney (1760-1848), and Ozias Humphrey (1742-1810); several theatrical prints; and a marble bust by Anne Seymour Damer (1748/49-1828).[8]

The Knight-Bartolozzi stipple is a comparatively large format for the medium and a grand production in its own right, matching the bravura quality of Lawrence's painting. The reasons for the switch of engravers' names are not known; but it is known that many prints that bear Bartolozzi's name were the work of his assistants. Godfrey asserts that his name really became "the nature of a trademark."[9] One commentator suggests that after Lawrence's oil had achieved such a great success, Bartolozzi imposed his signature in place of Knight's in order to claim the credit.[10] From the date, which is over ten months prior to the earliest Bartolozzi publication (by the same publisher), Knight would seem to have actually published his state of the print. However, the possibility of a hiatus in the actual production of the print cannot be discounted. Knight engraved another smaller version of this portrait in 1813.[11]

The artistic changes between the two Cincinnati impressions of *Miss Farren* illuminate the stipple process. The first state of the print by Knight has quite a few unfinished areas. It appears to be totally etched, before final areas of shading were added by further etched stipple tones and engraved lines. The slightly darker area around the head and shoulders appears to be an indication of the intended final appearance of the sky. Very finely textured objects – her muff, fur collar, and hair – are only preliminarily etched, and it is in areas such as these that the contrast between the two states is most easily observed.

By the time that the second Cincinnati impression was made, the overall effect of the print had been darkened and the contrasts had been considerably softened. The sky in this impression is more evenly toned (the clouds are less evident), and the texture of the articles of fur is rendered in finer detail. The volume of the dress has been accentuated with engraved lines that regularize the shading. Both Cincinnati states are beautifully preserved brilliant impressions, printed in black ink. Other impressions of the final state are printed in color, imitative of the Lawrence painting. These latter show the subject wearing a white dress with gray fur trim, a blue ribbon at her neck, carrying brownish red gloves, with effectively rendered flesh tones, pink cheeks and lips, and blue eyes.[12] – DPB

1. Antony Griffiths, *Prints and Printmaking* (London: British Museum, 1980), 83.

2. For another instance of the head of a printmaking studio asserting his name over the work of an assistant, see Larmessin, cat. 99. In addition to the primary state difference between Knight's etching and Bartolozzi's considerable additions, a number of changes appear in the engraved captions below the image. Vesme and Calabi list six states, as does E. Barrington Nash in his article "Miss Farren," *Magazine of Art* 9 (1886): 143. This writer believes there are at least seven, perhaps more, states, based on the comparison of photographs of both Cincinnati impressions with six other impressions in the Yale Center for British Art, New Haven, and one in the Frick Collection, New York. The primary new state addition seems to be the date of the later Cincinnati impression (1943.476): January 1, 1792; two impressions of otherwise virtually the same state in the British Art Center (B1970.3.454 and .456) are dated January 2, 1792.

3. Kenneth Garlick, *Sir Thomas Lawrence – A Complete Catalogue of the Paintings* (Oxford: University Press, 1989), 187, no. 294(a), illustrated in color pl. 5; also illustrated in color in Howard Hibbard, *The Metropolitan Museum of Art* (New York: Metropolitan Museum of Art, 1980), 378, fig. 680. A preliminary oil sketch of Miss Farren's head is illustrated in Garlick, *Sir Thomas Lawrence*, 187, no. 294(b).

4. Garlick, *Sir Thomas Lawrence*, 168, no. 186, illustrated in color pl. 4.

5. *The Public Advertiser*, April 30, 1790, as quoted in Michael Levey, London 1979, no. 4.

6. Letter to the artist, quoted in Levey, London 1979.

7. See Freeman O'Donoghue, *Catalogue of Engraved British Portraits. . . in the Department of Prints and Drawings in the British Museum* (London: British Museum, 1908-22), 2:39-40, where a total of sixteen portrait engravings of Miss Farren are catalogued.

8. Richard Ormond and Malcolm Rogers, eds., *Dictionary of British Portraiture*, comp. Elaine Kilmurray (New York: Oxford University Press, 1979), 2:62.

9. Richard T. Godfrey, *General History of British Printmaking* (Oxford: Oxford University Press, 1978), 55.

10. Nash, "Miss Farren," 143.

11. Garlick, *Sir Thomas Lawrence*, 187.

12. Color impressions are in the Frick Collection and the Yale Center for British Art. The latter collection also owns an impression printed in brown ink.

Philibert-Louis Debucourt

Paris 1755-1832 Paris

115. The Public Promenade 1792.

Color etching, engraving, and aquatint (four plates) on antique laid paper 46.3 x 64.2 cm (platemark).
Fenaille 33 i/iii; I.F.F. 1700 VI.175.26.
Watermark: T [well-tower] DUPUY/AUVERGNE 1742[1]
Provenance: Cortlandt F. Bishop (Lugt s. 2770b); (his sale Anderson Galleries, New York, November 21, 1935, lot 50); (purchased from M. Knoedler, New York, December 16, 1935, for $5,610). Bequest of Herbert Greer French, 1943.420.
Exhibitions: Cincinnati 1941, no. 215; Minneapolis 1956

Philibert-Louis Debucourt originally trained as a painter under Joseph-Marie Vien (1716-1809) and was admitted to the Royal Academy in 1781. At that time he also executed his first prints, eventually producing over five hundred. In 1785 Debucourt issued his first color prints, eventually becoming an extremely accomplished master of the medium. Many of his most successful color prints were designed after his own compositions, but he also worked after other artists. His oeuvre forms a conspectus of the changing artistic tastes of the era, extending from his earliest pictures of Parisian society, through severe revolutionary allegories, to prints after early Romantic artists, such as Carle Vernet (1758-1836).[2]

The Public Promenade, with considerable justification, is often considered to be Debucourt's masterpiece and one of the supreme accomplishments of eighteenth-century French printmaking. Debucourt's mastery of the multiple-plate color-printing process is displayed to its fullest advantage in this view of Parisian society during the early years of the Revolution through the play of fabrics, foliage, and foppery. At the time of Debucourt's rendering, Parisian society was vainly attempting to hold on to its privileges, yet in the same year, in August and September 1792, the full force of revolutionary terror was to begin in earnest with the imprisonment of the royal family and the massacre of hundreds of prisoners.

Debucourt daringly portrayed several well-known individuals in his print, which is closely related to his own gouache, now in the Metropolitan Museum of Art, New York.[3] Among those identified are the dandified duc d'Aumont, dressed in pink and sprawling across three chairs, and the duc de Chartres (the future King Louis-Philippe), blowing kisses to the group of parading women in the center of the print.[4] The young woman in a yellow dress with a black bodice is identified as Manola, a favorite model of Fragonard who was recommended to him by Goya; the very tall woman at the right edge wearing her native headdress is La Cauchoise, "a rising beauty." Debucourt has even included family friends in the scene.[5]

His palette is appropriately dominated by patriotic blues, reds, and whites. The actual locality is the grounds of the Palais Royal, a favorite gathering place for public exhibitions of the latest fashions and liaisons.

Debucourt executed another elaborate color view of this public "spectacle" on the same spot some five years earlier in his view of the *Palais Royal Gallery's Walk* (Fenaille 11), itself a pendant to the *Palais Royal Garden Walk* of the same year, engraved by Louis Le Coeur (cat. 113). The owner of the palace, the duc d'Orléans, opened the grounds to the public, allowing boutiques and cafés to operate and soon creating a haven for society of all levels where the police were barred from entering.[6] Debucourt was assuredly dependent for his conception of *The Public Promenade* and for his earlier print, *Palais Royal Gallery's Walk*, on a similar panorama by Thomas Rowlandson of the Vauxhall Gardens in London, issued in 1785.[7] As Rowlandson before him, Debucourt effectively managed a humorous, gently mocking portrayal without injecting harsh sarcasm or caricature into these hapless society types. Amidst the fun is quite an accurate portrayal of dress and social custom; the grounds of the palace are accurately portrayed. Groups, especially one at the lower right, apparently earnestly discuss the latest events of the day, resisting the temptation to view the frivolity on parade.[8] *The Public Promenade* is a deceptively simple portrayal of a very complicated moment.

Debucourt used a combination of aquatint and hand tools to create the plates for this print. The layers and subtleties of application of the aquatint washes are remarkable, and a formidable task of registration was necessary to print four plates of such a great size (a black "key" plate, along with red, yellow, and blue color plates). John Ittmann determined that aquatint was used only in the black plate to achieve a fuller range of shadows; more traditional tools were utilized to manually prepare the three color plates.[9] The totality of this brilliant effect resembles a movie set — the opening scene slowly panned for the viewer before individual and collective dramas are played out.

The Museum's impression is one of perhaps only three impressions in this state, before all inscriptions and the artist's initials and date were added. The colors are at their freshest and most luminous.[10] This print, one of Mr. French's most costly purchases in the eighteenth-century field, was acquired along with several other of his most-noted prints from this period from the famous Cortlandt F. Bishop sale in New York in 1935 (see Moreau, cat. 106, Baquoy, cat. 107a, Janinet, cat. 111, De Launay, cat. 110, and Bonnet, cat. 105).[11] French acquired a total of eleven prints from the Bishop Collection, for a total cost of some $16,042. As for Debucourt alone, in addition to *The Public Promenade*, *The Poorly Defended Rose* (Fenaille 27), and *The Wedding at the Chateau* (Fenaille 21) purchased from the Bishop Collection, Mr. French acquired the pair of *The Rose* and *The Hand* (Fenaille 17-18). — DPB

1. See Pierrette Jean-Richard, *L'Oeuvre gravé de François Boucher dans la collection Edmond de Rothschild* (Paris: Editions des Musées Nationaux, 1978), s.v. "Filigranes – Dupuy."

2. The basic Debucourt reference is Maurice Fenaille, *L'Oeuvre gravé de P. L. Debucourt* (Paris: Damascène Morgand, 1899), which lists 577 prints by and after Debucourt. See also I.F.F. 1700 VI:162-91 and I.F.F. 1800 VI:68-69. For reproductions of several of his revolutionary allegories, see Los Angeles 1988, nos. 127, 136-37, 187.

3. John Ittmann, Baltimore 1984, 290. Reproduced in Paris 1920, no. 31 and pl. 31 in separate "album."

4. However, Jean-Richard casts doubt on the latter identification, asserting that the duc de Chartres was never in Paris during the summers of either 1791 or 1792 (Paris 1985, 112, under no. 146), not a fact that would have necessarily prevented Debucourt from including him in his print.

5. See [Edward Clayton] *French Engravings of the Eighteenth Century in the Collection of Joseph Widener, Lynnewood Hall* (London: Chiswick Press, 1923), 159, who quotes Edmond and Jules de Goncourt, who discuss this print in great detail in their *Art of the Eighteenth Century.*

6. Both prints are reproduced and discussed in Baltimore 1984, 279-82, nos. 99-100.

7. Reproduced in A. Hyatt Mayor, *Prints and People* (New York: Metropolitan Museum of Art, 1971), no. 605.

8. For a discussion of this print within the tradition of caricature, see Los Angeles 1988, 260, no. 174.

9. Baltimore 1984, 290. Ittmann also states that this print is the "only major example of multiple-plate color printing of the period to use aquatint."

10. See [Clayton] *French Engravings*, 157-61, where it is stated that there were three impressions of this state printed in black ink only and three printed in color. The Bibliothèque Nationale in Paris owns impressions of both the color and black-only variations (I.F.F. 1700 VI:175.26).

11. Trained as a lawyer, Bishop (1870-1935) never practiced; instead he devoted his life to collecting, primarily eighteenth-century books and prints but including other areas of the book arts. In a desire to see New York become more of a center of art auction activity, Bishop also acquired the American Art Association and Anderson Galleries, among the forerunners of Sotheby Parke-Bernet, Inc. See Lugt, S., no. 2770b.

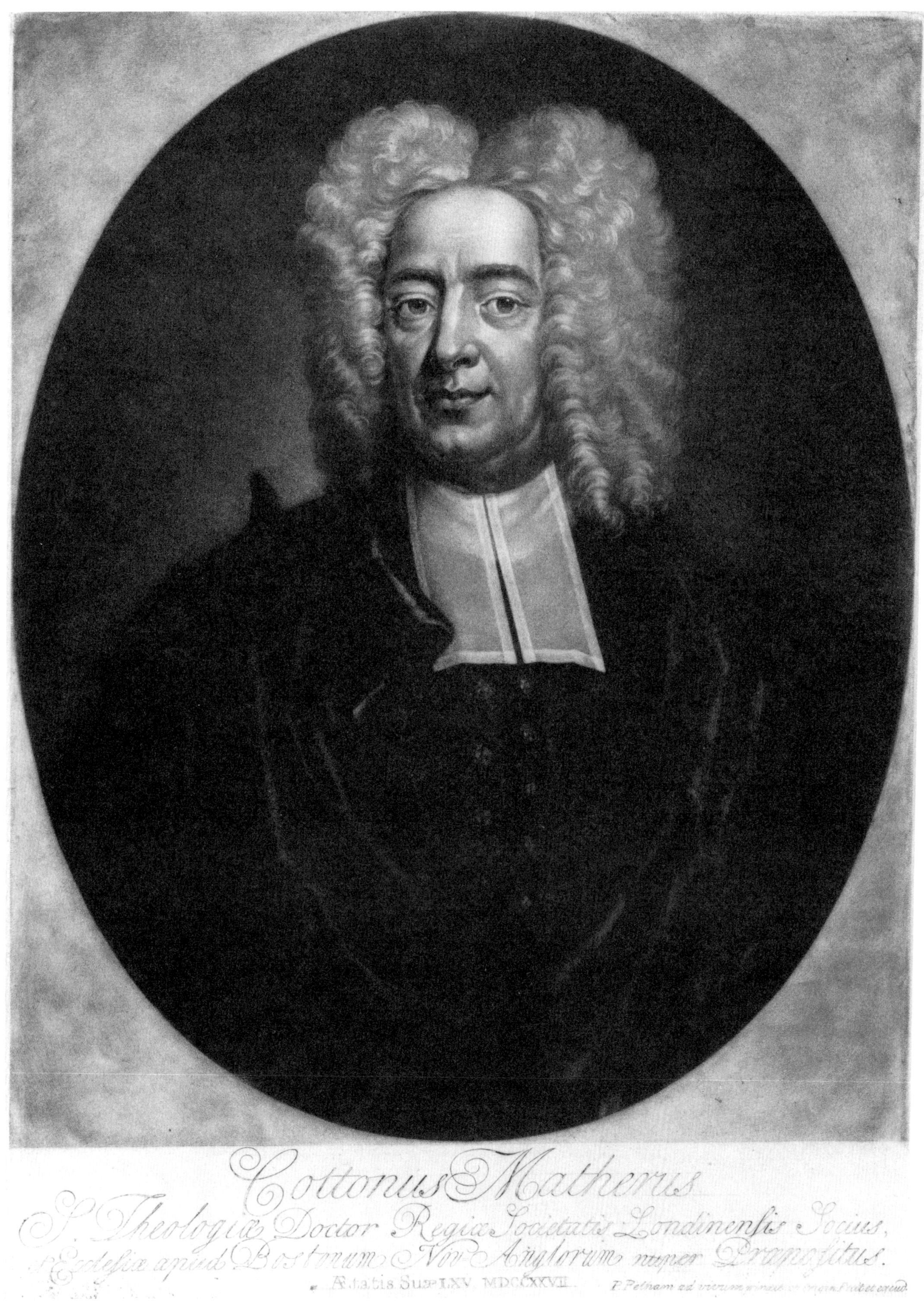

Plate 98. Peter Pelham, *Cotton Mather*, 1727.

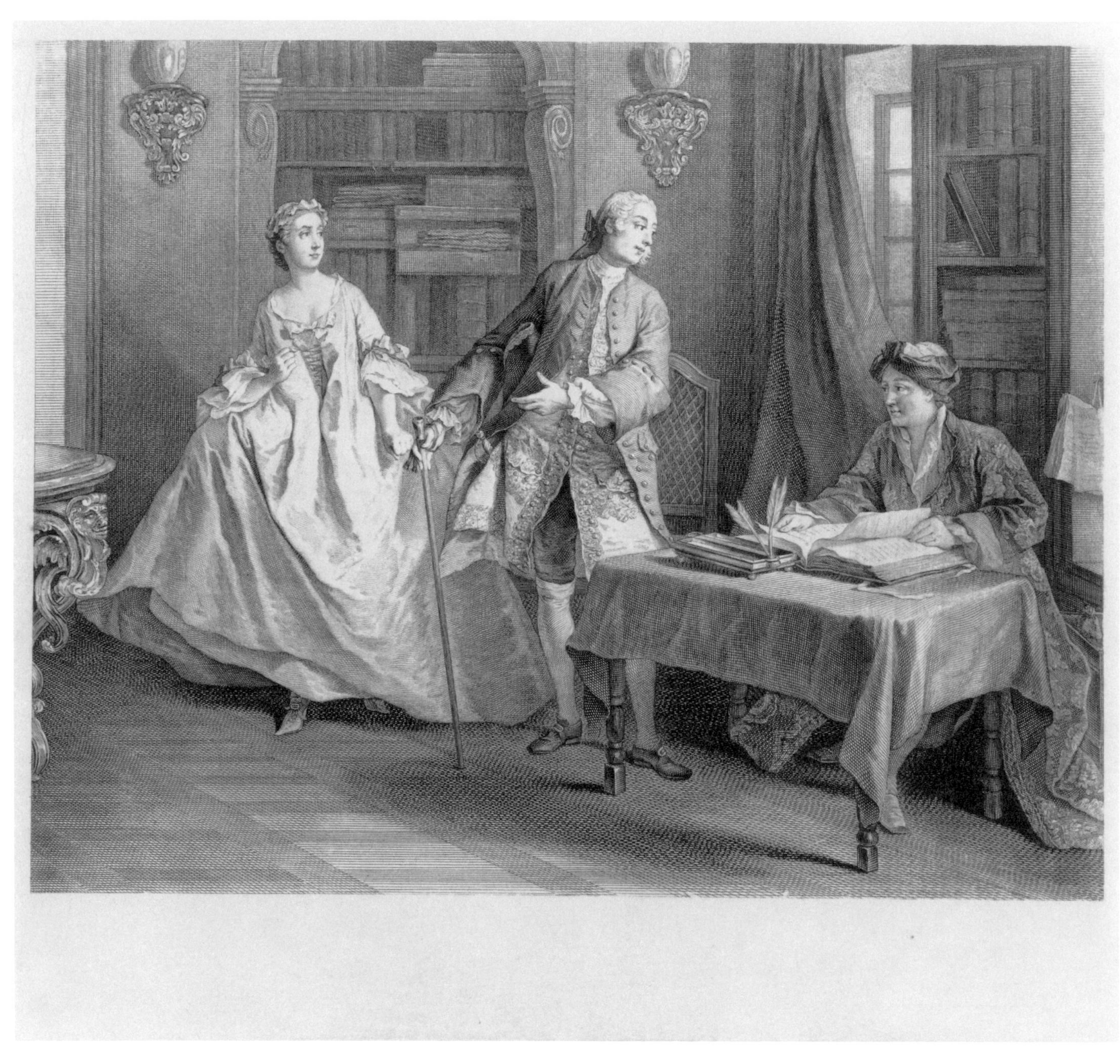

Plate 99. Georg Friedrich Schmidt and Nicolas de Larmessin, *The Avaricious Wife and the Gallant Swindler*, 1738.

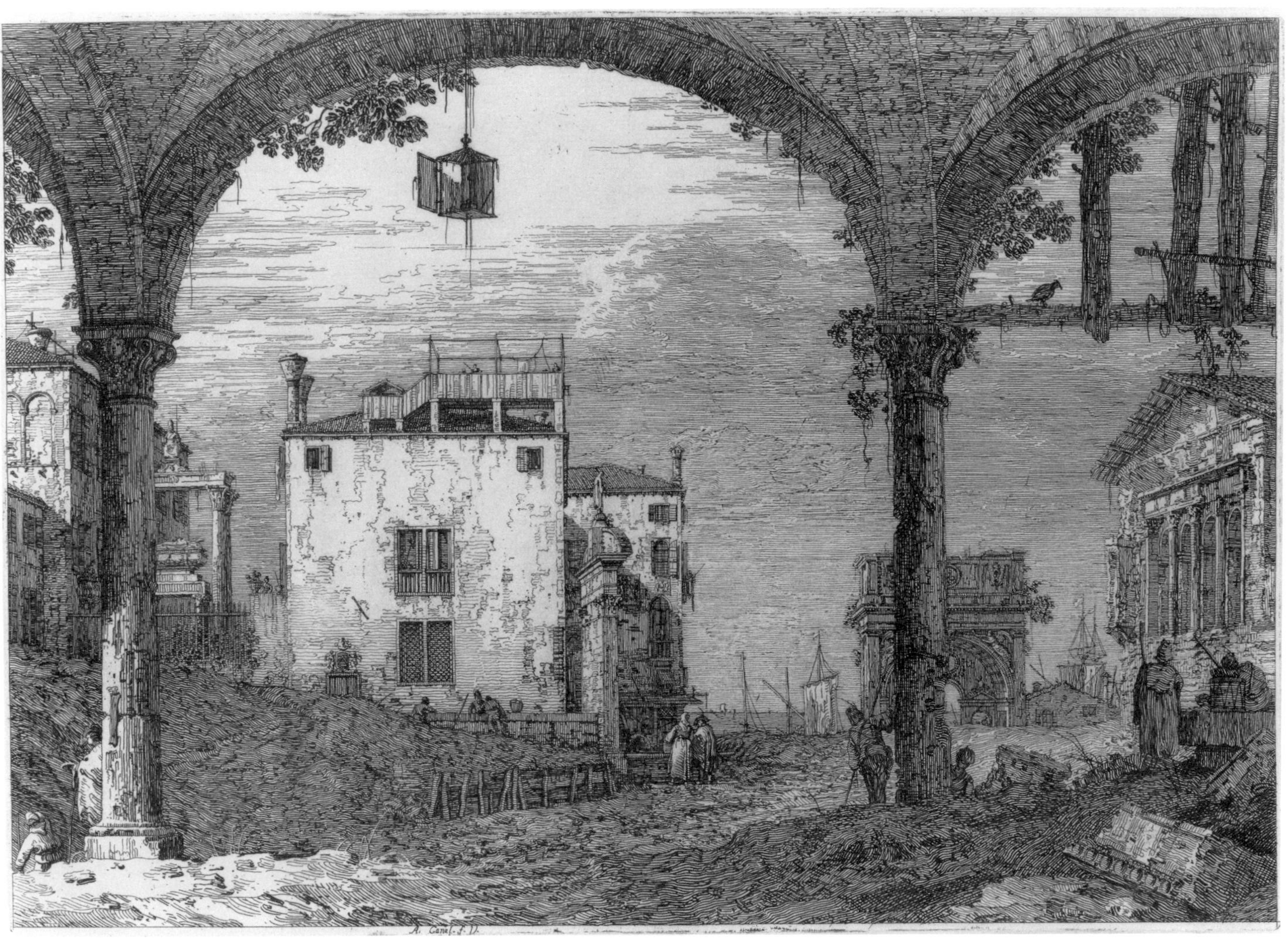

Plate 100. Giovanni Antonio Canal called Canaletto, *The Portico with the Lantern*, early 1740s.

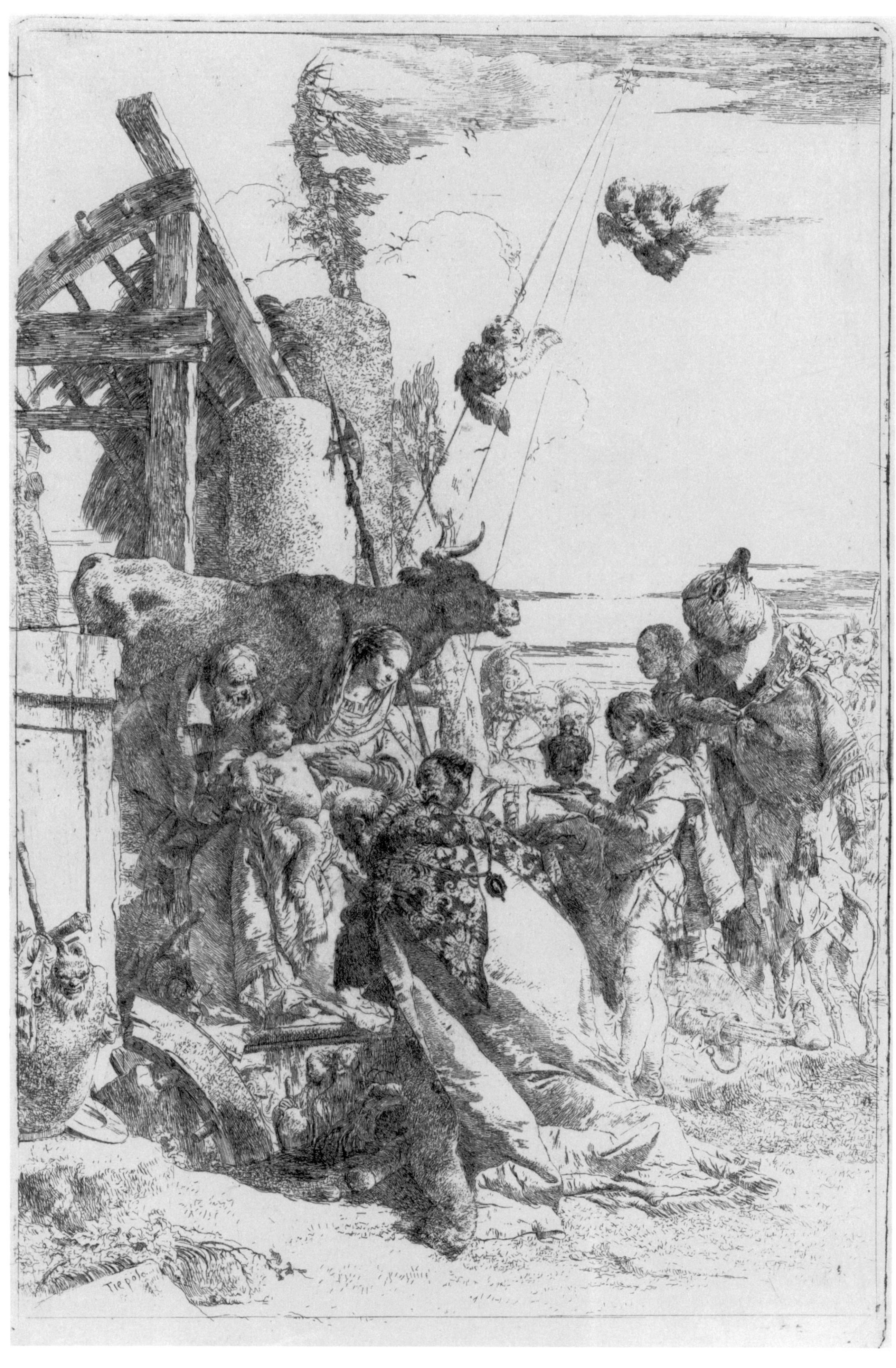

Plate 101. Giovanni Battista Tiepolo, *Adoration of the Magi*, 1740s.

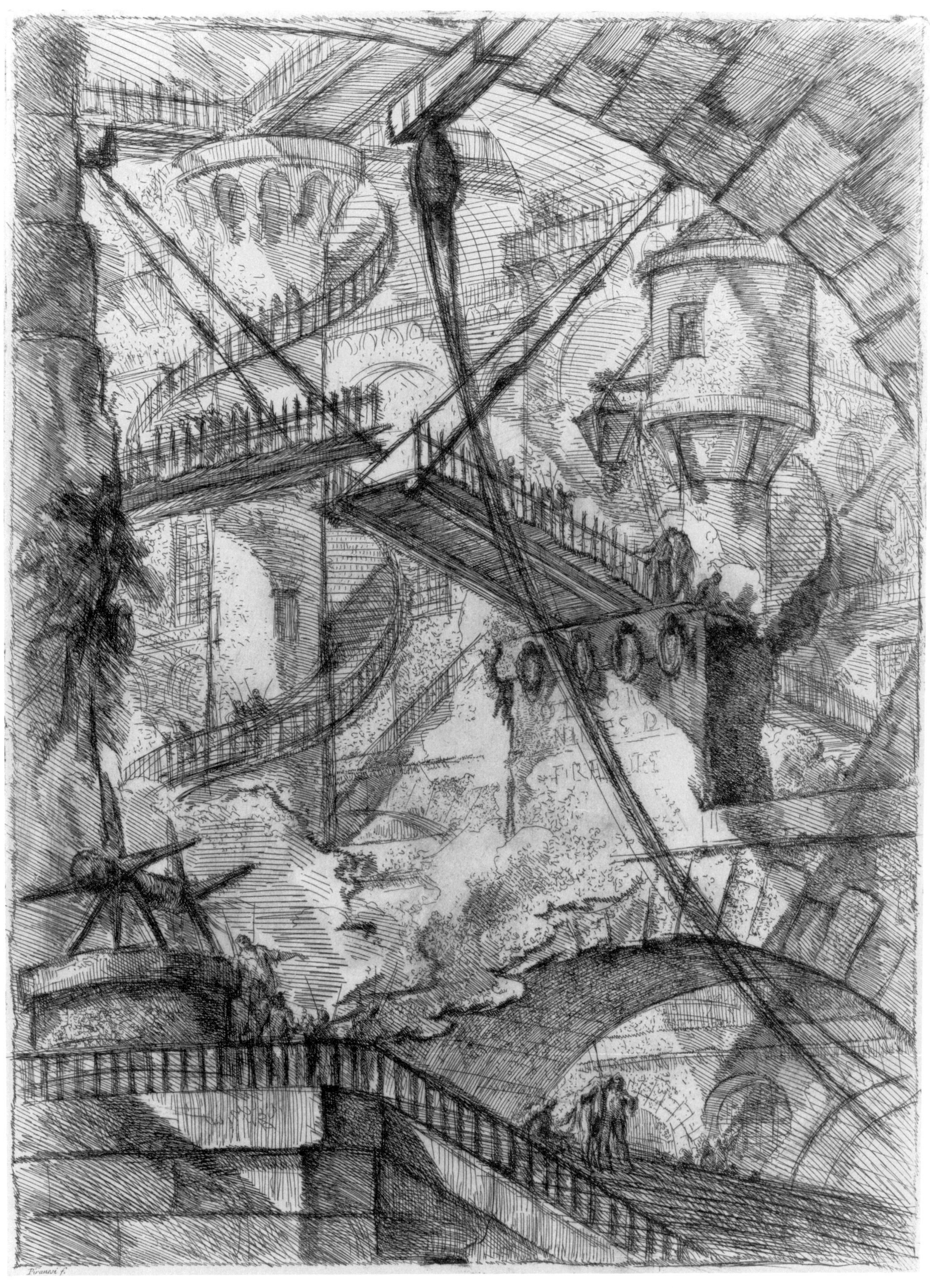

Plate 102a. Giovanni Battista Piranesi, *The Drawbridge*, 1749-50.

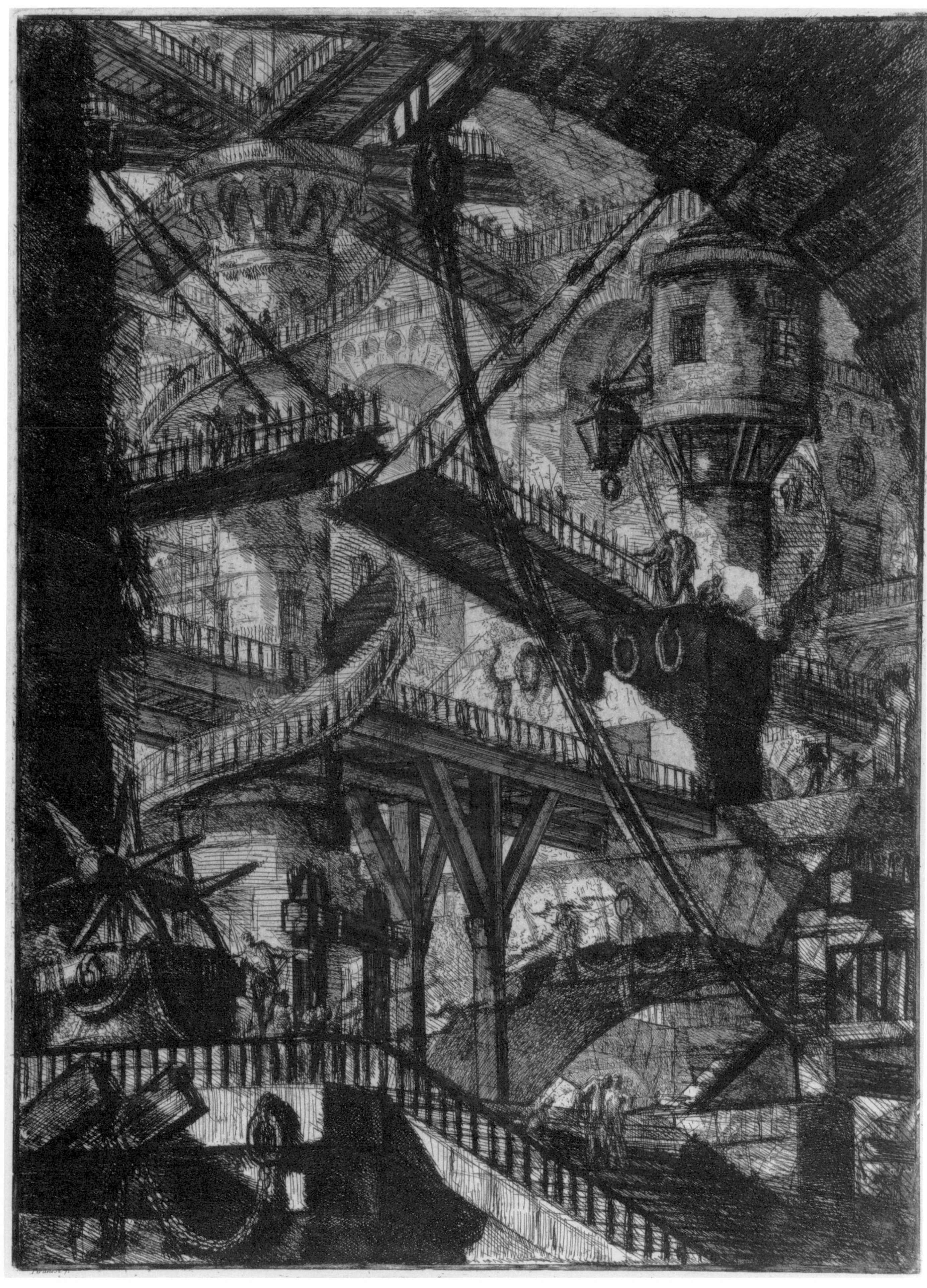

Plate 102b. Giovanni Battista Piranesi, *The Drawbridge*, 1761.

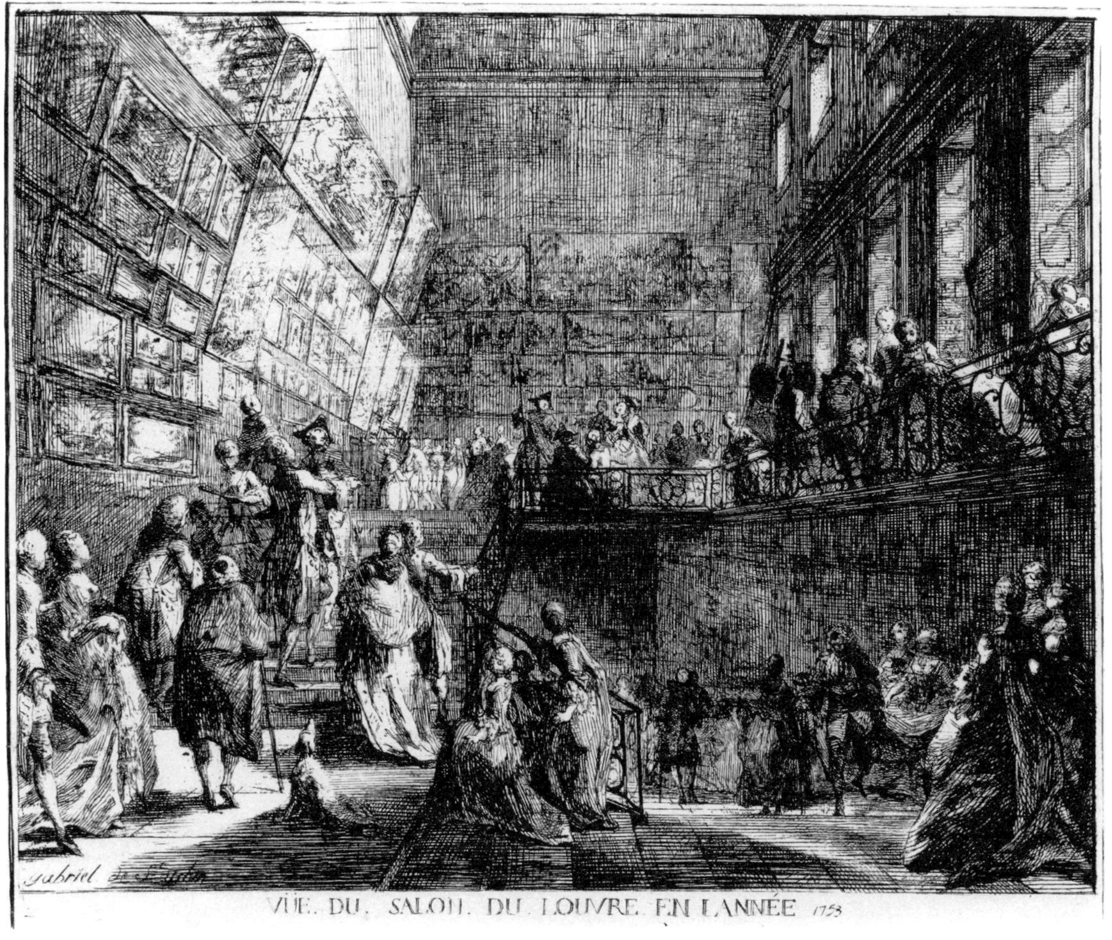

Plate 103. Gabriel-Jacques de Saint-Aubin, *View of the 1753 Salon at the Louvre,* 1753.

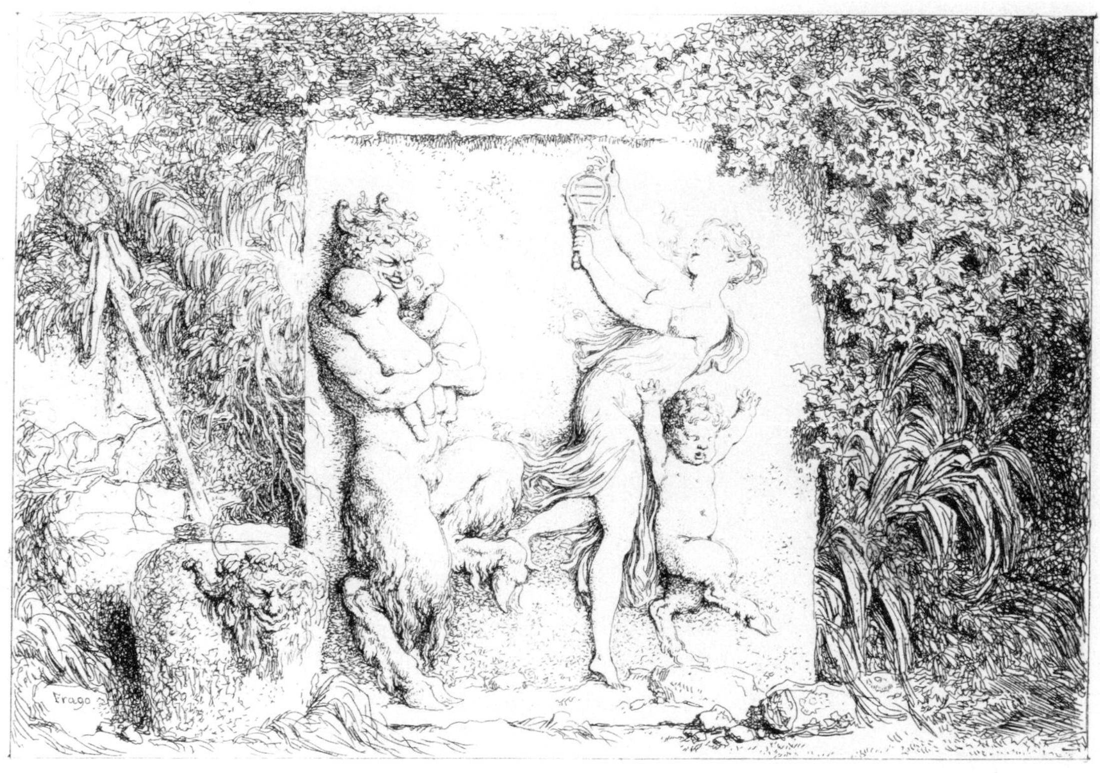

Plate 104. Jean-Honoré Fragonard, *Dance of the Satyrs,* 1763.

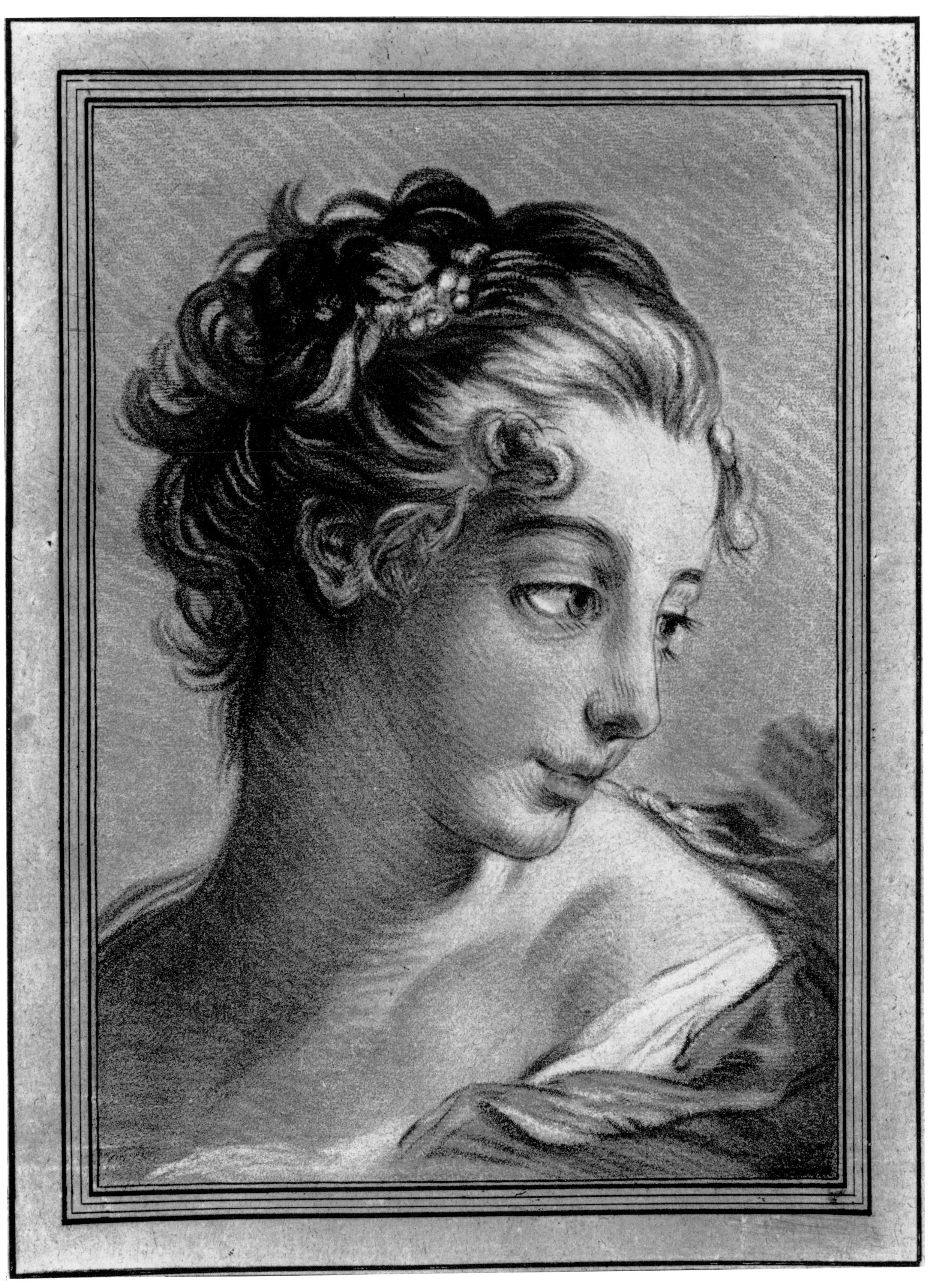

Plate 105. Louis-Marin Bonnet, *Head of a Young Woman*, 1767.

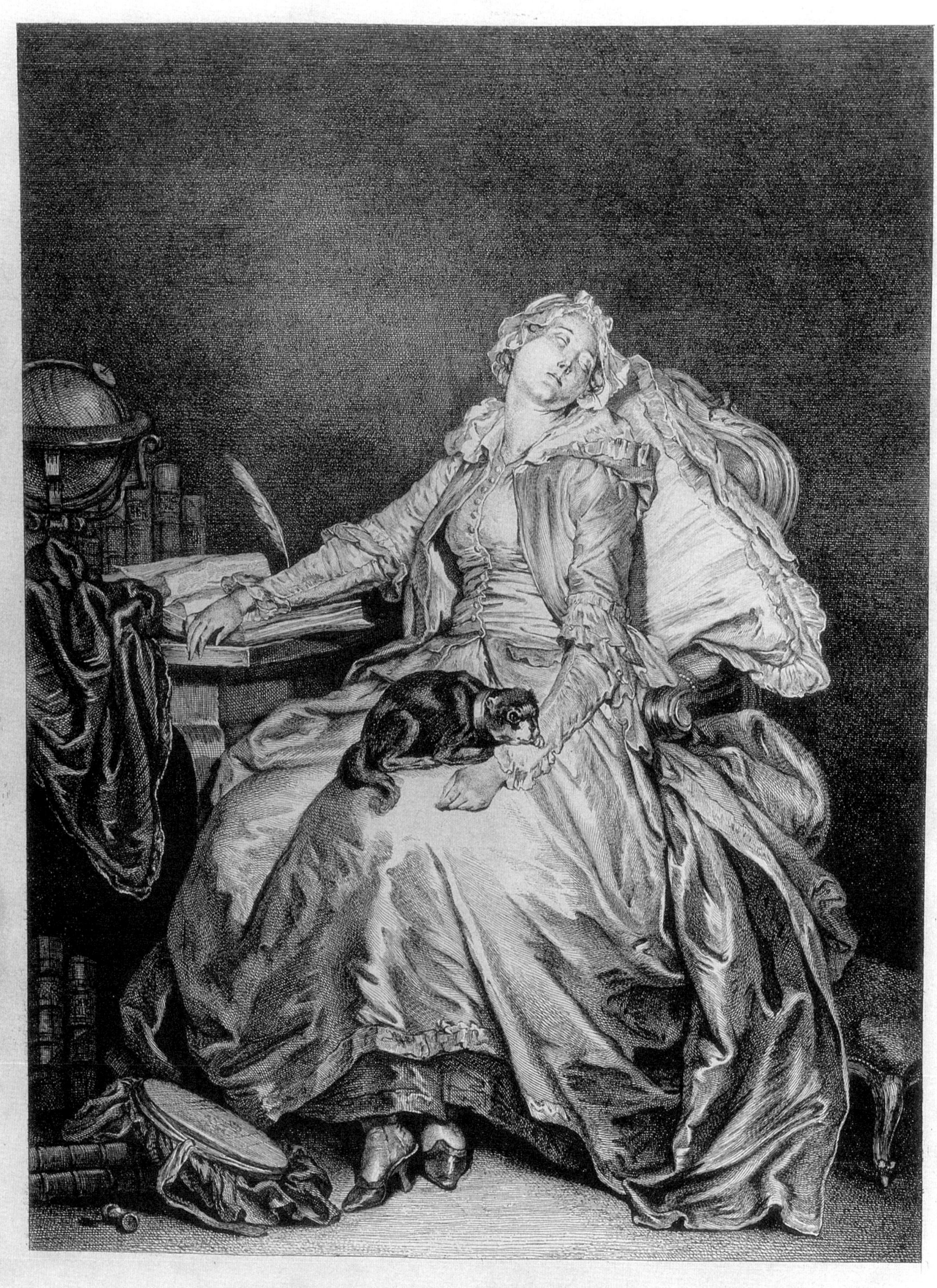

Plate 106. Jean-Michel Moreau *le jeune*, *Philosophy Asleep*, 1778.

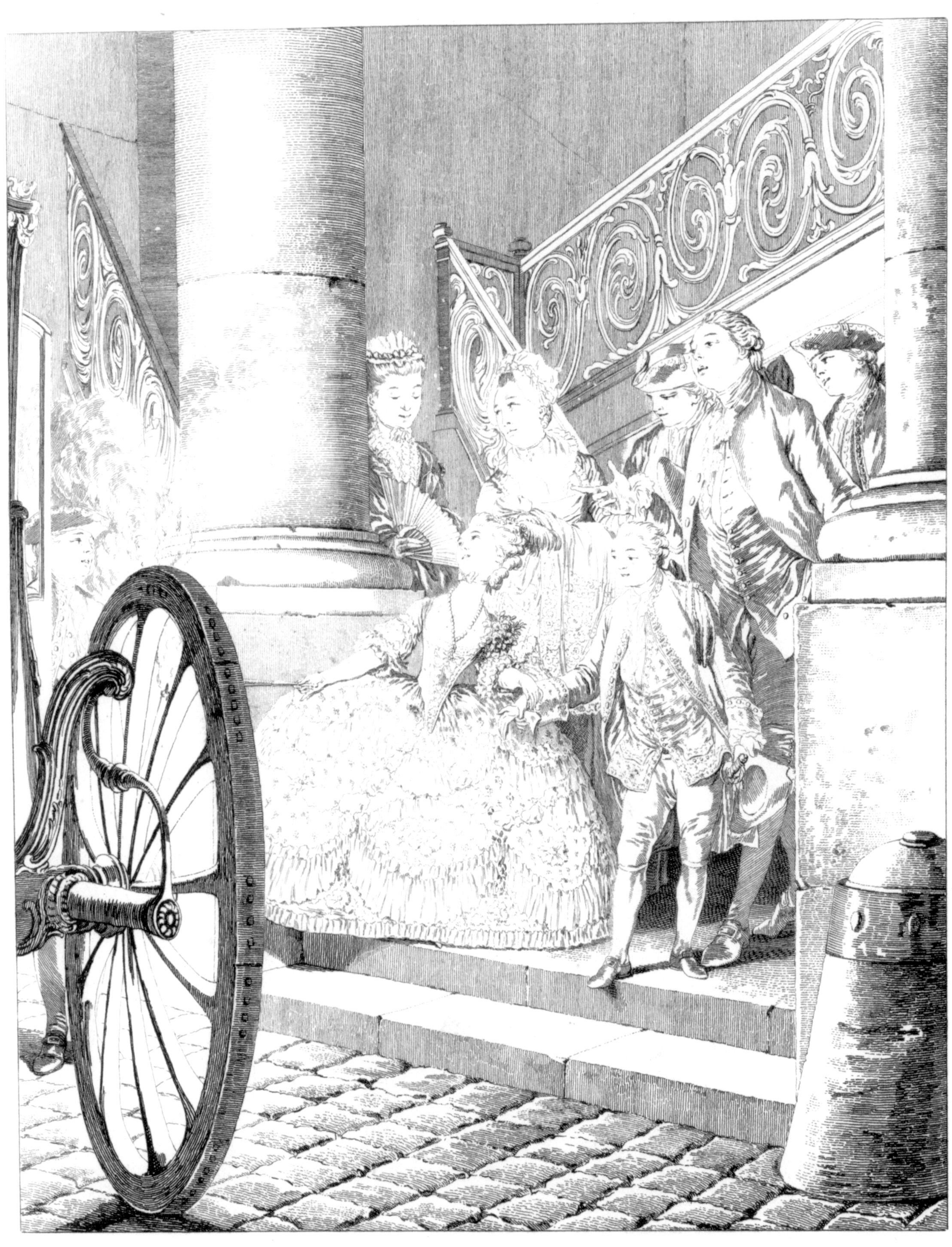

Plate 107a. Jean-Charles Baquoy, *The Little Godparents*, 1777.

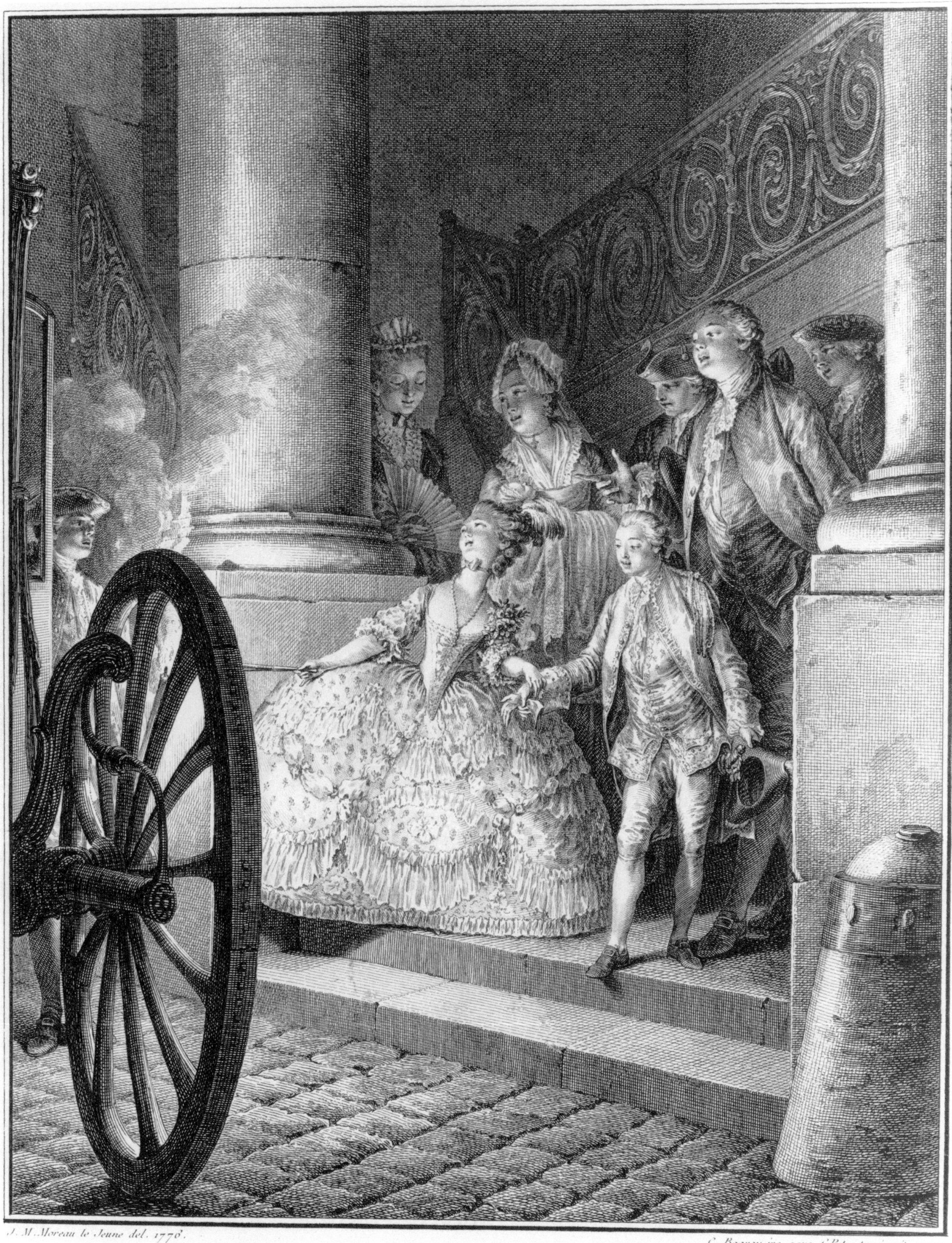

Plate 107b. Jean-Charles Baquoy and Charles-Emmanuel Patas, *The Little Godparents*, 1777.

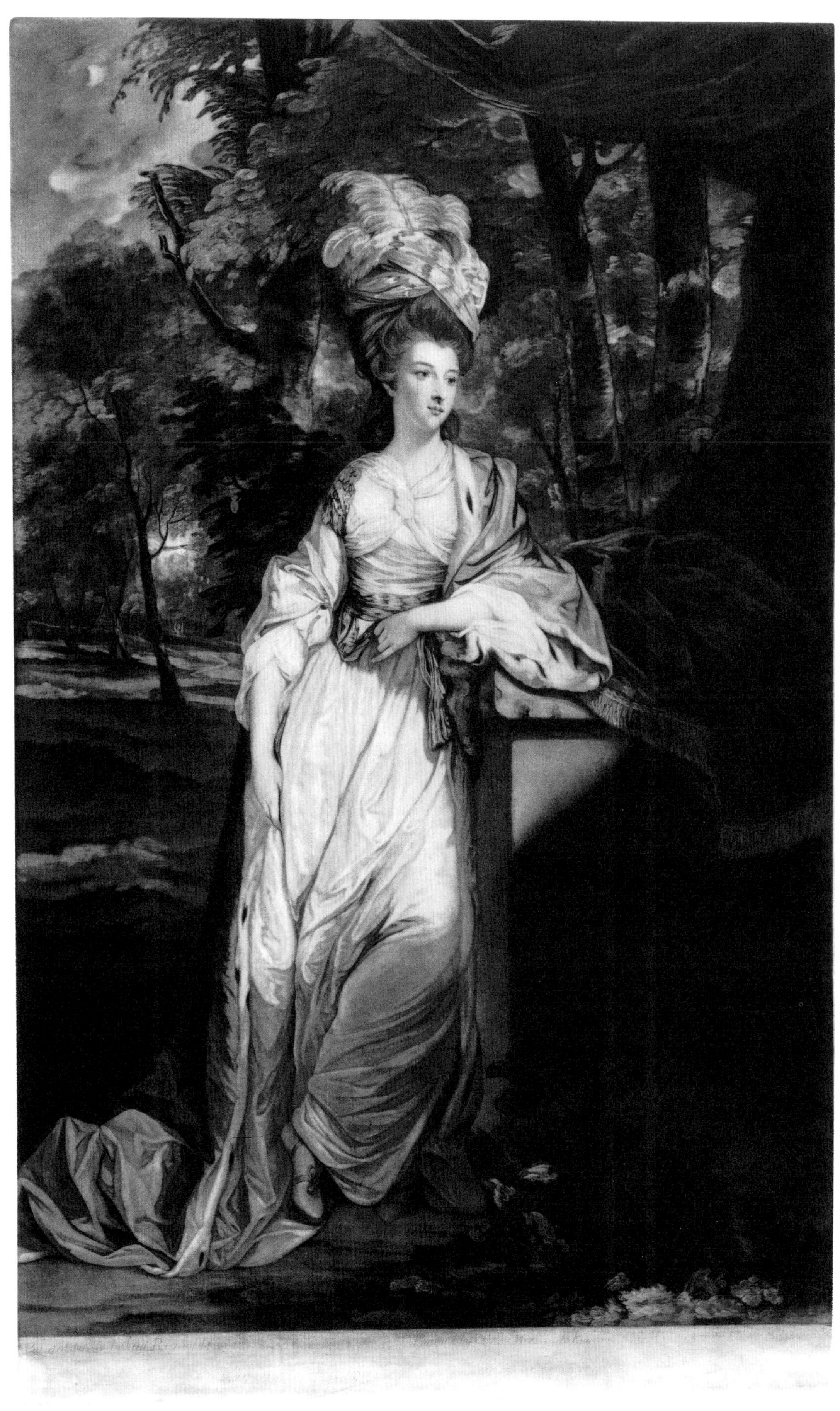

Plate 108. Valentine Green, *Mary Isabella, Duchess of Rutland*, 1780.

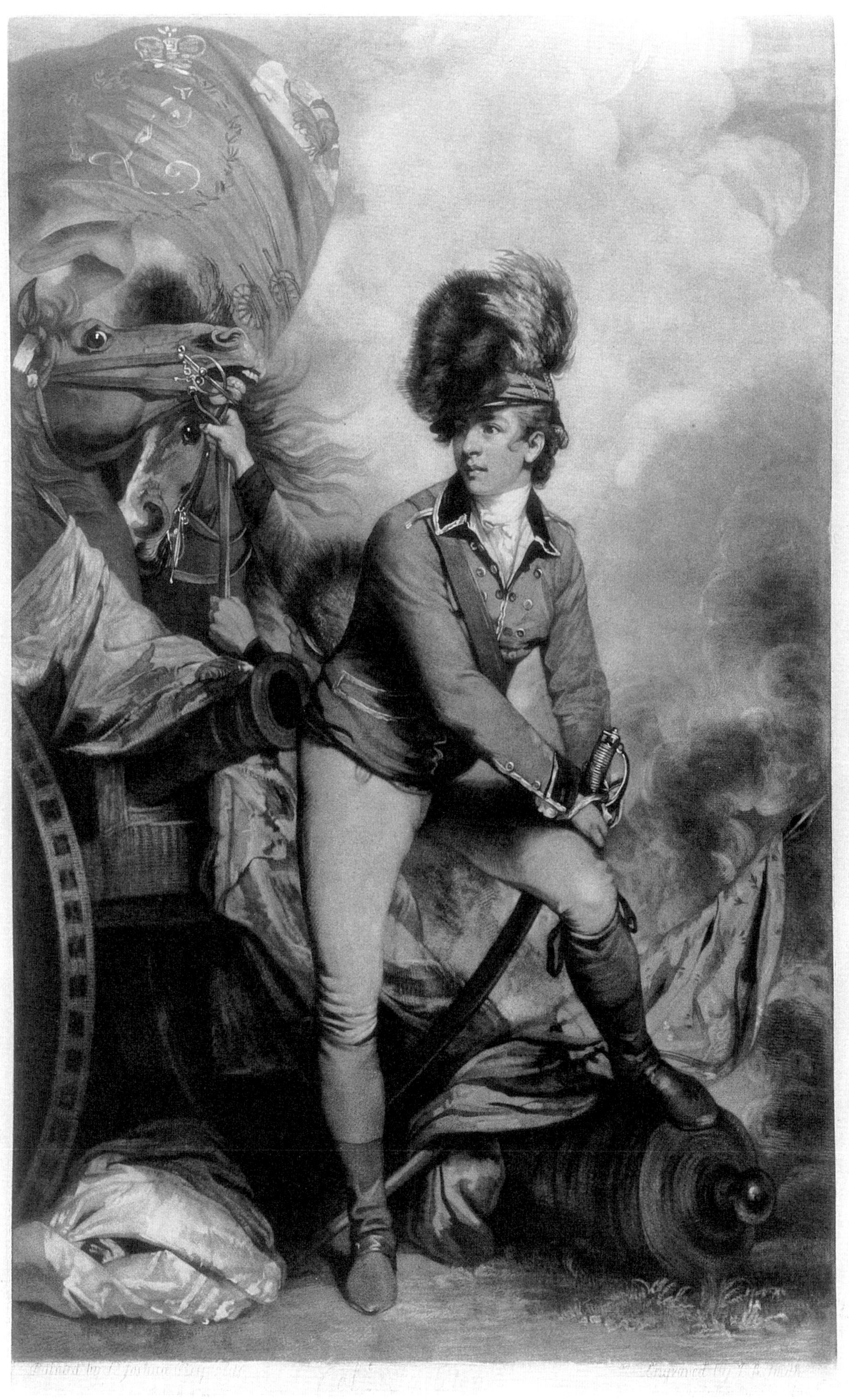

Plate 109. John Raphael Smith, *Lieutenant Colonel Sir Banastre Tarleton*, 1782.

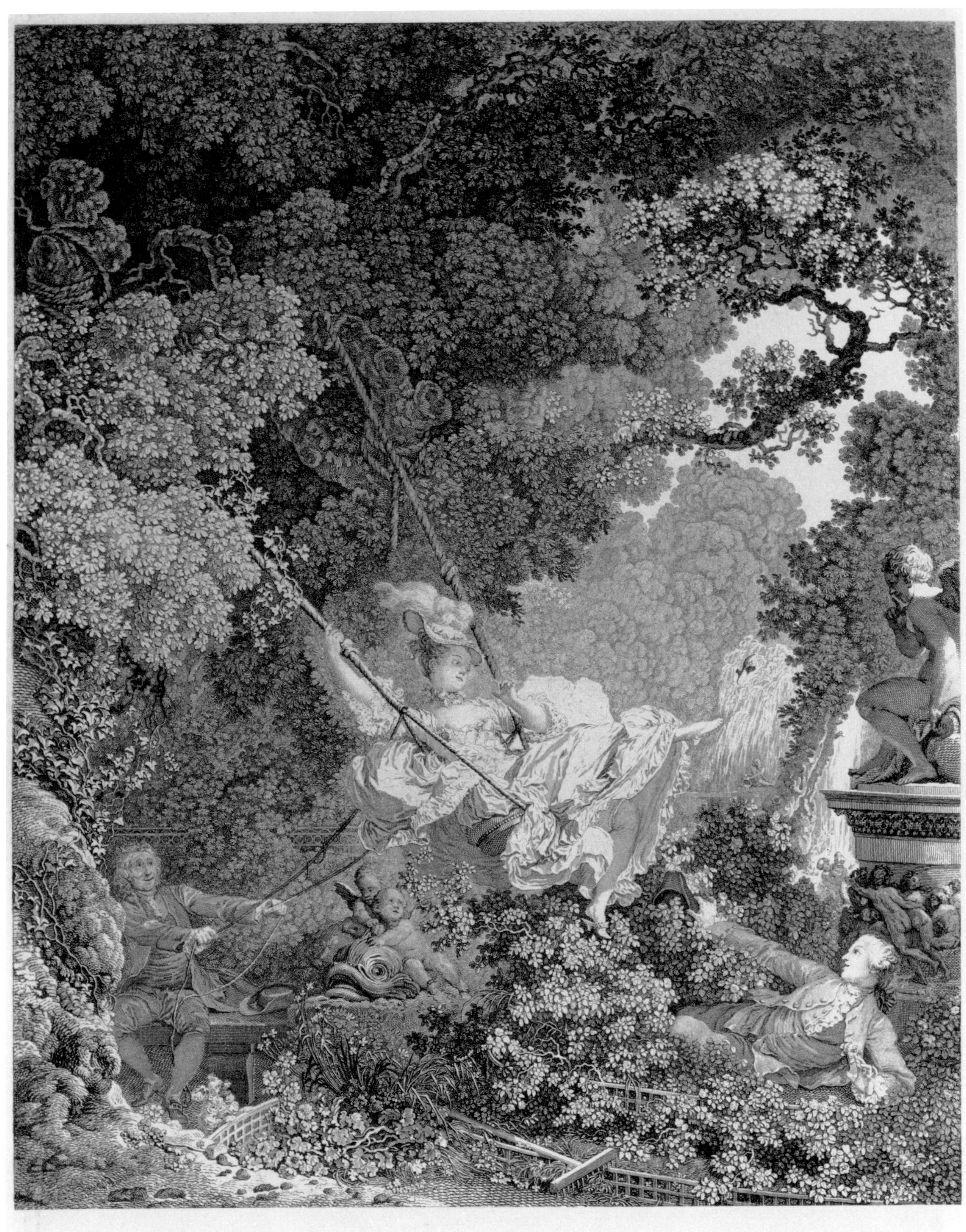

Plate 110. Nicolas de Launay, *The Swing's Lucky Chances*, 1782.

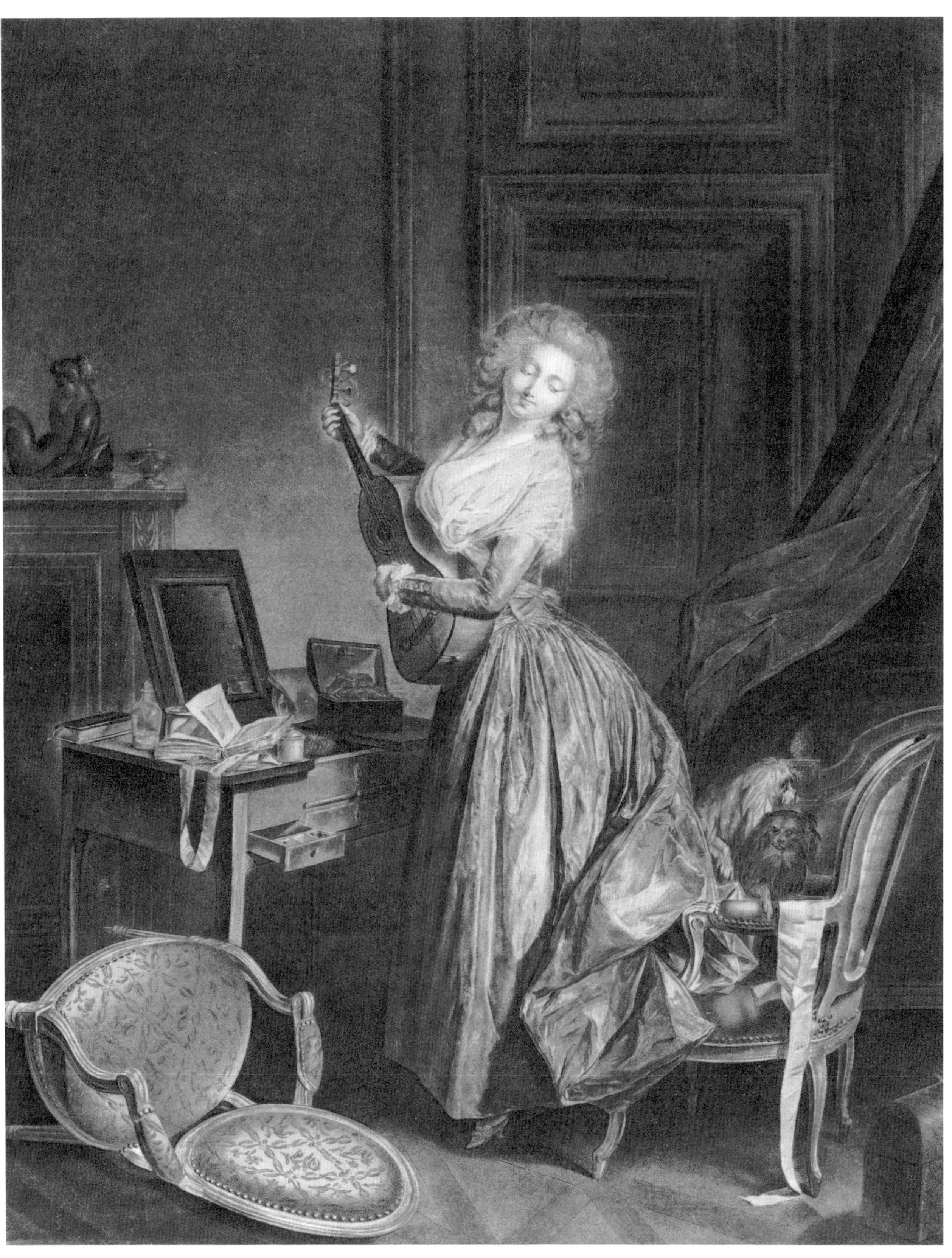

Plate III. Jean-Francois Janinet, *The Guitar Player*, 1788-89.

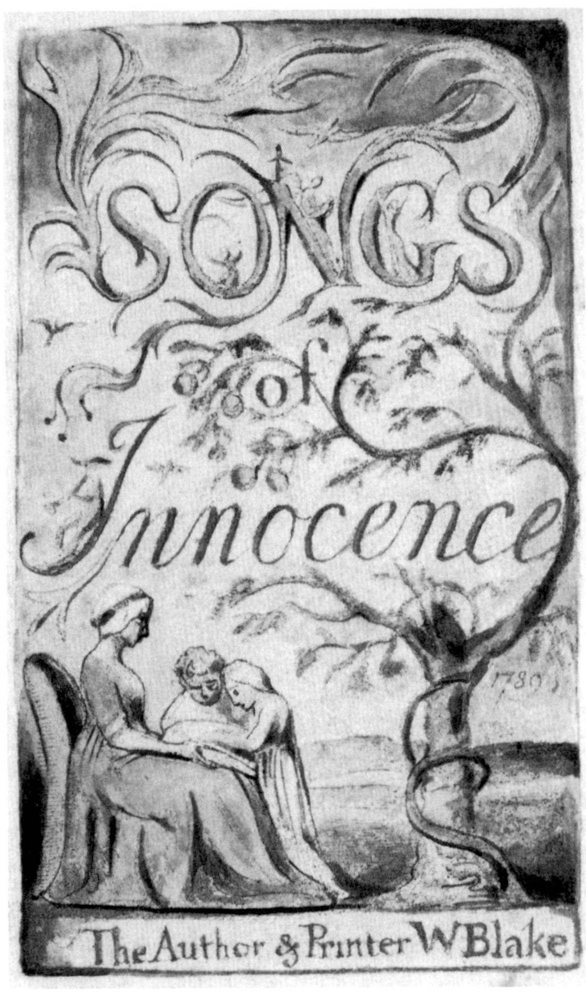

Plate 112a. William Blake, *Title Page, plate 2,*
from *Songs of Innocence,* ca. 1789.

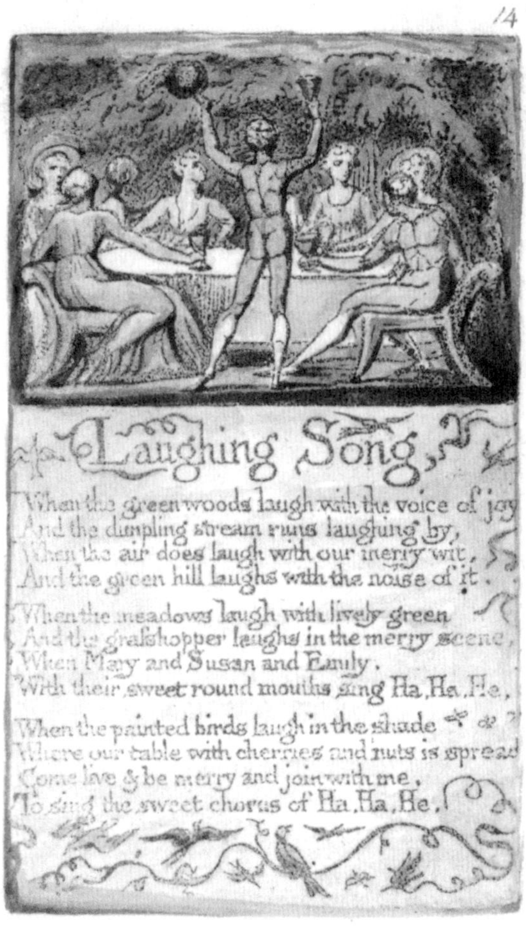

Plate 112b. William Blake, *Laughing Song, plate 14,*
from *Songs of Innocence,* ca. 1789.

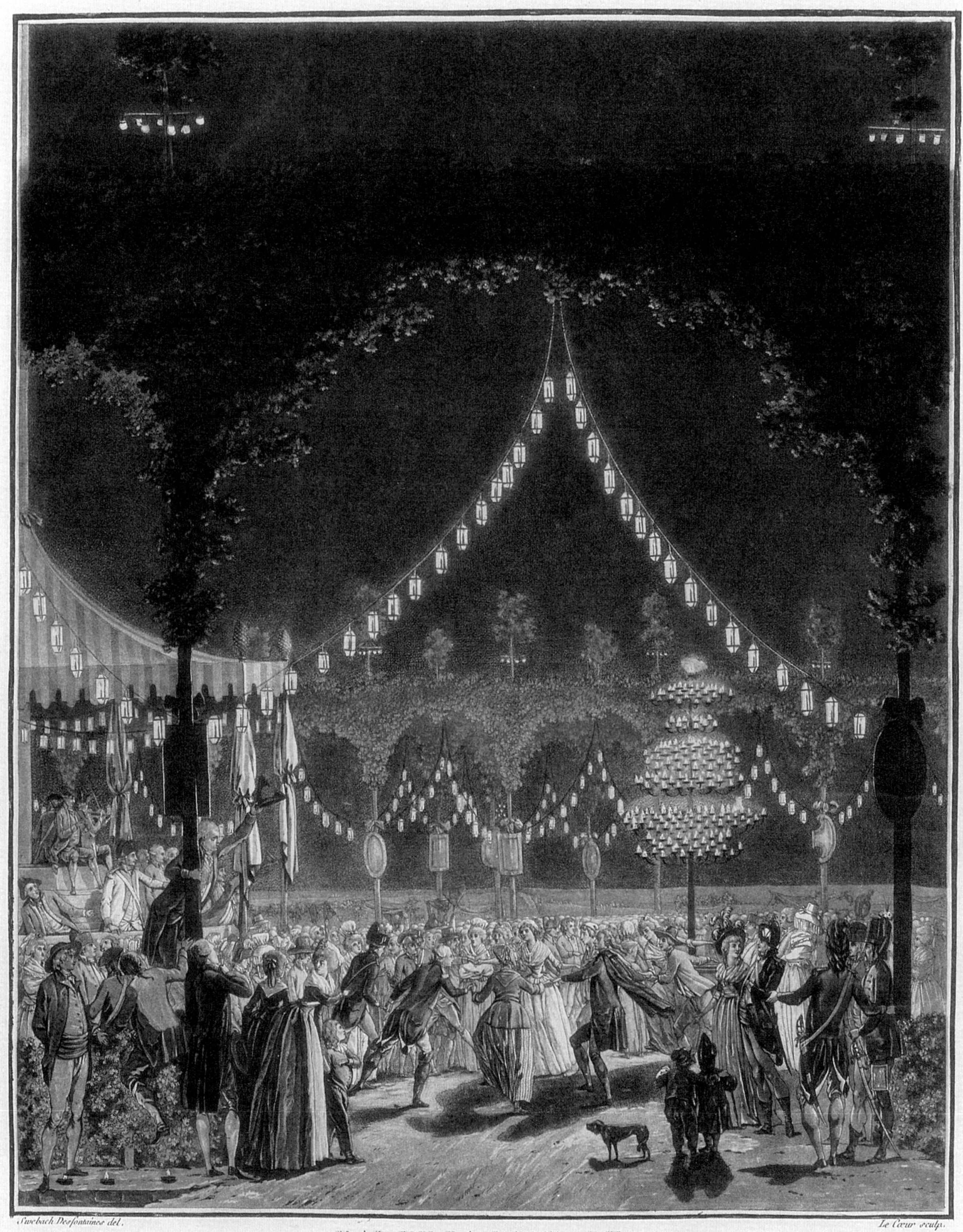

Plate 113. Louis le Coeur, *The Bastille Ball*, 1790.

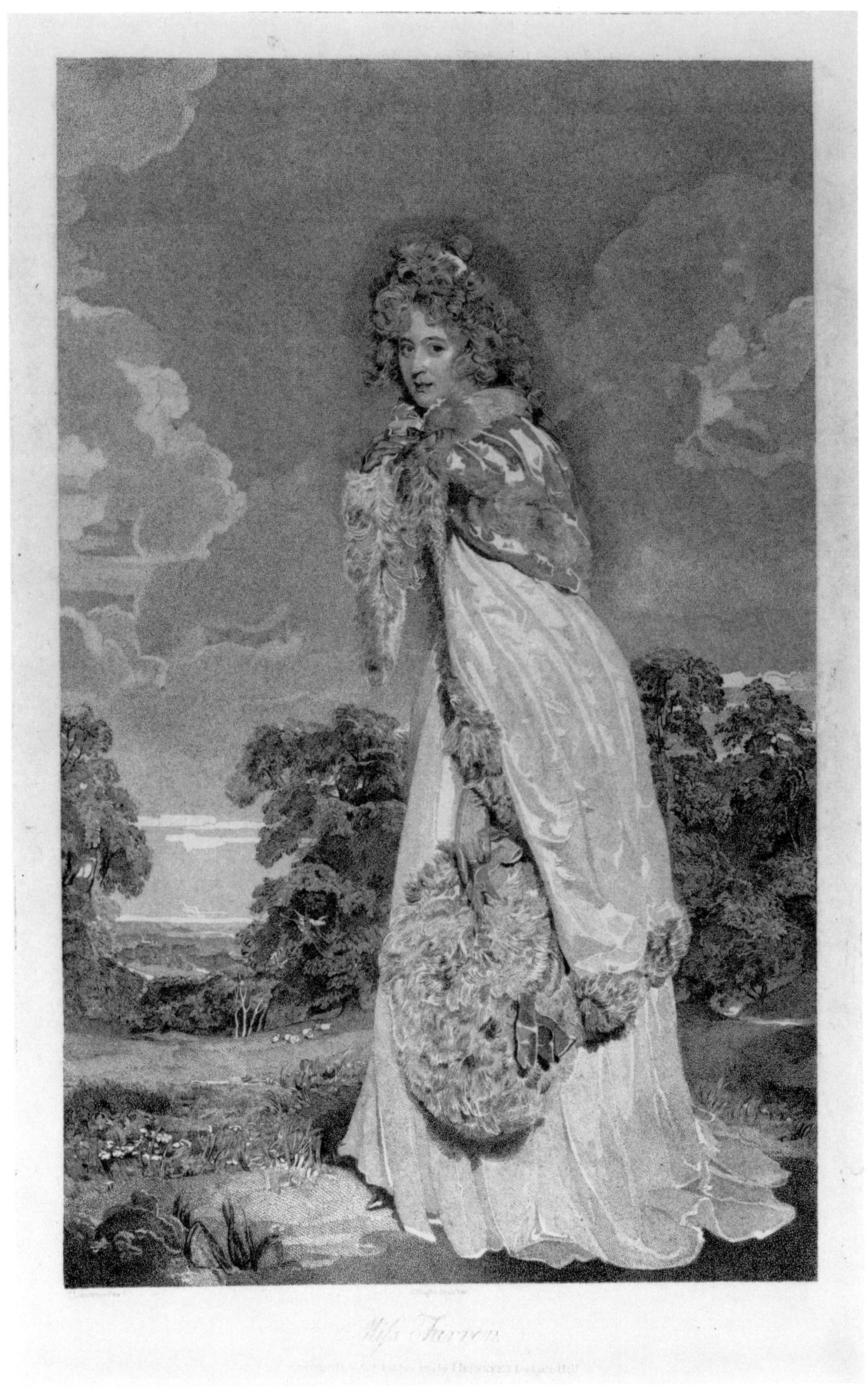

Plate 114a. Charles Knight, *Miss Farren*, 1791.

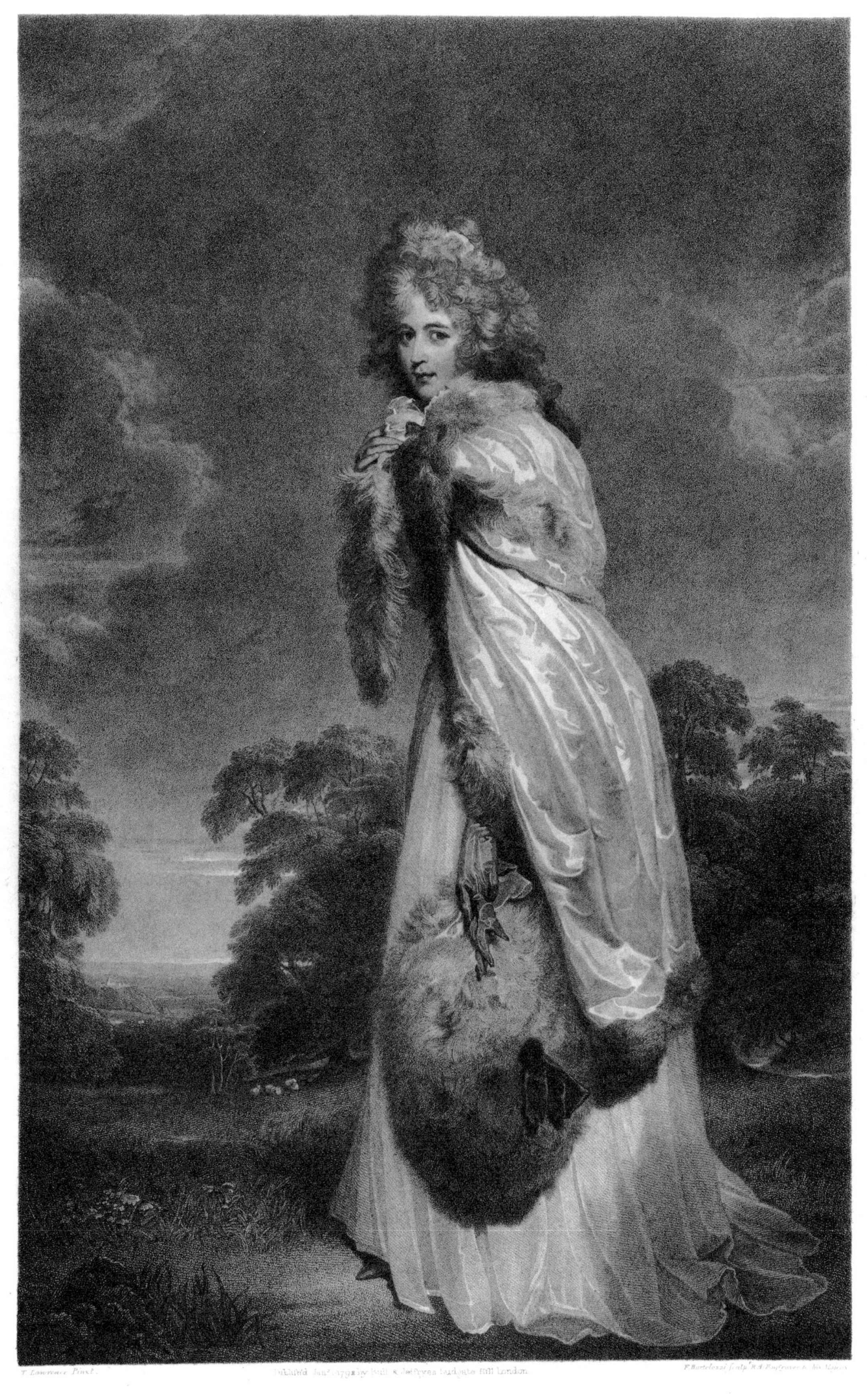

Plate 114b. Charles Knight and Francesco Bartolozzi, *Miss Farren*, 1791-92.

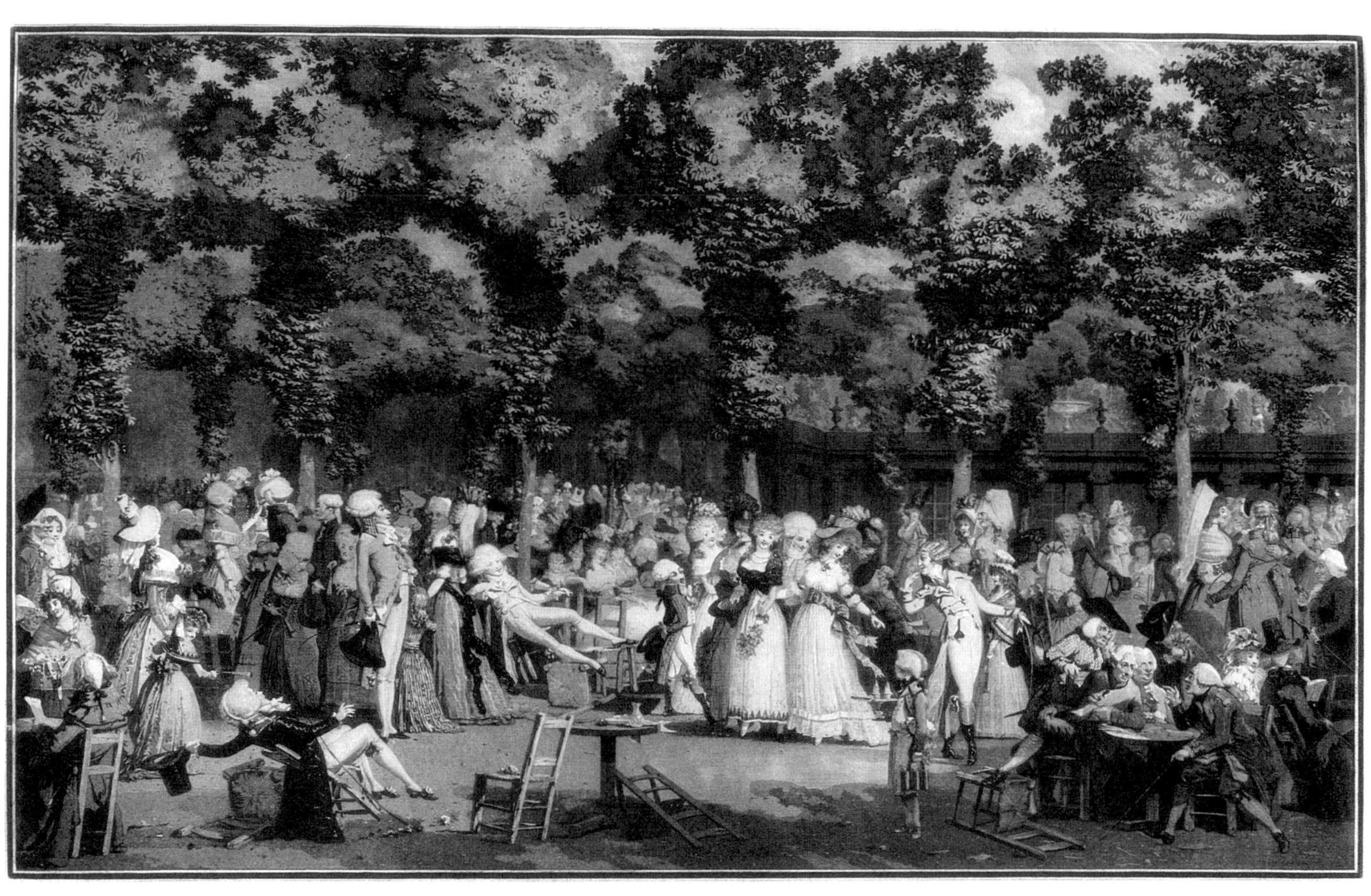

Plate 115. Philibert-Louis Debucourt, *The Public Promenade*, 1792.

Francisco José Goya y Lucientes

Fuendetodos 1746-1828 Bordeaux

116. Blind Man Tossed on the Horns of a Bull

ca. 1800-04.
Etching, aquatint, and drypoint on antique laid paper, 17.5 x 21.6 cm (platemark).
Del. 24 i/iii; Harris 25.I.2.
Watermark: SERRA
Provenance: Georges Provôt?; (his sale Paris, April 10, 1935, lot 20?); (Maurice Gobin, Paris, consigned to Knoedler, July 10, 1935); (purchased from M. Knoedler, New York, October 28, 1935, for $221).
Bequest of Herbert Greer French, 1943.527.

Francisco José de Goya y Lucientes died in Bordeaux in 1828 at the age of eighty-two, in exile from his native Spain. He witnessed the promise of the Enlightenment for socioeconomic betterment and ecclesiastical reform that Ferdinand VII extinguished. Against this backdrop Goya's unique genius matured into the foremost Spanish painter and one of the world's great printmakers.

Goya was born in the province of Aragon on March 30, 1746, the son of Doña Garcia Lucientes of Fuendetodos, who could claim noble blood, and José de Goya, a master gilder, just as the Bourbon king Ferdinand VI succeeded to the Spanish throne. At the age of fourteen he entered the studio of José Luzán y Martinez, a respected Neapolitan-trained painter, remaining four years. In 1763 and again in 1766 Goya competed unsuccessfully in the drawing competition for travel scholarships given by the Academia de Bellas Artes de San Fernando in Madrid. In the interim he entered the studio of the Aragonese painter Francisco Bayeu in Madrid, at a time when the king called the great Venetian rococo master Giovanni Battista Tiepolo and his antithesis, the German neoclassicalist Anton Raffael Mengs, to Madrid to undertake decorative schemes for the royal palaces. Undaunted by a lack of financial support, the aspiring artist traveled to Italy in 1770-71, where he won an honorable mention at the Royal Academy of Fine Arts in Parma. Other details of his activity in Italy remain a mystery. Upon his return to Spain, he secured his first important commission: the decoration of the choir ceiling of Santa María del Pilar in Zaragoza, where he demonstrated that he was already an accomplished fresco painter. In 1773 he married Josefa Bayeu, the sister of Francisco Bayeu, who was then the most prominent painter in Spain and Mengs' protégé. Upon Bayeu's recommendation, he was called to Madrid by Mengs to design his first series of tapestry cartoons: hunting scenes to be executed by the Real Fábrica de Tapices de Santa Bárbara for the Escorial. Between 1775 and 1792 he painted models and cartoons for approximately sixty genre tapestries for various royal residences.

About 1771 Goya executed his first known etching, *The Flight into Egypt*. This religious print may have been made in Italy or shortly thereafter given the Italianate style of signature. Before Goya, Spain had no established tradition of original printmaking or print collecting. While foreign prints – French, Flemish, and Italian – flooded the country, printmaking in Spain during the late seventeenth and early eighteenth century tended to serve utilitarian needs for religious, topographic, illustrative, and reproductive prints. In 1752, when the academia was established in Madrid, printmaking was added to the curriculum. A decade later in 1861 Don Manuel de Rueda wrote the first printmaking manual in Spanish. Antonio Ponz Piquer, a painter turned art historian, discussed the royal collections in his book *Viaje de España* (1776) and lamented public ignorance of the paintings of Diego Velázquez (1599-1660) and other artists. Goya took up this challenge. On July 28, 1778, he advertised in the *Gazeta de Madrid* nine reproductive etchings after Velázquez, demonstrating that he had mastered the process.[1]

The equestrian portraits sold for six reales and the others for three. Goya used an unusual method to transfer his preparatory chalk drawings to the copperplate. The paper was dampened and placed facedown on the grounded plate, then it was run through the press. Sufficient chalk transferred to the protective waxy coating to serve as a guide to begin working on the plate. Additional prints after Velázquez followed, including some of the earliest aquatints in Spain.[2] Goya's prints after Velázquez are reinterpretations with line and tone rather than dry mechanical copies. Of the 269 intaglio prints executed by Goya, only 130 were published, some in extremely limited editions.

In 1780 Goya was elected to the academia. At the age of thirty-seven he painted his first official portrait of the minister of state, *Conde de Floridablanca* (1783), which was followed almost immediately by *The Family of the Infante Don Luis* (1784). Thus began Goya's distinguished and remunerative career as a society portraitist. In 1789, when Carlos IV came to the throne, he was appointed court painter, and a series of royal portraits was commissioned culminating in *The Family of Carlos IV* (1800-01). In 1792-93 Goya suffered a serious illness that left him permanently deaf. Although he was appointed director of painting at the academia in 1795, he resigned two years later because of his affliction.

Goya executed four major print series, but only two were publicly issued during his lifetime. The *Caprichos* (*Los Caprichos*) was advertised in the *Diario de Madrid* on February 6, 1799.[3] This series of eighty etchings and aquatints executed between 1797-98 sold for 320 reales (an ounce of gold). These prints, reflecting a variety of artistic, literary, and iconographical sources, mirror the enlightened thinking and writing of Goya's friends during politically turbulent times. Cognizant of the power of political and social caricature, Goya's ad carried the disclaimer that none of the prints was intended "to ridicule the particular defects of any one individual."[4] He stressed that censure of errors and vices was legitimate subject matter and that he *chose* as his subjects society's follies and wrongdoings.[5] Although it is impossible to pinpoint the objects of Goya's derision in *Los Caprichos*, because he was intentionally ambiguous, his contemporaries interpreted his bold humor and mordant satire as indictments against the Church, the Inquisition, the government, and the royal family.

The *Tauromaquia* (*Bullfights*), Goya's second major series, was published when the artist was seventy. It was advertised in the *Diario de Madrid* on October 28, 1816.[6] Of the forty-four subjects ultimately executed, a first edition set of thirty-three prints was published for three hundred reales. As first issued, the series begins with thirteen prints depicting the origins of bullfighting and the extraordinary men who turned it into an art; it culminates with prints of the valor and skill of Goya's celebrated contemporaries. Three of the plates are dated 1815, and it is believed that Goya began the series when the abrogation of the constitution of 1812 by Fernando VII began a period of repressive rule (1814-20) that made it impossible to publish the *Disasters of War* or the *Disparates* (*Follies*).

There are few historic precedents for the *Tauromaquia*. The close parallel of the captions suggests a relationship with Don Nicolás Fernández de Moratín's *Carta histórica sobre el origen y progresos de las fiestas de toros en España* (Historical Paper on the Origin and Progress of the Festival of Bulls in Spain).[7] In 1790 Antonio Carnicero published a set of hand-colored etchings with the title *Coleccion de las principales suertes de una corrida de toros* (*Set of the Principal Maneuvers in a Bullfight*)[8] and, in 1804, there appeared a revised and illustrated second edition of the great matador "Pepe Hillo's" *Tauromaquia, o arte de torear á caballo y á pie* (*The Bullfight, or the Art of Contesting Bulls, Mounted and on Foot*).[9] With great imagination and flare Goya celebrates this fashionable and popular national sport. He transcends the work of his predecessors with incisive design, dramatic action, and painterly shading in etching and aquatint. One would think that *Blind Man Tossed on the Horns of a Bull* was executed closer to 1815; however, Domenico Tiepolo, who died in 1804, owned an early working proof.[10] This may be the impression from the Georges Provôt Collection that was sold in 1935, the year French bought the print.[11] The copy of the *Tauromaquia* that Goya gave his friend the art historian Juan Augustín Ceán Bermúdez to draft titles, now in the British Museum, has an impression of *Blind Man Tossed on the Horns of a Bull* pasted as a frontispiece opposite the table of plates.[12] This working proof carries the title, possibly in Goya's hand: *Barbara diversion* (*Barbarous Entertainment*).[13] Below there is a pencil commentary closely resembling the ink calligraphy of the title page, *Esta es la voz del Publico racional, religioso e ilustrado de España.* (This is the voice of the rational, religious and enlightened people of Spain.)[14] The original red crayon drawing (fig. 116-1), now in the Museo del Prado, is inscribed "*Dios se lo pague a usted*" ("May God repay you").[15] Like most of Goya's other drawings, it shows a platemark, indicating that it was used to transfer the design

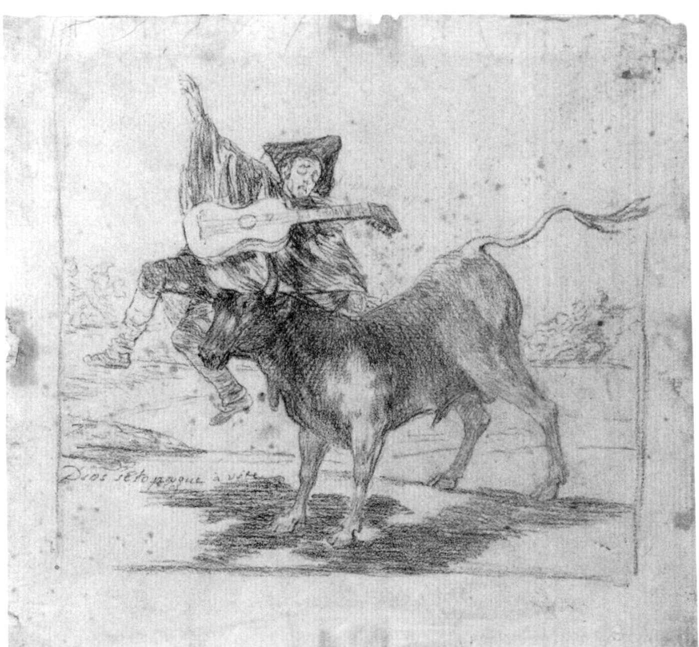

Figure 116-1. Francisco José Goya y Lucientes, *Dios se lo paque a Usted*, 1800-04, red crayon. Museo del Prado, Madrid.

to the copperplate, which is currently owned by Dr. Zdenko Bruck of Buenos Aires.[16] The most significant difference between the drawing and print is Goya's simplification of the landscape to focus on the activity in the foreground. Juliet Wilson Bareau has pondered whether the *Tauromaquia* prints have satirical or allegorical connotations and whether Goya's use of this print as a frontispiece was "intended as a criticism of the people who enjoy the brutal spectacle or of the bull which tosses a personification of poor, blind Spain on his horns."[17] This print was not published until after Goya's death, when the *Gazette des Beaux-Arts* in 1867 published an impression printed by Delâtre with the title *Aveugle enlevé sur les cornes d'un taureau*, fanning French passion for Goya on the heels of the first posthumous editions of the *Disasters of War* (1863) and "*Los Proverbios*" (1864).[18] – KLS

1. Eleanor Sayre, Boston 1974, 19-20.
2. Sayre, Boston 1974, 23.
3. Tomás Harris, *Goya Engravings and Lithographs* (Oxford: Bruno Cassirer, 1964), 95.
4. Harris, *Goya Engravings*, 95.
5. Harris, *Goya Engravings*, 99.
6. Harris, *Goya Engravings*, 174.
7. Sayre, Boston 1974, 201.
8. Sayre, Boston 1974, 197.
9. Sayre, Boston 1974, 202. The real name of "Pepe Hillo" was Josef Delgado.
10. Harris, *Goya Engravings*, 12, 45.
11. Harris, *Goya Engravings*, 45.
12. Pierre Gassier and Juliet Wilson, *The Life and Complete Work of Francisco Goya* (New York: William Morrow, 1971), 166.
13. Gassier and Wilson, *The Life*, 166.
14. Harris 25; Juliet Wilson Bareau, *Goya's Prints: The Tomás Harris Collection in the British Museum* (London: British Museum Publication, Ltd., 1981), 62.
15. Pierre Gassier, *Dibujos de Goya: Estudios para Grabados y Pinturas* (Barcelona: Editorial Noyner, 1974), 199.
16. Gassier and Wilson, *The Life*, 166.
17. Bareau, *Goya's Prints*, 75.
18. GBA. 22 (1867), 388.

Joseph Mallord William Turner

London 1775-1851 London

117. Junction of Severn and Wye 1811.

Plate 28 from *Liber Studiorum*.
Etching, mezzotint, and aquatint on wove paper, 20.8 x 29.0 cm (platemark).
Rawlinson 28 i/iii.
Inscribed in plate upper center: EP; signed and dated lower center: *Drawn, Etched & Engraved by J.M.W. Turner Esq. R.A. / Published June 1811, by J.M.W. Turner, Queen Ann Street West.*
Provenance: (Purchased from M. Knoedler, New York, May 31, 1930, for $140).
Bequest of Herbert Greer French, 1943.533.

During the year 1806, J. M. W. Turner was a frequent guest at the cottage of William Frederick Wells at Knockholt in Kent. One of Turner's closest friends, Wells was a landscape artist and drawing master who that very year had become president of the Old Water-Colour Society.[1] According to Wells' daughter Clara, it was at Knockholt that her father urged Turner to begin the *Liber Studiorum*, a series of prints intended to display the artist's versatility and range in the various categories of landscape composition. Although Turner was somewhat reluctant about the project, Wells' persistence eventually won him over:

> For your own credit's sake Turner you ought to give a work to the public which will do you justice – if after your death any work

injurious to your fame should be executed, it then could be compared with the one you yourself gave to the public.[2]

Turner was at a peak in his career, having already been recognized as the leading landscape and marine painter of his day. A project such as the *Liber* would undoubtedly broaden his audience and therefore strengthen his current status. Gerald Wilkinson also notes that although he was financially well off, "Turner was so determined to sell his work. . . . It is part, but a curious part, of the complexity and energy which made him a genius."[3]

The idea for the *Liber Studiorum* was inspired by Claude Lorrain's *Liber Veritatis*, a group of 195 sketches that was successfully reproduced as mezzotint engravings by Thomas Earlom in 1777.[4] While Claude's book was initially created as a personal record of his paintings, with no intention of being seen by the public, Turner wanted his *Liber* to include "fully-finished pictures," with the sole purpose of exploiting the complete range of his skills.

The original plan for Turner's *Liber* called for one hundred engravings divided into groupings of five plates with the following headings (and abbreviations): Historical (H), Mountainous (Ms or M), Pastoral (P), Marine (M), and Architectural (A). A sixth category, using the initials "EP," was also included and possibly refers to either Epic, Elegant, Elevated and/or Elegiac Pastoral.[5] Turner created the basic design and etched outline that was later sent to an engraver who, under Turner's close supervision and with the aid of a related wash drawing, added the desired tonal effects.[6]

According to W. G. Rawlinson, Turner initially selected aquatint as the medium for the *Liber*, but because of an apparent financial dispute with his engraver, F. C. Lewis, switched instead to the more traditional medium of mezzotint.[7] Luke Herrmann feels, however, that Turner was undecided and experimented with several engravers and engraving techniques before finally selecting Charles Turner, his namesake and fellow student at the Royal Academy, who had earlier produced an impressive mezzotint engraving of the artist's painting *The Shipwreck*.[8] Furthermore, mezzotint had been used by Thomas Earlom in his execution of the *Liber Veritatis*, a fact that undoubtedly played an important role in Turner's final decision. Nonetheless, aquatint was still used in several instances, including the *Junction of Severn and Wye*, as Herrmann notes, "thereby adding to the subtlety of the tones."[9]

Seventy-one prints were eventually published from 1807 until 1819, when Turner apparently decided to discontinue the series.[10] Although Charles Turner was originally commissioned to work on the entire project, he departed after completing only twenty plates, leaving the remaining images to a number of other engravers hired at various times during the twelve-year period.[11] Turner himself was responsible for eleven mezzotint engravings (as well as the drawings and etchings), the first and very possibly the finest of which was the *Junction of Severn and Wye* in 1811. Listed under the EP category in part VI,[12] which uses the depiction of water as its didactic theme, the print consists of several horizontal bands of light and dark that elicit an effective if not dramatic sense of depth as the hill recedes into the gorge below where the Wye River winds its way to the Severn. Thirteen years earlier, Turner made a much simpler drawing of the subject in his "Hereford Court" sketchbook that he later formalized with the addition of the trees, castle, and figure in his version for the *Liber Studiorum*. Wilkinson notes that "his preoccupation with classical composition led him into a different sort of faithlessness to his originals."[13]

The Museum has an outstanding first-state impression of the *Junction of Severn and Wye* printed on a medium wove paper. The deeply etched outlines, which appear embossed on the verso of the paper, together with Turner's own mezzotint technique and subtle use of aquatint in the sky, create an idyllic vision of a brisk June morning as the freshly lit sky shimmers across the beatific landscape. Turner had been concerned about the low opinion the Royal Academy and its first president, Sir Joshua Reynolds, had of landscape painting. According to Eric Shanes, Reynolds "did not think the genre capable of much complexity, and certainly not those dimensions of humanistic meaning" that a history painting could express.[14] With a plate such as the *Junction of Severn and Wye*, however, Turner proved that landscape had limitless range and was capable of being "elevated" to a higher and more creative plane. – DK

1. For a complete account of Turner and the *Liber Studiorum*, see W. G. Rawlinson, *Turner's Liber Studiorum*, 2nd ed. (New York: MacMillan Company, 1906), and Luke Herrmann, *Turner's Prints* (Washington Square: New York University Press, 1990), 24-71.

2. Rawlinson, *Turner's Liber*, xii-xiii.

3. Gerald Wilkinson, *Turner Sketches 1802-20* (New York: Watson-Guptill, 1974), 28.

4. Earlom worked on the mezzotint engravings between 1774 and 1776. They were published by Boydell in two magnificent volumes dedicated to the duke of Devonshire, who then owned Claude's original sketches. See Herrmann, *Turner's Prints*, 27.

5. Herrmann, *Turner's Prints*, 29. According to Herrmann, this latter category "could be used in referring to a Claudian landscape, and it is their Claudian characteristics that unite the fifteen compositions which were ultimately published under the heading EP."

6. Once the proof was approved, the plate was sent to what we refer to today as a master printer, who produced the impressions to be sold. The *Liber* plates were printed by James Lahee of Castle Street. See Rawlinson, *Turner's Liber*, xlii.

7. Rawlinson, *Turner's Liber*, xxi-xxiv. Herrmann also notes that "it comes as no surprise that Turner was considering aquatint, popularized by Paul Sandby thirty years earlier, and at this time producing far more satisfactory results in the representation of landscape subjects than the more traditional copper engraving." See Herrmann, *Turner's Prints*, 25-26.

8. By 1804 Turner had added a gallery to his house at 64 Harley Street. The most important painting in his first exhibition held there in May 1805 was *The Shipwreck*.

9. Herrmann, *Turner's Prints*, 28.

10. Turner personally handled the advertising and publishing of the series and charged fourteen guineas for each set of five prints. See Jack Lindsay, *J. M. W. Turner: His Life and Work* (Greenwich: New York Graphic Society, 1966), 259.

11. Along with Charles Turner, the mezzotint engravers who were hired by J. M. W. Turner to work on the *Liber* were William Say, Thomas Goff Lupton, William Annis, Robert Dunkarton, James Easline, Henry Dawe, S. W. Reynolds, George Clint, and Thomas Hodgetts.

12. Part VI was published simultaneously with Part VII on June 1, 1811. The four other plates that accompanied the *Junction of Severn and Wye* were *Near Blair Athol* (Ms), *Lauffenbourgh on the Rhine* (A), *Windmill and Lock* (P), and *Marine Dabblers* (M). See Herrmann, *Turner's Prints*, 50.

13. "Hereford Court" was Turner's abbreviation for Hampton Court, Hereford. See Gerald Wilkinson, *Turner's Early Sketchbooks* (New York: Watson-Guptill, 1974), 62.

14. Eric Shanes, *Turner's England: A Survey in Watercolors* (North Pomfret: Trafalgar Square Publishing, 1990), 18.

Jean-Auguste-Dominique Ingres

Montauban 1780-1867 Paris

118. Gabriel Cortois de Pressigny 1816.

Etching and engraving on wove paper, 30.8 x 21.3 cm (platemark). Del.1 iii/iii; I.F.F.1800 1.
Signed and dated in plate lower left: J. D. INGRES, FECIT ROMAE. *1816*; inscribed lower center: *Exquise politesse, entretien noble, affable, / Dignité sûre, esprit, piété véritable, / Style animé, bon coeur, tendre amour pour le Roi: / Dans ce Portrait, Lecteur, j'ai dit ce que tu vois.*
Provenance: Loys-Henry Delteil (Lugt 773); (his sale Le Garrec, Paris, June 13-15, 1928, lot 252); (purchased from M. Knoedler, New York, February 1, 1929, for $725).
Bequest of Herbert Greer French, 1943.528.
Exhibitions: Cincinnati 1930, no. 31.

Known equally for his paintings and his superbly rendered graphite portrait drawings, Ingres very rarely worked in any printmaking medium. Born in the southern French city of Montauban, Ingres received his first artistic training from his father and later studied in Toulouse from 1792 until 1796. In 1796 he went to Paris and entered the studio of Jacques-Louis David (1748 – 1825). He won the Prix de Rome in 1801 but had to wait until 1805 for his stipend for a Roman stay, which he began the next year. After his pension at the French Academy in Rome ended in 1810, Ingres continued to work and study in Rome, receiving occasional commissions from French governmental officials and sending paintings back to the Paris Salons. After the fall of the Napoleonic empire in 1814 (and the end of French control of Rome), Ingres found himself with little institutional support, but he executed numerous private portrait commissions to manage a living. After a four-year stay in Florence, Ingres returned to Paris. Except for a six-year stint as director of the French Academy in Rome from 1835 to 1841, he worked there for the rest of his life.

This portrait of the influential French cleric Gabriel Cortois de Pressigny (1745-1823) was executed in Rome during Ingres' first extended stay there after winning the Prix de Rome. In 1816 Cortois de Pressigny was the French ambassador to Rome, involved in negotiating an alliance with the pope on behalf of the new government of Louis XVIII. Born to a family well situated within the royal administration, Cortois de Pressigny progressed through the ranks of the church, being appointed bishop of Saint-Malo in 1786 by Louis XVI. Forced into exile during the Revolution for his royalist sympathies, he returned to France in 1801, was appointed ambassador to Rome in 1814, and became archbishop of Besançon in 1817, a position that he held until his death.

Ingres' etching reproduces a graphite portrait drawing of Cortois de Pressigny executed in the same year, presumably before the sitter's departure from Rome at the end of May.[1] The print is in reverse to the drawing, but the inherent reversal in the printmaking process was anticipated by Ingres, who switched the bishop's ring between the drawing and the print in order that it remain on the sitter's right hand. A graphite sketch for the bishop's right hand is in the Musée Ingres, Montauban.[2] The rarity of prints actually executed by Ingres, coupled with the great number of reproductive prints produced after his portrait drawings that have been attributed to him, has led to much scholarly discussion concerning the extent of his genuine printmaking oeuvre. Articles by Heinrich Schwarz and Hans Naef have generally established that this single etching and some four lithographs are the only agreed-upon prints by Ingres himself.[3]

The case for Ingres' own participation in this portrait etching is bolstered not only by the above-mentioned care in switching the ring in order to render the print version ecclesiastically correct but also by an impression of the print in the Bibliothèque Municipale in Versailles that carries a dedication and inscription by Ingres specifying that he both drew and etched it.[4] The copperplate for the print is now in the Calcographia Nazionale in Rome.[5] The actual motive for producing this etched reproduction of the bishop's portrait remains obscure, but it is known to have served as a gift for members of the French diplomatic circle in Rome.[6] The etching reproduces Ingres' graphite drawing successfully by transforming soft graphite shading into cross-hatched textures. A certain awkwardness or dryness of the etched lines testifies to the work of someone not used to the medium; however, the characterization of the subject's face and expression has been admirably transferred from drawing to print.

It is not known where or from whom Ingres learned to etch. The mastery of Ingres' portrait draftsmanship is evident in this subject, which concentrates on the face and head and radiates outward through the dress and accessories, despite a totally blank background. This example of Ingres' command of portrait draftsmanship originated during one of his most prolific periods of drawing portrait studies, which remain, in themselves, classic achievements in the genre.[7] His graphite portraits have a firmly established place in the history of drawing, in a tradition that includes such artists as Anthony van Dyck (cats. 72-73) and Edgar Degas (cat. 127).

Ingres' choice of the etching medium does stand as an anomaly within this particular period of French printmaking. The favored print media for portraits were engraving (at times combined with etching or aquatint) and lithography, itself invented less than twenty years previously. The romantic etching tradition of Eugène Delacroix, Théodore Chassériau, and others was still some years in the future. During the late eighteenth century in France, etching, for the most part, was a mark of the independent, original (as opposed to reproductive) printmaker, represented by Jean-Jacques de Boissieu (1736-1810) or amateurs such as the Baron Dominique-Vivant Denon (1747-1825). For precedents one perhaps needs to look to the strong tradition of etching in Italy, among students at the French Academy in Rome, and even further to Dutch and Flemish etched portraits by Jan Lievens, Rembrandt, and Van Dyck. Indeed, this etching of Cortois de Pressigny may have been a conscious attempt to evoke the spirit of Van Dyck's own etched portraits connected with his *Iconography*.

Like the *Iconography*, that series of seventeenth-century portraits of notables, Ingres appended a four-line inscription extolling the many virtues of his subject. Its clumsy style has led authorities to assume it was composed by Ingres himself.[8] Definitely not clumsy, however, is the artist's evocation of an influential, conservative, worldly, and perhaps somewhat stern cleric. The Museum's impression is of the still comparatively rare third, completed state with the inscriptions. The first two states are of the greatest rarity; the Bibliothèque Nationale owns impressions of all three (I.F.F. 1800 XI:41.1). – DPB

1. Now in a private collection, the drawing is reproduced and discussed in Hans Naef, *Die Bildniszeichnungen von J.-A.-D. Ingres* (Bern: Benteli, 1977 – 80), vol. 4, no. 170.

2. Naef, *Bildniszeichnungen*, 4:312.

3. See, in particular, Heinrich Schwarz, "Ingres graveur," GBA., 6th per., 54 (December 1959): 329-42. For this etching, see Hans Naef, "Deux dessins d'Ingres, Monseigneur Cortois de Pressigny et le chevalier de Fontenay," *La Revue des arts* 6 (November-December 1957): 243-45, and the bibliography for the related drawing in Naef, *Bildniszeichnungen*, 4:312. A. Hyatt Mayor attributed another lithograph to Ingres in "An Unidentified Ingres Lithograph," *Burl. M.* 109 (October 1967): 583.

4. Reproduced in Schwarz, "Ingres graveur," 334, fig. 5. See also the discussion in I.F.F. 1800 XI:40, where the authors cast doubt on the attribution as scarcely believable, a "debut" effort not in accord with contemporary etching style. They even venture another attribution, to Claude Dien (1787-1865), but do agree that the Versailles proof of the portrait argues in favor of Ingres' participation.

5. First published by Campbell Dodgson in "Quarterly Notes," PCQ. 22, n. 4 (October 1935): 281.

6. The impression cited in n. 4 above is dedicated to "Chevalier de Fontenay." In their biography of the reproductive engraver Henriquel-Dupont, the authors of I.F.F. 1800 (X :281) include an intriguing but far-fetched reference to *Cortois de Pressigny* having been intended for a commemorative publication of the coronation of Charles X, which did not take place until 1824.

7. For studies of Ingres's portrait drawings, in addition to Naef (*Bildniszeichnungen*), see the classic exhibition catalogue by Agnes Mongan and Hans Naef, Cambridge 1967.

8. Naef, *Bildniszeichnungen*, 2:113. The verses translate: "Refined civility, noble and affable conversation, / Unfailing dignity, spirit and true piety, / An animated spirit, good heart, and tender love for the king: / In this portrait, Reader, I have described what you see."

Francisco José Goya y Lucientes

Fuendetodos 1746-1828 Bordeaux

119. Disparate alegre (Merry Folly) ca. 1816-17.
Plate [12] from the *Disparates*
Etching, burnished aquatint, and drypoint on wove paper,
24.3 x 35.4 cm (platemark).
Del. 213 i/iii; Harris 259 II.
Provenance: (Maurice Gobin, Paris, consigned to Knoedler, July 10,
1935); (purchased from M. Knoedler, New York, October 28, 1935,
for $221).
Bequest of Herbert Greer French, 1943.526.

Francisco Goya never published editions of his later series the
Disasters of War (1810-14, 1820-23) and the *Disparates* (ca. 1816-17)
during his lifetime because of the fluctuating political climate. In
1814, two years after the duke of Wellington's victory over
Napoleon in the Spanish War of Independence, Ferdinand VII
returned to power and subjected Spain to a very repressive regime.
Although Goya probably intended to publish the *Disasters of War*,
the swing of the political pendulum in 1814 forced him to go
underground with his printmaking, except for the *Tauromaquia*,
which he published in 1816.

Before Goya expatriated himself to Bordeaux in 1824, the
copperplates for *Disasters of War* were safely stored by his son
Francisco Javier, who died in 1854. Goya's grandson, Mariano
Goya, brought the virtually unknown drawings, plates, and proofs
to light.[1] The Academia de Bellas Artes de San Fernando published
the first edition of the eighty aquatint etchings in 1863, thirty-five
years after the artist's death, under the title *Disasters of War* (*Los
Desastres de la Guerra*). This series documented the Napoleonic war
against Spanish guerrillas and traces Goya's shifting perspective on
the political situation from patriotism to grim reality and finally to
postwar political repression. The prints are generally grouped as war
subjects representing herioc deeds and mindless atrocities, which had
their genesis at Saragossa (pls. 2-47); Madrid famine scenes from
1811-12 (pls. 48-64); and violently anticlerical *caprichos enfáticos*
(pls. 65-80), which were probably begun after the war (1814) when
quality copperplates were again available.Goya gave a bound set of
the *Disasters* with manuscript title and plate number to the critic
Ceán Bermúdez to edit. It was this set that the academia used in 1863
as its model for the first published edition of the *Disasters*.

The *Disparates* remains shrouded in mystery. None of the plates
were dated nor can they be pinpointed to external events. One of the
plates, *Modo de Volar* (*Method of Flying*), was included in the
bound copy of *Tauromaquia* given by Goya to Ceán Bermúdez,
suggesting that the series was in progress as early as 1816.[2] Most
recently Eleanor Sayre has suggested that the plates date from circa
1816-17.[3] From 1820 to 1823 the short-lived constitutional
monarchy drove out the Jesuits, for the second time secularized
much Church property, and abolished the Inquisition. In 1823, when
Ferdinand VII revoked the constitution for the second time and
reinstated his oppressive autocratic regime, thousands of Spanish
liberals were pursued and prosecuted. Fearing that this series would
further compromise his safety, Goya suppressed the material,
abandoned the plates, and sought a legitimate excuse to flee Spain in
1824. The plates were stored at Goya's country home along with
those for the *Disasters of War*. Not only are there no certainties
concerning dates of the plates, but we have no information
concerning their sequence or their meaning. In 1864 the Real
Academia of San Fernando published an edition of eighteen of the
Disparates plates under the title "Los Proverbios." According to

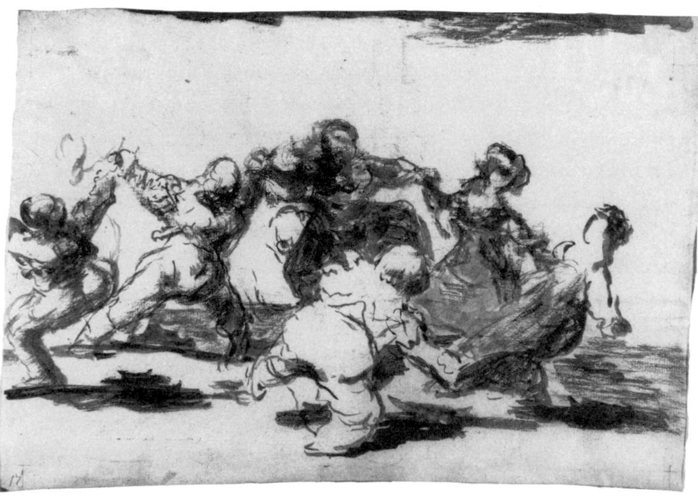

Figure 119-1. Francisco José Goya y Lucientes, *Disparate alegre*, 1815-24,
sanguine wash over red chalk. Museo del Prado, Madrid.

Sayre, there is no proof that the order was based on Goya; instead,
the sequence was probably based on an earlier posthumous edition
of 1848, now in the Boston Museum of Fine Arts.[4] The academia
edition did not include an additional four subjects that surfaced in
the collection of the Spanish painter Eugenio Lucas printed for the
French periodical *L'Art* by Liénard in 1877.[5] In addition, three
drawings have transfer platemarks identical in style and technical
characteristics, implying that the series could even have been larger.[6]

The drawings for the series, executed with brush and sanguine
wash over red chalk, have a breathtaking freedom and
impressionistic vitality. In some instances, radical alterations were
made to the original design in the process of executing the plate. The
original drawing for *Disparate alegre* (*Merry Folly*) (fig. 119-1) in the
Museo del Prado is close to the print. In the drawing, the dancer's
hands are joined rather than individually dancing with castanets as
in the print. The center *maja*'s active stance has been redrawn in a
restrained pose for the print. The drawing carries the number
seventeen in the lower left corner.

In 1918 thirteen contemporary working proofs with manuscript
titles sharing the word *disparate*, generally accepted to be by Goya,
were described and published by Beruete.[7] Subsequent historians
accepted his series title the *Disparates* as more appropriate than the
academia's *Los Proverbios*. The Spanish word *disparate* in English
means "folly." It provides the only clue to the interpretation of the
prints. In 1973 the Boston Museum of Fine Arts acquired the only
known working proof for this print with the manuscript title
Disparate alegre and the marginal numbers *eight* and *nineteen*.[8] The
Museum's impression may be the Georges Provôt trial proof that
was sold at auction in 1935, since French acquired it shortly
thereafter.[9] Like all the *Disparates*, the full qualities of this subject
can only be appreciated in an early impression. Unlike the 1864
edition impressions, which were printed with plate tone by
Laurenciano Potenciano for the academia in deference to the
purveyors of the etching revival, this impression, printed in black, is
cleanly wiped with no tone on the highlights as is the working proof
in the Boston Museum of Fine Arts. The aquatint in the foreground
and background does not have the splotchy appearance of the
published edition nor has the aquatint on the skirt of the right *maja*
lost its duotone quality. The areas of drypoint on the head and jacket
of the dwarf *majo* still print strongly. The facing *majo* and *maja* are
relegated to the background by light strokes of parallel drypoint
hatching. The clean wiping intensifies the syncopated frenzy of the
dance. The copperplate is now in the Calcograía National, Madrid.[10]

In the *Disparates* Goya distills, transforms, and twists the social, political, and religious significance of a subject to the point that it defies explanation. His evocative titles and innovative themes remain the most ambiguous and enigmatic of any of his print series. Here, the six figures dancing in a circle are no longer the gay, youthful *majos* and *majas* gracefully frolicking on the banks of the Manzanares in Goya's 1777 tapestry cartoon.[11] They now stiffly totter as if sentenced to dance eternally in a situation laden with lustful erotic overtones. As an appropriate equivalent to this image, Tomás Harris proposed the nineteenth-century proverb *Si Marina bayló, tome los que halló (If Marion Will Dance, Then She Has to Take the Consequences)*.[12] More recently Armstrong Roche has suggested Goya's enlightened liberal stance that satirizes the fate of the nobility who offer society no merit or service for their honorific and hereditary titles.[13] Unfortunately we do not have the benefit of contemporary manuscript interpretations as with *Los Caprichos*. In 1828 Goya died exiled in Bordeaux. – KLS

1. Tomás Harris, *Goya Engravings and Lithographs* (Oxford: Bruno Cassirer, 1964), 1:141.
2. Harris, *Goya Engravings*, 1:193.
3. Eleanor Sayre in Boston 1989a, cxvii.
4. Eleanor Sayre in Boston 1989a, cxvii.
5. Harris, *Goya Engravings*, 2:389.
6. Harris, *Goya Engravings*, 2:408-10, nos. 296 a-c.
7. Harris, *Goya Engravings*, 1:193.
8. Eleanor Sayre, Boston 1974, 267-68.
9. The collection of Monsieur P. G. (Georges Provôt), Hôtel Drouot, Paris, April 10, 1935.
10. Pierre Gassier and Juliet Wilson, *The Life and Complete Work of Francisco Goya* (New York: William Morris and Co., Inc., 1971), 325.
11. Gassier and Wilson, *The Life*, 85, no. 74.
12. Harris, *Goya Engravings*, 2:393, no. 259.
13. Michael Armstrong Roche in Boston 1989a, no. 140.

Ferdinand-Victor-Eugène Delacroix

Charenton-Saint-Maurice 1798-1863 Paris

120. Turk Mounting a Horse ca. 1824.

Aquatint on wove paper, 23.0 x 27.1 cm (sheet).
Del. 11 ii?/ii;[1] I.F.F. 1800 9.
Condition: Trimmed within platemark.
Provenance: (Purchased from F.H. Bresler, Milwaukee, February 15, 1929, for $340).
Bequest of Herbert Greer French, 1943.669.

After receiving his principal artistic training in the studio of Pierre Guérin (1774-1833), beginning in 1816, and at the École des Beaux-Arts, Delacroix quickly achieved a major and influential position as a richly innovative painter. His first official triumph, the government's purchase of *Dante and Virgil in Hell*, occurred at the Salon exhibition of 1822. Delacroix produced other major paintings in the 1820s, including *The Massacre at Chios* (1823) and *The Death of Sardanapalus* (1827). With paintings such as these, Delacroix came to be considered the leader of the romantic school of French painting in reaction to the classical tradition of Jacques-Louis David (1748-1825) and J.-A.-D. Ingres (cat. 118).

Delacroix was also among the most prolific and inventive of painter-printmakers in nineteenth-century France. His more than one hundred lithographs extended from 1817, during the beginning of the lithography era in Paris (it had only been invented some twenty years previously), through the 1840s. His series of illustrations for a French translation of Goethe's *Faust* (Del. 57-74) in 1828 is credited with being the prototype for the modern artist's

illustrated book (*livre de peintre*). In 1843 he published a set of lithographs illustrating Shakespeare's *Hamlet* (Del. 103-18).

His first efforts at line etching – two crude sketch-plates (Del. 1 – 2) – perhaps date from 1814. These were followed by beginning efforts at mastering aquatint (itself a relatively new technique), probably during the early 1820s. He subsequently executed over twenty intaglio prints, although they did not play as major a part in his work as the lithographs. *Turk Mounting a Horse* is one of three Delacroix aquatints of similar format, technique, and subject matter, featuring portraits of horsemen with their horses (the two others are *Turk Saddling a Horse* [Del. 9] and *Mameluke Restraining a Horse* [Del. 10]).

Amidst the current rage for orientalist subjects, the group complements both Delacroix's own interest in the subject and his consistent study of and fascination with animal motifs, especially the motif of horse and rider.[2] His interest in the Near East and Africa had begun as early as the mid-1810s. He eagerly read accounts of journeys to that region, interviewed returning travelers, and visited collectors who owned artifacts and costumes so that he might sketch them.[3] Among Delacroix's numerous paintings and watercolors of such subjects, none is recorded that is a direct study for any of the aquatints. Three tantalizing references in Delacroix's journal for March and April 1824 speak of a work titled *Turk Mounting a Horse*, perhaps a related painting or watercolor.[4]

Among the related works closest in feeling to the three aquatints are two finished watercolors in the Art Institute of Chicago and the Louvre, both of mounted Turkish horsemen.[5] The isolation of the monumentally conceived horse and rider against a relatively blank background is comparable to the watercolors, as are the carefully observed details of costume. At least three oil paintings dated from 1825 to circa 1826 are closely related in subject matter and treatment: *Turk in a Red Cape, Indian Warrior with Tethered Horse*, and *Young Turk Stroking his Horse*.[6] Similar subjects were of course being explored by many other artists of the period, in all media, including prints. *Desert Arab* (1817) by Baron Antoine-Jean Gros (1771-1835) or Gericault's own numerous prints of horses, especially a print such as his *Arabian Horse* of 1821 (Del. 37), would surely have inspired Delacroix's efforts on this relatively intimate scale: he is recorded as owning prints by both.[7]

In conjunction with the dating of the watercolors and the paintings of Turkish horsemen to the early and mid-1820s, a date of circa 1824 or a bit later would be logical for the aquatint horsemen series.[8] It is difficult to determine precisely when and where Delacroix first attempted to learn aquatint and, more importantly, when he achieved such superlative control of the medium. Only two tantalizing references to working in aquatint appear in his journal, both for the year 1824 (May 4 and June 13).[9] Jean Adhémar has stated that Delacroix received advice in etching from his friend Frédéric Villot (1809-1875) and from the reproductive engraver Louis-Pierre Henriquel-Dupont (1797-1892).[10] However, as Delacroix's friendship with Villot did not begin until 1827, it is unlikely that Villot was involved in helping Delacroix with this group of prints.[11] Henriquel-Dupont, who was executing quite sophisticated aquatints from at least 1826, could be a source for Delacroix's mastery of the extremely tricky medium; he also trained in Guérin's studio.[12]

A more likely connection for Delacroix's knowledge of aquatint would have been the Fielding brothers, British artists residing in Paris with whom Delacroix was very close during this period. There has always been confusion as to which brother is referred to at any one time in Delacroix's brief journal entries, but perhaps the closest to him was Thales Fielding (1793-1837), whose studio Delacroix eventually took over when Thales moved back to England in

October 1824.[13] Thales and his brothers Theodore (1781-1851) and Newton (1799-1856) were all executing extremely sophisticated aquatints in Paris for both French and English publishers from the early 1820s, usually reproducing watercolors. Almost every day from June 13-21, 1824, when Delacroix mentions beginning his aquatint and working on his "plate," he also mentions being at "Fielding's."[14] Significantly, one of the Parisian publishers for whom the Fieldings worked was J. F. Ostervald, whose name has been linked in early catalogues with Delacroix's horsemen series of aquatints.[15]

Turk Mounting a Horse is a virtual textbook lesson in the process of staged bitings of aquatint in order to achieve subtle gradations of tone and shadow. While the white highlights of the figure's headdress and in the folds of his clothing would have been protected from the action of the acid throughout the entire process (therefore showing only the bright white of the paper), the darkest areas of black tonality in the horse's mane and in the shadows cast on its body would have received the greatest exposure to acid. The intermediate tones would have been carefully protected by brushing varnish that was impervious to acid onto the surface of the plate. Remarkable control was necessary to achieve a dozen or so successful immersions in the acid. Areas of the subtlest tone changes in the sky and the flanks of the horse reveal the possibilities inherent in the process.

It remains an open question as to why the three aquatint horsemen were never published in an edition. Delacroix later allowed another masterful aquatint to be published in 1833, *The Blacksmith* (Del. 19). Impressions of *Turk Mounting a Horse* are exceedingly rare; others are recorded in the Princeton University Art Museum (first state); the Metropolitan Museum of Art, New York (trimmed similarly to the Cincinnati impression); and Bibliothèque Nationale, Paris, which owns two impressions of the first state. – DPB

1. The difference between the first and second state is merely the presence of some aquatint trials in the margins in the first state, which were burnished out by the second. The Museum's impression has been trimmed to just within the area of those trials, so it is not possible with certainty to determine if it could be a first state (although there seems to be a very tiny area of aquatint at the edge of the sheet at the lower left not present in the Metropolitan Museum's impression). There is no artistic difference between the states, and it is possible that the Museum's impression is of the first. Some confusion in the literature exists. Delteil apparently reproduces a second-state impression but indicates that it is a first. On the other hand, the Princeton impression of the first state is illustrated in Frankfurt am Main 1987, 133, no. H3, where it is correctly numbered but described as the second state.

2. For numerous such sketches of horses and riders, see Maurice Sérullaz et al., *Dessins d'Eugène Delacroix*, Musée du Louvre, Cabinet des Dessins, *Inventaire général des dessins – école française* (Paris: Editions de la Réunion des Musées Nationaux, 1984), vol. 1, nos. 978-1044.

3. Frank A. Trapp, *The Attainment of Delacroix* (Baltimore and London: John Hopkins Press, 1971), 36-39; also see, for instance, Delacroix's journal entry for May 4, 1824, where he lists several books on the "orient" and Turkish costumes that he had purchased or consulted (André Joubin, ed., *Journal de Eugène Delacroix* [Paris: Librairie Plon, 1932], 1:92-93).

4. [March 15, 1824]: "Made the sketch [? – "trait"] for a *Turk Mounting a Horse*"; [March 18, 1824 – the same day in which he bought Gericault lithographs]: "Finished the *Turk Mounting a Horse*"; [April 18, 1824] "M. Lemâle came and bought the *Turk Mounting a Horse*." (Joubin, ed., *Journal*, 1:61-62 and 80, respectively) Joubin specifically relates these references to the aquatint (Joubin, ed., *Journal*, 61, n. 1; 80, n. 1), but it cannot be automatically assumed to be so. Delacroix's journal for May 10, 1824 (Joubin, ed., *Journal*, 98) also specifically mentions a watercolor of a "Mameluke holding a horse by the bridle," which does seem to describe the subject of the related aquatint (Del. 10). See also the entry for June 4 (Joubin, ed., *Journal*, 109), in which Delacroix mentions work on a "Turk on a horse."

5. The Chicago watercolor is illustrated in Frankfurt am Main 1987, no. H5; the Louvre's in Sérullaz et al., *Dessins*, 2: 96, no. 1505. The respective authors date the works to 1828-30 and 1826-28.

6. Lee Johnson, *The Paintings of Eugène Delacroix – A Critical Catalogue* (Oxford: Clarendon Press, 1981), 1:26-28, nos. 36-38; reproduced in vol. 2, pls. 31-33. Johnson's entry for *Indian Warrior with Tethered Horse* clears up a curious inscription on the mat of the Cincinnati aquatint: "Plate bitten by Bracquemond." As Bracquemond (cat. 124)

was not born until 1833, he could hardly have worked on Delacroix's plate. However, in 1857 he did etch a reproduction of the *Indian Warrior* painting; it was never published, probably because of Delacroix's severe criticism of it (Johnson, *Eugène Delacroix*, 1:27). For the Bracquemond etching, see Jean-Paul Bouillon, *Félix Bracquemond, le réalisme absolu – oeuvre gravé 1849-1859* (Geneva: Skira, 1987), 166, no. *Ae 40, repr.

7. In his journal for May 9, 1824, Delacroix mentions purchasing prints on the Rue des Saints-Pères for five francs, including oriental costumes, primitive "instruments," and an "old lithograph" by Gericault (Joubin, ed., *Journal*, 94). The next day he purchased a Gros lithograph, depicting North African horsemen (Gros made only two prints in all, both of such subjects – -I.F.F. 1800 IX:422). Mention should also be made of a lithograph attributed to Delacroix himself quite similar to the aquatint series of horsemen, *Negro on a Horse* (Del. 39), dated by Delteil to 1823. It features a horseman placed against a comparatively flat, expansive landscape and perhaps reflects an experiment to see which medium would be more suitable to reproduce his watercolors of the subject.

8. Following Alfred Robaut, Delteil dated them to 1828, with no specific supporting evidence.

9. Joubin, ed., *Journal*, 1:92, 112 [May 4, 1824]: "While returning, dreamed with Soulier about making aquatints together after my drawings"; [June 13, 1824] "Began my aquatint." His first accomplished aquatint, *Interior of a Military Hospital* (Del. 8), was probably inspired by a composition of Gericault's and was perhaps executed about the time of the latter's death in January 1824; indeed, the figure of the wounded soldier bears more than a passing resemblance to Gericault. It was at this time that Delacroix was making several drawn studies after the *Caprichos* of Goya, themselves aquatints; therefore, 1824 would be a logical date for his own aquatint after Goya's *The Bogeyman* (Harris 38). The authors of Frankfurt am Main 1987 (p. 4) have also placed that print (Del. 7) to the first half of the 1820s rather than accepting Delteil's date of 1819.

10. In Paris 1963, above no. 1.

11. See Johnson, *Eugène Delacroix*, 3:36, no. 217, for a brief overview of their friendship and Villot's career.

12. For Henriquel-Dupont, see I.F.F. 1800 X:281-92, esp. p. 284, nos. 26-29, and Ber. 8:77ff.

13. For further information and a portrait of Thales, see Johnson, *Eugène Delacroix*, 1:45-46, no. 70, illustrated as pl. 63. The most extensive treatment of the Fielding brothers is included in Marcia R. Pointon, *The Bonington Circle – English Watercolour and Anglo-French Landscape 1790-1855* (Brighton: Hendon Press, 1985).

14. Joubin, ed., *Journal*, 112-15 [June 13, 1824]: "Dinner with Soulier and Fielding at *Butter Mill*. – Began my aquatint"; [June 16, 1824]: "The morning at Fielding's. Began the plate at the studio"; [June 17, 1824]: "Fielding the morning. – The plate. At noon the studio"; [June 18, 1824]: "The morning, at Fielding's. – and my plate"; [June 20, 1824]: "The day at Fielding's. – Finished my plate"; [June 21, 1824]: "Carried my plate to the printer." Joubin identifies the "plate" in these instances with *Turk Mounting a Horse*, but he offers no concrete evidence for its identification. Mention should also be made of a contemporaneous aquatint *formerly* attributed to Delacroix but now given to his friend Jean-Baptiste Pierret (1795-1854). Pierret is said to have executed it with Newton Fielding (Del., "Doubtful or falsely attributed works," no. 2). An aquatint by Newton is reproduced in Malcolm Cormack, *Bonington* (Oxford: Phaidon, 1989), 54, fig. 38. Pointon (*Bonington Circle*, 73) directly asserts Delacroix's knowledge of aquatint with the Fieldings. She also states that a reference in his journal from March 7, 1824 (Joubin, ed., *Journal*, 1:60), to Fielding having helped Delacroix with the "ground" (*fond*) refers to an aquatint ground; it could, however, refer to the background of a painting.

The sophisticated use of the medium evident in Delacroix's print is indeed quite comparable to the aquatint work of the Fieldings. For instance, very similar "spotted" effects in stopping-out as seen in the foreground of *Turk Mounting a Horse* are seen in several plates in T. H. A. Fielding, *Cumberland, Westmoreland, and Lancashire, Illustrated. . . the Scenery of the Lakes* (London: Thomas M'Lean, 1822), particularly pls. 5, 23, and 20 [copy in Yale Center for British Art]. The possibility that the Fieldings played more of a role in the aquatints than mentors must be considered, but lack of any documentation thus far prevents a clear determination either way.

15. See the first catalogue of Delacroix's prints, included in Adolphe Moreau, *E. Delacroix et son oeuvre* (Paris: Librairie des bibliophiles, 1873), nos. 6-8; Alfred Robaut, *L'Oeuvre complet de Eugène Delacroix* (Paris: Charavay, 1885; reprint, New York: Da Capo, 1969), 78-79, nos. 283-85; and Del. 9-11. All state that "[the group,] at first executed for Osterwald [sic], [was] not published." Among other projects, the Fielding brothers between them executed at least twenty-six aquatint plates (out of ninety-two) for Achille Gigault de la Salle, *Voyage pittoresque en Sicile*, 2 vols. (Paris: Didot, 1822-26); see *Travel in Aquatint and Lithography 1770-1860 from the Library of J. R. Abbey* (Folkestone and London: Dawsons of Pall Mall, 1972), 1:231 – 35, no. 262. Ostervald was the publisher and editor; see also Pointon, *Bonington Circle*, 67, n. 30, for information about Ostervald's publishing activity.

William Blake

London 1757-1827 London

121. Satan Before the Throne of God 1825.

Plate 2 from *Illustrations of the Book of Job*.
Engraving on Chine collé mounted on wove paper 21.8 x 17.0 cm (platemark).
Binyon 107 (proof edition).
Signed and dated in plate lower center: *London Published as the Act directs March 8, 1825 by William Blake N 3 Fountain Court Strand*; lower right: *Proof*.
Provenance: (Book purchased from M.A. McDonald, New York, July 20, 1936, for $450).
Bequest of Herbert Greer French, 1943.583b.

During the last seven years of his life, William Blake produced three of his most outstanding works: his only wood engravings, *The Pastorals of Virgil with a Course of English Reading, Adapted for Schools. . . by Robert John Thornton*; the plates based on Dante's *Divine Comedy*, of which only seven were completed before his death; and twenty-two engravings for *Illustrations of the Book of Job*, considered by many to be his finest achievement as a graphic artist.

Throughout his life, Blake was fascinated with the story of Job and often identified with his struggles. The Old Testament describes Job as a man "who never faltered in his faith in God. . . and who at last was rewarded with the fullness of God's blessing."[1] Blake completed his first Job-inspired piece in 1785, a pen-and-wash drawing showing the biblical character surrounded by his wife and three accusing friends. Approximately twenty years later, he produced a set of watercolors on the subject for Thomas Butts, a clerk in the Office of the Commissary General of Musters and an important patron of his paintings.[2] These watercolors were eventually seen by the landscape painter John Linnell, who persuaded Blake to create a second set of Job watercolors, this time with the addition of text. Linnell contributed to the project by making traced outlines of the Butts series and by adding some of the brushstrokes. The two parties eventually signed a contract calling for the production of twenty engravings (later extended to twenty-two) based on this new group of watercolors.

The twenty-six-year-old Linnell played an influential role in the last decade of Blake's career. The two were introduced in 1818 by a son of Blake's good friend George Cumberland at a time when Blake was experiencing serious financial difficulties. Production and sales of his graphic works had slackened considerably as had his patronage with Thomas Butts. Linnell purchased and promoted Blake's single prints and illuminated books and introduced him to a number of new customers. Because of Linnell's patronage, Blake's production level throughout the 1820s increased considerably.[3]

Inspired by his lifelong interest in Old Master prints, the *Job* series marked a return by Blake to the traditional medium of line engraving. In preparation for the printing, reduced pencil drawings were made from the watercolors and were later transferred to copperplates. All twenty-two plates existed in proof states by March 1825, but publication did not occur until the following year. Two hundred fifteen proof sets were printed, followed by an additional hundred lacking the word "Proof."

As noted in the Museum's "proof" impression of *Satan before the Throne of God* (plate 2), an engraving on chine collé,[4] the basic format for the series consists of a highly finished central panel surrounded by a sparsely designed border/text arrangement that complements the individual theme. Blake's linear approach was probably influenced by the engravings he had collected in his youth as well as by works of early Italian masters like Marcantonio Raimondi (cat. 32) and Julio Bonasoni, whose compositions could be found in the extensive print collection of George Cumberland.[5] In plate 2, Satan, represented as a young and energetic figure running through blazing flames directly below the image of God, is challenging God's declaration of Job's perfection. As God, who is portrayed in Job's likeness, points downward, Job and his wife appear in a curtain of fire, an indication of the torment Satan has planned for them. Blake's portrayal of the "master of Hell" is very similar to his earlier figural study of Orc, drawn with expressive movement and his own youthful energy from plate 3 of *The Book of Urizen*, completed in 1794. In defense of Job, a number of angels appear at his side with scrolls containing lists of his benevolent works and deeds.

Blake was extremely fond of Gothic art, especially the graphic work of Albrecht Dürer. Essick notes that by studying Dürer's prints, Blake learned how to unify individual lines and a variety of linear patterns "through the harmonious interplay of tones and textures."[6] Dürer's *Melencolia I* (1514) (cat. 49), one of the few prints that Blake retained from the sale of his collection in the early 1820s, was especially influential. Seven plates in the *Job* series, including *Satan before the Throne of God*, contain a variation in the radiating line/sunburst motif found in the upper left corner of the Dürer engraving. In his design for plate 2, Essick maintains it was Blake's "desire for a restrained and antique style that prompted [him] to eliminate. . . the rays of light breaking through the sharp edge of the halo in the earlier states."[7]

Blake separated his image of God and the other spiritual figures from the earthly scene below with a ring of cumulus clouds, a compositional device he may have also borrowed from Dürer.[8] In the lower portion, Job is surrounded by his wife and family while being confronted by two angels. This figural arrangement has no biblical reference but was derived in reverse from Blake's pen, pencil, and watercolor drawing *Enoch Walked with God?*, circa 1780-85, in the Museum's permanent collection (CAM 1977.214) (fig. 121-1). The title of the watercolor is based on a quotation found in his Enoch lithograph (ca. 1807), which used a similar composition. Both the lithograph and the drawing have also been identified as Job and his family in prosperity.[9] – DK

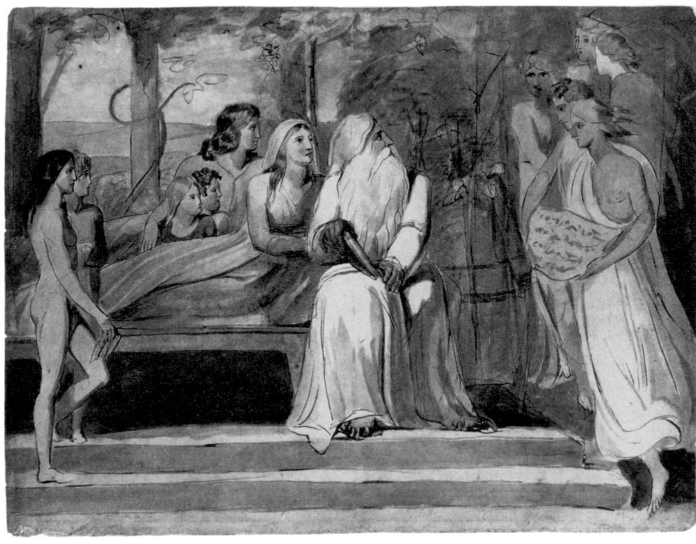

Figure 121-1. William Blake, *Enoch Walked with God(?)*, ca. 1780-85, pen and black ink, watercolor over traces of pencil. Cincinnati Art Museum, Gift of Mr. and Mrs. John W. Warrington (1977.214).

1. Alan N. Owen, "Two of the Best Illustrated Books: John Audubon's *Birds of America* and William Blake's *Book of Job*," *Connoisseur* 215 (August 1985), 116.

2. Besides the Job watercolors, Butts also commissioned Blake to produce a series of tempera paintings (ca. 1799-1800) and watercolor illustrations (ca. 1800-09) to the Bible as well as several sets of illustrations to Milton (from 1808 onward). See Martin Butlin, *William Blake* (London: Tate Gallery Publications Department, 1978), 22-23.

3. Linnell introduced Blake to John Varley (1778-1842) in 1818, Samuel Palmer (1805-1881) in 1824, George Richmond (1809-1896) in 1825, Edward Calvert (1799-1883) in 1826, and William Young Ottley in 1827. Besides the second set of watercolors and the *Job* engravings, Linnell commissioned the Dante illustrations (1824-27) and a number of other works. Because of these projects, Blake received regular payments up until his death. See Butlin, *William Blake*, 133.

4. The Museum's copy of the *Book of Job* includes a title page and twenty-one "proof" impressions printed on India paper. Mr. French purchased this set in its original binding in 1936.

5. Since Blake and Cumberland were good friends, he undoubtedly was aware of the latter's collection, which contained over eighty early printmakers. Cumberland also published *Some Anecdotes of the Life of Julio Bonasoni* in 1793.

6. For a detailed account of Dürer's influence on Blake and the *Job* series, see Essick, 244-48.

7. Essick, 246.

8. A total of six plates in *Illustrations of the Book of Job* use this compositional device, which relates to eight of Dürer's woodcuts in the *Apocalypse* (cat. 23) and to the *Resurrection* in the *Large Passion* (1511). See Essick, 245.

9. Martin Butlin, *The Paintings and Drawings of William Blake* (New Haven: Yale University Press, 1981), 55.

Honoré Daumier
Marseilles 1808-1879 Valmondois

122. Rue Transnonain, Le 15 Avril 1834.

Plate 24 from *L'Association mensuelle*.
Lithograph (crayon and scraper) on *chine appliqué*,
28.6 x 44.1 cm (image).
Del. 135.
Signed in stone lower left: H.-D.; inscribed in upper left margin: 24.
Dessing de la Lithographie Mensuelle.; in lower left margin: *Au bureau, galerie véro dodat.*; lower center: RUE TRANSNONAIN, LE 15 AVRIL 1834; lower right: *Litho. de Delaunois.*
Provenance: (Purchased from M. Knoedler, New York, November 18, 1937, for $583).
Bequest of Herbert Greer French, 1943.677.

Honoré Daumier was born in Marseille on February 26, 1808. His career as a printmaker, painter, and sculptor should be seen against the complex and shifting background of violence and revolution in nineteenth-century France. The son of Jean-Baptiste Daumier, a glazier and framemaker with literary aspirations, Daumier moved to Paris at the age of eight, where his father hoped to further his literary fortune during the early days of the Restoration following the overthrow of Napoleon. During his lifetime Daumier would witness and record the turbulent events of the revolution of 1848, the fall of Louis-Napoleon, the Crimean War, the Franco-Prussian War, and the catastrophic Paris commune. The events immediately following the Glorious Revolution of July 1830 launched Daumier's career as a political cartoonist. Between 1832 and 1870 he set the standard for political and social satire, producing nearly four thousand lithographs and one thousand wood engravings for newspapers and illustrated books.

Daumier's first signed lithograph was published in the weekly satirical periodical *La Silhouette* on July 22, 1830 (Del. 1), shortly before the overthrow of the Bourbon monarch Charles X.[1] At the age of twenty-two, Daumier's life became inextricably linked with Charles Philipon (1800-1862), the master republican strategist who adopted the new, inexpensive technology of lithography to capture the emerging bourgeois market for weekly and daily newspapers. The entrepreneurial Philipon opened La Maison Aubert in 1829 with his brother-in-law, Gabriel Aubert, to publish and sell caricatures and launched two satirical illustrated newspapers, the weekly *La Caricature* (1830-35) and the daily *Le Charivari* (1832). Philipon's political agenda brought together a new generation of journalists and artists who ridiculed the despised regime of Charles X and then turned on Louis-Philippe and his government for reneging on promised political freedom and social reforms and for following the censorial footsteps of their Bourbon predecessor. Knowing that images speak louder than words, Philipon invented the physiognomic comparison of the citizen king Louis-Philippe to *la poire*, or "pear," a satirical symbol that immediately fixed itself in the popular consciousness.[2]

In 1830 Daumier began supplying independent lithographs for La Maison Aubert. His early work was derivative of other lithographers in Philipon's stable, but one year later Daumier was catapulted into the limelight. On December 15, 1831, La Maison Aubert published Daumier's virulent caricature of a bloated Louis-Philippe as Rabelais' folk hero *Gargantua* (Del. 34). Sitting on a *chaise percé* (toilet seat), fed baskets of money by poor downtrodden workers, Gargantua defecates "peerages, army commissions, prefectural positions, and crosses of the Legion of Honor" in front of the National Assembly.[3] The target of this lithograph was the "civil list," a proposed budget for the support of the king and his family. The *guisquetaires* raided La Maison Aubert, seized the lithographic stone, and summoned Aubert, Delaporte (the lithographer) and Daumier to trial. All three defendants were sentenced by the *Cour d'Assises* to six months in prison and given a five-hundred-franc fine for defamation of Louis-Philippe on February 23, 1832.[4] During the six months prior to serving his prison term, Daumier executed several cartoons for *Le Caricature*. Daumier was incarcerated at Sainte-Pélagie on August 27, 1832, where he met important republicans of the resistance movement. He was transferred after two months to Dr. Pinel's *maison de sante*, where he completed his term, carrying on as usual in the company of Philipon, who had been imprisoned there for publishing one of his own caricatures in *La Caricature*.

In December 1832 Philipon founded the daily *Le Charivari*, featuring a lithograph in each issue to further aggravate Louis-Philippe and his assembly. Raids, seizures, and trials, while evidence of the effectiveness of Philipon's campaign, were financially taxing. To provide a reserve fund to pay fines for press offenses, he formed *L'Association Mensuelle* (Print of the Month Club) in August 1832. Middle-class subscribers received large-scale framable political caricatures, thereby mixing connoisseurship with opposition politics. The climax of *L'Association Mensuelle*, which overshadowed all of Philipon's other caricatures, was five lithographs by Daumier. His attack on the National Assembly, *Le Ventre législatif* (*The Legislative "Belly"*) (Del. 131), appeared in January 1834, followed by *Très hauts et très puissans Moutards et Moutardes légitimes* (*Very Naughty and Very Mighty Legitimist Brats*) (Del. 132); *Liberté de la Presse: Ne vous y frottez pas* (*Liberty of the Press: Don't Meddle with It*) (Del. 133); *Enfoncé Lafayette! Attrappé, mon Vieux!* (*You are finished, Lafayette! Trapped, old man!*) (Del. 134), culminating with his masterpiece, *Rue Transnonain, le 15 avril 1834*. The latter was released six months after the actual event had taken place, accompanied by Philipon's commentary.

This lithograph is shocking to see, frightful as the ghastly scene which it relates. Here lie an old man slaughtered, a woman murdered, the corpse of a man who, riddled with wounds, fell on the body of a poor child which lies under him, with its skull crushed. This indeed is not caricature;. . .it is a page of our modern history besplattered with blood, a page drawn with a powerful hand and dictated by a noble anger. In creating his drawing, Daumier raised himself to a high eminence. He has made a picture which, though executed in black on a sheet of paper, will not be the less esteemed nor will it be the less enduring. The murders of the Rue Transnonain will be a permanent blot of shame on all who allowed them to happen. This lithograph which we cite will be the medal struck at the time to perpetuate the recollection of the victory won over fourteen old men, women, and children.[5]

The sober realism of Daumier's *Rue Transnonain* is more powerful than the exaggerated satire of his other political lithographs. When the government moved against the weavers' revolt in Lyon, the riots spread to the workers' district in Paris. Innocent citizens were massacred when soldiers retaliated for sniper fire from no. 12 Rue Transnonain. A shaft of light striking the foreshortened body of the martyred father lying on top of his child intensifies the sense of quiet outrage. Against the violence of the disheveled bed and overturned chair, Daumier carefully renders the dead figures, then selectively scratches the crayon to texture the dark and to intensify the coloristic power of the lithograph. People crowded the window of La Maison Aubert to see the lithograph, which was later seized by the government. On the fifth anniversary of the July revolution, an assassination attempt on the king's life accelerated press laws terminating opposition political caricature. The September Laws of 1835 increased penalties and security deposits and reintroduced prior censorship of caricature. – KLS

1. Peter Morse, "Daumier's Early Lithographs," in Andrew Stasik, ed., *Honoré Daumier: A Centenary Tribute* (New York: Pratt Graphic Center, 1980), 6-7.

2. James Bash Cuno, *Charles Philipon and La Maison Aubert: The Business Politics, and Public of Caricature in Paris, 1820-1840* (Ann Arbor: UMI, 1985), 193-258. Cuno gives a full discussion of the meaning.

3. Morse, "Daumier's Early Lithographs," 35.

4. Howard P. Vincent, *Daumier and His World* (Evanston: Northwestern University Press, 1968), 29.

5. Vincent, *Daumier and His World*, 59.

Charles Meryon

Paris 1821-1868 Charenton

123. Le Petit Pont (The Little Bridge) 1850.

Etching with engraving on greenish toned laid paper, 26.0 x 18.8 cm (platemark).

D.-W. 24 iii/vii; Schneiderman *Meryon* 20 iii/ix.[1]

Initialled in plate upper right: C.M.

Provenance: (Purchased from Robert Dunthorne & Son, London, June 24, 1931, for $1,702).

Bequest of Herbert Greer French, 1943.614.

Exhibitions: Cincinnati 1934, no. 76.

The etchings of Charles Meryon were among the most sought-after prints in this country during the first decades of this century. After Rembrandt, Dürer, and Van Dyck, the only "modern" intaglio printmakers on everyone's list of desiderata were Whistler (cat. 128) and Meryon. This phenomenon, helped by the coincidental dispersal of the largest private collection of Meryon prints and drawings ever assembled, that of Bernard B. Macgeorge (Knoedler, New York, 1917), led to the remarkably rich holdings of Meryon prints in U.S. collections. Mr. French, no exception to this rule, assembled a very fine selection of thirteen Meryon works, including nine of his most celebrated views of Paris.

Meryon was the illegitimate child of a French actress and an English doctor/naturalist. After early schooling in Paris, Meryon attended naval school in Brest from 1837. During the next decade, he completed two long sea voyages: one around the Mediterranean; the other to South America and the South Pacific. Upon his return to Paris in 1846, Meryon decided to pursue an artistic career and began studies in painting. However, the discovery that he was color-blind led him to printmaking and a two-year apprenticeship with the landscape etcher Eugène Bléry (1805-1887). *Le Petit Pont* was Meryon's first original print and the first of his *Etchings of Paris*, upon which he worked for the next four years. He also etched views of the city of Bourges. In the mid-1850s Meryon began to suffer from increasingly severe mental disturbances, which brought on a stay in an asylum at Charenton in 1858. During the 1860s he was only capable of producing a few commissioned reproductive etchings, although he did work on a series of views and vignettes drawn from his South Pacific voyage. He was readmitted to Charenton in 1866 and died there two years later.

Although consistently impoverished and lacking significant critical recognition, Meryon was favorably received during his lifetime by such writers as Charles Baudelaire and Victor Hugo. The noted collector and critic Philippe Burty (see provenance under cat. 125) published a catalogue and appreciation of Meryon's prints in the *Gazette des Beaux-Arts* in 1863. Meryon's etched work, particularly his Paris views, strongly influenced an etching revival that began in earnest in France and England during the 1860s in which printmakers from Whistler to Haden (cat. 129) and Bracquemond (cat. 124) emulated the clarity and finesse of his etching technique.

In its final published form, Meryon's *Etchings of Paris* consisted of twelve large views and several smaller vignettes, with incidental verses by Meryon himself.[2] Bracquemond's etched portrait of Meryon, as if on a carved stone relief, was also included. The whole series was then enclosed in color paper wraps, with the title plate printed on the upper cover sheet.[3] The genesis of Meryon's idea for the group of views is unclear; his choice of subjects, their original order of execution, and even the original conception as a connected series are not known.[4] Meryon is supposed to have issued the earliest printings of the series himself in three parts between 1852 and 1854.

With two exceptions, the artist was reluctant to acknowledge any artistic precedent for his project. Victor Hugo's evocation of the medieval city in his famed novel *Notre-Dame de Paris*, which appeared in 1831, was a clear source: in particular, a chapter delineating a bird's-eye view of the city from Notre Dame's cathedral towers was emulated by Meryon in his own aerial view, *The Vampire* (D.-W. 23, an impression of which is in the Museum's Herbert Greer French Collection, CAM 1943.618). Meryon's etched views of the city are equally dominated by Notre Dame, *Le Petit Pont* literally so. Meryon's etched dedication of the series to the seventeenth-century etcher Reinier Nooms, called "Zeeman" (cat. 88), states his debt to the earlier artist's set of etched views of Paris, several of which were copied by Meryon.

Meryon's set of city views has been seen as a lament for the destruction of the old city by urban renewal efforts undertaken before and during the Second Empire, a reflection of the contemporary romantic interest in the Gothic and a visualization of the horrors of city life and its vices.[5] Begun just after the convulsions of the 1848 revolution, Meryon's series manages to capture a sense of a city caught in a time of flux with an emotional and hyperreal treatment beyond that of all contemporaries or modern imitators.

Le Petit Pont was finished sometime during the summer of 1850: Meryon sent an impression of it to his father in August, and another was exhibited in the Salon of that year, which opened on December 30.[6] The view is taken from the left (south) bank of the Seine, eastward toward the cathedral and the Île de la Cité. Meryon combined two vantage points in his composition, delineating the houses and the bridge from the level of the river and then moving up to street level for a more prominent view of the two cathedral towers. This conflation of viewpoints is clearly revealed in the earliest study for this etching, now at the Toledo Museum of Art: a graphite study on tracing paper made with the aid of a *camera lucida*. The camera lucida, essentially an early box "camera," substitutes a sheet of drawing paper for photographic film, thus enabling the artist to trace an image. The Toledo study shows the much-reduced height of the towers as seen from water level, with the final composition compressing the bridge and raising the towers roughly sketched on top.[7] In numerous other studies for the etching, Meryon minutely depicted each detail for the final print, recording careful notes on building construction and materials.[8]

The unique qualities of Meryon's vision are apparent in this, his first mature print. Such features as the harsh sunlight, strong contrasts, claustrophobic atmosphere, and very low viewpoint (lower than the passersby on the street above) recur often in his later Paris etchings. The eerily photographic aspect of this scene serves as a reminder that Meryon was indeed familiar with the new art of photography and that he utilized it at times in composing his prints.[9] A few tiny specks of birds in the sky and the pinpoint figures on the towers forebode Meryon's later skies, which are often filled with menacing birds as are most spectacularly seen in his *Naval Ministry* of 1865 (D.-W. 45) (CAM 1943.625), an impression of which is in the Museum's Herbert Greer French Collection. In a remark recorded by Charles Baudelaire in 1860, the artist noted the unintentional resemblance of the shadow cast by the house porch at the left end of the Petit Pont to the profile of a sphinx, thus drawing an after-the-fact connection with Louis Napoleon, who had seized power in 1851, inaugurating the Second Empire in France.[10]

Meryon printed most of the earliest impressions of his etchings himself, experimenting with different papers and with the subtleties of inking his plates. As is the case in this impression, he often printed his Paris views on greenish-toned paper in order to mute his sharply contrasted shadows, imparting at times a misty, almost melancholy atmosphere to them. The Museum's is a rich impression of the third state of nine, before the addition of marginal inscriptions. The plate is printed with full clarity and with the darkest areas of the cathedral towers solidly black, anchoring the upper center of this powerfully architectonic composition. – DPB

1. Although Schneiderman lists the Museum's impression as the fourth state, this writer sees no evidence of the cited drypoint lines at upper left and, therefore, places it as the third state. See David P. Becker, "Meryon [review of Schneiderman]," PQ. 8, no. 1 (March 1991): 94, no. S. 20.

2. For a complete listing of the prints in the set, see D.-W., under no. 17.

3. Bracquemond's portrait has been often miscatalogued as having been etched by Meryon; in reality, only the verses on the later states are by him. See D.-W. 17A and Jean-Paul Bouillon, *Félix Bracquemond le réalisme absolu – oeuvre gravé 1849-1859* (Geneva: Skira, 1987), no. Aa 15.

4. The etched title to the series (D.-W. 17) was not executed until 1852; and numbers were not added to the large views in the set until an 1861 edition of the plates was printed by Auguste Delâtre (see individual entries in D.-w.).

5. For further discussion and bibliography, see Adele M. Holcomb, "*Le Stryge de Notre-Dame*: Some Aspects of Meryon's Symbolism," *Art Journal* 31, no. 2 (1971-72): 150-57; James D. Burke, New Haven 1974; Frankfurt am Main 1975; and Bonnie L. Grad and Timothy A. Riggs, Worcester 1982, esp. 118-29.

6. Paris 1968, under no. 724, for excerpts from the letter.

7. Reproduced in Burke, New Haven 1974, no. 14. It is inscribed by Meryon "pris sur nature à la chambre claire" ("taken from life in the light chamber"). See also a photograph of this view taken in 1852 from street level by Henri Le Secq (reproduced in Frankfurt am Main 1975, no. P3).

8. Two of the detail studies at Toledo are reproduced in Burke, New Haven 1974, nos. 15-16. Three others are known in the Bibliothèque Nationale, Paris (Inv. A.C. 8524), and the National Gallery of Art, Washington (Inv. B. 8690 and 8691).

9. See especially Eugenia P. Janis, "Charles Meryon und die Photographen von Paris," Frankfurt am Main 1975, 139-44.

10. Baudelaire's letter is partially translated in Burke, New Haven 1974, 40.

Félix Bracquemond
Paris 1833-1914 Paris

124. The Top of a Swinging Door 1852.
Etching on laid paper, 29.3 x 39.1 cm (sheet).
Ber.110 iii/v; Bouillon **Ac 1 iii/x.
Watermark: Cursive monogram GP?
Signed and dated in plate lower right: *fBracquemond / inv & fec / 1852*; lower center: *Le Haut d'un battant de porte*; lower center (partially trimmed): *Imp Delâtre rue de Bièvre 19 Paris.*
Condition: Trimmed within platemark.
Provenance: (Purchased from M. Knoedler, New York, June 19, 1940, for $50).
Bequest of Herbert Greer French, 1943.773.

Essentially self-trained as an etcher, Bracquemond became one of the most celebrated printmakers of the second half of the nineteenth century, garnering countless prizes in official exhibitions, founding societies for the promulgation of etching, and collaborating with many noted artists of his time. Apprenticed to a lithographic printer at the age of fifteen, he began to learn drawing and then studied painting with Joseph Guichard (1806-1880). Guichard had been a student of both Ingres and Eugène Delacroix. Although he began exhibiting as a painter in 1852, it was as an etcher that Bracquemond began to establish his reputation; indeed, after 1869 he ceased showing paintings altogether.

Bracquemond began etching in 1849 and quickly mastered an astonishing technique and sure draftsmanship, finishing *The Top of a Swinging Door*, often considered his master print, a mere three years later. Clearly the prints of such etchers as Charles Jacque and Charles Meryon (cat. 123) furnished strong examples for his style, but in his turn, Bracquemond influenced many after him. He rapidly made numerous acquaintances among the writers and artists of Paris, including the emerging impressionists.[1] He exhibited both with that group and in official Salons.

Bracquemond combined traditional etching skills with a willingness to push the technique in innovative ways that, at times, approached an impressionist printmaking aesthetic.[2] In addition to executing both original prints and prints after the paintings of others, Bracquemond actively designed for decorative objects, particularly ceramics. He was an ardent admirer of Japanese prints, fostering their popularity and influence in French art from the late 1850s. He was one of the founders of the Société des Aquafortistes (Society of Etchers) in 1862 and the Société des Peintres-graveurs (Society of Painter-Engravers) at the turn of the century. Bracquemond etched almost nine hundred prints during his career, including lithographs and drypoints in addition to pure etchings. His work is extremely well represented in museums in the United States, three of the five largest collections of his prints being in the New York Public Library, the Baltimore Museum of Art, and the College of Wooster Art Museum, Ohio.[3]

The Top of a Swinging Door immediately caught critics' attention when it appeared at the International Exhibition in Paris in 1855, astonishing viewers with its combination of unusual perspective, hyperreal bravura technique, and enigmatically morbid subject. Bracquemond's son Pierre wrote that his father had seen birds pinioned on a farm gate in the village of Villers-Cotterêts, northwest of Paris near Soissons.[4] An undated sketch and two studies for individual birds in the print, dated September 16 and 19, 1852, serve to determine the print's exact genesis.[5] Etched in December, an impression was officially deposited in the Bibliothèque Nationale, Paris, on January 6, 1853.

The print depicts a crow, or raven, at the upper left, an owl at upper right, a small long-eared bat between them, and a sparrow hawk below. Amidst many attempts to explain the iconography of the subject, Bouillon stresses that no account can avoid considering the four-line verse that Bracquemond added to his plate in the fifth state as a sort of motto or explication (the Museum's impression is of the third state). In translation, it reads: "Here you see sadly suspended / Predatory and covetous birds. . . / In order to inform their equals / That flying and plundering are different."[6] The last line contains a pun on the word *voler*, which can mean either "to fly" or "to steal." The poem is inserted as if inscribed on a small wooden placquette hanging on the door to the lower right. Pointing out that other artists of the time often appended explanations or poems to their works, Bouillon feels that in addition to reflecting both Bracquemond's still-developing personality and "a certain sadism found in other youthful works," it is necessary to view the print as both a bravura exercise in realistic observation and a moralization.[7]

The unusual treatment of the pictorial space that pushes the visual plane right up against the actual surface of the print, thus isolating the detailed figures of the birds and bat against a nearly blank background, has prompted several commentators to see an influence from Japanese prints.[8] However, as Bracquemond is not known to have actually seen his first Japanese print until 1856 (an illustrated book by Hokusai), this hypothesis must be discounted. Bouillon declares that Bracquemond's composition is essentially "empirical," being assembled after studies of each of the birds were separately compiled.[9]

Bracquemond's patient skill in translating the qualities of a highly detailed drawing foretells his immense success in adapting the medium of etching to reproduce all manner and means of paintings and drawings by other artists. The creator of *Swinging Door* obviously took pleasure in depicting the qualities of feather and fur (and wooden door) in a duplicatible print medium (one is reminded of Hollar [cat. 79]). Although initially a commercial failure, the print was an immediate artistic success. The critic Philippe Burty, writing in 1875, declared that it would be as sought-after in the future as the most famous Dutch prints were at that time.[10] Indeed, its fame has tended to overshadow Bracquemond's later work, to its detriment.

The Museum's impression of *Swinging Door* was printed by the well-known Parisian printer Auguste Delâtre (1822-1907). Delâtre printed for many of the major French etchers of the time, including Meryon, Millet (cat. 126), and Corot (cat. 132), to name only a few. It is printed with an almost black ink, as in the birds, with a light brown tone of ink left on the surface of the plate. Other impressions of this state range from a genuinely black ink to one of a distinctly more brownish tone. Impressions of the third state are comparatively rare; Beraldi stated that there were only some thirty.[11] Later states were printed in many impressions, including an edition in the third annual publication of the Société des Aquafortistes (1865), with subsequent editions in 1872 and 1874, by which time the plate had become significantly worn. Mr. French acquired only one other Bracquemond print, a reproduction of a portrait of Erasmus by Hans Holbein the Younger (1497/98-1543) (Ber. 39). Ironically, it was this extremely straightforward etching of 1863, which, when rejected by the official Salon jury (some say by envious engravers), prompted Bracquemond happily to show it in the famed Salon des Refusés of that year. – DPB

1. The extent of his circle can be appreciated in Jean-Paul Bouillon, "La correspondance de Félix Bracquemond," GBA. 6th per., 82 (December 1973): 351-86. Among others, Bracquemond taught Edouard Manet how to etch.

2. See Paris 1974, 67-72.

3. The most complete reference and bibliography for the first ten years of Bracquemond's career is Jean-Paul Bouillon, *Félix Bracquemond le réalisme absolu – oeuvre gravé 1849-1859 catalogue raisonné* (Geneva: Skira, 1987); the most complete catalogue for all of his prints is still Henri Beraldi (Ber. 111). Another good biographical and technical source is Wooster 1974.

4. Such scenes were apparently not uncommon. Referring to an enforced home stay due to illness, Millet (cat. 126) remarked in an 1868 letter that, "Once more, I find myself nailed like an old owl to the door of a barn" (Boston 1984, 247).

5. The drawing of September 19, depicting the crow at the upper left of the print, is in the Minneapolis Institute of Arts (reproduced in Bouillon, *Bracquemond*, 78).

6. "Ici tu vois tristement pendre / Oiseaux pillards et convoiteux. . . / A leur pareils c'est pour apprendre / Que voler et voler sont deux." For his extensive discussion of this print, see Bouillon, *Bracquemond*, 76-81. For a later printing in 1865, Bracquemond changed the date from 1852 to that year.

7. Bouillon, *Bracquemond*, 78.

8. See Wooster 1974, 21-22; and Katharine A. Lochnan, *The Etchings of James McNeill Whistler* (New Haven and London: Yale University Press, 1984), 92 – 93.

9. Bouillou, *Bracquemond*, 80.

10. Bouillou, *Bracquemond*, 80.

11. The first state, containing only the birds and bat, is known in only two impressions (British Museum, London, and Prouté Archives, Paris); the second, with the background filled in but before inscriptions, is unlocated by Bouillon.

Charles Meryon

Paris 1821-1868 Charenton

125. The Morgue 1854.

Etching with touches of drypoint on laid paper, 23.1 x 20.5 cm (platemark).
D.-W. 36 iii/vii; Schneiderman *Meryon* 42 iii/vii.
Watermark: Initials G D T.
Provenance: Philippe Burty (Lugt 2071); Albert W. Scholle (Lugt S.2923a); Theodore DeWitt; (purchased from M. Knoedler, New York, January 10, 1928, for $2,900).
Bequest of Herbert Greer French, 1943.622.
Exhibitions: Cincinnati 1930, (no. 45); Cincinnati 1934, no. 81.

During the nineteenth century, the Paris morgue stood on the southern side of the Île de la Cité, not far from the cathedral of Notre-Dame, which would be to the viewer's right beyond the margin of this print. This view is taken just downstream from the vantage point seen in *Le Petit Pont* (cat. 123); the triangular shadow at lower left is probably that of the Pont Saint-Michel. The building was built in 1568 and was formerly used as a slaughterhouse, a fact that may have influenced Meryon's depiction.[1] It was used to temporarily house the bodies of deaths resulting from murder, suicide, and accident, placing them on view to be claimed. As expressed in a contemporary tourist guide, it was a must-see attraction: "Ask some French friend to show you the *morgue* in the morning, and to give you the history – you will never pass the quays after dark."[2] In a lively discussion of the sights and social life of Paris in 1835, Frances Trollope also described a visit to the morgue:

> No visit to a tomb, however solemn or however sad, can approach in thrilling horror to the sensation caused by passing the threshold of this charnel-house. . . . I was steadfast in my will to visit it, and I have done it. The building is a low, square, carefully-whited structure, situated on the Quai de la Cité. It is open to all; and it is fearful to think how many anxious hearts have entered, how many despairing ones have quitted it.[3]

Meryon's print is justly famed for its macabre atmosphere and oppressively constructed composition. The viewer's eye focuses on the scene as if through a telescopic lens that flattens the picture plane and allows neither relief nor escape. Although the morgue had been rendered by other artists, Meryon's particular synthesis of harsh light, disorienting jumble of surfaces, and seemingly matter-of-fact reportage has evoked a great deal of commentary.[4] Meryon composed and etched a poem that he printed with a few impressions of his view. Entitled "L'Hôtellerie de la mort" ("The Hostel of Death"), the verses are a bleak and satiric recitation of the miseries of the urban underclass who receive "free bed and board" only in the city morgue before finding their final (and only) peace in a "saintly halo of Love and Happiness."[5]

Meryon's champion and collector Philippe Burty (once the owner of the Museum's impression of *The Morgue*) wrote at the time:

> This pile of roofs, these colliding angles, this blinding light which serves to throw up in greater relief the contrasts between the various shadows, and this old building which under the needle of the artist assumes a vague resemblance to an antique tomb, combine to form an enigma of which the sinister solution is provided by the group of people.[6]

What should be a scene of anguish – the transport of a recently deceased person to the morgue – is dispassionately played out in the harsh daylight on the quay at lower left. The indifference of the line of unconcerned citizens above, who snidely observe the isolated, grieving figures bearing the body, underscores the human cost of living in the dark city. Meryon's view undoubtedly reflects his attitudes about the "underside" of city life in nineteenth-century Paris. The dense overcrowding in cities is amply represented by the perspective of the cramped buildings and the figures who inhabit them. The filthy smoke rising from the morgue, the stains running down its walls, the sewer emptying its contents into the river below the stairs, and the laundering seen immediately below all combine to emphasize the pollution inherent in cities of the time.[7] There is even a fire burning unnoticed in a window in the shadows at the extreme left of the composition. Meryon expressed his sympathy for city dwellers and their need for fresh air and sunlight in an etching of 1855, *La Loi solaire* (*The Solar Law*) (D.-W. 93), in which he declared those two necessities able to prevent the "idleness, avarice, vice, luxury, and other evil passions" that are inevitably bred in urban areas.[8]

One drawn study for the entire composition is now in the Bibliothèque Nationale, Paris.[9] The Museum's impression is of the third state of seven: the image is complete, but it lacks the artist's signature and date. In later states, Meryon changed the inscribed date to 1850 and added various inscriptions on the walls of several buildings. Meryon's own printings of this plate were quite varied, ranging from very cleanly wiped impressions with brightly lit effects to more heavily inked impressions (often printed on duskier papers) with a distinctly gloomier atmosphere. The Museum's impression is quite richly printed, with very bright highlights; in some areas Meryon intentionally left some of the ink on the plate that had been pulled out of the lines as he wiped the plate, a technique called *retroussage* (pulling up), thus softening the lines and creating rich mini-shadows. For instance, the slightly more inky treatment in printing makes the stains that drip from the morgue's windows more effectively "dirty." In his own manuscript commentary on his prints, "My Observations," Meryon reveals the obsessive concern he had for the atmosphere of this print. He cites several mysterious strokes of the engraving burin that "maliciously disfigured" the mood of one of the men carrying the corpse from one of commiseration to that of disgust; he often attributed such changes in his plates to occult powers.[10] – DPB

1. James D. Burke, New Haven 1974, 69.

2. F. Coghlin, *A Visit to Paris, or, The Stranger's Guide to Every Object Worthy of Notice in that Gay City* (London, 1830), 17. [I am grateful to Edgar Munhall for this notice.]

3. Frances Trollope, *Paris and the Parisians in 1835* (New York: Harper and Brothers, 1836), 194.

4. Another contemporary, quite pedestrian view of the morgue is reproduced in Frankfurt am Main 1975, 89, upper right. Other views are cited in Burke, New Haven 1974, 70. An extremely macabre nocturnal drawing of a beggar woman in front of the morgue by François Bonvin is in the Ackland Art Museum, Chapel Hill (reproduced in *The Ackland Art Museum – A Handbook* [Chapel Hill: Ackland Art Museum, 1983], no. 110).

5. The entire text is transcribed and translated in D.-W., under no. 37, and Burke, New Haven 1974, 71-74.

6. D.-W., under no. 37. A particularly poetic description of *The Morgue* has been written by the graphic artist Leonard Baskin in his *Five Addled Etchers* (Hanover: Dartmouth Publications, 1969), 44-47.

7. See Worcester 1982, 126.

8. His quite incoherent ramblings on the moral health of cities prompted by his depiction of the morgue are quoted in Philippe Verdier, "Charles Meryon – *Mes observations (1863)*," GBA. 102, no. 1378 (November 1983): 234, n. 44.

9. Illustrated in Del. II, under no. 36.

10. Verdier, "*Mes observations*," 225, 233, n. 43.

Jean-François Millet
Gruchy (Gréville) 1814-1875 Barbizon

126. The Diggers 1855-56.
Etching on wove paper, 23.7 x 33.6 cm (platemark).
Del. 13 i/iv; Melot 13 i/iv.
Signed in plate upper right: *J.F. Millet*.
Provenance: Loys-Henry Delteil (Lugt 773); (his sale, Drouet, Paris, June 13-15, 1928, lot 322); (purchased from M. Knoedler, New York, October 6, 1928, for $1,450).
Bequest of Herbert Greer French, 1943.700.
Exhibitions: Cincinnati 1930, (no. 49); Cincinnati 1934, no. 90.

Raised on his family's farm on the coast of Normandy near Cherbourg, Millet pursued his early painting studies in that city until 1837, when a municipal stipend enabled him to enter the École des Beaux-Arts in Paris. His first submission to an official Salon exhibition was rejected, and he returned to Cherbourg as a portrait painter in 1840. During the next few years, Millet moved between Normandy and Paris, attempting to gain recognition but finding it elusive. By the end of the decade, he had built up a circle of admirers and fellow painters, including Honoré Daumier (cats. 122, 130), Théodore Rousseau (1812 – 1867), and Charles Jacque. During 1849 Millet received his first state commission – a large painting of *The Harvesters* (Louvre, Paris) – and in that year moved to the town of Barbizon.

During the 1840s the Forest of Fontainebleau southeast of Paris became the center of a group of primarily landscape and genre painters that was to have an important influence on the development of realist art in France and elsewhere. Situated on the edge of the forest, Barbizon gave its name to the "school" of painting that evolved there. The leading members of the group were Jacque, Rousseau, and Millet, with Charles-François Daubigny (1817-1878), Corot (cat. 132), and Narcisse Diaz (1808-1876) often associated with it. It was in this setting that Millet would fully develop his highly personal sense of portraying the daily life of rural workers and the landscape in which they lived. His works were very influential and have been subject to interpretations ranging from romantically elegiac to spiritual to intensely political. Certain paintings, such as *The Sower* (Museum of Fine Arts, Boston) and *The Angelus* (Louvre, Paris), have become virtual icons.[1] The Cincinnati Art Museum owns two important Millet paintings, *Going to Work* of 1851-53 (CAM 1927.411) and *The Knitter* of 1856 (CAM 1940.984).[2] Millet's work influenced many subsequent artists, including Vincent van Gogh and Georges Seurat.

Millet executed only some thirty-four prints, of which a relatively small group of etchings represent his most intense involvement with printmaking.[3] After a few early trials, he set out in 1855 to etch a series of subjects that he could circulate to prospective collectors and in which he could explore themes before attempting them in painting.[4] Millet is recorded as making "frequent trips to Paris to learn the art of etching" during the fall and winter of 1855-56.[5] One of Millet's closest friends in Barbizon was the painter-printmaker Charles Jacque, who surely would have aided his friend in the etching process. The decade of the 1850s saw the beginning of an etching revival, with Jacque, Bracquemond (cat. 124), and others championing the directness of the medium and its attraction for collectors who could not afford paintings.

The small group of developed etchings that Millet executed at this time were eventually printed and published in 1858 by Auguste Delâtre, the well-known Paris printer.[6] Including such images as *Woman Churning Butter* (Del. 10) (CAM 1943.699), *Man with a Wheelbarrow* (Del. 11) (CAM 1943.702), and *The Gleaners* (Del. 12) (CAM 1943.701) – all of which are in the Museum's French Collection – this series of etchings well represents major themes that preoccupied Millet. He often returned later to subjects explored in his etchings for pastels and paintings.

The Diggers is but one work in an almost twenty-year-long exploration of this particular composition by Millet. It represents the deadeningly monotonous labor of turning over the hard-packed soil after the harvest, before the new planting. One of Millet's first compositions involving diggers is a painting of a single digger (close in pose to the figure on the right in this etching), datable perhaps as early as 1847. This date is significant because it shows that the painting was made before the revolutionary struggles of 1848, which are generally credited as inspiring so many artists to depict the plight of the urban and rural poor.[7] Alexandra Murphy and Robert Herbert list many preliminary studies and works related to this painting, the etching, and a major pastel of the subject from 1866.[8] This etching, however, seems to have been executed as an end in itself rather than as a reproduction of a finished painting, indicating Millet's belief that printmaking was a worthy medium.[9]

In *The Diggers*, Millet developed his recently acquired knowledge of etching into a robust yet subtle adaptation of his draftsmanship. After exploring the poses and the relationship of the two figures in a series of studies, he then transferred the figures to the plate and added the background and distant landscape, which depicts the flat plain of Chailly near Barbizon.[10] The immensity of the men's task is amply indicated by the huge unworked area behind them; the monumentality of their poses uncompromisingly confronts the viewer. Herbert compares the rhythmic poses of the two figures to Parthenon friezes, the diggers in Pieter Bruegel the Elder's engraving *Spring* (an impression of which Millet owned), and the sculptural force of Nicolas Poussin's figures.[11] The particular social denial often seen in the nineteenth century is revealed in critic Philippe Burty's comments on this print: "The silhouettes of these humble laborers are marked by a touching simplicity, but there is no vulgarity of pose or clothing."[12]

Millet adapted a system of short strokes and dots to define his surfaces and volumes, showing apparently little variation in degrees of biting with the acid.[13] This impression of the first state of four is printed in black ink with a very light tone of ink left on the plate. The clarity of his line and the lightness of the printing in this early impression conveys the light reflected on the figures' chests from the

ground, an effect lost in later printings. An area of pitting in the lower left has been skillfully adapted to believably assume the texture of the dirt itself. In later states, such as one of the fourth and final state, also in the Cincinnati Art Museum (CAM 1930.134), the inking of the plate tends to become heavier, especially in the figures, rendering them less three-dimensional. Millet is known to have preferred more lightly printed examples of his etchings.[14] Other impressions of the first state are recorded only in the Art Institute of Chicago, Yale University Art Gallery, New Haven, and the Bibliothèque Nationale, Paris. This impression was once owned by the Paris print dealer, scholar, and publisher Loys Delteil, who wrote the first illustrated catalogue of Millet's prints. – DPB

1. Excellent overviews of Millet's life and work are present in these exhibition catalogues: Robert Herbert, Paris 1975, and Alexandra R. Murphy, Boston 1984, the latter documenting the eminent collection of Millet's work in the Museum of Fine Arts and in other Boston collections. See also Griselda Pollock, *Millet* (London: Oresko, 1977), and the chapter on Millet in T. J. Clark, *The Absolute Bourgeois – Artists and Politics in France 1848-1851* (Princeton: Princeton University Press, 1982), 72-98, for more in-depth views of the political setting of the time.

2. Illustrated in Herbert, Paris 1975, nos. 70 and 82, respectively.

3. Perhaps the finest collection of Millet's prints is in the Art Institute of Chicago, based upon the intact collection of Alfred Lebrun, one of Millet's contemporaries and one of his first cataloguers.

4. Murphy, Boston 1984, 87, where she disputed Michel Melot's dating of three early trial etchings to the late 1840s.

5. Edward Wheelwright, "Personal Recollections of Jean François Millet," *The Atlantic Monthly* 38 (September 1876): 271.

6. For many details concerning Delâtre's printing of these plates (handled by Millet's friend Alfred Sensier as middleman), see Michel Melot, *Graphic Art of the Pre-Impressionists* (New York: Abrams, 1980), 288-89. Evidently there was one printing of these plates in 1860 by Charles Meryon (cats. 123, 125).

7. Museum of Fine Arts, Boston, reproduced in Murphy, Boston 1984, no. 17. Murphy writes that an X-ray of the painting reveals that originally a second figure very similar to that in the etching had been painted over.

8. See Murphy, Boston 1984, 29, 105, 175. Herbert (Paris 1975, 159 – 66) reproduces several of the related subjects in his dossier on *The Diggers*.

9. Although Wheelwright ("Recollections," 271) states that this print is a "reproduction of the picture of two men digging," he described that painting actually as only "begun," lacking color and existing only in outline sketch. That work has been identified with the unfinished oil in the Tweed Gallery, University of Minnesota, Duluth (reproduced in Herbert, Paris 1975, no. 123).

10. Murphy, Boston 1984, 29.

11. Herbert, Paris 1975, 159.

12. Quoted in Ber. 10.67-68.14.

13. Wheelwright ("Recollections," 272) recounts a trip Millet made to Paris "to learn the important process of 'biting', – for which, he playfully added, he was not particularly well qualified by nature."

14. Murphy, Boston 1984, 98-99.

Hilaire-Germain-Edgar Degas

Paris 1834-1917 Paris

127. The Engraver Joseph Tourny 1857.

Etching on wove paper, 23.1 x 14.3 cm (platemark).
Del. 4; Reed and Shapiro 5 (only state, fifth printing).
Provenance: Degas atelier (Lugt 657); (atelier sale Paris, November 22-23, 1918); (M. Knoedler, New York, 1919); The Metropolitan Museum of Art (Lugt 1943 [inv. no. 19.29.1], purchased from Knoedler 1919, and Lugt s.1808h, exchanged to Knoedler, January 17, 1931); (purchased from M. Knoedler, New York, May 19, 1937, for $950).
Bequest of Herbert Greer French, 1943.679.
Exhibitions: Chicago 1964, no. 8.

Originally trained as a history and portrait painter in the classical tradition of Ingres (cat. 118), Degas developed into an artist who cannot be readily categorized. A three-year sojourn in Italy from

1856 to 1859 was crucial in allowing him to break away from his classical training and to evolve his own personal style. He was considerably influenced by the painter Gustave Moreau (1826 – 1898), whom he met in Italy, and later by his friendship with (and reactions to) the emerging Impressionist group, particularly Edouard Manet (1832-1883), whom he met in 1862.

Aside from a six-month stay in New Orleans in 1872-73 and periodic visits to Italy on family business, Degas worked in Paris during his entire career, living until almost the end of the First World War. He appeals greatly to modern viewers because of his deep concentration upon a few themes, his refusal to court styles, and the sense of mystery that revolves around his extreme privacy and his often enigmatic subjects. His subject matter included portraiture, portrayals of the theater and ballet, landscape, and individual figural studies. In addition to his paintings, pastels, drawings, and other graphic work, Degas executed a significant number of sculptural studies of horses and the human figure.[1]

Although Degas worked in various printmaking media from the mid-1850s, he executed fewer than seventy prints, many of them almost unique early works or trials. Printmaking was essentially a private activity for him. Only four of his images were published in the conventional sense, and he rarely used professional printers. The vast majority of impressions were kept in his studio and only became known through the sale of the contents of his studio in 1918. Consistently fascinated with exploring new techniques for achieving artistic ends, Degas maintained an intense interest in the unique ability of prints to permanently record the permutations of a developing image through printing progressive states of a plate.[2] In that respect he has often been compared with Rembrandt (see cat. 83), both artists regarding the "etched plate [as] a sort of meditational forum, subject to significant pictorial changes, great and small."[3]

During 1855-56, Degas received his first simple lessons in etching from Prince Grégoire Soutzo (1818-1869), a family friend, amateur engraver, and collector, who also shared his rich collection of Old Master prints with the young artist. Three very small exercises in etching (Reed and Shapiro 1-3) are recorded from this period. Degas developed his etching activity further during his stay in Italy, stimulated by his friendship with Joseph-Gabriel Tourny (1817-1880), an older engraver and watercolorist who was then working in Rome. Among other projects, Tourny copied the Sistine Ceiling in watercolor for a French patron.[4] In addition to this etched portrait of Tourny, Degas used his older friend as a model for other works, including a painting of Dante and Virgil.[5] The two continued to keep in touch through the years. It was Tourny who introduced the artist Mary Cassatt to Degas in 1877.[6]

Degas' portrait of Tourny, his first confidently executed print, clearly reflects both his finely modulated draftsmanship in the Ingres tradition and his study and love of the portrait etchings of Rembrandt. The sitter's pose recalls most clearly Rembrandt's *Self-Portrait Drawing at a Window* of 1648 (B. 22), in which he is seated at a table drawing, his face illuminated by the light from a window at the left.[7] Degas placed Tourny identically, originally portraying him in three-quarter length (as in many Ingres graphite drawings) but then drawing a horizontal line just underneath the edge of the table at which he sits, directly evoking the format of Rembrandt's self portrait. He placed a soft felt hat on his subject's head, reminiscent of several other Rembrandt portraits.[8] At the base of Tourny's portrait, he included two profile studies of a male with a skull cap (perhaps also Tourny), probably as trials to judge his etching technique as he was working on his major portrait.[9]

While Degas made no changes in the image on the etching plate after he first completed it in 1857, he subsequently printed impressions from it at various times. During the mid-1860s, he experimented with variant inkings, leaving painterly tones of ink on the surface of the plate in order to achieve more dramatic effects of lighting in the composition, transforming it in the process from a pure line etching to a virtual monotype.[10] In a careful analysis of the papers used for different impressions and the accidental scratches that inevitably accumulated on the surface of the plate, Reed and Shapiro place the Museum's impression as from the fifth printing of six. For the sixth and last printing, Degas (or a skillful professional printer) carefully polished the surface of the plate, eliminating most of the scratches still visible in the Museum's impression. The latter is one of only five impressions of this particular printing known, and only twenty impressions in all of this plate are recorded by Reed and Shapiro.

Like Ingres and Rembrandt before him, Degas concentrated his delineation on a meticulous modeling of the head, with the rest of the body and the setting more cursorily indicated. While certainly reflective of earlier traditions and Degas' developing artistic personality, this portrait of his friend Tourny is yet very characteristic of his portraiture throughout his career, a quite dispassionate, unprettified look that reveals nothing of the sitter to the viewer. In speaking of this print (probably this impression, as he had acquired it for the Metropolitan Museum of Art), William Ivins compared its "simplicity of attack" to Van Dyck's portraits (see cats. 72-73) but declared that Degas' "uncompromising directness of thought. . . lay far beyond the mental capacity of the seventeenth-century artist."[11] Significantly, the next etching Degas executed, probably soon after *The Engraver Joseph Tourny*, was his technically freer and more sophisticated self-portrait (Reed and Shapiro 8). – DPB

1. For a detailed chronology of his career and large-scale discussion of works in other media, see New York 1988b. An excellent biography is Roy McMullen, *Degas – His Life and Work* (Boston: Houghton Mifflin, 1984). For an introduction to a more penetrating social analysis of Degas' art, see Eunice Lipton's review of the 1988 exhibition, "Anxiety at the Met," *Artforum* 27 (October 1988): 100 – 104, with references to other literature by herself and others.

2. The most recent and fullest treatment of Degas' prints is in Reed and Shapiro, essentially a catalogue raisonné. See also the revelatory exhibition catalogue by Eugenia Janis, Cambridge 1968. Degas was also an avid collector of prints by his contemporaries, from Delacroix, to Gavarni, to Gauguin.

3. Eugenia P. Janis, "The Argument of the Eye [review of Reed and Shapiro]," PQ 2, no. 2 (June 1985): 138.

4. For Tourny, see New York 1988b, 71. Tourny's surviving correspondence supplies intriguing hints into the youthful Degas' personality: "We are always thinking of the Degas who grumbles and the Edgar who growls" (from a letter to Degas, July 13, 1858, quoted in New York 1988b, 50).

5. See Reed and Shapiro, 30. The Cincinnati Art Museum owns a graphite study for this painting (Cincinnati 1978, no. 37, illus.).

6. McMullen, *Degas*, 293.

7. An impression is in the French Collection (CAM 1943.313). Theodore Reff ("New Light on Degas's Copies," *Burl. M.* 106, no. 735 [June 1964]: 251) suggests that Degas "discovered" Rembrandt in Italy, thanks to Tourny's influence. While Tourny undoubtedly avidly fostered his admiration, it is probable, however, that Degas already had seen Rembrandt etchings in Prince Soutzo's collection, if not elsewhere.

8. B. 17, 20, 21, 26, and 268, the last of which Degas copied directly in another etching at this period (Reed and Shapiro 6 – see their discussion of this print and other Degas copies after Rembrandt, Reed and Shapiro, 20-21).

9. Suggesting these heads as clerics, Paul Moses associated them with Degas' "Dantesque themes of this period" (Chicago 1964, under no. 8).

10. Three such impressions are known (illustrated in Reed and Shapiro, 14-16).

11. William M. Ivins, Jr., *Prints and Books – Informal Papers* (Cambridge: Harvard University Press, 1927; reprint, New York: Da Capo, 1969) 233.

James Abbott McNeill Whistler

Lowell, Massachusetts 1834-1903 London

128. The Kitchen 1858.

From "Twelve Etchings from Nature."
Etching on yellow *chine appliqué*, 22.7 x 15.6 cm (platemark).
K. 24 ii/iii; Mansfield 24 ii/iii.
Signed in plate lower right: *Whistler / Imp. Delatre Rue St. Jacques*
171; signed with pencil in margin lower right: Butterfly and *imp*.
Provenance: John H. Wrenn (Lugt 1475); (purchased from M.
Knoedler, New York, April 16, 1928, for $1,900).
Bequest of Herbert Greer French, 1943.599.

At the age of fifteen, James Abbott McNeill Whistler decided to
become an artist. On January 26, 1849, he wrote to his father, Major
George Washington Whistler, in Russia: "I hope, dear father, you
will not object to my choice, viz: a painter, for I wish to be one so
very much and I don't see why I should not, many others have done
so before."[1] In spite of his parents' efforts to channel his artistic
leanings into a practical occupation, Whistler never wavered in his
desire to become an artist. His career began in Paris at the age of
twenty-one; however, his printmaking activities can be traced to an
earlier date. From the beginning printmaking was a primary medium
for Whistler. Between 1855 and 1901 he executed nearly four
hundred fifty etchings and more than one hundred fifty lithographs.
In the 1860s and 1870s he played a key role in the etching revival that
swept France and Britain. Likewise, beginning in the late 1870s, he
was an important figure in the resurgence of the original lithograph.
Since his death, appreciation of his preeminent position as a late
nineteenth-century experimental printmaker has continued to rise.

On July 10, 1834, Whistler was born to Major Whistler, a civil
engineer, and his second wife, Anna Mathilda McNeill. In 1842
Whistler's father accepted an invitation by Tsar Nicholas I of Russia
to build a railroad between Saint Petersburg and Moscow. The
Major was joined by his family the following year. In 1845 Whistler
enrolled in the Imperial Academy of Fine Arts in Saint Petersburg,
where he received regular drawing lessons. In October 1847 his half-
sister, Deborah, married a surgeon, Francis Seymour Haden, who
became a noted print connoisseur and accomplished amateur etcher.
During the following school year, Whistler stayed with the Hadens
in London. He was exposed not only to ideas about art but to the
etchings of Rembrandt and the seventeenth-century Dutch painting
school. After the sudden death of Major Whistler in a cholera
epidemic in 1849, his mother returned to America.

Whistler bided his time by following in his father's footsteps at
West Point. He excelled in drawing but was finally expelled for a
deficiency in chemistry. Through a family connection, he received an
appointment in the U.S. Coast Survey Office in Washington in
November 1854. There he learned the rudiments of etching in order
to make plates for maps and topographic plans. Within four months
he resigned and counted the final days until his twenty-first birthday
when he would come into a modest inheritance that would allow
him to study in Paris.

Although he always considered himself an American, Whistler
spent the rest of his life as an expatriate. In the fall of 1855, after a
month with the Hadens in London, Whistler moved to Paris where
he enrolled at the École Impériale et Spéciale de Dessin and six
months later at the popular Academie Gleyre. While encouraging
individuality, Charles Gleyre taught in the French classical tradition,
which emphasized the ideal over nature in both drawing and
painting. Fluent in French, learned in the Russian court, the young
truant's classroom became the Louvre. At the Louvre, Whistler was
commissioned by Americans to paint copies of its collections. He

also painted scenes of the streets and cafés in the Latin Quarter.
George Du Maurier based his character "the idle apprentice" in his
novel *Trilby* on Whistler.

To launch his career, Whistler conceived of a set of etchings.
Although popularly known as the *French Set*, Whistler's group of
etchings was published in 1858 under the title "Twelve Etchings
from Nature." This set, which marks the start of his mature artistic
career, demonstrates Whistler's precocity with etching needles and
places him in the forefront of the etching revival of the 1850s. It
established Whistler's affiliation with the realist current of the
naturalist movement and associated him with the avant-garde anti-
academic stance of Gustave Courbet and his followers. The subjects
were executed in one year, and while uneven, they reveal his rapid
development as a draftsman and the range of his realist repertoire.
The set contains two portraits of his niece and nephew, which were
executed between January and April while Whistler was
convalescing at the Hadens. Upon his return to Paris in April,
Whistler began a series portraying lower class Parisian working
women, but from mid-August through September he interrupted this
work to take a trip through Alsace and up the Rhine with his
Bohemian friend Ernest Delannoy. On his trip, Whistler worked
directly from nature. *The Kitchen*, considered during Whistler's
lifetime as one of the most beautiful of his early etchings, was
conceived on this journey. He executed a drawing and a watercolor
of the subject in Lutzelbourg but waited until his return to Paris to
execute the plate.[2] The subject is the mirror image of the preliminary
drawing, the result of translating the idea directly to the plate
without reversal. The orthogonals and spatial recession focus
attention on the silhouette of a peasant woman in a sparsely
furnished room who gazes out a foliage-covered window. The strong
emphasis on light and dark patterns is carried over from the
watercolor to the etching. A Rembrandtesque web of cross-hatching
reinforces the dramatic impact of the composition.

Katharine Lochnan has proposed that "Whistler would have
intended his contemporaries to see in this set not only a commitment
to naturalism, but an admiration for certain of its adherents."[3] He
studied Dutch seventeenth-century painting in the Louvre and
traveled across the Channel to see the widely acclaimed Manchester
Art Treasure exhibition with its outstanding selection of Dutch
masters and a major survey of the history of printmaking with a
special section of Rembrandt.

The *French Set* reveals Whistler's debt to the Dutch seventeenth-
century school, the contemporary realist painters François Bonvin
and Gustave Courbet, and the Barbizon printmakers Charles Jacque
and Jean-François Millet (cat. 126). Upon his return to Paris in
October 1858, Whistler took his plates to Auguste Delâtre for
proofing. Delâtre had established a reputation as a printer for early
members of the etching revival. They experimented with a variety of
papers, but the final *French Set* was ultimately printed on *chine
appliqué*. The Museum's impression on a yellow *chine appliqué*
comes from the London edition rather than the Paris edition.[4] The
pencil butterfly signature on the mount must have been added at a
later date because Whistler did not begin to use it until 1869. In 1884
Whistler reworked the plate, and an edition of fifty impressions was
published by the Fine Art Society.[5] "Twelve Etchings from Nature"
represents Whistler's first major body of work. One of the etchings
was shown in the Paris Salon in 1859; however, his first major
painting, *At the Piano*, was rejected.[6] – KLS

1. Katharine A. Lochnan, *The Etchings of James McNeill Whistler* (New Haven and
London: Yale University Press, 1984), 7.
2. David Park Curry, *James McNeill Whistler at the Freer Gallery of Art* (New York
and London: W. W. Norton and Company, 1984), 180.
3. Lochnan, *The Etchings*, 58.

4. Robert H. Getscher, Oberlin 1977, 20.

5. Ruth E. Fine, Los Angeles 1984, 39.

6. The painting is now in the collection of the Taft Museum, Cincinnati.

Sir Francis Seymour Haden

Chelsea 1818-1910 Hampshire

129. On the Test 1859.

Etching and drypoint on Japanese paper, 15.1 x 22.5 cm (platemark).
Harrington 20; Schneiderman *Had.* 24 vi/vii.
Resigned in plate lower right: *Seymour Haden.*
Provenance: (Purchased from M. Knoedler, New York, September 12, 1927, for $110).
Bequest of Herbert Greer French, 1943.721.

Francis Seymour Haden was one of the most influential landscape etchers of the late nineteenth century. Together with James McNeill Whistler (cat. 128), his brother-in-law, he was instrumental in the revival of etching as a fine art. His strong convictions on the subject of etching led to numerous articles, books, and lectures. Haden's work was much admired at home and abroad, receiving, among its many adulations, early praise from the renowned French art critic Philippe Burty.[1]

As an artist, Seymour Haden was considered an amateur; his chosen profession was medicine. Born in Chelsea in 1818, Haden took several drawing classes while still a medical student in Paris as an experiment to perfect his surgical skills. After graduation, he produced his first half-dozen etchings after drawings he had made of the Italian countryside in 1843-44. Once again, Haden's approach was academic, but his interest in etching proved to be more than just a passing fancy. A year later he began a firsthand study of Old Master prints, eventually forming an important collection of his own that specialized in Rembrandt and his circle. Haden became an expert on the Dutch master and later recatalogued all of his works for a major exhibition at the Burlington Fine Arts Club in 1877.

In 1847 Seymour Haden married Deborah "Dasha" Delano, Whistler's older half-sister. Eleven years later, after leaving America and studying art in Paris, Whistler lived with the Hadens for a brief time in London. While Haden's renewed interest in making etchings was stimulated by his brother-in-law's visit, Whistler, on the other hand, found much artistic inspiration in the extensive Rembrandt collection to which he now had easy access.

Although Haden's early etchings, like Whistler's at the time, were portraits, his real interest was landscape. He soon found himself out-of-doors, attempting to capture the fleeting qualities of nature and creating a *plein-air* style that would later be indicative of his most mature work. Haden and Whistler developed a close but trying artistic relationship that occasionally saw them working side by side.[2]

Beginning in 1859, Haden took a number of prepared copperplates with him on day-long excursions. It was during one of these trips that he produced *On the Test*, a tranquil view of a famous trout stream (in Hampshire) located near the market town of Romsey. A study of the first state of *On the Test*, as described by Richard Schneiderman, indicates that, in this instance, when Haden worked "directly from nature" he concentrated primarily on the essential elements of the scene: the River Test, the beginnings of a somewhat threatening sky, a smaller set of trees on the left, and a much clearer depiction of the figure and bridge. Haden later took the plate through a number of states until he captured, to his satisfaction, the appropriate mood, atmosphere, and time of day.

This is evident in the Museum's print, a very fine impression in the sixth state[3] where Haden added some new features: a flock of sheep in the lower right foreground, three tall cedars on the right, a number of cottages at center background, and several birds in flight. By reworking many of these areas and the foreground rushes in drypoint and by incorporating an expressive series of vertical and horizontal lines throughout the stream, Haden created a pensive ambience typical of a late evening sunset and approaching storm. Printed on thin laid Japanese paper, the Museum's impression has a soft, velvetlike finish that further intensifies the overall effect. The sheep and nondescript figure on the bridge are dominated by the entire landscape, a pictorial device inspired by Rembrandt and possibly his etching of *The Three Trees* (cat. 81).

Seymour Haden created more than two hundred fifty prints throughout his career, the majority of which were made between 1859 and 1865. In 1860 he was elected to the "Old" Etching Club, one of the first serious etching organizations in England. During the next four years Haden exhibited over a dozen prints at the Royal Academy, and in 1878-79 the Fine Art Society honored him with a special exhibition of his work. When his eyesight began to fail him in 1881, he spent several years on the lecture circuit in America, successfully promoting his views on the art of etching. Cincinnati was one of Haden's lecture stops. According to the *Cincinnati Gazette*, December 5, 1882, "Mr. Haden arrived in the city yesterday morning at an early hour by the train from Boston, and was met and welcomed at the railway station by Mr. Herman Goepper. Yesterday he visited the Merchant's Exchange. Today he will visit Rookwood Pottery and other places of interest, leaving the city on Wednesday morning."[4]

In 1880 Haden founded the Society of Painter-Etchers, which received a royal charter at the end of the decade. For his lifelong contributions to art, Seymour Haden was knighted in 1894. He remained president of the Society of Painter-Etchers until his death in 1910. — DK

1. For a detailed account of Haden's life as an artist, see Schneiderman *Had.*

2. With two very strong egos, it was not surprising that by 1863 both men had become weary of each other's company. Among other things, Whistler may have been jealous of Burty's praise for his brother-in-law; Haden was outraged by Whistler's illicit relationship with Joanna Hiffernan. The split finally came in a café in Paris in 1867. Whistler argued with Haden over his treatment of the latter's partner, James Reeves Traer, who drank heavily and was found dead in a brothel. A fight broke out and Whistler supposedly pushed Haden through a plate glass window. After this incident, the two no longer spoke, and Whistler was forced to meet with his sister surreptitiously. See Lochnan, 143-46.

3. Haden worked with William R. Drake on his book *A Descriptive Catalogue of the Etched Work of Francis Seymour Haden* (London: MacMillan and Co., 1880) and assisted H. Nazeby Harrington with *A Supplement to Sir William Drake's Catalogue of the Etched Work of Francis Seymour Haden* (London, 1903) and with *The Engraved Work of Sir Francis Seymour Haden* (Liverpool, 1910). Both authors followed Haden's recommendations concerning "trial" or "artist's proofs" (changes made to the plate while in progress) and "states" (the finished or published plate). The Museum's impression, therefore, qualifies as a first state in their catalogues (Drake, *A Descriptive Catalogue*, no. 19; Harrington, *A Supplement*, no. 20). Schneiderman, however, uses the modern terminology of "state" (any deliberate changes made to the plate) and has classified Cincinnati's *On the Test* as a sixth state (Schneiderman *Had.*, no. 24). See Drake, *A Descriptive Catalogue*, vii-viii, and Schneiderman *Had.*, 36-37, 87.

4. Schneiderman *Had.*, 32, n. 52.

Honoré Daumier

Marseilles 1808-1879 Valmondois

130. Nadar Elevating Photography to Artistic Heights 1862.

Lithograph on *chine appliqué*, 26.7 x 22.1 cm (image).
Del. 3248.
Signed in stone lower left: *h.D.*; titled in upper left margin: *Souvenirs d'Artistes*; upper right: *367*; lower center: IMP BERTAUTS, PARIS. / NADAR *élevant le Photographie à la hauteur de l'Art.*

Provenance: (Maurice Gobin, Paris, 1928); The Metropolitan Museum of Art (Lugt 1943 [inv. no. 28.92.5], purchased from Gobin, 1928, and Lugt s. 1808h, exchanged with Knoedler, January 17, 1931); (gift from M. Knoedler, New York, September 21, 1936). Bequest of Herbert Greer French, 1943.675.
Exhibitions: Cincinnati 1948, no. 14.

Between 1835 and 1881, except during the hiatus of the Second Republic (1848-52) and the early days of the Third Republic (1870-71), censorship of political caricature was enforced by the September Laws of 1835. Under the constant threat of repression, Daumier played a major role in implementing Charles Philipon's new strategy to express political attitudes through social satire by the creation of imaginary bourgeois types. He created for *Le Charivari* three emblematic characters: Robert Macaire (1835-38), Ratapoil (1850-52), and Joseph Prudhomme (1852-70). Adopted from the theatre, Macaire was the quintessential con man who, through his many professional guises, personified the exploitative activities of the July monarchy with which the public vicariously empathized. In anticipation of the fall of the Second Republic after the ouster of Louis-Philippe in 1848, Daumier invented the sinister character Ratapoil, a hired bully and secret agent who agitated for the *coup d'état* of Louis-Napoleon. During the Second Empire, Daumier drew again from the theatre to create his bourgeois antihero, Prudhomme.

For thirty years, through his many series, Daumier succeeded in portraying the dynamics of the emerging bourgeoisie that was his subject and audience. By the late 1850s, repetitiveness and lack of verve saw his popularity wane. He was dropped from *Le Charivari* after Philipon departed for *Le Journal amusant* and turned his attention to painting, which was, for Daumier, an irregular source of income. During his respite from political satire, he contributed wood engravings to *Le Temps* and *Le Monde Illustré*. He was commissioned by his friend the caricaturist, writer, and photographer Étienne Carjat to become a regular contributor to his new weekly illustrated paper, *Le Boulevard*. In *Le Boulevard*, Daumier was given free rein to explore the changing times of Paris and the transformation of bourgeois habits. He satirized photography eight times between 1840 and 1865.[1]

The French painter and dioramist Louis Jacques Mandé Daguerre discovered the first practicable photographic process. François Arago announced the discovery to the French Académie des Sciences on January 7, 1839, and Daguerre followed the announcement with a public demonstration on August 19.[2] On July 2, 1840, *La patience est la vertu des ânes* (Patience Is the Virtue of Asses) (Del. 805) appeared in *Le Charivari* as part of a series entitled *Proverbs et Maximes*. It humorously comments on Daguerre holding a watch and on the length of time required for a successful daguerreotype exposure. Daumier followed this caricature with a series of satires on public vanity in front of the camera and the tortuous medieval apparatus required to take a likeness. For the May 25, 1862, issue of *Le Boulevard*, he executed *Nadar élevant la Photographie à la hauteur de L'Art* (Nadar Elevating Photography to Artistic Heights), the only other lithograph in which Daumier pays homage to an identifiable photographer. Nadar (Gaspard-Félix Tournachon) was a flamboyant photographer and daredevil aeronaut. Shortly after receiving his October 23, 1858, patent for aerial photography, he coined the phrase "*élever la photographie à la hauteur de l'art*" for an advertisement that appeared in *Le Journal Amusant* on November 6, 1858.[3]

Although Nadar attempted aerial photography as early as 1855, he was unsuccessful in recording even a faint image until the early winter of 1858 and had no further success until 1862. Unconvinced of its validity and usefulness, Daumier punned the concept of photography as art. He portrayed Nadar with top hat suspended in a wicker balloon basket against a bird's-eye view of the pre-Haussmann metropolis, where the proliferation of photographic trade advertising attests to the frightening expansiveness of the new vogue. The unusual point of view, selective cropping, and fluid rendering affirm Daumier's brilliance as draftsman. Nadar used a Dallmeyer camera and the cumbersome "wet collodion" process. In order for the light-sensitive emulsion to remain moist and tacky, he prepared plates in a special airborne darkroom tent immediately before use and developed the negatives immediately after exposure. In turn both Carjat and Nadar took notable portraits of Daumier.

In 1863 Daumier was offered a new contract from *Le Charivari* and returned to parodying familiar bourgeois subjects until Napoleon III optimistically lifted the censorship laws in 1866. In the final years before the Franco-Prussian War, preferring issues to personalities, Daumier made heroic efforts to warn the masses of the impending disaster that threatened peace through political allegories played out on the international stage. In 1867 he introduced the symbolic jester, a self-portrait as critic-at-large, who entertained through wit and confrontations while fighting a losing battle for the republic. With failing eyesight, Daumier finally retired to Valmondois in 1872. His friends, among them the novelist Victor Hugo, the romantic Barbizon landscapist Charles Daubigny, and Nadar, organized a major retrospective of his paintings, drawings, sculpture, and a sampling of his lithographs at the Galerie Durand-Ruel in 1878, where his work was enthusiastically received by critics. Within a year of this exhibition, Daumier died, leaving a legacy of political and social caricature matched only by Goya. – KLS

1. The lithographs are the following: Del. 805 (1840), Del. 1287 (1844), Del. 1504 (1846), Del. 1525 (1847), Del. 2445 (1853), Del. 2803 (1856), and Del. 3416 (1865).
2. Helmut Gernsheim and Alison Gernsheim, *The History of Photography from the Camera Obscura to the Beginning of the Modern Era* (New York, St. Louis, and San Francisco: McGraw-Hill, 1969), 68-70.
3. Gernsheim and Gernsheim, *The History of Photography*, 507.

James Abbott McNeill Whistler
Lowell, Massachusetts 1834-1903 London

131. Weary 1863.
Drypoint on Japanese paper, 19.9 x 13.1 cm (platemark).
K. 92 ii/iii; Mansfield 92 ii/iii.
Signed and dated in plate lower left: *Whistler / 63*.
Provenance: (Purchased from M. Knoedler, New York, April 1, 1935, for $139).
Bequest of Herbert Greer French, 1943.603.
Exhibitions: Indianapolis 1965.

In 1859 Whistler made the decision to move to London, effectively ending his student years. He returned to London in May to see two of his etchings exhibited at the Royal Academy. During the spring of 1859, Whistler and two French artists, Henri Fantin-Latour and Alphonse Legros, formed a short-lived Société des Trois and "set out to create the 'art of the future'," employing styles and subjects that would demonstrate their admiration for Courbet's realism while retaining their own individuality.[1] At this time, Whistler's etchings took a new direction, away from his early style based on Rembrandtesque naturalism, toward realism. During the late summer, he took up a radically new subject matter and explored new methods of constructing pictorial space. His picturesque etchings of the squalid and unsavory docks and warehouses around Wapping and Rotherhithe, bounding the Thames, were truly revolutionary and anti-academic. Whistler recorded the city's commercial environment that would be drastically altered by the proposed embanking of the river. At this time the growing professional rivalry between Whistler and his brother-in-law, Haden, derailed a possible joint portfolio.

During the fall of 1859, Whistler explored the unique qualities of drypoint while still in Paris. He was undoubtedly attracted to the aura of rarity associated with the medium since few impressions are possible from a drypoint plate because the burr, which produces the soft velvety line, wears down during repeated printings. At the time, the medium was rarely used in either England or France. Of the twelve drypoints that he executed in Paris, nine were portraits that focused on the essence of the sitter's personality. His male portraits reveal an ongoing interest in the work of Rembrandt and in Anthony van Dyck's famous series of portrait etchings, the *Iconographia* (cats. 72-73). Whistler adopted the refined aesthetic style of Van Dyck and used it in the first states of a number of his portraits. He focused on the head, utilizing only a few descriptive lines for the torso. Notable among this group were his portraits of the writer Austruc, the musician Becquet, and the sculptor Drouet. His female portraits hint at his future association with aestheticism. His full-length portraits *Finette* (K. 58) and *Annie Haden* (K. 62) reveal a growing interest in texture, color, and elegance. Portraits of beautiful men and women remained a constant theme throughout the rest of his career.

During the 1860s, a red-haired Irish beauty named Joanna Hiffernan became his model and mistress. She appears in many of Whistler's paintings: *Wapping* (1860-64), *Symphony in White, No. 1: The White Girl* (1862), *Symphony in White, No. 2: The Little White Girl* (1864), and *Symphony in White, No. 3* (1867).[2] In his 1861 drypoint *Jo's Bent Head* (K. 78), the audaciously abbreviated left profile centered at the top of the plate is one of the artist's sparest portraits: only a few lines indicate the contour of her dress. *Weary* is Whistler's most Pre-Raphaelite etching. The avant-garde Pre-Raphaelite Brotherhood formed in 1848 was the English counterpart to the French realist movement. Although they were interested in historical, literary, and religious themes, their stance was antiacademic and their models were personal acquaintances. In 1855 several members of the brotherhood exhibited at the Exposition Universelle in Paris. Whistler met the Pre-Raphaelite poet and painter Dante Gabriel Rossetti on July 28, 1862. Not only were they Chelsea neighbors, but they shared a passion for Japanese *ukiyo-e* woodcuts, blue and white porcelain, and beautiful women. In *Weary* Whistler transforms Jo into a lithe beauty whose spiritual pathos and languid melancholy recall Rossetti's Pre-Raphaelite ideal. In a semirecumbent pose, her abundant tresses strewn across the back of the chair frame her face. The head relates closely to Whistler's crayon drawing of Jo in the Rosenwald Collection at the National Gallery of Art.[3] The long-sweeping drypoint lines of the gown echo the enveloping curve of the chair back and focus all attention on the mysterious, sensuous beauty. The delicacy and fragility of the figure is reinforced by Whistler's use of a thin Japanese paper. As the drypoint burr wears down the portrait becomes more ethereal. The head at the bottom of the plate was abandoned but not fully erased.

With the critical success of his *Symphony in White, No. 1: The White Girl* in the Paris Salon des Refusés in 1863, Whistler turned his attention to painting. He no longer looked for realist themes; instead he pursued "an art which, while based on nature, was governed by beauty, the imagination, and artistic temperament."[4] The recumbent female was a theme that Whistler returned to in his lithographs during his later years. – KLS

1. Katharine A. Lochnan, "'The Thames from Its Source to the Sea': An Unpublished Portfolio by Whistler and Haden," in Ruth E. Fine, ed., *Studies in the History of Art* (Washington: National Gallery of Art, 1987), 19:33.

2. Andrew McLaren Young, Margaret MacDonald, and Robin Spencer, *The Paintings of James McNeill Whistler* (New Haven and London: Yale University Press, 1980), 14-15, no. 35; 17-20, no. 38; 28-29, no. 52; 34-36, no. 61.

3. Denys Sutton, *James McNeill Whistler: Paintings, Etchings, Pastels, and Watercolors* (London: Phaidon Press, 1966), 187, no. 27, illustrated. There is also another study in the Sterling and Francine Clark Art Institute, Williamstown, Massachusetts.

4. Katharine A. Lochnan, *The Etchings of James McNeill Whistler* (New Haven and London: Yale University Press, 1984), 155.

Jean-Baptiste-Camille Corot

Paris 1796-1875 Paris

132. The Environs of Rome 1866.

Etching on laid paper, 31.3 x 23.2 cm (platemark).
Del.6 i/iii; Melot 6 i/iii.
Provenance: Alfred Beurdeley (Lugt 421); (his sale Paris, November 5-6, 1920, lot 196, illus., for FR 2,000); (purchased from Robert Dunthorne & Son, London, November 16, 1927, for $375).
Bequest of Herbert Greer French, 1943.665.

The influential landscape painter Corot abandoned a career as a cloth merchant to take up art full-time at the age of twenty-six, studying with the landscape painter Victor Bertin (1755-1842). He spent three years in Italy from 1825 to 1828, a period that strongly influenced his direct observation of nature and the evocation of classical themes in his works. His landscapes at the time were sharply lit and remarkably "realist," indeed anticipatory of the soon-to-be announcement of photography.[1] Although he devoted considerable efforts to figurative compositions and portraits, especially later in his career, Corot was known primarily for his atmospheric depiction of pastoral landscape motifs. His landscapes were often labeled "poetic," a quality defined in the nineteenth century by Théophile Thoré as "the opposite of imitation. . . . Poetry is not nature, but the feeling [*sentiment*] that nature inspires in the artist."[2]

Corot exhibited in the official Salons from the 1830s and gradually accumulated popular and critical success, including bestowal of the Legion of Honor in 1846 and numerous public and private commissions. Customarily, his output is divided between smaller, more personal treatments of landscape (often painted outdoors and not widely exhibited) and larger, more formal submissions to the Salon. His later works became more and more ethereal in effect and technique and were often imitated and even forged in sizable numbers. During the 1850s and 1860s Corot maintained friendships with several members of the Barbizon school, in particular Charles-François Daubigny (1817-1878), with whom he often went on painting trips. Corot spent much of his life on his family's property in Ville d'Avray, southwest of Paris.

His print oeuvre consists of some fourteen etchings, ten lithographs, and over sixty *clichés-verre*. Corot was particularly attracted to the latter technique (literally translated as "glass-negative"), which was a combination of drawing and photographic techniques, produced by exposing a light-sensitive paper under a blackened glass plate whose surface had been scratched with a drawing tool).[3] Its fluidity and the ease of preparing the matrix appealed to the artist, and it is surmised that the relatively indirect methods of lithography and etching did not so much attract him; in fact, most of his few etchings were done for specific commissions. After his first assay in drawing on an etching plate about 1845 (perhaps stimulated by Charles-Emile Jacque's example), Corot didn't touch another until the 1860s, when Bracquemond (see cat. 124) discovered the earlier effort, never bitten, and persuaded Corot to allow him to etch it.[4] It was at this time that Bracquemond and others were founding the Société des Aquafortistes (Society of Etchers) and hoped to attract the very influential older artist to submit a work for their portfolios.

Under the aegis of the printseller-publisher Alfred Cadart (1828-1875) and the well-known etching printer Auguste Delâtre (1822-1907), the Société eventually issued monthly portfolios of original etchings, titled *Eaux-fortes modernes* (*Modern Etchings*) over a period of five years from 1862 to 1867, encompassing in all some three hundred separate plates.[5] Corot, Delacroix, and Edouard Manet (1832-1883) were perhaps the most famous painter-etchers represented, but many well-known etchers such as Bracquemond, Alphonse Legros (1837-1911), Meryon (cats. 123, 125), Daubigny, Adolphe Appian (1818-1898), and Maxime Lalanne (1827-1886) were included.

Three etchings by Corot appeared in the Société's publications: *Remembrance of Italy*, *The Environs of Rome*, and *Italian Landscape* (Del. 5-7). All date from the 1860s, and all are rather nostalgic evocations of Corot's Italian experiences. *The Environs of Rome* was in the April 1866 part-issue of the fourth annual volume of *Modern Etchings*, and it was concurrently exhibited in the Salon of 1866 (one of eleven etchings exhibited there by members of the Société).[6] At the time, the critic Philippe Burty declared that "The etching triumphs in every way this year, and this Salon could be called 'The Salon of the Etchers'."[7] It was also in 1866 that Maxime Lalanne's influential etching manual, *Traité de la gravure de l'eau-forte*, was published by Cadart; that year also saw Cadart's journey to the United States to promote the art of etching and to organize an exhibition of contemporary French etchings.[8] The latter was a strong impetus for the etching revival that reached its peak in the United States some twenty years later.

The motifs of Corot's etchings accord well with his work in other media, but their specific draftsmanship reveals a certain influence from his experiments with cliché-verre, which he had been exploring in depth since the mid-1850s. His etchings are similarly built up with many fluid, sketchy strokes of the needle, combining elements of landscape in an overall linear texture. The trees in the middle distance of *The Environs of Rome* are indicated primarily with broad strokes of line; not a leaf is individually described. Corot very carefully placed a restricted number of landscape elements: strongly silhouetted trees, a broadly delineated hillside, and a hazy view of a distant monument. The combination of his fluid lines and Bracquemond's skill in the staged bitings of this plate produced an evanescent atmosphere suffused with a soft sunlight. Even if ultimately derived from an actual view, Corot's prints were not meant to be particularized scenes.

As Melot points out, Corot only drew one state on the plate itself, the recorded changes being in the lettering in the margins. Melot states that various retouchings in the plate in the background and foliage were necessitated by the extensive printings for Société editions, although "nothing proves that they were from the hand of the artist himself."[9] The plate for *The Environs of Rome* was reprinted twice by Cadart in 1872 and 1874 and was formerly in the possession of the New York print dealer Frederick Keppel.

This impression acquired by Mr. French is of the very rare first state before any inscriptions or retouchings. It is marked by distinctly more atmosphere in the dark areas of the foreground landscape at the bottom of the plate, areas that become murky and flat in later printings.[10] There is more plate tone in the sky of this impression, rendering a softer effect overall, with more depth to the landscape and the far distant vista. It is printed on a dark cream-colored paper, enhancing the warm tone. Later impressions are marked by a greater contrast between the trees and darker landscape elements and the sky. This impression was once part of one of the finest and probably

the largest contemporary collections of nineteenth-century French prints, that of Alfred Beurdeley (1847-1919), consisting of some twenty-eight thousand works.[11] – DPB

1. See Peter Galassi, New York 1981; see also idem, *Corot in Italy: Open-air Painting and the Classical Landscape Tradition* (New Haven: Yale University Press, 1991).

2. Quoted in Richard Shiff, *Cézanne and the End of Impressionism* (Chicago and London: University of Chicago Press, 1984), 102. Shiff (102-08) includes a useful analysis of an early and a late painting in Corot's career, elucidating his role as an important precursor to the impressionist landscape painters. See also Bonnie L. Grad and Timothy A. Riggs, Worcester 1982, 160.

3. See Elizabeth Glassman and Marilyn F. Symmes, Detroit 1980, esp. 52-68.

4. See Michel Melot, *Graphic Art of the Pre-Impressionists* (New York: Abrams, 1980), 257.

5. See the extensive history of the Société and its annual publications: Janine Bailly-Herzberg, *L'Eau-forte de peintre au dix-neuvième siècle – La Société des Aquafortistes (1862-1867)*, 2 vols. (Paris: Leonce Laget, 1972).

6. See Bailly-Herzberg, *L'Eau-forte*, 1:184, no. 211 (reproduced on p. 202).

7. Bailly-Herzberg, *L'Eau-forte*, 210.

8. Bailly-Herzberg, *L'Eau-forte*, 211-16.

9. Melot, *Pre-Impressionists*, 258, under no. C 6.

10. An impression of the second state, from the Société printing for the 1866 publication of *Eaux-fortes modernes*, is in the Cincinnati Art Museum collection (CAM 1962.662).

11. See Lugt, 72-75, for a biography and description of the highlights of Beurdeley's collection.

Samuel Palmer

London 1805-1881 Surrey

133. The Lonely Tower 1879.

Etching on wove paper, 18.9 x 25.3 cm (platemark).
Alexander 12 vi/vi; Lister E 12 vi/vii.
Signed in image lower left: *Sam¹ Palmer;* in plate lower left: *16;* signed with pencil lower right: *Samuel Palmer.*
Provenance: (Purchased from Kennedy, New York, September 13, 1927, for $260).
Bequest of Herbert Greer French, 1943.718.

> Or let my lamp at midnight hour,
> Be seen in some high lonely tow'r,
> Where I may oft out-watch the Bear,
> With thrice-great Hermes.[1]

In 1863 Leonard Rowe Valpy, John Ruskin's solicitor, purchased a small painting by Samuel Palmer entitled *Twilight: The Chapel by the Bridge* from the winter exhibition of the Old Watercolour Society. Valpy disliked certain aspects of the lighting and asked Palmer if he would make the appropriate changes. The artist agreed that the lights in the windows "glare a little and should rather glimmer."[2] Sometime later Valpy commissioned a project that Palmer had been considering for years: a series of designs illustrating Milton's "L'Allegro" and "Il Penseroso."

Palmer had a lifelong interest in Milton. As a small child, he was first introduced to Milton's poems by his nurse, Mary Ward, who, on her deathbed in 1837, also gave Palmer a personal volume of the poet's works. It was a special gift that he cherished, carrying it on many drawing expeditions. He made constant references to Milton in letters and conversations throughout his life. Palmer, therefore, enthusiastically accepted the Valpy commission to illustrate *The Shorter Poems of John Milton*, which initially began with a series of eight large watercolors. While preparing some of the smaller working drawings for the project, Palmer also decided to produce a set of etchings for the series, similar in scale to Turner's *Liber Studiorum* (cat.117).[3] Although a series of plates was planned, only two etchings, *The Bellman* and *The Lonely Tower*, were actually completed prior to his death in 1881.[4]

The Lonely Tower is a very powerful and moving composition. It achieves Palmer's highest ideal: a blending of romance with "an intense, constant, and absorbing study of nature."[5] Under a moonlit sky, with the constellations of the Great Bear and the Heavenly Twins glowing from above, two shepherds, with their flock sleeping soundly underneath a group of hawthorne trees, stare reverently at the bright light coming from the tower. On the other side, a mysterious figure seeks the tower by foot; another, with a similar destination in mind, rides in a covered wagon along a narrow road.

According to Raymond Lister, "Blake's influence on Palmer is clearest in *The Lonely Tower*." Along with the waning moon, "the distant trilithons silhouetted against the sky, the deep fissure dividing the dreaming shepherds from the hill and the tower, and the tower itself, its window like a beacon, could have been suggested by Blake's symbolism."[6] Throughout his career, Palmer greatly admired William Blake both as a man and an artist. They met when Palmer was only nineteen, introduced by the landscape painter John Linnell, who would later become Palmer's father-in-law. Palmer was encouraged by the artist/poet to continue with his unique and imaginative approach to portraying nature. Later in his etchings, he remembered what Blake had once written about the "great and golden rule of art, as well as life: that the more distinct, sharp and wiry the bounding line, the more perfect the work of art."[7] Palmer used a complex myriad of deeply etched, diagonal, zigzagged, and cross-hatched lines to create the tone and night ambiance found in *The Lonely Tower*. The effect of light, or the "flicker of light and shade," was also an important part of this process. Palmer always felt "that the charm of linear etching is the glimmering through of the paper even in the shadows, so that almost everything either sparkles or suggests sparkle."[8]

Palmer had a difficult and problematic career. The paintings and drawings from the years he spent at Shoreham in Kent show a vision and poetic insight that many feel he was never able to recapture. According to Lister, the "early visionary work remains the most important section of Palmer's 'oeuvre'."[9] Nonetheless, some of this enthusiasm and creativity did return and can be found in many of the etchings as well as in the drawings produced during the last thirty years of his life.

Palmer worked up a number of preliminary studies for both the watercolor and the etching of *The Lonely Tower*. One of these studies, a wash drawing from circa 1864,[10] is now in the Museum's collection (CAM 1953.82) (fig. 133-1). According to A. H. Palmer's inscription on the verso, the piece was used as the working design for the commissioned watercolor.[11] Because of the similarity in size and composition,[12] it probably became the model for the etching as well. With a mountainous vista similar to Palmer's studies in the Apennines, Lister notes that the "mood and mastery of technique in this design recall Palmer's earlier Shoreham work."[13] Furthermore, with a composition such as *The Lonely Tower*, "if we are to see in Palmer's etchings a return to visionary work, it is here above all."[14] – DK

1. *The Shorter Poems of John Milton* (London: Seeley and Company, 1889), 27.

2. Raymond Lister, "Milton Watercolours," *Connoisseur* 194 (January 1977): 17.

3. In a letter sent to Valpy dated October 20, 1864, Palmer explained how the etching idea came to him:

> The Etching dream came over me in this way. I am making my working sketches a quarter of the size of the drawings, and was surprised and not displeased to notice the variety – the difference of each from all the rest. I saw within, a set of highly-finished etchings the size of Turner's *Liber Studiorum*.

See A. H. Palmer, *The Life and Letters of Samuel Palmer* (London: Seeley and Co., Limited, 1892), 261.

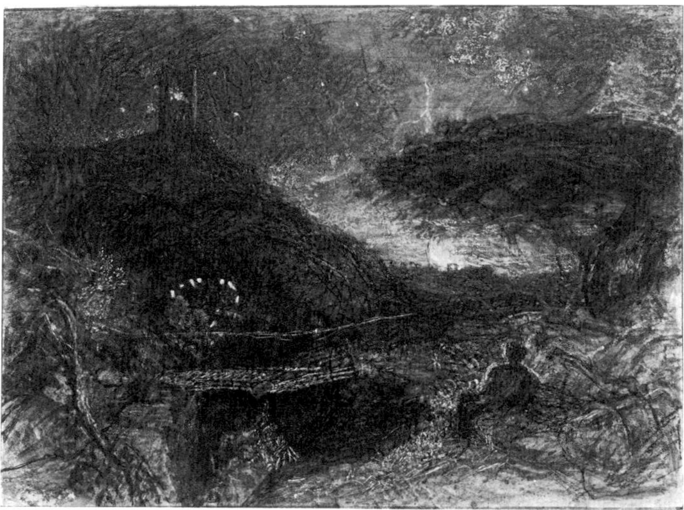

Figure 133-1. Samuel Palmer, *The Lonely Tower*, ca. 1864, bistre ink wash and crayon with scraped highlights, charcoal and white chalk. Cincinnati Art Museum, Gift of Emily Poole (1953.82).

4. Palmer was a perfectionist and, therefore, an extremely slow worker. Consequently, during his printmaking years between 1850-81, he completed only thirteen etchings.

5. Martin Hardie, "The Etched Work of Samuel Palmer," PCQ. 3 (1913): 219.

6. Lister, "Milton Watercolours," 17.

7. Raymond Lister, "A Vision Recaptured: The Etchings and the Designs for Milton and Virgil," in *Samuel Palmer: A Vision Recaptured* (London: Trianon Press Facsimiles, 1978), 23.

8. Hardie, "The Etched Work of Samuel Palmer," 215-16.

9. Raymond Lister, *Samuel Palmer and His Etchings* (New York: Watson-Guptill Publications, 1969), 15.

10. Palmer used a combination of bistre ink, crayon with scraped highlights, charcoal, and white chalk in executing the Museum's wash-drawing. Other related studies include a watercolor and gouache, 1868, in the Paul Mellon Collection, Yale Center for British Art, and a watercolor, after 1864?, in the Huntington Library and Art Gallery, San Marino, California.

11. A. H. Palmer, Samuel Palmer's son, wrote the following inscription on the back of the drawing: "The First design for the 'Lonely Tower' Milton Drawing. Never Exhibited/See my note No. 145 in the Catalogue of the Victoria & Albert Museum/Exhibition page 51 as to the occational discordent use of white. A.H.P."

12. The etching of *The Lonely Tower* is slightly smaller than the Museum's wash-drawing.

13. Raymond Lister, "Catalogue: The Designs for Virgil and Milton," in *Samuel Palmer: A Vision Recaptured*, 73.

14. Lister, *Samuel Palmer and His Etchings*, 87.

Ignace-Henri-Jean-Théodore Fantin-Latour

Grenoble 1836-1904 Buré

134. Bouquet of Roses 1879.

Transfer lithograph (crayon and scraper) on *chine appliqué*, 41.7 x 35.6 (image).
Hédiard 26 ii/ii.
Signed and dated in stone upper left: *Fantin 79*; printed in lower center: *Impr. Lemercier & C*ᶦᵉ, Paris; signed with pencil lower right margin: *h. Fantin*.
Provenance: Marcel Louis Guérin (Lugt s. 1872b); Marcel Mirault (Lugt s. 1892a); (purchased from M. Knoedler, New York, January 20, 1939, for $325).
Bequest of Herbert Greer French, 1943.683.
Exhibitions: Cincinnati 1948, no. 26.

Inspired by the new choral music of Robert Schumann, Hector Berlioz, Johannes Brahms, and the controversial Richard Wagner,

Fantin's lithographs were almost solely responsible for the resurgence of enthusiasm for original lithographs in the 1880s. In 1862 the critic Philippe Burty championed the revival of etching and the formation of the *Société des Aquafortistes* by Alfred Cadart. Burty likewise observed that lithography was dying through the disinterest of painters who, in the heyday of chromolithography, viewed the medium as unsuitable for original prints.[1] Cadart, who was preparing the first issue of *Eaux-fortes modernes*, the main publication of the Société des Aquafortistes, bypassed older established lithographers Eugène Delacroix, Honoré Daumier, and Gavarni, providing five younger founding members of the *Société*, Edouard Manet, Alphonse Legros, Félix Bracquemond, Augustin Ribot, and Fantin, with lithographic stones in their stead.[2] This was Fantin's first experience with lithography. He drew four subjects on three stones. The most ambitious composition was the first version of *Tannhauser: Venusberg* (Hédiard 1), loosely and energetically executed using lithographic crayon, scraper, and stump. This Wagnerian subject, with its unorthodox lack of finish, was a major departure from the carefully rendered lithographs of the 1820s and 1830s. Along with those of the other four artists, Cadart found Fantin's lithograph too radical and so abandoned his publication.

Fantin returned seriously to lithography in 1873. Although he had originally contemplated a major painting in homage to Schumann for the Salon, illness intervened and he produced instead *A la mémoire de Robert Schumann* (Hédiard 5) to commemorate the unveiling of a monument to the composer in Bonn in August 1873. Fantin produced over 190 lithographs throughout the remainder of his career. They became an embryonic testing ground for the majority of his ambitious paintings, which were inspired by a personal pantheon of composers to whose musical themes of hidden ecstasy Fantin obsessively returned again and again. His two chief gods were Wagner and Berlioz. The choice of Wagner is surprising in the wake of the France's crushing defeat in the Franco-Prussian War, yet the popularity of the composer's cult rose steadily until the end of the century.

Fantin was a technical innovator. After his first attempts to draw directly on the stone, he perfected a method of working with transfer paper on a number of textured surfaces to achieve a variety of textures, thus setting the tone for a particular image. He often enhanced his finest lithographs with a full range of gradations from white to black by printing them on a variety of papers. He introduced further subtleties by stumping the chalk to provide tonal transitions and by vigorously scraping the drawing on the stone to create highlights. While the germ of his experimental technique could have had many sources, Delacroix, one of Fantin's heros whose lithographs he collected, used this process in his work.

A painter for the intellectual bourgeoisie, Fantin's subjects were limited to still lifes, portraits, and imaginary moments of great music. His ambitions were those of a romantic; his great talents were those of a realist. For thirty-five years Fantin supported himself and his family by painting still lifes and portraits, but it was as an eminent specialist in flower painting that he first gained attention in Victorian England.

Ignace-Henri-Jean-Théodore Fantin-Latour was born on January 14, 1836, in Grenoble, the son of a French portrait painter and a Russian mother. When Fantin was ten, his father gave him his first drawing lessons. In 1850, three months shy of his fifteenth birthday, he attended the classes of Lecoq-de-Boisbaudran at the École de Dessin, where the emphasis was on interpreting nature through drawing and painting from memory rather than from life. He left Lecoq's class for the École des Beaux-Arts, where after a three-month probationary period, he failed to gain admission. Like many painters of his generation, he served his apprenticeship by copying

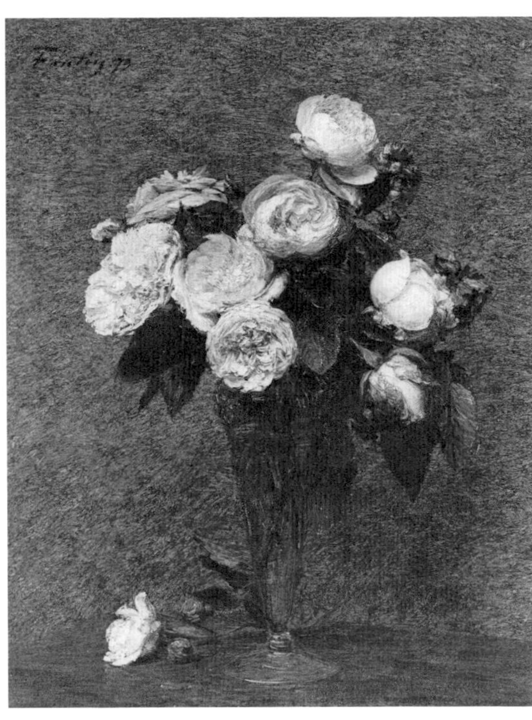

Figure 134-1. Ignace-Henri-Jean-Théodore Fantin-Latour, *Tea and Tea-Noisette Roses*, 1879, oil on canvas. Manchester City Art Galleries.

paintings of the great masters in the Louvre for the next twelve years. His copies for American and British clients were a major source of income. The Louvre was an important social forum where he met artists, including Edouard Manet, Berthe Morisot and Whistler.

In 1858 Whistler (cat. 131), Legros, a former classmate from the École de Dessin, and Fantin formed the Société des Trois, a mutual admiration and financial aid society. At Whistler's invitation, Fantin first visited England in 1859. On his subsequent visit he stayed with Ruth and Edwin Edwards, an etcher-lawyer who eventually became Fantin's dealer of still lifes in England. Fantin made his debut in the Paris Salon in 1861 with three studies after nature. Inspired by Delacroix's death, he painted his first group portrait, *Hommage à Delacroix*, which was shown in the Salon of 1864. This group portrait was followed by *The Toast! Homage to Truth* (Salon 1865), which he subsequently destroyed, *Atelier in the Batignolles* (Salon 1870) and *Le Coin de Table* (Salon 1872), and *Mr. and Mrs. Edwin Edwards* (Salon 1875), for which he won a second-class medal. In 1879 Fantin was made chevalier of the Legion of Honor and was designated *hors concours* at the Salon. One of the lithographs for which he received an honorable mention at the Salon of 1880, an anomaly in his lithographic oeuvre, was *Bouquet of Roses*. Considered the artist's lithographic masterpiece in Mr. French's day, this vase of roses is remarkably close in subject and size to his 1879 painting *Tea and Tea-Noisette Roses* (fig. 134-1), now in the collection of the City of Manchester Art Galleries.[3] The lithograph was undoubtedly intended for the English market, which had become the world leader in rose cultivation. From the mid-1870s on, the Edwardses provided Fantin with fashionable glass vases, popular with English collectors. Although *Bouquet of Roses* may have begun as a tracing on thin transfer paper, Fantin combined crayon and scraper to transcend the mere reproduction from color to black and white as he translated the image from one medium to another. To capture the delicacy and translucency of the open blossoms he scraped the flowers and, at the same time, scraped the highlighting of the trumpet-shaped glass vase to capture its hard reflective surface. Fantin modulated the medium-tone background with the scraper and lightened the value of the table corner on which the vase sits.

The critic for *The Athenaeum* lauded its "remarkable. . . breadth of effect and richness of touch" when it was shown in the 1880 Black and White Exhibition at the Dudley Gallery in London.[4] The still life appears again in Fantin's *Portrait of Madame Henri Lerolle*, now in the Cleveland Museum of Art.[5]

From the 1880s onward, imaginary music-inspired compositions played an increasingly important role in Fantin's paintings and lithographs. In the 1890s he benefited from the renewed popularity of lithography, popularity that culminated in the critical success of his 1899 one-man exhibition, arranged by Léonce Bénédite, director of the Luxembourg. Two years after his death, a major exhibition of his work in all media was organized at the Palais d'École Nationale des Beaux-Arts, which revealed Fantin to be equally a realist and a romantic who had no kinship with the subjects and techniques of his insurgent impressionist contemporaries. – KLS

1. Philippe Burty, "La Gravure et la lithographie a l'Exposition de 1861," GBA. II (August 1861): 177-78.
2. Hédiard, 15.
3. Hédiard, 20; Douglas Druick, Ottawa 1983, 265-66.
4. Quoted in Ottawa 1983, 266.
5. Cynthia Nadelman, "Henri Fantin-Latour: 'Tea and Tea-Noisette Roses'," *Art News* 89 (October 1990): 110.

James Abbott McNeill Whistler
Lowell, Massachusetts 1834-1903 London

135. Nocturne 1879-80.
From *Venice: Twelve Etchings*.
Etching and drypoint on antique laid paper, 19.9 x 29.5 cm (platemark).
K. 184 v/v; Mansfield 181 iv/iv.
Watermark: Shield with horn surmounted by crown.
Signed with pencil on tab lower left: butterfly and *imp*.
Provenance: R. C. Fisher, Jr.; (purchased from F.H. Bresler, Milwaukee, February 20, 1928, for $4,850).
Bequest of Herbert Greer French, 1943.596.
Exhibitions: Indianapolis 1965.

In July 1876 Whistler recorded orders from dealers P. and G. Colnaghi, London, and M. Knoedler, New York, among others, for a series of etchings of Venice in connection with a trip that he intended to take in the fall.[1] The trip, however, never materialized. At that time, Whistler was occupied with painting the "Peacock Room" for Frederick R. Leyland, a Liverpool shipping tycoon. Leyland refused to pay time and materials to the artist because Whistler exceeded his mandate. In addition, social improprieties led Leyland to terminate their business relationship. During the same month, Whistler's painting *Nocturne in Black and Gold: The Falling Rocket* was viciously attacked by the art critic John Ruskin in *Fors Clavigera*: "I have seen and heard much of cockney imp[r]udence before now; but never expected to hear a coxcomb ask two hundred guineas for flinging a pot of paint in the public's face."[2] Whistler sued Ruskin for libel. Although he won the trial, the lawsuit and the construction costs for "White House," designed by the dean of the aesthetic movement, E. W. Goodwin, forced Whistler to declare bankruptcy in May 1879.

On September 9, 1879, the Fine Art Society came to Whistler's rescue. Given a subsidy of 150 pounds, Whistler would finally embark on his trip to Venice. He etched twelve plates in Venice over a four-month period that were to be published in December of that year. Whistler maximized his opportunity in Venice by staying a year longer than he had anticipated, thereby completing fifty rather than

twelve etchings in addition to a few watercolors, a few oil sketches, and ninety pastels.

In 1879 Ruskin, in *The Stones of Venice*, described the unique qualities of the ancient city:

> Her successor, like her in perfection of beauty, though less in endurance of dominion, is still left for our beholding in the final period of her decline: a ghost upon the sands of the sea, so weak – so quiet – so bereft of all but her loveliness, that we might well doubt, as we watched her faint reflections in the mirage of the lagoon, which was the City, and which the Shadow.[3]

Whistler's Venice is not the familiar *vedute* of his eighteenth-century predecessors Canaletto and Guardi. Instead of popular tourist views like San Marco and the Grand Canal, he captured the essence of anonymous doorways, back canals, palace facades, and picturesque plazas.

Of all Whistler's Venice subjects, his evocative and poetic *Nocturne* exhibits the most variation among impressions. The first etched state was executed directly from nature. Across the bay, San Giorgio appears on the right and the Church of the Redemptor to the left (the reversal the result of the printing process). Kennedy describes five states (K. 184). Since the plate was never steelfaced, its drypoint lines wore down quickly.[4] All changes beyond the first state were executed in drypoint; therefore, additional drypoint states may exist because Whistler tried to keep the plate in shape for an edition of one hundred. In the second state, two large gondolas were added in front of the ship; three smaller ones in the middle distance at the right; one at the left. In the third state, the two large gondolas were removed. Through the third state, the impressions were printed in black. The final two states were printed in brown. Manipulating the film of ink on the plate, Whistler altered the mood and the time of day from dawn to midnight.

The impression of *Nocturne* selected by Mr. French suggests the calm at dawn or dusk. Hand wiping in the sky and water perpendicular to the distant shoreline reveals either the first decisive rays of the sun or the day's final dissolve into palpable darkness. The two rightmost gondolas have become a mere blur; the one left of the ship has almost disappeared; and unlike other impressions, Whistler did not wipe the ink clean from the aureoles of the ship's lantern.

Whistler's Venice etchings, mysterious and magical, were a logical outgrowth of his painted nocturnes of the late 1870s. *Nocturne* was one of the first prints Whistler made in Venice. At the University of Glasgow there is an impression inscribed "1st State – 1st Proof – Venice 1879."[5]

Once in Venice, Whistler immersed himself in the social life of the cafés and the English-speaking community. During the summer, he met Frank Duveneck and his "boys" and moved to join them at Casa Jankovitz, where he experienced not only adulation and camaraderie but had access to Otto Bacher's portable etching press for his initial proofing. In November 1880, Whistler returned to London. There he proofed and selected twelve plates for *Venice: Twelve Etchings*, also known as "the First Venice Set," which included *Nocturne*. The etchings were printed by Whistler and his assistants on scavenged eighteenth-century Dutch laid paper. By trimming his prints to the platemark to conserve paper and to needle snobbish collectors who often acquired prints for their margins rather than their quality, Whistler turned a necessity into an aesthetic virtue. For his butterfly signature he left a tab on the lower edge, strategically placed to balance the composition. The set was shown at the Fine Art Society in December 1880 to mixed reviews. On December 7, 1880, a reviewer from the *Daily News* observed:

On the Whole, we think that London Fogs and the Muddy old Thames supply Whistler's needle with subjects more congenial than do the Venetian palaces and lagoons.[6]

On December 10, 1889, another reviewer wrote in the *British Architect*:

"Nocturne" is different in treatment to the rest of the prints, and can hardly be called, as it stands, an etching; the bones consist of some shipping and distant objects, and then over the whole of the plate ink has apparently been smeared. We have seen a great many representations of Venetian skies, but never saw one before consisting of brown smoke with clots of ink in diagonal lines.[7]

Unfortunately, the publication of the "First Venice Set" at two guineas each did not reestablish Whistler's solvency nor did it improve his reputation with the general public after Ruskin's libelous criticism. Whistler's exhibition of fifty-three pastels at the Fine Art Society Gallery in January 1881 was by comparison a tremendous success and produced many sales. Two years later he showed fifty-one etchings, primarily Venetian, accompanied by a witty catalogue. For all three of his shows, Whistler planned innovative displays in restricted detail and color to counter prevailing Victorian tastes. A selection of Whistler's remaining Venetian plates was finally published by Dowdeswell and Dowdeswell under the title *A Set of Twenty-Six Etchings*, also known as the "Second Venice Set." Although the editioning of this set of thirty was completed, some of the editions of the "First Venice Set" remained unfinished at the artist's death because Whistler could not bear to surrender his plates to a professional printer.

In spite of Ruskin's harsh criticisms, Whistler's contemporaries viewed his Venetian work as modern and revolutionary, the embodiment of a new aesthetic. – KLS

1. Katharine A. Lochnan, *The Etchings of James McNeill Whistler* (New Haven and London: Yale University Press, 1984), 181, 298.
2. Elizabeth Robins Pennell and Joseph Pennell, *The Life of James McNeill Whistler*, 2 vols. (Philadelphia: J. B. Lippincott; London: William Heinemann, 1908), 213.
3. Quoted in Lochnan, *The Etchings*, 187.
4. Ruth E. Fine, Los Angeles 1984, 23.
5. Robert H. Getscher, Oberlin 1977, 95.
6. Quoted in Los Angeles 1984, 23.
7. Fine, Los Angeles 1984, 133.

Frank Duveneck

Covington, Kentucky 1848-1919 Cincinnati

136. Riva degli Schiavoni, Number Two

(upright plate) 1880.
Etching on antique laid paper, 33.4 x 21.5 cm (platemark).
Poole 13.
Watermark: Anvil with hammer.
Monogrammed and dated lower left: FD (in ligature) *Venice/1880*.
Provenance: (Purchased from Clossons, Cincinnati, 1926?).
Bequest of Herbert Greer French, 1943.802.

The Museum owns the world's most comprehensive collection of Frank Duveneck's paintings and the only complete set of his etchings. Duveneck took up etching on his second visit to Venice in 1880, having been inspired to do so by Otto Bacher, one of his Munich students. Bacher provided technical advice, quality materials, and proofing assistance, via a portable wooden press, for both Duveneck and James McNeill Whistler (cat. 135), who arrived in Venice a month or so later. The famous London beauty, Gertrude

Elizabeth Blood (later Lady Colin Campbell), unbeknownst to Duveneck, sent three views of the Riva – *Laguna, Venice*; *Riva degli Schiavoni, Number one*; and *Riva degli Schiavoni, Number two* – to the first exhibition of the newly formed Society of Painter-Etchers in London. Joseph Pennell, writing in *Etching and Etchers*, states that though "abominably printed [they] were the success of the season."[1] Whistler was beside himself when he discovered that his brother-in-law, Sir Seymour Haden (cat. 129), along with the French painter Alphonse Legros, suspected that the prints by the unknown Duveneck were his [Whistler's] work exhibited under an alias, a serious violation of his contract with the Fine Art Society. This slur to Whistler's integrity, in addition to a less-than-enthusiastic reception for twelve of his etchings then being exhibited at the Fine Art Society, touched off "a storm in an aesthetic teapot." Letters to the press were dutifully recorded by the infuriated Whistler in *The Gentle Art of Making Enemies*.[2] Unlike Whistler, Duveneck did not capitalize on this unexpected publicity by systematically merchandising his etchings. Only four of his prints were ever formally published.

Of the thirty etchings executed by Duveneck between 1880 and 1885, twenty-five were Venetian subjects. During his first Venice period, between 1880 and 1881, he executed eight etchings that differ stylistically from a second group executed between 1883 and 1885 after his brief sojourn back to America. According to Bacher, "It is only fair to say that Duveneck made the etchings of the Riva before Whistler made his. Whistler saw them as I was helping Duveneck bite the plates, and frankly said: Whistler must do the Riva also."[3] Within two weeks after his arrival in Venice, Whistler had moved into Casa Jankovitz, where both he and Duveneck pulled proofs on Bacher's press.

Riva degli Schiavoni, Number two, also known as *The Riva, looking towards the Caserna*, a print that scholars and collectors rank as Duveneck's most important, was probably done prior to Whistler's etchings. It was drawn from the balcony of the Casa Kirsch, where Duveneck lodged, looking east toward the Giardini Pubblici, which Napoleon laid out in 1807. This plate, an ambitious composition for a painter who had difficulty with complex figure compositions, evolved through four states before the final published state was issued. In the first state 6.3 cm at the bottom remained unworked (CAM 1913.860, 1913.861). In the second state (fig. 136-1), all but two figure groups in the center were completed (CAM 1983.28). In the third state, the artist finished the composition and signed it in the lower left corner with his monogram and the inscription *Venice 1880* (CAM 1917.409). A flaw in the lower center remained until the fourth state (CAM 1915.509, 1917.408). In 1882 Robert Dunthorne published an edition of forty impressions in London printed by Frederick Goulding under the alternate title *Riva, Looking toward the Caserna*. Robert Getscher points out that Emily Poole, who catalogued Duveneck's etchings, incorrectly identified this etching as *Riva, Looking toward the Grand Ducal Palace* instead of *Riva, Looking toward the Caserna*.[4] Only twenty-five of the forty impressions were signed by the artist; for various reasons, Dunthorne was never successful in getting the artist to sign the remaining impressions.[5] In 1920 the publisher donated the canceled copperplate to the Museum (CAM 1920.92).

In 1848 Frank Decker was born in Covington, Kentucky, at the juncture of the Licking and Ohio rivers opposite Cincinnati. A year later, his widowed mother, Katherine Siemers Decker, married a businessman named "Squire" Joseph Duveneck, whose surname Frank took but did not legally adopt until 1886. The boy's artistic talents soon became evident. He was apprenticed to church decorators Johann Schmitt and later Wilhelm Lamprecht. In 1869, at the age of twenty, Duveneck traveled to Munich, where he enrolled

Figure 136-1. Frank Duveneck, *Riva degli Schiavoni Number Two*, 1880, etching, state II. Cincinnati Art Museum, The Albert P. Strietmann Collection and Deaccession Funds (1983.28).

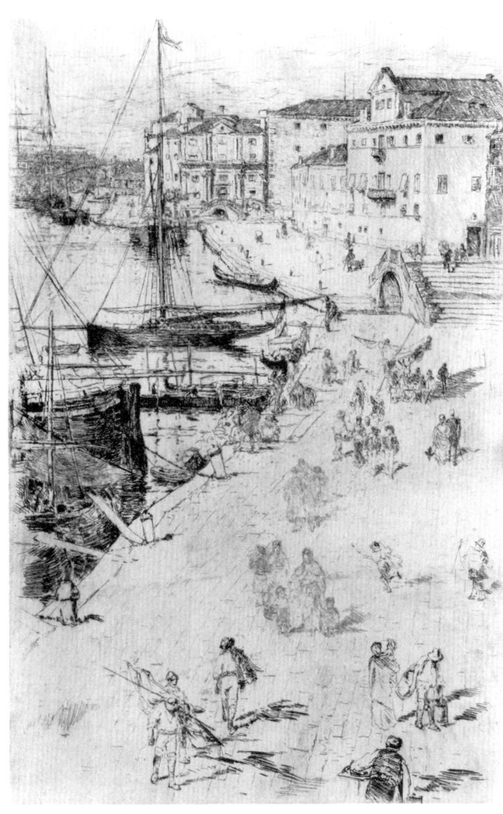

in the Royal Academy of Fine Arts. He progressed rapidly through the prerequisite curricula and became the student of Wilhelm Diez. In 1872 he painted his first masterpiece, *Whistling Boy*, with a vigorous *alla prima* realism that electrified his peers and professors. Disappointed at the lack of recognition and commissions after two years in Cincinnati, he returned to Munich in 1875, assuming the role of instructor to a younger group of American students in 1878. One year later, in 1879, he and his followers, the Duveneck "boys," moved to Italy, spending the winters in Florence and the summers in Venice. By 1883 he had broken with the tenebrous Munich portrait style and begun to paint outdoor subjects with a lighter palette and brighter color. He married his long-time pupil and admirer Elizabeth Booth, the daughter of expatriate Bostonian Francis Booth, in 1886. Two years later in Paris, after the birth of their son, Francis, their marriage ended tragically with her sudden death. After a twenty-year European sojourn, Duveneck returned to his hometown and joined the faculty of the Art Academy of Cincinnati in 1900. He remained there, a highly regarded and influential teacher, until his death. In his later years, he painted many nudes and landscapes in Gloucester, Massachusetts. During his final years, he was elected to the National Academy of Design (1905) and showed in major exhibitions in Chicago (1893) and in Buffalo (1901). His paintings and prints were exhibited in a special gallery at the Panama-Pacific International Exposition in San Francisco (1915), where he was unanimously awarded a special gold medal by an international jury of artists and critics in recognition of his contribution to American art. – KLS

1. Joseph Pennell, *Etchers and Etching* (New York: Macmillan Co., 1926), 102.

2. James McNeill Whistler, *The Gentle Art of Making Enemies*, ed. Sheridan Ford (New York: Frederick Stokes and Brother, 1890), 71-82.

3. Otto H. Bacher, *With Whistler in Venice* (New York: Century Co., 1908), 144.

4. Robert H. Getscher, Oberlin 1977, 157; Emily Poole, "Catalogue of the Etchings of Frank Duveneck," in PCQ. 25 (December 1938), 451.

5. R. Gordon Dunthorne, letter to J. H. Gest, December 29, 1922. Duveneck Scrapbook, CAM Library.

August Rodin

Paris 1840-1917 Meudon

137. Victor Hugo, Front View (Victor Hugo, de Face)

1885.
Drypoint on laid paper, 22.3 x 17.7 cm (platemark).
Del.7 i/vii; Thorson 9 i/ix.
Watermark: initials M B M.[1]
Provenance: Albert Pontremoli; (purchased from M. Knoedler, New York, April 16, 1928, for $1,480).
Bequest of Herbert Greer French, 1943.794.
References: Thorson 1975, no. 46 (as location unknown).

Rodin's formal training began in 1854 in the studio of Horace Lecoq de Boisbaudran (1802-1897), a rigorous drawing teacher who emphasized being able to draw from memory and whose tutelage influenced many artists of the time. One of Rodin's fellow students was Alphonse Legros (1837-1911), who was to become a lifelong friend. Having determined to work in sculpture, Rodin attempted several times, unsuccessfully, to be admitted to the École des Beaux-Arts to study that discipline.

Forced outside the academy, Rodin endured a long period of obscurity. He worked for many commercial and decorative jobs, assisted the popular sculptor Ernest Carrier-Belleuse (1824-1887), collaborated with a Belgian sculptor on several large projects, and perfected his own craft on the side. After a trip to Italy in 1874-1875, Rodin achieved his first success at the official Salon of 1877 with his statue of a nude male, *The Age of Bronze*. During the 1880s and 1890s Rodin finally gained recognition and private and public commissions. Such later monumental works as *St. John the Baptist Preaching*, *The Gates of Hell*, *The Thinker*, and *The Burghers of Calais* have become enormously influential icons of modern sculpture.[2]

Rodin's printmaking activity was restricted to only thirteen drypoints executed during the mid-1880s and one lithograph dating from the turn of the century. Legros, an avid practitioner of drypoint engraving, taught Rodin the technique in 1881 or 1882, while the latter was visiting London as Legros' guest. It is said that Rodin's first drypoint, *Love Turning the World* (Thorson 1), was scratched on one of Legros' plates with a sewing needle.[3] Victoria Thorson traces the origin of Rodin's distinctively vigorous attack seen in his drypoint prints to his concurrent work incising decorative detailing on ceramic works at the Sèvres porcelain factory outside Paris. His drawing style at the time was characterized also by quite bold black pen-and-ink outlines.[4] Writing in 1902, Roger Marx stressed the sculptor's immediate grasp of the potential of the technique, comparing the physical effort of "chiseling" the image in the plate to carving marble and noting that the drypoint lines "transparently reveal the artist's battle."[5] Given the rarity of sculptors working in the printmaking medium, it is all the more remarkable that Rodin's enduring reputation as an original printmaker rests on but four portrait busts: Victor Hugo (two versions), Henri Becque, and Antonin Proust (Thorson, nos. 7-10). All were based on sculptures and were executed between 1883 and 1888.

The famed French writer and national hero Victor Hugo (1802-1885) had rebuffed repeated requests from Rodin to model for him, but in 1883 he finally agreed to allow the sculptor to visit and observe him at home. Without the leisure of a formal sitting, Rodin was reduced to making dozens of rapid sketches of the old man at his dinner table or his desk, then rushing out to the balcony, where he had set up a portable modeling stand. His earliest drawings were done on small squares of cigarette paper.[6] Rodin's first impressions of Hugo were dominated by the poet's deepset eyes, which are also very prominent in the drypoint portraits:

> The first time I saw Victor Hugo, he made a profound impression on me; his eye was magnificent; he seemed terrible to me. . . . I thought I had seen a French Jupiter; when I knew him better he seemed more like Hercules.[7]

A bronze bust exhibited in the Salon of 1884 (fig. 137-1) and two drypoint portraits (full face and three-quarter views) resulted from these sessions. Thorson maintains that the drypoints were drawn from the bronze or from an intermediate drawing after it (i.e., that they were not independently made from Rodin's first sketches), by pointing out the reversal inherent in the printmaking process of several features of the bust.[8] Both prints emphasize a viewpoint seen from below.

The two drypoints were both probably executed in 1885; the three-quarter view was published in *L'Artiste* in February of that year. Thorson regards the full-frontal view as the second in order of execution, in which Rodin refined the more monumental three-quarter view and concentrated more on the prominent eyes. The first states of the three-quarter view also reveal several other trial positions of the head on the plate, whereas the full-frontal view seems more confidently placed from the beginning. She speculates that the "more-dignified" front view was perhaps executed in response to Hugo's death on May 22, 1885.[9] At least two intriguing photographs of a clay version of the sculpture of Hugo reveal pen lines drawn over the photograph by the artist, one specifically emphasizing the intense shadows in his deepset eyes.[10] The photographs were probably taken while Rodin was working on the bust at Hugo's home.[11] Rodin worked for years on a projected public monument for Hugo but successfully completed only several fragments.[12]

The Cincinnati impression of *Victor Hugo – Full Face* is the only recorded impression of the first state of this plate. It was known to Thorson only from Delteil's reproduction in his 1910 catalogue; she was unaware of its location in Cincinnati at the time of her 1975 catalogue raisonné of Rodin's prints. The earliest states of the drypoint portraits were printed in very few impressions and were often inscribed to artist friends, such as Legros and Bracquemond.[13]

This impression is at the height of its freshness; the strokes of velvety ink, reminiscent of broad pen- or brush-and-ink lines, almost threaten to overwhelm the subtler draftsmanship in the sculptor's drypoint lines. A rich gray tone of ink has been left on the surface of the plate. Rodin made only the slightest of changes in the plate after this state, adding a curvature to the back of the lower head and some lines of shading elsewhere. The later printings, while still preserving much of the sculptural strength of Rodin's conception, are reduced in richness and are grayish in tonality. The metal burr created on the plate in the drypoint process wears down extremely quickly in repeated printings, gradually losing its ability to retain the quantities of ink so important to the rich effects possible with drypoint. Indeed, after the first few impressions, the plate was steel-faced electrolytically to enable it to hold up to the large edition printings. The sixth state was printed in the March 1889 issue of *Gazette des Beaux-Arts*; the seventh, in a separate publication by Roger Marx on Rodin's drypoints in 1902. – DPB

1. See Roy L. Perkinson, "Degas's Printing Papers," in Reed and Shapiro, 260, no. 10, illus.

2. For introductions to Rodin's career and works, see Albert E. Elsen, *Rodin* (New York: Museum of Modern Art, 1963); Albert E. Elsen and Kirk T. Varnedoe, *The Drawings of Rodin* (New York: Praeger, 1971), and Washington 1981, to name only a few from a very large bibliography.

3. Thorson, 18-21.

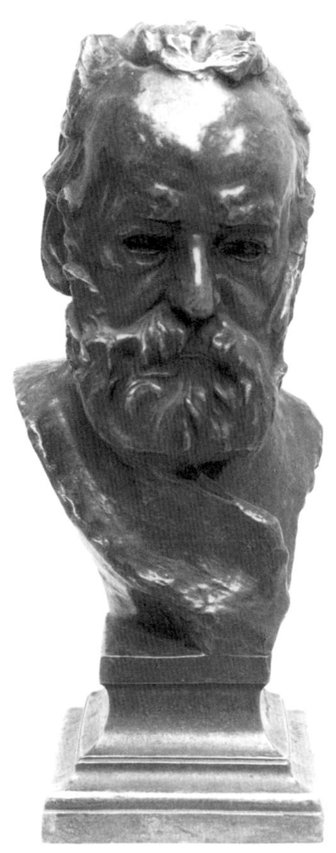

Figure 137-1. Auguste Rodin, *Victor Hugo*, 1884, bronze. The Fine Arts Museums of San Francisco, Gift of Alma de Bretteville Spreckels, 1942.38.

4. Thorson, 13.

5. Roger Marx, *Les pointes sèches de Rodin* (Paris: Gazette des Beaux-Arts, 1902), 10 (reprinted from an article in the *GBA*. 27, no. 1 [March 1902]: 204-08).

6. Several sketches are reproduced in Thorson, 51-52, figs. 40 – 44. Some of Rodin's first "cigarette paper" studies, including attempts to gauge the shape of Hugo's head from above, are reproduced in Claudie Judrin, Paris 1976, 80-85.

7. Albert E. Elsen, *In Rodin's Studio – A Photographic Record of Sculpture in the Making* (Ithaca: Cornell University Press, 1980), 177; see also Thorson, 48.

8. Thorson, 49-50.

9. Thorson, 49.

10. Elsen, *In Rodin's Studio*, pls. 86-87.

11. Elsen, *In Rodin's Studio*, 177.

12. See Jane Mayo Roos, "Rodin's *Monument to Victor Hugo*: Art and Politics in the Third Republic," *AB*. 68, no. 4 (December 1986): 632-56, for a review of this project.

13. Second states of the *Hugo – Three-Quarters View* (Thorson 8) are inscribed to Legros (Bibliothèque Nationale) and Bracquemond (Private Collection); a third state of the *Henri Becque* (Thorson 7) is inscribed to Bracquemond (location unknown).

James Abbott McNeill Whistler

Lowell, Massachusetts 1834-1903 London

138. The Embroidered Curtain 1889.

Etching and drypoint on antique laid paper, 24.1 x 16.0 cm (platemark).

K. 410 i-ii/vii; Mansfield 411 ii/vii.

Signed in plate on building upper left with butterfly; signed with pencil on tab lower left: butterfly and *imp*.

Provenance: (Purchased from M. Knoedler, New York, April 27, 1939, for $850).

Bequest of Herbert Greer French, 1943.611.

Exhibitions: Indianapolis 1965.

Etching and drawing became synonymous in Whistler's graphic oeuvre after his Venice period. Between 1887 and 1889 he executed approximately one-fourth of his etched compositions. Most of these etchings were small, spontaneous on-the-spot vignettes of streets, shops, and children. This spurt of printmaking received impetus from the increasing demand for his etchings in Europe and America; thus, with the collecting market in mind, he traveled to Brussels (1887), Touraine (1888), and Amsterdam (1889), taking with him prepared plates on which to sketch directly. Disdaining popular tourist views, Whistler sought instead picturesque dilapidation.

In the fall of 1887 he executed nineteen plates on a tour of Holland and Belgium. Architectural subjects that were rendered during this excursion, *Grand Palace, Brussels* (K. 362) and *Palaces, Brussels* (K. 361), for example, begin in the center and spread to the outside a basic linear skeleton. The solidity of architectural forms dissolves in the play of light and shade. Unlike his earlier Venice etchings in which he manipulated surface plate tone, Whistler cleanly wiped the plate in his late etchings, leaving only a trace of ink film.

On August 11, 1888, Whistler married the wealthy widow of E. W. Godwin, the architect of the "White House." Beatrice ("Trixie"), a competent painter and amateur etcher, encouraged his involvement in printmaking, particularly lithography. Their honeymoon took them to the chateaux of the Loire and to the towns of Touraine. He focused his etchings on French Renaissance architecture, with its flat, volumetric surfaces and localized ornament. His choices of subject were characterized by picturesque yet intimate vignettes of doors and windows. As a teaser for collectors, Whistler sent a few words about his trip to the *Pall Mall Gazette* through Charles Hanson, his illegitimate son who was acting as his London agent:

> Mr. Whistler, we hear, has in his journeying to France, not been idle – He brings back with him some fifty new etchings of the finest quality. Those who have seen them in Paris say that the elegances of French Renaissance have never been so exquisitely rendered as in these fairy-like plates.[1]

Like the Brussels etchings, Whistler never published the Renaissance plates as a set, and it appears that only a limited number of impressions were pulled. A selection of these etchings was displayed at the Exposition Universelle in Paris, only to be overshadowed by his brother-in-law, Haden, whose work won the grand prix.

The climax of his total oeuvre, Whistler's Amsterdam etchings constituted the last of his prints planned as a set. His first pilgrimage to Rembrandt's city, planned for 1858, was thwarted by lack of money. He finally visited the city in 1863, accompanied by Alphonse Legros, and returned again in 1884. These two visits did not quell his "expressed wish to return to Holland and portray, with their fascinating reflections, some of the picturesque old houses on the canals of Amsterdam."[2] In August 1889 he and his wife traveled to Amsterdam, where he was awarded a gold medal at the International Exhibition, which included his painting *Arrangement in Grey and Black: Portrait of the Painter's Mother* (1871). Although he did a few oils and sketches, his etchings were the important output of the trip. On September 3 he wrote to Marcus Huish at the Fine Art Society with a proposal for the purchase and exhibition of his new prints.

> I find myself doing far finer work than anything I have hitherto produced. . . the beauty and importance of these plates, you can only estimate. . . [They combine] a minuteness of detail, always referred to with sadness by Critics, who hark back to the Thames etchings. . . and with greater freedom and more beauty of execution than even the Venice, or the last Renaissance lot can pretend to.[3]

His draft contract offered thirty impressions of each plate to the Fine Art Society, with one additional proof going to the British Museum and five proofs to the artist. Whistler priced the ten plates at two thousand guineas, with individual prints starting at ten guineas. Although neither the Fine Art Society nor Kennedy and Company in New York pursued this opportunity, Whistler was not discouraged: he executed thirteen etchings in Amsterdam and a pure landscape at Zaandam.

The Embroidered Curtain represents Whistler's final stage along the road toward abstraction. It is an early impression of one of Whistler's most intricate and highly finished designs – the perfect synthesis of the lessons he learned from the Dutch and Japanese. In it he returned to Rembrandtesque chiaroscuro and balanced it with a complex mosaic of surface pattern. Whistler flattened the space into a narrow street along the canal and played the asymmetric arrangement of windows and doors off against the visual richness and surface vitality reflected in water and glass. Whistler's virtuoso technique with the etching needle allowed him to juxtapose a rich vocabulary of linear patterns and textures – small zigzag strokes and random layering of cross-hatching. The patterns of dark openings suggest a life beyond the embroidered curtain as the activity along the canal front takes on a new life in a mirage of reflections.

Although Kennedy records seven changes in states, Whistler seems to have continually reworked the figures and reflections in drypoint. As with his Venetian etchings, Whistler signed the print with his butterfly signature, which he also inserted as a plaque on the building at the upper left. This impression appears to be an intermediate state between the first (fig. 138-1) and second. The little girl at the right has the drypoint work as in the second state – she has gained a face and she has a shadow blob at her waist. The man in the door above her has delicate shading between his legs, but it is not heavy and velvety. The water, however, is not as elaborately worked in the reflections, especially at the lower right, as compared with the second state illustrated in Kennedy (440 ii). The copperplate belongs to the Hunterian Art Gallery of the University of Glasgow.

The Amsterdam etchings were exhibited at Dunthorne's Gallery in London and the Grolier Club in New York. Joseph Pennell, who

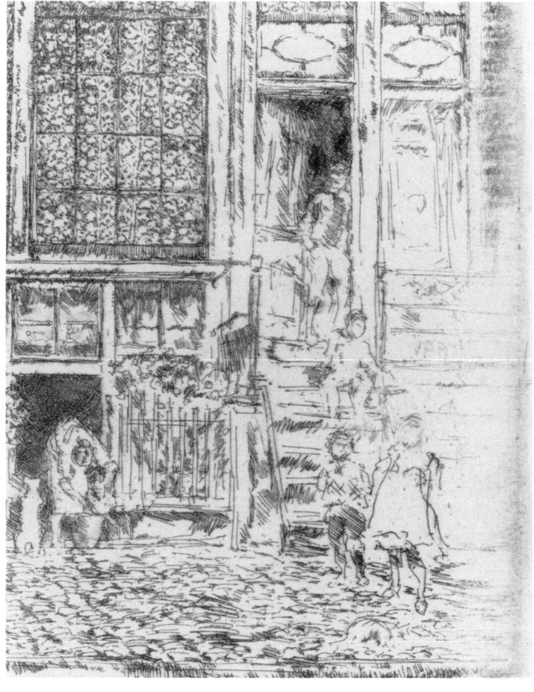

Figure 138-1. James McNeill Whistler, *Embroidered Curtain* (detail), 1889, etching and drypoint, K. 410 i. The Metropolitan Museum of Art, New York, Gift of Mrs. Charles Platt, 1957.

with his wife, Elizabeth, would be Whistler's future biographer, succeeded George Bernard Shaw as art critic at the London *Star*. Upon seeing the show Pennell wrote, "Had Mr. Whistler never put brush to canvas, he has done enough in these plates to be able to say that he will not altogether die."[4]

Whistler continued to make prints right up to the end; however, his wife's death (1896) and poor health slowed his productivity. His last etchings, of Corsica, are dated 1900-1901. Late in his life, Whistler began to receive the recognition he was due. In 1898 the International Society of Sculptors, Painters and Gravers elected him president. After nearly half a century, Whistler's printmaking legacy set the course for future radical experimentation and influenced a generation of British and American artists, including D.Y. Cameron (cats. 143-44), James McBey (cats. 145, 148), Joseph Pennell, and John Marin. – KLS

1. Quoted in Katharine A. Lochnan, *The Etchings of James McNeill Whistler* (New Haven and London: Yale University Press, 1984), 248.

2. Howard Mansfield, "Whistler in Belgium and Holland," *PCQ*. 6 (1916): 382.

3. Lochnan, *The Etchings*, 251.

4. Elizabeth R. Pennell and Joseph Pennell, *The Life of James McNeill Whistler*, 2 vols. (Philadelphia: J. B. Lippincott Company; London: William Heinemann, 1908), 86.

Henri de Toulouse-Lautrec

Albi 1864-1901 Malromé

139. At the Ambassadeurs – Café Concert Singer 1894.

From sixth album of *L'Estampe originale*.
Color lithograph (crayon, tusche, and splatter) on wove paper, 30.6 x 24.6 cm (image).
Del. 68; Adhémar 73; Wittrock 58.
Monogrammed on stone lower left: Ⓗ ; signed with pencil lower left margin: *HT Lautrec*.
Provenance: (Purchased from Albert Roullier, Chicago, December 5, 1939, for $112).
Bequest of Herbert Greer French, 1943.685.

The heir apparent of an ancient aristocratic family from southern France, Henri Marie Raymond de Toulouse-Lautrec-Monfa was born in Albi on November 24, 1864. His parents, Count Alphonse de Toulouse-Lautrec Monfa and Adèle Tapié de Céleyran, were first cousins. The cruel legacy of their families' frequent intermarriages to preserve land holdings and ensure proper lineage revealed itself in 1878 and 1879 when Lautrec broke both legs in separate incidents: all growth stopped, leaving him a 4½-foot dwarf. During his convalescence he entertained himself by sketching everything around him. He received art lessons from René Princeteau, a deaf-mute painter of horses and sporting subjects. In 1881, upon completion of his baccalaureate, he was not expected to undertake further study. Born into a lifestyle of inherited wealth, his handicap rendered him unsuited for the usual occupations of the noble rich: army officer, equestrian hunter, or fashionable dandy promenading in the Bois de Boulogne.

Lautrec's formal art studies began in 1882 when his parents reluctantly enrolled him in the atelier of Léon Bonnat, a popular Parisian society painter. He transferred to the atelier of Fernand Cormon, a successful academic history painter, by the end of the year, and there met Louis Anquetin, Emile Bernard, and Vincent van Gogh. Cormon invited Lautrec to assist him in preparing illustrations for a deluxe edition of Victor Hugo's *La Légende des siècles*, which in the end were not used.

Rather than spending his life as a dilettante, Lautrec pursued a career as a working artist by illustrating popular journals and song sheet covers. In the beginning he used pseudonyms to shield his conservative and snobbish aristocratic family from the disgrace that he worked. By 1889 he had settled on a signature: "H. T. Lautrec" or a circular monogram "HTL," inspired by Japanese woodcut seals. Perhaps more scandalizing than working for a living was his plunge into the bohemian life of Montmartre, where he maintained his residence and studio from the mid-1880s until his death. Montmartre in the 1880s and 1890s, with its growing number of commercialized theaters, café-concerts, cabarets, and dance halls, was the hub of the artistic, intellectual, and literary avant-garde. Lautrec portrayed the mood and the atmosphere of these nocturnal haunts of Parisian entertainment by discarding the inflexible compositional restraints and finish of his academic training.

In 1891 the twenty-seven-year-old painter was commissioned by Charles Zidler, manager of the music hall Moulin Rouge, to design a color lithograph poster. Lautrec's poster made an overnight success of the café and the artist. His three-color plus black lithograph was heir to Christoph Le Blon's invention (cat. 97). Color lithography emerged in the latter half of the 1880s as a separate aesthetic force in French art in the lithographs of Jules Chéret, who produced the first poster for the newly opened Moulin Rouge in 1889. Lautrec's *Moulin Rouge – La Goulue* (W. Pl) was a dramatic break with the past. His emphasis on curvaceous, two-dimensional design, shallow pictorial space, and bright, flat colors, synthesized with hand lettering, was inspired by the formal compositional effects of Japanese color woodcuts of which he was an enthusiastic aficionado. The art critic André Mellerio, in his 1898 book, *La Lithographie originale en couleurs*, recognized the revolutionary importance of Lautrec's contribution to color lithography both as an artistic and commercial medium.

> *Ce n'est plus de l'affiche, ce n'est pas encore complètement de l'estampe, oeuvre de saveur hybride participant des deux, ou plutôt si – c'est l'estampe en couleurs moderne.*[1]
> (This is no longer just a poster, and it is not yet quite a print; a work of a hybrid pungency deriving from the two, or rather, it *is* the modern color print.)[2]

Between 1891 and his death at thirty-seven in 1901, Lautrec created thirty posters, 325 lithographs, nine drypoints, and four monotypes. He was just one of a young group of avant-garde artists who used color lithography as a vehicle for innovative printmaking in the 1890s. Lautrec received many commissions for song sheets, menus, theater programs, book covers, journals, and exhibition posters. We follow his infatuation with popular café singers, dance hall performers, and theater celebrities, such as Jane Avril, Yvette Guilbert, Sarah Bernhardt, Loie Fuller, and Aristide Bruant, across the stages of Moulin Rouge, Moulin de la Galette Elysée, Montmartre, and Mirliton. In 1893 André Marty, director of the *Journal des artistes*, launched a quarterly publication, *L'Estampe originale*, with a preface by the art critic Roger Marx. Marty's quarterly offered an impressive cross section of the various aesthetic attitudes of French avant-garde *fin de siècle* printmaking.[3] Of the ninety-five prints by seventy-four artists ultimately published in *L'Estampe originale*, sixty were lithographs. Thirty-three of the sixty were in color: a testament to the impact of the color revolution.

The quarterly was published in editions of one hundred. Lautrec contributed three color lithographs. His cover for the first issue in 1893 shows the dancer Jane Avril in Ancourt's workshop examining a proof that Père Cotelle printed on the hand-operated press. His second color lithograph, *At the Ambassadeurs – Café Concert Singer*, in the sixth issue of April-June 1894, depicts a singer performing at one of Paris' most elegant café-concerts. The unidentified performer is voyeuristically observed from backstage. In 1893 the Ambassadeurs installed a movable roof, permitting audience comfort and regular performances regardless of the weather.[4] This may account for the columns and latticework partition across the lower third of the composition. Using six colors, Lautrec combined lithographic crayon, tusche, and *crachis*, a technique of covering large areas with splatter. The flattened pictorial space, emphasis on surface pattern, and juxtaposition of vivid color forms in blue, salmon pink, and yellow betray the continued influence of Japanese *ukiyo-e* woodcuts. Lautrec signed the print in the lower left with his monogram. In 1876-77 Edgar Degas used a comparable vantage point for his lithograph *Singer at a Café-Concert* (Reed and Shapiro 26). Lautrec executed the cover for the final issue of *L'Estampe original* in 1895. – KLS

1. André Mellerio, *La Lithographie originale en couleurs* (Paris: L' Estampe et l'affiche, 1898), 8.
2. Margaret Needham, trans., in New Brunswick 1978, 82.
3. New York 1970, 13.
4. Charles Rearick, *Pleasures of the Belle Epoche* (New Haven and London: Yale University Press, 1985), 153.

Odilon Redon

Bordeaux 1840-1916 Paris

140. Béatrice 1897.

From *L'Album d'estampes originales de la Galerie Vollard*, 1897
Color lithograph (crayon and tusche) on *chine appliqué*,
33.3 x 29.4 cm (image).
Mellerio 168.
Monogrammed in stone upper right: OR (in ligature).
Provenance: (Purchased from Kennedy, New York, June 13, 1941, for $121).
Bequest of Herbert Greer French, 1943.662.
Exhibitions: Cincinnati 1948, no. 42.

The young critic Emile Hennequin wrote perceptively of Redon's second one-man exhibition of charcoal drawings and lithographs, which was held at the office of the national daily *Le Gaulois* in 1882.

> Odilon Redon should be seen as one of our masters. . . . Except for Goya, there is no one past or present who can be compared with this master. He has conquered a deserted territory on the border between dreams and reality. This region has been filled with the combined presence of fearful ghosts, monsters, and microorganisms and the fearfulness of all human evils, animal degradations, and impotent but harmful things. . . . Like Baudelaire, Redon deserves the highest praise for having created new terrors.[1]

Redon's boyhood years were spent on the family's sixteenth-century estate Peyrelebade (Gironde), the source to which many of his drawings and lithographs owed their genesis. He was born Bertrand-Jean Redon (called Odilon) on April 22, 1840, his father, Bertrand, with his pregnant Creole wife, having recently returned to France from New Orleans, where he had recouped his fortune. Left to his own devices, Redon grew up at Peyrelebade surrounded by vineyards and grim uncultivated landscape that had once been a sea bed. At the age of fifteen he began studying drawing with Stanislas Gorin, who awakened his interest in Delacroix and romantic painting. At the urging of his father, upon graduation in 1857, he began studying architecture rather than painting under the neoclassic architect Louis-Hippolyte Lebas.

Through his friendship with the botanist Armand Clavaud, he was introduced to Darwin's theory of evolution, to poetry, to philosophy, and to the works of contemporary writers – Flaubert, Baudelaire, and Poe. In Paris in 1862 he failed the oral examination for admission to the architecture section of the École des Beaux-Arts and followed this defeat with an unsuccessful attempt to study sculpture in Bordeaux. He returned to Paris in 1864 and enrolled in the atelier of Jean-Léon Gérôme only to rebel against the atelier's inflexible academic program. The most decisive influence on Redon at this time was his friendship with the bohemian artist Rodolphe Bresdin (1822-1885), who stimulated Redon's future direction. From Bresdin he learned the techniques of etching and lithography. In addition, he was introduced to the graphic achievements of Dürer (cat. 23) and Rembrandt (cat. 77). At last Redon had found a mentor who likewise was exploring the visionary potential of black and white.

In 1868 he reviewed the Paris Salon for the Bordeaux newspaper, *La Gironde*. Redon voiced concern over the increased number of realistic landscapes in the exhibition that seemed to be, in Redon's opinion, merely an end in themselves; at the same time, he justified his position on the indispensable and transcendent role of imagination and poetic vision in art. It was only after his service in the Franco-Prussian War (1870-71) that Redon's productive mature phase began.

First in his charcoal drawings and later in his lithographs, both of which he referred to as *noirs*, he synthesized fantastic and allegorical imagery with visible logic. He saw black as an effective color with which to translate haunting, apparitional, and disquieting enigmatic images.

At the salon of Madame de Rayssac, he met Henri Fantin-Latour (cat. 134), who suggested that he use transfer lithography to multiply his drawings. In 1878, shortly after Redon took up this new method of working with lithographic crayon on transfer paper, he recognized the intrinsic aesthetic possibilities of the medium and its potential to increase public exposure. His first album, called *Dans le Rêve (Dreaming)* (Mellerio 26-36), appeared in 1879. The lithographs that Redon made after his charcoal drawings were in direct defiance to the mimetic fidelity of nature advocated by the impressionists. Between 1882 and 1899 Redon produced in rapid succession twelve albums of lithographs, including three based on Flaubert's *La Tentation de Saint-Antoine (The Temptation of Saint Anthony)*, culminating in the *Apocalypse de Saint-Jean (The Revelation of St. John the Divine)*. Although Redon exhibited in the Paris Salon in 1867, he remained a virtual unknown until his second solo exhibition held at the offices of *Le Gaulois* (1882). His newest album, *A Edgar Poë (To Edgar Allan Poe)* (Mellerio 37-43), attracted the enthusiastic attention of the critics Emile Hennequin and Joris-Karl Huysmans. In 1884 it was Huysmans' book *A Rebours (Against Nature)* with Redon's accompanying macabre imagery that thrust the artist into the limelight. Redon became the hero of the avant-garde symbolists (artists, critics, and writers), including Stéphane Mallarmé, who interpreted Redon's images to suit symbolist aims and ideas. Their enthusiasm was an important catalyst in the development of Redon's style and reputation. Each new album presented an occasion for reviews, and Redon enticed or rewarded his French and Belgian critics and patrons with autographed copies or special proofs.[2]

He participated in the first Salon des Artistes Indépendants in 1884 and the first exhibition of the Peintre-Graveurs in 1889. It was not until the age of fifty-four that he was given a major retrospective: 130 drawings, oils, pastels, and lithographs were exhibited at the avant-garde Galeries Durand-Ruel with an accompanying cataiogue prefaced by the critic André Mellerio.

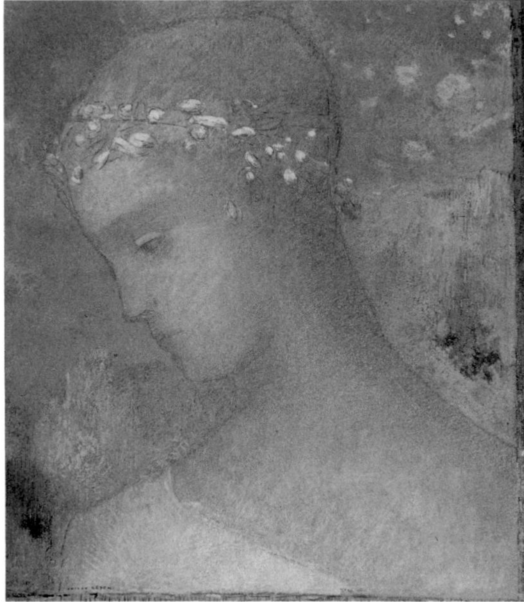

Figure 140-1. Odilon Redon, *Béatrice*, 1895, pastel and pencil on paper. The Woodner Family Collection, New York.

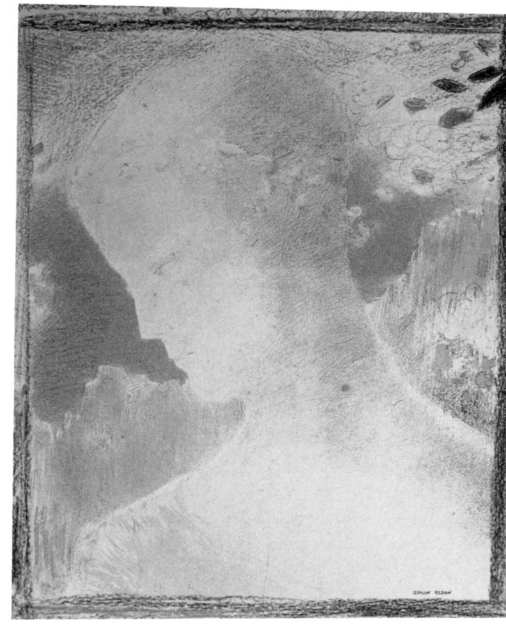

Figure 140-2. Odilon Redon, *Béatrice*, 1897, color lithograph reworked with pastel and pencil. Rijksprentenkabinet, Amsterdam.

A major turning point in his life occurred in 1897 when his family estate at Peyrelebade, the source of his early *noirs*, was sold. The early 1890s constituted a transitional period for Redon, who began to move away from black and white to color and away from macabre pessimism to lyrical optimism. In 1897 he executed several two-color lithographs: *La Sulamite* (*The Shulamite*) (Mellerio 167) and *Tête d'enfant avec fleurs* (*Child's Head with Flowers*) (Mellerio 169) for Gustave Pellet and *Béatrice* for the budding impresario Ambroise Vollard (1867-1939). All three were printed by August Clot. Having successfully opened a gallery at No. 6 Rue Lafitte, Vollard decided to commission and publish original prints, particularly color lithographs. Vollard commissioned *Béatrice* for his second album, which contained prints by thirty-two artists under the revised title *L'Album d'estampes originales de la Galerie Vollard* and which he published in December 1897. We may never know the exact nature of the commission, although two letters to Clot survive which shed some light on the project. On December 14, 1896, Madame Redon wrote, *"Eh la Béatrice! Vous semblez l'oublier? Voilà six semaines que vous l'avec"*[3] (And Béatrice! It seems you have forgotten it. You have had it for six weeks.). Five months later on April 13, 1897, Redon himself wrote to Clot:

Je crois qu'il sera bien que je sois présent aux essais du pastel réproduit de M. Vollard. Il y aura sans doute quelque couleurs à changer ou à modifier.[4]
(I think it will be as well for me to be present at the proofing of the reproduced pastel of M. Vollard. Undoubtedly there will be some colour changes or modifications to do.[5])

Considering the length of time that it took Auguste Clot to translate Vollard's pastel *Béatrice* (fig. 140-1), now in the Ian Woodner Family Collection,[6] into color separations, it is obvious that the end result was a stilted interpretation of the pastel.[7] Clearly Redon was present and became creatively involved in the printing process. He distilled the lithograph into an ethereal essence of feminine beauty by altering and eliminating color and detail. The Rijksprentenkabinet, Amsterdam, has a hand-worked proof (fig. 140-2) that eliminates the outline of the figure and the blue in the background and introduces leaves in the upper right corner.[8] This ethereal lithograph is considered one of the high points in the career of this visionary talent. The simple linear silhouette extracted from the Italian Renaissance portrait type of Piero dell Francesca and Botticelli creates an icon of womanhood and aesthetic beauty that transcends Dante's literary heroine.

During Redon's final years, he continued to explore a wide range of visionary iconography and inventive color. In 1913 his international reputation increased with his extensive representation in the Armory Show in New York. For the twentieth century, his work provided a vital link between the romantics and the surrealists. – KLS

1. Kunio Motoé, "Odilon Redon: Light and Darkness" in Tokyo 1989, 12.
2. Ted Gott, *The Enchanted Stone: The Graphic Worlds of Odilon Redon* (Melbourne: National Gallery of Victoria, 1990), 48-56; Ted Gott, "Silent Messengers: Odilon Redon's Dedicated Lithographs and the Politics of Gift Giving," PCN. 19, no. 3 (July-August 1988): 92-101.
3. Pat Gilmour, "Cher Monsieur Clot," in Pat Gilmour, ed., *Lasting Impressions: Lithography as Art* (London: Alexandria Press, 1988): 372, n. 107.
4. Gilmour, "Cher Monsieur Clot," 372, n. 107.
5. Translation by Mark Henshaw supplied by Pat Gilmour.
6. Gott, *The Enchanted Stone*, 132, illus.
7. Claude Roger-Marx, *La Gravure originale au XIXᵉ siècle* (Paris: Somogy, 1962), 135, illus.
8. Irene M. de Groot, "Béatrice: Een prent door Odilon Redon," BvHR. (August 1972): 92-101, illus. 100; Gott, *The Enchanted Stone*, 132, illus.

Anders Zorn

Mora, Sweden 1860-1920 Mora

141. King Oscar II (second plate) 1898.

Etching on laid paper, 24.6 x 17.7 cm (platemark).
Del. 130 i/ii; Asplund 132 i/ii; Brummer 88 i/ii.
Watermark: VAN GELDER.
Signed and dated in plate lower right: *1898* ZORN; inscribed with pencil lower left margin: *Unique proof 1st state*; lower right: *Zorn*.
Provenance: Charles B. Eddy (Lugt 499); (purchased from M. Knoedler, New York, February 4, 1928, for $610).
Bequest of Herbert Greer French, 1943.689.

Anders Zorn was an acclaimed painter and master etcher both at home in Sweden and in the cosmopolitan art centers of Paris, London, and the United States. His elegant portraits chronicle an entire generation of creative talent, social matrons, business tycoons, and statesmen.

Zorn's unpropitious life began as the illegitimate child of Leonard Zorn, a Bavarian brew master who managed a plant in Uppsala, and Anna Andersdotter, a peasant girl who had left her rural home to find employment in the brewery. Anna returned to her native town of Mora, in the province of Dalarna in central Sweden, where she gave birth to Anders Leonard Zorn on February 18, 1860. Returning to Uppsala to work, she left Anders in the care of her parents until he was twelve. At twelve, she enrolled him in a secondary school in Enköping, near Stockholm. His father's interest in his education was continued by a stipend from the Zorn family, which Anders began to receive after his father's death in 1872.

Zorn enrolled in the Stockholm Academy of Art in 1875. At a memorial exhibition of the work of the Swedish painter Egron Lundgren (1815-1875), he discovered watercolor. He immediately purchased a set and began experimenting. By 1879 Zorn developed such proficiency that he could charge fifty crowns for watercolor portraits to support his school expenses. The following year his watercolor of a beautiful woman with a veil, *In Mourning*, was exhibited at the academy and sold, but not before it had attracted the attention of the art critic Carl Rupert Nyblom and King Oscar II of Sweden, for whom he painted a similar piece in 1883.[1] Bolstered by this recognition and by his successful commissions as a watercolor portraitist, Zorn abandoned the conservative attitudes of the academy and his studies, which he had been neglecting, and pursued his career in the spring of 1881. He made his first journey abroad, stopping in London and Paris before spending the winter in Spain. In Spain, while still under the influence of Lundgren, he honed his skills as a landscape watercolorist. In 1882 he returned to London, where he stretched his financial resources to impress prospective clients by acquiring a portrait studio at a fashionable address on Brock Street. Although it was a struggle, sales of his Spanish landscapes and commissions from members of the Swedish legation, the British aristocracy, and rich Americans kept him financially afloat. In the same year he befriended fellow countryman Axel Herman Haig (1835-1921), an architectural etcher who taught him the rudiments of the medium that became an important part of his oeuvre circa 1890. Although repeated travels to Paris and Spain were important for his education, Zorn maintained his London studio until his marriage to Emma Lamm, the daughter of a Stockholm textile merchant, in 1885. On their wedding trip, the Zorns traveled to Turkey via Hungary and Germany. In Turkey, Zorn became gravely ill with typhus and eventually returned to Sweden through Greece, Italy, and Paris.

His watercolors from the 1880s range in diversity from "Victorian" themes and travel vignettes to genre scenes from Sweden and abroad. In 1887 he traveled to Spain and North Africa, where he completed a commission from Oscar II to paint the Algiers Harbor.[2] Upon his return he spent the fall in the artists' colony at St. Ives in Cornwall, where he mastered the use of oils. His large canvas, *Fisherman at St. Ives*, a brilliant example of *plein-air* painting, won an honorable mention at the Paris Salon in 1888 and was acquired by the state for the Musée de Luxembourg.[3] Welcomed into the city's most influential art circle, the Zorns moved to Paris, remaining there until 1896. In Paris, Zorn maintained studios first on Rue Daubigny, then on Boulevard de Clichy; there he renewed his acquaintance with Whistler, met the impressionists, and reveled in the attention of the art critic and publisher Armand Dayot, who acclaimed his work in *Art et les Artistes*. He undertook two commissioned portraits for

Antonin Proust, the minister of Fine Arts. His painting of the celebrated dancer Rosita Mauri (1889) and its subsequent reinterpretation as an etching (Asplund 34), executed for Proust, constituted the first high point in his etching oeuvre. Between 1882 and 1888 Zorn executed twenty-nine etchings. Beginning in 1889, he became caught up in the etching revival. His total graphic oeuvre, many of which were related to his watercolors and oil paintings, totaled nearly three hundred.

An admirer of Rembrandt (cat. 77), Zorn brought to etching a painterly technique. He used a "shower" of broad-slashing parallel hatching to define form and color. Raking light animated his subjects and conveyed moods. In his etching *Rosita Mauri*, he merged shadow and figure eliminating contour, creating the first in a line of unqualified successes when shown at Société de Peintres-graveurs in 1891.[4]

At the urging of the art commissioner, Halsey C. Ives, Zorn organized a representative selection of Swedish artists to bring to the 1893 World's Columbian Exposition in Chicago. This trip, the first of seven trips that Zorn would take to America between 1893 and 1911, enabled him to establish long-standing friendships with wealthy American clients, among them the Deerings of Evanston, the Palmers of Chicago, and Isabella Stewart Gardner of Boston.[5] He was asked to paint and etch portraits of three presidents: Grover Cleveland in 1899 (Asplund 143-44), Theodore Roosevelt in 1905 (Asplund 189), and William Howard Taft in 1911 (Asplund 239).

The New York dealer Frederick Keppel arranged for his first American print exhibition in 1893; others followed in 1899 and 1907. In 1906 he was given a major retrospective of his paintings, prints, and sculpture at the avant-garde Gallery Durand-Ruel in Paris.

Zorn returned to his hometown, Mora, in 1896. He settled and built a studio there, beginning a period of nationalist sentiment that particularly focused on the folk art and culture of Dalarna, which he began collecting. He continued his preoccupation with the theme of the nude, unabashed in its nakedness, stripped of all literary and symbolic allusions. He did not abandon his international clientele and continued to act as portraitist to notable aristocrats, adding kings and princes to his list of subjects, until the outbreak of World War I in 1914. He etched portraits of five members of the Swedish royal family, Princess Ingeborg, Crown-Princess Margaret, Queen Sophia, King Oscar II, and King Gustav V.

His portrait of his former patron, Oscar Frederik (1829-1907), king of Sweden from 1872 to 1907, was executed during the summer of 1898 on the king's yacht, "Drott."[6] Honored by the opportunity to paint his sovereign, Zorn would not accept payment and etched the portrait as a gift. The first plate failed to satisfy Zorn, so he executed another. The Museum's impression of the second plate is a rare first state, before the addition of a light aquatint covering the background and a darker, coarser aquatint across the lower part of the coat and chair arm in the lower left corner. Further details were added in the second state to the boat to the right of the figure (fig. 141-1). There is a preliminary drawing for the etching in the Waldemarsudde, Stockholm. The canceled plate is in the Zornsamlingarna, Mora.[7]

Six years after Zorn's death, M. Knoedler, New York, mounted the largest show of his prints ever exhibited in America, followed in 1935 by a show at Kennedy Gallery, New York. Despite the depression, Zorn's etchings continued to sell at high prices. Mr. French sought out some of his best-known subjects, *Fisherman at St. Ives* (Asplund 53), *Ernst Renan* (Asplund 73), and *Cercles d'Eau* (Asplund 213), confident that they would withstand the vicissitudes of taste.

The new wave of modernism that swept Europe and America in the early twentieth century consigned Zorn's work and that of other

Figure 141-1. Anders Leonard Zorn, *King Oscar II* (second plate), 1898, etching and aquatint, Asplund 132 ii. The Art Institute of Chicago, Charles Deering Collection.

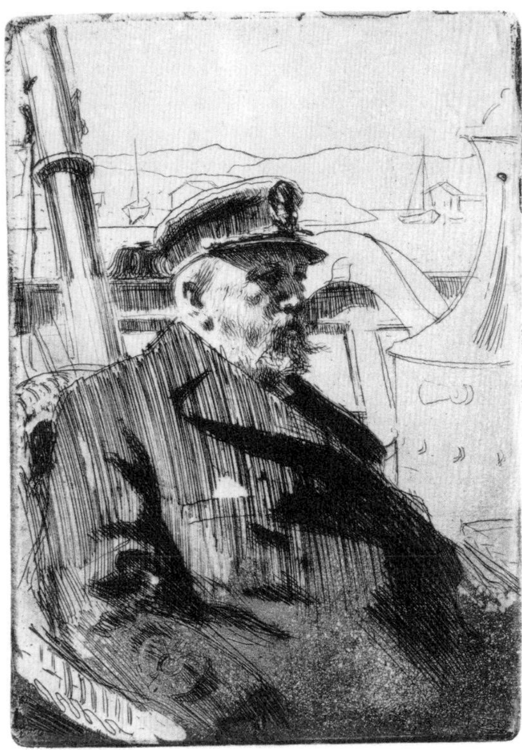

society painters of the gilded era to oblivion. Since the mid-1970s, a reexamination of American impressionists has refocused critical attention on Zorn, renewing our appreciation of his technical virtuosity as an etcher and a painter. – KLS

1. Anne B. Morris, "Anders Zorn Bibliography" in Long Beach 1984, 12.
2. Evert J. M. Douwes, Jr., *Anders Zorn: The Artist as Peintre-Graveur* (London: Gebr. Douwes Fine Art, 1991), 9.
3. Morris, Long Beach 1984, 14.
4. Elizabeth Broun, Lawrence 1979, 11.
5. Carrell Shaw, "*Anders Zorn American Patronage,*" in Long Beach 1984, 18.
6. Evert J. M. Douwes, Jr., *Anders Zorn: "The Artist as Peintre-Graveur*," 9.
7. Brigitta Sandström, Zornsamlingarna, Mora, letter to Kristin Spangenberg, September 4, 1991.

Henri de Toulouse-Lautrec

Albi 1864-1901 Malromé

142. The Jockey 1899.

Color lithograph (crayon, tusche, and splatter) on china paper, 51.5 x 35.9 cm (image).
Del. 279; Adhémar 365; Wittrock 308 ii/ii.
Signed and dated in stone lower right: ⓕⓛ /1899 (date reversed).
Provenance: (Purchased from Albert Roullier, Chicago, December 5, 1939, for $180).
Bequest of Herbert Greer French, 1943.686.

In the fall of 1893, when major entertainers began to leave Montmartre for other parts of the city, Lautrec shifted his attention to the theatre. He spent his evenings at the Opéra, Comédie Française, and avant-garde theater. Lautrec's theatrical subjects carried over to his commercial work, at times with no relationship to the product being advertised. *At the Concert* (W. 28), for example, was an advertising poster for the Ault and Wiborg lithographic ink company of Cincinnati, New York, and Chicago. To attract

attention to the product, Lautrec used a beautiful woman and her escort in a loge. The artist's only American commission, it was executed in 1896 on zinc plates rather than on lithographic stones to facilitate shipment to the States.

Women figure prominently in another important milestone of Lautrec's career, the portfolio *Elles*, which was published in 1896 by Gustave Pellet. Between 1892 and 1895, Lautrec lived with and painted prostitutes in the *maisons closes* of Rue d'Amboise, Rue des Moulins, and Rue Joubert. With unsensational objectivity he portrayed the women going about their daily routines of eating, grooming, and dressing. Lautrec fell back on Japanese aesthetics for compositional choices and iconographic solutions. *Elles*, a portfolio with ten color lithographs, was issued for collectors of quasi-erotica, a subcategory of the print market to which Pellet catered. Lacking blatant erotic and prurient overtones, the portfolio ended up a financial failure.

The years between 1892 and 1896 marked a period of intense productivity in Lautrec's career; however, his increasing dependency on alcohol and his instability led to his hospitalization in February 1899. Late in his convalescence the publisher Pierrefort, accompanied by his printer Henri Stern, visited Lautrec at the clinic in Neuilly. He suggested that Lautrec execute a series of lithographs devoted to horse racing to be issued under the title *Courses*. Four prints were completed: *The Jockey, The Trainer and His Jockey* (W. 309), *The Paddock* (W. 310), and *The Jockey Going to the Post* (W. 311). *The Jockey* was the only lithograph published, first in a black and white, then in a color edition, both in 1899. These late works again give expression to Lautrec's early interest in dogs and horses, animals that surrounded him on family estates in southern France during his boyhood and during his first instruction under Princeteau.

Fashionable gatherings at tracks and horse racing at the Bois de Boulogne or Longchamp were appropriate subjects of contemporary life. Racing scenes in the work of Edouard Manet and Edgar Degas, both of whom Lautrec admired, were possible models. Lautrec probably knew Théodore Gericault's *Races at Epsom*, which had been acquired by the Louvre in 1866, and Manet's lithograph *The Races* (M.N. 85) and *The Races in the Bois de Boulogne* (1872), both of which were shown in the memorial Exposition des Oeuvres d'Edouard Manet at the École Nationale des Beaux-Arts in 1884.[1] In addition, Lautrec would have been familiar with the rocking-horse convention seen in English and French sporting prints of the time.

During the late 1870s and early 1880s, Eadweard Muybridge in Palo Alto, California, and Étienne-Jules Marey in Paris used photography to explore animal locomotion. On November 26, 1881, the French history painter, Jean-Louis-Ernst Meissonier gave a sensational reception for Muybridge at his Paris home.[2] Among the influential painters and critics of the official art establishment at this reception was Lautrec's future teacher Léon Bonnat. "They all witnessed the photographic proof that the horse had, indeed, all four legs off the ground during one phase of the gallop;. . . with all four legs bunched together under its body."[3] Discussed by many newspapers and journals, the analysis and representation of movement became one of the hotly debated topics in artistic and scientific circles of the day. Lautrec could have seen lithographs after Muybridge's photographs in *The Horse in Motion* (1882) by J. B. D. Stillman or in photographic reproductions in *The Attitudes of Animals in Motion* (1881) or in *Animal Locomotion* (1887), published by the University of Pennsylvania.

The windmill on the hill in *The Jockey* identifies this racetrack as the Bois de Boulogne.[4] Just as Manet used a radical perspective of horses racing toward the spectators in his lithograph *The Races*, Lautrec's horses lunge down the track at a diagonal. The dynamism of the subject is heightened by the close-up cropping of the horses

Continued on page 315.

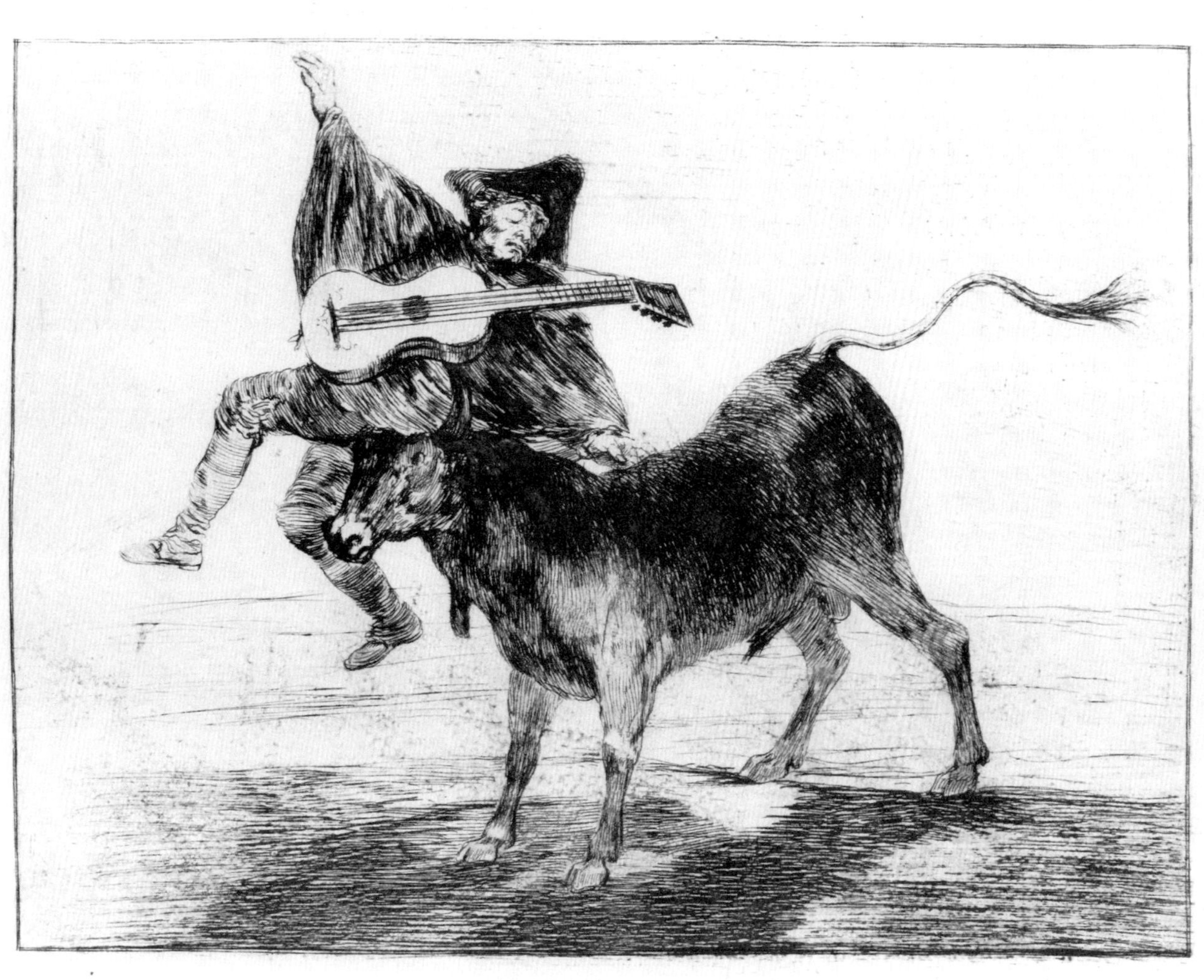

Plate 116. Francisco José Goya y Lucientes, *Blind Man Tossed on the Horns of a Bull*, ca. 1800-04.

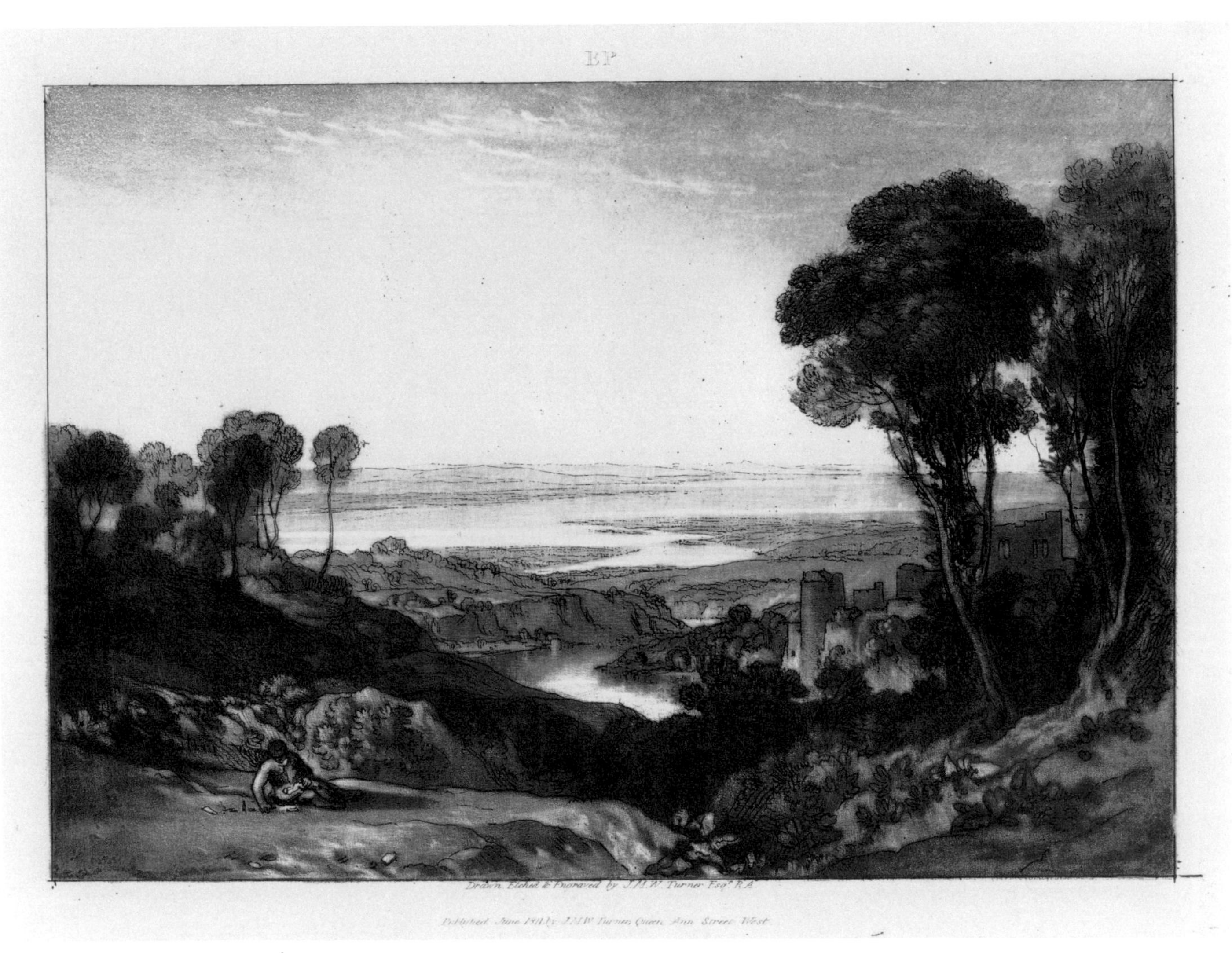

Plate 117. Joseph Mallord William Turner, *Junction of Severn and Wye*, 1811.

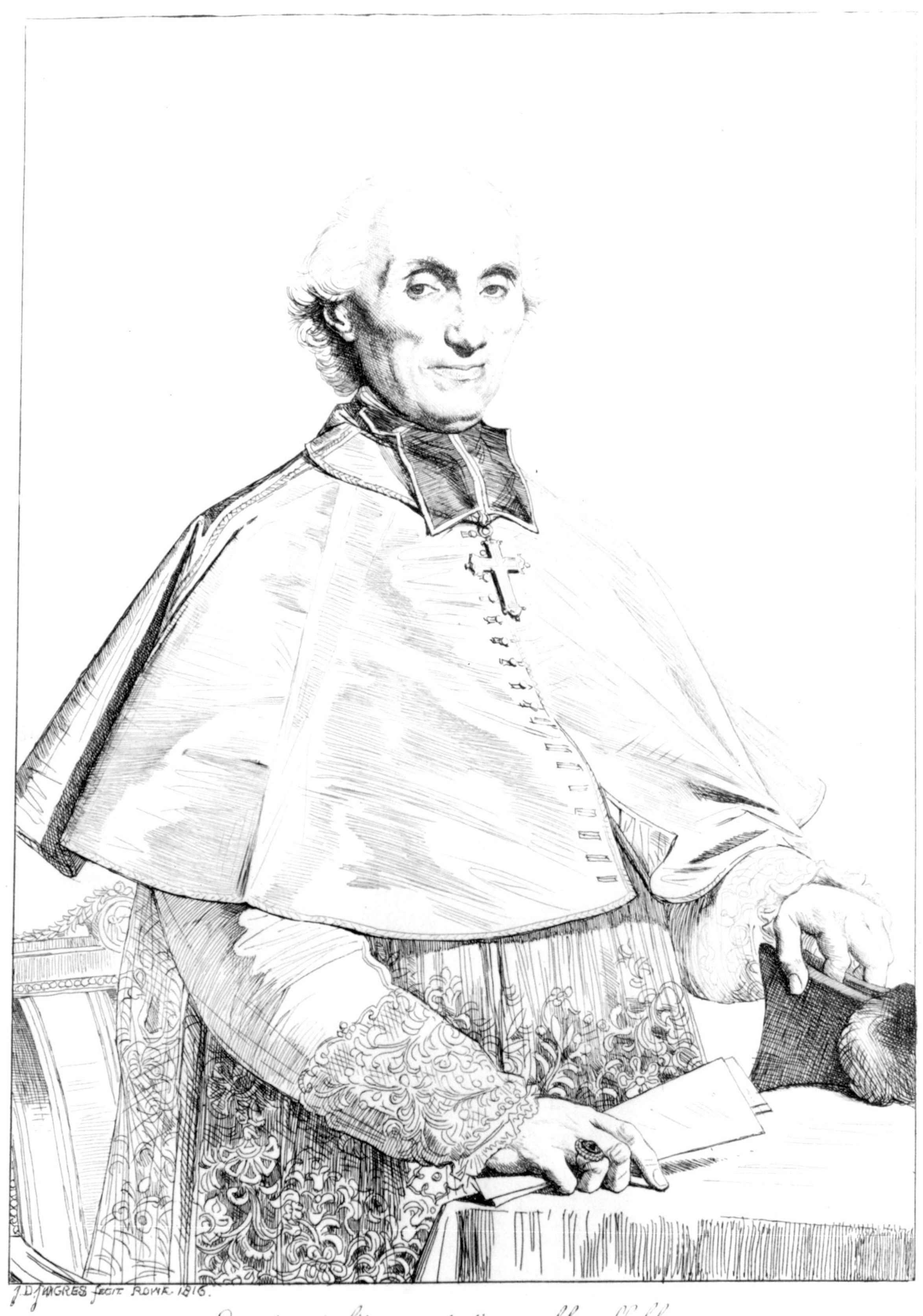

Plate 118. Jean-Auguste-Dominique Ingres, *Gabriel Cortois de Pressigny*, 1816.

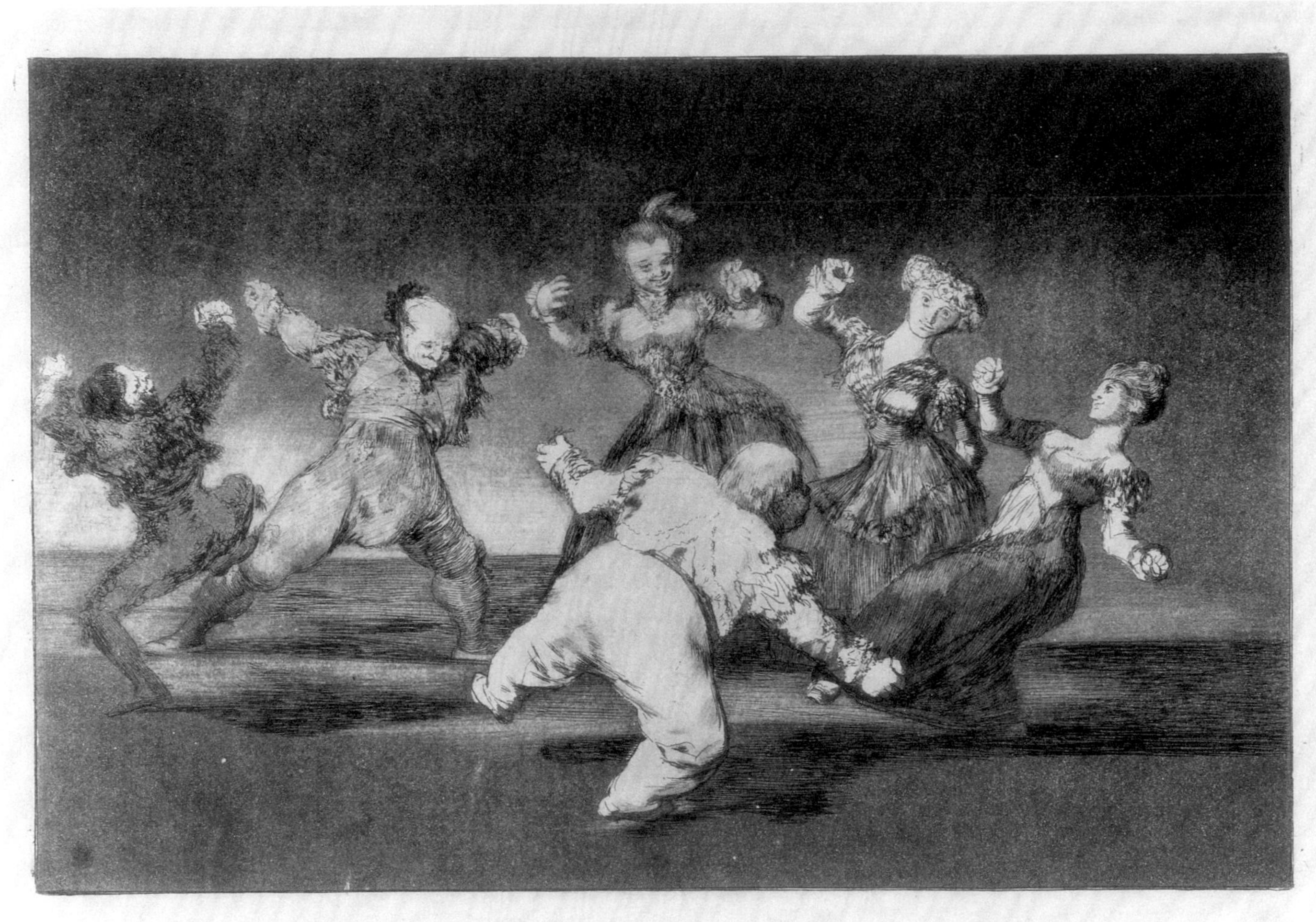

Plate 119. Francisco José Goya y Lucientes, *Disparate alegre (Merry Folly)*, ca. 1816-17.

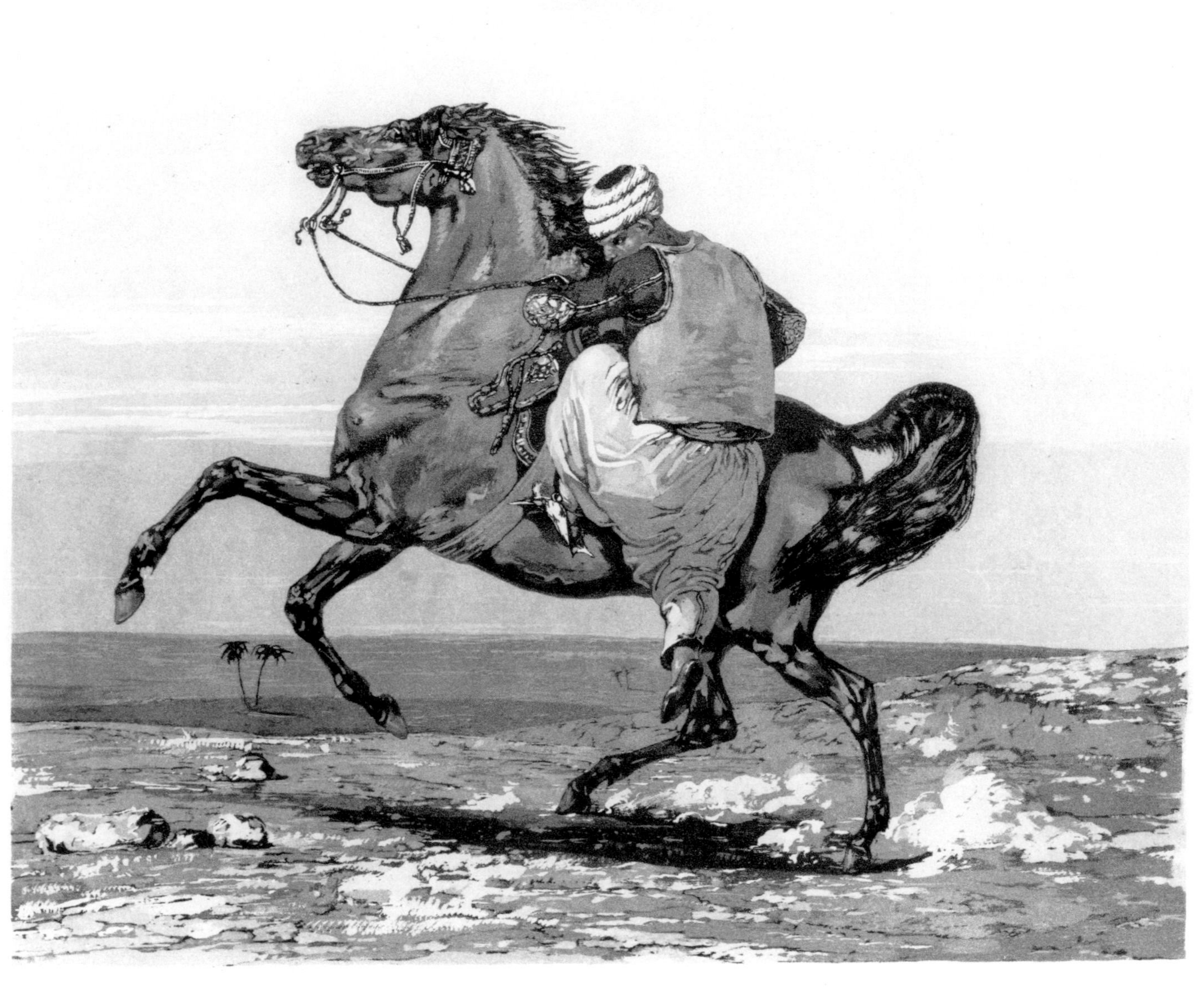

Plate 120. Ferdinand-Victor-Eugène Delacroix, *Turk Mounting a Horse*, ca. 1824.

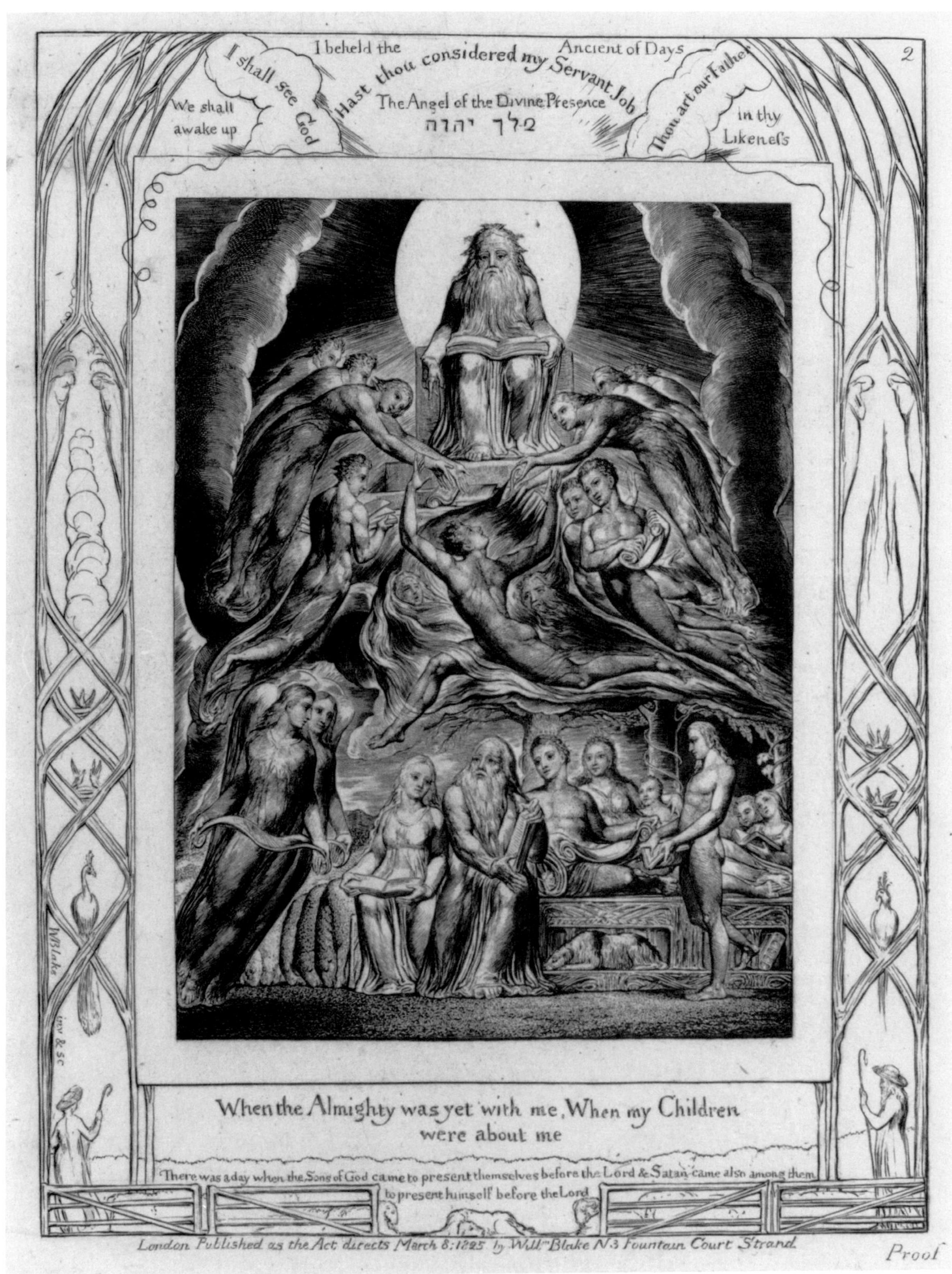

Plate 121. William Blake, *Satan Before the Throne of God*, 1825.

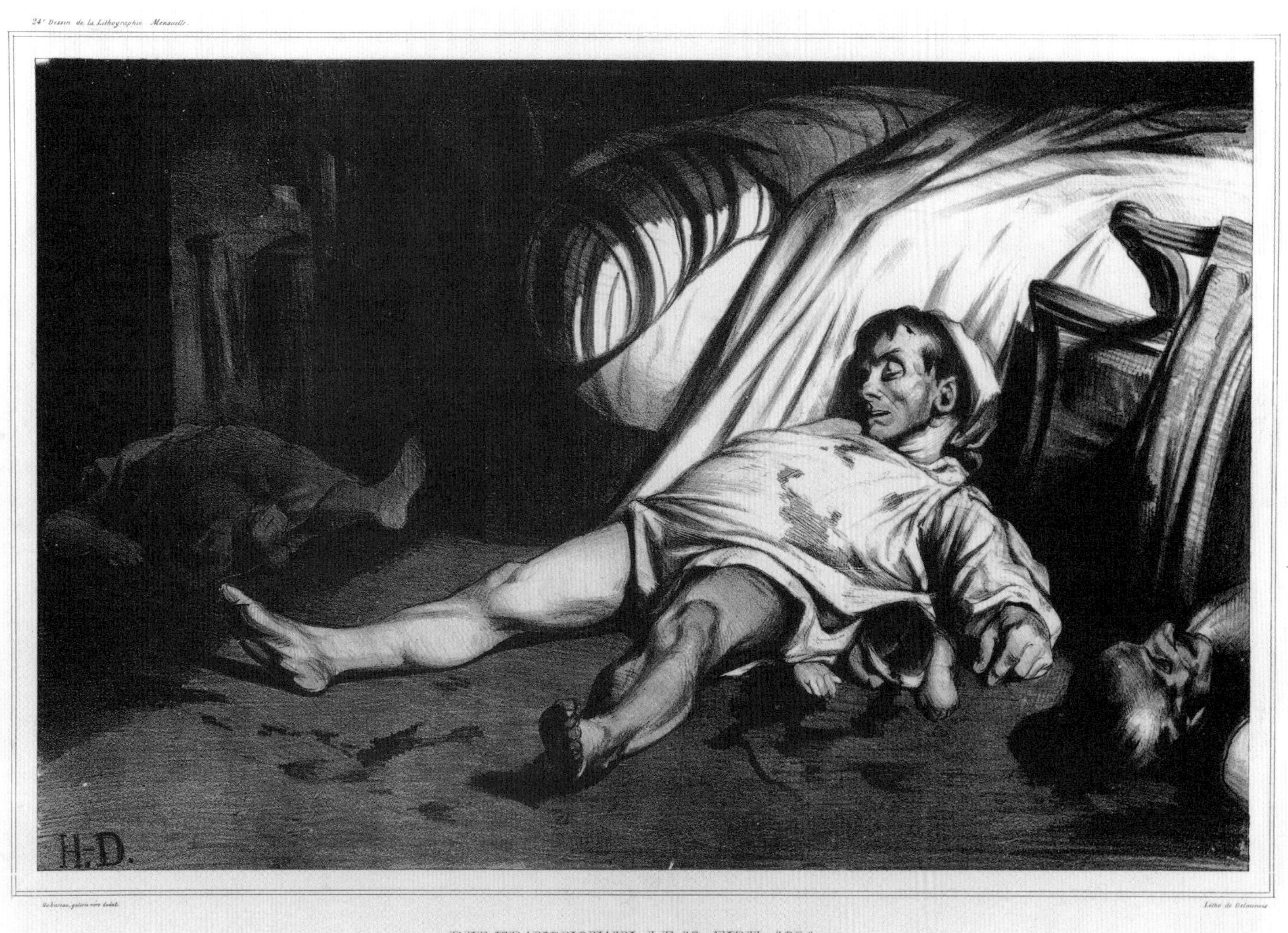

Plate 122. Honoré Daumier, *Rue Transnonain, April 25, 1834.*

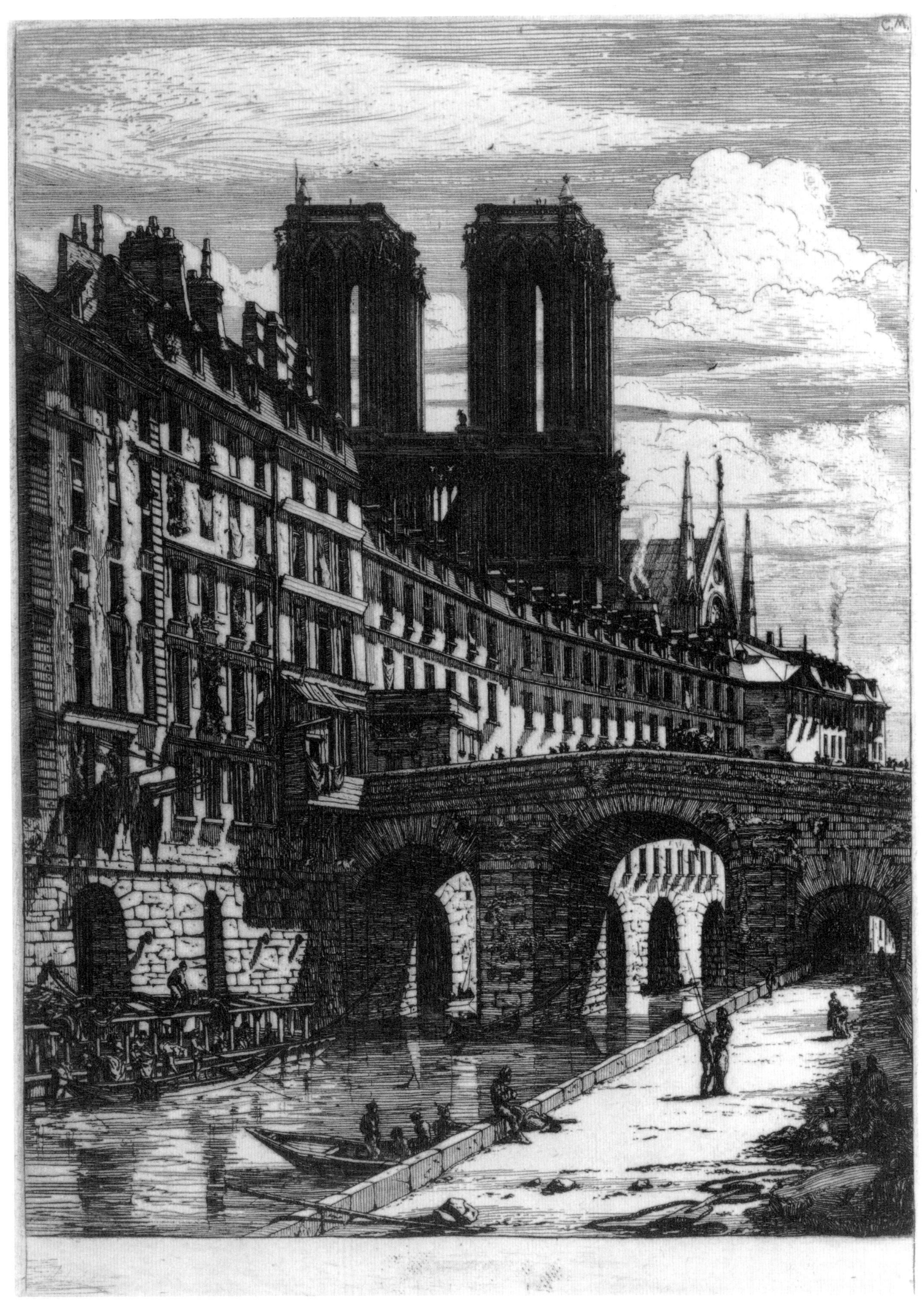

Plate 123. Charles Meryon, *Le Petit Pont (The Little Bridge)*, 1850.

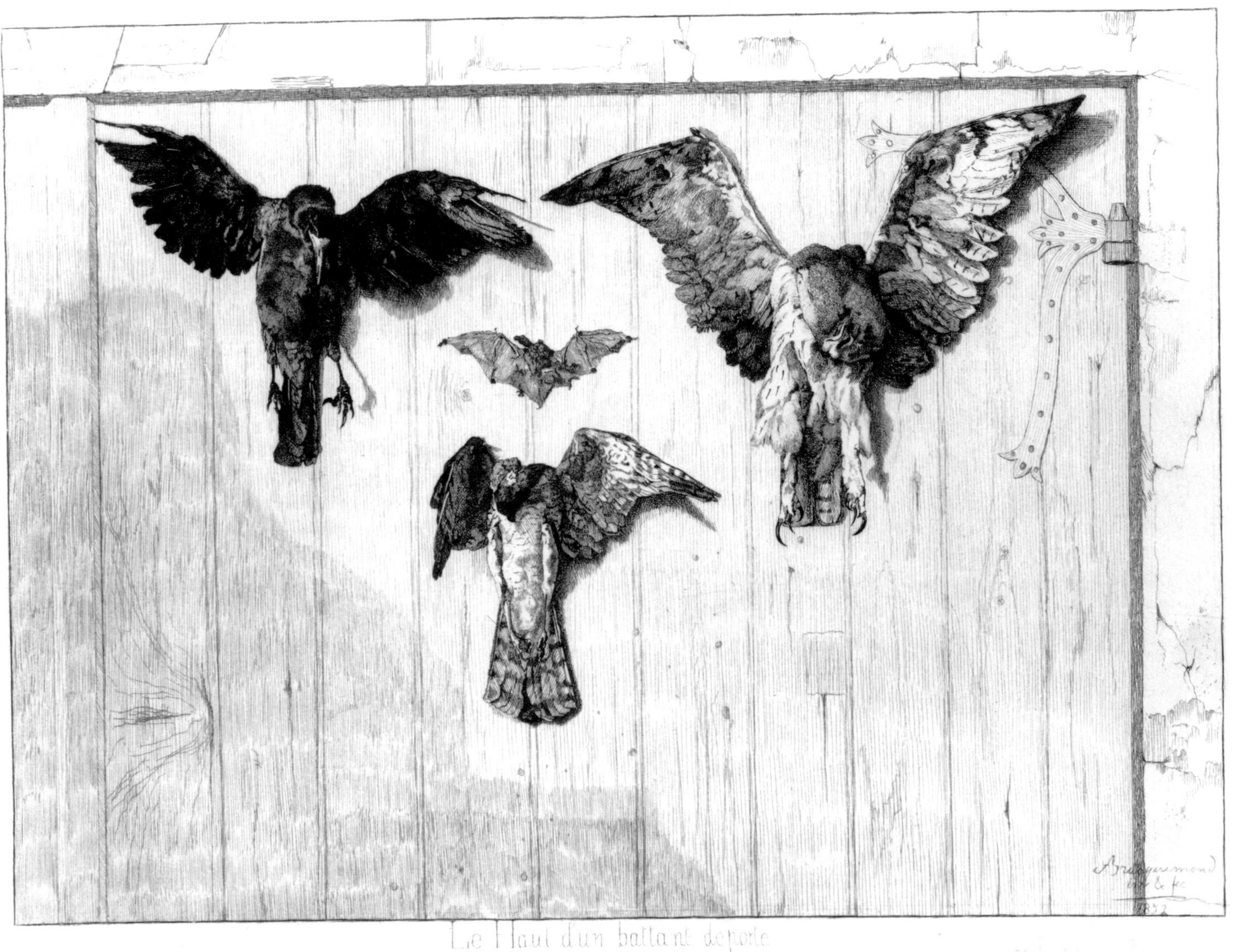

Plate 124. Félix Bracquemond, *The Top of a Swinging Door*, 1852.

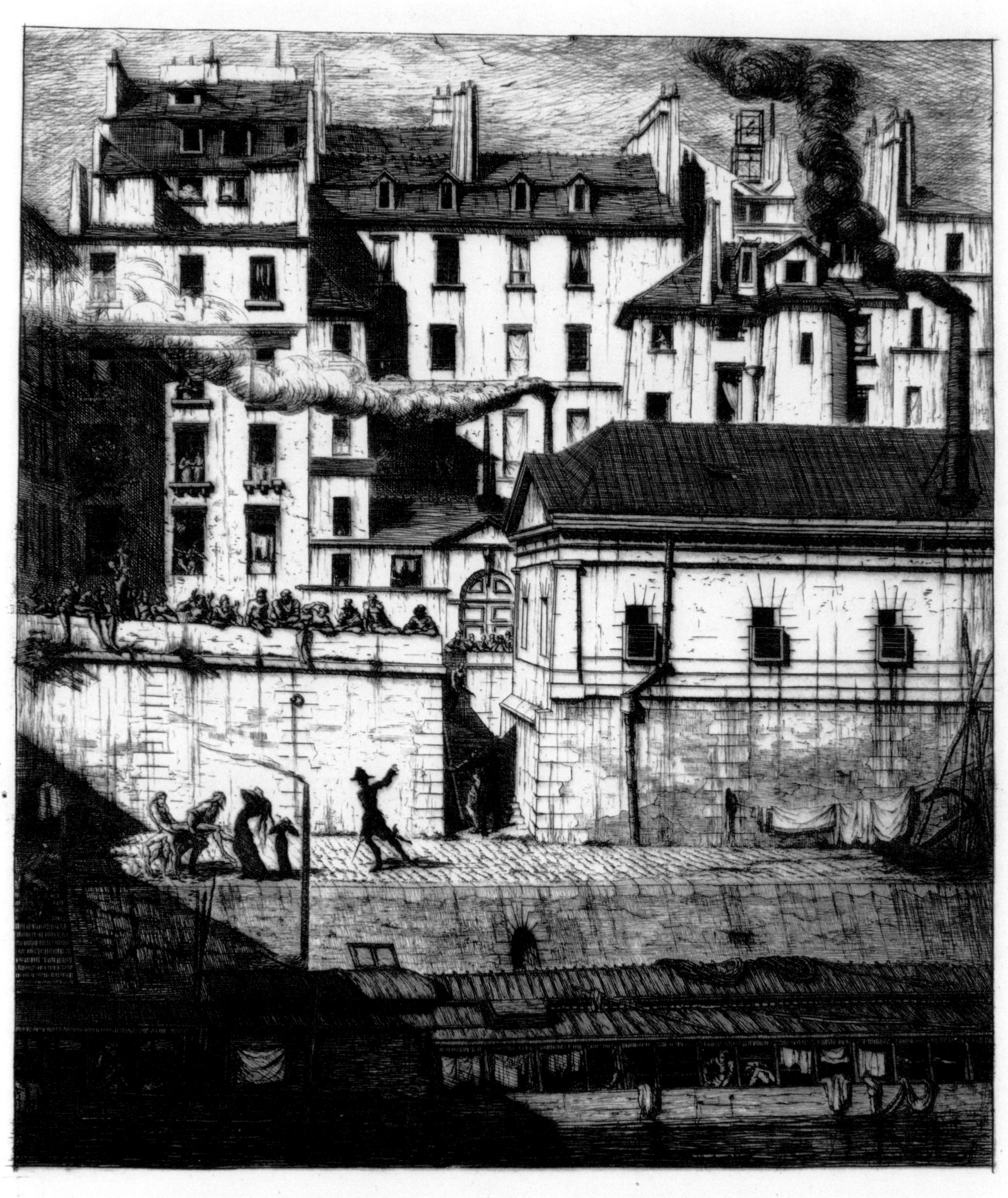

Plate 125. Charles Meryon, *The Morgue*, 1854.

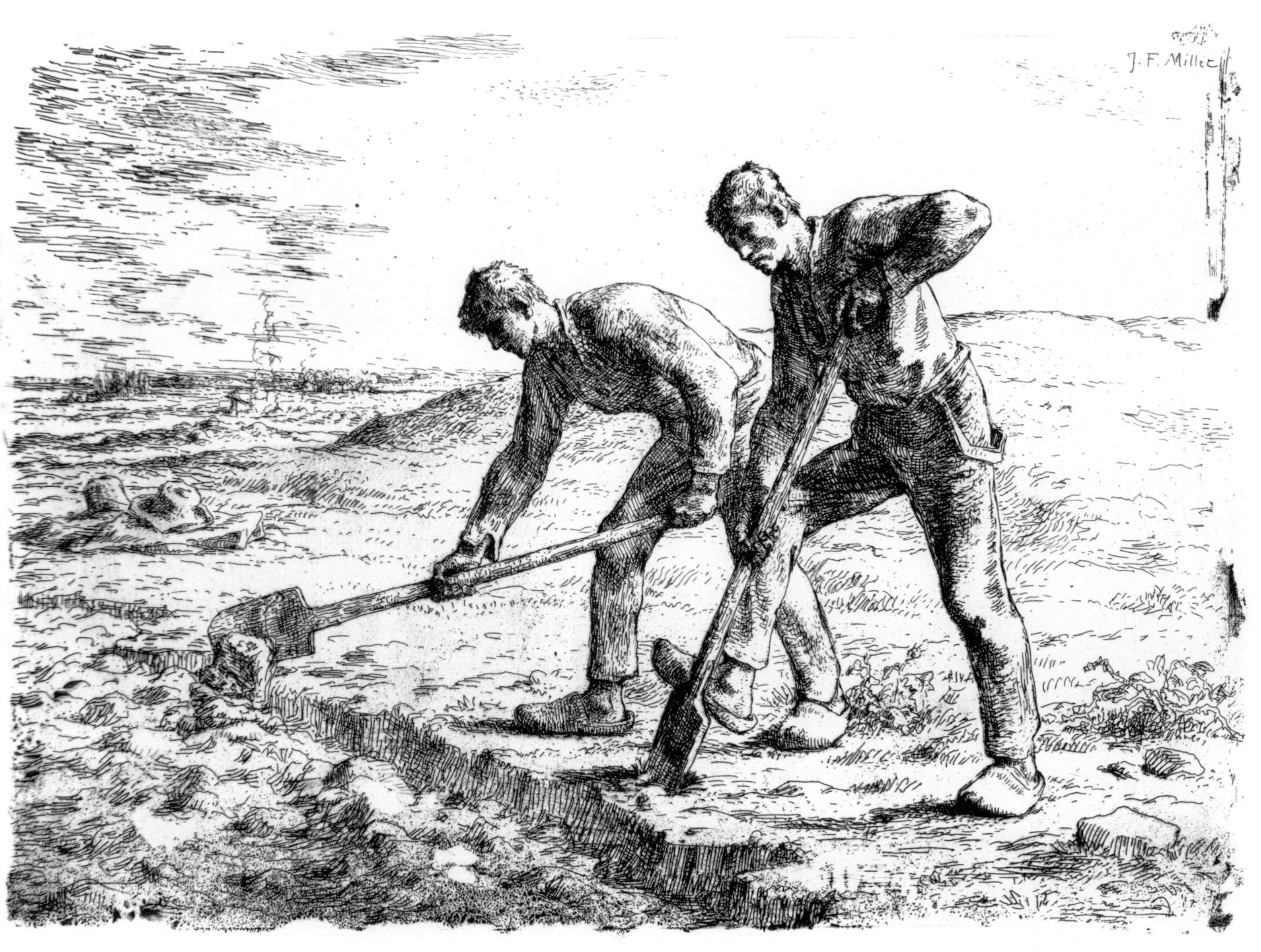

Plate 126. Jean-François Millet, *The Diggers*, 1855-56.

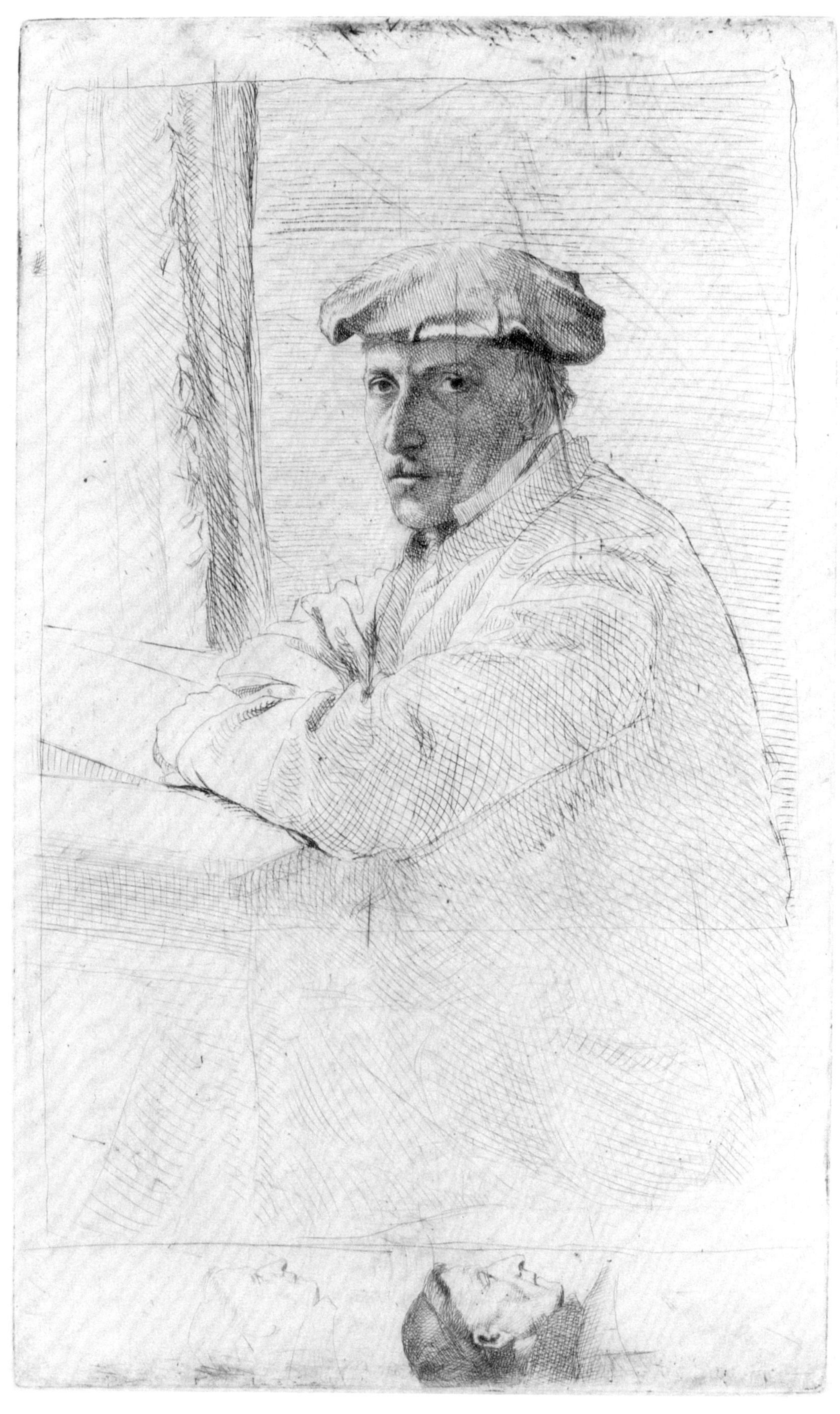

Plate 127. Hilaire-Germain-Edgar Degas, *The Engraver Joseph Tourny*, 1857.

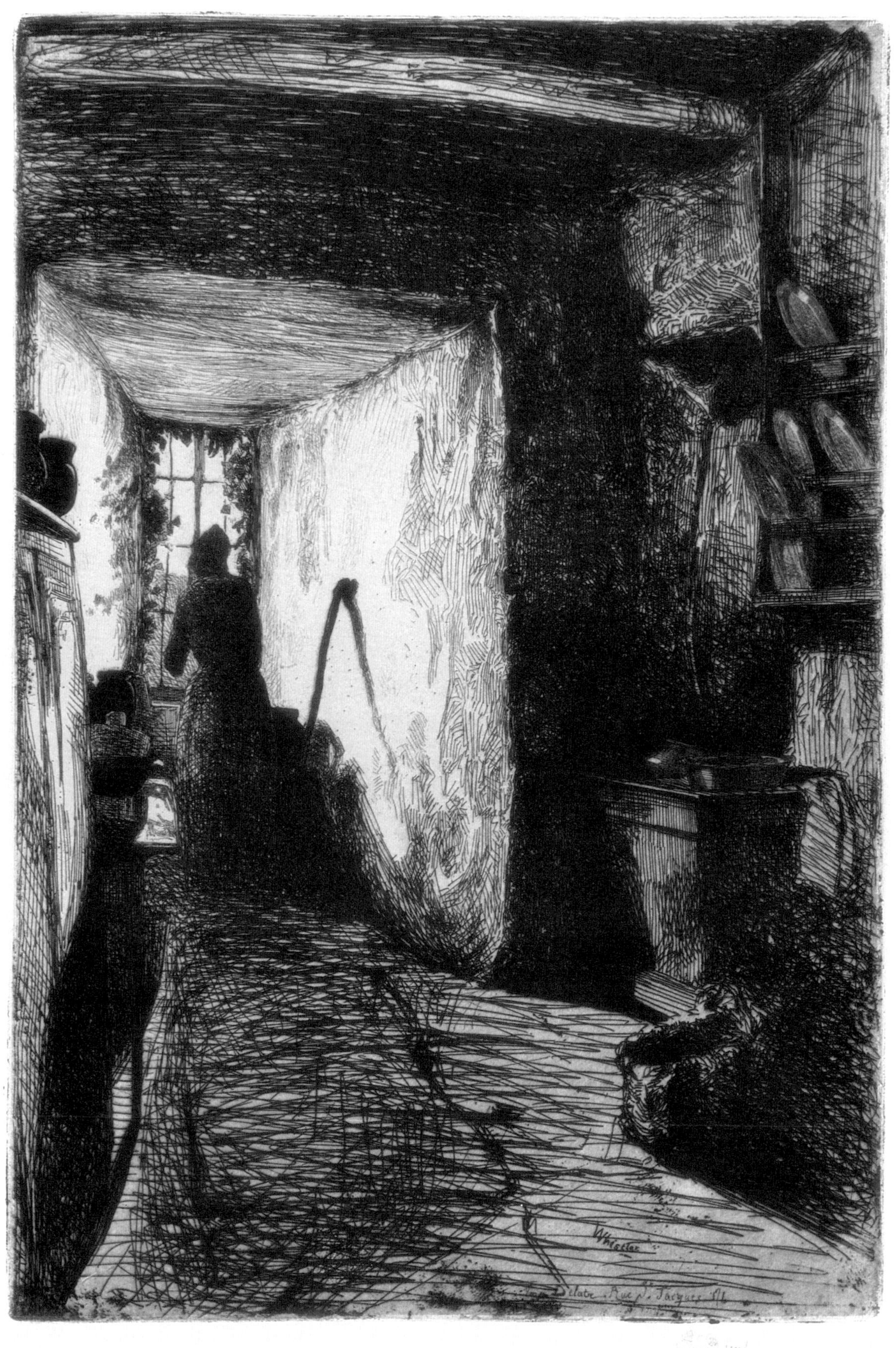

Plate 128. James Abbott McNeill Whistler, *The Kitchen*, 1858.

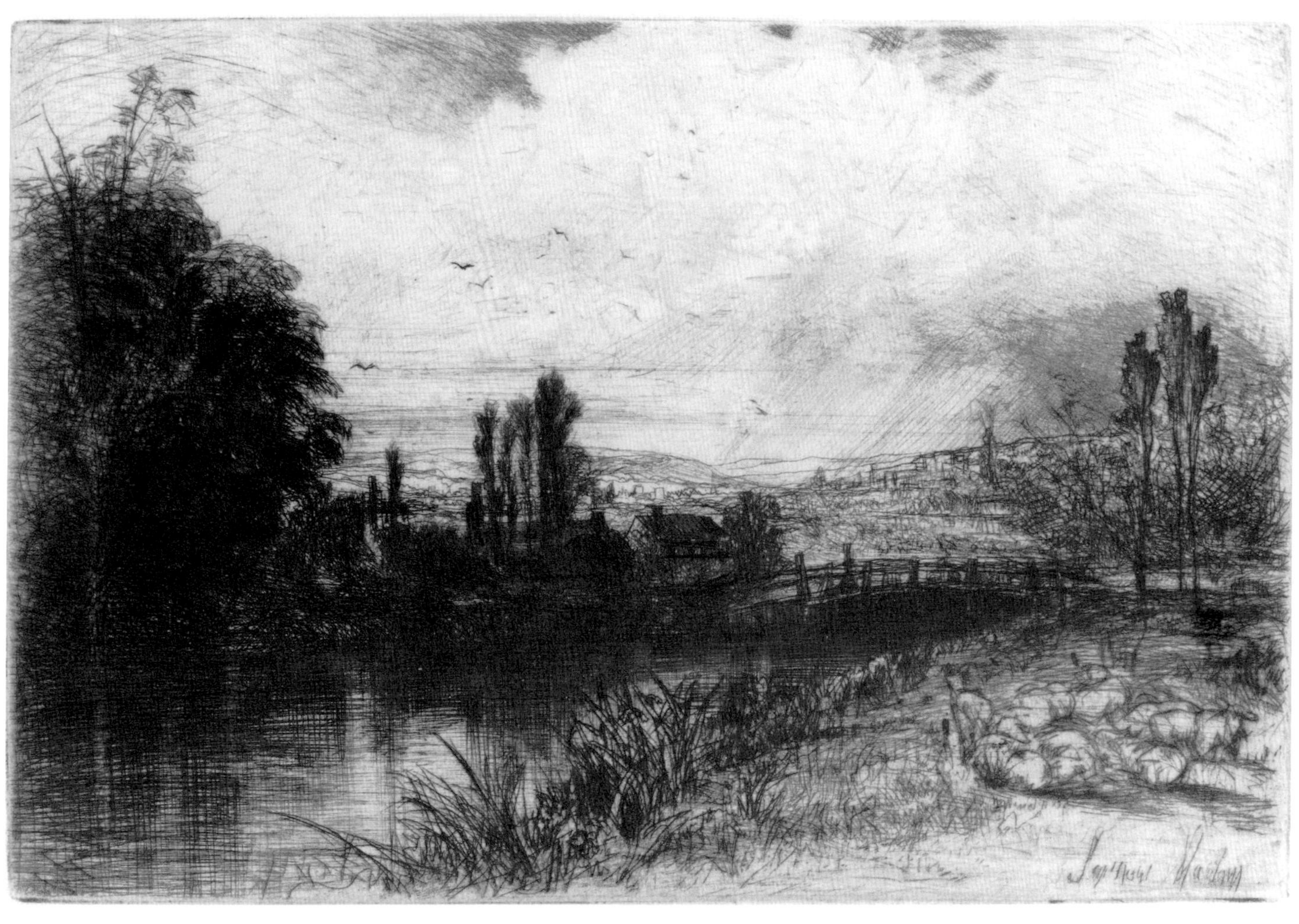

Plate 129. Sir Francis Seymour Haden, *On the Test*, 1859.

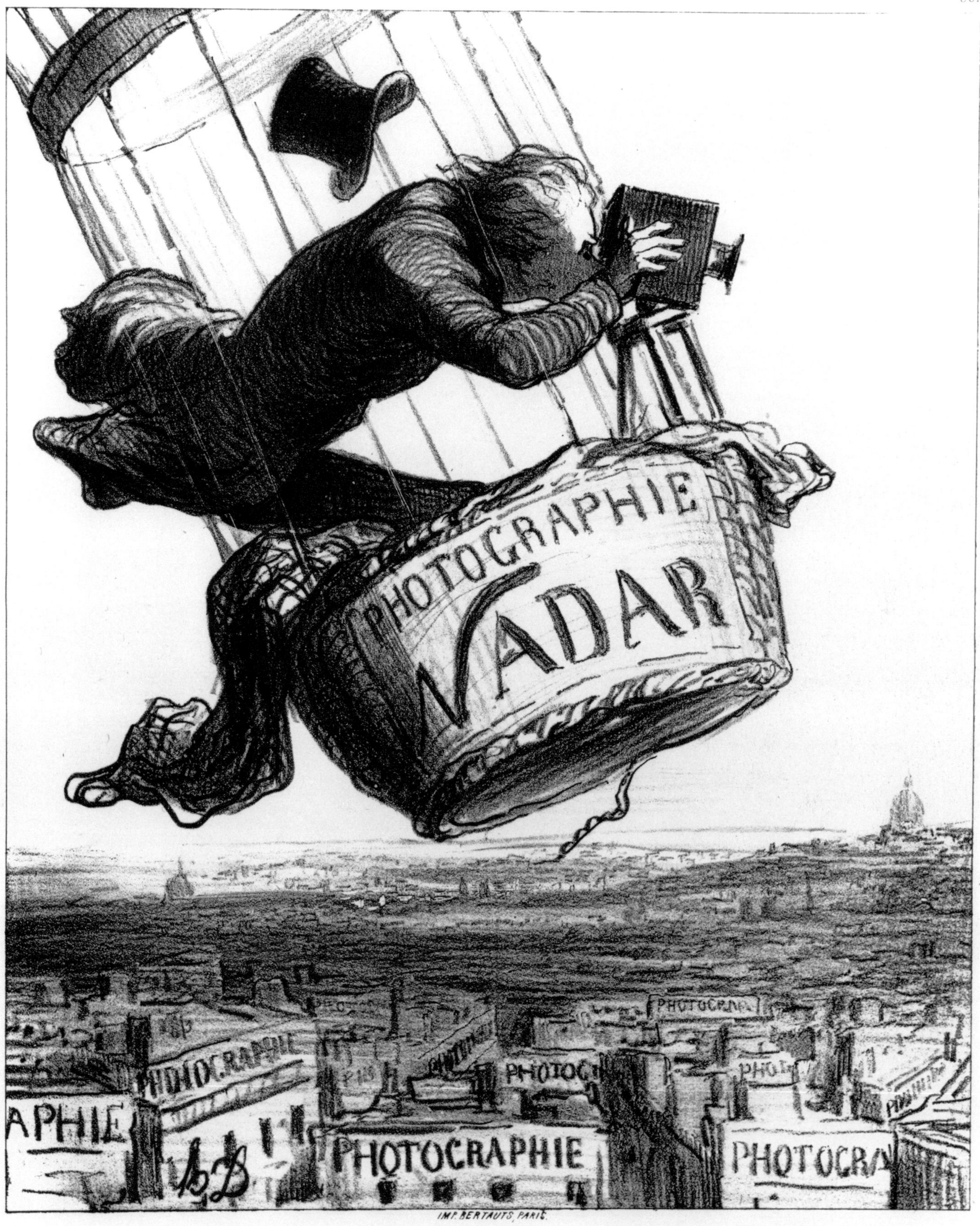

NADAR élevant la Photographie à la hauteur de l'Art

Plate 130. Honoré Daumier, *Nadar Elevates Photography to Artistic Heights*, 1862.

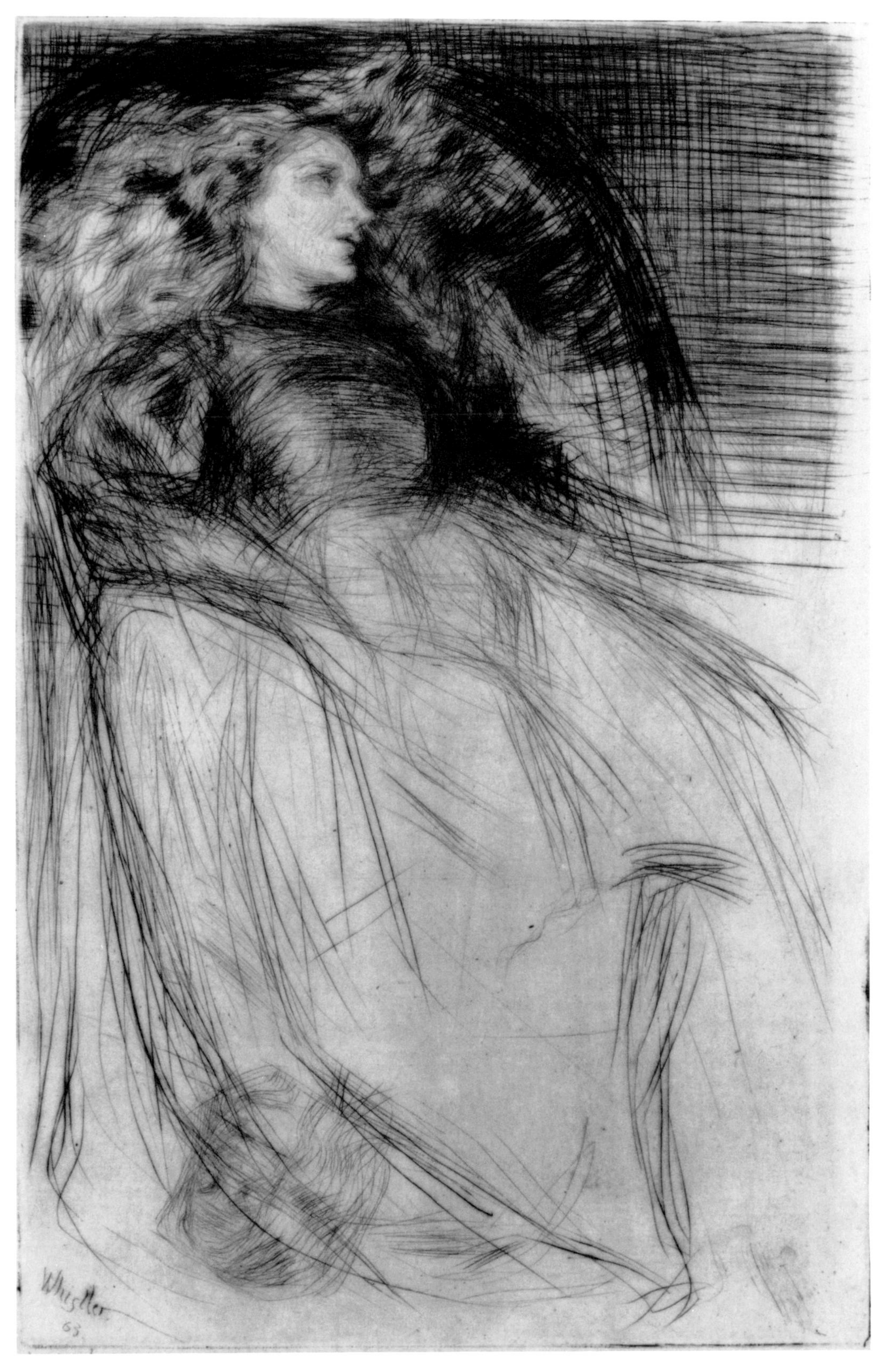

Plate 131. James Abbott McNeill Whistler, *Weary*, 1863.

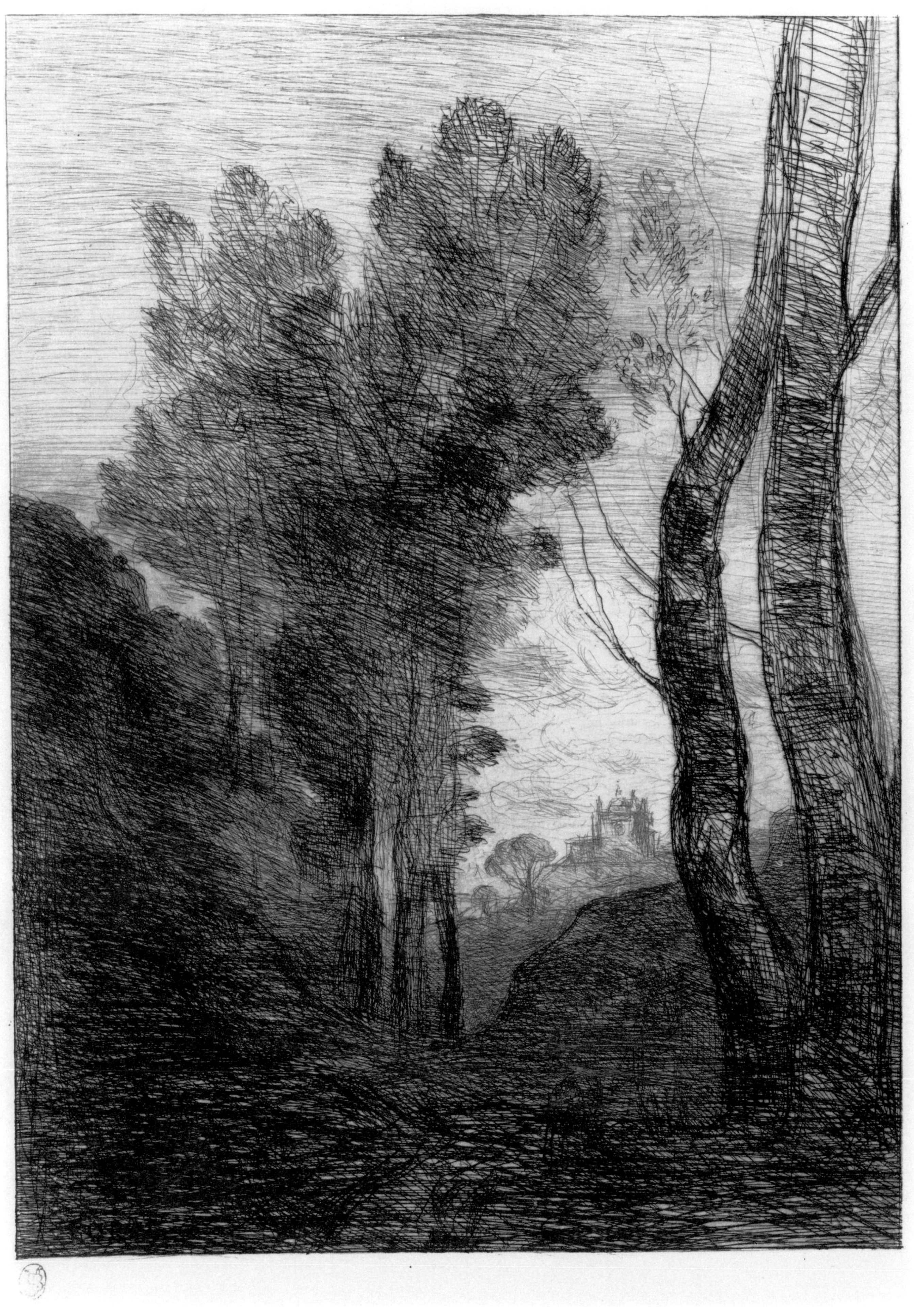

Plate 132. Jean-Baptiste-Camille Corot, *The Environs of Rome*, 1866.

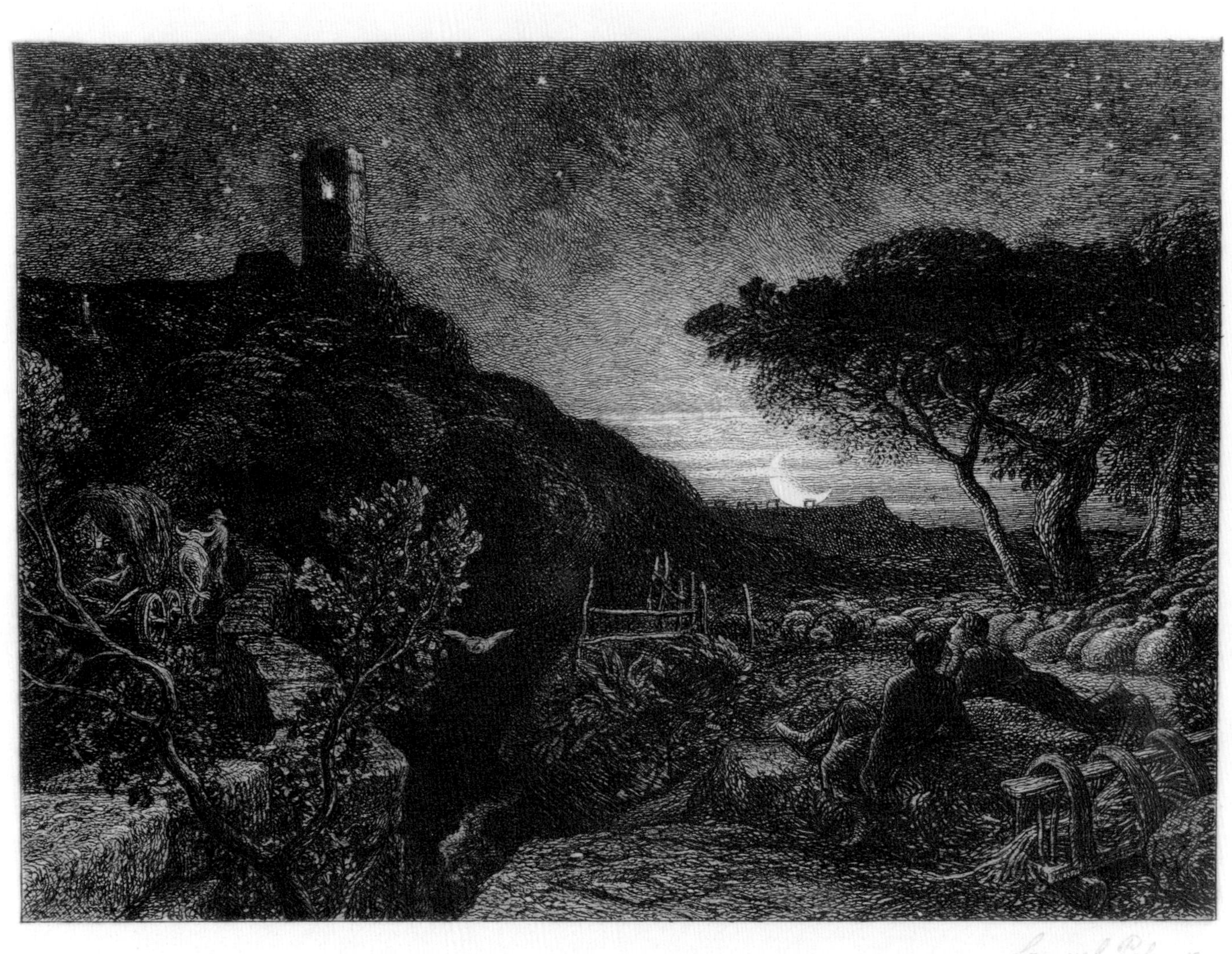

Plate 133. Samuel Palmer, *The Lonely Tower*, 1879.

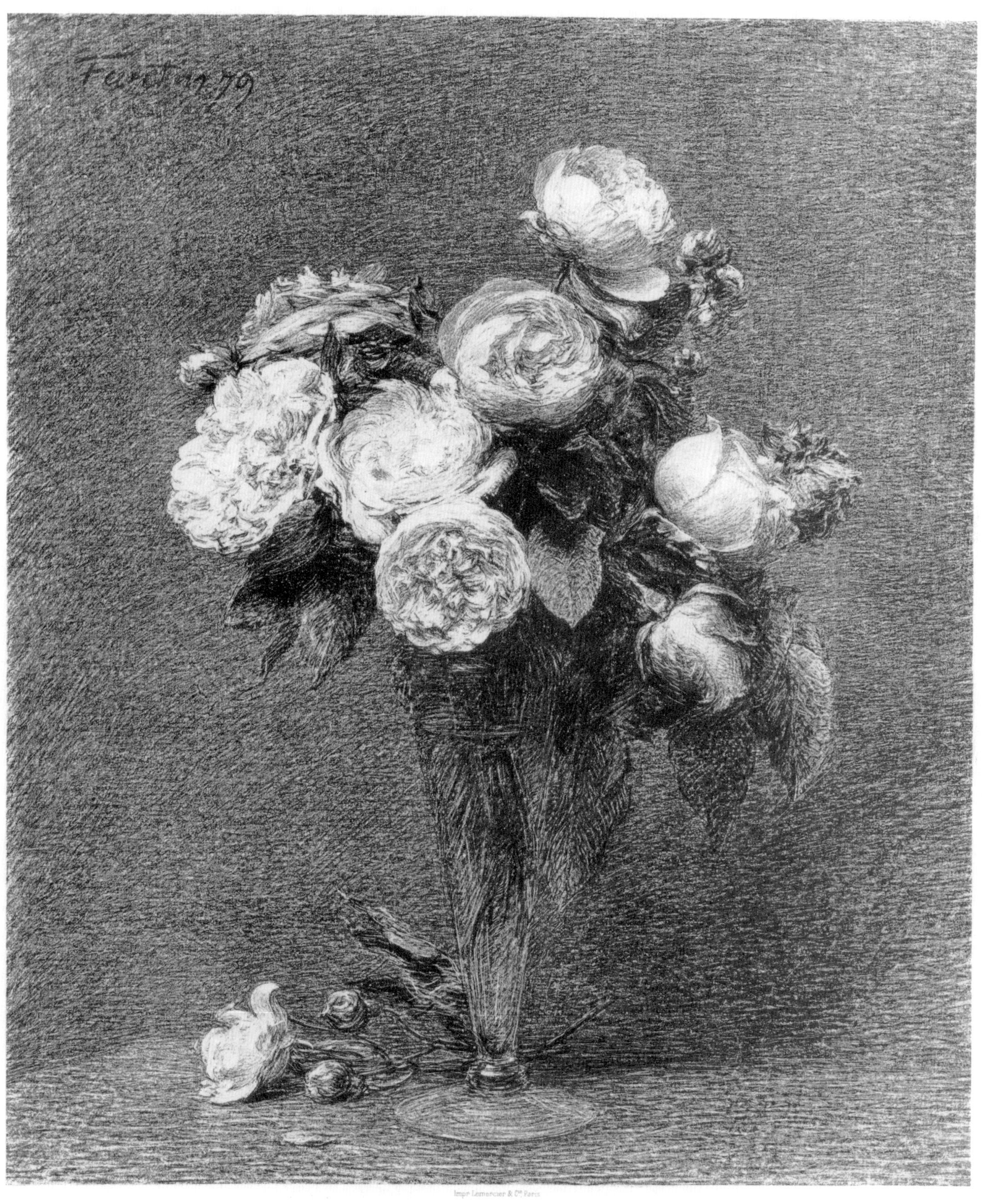

Plate 134. Ignace-Henri-Jean-Théodore Fantin-Latour, *Bouquet of Roses*, 1879.

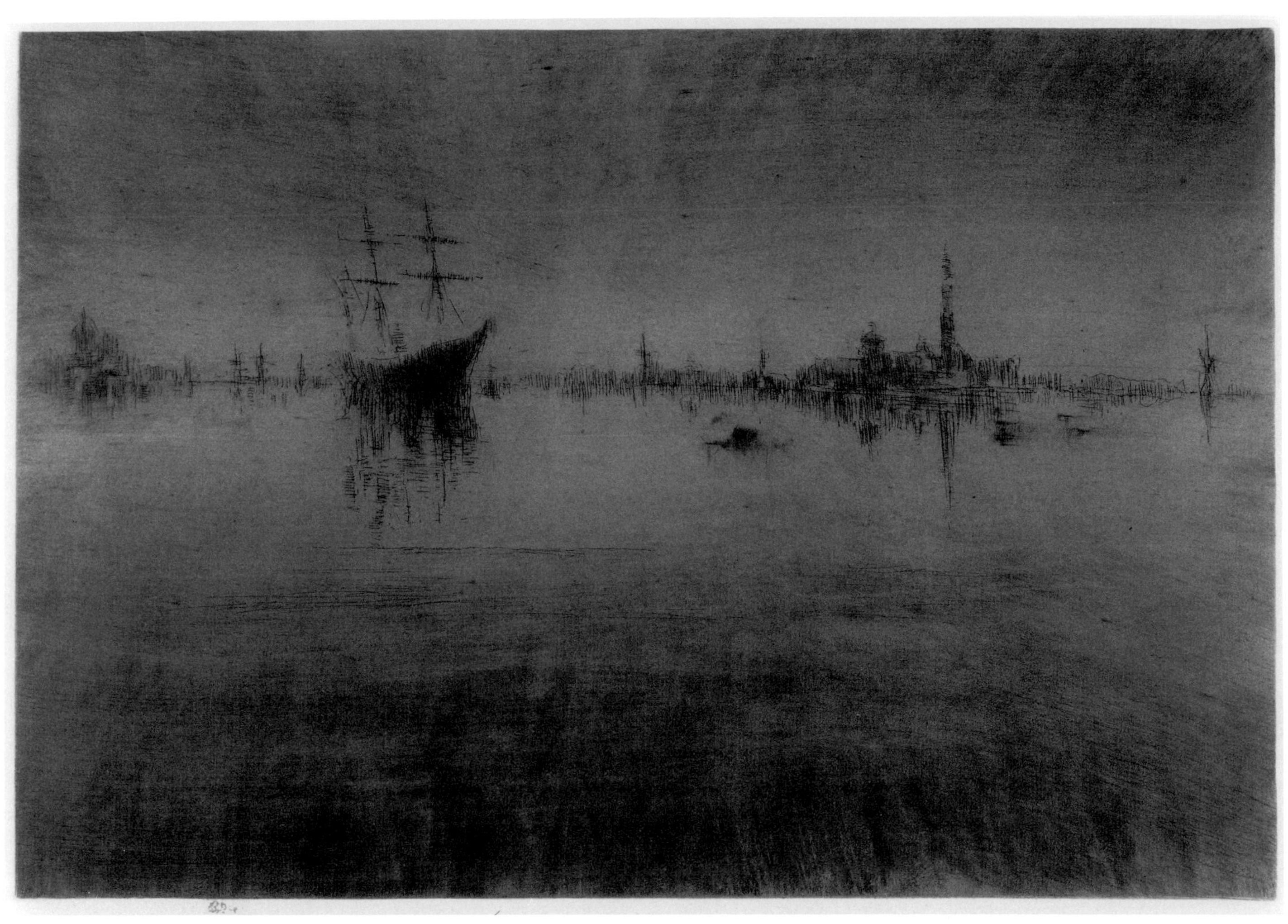

Plate 135. James Abbott McNeill Whistler, *Nocturne, 1879-80.*

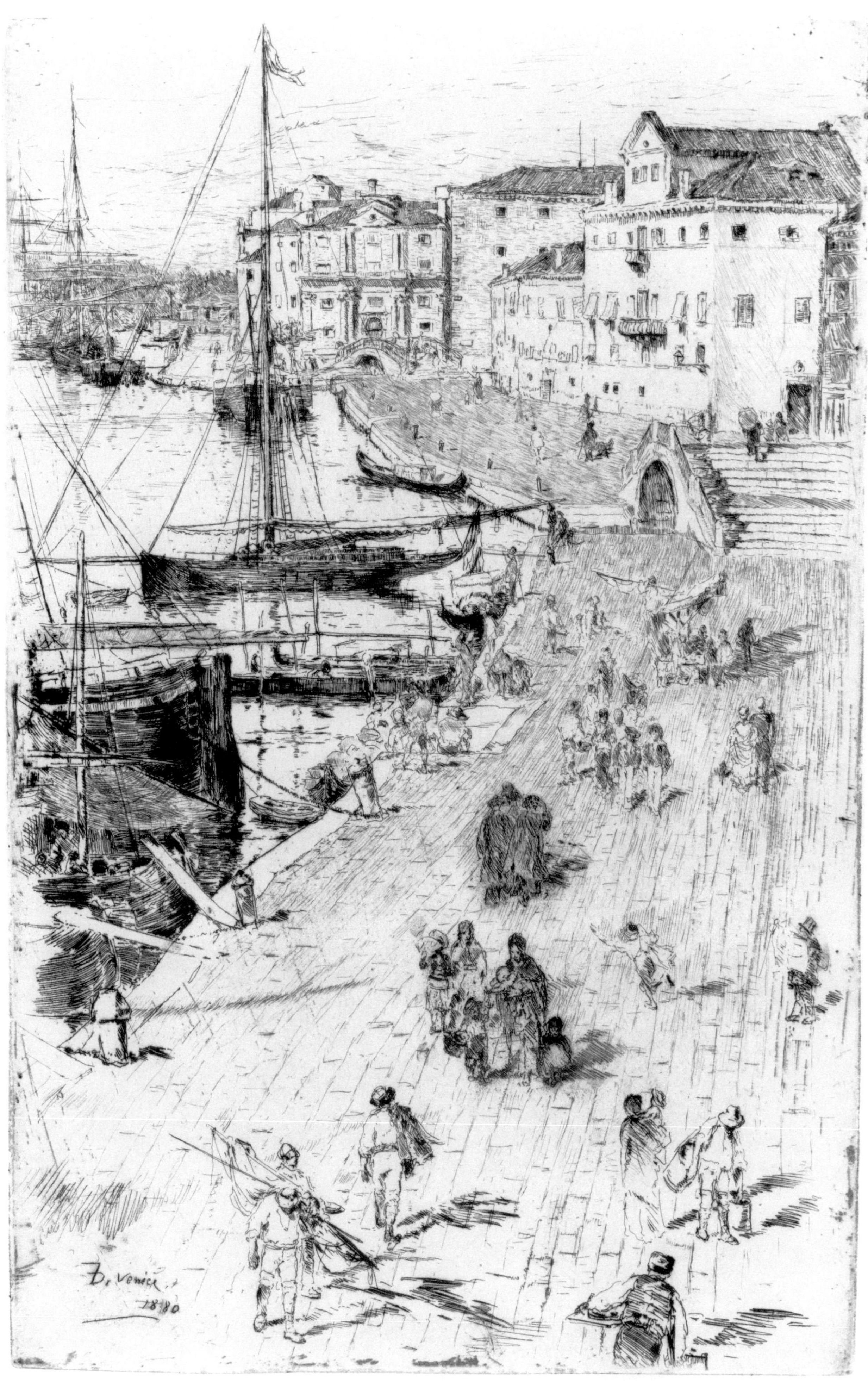

Plate 136. Frank Duveneck, *Riva degli Schiavoni, Number Two*, (upright plate), 1880.

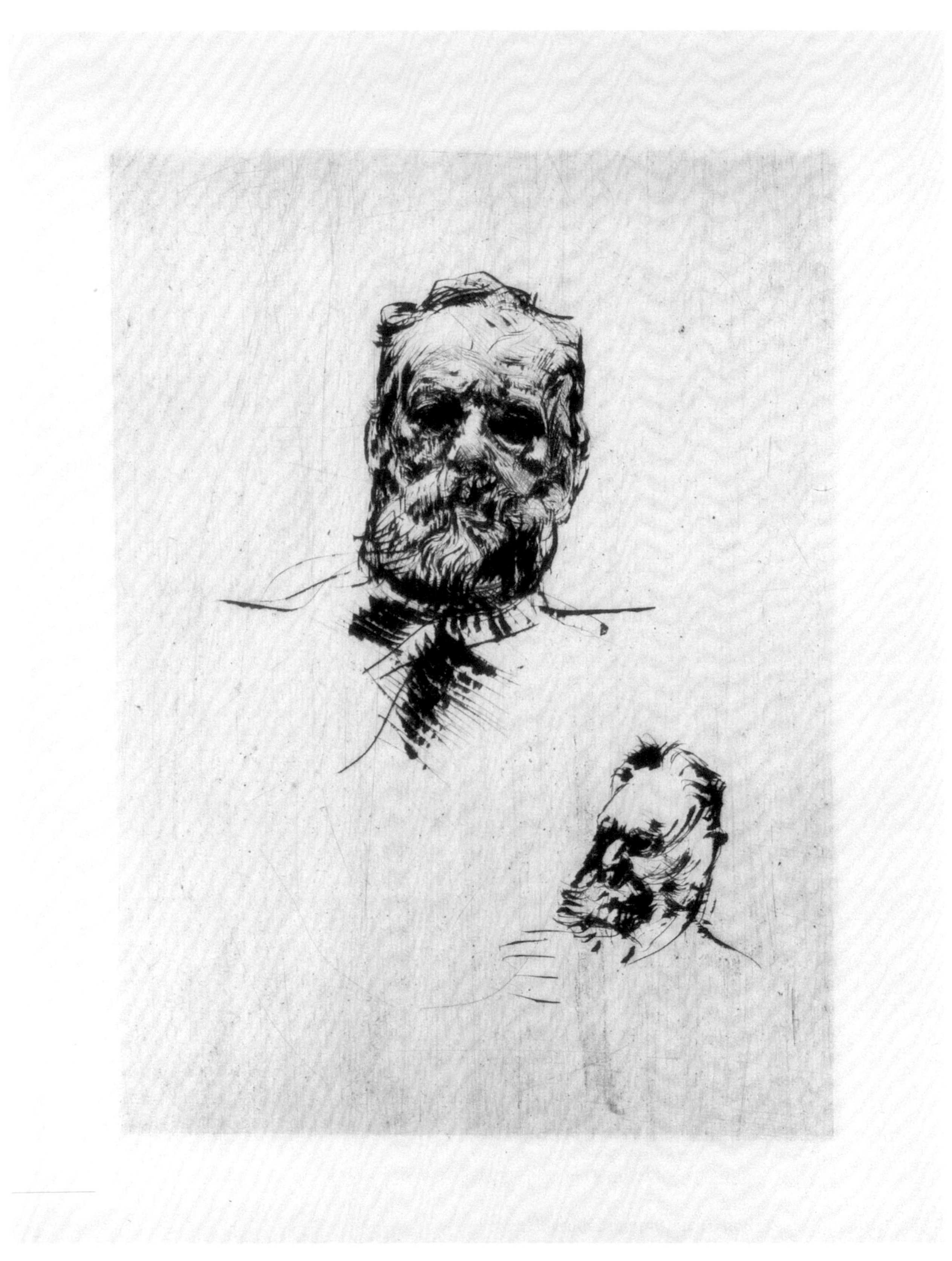

Plate 137. August Rodin, *Victor Hugo, Front view (Victor Hugo, de Face)*, 1885.

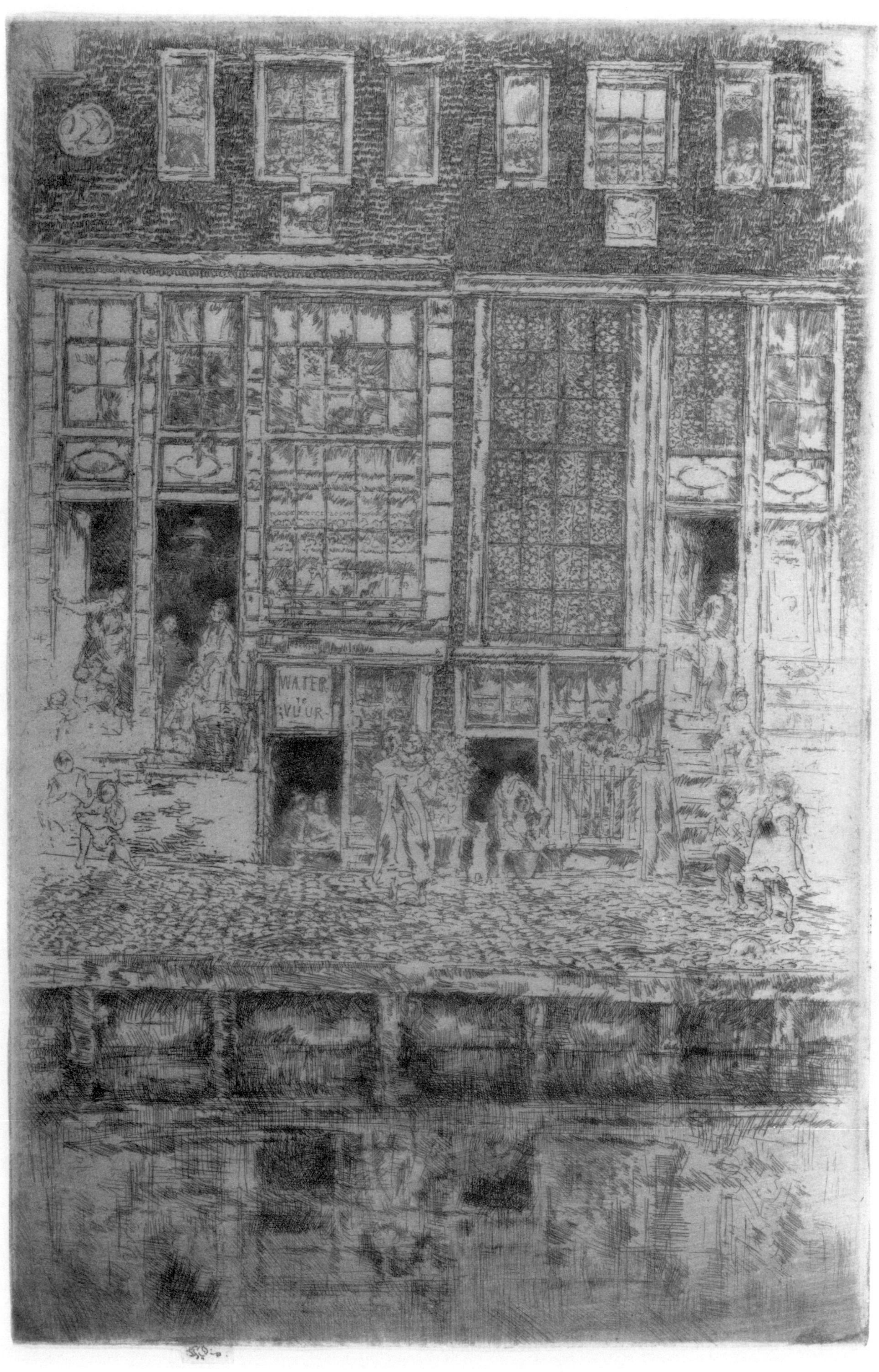

Plate 138. James Abbott McNeill Whistler, *The Embroidered Curtain*, 1889.

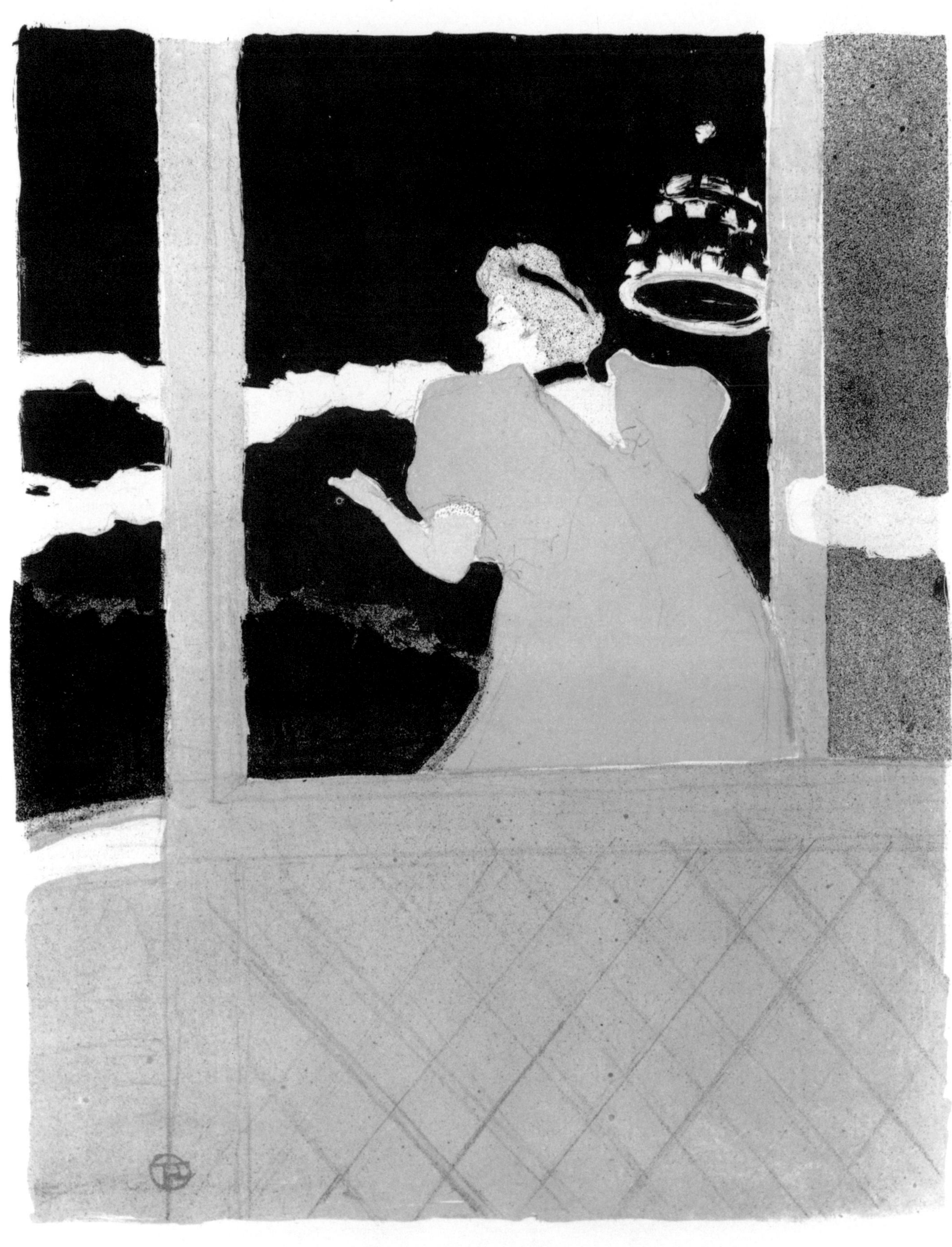

Plate 139. Henri de Toulouse-Lautrec, *At the Ambassadeurs – Café Concert Singer*, 1894.

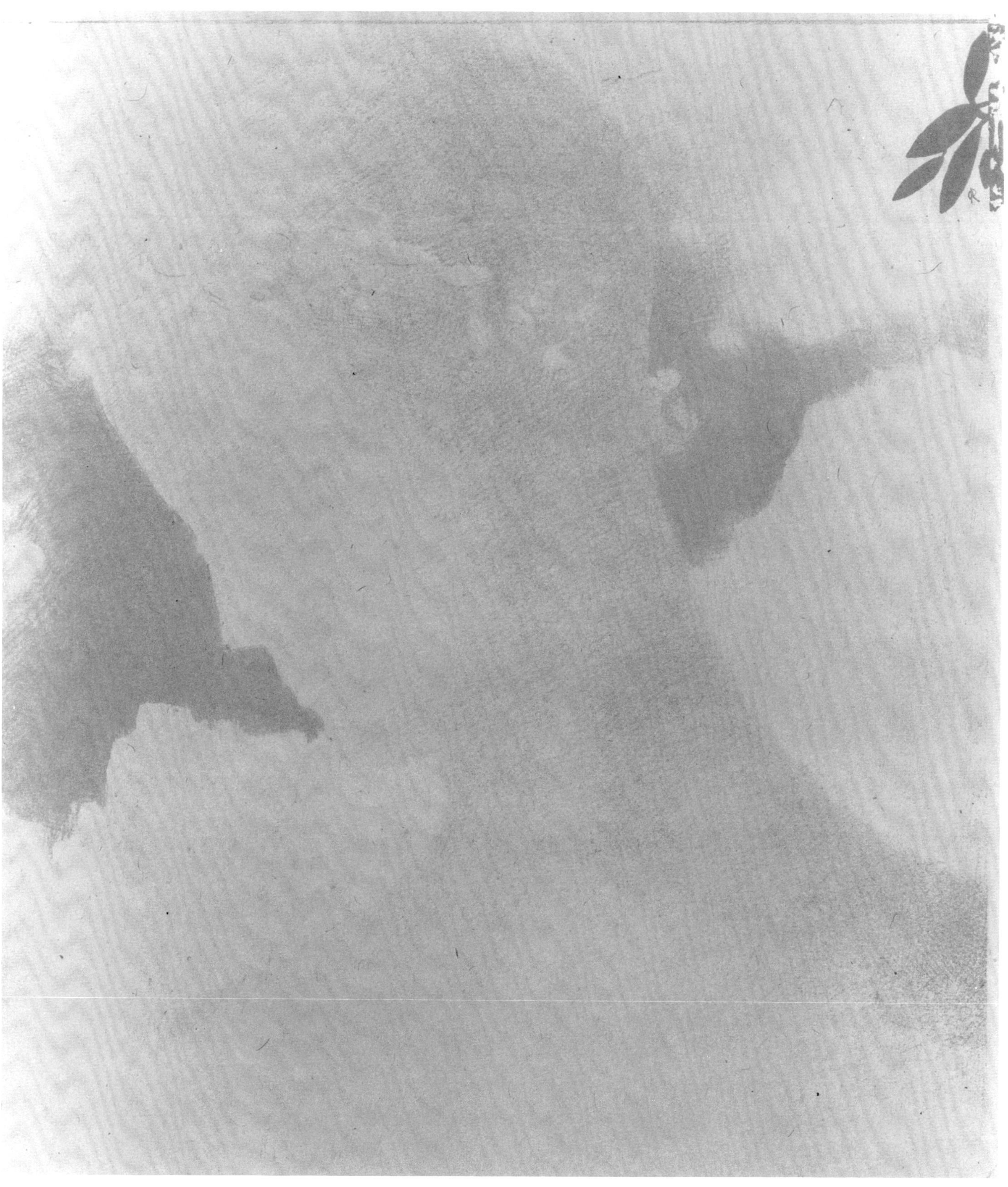

Plate 140. Odilon Redon, *Béatrice*, 1897.

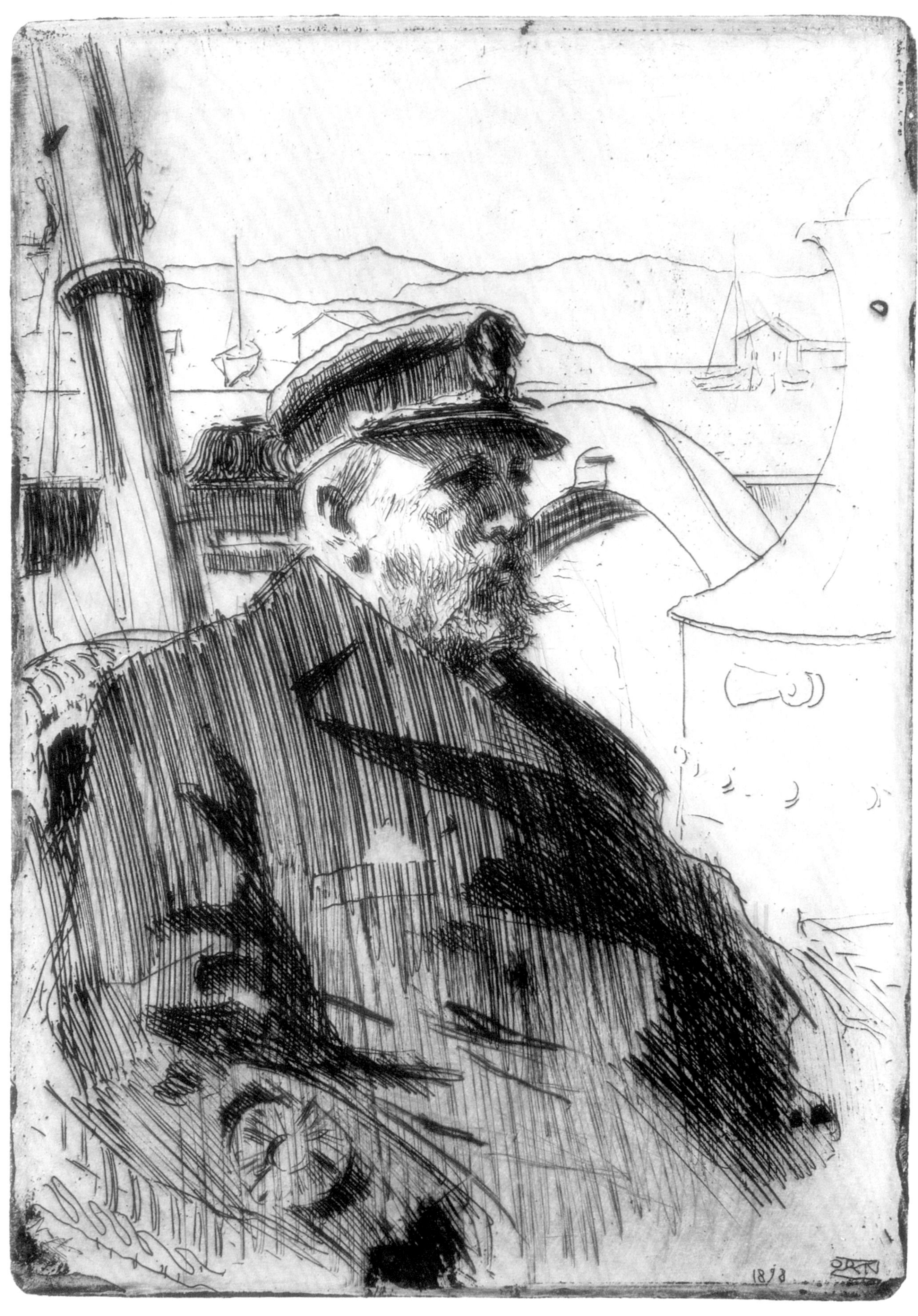

Plate 141. Anders Zorn, *King Oscar II*, 1898.

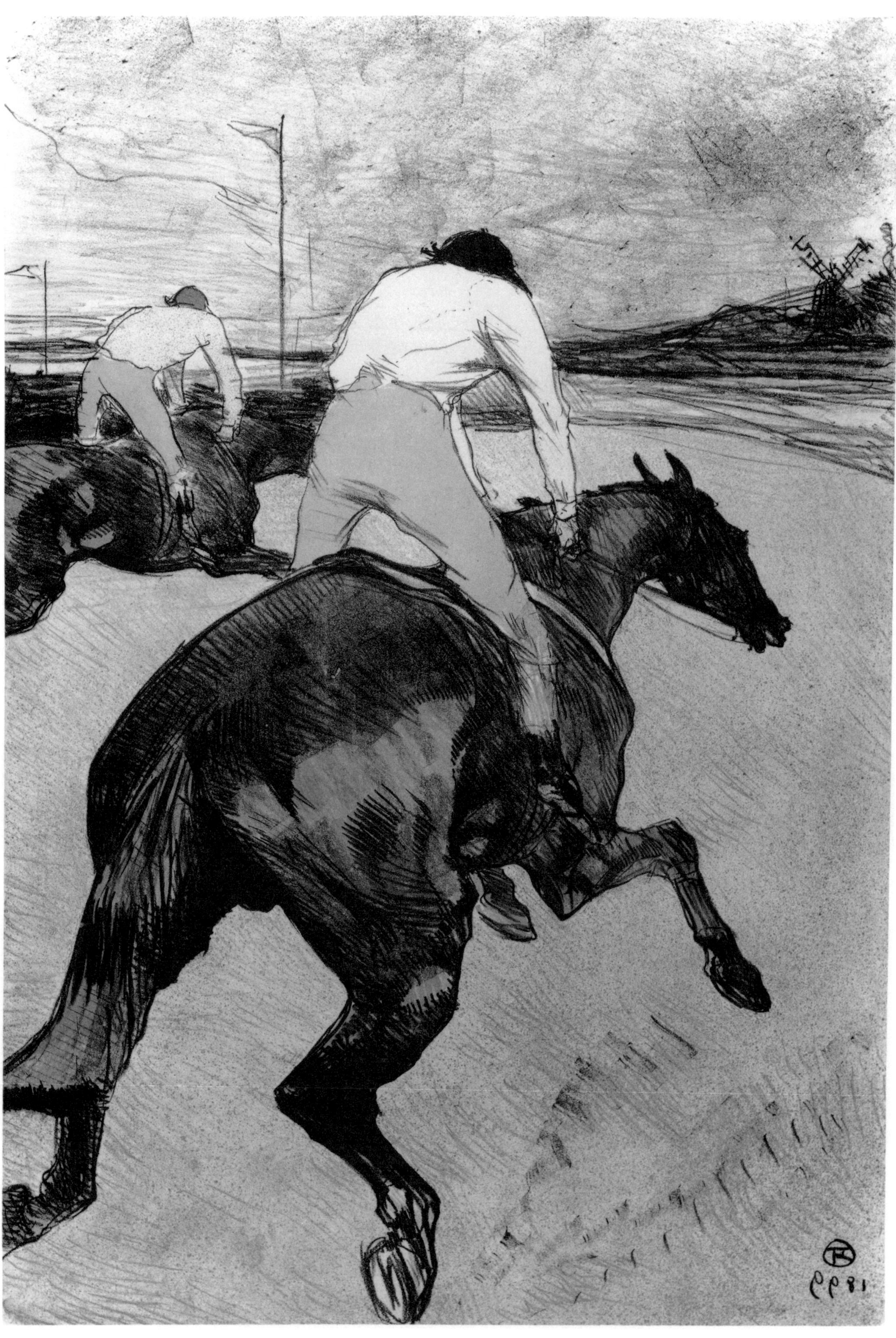

Plate 142. Henri de Toulouse-Lautrec, *The Jockey*, 1899.

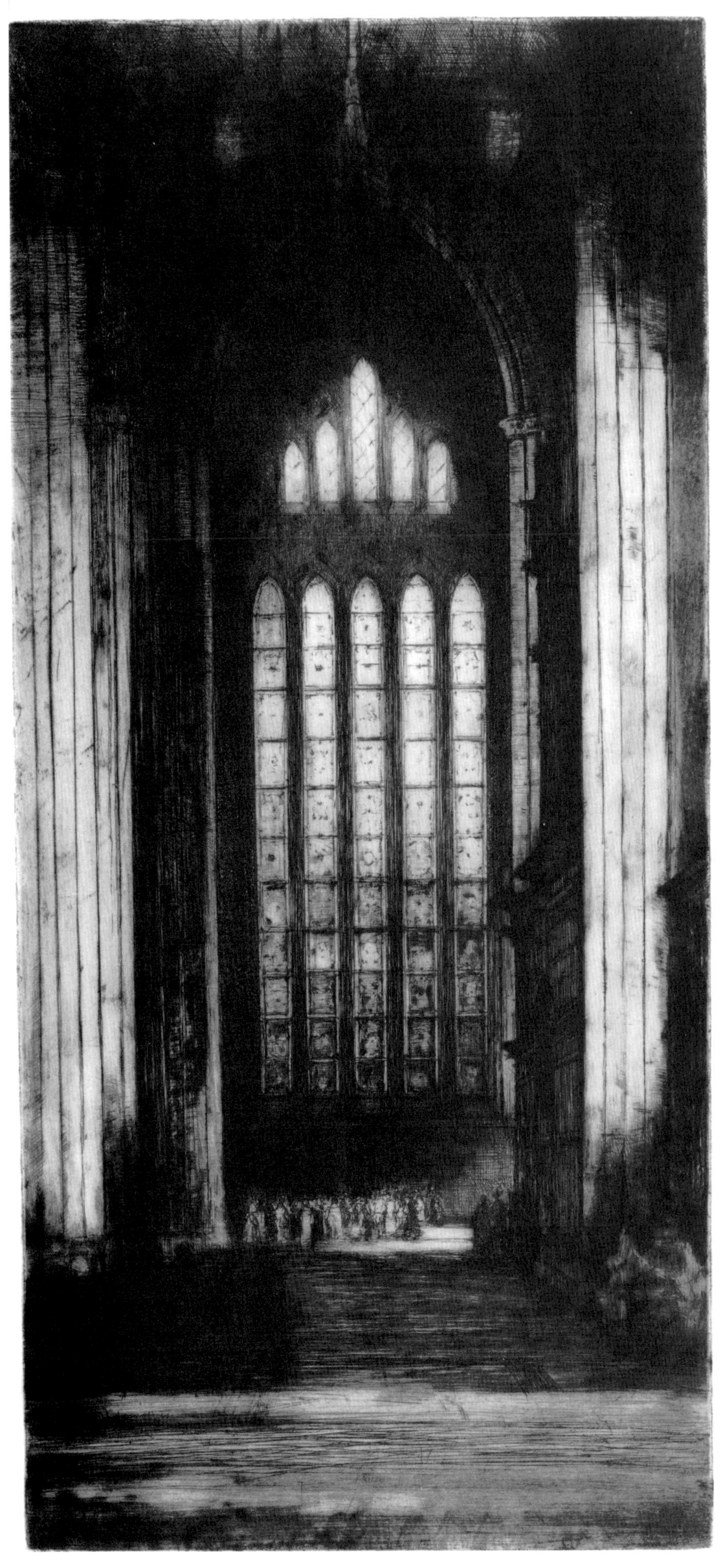

Plate 143. Sir David Young Cameron, *The Five Sisters, York Minster*, 1907.

viewed from an elevated position. The viewer is so effectively drawn into the composition that one does not realize that Lautrec retained the conventional hobbyhorse position rather than the contracted position with all four feet off the ground. The second edition of *The Jockey* was actually printed with seven rather than six colors. This is clearly evident in the trial proof in the Rosenwald Collection at the National Gallery of Art.[5] In the regular edition, the two browns on the horse, one in crayon and one in tusche, are close in value and hue and can be overlooked by the casual viewer.

Within months of his release from the hospital, Lautrec lapsed into his old habit of drinking. In August 1901 he suffered a stroke and was partially paralyzed. He returned to his mother's estate, where he died on September 9, 1901.

Lautrec exhibited in almost every Salon des Artistes Indépendants from 1889 and in other avant-garde exhibitions in Paris and in Les XX in Brussels. In 1898, three years before his death, the debate concerning whether color lithography should be admitted into the Salon still raged.[6] Lautrec's revolutionary color lithography revitalized graphic design. He did not need traditional venues or rogue salons to reach the public: the intellectual and popular media and the walls lining Parisian streets constituted Lautrec's Salon. – KLS

1. New York 1983, nos. 100, 132.
2. Françoise Foster-Hahn, Stanford 1972, 85.
3. Foster-Hahn, Stanford 1972, 85.
4. New York 1983, 338.
5. New York 1985, 217-18, illus.
6. Philip Dennis Cate, New Brunswick 1978, 1.

Twentieth Century

Sir David Young Cameron
Glasgow 1865-1945 Perth

143. The Five Sisters, York Minster 1907.
Etching and drypoint on Japanese paper, 39.1 x 18.1 cm (platemark). Rinder 397 iv/iv.
Signed in plate lower left: *D.Y. Cameron*; signed with pencil lower right margin: *D.Y. Cameron*.
Provenance: (Purchased from Schwartz Galleries, New York, November 18, 1930, for $3,960).
Bequest of Herbert Greer French, 1943.728.

The work of James McNeill Whistler and Sir Francis Seymour Haden created an interest and enthusiasm for etching that reached an all-time high during the first three decades of the twentieth century. To meet the demands of collectors, artists like Sir David Young Cameron, Sir Muirhead Bone, and James McBey produced a steady flow of work until England felt the effects of the stock market crash in 1929.[1]

Cameron was one of the most prominent etchers of this period. The third son of the reverend Robert Cameron, he was born in Glasgow, Scotland, in 1865. At age sixteen, he left the Glasgow Academy to work in the office of a local iron foundry. To satisfy his creative needs, he attended daily classes before and after work at the Glasgow School of Art, one of the most liberal schools in Britain. Cameron soon befriended those students who rebelled against the tradition of the Academy. In 1885 he quit his job at the foundry and enrolled full time in the Edinburgh School of Art, becoming a member of the Scottish Atelier Society later that same year.

Impressed with Cameron's pen-and-ink drawings, George Stevenson, a good friend of Seymour Haden's, encouraged him to try etching in 1887. As his only instructor,[2] Stevenson, like Haden, was an avid print collector who gave his students the unique opportunity to study fine printmaking. By 1889 Cameron had matured as an artist and was elected an associate, and later a fellow, of the Royal Society of Painter-Etchers. By the time he resigned in 1903 over a disagreement concerning the display of reproductive prints, Cameron had exhibited more than one hundred twenty etchings at the Royal Society.

For his subject matter and technique, David Young Cameron was inspired by Haden and Whistler as well as the architectural renderings of the great French etcher Charles Meryon (cat. 123). The gloomy, dark shadows that are characteristic of many of Meryon's prints can especially be seen in *The Five Sisters, York Minster* from 1907. With its well-defined clustered columns, magnificent space of the transept and Gothic arch, and glimmering lancet windows, the entire composition can be viewed as an elaborate extension of the doorway series Whistler created in Venice.

The Five Sisters window, built around 1280 as part of the north transept of York Minster, is considered by many to be the *pièce de résistance* of the entire cathedral. The slender lancets, fifty-three feet high and only five feet wide, are filled with the finest grouping of thirteenth-century grisaille glass in Europe.[3] By treating the entire wall of the transept as a unit, the window led the way to the great traceried windows of the late Gothic style in England.[4]

Throughout his career, Cameron etched a considerable number of cathedral interiors. W. P. Robins wrote in the 1931 edition of *The Print-Collector's Bulletin* that *The Five Sisters, York Minster* was his masterpiece: "The tremendous effect of height and suggestion of the glorious colour of the stained glass place the print among the finest modern etchings."[5]

The Museum's print is a very fine impression in the fourth state. Printed on thin Japanese paper, Cameron's effective use of drypoint throughout the area of the arch and the additional burnishing around the upper windows create a variety of subtle lighting effects that filter through the murky haze of the transept. The group of figures at the base of *The Five Sisters* increases the scale of the window considerably, intensifying the spiritual quality of the scene. According to Frank Rinder, in his catalogue raisonné of Cameron's etchings,

in the art of stained glass, it has been said, man fashions the form into which God breathes the life. Something of that activity was

Cameron's when, as an image of aspiration, he etched the light-suffused window in the north transept of York Minster.[6]

– DK

1. Because of the demand, prices for Cameron's prints were generally high. Mr. French purchased *The Five Sisters, York Minster* in 1930 for $3960. This was more than he paid for Dürer's *Melencolia I* ($2700) and *St. Jerome in His Study* ($2800) the previous year. In total Mr. French acquired ten prints by this popular contemporary printmaker.

2. According to Frank Rinder, "Mr. Stevenson did not confine himself to counsel and encouragement, for, though the fact be not generally known, he actually worked upon many of the early plates, including some of the 'Clyde Set' (nos. 30-49) and helped with the biting." See Frank Rinder, *D. Y. Cameron: An Illustrated Catalogue of His Etchings and Drypoints, 1887-1932* (Glasgow: Jackson, Wylie and Company, 1932), xxxii.

3. Wim Swaan, *The Gothic Cathedral* (New York: Park Lane, 1981), 208. "The legend repeated in 'Nicholas Nickelby' that five maiden embroidery-workers made the designs and sent them abroad to be carried out in glass cannot be credited." See Rinder, *D. Y. Cameron*, 217.

4. Peter Kidson, Peter Murray, and Paul Thompson, *A History of English Architecture* (Middlesex: Pelican Books, 1965), 91.

5. *The Print-Collector's Bulletin: An Illustrated Catalogue for Museums and Collectors* (New York: M. Knoedler and Company, 1931), 117.

6. Rinder, *D. Y. Cameron*, xlv.

Sir David Young Cameron

Glasgow 1865-1945 Perth

144. Ben Ledi 1911.

Etching and drypoint on Japanese paper, 37.9 x 30.0 cm (platemark).
Rinder 424 i/iii.
Signed in plate lower right: D.Y.C.; signed with pencil in lower right margin: *D.Y. Cameron*.
Provenance: (Purchased from M. Knoedler, New York, September 15, 1930, for $4,500).
Bequest of Herbert Greer French, 1943.732.

David Young Cameron's printmaking oeuvre falls basically into two main categories: architecture and landscape. Although his reputation was established primarily through his architectural images, many historians feel that Cameron's most creative work can be found in his landscape etchings and drypoints. Malcolm Salaman, for example, in his introduction on Cameron for the *Modern Masters of Etching* series, states that the artist's "interpretation of landscape offers fuller scope for the authentic expression of his artistic self than his presentation of any building."[1] Cameron began the first of his many landscape prints in 1888 with *Speyside*, a sharply defined rendering of a stream and wooded banks. The second state of this plate, completed four years later, shows a definite "change of attitude" and an indication of the direction he was hoping to follow. Experimenting with his subject matter and feeling that his approach "had to be somewhat ruthless in character,"[2] Cameron added heavy drypoint lines to the trees and rushes, giving the composition a much freer and more expressive quality. *A Lowland River: A Dry-Point* and *Landscape with Trees: A Dry-Point*, two other landscape prints completed in 1892, were likewise emotional interpretations, both focusing on an interplay between light and dark patterns.

Cameron worked on this approach periodically during the next two decades. Although he would later become one of the most popular etchers in the early part of the twentieth century,[3] initial demand for his prints was low. As a result, many of Cameron's plates during this particular period show the restraints of commissioned work. Nonetheless, *The Vale of Clyde* (1898) and especially *Elcho on the Tay* (1900) are two examples of his continued

experimentation and search for a personal and more emotional response to the landscape setting.

In 1911 Cameron made an important advance in this direction when he produced the abstract rendering *Ben Ledi*, a composition again balanced by the opposing forces of light and dark. At the turn of the century, he decided to return to his native Scotland and take up permanent residence in Kippen, a town ten miles out of Stirling. His new home, where Cameron more than likely executed this plate, was situated high above the Firth of Forth[4] and had a remarkable view of Ben Ledi and the outposts of the Highlands. The name Ben Ledi, Gaelic for "Hill of God," is said "to have originated in the Beltane mysteries celebrated on its summit on the first day of May."[5]

The Museum has an excellent first state impression of *Ben Ledi* on thin Japanese paper. In the second state, Cameron would divide the lower portion of the oblong shadow on the water to the right and add drypoint lines throughout. The heads of the grasses were added in the lower right foreground in the third state. Because Cameron was influenced by the work of Rembrandt, it is quite possible that a print such as *The Three Trees* (cat. 81) was his inspiration for this landscape. Through an aggressive and vigorous use of etched and drypoint lines, he shifted the focus of the composition to its abstract patterns and shapes. Specific details, such as the row of trees and houses in the midground, become secondary objects, visible only after a more serious study of the overall scene.

Ben Ledi has often been regarded as Cameron's attempt to bring out "a truer sense of his personality." Hind feels that the print "reflects the very essence of Cameron's genius." He further states that

> the noble simplicity of design at once compels admiration, but this is but a part of its lasting allure, which consists equally in the subtle beauties of detail, richly spread, but veiled with the unerring instinct of a master of harmony.[6]

– DK

1. Malcolm C. Salaman, *Modern Masters of Etching: Sir D.Y. Cameron, R.A.* (London: The Studio, 1925), 1-2.

2. Frank Rinder, *D.Y. Cameron: An Illustrated Catalogue of His Etchings and Drypoints, 1887-1932* (Glasgow: Jackson, Wylie and Company, 1932), xlvi.

3. Cameron's prints were extremely popular between 1910 and 1930. Individual impressions generally sold in London for several hundred pounds. See Robert H. Getscher, "David Young Cameron" in *The Stamp of Whistler* (Oberlin: Oberlin College, 1977), 232. On several occasions, Mr. French paid more for a Cameron print than he did for a Rembrandt or Dürer.

4. The Firth of Forth is an inlet of the North Sea extending about fifty miles into southeastern Scotland.

5. Rinder, *D.Y. Cameron*, 237.

6. Arthur M. Hind, *The Etchings of D.Y. Cameron* (London: Halton and Truscott Smith, Ltd., 1924), 28.

James McBey

Newmill 1883-1959 Tangier

145. The Pianist 1920.

Drypoint on laid paper, 17.6 x 32.9 cm (platemark).
Hardie 190 vii/vii (British edition).
Watermark: indecipherable.
Signed and dated in plate lower left: *McBEY 28 February 1920*; inscribed with pen and ink lower left margin: III; signed lower right: *James McBey*.
Provenance: (Purchased from Albert Roullier, Chicago, March 16, 1927, for $675).
Bequest of Herbert Greer French, 1943.738.
Exhibitions: Cincinnati 1930, (no. 39).

In 1916, after several successful years as an etcher, James McBey was ordered to report to France to begin military service. Despite wartime regulations that prohibited outdoor sketching, McBey continued to secretly collect ideas for his plates by making thumbnail notes, doodling on the palm of his hand, and even drawing on the inside of his coat pocket.[1] After hearing that David Cameron, Muirhead Bone, and several of his other colleagues had been hired as "official artists," McBey decided to take his next leave drawing at the front. Documenting the tragedy of war in five plates, his etchings invariably led to his appointment as Official Artist in Egypt by the war office in the summer of 1917. Throughout the following year, McBey traced the history of the Palestine campaign as well as his experiences with the Australian Camel Patrol. Selections of this work were then included in three sets of etchings published yearly from 1920 to 1923.

After the war ended and the "First Palestine Set" was published, McBey spent some quiet time in London in his new Holland Park Avenue studio, where he turned his attention to portraiture.[2] Using his close friends Dr. and Mrs. William Murray and their daughter Margot as subjects, he produced three rather sedate images in 1920 titled *The Silk Dress*, *Margot as Lopokova*, and *Margot*. With *The Pianist*, however, a fourth print in the series, McBey discovered a renewed sense of vigor and created what many considered to be one of his most expressive works. In fact, Martin Hardie, in his catalogue raisonné, *Etchings and Dry Points from 1902 to 1924 by James McBey*, feels that McBey had never been "so happy in rhythm and balance of design, or so quick and sure in rapid presentment of his subject" as he was in *The Pianist*. Hardie even went so far as to call this print "the pinnacle of McBey's achievements."[3]

The Pianist shows Dr. Murray relaxing in a chair at the end of a grand piano. Seated upright on the arm of a settee is his wife. Both of them are obviously enjoying a number being played by Benno Schonberger, a distinguished-looking man with gray hair who was also a friend of the Murrays and McBey. Printed on an antique laid paper that McBey was very fond of using,[4] the Museum's impression is extremely fine. The quality of the drypoint lines, especially in the forced diagonal and vertical zigzags of Dr. Murray's coat, the side of the grand piano, and Benno Schonberger's arms and hands, creates a blurred yet extremely rich surface texture that gives the illusion of rhythm and movement. We can virtually see Schonberger's fingers moving rapidly up and down the keyboard while Dr. Murray sways melodically to the beat. Because McBey admired the work of Rembrandt and Whistler, *The Pianist* has a free and spontaneous style that is both aggressive and powerful.

James McBey was born in Newmill, a small fishing village near Aberdeen, Scotland. At fifteen, he was hired as a clerk in the Aberdeen branch of the North of Scotland Bank. He perfected his drawing skills during his free time and read as many books on art as possible. One book in particular, Maxime Lalanne's *Traité de la gravure a l'eau-forte* (translated by S. R. Koehler) aroused his interest in etching. By the time McBey was seventeen, he was pulling proofs from pieces of unpolished plumber's copper. During this first phase of his career, which lasted until he left the bank in 1910, McBey produced sixty prints that focused on his experiences in both Aberdeen and Edinburgh. It was at this time that he made the first of two trips to Holland to visit the land of Rembrandt. Inspired by the windmills, canals, and beautiful skies, McBey produced a Dutch series consisting of twenty-one etchings. After briefly returning to Scotland in 1911, he became more adventuresome and traveled to Spain; later the next year, he journeyed to Morocco in search of new ideas and subject matter.

The year 1911 marked a turning point in McBey's career. His first exhibition, consisting of fifty-five prints, was held at the gallery of

Messrs. Goupil & Co. in London. The show was a critical and financial success. With all this attention, McBey quickly became a major force in the field of etching, reaching the height of his fame in the late 1920s, when his prints sold for extremely high prices. Mr. French was very fond of McBey's work and acquired eleven prints for his collection between 1926-28, paying as much as $1850 for the etching *Gamrie* (CAM 1943.744). He bought *The Pianist* in 1927 for $675, considerably more than he paid for Rembrandt's *Self Portrait with Raised Sabre* (CAM 1943.305) ($485) and *Second Oriental Head* (CAM 1943.306) ($339), both purchased the same year. – DK

1. McBey was obviously very cautious this time around because he had gotten into what could have been serious trouble for sketching out of doors two years before. Several weeks after World War I began, he traveled to northern England, where there were no drawing restrictions. After sketching on the coast for two hours, McBey stood up and stretched his arms. He was later arrested by the coastguard and accused of sending secret messages to an unspecified German submarine. McBey was further humiliated when he was asked if he "could speak English." See Martin Hardie, *Etchings and Dry Points from 1902 to 1924 by James McBey* (London: P. & D. Colnaghi & Co., 1925), xiv.

2. McBey first experimented with portraiture in 1912 when he etched the unpublished portraits of *Malcolm Salaman (No. 1)* and *James Torn Reid*. Over the next few years his output in this area, which was extremely sporadic, consisted of *Christmas Card*, 1913; *Disquietude (Portrait of Mrs. Martin Hardie)*, 1914; *Portrait of Martin Hardie (No. 1)*, 1915; *Portrait of Malcom Salaman (No. 2)*, 1915; *Portrait of Frank Gibson*, 1915; *Disraeli*, 1916; and *Portrait of Martin Hardie (No. 2)*, 1916.

3. Hardie, *Etchings*, xvi-xvii.

4. The paper used for the Museum's impression of *The Pianist* contains a watermark that is indecipherable. McBey was an avid collector of antique paper because "it had qualities of tone and texture and durability that made it desirable for printing." He once stated that "the skin of old paper has become soft and velvety, due to the action of time on the surface size, while the strength of the actual paper has not been impaired." His collection consisted of sheets from Holland, Rouen, Egypt, the slums of Barcelona, and Toledo as well as the back rooms of London bookstores. Hardie, *Etchings*, xx.

Pablo Ruiz Picasso
Málaga 1881-1973 Mougins

146. The Three Graces, II 1923.
Etching on wove paper, 32.5 x 19.7 cm (platemark).
Bloch 59; Geiser 105b.
Watermark: Indecipherable fragment.
Signed and numbered with pencil in lower right margin:
25/100 Picasso.
Provenance: (Purchased from Albert Roullier, Chicago, January 2, 1941, for $83).
Bequest of Herbert Greer French, 1943.811.

In 1899, at the age of eighteen, Picasso executed his first etching, *Le Zurdo (The Left Handed Man)*, a picador with his lance in his left rather than his right hand, betraying a typical beginner's mistake by not realizing that the image on the plate would reverse left to right.[1] During the first three-quarters of the twentieth century Picasso executed approximately twenty-five hundred prints, employing a wide spectrum of technical means, from etching and aquatint to lithography and linoleum cut. He used printmaking both as a means to explore themes and ideas in depth and as a major vehicle of his oeuvre.

Pablo Ruiz Picasso was born in Málaga on October 25, 1881. He was the first child of Don José Ruiz Blasco, a painter and drawing instructor, and Doña Maria Picasso y Lopéz. Although he began his instruction as his father's pupil (1888), he later studied drawing and painting in La Coruña (1891-95), Barcelona (1895-97), and Madrid (1897). In the winter of 1897, he abandoned further academic study.

He had his first Parisian exhibition in 1901 at the Galeries Vollard and became part of the Spanish bohemian set. He did not take up printmaking again until he settled in Paris in 1904. In September 1904 he executed *Le Repas frugal (The Frugal Repast)* (Bloch 1), his first etched masterpiece. In this early etching, Picasso confronted the brutal reality of loneliness and the blindness of one human being to the suffering of another. He worked in Auguste Delâtre's workshop, where at least two impressions of this etching were printed in the blue tones so pervasive in his paintings of the period. Fifteen of Picasso's etching and drypoint plates executed between the end of 1904 and 1906 were acquired by Ambroise Vollard and published in 1914 in an edition known as *La Suite des Saltimbanques* (Bloch 1-15).

There are no prints related to Picasso's famous paintings *Les Demoiselles d'Avignon* (1907), now in the Museum of Modern Art, and *Three Women* (1908), now in the Hermitage Museum. Although he acquired a small handpress in 1907 to proof his images as they progressed through various states, it took two years to master the new pictorial vocabulary of analytical cubism, which he and Georges Braque invented.[2] Picasso's experimental prints executed between 1907 and 1914 interpret faceting, overlapping, and dissolving planes, ambiguous space, and shifting perspective. The declaration of war in 1914 dispersed his artist friends and cut short his experiments. During World War I, Picasso developed a style of simple linear elegance, which pays homage to the paintings of Ingres. This "classical" style alternated with his cubist mode until 1917, when the classic overtook the cubist.

In 1917 Picasso traveled to Rome, where he designed the sets and costumes for Diaghilev's ballet *Parade*. His visit to Italy had a profound effect on his career. He had the opportunity to study the great frescoes of the High Renaissance and ancient Roman murals from Herculaneum and Pompeii. Once exposed to the antique, he was attracted to his predecessors whose style conformed to a similar classical ethos. At the same time, his involvement with the ballet and his marriage to the Ingresque dancer Olga Koklova in 1918 revived his appreciation for graceful human movement.

The antique trinity of the three Graces and the theme of three women appear frequently in Picasso's drawings and prints circa 1922-23. He did not literally quote the ancient configuration of heraldically posed nudes whose center figure has her back to the viewer and whose two side figures face forward.[3] He would have seen this iconography on Greek vases, Roman sarcophagi, and Renaissance sepulchral sculpture. Hesiod's *Theogony* describes the three Greek Charities as youthful goddesses who bestowed pleasure and benefit on nature and society: fertility and growth, beauty in the arts, and harmonious reciprocity among men. He identified them as the daughters of Zeus and Eurynome, naming them Aglaia (Beauty), Euphrosyne (Mirth), and Thalia (Abundance). In Picasso's etching, the three Charities, or Graces as they were called by the Romans, are without their vegetative attributes.

Picasso's classical borrowings and his debt to ancient art and mythology are hard to assess because of his talented inventions and interpretations. As stated earlier, while Picasso did not copy the heraldic pose, he used its inspiration as a means to explore figural and compositional relationships. His three-figure compositions began in 1908 with a series of studies for a painting, *Three Women* (1908). He returned to the subject in 1923, executing four prints (Bloch 58-61) and seven drawings during a summer in Antibes (Zervos 98-104). In these compositions he inverted the ancient heraldic relationship so that the central figure faces the viewer in a setting implied by a single horizon line.[4]

In *The Three Graces, II*, Picasso's sculpturesque, classically contoured goddesses represent an exquisite variation on the theme of feminine relationships. During the following decades, this subject would reappear in groupings of two, three and four women. Although this plate was executed circa 1922-23, it was not editioned until 1929.[5]

Between 1927 and 1933 Picasso spent a major portion of his time on book illustrations: his classic linear style is still evident in his illustrations for Honoré Balzac's *Le Chef-d'Oeuvre Inconnu* (1931) (Bloch 82-94) and *Les Métamorphoses d'Ovide* (1931) (Bloch 99-128) and reached its lyrical culmination in *The Suite Vollard* (1930-37) (Bloch 134-233).

From traditional beginnings, Picasso went on in the 1930s to exploit prodigiously the expressive possibilities latent in various graphic media. In 1935 the printer Roger Lacourière taught Picasso the painterly sugar-lift aquatint technique, which he used in 1941-42 with great verve for Buffon's *L'Histoire naturalle* (Bloch 328-58). That same year he created his masterpiece *Minotauromachy* (Bloch 288). His graphic output was disrupted by the Spanish civil war, during which he painted *Guernica*, and World War II. In the postwar years, beginning in 1945, he took up lithography in the workshop of Fernand Mourlot. Between 1955 and 1963 he tackled the linoleum cut, inventing a unique one-block color method. Over the decades he sustained an interest in the potential of various intaglio techniques, executing in 1968 at the age of eighty-seven with dazzling brio his *347 Suite* (Bloch 1481-1827).

Throughout the years the important women in Picasso's life, beginning with Olga, Marie-Térèse Walter, Dora Maar, Françoise Gilot and ending with Jacqueline, have played important roles as models and muses both real and symbolic. The vital creative force of Picasso's fertile invention, his dizzy virtuosity, and fluent execution, coupled with his unique affinity, comprehension, and love for plate, stone, and block, made him one of the great printmakers of our time. – KLS

1. Geiser 1.
2. Bernard Geiser, Los Angeles 1966, 12.
3. Nancy Lodge Webbe, "The Three Graces in Renaissance Art: Origins and Transformations of a Theme," (Ph.D. diss., Boston University, 1986), 9.
4. Bloch 58-62; Christian Zervos, *Pablo Picasso* (Paris: Editions Cahiers d'Art, 1952), vol. 5, nos. 98-104.
5. Geiser no. 105. The plate was printed by Leblanc and Trautmann for Édition Marcel Guiot.

Frederick Landseer Griggs
Hitchin 1876-1938 Campden

147. The Almonry 1925.
Etching on antique laid paper, 24.5 x 17.0 cm (platemark).
Comstock 34 v/vii.
Signed in plate lower right: FLG; signed with pencil lower right margin: *LFGriggs*; verso stamped in black: DHP (Dover House Press in ligature).
Provenance: (Purchased from Albert Roullier, Chicago, April 9, 1927, for $675).
Bequest of Herbert Greer French, 1943.758.
Exhibitions: Cincinnati 1930, (no. 25); Cincinnati 1934, no. 100.

Born in Hitchin, Hertfordshire, Frederick Landseer Griggs formed an early interest in drawing, influenced very possibly by his maternal grandfather, Thomas Houghton Bailey, an amateur painter.[1] He was educated at the Bancroft House School and given private lessons in art by a local architect and watercolorist. When not in school, Griggs spent his free time studying Old Master prints in the library of Lawson Thompson, an avid print collector and self-taught art

historian. It was the work as well as the philosophy of Samuel
Palmer, however, whose book illustrations Griggs discovered at the
Hitchin Mechanics Institute, that would prove most influential to his
career. Like Palmer, Griggs felt strongly about "the inseparability of
the arts from true civilisation. And his passion for creation was
equalled by his passion for preservation."[2] By remaining in Hitchin
for the first twenty-eight years of his life, he became extremely
devoted to his small town, the countryside, and its architecture.

Griggs initially experimented with printmaking in 1896. Not
having access to proper equipment, however, left him somewhat
dissatisfied with the process. As a result, he didn't pick up a
copperplate again until 1912. Turning his attention to architecture
instead, Griggs spent the next two years studying under the tutelage
of Charles Edward Mallows, a well-respected architect and
draftsman in the area. Mallows and several of Griggs' friends,
including Joseph Pennell, were so impressed with his drawing skills
that they encouraged him to abandon architecture for a career in
painting and illustration. Following their advice, Griggs spent the
next several years working on commissions from architectural
journals, books, and magazines. His drawings for thirteen volumes
of *Highways and Byways*, which he worked on from 1902 until
1918, gained him praise and notoriety. Traveling from town to town
throughout the duration of the project did much to deepen his
knowledge and love of the English countryside and its architecture.
Griggs' etchings would later echo his belief that Gothic art was "the
truest expression of all that mediaeval England stood for. . . [and] the
nearest approach to perfection which civilisation has yet seen."[3]

This devotion to the noble achievements of the past struck a
responsive chord with the public when *The Almonry* was exhibited
at the Royal Society of Painter-Etchers and Engravers in 1925. Its
appealing holiday sentiment, together with Griggs' superb handling
of the etched line, made this his most popular print. The partial view
of the snow-covered cathedral, the lady chapel, chapter room, and
almonry are all variations by Griggs of church architecture in
England as it may have appeared during the fifteenth century.
Several singers and musicians are performing in a courtyard that
overlooks a river. Walking across a bridge to the left is a woman
carrying a child and a man with a bag full of gifts, the latter
presumably to be received in the almonry on the right. Griggs
worked long hours on the plate, taking it through a number of states
and later claiming that it was "coaxed and cajoled and patted and
stroked until I got the wintry atmosphere I wanted."[4]

The Museum's impression, on antique laid paper, is the fifth of
seven states. Griggs focused much of his attention on the roof lines:
lowering ridges, modeling the snow, and adding a series of faint lines
to create an illusion of gray. In this state, he changed the roof over
the entrance to the almonry, which had previously been straight, and
sloped it downward half-way to the margin. With an expressive use
of close cross-hatching, a strong foreground motif, and the delicate
etching of the cathedral, Griggs created a brisk, serene midday
environment that appropriately fit the mood of the Christmas
season.

Frederick Landseer Griggs was a multifaceted artist. Although he
is noted primarily for his etchings and book illustrations, he was also
actively involved with building and furniture design, the latter with
his friend Ernest Gimson. In addition, Griggs created the designs for
bookplates, needlework, altar furnishings, typefaces, and several
outdoor sculptures, to name just a few of his accomplishments. In
recognition of his artistic achievements, he was elected an associate
member and fellow of the Royal Society of Painter-Etchers and
Engravers in 1916 and 1918, respectively. In 1920 Griggs was invited
to be a member of the Society of the Royal Council and, in the same
year, joined the Council of the Graphic Art Society. After his election

as associate engraver by the Royal Academy in 1922, he was finally
elevated to the status of royal academician in 1931. – DK

1. For a detailed account of Griggs' life as an artist see Comstock.
2. Comstock, 2.
3. Harold J. L. Wright, *The Etched Work of F. L. Griggs* (London: The Print
Collectors' Club, 1941), 10.
4. Letter to Russell Alexander, July 27, 1925, in Comstock, 157.

James McBey
Newmill 1883-1959 Tangier

148. Barcarole 1926.
Etching and drypoint on pale blue laid paper, 37.6 x 21.3 cm
(platemark).
Hardie 233 (American edition of 20).
Watermark: Strasburg bend and lily.
Signed and dated in plate at lower left: *McBey Venice September
1925*; inscribed with pen and ink lower left margin: A1; signed lower
right margin: *James McBey*.
Provenance: (Purchased from M. Knoedler, New York, September
12, 1927, for $1,310).
Bequest of Herbert Greer French, 1943.737.
Exhibitions: Cincinnati 1930, (no. 40); Cincinnati 1934, no. 97.

James McBey reached the height of his etching career in the late
1920s.[1] His most important work during this period consisted of
thirty-two plates made after an extensive stay in Venice in 1925.
Having greatly admired the work of both Rembrandt and Whistler
and having already visited Rembrandt's homeland, he felt compelled
to see Venice, the mysterious city of canals and palaces that Whistler
had so beautifully portrayed in his prints.

While in Venice, McBey preferred working in the early hours of
the morning or late at night, when normally harsh details were often
hazy and indistinct and when the atmosphere, or climate, was more
conducive to his spontaneous style of etching. He was often seen
sketching at the end of the Rialto, at a table in the Piazzetta, or in a
gondola on the canals, using several tallow candles in an old tin
when it became too dark to see his drawing paper or copperplate.[2]

Several of the prints in the Venice series show McBey's strong
devotion to Whistler. *Barcarole*, in particular, with its slashing
drypoint lines, angular composition, and manipulated plate tone,
borrows heavily from Whistler's *Nocturne: Palaces*. McBey did not
like Whistler's method of printing his images in reverse, a situation
that resulted from working directly on copper. In an attempt to
avoid this problem and to achieve exact topographical accuracy,
McBey set up his composition in a rearview mirror that he
conveniently took from an automobile and attached to his drawing
board.

According to Martin Hardie, McBey's *Barcarole* portrays "the
very soul and spirit of Venice, its moonlight and mystery, its poetry
and romance."[3] The title of the print is very appropriate. The
barcarole is the traditional song of the Venetian gondolier, a song
that has a rhythm suggestive of rowing. Here, as the gondola moves
slowly round the bend of the canal, one can imagine the sound of the
gondolier's melodic voice as it echoes off the palace walls. In the
Museum's impression, the effect of the soft moonlit glow is further
enhanced by the rich burr of the drypoint as it yields itself to the
surface of the pale blue antique paper. McBey was fond of the
warmth, sensitivity, and variations often found in "the skin of old
paper,"[4] and throughout his career, he collected different papers
during his many travels. The laid paper he selected for the Museum's

Barcarole has a watermark that is partially visible and appears to be a variation of the Strasburg bend and lily.

Charles Carter, director of the Aberdeen Art Gallery, feels that McBey's Venetian plates were the "consummation of his career as an etcher, his last major achievement in the medium." This assessment is accurate primarily because of the American Depression, which virtually put an end to the etching boom. McBey, nonetheless, had already turned his attention to painting in the mid-1920s and, as a result, made very few prints during the remaining years of his life.[5] In 1931 he married Marguerite Loeb of Philadelphia and ten years later became an American citizen. He spent his remaining years not only in America but also in his London studio on Holland Park Avenue and especially at his home in Tangier, where he died in 1959. – DK

1. Mr. French purchased eleven McBey prints between 1926-28.

2. For more information concerning McBey's Venetian period, see Martin Hardie, "The Etched Work of James McBey, 1925-1937," with a catalogue, PCQ. 25, no. 4 (December 1938): 421-45.

3. Hardie, "The Etched Work," 429.

4. Martin Hardie, *Etchings and Dry Points from 1902 to 1924 by James McBey* (London: P. & D. Colnaghi & Co., 1925), xx.

5. As McBey got older, it not only became more difficult for him to etch a plate, but after America entered the war, copper was soon in short supply. See Charles Carter, *Etchings and Dry Points from 1924 by James McBey* (Aberdeen: Aberdeen Art Gallery, 1962), xiv-xv.

Martin Lewis

Castlemaine, Australia 1881-1962 New York

149. Subway Steps 1930.

Drypoint on wove paper, 34.5 x 20.8 cm (platemark).
McCarron 96.
Signed in plate lower left: MARTIN LEWIS; signed with pencil in lower right margin: *Martin Lewis-*.
Provenance: (Purchased from Kennedy, New York, December 1, 1932, for $27).
Bequest of Herbert Greer French, 1943.788.

Today we recognize Martin Lewis as an urban regionalist who captured with stop action precision the drama of street life in a modern megalopolis. He had no peer on either side of the Atlantic when interpreting the dynamic pulse, fleeting moods, and picturesque moments of New York. He came to his adopted city from halfway around the globe by way of a variety of experiences. He was born in Castlemaine, Australia, on June 7, 1881. Running away from home at the age of fifteen, he supported himself with various jobs as he traveled and sketched in the outback, New South Wales, and New Zealand, before settling in a bohemian colony overlooking Sydney harbor in 1898. In Sydney he studied briefly at the Julian Ashton Art School before emigrating to America. When he arrived in San Francisco in 1900 his first job was painting decorations for William McKinley's presidential campaign. He had worked and sketched his way to New York City by 1901, where he pursued a successful career in commercial art.

During his first decade in New York, Lewis encountered several art movements that had varying degrees of influence on his painting and his future printmaking. He was exposed to the fragmented strokes and broken color of the American impressionists; the filmy light and dreamy mood of the tonalists; and the realist depictions of the ashcan school, whose landmark exhibition of New York people and life took place at the MacBeth Gallery in 1908. Particularly germane to Lewis' early prints were the soft focus and painterly technique of the photo secession photographers under the leadership of Alfred Stieglitz. American printmakers between the two world wars had little interest in the European avant-garde, preferring as their standard of excellence British etchers, such as Muirhead Bone, David Cameron, and James McBey, and the earlier continental printmakers Alphonse Legros and Charles Meryon and their successor Jean-Louis Forain. Perhaps it was his 1910 trip to England and Wales that inspired him to take up printmaking. A self-taught printmaker, Lewis executed 146 prints between 1915 and 1940. His first print, *Smoke Pillar, Weehawken* (1915), was a success. Edward Hopper asked him for etching tips. Between 1915 and 1919, Lewis experimented with etching, aquatint, mezzotint, and drypoint. Lewis' printmaking activity was interrupted in 1920 by a two-year painting and sketching sojourn to Japan, which had a significant impact on his aesthetic development. The Japanese trip enhanced his appreciation and understanding of genre subjects. He undoubtedly studied Japanese *ukiyo-e* prints, particularly the color woodcuts of Hiroshige. From this time forward he adopted a tight compositional formula that incorporated diagonal recession, asymmetrical arrangement, and rhythmic design. He modulated this rigorous structure with light and atmosphere. By the time he resumed printmaking in 1925, he had abandoned impressionism, tonalism, and pictorialism in favor of greater realism.

One of the first New York galleries to promote British printmakers regularly alongside of contemporary American artists was Kennedy and Company. Lewis was one of the earliest artists that Kennedy promoted. Kennedy exhibited his watercolors in 1926 and 1927 and his prints in 1928. In 1929 the gallery mounted a major retrospective of Lewis' work in all media, which attracted wide critical acclaim. At the same time Kennedy began to publish prints by Lewis. One of the sixteen prints Kennedy published was *Subway Steps*. It reveals the rich, resonant vocabulary of drypoint line and burr that Lewis exploited almost exclusively after 1925 through the sensitive manipulation of pressure, angle, and tool. Steelfacing permitted Lewis the freedom to explore drypoint beyond the

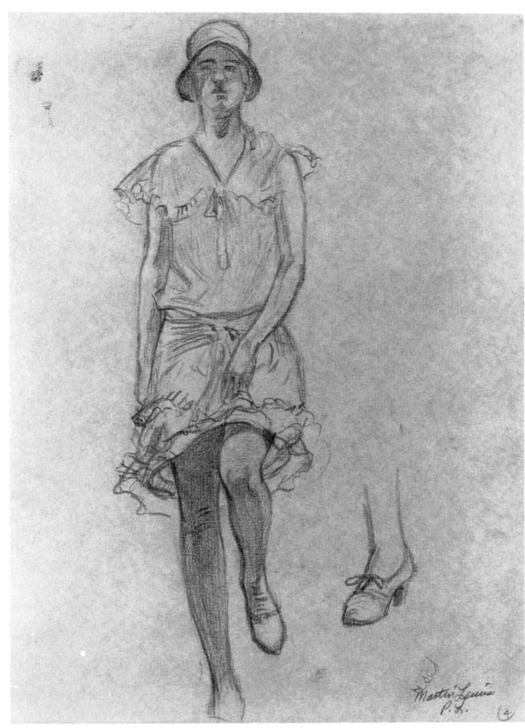

Figure 149-1. Martin Lewis, study for *Subway Steps*, ca. 1930, pencil and orange pastel on green paper. The Detroit Institute of Arts, promised gift of Mr. and Mrs. Robert M. Katzman in honor of Sidney and Betty Katzman and their children, Ellen and Laura, from the collection assembled by Patricia Lewis.

Figure 149-2. Martin Lewis, *Subway Steps*, 1930, drypoint, McCarron 96 i. The Detroit Institute of Arts, promised gift of Mr. and Mrs. Robert M. Katzman in honor of Sidney and Betty Katzman and their children, Ellen and Laura, from the collection assembled by Patricia Lewis.

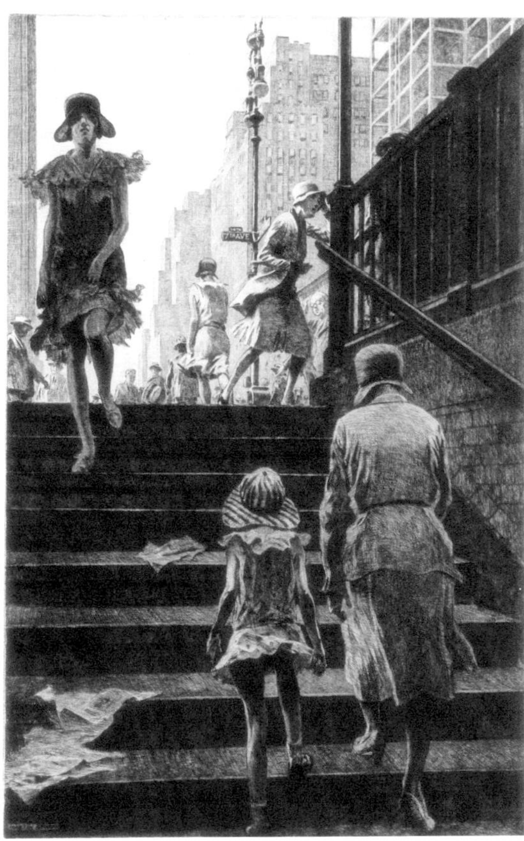

traditional parameters of the medium by allowing him to overlay successive layers of lines, patterns, and textures that he might or might not burnish away.

Lewis frequently made separate drawings of individual figures and settings. Two preparatory drawings exist for *Subway Steps*. A drawing of the woman coming down the steps (fig. 149-1) has been recently made a promised gift to the Detroit Institute of Arts,[1] and a pencil study of the girl climbing the steps (fig. 149-2) was sold by the June 1 Gallery in 1984.[2] Recently there appeared on the market an impression of the plate before it was cut down 1.9 cm. This rare first state carried this inscription: "Trial proof – No. 2 before cutting plate – additional work on farther buildings – changed arms & hands of child also added work on figures/in foreground – /proof on Whatman paper – Frankfort black & little brn't sienna – ."[3] Comparison of the Museum's second-state impression with the first state shows that these changes had been made earlier, suggesting that there should be an earlier state. The only difference between the two states is the additional work on the upper skirt of the woman descending the stairs.

In December 1931, at the height of the Great Depression, Kennedy and Company announced the publication of five new prints by Lewis, including *Subway Steps*, at a price of thirty dollars.[4] Mr. French was one of the early subscribers. Today this drypoint is considered one of Lewis' quintessential subjects. Using a low vantage point, Lewis carefully heightened the dynamic pulse and focus of the subject when he deliberately cut down the plate. The mechanical repetition of the stairs and the diagonal thrust of the building are enlivened by the chicly dressed women ascending and descending the stairs and the windswept figures on the corner of Seventh Avenue and Thirty-fourth Street. A wizard with light dark, Lewis

manipulated the drypoint line to achieve a full scale of grays and a wide range of textures, from transparent, fluttering fabric to cold, hard cement. He further tied the subject together by the visual ascent from deep shadow into an all-pervasive light. Lewis remained a quiet observer and did not editorialize about the despair and hardships of the Depression.

However, he sold his residence and moved out of the city from 1930 to 1936 to a small town in Connecticut, where his subjects reflect a slower rural pace. In 1934 he joined forces with the lithographic printer George Miller and the printmaker Armin Landeck to open a short-lived school for printmaking on East Fourteenth Street. Upon his return to New York, he continued to execute prints on a regular basis until 1940. In 1944 he secured a teaching post at the Art Students' League, where he taught until he retired in 1951. After a decade of poor health, Lewis died in relative obscurity in 1962, his modern realism eclipsed by abstraction. Today critical reevaluation of American printmaking in the 1920s and 1930s has focused new attention on his talents. – KLS

1. The Detroit Institute of Arts, promised gift of Mr. and Mrs. Robert M. Katzman in honor of Sidney and Betty Katzman and their children Ellen and Laura, from the collection of Martin Lewis prints and drawings assembled by Patricia Lewis.

2. *Martin Lewis – American Master*, June 1 Gallery, Bethlehem, Connecticut (November-December, 1984), no. 57. According to Norman Kraeft, this drawing on orange-brown paper, 25.4 x 7.6 cm, was of the little girl. Current location unknown.

3. *Contemporary, American and Modern Prints and Illustrated Books*, Christies' New York, Sale 7348, (November 4, 1991) lot 294.

4. Kennedy and Company subscription brochure, December 1931. Artists' files, Prints Department, New York Public Library.

John Taylor Arms
Washington, D.C. 1898-1953 New York

150. Gloria Ecclesiae Antiquae 1937.
Etching on antique laid paper, 35.5 x 22.0 cm (platemark).
Arms 312 iii; Fletcher 307 iii/iv.
Watermark: ENGLAND.
Titled in plate lower center: *Gloria Ecclesiae Antiquae*; inscribed with pencil in lower left margin: III *To my friend Herbert Greer French, with deepest appreciation/John Taylor Arms-1938*; below: *"Gloria" (Church at St. Riquiar, France)./Third State, before the decorative panel with inscription was cut off*; signed lower right: *John Taylor Arms - 1938*.
Provenance: Gift of John Taylor Arms, 1938.
Bequest of Herbert Greer French, 1943.806.

The physical beauty of mass, proportion, and the balanced handling of light and shade found in the world's great structural monuments always held a special appeal for John Taylor Arms. He considered beauty as possessing universal significance, waiting to be discovered, interpreted, and shared with others. He once wrote:

> To me the Gothic represents the most spiritual and significant expression of his aspirations that man has yet created in terms of stone and glass and metal, and so for years I have followed its trail, through France and England, Italy and Spain. . . .I have not tried to express abstract ideas. . .but rather to state, in terms as lucid, comprehensive, and intelligible as lay within my power, exactly what moved me deeply. Convinced that I could not possibly create anything more beautiful than what I saw, I have tried only to recreate in my prints, that those who saw them might see it too – with me.[1]

Recognized as one of America's most eminent printmakers, Arms' career spanned nearly four decades, from 1915 until his death in 1953. His graphic work comprises 448 prints, mainly etchings and aquatints, but includes one mezzotint done in 1920 and eight lithographs done in 1921. Most of his work interprets architecture in one form or another, whether it be a gargoyle perched high on a cathedral wall, an impressive portal or facade, or an entire majestic cathedral.

Born in Washington, D.C., in 1887, Arms was the first in his family to pursue a career in art. After his graduation, he studied law at Princeton University for two years, prior to transferring to the Massachusetts Institute of Technology, where he studied with Désiré Despradelle, head of the design department of the school of architecture. A graduate of the École des Beaux-Arts, Paris, and winner of the Grand Prix de Rome, Despradelle emphasized classical designs and schooled his students in draftsmanship. Arms practiced as an architectural draftsman for two years with the New York firm Carrère and Hastings after graduating from M.I.T. with B.S. and M.S. degrees in 1911 and 1912, respectively. He formed his own architectural firm in partnership with Cameron Clark, which functioned until the outbreak of World War I. His interest in printmaking was stimulated by the purchase of a print by Ernest Lumsden and the gift of a twelve-dollar etching kit for Christmas from Dorothy Noyes, whom he married in 1913. During the war he served in the U.S. Navy as a navigation officer on convoy duty. Following his discharge in January 1919, Arms decided to make printmaking his life's work. By the time he made his first original print in 1915, the status of etching had outstripped reproductive wood engraving as an important artist medium in America. Unlike the etchings of his contemporaries John Sloan and Edward Hopper, which focused on the realities of urban American life, Arms and others, among them Samuel Chamberlain and John W. Winkler, turned from life in the industrial age to extol the hallowed architectural monuments of Europe's past. His unquestioned belief that Gothic architecture exemplified mankind's highest achievement in unifying spiritual and aesthetic values inspired Arms to begin his ambitious series of prints to record the Gothic churches of Spain, France, and Italy. The fifteen prints in his *Spanish Church Series* (1923-50) interpret the cathedrals of Burgos, Segovia, Gerona and Palencia. Arms began his *French Cathedral Series* in 1924, continually adding images throughout his lifetime for a total of fifty-five plates. The twenty-seven prints in his *Italian Series* (1925-35) depict not only churches but street scenes, hilltop towns, and Venetian locales. During the 1920s he executed 186 prints, the large majority dedicated to his "beloved Gothics." In the 1930s his printmaking continued, in spite of his new role as the foremost proselytizer for etching and printmaking in America as president of the Society of American Etchers and through numerous demonstrations, exhibitions, and publications. In 1933 and 1935 Arms lectured to the Cincinnati Print and Drawing Circle, of which Mr. French was president. Arms is the only artist from whom French acquired a print directly.

Gloria Ecclesiae Antiquae (1937) is the thirty-ninth print in the *French Church Series*. This interpretation of Saint Riquiar's highly ornate facade provides a glimpse into "the crystal-clear and logical splendor of the French mentality."[2] The Museum's impression is in the third state, prior to the removal of the panel across the bottom. Like all of Arms' etchings it is a tour de force of linear and textural detail and illusions of light and shadow. With the aid of a magnifying glass, Arms executed microscopic lines and dots with ordinary sewing needles (ranging in size from 5 to 10). In November 1937 Kennedy and Company, New York, advertised the third state in a sales brochure, along with the work of Armin Landeck and Martin

Lewis, at a price of thirty-six dollars.[3] Yet when Arms dedicated this impression to Mr. French, he dated it 1938.

Over the years Arms wrote more than fifty articles on printmaking and printmakers and in 1934 he published his influential *Handbook of Print Making and Print Makers*. Six years later he became contributing editor of *Print* magazine. During World War II, he visited Mexico and the Yucatan, but as soon as he was able, he rededicated himself to Gothic themes. In 1952, shortly before he died, Arms returned to Cincinnati and gave one of his demonstration talks. The drawing, proofs, and plate for *Abbaye de St. Paul-au-Bois* (CAM 1952.403) were gifts of the artist to the Museum. – KLS

1. John Taylor Arms, "Self Estimate," in *Twenty-One Years of Drawing: A Retrospective Exhibition of the Work of John Taylor Arms* (New York: Grand Central Art Galleries, 1938), 10.

2. S. William Pelletier, "John Taylor Arms: An American Mediaevalist," *The Georgia Review* 30, no. 4 (Winter 1976): 923.

3. Artist's file, Print Division, New York Public Library.

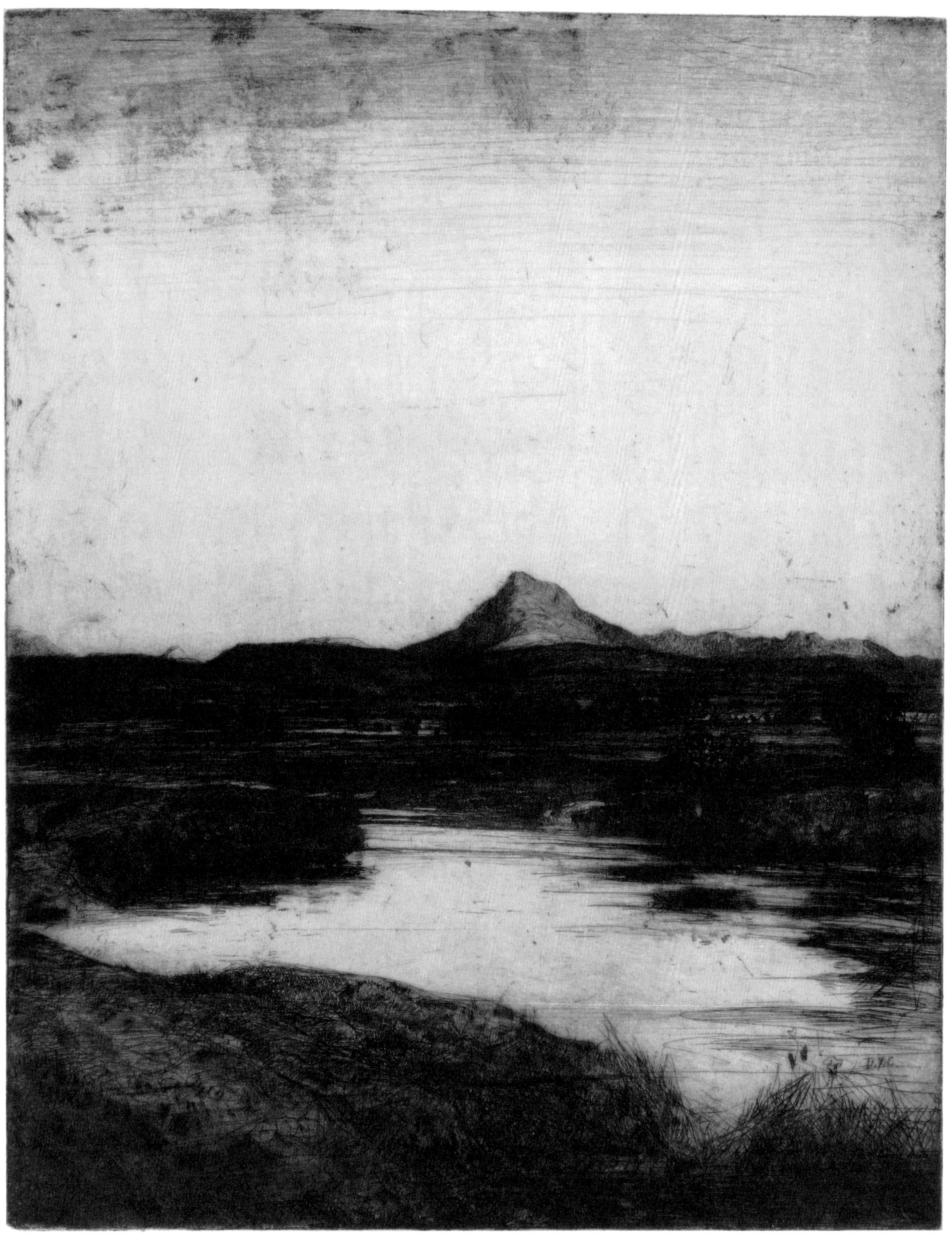

Plate 144. Sir David Young Cameron, *Ben Ledi*, 1911.

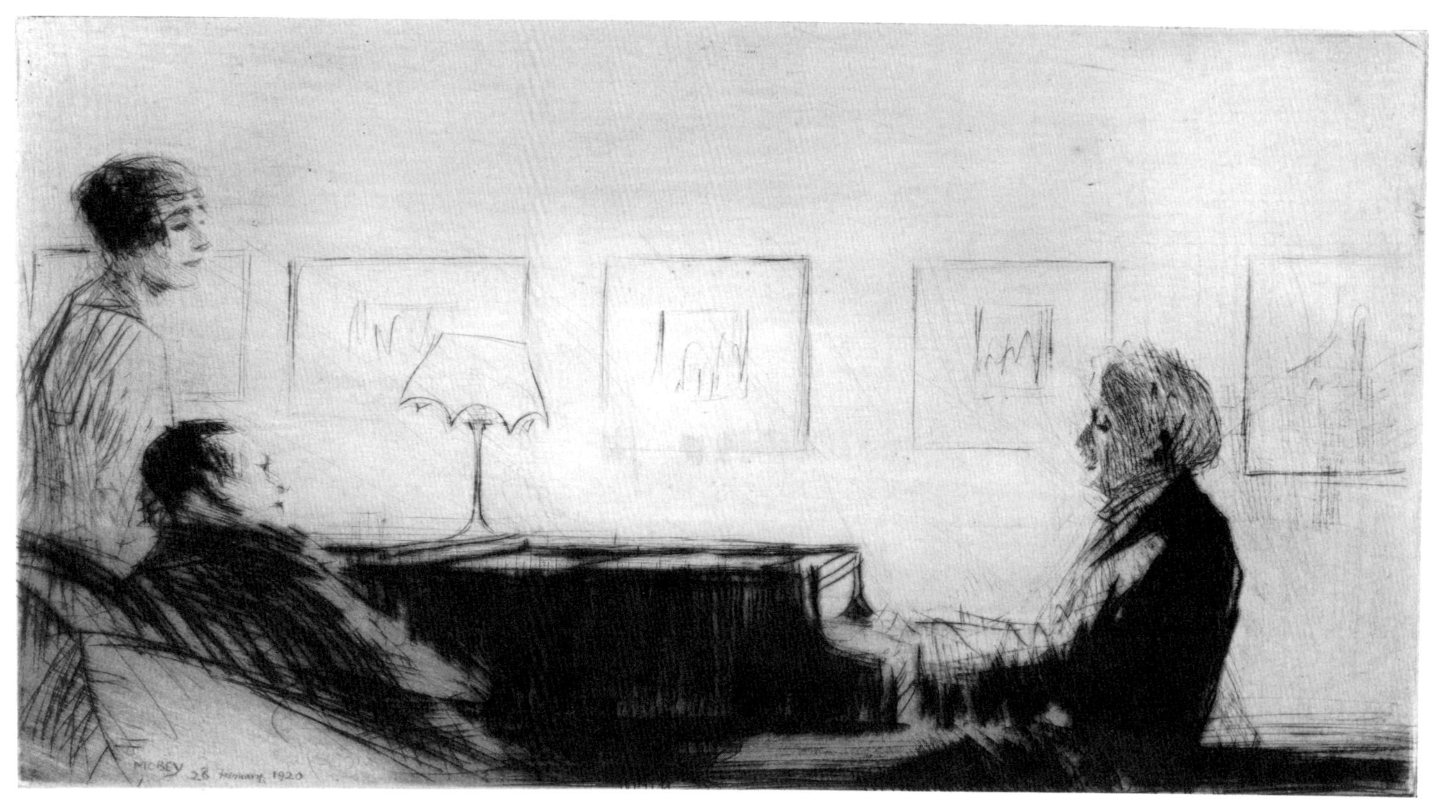

Plate 145. James McBey, *The Pianist*, 1920.

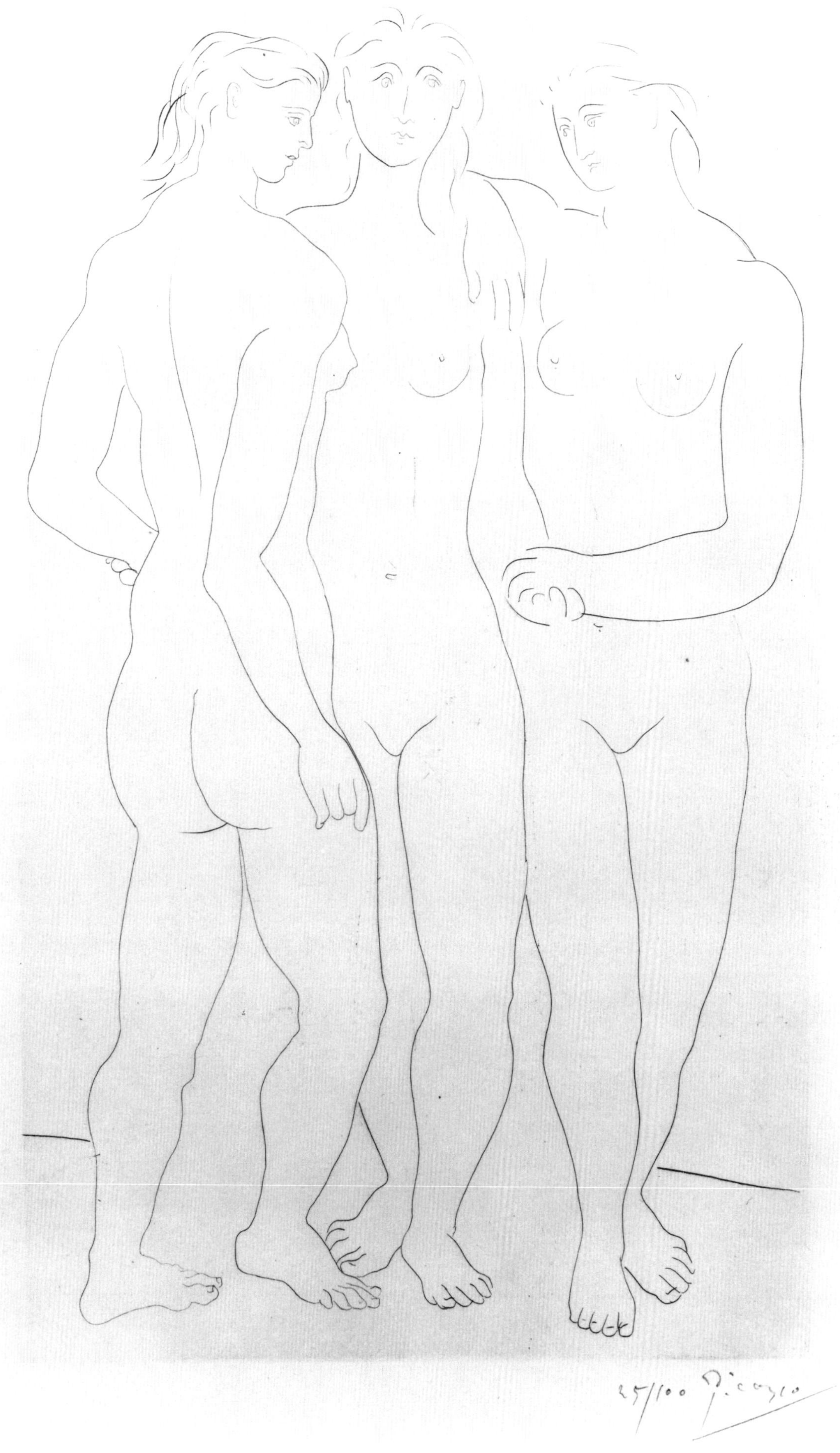

Plate 146. Pablo Ruiz Picasso, *The Three Graces*, 1923.

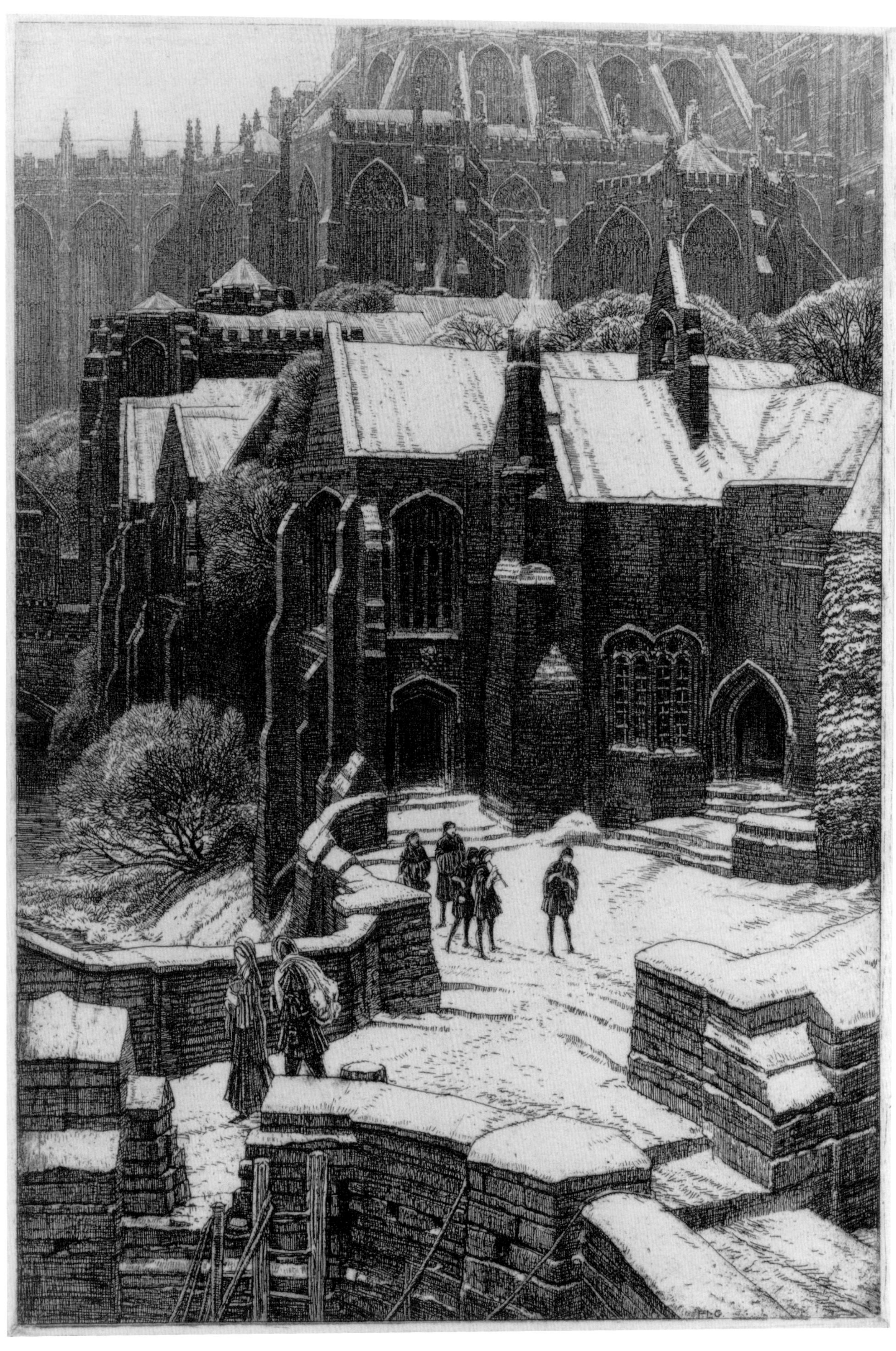

Plate 147. Frederick Landseer Griggs, *The Almonry*, 1925.

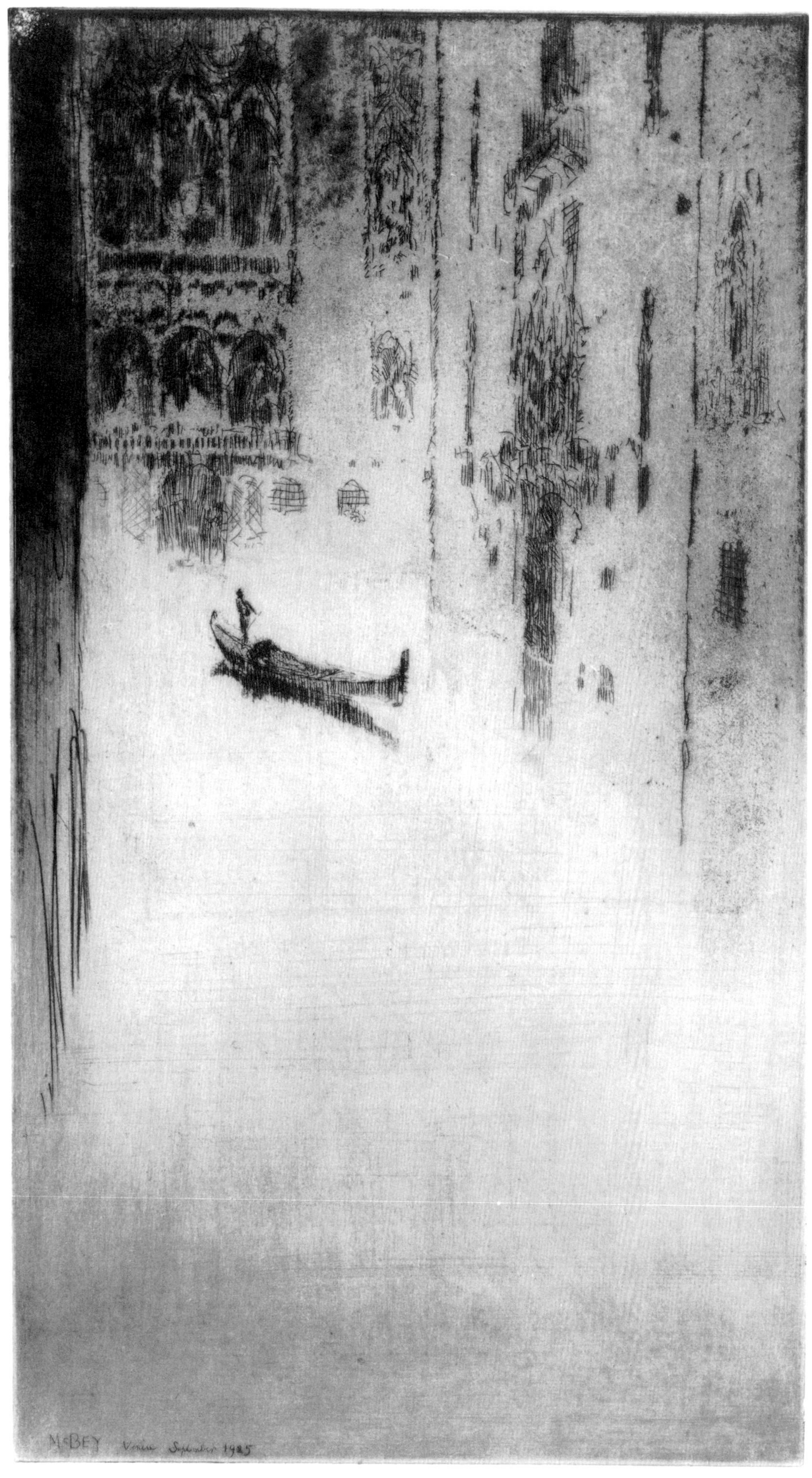

Plate 148. James McBey, *Barcarole*, 1926.

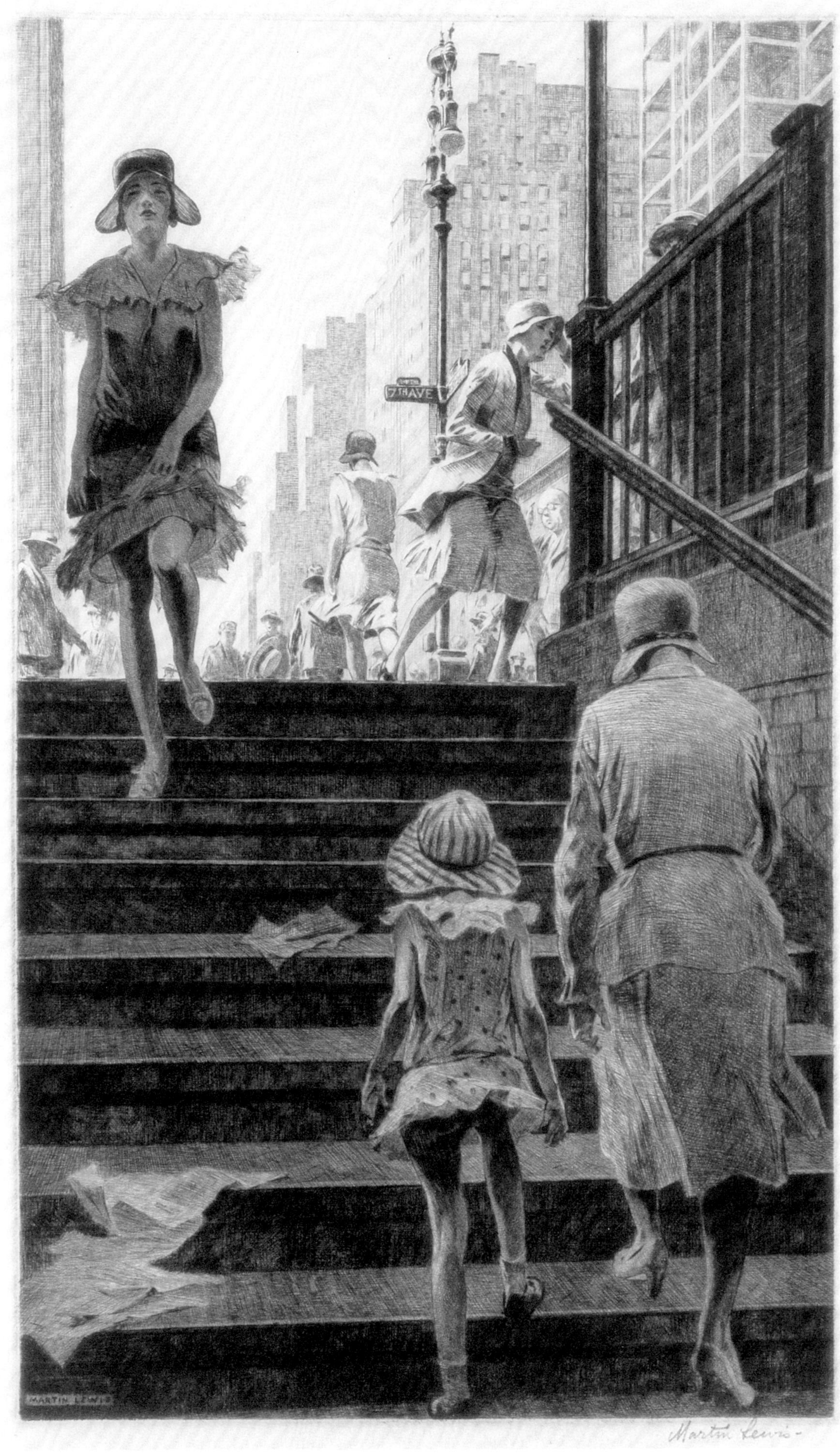

Plate 149. Martin Lewis, *Subway Steps*, 1930.

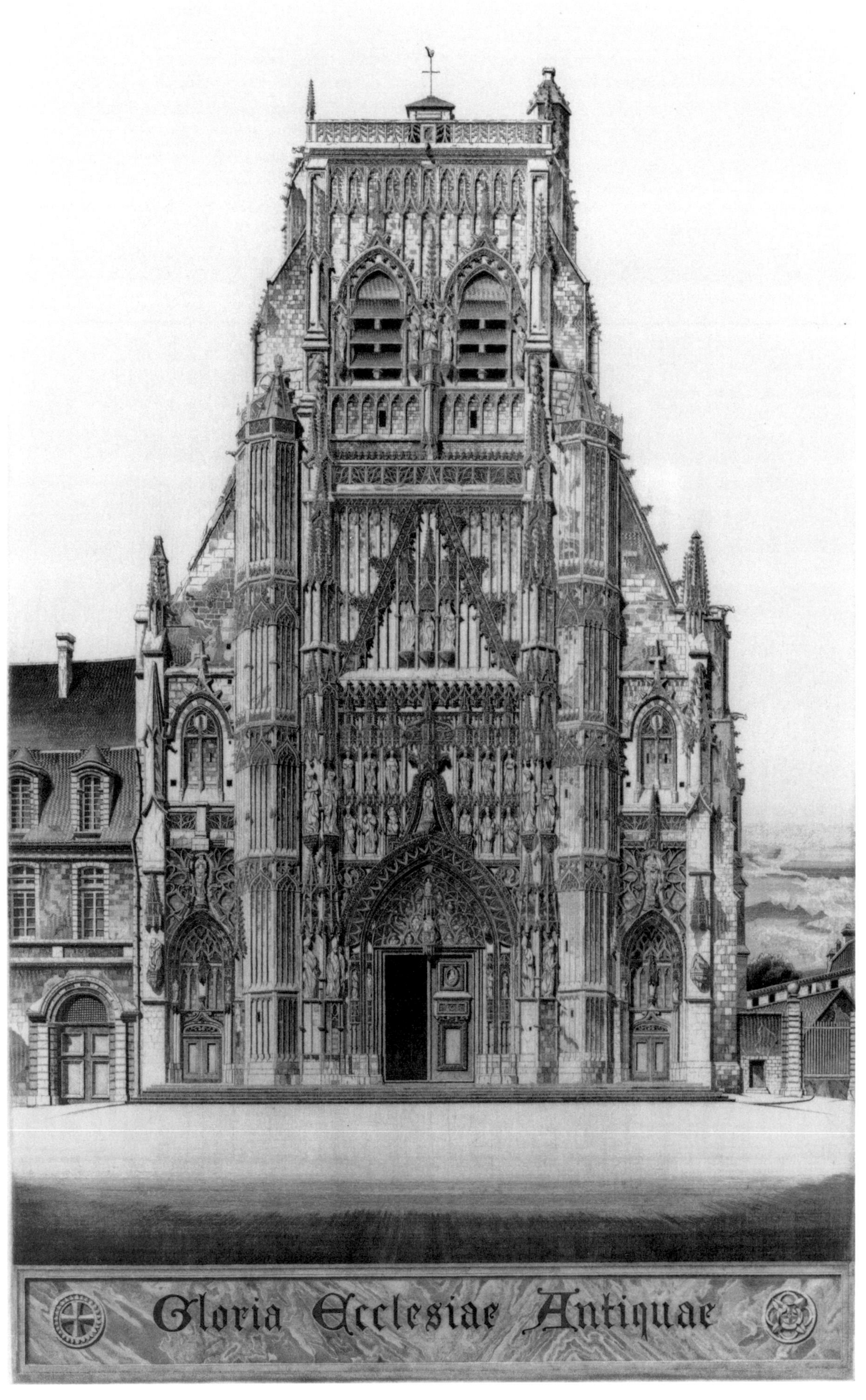

Plate 150. John Taylor Arms, *Gloria Ecclesiae Antiquae*, 1937.

Contributors

David P. Becker is an independent curator specializing in the graphic arts. He formerly served as acting curator of prints at the Fogg Art Museum, Harvard University (1987-89) and as assistant curator in the Department of Prints, Drawings, and Photographs at the Museum of Fine Arts, Boston (1984-86). His recent publications include *Old Master Drawings at Bowdoin College* (1985), *Drawings for Book Illustrations — The Hofer Collection* (1980), and *500 Years of Printmaking — Prints and Illustrated Books at Bowdoin College* (1978). Becker has been a contributing author to *Italian Etchers of the Renaissance and Baroque* (1989) and *Regency to Empire: French Printmaking 1715-1814* (1984).

Suzanne Boorsch is associate curator of prints and illustrated books at The Metropolitan Museum of Art. She was a contributing author on printmaking by the School of Mantegna for *Andrea Mantegna* (1992). Her publications include *The Engravings of Giorgio Ghisi* (1985) and volumes 28, 29, and 31 on sixteenth-century Italian printmakers for *The Illustrated Bartsch*.

Jane Campbell Hutchison is a professor of art history at the University of Wisconsin-Madison. She specializes in German, Dutch, and Flemish painting and graphic art of the fifteenth through seventeenth centuries. Her books include *Albrecht Dürer: A Biography* (1990) and *The Master of the Amsterdam Cabinet* (1972). She has authored volumes 8 and 9 on fifteenth-century German masters for *The Illustrated Bartsch*, including Master E.S., Martin Schongauer, and Israhel van Meckenem.

George S. Keyes is curator of painting at the Minneapolis Institute of Arts. He collaborated on volumes 23 through 25 and 27 through 29 of F. W. H. Hollstein's *Dutch and Flemish Etchings, Engravings and Woodcuts 1450-1700* and has written books on Cornelis Vroom, Pieter Bast, and Esais van de Velde. Keyes has most recently completed *Mirror of the Empire: Dutch Marine Art of the Seventeenth Century* (1990).

Dennis Kiel is associate curator in the Department of Prints, Drawings, and Photographs at the Cincinnati Art Museum. He has been a contributing author to *The Fine Art of Folk Art* (1990) and *Photographic Treasures from the Cincinnati Art Museum* (1989). He organized *The Hollywood Photographs of George Hurrell* (1987), which was subsequently toured by the Smithsonian Institution Traveling Exhibition Service. He has organized numerous print exhibitions ranging from Old Master to modern.

Jane S. Peters is professor of art history at the University of Kentucky in Lexington. Her publications include volumes 18 through 20 on sixteenth-century German printmakers for *The Illustrated Bartsch*, including Augustin Hirschvogel, Hanns Lautensack, and Jost Amman. Peters has contributed scholarly articles to *The Dictionary of Art, Anzeiger des Germanischen Nationalmuseums*, and *Master Drawings*.

Timothy A. Riggs, former curator of prints and drawings at the Worcester Art Museum, is currently assistant director of the Ackland Art Museum at the University of North Carolina, Chapel Hill. His publications include *The Print Council Index to Oeuvre-Catalogues of Prints by European and American Artists* (1983), *Visions of City and Country: Prints and Photographs of Nineteenth-Century France* (1982), and *Hieronymous Cock, Printmaker and Publisher* (1977).

Kristin L. Spangenberg is curator of prints and drawings, and heads the Department of Prints, Drawings, and Photographs at the Cincinnati Art Museum. She is editor of this catalogue and coordinating curator of the corresponding exhibition. Her publications include *Innovation and Tradition: Twentieth Century Japanese Prints from the Howard and Caroline Porter Collection* (1990), *Photographic Treasures from the Cincinnati Art Museum* (1989), *French Drawings, Watercolors, and Pastels 1800-1950* (1978), and *Eastern European Printmakers* (1975).

Mark J. Zucker is professor of art history at Louisiana State University. He is author of volume 25 and the forthcoming volume 24 on fifteen-century Italian printmakers from Florence, Ferrarese, and Lombardy for *The Illustrated Bartsch*. His numerous scholarly articles have appeared in *Master Drawing, Art Bulletin, Print Quarterly*, and *Metropolitan Museum Journal*.

H.G. French Bibliography

1930 *Catalogue of an Exhibition of Etchings and Engravings Loaned by Herbert Greer French*, Cincinnati Art Museum, January 13, 1930.

French, Herbert Greer, "The Art Museum and the Institute of Fine Arts," *Bulletin of the Cincinnati Art Museum* (April 1930) 23-32.

1932 Poole, Emily, "An Exhibition of Prints of Six Centuries," *Bulletin of the Cincinnati Art Museum* 3 (April 1932): 47-64.

1934 French, Herbert Greer, "One Hundred Selected Prints," *Bulletin of the Cincinnati Art Museum* 5 (April 1934): 35-45.

Catalogue of a Loan Exhibition from the Print Collection of Herbert Greer French, Cincinnati Art Museum, January 6-March 5, 1934.

1935 French, Herbert Greer, "Rembrandt – Master Etcher," *Bulletin of the Cincinnati Art Museum* 6 (January 1935): 3-19.

1936 French, Herbert Greer, "Albrecht Dürer: Engraver," *Bulletin of the Cincinnati Art Museum* 7 (January 1936): 9-15.

1940 "The Allyn Poole Collection," *The Art Digest* 14 (August 1, 1940): 18.

"Cincinnati: Poole Print Collection," *Art News* 39 (October 5, 1940): 14.

Poole, Emily, "Notes on the Print Collection of Allyn C. Poole," *Bulletin of the Cincinnati Art Museum* 11 (July 1940): 100-16.

1941 Siple, Walter H., "An Exhibition of Prints of the Fifteenth, Sixteenth, Seventeenth, and Eighteenth Centuries," *Bulletin of the Cincinnati Art Museum* 12 (October 1941): 70-71.

"Herbert Greer French Prints Exhibited," *The Art Digest* (October 1, 1941): 6.

"Prize Prints of the Past: Cincinnati Connoisseur's Collection: 1st View," *Art News* 39 (October 15, 1941): 13.

Siple, Walter H., foreword, *Exhibition of Prints of the Fifteenth, Sixteenth, Seventeenth, and Eighteenth Centuries from the Collection of Herbert Greer French*, Cincinnati Art Museum, September 27-November 2, 1941.

1942 "Cincinnati Gets French Collection of Prints," *The Museum News*, 20 (September 1, 1942): 1.

Comstock, Helen, "The Connoisseur in America: The Herbert Greer French Collection of Prints," *Connoisseur* 109 (March 1942): 60-62.

"French Collection for Cincinnati," *Antiques* (September 1942) 149-50.

Siple, Walter H., "Herbert Greer French," *Cincinnati Museum News* 1 (November 1942): n.p.

1943 Wright, Harold J. L., "The Albert H. Wiggen and Herbert Greer French Collection: Part I," *Apollo* 37 (February 1943): 25-27.

__________. "The Herbert Greer French Collection, Cincinnati Art Museum: Part II, *Apollo* 37 (March 1943): 57-59.

"Cincinnati (Ohio) Art Museum: The Herbert Greer French Print Collection," *The Museums Journal* 43 (May 1943): 26.

1950 "Rare and Unusual Prints from the Herbert Greer French Collection," *Magazine of Art – The Cincinnati Art Museum Edition* 5 (May 1950): iii-iv.

1971 "Masterpieces of the Print-Makers Art," *Apollo* 93 (April 1971): 30-33.

Baskett, Mary W., "A Print Collector of Yesterday: Herbert Greer French," *Auction* 4 (March 1971): 50-52.

1976 Spangenberg, Kristin L., "The Print Collection of the Cincinnati Art Museum," *Print Review* 6 (1976): 27-38.

Select Bibliography

Periodicals

AB.   *Art Bulletin*
AH.   *Art History*
AQ.   *Art Quarterly*
BVHR.   *Bulletin van het Rijksmuseum*
Burl.M.   *The Burlington Magazine.*
GBA.   *Gazette des Beaux-arts.*
JprK.   *Jahrbuch der königlich-preussischen Kunstsammlungen.*
JWarb.   *Journal of the Warburg and Courtauld Institutes.*
MGvk.   *Mitteilungen der Gesellschaft für vervielfältigende Kunst.*
PCN.   *Print Collector's Newsletter.*
PCQ.   *The Print Collector's Quarterly.*
P.Conn.   *The Print Connoisseur.*
PQ.   *Print Quarterly*
Rep.Kw.   *Repertorium für Kunstwissenschaft.*

Books and Catalogue Raisonnés

Adhémar
Adhémar, Jean. *Toulouse-Lautrec: His Complete Lithographs and Drypoints.* New York: Harry N. Abrams, 1965.

AKL
Allgemeines Kunstlerlexikon. Die Bildenden Kunstler aller zeiten und völker. Munich and Leipzig: K. G. Saur, 1992.

Alexander
Alexander, R. G. *A Catalogue of the Etchings of Samuel Palmer.* London: Print Collector's Club, 1937.

A.
Andresen, Andreas. *Der deutsche Peintre-graveur.* 5 vols. Leipzig: Rudolph Weigel, Alexander Danz, 1864-78.

Arms
Arms, John Taylor, and Dorothy Noyes Arms. "Descriptive Catalogue of the Etchings of John Taylor Arms." In Ben L. Bassham. *John Taylor Arms, American Etcher.* Madison, Wisconsin: Elvehjem Art Center, University of Wisconsin-Madison, 1975.

Asplund
Asplund, Karl. *Zorn's Engraved Work: A Descriptive Catalogue.* 2 vols. Translated by Edward Adams-Ray. 2 vols. Stockholm: A.-B. H. Buckowskis Konsthandel, 1920.

B.
Bartsch, Adam. *Le Peintre graveur.* 21 vols. Vienna: J. V. Degen, 1803-21.

B. *Rem.*
Bartsch, Adam. *Catalogue raisonné de toutes les estampes qui forment l'oeuvre de Rembrandt et ceux de ses principaux imitateurs.* 2 vols. Vienna: A. Blumauer, 1797.

Basan
Basan, Pierre François. "Catalogue des estampes gravées d'aprés P. P. Rubens." In vol. 3 *of Dictionnaire des graveurs anciens et modernes depuis l'origine de la gravure.* Paris: De Lormel, Saillant, 1767.

Ber.
Beraldi, Henri. *Les graveurs du XIXᵉ siècle, guide de l'amateur d'estampes modernes.* 12 vols. Paris: Librairie L. Conquet, 1885-92.

Bialostocki
Bialostocki, Jan. *Dürer and His Critics 1500-1971.* Vol. 7 of *Saecula Spiritalia.* Baden-Baden: V. Koerner, 1986.

Bloch
Bloch, Georges. *Pablo Picasso: Catalogue of the Printed Work 1904-1967.* Berne: Kornfeld & Klipstein, 1968.

Bober & Rubenstein
Bober, Phyllis Pray, and Ruth Rubinstein. *Renaissance Artists and Antique Sculpture: A Handbook of Sources.* London: Harvey Miller Publishers, Oxford University Press, 1986.

Bocher
Bocher, Emmanuel. *Les graveurs françaises du XVIIIᵉ siècle.* 6 vols. Paris: Librairie des Bibliophiles, 1875-82.

Bouillon
Bouillon, Jean-Paul. *Félix Bracquemond le réalisme absolu-oeuvre gravé 1849-1859 catalogue raisonné.* Geneva: Skira, 1987.

Br.
Bredius, A. *Rembrandt: The Complete Edition of the Paintings.* Revised and edited by H. Gerson. London: Phaidon, 1969.

Briquet
Briquet, C. M. *Les filigranes.* 4 vols. Amsterdam: The Paper Publications Society, 1968.

Bromberg
Bromberg, Ruth. *Canaletto's Etchings.* London and New York: Sotheby Parke Bernet, 1974.

Brummer
Brummer, Henrick. *Zorn Engraving.* Uppsala, Sweden: Hject & Hject, 1980.

Churchill
Churchill, W. A. *Watermarks in Paper: In Holland, England, France, etc., in the XVII and XVIII Centuries and Their Interconnection.* Amsterdam: Menno Hertzberger & Co., 1935.

Comstock
Comstock, Francis Adams. *A Gothic Vision: F. L. Griggs and His Work.* Boston: Boston Public Library; Oxford (England): Ashmolean Museum, 1966.

Dacier 1914
Dacier, Émile. *L'Oeuvre gravé de Gabriel de Saint-Aubin; notice biographique et catalogue raisonné.* Paris: Société pour l'étude de la Gravure française, 1914.

Dacier 1931
Dacier, Émile. *Gabriel de Saint-Aubin, peintre, dessinateur et graveur.* 2 vols. Paris: G. van Oest, 1929-31.

Davidsohn
Davidsohn, Paul. *Adriaen van Ostade, 1610-1685, Verzeichnis seiner Original-Radierungen.* Leipzig: C. G. Boerner, 1922.

Delaborde
Delaborde, Henri. *Marc-Antoine Raimondi; étude historique et critique suivie d'un catalogue raisonné.* Paris: Librarie de l'Art, 1887.

Del.
Delteil, Loys. *Le peintre-graveur illustré.* 31 vols. Paris: Loys Delteil, 1906-26.

D.-W.
Delteil, Loys, and Harold J. L. Wright. *Catalogue Raisonné of the Etchings of Charles Meryon.* New York: Winfred Porter Truesdell, 1924.

DBI.
Dizionario biografico degli italiani. 38 vols. Rome: Instituto della Enciclopedia Italiana, 1960-90 (in progress).

Dodgson
Dodgson, Campbell. *Albrecht Dürer: Engravings and Etchings.* London, 1926.

Dodgson B.M.
Dodgson, Campbell. *Catalogue of Early German and Flemish Woodcuts Preserved in the Department of Prints and Drawings in the British Museum.* 2 vols. London, 1903-11.

Dut.
Dutuit, Eugène. *Manuel de l'amateur d'estampes.* Vols. 1, 4-6. Paris: A. Lévy, 1884-85. (Other volumes not published.)

Eisler
Eisler, Colin Tobias. *The Master of the Unicorn: The Life and Work of Jean Duvet.* New York: Abaris Books, 1979.

Essick
Essick, Robert N. *William Blake Printmaker.* Princeton: Princeton University Press, 1980.

Fenaille
Fenaille, Maurice. *L'Oeuvre gravé de P. L. Debucourt (1755-1832).* Paris: Librarie Damascène Morgand, 1899.

Fletcher
    Fletcher, William Dolan. *John Taylor Arms, A Man for All Times: The Artist and His Work.* N.p.: The Sign of the Arrow, 1982.
Focillon
    Focillon, Henri. *Giovanni Battista Piranesi.* Translated by Giuseppi Guglielmi. Bologna: Alfa, 1967.
Fr.-v.d.ᴋ.
    Franken, Daniel, and Johan Philip van der Kellen. *L'Oeuvre de Jan van de Velde, gravure hollandais 1591-1641.* Amsterdam: Frederik Muller et Cie; Paris: Rapilly, 1883. Reprint. Amsterdam. G. W. Hissink en Co., 1968.
Ge.
    Geisberg, Max. *Der deutsche Einblatt-Holzschnitt in der ersten Hälfte des 16. Jahrhunderts.* 43 portfolios and index vol. Munich: Hugo Schmidt Verlag, 1923-31.
Geisberg 1909
    Geisberg, Max. *Die Anfänge des deutschen Kupferstiches und der Meister E.S. Meister der Graphik II.* Leipzig, 1909.
Geisberg 1924
    Geisberg, Max. *Der Meister E.S. Meister der Graphik X.* Leipzig, 1924.
Geisberg/Strauss
    Geisberg, Max. *The German Single-Leaf Woodcut 1500-1550.* Revised and edited by Walter L. Strauss. 4 vols. New York: Abaris Books, 1974.
Geiser
    Geiser, Bernhard. *Picasso, peintre-graveur; catalogue illustré de l'oeuvre gravé et lithographié 1899-1931.* Berne: Bernhard Geiser, 1955.
Godefroy
    Godefroy, Louis. *The Complete Etchings of Adriaen van Ostade.* Reprint and translation. San Francisco: Alan Wofsy Fine Arts, 1990.
Hain
    Hain, Ludwig. *Repertorium bibliographicum.* 2 vols. in 4. Stuttgart: J. G. Cotta, 1826-38.
Hardie
    Hardie, Martin. *Etchings and Drypoints from 1902 to 1924 by James McBey.* London: P. and D. Colnaghi and Co., 1925.
Harrington
    Harrington, H. Nazeby. *The Engraved Work of Sir Francis Seymour Haden.* Liverpool: Henry Young & Sons, 1910.
Harris
    Harris, Tomás. *Goya Engravings and Lithographs.* Oxford: Bruno Cassirer, 1964.
ʜʙ.
    Haverkamp-Begemann, Egbert. *Hercules Segers: The Complete Etchings.* Amsterdam: Scheltema and Holkema; The Hague: Martinus Nijhoff, 1973.
Heawood
    Heawood, Edward. *Watermarks Mainly of the 17th and 18th Centuries.* Vol. I of *Monumenta Chartae Papyraceae, Historium Illustrantia.* Hilversum, Holland: The Paper Publications Society, 1950.
Hédiard
    Hédiard, Germain. *Fantin-Latour, catalogue de l'oeuvre lithographique du maître.* Paris: Librairie de l'Art Ancien et Moderne, 1906.
Hérold
    Hérold, Jacques. *Louis-Marin Bonnet (1756-1793), catalogue de l'oeuvre gravé.* Paris: Société pour l'étude de la Gravure française, 1935.
Hind
    Hind, Arthur M. *Early Italian Engraving; A Critical Catalogue with Complete Reproduction of All the Prints Described.* 7 vols. London: Bernard Quatrich Ltd., 1938-48.
Hind *B.M.*
    Hind, Arthur M. *Catalogue of Early Italian Engravings Preserved in the Department of Prints and Drawings in the British Museum.* Edited by Sidney Colvin. London: British Museum, 1910.
Hind *Pir.*
    Hind, Arthur M. *Giovanni Battista Piranesi: A Critical Study.* London: The Cotswold Gallery, 1922.
Hind *Rem.*
    Hind, Arthur M. *A Catalogue of Rembrandt's Etchings.* 2 vols. London: Methuen and Co., Ltd., 1923.

Hirschmann
    Hirschmann, Otto. *Verzeichnis des graphischen Werks von Hendrick Goltzius (1558-1617).* Leipzig: Verlag von Klinkhardt und Biermann, 1921.
H. *Ger.*
    Hollstein, F. W. H., et al. *German Engravings, Etchings and Woodcuts ca. 1400-1700.* 29 vols. Amsterdam: Menno Hertzberger, 1954-92, (in progress).
H. *Neth.*
    Hollstein, F. W. H., et al. *Dutch and Flemish Etchings, Engravings and Woodcuts, ca. 1450-1700.* 36 vols. Amsterdam: Menno Hertzberger, 1949-1992, (in progress).
Hutchison
    Hutchison, Jane C. *Albrecht Dürer: A Biography.* Princeton: Princeton University Press, 1990.
ɪ.ꜰ.ꜰ. 1500
    Bibliothèque Nationale, Paris [André Linzeler and Jean Adhémar, compilers]. *Inventaire du fonds français; graveurs du seizème siècle.* 2 vols. Paris: M. Le Garrec, 1932-35.
ɪ.ꜰ.ꜰ. 1600
    Bibliothèque Nationale, Paris [Roger-Armand Weigert, compiler]. *Inventaire du fonds français: Graveurs du XVIIe siècle.* 10 vols. Paris: Bibliothèque Nationale, 1939-89, (in progress).
ɪ.ꜰ.ꜰ. 1700
    Biliothèque Nationale, Paris [Marcel Roux et al., compilers]. *Inventaire du fonds français: Graveurs du dix-huitième siècle.* 14 vols. Paris: Maurice Le Garrec, 1930-77, (in progress).
ɪ.ꜰ.ꜰ. 1800
    Bibliothèque Nationale, Paris [Jean Laran et al., compilers]. *Inventaire du fonds français après 1800.* 15 vols. Paris: Maurice Le Garrec, 1930-85, (in progress).
K.
    Kennedy, Edward G. *The Etched Work of Whistler.* New York: The Grolier Club, 1910.
Koepplin and Falk
    Koepplin, Dieter, and Tilman Falk. *Lucas Cranach. Gemälde Zeichnungen, Druckgraphik.* Basel: Birkhäuser Verlag, 1974.
ʟ.ᴅ.
    Lawrence, H. W., and Basil Lewis Dighton. *French Line Engravings of the Late Eighteenth Century.* London: Lawrence and Jellicoe, Ltd., 1910.
Lehrs
    Lehrs, Max. *Geschichte und kritischer Katalog des deutschen, niederländischen und französischen Kupferstichs im XV. Jahrhundert.* 9 vols. Vienna: Gesellschaft für vervielfältigende Kunst, 1908-34.
Lieure
    Lieure, J. *Jacques Callot.* 5 vols. Paris: Editions de la Gazette des Beaux-Arts, 1924-27.
Lister
    Lister, Raymond. *Catalogue Raisonné of the Works of Samuel Palmer.* Cambridge: Cambridge University Press, 1988.
Lochnan
    Lochnan, Katharine A. *The Etchings of James McNeill Whistler.* New Haven and London: Yale University Press, 1984.
Lugt
    Lugt, Fritz. *Les marques de collections de dessins et d'estampes.* Amsterdam, 1921 Reprint. The Hague: Martinus Nijhoff, 1956.
Lugt S.
    Lugt, Fritz. *Les marques de collections de dessins et d'estampes. Supplément.* The Hague: Martinus Nijhoff, 1956.
McCarron
    McCarron, Paul. *Martin Lewis: The Graphic Work.* New York: Kennedy Galleries, 1973.
Mannocci
    Mannocci, Lino. *The Etchings of Claude Lorrain.* New Haven and London: Yale University Press, 1988.
Mansfield
    Mansfield, Howard. *A Descriptive Catalogue of the Etchings and Drypoints of James McNeill Whistler.* Chicago: The Coxton Club, 1909.

MH. *Wierix*
Mauquoy-Hendrickx, Marie. *Les Estampes des Wierix*. 3 vols. in 4 sec. Brussels: Bibliothèque Royal Albert Ier., 1978-83.

Mauquoy-Hendrickx
Mauquoy-Hendrickx, Marie. *L'Iconographie d'Antoine van Dyck, catalogue raisonné*. 2 vols. Brussels: Palais des Académies, 1956.

Meder
Meder, Joseph. *Dürer-Katalog. Ein Handbuch über Albrecht Dürers Stiche, Radierungen, Holzschnitte, deren Zustände, Ausgaben und Wasserzeichen*. Vienna: Verlag Gilhofer und Ranschburg, 1932.

Mellerio
Mellerio, André. *Odilon Redon*. Paris: Société pour l'étude de la Gravure française, 1913.

Melot
Melot, Michel. *Graphic Art of the Pre-Impressionists*. Translated by Robert Erich Wolf. New York: Harry N. Abrams, 1980.

Mende
Mende, Matthias. *Hans Baldung Grien. Das Graphische Werk*. Unterschneidheim: Dr. Alfons Uhl, 1978.

M.N.
Moreau-Nelaton, Étienne. *Manet graveur et lithographe*. Paris: L. Delteil, 1906.

Münz
Münz, Ludwig. *Rembrandt's Etchings*. London: Phaidon Press, 1952.

NGA
Levenson, Jay A., Konrad Oberhuber, and Jacquelyn L. Sheehan. *Early Italian Engravings from the National Gallery of Art*. Washington: National Gallery of Art, 1973.

Nagler
Nagler, G. K. *Neues allgemeines Künstler-Lexicon*. 22 vols. Munich: E. A. Fleischmann, 1835-52. 2d ed. 25 vols. Linz (Austria): E. Mareis, 1904-14.

Nagler, *Mon.*
Nagler, G. K. *Die Monogrammisten*. 5 vols. Munich: G. Franz, 1858-79.

N. *Arch.*
[Naumanns] *Archiv für die zeichnenden Künste mit besonderer Beziehung auf Kupferstecher- und Holzschneidekunst und ihre Geschichte. . . hrsg. von Dr. Robert Naumann*. 16 vols. (1855-70).

Panofsky
Panofsky, Erwin. *The Life and Art of Albrecht Dürer*. Princeton: Princeton University Press, 1971.

Parthey
Parthey, Gustav. *Wenzel Hollar. Beschreibendes Verzeichniss seiner Kupferstiche*. Berlin: Verlag der Nicolaischen Buchhandlung, 1953.

P.
Passavant, Johann David. *Le peintre-graveur*. 6 vols. Leipzig: Rudolph Weigel, 1860-64.

Pennington
Pennington, Richard. *A Descriptive Catalogue of the Etched Work of Wenceslaus Hollar, 1607-1677*. Cambridge: Cambridge University Press, 1982.

Poole
Poole, Emily. "The Etchings of Frank Duveneck." PCQ. 25 (1938): 12-31, 446-63.

Popham
Popham, A. E. "The Engravings and Woodcuts of Dirick Vellert." PCQ. 12 (1925): 343-68.

Popham & Pouncey.
Popham, A. E., and Philip Pouncey. *Italian Drawings in the Department of Prints and Drawings in the British Museum: The Fourteenth and Fifteenth Centuries*. 2 vols. London: British Museum, 1950.

Portalis & Béraldi
Portalis, Baron Roger, and Henri Béraldi. *Les graveurs du dix-huitième siècle*. 6 vols. Paris: Damascène Morgand and Charles Fatout, 1880-82.

Rawlinson
Rawlinson, W. G. *Turner's Liber Studiorum: A Description and a Catalogue*. 2d ed., rev. New York: The Macmillan Company, 1906.

Reed and Shapiro
Reed, Sue Welsh, Barbara Stern Shapiro et al. *Edgar Degas: The Painter as Printmaker*. Boston: Museum of Fine Arts, 1984.

Riggs
Riggs, Timothy A. *Hieronymus Cock, Printmaker and Publisher*. New York: Garland Publishing, Inc., 1977.

Rinder
Rinder, Frank. *D. Y. Cameron: An Illustrated Catalogue of His Etchings and Drypoints, 1887-1932*. Glasgow: Jackson, Wylie and Company, 1932.

Rizzi
Rizzi, Aldo. *The Etchings of the Tiepolos*. New York: Phaidon, 1971.

RD.
Robert-Dumesnil, A. P. F. *Le peintre-graveur français*. 11 vols. Paris: Gabriel Warée, Mme Huzard, etc., 1835-71.

Robison
Robison, Andrew. *Piranesi's Early Architectural Fantasies: A Catalogue Raisonné of the Etchings*. Washington: National Gallery of Art; Chicago and London: University of Chicago Press, 1986.

Romano
Romano, Serena. *Ritrattto di fanciullo di Girolamo Mocetto*. Modena: Edizione Panini, 1985.

Rov.
Rovinski, Dmitri. *L'Oeuvre gravé des élèves de Rembrandt et des maîtres qui ont gravé dans son goût*. 3 vols. St. Petersburg: Imprimerie de l'Academie Impériale des Sciences, 1894.

Schmitt
Schmitt, Annegrit. *Hanns Lautensack*. Vol. 4 of *Nürnberger Forschungen*. Nuremberg, 1957.

Schneiderman *Had.*
Schneiderman, Richard S. *A Catalogue Raisonné of the Prints of Sir Francis Seymour Haden*. London: Robin Garton, 1983.

Schneiderman *Meryon.*
Schneiderman, Richard S. *The Catalogue Raisonné of the Prints of Charles Meryon*. London: Garton & Co., 1990.

Schreiber
Schreiber, Wilhelm Ludwig. *Manuel de l'amateur de la gravure sur bois et sur metal au 15e siècle*. 5 vols. Leipzig: Otto Harrassowitz, 1902.

Schreiber, *Metallschneidekunst*
Schreiber, Wilhelm Ludwig. *Die Meister der Metallschneidekunst nebst einem nach Schulen geordneten Katalog ihrer Arbeiten*. Studien zur deutschen Kunstgeschichte, 241. Strasbourg: J. H. Ed. Heitz, 1926.

Schwarz
Schwarz, Karl. *Augustin Hirschvogel; ein deutscher Meister der Renaissance*. Berlin: Verlag von Julius Bard, 1917. Reprint. 2 vols. New York: Collectors Editions, 1977.

Singer
Singer, Hans W. "Jacob Christoffel Le Blon." *MGvK.* (1901): 1-21.

Sm.
Smith, John Chaloner. *British Mezzotinto Portraits*. 5 vols. London: Henry Sotheran and Co. 1883-84.

Springer
Springer, Jaro. *Die Radierungen des Herkules Seghers*. 3 vols. *Graphische Gesellschaft*, 13, 14, 16. Berlin: B. Cassier, 1910-12.

Strauss
Strauss, Walter L. *Hendrik Goltzius 1558-1617: The Complete Engravings and Woodcuts*. 2 vols. New York: Abaris Books, 1977.

Strauss *Chiaroscuro*
Strauss, Walter L. *Chiaroscuro: The Clair-Obscur Woodcuts by the German and Netherlandish Masters of the XVIth and XVIIth Centuries*. Greenwich, Connecticut: New York Graphic Society, Ltd., 1973.

ThB.
Thieme, Ulrich, Felix Becker et al. *Allgemeines Lexicon der bildenden Künstler von der Antike bis zur Gegenwart*. 37 vols. Leipzig: Verlag von E. A. Seemann, 1907-50.

Thorson
Thorson, Victoria. *Rodin Graphics: A Catalogue Raisonné of Drypoints and Book Illustrations*. San Francisco: Fine Arts Museums, 1975.

TIB.

Strauss, Walter L., and John Spike, eds. *The Illustrated Bartsch.* 165 vols. (Projected). New York: Abaris Books. 1978-92 (in progress).

Tuer

Tuer, Andrew W. *Bartolozzi and His Works.* 2 vols. London: Field and Tuer; New York: Scribner and Welford, 1882.

Vesme

Vesme, Alexandre de [Baudi di Vesme, Alessandro]. *Le peintre-graveur italien.* Milan: Ulrico Hoepli, 1906.

Vesme & Calabi

Calabi, A. *Francesco Bartolozzi; catalogue des estampes et notice biographique d'après les manuscrits de A. de Vesme.* Milan: Guido Modiano, 1928.

Wax

Wax, Carol. *The Mezzotint: History and Technique.* New York: Harry N. Abrams, Inc., 1990.

Wildenstein

Wildenstein, Georges. *Fragonard acqua-fortiste.* Paris: Les Beaux-Arts, 1956.

Winkler

Winkler, Friedrich. *Die Zeichnungen Albrecht Dürers.* 4 vols. Berlin, 1936-39.

Winzinger

Winzinger, Franz. *Albrecht Altdorfer. Graphik, Holzschnitte, Kupferstiche, Radierungen.* Munich: R. Piper & Co. Verlag, 1963.

Wittrock

Wittrock, Wolfgang. *Toulouse-Lautrec: The Complete Prints.* 2 vols. London: Sotheby's Publications, Ltd., 1985.

W.

Wurzbach, Alfred von. *Niederländisches Künstler-Lexikon.* 3 vols. Vienna: Verlag von Halm und Goldmann, 1906-11.

Exhibitions

Amsterdam 1981

Schatborn, Peter. *Dutch Figure Drawing from the Seventeenth Century.* Rijksprentenkabinet, Rijksmuseum, Amsterdam; National Gallery of Art, Washington, 1981-82.

Amsterdam 1984

Thiel, P. J. J. van, and C. J. de Bryn Kops. *Prijst de Lijst. De Hollandse schilderjlijst in de zeventiende eeuw.* Rijksmuseum, Amsterdam; Staatsuitgeverij, The Hague, 1984.

Amsterdam 1985

Schatborn, P. *Drawings by Rembrandt in the Rijksmuseum.* Rijksprentenkabinet, Rijksmuseum, Amsterdam, 1985.

Amsterdam 1987

Sutton, Peter C., et al. *Masters of 17th-Century Dutch Landscape Painting.* Rijksmuseum, Amsterdam; Museum of Fine Arts, Boston; Philadelphia Museum of Art, 1987-88.

Ann Arbor 1960

Rembrandt Prints. The University of Michigan Museum of Art, Ann Arbor, 1960.

Ann Arbor 1975

Reflections of an Era of Change: The Art of France, 1774-1830. The University of Michigan Museum of Art, Ann Arbor, 1975.

Austin 1983

Smith, Jeffrey Chipps. *Nuremberg: A Renaissance City 1500-1618.* Archer M. Huntington Art Gallery, Austin, 1983.

Austin 1988

Norris, Andrea, and Kendall Curlee. *The Sforza Court: Milan in the Renaissance 1450-1535.* Archer M. Huntington Art Gallery, Austin; University Art Museum, Berkeley, CA; Yale University Art Gallery, New Haven, 1988-89.

Avignon 1979

Schnapper, Antoine. *Mignard d'Avignon (1606-1668).* Palais des Papes, Avignon, 1979.

Baltimore 1984

Carlson, Victor I., John W. Ittmann et al. *Regency to Empire: French Printmaking, 1715-1814.* The Baltimore Museum of Art; Museum of Fine Arts, Boston; The Minneapolis Institute of Arts, 1984-85.

Basel 1974

Koepplin, Dieter, and Tilman Falk, eds. *Lukas Cranach. Gemälde, Zeichnungen, Druckgraphik.* 2 vols. Kunstmuseum, Basel, 1974.

Basel 1978

Boerlin, Paul H., Tilman Falk, Richard W. Gassen, and Dieter Koepplin. *Hans Baldung Grien im Kunstmuseum Basel.* Kunstmuseum, Basel, 1974.

Berlin 1984

Mielke, Hans. *Wenzel Hollar. Radierungen und Zeichnungen aus dem Berliner Kupferstichkabinett.* Kupferstichkabinett, Staatliche Museen Preussischer Kulturbesitz, Berlin, 1984.

Berlin 1988

Mielke, Hans, ed. *Albrecht Altdorfer: Zeichnungen, Deckfarbenmalerei, Druckgraphik.* Kupferstichkabinett. Staatliche Museen Preussischer Kulturbesitz, Berlin; Museen der Stadt Regensburg, Regensburg, 1988.

Berlin 1991

Krohm, Hartmut, and Jan Nicolaisen. *Martin Schongauer Druckgraphik im Berliner Kupferstichkabinett.* Kupferstichkabinett, Staatliche Museen Preussischer Kulturbesitz, Berlin, 1991.

Bocholt 1953

Geisberg, Max, Paul Pieper, Paul Vogt, and Heinrich Kohlhausen. *Israhel van Meckenem. Goldschmied und Kupferstecher. Zur 450. Wiederkehr seines Todestages herausgegeben von der Stadt Bocholt.* Kunsthaus der Stadt Bocholt, Bocholt, 1953.

Bocholt 1972

Broker, Elisabeth, ed. *Israhel van Meckenem und der deutsche Kupferstich des 15. Jahrhunderts. 750 Jahre Stadt Bocholt 1222-1972.* Kunsthaus der Stadt, Bocholt, 1972.

Bologna 1988

Faietti, Marzia, and Corinna Giudici. *Bologna e l'umanesimo 1490-1510.* Pinacoteca Nazionale, Bologna; Graphische Sammlung Albertina, Vienna, 1988.

Boston 1969

Sayre, Eleanor A., and Felice Stampfle. *Rembrandt: The Experimental Etcher.* Museum of Fine Arts, Boston; Pierpont Morgan Library, New York, 1969-70.

Boston 1971

Department of Prints and Drawings. *Albrecht Dürer: Master Printmaker.* Museum of Fine Arts, Boston, 1971-72.

Boston 1974

Sayre, Eleanor A. *The Changing Image: Prints by Francisco Goya.* Museum of Fine Arts, Boston, 1974.

Boston 1980

Ackley, Clifford S. *Printmaking in the Age of Rembrandt.* Museum of Fine Arts, Boston; St. Louis Art Museum, 1980-81.

Boston 1984

Murphy, Alexandra R., et al. *Jean François Millet.* Museum of Fine Arts, Boston, 1984.

Boston 1989a

Sánchez, Alfonso E. Pérez, and Eleanor A. Sayre, eds. *Goya and the Spirit of Enlightenment.* Museo del Prado, Madrid; Museum of Fine Arts, Boston; The Metropolitan Museum of Art, New York, 1988-89.

Boston 1989b

Reed, Sue Welsh, and Richard Wallace, eds. *Italian Etchers of the Renaissance and Baroque.* Museum of Fine Arts, Boston; The Cleveland Museum of Art; National Gallery of Art, Washington, 1989.

Braunschweig 1987

Das gestochene Bild: Von der Zeichnung Kupferstich. Herzog Anton Ulrich-Museum, Braunschweig, 1987.

Brussels 1968

Hasselt, Carlos van. *Dessins des Paysagistes Hollandais du XVIIᵉ siècle.* Bibliothèque Albert Ier, Brussels; Musée Boymans-van Beuningen, Rotterdam; Institut Néerlandais, Paris; Musée des Beaux-Arts, Berne, 1968-69.

Cambridge 1930
Loan Exhibition of Works of William Blake. Fogg Art Museum, Cambridge, MA, 1930 (no catalogue).

Cambridge 1967
Mongan, Agnes, and Hans Naef. *Ingres Centennial Exhibition, 1867-1967: Drawings, Watercolors, and Oil Sketches from American Collections.* Fogg Art Museum, Cambridge, MA, 1967.

Cambridge 1968
Janis, Eugenia P. *Degas Monotypes.* Fogg Art Museum, Cambridge, MA, 1968.

Cambridge 1970
Knox, George. *Tiepolo: A Bicentenary Exhibition 1770-1970.* Fogg Art Museum, Cambridge, MA, 1970.

Chicago 1941
Mongan, Elizabeth, and Carl O. Schniewind. *The First Century of Printmaking 1400-1500.* The Art Institute of Chicago, 1941.

Chicago 1964
Moses, Paul. *An Exhibition of Etchings by Edgar Degas.* The University of Chicago, 1964.

Cincinnati 1930
Catalogue of an Exhibition of Etchings and Engravings Loaned by Herbert Greer French. Cincinnati Art Museum, 1930.

Cincinnati 1934
Catalogue of a Loan Exhibition from the Print Collection of Herbert Greer French. Cincinnati Art Museum, 1934.

Cincinnati 1941
Exhibition of Prints of the Fifteenth, Sixteenth, Seventeenth, and Eighteenth Centuries from the Collection of Herbert Greer French. Cincinnati Art Museum, 1941.

Cincinnati 1948
Groschwitz, Gustave von. *One Hundred and Fifty Years of Lithography.* Cincinnati Art Museum, 1948.

Cincinnati 1978
Spangenberg, Kristin L. *French Drawings, Watercolors, and Pastels, 1800-1950.* Cincinnati Art Museum, 1979.

Cleveland 1978
Pillsbury, Edmund P., and Louise S. Richards. *The Graphic Art of Federico Barocci.* The Cleveland Museum of Art; Yale University Art Gallery, New Haven, 1978.

Coburg 1972
Maedebach, Heino, ed. *Lucas Cranach d. Ae. 1472-1553, Graphik.* Veste Coburg, Coburg, 1972.

Colmar 1991
Anzelewsky, Fedja, Pantixka Béguerie, Georges Bischoff, Albert Châtelet, Tilman Falk, Fritz Koreny, Maxime Préaud, Helmut F. Reichwald, and Emmanuel Starcky. *Le beau Martin: Gravures et dessins de Martin Schongauer.* Musée d'Unterlinden, Colmar, 1991.

Cologne 1970
Osten, Gert von der, Anton C.-F. Koch, Günther Albrecht, Friedrich Gerissen, Harald Kümmerling, Rolf Wallrath, Heribert Meurer, Johann Michael Fritz, Hella Robels et al. *Herbst des Mittelalters. Spätgotik in Köln und am Niederrhein.* Kunsthalle, Cologne, 1970.

Detroit 1958
Grigaut, Paul L. *Decorative Arts of the Italian Renaissance 1400-1600.* The Detroit Institute of Arts, 1958-59.

Detroit 1980
Glassman, Elizabeth, and Marilyn F. Symmes. *Cliché-verre: Hand-Drawn, Light-Printed: A Survey of the Medium from 1839 to the Present.* The Detroit Institute of Arts; The Museum of Fine Arts, Houston, 1980.

Detroit 1983
Andersson, Christiane, and Charles Talbot, eds. *From a Mighty Fortress: Prints, Drawings, and Books in the Age of Luther 1483-1546.* The Detroit Institute of Arts; National Gallery of Canada, Ottawa; Kunstsammlungen der Veste Coburg, Coburg, 1981-82.

Ferrara 1987
Berti, Giordano, and Andrea Vitali, eds. *I. Tarocchi, Le Carte di corte: Gioco e magia alla corte degli Estensi.* Castello Estense, Casa di Stella dell'Assassino, Ferrara, 1987-88.

Frankfurt-am-Main 1975
Charles Meryon. Paris um 1850, Zeichnungen, Radierungen, Photographien. Städelsches Kunstinstitut und Städtische Galerie, Frankfurt-am-Main; Kunsthalle, Hamburg, 1975.

Frankfurt-am-Main 1987
Stuffmann, Margret, et al. *Eugène Delacroix: Themen und Variationen Arbeiten auf Papier.* Städtische Galerie im Städelschen Kunstinstitut, Frankfurt-am-Main, 1987-88.

The Hague 1986
Filedt Kok, J. P., W. Halsema-Kubes, and W. Th. Kloek. *Kunst voor de beeldenstorm.* Staatsuitgeverij, The Hague; Rijksmuseum, Amsterdam, 1986.

Hamburg 1983
Hofman, Werner. *Luther und die Folgen für die Kunst.* Hamburger Kunsthalle, 1983-84.

Hanover 1990
Goldfarb, Hilrard T., and Reva Wolf. *Fatal Consequences: Callot, Goya, and the Horrors of War.* Hood Museum of Art, Hanover, NH, 1990.

Hartford 1976
Munhall, Edgar. *Jean-Baptiste Greuze 1725-1805.* Wadsworth Athenaeum, Hartford; California Palace of the Legion of Honor, San Francisco; Musée de Beaux-Arts, Dijon, 1976-77.

's-Hertogenbosch 1990
Koldewij, A. M. *In Buscoducis 1450-1629: Kunst uit de Bourgondische tijd te 's-Hertogenbosch.* Noord-Brabants Museum, 's-Hertogenbosch, 1990.

Houston 1960
MacAgy, Jermayne. *The Lively Arts of the Renaissance.* The Museum of Fine Arts, Houston, 1960.

Indianapolis 1965
Etchings by Whistler. Herron Museum of Art, Indianapolis, 1965 (no catalogue).

Innsbruck 1969
Ausstellung Maximilian I. Innsbruck. Zeughaus des Kaisers, Innsbruck, 1969.

Ithaca 1973
Schlesinger, Ruth H. *Fifteenth- and Sixteenth-Century Prints of Northern Europe from the National Gallery of Art Rosenwald Collection.* Herbert F. Johnson Museum of Art, Ithaca, 1973.

Karlsruhe 1959
Hans Baldung Grien, Staatliche Kunsthalle, Karlsruhe, 1959.

Karlsruhe 1986
Die Renaissance im deutschen Südwestern zwischen Reformation und dreissigjährigem Krieg. 2 vols. Badisches Landesmuseum, Karlsruhe, 1986.

Langres 1985
May, R., et al. *Jean Duvet, le Maitre à licorne.* Musée de l'Hotel du Breuil de St. Germain, Langres, 1985.

Lawrence 1979
Broun, Elizabeth. *The Prints of Anders Zorn.* Spencer Museum of Art, Lawrence. KS; Sterling and Francine Clark Institute, Williamstown, MA; Georgia Museum of Art, The University of Georgia, Athens; Flint Institute of Arts, Michigan, 1979-80.

Lawrence 1981
Shoemaker, Innis H., and Elizabeth Broun. *The Engravings of Marcantonio Raimondi.* Spencer Museum of Art, Lawrence, KS; The Ackland Art Museum, Chapel Hill, NC; The Wellesley College Art Museum, Wellesley, MA, 1981-82.

Lawrence 1988
Emison, Patricia A., Stephen H. Goddard, and Janet L. Levy. *The World in Miniature: Engravings by the German Little Masters 1500-1550.* Stephen H. Goddard, ed. Spencer Museum of Art, Lawrence, KS; Yale University Art Gallery, New Haven; The Minneapolis Institute of Arts; Grunwald Center for the Graphic Arts, Los Angeles, 1988-89.

Leningrad 1977
Novoselskaia, I. N. *Jean-Baptiste Greuze: Drawings from the Hermitage Collection.* Hermitage, Leningrad, 1977.

London 1968
  Sutton, Denys. *France in the Eighteenth Century*. Royal Academy of Arts, London, 1968.
London 1977
  Rowlands, John. *Rubens: Drawings and Sketches: Catalogue of an Exhibition at the Department of Prints and Drawings in the British Museum*. British Museum, London, 1977.
London 1979
  Levey, Michael. *Sir Thomas Lawrence 1769-1830*. National Portrait Gallery, London, 1979.
London 1982
  Millar, Oliver. *Van Dyck in England*. National Gallery, London, 1982.
London 1983a
  Martineau, Jane, and Charles Hope, eds. *The Genius of Venice*. Royal Academy of Arts, London, 1983.
London 1983b
  Griffiths, Antony, and Gabriela Kesnerová. *Wenceslaus Hollar: Prints and Drawings from the Collections of the National Gallery, Prague, and the British Museum, London*. British Museum, London, 1983.
London 1986
  Brown, Christopher. *Dutch Landscape: The Early Years, Haarlem and Amsterdam 1590-1650*. National Gallery, London, 1986.
London 1992
  Boorsch, Suzanne, Keith Christiansen, David Ekserdjian, Charles Hope, David Landau et al. *Andrea Mantegna*. Jane Martineau, ed. Royal Academy of Arts, London; The Metropolitan Museum of Art, New York, 1992.
Long Beach 1984
  Bledsoe, Jane K. *Anders Zorn Rediscovered*. University Art Museum, California State University, Long Beach, 1984.
Los Angeles 1966
  Picasso: Sixty Years of Graphic Work. Los Angeles County Museum of Art, 1966.
Los Angeles 1984
  Fine, Ruth E. *Drawing Near: Whistler Etchings from the Zelman Collection*. Los Angeles County Museum of Art; University Art Museum, Berkeley, CA; Elvehjem Museum of Art, Madison, WI; Dallas Museum of Art; University of Maryland Art Gallery, College Park, 1984-85.
Los Angeles 1988
  Cuno, James et al. *French Caricature and the French Revolution, 1789-1799*. Grunwald Center for the Graphic Arts, Los Angeles, 1988.
Middletown 1975
  Carlson, Victor, Ellen D'Oench, and Richard S. Field. *Prints and Drawings by Gabriel de Saint-Aubin 1724-1780*. Davison Art Center, Wesleyan University, Middletown, CT; Baltimore Museum of Art, 1975.
Milan 1991
  Molfino, Alessandra Mottola, and Mauro Natale, eds. *Le Muse e il principe: Arte di corte nel Rinascimento primo*. Museo Poldi Pezzoli, Milan, 1991.
Minneapolis 1956
  Joachim, Harold. *Prints: 1400-1900*. The Minneapolis Institute of Arts; The Cleveland Museum of Art; The Art Institute of Chicago, 1956-57.
Munich 1965
  Hébert, Michél, and Marie-Christins Angebault. *Les plus belles gravures du monde occidental 1410-1914*. Haus der Kunst, Munich; Bibliothèque Nationale, Paris; Rijksmuseum, Amsterdam, 1965-66.
Munich 1986
  Bevers, Holm. *Meister E.S. Ein oberrheinischer Kupferstecher der Spätgotik*. Staatliche Graphische Sammlung, Munich; Kupferstichkabinett, Staatliche Museen Preussischer Kulturbesitz, Berlin, 1986-87.
Münster 1982
  Dethlefs, Gerd, Robert Stupperich, and Joachim Fest. *Die Wiedertäufer in Münster*. Stadtmuseum, Münster, 1982.
Münster 1985
  Heinrich Aldegrever und die Bildnisse der Wiedertäufer. Westfälisches Landesmuseum für Kunst und Kulturgeschichte, Münster, 1985.

New Brunswick 1978
  Cate, Phillip Dennis, and Sinclair Hamilton Hitchings. *The Color Revolution: Color Lithography in France, 1890-1900*. Rutgers University Art Gallery, The State University of New Jersey, New Brunswick; The Baltimore Museum of Art; Boston Public Library, 1978-79.
New Brunswick 1983
  Hofrichter, Frima Fox. *Haarlem: The Seventeenth Century*. The Jane Voorhees Zimmerli Art Museum, New Brunswick, 1983.
New Haven 1969
  Talbot, Charles, and Alan Shestack. *Prints and Drawings of the Danube School: An Exhibition of South German and Austrian Graphic Art of 1500-1560*. Yale University Art Gallery, New Haven; City Art Museum of St. Louis; Philadelphia Museum of Art, 1969-70.
New Haven 1974
  Burke, James D. *Charles Meryon Prints and Drawings*. The Toledo Museum of Art; Yale University Art Gallery, New Haven; The St. Louis Museum of Art, 1974-75.
New Haven 1976
  Bayard, Jane, and Ellen D'Oench. *Darkness into Light: The Early Mezzotint*. Yale University Art Gallery, New Haven, 1976.
New Haven 1978
  Pillsbury, Edmund P., and Louise S. Richards. *The Graphic Art of Federico Barocci: Selected Drawings and Prints*. Yale University Art Gallery, New Haven; The Cleveland Museum of Art, 1978.
New Haven 1981
  Shestack, Alan, Charles W. Talbot, and Linda C. Hults. *Hans Baldung Grien: Prints and Drawings*. National Gallery of Art, Washington; Yale University Art Gallery, New Haven, 1981.
New Haven 1986
  Emison, Patricia A. *The Art of Teaching: Sixteenth-Century Allegorical Prints and Drawings*. Yale University Art Gallery, New Haven, 1986-87.
New York 1959
  French Drawings from American Collections: Clouet to Matisse. The Metropolitan Museum of Art, New York, 1959.
New York 1981
  Galassi, Peter. *Before Photography: Painting and the Invention of Photography*. The Museum of Modern Art, New York, 1981.
New York 1983
  Cachin, François, Charles S. Moffett, Michel Melot et al. *Manet 1832-1883*. Grand Palais, Paris; The Metropolitan Museum of Art, New York, 1983.
New York 1985
  Castleman, Riva, and Wolfgang Wittrock. *Henri de Toulouse-Lautrec: Images of the 1890s*. The Museum of Modern Art, New York, 1985.
New York 1986
  Wednerhorst, Alfred, Hermann Maué, Rainer Brandl, Rainer Kahsnitz, William D. Wixom, Kurt Löcher, Rainer Schoch, Johannes Willer et al. *Gothic and Renaissance Art in Nuremberg 1300-1550*. The Metropolitan Museum of Art, New York, 1986.
New York 1988a
  Rosenberg, Pierre. *Fragonard*. The Metropolitan Museum of Art, New York, 1988.
New York 1988b
  Boggs, Jean Sutherland, Henri Loyrette, Michael Pantazzi, and Gary Tinterow. *Degas*. The Metropolitan Museum of Art, New York; The National Gallery of Canada, Ottawa, 1988.
Nuremberg 1961
  Strieder, Peter, ed. *Meister um Albrecht Dürer: Ausstellung im Germanischen Nationalmuseum*. Germanisches Nationalmuseum, Nuremberg, 1961.
Nuremberg 1971
  Wilckens, Leonie von, ed. *Albrecht Dürer 1471-1971*. Germanisches Nationalmuseum, Nuremberg, 1971.
Nuremberg 1978
  Vorbild Dürer: Kupferstiche und Holzschnitte Albrecht Dürers im Spiegel der europäischen Druckgraphik des 16.Jahrhunderts. Peter Strieder and Arno Schönberger, eds. Germanisches Nationalmusuem, Nuremberg, 1978.

Nuremberg 1983
    Irsigler, F., H. Boockmann, F. Machilek, B. Lohse, H. Rabe, B. Moeller,
    H. Immenkötter, V. Press, K. Hoffman, G. Seebass, K. Stackmann, J.
    Schilling, M. Jenny, D. Koepplin, E. W. Zeeden, K. Löcher, and K. J.
    Dorsch. *Martin Luther und die Reformation in Deutschland.*
    Germanisches Nationalmuseum, Nuremberg, 1983.
Oberlin 1977
    Getscher, Robert H. *The Stamp of Whistler.* Allen Memorial Art
    Museum, Oberlin; Museum of Fine Arts, Boston; Philadelphia Museum
    of Art, 1977-78.
Ottawa 1976
    Knox, George. *Etchings by the Tiepolos.* The National Museum of
    Canada, Ottawa, 1976.
Ottawa 1983
    Druick, Douglas, and Michael Hoog. *Fantin-Latour.* Grand Palais, Paris;
    The National Museum of Canada, Ottawa; California Palace of the
    Legion of Honor, San Francisco, 1983.
Paris 1920
    Exposition Debucourt. Musée des Arts Decoratifs, Paris, 1920.
Paris 1963
    Delacroix et la gravure romantique. Bibiliothèque Nationale, Paris, 1963.
Paris 1968
    Ducros, J. *Charles Meryon officier de marine peintre-graveur 1821-1868.*
    Musée de la Marine, Paris, 1968.
Paris 1974
    Melot, Michel. *L'Estampe impressioniste.* Bibliothèque Nationale, Paris,
    1974.
Paris 1975
    Herbert, Roger. *Jean-François Millet.* Grand Palais, Paris, 1975.
Paris 1976
    Judrin, Claudie. *Rodin et les écrivains de son temps.* Musée Rodin, Paris,
    1976.
Paris 1984
    Guillaud, Jacqueline, and Maurice Guillaud, eds. *Altdorfer and Fantastic
    Realism in Art.* Centre Culturel du Marais, Paris, 1984.
Paris 1985
    Graveurs français de la seconde moitié du xviiie siècle. Musée du Louvre,
    Paris, 1985.
Paris 1989a
    Jean-Richard, Pierrette, and Gilbert Mondin. *Un collectionneur pendant
    la Révolution: Jean Louis Soulavie (1752-1813).* Musée du Louvre, Paris,
    1989.
Paris 1989b
    La Révolution française et L'europe 1789-1799. Grand Palais, Paris,
    1989.
Paris 1991
    Renouard de Bussierre, Sophie. *Martin Schongauer, maître de la gravure
    rhénane vers 1450-1491.* Petit Palais, Paris, 1991-92.
Passau 1953
    Halm, Peter. *Wolf Huber Gedächtnisausstellung zum 400. Todesjahr.*
    Oberhausmuseum, Passau, 1953.
Philadelphia 1967
    Shestack, Alan. *Master E.S.: 500th Anniversary.* Philadelphia Museum of
    Art, 1967.
Philadelphia 1984
    Sutton, Peter C., et al. *Masters of Seventeenth Century Dutch Genre
    Painting.* Philadelphia Museum of Art; Gemäldegalerie, Staatliche
    Museen Preussischer Kulturbesitz, Berlin; Royal Academy of Art,
    London, 1984.
Rotterdam 1974
    Haverkamp-Begeman, Egbert, et al. *Willem Buytewech 1591-1624.*
    Museum Boymans-van Beuningen, Rotterdam; Institut Néerlandais,
    Paris, 1974-75.
Santa Barbara 1979
    Wallen, Burr. *The William A. Gumberts Collection of Canaletto
    Etchings.* Santa Barbara Museum of Art, 1979.
Stanford 1972
    Mozley, Anita Ventura, Robert Bartlett Haas, and Françoise Forster-

Hahn. *Eadweard Muybridge: The Stanford Years, 1872-1882.* Stanford
    University Museum of Art; E. B. Crocker Art Gallery, Sacramento;
    University Galleries, University of Southern California, Los Angeles,
    1972-73.
Stuttgart 1973
    Falk, Tilman, Rolf Biedermann, and Heinrich Geissler. *Hans Burgkmair:
    Das Graphische Werk.* Graphische Sammlung, Staatsgalerie, Stuttgart;
    Städtische Kunstsammlungen, Augsburg, 1973.
Stuttgart 1979
    Geissler, Heinrich, ed. *Zeichnung in Deutschland: Deutsch Zeichner
    1540-1640.* 2 vols. Staatsgalerie, Stuttgart, 1979.
Tokyo 1989
    Motoé, Kunio. *Odilon Redon.* The National Museum of Art, Tokyo; The
    Hyogo Prefectural Museum of Art; Aichi Prefectural Art Gallery, 1989.
Unna 1986
    *Heinrich Aldegrever: Die Kleinmeister und das Kunsthandwerk der
    Renaissance.* Evangelische Stadtkirche, Unna, 1986.
Vienna 1953
    Katalog der Gedenkschau Augustin Hirschvogel (1503-1553).
    Historisches Museum, Vienna, 1953.
Vienna 1967
    Oberhuber, Konrad. *Zwischen Renaissance und Barock: Das Zeitalter
    von Bruegel und Bellange.* Die Kunst der Graphik IV. Graphische
    Sammlung Albertina, Vienna, 1967. Reprint. New York: Arno/
    Worldwide, 1968.
Washington 1949
    Early Italian Engravings. National Gallery of Art, 1949 (no catalogue).
Washington 1967
    Shestack, Alan. *Fifteenth Century Engravings of Northern Europe.*
    National Gallery of Art, Washington, 1967-68.
Washington 1971
    Talbot, Charles, Gaillard F. Ravenel, and Jay A. Levenson. *Dürer in
    America: His Graphic Work.* National Gallery of Art, Washington, 1971.
Washington 1972
    Russell, H. Diane. *Rare Etchings by Giovanni Battista and Giovanni
    Domenico Tiepolo.* National Gallery of Art, Washington, 1972.
Washington 1973
    Levenson, Jay A. *Prints of the Italian Renaissance: A Handbook of the
    Exhibition.* National Gallery of Art, Washington, 1973.
Washington 1975
    Russell, H. Diane, et al. *Jacques Callot: Prints and Related Drawings.*
    National Gallery of Art, Washington, 1975.
Washington 1976
    Rosand, David, and Michelangelo Muraro. *Titian and the Venetian
    Woodcut.* National Gallery of Art, Washington; Dallas Museum of Fine
    Arts; The Detroit Institute of Arts, 1976.
Washington 1979
    Bohlin, Diane DeGrazia. *Prints and Related Drawings by the Carracci
    Family: A Catalogue Raisonné.* National Gallery of Art, Washington,
    1979.
Washington 1981
    Elsen, Albert E., ed. *Rodin Rediscovered.* National Gallery of Art,
    Washington, 1981.
Washington 1982
    Russell, H. Diane. *Claude Lorrain 1600-1682.* National Gallery of Art,
    Washington, 1982-83.
Washington 1983
    Jacobowitz, Ellen S., and Stephanie Loeb Stepanek. *The Prints of Lucas
    van Leyden and His Contemporaries.* National Gallery of Art,
    Washington; Museum of Fine Arts, Boston, 1983.
Washington 1984
    Old Master Drawings from the Albertina. National Gallery of Art,
    Washington; The Pierpont Morgan Library, New York, 1984-85.
Washington 1988
    Cafritz, Robert C., Lawrence Gowing, and David Rosand. *Places of
    Delight: The Pastoral Landscape.* National Gallery of Art and The
    Phillips Collection, Washington, 1988-89.

Washington 1990a

Schneider, Cynthia P., Boudwijn Bakker, Nancy Ash, and Shelley Fletcher. *Rembrandt's Landscapes: Drawings and Prints*. National Gallery of Art, Washington, 1990.

Washington 1990b

Russell, H. Diane, and Bernadine Barnes. *Eva/Ave: Women in Renaissance and Baroque Prints*. National Gallery of Art, Washington, 1990-91.

Washington 1990c

Wheelock, Arthur K., Susan J. Barnes, Julius S. Held et al. *Anthony van Dyck*. National Gallery of Art, Washington, 1990-91.

Washington 1991

Levenson, Jay A., ed. *Circa 1492: Art in the Age of Exploration*. National Gallery of Art, Washington, 1991-92.

Wooster 1974

Getscher, Robert H. *Félix Bracquemond and the Etching Process*. College of Wooster Art Center Museum, Wooster, OH; John Carroll University Fine Arts Gallery, Cleveland, 1974.

Worcester 1982

Grad, Bonnie L., and Timothy A. Riggs. *Visions of City and Country: Prints and Photographs of Nineteenth Century France*. National Gallery of Art, Washington; Worcester Art Museum, MA; The Ackland Art Museum, Chapel Hill, NC, 1982.

Index

References to pages that contain illustrations are printed in **bold** type.

Photograph Credits